Exploring Philosophy

An Introductory Anthology

SEVENTH EDITION

Edited By

STEVEN M. CAHN

New York   Oxford

OXFORD UNIVERSITY PRESS

Oxford University Press is a department of the University of Oxford. It furthers the University's objective of excellence in research, scholarship, and education by publishing worldwide. Oxford is a registered trade mark of Oxford University Press in the UK and certain other countries.

Published in the United States of America by Oxford University Press
198 Madison Avenue, New York, NY 10016, United States of America.

For titles covered by Section 112 of the US Higher Education Opportunity Act, please visit www.oup.com/us/he for the latest information about pricing and alternate formats.

Library of Congress Cataloging-in-Publication Data
Names: Cahn, Steven M., editor.
Title: Exploring philosophy : an introductory anthology / edited by Steven M. Cahn.
Description: Seventh edition. | New York, NY, United States of America : Oxford University Press, 2021. | Includes bibliographical references and index. | Summary: "Exploring Philosophy: An Introductory Anthology is the most accessible yet still comprehensive topically organized introduction to philosophy. Steven Cahn has carefully selected extraordinarily clear, recent essays by noted philosophers and has supplemented these with influential historical sources. Most importantly, the articles have been carefully edited to focus on their core content and arguments, making them understandable to students studying philosophy for the first time. The topics are drawn from across the major fields of philosophy and include knowledge and skepticism, mind and body, freedom and determinism, the existence of God, the problem of evil, ethical reasoning, abortion, euthanasia, world hunger, democracy, capital punishment, and affirmative action. The readings are enhanced by concise introductions, explanatory notes, and suggestions for further reading. In the 5th edition Cahn greatly increased the number of readings by women, and this feature was very positively received by instructors. This edition has become the 2nd or 3rd best-selling reader for the intro course, after our own #1 reader by Perry. The 6th edition will be revised in light of the reviews"—Provided by publisher.
Identifiers: LCCN 2020010439 | ISBN 9780190089580 (paperback) | ISBN 9780190089610 | ISBN 9780190089603 (ebook) | ISBN 9780190089597 (ebook)
Subjects: LCSH: Philosophy—Textbooks.
Classification: LCC BD21 .E96 2020 | DDC 100—dc23
LC record available at https://lccn.loc.gov/2020010439

Printing number: 9 8 7 6 5 4 3 2

Printed by LSC Communications, Inc.
United States of America

To the memory of my mother,
Evelyn Baum Cahn

CONTENTS

PREFACE

Those who begin the study of philosophy may easily become discouraged. Many classic texts are daunting in their complexity, and much contemporary writing is intended primarily for a professional audience.

A few prominent philosophers of our day write in a style understandable by all, but nonspecialists are often left unaware of this work. They may never realize that serious discussion of central problems of philosophy can proceed without arcane terminology, unexplained references, or convoluted arguments.

The guiding principle of this book is that reading clear, concise essays by recent philosophers offers an inviting avenue to understanding philosophical inquiry. While some of the articles are reprinted in their entirety, many are shortened to sharpen their focus and enhance their accessibility.

For readers who wish to understand the development of philosophy over the centuries, I have included a substantial number of historical sources, including without abridgement Plato's *Defence of Socrates, Crito,* and *Meno,* as well as substantial segments from his *Republic,* Descartes' *Meditations on First Philosophy,* and Hume's *An Enquiry Concerning Human Understanding* and *Dialogues Concerning Natural Religion.* Most of these are identified by the name of the work from which the selection is drawn, while with regard to some of the recent essays, I have taken the liberty of developing short, descriptive titles.

NEW TO THIS EDITION

- Complete text of Plato's *Meno.*
- New essays on antiscientism, the concept of knowledge, free will, the problem of evil, reparations, sexual harassment, the divestiture puzzle, and the afterlife.
- A revision of the essay on the elements of argument.
- One-third of the contemporary essays are authored or coauthored by women.

READINGS ADDED TO THE NEW EDITION

Gillian Barker and Philip Kitcher, "Antiscientism"
Jennifer Nagel, "Knowing vs. Thinking"
Plato, *Meno*
Patricia Churchland, "Do We Have Free Will?"
Bernard R. Boxill, "The Morality of Reparation"
Chandran Kukathas, "Reparation and the Problem of Agency"
N. Ann David, "Sexual Harassment in the University"
Margaret Crouch, "Sexual Harassment in Public Places"
Steven M. Cahn, "The Divestiture Puzzle"
Samuel Scheffler, "The Afterlife"
Harry G. Frankfurt, "How the Afterlife Matters"
Susan Wolf, "The Significance of Doomsday"

Omitted after inclusion in the previous edition are selections by Marilyn McCord Adams, Christine Vitrano, Jean-Paul Sartre, Rosalind Hursthouse, James Rachels, Bonnie Steinbock, John Locke, Morris Weitz, Thomas Nagel, Shelly Kagan, and two each by Tom Regan and Mary Anne Warren.

INSTRUCTOR'S MANUAL
AND COMPANION WEBSITE

An Instructor's Manual and Companion Website (www.oup.com/us/cahn) for both Instructors and Students accompany *Exploring Philosophy*. The Instructor's Manual features PowerPoint lecture outlines, reading summaries, a glossary, and a Test Bank of objective and essay questions. A link to the instructor materials can be found on the Companion Website along with student resources such as self-test questions with answers, suggested readings, and helpful web links.

ACKNOWLEDGMENTS

I am grateful to my former editor, Robert Miller, for having helped me develop this book, and to my current editor, Andrew Blitzer, for his support and advice in planning this new edition. I also wish to thank assistant editors Anna Deen and Molly Zimetbaum for their generous help, production editor Marianne Paul for her conscientiousness, as well as numerous other members of the staff at Oxford University Press for their thoughtful assistance throughout production.

In planning this new edition I have been guided in part by suggestions from reviewers chosen by the Press. I would like to thank them individually:

Justin Garson, *Hunter College-CUNY*
Joshua Smith, *Central Michigan University*
Eugenio E. Zaldivar, *Santa Fe College*

Keith Hess, *College of Southern Nevada*
Heath Allen, *Oklahoma State University*
Erik M. Hanson, *University of Colorado, Colorado Springs*
Brad Rives, *Indiana University of Pennsylvania*
Brent Franklin, *Rowan College at Burlington County*
Laurence Carlin, *University of Wisconsin Oshkosh*

My editorial commentary reflects, as usual, stylistic pointers offered by my brother, Victor L. Cahn, playwright, critic, and Professor Emeritus of English at Skidmore College. The title of this book was originally proposed by my wife, Marilyn Ross, MD, to whom I owe so much more.

NOTE

Some of the materials throughout the book were written when the custom was to use the noun "man" and the pronoun "he" to refer to all persons, regardless of gender, and I have retained the author's original wording. With this proviso, let us embark on exploring philosophy.

PART 1

Introduction

What Is Philosophy?

Monroe C. Beardsley and Elizabeth Lane Beardsley

The study of philosophy is unlike the study of any other subject. No dates, formulas, or rules need be memorized. No field work is necessary, and no technical equipment required. The only prerequisite is an inquiring mind.

About what do philosophers inquire? The word *philosophy* is of Greek origin and literally means "the love of wisdom." But what sort of wisdom do philosophers love?

The answer is provided in our first selection. Its authors are Elizabeth Lane Beardsley (1914–1990), who taught at Lincoln University and then Temple University, and her husband, Monroe C. Beardsley (1915–1985), who taught at Swarthmore College and then Temple University.

While the best way to understand the nature of philosophical inquiry is to consider some specific philosophical issues, an overview of the subject is helpful, and that is what the Beardsleys provide.

Philosophical questions grow out of a kind of thinking that is familiar to all of us: the thinking that we do when we ask ourselves whether something that we believe is reasonable to believe. "Reasonable" has a broad, but definite, meaning here: a reasonable belief is simply a belief for which a good reason can be given. Reasonable beliefs are logically justifiable. It would seem that a belief that is reasonable stands a better chance of being true than one that is not, so anyone who is interested in the truth of his beliefs should be concerned about their reasonableness.

All of us have known, long before we approached the systematic study of philosophy, what it is like to want to make a belief reasonable, and also what it is like not to care whether a belief is reasonable or not. We have all had the experience of accepting beliefs without worrying about their logical justification, for we have all been children. We absorbed the beliefs of our parents, or the opinions current in our society or culture, without thinking about them very much or looking at them with a critical eye. We may not even have been fully aware that we had them; we may have acted on them without ever having put them into words. As long as our own experience did not seem to conflict with those early beliefs, or those beliefs did not seem to clash with one another, it did not occur to us to question them or to inquire into the reasons that could be given for them.

From *Philosophical Thinking: An Introduction*, by Monroe C. Beardsley and Elizabeth L. Beardsley.

But a growing individual cannot grow for very long without sometimes wondering whether his most cherished beliefs have any foundation. This experience, too, dates back to childhood. When, for example, a child notices that the Santa Claus on the street corner is about as tall as his father, while the one in the department store is a good deal taller, and is moved to ask questions about Santa's location and stature, he is looking critically at a belief and inquiring into its reasons.

As we emerge from childhood, we continue to have experiences of this kind and to acquire further beliefs. Some beliefs we go on accepting without checking up on their reasonableness; other beliefs we do question, some of them very seriously. But two things happen to many of us. First, the questioned beliefs increase in proportion to the unquestioned beliefs. And second, the questioning process, once begun, is carried on for longer and longer times before it is allowed to end. The child who is told that the department store Santa is "really" Santa Claus, while those in the street are merely trusted helpers, may be satisfied for a time, but at some later stage he will probably ask himself what reason there is for believing *this* to be true, especially if he compares notes with his cousin from another city, who has been provided with a different candidate for the "real Santa Claus." The junior high school student who has been told he should accept what his science teacher says because the latter knows his subject may wonder why the teacher is judged to be a qualified authority in this field. If provided with satisfactory assurances, he will call a halt to his questioning process at that stage; but later on, perhaps in college, he may be moved to ask why we should ever accept anything told us by "authorities," no matter how well qualified. Should we not rely entirely on our own firsthand experience? Is anything else really *knowledge?*

The search for good reasons for our beliefs, and for good reasons for the reasons, can be carried as far as we wish. If it is carried far enough, the searcher finds himself confronted by questions of a peculiar kind: the questions of philosophy. Among these questions you will find some that you have already thought about, as well as others that will be unfamiliar to you. Many of them, however, originally came to be asked because someone undertook a critical examination of his ordinary beliefs.

As our first example, let us trace the origin of a few philosophical questions that arise out of the moral aspects of life. People sometimes say, "He ought to be put in jail for that." Sometimes this is only an exclamation of anger at some instance of meanness or brutality; sometimes it leads to action, however, for juries do put people in jail because (if the jurors are conscientious) they believe that this punishment is just. Suppose you hear a friend remark, about the recent conviction of someone who has violated the law—a holdup man, a venal judge, an industrialist who has conspired to fix prices, a civil rights demonstrator who has blocked a construction site—that the jail sentence is deserved. After you hear all the relevant details, you may agree with him. But even so, you might still wonder whether you are right, and—not because you plan to do anything about the case, but merely because you would like to be sure you *are* right—you may begin to ask further, more searching, questions.

Why does the man deserve to be sent to jail? Because he committed a crime, of course. Yes, but why should he be sent to jail for committing a crime? Because to disobey the laws of the state is wrong. But *why?* Just because certain people you don't even know, perhaps people who died years before you were born, passed a law against, let us say, spitting in the subway or disorderly conduct, how does that obligate you to obey the law? This line of questioning, as we can foresee, will, if carried far, lead into some perplexing questions about the moral basis of the law, the tests of right and wrong, and the purposes of government and society. For example, we may discover that in approving the jail sentence we are assuming that the existence of a government is so important to maintain that governments have the right, under certain conditions, to deprive any citizen of his liberties. This assumption is a philosophical belief. And when we ask whether or not it is true, we are asking a philosophical question.

But consider how the questioning might turn into a different channel. Granted that the act was illegal, there still remains the question whether the man should be punished. Sometimes people do wrong things because they are feeble-minded or mentally ill, and we do not regard them as punishable. Well, in this case, it might be said, the man is responsible for his action. Why responsible? Because he was free when he committed it—free to commit the act or to refrain from committing it. He had, some would say, free will. Indeed, all men have free will—though they do not always exercise it. Then what reason is there to believe that this, in turn, is true? How do we know there is such a thing as free will? Again, we seem to have uncovered an underlying belief that lies deeper than the lawyer's or the juror's immediate problems, something they do not themselves discuss, but (according to one theory) take for granted. We have reached another belief that can be called philosophical, and exposed another philosophical question: do human beings have free will? . . .

Here are two more samples of thinking that begin with a nonphilosophical belief but lead gradually but directly into philosophy. We present them in the form of brief dialogues.

Dialogue I

A: You ought to have written to your parents last Sunday.
B: Why?
A: Because you promised you would write every Sunday.
B: I know I did, but I've been awfully busy. Why was it so important to keep my promise?
A: Not just *that* promise—*any* promise. It's wrong ever to break a promise.
B: Well, I used to think that, but now I'm not sure. What makes you think it's always wrong to break promises?
A: My reason is simply that most people in our society disapprove of it. You know perfectly well that they do.
B: Of course I know that most people in our society disapprove of breaking promises, but does that prove it really is always wrong to do it? The majority

opinion in our society could be mistaken, couldn't it? I don't see why it should be taken for granted that what most Americans *think* is wrong and what really *is* wrong should always coincide. What's the connection between the two?

Dialogue II

A: In my paper for political science I had to define "democracy." "Democracy" means "government by the people collectively."

B: What made you choose that definition?

A: I looked up the word in the dictionary, of course.

B: How do you know your dictionary is right? My dictionary doesn't always give the same definitions as yours.

A: Oh, but mine is larger and more recent, so it's bound to be more reliable.

B: Yes, but language is constantly changing, and words like "democracy" are used in lots of different ways. I think one shouldn't feel bound by any dictionary definition. Every writer should feel free to define any word as he wishes.

A: But that would be chaotic. Besides, you wouldn't really have definitions at all, in that case.

B: Why wouldn't you have definitions? There's no such thing as *the* "one true meaning" of a word, is there? Words mean whatever people make them mean, so why shouldn't I select my own meanings and put them in definitions of my own?

Very different topics are discussed in these brief conversations, but they follow a similar pattern. In each case, speaker A makes an opening remark of a fairly specific sort, speaker B asks A to give a good reason for his opening statement, and A does provide what, on the level of ordinary common-sense thinking, would be regarded as a satisfactory reason. Many conversations would end at this stage; but B is disposed to probe more deeply, to uncover the assumptions underlying A's reasons, and to ask whether these more basic assumptions, in turn, are reasonable. Notice how the beliefs being questioned become more general and more fundamental as the questioning goes on. In each of the little dialogues, B pushes A over the brink into philosophy. At the end of each, he raises a question concerning the truth of a philosophical belief—and there the matter is left, for the time being.

But you may not be content to leave it at that. If you feel some frustration or impatience with the way A and B are arguing, you are on the verge of doing some philosophical thinking yourself. Wouldn't you like to ask B some searching questions—for example, about the way in which he is using some of his key words? This would all be a lot clearer, you may have said to yourself while you were reading Dialogue I, if we were sure just what the word "wrong" means here. Maybe it means simply "disapproved by a majority of people in one's own society." In that case, what happens to B's final question? Isn't he confused? But *does* "wrong" mean only this? And take the term "free will," which was used in one of the other examples of philosophical thinking discussed above. How can we decide whether it is reasonable to believe that human beings have this mysterious thing without saying precisely what it is?

If you have been thinking for yourself along these lines, or (even if you haven't) if you can now see the sense in raising these questions about the meaning of key words, you will be able to sympathize with a good deal of what contemporary philosophers have been doing. . . .

Increased clearness in your own beliefs is, then, one of the three chief benefits you can derive from a study of philosophy—if, as we hope, you are not content merely to learn about the theories and arguments of the great philosophers (interesting and valuable as that is), but will make this study an active exercise in philosophical thinking.

The second benefit, partly dependent on the first, is increased assurance that your beliefs are reasonable. A belief whose reasons have been examined deeply enough to reach the level of philosophical questioning rests on a firmer foundation than one that has been examined less thoroughly. . . . Admittedly, the philosopher's desire to base his beliefs on good reasons is unusually persistent and intense. . . . But all of us who want assurance that our beliefs are well grounded should do some philosophical thinking about some of them, at least, in order to secure the firmest possible grounds.

The third benefit which the study of philosophy can confer upon our beliefs is increased consistency. For philosophical thinking forces each of us to see whether his fundamental beliefs in different areas of experience form a logically coherent whole. . . .

The three values we have cited—clarity, reasonableness, and consistency—are basic intellectual values. But perhaps you are saying to yourself something like this: "I can see that studying philosophy may help me improve my beliefs, but, after all, there is more to life than thinking and believing. What I most want from my education is to improve my *actions*. How can philosophical thinking help me to *live* better?"

Part of our answer here is that we must beware of drawing too sharp a line between beliefs and actions. Our beliefs—including philosophical beliefs—have a considerable influence on our actions. This influence can be seen most directly in one area of philosophy, where we are concerned with questions of value, but answers to some other basic philosophical questions may also possess some power to affect, however indirectly, the way we live. Although knowledge may be valuable for its own sake, as well as for its practical consequences, it is not wrong to expect philosophy to have its effects. It would be wrong, however, to ask every philosophical belief to show a direct and simple connection with human action. Perhaps the growing appreciation of the importance of basic research in science may foster an appreciation of the quest for answers to other highly fundamental questions, without insistence on immediate practical results.

In saying that beliefs influence actions, we do not mean to lose sight of the effect of emotions on human conduct. Temporary emotions, as well as more enduring emotional attitudes, are often powerful enough to make us behave in ways counter to what we believe intellectually. Philosophical thinking can do a great deal to clarify and harmonize our beliefs at all levels, and to strengthen their foundations. But the philosopher is no substitute for the psychiatrist, or for the parents and teachers of our early years who help create our emotional make-up. Yet many philosophers have claimed that the experience of thinking about philosophical questions can affect our emotional attitudes as well as our beliefs.

When we detach our minds from immediate practical matters and from the limited boundaries of particular fields of specialization, we experience a kind of release from petty and provincial concerns. The experience of thinking as human beings who are trying to understand themselves and their universe may produce a serenity and breadth of mind that can in time become enduring attitudes.

STUDY QUESTIONS

1. According to the Beardsleys, what is a philosophical question?
2. Construct a brief dialogue of your own, like Dialogues I and II, that illustrates how a philosophical issue can arise in the course of an ordinary conversation.
3. According to the Beardsleys, what are the three chief benefits to be derived from the study of philosophy?
4. Present an example of a philosophical belief that has influenced action.

The Value of Philosophy

BERTRAND RUSSELL

As we begin the study of philosophy, you may wonder whether the value of the subject can be explained briefly. Here is an insightful, inspirational statement from Bertrand Russell (1872–1970), the English philosopher, mathematician, and social activist, winner of the 1950 Nobel Prize for Literature, and one of the most prominent figures of the twentieth century.

....

... [I]t will be well to consider ... what is the value of philosophy and why it ought to be studied. It is the more necessary to consider this question, in view of the fact that many men, under the influence of science or of practical affairs, are inclined to doubt whether philosophy is anything better than innocent but useless trifling, hair-splitting distinctions, and controversies on matters concerning which knowledge is impossible.

This view of philosophy appears to result, partly from a wrong conception of the ends of life, partly from a wrong conception of the kind of goods which philosophy strives to achieve. Physical science, through the medium of inventions, is useful to innumerable people who are wholly ignorant of it; thus the study of physical science is to be recommended, not only, or primarily, because of the effect on the student, but rather because of the effect on mankind in general. Thus utility does not belong to philosophy. If the study of philosophy has any value at all for others than students of philosophy, it must be only indirectly, through its effects upon the lives of those who study it. It is in these effects, therefore, if anywhere, that the value of philosophy must be primarily sought.

But further, if we are not to fail in our endeavour to determine the value of philosophy, we must first free our minds from the prejudices of what are wrongly called "practical" men. The "practical" man, as this word is often used, is one who recognizes only material needs, who realizes that men must have food for the body, but is oblivious of the necessity of providing food for the mind. If all men were well off, if poverty and disease had been reduced to their lowest possible point, there would still remain much to be done to produce a valuable society; and even in the existing world the goods of the mind are at least as important as the goods of the body. It is exclusively among the goods of the mind that the value of philosophy is to be found; and only those who are not indifferent to these goods can be persuaded that the study of philosophy is not a waste of time.

Philosophy, like all other studies, aims primarily at knowledge. The knowledge it aims at is the kind of knowledge which gives unity and system to the body of the sciences, and the kind which results from a critical examination of the grounds of our convictions, prejudices, and beliefs. But it cannot be maintained that philosophy has had any very great measure of success in its attempts to provide definite answers to its questions. If you ask a mathematician, a mineralogist, a historian, or any other man of learning, what definite body of truths has been ascertained by his science, his answer will last as long as you are willing to listen. But if you put the same question to a philosopher, he will, if he is candid, have to confess that his study has not achieved positive results such as have been achieved by other sciences. It is true that this is partly accounted for by the fact that, as soon as definite knowledge concerning any subject becomes possible, this subject ceases to be called philosophy and becomes a separate science. The whole study of the heavens, which now belongs to astronomy, was once included in philosophy; Newton's great work was called "the mathematical principles of natural philosophy." Similarly, the study of the human mind, which was a part of philosophy, has now been separated from philosophy and has become the science of psychology. Thus, to a great extent, the uncertainty of philosophy is more apparent than real: those questions which are already capable of definite answers are placed in the sciences, while those only to which, at present, no definite answer can be given will remain to form the residue which is called philosophy.

This is, however, only a part of the truth concerning the uncertainty of philosophy. There are many questions—and among them those that are of the profoundest interest to our spiritual life—which, so far as we can see, must remain insoluble to the human intellect unless its powers become of quite a different order from what they are now. Has the universe any unity of plan or purpose, or is it a fortuitous concourse of atoms? Is consciousness a permanent part of the universe, giving hope of indefinite growth in wisdom, or is it a transitory accident on a small planet on which life must ultimately become impossible? Are good and evil of importance to the universe or only to man? Such questions are asked by philosophy, and variously answered by various philosophers. But it would seem that, whether answers be otherwise discoverable or not, the answers suggested by philosophy are none of them demonstrably true. Yet, however slight may be the hope of discovering an answer, it is part of the business of philosophy to continue the consideration of such questions, to make us aware of their importance, to examine all the approaches to them, and to keep alive that speculative interest in the universe which is apt to be killed by confining ourselves to definitely ascertainable knowledge. . . .

The value of philosophy is, in fact, to be sought largely in its very uncertainty. The man who has no tincture of philosophy goes through life imprisoned in the prejudices derived from common sense, from the habitual beliefs of his age or his nation, and from convictions which have grown up in his mind without the co-operation or consent of his deliberate reason. To such a man the world tends to become definite, finite, obvious; common objects rouse no questions, and unfamiliar possibilities are contemptuously rejected. As soon as we begin to philosophize, on the contrary, we find . . . that even the most everyday things lead to problems to which only very incomplete answers can be given. Philosophy, though unable to tell us with certainty what is the true answer to the doubts which it raises, is able to suggest many possibilities which enlarge our thoughts and free them from the tyranny of custom. Thus, while diminishing our feeling of certainty as to what things are, it greatly increases our knowledge as to what they may be; it removes the somewhat arrogant dogmatism of those who have never travelled into the region of liberating doubt, and it keeps alive our sense of wonder by showing familiar things in an unfamiliar aspect.

Apart from its utility in showing unsuspected possibilities, philosophy has a value—perhaps its chief value—through the greatness of the objects which it contemplates and through the freedom from narrow and personal aims resulting from this contemplation. The life of the instinctive man is shut up within the circle of his private interests: Family and friends may be included, but the outer world is not regarded except as it may help or hinder what comes within the circle of instinctive wishes. In such a life there is something feverish and confined, in comparison with which the philosophic life is calm and free. The private world of instinctive interests is a small one, set in the midst of a great and powerful world which must, sooner or later, lay our private world in ruins. Unless we can so enlarge our interests as to include the whole outer world, we remain like a garrison in a beleaguered fortress, knowing that the enemy prevents escape and that ultimate surrender is inevitable. In such a life there is no peace, but a constant strife between the insistence of desire and the powerlessness of will. In one way or another, if our life is to be great and free, we must escape this prison and this strife. . . .

Thus, to sum up our discussion of the value of philosophy: Philosophy is to be studied, not for the sake of any definite answers to its questions, since no definite answers can, as a rule, be known to be true, but rather for the sake of the questions themselves; because these questions enlarge our conception of what is possible, enrich our intellectual imagination and diminish the dogmatic assurance which closes the mind against speculation; but above all because, through the greatness of the universe which philosophy contemplates, the mind also is rendered great, and becomes capable of that union with the universe which constitutes its highest good.

STUDY QUESTIONS

1. Do you agree with Russell that the goods of the mind are at least as important as the goods of the body?
2. According to Russell, who are wrongly called "practical men"?
3. What value does Russell find in uncertainty?
4. According to Russell, what is the mind's highest good?

HISTORICAL SOURCE

Defence of Socrates

PLATO

Philosophers build on the work of their predecessors, and the intellectual links that form the chain of the history of philosophy extend back to ancient Greece, more than five centuries before the Christian era. While only tantalizing fragments remain from the writings of the earliest philosophers, three men made such enormous contributions to the development of the subject that their overwhelming impact is widely acknowledged: Socrates (c. 470–399 B.C.E.), Plato (c. 429–347 B.C.E.), and Aristotle (384–322 B.C.E.).

Their relationship is unusual. Socrates wrote nothing, but in conversation was able to befuddle the most powerful minds of his day. Plato, his devoted student, responded to Socratic teaching not, as one might suppose, by being intimidated but by becoming the greatest of philosophical writers, whose *Dialogues,* mostly featuring the character Socrates, form the foundation of all subsequent Western philosophy. Such a towering figure as Plato could have been expected to produce mere disciples, but, after studying with Plato for more than two decades, Aristotle developed his own comprehensive philosophical system, opposed in many respects to that of Plato, and so powerful in its own right that throughout history its impact has rivaled that of Plato. Surely Socrates and Plato were remarkable teachers as well as philosophers.

The *Defence of Socrates* (or *Apology* as it is sometimes titled) is an account of the trial of Socrates, who, after having been found guilty of impiety, was put to death by the Athenian democracy. Socrates' speech to the jury, as related by Plato, has come down through the ages as an eloquent defense of not only Socrates' life but also philosophy itself.

Are the words actually those Socrates spoke? Scholars disagree, but a plausible answer is provided by David Gallop, Professor Emeritus of Philosophy at Trent University in Ontario, Canada, the author of the translation from the Greek that we are using:

> [I]t is inconceivable that any speaker could have improvised before a real court such an artfully structured, nuanced, and polished composition as Plato's *Defence of Socrates.* That is not to say that the work falsifies any biographical facts about Socrates, still less that its content is wholly invented. For we all know to the contrary, it may even in some places faithfully reproduce what Socrates said in court. But whatever blend of fact and fiction it contains, the speech as a whole is a philosophical memoir, intended to convey a sense of Socrates' mission and the supreme injustice of his conviction. It remains, above all, an exhortation to the practice of philosophy. No less than Plato's dramatic dialogues, it is designed to draw its readers into philosophical reflection, so that they may recover for themselves the truths to which the master had borne witness.
>
> If that is the chief aim of the *Defence,* its fidelity to fact becomes a secondary issue.

To assist you in reading the *Defence,* Notes and an Index of Names prepared by the translator are provided at the end.

....

I don't know[1] how you, fellow Athenians, have been affected by my accusers, but for my part I felt myself almost transported by them, so persuasively did they speak. And yet hardly a word they have said is true. Among their many falsehoods, one especially astonished me: their warning that you must be careful not to be taken in by me, because I am a clever speaker. It seemed to me the height of impudence on their part not to be embarrassed at being refuted straight away by the facts, once it became apparent that I was not a clever speaker at all—unless indeed they call a "clever" speaker one who speaks the truth. If that is what they mean, then I would admit to being an orator, although not on a par with them.

As I said, then, my accusers have said little or nothing true; whereas from me you shall hear the whole truth, though not, I assure you, fellow Athenians, in language adorned with fine words and phrases or dressed up, as theirs was: you shall hear my points made spontaneously in whatever words occur to me—persuaded as I am that my case is just. None of you should expect anything to be put differently, because it would not, of course, be at all fitting at my age, gentlemen, to come before you with artificial speeches, such as might be composed by a young lad.

One thing, moreover, I would earnestly beg of you, fellow Athenians. If you hear me defending myself with the same arguments I normally use at the bankers' tables in the market-place (where many of you have heard me) and elsewhere, please do not be surprised or protest on that account. You see, here is the reason: This is the first time I have ever appeared before a court of law, although I am over 70; so I am literally a stranger to the diction of this place. And if I really were a foreigner, you would naturally excuse me, were I to speak in the dialect and style in which I had been brought up; so in the present case as well I ask you, in all fairness as I think, to disregard my manner of speaking—it may not be as good, or it may be better—but to consider and attend simply to the question whether or not my case is just; because that is the duty of a judge, as it is an orator's duty to speak the truth.

To begin with, fellow Athenians, it is fair that I should defend myself against the first set of charges falsely brought against me by my first accusers, and then turn to the later charges and the more recent ones. You see, I have been accused before you by many people for a long time now, for many years in fact, by people who spoke not a word of truth. It is those people I fear more than Anytus and his crowd, though they too are dangerous. But those others are more so, gentlemen: they have taken hold of most of you since childhood, and made persuasive accusations against me, yet without an ounce more truth in them. They say that there is one Socrates, a "wise man," who ponders what is above the earth and investigates everything beneath it, and turns the weaker argument into the stronger.[2]

Those accusers who have spread such rumour about me, fellow Athenians, are the dangerous ones, because their audience believes that people who inquire into those matters also fail to acknowledge the gods. Moreover, those accusers are numerous, and have been denouncing me for a long time now, and they also spoke to you at an age at which you would be most likely to believe them, when some of you were children or young lads; and their accusations simply went by default for lack of any defence. But the most absurd thing of all is that one cannot even get to know their names or say who they were—except perhaps one who happens to be a comic playwright.[3] The ones who have persuaded you by malicious slander, and also some who persuade others because they have been persuaded themselves, are all very hard to deal with: one cannot put any of them on the stand here in court, or cross-examine anybody, but one must literally engage in a sort of shadow-boxing to defend oneself, and cross-examine without anyone to answer. You too, then, should allow, as I just said, that I have two sets of accusers: one set who have accused me recently, and the other of long standing to whom I was just referring. And please grant that I need to defend myself against the latter first, since you too heard them accusing me earlier, and you heard far more from them than from these recent critics here.

Very well, then. I must defend myself, fellow Athenians, and in so short a time[4] must try to dispel the slander which you have had so long to absorb. That is the outcome I would wish for, should it be of any benefit to you and to me, and I should like to succeed in my defence—though I believe the task to be a difficult one, and am well aware of its nature. But let that turn out as God wills: I have to obey the law and present my defence.

Let us examine, from the beginning, the charge that has given rise to the slander against me—which was just what Meletus relied upon when he drew up this indictment. Very well then, what were my slanderers actually saying when they slandered me? Let me read out their deposition, as if they were my legal accusers:

"Socrates is guilty of being a busybody, in that he inquires into what is beneath the earth and in the sky, turns the weaker argument into the stronger, and teaches others to do the same."

The charges would run something like that. Indeed, you can see them for yourselves, enacted in Aristophanes' comedy: in that play, a character called "Socrates" swings around, claims to be walking on air,[5] and talks a lot of other nonsense on subjects of which I have no understanding, great or small.

Not that I mean to belittle knowledge of that sort, if anyone really is learned in such matters—no matter how many of Meletus' lawsuits I might have to defend myself against—but the fact is, fellow Athenians, those subjects are not my concern at all. I call most of you to witness yourselves, and I ask you to make that quite clear to one another, if you have ever heard me in discussion (as many of you have). Tell one another, then, whether any of you has ever heard me discussing such subjects, either briefly or at length; and as a result you will realize that the other things said about me by the public are equally baseless.

In any event, there is no truth in those charges. Moreover, if you have heard from anyone that I undertake to educate people and charge fees, there is no truth in that either—though for that matter I do think it also a fine thing if anyone *is* able to educate people, as Gorgias of Leontini, Prodicus of Ceos, and Hippias of Elis profess to. Each of them can visit any city, gentlemen, and persuade its young people, who may associate free of charge with any of their own citizens they wish, to leave those associations, and to join with them instead, paying fees and being grateful into the bargain.

On that topic, there is at present another expert here, a gentleman from Paros; I heard of his visit, because I happened to run into a man who has spent more money on sophists[6] than everyone else put together—Callias, the son of Hipponicus. So I questioned him, since he has two sons himself.

"Callias," I said, "if your two sons had been born as colts or calves, we could find and engage a tutor who could make them both excel superbly in the required qualities—and he'd be some sort of expert in horse-rearing or agriculture. But see-ing that they are actually human, whom do you intend to engage as their tutor? Who has knowledge of the required human and civic qualities? I ask, because I assume you've given thought to the matter, having sons yourself. Is there such a person," I asked, "or not?"

"Certainly," he replied.

"Who is he?" I said; "Where does he come from, and what does he charge for tuition?"

"His name is Evenus, Socrates," he replied; "He comes from Paros, and he charges 5 minas."[7]

I thought Evenus was to be congratulated, if he really did possess that skill and imparted it for such a modest charge. I, at any rate, would certainly be giving myself fine airs and graces if I possessed that knowledge. But the fact is, fellow Athenians, I do not.

Now perhaps one of you will interject: "Well then, Socrates, what is the dif-ficulty in your case? What is the source of these slanders against you? If you are not engaged in something out of the ordinary, why ever has so much rumour and talk arisen about you? It would surely never have arisen, unless you were up to some-thing different from most people. Tell us what it is, then, so that we don't jump to conclusions about you."

That speaker makes a fair point, I think; and so I will try to show you just what it is that has earned me my reputation and notoriety. Please hear me out. Some of you will perhaps think I am joking, but I assure you that I shall be telling you the whole truth.

You see, fellow Athenians, I have gained this reputation on account of nothing but a certain sort of wisdom. And what sort of wisdom is that? It is a human kind of wisdom, perhaps, since it might just be true that I have wisdom of that sort. Maybe the people I just mentioned possess wisdom of a superhuman kind; oth-erwise I cannot explain it. For my part, I certainly do not possess that knowledge; and whoever says I do is lying and speaking with a view to slandering me.

Now please do not protest, fellow Athenians, even if I should sound to you rather boastful. I am not myself the source of the story I am about to tell you, but I shall refer you to a trustworthy authority. As evidence of my wisdom, if such it actually be, and of its nature, I shall call to witness before you the god at Delphi.[8]

You remember Chaerephon, of course. He was a friend of mine from youth, and also a comrade in your party, who shared your recent exile and restoration.[9] You recall too what sort of man Chaerephon was, how impetuous he was in any undertaking. Well, on one occasion he actually went to the Delphic oracle, and had the audacity to put the following question to it—as I said, please do not make a disturbance, gentlemen—he went and asked if there was anyone wiser than myself, to which the Pythia responded that there was no one. His brother here will testify to the court about that story, since Chaerephon himself is deceased.

Now keep in mind why I have been telling you this: it is because I am going to explain to you the origin of the slander against me. When I heard the story,

I thought to myself: "What ever is the god saying? What can his riddle mean? Since I am all too conscious of not being wise in any matter, great or small, what ever can he mean by pronouncing me to be the wisest? Surely he cannot be lying: For him that would be out of the question."

So for a long time I was perplexed about what he could possibly mean. But then, with great reluctance, I proceeded to investigate the matter somewhat as follows. I went to one of the people who had a reputation for wisdom, thinking there, if anywhere, to disprove the oracle's utterance and declare to it: "Here is someone wiser than I am, and yet you said that I was the wisest."

So I interviewed this person—I need not mention his name, but he was someone in public life; and when I examined him, my experience went something like this, fellow Athenians: in conversing with him, I formed the opinion that, although the man was thought to be wise by many other people, and especially by himself, yet in reality he was not. So I then tried to show him that he thought himself wise without being so. I thereby earned his dislike, and that of many people present; but still, as I went away, I thought to myself: "I am wiser than that fellow, anyhow. Because neither of us, I dare say, knows anything of great value; but he thinks he knows a thing when he doesn't; whereas I neither know it in fact, nor think that I do. At any rate, it appears that I am wiser than he in just this one small respect: if I do not know something, I do not think that I do."

Next, I went to someone else, among people thought to be even wiser than the previous man, and I came to the same conclusion again; and so I was disliked by that man too, as well as by many others.

Well, after that I went on to visit one person after another. I realized, with dismay and alarm, that I was making enemies; but even so, I thought it my duty to attach the highest importance to the god's business; and therefore, in seeking the oracle's meaning, I had to go on to examine all those with any reputation for knowledge. And upon my word,[10] fellow Athenians—because I am obliged to speak the truth before the court—I truly did experience something like this: As I pursued the god's inquiry, I found those held in the highest esteem were practically the most defective, whereas men who were supposed to be their inferiors were much better off in respect of understanding.

Let me, then, outline my wanderings for you, the various "labours" I kept undertaking,[11] only to find that the oracle proved completely irrefutable. After I had done with the politicians, I turned to the poets—including tragedians, dithyrambic poets,[12] and the rest—thinking that in their company I would be shown up as more ignorant than they were. So I picked up the poems over which I thought they had taken the most trouble, and questioned them about their meaning, so that I might also learn something from them in the process.

Now I'm embarrassed to tell you the truth, gentlemen, but it has to be said. Practically everyone else present could speak better than the poets themselves about their very own compositions. And so, once more, I soon realized this truth about them too: it was not from wisdom that they composed their works, but from a certain natural aptitude and inspiration, like that of seers and sooth-sayers—because those people too utter many fine words, yet know nothing of the matters on which they pronounce. It was obvious to me that the poets were in much the same situation; yet at the same time I realized that because of their compositions they thought themselves the wisest people in other matters as well, when they were not. So I left, believing that I was ahead of them in the same way as I was ahead of the politicians.

Then, finally, I went to the craftsmen, because I was conscious of knowing almost nothing myself, but felt sure that amongst them, at least, I would find much valuable knowledge. And in that expectation I was not disappointed: They did have knowledge in fields where I had none, and in that respect they were wiser than I. And yet, fellow Athenians, those able craftsmen seemed to me to suffer from the same failing as the poets: because of their excellence at their own trade, each claimed to be a great expert also on matters of the utmost importance; and this arrogance of theirs seemed to eclipse their wisdom. So I began to ask myself, on the oracle's behalf, whether I should prefer to be as I am, neither wise as they are wise, nor ignorant as they are ignorant, or to possess both their attributes; and in reply, I told myself and the oracle that I was better off as I was.

The effect of this questioning, fellow Athenians, was to earn me much hostility of a very vexing and trying sort, which has given rise to numerous slanders, including this reputation I have for being "wise"—because those present on each occasion imagine me to be wise regarding the matters on which I examine others. But in fact, gentlemen, it would appear that it is only the god who is truly wise; and that he is saying to us, through this oracle, that human wisdom is worth little or nothing. It seems that when he says "Socrates," he makes use of my name, merely taking me as an example—as if to say, "The wisest amongst you, human beings, is anyone like Socrates who has recognized that with respect to wisdom he is truly worthless."

That is why, even to this day, I still go about seeking out and searching into anyone I believe to be wise, citizen or foreigner, in obedience to the god. Then, as soon as I find that someone is not wise, I assist the god by proving that he is not. Because of this occupation, I have had no time at all for any activity to speak of, either in public affairs or in my family life; indeed, because of my service to the god, I live in extreme poverty.

In addition, the young people who follow me around of their own accord, the ones who have plenty of leisure because their parents are wealthiest, enjoy listening to people being cross-examined. Often, too, they copy my example themselves, and so attempt to cross-examine others. And I imagine that they find a great abundance of people who suppose themselves to possess some knowledge, but really know little or nothing. Consequently, the people they question are angry with me, though not with themselves, and say that there is a nasty pestilence abroad called "Socrates," who is corrupting the young.

Then, when asked just what he is doing or teaching, they have nothing to say, because they have no idea what he does; yet, rather than seem at a loss, they resort to the stock charges against all who pursue intellectual inquiry, trotting out "things in the sky and beneath the earth," "failing to acknowledge the gods," and "turning the weaker argument into the stronger." They would, I imagine, be loath to admit the truth, which is that their pretensions to knowledge have been exposed, and they are totally ignorant. So because these people have reputations to protect, I suppose, and are also both passionate and numerous, and have been speaking about me in a vigorous and persuasive style, they have long been filling your ears with vicious slander. It is on the strength of all this that Meletus, along with Anytus and Lycon, has proceeded against me: Meletus is aggrieved for the poets, Anytus for the craftsmen and politicians, and Lycon for the orators. And so, as I began by saying, I should be surprised if I could rid your minds of this slander in so short a time, when so much of it has accumulated.

There is the truth for you, fellow Athenians. I have spoken it without concealing anything from you, major or minor, and without glossing over anything. And yet I am virtually certain that it is my very candour that makes enemies for me—which goes to show that I am right: The slander against me is to that effect, and such is its explanation. And whether you look for one now or later, that is what you will find.

So much for my defence before you against the charges brought by my first group of accusers. Next, I shall try to defend myself against Meletus, good patriot that he claims to be, and against my more recent critics. So once again, as if they were a fresh set of accusers, let me in turn review their deposition. It runs something like this:

"Socrates is guilty of corrupting the young, and of failing to acknowledge the gods acknowledged by the city, but introducing new spiritual beings instead."

Such is the charge: let us examine each item within it.

Meletus says, then, that I am guilty of corrupting the young. Well I reply, fellow Athenians, that Meletus is guilty of trifling in a serious matter, in that he brings people to trial on frivolous grounds, and professes grave concern about matters for which he has never cared at all. I shall now try to prove to you too that that is so.

Step forward, Meletus, and answer me. It is your chief concern, is it not, that our younger people shall be as good as possible?

—It is.

Very well, will you please tell the judges who influences them for the better—because you must obviously know, seeing that you care? Having discovered me, as you allege, to be the one who is corrupting them, you bring me before the judges here and accuse me. So speak up, and tell the court who has an improving influence.

You see, Meletus, you remain silent and have no answer. Yet doesn't that strike you as shameful, and as proof in itself of exactly what I say—that you have never cared about these matters at all? Come then, good fellow, tell us who influences them for the better.

—The laws.

Yes, but that is not what I'm asking, excellent fellow. I mean, which *person*, who already knows the laws to begin with?

—These gentlemen, the judges, Socrates.

What are you saying, Meletus? Can these people educate the young, and do they have an improving influence?

—Most certainly.

All of them, or some but not others?

—All of them.

My goodness, what welcome news, and what a generous supply of benefactors you speak of! And how about the audience here in court? Do they too have an improving influence, or not?

—Yes, they do too.

And how about members of the Council?[13]

—Yes, the Councillors too.

But in that case, how about people in the Assembly, its individual members, Meletus? They won't be corrupting their youngers, will they? Won't they all be good influences as well?

—Yes, they will too.

So every person in Athens, it would appear, has an excellent influence on them except for me, whereas I alone am corrupting them. Is that what you're saying?

—That is emphatically what I'm saying.

Then I find myself, if we are to believe you, in a most awkward predicament. Now answer me this. Do you think the same is true of horses? Is it everybody who improves them, while a single person spoils them? Or isn't the opposite true: A single person, or at least very few people, namely the horse-trainers, can improve them; while lay people spoil them, don't they, if they have to do with horses and make use of them? Isn't that true of horses as of all other animals, Meletus? Of course it is, whether you and Anytus deny it or not. In fact, I dare say our young people are extremely lucky if only one person is corrupting them, while everyone else is doing them good.

All right, Meletus. Enough has been said to prove that you never were concerned about the young. You betray your irresponsibility plainly, because you have not cared at all about the charges on which you bring me before this court.

Furthermore, Meletus, tell us, in God's name, whether it is better to live among good fellow citizens or bad ones. Come sir, answer: I am not asking a hard question. Bad people have a harmful impact upon their closest companions at any given time, don't they, whereas good people have a good one?

—Yes.

Well, is there anyone who wants to be harmed by his companions rather than benefited?—Be a good fellow and keep on answering, as the law requires you to. Is there anyone who wants to be harmed?

—Of course not.

Now tell me this. In bringing me here, do you claim that I am corrupting and depraving the young intentionally or unintentionally?

—Intentionally, so I maintain.

Really, Meletus? Are you so much smarter at your age than I at mine as to realize that the bad have a harmful impact upon their closest companions at any given time, whereas the good have a beneficial effect? Am I, by contrast, so far gone in my stupidity as not to realize that if I make one of my companions vicious, I risk incurring harm at his hands? And am I, therefore, as you allege, doing so much damage intentionally?

That I cannot accept from you, Meletus, and neither could anyone else, I imagine. Either I am not corrupting them—or if I am, I am doing so unintentionally;[14] so either way your charge is false. But if I am corrupting them unintentionally, the law does not require me to be brought to court for such mistakes, but rather to be taken aside for private instruction and admonition—since I shall obviously stop doing unintentional damage, if I learn better. But you avoided association with me and were unwilling to instruct me. Instead you bring me to court, where the law requires you to bring people who need punishment rather than enlightenment.

Very well, fellow Athenians. That part of my case is now proven: Meletus never cared about these matters, either a lot or a little. Nevertheless, Meletus, please tell us in what way you claim that I am corrupting our younger people. That is quite obvious, isn't it, from the indictment you drew up? It is by teaching them not to acknowledge the gods acknowledged by the city, but to accept new spiritual beings instead? You mean, don't you, that I am corrupting them by teaching them that?

—I most emphatically do.

Then, Meletus, in the name of those very gods we are now discussing, please clarify the matter further for me, and for the jury here. You see, I cannot make out what you mean. Is it that I am teaching people to acknowledge that some gods exist—in which case it follows that I do acknowledge their existence myself as well and am not a complete atheist, hence am not guilty on that count—and yet that those gods are not the ones acknowledged by the city, but different ones? Is that your charge against me—namely, that they are different? Or are you saying that I acknowledge no gods at all myself and teach the same to others?

—I am saying the latter: you acknowledge no gods at all.

What ever makes you say that, Meletus, you strange fellow? Do I not even acknowledge, then, with the rest of mankind, that the sun and the moon are gods?[15]

—By God, he does not, members of the jury, since he claims that the sun is made of rock, and the moon of earth!

My dear Meletus, do you imagine that it is Anaxagoras you are accusing?[16] Do you have such contempt for the jury, and imagine them so illiterate as not to know that books by Anaxagoras of Clazomenae are crammed with such assertions? What's more, are the young learning those things from me when they can acquire them at the bookstalls, now and then, for a drachma at most, and so ridicule Socrates if he claims those ideas for his own, especially when they are so bizarre? In God's name, do you really think me as crazy as that? Do I acknowledge the existence of no god at all?

—By God no, none whatever.

I can't believe you, Meletus—nor, I think, can you believe yourself. To my mind, fellow Athenians, this fellow is an impudent scoundrel who has framed this indictment out of sheer wanton impudence and insolence. He seems to have devised a sort of riddle in order to try me out: "Will Socrates the Wise tumble to my nice self-contradiction?[17] Or shall I fool him along with my other listeners?" You see, he seems to me to be contradicting himself in the indictment. It's as if he were saying: "Socrates is guilty of not acknowledging gods, but of acknowledging gods"; and yet that is sheer tomfoolery.

I ask you to examine with me, gentlemen, just how that appears to be his meaning. Answer for us, Meletus; and the rest of you, please remember my initial request not to protest if I conduct the argument in my usual manner.

Is there anyone in the world, Meletus, who acknowledges that human phenomena exist, yet does not acknowledge human beings?—Require him to answer, gentlemen, and not to raise all kinds of confused objections. Is there anyone who does not acknowledge horses, yet does acknowledge equestrian phenomena? Or who does not acknowledge that musicians exist, yet does acknowledge musical phenomena?

There is no one, excellent fellow: if you don't wish to answer, I must answer for you, and for the jurors here. But at least answer my next question yourself. Is there anyone who acknowledges that spiritual phenomena exist, yet does not acknowledge spirits?

—No.

How good of you to answer—albeit reluctantly and under compulsion from the jury. Well now, you say that I acknowledge spiritual beings and teach others to do so. Whether they actually be new or old is no matter: I do at any rate, by your account, acknowledge spiritual beings, which you have also mentioned in your sworn deposition. But if I acknowledge spiritual beings, then surely it follows quite inevitably that I must acknowledge spirits. Is that not so?—Yes, it is so: I assume your agreement, since you don't answer. But we regard spirits, don't we, as either gods or children of gods? Yes or no?

—Yes.

Then given that I do believe in spirits, as you say, if spirits are gods of some sort, this is precisely what I claim when I say that you are presenting us with a riddle and making fun of us: you are saying that I do not believe in gods, and yet again that I do believe in gods, seeing that I believe in spirits.

On the other hand, if spirits are children of gods,[18] some sort of bastard offspring from nymphs—or from whomever they are traditionally said, in each case, to be born—then who in the world could ever believe that there were children of gods, yet no gods? That would be just as absurd as accepting the existence of children of horses and asses—namely, mules—yet rejecting the existence of horses or asses!

In short, Meletus, you can only have drafted this either by way of trying us out, or because you were at a loss how to charge me with a genuine offense. How could you possibly persuade anyone with even the slightest intelligence that someone who accepts spiritual beings does not also accept divine ones, and again that the same person also accepts neither spirits nor gods nor heroes? There is no conceivable way.

But enough, fellow Athenians. It needs no long defence, I think, to show that I am not guilty of the charges in Meletus' indictment; the foregoing will suffice. You may be sure, though, that what I was saying earlier is true: I have earned great hostility among many people. And that is what will convict me, if I am convicted: not Meletus or Anytus, but the slander and malice of the crowd. They have certainly convicted many other good men as well, and I imagine they will do so again; there is no risk of their stopping with me.

Now someone may perhaps say: "Well then, are you not ashamed, Socrates, to have pursued a way of life which has now put you at risk of death?"

But it may be fair for me to answer him as follows: "You are sadly mistaken, fellow, if you suppose that a man with even a grain of self-respect should reckon up the risks of living or dying, rather than simply consider, whenever he does something, whether his actions are just or unjust, the deeds of a good man or a bad one." By your principles, presumably, all those demigods who died in the plain of Troy[19] were inferior creatures—yes, even the son of Thetis,[20] who showed so much scorn for danger, when the alternative was to endure dishonour. Thus, when he was eager to slay Hector, his mother, goddess that she was, spoke to him—something like this, I fancy:

My child, if thou dost avenge the murder of thy friend, Patroclus,
And dost slay Hector, then straightway [so runs the poem]
Shalt thou die thyself, since doom is prepared for thee
Next after Hector's.

But though he heard that, he made light of death and danger, since he feared far more to live as a base man, and to fail to avenge his dear ones. The poem goes on:

Then straightway let me die, once I have given the wrongdoer
His deserts, lest I remain here by the beak-prowed ships,
An object of derision, and a burden upon the earth.

Can you suppose that he gave any thought to death or danger?

You see, here is the truth of the matter, fellow Athenians. Wherever a man has taken up a position because he considers it best, or has been posted there by his commander, that is where I believe he should remain, steadfast in danger, taking no account at all of death or of anything else rather than dishonour. I would therefore have been acting absurdly, fellow Athenians, if, when assigned to a post at Potidaea, Amphipolis, or Delium[21] by the superiors you had elected to command me, I remained where I was posted on those occasions at the risk of death, if ever any man did; whereas now that the god assigns me, as I became completely convinced, to the duty of leading the philosophical life by examining myself and others, I desert that post from fear of death or anything else. Yes, that would be unthinkable; and then I truly should deserve to be brought to court for failing to acknowledge the gods' existence, in that I was disobedient to the oracle, was afraid of death, and thought I was wise when I was not.

After all, gentlemen, the fear of death amounts simply to thinking one is wise when one is not: it is thinking one knows something one does not know. No one knows, you see, whether death may not in fact prove the greatest of all blessings for mankind; but people fear it as if they knew it for certain to be the greatest of evils. And yet to think that one knows what one does not know must surely be the kind of folly which is reprehensible.

On this matter especially, gentlemen, that may be the nature of my own advantage over most people. If I really were to claim to be wiser than anyone in any respect, it would consist simply in this: just as I do not possess adequate knowledge of life in Hades, so I also realize that I do not possess it; whereas acting unjustly in disobedience to one's betters, whether god or human being, is something I *know* to be evil and shameful. Hence I shall never fear or flee from something which may indeed be a good for all I know, rather than from things I know to be evils.

Suppose, therefore, that you pay no heed to Anytus, but are prepared to let me go. He said I need never have been brought to court in the first place; but that once I had been, your only option was to put me to death. He declared before you that, if I got away from you this time, your sons would all be utterly corrupted by practising Socrates' teachings. Suppose, in the face of that, you were to say to me:

"Socrates, we will not listen to Anytus this time. We are prepared to let you go—but only on this condition: you are to pursue that quest of yours and practise philosophy no longer; and if you are caught doing it any more, you shall be put to death."

Well, as I just said, if you were prepared to let me go on those terms, I should reply to you as follows:

"I have the greatest fondness and affection for you, fellow Athenians, but I will obey my god rather than you; and so long as I draw breath and am able, I shall never give up practising philosophy, or exhorting and showing the way to any of you whom I ever encounter, by giving my usual sort of message. 'Excellent friend,' I shall say; 'You are an Athenian. Your city is the most important and renowned for its wisdom and power; so are you not ashamed that, while you take care to acquire as much wealth as possible, with honour and glory as well, yet you take no care or thought for understanding or truth, or for the best possible state of your soul?'

"And should any of you dispute that, and claim that he does take such care, I will not let him go straight away nor leave him, but I will question and examine and put him to the test; and if I do not think he has acquired goodness, though he says he has, I shall say, 'Shame on you, for setting the lowest value upon the most precious things, and for rating inferior ones more highly!' That I shall do for anyone I encounter, young or old, alien or fellow citizen; but all the more for the latter, since your kinship with me is closer."

Those are my orders from my god, I do assure you. Indeed, I believe that no greater good has ever befallen you in our city than my service to my god; because all I do is to go about persuading you, young and old alike, not to care for your bodies or for your wealth so intensely as for the greatest possible well-being of your souls. "It is not wealth," I tell you, "that produces goodness; rather, it is from goodness that wealth, and all other benefits for human beings, accrue to them in their private and public life."

If, in fact, I am corrupting the young by those assertions, you may call them harmful. But if anyone claims that I say anything different, he is talking nonsense. In the face of that I should like to say: "Fellow Athenians, you may listen to Anytus or not, as you please; and you may let me go or not, as you please, because there is no chance of my acting otherwise, even if I have to die many times over."

Stop protesting, fellow Athenians! Please abide by my request that you not protest against what I say, but hear me out; in fact, it will be in your interest, so I believe, to do so. You see, I am going to say some further things to you which may make you shout out—although I beg you not to.

You may be assured that if you put to death the sort of man I just said I was, you will not harm me more than you harm yourselves. Meletus or Anytus would not harm me at all; nor, in fact, could they do so, since I believe it is out of the question for a better man to be harmed by his inferior. The latter may, of course, inflict death or banishment or disenfranchisement; and my accuser here, along with others no doubt, believes those to be great evils. But I do not. Rather, I believe it a far greater evil to try to kill a man unjustly, as he does now.

At this point, therefore, fellow Athenians, so far from pleading on my own behalf, as might be supposed, I am pleading on yours, in case by condemning me you should mistreat the gift which God has bestowed upon you—because if you put me to death, you will not easily find another like me. The fact is, if I may put the point in a somewhat comical way, that I have been literally attached by God to our city, as if to a horse—a large thoroughbred, which is a bit sluggish because of its size, and needs to be aroused by some sort of gadfly. Yes, in me, I believe, God has attached to our city just such a creature—the kind which is constantly alighting everywhere on you, all day long, arousing, cajoling, or reproaching each and every one of you. You will not easily acquire another such gadfly, gentlemen; rather, if you take my advice, you will spare my life. I dare say, though, that you will get angry, like people who are awakened from their doze. Perhaps you will heed Anytus and give me a swat: you could happily finish me off, and then spend the rest of your life asleep—unless God, in his compassion for you, were to send you someone else.

That I am, in fact, just the sort of gift that God would send to our city, you may recognize from this: it would not seem to be in human nature for me to have neglected all my own affairs, and put up with the neglect of my family for all these years, but constantly minded your interests, by visiting each of you in private like a father or an elder brother, urging you to be concerned about goodness. Of course, if I were gaining anything from that, or were being paid to urge that course upon you, my actions could be explained. But in fact you can see for yourselves that my accusers, who so shamelessly level all those other charges against me, could not muster the impudence to call evidence that I ever once obtained payment or asked for any. It is I who can call evidence sufficient, I think, to show that I am speaking the truth—namely, my poverty.

Now it may perhaps seem peculiar that, as some say, I give this counsel by going around and dealing with others' concerns in private, yet do not venture to appear before the Assembly, and counsel the city about your business in public. But the reason for that is one you have frequently heard me give in many places: it is a certain divine or spiritual sign[22] which comes to me, the very thing to which Meletus made mocking allusion in his indictment. It has been happening to me ever since childhood: a voice of some sort which comes and which always— whenever it does come—restrains me from what I am about to do, yet never gives positive direction. That is what opposes my engaging in politics—and its opposition is an excellent thing, to my mind; because you may be quite sure, fellow Athenians, that if I had tried to engage in politics, I should have perished long since and should have been of no use either to you or to myself.

And please do not get angry if I tell you the truth. The fact is that there is no person on earth whose life will be spared by you or by any other majority, if he is genuinely opposed to many injustices and unlawful acts and tries to prevent their occurrence in our city. Rather, anyone who truly fights for what is just, if he is going to survive for even a short time, must act in a private capacity rather than a public one.

I will offer you conclusive evidence of that—not just words, but the sort of evidence that you respect, namely, actions. Just hear me tell my experiences, so that you may know that I would not submit to a single person for fear of death, contrary to what is just; nor would I do so, even if I were to lose my life on the spot. I shall mention things to you which are vulgar commonplaces of the courts, yet they are true.

Although I have never held any other public office in our city, fellow Athenians, I have served on its Council. My own tribe, Antiochis, happened to be the presiding commission[23] on the occasion when you wanted a collective trial for the ten generals who had failed to rescue the survivors from the naval battle.[24] That was illegal, as you all later recognized. At the time I was the only commissioner opposed to your acting illegally, and I voted against the motion. And though its advocates were prepared to lay information against me and have me arrested, while you were urging them on by shouting, I believed that I should face danger in siding with law and justice, rather than take your side for fear of imprisonment or death, when your proposals were contrary to justice.

Those events took place while our city was still under democratic rule. But on a subsequent occasion, after the oligarchy had come to power, the Thirty summoned me and four others to the round chamber,[25] with orders to arrest Leon the Salaminian and fetch him from Salamis[26] for execution; they were constantly issuing such orders, of course, to many others, in their wish to implicate as many as possible in their crimes. On that occasion, however, I showed, once again not just by words but by my actions, that I couldn't care less about death—if that would not be putting it rather crudely—but that my one and only care was to avoid doing anything sinful or unjust. Thus, powerful as it was, that regime did not frighten me into unjust action: when we emerged from the round chamber, the other four went off to Salamis and arrested Leon, whereas I left them and went off home. For that I might easily have been put to death, had the regime not collapsed shortly afterwards. There are many witnesses who will testify before you about those events.

Do you imagine, then, that I would have survived all these years if I had been regularly active in public life and had championed what was right in a manner worthy of a brave man, and valued that above all else, as was my duty? Far from it, fellow Athenians: I would not, and nor would any other man. But in any public undertaking, that is the sort of person that I, for my part, shall prove to have been throughout my life; and likewise in my private life, because I have never been guilty of unjust association with anyone, including those whom my slanderers allege to have been my students.[27]

I never, in fact, was anyone's instructor[28] at any time. But if a person wanted to hear me talking, while I was engaging in my own business, I never grudged that to anyone, young or old; nor do I hold conversation only when I receive payment, and not otherwise. Rather, I offer myself for questioning to wealthy and poor alike, and to anyone who may wish to answer in response to questions from me. Whether any of those people acquires a good character or not, I cannot fairly be held responsible, when I never at any time promised any of them that they would learn anything from me, nor gave them instruction. And if anyone claims that he ever learnt anything from me, or has heard privately something that everyone else did not hear as well, you may be sure that what he says is untrue.

Why then, you may ask, do some people enjoy spending so much time in my company? You have already heard, fellow Athenians: I have told you the whole truth—which is that my listeners enjoy the examination of those who think themselves wise but are not, since the process is not unamusing. But for me, I must tell you, it is a mission which I have been bidden to undertake by the god, through oracles and dreams[29] and through every means whereby a divine injunction to perform any task has ever been laid upon a human being.

That is not only true, fellow Athenians, but is easily verified—because if I do corrupt any of our young people, or have corrupted others in the past, then presumably, when they grew older, should any of them have realized that I had at any time given them bad advice in their youth, they ought now to have appeared here themselves to accuse me and obtain redress. Or else, if they were unwilling to come in person, members of their families—fathers, brothers, or other relations—had their relatives suffered any harm at my hands, ought now to put it on record and obtain redress.

In any case, many of those people are present, whom I can see: first there is Crito, my contemporary and fellow demesman, father of Critobulus here; then Lysanias of Sphettus, father of Aeschines here; next, Epigenes' father, Antiphon from Cephisia, is present; then again, there are others here whose brothers have spent time with me in these studies: Nicostratus, son of Theozotides, brother of Theodotus—Theodotus himself, incidentally, is deceased, so Nicostratus could not have come at his brother's urging; and Paralius here, son of Demodocus, whose brother was Theages; also present is Ariston's son, Adimantus, whose brother is Plato here; and Aeantodorus, whose brother is Apollodorus here.

There are many others I could mention to you, from whom Meletus should surely have called some testimony during his own speech. However, if he forgot to do so then, let him call it now—I yield the floor to him—and if he has any such evidence, let him produce it. But quite the opposite is true, gentlemen: you will find that they are all prepared to support me, their corruptor, the one who is, according to Meletus and Anytus, doing their relatives mischief. Support for me from the actual victims of corruption might perhaps be explained; but what of the uncorrupted—older men by now, and relatives of my victims? What reason would they have to support me, apart from the right and proper one, which is that they know very well that Meletus is lying, whereas I am telling the truth?

There it is, then, gentlemen. That, and perhaps more of the same, is about all I have to say in my defence. But perhaps, among your number, there may be some-one who will harbour resentment when he recalls a case of his own: he may have faced a less serious trial than this one, yet begged and implored the jury, weeping copiously, and producing his children here, along with many other relatives and loved ones, to gain as much sympathy as possible. By contrast, I shall do none of those things, even though I am running what might be considered the ultimate risk. Perhaps someone with those thoughts will harden his heart against me; and enraged by those same thoughts, he may cast his vote against me in anger. Well, if any of you are so inclined—not that I expect it of you, but if anyone *should* be—I think it fair to answer him as follows:

"I naturally do have relatives, my excellent friend, because—in Homer's own words—I too was 'not born of oak nor of rock,' but of human parents; and so I do have relatives—including my sons,[30] fellow Athenians. There are three of them: one is now a youth, while two are still children. Nevertheless, I shall not produce any of them here, and then entreat you to vote for my acquittal."

And why, you may ask, will I do no such thing? Not out of contempt or disre-spect for you, fellow Athenians—whether or not I am facing death boldly is a dif-ferent issue. The point is that with our reputations in mind—yours and our whole city's, as well as my own—I believe that any such behaviour would be ignominious, at my age and with the reputation I possess; that reputation may or may not, in fact, be deserved, but at least it is believed that Socrates stands out in some way from the run of human beings. Well, if those of you who are believed to be pre-eminent in wisdom, courage, or any other form of goodness are going to behave like that, it would be demeaning.

I have frequently seen such men when they face judgment: they have sig-nificant reputations, yet they put on astonishing performances, apparently in the belief that by dying they will suffer something unheard of—as if they would be immune from death, so long as you did not kill them! They seem to me to put our city to shame: they could give any foreigner the impression that men preeminent among Athenians in goodness, whom they select from their own number to govern and hold other positions, are no better than women.[31] I say this, fellow Athenians, because none of us who has even the slightest reputation should behave like that; nor should you put up with us if we try to do so. Rather, you should make one thing clear: you will be far more inclined to convict one who stages those pathetic charades and makes our city an object of derision than one who keeps his composure.

But leaving reputation aside, gentlemen, I do not think it right to entreat the jury, nor to win acquittal in that way, instead of by informing and persuading them. A juror does not sit to dispense justice as a favour, but to determine where it lies. And he has sworn, not that he will favour whomever he pleases, but that he will try the case according to law. We should not, then, accustom you to transgress your oath, nor should you become accustomed to doing so: neither of us would be showing respect towards the gods. And therefore, fellow Athenians, do not require behaviour from me towards you which I consider neither proper nor right nor pious—more especially now, for God's sake, when I stand charged by Meletus here with impiety: because if I tried to persuade and coerce you with entreaties in spite of your oath, I clearly *would* be teaching you not to believe in gods; and I would stand literally self-convicted, by my defence, of failing to acknowledge them. But that is far from the truth: I do acknowledge them, fellow Athenians, as none of my accusers do; and I trust to you, and to God, to judge my case as shall be best for me and for yourselves.

For many reasons, fellow Athenians, I am not dismayed by this outcome[32]—your convicting me, I mean—and especially because the outcome has come as no surprise to me. I wonder far more at the number of votes cast on each side, because I did not think the margin would be so narrow. Yet it seems, in fact, that if a mere thirty votes had gone the other way, I should have been acquitted.[33] Or rather, even as things stand, I consider that I have been cleared of Meletus' charges. Not only that, but one thing is obvious to everyone: if Anytus had not come forward with Lycon to accuse me, Meletus would have forfeited 1,000 drachmas, since he would not have gained one-fifth of the votes cast.

But anyhow, this gentleman demands the death penalty for me. Very well, then: what alternative penalty[34] shall I suggest to you, fellow Athenians? Clearly, it must be one I deserve. So what do I deserve to incur or to pay, for having taken it into my head not to lead an inactive life? Instead, I have neglected the things that concern most people—making money, managing an estate, gaining military or civic honours, or other positions of power, or joining political clubs and parties which have formed in our city. I thought myself, in truth, too honest to survive if I engaged in those things. I did not pursue a course, therefore, in which I would be of no use to you or to myself. Instead, by going to each individual privately, I tried to render a service for you which is—so I maintain—the highest service of all. Therefore that was the course I followed: I tried to persuade each of you not to care for any of his possessions rather than care for himself, striving for the utmost excellence and understanding; and not to care for our city's possessions rather than for the city itself; and to care about other things in the same way.

So what treatment do I deserve for being such a benefactor? If I am to make a proposal truly in keeping with my deserts, fellow Athenians, it should be some benefit; and moreover, the sort of benefit that would be fitting for me. Well then, what *is* fitting for a poor man who is a benefactor, and who needs time free for exhorting you? Nothing could be more fitting, fellow Athenians, than to give such a man regular free meals in the Prytaneum;[35] indeed, that is far more fitting for him than for any of you who may have won an Olympic race with a pair or a team of horses: that victory brings you only the appearance of success, whereas I bring you the reality; besides, he is not in want of sustenance, whereas I am. So if, as justice demands, I am to make a proposal in keeping with my deserts, that is what I suggest: free meals in the Prytaneum.

Now, in proposing this, I may seem to you, as when I talked about appeals for sympathy, to be speaking from sheer effrontery. But actually I have no such motive, fellow Athenians. My point is rather this: I am convinced that I do not treat any human being unjustly, at least intentionally—but I cannot make you share that conviction, because we have conversed together so briefly. I say this, because if it were the law here, as in other jurisdictions, that a capital case must not be tried in a single day, but over several,[36] I think you could have been convinced; but as things stand, it is not easy to clear oneself of such grave allegations in a short time.

Since, therefore, I am persuaded, for my part, that I have treated no one unjustly, I have no intention whatever of so treating myself, nor of denouncing myself as deserving ill, or proposing any such treatment for myself. Why should I do that? For fear of the penalty Meletus demands for me, when I say that I don't know if that is a good thing or a bad one? In preference to that, am I then to choose one of the things I know very well to be bad, and demand that instead? Imprisonment, for instance? Why should I live in prison, in servitude to the annually appointed prison commissioners? Well then, a fine, with imprisonment until I pay? That would amount to what I just mentioned, since I haven't the means to pay it.

Well then, should I propose banishment? Perhaps that is what you would propose for me. Yet I must surely be obsessed with survival, fellow Athenians, if I am so illogical as that. You, my fellow citizens, were unable to put up with my discourses and arguments, but they were so irksome and odious to you that you now seek to be rid of them. Could I not draw the inference, in that case, that others will hardly take kindly to them? Far from it, fellow Athenians. A fine life it would be for a person of my age to go into exile, and spend his days continually exchanging one city for another, and being repeatedly expelled—because I know very well that wherever I go, the young will come to hear me speaking, as they do here. And if I repel them, they will expel me themselves, by persuading their elders; while if I do not repel them, their fathers and relatives will expel me on their account.

Now, perhaps someone may say: "Socrates, could you not be so kind as to keep quiet and remain inactive, while living in exile?" This is the hardest point of all of which to convince some of you. Why? Because, if I tell you that that would mean disobeying my god, and that is why I cannot remain inactive, you will disbelieve me and think that I am practising a sly evasion. Again, if I said that it really is the greatest benefit for a person to converse every day about goodness, and about the other subjects you have heard me discussing when examining myself and others—and that an unexamined life is no life for a human being to live—then you would believe me still less when I made those assertions. But the facts, gentlemen, are just as I claim them to be, though it is not easy to convince you of them. At the same time, I am not accustomed to think of myself as deserving anything bad. If I had money, I would have proposed a fine of as much as I could afford: that would have done me no harm at all. But the fact is that I have none—unless you wish to fix the penalty at a sum I could pay. I could afford to pay you 1 mina, I suppose, so I suggest a fine of that amount—

One moment, fellow Athenians. Plato here, along with Crito, Critobulus, and Apollodorus, is urging me to propose 30 minas,[37] and they are saying they will stand surety for that sum. So I propose a fine of that amount, and these people shall be your sufficient guarantors of its payment.

For the sake of a slight gain in time, fellow Athenians, you will incur infamy and blame from those who would denigrate our city, for putting Socrates to death[38]—a "wise man"—because those who wish to malign you will say I am wise, even if I am not; in any case, had you waited only a short time, you would have obtained that outcome automatically. You can see, of course, that I am now well advanced in life, and death is not far off. I address that not to all of you, but to those who condemned me to death; and to those same people I would add something further.

Perhaps you imagine, gentlemen, that I have been convicted for lack of arguments of the sort I could have used to convince you, had I believed that I should do or say anything to gain acquittal. But that is far from true. I have been convicted, not for lack of arguments, but for lack of brazen impudence and willingness to address you in such terms as you would most like to be addressed in—that is to say, by weeping and wailing, and doing and saying much else that I claim to be unworthy of me—the sorts of thing that you are so used to hearing from others. But just as I did not think during my defence that I should do anything unworthy of a free man because I was in danger, so now I have no regrets about defending myself as I did; I should far rather present such a defence and die than live by defending myself in that other fashion.

In court, as in warfare, neither I nor anyone else should contrive to escape death at any cost. On the battlefield too, it often becomes obvious that one could avoid death by throwing down one's arms and flinging oneself upon the mercy of one's pursuers. And in every sort of danger there are many other means of escaping death, if one is shameless enough to do or to say anything. I suggest that it is not death that is hard to avoid, gentlemen, but wickedness is far harder, since it is fleeter of foot than death. Thus, slow and elderly as I am, I have now been overtaken by the slower runner; while my accusers, adroit and quick-witted as they are, have been overtaken by the faster, which is wickedness. And so I take my leave, condemned to death by your judgment, whereas they stand for ever condemned to depravity and injustice as judged by Truth. And just as I accept my penalty, so must they. Things were bound to turn out this way, I suppose, and I imagine it is for the best.

In the next place, to those of you who voted against me, I wish to utter a prophecy. Indeed, I have now reached a point at which people are most given to prophesying—that is, when they are on the point of death. I warn you, my executioners, that as soon as I am dead retribution will come upon you—far more severe, I swear, than the sentence you have passed upon me. You have tried to kill me for now, in the belief that you will be relieved from giving an account of your lives. But in fact, I can tell you, you will face just the opposite outcome. There will be more critics to call you to account, people whom I have restrained for the time being though you were unaware of my doing so. They will be all the harder on you since they are younger, and you will rue it all the more—because if you imagine that by putting people to death you will prevent anyone from reviling you for not living rightly, you are badly mistaken. That way of escape is neither feasible nor honourable. Rather, the most honourable and easiest way is not the silencing of others, but striving to make oneself as good a person as possible. So with that prophecy to those of you who voted against me, I take my leave.

As for those who voted for my acquittal, I should like to discuss the outcome of this case while the officials are occupied, and I am not yet on the way to the place where I must die. Please bear with me, gentlemen, just for this short time: there is no reason why we should not have a word with one another while that is still permitted.

Since I regard you as my friends, I am willing to show you the significance of what has just befallen me. You see, gentlemen of the jury—and in applying that term to you, I probably use it correctly—something wonderful has just happened to me. Hitherto, the usual prophetic voice from my spiritual sign was continually active, and frequently opposed me even on trivial matters, if I was about to do anything amiss. But now something has befallen me, as you can see for yourselves, which one certainly might consider—and is generally held—to be the very worst of evils. Yet the sign from God did not oppose me, either when I left home this morning, or when I appeared here in court, or at any point when I was about to say anything during my speech; and yet in other discussions it has very often stopped me in mid-sentence. This time, though, it has not opposed me at any moment in anything I said or did in this whole business.

Now, what do I take to be the explanation for that? I will tell you: I suspect that what has befallen me is a blessing, and that those of us who suppose death to be an evil cannot be making a correct assumption. I have gained every ground for that suspicion, because my usual sign could not have failed to oppose me, unless I were going to incur some good result.

And let us also reflect upon how good a reason there is to hope that death is a good thing. It is, you see, one or other of two things: either to be dead is to be nonexistent, as it were, and a dead person has no awareness whatever of anything at all; or else, as we are told, the soul undergoes some sort of transformation, or exchanging of this present world for another. Now if there is, in fact, no awareness in death, but it is like sleep—the kind in which the sleeper does not even dream at all—then death would be a marvellous gain. Why, imagine that someone had to pick the night in which he slept so soundly that he did not even dream, and to compare all the other nights and days of his life with that one; suppose he had to say, upon consideration, how many days or nights in his life he had spent better and more agreeably than that night; in that case, I think he would find them easy to count compared with his other days and nights—even if he were the Great King of Persia,[39] let alone an ordinary person. Well, if death is like that, then for my part I call it a gain; because on that assumption the whole of time would seem no longer than a single night.

On the other hand, if death is like taking a trip from here to another place, and if it is true, as we are told, that all of the dead do indeed exist in that other place, why then, gentlemen of the jury, what could be a greater blessing than that? If upon arriving in Hades, and being rid of these people who profess to be "jurors," one is going to find those who are truly judges, and who are also said to sit in judgment there[40]—Minos, Rhadamanthys, Aeacus, Triptolemus, and all other demigods who were righteous in their own lives—would that be a disappointing journey?

Or again, what would any of you not give to share the company of Orpheus and Musaeus, of Hesiod and Homer? I say "you," since I personally would be willing to die many times over, if those tales are true. Why? Because my own sojourn there would be wonderful, if I could meet Palamedes, or Ajax, son of Telamon, or anyone else of old who met their death through an unjust verdict. Whenever I met them, I could compare my own experiences with theirs—which would be not unamusing, I fancy—and best of all, I could spend time questioning and probing people there, just as I do here, to find out who among them is truly wise, and who thinks he is without being so.

What would one not give, gentlemen of the jury, to be able to question the leader of the great expedition against Troy,[41] or Odysseus, or Sisyphus, or countless other men and women one could mention? Would it not be unspeakable good fortune to converse with them there, to mingle with them and question them? At least that isn't a reason, presumably, for people in that world to put you to death—because amongst other ways in which people there are more fortunate than those in our world, they have become immune from death for the rest of time, if what we are told is actually true.

Moreover, you too, gentlemen of the jury, should be of good hope in the face of death, and fix your minds upon this single truth: nothing can harm a good man, either in life or in death; nor are his fortunes neglected by the gods. In fact, what has befallen me has come about by no mere accident; rather, it is clear to me that it was better I should die now and be rid of my troubles. That is also the reason why the divine sign at no point turned me back; and for my part, I bear those who condemned me, and my accusers, no ill will at all—though, to be sure, it was not with that intent that they were condemning and accusing me, but with intent to harm me—and they are culpable for that. Still, this much I ask of them. When my sons come of age, gentlemen, punish them: give them the same sort of trouble that I used to give you, if you think they care for money or anything else more than for goodness, and if they think highly of themselves when they are of no value. Reprove them, as I reproved you, for failing to care for the things they should and for thinking highly of themselves when they are worthless. If you will do that, then I shall have received my own just deserts from you, as will my sons.

But enough. It is now time to leave—for me to die, and for you to live—though which of us has the better destiny is unclear to everyone, save only to God.

NOTES

1. It is striking that the *Defence of Socrates* begins, as it ends, with a disavowal of knowledge.
2. Socrates' reputation for skill in argument enabled Aristophanes to caricature him as an instructor in logical trickery. Cf. *Clouds* (112–15).
3. The reference is to Aristophanes.
4. Speeches in Athenian lawcourts were timed.
5. This describes Socrates' first appearance in the *Clouds* (223–5), where he is swung around in a basket in the air, and he says he is walking on air and thinking about the sun.
6. Professional educators who offered instruction in many subjects.
7. A mina equalled 100 silver drachmas. At the end of the fifth century a drachma was roughly equivalent to one day's pay for a man employed in public works. Evenus' fees were therefore not as "modest" as Socrates pretends.
8. The god Apollo, though nowhere named in the *Defence,* is the deity whose servant Socrates claims to be. In what follows, however, when he speaks of "the god," it is not always clear whether he means Apollo or a personal God distinct from any deity of traditional Greek religion.
9. Politicians of the democratic party had fled from Athens during the regime of the Thirty Tyrants. They returned under an amnesty in 403 B.C. when the Thirty were overthrown.
10. Literally, "by the dog," a favourite Socratic oath, which may have originated as a euphemism.
11. Socrates alludes to the labours of Heracles, twelve tasks of prodigious difficulty imposed upon a hero of legendary strength and courage.
12. The dithyramb was an emotionally powerful lyric poem, performed by a chorus of singers and dancers.
13. The Athenian Council was a body of 500, with fifty members from each of the ten tribes, elected annually by lot from citizens over the age of 30. In conjunction with the magistrates, it carried on state business and prepared an agenda for the Assembly.
14. Socrates' denial that he corrupts the young intentionally relies upon the principle that human beings never intentionally follow a course of action which they know or believe to be harmful to themselves. Since, in Socrates' view, all wrongdoing is harmful to the agent, it follows that all wrongdoing is unintentional and is curable by the removal of ignorance. This doctrine, one of the so-called Socratic Paradoxes, is often summarized in the slogan "Virtue Is Knowledge." It is elaborated in the *Meno*.
15. The sun and moon, even though not the objects of an official cult at Athens, were widely believed to be divine.
16. According to one tradition, Anaxagoras had been prosecuted for heresies regarding the composition of the sun and moon.

17. The "riddle" which Socrates attributes to Meletus consists in the self-contradictory statement "Socrates acknowledges gods and does not acknowledge gods." Greek riddles often take the form of paradoxes generated by apparent self-contradiction.
18. Spirits were sometimes begotten by gods through union with nymphs or mortals.
19. Site of the legendary war between the Greeks and Trojans, which is the context of Homer's *Iliad*.
20. Achilles, heroic Greek warrior in the Trojan War. As the offspring of a goddess mother by a mortal father, he is referred to as a "demigod."
21. Potidawa, in Thrace, was the scene of a campaign in 432 B.C.
22. Socrates here confirms that his well-known mysterious "sign" had been used to substantiate the charge of "introducing new spiritual realities."
23. Fifty representatives from each of the ten tribes who made up the Council took turns during the year to provide an executive for the entire body.
24. In 406 B.C., after a sea battle off the Ionian coast at Arginusae, several Athenian commanders were charged for their failure to rescue the shipwrecked survivors and recover the dead. A motion to try them collectively was endorsed by the Council and referred to the Assembly. Although a collective trial was unconstitutional, the motion was passed by the Assembly after a stormy debate, and six surviving commanders were convicted and executed.
25. A building also called the "sun-shade" from its shape. It was commandeered as a seat of government by the Thirty.
26. An island separated by a narrow channel from the coast of Africa.
27. Socrates is probably alluding, especially, to two of his former associates who had become notorious enemies of the Athenian democracy, Alcibiades and Critias. The former was a brilliant but wayward politician, who had turned against Athens and helped her enemies. The latter was an unscrupulous oligarch, who had become a leading member of the Thirty Tyrants.
28. Socrates here, in effect, contrasts himself with the sophists, in that he did not set himself up as a professional teacher.
29. For example, the Delphic oracle, whose answer had led Socrates to undertake his mission. Dreams had long been believed to be a source of divine communication with human beings, and are often so treated by Plato.
30. At the time of the trial Socrates had two little boys, Sophroniscus and Menexenus, and an older son, Lamprocles.
31. This is one of many disparaging remarks in Plato about women. Open displays of emotion, especially grief, are regarded as distinctively female, an indulgence of the "female side" of our nature.
32. The verdict was "Guilty." Socrates here begins his second speech, proposing an alternative to the death penalty demanded by the prosecution.
33. With a jury of 500, this implies that the vote was 280–220, since at the time of Socrates' trial an evenly split vote (250–250) would have secured his acquittal.
34. The court had to decide between the penalty demanded by the prosecution and a counter-penalty proposed by the defence, with no option of substituting a different one.
35. The Prytaneum was the building on the north-east slope of the Acropolis, in which hospitality was given to honoured guests of the state as well as to Olympic victors and other sports heroes.
36. This was the law at Sparta, because of the irrevocability of capital punishment.
37. This seems to have been a normal amount for a fine and was a considerable sum.

38. The jury has now voted for the death penalty, and Socrates begins his final speech.

39. This monarch embodied the popular ideal of happiness.

40. It is not clear whether Socrates envisages them merely as judging disputes among the dead, or as passing judgment upon the earthly life of those who enter Hades.

41. Agamemnon, chief of the Greek forces in the Trojan War.

INDEX OF NAMES

Adimantus: older brother of Plato.

Aeacus: one of the three judges in Hades. He also appears as a judge and lawgiver of the island Aegina and as an arbiter of disputes among the gods.

Aeantodorus: brother of APOLLODORUS, but otherwise unknown.

Aeschines: devotee of Socrates, who wrote speeches for the lawcourts, taught oratory, and was admired as an author of Socratic dialogues. A few fragments of his writings are extant.

Ajax: Greek hero of the Trojan War, mentioned as a victim of an "unjust verdict." This refers to the award of Achilles' armour to ODYSSEUS in a contest with Ajax. The latter's resulting madness and suicide are the subject of *Ajax,* one of the extant tragedies by Sophocles.

Anaxagoras: Presocratic philosopher, originally from Clazomenae in Ionia. Important fragments of his work are extant. He spent many years in Athens and was prominent in Athenian intellectual life.

Antiphon: from Cephisia, father of EPIGENES and supporter of Socrates at his trial, but not otherwise known.

Anytus: leading Athenian democratic politician and accuser of Socrates as well as the main instigator of the prosecution.

Apollodorus: ardent devotee of Socrates, notorious for his emotional volatility.

Ariston: Athenian of distinguished lineage and father of Plato.

Aristophanes: *c.* 450–385. The most famous playwright of Athenian Old Comedy. Eleven of his plays and many fragments are extant.

Callias: wealthy Athenian patron of sophistic culture.

Cebes: citizen of Thebes in Boeotia, who had studied there with the Pythagorean philosopher Philolaus. A disciple of Socrates.

Chaerephon: long-time faithful follower of Socrates. Expelled from Athens in 404 during the regime of the Thirty Tyrants, he returned when the democracy was restored in the following year. The comic poets nicknamed him "the bat" from his squeaky voice.

Crito: Socrates' contemporary, fellow demesman, and one of his closest friends.

Critobulus: son of CRITO and member of the Socratic circle, who was present at Socrates' trial and death.

Cronus: mythical son of URANUS (Heaven) and Gaea (Earth), father of ZEUS, and his predecessor as chief among the gods. He mutilated his father, married his sister Rhea, and devoured his children, except for Zeus, who overthrew him.

Daedalus: legendary artist, craftsman, and inventor. His many marvellous works included the labyrinth for the Minotaur in the palace of King Minos of Crete, along with wings for himself and his son, Icarus. He was also believed to have made statues that could open their eyes, walk, and move their arms.

Demodocus: father of THEAGES.

Epigenes: an associate of Socrates. He was present at Socrates' death.

Euthyphro: self-proclaimed expert on religious law. Since Plato portrays him as somewhat eccentric, it is a nice irony that his name should mean "Straight-Thinker" or "Right-Mind."

Evenus: a professional teacher of human excellence, or "sophist."

Gorgias: c. 480–376, from Leontini in Sicily; commonly but perhaps wrongly classified as a "sophist." He cultivated an artificial but influential prose style and gave lessons in rhetoric, or effective public speaking.

Hades: the underworld inhabited by the dead. The name belongs, properly, to the mythical king of that realm, who was the brother of ZEUS and Poseidon.

Hector: son of Priam, and leading Trojan hero in the war between Greece and Troy. In HOMER's *Iliad* he kills PATROCLUS, squire of Achilles, who in turn avenges his friend's death by slaying Hector.

Hephaestus: lame god of fire and of the forge. He is associated with volcanoes in Greek mythology and was cast out of heaven by his mother HERA because he was deformed. In revenge he sent her a golden throne to which she was chained with invisible bonds when she sat upon it.

Hera: daughter of CRONUS, wife and sister of ZEUS, and mother of HEPHAESTUS.

Hesiod: one of the earliest extant Greek poets. His *Theogony* contains an account of the origin of the traditional gods. His *Works and Days* is a didactic poem giving moral and practical precepts about rural life.

Hippias: itinerant teacher or "sophist," probably a close contemporary of Socrates, who claimed expertise in many subjects.

Hipponicus: member of wealthy Athenian family and the father of CALLIAS.

Homer: greatest epic poet of Greece and composer of the *Iliad* and the *Odyssey*. The *Iliad* contains episodes from the legendary Trojan War, while the *Odyssey* recounts the travels and adventures of the hero ODYSSEUS during his journey home after the war.

Leon: resident of Salamis, unjustly arrested and murdered by the Thirty Tyrants in 404.

Lycon: Athenian politician and co-accuser of Socrates with MELETUS and ANYTUS.

Lysanias: of Sphettus, father of AESCHINES, but otherwise unknown.

Meletus: youthful co-accuser of Socrates with ANYTUS and LYCON. He drew up the indictment against Socrates, but was evidently a mere tool of Anytus.

Minos: legendary king of Crete and also a traditional judge in the underworld.

Musaeus: mythical bard or singer, closely connected with ORPHEUS.

Nicostratus: supporter of Socrates, present at his trial but otherwise unknown.

Odysseus: legendary hero in HOMER's *Iliad* and also a central figure in the *Odyssey*, which recounts his wanderings after the Trojan War.

Orpheus: legendary bard and founder of the archaic mystical or religious movement known as "Orphism."

Palamedes: Greek hero of the Trojan War, credited with invention of the alphabet.

Paralius: supporter of Socrates who was present at his trial but is not otherwise known.

Patroclus: squire and close friend of Achilles in HOMER's *Iliad*, slain by HECTOR and avenged by Achilles.

Prodicus: itinerant teacher from Ceos and also one of the sophists.

Proteus: mythical "old man of the sea," who eluded all attempts at capture by constantly changing his form.

Rhadamanthys: with AEACUS and MINOS one of the three traditional judges in the underworld.

Simmias: citizen of Thebes and follower of Socrates. He was prepared to finance Socrates' escape.

Sisyphus: mythical wrongdoer, famous for his endless punishment in the underworld. His task was to push a boulder up to the top of a hill, from which it always rolled down again.

Tantalus: mythical king of Phrygia, possessing proverbial wealth. In one tradition he tried to make himself immortal by stealing the food of the gods. For this he was punished by being made to stand in water which receded as soon as he stooped to drink, and to stretch out for fruit which the wind always blew away from his grasp.

Telamon: legendary king of Salamis and father of AJAX.

Theages: disciple of Socrates, whose brother PARALIUS was present at the trial, though Theages himself was already dead.

Theodotus: associate of Socrates who died before his trial but is not otherwise known.

Theozotides: father of NICOSTRATUS and THEODOTUS. Though deceased by the time of Socrates' trial, he is known to have introduced two important democratic measures after the fall of the Thirty Tyrants. Plato may therefore have mentioned him to counter suspicion that Socrates had antidemocratic leanings.

Thetis: sea-nymph or goddess, given in marriage to the mortal Peleus. Achilles was her only child.

Triptolemus: mythical agricultural hero from Eleusis, as well as a central figure in its mystery cults.

Uranus: heaven or the sky, conceived in mythology as child and husband of Gaea (earth). Chief deity before his son CRONUS.

Zeus: son of CRONUS, as well as chief among the Olympian gods.

STUDY QUESTIONS

1. According to Socrates, why did the Delphic oracle declare that no one was wiser than Socrates?
2. According to Socrates, what mistake is involved in the fear of death?
3. Why is Socrates unwilling to give up the study of philosophy?
4. According to Socrates, what is far harder to avoid than death?

PART 2

Reasoning

The Elements of Argument

✦

Steven M. Cahn, Patricia Kitcher, and George Sher

To assert a belief is simple; defending it is far more difficult. Yet if a belief is not defended adequately, why accept it?

Saying something is true does not make it true. Suppose Smith says that both Charles Darwin, who developed the theory of evolution, and Abraham Lincoln were born on February 12, 1809. Jones denies this claim. If saying something is true proves it true, then what Smith says is true and what Jones says is also true—which is impossible, because one of them denies exactly what the other affirms. Their statements are contradictory, and asserting both of them amounts to saying nothing at all. (Incidentally, Smith is correct.)

To reason effectively, we need to avoid contradiction and accept beliefs that are adequately defended. But what are the appropriate standards by which we can determine if our beliefs are consistent and well-confirmed by the available evidence? Logic is the subject that offers answers to these questions, and the scope of logic is explained in the following essay that I coauthored with Patricia Kitcher, Professor of Philosophy at Columbia University, and George Sher, Professor of Philosophy at Rice University. At one time we were colleagues in the Department of Philosophy at the University of Vermont.

....

We reason every day of our lives. Whether the topic is politics, morality, movies, or sports, we offer arguments to convince others that our views are reasonable. But what is an argument, and which arguments should be accepted?

ARGUMENTS

In ordinary parlance, an argument is simply a dispute. To philosophers, however, an argument is a collection of sentences consisting of one or more *premises* and a *conclusion*. The evidence you cite is your premise or premises; the statement you defend is your conclusion. Whenever you construct an argument, you need to take some claim as your premise. Of course, assuming the truth of a controversial claim in order to argue for what is obvious would be unconvincing. The direction of sensible argumentation is always from the more obvious to the less. Ideally, a reasoner

This essay, modified by the editor, is from Steven M. Cahn, Patricia Kitcher, and George Sher, "The Uses of Argument," in *Philosophical Horizons: Introductory Readings*, second edition, eds. Steven M. Cahn and Maureen Eckert. Copyright © 2012. Reprinted by permission of Wadsworth/Cengage Learning.

will choose premises that are uncontroversial and argue that a more disputed, perhaps even surprising, conclusion follows from those unproblematic assumptions.

Logic is the branch of philosophy that studies the relations between premises and conclusion, establishing guidelines about which claims can be inferred from others. This task has been carried out with great success for deductive inference.

Deductive Arguments

The central concept of deductive logic is *validity*. An argument is valid whenever the truth of the premises guarantees the truth of the conclusion. In other words, in a valid argument the conclusion follows from the premises; that is, the conclusion cannot be false if the premises are true. Logic is not concerned with the truth of the premises or the truth of the conclusion but only with the relation between the premises and the conclusion.

In ordinary English "valid" and "true" are often used synonymously, yet their technical meanings are different. In philosophical terminology, statements are true or false, not valid or invalid. Arguments, however, are valid or invalid, not true or false. Thus you can make a true statement or present a valid argument, but you can't speak validly or argue truthfully.

Note that a valid argument can have true or false premises, and they may be as numerous as wished. Here, for example, is a valid argument with true premises (such an argument is referred to as a *sound argument*):

Premise 1   The capital of Massachusetts is Boston.
Premise 2   Boston is the home of the Boston Red Sox.
Conclusion   The capital of Massachusetts is the home of the Boston Red Sox.

In this example the two premises are true, and the conclusion follows from the premises.

Here is another valid argument, but in this case the first premise is false and the second is true.

Premise 1   All playwrights lived in Greece.
Premise 2   Shakespeare was a playwright.
Conclusion   Shakespeare lived in Greece.

Although the first premise is false, the argument is nevertheless valid, because the conclusion follows from the premises. In other words, whether the premises are true, they imply the conclusion.

Now here is another valid argument, but this time both premises are false, yet they imply a true conclusion:

Premise 1   All canaries are polar bears.
Premise 2   All polar bears have feathers.
Conclusion   All canaries have feathers.

Note also that even if the premises of an argument are all true and the conclusion is true, the argument may not be valid, as in this case:

Premise 1	Some roses are red.
Premise 2	Some violets are blue.
Conclusion	Flowers give some people hay fever.

The problem is that while all the statements are true, the truth of the premises does not guarantee the truth of the conclusion, and that relation is the hallmark of a valid argument.

Thus a compelling deductive argument should be valid. Otherwise the premises will not lead us to accept the conclusion.

Deductive arguments, however, are not the only form of effective reasoning. We turn next to non-deductive arguments.

Non-Deductive Arguments

We encounter many good but non-deductive inferences in everyday and scientific discussions. Suppose, for example, that a particular drug is given a hundred thousand trials across a wide variety of people, and it never produces serious side effects. Even the most scrupulous researcher would conclude that the drug is safe. Still, this conclusion cannot be deductively inferred from the data. Here is the argument:

Premise	In 100,000 trials, drug X produced no serious side effects.
Conclusion	Drug X does not have any serious side effects.

Because a serious side effect may appear on the 100,001st trial, the premise could be true even though the conclusion is false. Hence the argument is deductively invalid, yet it is strong and should be accepted.

We can present many more good but deductively invalid arguments. Here is another example.

Premise 1	The dining room window is shattered.
Premise 2	A baseball is lying in the middle of the glass on the dining room floor.
Premise 3	A baseball bat is found on the ground in the yard outside the dining room.
Conclusion	The dining room window was shattered by being hit with a baseball.

If we recognize only the standard of deductive validity, then the previous arguments—and all other arguments like these—will have to be dismissed as bad reasoning. That constraint on argumentation, however, is unacceptable. Why should we demand that the truth of the premises guarantees the truth of the conclusion? After all, we often suppose that a claim is not certain but highly probable. For instance, we would be willing to place a sizable bet that a roulette ball will not land on number 7 twenty times in a row. Yet no true premises about how roulette is played render that result impossible. Logic, therefore, has a second task. It needs to provide criteria for evaluating good but non-deductive inferences.

INDUCTION

We believe that if a dry piece of paper is placed into the flame of a candle, the paper will burn. Why do we hold this belief? We reason that in the past dry paper placed into the flame of a candle always burned, so we infer that it will burn in the present case. This common type of reasoning is called *induction*. In it, we rely on similar, observed cases to infer that the same event or property will recur in as *yet* unobserved cases.

Of course, in different instances we have different amounts of evidence on which to draw. If only ten cases of a disease have been observed, then we will have much less confidence in predicting the course of the disease than if we had observed ten thousand cases. Philosophers often refer to our confidence in a claim as our *strength of belief*. Surely it should increase with the number of positive instances of the claim. Hence, for example, if you arrive in a new town and notice that all the buses you see on your first day are green, then as the days pass and you continue to observe only green buses, the strength of your belief that all the buses in town are green will increase.

While positive instances gradually confirm an inductive generalization, rendering it more and more reasonable, a negative instance defeats the generalization. To take a dramatic twentieth-century example, with the splitting of the first atom, the long-standing claim that atoms are indivisible particles of matter had to be relinquished.

Beside the sheer number of positive instances, another criterion for good inductive reasoning is that the evidence be varied. If you have observed buses in many different parts of town, then you are more justified in claiming that the town's buses are all green than if you have only considered the buses on your own street.

HYPOTHESIS TESTING

All of us, especially scientists, test hypotheses as a form of inductive reasoning. For example, imagine that a problem has developed in a small rural town, where residents are falling sick at an alarming rate. The local doctor hypothesizes that the trouble has been caused by the opening of a new chemical plant that is emptying waste within a mile of one of the lakes that yields the town's supply of drinking water. The hypothesis can be tested in a number of different ways. For instance, the residents might check the consequences of drinking water only from a lake not close to the chemical plant. Granted, the doctor's hypothesis would fail such a test if, despite using water from a different lake, the sickness continued to spread. Yet the hypothesis might pass the test if drinking water from a different lake leads to the illness disappearing. This case indicates the way in which a hypothesis can be tested. Frequently we advance a claim whose truth or falsity we are unable to ascertain by direct observation. We cannot just look and see if the earth moves, or if the continents were once part of a single land mass, or if the butler committed the crime. In evaluating such hypotheses, we consider what things we would expect to observe if the hypothesis were true. Then we investigate to see if these expectations are confirmed. If so, then the hypothesis passes the test, and its success counts in its favor; if not, then the failure counts against the hypothesis.

INFERENCE TO THE BEST EXPLANATION

Another common and indispensable type of non-deductible inference should be familiar to readers of detective stories. Sherlock Holmes, for instance, uses this type of reasoning in his first encounter with Dr. Watson in *A Study in Scarlet.*

> I *knew* you came from Afghanistan. From long habit the train of thoughts ran so swiftly through my mind that I arrived at the conclusion without being conscious of intermediate steps. There were such steps, however. The train of reasoning ran, 'Here is a gentleman of a medical type, but with the air of a military man. Clearly an army doctor, then. He has just come from the tropics, for his face is dark, and that is not the natural tint of his skin, for his wrists are fair. He has undergone hardship and sickness, as his haggard face says clearly. His left arm has been injured. He holds it in a stiff and unnatural manner. Where in the tropics could an English army doctor have seen much hardship and got his arm wounded? Clearly in Afghanistan.' The whole train of thought did not occupy a second. I then remarked that you came from Afghanistan, and you were astonished.[1]

Holmes' argument is deductively invalid. Even though Watson has a deep tan and a wounded arm, perhaps he has never been in Afghanistan but obtained the tan in Argentina and the wound in a knife fight in Peru. Yet Holmes' argument does provide considerable support for his claim that Watson had been in Afghanistan. Here is how Holmes' reasoning works. He lists various facts, such as the military bearing, the tan, and the wounded arm. Then he uses them to infer a conclusion that would explain all of them. In this case, if Watson is a military doctor who just returned from active service in Afghanistan, that conclusion would explain why he has a tan, an injured arm, and so forth. The name for this type of reasoning is *argument by inference to the best explanation,* and it is closely related to hypothesis testing. There a hypothesis is supported when observations that can be deduced from the hypothesis are borne out. In argument by inference to the best explanation, the hypothesis is supported when it explains given facts. In either case the results can yield high probabilities, although not certainties.

ARGUMENT ANALYSIS

Having examined various types of inference, let us now consider how this information may be used in analyzing reasoning. The basic task of argument analysis is to provide a clear formulation of the chain of argumentation presented in a piece of prose. After all, arguments do not come neatly packaged with labels clearly identifying the premises and the conclusion. A critic needs to find the optimal version of an argument before evaluating it. Perhaps surprisingly, the first step to assess reasoning is finding the conclusion. It may occur at the beginning, at the end, or in the middle of a passage. Indeed, the conclusion may not be stated at all.

Thus to find it, you need to ask: "What is the author trying to persuade us to believe?"

After locating the conclusion, the next step is to list the premises. To find them, you need to consider the author's starting places. Once they are found, you are ready to try to trace a plausible route from the premises to the conclusion. Here you need to clarify the meanings of key terms and consider the criteria for different types of inference. Once you have reconstructed the argument, you can appraise its success or failure.

Evaluating reasoning is a complex task, because human language is rich and fluid, and facts can be connected in many ways. Yet while the task is difficult, the alternative is unacceptable. For if we give up trying to understand reasoning, then we must either naively accept what others assert or abandon the possibility of assessing their claims.

NOTE

1. *A Study in Scarlet*, in Arthur Conan Doyle, *The Complete Sherlock Holmes* (Garden City, N.Y.: Doubleday, n.d.), p. 24.

STUDY QUESTIONS

1. Can a valid deductive argument have true premises and a false conclusion?
2. Can a valid deductive argument have false premises and a true conclusion?
3. Give your own example of hypothesis testing.
4. Give your own example of arguing by inference to the best explanation.

Improving Your Thinking

Stephen F. Barker

Effective reasoning calls for avoiding fallacious arguments and clarifying ambiguous terms. Both these issues are addressed in our next selection, written by Stephen F. Barker (1927–2019), who was Professor of Philosophy at Johns Hopkins University.

You can strengthen your own thinking by being alert to some commonly used words that are so notoriously vague that their appearance in any argument signals trouble. Here are some examples: subjective, natural, relative, pragmatic, diverse. Next time you hear someone use one of these terms, ask what it means. Everyone will benefit from the clarification.

....

1. FALLACIES

If we want to become more skillful at playing chess, or football, or any other game, it is a good idea to study not only the shrewd moves that experts make, but also the poor moves that less experienced players make—we can learn from their mistakes. Similarly, as we try to improve our ability to reason logically, we should not confine our attention to specimens of good reasoning; we should also consider plenty of tempting examples of bad reasoning. By becoming more aware of how these bad arguments are bad, we strengthen our ability to distinguish between good and bad reasoning.

In ordinary talk the term "fallacy" is often loosely applied to any sort of mistaken belief or untrue sentence. "It's a fallacy to believe that handling a toad causes warts," people say. Here the thing being called a fallacy is just a belief, not a piece of reasoning. But in logic the term "fallacy" is restricted to mistakes in reasoning: a *fallacy* is a logical mistake in reasoning, especially one that it is tempting to make. There is a logical fallacy only when there are premises and a conclusion which is erroneously thought to be proved by them.

Many types of fallacies have been given special names, especially those types that are rather tempting and likely to deceive people. . . .

An argument is called a *petitio principii* (or begging of the question) if the argument fails to prove anything because it somehow takes for granted what it is supposed to prove. Suppose a man says "Jones is insane, you know," and we reply "Really? Are you sure?" and he responds, "Certainly, I can prove it. Jones is demented; therefore he is insane." This is a valid argument in the sense that if the premise is true, the conclusion must be true too; but the argument is unsatisfactory, for it does not really prove anything. The premise is merely another statement of the conclusion, so that practically anyone who doubts the truth of the conclusion ought to be equally doubtful about the truth of the premise, and the argument is useless for the purpose of convincing us of the truth of the conclusion. Thus the argument takes for granted just what it is supposed to prove; it begs the question. . . .

One important type of fallacy . . . is the *ad hominem* fallacy. An argument is *ad hominem* (Latin: "to the man") if it is directed at an opponent in a controversy rather than being directly relevant to proving the conclusion under discussion. Such arguments are often, but not always, fallacious. For example, suppose someone argues: "Of course Karl Marx must have been mistaken in maintaining that capitalism is an evil form of economic and social organization. Why, he was a miserable failure of a man who couldn't even earn enough money to support his family." This is an *ad hominem* argument, for it attacks Marx the man instead of offering direct reasons why his views are incorrect. . . .

Another quite different fallacy of irrelevance is the appeal to unsuitable authority. . . . We commit this fallacy when we appeal to some admired or famous person as if that person were an authority on the matter being discussed—but when we have no good reason for thinking that the person is a genuine authority on it. Of course it is not always fallacious to appeal to authorities, but we are not entitled to appeal to persons as authorities unless there are good reasons for believing them to be authorities, and we should not trust an authority outside his or her special proven field of competence. A famous guitarist may be an expert on one type of music, but this does not make her an authority on philosophy of life. A movie star may be an authority on how to look attractive to the opposite sex, but is not likely to be an authority on which pain reliever is most healthful or which toothpaste tastes best. . . .

We conclude with . . . the fallacy of *black-and-white* thinking. A wife may say to her husband "So you think the soup is too cold, do you? Well, I suppose you would like to have had it scalding hot then, instead." The second remark is presented as if it followed logically from the first, and yet there is no logical connection whatever. But people find it very easy to fall into this sort of thinking in extremes, especially in the heat of controversy.

2. DEFINITIONS

When we encounter words that cause confusion because their meanings are ambiguous, it is often helpful to define them. . . .

Definitions that are useful in preventing ambiguity may be subdivided into two types. Some of them serve the purpose of describing the meaning that a word already has in language. We might call these *analytical* definitions. In giving this kind of definition of a word, the speaker does not aim to change its meaning; he aims only to characterize the meaning it already has. Dictionary definitions are of this type. When a definition has this purpose, we can properly ask whether the definition is correct or incorrect.

In order to be correct in its description of the meaning of a word, an analytical definition must not be *too broad;* that is, it must not embrace things that do not really belong. (To define "pneumonia" as "disease of the lungs" would be too broad, for there are many lung diseases besides pneumonia.) Also, in order to be correct in its description of the meaning of a word, an analytical definition must not be *too narrow;* that is, it must not exclude things that really belong. (To define "psychosis" as "schizophrenia" would be too narrow, for there are other kinds of psychoses. . . .)

Finally, a definition cannot serve much useful purpose if it is circular. . . . For example, to define "straight line" as "the line along which a ray of light travels when it goes straight" is circular and uninformative. . . .

A second type of definition useful in preventing ambiguity is the *stipulative* definition, whose purpose is to declare how a speaker intends that a certain word, phrase, or symbol shall be understood ("Let '*S*' mean 'Samoans'"; "Let 'heavy truck' mean 'truck that can carry a load of 5 tons or more'"; etc.). Perhaps the expression being defined is one that previously had no meaning, or perhaps it had a different or a vaguer meaning. At any rate, the point of the stipulative definition is that the expression now is deliberately endowed with a particular meaning. Obviously, a stipulative definition cannot be of much use if it is unclear or circular. However, we do not have to worry about whether it is too broad or too narrow, for that sort of correctness cannot pertain to stipulative definitions. A stipulative definition is arbitrary, in that it expresses only the speaker's intention to use the word in the stipulated manner, and the speaker is, after all, entitled to use it in any desired way, so long as it does not cause confusion.

In order to avoid causing confusion, however, a stipulative definition should not assign to a word that already has an established meaning some new meaning that is likely to be confused with it. Consider the following dialogue:

SMITH: General Green is insane, you know. He ought to be dismissed.

JONES: He is? I agree that we should not have insane persons serving in the Army. But how do you know he's insane?

SMITH: It's obvious. He says he believes in extrasensory perception, and according to my definition—surely I'm entitled to use words as I please—anyone who does that is insane.

Here the stipulative definition is used to promote ambiguity rather than to prevent it. In the ordinary sense of the term "insane," Jones agrees with Smith that insane persons ought not to be generals. But Smith offers no evidence that General Green is insane in this sense. All that Smith shows is that the general is "insane" in a special, idiosyncratic sense of the word. From that, nothing follows about whether he ought to be dismissed. Smith is causing confusion by failing to keep distinct these two very different senses of the word; this happens because he fails to recognize the difference here between a stipulative and an analytical definition. . . .

The two kinds of definitions mentioned so far both aim to inform us about verbal usage. . . . It would be a mistake, however, to suppose that everything called a definition belongs to one of these two kinds. In fact, the profoundest and most valuable definitions usually do not fit tidily into either kind. When Newton defined force as the product of mass times acceleration, when Einstein defined simultaneity of distant events in terms of the transmission of light rays . . . [w]hat these definitions did was to propose new verbal usages growing out of the previously established usages. It was felt that these new usages perfected tendencies of thought implicit in the old usages and offered more insight into the subject matter being treated.

We might give the name *revelatory* definitions to definitions like these, which do not fit into either of the two categories of stipulative and analytical. Revelatory definitions constitute a third category. Further examples of revelatory definitions can be found in other, diverse fields. For example, when a nineteenth-century writer defined architecture as frozen music, he was not trying to describe how the word "architecture" is used in our language. (He took it for granted that his readers would know what kinds of constructions are considered architecture.) Nor was he proposing some arbitrary new usage. We should not censure his definition on the ground that it is unhelpful for the purpose of preventing ambiguity; that is not the purpose of this kind of definition. This definition is a metaphor, and it suggests a new way of looking at architecture, comparing the structural organization of the parts of a building with the structural organization of the parts of a musical composition. In trying to decide whether the definition is a good one or not, we must reflect about the extent and validity of this comparison between music and buildings; the definition is a good one if and only if the comparison is revealing. . . .

How frequently are definitions needed? People sometimes think that one always should define one's terms at the beginning of any discussion. But this idea becomes absurd if carried too far. Suppose that we as speakers did undertake to define all our terms in noncircular ways. However far we proceeded, we would always still have . . . undefined terms; therefore this task is an impossible one to complete. Moreover, we do have a fairly adequate understanding of the meanings of many words that we have never bothered to define and also of many words that we would not know how to define satisfactorily even if we tried. Thus, it would be foolish to try indiscriminately to define all or even most of our terms before proceeding with our thinking. What we should do at the beginning of a discussion is seek definitions of those particular words which are especially likely to make trouble in the discussion because they are harmfully ambiguous, obscure, or vague.

This is especially true with regard to discussions in which confusion is caused by failure to notice the different meanings of a term. A *verbal dispute* is a dispute arising solely from the fact that some word is being used with different meanings; this kind of dispute can be settled merely by giving the definitions that clarify the situation (though this is not to say that such disputes always are *easy* to settle).

The American philosopher William James gives a classic example of such a verbal dispute. . . . Suppose there is a squirrel on the trunk of a tree, and a man walks around the tree. The squirrel moves around the tree trunk so as to stay out of sight, always facing the man but keeping the tree between them. Has the man gone around the squirrel or not? Some of James's friends disputed hotly for a long time about this question. Here is a purely verbal dispute; it can be settled by pointing out that in one sense the man has gone "around" the squirrel, for he has moved from the north to the west and then to the south and east of the squirrel's location, but in another sense the man has not gone "around" the squirrel, for the squirrel has always been facing him. Once we have pointed out these two different senses of the word, we have done all that can reasonably be done; there is nothing more worth discussing (though this does not ensure that discussion will cease). With a verbal dispute like this, giving definitions is the way to resolve the dispute. But it would be utterly wrong to assume that all disputes are verbal in this way. There are many serious problems for the settling of which definitions are not needed, and there are many other problems where if definitions help, they mark only the beginning of the thinking needed to resolve the issue.

STUDY QUESTIONS

1. Give an example of an argument that begs the question.
2. Give your own example of an *ad hominem* argument.
3. Explain the danger involved in offering a stipulative definition that uses an ordinary word in an idiosyncratic manner.
4. Give your own example of a purely verbal dispute.

Necessary and Sufficient Conditions

Steven M. Cahn

One key to effective thinking is understanding the concepts of necessary and sufficient conditions. In the next selection I explain their proper and improper uses.

One state of affairs, A, is a necessary condition for another state of affairs, B, if B cannot occur without A occurring. For instance, in the United States a person must be at least eighteen years old before being entitled to vote. In other words, being eighteen is a necessary condition for being entitled to vote.

One state of affairs, A, is a sufficient condition for another state of affairs, B, if the occurrence of A ensures the occurrence of B. For instance, in an American presidential election for a candidate to receive 300 electoral votes ensures that candidate's election. In other words, receiving 300 electoral votes is a sufficient condition for winning the election.

Note that even if A is a necessary condition for B, A need not be a sufficient condition for B. For instance, even if you need to be eighteen to vote, you also need to be a citizen of the United States. Thus being eighteen is necessary but not sufficient for voting.

Similarly, even if A is a sufficient condition for B, A need not be a necessary condition for B. For instance, if a presidential candidate receives 300 electoral votes, then that candidate is elected, but receiving 300 electoral votes, while sufficient for election, is not necessary, because a candidate who receives 299 votes is also elected.

Confusing necessary and sufficient conditions is a common mistake in reasoning. If one individual argues that extensive prior experience in Washington, DC, is required for a person to be a worthy presidential candidate, that claim is not refuted by pointing out that many candidates with such experience have not been worthy. To refute the claim that experience is necessary for worthiness requires demonstrating not that many with experience have been unworthy but that a person without experience *has* been worthy. After all, the original claim was that experience is necessary, not sufficient.

Suppose A is both necessary and sufficient for B. For example, being a rectangle with all four sides equal is necessary and sufficient for being a square. In other words, a geometric figure cannot be a square unless it is a rectangle with all four sides equal, and if a rectangle has all four sides equal, then it is a square. Thus a satisfactory definition of "square" is "rectangle with all four sides equal."

Now here is an additional twist that may be surprising. What is the difference between asserting that A is a necessary condition for B and that B is a sufficient condition for A? Nothing. These are two ways of saying that the occurrence of B ensures the occurrence of A. Furthermore, what is the difference between asserting that A is a sufficient condition for B and that B is a necessary condition for A? Again, nothing. These are two ways of saying that the occurrence of A ensures the occurrence of B.

The critical mistake is thinking that if A is necessary for B, then A is sufficient for B. Or that if A is sufficient for B, then A is necessary for B. These are fallacies.

Hence the next time you hear someone say, for example, that you can be well educated without knowing any logic, because some people who know logic are not well educated, you can point out that the speaker has confused necessary and sufficient conditions. Just because some people who know logic are not well educated does not prove that you can be well educated without knowing logic. That conclusion would only follow if some people who don't know logic are nevertheless well educated.

If you're on the lookout for this fallacy, you'll find it committed far more often than you might suppose.

STUDY QUESTIONS

1. If A is a necessary condition for B, is B always a necessary condition for A?
2. If A is a necessary condition for B, is B always a sufficient condition for A?
3. Is the claim that the study of philosophy is necessary for happiness undermined by presenting cases of unhappy people who have studied philosophy?
4. Present your own example of the fallacy of confusing necessary and sufficient conditions.

Scientific Inquiry

CARL G. HEMPEL

The scientific method of explanation involves formulating a hypothesis and testing it, then accepting, rejecting, or modifying it in light of the experimental results. But how do we test a hypothesis? That is the subject of the following selection by philosopher of science Carl G. Hempel (1905–1997), who was Professor of Philosophy at Princeton University.

As you read about hypothesis testing, you may wonder how hypotheses are developed. What is their source? No mechanical procedures are available; the answer lies in creative imagination. While giving free rein to ingenuity, however, scientific method requires that our intuitions be accepted only if they pass the rigors of careful testing.

....

1. A CASE HISTORY AS AN EXAMPLE

As a simple illustration of some important aspects of scientific inquiry, let us consider Semmelweis' work on childbed fever. Ignaz Semmelweis, a physician of Hungarian birth, did this work during the years from 1844 to 1848 at the Vienna General Hospital. As a member of the medical staff of the First Maternity Division in the hospital, Semmelweis was distressed to find that a large proportion of the women who were delivered of their babies in that division contracted a serious and often fatal illness known as puerperal fever or childbed fever. In 1844, as many as 260 out of 3,157 mothers in the First Division, or 8.2 per cent, died of the disease; for 1845, the death rate was 6.8 per cent, and for 1846, it was 11.4 per cent. These figures were all the more alarming because in the adjacent Second Maternity Division of the same hospital, which accommodated almost as many women as the First, the death toll from childbed fever was much lower: 2.3, 2.0, and 2.7 per cent for the same years. In a book that he wrote later on the causation and the prevention of childbed fever, Semmelweis describes his efforts to resolve the dreadful puzzle.[1]

He began by considering various explanations that were current at the time; some of these he rejected out of hand as incompatible with well-established facts; others he subjected to specific tests.

One widely accepted view attributed the ravages of puerperal fever to "epidemic influences," which were vaguely described as "atmospheric–cosmic– telluric changes" spreading over whole districts and causing childbed fever in women in confinement. But how, Semmelweis reasons, could such influences have plagued the First Division for years and yet spared the Second? And how could this view be reconciled with the fact that while the fever was raging in the hospital, hardly a case occurred in the city of Vienna or in its surroundings: a genuine epidemic, such as cholera, would not be so selective. Finally, Semmelweis notes that some of the women admitted to the First Division, living far from the hospital, had been overcome by labor on their way and had given birth in the street: yet despite these adverse conditions, the death rate from childbed fever among these cases of "street birth" was lower than the average for the First Division.

On another view, overcrowding was a cause of mortality in the First Division. But Semmelweis points out that in fact the crowding was heavier in the Second Division, partly as a result of the desperate efforts of patients to avoid assignment to the notorious First Division. He also rejects two similar conjectures that were current, by noting that there were no differences between the two Divisions in regard to diet or general care of the patients.

In 1846, a commission that had been appointed to investigate the matter attributed the prevalence of illness in the First Division to injuries resulting from rough examination by the medical students, all of whom received their obstetrical training in the First Division. Semmelweis notes in refutation of this view that (a) the injuries resulting naturally from the process of birth are much more extensive than those that might be caused by rough examination; (b) the midwives who received their training in the Second Division examined their patients in much the same manner but without the same ill effects; (c) when, in response to the commission's report, the number of medical students was halved and their examinations of the women were reduced to a minimum, the mortality, after a brief decline, rose to higher levels than ever before.

Various psychological explanations were attempted. One of them noted that the First Division was so arranged that a priest bearing the last sacrament to a dying woman had to pass through five wards before reaching the sickroom beyond: the appearance of the priest, preceded by an attendant ringing a bell, was held to have a terrifying and debilitating effect upon the patients in the wards and thus to make them more likely victims of childbed fever. In the Second Division, this adverse factor was absent, since the priest had direct access to the sickroom. Semmelweis decided to test this conjecture. He persuaded the priest to come by a roundabout route and without ringing of the bell, in order to reach the sick chamber silently and unobserved. But the mortality in the First Division did not decrease.

A new idea was suggested to Semmelweis by the observation that in the First Division the women were delivered lying on their backs; in the Second Division, on their sides. Though he thought it unlikely, he decided "like a drowning man clutching at a straw," to test whether this difference in procedure was significant. He introduced the use of the lateral position in the First Division, but again, the mortality remained unaffected.

At last, early in 1847, an accident gave Semmelweis the decisive clue for his solution of the problem. A colleague of his, Kolletschka, received a puncture wound in the finger, from the scalpel of a student with whom he was performing an autopsy, and died after an agonizing illness during which he displayed the same symptoms that Semmelweis had observed in the victims of childbed fever. Although the role of microorganisms in such infections had not yet been recognized at the time, Semmelweis realized that "cadaveric matter" which the student's scalpel had introduced into Kolletschka's blood stream had caused his colleague's fatal illness. And the similarities between the course of Kolletschka's disease and that of the women in his clinic led Semmelweis to the conclusion that his patients had died of the same kind of blood poisoning: he, his colleagues, and the medical students had been the carriers of the infectious material, for he and his associates used to come to the wards directly from performing dissections in the autopsy room, and examine the women in labor after only superficially washing their hands, which often retained a characteristic foul odor.

Again, Semmelweis put his idea to a test. He reasoned that if he were right, then childbed fever could be prevented by chemically destroying the infectious material adhering to the hands. He therefore issued an order requiring all medical students to wash their hands in a solution of chlorinated lime before making an examination. The mortality from childbed fever promptly began to decrease, and for the year 1848 it fell to 1.27 per cent in the First Division, compared to 1.33 in the Second.

In further support of his idea, or of his hypothesis, as we will also say, Semmelweis notes that it accounts for the fact that the mortality in the Second Division consistently was so much lower: the patients there were attended by midwives, whose training did not include anatomical instruction by dissection of cadavers.

The hypothesis also explained the lower mortality among "street births": women who arrived with babies in arms were rarely examined after admission and thus had a better chance of escaping infection.

Similarly, the hypothesis accounted for the fact that the victims of childbed fever among the newborn babies were all among those whose mothers had contracted the disease during labor; for then the infection could be transmitted to the baby before birth, through the common bloodstream of mother and child, whereas this was impossible when the mother remained healthy.

Further clinical experiences soon led Semmelweis to broaden his hypothesis. On one occasion, for example, he and his associates, having carefully disinfected their hands, examined first a woman in labor who was suffering from a festering cervical cancer; then they proceeded to examine twelve other women in the same room, after only routine washing without renewed disinfection. Eleven of the twelve patients died of puerperal fever. Semmelweis concluded that childbed fever can be caused not only by cadaveric material, but also by "putrid matter derived from living organisms."

2. BASIC STEPS IN TESTING A HYPOTHESIS

We have seen how, in his search for the cause of childbed fever, Semmelweis examined various hypotheses that had been suggested as possible answers.... [L]et us examine how a hypothesis, once proposed, is tested.

Sometimes, the procedure is quite direct. Consider the conjectures that differences in crowding, or in diet, or in general care account for the difference in mortality between the two divisions. As Semmelweis points out, these conflict with readily observable facts. There are no such differences between the divisions; the hypotheses are therefore rejected as false.

But usually the test will be less simple and straightforward. Take the hypothesis attributing the high mortality in the First Division to the dread evoked by the appearance of the priest with his attendant. The intensity of that dread, and especially its effect upon childbed fever, are not as directly ascertainable as are differences in crowding or in diet, and Semmelweis uses an indirect method of testing. He asks himself: Are there any readily observable effects that should occur if the hypothesis were true? And he reasons: *If* the hypothesis were true, *then* an appropriate change in the priest's procedure should be followed by a decline in fatalities. He checks this implication by a simple experiment and finds it false, and he therefore rejects the hypothesis.

Similarly, to test his conjecture about the position of the women during delivery, he reasons: *If* this conjecture should be true, *then* adoption of the lateral position in the First Division will reduce the mortality. Again, the implication is shown false by his experiment, and the conjecture is discarded.

In the last two cases, the test is based on an argument to the effect that *if* the contemplated hypothesis, say H, is true, *then* certain observable events (e.g., decline in mortality) should occur under specified circumstances (e.g., if the priest refrains from walking through the wards, or if the women are delivered in lateral position); or briefly, if H is true, then so is I, where I is a statement describing the observable occurrences to be expected. For convenience, let us say that I is inferred from, or implied by, H; and let us call I a *test implication of the hypothesis H....*

In our last two examples, experiments show the test implication to be false, and the hypothesis is accordingly rejected. The reasoning that leads to the rejection may be schematized as follows:

(2a)   If H is true, then so is I.
        But (as the evidence shows) I is not true.
        H is not true.

Any argument of this form, called *modus tollens* in logic, is deductively valid; that is, if its premises (the sentences above the horizontal line) are true, then its conclusion (the sentence below the horizontal line) is unfailingly true as well. Hence, if the premises of (2a) are properly established, the hypothesis H that is being tested must indeed be rejected.

Next, let us consider the case where observation or experiment bears out the test implication *I*. From his hypothesis that childbed fever is blood poisoning produced by cadaveric matter, Semmelweis infers that suitable antiseptic measures will reduce fatalities from the disease. This time, experiment shows the test implication to be true. But this favorable outcome does not conclusively prove the hypothesis true, for the underlying argument would have the form

> (2*b*)   If *H* is true, then so is *I*.
> (As the evidence shows) *I* is true.
> *H* is true.

And this mode of reasoning, which is referred to as the *fallacy of affirming the consequent*, is deductively invalid, that is, its conclusion may be false even if its premisses are true. This is in fact illustrated by Semmelweis' own experience. The initial version of his account of childbed fever as a form of blood poisoning presented infection with cadaveric matter essentially as the one and only source of the disease; and he was right in reasoning that if this hypothesis should be true, then destruction of cadaveric particles by antiseptic washing should reduce the mortality. Furthermore, his experiment did show the test implication to be true. Hence, in this case, the premisses of (2*b*) were both true. Yet, his hypothesis was false, for as he later discovered, putrid material from living organisms, too, could produce childbed fever.

Thus, the favorable outcome of a test, that is, the fact that a test implication inferred from a hypothesis is found to be true, does not prove the hypothesis to be true. Even if many implications of a hypothesis have been borne out by careful tests, the hypothesis may still be false. The following argument still commits the fallacy of affirming the consequent:

> (2*c*)   If *H* is true, then so are $I_1, I_2, \ldots, I_n$.
> (As the evidence shows) $I_1, I_2, \ldots, I_n$ are all true.
> *H* is true.

This, too, can be illustrated by reference to Semmelweis' final hypothesis in its first version. As we noted earlier, his hypothesis also yields the test implications that among cases of street births admitted to the First Division, mortality from puerperal fever should be below the average for the Division, and that infants of mothers who escape the illness do not contract childbed fever; and these implications, too, were borne out by the evidence—even though the first version of the final hypothesis was false.

But the observation that a favorable outcome of however many tests does not afford conclusive proof for a hypothesis should not lead us to think that if we have subjected a hypothesis to a number of tests and all of them have had a favorable outcome, we are no better off than if we had not tested the hypothesis at all. For each of our tests might conceivably have had an unfavorable outcome and might have led to the rejection of the hypothesis. A set of favorable results obtained by testing different test implications, $I_1, I_2, \ldots, I_n$, of a hypothesis shows that as far as these particular implications are concerned, the hypothesis has been borne out; and while this result does not afford a complete proof of the hypothesis, it provides at least some support, some partial corroboration or confirmation for it.

NOTE

1. The story of Semmelweis' work and of the difficulties he encountered forms a fascinating page in the history of medicine. A detailed account, which includes translations and paraphrases of large portions of Semmelweis' writings, is given in W. J. Sinclair, *Semmelweis: His Life and His Doctrine* (Manchester, England: Manchester University Press, 1909). Brief quoted phrases in this chapter are taken from this work. The highlights of Semmelweis' career are recounted in the first chapter of P. de Kruif, *Men Against Death* (New York: Harcourt, Brace & World, Inc., 1932).

STUDY QUESTIONS

1. Give your own example of testing a hypothesis by use of scientific method.
2. Give your own example of an argument in the form of *modus tollens*.
3. If an implication inferred from a hypothesis is found to be true, is the hypothesis thereby proven to be true?
4. What is the value of a partial confirmation of a hypothesis?

Antiscientism

GILLIAN BARKER AND PHILIP KITCHER

Gillian Barker is Assistant Professor of Philosophy at the University of Western Ontario, and Philip Kitcher is Professor of Philosophy at Columbia University. They explore the reasons why hostility toward science is not uncommon.

... [T]he world clearly contains genuinely antiscience sentiment: attitudes of hostility or contempt for science that have important effects on public decision making about science policy and hobble our ability to make good use of scientific knowledge.... Worries about the human implications of the scientific worldview

From *Philosophy of Science: A New Introduction*, Oxford University Press, 2014. Reprinted by permission of the publisher.

and the scientific conception of knowledge go back to the early modern period when physics achieved its earliest successes.

The triumph of the "mechanical philosophy" in the eighteenth century provoked worries that science had given us a world that is soulless, meaningless, and devoid of all the things that matter to people. Before the Scientific Revolution, Europeans lived in a world that they understood to be filled with meaning and purpose, one in which the place of humankind was (in every sense) central. They were "at home" in the universe. The cosmos as they conceived it was of a reassuringly human scale, and its history stretched back only a few hundred human generations. Their knowledge about the world—about its structure and history—was at the same time knowledge about the meanings and purposes of their lives and actions, knowledge about how to live. Other traditional systems of belief have shared many of these features, although, of course, the details have varied widely. But the world revealed by the new sciences of the seventeenth century was quite different. The Earth was no longer the center of the universe, but just one planet among many. The universe was vast and impersonal, and devoid of the qualities most familiar to us; the homely world of our sensory and emotional experience came to be seen as an illusion laid over an austere reality—atoms moving through the void. Knowledge, as the new sciences came to conceive it, is a dispassionate knowledge of the facts of this austere world, and nothing more. It cannot help us to understand our place in the universe, the meaning or purpose of our actions or of larger events. Indeed, as the new sciences matured, they seemed more and more strongly to suggest that there are no meanings or purposes at all, except those that we invent; no truths about what we should do or how we should live, beyond our conflicting desires and opinions. In an image repeated again and again in writings by scientists and philosophers, we heirs of the Scientific Revolution found ourselves alone, in a "disenchanted" world, a world that cares nothing for us, a world unimaginably vast, empty, and cold.

The scientific developments of the ensuing centuries offer no new comfort. Quantum physics has given us a world that is far stranger and less comprehensible than that offered by the mechanical philosophy, but no more humane. And most important, evolutionary biology, cognitive science, and neuroscience have combined to bring the full force of the scientific worldview to bear on our understanding of ourselves. Descartes and the other mechanical philosophers abolished the idea of organisms as beings endowed with their own purposes and meaningful structure, but though they saw other organisms and human bodies as elaborate machines, they held that the machine that is a human body is connected to a soul. The new sciences of our era turn even the soul into part of the machine.

Defenders of science have little patience with these complaints. We should stand firm, they say, even if the truth is hard to face. If we give up the cozy illusions of the past, we may come to a different kind of fulfilling experience, one reported by scientists from Galileo to Richard Dawkins, achieving the thrilling sense of intellectual freedom science offers and appreciating the awe-inspiring beauty, order, and richness of the world it reveals. A clear-eyed vision of reality more than compensates us for the loss of our prescientific illusions. We should also remember that the sense of meaning and purpose inherent in the worldview of prescientific Europe was deeply involved in the justification of a social order marked by an oppressive class structure and dogmatic religious belief. Liberating people from the "purposes" of such a social order was a great achievement, one made possible by the emergence of modern science.

Many people are not convinced by defenses of science along these lines. They have a deep sense of loss, one not to be assuaged by urging them to share the thrill of understanding nature without illusions. . . . Although they may respect areas of science bountiful in offering predictions and interventions that make their lives go better, they seek ways of interpreting the theoretical bases for the practical successes that allow them to retain comforting beliefs: If the cosmologists tell them that the universe originated in a "big bang," they continue to envisage a creator who lit the fuse. And where predictions and interventions are less successful, they are apt to be skeptical of scientists' claims. As they focus attention on human sciences, they recognize forecasting failures and misguided interventions—the economists are far less sure-footed than their counterparts in chemistry. Especially with those sciences that deal with complex systems—historical sciences like evolutionary biology as well as studies of ecosystems and of the Earth's atmosphere, where precise predictions and impressive interventions are hard to come by—there might seem to be grounds for doubt. If the standard of success is prediction and control, then many alleged sciences appear to fail the test. Especially when these sciences clash sharply with firmly held views about the place of humanity in the cosmos, they are apt to face firm rejection.

Public disagreement among scientists exacerbates the situation, perhaps because many people have expected that science would offer certainty. Even when, as in the case of climate change, thousands of experts agree, the force of the consensus can be blunted when people perceive that "other experts" (typically not specialists in climate science; typically with well-concealed sources of support from industrial conglomerates) offer an "alternative viewpoint." It is not hard to hang on to your cherished convictions when the science you are asked to accept has little to offer in the way of spectacular interventions or precise predictions, and when the debates carried on in the media seem to make it clear that there are two sides to the story.

Antiscience is not exactly wishful thinking, but it grows out of a desire to preserve what the sciences seem to threaten. Its growth is facilitated when the most striking markers of scientific success are absent, and when the clashing "experts" seem to show that the issue remains controversial. Instead of thinking of antiscience sentiments as wholly irrational, we might view them as expressions of natural reasonableness in a social environment that hinders the transmission of well-supported findings. Central aspects of people's ways of life are threatened—they are asked to give up their normal practices (e.g., of energy consumption), their commonsense beliefs about the world, or (even worse) the deity in whom they put their trust. The exhortations to find fulfillment in the bracing experience of looking truth in the face make little contact with the realities of most human lives. The evidence that supports the threatening sciences is subtle and delicate, difficult to explain thoroughly and lucidly. And finally, what percolates through the channels of information transmission is not even an approximation to a simplified version of the evidential situation, but a cacophony of voices in which the experts cannot be distinguished from the ignorant or from those whose verdicts have been bought. No wonder, then, that antiscience is one result.

STUDY QUESTIONS

1. Should those who are suspicious of science reject new medical treatments?
2. Should those who are suspicious of science reject findings made through telescopes or microscopes?
3. Is belief in the efficacy of science compatible with religious commitment?
4. Is knowing the truth always beneficial?

PART 3

Knowledge

Caring and Epistemic Demands

ᘒ

LINDA ZAGZEBSKI

We now turn to a fundamental field of philosophy: the theory of knowledge, or, as philosophers often refer to it, "epistemology," from the Greek word *epistēmē*, meaning "knowledge." Why should we care whether we hold true beliefs? An answer is provided in the following selection by Linda Zagzebski, Professor of Philosophy at the University of Oklahoma.

....

We all care about a lot of things. Even if it were possible not to care about anything, we would not have a good life if we did not care. Caring about many things is not only natural, but is part of any life we would care to live. But if we care about anything, we must care about having true beliefs in the domains we care about. If I care about my children's lives and I am minimally rational, I must care about having true beliefs about my children's lives. If I care about football, I must care about having true beliefs about football. I'll call a belief that is governed by a concern for truth a *conscientiously* held belief. I assume that conscientiousness is something that comes in degrees, and I propose that (with some qualifications) the more we care about something, the more conscientious we must be.

I think that caring imposes a demand for conscientious belief on us in two ways. First, there is a demand to be conscientious in whatever beliefs we have in that domain, and second, there is a demand to acquire conscientious beliefs in the domain. The first demand is no doubt stronger than the second because our ability to care probably extends beyond our ability to form beliefs, although our inability to form beliefs in some domain probably limits our ability to care. For example, we may care about the personal well-being of all the victims of a hurricane, but since there are so many of them, none of us can acquire beliefs about very many of those people. I suspect that this limits our ability to care about them individually. What we tend to do is get beliefs about them as a class, and if that is all we have, then I suspect that we can only care about them as a class. That is probably why photojournalists try to put a face on disastrous events; it aids us in caring about the victims as individuals.

I am suggesting, then, that not only do we commit ourselves to conscientiously getting beliefs about those things we care about, but if we don't or can't do it, that tends to weaken our caring. And if we need to care about many things to

From Linda Zagzebski, *On Epistemology*, Wadsworth/CENGAGE Learning, 2009. Reprinted by permission of the publisher.

have a good life, the limitations of our ability to form beliefs conscientiously limit the desirability of our lives.

There are some qualifications on the demand to acquire beliefs in the domains we care about. Sometimes having beliefs in a domain we care about conflicts with something else we care about. Even if you care about your friends' personal happiness, if you also care about their privacy, you will not care about having beliefs about the most personal aspects of their lives, at least not many detailed beliefs. So there are exceptions to the demand to conscientiously acquire beliefs in the domains of what we care about, but the exceptions also arise from something we care about, such as the privacy of other people. (This is one reason why curiosity can be a vice.)

Another qualification is that the desire to acquire beliefs about what we care about can sometimes be counterproductive. For example, health is clearly an important component of a desirable life, but obsession with one's health can detract from the desirability of one's life because getting too much information about health can impair your health. But aside from these qualifications, I think that in general, if we care about something, merely being conscientious in whatever beliefs we happen to have in that domain is not enough. We also need to get beliefs in those domains.

So we care about many things, and caring about anything imposes a demand on us to care about true belief in the domains of what we care about, and that includes a demand to acquire beliefs conscientiously in those domains. But the logic of caring demands something more than conscientious belief for a variety of reasons. For one thing, we are often agents in the domains of what we care about. We want beliefs that can serve as the ground of action, and that requires not only true beliefs, but confidence that the particular beliefs we are acting upon are true. The degree of confidence needed varies with the context. Acting involves time, usually effort, and sometimes risk or sacrifice, and it is not rational to engage in action without a degree of confidence in the truth of the beliefs upon which we act that is high enough to make the time, effort, and risk involved in acting worthwhile. Sometimes the degree of confidence we need amounts to certainty, but usually it does not.

We also know that we have false beliefs, if for no other reason than that we sometimes have beliefs that conflict, and since we do not want false beliefs in the domains of what we care about, we want mechanisms to sort out the false beliefs from the true ones. Imagine you are digging for a precious substance such as gold. (Ignore the fact that these days you are not likely to find any.) Suppose that as you dig for gold, you find lots of gold nuggets, but you also find lots of Fool's Gold, which we will imagine is hard to distinguish from real gold. Imagine also that you discover that some of the nuggets you have kept in the past are actually Fool's Gold, so even though you are pretty sure that you have lots of real gold, you are not sure which is which. Even though you have some valuable gold, it is not very helpful to have it if it is mixed up with Fool's Gold. You not only want gold, but you also want to distinguish the real gold from the fake gold. Similarly, we not only want true beliefs, but we also want to distinguish the true beliefs from the false ones. It diminishes the value of our true beliefs if they are mixed up with too many false beliefs.

Among the things we care about is caring that others care about what we care about, which means that we care about their having true beliefs about what we care about, and we also care to some extent about what they care about. So we care about being good informants to others. We want the ability to convey true beliefs and not false beliefs to others.

Conscientiousness requires self-trust. Being conscientious is all I can do to get true beliefs, but there is no guarantee that being conscientious gives me the truth. I can be careful, be thorough in seeking and evaluating evidence, be open-minded, listen to those with a contrary view, and so forth, but there are no guarantees. So I need trust that there is a close connection between conscientious belief and true belief. If I did not trust, and my lack of trust led me to have fewer conscientious beliefs in the domains I care about, I would care less about what I care about and that would give me a less desirable life, a life I would not care to have. Furthermore, since I depend upon other people for most of my beliefs, I need another sort of trust. I am not often in a position to confirm that other people are conscientious, so I need to trust that they are. And again, if I don't trust them, I will have fewer beliefs about what I care about and that will give me a less desirable life.

The logic of caring requires that we live in a community of epistemic trust, the importance of which is dramatically described in the Greek legend of Cassandra. According to that myth, Apollo gave Cassandra the gift of prophecy as part of a scheme to seduce her. When she rebuffed him, he did not take back his gift, but did something much worse. He allowed her to continue to see the future, but she was fated never to be believed. Cassandra's curse meant that her warning that the Trojan horse was a trick went unheeded, with disastrous results for the Trojans, but its effect on her was terrible in a different way. She was the ultimate voiceless woman. Aeschylus tells us it drove her mad.

Cassandra was disbelieved only in her predictions about the future, but imagine what it would be like to be disbelieved about everything you say. You would be epistemically isolated in such an extreme way that you would probably be isolated in every other way as well. Every attempt at communication would be futile, so there would be no point in trying to talk with anybody about anything. You could not make plans with others, successfully express your feelings to them, or even do the minimum that it takes to carry on practical life. We need trust, but trust breaks down when people are thought to be untrust*worthy*. Living in a community of epistemically trusting and trustworthy people is an important requirement of any worthwhile life.

Another thing we care about is not being surprised at what happens next. We want to be able to predict the way the world will be tomorrow. We probably want that anyway, but we certainly want to be able to predict the way the world will be in ways that impinge on what we care about. That is one reason science has so much status. It allows us to explain the future as well as the past.

I have mentioned a series of epistemic values that we have because we care about many things and caring about things is part of living a life we would care to live. These values include true belief, the ability to distinguish true from false belief, certainty or at least confidence in our beliefs, credibility, trust and trustworthiness, and predictability. Each of these things is desirable within a domain of what we care about because we care about that domain. Caring imposes these demands on us, which means we impose these demands on ourselves by caring. Some of these values may be components of knowledge, but knowledge might be something else. In any case, knowledge also is something we want in the domains of what we care about, and we might also want knowledge for its own sake.

STUDY QUESTIONS

1. According to Zagzebski, in what two ways does caring impose a demand for conscientious belief?
2. What does Zagzebski mean by "a community of epistemic trust"?
3. What lesson does Zagzebski draw from the legend of Cassandra?
4. If some of your beliefs turned out to be false, would you care, and, if so, why?

Knowing vs. Thinking

⟶

JENNIFER NAGEL

How does knowing that something is the case differ from merely thinking it so? A crucial difference is that you can think that a falsehood is true but not know that it is true. Thus, knowledge is linked to truth. The matter is discussed by Jennifer Nagel, Professor of Philosophy at the University of Toronto.

....

...[H]ow is 'know' different from the contrasting verb 'think'? Everyday usage provides some clues. Consider the following two sentences:

Jill knows that her door is locked.
Bill thinks that his door is locked.

We immediately register a difference between Jill and Bill—but what is it? One factor that comes to mind has to do with the truth of the embedded claim about the door. If Bill just thinks that his door is locked, perhaps this is because Bill's door is not really locked. Maybe he didn't turn the key far enough

From Jennifer Nagel, *Knowledge: A Very Short Introduction* (Oxford: Oxford University Press, 2014). Reprinted by permission of the publisher.

this morning as he was leaving home. Jill's door, however, must be locked for the sentence about her to be true: you can't ordinarily say, 'Jill knows that her door is locked, but her door isn't locked.' Knowledge links a subject to a truth. This feature of 'knowing that' is called *factivity*: we can know only facts, or true propositions. 'To know that' is not the only factive construction: others include 'to realize that', 'to see that', 'to remember that', 'to prove that'. You can realize that your lottery ticket has won only if it really has won. One of the special features of 'know' is that it is the most general such verb, standing for the deeper state that remembering, realizing, and the rest all have in common. Seeing that the barn is on fire or proving that there is no greatest prime number are just two of the many ways of achieving knowledge.

Of course, it's possible to *seem* to know something that later turns out to be false—but as soon as we recognize the falsity, we have to retract the claim that it was ever known. ('We thought he knew that, but it turned out he was wrong and didn't know.') To complicate matters, it can be hard to tell whether someone knows something or just seems to know it. This doesn't erase the distinction between knowing and seeming to know. In a market flooded with imitations it can be hard to tell a real diamond from a fake, but the practical difficulty of identifying the genuine article shouldn't make us think there is no difference out there: real diamonds have a special essence—a special structure of carbon atoms—not shared by lookalikes.

The dedicated link to truth is part of the essence of knowledge. We speak of 'knowing' falsehoods when we are speaking in a non-literal way (just as we can use a word like 'delicious' sarcastically, describing things that taste awful). Emphasis—in italics or pitch—is one sign of non-literal use. 'That cabbage soup smells *delicious*, right?' 'I *knew* I had been picked for the team. But it turned out I wasn't.' This use of 'knows' has been called the 'projected' use: the speaker is projecting herself into a past frame of mind, recalling a moment when it seemed to her that she knew. The emphasis is a clue that the speaker is distancing herself from that frame of mind: she didn't literally or really know (as our emphatic speaker didn't really like the soup). The literal use of 'know' can't mix with falsehood in this way.

By contrast, belief can easily link a subject to a false proposition: it's perfectly acceptable to say, 'Bill thinks that his door is locked, but it isn't.' The verb 'think' is *non-factive*. (Other non-factive verbs include 'hope', 'suspect', 'doubt', and 'say'—you can certainly say that your door is locked when it isn't.) Opinions being non-factive does not mean that opinion is always wrong: when Bill just thinks that his door is locked, he could be right. Perhaps Bill's somewhat unreliable roommate Bob occasionally forgets to lock the door. If Bill isn't entirely sure that his door is locked, then he could think that it is locked, and be right, but fail to know that it is locked. Confidence matters to knowledge.

Knowledge has still further requirements, beyond truth and confidence. Someone who is very confident but for the wrong reasons would also fail to have knowledge. A father whose daughter is charged with a crime might feel utterly certain that she is innocent. But if his confidence has a basis in emotion rather than evidence (suppose he's deliberately avoiding looking at any facts about the case), then even if he is right that his daughter is innocent, he may not really know that she is. But if a confidently held true belief is not enough for knowledge, what more needs to be added? This question turns out to be surprisingly difficult. . . .

STUDY QUESTIONS

1. Can you think what is false?
2. Can you know what is false?
3. Explain the distinction between knowing and seeming to know.
4. How does holding a belief on the basis of emotion differ from holding it on the basis of evidence?

Is Justified True Belief Knowledge?

EDMUND L. GETTIER

Suppose a belief is true, you believe it confidently, and your belief has a basis in evidence. Might you still not know that the belief is true? Perhaps not. A much-discussed example is found in an article by Edmund L. Gettier, Professor Emeritus of Philosophy at the University of Massachusetts at Amherst. He begins by referring to A. J. Ayer (1910–1989), who was Professor of Philosophy at the University of Oxford and one of the best-known philosophers of the twentieth century.

....

Ayer has stated the necessary and sufficient condition for [S knows that P] as follows:

(i) P is true,
(ii) S is sure that P is true, and
(iii) S has the right to be sure that P is true.

I shall argue that the conditions stated therein do not constitute a *sufficient* condition for the truth of the proposition that S knows that P. . . .

Suppose that Smith and Jones have applied for a certain job. And suppose that Smith has strong evidence for the following conjunctive proposition:

(d) Jones is the man who will get the job, and Jones has ten coins in his pocket.

From Edmund L. Gettier, *Analysis,* 23 (1963). Reprinted by permission of the author.

Smith's evidence for (d) might be that the president of the company assured him that Jones would in the end be selected, and that he, Smith, had counted the coins in Jones's pocket ten minutes ago. Proposition (d) entails:

(e)   The man who will get the job has ten coins in his pocket.

Let us suppose that Smith sees the entailment from (d) to (e), and accepts (e) on the grounds of (d), for which he has strong evidence. In this case, Smith is clearly justified in believing that (e) is true.

But imagine, further, that unknown to Smith, he himself, not Jones, will get the job. And, also, unknown to Smith, he himself has ten coins in his pocket. Proposition (e) is then true, though proposition (d), from which Smith inferred (e), is false. In our example, then, all of the following are true: (*i*) (e) is true, (*ii*) Smith believes that (e) is true, and (*iii*) Smith is justified in believing that (e) is true. But it is equally clear that Smith does not *know* that (e) is true; for (e) is true in virtue of the number of coins in Smith's pocket, while Smith does not know how many coins are in Smith's pocket, and bases his belief in (e) on a count of the coins in Jones's pocket, whom he falsely believes to be the man who will get the job.

STUDY QUESTIONS

1. What is the point of Gettier's example?
2. Is Smith justified in believing that the man who will get the job has ten coins in his pocket?
3. Does Smith know that Jones will get the job?
4. Can you develop your own example along the same lines as Gettier's case?

Conditions for Knowledge

᪣

Robert Nozick

Many philosophers have proposed revised definitions of knowledge in an effort to deal with cases like the one Gettier presents. An intriguing suggestion is developed by Robert Nozick (1938–2002), who was Professor of Philosophy at Harvard University.

....

From *Philosophical Explanations* by Robert Nozick. Copyright © 1981 by Robert Nozick. Reprinted by permission of The Belknap Press of Harvard University Press. The symbolism is simplified.

In knowledge, a belief is linked somehow to the fact believed; without this linkage there may be true belief but there will not be knowledge. Plato first made the point that knowledge is not simply a belief that is true, if someone knowing nothing about the matter separately tells you and me contradictory things, getting one of us to believe p while the other believes not-p, although one of us will have a belief that happens to be true, neither of us will have knowledge. Something more is needed for a person S to know that p, to go alongside

(1) p is true.
(2) S believes that p.

This something more, I think, is not simply an additional fact, but a way that 1 and 2 are linked. . . .

Our task is to formulate further conditions to go alongside

(1) p is true.
(2) S believes that p.

We would like each condition to be necessary for knowledge, so any case that fails to satisfy it will not be an instance of knowledge. Furthermore, we would like the conditions to be jointly sufficient for knowledge, so any case that satisfies all of them will be an instance of knowledge. . . .

Let us consider. . . .

(3) If p weren't true, S wouldn't believe that p.

The subjunctive condition 3 serves to exclude cases of the sort first described by Edmund Gettier, such as the following. Two other people are in my office and I am justified on the basis of much evidence in believing the first owns a Ford car; though he (now) does not, the second person (a stranger to me) owns one. I believe truly and justifiably that someone (or other) in my office owns a Ford car, but I do not know someone does. Concluded Gettier, knowledge is not simply justified true belief.

The following subjunctive, which specifies condition 3 for this Gettier case, is not satisfied: if no one in my office owned a Ford car, I wouldn't believe that some-one did. The situation that would obtain if no one in my office owned a Ford is one where the stranger does not (or where he is not in the office); and in that situation I still would believe, as before, that someone in my office does own a Ford, namely, the first person. So the subjunctive condition 3 excludes this Gettier case as a case of knowledge. . . .

Despite the power and intuitive force of the condition that if p weren't true the person would not believe it, this condition does not (in conjunction with the first two conditions) rule out every problem case. There remains, for exam-ple, the case of the person in [a] tank who is brought to believe, by direct elec-trical and chemical stimulation of his brain, that he is in the tank and is being brought to believe things in this way; he does not know this is true. However, the subjunctive condition is satisfied: if he weren't floating in the tank, he wouldn't believe he was.

The person in the tank does not know he is there, because his belief is not sensitive to the truth. Although it is caused by the fact that is its content, it is not sensitive to that fact. The operators of the tank could have produced any belief, including the false belief that he wasn't in the tank; if they had, he would have believed that. Perfect sensitivity would involve beliefs and facts varying together. We already have one portion of that variation, subjunctively at least: if p were false, he wouldn't believe it. This sensitivity as specified by a subjunctive does not have the belief vary with the truth or falsity of p in all possible situations, merely in the ones that would or might obtain if p were false.

The subjunctive condition 3 . . . tells us only half the story about how his belief is sensitive to the truth-value of p. It tells us how his belief state is sensitive to p's falsity, but not how it is sensitive to p's truth; it tells us what his belief state would be if p were false, but not what it would be if p were true.

To be sure, conditions 1 and 2 tell us that p is true and he does believe it, but it does not follow that his believing p is sensitive to p's being true. This additional sensitivity is given to us by a further subjunctive: if p were true, he would believe it.

(4)   If p were true, S would believe that p.

A person knows that p when he not only does truly believe it, but . . . if it weren't true he wouldn't believe it, and if it were true he would believe it. To know that p is to be someone who would believe it if it were true, and who wouldn't believe it if it were false.

It will be useful to have a term for this situation when a person's belief is thus subjunctively connected to the fact. Let us say of a person who believes that p, which is true, that when 3 and 4 hold, his belief *tracks* the truth that p. To know is to have a belief that tracks the truth. Knowledge is a particular way of being connected to the world, having a specific real factual connection to the world: tracking it.

STUDY QUESTIONS

1. What task does Nozick set for himself?
2. What two subjunctive conditions for knowledge does he offer?
3. Are both conditions needed to exclude Gettier's case?
4. What does Nozick mean by "a belief that tracks the truth"?

Appearance and Reality

Bertrand Russell

An ancient philosophical question is whether we know the world as it is or only as we experience it from a limited perspective. The relation between what appears to be the case and what is the case, between appearance and reality, is the theme of our next selection. Its author is Bertrand Russell, whose work we read previously.

....

Is there any knowledge in the world which is so certain that no reasonable man could doubt it? This question, which at first sight might not seem difficult, is really one of the most difficult that can be asked. When we have realized the obstacles in the way of a straightforward and confident answer, we shall be well launched on the study of philosophy—for philosophy is merely the attempt to answer such ultimate questions, not carelessly and dogmatically, as we do in ordinary life and even in the sciences, but critically, after exploring all that makes such questions puzzling, and after realizing all the vagueness and confusion that underlie our ordinary ideas.

In daily life, we assume as certain many things which, on a closer scrutiny, are found to be so full of apparent contradictions that only a great amount of thought enables us to know what it is that we really may believe. In the search for certainty, it is natural to begin with our present experiences, and in some sense, no doubt, knowledge is to be derived from them. But any statement as to what it is that our immediate experiences make us know is very likely to be wrong. It seems to me that I am now sitting in a chair, at a table of a certain shape, on which I see sheets of paper with writing or print. By turning my head I see out of the window buildings and clouds and the sun. I believe that the sun is about ninety-three million miles from the earth; that it is a hot globe many times bigger than the earth; that, owing to the earth's rotation, it rises every morning, and will continue to do so for an indefinite time in the future. I believe that, if any other normal person comes into my room, he will see the same chairs and tables and books and papers as I see, and that the table which I see is the same as the table which I feel pressing against my arm. All this seems to be so evident as to be hardly worth stating, except in answer to a man who doubts whether I know anything. Yet all this may be reasonably doubted, and all of it requires much careful discussion before we can be sure that we have stated it in a form that is wholly true.

To make our difficulties plain, let us concentrate attention on the table. To the eye it is oblong, brown and shiny, to the touch it is smooth and cool and hard;

when I tap it, it gives out a wooden sound. Any one else who sees and feels and hears the table will agree with this description, so that it might seem as if no difficulty would arise; but as soon as we try to be more precise our troubles begin. Although I believe that the table is "really" of the same colour all over, the parts that reflect the light look much brighter than the other parts, and some parts look white because of reflected light. I know that, if I move, the parts that reflect the light will be different, so that the apparent distribution of colours on the table will change. It follows that if several people are looking at the table at the same moment, no two of them will see exactly the same distribution of colours, because no two can see it from exactly the same point of view, and any change in the point of view makes some change in the way the light is reflected.

For most practical purposes these differences are unimportant, but to the painter they are all-important: the painter has to unlearn the habit of thinking that things seem to have the colour which common sense says they "really" have, and to learn the habit of seeing things as they appear. Here we have already the beginning of one of the distinctions that cause most trouble in philosophy—the distinction between "appearance" and "reality," between what things seem to be and what they are. The painter wants to know what things seem to be, the practical man and the philosopher want to know what they are; but the philosopher's wish to know this is stronger than the practical man's, and is more troubled by knowledge as to the difficulties of answering the question.

To return to the table. It is evident from what we have found, that there is no colour which preeminently appears to be *the* colour of the table, or even of any one particular part of the table—it appears to be of different colours from different points of view, and there is no reason for regarding some of these as more really its colour than others. And we know that even from a given point of view the colour will seem different by artificial light, or to a colour-blind man, or to a man wearing blue spectacles, while in the dark there will be no colour at all, though to touch and hearing the table will be unchanged. This colour is not something which is inherent in the table, but something depending upon the table and the spectator and the way the light falls on the table. When, in ordinary life, we speak of *the* colour of the table, we only mean the sort of colour which it will seem to have to a normal spectator from an ordinary point of view under usual conditions of light. But the other colours which appear under other conditions have just as good a right to be considered real; and therefore, to avoid favouritism, we are compelled to deny that, in itself, the table has any one particular colour.

The same thing applies to the texture. With the naked eye one can see the grain, but otherwise the table looks smooth and even. If we looked at it through a microscope, we should see roughnesses and hills and valleys, and all sorts of differences that are imperceptible to the naked eye. Which of these is the "real" table? We are naturally tempted to say that what we see through the microscope is more real, but that in turn would be changed by a still more powerful microscope. If, then, we cannot trust what we see with the naked eye, why should we trust what we see through a microscope? Thus, again, the confidence in our senses with which we began deserts us.

The *shape* of the table is no better. We are all in the habit of judging as to the "real" shapes of things, and we do this so unreflectingly that we come to think we actually see the real shapes. But, in fact, as we all have to learn if we try to draw, a given thing looks different in shape from every different point of view. If our table is "really" rectangular, it will look, from almost all points of view, as if it had two acute angles and two obtuse angles. If opposite sides are parallel, they will look as if they converged to a point away from the spectator; if they are of equal length, they will look as if the nearer side were longer. All these things are not commonly noticed in looking at a table, because experience has taught us to construct the "real" shape from the apparent shape, and the "real" shape is what interests us as practical men. But the "real" shape is not what we see; it is something inferred from what we see. And what we see is constantly changing in shape as we move about the room; so that here again the senses seem not to give us the truth about the table itself, but only about the appearance of the table.

Similar difficulties arise when we consider the sense of touch. It is true that the table always gives us a sensation of hardness, and we feel that it resists pressure. But the sensation we obtain depends upon how hard we press the table and also upon what part of the body we press with; thus the various sensations due to various pressures or various parts of the body cannot be supposed to reveal *directly* any definite property of the table, but at most to be *signs* of some property which perhaps *causes* all the sensations, but is not actually apparent in any of them. And the same applies still more obviously to the sounds which can be elicited by rapping the table.

Thus it becomes evident that the real table, if there is one, is not the same as what we immediately experience by sight or touch or hearing. The real table, if there is one, is not *immediately* known to us at all, but must be an inference from what is immediately known. Hence, two very difficult questions at once arise; namely, (1) Is there a real table at all? (2) If so, what sort of object can it be?

It will help us in considering these questions to have a few simple terms of which the meaning is definite and clear. Let us give the name of "sense-data" to the things that are immediately known in sensation: such things as colours, sounds, smells, hardnesses, roughnesses, and so on. We shall give the name "sensation" to the experience of being immediately aware of these things. Thus, whenever we see a colour, we have a sensation *of* the colour, but the colour itself is a sense-datum, not a sensation. The colour is that *of* which we are immediately aware, and the awareness itself is the sensation. It is plain that if we are to know anything about the table, it must be by means of the sense-data—brown colour, oblong shape, smoothness, etc.—which we associate with the table; but, for the reasons which have been given, we cannot say that the table *is* the sense-data, or even that the sense-data are directly properties of the table. Thus a problem arises as to the relation of the sense-data to the real table, supposing there is such a thing....

In fact, almost all philosophers seem to be agreed that there is a real table: they almost all agree that, however much our sense-data—colour, shape, smoothness, etc.—may depend upon us, yet their occurrence is a sign of something existing independently of us, something differing, perhaps, completely from our sense-data, and yet to be regarded as causing those sense-data whenever we are in a suitable relation to the real table....

[I]t will be well to consider for a moment what it is that we have discovered so far. It has appeared that, if we take any common object of the sort that is supposed to be known by the senses, what the senses *immediately* tell us is not the truth about the object as it is apart from us, but only the truth about certain sense-data which, so far as we can see, depend upon the relations between us and the object. Thus what we directly see and feel is merely "appearance," which we believe to be a sign of some "reality" behind. But if the reality is not what appears, have we any means of knowing whether there is any reality at all? And if so, have we any means of finding out what it is like?

Such questions are bewildering, and it is difficult to know that even the strangest hypotheses may not be true. Thus our familiar table, which has roused but the slightest thoughts in us hitherto, has become a problem full of surprising possibilities. The one thing we know about it is that it is not what it seems.

STUDY QUESTIONS

1. By what reasoning does Russell reach the conclusion that the table has no particular color?
2. By what reasoning does Russell reach the conclusion that the table has no particular shape?
3. What does Russell mean by "sense-data"?
4. Has Russell proven that the table is not what it seems?

What Can I Know?

D. Z. PHILLIPS

Philosophers often test fundamental beliefs by raising doubts about them, then considering possible ways of resolving the doubts. The previous selection, by Bertrand Russell, raised doubts about the evidence of the senses and concluded that a familiar table is not what it seems. Our next article, authored by D. Z. Phillips (1934–2006), who was Professor of Philosophy at the University of Wales, Swansea, maintains that Russell's doubts can be answered and that we do know the table as it is.

Here is a typical instance of philosophers disagreeing. Which, if either, is correct? Just as each member of a jury at a trial needs to make a decision and defend a view after considering all the relevant evidence, so each philosophical inquirer needs to make a decision and defend a view after considering all the relevant arguments. The challenge and excitement of philosophy is that, after taking account of the work others have done, the responsibility for reaching conclusions is your own.

....

What is philosophy about? Before I went to university, but knowing that philosophy was going to be one of the subjects I was to study there, I read a well-known introduction to philosophy in the hope of answering that question. My first impression was that the philosopher is an ultra-cautious person. Philosophers do not rush into saying that we know this or that, as most people do. They step back and think about things. Although we say we know all sorts of things, strictly speaking—philosophers conclude—we do not.

Given this view of philosophy, it seemed to me that the usefulness of philosophy was evident. Philosophy is a way of sharpening our thinking. It teaches us to be cautious, and not to be over-hasty in reaching our conclusions. By imposing its strict demands, philosophy tightens up our standards of knowledge. Our day-to-day assumptions are shot through with contradictions and inconsistencies. A great deal of reflection is necessary before we can arrive at what we really know. Philosophy is an indispensable guide in this reflection. This view of the usefulness of philosophy was reflected in the views of many educationalists, and this is still the case. They favour introductory classes in philosophy even for those whose primary intentions are to study other subjects. The pencil needs to be sharpened before it can write with sufficient care about other topics.

This straightforward view of philosophy was given a severe jolt, however, when I read further and discovered the kinds of things that many philosophers were prepared to doubt.[1] They doubt things that we ordinarily would not doubt. The list that I read in the introduction to philosophy was surprising, to say the least. The philosopher told me that it seemed to him, at a certain moment, that he was sitting in a chair at a table which had a certain shape, on which he saw sheets of paper with writing or print on them. By turning his head he could see buildings, clouds, and the sun through the window. He believed that the sun is about ninety-three million miles away from the Earth and that, owing to the Earth's rotation, it rises every morning and will continue to do so for an indefinite time in the future. He believed that if any other normal person came into the room, that person would see the same chairs, tables, books, and papers as he saw. Further, he believed that the table he saw was the same table as he felt pressing against his arm.

What puzzled me was this: on the one hand, the philosopher wrote that all these things seemed so evident as to be hardly worth stating; but on the other hand, he said that all these facts could be reasonably doubted and that much reflection is needed before we can arrive at a description of the situation which would be wholly true. Of course, he was quite prepared to admit that most people would not bother to question these facts. They would see no point in doing so. My initial reaction was to think that the majority were correct on this issue. Suddenly, in view of what the philosopher was prepared to doubt, philosophy, so far from appearing to be a useful subject, now appeared to be a complete waste of time. The philosophical doubt seemed to be, not a tightening up of standards, but a trivial game; the kind of game which irritates parents when, on the first visit home after commencing the subject, budding philosophers confront them with the question, "So you think there's a table here, do you?" Recently, some philosophers have reacted in the same way to philosophers' doubts. They have asked why philosophers should give young people doubts that they would never have had in the first place if the philosophers had not opened their mouths. On this view, philosophy does not clarify our confusions—it creates them.

My new reaction, however, simply led to a new puzzle. Why should we doubt what seems so evident as to not need stating? Surely, it is not enough simply to accuse philosophers of indulging in trivial pursuits. They take their doubts seriously. I felt there was something wrong about these doubts, but did not know why. Whether we like it or not, people have always been puzzled about the doubts that philosophers discuss. I felt it was insufficient to say to someone who has doubts about whether we *know* something, "Well, we *do*, so that's that." Even if we feel that there is something odd about the philosophical doubts, that response will not help the doubter. The doubter is not going to accept the answer on authority. If the doubt is misplaced, we have to show the route by which it is reached. Unless we show the road to confusion, there is no road back from it. . . .

How do I come to know anything? Before I know anything, my mind must have been like an empty receptacle, waiting to receive knowledge. Where is this knowledge to come from? Surely, from something outside myself, something which will furnish my mind with knowledge. How else am I to become acquainted with "yellow," "red," "hardness," "softness," "hot," "cold," "sweetness," "bitterness," and so on? These are experiences that I receive as a result of my interaction with the external world. I call the experiences that I have "ideas," "impressions," or "sensations." These are the furnishings of my mind, the data on which any knowledge I have relies.

But, now, a sceptical worry surfaces. If the sensory experiences of my mind are my necessary starting-point in my search for knowledge, how do I ever get beyond them? I say that these experiences come from an external world, but how do I know this? If my mind is acquainted only with its own ideas, how do I know—how can I know—whether these ideas refer to anything? How can I know that they refer to an external world? The very *possibility* of knowledge of an external world seems thrown into question.

Consider "seeing" as an example; seeing a table, let us say. I want to say that this experience came about as a result of something external to itself, namely, the table. But how can I ever know that? How do I get from my experience, my idea of the table, to the real table? If I have an experience called "seeing a table," I have an obvious interest in knowing whether it refers to a table. My experience may have been caused by some other object, or by no object at all. Light conditions may create the illusion that I am seeing a table. But how can I find out whether my experience does refer to a table, or to some other object, or whether it is illusory? If I want to know what causes the bulge in my sock, I can take out the object causing the bulge, a golf ball, let us say, and find out by doing so. In this example I have an independent access to the cause of the bulge in my sock. But when I want to know the cause of the ideas in my mind, I can have no independent access to their cause. But in that case, how do I know that they are caused by anything or refer to anything? I seem to be locked in the circle of my own ideas.

Let us suppose that my mental experience takes the form of an image of an apple. How can I know whether I am seeing an apple or imagining an apple? If I am imagining an apple, my experience makes no contact with a real apple. But, once again, I can only check this if I have independent access to the apple, the very access which seems to be denied to me. How on Earth am I going to get out of this predicament? ...

Perhaps we ought to question the initial starting point of the challenge, the assumption that all I am acquainted with are the ideas of my own mind. What is it that makes this assumption attractive? Think of examples such as hearing a car in the distance. It may be said that to say I hear a car is to say more than I know, strictly speaking. I am going beyond the immediate datum of my experience. That immediate datum is a sound. That is what I can be said to know. In saying that it is the sound of a car, I am interpreting the sound, perhaps by association with other occasions, and so on.

For examples such as these, the illegitimate assumption is made that *all* our experiences are based on minimal, immediate data. Thus, although there is nothing wrong in saying that I see a book, I am told that this is a very complex claim. What I experience immediately, it is said, is not a book, but a certain diversity of light and colour. These immediate data are self-authenticating. We cannot be mistaken about them. They are called *sense-data*. When we say that we see tables and chairs we are clearly going beyond our immediate experience of sense-data. The sceptical challenge can now be reformulated in these terms: What is the relation between our experience of sense-data and our claim to experience an external world? How can we ever get from sense-data to knowledge of the external world? Claims about the external world always stand in need of evidence. Sense-data, on the other hand, provide the evidence. But the problem is that sense-data can never provide sufficient justification for saying that we are in contact with an external world. Let us see why.

What qualifies as an example of an indubitable immediate experience? "I hear a car" clearly does not qualify, since that is a claim that I could be mistaken about. But "I hear a purring engine-like noise" will not qualify either, since I could be mistaken about that too. I may have forgotten that I have cotton-wool in my ears, and the noise may, in fact, be quite a loud one. Will "I hear a noise" qualify as a minimal, immediate experience? No, because I may be mistaken about that too. What I am hearing is simply noises in my head. And so we arrive at a minimal sense-datum: "It seems to me now as if I were hearing a noise."

The outcome of our quest for an example of a minimal sense-experience is not encouraging. We must not forget that the purpose of locating such data was to provide evidence for claims concerning the external world. We were supposed to be enabled to *advance* from such data to statements concerning the external world. But the location of such data constitutes not an advance to, but a retreat from, any claims about the external world. In terms of our example, the retreat takes the following form: "I hear a car"—"I seem to hear a car"—"It seems to *me* I hear a car"—"It seems to me *now* that I hear a purring noise"—"It seems to me now as though I were hearing a purring noise."

Why did we go in search of minimal sense-data in the first place? We did so because we felt that any statement about an external world can always be doubted, and thus stands in need of evidence. What we know immediately are minimal sense-data. But is this true? . . . [W]e doubt in circumstances that we call unfavourable. But what of favourable circumstances? Can I doubt that I hear a car in these? The car may be coming directly towards me. I may be sitting in the car or driving it. There may be no room for doubt at all. It would be absurd to suggest that there is always room for doubt because I may have forgotten that I had cotton-wool in my ears. It would be odd to say that any kind of judgement or verdict on the basis of sense-data is necessary when, in favourable circumstances, we hear a car. Verdicts are needed, for the most part, when we are not in a position to hear or see things clearly. But if I am sitting at a table, leaning on it, and so on, I am not giving a verdict on anything. My sitting at a table is not a claim which stands in need of evidence. It is not a claim at all. When I see a book, select it, pick it up, turn its pages, and read it, I am not verifying anything. I am simply seeing, selecting, picking up, turning the pages, and reading a book.

Whether a statement stands in need of evidence depends on the circumstances in which it is made. Once this is admitted, we can see that there is no absolute distinction between two kinds of statement—one kind of statement which always stands in need of evidence, and another kind of statement which always provides evidence. So we cannot say that any statement about the external world stands in need of evidence and that it is the function of statements about sense-data to provide such evidence. But once this absolute distinction is rejected, we reject the terms of the sceptical challenge at the same time. It can no longer be said that we *must* show how knowledge of an external world can be arrived at on the basis of the immediate data of our experience. Indeed, when circumstances are favourable, the onus is not on us to say when we can stop doubting and be able to assert "I see a book." The onus is on the sceptic to tell us why we should have started to doubt in the first place. . . .

[W]e are sometimes mistaken about what we think we perceive. I see a stick partly immersed in water and think it is bent. Later I find out that I was mistaken. The stick was not bent. But what I saw was bent. What, then, did I see? It is tempting to reply, "Not the stick, but the appearance of the stick." What "appears," the sense-datum, does not guarantee any reference to what is really the case. By such an argument, experiences become a "something" between me and objects in the external world. In the case of illusions the "something" that I experience does not refer to anything, whereas in the case of perceptions it does.

But this conception of a sense-datum, the necessary object of my experience, is a confused one. If I think I see a bent stick which later turns out to be straight, I do not need to postulate anything other than the stick to account for my mistake. I do not see "the appearance" of the stick. It is the stick that looks bent. It is the *same* thing, namely, the stick, which—in certain conditions—appears to be bent when it is not. The phenomenon of deception does not necessitate the postulation of two realms, one of sense-data and the other of physical objects. That being so, we are not faced with the task of showing how we move from the first realm to the second.

NOTE

1. [S]ee Russell, *The Problems of Philosophy,* one of the most famous introductions to philosophy.

STUDY QUESTIONS

1. How do you know whether you are seeing an apple or imagining an apple?
2. According to Phillips, are you acquainted with more than the contents of your own mind?
3. According to Phillips, does every statement about the external world stand in need of evidence?
4. According to Phillips, why is "sense-datum" a confused notion?

The Problem of Induction

BERTRAND RUSSELL

We now return to the writings of Bertrand Russell and consider a different problem about knowledge. This one is raised by reflecting on our common practice of assuming that the laws of nature that have held in the past will continue to hold in the future.

We have learned that bread nourishes us; stones do not. But do we have good reason to believe that the laws of nature will remain constant? Starting tomorrow, might stones nourish us and bread be inedible? That is the question Russell challenges us to answer.

He is not urging that we change our basic beliefs but that we seek to understand their justification. In other words, he asks that we engage in philosophical inquiry.

....

It is obvious that if we are asked why we believe that the sun will rise tomorrow, we shall naturally answer, "Because it always has risen every day." We have a firm belief that it will rise in the future, because it has risen in the past. If we are challenged as to why we believe that it will continue to rise as heretofore, we may appeal to the laws of motion: the earth, we shall say, is a freely rotating body, and such bodies do not cease to rotate unless something interferes from outside, and there is nothing outside to interfere with the earth between now and tomorrow. Of course it might be doubted whether we are quite certain that there is nothing outside to interfere, but this is not the interesting doubt. The interesting doubt is as to whether the laws of motion will remain in operation until tomorrow. If this doubt is raised, we find ourselves in the same position as when the doubt about the sunrise was first raised.

The *only* reason for believing that the laws of motion will remain in operation is that they have operated hitherto, so far as our knowledge of the past enables us to judge. It is true that we have a greater body of evidence from the past in favour of the laws of motion than we have in favour of the sunrise, because the sunrise is merely a particular case of fulfilment of the laws of motion, and there are countless other particular cases. But the real question is: Do *any* number of cases of a law being fulfilled in the past afford evidence that it will be fulfilled in the future? If not, it becomes plain that we have no ground whatever for expecting the sun to rise tomorrow, or for expecting the bread we shall eat at our next meal not to poison us, or for any of the other scarcely conscious expectations that control our daily lives. It is to be observed that all such expectations are only *probable*; thus we have not to seek for a proof that they *must* be fulfilled, but only for some reason in favour of the view that they are *likely* to be fulfilled.

Now in dealing with this question we must, to begin with, make an important distinction, without which we should soon become involved in hopeless confusions. Experience has shown us that, hitherto, the frequent repetition of some uniform succession or coexistence has been a *cause* of our expecting the same succession or coexistence on the next occasion. Food that has a certain appearance generally has a certain taste, and it is a severe shock to our expectations when the familiar appearance is found to be associated with an unusual taste. Things which we see become associated, by habit, with certain tactile sensations which we expect if we touch them; one of the horrors of a ghost (in many ghost stories) is that it fails to give us any sensations of touch. Uneducated people who go abroad for the first time are so surprised as to be incredulous when they find their native language not understood.

And this kind of association is not confined to men; in animals also it is very strong. A horse which has been often driven along a certain road resists the attempt to drive him in a different direction. Domestic animals expect food when they see the person who usually feeds them. We know that all these rather crude expectations of uniformity are liable to be misleading. The man who has fed the chicken every day throughout its life at last wrings its neck instead, showing that more refined views as to the uniformity of nature would have been useful to the chicken.

But in spite of the misleadingness of such expectations, they nevertheless exist. The mere fact that something has happened a certain number of times causes animals and men to expect that it will happen again. Thus our instincts certainly cause us to believe that the sun will rise tomorrow, but we may be in no better a position than the chicken which unexpectedly has its neck wrung. We have therefore to distinguish the fact that past uniformities *cause* expectations as to the future, from the question whether there is any reasonable ground for giving weight to such expectations after the question of their validity has been raised.

The problem we have to discuss is whether there is any reason for believing in what is called "the uniformity of nature." The belief in the uniformity of nature is the belief that everything that has happened or will happen is an instance of some general law to which there are *no* exceptions. The crude expectations which we have been considering are all subject to exceptions, and therefore liable to disappoint those who entertain them. But science habitually assumes, at least as a working hypothesis, that general rules which have exceptions can be replaced by general rules which have no exceptions. "Unsupported bodies in air fall" is a general rule to which balloons and airplanes are exceptions. But the laws of motion and the law of gravitation, which account for the fact that most bodies fall, also account for the fact that balloons and airplanes can rise; thus the laws of motion and the law of gravitation are not subject to these exceptions.

The belief that the sun will rise tomorrow might be falsified if the earth came suddenly into contact with a large body which destroyed its rotation; but the laws of motion and the law of gravitation would not be infringed by such an event. The business of science is to find uniformities, such as the laws of motion and the law of gravitation, to which, so far as our experience extends, there are no exceptions. In this search, science has been remarkably successful, and it may be conceded that such uniformities have held hitherto. This brings us back to the question: Have we any reason, assuming that they have always held in the past, to suppose that they will hold in the future?

It has been argued that we have reason to know that the future will resemble the past, because what was the future has constantly become the past, and has always been found to resemble the past, so that we really have experience of the future, namely of times which were formerly future, which we may call past futures. But such an argument really begs the very question at issue. We have experience of past futures, but not of future futures, and the question is: Will future futures resemble past futures? This question is not to be answered by an argument which starts from past futures alone. We have therefore still to seek for some principle which shall enable us to know that the future will follow the same laws as the past.

STUDY QUESTIONS

1. Do we have good reason to expect the sun to rise tomorrow?
2. What is "the uniformity of nature"?
3. Does our belief that the sun will rise tomorrow depend on our believing in the uniformity of nature?
4. Do we have any alternative to relying on inductive reasoning?

Induction Without a Problem

৵

P. F. STRAWSON

In response to Russell, P. F. Strawson (1919–2006), who taught at the University of Oxford, argues that seeking a justification for induction is not sensible, because any successful method of finding things out necessarily has inductive support.

....

I want to point out that there is something a little odd about talking of "the inductive method," or even "the inductive policy," as if it were just one possible method among others of arguing from the observed to the unobserved, from the available evidence to the facts in question. If one asked a meteorologist what method or methods he used to forecast the weather, one would be surprised if he answered: "Oh, just the inductive method." If one asked a doctor by what means he diagnosed a certain disease, the answer "By induction" would be felt as an impatient evasion, a joke, or a rebuke. The answer one hopes for is an account of the tests made, the signs taken account of, the rules and recipes and general laws applied. When such a specific method of prediction or diagnosis is in question, one can ask whether the method is justified in practice; and here again one is asking whether its employment is inductively justified, whether it commonly gives correct results. This question would normally seem an admissible one. One might be tempted to conclude that, while there are many different specific methods of prediction, diagnosis, &c., appropriate to different subjects of inquiry, all such methods could properly be called "inductive" in the sense that their employment rested on inductive support; and that, hence, the phrase "non-inductive method of finding out about what lies deductively beyond the evidence" was a description without meaning, a phrase to which no sense had been given; so that there could be no question of justifying our selection of one method, called "the inductive," of doing this.

However, someone might object: "Surely it is possible, though it might be foolish, to use methods utterly different from accredited scientific ones. Suppose a man, whenever he wanted to form an opinion about what lay beyond his observation or the observation of available witnesses, simply shut his eyes, asked himself the appropriate question, and accepted the first answer that came into his head. Wouldn't this be a non-inductive method?" Well, let us suppose this. The man is asked: "Do you usually get the right answer by your method?" He might answer: "You've mentioned one of its drawbacks; I never do get the right answer; but it's an extremely easy method." One might then be inclined to think that it was not a method of finding things out at all. But suppose he answered: Yes, it's usually (always) the right answer. Then we might be willing to call it a method of finding out, though a strange one. But, then, by the very fact of its success, it would be an inductively supported method. For each application of the method would be an application of the general rule, "The first answer that comes into my head is generally (always) the right one"; and for the truth of this generalization there would be the inductive evidence of a long run of favourable instances with no unfavourable ones (if it were "always"), or of a sustained high proportion of successes to trials (if it were "generally").

So every successful method or recipe for finding out about the unobserved must be one which has inductive support; for to say that a recipe is successful is to say that it has been repeatedly applied with success; and repeated successful application of a recipe constitutes just what we mean by inductive evidence in its favour. Pointing out this fact must not be confused with saying that "the inductive method" is justified by its success, justified because it works. This is a mistake, and an important one. I am not seeking to "justify the inductive method," for no meaning has been given to this phrase. *A fortiori*, I am not saying that induction is justified by its success in finding out about the unobserved. I am saying, rather, that any successful method of finding out about the unobserved is necessarily justified by induction. . . . The phrase "successful method of finding things out which has no inductive support" is self-contradictory. Having, or acquiring, inductive support is a necessary condition of the success of a method.

STUDY QUESTIONS

1. According to Strawson, why is it "a little odd" to talk about the inductive method?
2. Why would anyone decide not to use inductive reasoning?
3. According to Strawson, what mistake is involved in claiming that the inductive method is justified by its success?
4. Do you agree with Strawson that every successful method of finding out about the unobserved must have inductive support?

Puzzling Out Knowledge

⚜

SUSAN HAACK

Susan Haack is Professor of Philosophy and of Law at the University of Miami. She draws an analogy between enhancing knowledge and solving crossword puzzles.

....

From Susan Haack, *Putting Philosophy to Work: Essays on Science, Religion, Law, Literature, and Life*, Prometheus Books, 2013. Reprinted by permission of the publisher.

Evidence is complex and ramifying, often confusing, ambiguous, or misleading. Think of the controversy over that four-billion-year-old meteorite discovered in 1984 Antarctica, thought to have come from Mars about eleven thousand years ago, and containing what might possibly be fossilized bacteria droppings. Some space scientists thought this was evidence of bacterial life on Mars; others thought the bacterial traces might have been picked while the meteorite was in Antarctica; and others again believed that what look like fossilized bacteria droppings might be merely artifacts of the instrumentation. How did they know that giving off these gases when heated indicates that the meteorite comes from Mars? that the meteorite is about four billion years old? that this is what fossilized bacteria droppings look like?—like crossword entries, reasons ramify in all directions.

How reasonable a crossword entry is depends on how well it is supported by its clue and any already completed intersecting entries; how reasonable those other entries are, independent of the entry in question; and how much of the crossword has been completed. How justified a belief is, similarly, depends on how well it is supported by experiential evidence and by reasons, i.e., background beliefs; how justified those background beliefs are, independent of the belief in question; and how much of the relevant evidence the evidence includes.

The quality of the evidence for a claim is objective, depending on how supportive it is of the claim in question, how comprehensive, and how independently secure. A person's judgments of the quality of evidence, however, are perspectival, depending on his background beliefs. Suppose you and I are working on the same crossword puzzle, but have filled in some long, much-intersected entry differently; you think a correct intersecting entry must have an "F" in the middle, while I think it must have a "D" there. Suppose you and I are on the same appointments committee, but you believe in graphology, while I think it's bunk; you think how the candidate writes his gs is relevant to whether he can be trusted, while I scoff at your "evidence." Or, to take a real example: in 1944, when Oswald Avery published his results, even he hedged over the conclusion to which they pointed, that DNA is the genetic material; for the then-accepted wisdom was that DNA is composed of the four nucleotides in regular order, and so is too stupid, too monotonous, a molecule to carry the necessary information. But by 1952, when Hershey and Chase published their results, the tetranucleotide hypothesis had been discredited; and then it could be seen that Avery already had good evidence in 1944 that DNA, not protein, is the genetic material.

Inquiry can be difficult and demanding, and we very often go wrong. Sometimes the obstacle is a failure of will; we don't really want to know the answer badly enough to go to all the trouble of finding out, or we really *don't* want to know, and go to a lot of trouble *not* to find out. I think of the detective who doesn't really want to know who committed the crime, just to collect enough evidence to get a conviction; of the academic who cares less about discovering the causes of racial disharmony than about getting a large grant to investigate the matter—and of my own disinclination to rush to the library to check out the article that might oblige me to redo months of work.

Other things being equal, inquiry goes better when the will and the intellect, instead of pulling in different directions, work together; that's why intellectual integrity is valuable. But even with the best will in the world, even when we really want to find out, we often fail. Our senses, imaginations, and intellects are limited; we can't always see, or guess, or reason, well enough. With ingenuity, we can devise ways of overcoming our natural limitations, from cupping our ears to hear better, through tying knots in rope or cutting notches in sticks to keep count, to highly sophisticated electron microscopes and techniques of computer modelling. Of course, our ingenuity is limited too.

Everyone who looks into how some part or aspect of the world is—the physicist and the detective, the historian and the entomologist, the quantum chemist and the investigative journalist, the literary scholar and the X-ray crystallographer—works on part of a part of the same vast crossword. Since they all investigate the same world, sometimes their entries intersect: a medical researcher relies on an amateur historian's family tree in his search for the defective gene responsible for a rare hereditary form of pancreatitis; ancient historians use a technique devised for the detection of breast cancer to decipher traces on the lead "postcards" on which Roman soldiers wrote home. . . .

Progress in the sciences is ragged and uneven, and each step, like each crossword entry, is fallible and revisable. But each genuine advance potentially enables others, as a robust crossword entry does; "nothing succeeds like success" is the phrase that comes to mind. . . .

Just about every inquirer, in the most mundane of everyday inquiries, depends on others; otherwise, each would have to start on his part of the crossword alone and from scratch. Natural-scientific inquiry is no exception; in fact, it is more so—the work, cooperative and competitive, of a vast intergenerational community of inquirers, a deeply and unavoidably social enterprise.

STUDY QUESTIONS

1. According to Haack, in what ways is enhancing knowledge akin to solving a crossword puzzle?
2. Can you present your own example of how you enhanced your knowledge in a manner akin to solving a crossword puzzle?
3. What does Haack mean by "intellectual integrity"?
4. Do we sometimes not want knowledge?

Meno

➳

PLATO

The *Meno* combines many Platonic themes in accessible form. It opens abruptly with the question of whether virtue can be taught, then explores among many other issues the concept of definition, the role of inquiry, and the nature of knowledge. The translation from the Greek is by the noted scholar R. E. Allen (1931–2007), who was Professor of Classics and Philosophy at Northwestern University. He considers a lesson of the *Meno* to be that "definition is necessary, that in order to talk, it is good to know what one is talking about." Although the dialogue ends in perplexity, Allen maintains that the work reveals the nature of mind "as containing within its depths the essential nature of all that is."

....

MENO: Can you tell me, Socrates, whether virtue is taught? Or is it not taught but acquired by practice? Or is it neither acquired by practice nor learnt, but present in men by nature or some other way?[1]

SOCRATES: Meno, it used to be that Thessalians were famous among the Greeks for their wealth and skill with horses, but it seems now that they are admired for their wisdom, and not least among them the Larisians, fellow citizens of your comrade Aristippus. Gorgias[2] is the reason. He came to Larisa and made the first men of the city eager for his wisdom—your friend Aristippus among them, and the foremost among the other Thessalians too. Specifically, he gave you your habit of answering any question fearlessly, in the style of men who know; for he offers himself for questioning to any Greek who wishes, on any subject he pleases, and there is no one he does not answer. But Meno, my friend, things are just the opposite here in Athens. There is, as it were, a drought of wisdom; very likely she has left our borders for yours. At any rate, if you mean to ask that kind of question of anyone here, he will laugh and say, "Stranger, you must think me fortunate indeed, if you suppose I know whether virtue is taught, or how it comes to be present. So far am I from knowing whether or not it is taught, I don't even know what it is at all."

Now, I'm that way too, Meno. I share this poverty of my fellow citizens, and reproach myself for knowing nothing at all about virtue. And if I don't know what something is, how am I to know what pertains to it? Or do you think someone could determine, for instance, whether Meno is handsome or wealthy or wellborn, or the opposite of these things, without knowing at all who Meno is? Does that seem possible to you?

MENO: Not to me. But Socrates, is it really true that you don't know what virtue is? Is this the report I am to carry home about you?

SOCRATES: Not only that, my friend, but also that I never met anyone else I thought did know.

MENO: Really? Didn't you meet Gorgias when he was here?

SOCRATES: I did.

MENO: Well, didn't you think he knew?

SOCRATES: I have a poor memory, Meno. I can't say at present what I thought then. Perhaps he did know, and you know what he used to say. Remind me of it. Or if you will, tell me yourself, for no doubt you are in agreement with him.

MENO: Yes, I am.

SOCRATES: Then we may as well dismiss him, since he isn't here anyway. What do you say virtue is, Meno? Don't begrudge telling me, so that I may find, should it turn out that you and Gorgias know, that I was in most fortunate error when I said that I had never met anyone who knew.

MENO: No difficulty, Socrates. First of all, if it is the virtue of a man you want, that is easy: the virtue of a man is to be capable of managing the affairs of his city, and in this management benefiting his friends and harming his enemies, taking care to suffer no such harm himself. And if it is the virtue of a woman you want, that is not difficult to explain either: she should manage her house well, preserving what is in it, and obey her husband. There is another virtue for children, male and female; and for an old man, free or slave as you please. And there are a great many other virtues, so that there is no perplexity in saying what virtue is. For each of us, there is a virtue with respect to each particular activity and time of life, and in relation to each particular function. The same is also true of vice, Socrates.

SOCRATES: This is quite a stroke of luck, Meno. I was looking for one virtue, and here I've found a whole swarm of them settled at your side. But still, Meno, please keep to this image of a swarm. Suppose I were to ask you what it is to be a bee, about its nature and reality, and you replied that there are many different kinds of bees. What would your answer be if I then asked you, "Do you mean that there are many different kinds, and that they differ from each other in respect to being bees? Do they differ in that way, or in some other way—in beauty or size, for example, or something else like that." Tell me, how would you answer such a question?

MENO: Why, that *as* bees, one is not different from another.

SOCRATES: All right, suppose I went on and said, "Now that's the very thing I want you to tell me about, Meno: Just what do you say it is, in respect to which they do not differ but are the same?" You could surely tell me?

MENO: Of course.

SOCRATES: So too then with virtues. Even if there are many different kinds, they surely all have a certain single characteristic which is the same, through which they are virtues; it is on this that he who would make clear what virtue is should fix his gaze. Do you understand what I mean?

MENO: I think I do. But I still don't quite grasp the point of your question.

SOCRATES: Well Meno, do you think it is only true of virtue that it is one thing for a man, another for a woman, and so on? Or is this also true of health and size and strength? Do you think health is one thing for a man, and another for a woman? Or is health, if it is to be health, the same character everywhere, whether in man or anything else?

MENO: I would say that health is the same for both man and woman.

SOCRATES: What about size and strength then? If a woman is strong, will she not be strong by reason of the same character, the same strength? By "the same" I mean this: strength does not differ, in respect of being strength, whether it be in a man or a woman. Or do you think there is some difference?

MENO: No.

SOCRATES: Then will virtue differ, in respect of being virtue, whether it be in a woman or man, old man or child?

MENO: Somehow, Socrates, I don't think this is like those others any more.

SOCRATES: Really? Didn't you say that a man's virtue is to manage a city well, and a woman's a house?

MENO: Yes, I did.

SOCRATES: Well, is it possible to manage city, house, or anything else well, without managing it temperately and justly?

MENO: Surely not.

SOCRATES: Now, if people manage justly and temperately, they do so by reason of justice and temperance?

MENO: Necessarily.

SOCRATES: So both men and women alike have need of the same things, namely justice and temperance, if they are to be good.

MENO: It appears they do.

SOCRATES: What about a child or an old man. Could they be good if they were intemperate or unjust?

MENO: Surely not.

SOCRATES: Only if temperate and just?

MENO: Yes.

SOCRATES: Then all human beings are good in the same way: for they become good by obtaining the same things.

MENO: So it seems.

SOCRATES: But surely they would not be good in the same way unless they possessed the same virtue.

MENO: Of course not.

SOCRATES: Since they all possess the same virtue, try to recollect and tell me what Gorgias, and you with him, say it is.

MENO: Virtue is nothing else but ability to rule mankind, if you are after some one thing common to all cases.

SOCRATES: I am indeed. But does a child possess the same virtue, Meno, or a slave the ability to rule his master? Does it seem true to you that one who rules would still be a slave?

MENO: It surely doesn't, Socrates.

SOCRATES: No, not likely, my friend. And there is a further point to consider: you say "ability to rule." Are we not to add to that "justly, not unjustly"?

MENO: Yes, I think so. For justice is virtue, Socrates.

SOCRATES: Virtue, Meno? Or *a* virtue?

MENO: What do you mean by that?

SOCRATES: Something which holds generally. For example, take roundness if you will. I'd say that it is *a* figure, but not figure without qualification. The reason I'd say so is that there are other figures too.

MENO: Yes, and you'd be right. I also say there are other virtues besides justice.

SOCRATES: What are they? As I'd cite other figures for you, if you asked, so please cite other virtues for me.

MENO: Well, I think courage is a virtue, and temperance, and wisdom, and dignity. And there are a great many others.

SOCRATES: And now we're back where we started, Meno. Looking for one virtue, we've found many, though by a different way than a moment ago. But the one virtue which runs through them all we can't find.

MENO: No, for I can't yet do as you ask, Socrates, and grasp a single virtue common to all, as in the other cases.

SOCRATES: Naturally enough. But I'll try if I can to help us on. You understand, I suppose, that this holds generally: if someone asked you the question I put just now, "What is figure, Meno?" and you replied, "Roundness," and he then asked, as I did, "Is roundness figure or *a* figure?" you'd surely reply that it is *a* figure.

MENO: Of course.

SOCRATES: And for this reason, that there are other figures too?

MENO: Yes.

SOCRATES: And if he went on and asked you what they were, you'd tell him?

MENO: I would.

SOCRATES: And again, if he asked in the same way what color is, and you said "white," and he went on to ask whether white is color or *a* color, you would say that it is *a* color, because there are other colors too.

MENO: I would.

SOCRATES: And if he asked you to mention other colors, you'd mention others which are no less colors than white?

MENO: Yes.

SOCRATES: Suppose he pursued the argument as I did. Suppose he said, "We keep arriving at a plurality, and that's not what I want. Since you call that plurality by a single name and say that all of its members are figures even though they are opposite to each other, just what is this thing which encompasses the round no less than the straight and which you name figure, saying that the round is no more figure than the straight?" You do make that claim, don't you?

MENO: I do.

SOCRATES: When you do, do you mean that the round is no more round than straight, the straight no more straight than round?

MENO: Of course not, Socrates.

SOCRATES: Rather, you mean that the round is no more *figure* than the straight, and the straight no more than the round.

MENO: True.

SOCRATES: Well then, what is this thing of which "figure" is the name? Try and say. Suppose when asked this question about figure or color you said, "I don't understand what you want, Sir, nor do I know what you mean." Your questioner might well be surprised and say, "Don't you understand that I'm after what is the same over all these cases?" Would you have no reply, Meno, if someone asked, "What is it that is over the round and the straight and the rest, and which you call figure, as the same over all?" Try and answer, in order to get practice for your reply about virtue.

MENO: No, please, Socrates, you answer.

SOCRATES: You want me to gratify you?

MENO: Yes, indeed.

SOCRATES: And then you'll tell me about virtue?

MENO: I will.

SOCRATES: Then I must do my best, for it's worth it.

MENO: Yes, certainly.

SOCRATES: Come then, let us try to say what figure is. See if this will do: let figure alone among things which are be that which ever follows color.

Is that sufficient, or are you after something else? For my part, I'd be delighted to have you tell me about virtue even that way.

MENO: Yes, but surely this is foolish, Socrates.

SOCRATES: How do you mean?

MENO: According to your account, figure is what ever follows color. All right, suppose someone said he didn't know color, that he was as much at a loss there as he was about figure. What would you think of your answer then?

SOCRATES: That is the truth. And if my questioner were one of your contentious and eristical wise men, I'd tell him, "I've answered. If my answer is not good, it is your job to refute me." But with friends who wish to converse with each other, as in our case, a gentler answer is indicated, one more suited to dialectic. It is more dialectical not only to answer what is true, but to do so in terms which the questioner further agrees that he knows. So that's how I'll try to answer you. Tell me then, is there something you call an end? I mean something like a limit or a boundary—they are all about the same, though Prodicus[3] perhaps would disagree. But you surely call something limited and ended, and that is the kind of thing I mean—nothing fancy.

MENO: To be sure I do, and I think I understand what you mean.

SOCRATES: Well then, is there something you call a surface, and still another you call a solid, as in geometry?

MENO: Certainly.

SOCRATES: Then at this point you can understand what I say figure is. In respect of every figure, I say figure is that in which a solid terminates. More briefly, figure is the limit of a solid.

MENO: And what do you say color is, Socrates?

SOCRATES: You are outrageous, Meno. You put an old man to the trouble of answering, when you won't yourself recollect and say what Gorgias said virtue is.

MENO: You tell me this, Socrates, and I'll tell you that.

SOCRATES: A man could realize blindfolded, Meno, just from the way you converse, that you are handsome and still have admirers.

MENO: Why?

SOCRATES: Because you speak only to command, as spoiled favorites do, who play tyrant as long as the bloom of their beauty lasts. And at the same time you've probably noticed my weakness for the fair, so I'll gratify you and answer.

MENO: By all means do.

SOCRATES: Will you have me answer in the manner of Gorgias, which would be easiest for you to follow?

MENO: Why, of course.

SOCRATES: Well then, don't you and Gorgias talk about certain effluences among the things which are, in the same way as Empedocles?[4]

MENO:	Yes, emphatically.
SOCRATES:	And about pores or passages, into which and through which the effluences pass?
MENO:	Certainly.
SOCRATES:	And that some of the effluences fit certain of the pores, while some are too large or too small?
MENO:	That is so.
SOCRATES:	Again, there is something you call sight?
MENO:	There is.
SOCRATES:	Then "grasp what I tell you," as Pindar says.[5] Color is an effluence of figures, commensurable with sight, therefore perceptible.
MENO:	Socrates, I think you've found an answer which is simply superb!
SOCRATES:	No doubt because it is put in a way you're accustomed to. At the same time you realize, I suppose, that in a similar way you could say what sound is, and smell, and many other things of the sort.
MENO:	Of course.
SOCRATES:	It is a stately style of answer, Meno, and so you like it better than my answer about figure.
MENO:	Yes, I do.
SOCRATES:	And yet, son of Alexidemus, I myself am convinced the other answer was better, and I think you would come to agree too, if it weren't necessary for you, as you were saying yesterday, to leave before the mysteries are celebrated, and if you were able to stay to be initiated.[6]
MENO:	Socrates, I would make it a point to stay if you gave me many such answers as that.
SOCRATES:	Then I must spare no effort to do so, both for your sake and my own—though I'm afraid I may not be able to keep to a level like that for very long. But come, it's your turn to pay your promised debt and say what virtue as a whole is. And "stop making one into many," as the joke goes when somebody breaks something. Leave virtue whole and healthy and say what it is. Examples you have got from me.
MENO:	Well, I think, Socrates, that as the poet says, virtue is "to rejoice in things beautiful and be capable of them." And that, I claim, is virtue: desire for beautiful things and ability to attain them.
SOCRATES:	Do you say that to desire beautiful things is to desire good things?
MENO:	Yes, of course.
SOCRATES:	Then do some men desire evils, and others goods? Does it not seem to you, my friend, that *all* men desire goods?
MENO:	No, it doesn't.
SOCRATES:	Some desire evils?
MENO:	Yes.
SOCRATES:	Supposing the evils to be goods, you mean, or recognizing that they are evils and still desiring them?

MENO: Both, I think.

SOCRATES: You think, Meno, that anyone recognizes evils to be evils and still desires them?

MENO: Certainly.

SOCRATES: What do you mean by "desire"? Desire to possess?

MENO: Why yes, of course.

SOCRATES: Believing that evils benefit, or recognizing that evils harm, those who possess them?

MENO: Some believe evils benefit, others recognize that they harm.

SOCRATES: Does it seem to you that those who believe that evils benefit recognize evils to be evils?

MENO: No, I certainly don't think that.

SOCRATES: Then it is clear that these people, who do not recognize evils for what they are, do not desire evils; rather, they desire things they suppose to be good, though in fact those things are evil. Hence, these people, not recognizing evils to be evils, and supposing them to be goods, really desire goods. Not so?

MENO: Yes, very likely it is.

SOCRATES: Now what about those who, as you claim, desire evils believing that evils harm their possessor. Surely they recognize they will be harmed by them?

MENO: They must.

SOCRATES: Don't they suppose that people who are harmed are made wretched to the degree they are harmed?

MENO: Again, they must.

SOCRATES: And aren't the wretched unhappy?

MENO: I should think so.

SOCRATES: Now, does anyone wish to be wretched and unhappy?

MENO: I think not, Socrates.

SOCRATES: Then nobody wishes for evils, Meno, unless he wishes to be in that condition. For what else is it to be wretched, than to desire evils and get them?

MENO: You are very likely right, Socrates; nobody wishes for evils.

SOCRATES: Now, you were just saying that virtue is to wish for good things and to be able to get them?

MENO: Yes, I did.

SOCRATES: Well, of this claim, the wishing part applies to everybody, so in that respect, one person is no better than another.

MENO: So it appears.

SOCRATES: But it is clear that if one person is better than another, it must be in respect to ability.

MENO: Certainly.

SOCRATES: So it seems that, according to your account, virtue is the ability to attain good things.

MENO: You have now expressed my opinion precisely.

SOCRATES: Then let us consider this and see if you are right, as you very likely are. You say that being able to attain goods is virtue?

MENO: I do.

SOCRATES: And you call such things as health and wealth goods, do you not?

MENO: Yes, I count possession of gold and silver good, as well as civic honors and offices.

SOCRATES: And you don't count other things good besides those sorts of things?

MENO: No, only things such as those.

SOCRATES: Very well. Then to attain gold and silver is virtue—so says Meno, ancestral guest-friend of the Great King of Persia. Do you add "justly and piously" to that attainment, Meno, or does it make no difference? If someone attains them unjustly, do you call it virtue all the same?

MENO: Surely not, Socrates.

SOCRATES: Vice, rather?

MENO: Of course.

SOCRATES: So it seems that justice or temperance or holiness, or some other part of virtue, must be present in the attainment. Otherwise, it will not be virtue even if it provides goods.

MENO: No, for how could it be virtue without them?

SOCRATES: And failure to provide gold and silver for oneself or for another when it would not be just to do so—that is virtue too, that very failure and perplexity of provision?

MENO: So it seems.

SOCRATES: So the provision of such goods is no more virtue than the failure to provide them. Rather, it seems what is accompanied by justice is virtue, and what is without anything of the sort will be vice.

MENO: I think it must be as you say.

SOCRATES: Now we were saying a moment ago that justice and temperance and everything of the sort each are a part of virtue?

MENO: Yes.

SOCRATES: Then, Meno, you're making fun of me.

MENO: But why, Socrates?

SOCRATES: Because I just now begged you not to break virtue up into bits and pieces, and gave you examples of how you should answer, and here you are paying no attention to that, but telling me that virtue is the ability to attain good things with justice. And justice, you say, is a part of virtue?

MENO: Yes.

SOCRATES: So it follows from your own admissions that virtue is doing whatever one may do with a part of virtue, since you say that justice and the rest are parts of virtue. What do I mean by that?

Just this: I begged you to say what virtue is as a whole, but you, so far from saying what it is, claim that every action is virtue if it is done with a part of virtue—as though you already had said what virtue as a whole is, and I am at this point to understand even if you break it into parts. So it seems to me that you must start from the beginning with the same question, my dear Meno: What is virtue? For that is what is being said when someone says that every action done with justice is virtue. Don't you think you need to go back to the original question? Or do you think some-one knows what a part of virtue is, without knowing what virtue is?

MENO: I do not.

SOCRATES: No, for if you remember when I was answering you just now about figure, we discarded the sort of answer which is given in terms of what is still under investigation and not yet agreed upon.

MENO: Yes, and we were right to do so, Socrates.

SOCRATES: Then my friend, as long as what virtue is as a whole is still under in-vestigation, don't suppose that you will clarify virtue for anyone by answering in terms of its parts, or in any other terms which contain a similar obscurity. The original question needs to be answered. You talk about virtue—but what is it? Do I seem to be talking non-sense?

MENO: Most certainly not.

SOCRATES: Then answer again from the beginning: what do you and your comrade Gorgias say virtue is?

MENO: Socrates, I kept hearing before I ever met you that you are your-self in perplexity, and cause perplexity in others. And now I think you've cast a spell on me; I am utterly subdued by enchantment, so that I too have become full of perplexity. Am I allowed a small joke? You are both in appearance and other ways very like the stingray in the sea, which benumbs whatever it touches.[7] I think you've now done something of the sort to me. My tongue, my soul, are numb—truly—and I cannot answer you. And yet, I've said many things about virtue a thousand times, and to a host of people—and, as I thought, spoken well. But now I'm utterly at a loss to say even what it is. You do well, I think, not to journey abroad from here; for if you worked things like this as a stranger in another city, you might well be arrested as a sorcerer.

SOCRATES: Meno, you are quite unscrupulous. You very nearly fooled me.

MENO: How could I, Socrates!

SOCRATES: I see the motive in your comparison.

MENO: What do you think it is?

SOCRATES: You want a comparison in return. This I know of all you handsome types—you delight in being compared, because you make a profit on it; your beauty leads to beautiful comparisons. But I won't give you a comparison. As for myself, if the stingray numbs itself as it numbs others, I am like it; otherwise not. For I don't cause perplexity in others while free of perplexities myself; the truth is rather that I cause perplexity in others because I am myself perplexed. And so it is now with virtue. I don't know what it is, while you, who may have known before I touched you, are now in like way ignorant. Nevertheless, I wish to join with you in inquiring what it is.

MENO: And how will you inquire into a thing, Socrates, when you are wholly ignorant of what it is? What sort of thing among those you don't know will you set up as the object of your inquiry? Even if you happen to bump right into it, how will you know that it is the thing you didn't know?

SOCRATES: I understand what you want to say, Meno. Do you see what an eristical argument you're spinning? It is thus impossible for a man to inquire either into what he knows, or into what he does not know. He cannot inquire into what he knows; for he knows it, and there is no need for inquiry into a thing like that. Nor would he inquire into what he does not know; for he does not know what it is he is to inquire into.

MENO: Well, don't you think that's a good argument, Socrates?

SOCRATES: I do not.

MENO: Can you say why?

SOCRATES: Yes. For I have heard from men and women who are wise in things divine—

MENO: What was it they told?

SOCRATES: A noble truth, I think.

MENO: What was it? And who were they who told it?

SOCRATES: Some were priests and priestesses who wanted to explain their observances. But Pindar and as many other poets who are inspired have told it too. Here is their tale. See if you think it true. They say that the soul of man is immortal, sometimes reaching an end which men call dying, sometimes born again, but never perishing. Because this is so, one must live his whole life in utmost holiness; for from whomsoever

> Persephone shall accept requital for her ancient grief,
> Returning their souls in the ninth year to the upper light,
> Their term of banishment to darkness done:
>> From them illustrious kings shall spring,
>> Lords of rushing wisdom, and strength unsurpassed.
> In all remaining time they shall be known
> As heroes, and be sanctified by men.[8]

Seeing then that the soul is immortal, and has been born many times, and has beheld all things in this world and the world beyond, there is nothing it has not learnt: so it is not surprising that it can be reminded of virtue and other things which it knew before. For since the whole of nature is akin, and the soul has learned all things, there is nothing to prevent someone, upon being reminded of one single thing—which men call learning—from rediscovering all the rest, if he is courageous and faints not in the search. For learning and inquiry are then wholly recollection.[9] Therefore we need not be persuaded by the eristical argument, which would cause us to be idle; it is sweet only to the ear of the soft and weak, whereas this account induces industry and inquiry. I put my trust in its truth, and ask you to join me in inquiring what virtue is.

MENO: Yes, Socrates, but what do you mean by saying that we do not learn, that what we call learning is recollection? Can you teach me that this is so?

SOCRATES: Why Meno, I just said you were unscrupulous, and now you are asking me to teach you, when I claim there is no teaching but recollection, just so I can straightway prove myself inconsistent.

MENO: No, no, Socrates, that was surely not my aim. I just spoke from habit. If you can somehow prove it is as you say, please do so.

SOCRATES: Well, it is not easy, but still, for you I will make the effort. You have many of your attendants here. Summon for me whichwever one you please for the demonstration.

MENO: Certainly. (*Beckoning to a slave boy.*) You there, come here.

SOCRATES: He's a Greek, I assume, and speaks Greek?

MENO: Oh yes, he was born and raised in our house.

SOCRATES: Then pay close attention. See whether it appears to you that he recollects, or learns from me.

MENO: I certainly shall.

SOCRATES: (*Turning to the boy.*) Tell me, my boy. Do you recognize that this sort of figure is a square? (*Socrates traces square ABCD in the sand at his feet.*)

BOY: I do.

SOCRATES: Now, a square figure is one having all four of these sides equal? (*Indicating the sides.*)

BOY: Of course.

SOCRATES: And so is one having these lines drawn through the middle equal too? (*Socrates draws in transversals bisecting each side.*)

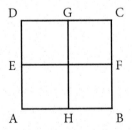

BOY: Yes.

SOCRATES: Now, a figure of this sort could be larger or smaller?

BOY: Of course.

SOCRATES: Now suppose that this side (AB) were two feet, and this one (AD) two feet. How many feet would the whole be? Look at it this way: if it were two feet this way (AB) and only one foot that way (AE), wouldn't the figure be two feet taken once?

BOY: (*Inspecting ABFE*) Yes.

SOCRATES: But since it is also two feet that way (AD), doesn't it become twice two?

BOY: It does.

SOCRATES: Therefore it becomes twice two feet?

BOY: Yes.

SOCRATES: Now, how many is twice two feet? Count and tell me. (*The boy looks at ABCD and counts the squares it contains.*)

BOY: Four, Socrates.

SOCRATES: Now could there be another figure twice the size of this one, but similar to it—that is, having four sides equal to each other?

BOY: Yes.

SOCRATES: How many feet will it be?

BOY: Eight.

SOCRATES: Come then. Try and tell me how long each side of it will be. Each side of this one (ABCD) is two feet. What about the side of a figure double this?[10]

BOY: Clearly it will be double, Socrates.

SOCRATES: Do you see, Meno, that I am teaching him nothing but am asking him all these things? And now he thinks he knows the length of the side from which the eight-foot figure will be generated. Do you agree?

MENO: I do.

SOCRATES: Well, does he know?

MENO: Of course not.

SOCRATES: He merely thinks it is generated from the doubled side?

MENO: Yes.

SOCRATES: Now watch him recollect serially and in order, as is necessary for recollection. (*Turning to the boy*) Tell me: are you saying that the doubled figure is generated from the doubled side? The figure I mean is not to be long one way and short the other; it is to be equal on all sides, as this one (ABCD) is, but double it, eight feet. See if you still think it will result from double the side.

BOY: I do.

SOCRATES: Now, this line (AB) becomes double (AX) if we add another of the same length here?

BOY: Of course.

SOCRATES: So there will be an eight-foot figure from it, you say, if four such sides are generated?

BOY: Yes.

SOCRATES: Then let us inscribe four equal sides from it. (*Socrates, beginning with base AX, inscribes AXYZ.*)

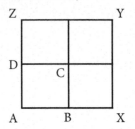

You say this would be eight feet?

BOY: Of course.

SOCRATES: Now, there are four squares in it, each of which is equal to this four-foot figure (ABCD)? (*Socrates completes the transversals begun by DC and BC above.*)

BOY: Yes.

SOCRATES: Then how big has it become? Four times as big?

BOY: Certainly.

SOCRATES: Now, is four times the same as double?

BOY: Surely not.

SOCRATES: How many?

BOY: Fourfold.

SOCRATES: Then from double the line, my boy, not a double but a four-fold figure is generated.

BOY: True.

SOCRATES: Since four times four is sixteen. Right?

BOY: Yes.

SOCRATES: Well, then, an eight-foot figure will be generated from what line? That one (AX) gave us a four-fold figure, didn't it? (i.e., AXYZ)

BOY: Yes.

SOCRATES: But half of it (AB) gave us four feet? (i.e., ABCD)

BOY: I agree.

SOCRATES: Very well. But an eight-foot figure is double this (ABCD), and half that (AXYZ)?

BOY: Yes.

SOCRATES: Then it will be from a side greater than this (AB) but smaller than that one there (AX), won't it?

BOY: Yes, I think so.

SOCRATES: Excellent. Always answer what you think. Now tell me: wasn't this line (AB) two feet, and that one (AX) four?

BOY: Yes.

SOCRATES: So the side of an eight-foot figure must be greater than this two-foot side here, but smaller than the four-foot side?

BOY: It must.

SOCRATES: Try and tell me how long you'd say it is.

BOY: Three feet.

SOCRATES: Now, if it is to be three feet, we'll add (to AB) half of this (BX), and it will be three feet; for this (AB) is two, and that (BM) is one. And in the same way over here, this (AD) is two and that (DN) is one; and the figure you speak of is generated. (*Socrates as he speaks marks M and N on BX and DZ, and then completes the square.*)

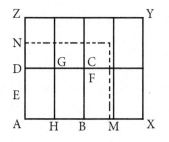

BOY: Yes.

SOCRATES: Now if this (AM) is three and that (AN) is three, the whole figure generated is thrice three feet?

BOY: That follows.

SOCRATES: And how many is thrice three?

BOY: Nine.

SOCRATES: But the double (of the original square) had to be how many feet?

BOY: Eight.

SOCRATES: So somehow the eight foot figure is not generated from the three-foot side either.

BOY: It certainly isn't.

SOCRATES: But from what, then? Try and tell us exactly. If you don't want to count it out, just point to it.

BOY: Socrates, I really don't know.

SOCRATES: (*Turning to Meno.*) Here again, Meno, do you see the progress in recollection he's made so far? At first he didn't know the side required for an eight-foot figure—and he still doesn't. But earlier he supposed he knew and answered confidently, and did not believe he was in perplexity. But now he *does* believe it, and as he doesn't know, neither does he suppose he knows.

MENO: You are right.

SOCRATES: So he is now better off with respect to the thing which he did not know?

MENO: I agree.

SOCRATES: Well, did we harm him any by numbing him like a stingray and making him aware of his perplexity?

MENO: I think not.

SOCRATES: We have at any rate done something, it seems, to help him discover how things are, for in his present condition of ignorance, he will gladly inquire into the matter, whereas before he might easily have supposed he could speak well, and frequently, and before large audiences, about doubling the square and how the side must be double in length.

MENO: So it seems.

SOCRATES: Well, do you think he would undertake to inquire into or learn what he thought he knew and did not, before he fell into perplexity and became convinced of his ignorance and longed to know?

MENO: I think not, Socrates.

SOCRATES: So numbing benefited him?

MENO: Yes.

SOCRATES: Then please observe what he will discover from this perplexity as he inquires with me—even though I will only ask questions and will not teach. Be on guard lest you find that I teach and explain to him, instead of questioning him about his own opinions. (*Socrates at this point rubs out the figures in the sand at his feet, leaving only rectangle ABCD, and turns to the boy.*) Now back to you. We've got this figure of four feet, don't we? Do you follow?

BOY: I do.

SOCRATES: And we can add here another equal to it? (*Inscribes it*)

BOY: Yes.

SOCRATES: And a third here, equal to each of those? (*Inscribes it*)

BOY: Yes.

SOCRATES: Now, we can fill in the one here in the corner? (*Inscribes it*)

BOY: Of course.

SOCRATES: So these four equal figures would be generated?

BOY: Yes.

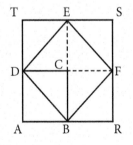

SOCRATES: Now then. How many times larger than this (ABCD) does this whole (ARST) become?

BOY: Four times.

SOCRATES: But we had to generate double. Do you recall?

BOY: Of course.

SOCRATES: Now take this line from corner to corner. (*Socrates inscribes BFED.*) Does it cut each of these figures in two?

BOY: Yes.

SOCRATES: Now, have we generated four equal lines here (BD, DE, EF, FE), enclosing this figure (BFED)?

BOY: We have.

SOCRATES: Then consider: how large is this figure?

BOY: I don't understand.

SOCRATES: Hasn't each of these lines cut off the inner half of these four squares?

BOY: Yes.

SOCRATES: Then how many (halves) of that size are in this (BFED)?

BOY: Four.

SOCRATES: And how many in this one (ABCD)?

BOY: Two.

SOCRATES: What is four to two?

BOY: Double.

SOCRATES: So this becomes how many feet?

BOY: Eight feet.

SOCRATES: From what line?

BOY: That one (BD).

SOCRATES: That is, from the line stretching from corner to corner of the four-foot figure?

BOY: Yes.

SOCRATES: Students of the subject call that the diagonal. So if that is the name for it, then you, Meno's slave, are stating as your view that the double figure would be generated from the diagonal.

BOY: Yes, certainly, Socrates.

SOCRATES: *(Turning to Meno)* Well, Meno, what do you think? Did he reply with any opinion not his own?

MENO: No, they were his.

SOCRATES: Yet he didn't *know,* as we were saying a little earlier.

MENO: True.

SOCRATES: Yet these opinions were *in* him, weren't they?

MENO: Yes.

SOCRATES: Therefore, while he is ignorant of these things he does not know, there are true opinions in him about these very things?

MENO: That follows.

SOCRATES: For the moment, these opinions have been stirred up in him as in a dream; but if he were repeatedly asked these same questions in different ways, you may rest assured that eventually he would know about these things as accurately as anyone.

MENO: It seems so.

SOCRATES: Then he will know without being taught but only questioned, recovering knowledge out of himself?

MENO: Yes.

SOCRATES: And his recovering knowledge which is in him is recollection?

MENO: Yes.

SOCRATES: The knowledge he now has he either gained at some time or always had?

MENO: Yes.

SOCRATES: Well, if he always had it, he always knew. And if he gained it at some time, he surely didn't do so in his present life. Or did someone teach him geometry? For he will do the very same thing all through geometry, and every other study. Is there anyone who has taught him all this? You ought to know, especially since he was born in your house and raised there.

MENO: I do know: no one ever taught him.

SOCRATES: But he has these opinions, does he not?

MENO: It appears he must, Socrates.

SOCRATES: Well, if he did not get them in his present life, is it not at this point clear he got and learned them at some other time?

MENO: It appears so.

SOCRATES: A time when he was not in human form?

MENO: Yes.

SOCRATES: So if we are to say that there are true opinions present in him both during the time when he is and is not a man, and that those opinions become knowledge when roused by questioning, then his soul will ever be in a state of having learned. For it is clear that through all time he either is or is not a man.

MENO: That follows.

SOCRATES: Now, if the truth of things is always in our soul, the soul is immortal. So it is right to try boldly to inquire into and recollect what you do not happen to know at present—that is, what you do not remember.

MENO: I think you are right, Socrates—how, I don't know.

SOCRATES: I think so too, Meno. There are other things about the argument I would not confidently affirm, but that we shall be better men, more courageous and less idle, if we think we ought to inquire into what we do not know, instead of thinking that because we cannot find what we do not know we ought not seek it—that I would do battle for, so far as possible, in word and deed.

MENO: Here again, I think you are right, Socrates.

SOCRATES: Then since we are agreed that there must be inquiry about what one does not know, shall we together undertake to investigate what virtue is?

MENO: By all means. But Socrates, what would please me most would be to take up the question I began with and hear you on it: whether virtue is something that is taught, or present by nature, or in what way it comes to be present in men.

SOCRATES: If I not only ruled myself, Meno, but also ruled you, we'd not consider whether virtue is or is not taught before first considering what it is. But since you do not even attempt to rule yourself—being a free man, after all—and yet still try to rule me, and do, I must perforce go along. What else can I do? It seems then that we must inquire of what sort virtue is, when we don't yet know what it is. But please relax your rule over me a little, and consent to inquire by means of a hypothesis whether it is taught. I mean the sort of thing geometers often use in their inquiries. When someone asks them, say, about an area, whether it is possible for a given area to be stretched as a triangle into a given circle, a geometer might say, "I don't know yet if it is possible, but I think there is, as it were, a hypothesis at hand to deal with the matter. It is this: if this area is such that, when applied along a line given for it, it falls short by an area of the same sort as the area which has already been applied. I think one thing follows: and a different thing follows in turn if it is impossible for the area to be so affected. So I wish to tell you what follows about the stretching out of it into the circle, whether it is possible or not, by using hypothesis."[11]

So too then for us about virtue. Since we know neither what it is nor what is true of it, let us use hypothesis in inquiring whether it is taught. As follows: among things of the soul, of what sort must virtue be if it is taught or if it is not taught? To begin with, if it is the same sort or a different sort than knowledge, is it or is it not taught?—or as we were just now saying, remembered? The name we use makes no difference here: is it taught? Or isn't it quite clear that a man is taught nothing but knowledge?

MENO: I think so.

SOCRATES: So if virtue is a kind of knowledge, it clearly would be taught.

MENO: Certainly.

SOCRATES: Then we have disposed of this point quickly: it is taught if it is of one sort, but not if of another.

MENO: Of course.

SOCRATES: The next step, it seems, is to inquire whether virtue is knowledge or of a sort other than knowledge.

MENO: I agree: that must be examined next.

SOCRATES: Well, then, do we say that virtue is good? Does that hypothesis stand fast for us, that it is good?

MENO: Certainly.

SOCRATES: Now, if something is good, but other than and separate from knowledge, virtue perhaps would not be a kind of knowledge. But if there is nothing good which knowledge does not encompass, we may rightly suspect that virtue is a kind of knowledge.

MENO: True.

SOCRATES: Again, it is by virtue that we are good?

MENO: Yes.

SOCRATES: And if good, beneficial. For all good things are beneficial, are they not?

MENO: Yes.

SOCRATES: So virtue is beneficial, then?

MENO: Necessarily, from what has been agreed.

SOCRATES: Then let us examine what sort of thing benefits us, taking particular examples. Health, we say, and strength, beauty, and no doubt wealth too—we hold that they and things like them are beneficial, do we not?

MENO: Yes.

SOCRATES: But we say that those same things sometimes also do harm. Do you dispute that?

MENO: No, it is true.

SOCRATES: Then let us consider what guides each of these things when they benefit us, and what guides them when they do harm. Don't they benefit us when there is right use, and harm us when there is not?

MENO: Certainly.

SOCRATES: Next, consider things having to do with the soul. Is there something you call temperance, and justice and courage and quick wits, and memory and nobility of character and so on?

MENO: There is.

SOCRATES: Then consider: do those among them which you think are not knowledge, but other than knowledge, sometimes benefit and sometimes harm? Take courage, for example. Suppose that courage is not wisdom but, as it were, a kind of boldness. When a man is bold without intelligence, he is harmed; with intelligence, he is benefited. Isn't that so?

MENO: Yes.

SOCRATES: And so similarly with temperance and quick wits. Things learned or acquired by training are beneficial when accompanied by intelligence, but harmful without it.

MENO: Very true indeed.

SOCRATES: To sum up then, everything that the soul undertakes or endures, when guided by wisdom, ends in happiness, and in the opposite when guided by folly?

MENO: It seems so.

SOCRATES: Therefore, if virtue is something among things in the soul, and is necessarily beneficial, it must be wisdom, since everything which has to do with the soul is in itself neither beneficial nor harmful, but becomes one or the other by the addition of wisdom or folly. According to this account, then, virtue, being beneficial, must be a kind of wisdom.

MENO: I agree.

SOCRATES: Returning then to the other things we just mentioned as sometimes good and sometimes harmful—I mean wealth, and so on—isn't the same true there? Just as wisdom, guiding the rest of the soul, makes things of the soul beneficial, while folly makes them harmful, so too with these: the soul, guiding and using them rightly, makes them beneficial; if not rightly, harmful.

MENO: Of course.

SOCRATES: But it is the wise soul which guides rightly, and the foolish soul which guides with error?

MENO: True.

SOCRATES: So this then is to be asserted generally: in man, all other things depend upon the soul; but things of the soul depend upon wisdom, if they are to be good. And by this account, the beneficial would be wisdom, while virtue, we say, is beneficial.

MENO: Quite so.

SOCRATES: Therefore, we say that virtue is wisdom, either all or some part?

MENO: I think these statements excellent, Socrates.

SOCRATES: Now if this is true, good men are not good by nature.

MENO: No.

SOCRATES: Otherwise, this would surely follow: if good men are good by nature, we would no doubt have among us people who could discern among our youth those whose natures are good; and we would take them, once revealed to us, and guard them in a lofty citadel, setting our seal upon them more surely than on our gold, so that no one might corrupt them. For when they reach maturity, they will be of service to their cities.

MENO: Very likely, Socrates.

SOCRATES: Then since good men are not good by nature, are they so by learning?

MENO: At this point, it seems necessary. And, Socrates, it is clear from the hypothesis, if virtue is knowledge, it is taught.

SOCRATES: To be sure. But perhaps it was improper to agree to that.

MENO: It surely seemed proper a moment ago.

SOCRATES: Yes, but if there is to be any soundness to it, shouldn't it seem proper not only "a moment ago," but now and in the future as well?

MENO: No doubt. But what do you see to make you uneasy? Why do you doubt that virtue is knowledge?

SOCRATES: I'll tell you, Meno. I'm not taking back as improper the claim that it is taught if it is knowledge. But consider whether you don't think it reasonable to doubt that it is knowledge. Just tell me this: if anything at all—not just virtue—is taught, must there not be teachers and students of it?

MENO: I think so.

SOCRATES: Then might we not reasonably conjecture that the opposite also holds—that should there be neither teachers nor students of it, it is not taught?

MENO: Yes. But don't you think there are teachers of virtue?

SOCRATES: Well at any rate I've often inquired if there are, and try as I might, I couldn't find them. And yet I inquired among many people, especially those I thought most experienced in the matter.

SOCRATES: But look now, Meno. Here is Anytus sitting down beside us, and just at the right time.[12] Let us make him a partner in our inquiry. It is reasonable that we should, for in the first place, he is the son of a wise and wealthy father, Anthemion, who became rich not by gift or accident, like Ismenias the Theban who has just recently come into the fortune of Polycrates,[13] but by his own diligence and skill. Then too, he seems to be a citizen who is not insolent, or pompous and offensive, but a man of good conduct and well-ordered life. Finally, he raised and educated his son here well, as the majority of Athenians think; at any rate, they choose him for their highest offices. It is right, then, to inquire with such a man whether or not there are teachers of virtue, and who they are. So Anytus, please join us—your guest-friend Meno here, and me—and inquire into this matter of who the teachers of virtue may be. Consider this: if we wished Meno here to become a good physician, to what teachers would we send him? To the physicians, I assume?

ANYTUS: Of course.

SOCRATES: What if we wished him to become a good cobbler. To the cobblers?

ANYTUS: Yes.

SOCRATES: And so in other cases?

ANYTUS: Of course.

SOCRATES: Then look again to the same examples and tell me this: We say we properly send him to the physicians if we wish him to become a physician. When we make that statement, do we mean that we'd be well advised to send him to people who lay claim to the art, rather than those who do not, and charge a fee precisely on that basis, declaring themselves teachers for anyone wishing to come and learn? Wouldn't this be our proper consideration in sending him?

ANYTUS: Yes.

SOCRATES: And isn't it just the same with flute playing and so on? It is the height of unreason, if we wish to make somebody a flute player, not to be willing to send him to people who promise to teach the art and charge for it, and instead to trouble others to teach him when they don't claim to be teachers and haven't got a single pupil in the subject. Don't you think that would be highly unreasonable?

ANYTUS: I do, and stupid to boot.

SOCRATES: Well said. Accordingly, you and I can now consult together about your guest-friend Meno here. He has been saying to me for some time, Anytus, that he desires the wisdom and virtue by which men properly order households and cities, and take care of their parents, and know how to welcome and take leave of fellow citizens and guest-friends in a manner worthy of a good man. To whom should we send him for this? Or is it clear from our account just now that we should send him to people who undertake to be teachers of virtue, declaring themselves available to any Greek who wishes to learn, and charging a set fee for it.

ANYTUS: And just who do you mean, Socrates?

SOCRATES: Why, you know as well as I do. The men people call sophists.

ANYTUS: Good Lord, don't blaspheme, Socrates. May none of my own, not family, not friends, no citizen, no guest, be seized with such madness as to go to these men and be ruined. For they clearly ruin and corrupt anyone who associates with them.

SOCRATES: Why Anytus, what do you mean? Do they therefore differ so much from others who claim to know how to work some good, that they alone not only provide no benefit, as the rest do, to what is placed in their hands, but on the contrary corrupt it? They openly demand a fee for doing *that*? I can scarcely believe you. Why, I know one man, Protagoras,[14] who made more money from that wisdom of his than did Phidias,[15] who produced such conspicuously beautiful work, and any ten other sculptors you please. People who mend old shoes and patch cloaks, if they were to hand back articles in worse condition than they got them, would not escape detection for thirty days and would quickly starve to death if they tried. You surely utter a portent, then, if Protagoras for more than forty years corrupted those who associated with him, sent them back in worse condition than he got them, and escaped detection by the whole of Greece. He was nearly seventy when he died, I think; he had been forty years in his art; and in all that time, and to the present day, esteem for him has been unceasing. And not just for Protagoras, either. There have been a host of others, some born before him and some still alive now. Are we to say according to your account that they led astray and ruined the youth knowingly, or that they were not even aware of it themselves? Shall we then deem them mad, whom some say are the wisest men of all?

ANYTUS: They are far from mad, Socrates. It is the youths who pay them money who are mad, still more the relatives who allow it, and most of all the cities which allow such men to enter and don't drive them out—whether they are foreigners or citizens.

SOCRATES: But Anytus, why are you so hard on them? Has one of the sophists wronged you?

ANYTUS: No indeed, I've never associated with any of them, nor permitted anyone of mine to do so.

SOCRATES: So you have no experience of the fellows?

ANYTUS: That's right. May it continue so.

SOCRATES: Then, my friend, how do you know whether this affair has good or mischief in it, when you have no experience of it?

ANYTUS: Easily. At any rate, I know who they are and what they are, whether I've had experience with them or not.

SOCRATES: You must have second sight, Anytus! I can't see how else you'd know about them, from what you've said. Still, we weren't asking where Meno can go to be corrupted. Let it be to the sophists, if you wish. Tell us instead about the others. Benefit this friend of your father's house and inform him to whom he should go in this great city to become distinguished in respect to the virtue I just described.

ANYTUS: Why don't you tell him yourself?

SOCRATES: Why, I did mention whom I thought were teachers of it, though it happens I was talking nonsense. So you say, at least, and perhaps you are right. But now it's your turn. Tell him to whom he should go among the Athenians. Mention any name you please.

ANYTUS: Why should he hear just one name? Any Athenian gentlemen he meets will make him better than would the sophists, provided he is willing to listen.

SOCRATES: But did they become fine gentlemen spontaneously? Without having learned from anyone, can they nonetheless teach others what they themselves did not learn?

ANYTUS: Why, I expect they learned from their elders, who were gentlemen too. Do you deny that there have been many good men in this city?

SOCRATES: No, Anytus, I think there are good men in political life here, and that their predecessors were not inferior to them. But have they been good teachers of their own virtue? Our discussion is about that; not whether there are good men here now, or formerly, but whether virtue is taught. We've been asking for some time, and to ask that is to ask this: Do good men, whether of our time or earlier, actually know how to hand down to someone else the virtue in which their goodness consists, or is it impossible for a man to hand it on or receive it from another? That's what Meno and I have been after for some time. On the basis of your own account, consider: would you say Themistocles was a good man?

ANYTUS: Of course. Eminently good.

SOCRATES: So if anyone else could teach his own virtue, you'd say he'd be a good teacher?

ANYTUS: I suppose so, at least if he wanted to.

SOCRATES: But don't you suppose he'd have wished others to become good men, especially his own son? Do you think he'd treat a son with grudging jealousy, and purposefully not hand on the virtue in which his own goodness consisted? Surely you must have heard how Themistocles[16] had his son Cleophantus taught to be a good horseman. Why, he could ride a horse standing bolt upright, and aim a javelin doing it, and he could do many other amazing things, because Themistocles educated him and made him skillful in everything which can be got from good teachers. Surely you've heard all this from your elders?

ANYTUS: I have.

SOCRATES: So no one could claim his son's nature was bad.

ANYTUS: Perhaps not.

SOCRATES: But what about this: Did you ever hear anybody, young or old, say that Cleophantus son of Themistocles was good and wise, as his father was?

ANYTUS: Certainly not.

SOCRATES: Well, are we to suppose that he wished to educate his son in other things, but not to make him any better than his neighbors in respect to the wisdom he himself possessed—that is, assuming virtue is taught?

ANYTUS: Hardly.

SOCRATES: So there's your teacher of virtue; yet even you agree he was one of the best men of past generations. But let's examine someone else then, Aristides son of Lysimachus.[17] Or don't you agree he was good?

ANYTUS: Of course I do.

SOCRATES: Well, he too gave his son Lysimachus the best education in Athens, so far as it could be got from teachers. Do you think it made him better than anybody at all? You've associated with him; you see what he's like. Or if you will, take Pericles—so splendidly wise a man.[18] You know he raised two sons, Paralus and Xanthippus?

ANYTUS: Yes.

SOCRATES: Then you also know he taught them to be horsemen inferior to none in Athens; he educated them in music and gymnastics and everything that could be got by art, and they excelled. Didn't he then wish to make them good men? I think he did, but perhaps this is not taught. But lest you think this has been impossible only for a few Athenians of a quite insignificant sort, think about Thucydides.[19] He also raised two sons, Melesius and Stephanus, educated them well in other things, and made them the best wrestlers in Athens. He had one of them trained by Xanthias and the other by Eudorus, who were reputed to be the best wrestlers of their time. You recall?

MENO: Yes, I've heard that.

SOCRATES: Well he clearly would never have gone to the expense needed to teach his children wrestling, and yet fail to teach them at no cost to himself the thing needed to make them good men—if it is taught. Was Thucydides perhaps insignificant, without a host of friends in Athens and among the Allies? To the contrary: he was great in house and great in power, in this city and in the rest of Greece. If the thing is taught, he'd certainly have found out who it was, fellow countryman or foreigner, who would make his sons good, if he himself lacked leisure due to cares of state. Anytus, my friend, it may well be that virtue is not taught.

ANYTUS: Socrates, it seems to me you slander men lightly. If you will be persuaded by me, I would advise you to beware. It may be that in other cities too it is easier to do evil to men than good. Certainly it is in this one. But then, I think you know that.

SOCRATES: Anytus seems angry, Meno. I'm not surprised. To begin with, he thinks I am disparaging these men; then too, he thinks he is one of them. If someday he should understand what slander really is, he will cease to be angry. At present, he does not know.

But Meno, you tell me: there are gentlemen in your country too, are there not?

MENO: Of course.

SOCRATES: Well then, are they willing to offer themselves as teachers to the young? Would they agree they are teachers and that virtue is taught?

MENO: Emphatically not, Socrates; rather, sometimes you hear them say it is taught, and sometimes not.

SOCRATES: Well, are we to say they are teachers of it, when they disagree on that very point?

MENO: I think not, Socrates.

SOCRATES: Then what about the sophists? They are the only ones who claim to be teachers of virtue. Do you think they are?

MENO: Socrates, that is why I especially admire Gorgias. You'd never hear him promise that: in fact, he laughs at those who do. He thinks it his business to make men clever speakers.

SOCRATES: Then you don't think the sophists are teachers?

MENO: Socrates, I can't say. Actually, I'm just like everybody else: sometimes I think so, sometimes not.

SOCRATES: But did you know that it's not just you and other people in public life who sometimes think it is taught and sometimes not? Even the poet Theognis said the same thing.[20]

MENO: Really? Where?

SOCRATES: In his Elegaics, where he says,

> Sit with them, eat with them, drink with them;
> Be pleasing unto those whose power is great,
> For the good will teach you to be good.
> Mix with evil and your mind will be lost.

You see that in those lines he says virtue is taught?

MENO: Yes, apparently so.

SOCRATES: But in others he shifts his ground a bit. I think it goes

> If thought were something to be made and put into a man,
> They would bear and carry many a fee and large.

Meaning by "they" the people who were able to do it. And again,

> Never is a bad son born of a good father,
> For he is persuaded by precepts of wisdom.
> But never by teaching will you make the bad man good.

You notice how he contradicts himself?

MENO: Apparently.

SOCRATES: Well, can you mention any other subject where those who claim to be teachers are not acknowledged as teachers, or even acknowledged to understand their own subject matter, but are thought to be bad at the very thing they claim to teach; whereas those acknowledged as accomplished in this subject matter sometimes claim it is taught and sometimes not. Can you in any proper sense say that people so confused are teachers?

MENO: Emphatically not.

SOCRATES: Now, if neither sophists nor gentlemen are teachers of the thing, then clearly no one else is.

MENO: I agree.

SOCRATES: And if no teachers, no students?

MENO: I think that's so.

SOCRATES: And we agreed that if there are neither teachers nor students of a thing, then it is not taught.

MENO: We did.

SOCRATES: Now, it turns out there are no teachers of virtue?

MENO: It does.

SOCRATES: And if no teachers, no students?

MENO: That follows.

SOCRATES: Therefore, virtue is not taught?

MENO: It seems not, provided that we've examined it correctly. But the result is that I really wonder, Socrates, whether there even are any good men, or how those who become good can do so.

SOCRATES: Very likely you and I are pretty poor types, Meno. Gorgias hasn't sufficiently educated you, nor Prodicus me. Beyond all else, we must pay close attention to ourselves and seek someone who will in some way make us better men. I say this with a view to the inquiry just concluded where we wittingly make ourselves ridiculous by neglecting the fact that it is not true that human affairs are carried on rightly and well only through the guidance of knowledge. That is perhaps why recognition of the way good men become good escapes us.

MENO: What do you mean, Socrates?

SOCRATES: This: we have agreed—and rightly, since it could hardly be otherwise—that good men must be beneficial.

MENO: Yes.

SOCRATES: And also that they will be beneficial if they guide matters rightly for us?

MENO: Yes.

SOCRATES: But that there cannot be right guidance unless there is understanding—to that, it seems, we agreed wrongly.

MENO: Really? Why do you say that?

SOCRATES: I'll tell you. Suppose someone who knew the road to Larisa[21] or any place you please, were to walk there and guide others. He would guide them rightly and well, wouldn't he?

MENO: Of course.

SOCRATES: But what if someone had right opinion as to the road, but had never taken it and did not know it. Wouldn't he guide rightly too?

MENO: Of course.

SOCRATES: And presumably as long as he has right opinion about matters of which the other has knowledge, he will be no worse a guide than the man who understands it, even though he only believes truly without understanding.

MENO: Quite so.

SOCRATES: Therefore true opinion, concerning rightness of action, is a guide not inferior to understanding; that is what we left out just now in our inquiry about what sort of thing virtue is. We said that understanding is the only guide to right action, whereas it seems there is also true opinion.

MENO: Yes, it seems so.

SOCRATES: So right opinion is no less beneficial than knowledge.

MENO: Except in this way, Socrates, that a man with knowledge will always hit upon the right answer, whereas a man with right opinion sometimes will and sometimes won't.

SOCRATES: How do you mean? Won't the man who always has right opinion always be right as long as his opinion is right?

MENO: It would appear he must. But Socrates, assuming this is true, I have to wonder that knowledge is much more highly valued than right opinion, and in what respect one is different from the other.

SOCRATES: Do you know why you're surprised, or should I tell you?

MENO: Tell me, please.

SOCRATES: It's because you haven't paid attention to the statues of Daedalus.[22] Maybe there aren't any in your country.

MENO: What are you getting at?

SOCRATES: Those statues, if they aren't bound, actually get up and run away; but if bound, they stay.

MENO: Well, so?

SOCRATES: It isn't worth a great deal, to own one of his creations if it's loose;
           like a runaway slave, it will not stay. But it is worth quite a great deal
           when bound, for his works are very beautiful. What am I getting at?
           This bears on true opinions. For in fact, true opinions, as long as
           they stay, are beautiful possessions and accomplish all that is good,
           but they are unwilling to stay very long. They run away from the
           soul of a man, so that they are not worth much until someone binds
           them by reflection on the reason for them. And that, my friend
           Meno, is recollection, as we agreed before. When bound, they in
           the first place become knowledge; and secondly, they abide. That
           is why knowledge is more to be valued than right opinion: Knowl-
           edge differs from right opinion by its bond.

MENO: Yes, Socrates, it certainly seems that way.

SOCRATES: Still, I speak as one who conjectures, not as one who knows. But that
           right opinion is other than knowledge I think is surely not conjecture:
           if I were to say I knew anything—and I would say it of very little—this
           one thing I would surely place among things I know.

MENO: Yes, and correctly, Socrates.

SOCRATES: Well, then, isn't it correct that in each action the guidance of true
           opinion accomplishes results in no way inferior to those accom-
           plished by knowledge?

MENO: There again, what you say seems true.

SOCRATES: So right opinion is not worse or less beneficial than knowledge in
           respect to action; nor is the man who has right opinion inferior to
           the man who knows.

MENO: True.

SOCRATES: Moreover, we've agreed that good men are beneficial.

MENO: Yes.

SOCRATES: Then since good men would benefit their cities, if they do, not only
           through knowledge but right opinion, and since neither of the two
           belongs to men by nature, but is acquired—or do you think either
           knowledge or right opinion is present by nature?

MENO: No, I don't.

SOCRATES: Then since they are not present by nature, good men are not good
           by nature.

MENO: Of course not.

SOCRATES: Since good men are not good by nature, we next considered if vir-
           tue is taught.

MENO: Yes.

SOCRATES: If virtue is wisdom, it seemed it would be taught.

MENO: Yes.

SOCRATES: And if taught, it would be wisdom?

MENO: Of course.

SOCRATES: And if there were teachers, it would be taught. If none, it would not be taught.

MENO: Yes.

SOCRATES: We have further agreed that there are no teachers of it?

MENO: That is so.

SOCRATES: Therefore, we have agreed that it is neither taught nor wisdom?

MENO: Of course.

SOCRATES: However, we surely agree that it is good.

MENO: Yes.

SOCRATES: And that which guides rightly is useful and good?

MENO: Of course.

SOCRATES: But only these two things, true opinion and knowledge, guide rightly, and a man guides rightly only if he has them. Things which occur rightly by chance occur through no human guidance, but wherever a man guides rightly, one of these two, true opinion or knowledge, is found.

MENO: I agree.

SOCRATES: Now, virtue no longer is knowledge, since it is not taught.

MENO: It appears not.

SOCRATES: Therefore, of two good and beneficial things, one has been ruled out: knowledge would not be a guide in political affairs.

MENO: I think not.

SOCRATES: So it is not by a kind of wisdom or because they are wise that men such as Themistocles, and those like him whom Anytus here just mentioned, guide their cities. For they cannot make others like themselves, since they are not what they are because of knowledge.

MENO: That seems to be true, Socrates, as you say.

SOCRATES: Then if not by knowledge, only true opinion is left. That is what men in political life use to direct their cities rightly, differing in no way from soothsayers and seers in respect to understanding. For the latter also say many things which are true, and understand nothing of what they are saying.

MENO: Very likely.

SOCRATES: Now, Meno, isn't it proper to call men divine, when without possessing intelligence they bring a multitude of important things to successful issue in what they do and say?

MENO: Of course.

SOCRATES: And therefore we rightly call those men divine whom we just mentioned—soothsayers and seers, and the whole race of poets. And surely we must say that our statesmen, by no means least among them, are divine and inspired. For when, by speaking, they bring a multitude of important things to successful issue without understanding what they are talking about, it is because they have been breathed upon and laid hold of by the god.

MENO: Of course.

SOCRATES: And surely that is the tale the women tell: they call good men divine. And the Spartans, when they sing the praises of a good man, say, "He is a man divine."

MENO: Yes, Socrates, it appears you are right. But Anytus here may be angry at you for saying it.

SOCRATES: That does not concern me. We shall doubtless talk with him another time, Meno. For the present, if this whole account of ours has been correctly examined and stated, virtue is neither present by nature nor taught: it comes to be present, in those to whom it comes, by divine apportionment, without intelligence—unless there is among statesmen a man who can make another man a statesman. If there is, that man might be said to be of the same sort among the living as Homer claimed Teiresias[23] was among the dead:

> Alone among those below he kept his wits.
> The rest are darting, fleeting shadows.

In the same way in this world with regard to virtue, such a man would be, as among shadows, a thing of reality and truth.

MENO: I think you put it most excellently, Socrates.

SOCRATES: Then from this it appears, Meno, that virtue comes to be present by divine apportionment in those to whom it comes. But we shall only know that with clear certainty when, before inquiring how virtue comes to be present in men, we first undertake to inquire what virtue is.

The hour is come for me to go. Please persuade your host Anytus here of the things of which you yourself are now persuaded, so that his anger may be allayed. If you persuade him, you may also do some benefit to the Athenians.

NOTES

1. Meno, a mercenary soldier, was a person of dubious character; hence, his questions carry a touch of irony.
2. Gorgias was one of the most famous of the Sophists, itinerant teachers of oratory who were paid for their services.
3. Prodicus was a Sophist, best known for his precision in drawing verbal distinctions.
4. Empedocles (c. 493–c. 433 B.C.E.) was a pre-Socratic philosopher, who thought that our perceptions are the result of effluences from physical objects entering our sense organs.
5. Pindar (518–438 B.C.E.) was a celebrated lyric poet.
6. Evidently the Athenians are about to celebrate the famous rites of the Eleusinian Mysteries, but Meno has to return to Thessaly before they fall due. Plato frequently plays upon the analogy between religious initiation, which bestowed a revelation of divine secrets, and the insight which comes from initiation into the truths of philosophy (translator's note).

7. The sting-ray, which paralyzed its victims, was a danger to Mediterranean swimmers.

8. The quotation is from Pindar (translator's note).

9. Recollection is related to, but not identical with, memory. A distinction between the two may be that knowledge based on experience is remembered, whereas knowledge not based on experience is recollected.

10. Socrates asks the slave boy to find a line whose length is the square root of eight, an irrational number.

11. The geometrical illustration is opaque. A cogent explanation of the mathematics that may be involved is provided by Judith I. Meyers in "Plato's Geometric Hypothesis: *Meno* 86E–87B," *Apeiron 21* (Fall 1988), 173–180 (editor's note).

12. Anytus, who helped restore Athenian democracy, was one of the three accusers of Socrates at his trial.

13. Ismenias (d. 382 B.C.E.) was a noted statesman. Polycrates (574–522 B.C.E.) was the tyrant of Samos.

14. Protagoras (c. 490–c. 420 B.C.E.) was one of the most prominent Sophists.

15. Phidias, active in the mid-fifth century B.C.E., was the most famous Athenian sculptor.

16. Themistocles (528–462 B.C.E.) was an Athenian statesman and general who helped defeat the Persians.

17. Aristides was an Athenian statesman and hero of the Persian War, renowned for his honesty.

18. Pericles (c. 495–429 B.C.E.), the most famous leader of democratic Athens, was celebrated for his incorruptible character.

19. Not the historian, but a political rival of Pericles (translator's note).

20. Theognis was a sixth-century B.C.E. elegiac poet from Megara.

21. Larissa was the principal city of Thessaly, the region of Meno's birth.

22. Daedalus, a legendary artist, craftsman, and inventor, made lifelike figures that moved.

23. Tiresias was a legendary blind Theban, gifted with the power of prophecy.

STUDY QUESTIONS

1. What does Socrates mean by the claim that learning is recollection?

2. What points are supposed to be made by use of the geometric example?

3. Is knowledge more than true opinion?

4. Do you believe virtue is taught?

Meditations on First Philosophy

的

RENÉ DESCARTES

The Frenchman René Descartes (1596–1650), mathematician, scientist, and philosopher, wrote one of the most influential of all philosophical works, his *Meditations on First Philosophy*, published in Latin in 1641. Its combination of personal narrative and rigorous argument is highly unusual.

Descartes is driven by his desire to place philosophy on an unshakable foundation. He searches for a starting point that can withstand all doubt. Because the evidence of our senses sometimes misleads us, it does not provide a secure basis for knowledge. Furthermore, we cannot be certain that we are awake and not dreaming. Nor can we be sure that we are not being systematically fooled by an evil genius who wishes to deceive us. Given such possibilities, can we be sure of any truth?

The *Meditations* is universally regarded as a philosophical classic, even by the many who do not accept all the steps in Descartes' argument. What continues to fascinate philosophers is the provocative manner in which Descartes formulated and pursued such crucial issues. To meditate along with him is as good a way as any to come to an understanding of philosophical inquiry.

What follows is the first of Descartes' six meditations. We shall return to the second meditation in the next section of the book.

....

FIRST MEDITATION

What Can Be Called into Doubt

Some years ago I was struck by the large number of falsehoods that I had accepted as true in my childhood, and by the highly doubtful nature of the whole edifice that I had subsequently based on them. I realized that it was necessary, once in the course of my life, to demolish everything completely and start again right from the foundations if I wanted to establish anything at all in the sciences that was stable and likely to last. But the task looked an enormous one, and I began to wait until I should reach a mature enough age to ensure that no subsequent time of life would be more suitable for tackling such inquiries. This led me to put the project off for so long that I would now be to blame if by pondering over it any further I wasted the time still left for carrying it out. So today I have expressly rid my mind of all worries and arranged for myself a clear stretch of free time. I am here quite alone,

From *Meditations on First Philosophy,* revised edition, translated by John Cottingham. Copyright © 1996 by Cambridge University Press. Reprinted by permission of the publisher.

and at last I will devote myself sincerely and without reservation to the general demolition of my opinions.

But to accomplish this, it will not be necessary for me to show that all my opinions are false, which is something I could perhaps never manage. Reason now leads me to think that I should hold back my assent from opinions which are not completely certain and indubitable just as carefully as I do from those which are patently false. So, for the purpose of rejecting all my opinions, it will be enough if I find in each of them at least some reason for doubt. And to do this I will not need to run through them all individually, which would be an endless task. Once the foundations of a building are undermined, anything built on them collapses of its own accord; so I will go straight for the basic principles on which all my former beliefs rested.

Whatever I have up till now accepted as most true I have acquired either from the senses or through the senses. But from time to time I have found that the senses deceive, and it is prudent never to trust completely those who have deceived us even once.

Yet although the senses occasionally deceive us with respect to objects which are very small or in the distance, there are many other beliefs about which doubt is quite impossible, even though they are derived from the senses—for example, that I am here, sitting by the fire, wearing a winter dressing-gown, holding this piece of paper in my hands, and so on. Again, how could it be denied that these hands or this whole body are mine? Unless perhaps I were to liken myself to madmen, whose brains are so damaged by the persistent vapours of melancholia that they firmly maintain they are kings when they are paupers, or say they are dressed in purple when they are naked, or that their heads are made of earthenware, or that they are pumpkins, or made of glass. But such people are insane, and I would be thought equally mad if I took anything from them as a model for myself.

A brilliant piece of reasoning! As if I were not a man who sleeps at night, and regularly has all the same experiences while asleep as madmen do when awake—indeed sometimes even more improbable ones. How often, asleep at night, am I convinced of just such familiar events—that I am here in my dressing-gown, sitting by the fire—when in fact I am lying undressed in bed! Yet at the moment my eyes are certainly wide awake when I look at this piece of paper; I shake my head and it is not asleep; as I stretch out and feel my hand I do so deliberately, and I know what I am doing. All this would not happen with such distinctness to someone asleep. Indeed! As if I did not remember other occasions when I have been tricked by exactly similar thoughts while asleep! As I think about this more carefully, I see plainly that there are never any sure signs by means of which being awake can be distinguished from being asleep. The result is that I begin to feel dazed, and this very feeling only reinforces the notion that I may be asleep.

Suppose then that I am dreaming, and that these particulars—that my eyes are open, that I am moving my head and stretching out my hands—are not true.

Perhaps, indeed, I do not even have such hands or such a body at all. Nonetheless, it must surely be admitted that the visions which come in sleep are like paintings, which must have been fashioned in the likeness of things that are real, and hence that at least these general kinds of things—eyes, head, hands, and the body as a whole—are things which are not imaginary but are real and exist. For even when painters try to create sirens and satyrs with the most extraordinary bodies, they cannot give them natures which are new in all respects; they simply jumble up the limbs of different animals. Or if perhaps they manage to think up something so new that nothing remotely similar has ever been seen before—something which is therefore completely fictitious and unreal—at least the colours used in the composition must be real. By similar reasoning, although these general kinds of things— eyes, head, hands and so on—could be imaginary, it must at least be admitted that certain other even simpler and more universal things are real. These are as it were the real colours from which we form all the images of things, whether true or false, that occur in our thought.

This class appears to include corporeal nature in general, and its extension; the shape of extended things; the quantity, or size and number of these things; the place in which they may exist, the time through which they may endure, and so on.

So a reasonable conclusion from this might be that physics, astronomy, medicine, and all other disciplines which depend on the study of composite things are doubtful; while arithmetic, geometry, and other subjects of this kind, which deal only with the simplest and most general things, regardless of whether they really exist in nature or not, contain something certain and indubitable. For whether I am awake or asleep, two and three added together are five, and a square has no more than four sides. It seems impossible that such transparent truths should incur any suspicion of being false.

And yet firmly rooted in my mind is the long-standing opinion that there is an omnipotent God who made me the kind of creature that I am. How do I know that he has not brought it about that there is no earth, no sky, no extended thing, no shape, no size, no place, while at the same time ensuring that all these things appear to me to exist just as they do now? What is more, just as I consider that others sometimes go astray in cases where they think they have the most perfect knowledge, how do I know that God has not brought it about that I too go wrong every time I add two and three or count the sides of a square, or in some even simpler matter, if that is imaginable? But perhaps God would not have allowed me to be deceived in this way, since he is said to be supremely good. But if it were inconsistent with his goodness to have created me such that I am deceived all the time, it would seem equally foreign to his goodness to allow me to be deceived even occasionally; yet this last assertion cannot be made.

Perhaps there may be some who would prefer to deny the existence of so powerful a God rather than believe that everything else is uncertain. Let us not argue with them, but grant them that everything said about God is a fiction. According to their supposition, then, I have arrived at my present state by fate or

chance or a continuous chain of events, or by some other means; yet since deception and error seem to be imperfections, the less powerful they make my original
cause, the more likely it is that I am so imperfect as to be deceived all the time.
I have no answer to these arguments, but am finally compelled to admit that there
is not one of my former beliefs about which a doubt may not properly be raised;
and this is not a flippant or ill-considered conclusion, but is based on powerful
and well thought-out reasons. So in the future I must withhold my assent from
these former beliefs just as carefully as I would from obvious falsehoods, if I want
to discover any certainty.

But it is not enough merely to have noticed this; I must make an effort to remember it. My habitual opinions keep coming back, and, despite my wishes, they
capture my belief, which is as it were bound over to them as a result of long occupation and the law of custom. I shall never get out of the habit of confidently
assenting to these opinions, so long as I suppose them to be what in fact they are,
namely, highly probable opinions—opinions which, despite the fact that they are
in a sense doubtful, as has just been shown, it is still much more reasonable to
believe than to deny. In view of this, I think it will be a good plan to turn my will
in completely the opposite direction and deceive myself, by pretending for a time
that these former opinions are utterly false and imaginary. I shall do this until the
weight of preconceived opinion is counter-balanced and the distorting influence
of habit no longer prevents my judgement from perceiving things correctly. In
the meantime, I know that no danger or error will result from my plan, and that
I cannot possibly go too far in my distrustful attitude. This is because the task
now in hand does not involve action but merely the acquisition of knowledge.

I will suppose therefore that not God, who is supremely good and the source
of truth, but rather some malicious demon of the utmost power and cunning has
employed all his energies in order to deceive me. I shall think that the sky, the air,
the earth, colours, shapes, sounds, and all external things are merely the delusions
of dreams which he has devised to ensnare my judgement. I shall consider myself
as not having hands or eyes, or flesh, or blood or senses, but as falsely believing
that I have all these things. I shall stubbornly and firmly persist in this meditation;
and, even if it is not in my power to know any truth, I shall at least do what is in my
power, that is, resolutely guard against assenting to any falsehoods, so that the deceiver, however powerful and cunning he may be, will be unable to impose on me
in the slightest degree. But this is an arduous undertaking, and a kind of laziness
brings me back to normal life. I am like a prisoner who is enjoying an imaginary
freedom while asleep; as he begins to suspect that he is asleep, he dreads being
woken up, and goes along with the pleasant illusion as long as he can. In the same
way, I happily slide back into my old opinions and dread being shaken out of them,
for fear that my peaceful sleep may be followed by hard labour when I wake, and
that I shall have to toil not in the light, but amid the inextricable darkness of the
problems I have now raised.

STUDY QUESTIONS

1. Can you ever be sure your senses are not deceiving you?
2. How can you tell that you are not now asleep?
3. Why does Descartes introduce the possibility of a malicious demon?
4. Can you doubt all your beliefs at once?

An Essay Concerning Human Understanding

ల్ల

JOHN LOCKE

Philosophers like Descartes, who base knowledge on reason alone rather than sense experience, are known as "rationalists." Those who base knowledge on sense experience rather than pure reason are known as "empiricists," and the leading historical exponents of empiricism are John Locke, George Berkeley, and David Hume.

Locke (1632–1704) argues that we can be mistaken in our beliefs about the external world; they fall short of Descartes' standard of absolute certainty. Nevertheless, our understanding of physical objects is a paradigm of knowledge, thus demonstrating that Descartes was mistaken in the standard he set.

Locke claims that all our ideas can be traced to two sources: sensation (i.e., sense perception) and reflection (i.e., awareness of the operations of our mind). Our knowledge of the world has its source in sensation. For example, I know a solid brown table is in front of me, and the basis for my knowledge is the evidence of my senses.

Locke draws a distinction between an object's primary and secondary qualities. The primary qualities are those inseparable from an object, such as its solidity, size, or velocity. The secondary qualities are powers in an object to produce sensations in us, for example, color, taste, and odor. So the solid brown table I see in front of me is in itself solid but only perceived as brown. If I looked at it in a different light, it would still be solid but might look black or some other color.

....

CONCERNING OUR SIMPLE IDEAS OF SENSATION

7. To discover the nature of our ideas the better, and to discourse of them intelligibly, it will be convenient to distinguish them as they are ideas or perceptions in our

From *An Essay Concerning Human Understanding* by John Locke (1690), Book II, Chapter VIII and Book IV, Chapter XI.

minds, and as they are modifications of matter in the bodies that cause such perceptions in us, that so we may not think (as perhaps usually is done) that they are exactly the images and resemblances of something inherent in the subject; most of those of sensation being in the mind no more the likeness of something existing without us, than the names that stand for them are the likeness of our ideas, which yet upon hearing they are apt to excite in us.

8. Whatsoever the mind perceives in itself, or is the immediate object of perception, thought, or understanding, that I call idea; and the power to produce any idea in our mind, I call quality of the subject wherein that power is. Thus a snowball having the power to produce in us the ideas of white, cold, and round, the power to produce those ideas in us, as they are in the snowball, I call qualities; and as they are sensations or perceptions in our understandings, I call them ideas; which ideas, if I speak of sometimes as in the things themselves, I would be understood to mean those qualities in the objects which produce them in us.

9. Qualities thus considered in bodies are, first, such as are utterly inseparable from the body, in what state soever it be; such as in all the alterations and changes it suffers, all the force can be used upon it, it constantly keeps; and such as sense constantly finds in every particle of matter which has bulk enough to be perceived and the mind finds inseparable from every particle of matter, though less than to make itself singly be perceived by our senses, e.g., take a grain of wheat, divide it into two parts, each part has still solidity, extension, figure, and mobility; divide it again, and it retains still the same qualities; and so divide it on till the parts become insensible, they must retain still each of them all those qualities. For division (which is all that a mill, or pestle, or any other body, does upon another, in reducing it to insensible parts) can never take away either solidity, extension, figure, or mobility from any body, but only makes two or more distinct separate masses of matter, of that which was but one before; all which distinct masses, reckoned as so many distinct bodies, after division, make a certain number. These I call original or primary qualities of body, which I think we may observe to produce simple ideas in us, viz., solidity, extension, figure, motion or rest, and number.

10. Secondly, such qualities which in truth are nothing in the objects themselves, but powers to produce various sensations in us by their primary qualities, i.e., by the bulk, figure, texture, and motion of their insensible parts, as colours, sounds, tastes, etc., these I call secondary qualities. To these might be added a third sort, which are allowed to be barely powers, though they are as much real qualities in the subject, as those which I, to comply with the common way of speaking, call qualities, but for distinction, secondary qualities. For the power in fire to produce a new colour or consistency in wax or clay, by its primary qualities, is as much a quality in fire as the power it has to produce in me a new idea or sensation of warmth or burning, which I felt not before, by the same primary qualities, viz., the bulk, texture, and motion of its insensible parts.

11. The next thing to be considered is, how bodies produce ideas in us; and that is manifestly by impulse, the only way which we can conceive bodies to operate in.

12. If then external objects be not united to our minds when they produce ideas therein, and yet we perceive these original qualities in such of them as singly fall under our senses, it is evident that some motion must be thence continued by our nerves or animal spirits, by some parts of our bodies, to the brain, or the seat of sensation, there to produce in our minds the particular ideas we have of them. And since the extension, figure, number, and motion of bodies of an observable bigness may be perceived at a distance by the sight, it is evident some singly imperceptible bodies must come from them to the eyes, and thereby convey to the brain some motion, which produces these ideas which we have of them in us.

13. After the same manner that the ideas of these original qualities are produced in us, we may conceive that the ideas of secondary qualities are also produced, viz., by the operations of insensible particles on our senses. For it being manifest that there are bodies and good store of bodies, each whereof are so small, that we cannot by any of our senses discover either their bulk, figure, or motion, as is evident in the particles of the air and water, and others extremely smaller than those, perhaps as much smaller than the particles of air and water, as the particles of air and water are smaller than peas or hailstones; let us suppose that the different motions and figures, bulk and number, of such particles, affecting the several organs of our senses, produce in us those different sensations which we have from the colours and smells of bodies; e.g., that a violet, by the impulse of such insensible particles of matter of peculiar figures and bulks, and in different degrees and modifications of their motions, causes the ideas of the blue colour and sweet scent of that flower to be produced in our minds; it being no more impossible to conceive that God should annex such ideas to such motions, with which they have no similitude, than that he should annex the idea of pain to the motion of a piece of steel dividing our flesh, with which that idea has no resemblance.

14. What I have said concerning colours and smells may be understood also of tastes and sounds, and other the like sensible qualities; which, whatever reality we by mistake attribute to them, are in truth nothing in the objects themselves, but powers to produce various sensations in us, and depend on those primary qualities, viz., bulk, figure, texture, and motion of parts, as I have said.

15. From whence I think it easy to draw this observation, that the ideas of primary qualities of bodies are resemblances of them, and their patterns do really exist in the bodies themselves; but the ideas produced in us by these secondary qualities have no resemblance of them at all. There is nothing like our ideas existing in the bodies themselves. They are in the bodies we denominate from them, only a power to produce those sensations in us; and what is sweet, blue, or warm in idea, is but the certain bulk, figure, and motion of the insensible parts in the bodies themselves, which we call so.

16. Flame is denominated hot and light; snow, white and cold; and manna, white and sweet, from the ideas they produce in us; which qualities are commonly thought to be the same in those bodies that those ideas are in us, the one the perfect resemblance of the other, as they are in a mirror; and it would by most men be judged very extravagant if one should say otherwise. And yet he that will consider

that the same fire that at one distance produces in us the sensation of warmth, does at a nearer approach produce in us the far different sensation of pain, ought to bethink himself what reason he has to say that this idea of warmth, which was produced in him by the fire, is actually in the fire; and his idea of pain, which the same fire produced in him the same way, is not in the fire. Why are whiteness and coldness in snow, and pain not, when it produces the one and the other idea in us; and can do neither, but by the bulk, figure, number, and motion of its solid parts?

19. Let us consider the red and white colours in porphyry: hinder light from striking on it, and its colours vanish, it no longer produces any such ideas in us; upon the return of light it produces these appearances on us again. Can any one think any real alterations are made in the porphyry by the presence or absence of light, and that those ideas of whiteness and redness are really in porphyry in the light, when it is plain it has no colour in the dark? It has, indeed, such a configuration of particles, both night and day, as are apt, by the rays of light rebounding from some parts of that hard stone, to produce in us the idea of redness, and from others the idea of whiteness; but whiteness or redness are not in it at any time, but such a texture that has the power to produce such a sensation in us.

23. The qualities, then, that are in bodies, rightly considered, are of three sorts.

First, the bulk, figure, number, situation, and motion or rest of their solid parts; those are in them, whether we perceive them or not; and when they are of that size that we can discover them, we have by these an idea of the thing as it is in itself, as is plain in artificial things. These I call primary qualities.

Secondly, the power that is in any body, by reason of its insensible primary qualities, to operate after a peculiar manner on any of our senses, and thereby pro-duce in us the different ideas of several colours, sounds, smells, tastes, etc. These are usually called sensible qualities.

Thirdly, the power that is in any body, by reason of the particular constitution of its primary qualities, to make such a change in the bulk, figure, texture, and motion of another body, as to make it operate on our senses differently from what it did before. Thus the sun has a power to make wax white, and fire to make lead fluid. These are usually called powers.

The first of these, as has been said, I think may be properly called real, origi-nal, or primary qualities, because they are in the things themselves, whether they are perceived or not; and upon their different modifications it is that the second-ary qualities depend.

The other two are only powers to act differently upon other things, which powers result from the different modifications of those primary qualities.

OF OUR KNOWLEDGE OF THE EXISTENCE
OF OTHER THINGS

1. The knowledge of our own being we have by intuition. The existence of a God reason clearly makes known to us. . . .

The knowledge of the existence of any other thing we can have only by sensa-tion: for there being no necessary connection of real existence with any idea a man has in his memory; nor of any other existence but that of God with the existence of any particular man: no particular man can know the existence of any other being, but only when, by actually operating upon him, it makes itself perceived by him. For the having the idea of anything in our mind no more proves the existence of that thing than the picture of a man evidences his being in the world, or the visions of a dream make thereby a true history.

2. It is therefore the actual receiving of ideas from without that gives us notice of the existence of other things, and makes us know that something does exist at that time without us which causes that idea in us, though perhaps we neither know nor consider how it does it. For it takes not from the certainty of our senses, and the ideas we receive by them, that we know not the manner wherein they are produced: e.g., while I write this, I have, by the paper affecting my eyes, that idea produced in my mind, which whatever object causes, I call white; by which I know that that quality or accident (i.e., whose appearance before my eyes always causes that idea) does really exist, and has a being without me. And of this, the greatest as-surance I can possibly have, and to which my faculties can attain, is the testimony of my eyes, which are the proper and sole judges of this thing; whose testimony I have reason to rely on as so certain, that I can no more doubt, whilst I write this, that I see white and black, and that something really exists that causes that sensa-tion in me, than that I write or move my hand; which is a certainty as great as human nature is capable of, concerning the existence of anything but a man's self alone, and of God.

3. The notice we have by our senses of the existing of things without us, though it be not altogether so certain as our intuitive knowledge, or the deduc-tions of our reason employed about the clear abstract ideas of our own minds; yet it is an assurance that deserves the name of *knowledge*. If we persuade ourselves that our faculties act and inform us right concerning the existence of those objects that affect them, it cannot pass for an ill-grounded confidence: for I think nobody can, in earnest, be so sceptical as to be uncertain of the existence of those things which he sees and feels. At least, he that can doubt so far (whatever he may have with his own thoughts) will never have any controversy with me; since he can never be sure I say anything contrary to his opinion. As to myself, I think God has given me assurance enough of the existence of things without me; since by their different application I can produce in myself both pleasure and pain, which is one great concern of my present state. This is certain, the confidence that our faculties do not herein deceive us is the greatest assurance we are capable of concerning the existence of material beings. For we cannot act anything but by our faculties, nor talk of knowledge itself, but by the help of those faculties which are fitted to appre-hend even what knowledge is. But besides the assurance we have from our senses themselves, that they do not err in the information they give us of the existence of things without us, when they are affected by them, we are farther confirmed in this assurance by other concurrent reasons.

4. First, It is plain those perceptions are produced in us by exterior causes affecting our senses, because those that want the organs of any sense never can have the ideas belonging to that sense produced in their minds. The organs themselves, it is plain, do not produce them; for then the eyes of a man in the dark would produce colours, and his nose smell roses in the winter: but we see nobody gets the relish of a pineapple till he goes to the Indies where it is, and tastes it.

5. Secondly, Because sometimes I find that I cannot avoid the having those ideas produced in my mind. For though when my eyes are shut, or windows fast, I can at pleasure recall to my mind the ideas of light or the sun, which former sensations had lodged in my memory; so I can at pleasure lay by that idea, and take into my view that of the smell of a rose, or taste of sugar. But if I turn my eyes at noon towards the sun, I cannot avoid the ideas which the light or sun then produces in me. So that there is a manifest difference between the ideas laid up in my memory, and those which force themselves upon me, and I cannot avoid having. And therefore it must be some exterior cause, and the brisk acting of some objects without me, whose efficacy I cannot resist, that produces those ideas in my mind, whether I will or not. Besides, there is nobody who does not perceive the difference in himself between contemplating the sun as he has the idea of it in his memory, and actually looking upon it: of which two, his perception is so distinct, that few of his ideas are more distinguishable one from another. And therefore he has certain knowledge that they are not both memory, or the actions of his mind, and fancies only within him; but that actual seeing has a cause without. . . .

7. Fourthly, Our senses, in many cases, bear witness to the truth of each other's report concerning the existence of sensible things without us. He that sees a fire may, if he doubt whether it be anything more than a bare fancy, feel it too, and be convinced by putting his hand in it; which certainly could never be put into such exquisite pain by a bare idea or phantom, unless that the pain be a fancy too; which yet he cannot, when the burn is well, by raising the idea of it, bring upon himself again.

Thus I see, while I write this, I can change the appearance of the paper; and by designing the letters, tell beforehand what new idea it shall exhibit the very next moment, barely by drawing my pen over it: which will neither appear (let me fancy as much as I will) if my hand stand still, or though I move my pen, if my eyes be shut: nor, when those characters are once made on the paper, can I choose afterwards but see them as they are; that is, have the ideas of such letters as I have made. Whence it is manifest that they are not barely the sport and play of my own imagination, when I find that the characters that were made at the pleasure of my own thoughts do not obey them; nor yet cease to be, whenever I shall fancy it, but continue to affect my senses constantly and regularly, according to the figures I made them. To which if we will add, that the sight of those shall, from another man, draw such sounds as I beforehand design they shall stand for, there will be little reason left to doubt that those words I write do really exist without me, when they cause a long series of regular sounds to affect my ears, which could not be the effect of my imagination, nor could my memory retain them in that order.

8. But yet, if after all this anyone will be so sceptical as to distrust his senses, and to affirm that all we see and hear, feel and taste, think and do, during our whole being, is but the series and deluding appearances of a long dream whereof there is no reality; and therefore will question the existence of all things or our knowledge of anything: I must desire him to consider, that if all be a dream, then he does but dream that he makes the question; and so it is not much matter that a waking man should answer him. But yet, if he pleases, he may dream that I make him this answer, that the certainty of things existing *in rerum natura* when we have the testimony of our senses for it, is not only as great as our frame can attain to, but as our condition needs. For our faculties being suited not to the full extent of being; nor to a perfect, clear, comprehensive knowledge of things free from all doubt and scruple; but to the preservation of us, in whom they are; and accommodated to the use of life: they serve to our purpose well enough, if they will but give us certain notice of those things which are convenient or inconvenient to us. For he that sees a candle burning, and has experimented the force of its flame by putting his finger in it, will little doubt that this is something existing without him, which does him harm and puts him to great pain. And if our dreamer pleases to try whether the glowing heat of a glass furnace be barely a wandering imagination in a drowsy man's fancy, by putting his hand into it, he may perhaps be awakened into a certainty, greater than he could wish, that it is something more than bare imagination. So that this evidence is as great as we can desire, being as certain to us as our pleasure or pain, i.e., happiness or misery; beyond which we have no concern, either of knowing or being. Such an assurance of the existence of things without us is sufficient to direct us in the attaining the good and avoiding the evil which is caused by them, which is the important concern we have of being made acquainted with them.

STUDY QUESTIONS

1. How does Locke distinguish primary from secondary qualities?
2. How can you decide if a quality is primary or secondary?
3. According to Locke, how do we know of a world outside ourselves?
4. How does Locke reply to those who would doubt that they have knowledge of the material world?

A Treatise Concerning the Principles of Human Knowledge

⚘

GEORGE BERKELEY

George Berkeley (1685–1753), born in Ireland, published his most important works during his twenties. At one time he lived in Rhode Island, then returned to his homeland to become bishop of Cloyne.

Berkeley accepts Locke's view of secondary qualities as mind-dependent and extends Locke's position to primary qualities, arguing that they "too" are mind-dependent. For example, an object that appears solid to one perceiver may not appear solid to another (the basis for many magic tricks).

But if both the primary and secondary qualities are mind-dependent, what remains of the material object? Berkeley's startling answer is: nothing. Physical objects exist but only as ideas in the minds of perceivers, who are themselves immaterial spirits. Does a table go out of existence when not being perceived by us? No, for it is being perceived by the "governing Spirit" we call God. He sends us our sensations in an orderly manner, thus giving rise to a world of sensations exhibiting the laws of nature.

Berkeley, after all, was a clergyman. So his epistemological and theological views are in harmony. Berkeley's idealism, his position that reality is fundamentally mental in nature, may not persuade many readers, but finding errors in his reasoning is no easy matter.

....

1. It is evident to anyone who takes a survey of the objects of human knowledge, that they are either ideas actually imprinted on the senses, or else such as are perceived by attending to the passions and operations of the mind, or lastly ideas formed by help of memory and imagination, either compounding, dividing, or barely representing those originally perceived in the aforesaid ways. By sight I have the ideas of light and colours with their several degrees and variations. By touch I perceive, for example, hard and soft, heat and cold, motion and resistance, and of all these more and less either as to quantity or degree. Smelling furnishes me with odours; the palate with tastes, and hearing conveys sounds to the mind in all their variety of tone and composition. And as several of these are observed to accompany each other, they come to be marked by one name, and so to be reputed as one thing. Thus, for example, a certain colour, taste, smell, figure and consistence

From *A Treatise Concerning the Principles of Human Knowledge* by George Berkeley (1710).

having been observed to go together, are accounted one distinct thing, signified by the name *apple*. Other collections of ideas constitute a stone, a tree, a book, and the like sensible things; which, as they are pleasing or disagreeable, excite the passions of love, hatred, joy, grief, and so forth.

2. But besides all that endless variety of ideas or objects of knowledge, there is likewise something which knows or perceives them, and exercises divers operations, as willing, imagining, remembering about them. This perceiving, active being is what I call *mind, spirit, soul* or *myself*. By which words I do not denote any one of my ideas, but a thing entirely distinct from them, wherein they exist, or, which is the same thing, whereby they are perceived; for the existence of an idea consists in being perceived.

3. That neither our thoughts, nor passions, nor ideas formed by the imagination exist without the mind is what everybody will allow. And it seems no less evident that the various sensations or ideas imprinted on the sense, however blended or combined together (that is, whatever objects they compose), cannot exist otherwise than in a mind perceiving them. I think an intuitive knowledge may be obtained of this, by anyone that shall attend to what is meant by the term *exist* when applied to sensible things. The table I write on, I say, exists, that is, I see and feel it; and if I were out of my study I should say it existed, meaning thereby that if I was in my study I might perceive it, or that some other spirit actually does perceive it. There was an odour, that is, it was smelled; there was a sound, that is to say, it was heard; a colour or figure, and it was perceived by sight or touch. This is all that I can understand by these and the like expressions. For as to what is said of the absolute existence of unthinking things without any relation to their being perceived, that seems perfectly unintelligible. Their *esse* is *percipi*, nor is it possible they should have any existence, out of the minds or thinking things which perceive them.

4. It is indeed an opinion strangely prevailing amongst men that houses, mountains, rivers, and in a word all sensible objects have an existence natural or real, distinct from their being perceived by the understanding. But with how great an assurance and acquiescence soever this principle may be entertained in the world; yet whoever shall find in his heart to call it in question, may, if I mistake not, perceive it to involve a manifest contradiction. For what are the forementioned objects but the things we perceive by sense, and what do we perceive besides our own ideas or sensations; and is it not plainly repugnant that any one of these or any combination of them should exist unperceived?

5. If we thoroughly examine this tenet, it will, perhaps, be found at bottom to depend on the doctrine of *abstract ideas*. For can there be a nicer strain of abstraction than to distinguish the existence of sensible objects from their being perceived, so as to conceive them existing unperceived? Light and colours, heat and cold, extension and figures, in a word the things we see and feel, what are they but so many sensations, notions, ideas or impressions on the sense; and is it possible to separate, even in thought, any of these from perception? For my part I might as easily divide a thing from itself. I may indeed divide in my thoughts or conceive

apart from each other those things which, perhaps, I never perceived by sense so divided. Thus I imagine the trunk of a human body without the limbs, or conceive the smell of a rose without thinking on the rose itself. So far I will not deny I can abstract, if that may properly be called *abstraction*, which extends only to the conceiving separately such objects, as it is possible may really exist or be actually perceived asunder. But my conceiving or imagining power does not extend beyond the possibility of real existence or perception. Hence as it is impossible for me to see or feel anything without an actual sensation of that thing, so is it impossible for me to conceive in my thoughts any sensible thing or object distinct from the sensation or perception of it.

6. Some truths there are so near and obvious to the mind that a man need only open his eyes to see them. Such I take this important one to be, to wit, that all the choir of heaven and furniture of the earth, in a word all those bodies which compose the mighty frame of the world, have not any subsistence, without a mind, that their being is to be perceived or known; that consequently so long as they are not actually perceived by me, or do not exist in my mind or that of any other created spirit, they must either have no existence at all, or else subsist in the mind of some eternal spirit: it being perfectly unintelligible and involving all the absurdity of abstraction, to attribute to any single part of them an existence independent of a spirit. To be convinced of which, the reader need only reflect and try to separate in his own thoughts the being of a sensible thing from its being perceived.

7. From what has been said, it follows, there is not any other substance than *spirit*, or that which perceives. But for the fuller proof of this point, let it be considered, the sensible qualities are colour, figure, motion, smell, taste, and such like, that is, the ideas perceived by sense. Now for an idea to exist in an unperceiving thing, is a manifest contradiction; for to have an idea is all one as to perceive; that therefore wherein colour, figure, and the like qualities exist, must perceive them; hence it is clear there can be no unthinking substance or *substratum* of those ideas.

8. But say you, though the ideas themselves do not exist without the mind, yet there may be things like them whereof they are copies or resemblances, which things exist without the mind, in an unthinking substance. I answer, an idea can be like nothing but an idea; a colour or figure can be like nothing but another colour or figure. If we look but ever so little into our thoughts, we shall find it impossible for us to conceive a likeness except only between our ideas. Again, I ask whether these supposed originals or external things, of which our ideas are the pictures or representations, be themselves perceivable or no? If they are, then they are ideas, and we have gained our point; but if you say they are not, I appeal to anyone whether it be sense, to assert a colour is like something which is invisible, hard or soft, like something which is intangible; and so of the rest.

9. Some there are who make a distinction betwixt *primary* and *secondary* qualities: by the former, they mean extension, figure, motion, rest, solidity or impenetrability and number: by the latter they denote all other sensible qualities, as colours, sounds, tastes, and so forth. The ideas we have of these they acknowledge

not to be the resemblances of anything existing without the mind or unperceived; but they will have our ideas of the primary qualities to be patterns or images of things which exist without the mind, in an unthinking substance which they call *matter*. By matter therefore we are to understand an inert, senseless substance, in which extension, figure, and motion, do actually subsist. But it is evident from what we have already shewn, that extension, figure and motion are only ideas existing in the mind, and that an idea can be like nothing but another idea, and that consequently neither they nor their archetypes can exist in an unperceiving substance. Hence it is plain that the very notion of what is called *matter* or *corporeal substance* involves a contradiction in it.

10. They who assert that figure, motion, and the rest of the primary or original qualities do exist without the mind, in unthinking substances, do at the same time acknowledge that colours, sounds, heat, cold, and such like secondary qualities, do not, which they tell us are sensations existing in the mind alone, that depend on and are occasioned by the different size, texture and motion of the minute particles of matter. This they take for an undoubted truth, which they can demonstrate beyond all exception. Now if it be certain that those original qualities are inseparably united with the other sensible qualities, and not, even in thought, capable of being abstracted from them, it plainly follows that they exist only in the mind. But I desire anyone to reflect and try, whether he can by any abstraction of thought, conceive the extension and motion of a body, without all other sensible qualities. For my own part, I see evidently that it is not in my power to frame an idea of a body extended and moved, but I must withal give it some colour or other sensible quality which is acknowledged to exist only in the mind. In short, extension, figure, and motion, abstracted from all other qualities, are inconceivable. Where therefore the other sensible qualities are, there must these be also, to wit, in the mind and nowhere else.

14. I shall farther add that after the same manner, as modern philosophers prove certain sensible qualities to have no existence in matter, or without the mind, the same thing may be likewise proved of all other sensible qualities whatsoever. Thus, for instance, it is said that heat and cold are affections only of the mind, and not at all patterns of real beings, existing in the corporeal substances which excite them, for that the same body which appears cold to one hand seems warm to another. Now why may we not as well argue that figure and extension are not patterns or resemblances of qualities existing in matter, because to the same eye at different stations, or eyes of a different texture at the same station, they appear various, and cannot therefore be the images of anything settled and determinate without the mind? Again, it is proved that sweetness is not really in the sapid thing because the thing remaining unaltered the sweetness is changed into bitter, as in case of a fever or otherwise vitiated palate. Is it not as reasonable to say that motion is not without the mind, since if the succession of ideas in the mind become swifter, the motion, it is acknowledged, shall appear slower without any alteration in any external object.

15. In short, let anyone consider those arguments, which are thought manifestly to prove that colours and tastes exist only in the mind, and he shall find they

may with equal force, be brought to prove the same thing of extension, figure, and motion? Though it must be confessed this method of arguing doth not so much prove that there is no extension or colour in an outward object, as that we do not know by sense which is the true extension or colour of the object. But the arguments foregoing plainly shew it to be impossible that any colour or extension at all, or other sensible quality whatsoever, should exist in an unthinking subject without the mind, or in truth, that there should be any such thing as an outward object.

16. But let us examine a little the received opinion. It is said extension is a mode or accident of matter, and that matter is the *substratum* that supports it. Now I desire that you would explain what is meant by matter's *supporting* extension: say you, I have no idea of matter, and therefore cannot explain it. I answer, though you have no positive, yet if you have any meaning at all, you must at least have a relative idea of matter; though you know not what it is, yet you must be supposed to know what relation it bears to accidents, and what is meant by its supporting them. It is evident *support* cannot here be taken in its usual or literal sense, as when we say that pillars support a building: in what sense therefore must it be taken?

17. If we inquire into what the most accurate philosophers declare themselves to mean by *material substance;* we shall find them acknowledge, they have no other meaning annexed to those sounds, but the idea of being in general, together with the relative notion of its supporting accidents. The general idea of being appeareth to me the most abstract and incomprehensible of all other; and as for its supporting accidents, this, as we have just now observed, cannot be understood in the common sense of those words; it must therefore be taken in some other sense, but what that is they do not explain. So that when I consider the two parts or branches which make the signification of the words *material substance*, I am convinced there is no distinct meaning annexed to them. But why should we trouble ourselves any farther, in discussing this material *substratum* or support of figure and motion, and other sensible qualities? Does it not suppose they have an existence without the mind? And is not this a direct repugnancy, and altogether inconceivable?

18. But though it were possible that solid, figured, moveable substances may exist without the mind, corresponding to the ideas we have of bodies, yet how is it possible for us to know this? Either we must know it by sense, or by reason. As for our senses, by them we have the knowledge only of our sensations, ideas, or those things that are immediately perceived by sense, call them what you will: but they do not inform us that things exist without the mind, or unperceived, like to those which are perceived. This the materials themselves acknowledge. It remains therefore that if we have any knowledge at all of external things, it must be by reason, inferring their existence from what is immediately perceived by sense. But what reason can induce us to believe the existence of bodies without the mind, from what we perceive, since the very patrons of matter themselves do not pretend there is any necessary connexion betwixt them and our ideas? I say it is granted on all hands (and what happens in dreams, phrensies, and the like, puts it beyond dispute) that it is possible we might be affected with all the ideas we have now, though no bodies existed without resembling them. Hence it is evident the supposition

of external bodies is not necessary for the producing our ideas: since it is granted they are produced sometimes, and might possibly be produced always in the same order we see them in at present, without their concurrence.

19. But though we might possibly have all our sensations without them, yet perhaps it may be thought easier to conceive and explain the manner of their production, by supposing external bodies in their likeness rather than otherwise; and so it might be at least probable there are such things as bodies that excite their ideas in our minds. But neither can this be said; for though we give the materialists their external bodies, they by their own confession are never the nearer knowing how our ideas are produced; since they own themselves unable to comprehend in what manner body can act upon spirit, or how it is possible it should imprint any idea in the mind. Hence it is evident the production of ideas or sensations in our minds can be no reason why we should suppose matter or corporeal substances, since that is acknowledged to remain equally inexplicable with or without this supposition. If therefore it were possible for bodies to exist without the mind, yet to hold they do so, must needs be a very precarious opinion; since it is to suppose, without any reason at all, that God has created innumerable beings that are entirely useless, and serve to no manner of purpose.

22. I am afraid I have given cause to think me needlessly prolix in handling this subject. For to what purpose is it to dilate on that which may be demonstrated with the utmost evidence in a line or two, to anyone that is capable of the least reflexion? It is but looking into your own thoughts, and so trying whether you can conceive it possible for a sound, or figure, or motion, or colour, to exist without the mind, or unperceived. This easy trial may make you see that what you contend for is a downright contradiction. Insomuch that I am content to put the whole upon this issue; if you can but conceive it possible for one extended moveable substance, or in general, for any one idea or anything like an idea, to exist otherwise than in a mind perceiving it, I shall readily give up the cause: and as for all that *compages* of external bodies which you contend for, I shall grant you its existence, though you cannot either give me any reason why you believe it exists, or assign any use to it when it is supposed to exist. I say, the bare possibility of your opinion's being true shall pass for an argument that it is so.

23. But you say, surely there is nothing easier than to imagine trees, for instance, in a park, or books existing in a closet, and nobody by to perceive them. I answer, you may so, there is no difficulty in it: but what is all this, I beseech you, more then framing in your mind certain ideas which you call *books* and *trees*, and at the same time omitting to frame the idea of anyone that may perceive them? But do not you yourself perceive or think of them all the while? This therefore is nothing to the purpose: it only shows you have the power of imagining or forming ideas in your mind; but it doth not shew that you can conceive it possible, the objects of your thought may exist without the mind: to make out this, it is necessary that you conceive them existing unconceived or unthought of, which is a manifest repugnancy. When we do our utmost to conceive the existence of external bodies, we are all the while only contemplating our own ideas. But the mind taking no

notice of itself, is deluded to think it can and doth conceive bodies existing un-thought of or without the mind; though at the same time they are apprehended by or exist in itself. A little attention will discover to anyone the truth and evidence of what is here said, and make it unnecessary to insist on any other proofs against the existence of material substance.

25. All our ideas, sensations, or the thing which we perceive, by whatsoever names they may be distinguished, are visibly inactive, there is nothing of power or agency included in them. So that one idea or object of thought cannot produce, or make any alteration in another. To be satisfied of the truth of this, there is nothing else requisite but a bare observation of our ideas. For since they and every part of them exist only in the mind, it follows that there is nothing in them but what is per-ceived. But whoever shall attend to his ideas, whether of sense or reflexion, will not perceive in them any power or activity; there is therefore no such thing contained in them. A little attention will discover to us that the very being of an idea implies passiveness and inertness in it, insomuch that it is impossible for an idea to do any-thing, or, strictly speaking, to be the cause of anything: neither can it be the resem-blance or pattern of any active being, as is evident from *Sect.* 8. Whence it plainly follows that extension, figure and motion, cannot be the cause of our sensations. To say therefore, that these are the effects of powers resulting from the configuration, number, motion, and size of corpuscles, must certainly be false.

26. We perceive a continual succession of ideas, some are a new excited, others are changed or totally disappear. There is therefore some cause of these ideas whereon they depend, and which produces and changes them. That this cause cannot be any quality or idea or combination of ideas is clear from the preceding section. It must therefore be a substance; but it has been shewn that there is no corporeal or material substance; it remains therefore that the cause of ideas is an incorporeal active substance or spirit.

27. A spirit is one simple, undivided, active being: as it perceives ideas, it is called the *understanding*, and as it produces or otherwise operates about them, it is called the *will*. Hence there can be no idea formed of a soul or spirit: for all ideas whatever, being passive and inert, *vide Sect.* 25, they cannot represent unto us, by way of image or likeness, that which acts. A little attention will make it plain to anyone that to have an idea which shall be like that active principle of motion and change of ideas is absolutely impossible. Such is the nature of *spirit* or that which acts that it cannot be of itself perceived, but only by the effects which it pro-duceth. If any man shall doubt of the truth of what is here delivered, let him but reflect and try if he can frame the idea of any power or active being; and whether he hath ideas of two principal powers, marked by the names *will* and *understand-ing*, distinct from each other as well as from a third idea of substance or being in general, with a relative notion of its supporting or being the subject of the afore-said powers, which is signified by the name *soul* or *spirit*. This is what some hold; but so far as I can see, the words *will, soul, spirit* do not stand for different ideas, or in truth, for any idea at all, but for something which is very different from ideas, and which being an agent cannot be like unto, or represented by, any idea

whatsoever. Though it must be owned at the same time that we have some notion of soul, spirit, and the operations of the mind, such as willing loving, hating, in as much as we know or understand the meaning of those words.

28. I find I can excite ideas in my mind at pleasure, and vary and shift the scene as oft as I think fit. It is no more than willing, and straightway this or that idea arises in my fancy: and by the same power it is obliterated and makes way for another. This making and unmaking of ideas doth very properly denominate the mind active. Thus much is certain, and grounded on experience: but when we talk of unthinking agents, or of exciting ideas exclusive of volition, we only amuse ourselves with words.

29. But whatever power I may have over my own thoughts, I find the ideas actually perceived by sense have not a like dependence on my will. When in broad daylight I open my eyes, it is not in my power to choose whether I shall see or no, or to determine what particular objects shall present themselves to my view; and so likewise as to the hearing and other senses, the ideas imprinted on them are not creatures of my will. There is therefore some other will or spirit that produces them.

30. The ideas of sense are more strong, lively, and distinct than those of the imagination; they have likewise a steadiness, order, and coherence, and are not excited at random, as those which are the effects of human wills often are, but in a regular train or series, the admirable connexion whereof sufficiently testifies the wisdom and benevolence of its Author. Now the set rules or established methods, wherein the mind we depend on excites in us the ideas of sense, are called the *Laws of Nature:* and these we learn by experience, which teaches us that such and such ideas are attended with such and such other ideas, in the ordinary course of things.

31. This gives us a sort of foresight, which enables us to regulate our actions for the benefit of the life. And without this we should be eternally at a loss: we could not know how to act anything that might procure us the least pleasure, or remove the least pain of sense. That food nourishes, sleep refreshes, and fire warms us; that to sow in the seed-time is the way to reap in the harvest, and, in general, that to obtain such or such ends, such or such means are conducive, all this we know, not by discovering any necessary connexion between our ideas, but only by the observation of the settled Laws of Nature, without which we should be all in uncertainty and confusion, and a grown man no more knows how to manage himself in the affairs of life than an infant just born.

32. And yet this consistent uniform working, which so evidently displays the goodness and wisdom of that governing spirit whose will constitutes the Laws of Nature, is so far from leading our thoughts to him that it rather sends them a wandering after second causes. For when we perceive certain ideas of sense constantly followed by other ideas, and we know this is not of our doing, we forthwith attribute power and agency to the ideas themselves and make one the cause of another, than which nothing can be more absurd and unintelligible. Thus, for example, having observed that when we perceive by sight a certain round luminous figure, we at the same time perceive by touch the idea of sensation called *heat,* we do from thence conclude the sun to be the cause of heat. And in like manner perceiving the

motion and collision of bodies to be attended with sound, we are inclined to think the latter an effect of the former.

33. The ideas imprinted on the senses by the Author of Nature are called *real things:* and those excited in the imagination being less regular, vivid and constant, are more properly termed *ideas,* or *images of things,* which they copy and represent. But then our sensations, be they never so vivid and distinct, are nevertheless *ideas,* that is, they exist in the mind, or are perceived by it, as truly as the ideas of its own framing. The ideas of sense are allowed to have more reality in them, that is, to be more strong, orderly, and coherent than the creatures of the mind; but this is no argument that they exist without the mind. They are also less dependent on the spirit, or thinking substance which perceives them, in that they are excited by the will of another and more powerful spirit: yet still they are *ideas,* and certainly no *idea,* whether faint or strong, can exist otherwise than in a mind perceiving it.

145. From what has been said it is plain that we cannot know the existence of other spirits otherwise than by their operations, or the ideas by them excited in us. I perceive several motions, changes, and combinations of ideas that inform me there are certain particular agents, like myself, which accompany them and concur in their production. Hence, the knowledge I have of other spirits is not immediate, as is the knowledge of my ideas, but depending on the intervention of ideas, by me referred to agents or spirits distinct from myself, as effects or concomitant signs.

146. But though there be some things which convince us human agents are concerned in producing them, yet it is evident to everyone that those things which are called "the works of nature," that is, the far greater part of the ideas or sensations perceived by us, are not produced by, or dependent on, the wills of men. There is therefore some other spirit that causes them; since it is repugnant that they should subsist by themselves. See sec. 29. But, if we attentively consider the constant regularity, order, and concatenation of natural things, the surprising magnificence, beauty, and perfection of the larger, and the exquisite contrivance of the smaller parts of the creation, together with the exact harmony and correspondence of the whole, but above all the never-enough-admired laws of pain and pleasure, and the instincts or natural inclinations, appetites, and passions of animals; I say if we consider all these things, and at the same time attend to the meaning and import of the attributes: one, eternal, infinitely wise, good, and perfect, we shall clearly perceive that they belong to the aforesaid spirit, "who works all in all," and "by whom all things consist."

147. Hence it is evident that God is known as certainly and immediately as any other mind or spirit whatsoever distinct from ourselves. We may even assert that the existence of God is far more evidently perceived than the existence of men; because the effects of nature are infinitely more numerous and considerable than those ascribed to human agents. There is not any one mark that denotes a man, or effect produced by him, which does not more strongly evince the being of that spirit who is the Author of Nature. For it is evident that in affecting other persons the will of man has no other object than barely the motion of the limbs of his body; but that such a motion should be attended by, or excite any idea in the mind of

another, depends wholly on the will of the Creator. He alone it is who, "upholding all things by the word of his power," maintains that intercourse between spirits whereby they are able to perceive the existence of each other. And yet this pure and clear light which enlightens everyone is itself invisible.

STUDY QUESTIONS

1. Do you believe that Berkeley succeeds in his attack on Locke's distinction between primary and secondary qualities?
2. How does Berkeley reply to the claim that nothing is easier to imagine than trees in a park with nobody there to perceive them?
3. How does Berkeley distinguish real things and images of things?
4. Why does Berkeley believe that the existence of God is evident?

An Enquiry Concerning Human Understanding

DAVID HUME

The Scotsman David Hume (1711–1776), essayist, historian, and philosopher, developed one of the most influential of all philosophical systems. He presented it first in his monumental *Treatise of Human Nature,* published when he was twenty-eight years old. Later he reworked the material to make it more accessible, and the selection that follows is from *An Enquiry Concerning Human Understanding,* which appeared in 1748.

The fundamental principle of Hume's philosophy is that our knowledge of the world depends entirely on the evidence provided by our senses. While this premise may appear uncontroversial, as developed by Hume it has startling consequences.

To use an example he offers, suppose you see one billiard ball hit a second, and then the second ball moves. You would say the first made the second move. Hume points out, however, that all you see is one event followed by another; you do not actually see any connection between them. You assume the connection, but the force of Hume's argument is that your assumption violates the principle that our knowledge rests only on the evidence of our senses, for you did not sense any necessary connection between the two events, but presumed it anyway.

From *An Enquiry Concerning Human Understanding* by David Hume (1748).

Hume extends this reasoning and argues that, so far as we know, the world consists of entirely separate events, some regularly following others but all unconnected. He concludes that our beliefs about the necessity of causation are instinctive, not rational.

Hume's arguments are among the most challenging in the history of philosophy, and in a later section we shall read more of his work.

....

SCEPTICAL DOUBTS CONCERNING THE OPERATIONS OF THE UNDERSTANDING

Part I

All the objects of human reason or inquiry may naturally be divided into two kinds, to wit, *relations of ideas,* and *matters of fact.* Of the first kind are the sciences of geometry, algebra, and arithmetic; and in short, every affirmation which is either intuitively or demonstratively certain. *That the square of the hypothenuse is equal to the squares of the two sides* is a proposition which expresses a relation between these figures. *That three times five is equal to the half of thirty* expresses a relation between these numbers. Propositions of this kind are discoverable by the mere operation of thought, without dependence on what is anywhere existent in the universe. Though there never was a circle or triangle in nature, the truths demonstrated by Euclid would forever retain their certainty and evidence.

Matters of fact, which are the second objects of human reason, are not ascertained in the same manner; nor is our evidence of their truth, however great, of a like nature with the foregoing. The contrary of every matter of fact is still possible; because it can never imply a contradiction, and is conceived by the mind with the same facility and distinctness, as if ever so conformable to reality. *That the sun will not rise tomorrow* is no less intelligible a proposition, and implies no more contradiction than the affirmation, *that it will rise.* We should in vain, therefore, attempt to demonstrate its falsehood. Were it demonstratively false, it would imply a contradiction and could never be distinctly conceived by the mind.

It may, therefore, be a subject worthy of curiosity to inquire what is the nature of that evidence which assures us of any real existence and matter of fact, beyond the present testimony of our senses or the records of our memory. This part of philosophy, it is observable, has been little cultivated, either by the ancients or moderns; and therefore our doubts and errors, in the prosecution of so important an inquiry, may be the more excusable; while we march through such difficult paths without any guide or direction. They may even prove useful, by exciting curiosity and destroying that implicit faith and security, which is the bane of all reasoning and free inquiry. The discovery of defects in the common philosophy, if any such there be, will not, I presume, be a discouragement, but rather an incitement, as is usual, to attempt something more full and satisfactory than has yet been proposed to the public.

All reasonings concerning matter of fact seem to be founded on the relation of *cause and effect*. By means of that relation alone, we can go beyond the evidence of our memory and senses. If you were to ask a man why he believes any matter of fact, which is absent; for instance, that his friend is in the country, or in France; he would give you a reason; and this reason would be some other fact; as a letter received from him, or the knowledge of his former resolutions and promises. A man finding a watch or any other machine in a desert island would conclude that there had once been men in that island. All our reasonings concerning fact are of the same nature. And here it is constantly supposed that there is a connection between the present fact and that which is inferred from it. Were there nothing to bind them together, the inference would be entirely precarious. The hearing of an articulate voice and rational discourse in the dark assures us of the presence of some person: Why? because these are the effects of the human make and fabric, and closely connected with it. If we anatomize all the other reasonings of this nature, we shall find that they are founded on the relation of cause and effect, and that this relation is either near or remote, direct or collateral. Heat and light are collateral effects of fire, and the one effect may justly be inferred from the other.

If we would satisfy ourselves, therefore, concerning the nature of that evidence, which assures us of matters of fact, we must inquire how we arrive at the knowledge of cause and effect.

I shall venture to affirm, as a general proposition, which admits of no exception, that the knowledge of this relation is not, in any instance, attained by reasonings a priori; but arises entirely from experience, when we find that any particular objects are constantly conjoined with each other. Let an object be presented to a man of ever so strong natural reason and abilities; if that object be entirely new to him, he will not be able, by the most accurate examination of its sensible qualities, to discover any of its causes or effects. Adam, though his rational faculties be supposed, at the very first, entirely perfect, could not have inferred from the fluidity and transparency of water that it would suffocate him, or from the light and warmth of fire that it would consume him. No object ever discovers, by the qualities which appear to the senses, either the causes which produced it, or the effects which will arise from it; nor can our reason, unassisted by experience, ever draw any inference concerning real existence and matter of fact.

This proposition, *that causes and effects are discoverable, not by reason but by experience,* will readily be admitted with regard to such objects, as we remember to have once been altogether unknown to us; since we must be conscious of the utter inability, which we then lay under, of foretelling what would arise from them. Present two smooth pieces of marble to a man who has no tincture of natural philosophy; he will never discover that they will adhere together in such a manner as to require great force to separate them in a direct line, while they make so small a resistance to a lateral pressure. Such events, as bear little analogy to the common course of nature, are also readily confessed to be known only by experience; nor does any man imagine that the explosion of gunpowder, or the attraction of a loadstone, could ever be discovered by arguments a priori. In like manner, when an effect is supposed to depend upon an intricate machinery or secret structure of parts, we make no difficulty in attributing all our knowledge of it to experience. Who will assert that he can give the ultimate reason why milk or bread is proper nourishment for a man, not for a lion or a tiger?

But the same truth may not appear, at first sight, to have the same evidence with regard to events, which have become familiar to us from our first appearance in the world, which bear a close analogy to the whole course of nature, and which are supposed to depend on the simple qualities of objects, without any secret structure of parts. We are apt to imagine that we could discover these effects by the mere operation of our reason, without experience. We fancy that were we brought a sudden into this world, we could at first have inferred that one billiard ball would communicate motion to another upon impulse; and that we needed not to have waited for the event in order to pronounce with certainty concerning it. Such is the influence of custom, that, where it is strongest, it not only covers our natural ignorance, but even conceals itself, and seems not to take place, merely because it is found in the highest degree.

But to convince us that all the laws of nature, and all the operations of bodies without exception, are known only by experience, the following reflections may, perhaps, suffice. Were any object presented to us, and were we required to pro-nounce concerning the effect, which will result from it, without consulting past observation; after what manner, I beseech you, must the mind proceed in this operation? It must invent or imagine some event, which it ascribes to the object as its effect; and it is plain that this invention must be entirely arbitrary. The mind can never possibly find the effect in the supposed cause, by the most ac-curate scrutiny and examination. For the effect is totally different from the cause, and consequently can never be discovered in it. Motion in the second billiard ball is a quite distinct event from motion in the first: nor is there anything in the one to suggest the smallest hint of the other. A stone or piece of metal raised into the air, and left without any support, immediately falls: but to consider the matter a priori, is there anything we discover in this situation which can beget the idea of a downward, rather than an upward, or any other motion, in the stone or metal?

And as the first imagination or invention of a particular effect, in all natural operations, is arbitrary, where we consult not experience, so must we also esteem the supposed tie or connection between the cause and effect, which binds them together and renders it impossible that any other effect could result from the operation of that cause. When I see, for instance, a billiard ball moving in a straight line towards another; even suppose motion in the second ball should by accident be suggested to me, as the result of their contact or impulse; may I not conceive that a hundred different events might as well follow from that cause? May not both these balls remain at absolute rest? May not the first ball return in a straight line, or leap off from the second in any line or direction? All these suppositions are consistent and conceivable. Why then should we give the preference to one, which is no more consistent or conceivable than the rest? All our reasonings a priori will never be able to show us any foundation for this preference.

In a word, then, every effect is a distinct event from its cause. It could not, therefore, be discovered in the cause, and the first invention or conception of it, a priori, must be entirely arbitrary. And even after it is suggested, the conjunction of it with the cause must appear equally arbitrary, since there are always many other effects, which, to reason, must seem fully as consistent and natural. In vain, therefore, should we pretend to determine any single event, or infer any cause or effect, without the assistance of observation and experience. . . .

Part II

But we have not yet attained any tolerable satisfaction with regard to the question first proposed. Each solution still gives rise to a new question as difficult as the foregoing, and leads us on to farther inquiries. When it is asked, *What is the nature of all our reasonings concerning matter of fact?* the proper answer seems to be that they are founded on the relation of cause and effect. When again it is asked, *What is the foundation of all our reasonings and conclusions concerning that relation?* it may be replied in one word, *experience*. But if we still carry on our sifting humor, and ask, *What is the foundation of all conclusions from experience?* this implies a new question, which may be of more difficult solution and explication. Philosophers, that give themselves airs of superior wisdom and sufficiency, have a hard task when they encounter persons of inquisitive dispositions, who push them from every corner to which they retreat, and who are sure at last to bring them to some dangerous dilemma. The best expedient to prevent this confusion is to be modest in our pretensions, and even to discover the difficulty ourselves before it is objected to us. By this means, we may make a kind of merit of our very ignorance.

I shall content myself, in this section, with an easy task and shall pretend only to give a negative answer to the question here proposed. I say then that, even after we have experience of the operations of cause and effect, our conclusions from that experience are *not* founded on reasoning, or any process of the understanding. This answer we must endeavor both to explain and to defend.

It must certainly be allowed that nature has kept us at a great distance from all her secrets and has afforded us only the knowledge of a few superficial qualities of objects, while she conceals from us those powers and principles on which the influence of those objects entirely depends. Our senses inform us of the color, weight, and consistence of bread; but neither sense nor reason can ever inform us of those qualities which fit it for the nourishment and support of a human body. Sight or feeling conveys an idea of the actual motion of bodies; but as to that wonderful force or power, which would carry on a moving body forever in a continued change of place, and which bodies never lose but by communicating it to others; of this we cannot form the most distant conception. But notwithstanding this ignorance of natural powers and principles, we always presume, when we see like sensible qualities, that they have like secret powers and expect that effects, similar to those which we have experienced, will follow from them. If a body of like color and consistence with that bread, which we have formerly eat, be presented to us, we make no scruple of repeating the experiment, and foresee, with certainty, like nourishment and support. Now this is a process of the mind or thought, of which I would willingly know the foundation. It is allowed on all hands that there is no known connection between the sensible qualities and the secret powers; and consequently, that the mind is not led to form such a conclusion concerning their constant and regular conjunction, by anything which it knows of their nature. As to past *experience,* it can be allowed to give *direct* and *certain* information of those precise objects only, and that precise period of time, which fell under its cognizance: but why this experience should be extended to future times, and to other objects, which, for aught we know, may be only in appearance similar; this is the main question on which I would insist. The bread, which I formerly eat, nourished me; that is, a body of such sensible qualities was, at that time, endued with such secret powers: but does it follow that other bread must also nourish me at another time and that like sensible qualities must always be attended with like secret powers? The consequence seems no wise necessary. At least, it must be acknowledged that there is here a consequence drawn by the mind; that there is a certain step taken, a process of thought, and an inference, which wants to be explained. These two propositions are far from being the same, *I have found that such an object has always been attended with such an effect,* and *I foresee that other objects, which are, in appearance, similar, will be attended with similar effects.* I shall allow, if you please, that the one proposition may justly be inferred from the other; I know, in fact, that it always is inferred. But if you insist that the inference is made by a chain of reasoning, I desire you to produce that reasoning. . . .

To say it is experimental is begging the question. For all inferences from experience suppose, as their foundation, that the future will resemble the past and that similar powers will be conjoined with similar sensible qualities. If there be any suspicion that the course of nature may change, and that the past may be no rule for the future, all experience becomes useless and can give rise to no inference or conclusion. It is impossible, therefore, that any arguments from experience can prove this resemblance of the past to the future, since all these arguments are founded on the supposition of that resemblance. Let the course of things be allowed hitherto ever so regular; that alone, without some new argument or inference, proves not that, for the future, it will continue so. In vain do you pretend to have learned the nature of bodies from your past experience? Their secret nature, and consequently all their effects and influence, may change, without any change in their sensible qualities. This happens sometimes, and with regard to some objects: Why may it not happen always, and with regard to all objects? What logic, what process of argument secures you against this supposition? My practice, you say, refutes my doubts. But you mistake the purport of my question. As an agent, I am quite satisfied in the point; but as a philosopher, who has some share of curiosity, I will not say scepticism, I want to learn the foundation of this inference. No reading, no inquiry has yet been able to remove my difficulty, or give me satisfaction in a matter of such importance. Can I do better than propose the difficulty to the public, even though, perhaps, I have small hopes of obtaining a solution? We shall, at least, by this means, be sensible of our ignorance, if we do not augment our knowledge. . . .

SCEPTICAL SOLUTION OF THESE DOUBTS

. . . Suppose a person, though endowed with the strongest faculties of reason and reflection, to be brought on a sudden into this world; he would, indeed, immediately observe a continual succession of objects, and one event following another; but he would not be able to discover anything farther. He would not, at first, by any reasoning, be able to reach the idea of cause and effect; since the particular powers, by which all natural operations are performed, never appear to the senses; nor is it reasonable to conclude, merely because one event, in one instance, precedes another, that therefore the one is the cause, the other the effect. Their conjunction may be arbitrary and casual. There may be no reason to infer the existence of one from the appearance of the other. And in a word, such a person, without more experience, could never employ his conjecture or reasoning concerning any matter of fact, or be assured of anything beyond what was immediately present to his memory and senses.

Suppose, again, that he has acquired more experience, and has lived so long in the world as to have observed familiar objects or events to be constantly conjoined together; what is the consequence of this experience? He immediately infers the existence of one object from the appearance of the other. Yet he has not, by all his experience, acquired any idea or knowledge of the secret power by which the one object produces the other; nor is it, by any process of reasoning, he is engaged to draw this inference. But still he finds himself determined to draw it: And though he should be convinced that his understanding has no part in the operation, he would nevertheless continue in the same course of thinking. There is some other principle which determines him to form such a conclusion.

This principle is *custom* or *habit*. For wherever the repetition of any particular act or operation produces a propensity to renew the same act or operation, without being impelled by any reasoning or process of the understanding, we always say that this propensity is the effect of *custom*. By employing that word, we pretend not to have given the ultimate reason of such a propensity. We only point out a principle of human nature, which is universally acknowledged and which is well known by its effects. Perhaps we can push our inquiries no farther, or pretend to give the cause of this cause, but must rest contented with it as the ultimate principle, which we can assign, of all our conclusions from experience. . . .

Custom, then, is the great guide of human life. It is that principle alone which renders our experience useful to us and makes us expect, for the future, a similar train of events with those which have appeared in the past. Without the influence of custom, we should be entirely ignorant of every matter of fact beyond what is immediately present to the memory and senses. We should never know how to adjust means to ends, or to employ our natural powers in the production of any effect. There would be an end at once of all action, as well as of the chief part of speculation....

What, then, is the conclusion of the whole matter? A simple one; though, it must be confessed, pretty remote from the common theories of philosophy. All belief of matter of fact or real existence is derived merely from some object, present to the memory or senses, and a customary conjunction between that and some other object. Or in other words; having found, in many instances, that any two kinds of objects—flame and heat, snow and cold—have always been conjoined together; if flame or snow be presented anew to the senses, the mind is carried by custom to expect heat or cold and to *believe* that such a quality does exist, and will discover itself upon a nearer approach. This belief is the necessary result of placing the mind in such circumstances. It is an operation of the soul, when we are so situated, as unavoidable as to feel the passion of love, when we receive benefits; or hatred, when we meet with injuries. All these operations are a species of natural instincts, which no reasoning or process of the thought and understanding is able either to produce or to prevent.

STUDY QUESTIONS

1. Explain Hume's distinction between "relations of ideas" and "matters of fact."
2. According to Hume, what is the foundation for all reasonings concerning matters of fact?
3. What does Hume mean by "custom"?
4. According to Hume, why is custom "the great guide of human life"?

Critique of Pure Reason

IMMANUEL KANT

Immanuel Kant (1724–1804), who lived his entire life in the Prussian town of Königsberg, is a preeminent figure in the history of philosophy, having made groundbreaking contributions in virtually every area of the subject. Kant seeks to show that the laws of nature are based in human reason. First, he distinguishes

From *The Critique of Pure Reason* by Immanuel Kant, translated by Norman Kemp Smith, 1929. Reprinted by permission of the publishers: Macmillan & Company, Ltd., London, and St. Martin's Press, Inc., New York.

between analytic and synthetic propositions. An analytic proposition, such as "all bachelors are unmarried," is true because its subject, "bachelor," contains its predicate, "unmarried"; in a synthetic proposition, such as "all bachelors are happy," the subject does not contain the predicate. Kant also distinguishes between *a posteriori* propositions, the truth of which can be determined only by the evidence of experience, and *a priori* propositions, the truth of which can be determined without such evidence.

Are any synthetic propositions true *a priori*? Kant thought so and maintained that, for example, "every event has a cause" is such a synthetic *a priori* proposition, an informative statement known to be true without appeal to the evidence of experience. Thus does Kant develop a strategy for responding to Hume's skepticism about human knowledge.

....

I. THE DISTINCTION BETWEEN PURE AND EMPIRICAL KNOWLEDGE

There can be no doubt that all our knowledge begins with experience. For how should our faculty of knowledge be awakened into action did not objects affecting our senses partly of themselves produce representations, partly arouse the activity of our understanding to compare these representations, and, by combining or separating them, work up the raw material of the sensible impressions into that knowledge of objects which is entitled experience? In the order of time, therefore, we have no knowledge antecedent to experience, and with experience all our knowledge begins.

But though all our knowledge begins with experience, it does not follow that it all arises out of experience. For it may well be that even our empirical knowledge is made up of what we receive through impressions and of what our own faculty of knowledge (sensible impressions serving merely as the occasion) supplies from itself. If our faculty of knowledge makes any such addition, it may be that we are not in a position to distinguish it from the raw material, until with long practice of attention we have become skilled in separating it.

This, then, is a question which at least calls for closer examination and does not allow of any off-hand answer:—whether there is any knowledge that is thus independent of experience and even of all impressions of the senses. Such knowledge is entitled *a priori*, and distinguished from the *empirical*, which has its sources *a posteriori*, that is, in experience.

The expression "*a priori*" does not, however, indicate with sufficient precision the full meaning of our question. For it has been customary to say, even of much knowledge that is derived from empirical sources, that we have it or are capable of having it *a priori*, meaning thereby that we do not derive it immediately from experience, but from a universal rule—a rule which is itself, however, borrowed by us from experience. Thus we would say of a man who undermined the foundations of his house, that he might have known *a priori* that it would fall, that is, that he need not have waited for the experience of its actual falling. But still he could not know this completely *a priori*. For he had first to learn through experience that bodies are heavy, and therefore fall when their supports are withdrawn.

In what follows, therefore, we shall understand by *a priori* knowledge, not knowledge independent of this or that experience, but knowledge absolutely independent of all experience. Opposed to it is empirical knowledge, which is knowledge possible only *a posteriori*, that is, through experience. *A priori* modes of knowledge are entitled pure when there is no admixture of anything empirical. Thus, for instance, the proposition, "every alteration has its cause," while an *a priori* proposition, is not a pure proposition, because alteration is a concept which can be derived only from experience.

II. WE ARE IN POSSESSION OF CERTAIN MODES OF *A PRIORI* KNOWLEDGE, AND EVEN THE COMMON UNDERSTANDING IS NEVER WITHOUT THEM

What we here require is a criterion by which to distinguish with certainty between pure and empirical knowledge. Experience teaches us that a thing is so and so, but not that it cannot be otherwise. First, then, if we have a proposition which in being thought is thought as *necessary*, it is an *a priori* judgement; and if, besides, it is not derived from any proposition except one which also has the validity of a necessary judgement, it is an absolutely *a priori* judgement. Secondly, experience never confers on its judgements true or strict, but only assumed and comparative *universality*, through induction. We can properly only say, therefore, that, so far as we have hitherto observed, there is no exception to this or that rule. If, then, a judgement is thought with strict universality, that is, in such manner that no exception is allowed as possible, it is not derived from experience, but is valid absolutely *a priori*. Empirical universality is only an arbitrary extension of a validity holding in most cases to one which holds in all, for instance, in the proposition, "all bodies are heavy." When, on the other hand, strict universality is essential to a judgement, this indicates a special source of knowledge, namely, a faculty of *a priori* knowledge. Necessity and strict universality are thus sure criteria of *a priori* knowledge and are inseparable from one another. But since in the employment of these criteria the contingency of judgements is sometimes more easily shown than their empirical limitation, or, as sometimes also happens, their unlimited universality can be more convincingly proved than their necessity, it is advisable to use the two criteria separately, each by itself being infallible.

Now it is easy to show that there actually are in human knowledge judgements which are necessary and in the strictest sense universal, and which are therefore pure *a priori* judgements. If an example from the sciences be desired, we have only to look to any of the propositions of mathematics; if we seek an example from the understanding in its quite ordinary employment, the proposition, "every alteration must have a cause," will serve our purpose. In the latter case, indeed, the very concept of a cause so manifestly contains the concept of a necessity of connection with an effect and of the strict universality of the rule, that the concept would be altogether lost if we attempted to derive it, as Hume has done, from a repeated association of that which happens with that which precedes, and from a custom of connecting representations, a custom originating in this repeated association, and constituting therefore a merely subjective necessity. Even without appealing to such examples, it is possible to show that pure *a priori* principles are indispensable for the possibility of experience, and so to prove their existence *a priori*. For whence could experience derive its certainty, if all the rules, according to which it proceeds, were always themselves empirical, and therefore contingent? Such rules could hardly be regarded as first principles. At present, however, we may be content to have established the fact that our faculty of knowledge does have a pure employment, and to have shown what are the criteria of such an employment.

Such *a priori* origin is manifest in certain concepts, no less than in judgements. If we remove from our empirical concept of a body, one by one, every feature in it which is [merely] empirical, the colour, the hardness or softness, the weight, even the impenetrability, there still remains the space which the body (now entirely vanished) occupied, and this cannot be removed. Again, if we remove from our empirical concept of any object, corporeal or incorporeal, all properties which experience has taught us, we yet cannot take away that property through which the object is thought as substance or as inhering in a substance (although this concept of substance is more determinate than that of an object in general). Owing, therefore, to the necessity with which this concept of substance forces itself upon us, we have no option save to admit that it has its seat in our faculty of *a priori* knowledge.

III. PHILOSOPHY STANDS IN NEED OF A SCIENCE WHICH SHALL DETERMINE THE POSSIBILITY, THE PRINCIPLES, AND THE EXTENT OF ALL *A PRIORI* KNOWLEDGE

But what is still more extraordinary than all the preceding is this, that certain modes of knowledge leave the field of all possible experiences and have the appearance of extending the scope of our judgements beyond all limits of experience, and this by means of concepts to which no corresponding object can ever be given in experience.

It is precisely by means of the latter modes of knowledge, in a realm beyond the world of the senses, where experience can yield neither guidance nor correction, that our reason carries on those enquiries which owing to their importance we consider to be far more excellent, and in their purpose far more lofty, than all that the understanding can learn in the field of appearances. Indeed we prefer to run every risk of error rather than desist from such urgent enquiries, on the ground of their dubious character, or from disdain and indifference. These unavoidable problems set by pure reason itself are *God, freedom,* and *immortality*.

The science which, with all its preparations, is in its final intention directed solely to their solution is metaphysics; and its procedure is at first dogmatic, that is, it confidently sets itself to this task without any previous examination of the capacity or incapacity of reason for so great an undertaking.

Now it does indeed seem natural that, as soon as we have left the ground of experience, we should, through careful enquiries, assure ourselves as to the foundations of any building that we propose to erect, not making use of any knowledge that we possess without first determining whence it has come, and not trusting to principles without knowing their origin. It is natural, that is to say, that the question should first be considered, how the understanding can arrive at all this knowledge *a priori*, and what extent, validity, and worth it may have. Nothing, indeed, could be more natural, if by the term "natural" we signify what fittingly and reasonably ought to happen. But if we mean by "natural" what ordinarily happens, then on the contrary nothing is more natural and more intelligible than the fact that this enquiry has been so long neglected. For one part of this knowledge, the mathematical, has long been of established reliability, and so gives rise to a favourable presumption as regards the other part, which may yet be of quite different nature. Besides, once we are outside the circle of experience, we can be sure of not being *contradicted* by experience. The charm of extending our knowledge is so great that nothing short of encountering a direct contradiction can suffice to arrest us in our course; and this can be avoided, if we are careful in our fabrications—which nonetheless will still remain fabrications. Mathematics gives us a shining example of how far, independently of experience, we can progress in *a priori* knowledge. It does, indeed, occupy itself with objects and with knowledge solely insofar as they allow of being exhibited in intuition. But this circumstance is easily overlooked, since this intuition can itself be given *a priori* and is therefore hardly to be distinguished from a bare and pure concept. Misled by such a proof of the power of reason, the demand for the extension of knowledge recognises no limits. The light dove, cleaving the air in her free flight, and feeling its resistance, might imagine that its flight would be still easier in empty space. It was thus that Plato left the world of the senses, as setting too narrow limits to the understanding, and ventured out beyond it on the wings of the ideas, in the empty space of the pure understanding. He did not observe that with all his efforts he made no advance—meeting no resistance that might, as it were, serve as a support upon which he could take a stand, to which he could apply his powers, and so set his understanding in motion. It is, indeed, the common fate of human reason to complete its speculative structures as speedily as may be, and only afterwards to enquire whether the foundations are reliable. All sorts of excuses will then be appealed to, in order to reassure us of their solidity, or rather indeed to enable us to dispense altogether with so late and so dangerous an enquiry. But what keeps us, during the actual building, free from all apprehension and suspicion, and flatters us with a seeming thoroughness, is this other circumstance, namely, that a great, perhaps the greatest, part of the business of our reason consists in analysis of the concepts which we already have of objects. This analysis supplies us with a considerable body of knowledge, which, while nothing but explanation or elucidation of what has already been thought in our concepts, though in a confused manner, is yet prized as being, at least as regards its form, new insight. But so far as the matter or content is concerned, there has been no extension of our previously possessed concepts, but only an analysis of them. Since this procedure yields real knowledge *a priori*, which progresses in an assured and useful fashion, reason is so far misled as surreptitiously to introduce, without itself being aware of so doing, assertions of an entirely different order, in which it attaches to given concepts others completely foreign to them, and moreover attaches them *a priori*. And yet it is not known how reason can be in position to do this. Such a question is never so much as thought of. I shall therefore at once proceed to deal with the difference between these two kinds of knowledge.

IV. THE DISTINCTION BETWEEN ANALYTIC AND SYNTHETIC JUDGEMENTS

In all judgements in which the relation of a subject to the predicate is thought (I take into consideration affirmative judgements only, the subsequent application to negative judgements being easily made), this relation is possible in two different ways. Either the predicate B belongs to the subject A, as something which is (covertly) contained in this concept A; or B lies outside the concept A, although it does indeed stand in connection with it. In the one case I entitle the judgement analytic, in the other synthetic. Analytic judgements (affirmative) are therefore those in which the connection of the predicate with the subject is thought through identity; those in which this connection is thought without identity should be entitled synthetic. The former, as adding nothing through the predicate to the concept of the subject, but merely breaking it up into those constituent concepts that have all along been thought in it, although confusedly, can also be entitled explicative. The latter, on the other hand, add to the concept of the subject a predicate which has not been in any wise thought in it, and which no analysis could possibly extract from it; and they may therefore be entitled ampliative. If I say, for instance, "All bodies are extended," this is an analytic judgement. For I do not require to go beyond the concept which I connect with "body" in order to find extension as bound up with it. To meet with this predicate, I have merely to analyse the concept, that is, to become conscious to myself of the manifold which I always think in that concept: The judgement is therefore analytic. But when I say, "All bodies are heavy," the predicate is something quite different from anything that I think in the mere concept of body in general; and the addition of such a predicate therefore yields a synthetic judgement.

Judgements of experience, as such, are one and all synthetic. For it would be absurd to found an analytic judgement on experience. Since, in framing the judgement, I must not go outside my concept, there is no need to appeal to the testimony of experience in its support. That a body is extended is a proposition that holds *a priori* and is not empirical. For, before appealing to experience, I have already in the concept of body all the conditions required for my judgement. I have only to extract from it, in accordance with the principle of contradiction, the required predicate, and in so doing can at the same time become conscious of the necessity of the judgement—and that is what experience could never have taught me. On the other hand, though I do not include in the concept of a body in general the predicate "weight," nonetheless this concept indicates an object of experience through one of its parts, and I can add to that part other parts of this same experience, as in this way belonging together with the concept. From the start I can apprehend the concept of body analytically through the characters of extension, impenetrability, figure, etc., all of which are thought in the concept. Now, however, looking back on the experience from which I have derived this concept of body, and finding weight to be invariably connected with the above characters, I attach it as a predicate to the concept; and in doing so I attach it synthetically, and am therefore extending my knowledge. The possibility of the synthesis of the predicate "weight" with the concept of "body" thus rests upon experience. While the one concept is not contained in the other, they yet belong to one another, though only contingently, as parts of a whole, namely, of an experience which is itself a synthetic combination of intuitions.

But in *a priori* synthetic judgements this help is entirely lacking [I do not here have the advantage of looking around in the field of experience.] Upon what, then, am I to rely, when I seek to go beyond the concept A, and to know that another concept B is connected with it? Through what is the synthesis made possible? Let us take the proposition, "Everything which happens has its cause." In the concept of "something which happens," I do indeed think an existence which is preceded by a time, etc., and from this concept analytic judgements may be obtained. But the concept of a "cause" lies entirely outside the other concept, and signifies something different from "that which happens," and is not therefore in any way contained in this latter representation. How come I then to predicate of that which happens something quite different, and to apprehend that the concept of cause, though not contained in it, yet belongs, and indeed necessarily belongs, to it? What is here the unknown = X which gives support to the understanding when it believes that it can discover outside the concept A a predicate B foreign to this concept, which it yet at the same time considers to be connected with it? It cannot be experience, because the suggested principle has connected the second representation with the first, not only with greater universality, but also with the character of necessity, and therefore completely *a priori* and on the basis of mere concepts. Upon such synthetic, that is, ampliative principles, all our *a priori* speculative knowledge must ultimately rest; analytic judgements are very important, and indeed necessary, but only for obtaining that clearness in the concepts which is requisite for such a sure and wide synthesis as will lead to a genuinely new addition to all previous knowledge.

STUDY QUESTIONS

1. Explain Kant's distinction between knowledge *a priori* and knowledge *a posteriori*.
2. Explain Kant's distinction between analytic and synthetic judgments.
3. According to Kant, why are analytic propositions important?
4. Do you agree with Kant that some propositions might be synthetic but known *a priori*?

PART 4

Mind

The Ghost in the Machine

✦

GILBERT RYLE

Philosophers sometimes consider questions about the fundamental nature of the world. Does every event have a cause? Do human beings possess free will? Does each person consist of a soul connected to a body? Such issues belong to the field of philosophy known as "metaphysics," a Greek term meaning "after physics," so called because when Aristotle's works were first catalogued more than two millennia ago, the treatise in which he discussed such matters was placed after his treatise on physics.

One of the central issues in metaphysics is commonly referred to by philosophers as "the mind–body problem." Are you identical with your body, your mind, or some combination of the two? If you are a combination, how are the mind and body connected so as to form one person?

An influential writer on these matters is Gilbert Ryle (1900–1976), who was Professor of Philosophy at the University of Oxford. He argues that it is a mistake to suppose that the mind is something inside the body, a "ghost in the machine." Such a misconception Ryle calls a "category mistake," the sort of error that would be committed by one who, having been shown a college's classrooms, offices, playing fields, and libraries, would then ask, "But where is the university?" The university, of course, is not a separate building that one can see, and Ryle believes that the mind is not a separate entity that one can sense.

....

THE OFFICIAL DOCTRINE

There is a doctrine about the nature and place of minds which is so prevalent among theorists and even among laymen that it deserves to be described as the official theory. Most philosophers, psychologists and religious teachers subscribe, with minor reservations, to its main articles and, although they admit certain theoretical difficulties in it, they tend to assume that these can be overcome without serious modifications being made to the architecture of the theory. It will be argued here that the central principles of the doctrine are unsound and conflict with the whole body of what we know about minds when we are not speculating about them.

The official doctrine, which hails chiefly from Descartes, is something like this. With the doubtful exceptions of idiots and infants in arms, every human being

From *The Concept of Mind,* by Gilbert Ryle, Hutchinson and Co., 1949. Reprinted by permission of Taylor & Francis Books UK and the Principal, Fellows and Scholars of Hertford College at Oxford University.

has both a body and a mind. Some would prefer to say that every human being is both a body and a mind. His body and his mind are ordinarily harnessed together, but after the death of the body his mind may continue to exist and function.

Human bodies are in space and are subject to the mechanical laws which govern all other bodies in space. Bodily processes and states can be inspected by external observers. So a man's bodily life is as much a public affair as are the lives of animals and reptiles and even as the careers of trees, crystals and planets.

But minds are not in space, nor are their operations subject to mechanical laws. The workings of one mind are not witnessable by other observers; its career is private. Only I can take direct cognisance of the states and processes of my own mind. A person therefore lives through two collateral histories, one consisting of what happens in and to his body, the other consisting of what happens in and to his mind. The first is public, the second private. The events in the first history are events in the physical world, those in the second are events in the mental world.

It has been disputed whether a person does or can directly monitor all or only some of the episodes of his own private history; but, according to the official doctrine, of at least some of these episodes he has direct and unchallengeable cognisance. In consciousness, self-consciousness and introspection he is directly and authentically apprised of the present states and operations of his mind. He may have great or small uncertainties about concurrent and adjacent episodes in the physical world, but he can have none about at least part of what is momentarily occupying his mind.

It is customary to express this bifurcation of his two lives and of his two worlds by saying that the things and events which belong to the physical world, including his own body, are external, while the workings of his own mind are internal. This antithesis of outer and inner is of course meant to be construed as a metaphor, since minds, not being in space, could not be described as being spatially inside anything else, or as having things going on spatially inside themselves. But relapses from this good intention are common and theorists are found speculating how stimuli, the physical sources of which are yards or miles outside a person's skin, can generate mental responses inside his skull, or how decisions framed inside his cranium can set going movements of his extremities.

Even when "inner" and "outer" are construed as metaphors, the problem how a person's mind and body influence one another is notoriously charged with theoretical difficulties. What the mind wills, the legs, arms and the tongue execute; what affects the ear and the eye has something to do with what the mind perceives; grimaces and smiles betray the mind's moods; and bodily castigations lead, it is hoped, to moral improvement. But the actual transactions between the episodes of the private history and those of the public history remain mysterious, since by definition they can belong to neither series. They could not be reported among the happenings described in a person's autobiography of his inner life, but nor could they be reported among those described in someone else's biography of that person's overt career. They can be inspected neither by introspection nor by laboratory experiment. They are theoretical shuttlecocks which are forever being bandied from the physiologist back to the psychologist and from the psychologist back to the physiologist.

Underlying this partly metaphorical representation of the bifurcation of a person's two lives there is a seemingly more profound and philosophical assumption. It is assumed that there are two different kinds of existence or status. What exists or happens may have the status of physical existence, or it may have the status of mental existence. Somewhat as the faces of coins are either heads or tails, or somewhat as living creatures are either male or female, so, it is supposed, some existing is physical existing, other existing is mental existing. It is a necessary feature of what has physical existence that it is in space and time; it is a necessary feature of what has mental existence that it is in time but not in space. What has physical existence is composed of matter, or else is a function of matter; what has mental existence consists of consciousness, or else is a function of consciousness.

There is thus a polar opposition between mind and matter, an opposition which is often brought out as follows. Material objects are situated in a common field, known as "space," and what happens to one body in one part of space is mechanically connected with what happens to other bodies in other parts of space. But mental happenings occur in insulated fields, known as "minds," and there is, apart maybe from telepathy, no direct causal connection between what happens in one mind and what happens in another. Only through the medium of the public physical world can the mind of one person make a difference to the mind of another. The mind is its own place and in his inner life each of us lives the life of a ghostly Robinson Crusoe. People can see, hear and jolt one another's bodies, but they are irremediably blind and deaf to the workings of one another's minds and inoperative upon them. . . .

THE ABSURDITY OF THE OFFICIAL DOCTRINE

Such in outline is the official theory. I shall often speak of it, with deliberate abusiveness, as "the dogma of the Ghost in the Machine." I hope to prove that it is entirely false, and false not in detail but in principle. It is not merely an assemblage of particular mistakes. It is one big mistake and a mistake of a special kind. It is, namely, a category mistake. It represents the facts of mental life as if they belonged to one logical type or category (or range of types or categories), when they actually belong to another. The dogma is therefore a philosopher's myth. . . .

I must first indicate what is meant by the phrase "category mistake." This I do in a series of illustrations.

A foreigner visiting Oxford or Cambridge for the first time is shown a number of colleges, libraries, playing fields, museums, scientific departments and administrative offices. He then asks, "But where is the University? I have seen where the members of the Colleges live, where the Registrar works, where the scientists experiment and the rest. But I have not yet seen the University in which reside and work the members of your University." It has then to be explained to him that the University is not another collateral institution, some ulterior counterpart to the colleges, laboratories and offices which he has seen. The University is just the way in which all that he has already seen is organized. When they are seen and when their coordination is understood, the University has been seen. His mistake lay in his innocent assumption that it was correct to speak of Christ Church, the Bodleian Library, the Ashmolean Museum *and* the University, to speak, that is, as if "the University" stood for an extra member of the class of which these other units are members. He was mistakenly allocating the University to the same category as that to which the other institutions belong.

The same mistake would be made by a child witnessing the march-past of a division, who, having had pointed out to him such and such battalions, batteries, squadrons, etc., asked when the division was going to appear. He would be supposing that a division was a counterpart to the units already seen, partly similar to them and partly unlike them. He would be shown his mistake by being told that in watching the battalions, batteries, and squadrons marching past he had been watching the division marching past. The march-past was not a parade of battalions, batteries, squadrons *and* a division; it was a parade of the battalions, batteries and squadrons *of* a division.

One more illustration. A foreigner watching his first game of cricket learns what are the functions of the bowlers, the batsmen, the fielders, the umpires and the scorers. He then says, "But there is no one left on the field to contribute the famous element of team spirit. I see who does the bowling, the batting and the wicket-keeping; but I do not see whose role it is to exercise *esprit de corps*." Once more, it would have to be explained that he was looking for the wrong type of thing. Team spirit is not another cricketing-operation supplementary to all of the other special tasks. It is, roughly, the keenness with which each of the special tasks is performed, and performing a task keenly is not performing two tasks. Certainly exhibiting team spirit is not the same thing as bowling or catching, but nor is it a third thing such that we can say that the bowler first bowls *and* then exhibits team spirit or that a fielder is at a given moment *either* catching *or* displaying *esprit de corps.*

These illustrations of category mistakes have a common feature which must be noticed. The mistakes were made by people who did not know how to wield the concepts *University, division* and *team spirit.* Their puzzles arose from inability to use certain items in the English vocabulary.

The theoretically interesting category mistakes are those made by people who are perfectly competent to apply concepts, at least in the situations with which they are familiar, but are still liable in their abstract thinking to allocate those concepts to logical types to which they do not belong. An instance of a mistake of this sort would be the following story. A student of politics has learned the main differences between the British, the French and the American Constitutions, and has learned also the differences and connections between the Cabinet, Parliament, the various Ministries, the Judicature and the Church of England. But he still becomes embarrassed when asked questions about the connections between the Church of England, the Home Office and the British Constitution. For while the Church and the Home Office are institutions, the British Constitution is not another institution in the same sense of that noun. So inter-institutional relations which can be asserted or denied to hold between the Church and the Home Office cannot be asserted or denied to hold between either of them and the British Constitution. "The British Constitution" is not a term of the same logical type as "the Home Office" and "the Church of England." In a partially similar way, John Doe may be a relative, a friend, an enemy or a stranger to Richard Roe; but he cannot be any of these things to the Average Taxpayer. He knows how to talk sense in certain sorts of discussions about the Average Taxpayer, but he is baffled to say why he could not come across him in the street as he can come across Richard Roe.

It is pertinent to our main subject to notice that, so long as the student of politics continues to think of the British Constitution as a counterpart to the other institutions, he will tend to describe it as a mysteriously occult institution; and so long as John Doe continues to think of the Average Taxpayer as a fellow citizen, he will tend to think of him as an elusive insubstantial man, a ghost who is everywhere yet nowhere.

My destructive purpose is to show that a family of radical category mistakes is the source of the double-life theory. The representation of a person as a ghost mysteriously ensconced in a machine derives from this argument.

STUDY QUESTIONS

1. What does Ryle mean by "the dogma of the Ghost in the Machine"?
2. What does Ryle mean by a "category mistake"?
3. According to Ryle, how does the dogma of the Ghost in the Machine involve a category mistake?
4. Present your own example of a category mistake.

Body and Soul

RICHARD TAYLOR

Dualism is the view that a person is a combination of a mind and a body. Materialism is the view that a person is just a body. If the materialist is correct, then how can a person think and feel? Can a mere body do that?

These issues are explored in the next article, by Richard Taylor (1919–2003), who was Professor of Philosophy at the University of Rochester.

From *Metaphysics*, 4th edition, by Richard Taylor. Copyright © 1992. Reprinted by permission of Pearson Education, Inc., Upper Saddle River, NJ.

All forms of dualism arise from the alleged disparity between persons and physical objects. People, it is rightly noted, are capable of thinking, believing, feeling, wishing, and so on, but bodies, it is claimed, are capable of none of these things, and the conclusion is drawn that people are not bodies. Yet it cannot be denied that they *have* bodies; hence, it is decided that a person is a nonphysical entity, somehow more or less intimately related to a body. But here it is rarely noted that whatever difficulties there may be in applying personal and psychological predicates and descriptions to bodies, precisely the same difficulties are involved in applying such predicates and descriptions to *anything whatever*, including spirits or souls. If, for example, a philosopher reasons that a body cannot think and thereby affirms that, since a person thinks, a person is a soul or spirit or mind rather than a body, we are entitled to ask how a spirit can think. For surely if a spirit or soul can think, we can affirm that a body can do so; and if we are asked *how* a body can think, our reply can be that it thinks in precisely the manner in which the dualist supposes a soul thinks. The difficulty of imagining how a body thinks is not in the least lessened by asserting that something else, which is not a body, thinks. And so it is with every other personal predicate or description. Whenever faced with the dualist's challenge to explain how a body can have desires, wishes, how it can deliberate, choose, repent, how it can be intelligent or stupid, virtuous or wicked, and so on, our reply can always be: The body can do these things, and be these things, in whatever manner one imagines the soul can do these things and be these things. For to repeat, the difficulty here is in seeing how *anything at all* can deliberate, choose, repent, think, be virtuous or wicked, and so on, and *that* difficulty is not removed but simply glossed over by the invention of some new thing, henceforth to be called the "mind" or "soul."

It becomes quite obvious what is the source of dualistic metaphysics when the dualist or soul philosopher is pressed for some description of the mind or soul. The mind or soul, it turns out in such descriptions, is just whatever it is that thinks, reasons, deliberates, chooses, feels, and so on. But the fact with which we began was that *human beings* think, reason, deliberate, choose, feel, and so on. And we do in fact have some fairly clear notion of what we mean by a human being, for we think of an individual person as existing in space and time, having a certain height and weight—as a being, in short, having many things in common with other objects in space and time, and particularly with those that are living, i.e., with other animals. But the dualist, noting that a human being is significantly different from other beings, insofar as he, unlike most of them, is capable of thinking, deliberating, choosing, and so on, suddenly asserts that it is not a person, as previously conceived, that does these things at all, but something else, namely, a mind or soul, or something that does not exist in space and time nor have any height and weight, nor have, in fact, any material properties at all. And then when we seek some understanding of what this mind or soul is, we find it simply described as a thing that thinks, deliberates, feels, and so on. But surely the proper inference should have been that people are like all other physical objects in some respects—e.g., in having size, mass, and location in space and time; that they are like some physical objects but unlike others in certain further respects—e.g., in being living, sentient, and so on; and like no other physical objects at all in still other respects—e.g., in being rational, deliberative, and so on. And of course none of this suggests that people are not physical objects, but rather that they are precisely physical objects, like other bodies in some ways, unlike many other bodies in other ways, and unlike any other bodies in still other respects.

The dualist or soul philosopher reasons that since people think, feel, desire, choose, and so on, and since such things cannot be asserted of bodies, then people are not bodies. Reasoning in this fashion, we are forced to the conclusion that people are not bodies—though it is a stubborn fact that they nevertheless *have* bodies. So the great problem then is to connect people, now conceived as souls or minds, to their bodies. But philosophically, it is just exactly as good to reason that, since people think, feel, desire, choose, etc., and since people are bodies—i.e., are living animal organisms having the essential material attributes of weight, size, and so on—then *some* bodies think, feel, desire, choose, etc. This argument is just as good as the dualist's argument and does not lead us into a morass of problems concerning the connection between soul and body. . . .

This point can perhaps be borne home to the imagination by the following sort of consideration: Suppose one feels, as probably everyone more or less does, that a *person* cannot be a mere *body*, and that no increase in the physical, biological, and physiological complexity of any body can bridge the gulf between being a body, albeit a complicated and living one, and being a person. Consider, then, a highly complex and living animal organism, physically and biologically identical in every respect to a living man, but lacking that one thing that is, we are supposing, still needed in order to convert this body into a person. Now just what can this extra essential ingredient be? What do we need to *add* to convert a mere body into a person?

Let us suppose it is a *soul*. If we add a soul to this living, complicated animal organism, let us suppose, then *lo!* it will cease to be a mere body and become a person. No one knows, however, exactly what a soul is or what properties it must possess in order to confer personality upon something. All we can say is that it is what distinguishes a person from a mere body, which of course tells us nothing here. So let us give it some definite properties. It does not matter what properties we give it, as we shall shortly see, so to make it simple and easy to grasp, let us suppose that this soul is a small round ball, about the size of a marble, transparent and indestructible. Now clearly, by implanting *that* anywhere in the living organism we get no closer to converting it from a mere body to a person. We manage only to add one further, trivial complication. But why so? Why are we now no closer to having a person than before? Is it just because the "soul" we added is itself a mere body? If that is the difficulty, then let us remove its corporeality. Let us suppose that the soul we add to this living animal organism is not a small round *physical* ball but a nonphysical one. This will permit us to retain its transparency. If, being nonphysical, it can no longer be described as a ball, then we can drop that part of the description too. Let the thing we add be, in short, anything one likes. Let it be a small hard ball, a small soft ball, an immaterial ball, or something that is neither material nor a ball. The point is that no matter *what* it is that is added, it goes not the least way toward converting what was a mere body into a person. If a small hard ball does not bridge the gap, then we get no closer to bridging it by simply removing its properties of hardness, smallness, and sphericity—by making it, in short, something that is merely *non*physical. What we need to do is state just what positive properties this extra thing must possess, in order to elevate an animal body to the status of a person, and no positive properties suggest themselves at all. We cannot give it psychological properties—by saying, for example, that this soul thinks, desires, deliberates, wills, believes, repents, and so on; for if the thing we are adding has *those* properties, then it is *already* a person in its own right, and there is no question of *adding* it to something in order to *get* a person. We could as easily have given *those* properties to the animal organism with which we began as to give them to something else and then superfluously amalgamate the two things. Plainly, there are no positive properties of any "soul" that will do the trick. The best we can do is to say that the extra something required—the soul, or the mind, or whatever we choose to call this additional thing—is that which, when added, makes up the difference between being a mere animal body and being a person. This is about as good a way as one could find for indicating that he has no idea what he is talking about.

STUDY QUESTIONS

1. According to Taylor, how do all forms of dualism arise?
2. Can a physical object think?
3. Because a person can think, does it follow that a person is more than a physical object?
4. What does Taylor mean by a "soul"?

The Mind–Body Problem

PAUL M. CHURCHLAND

Paul M. Churchland is Professor Emeritus of Philosophy at the University of California, San Diego. He explores different forms of dualism, concluding that none is persuasive.

From Paul M. Churchland, *Matter and Consciousness,* third edition, MIT Press, 2013. Reprinted by permission of the publisher.

The dualistic approach to mind encompasses several quite different theories, but they are all agreed that the essential nature of conscious intelligence resides in something *nonphysical*, in something forever beyond the scope of sciences like physics, neurophysiology, and computer science. Dualism is not the most widely held view in the current philosophical and scientific community, but it is the most common theory of mind in the public at large, it is deeply entrenched in most of the world's popular religions, and it has been the dominant theory of mind for most of Western history. It is thus an appropriate place to begin our discussion.

SUBSTANCE DUALISM

The distinguishing claim of this view is that each mind is a distinct nonphysical thing, an individual "package" of nonphysical substance, a thing whose identity is independent of any physical body to which it may be temporarily "attached." Mental states and activities derive their special character, on this view, from their being states and activities of this unique, nonphysical substance.

This leaves us wanting to ask for more in the way of a *positive* characterization of the proposed mind-stuff. It is a frequent complaint with the substance dualist's approach that his characterization of it is so far almost entirely negative. This need not be a fatal flaw, however, since we no doubt have much to learn about the underlying nature of mind, and perhaps the deficit here can eventually be made good. On this score, the philosopher René Descartes (1596–1650) has done as much as anyone to provide a positive account of the nature of the proposed mind-stuff, and his views are worthy of examination.

Descartes theorized that reality divides into two basic kinds of substance. The first is ordinary matter, and the essential feature of this kind of substance is that it is extended in space: any instance of it has length, breadth, and height and occupies a determinate position in space. Descartes did not attempt to play down the importance of this type of matter. On the contrary, he was one of the most imaginative physicists of his time, and he was an enthusiastic advocate of what was then called "the mechanical philosophy." But there was one isolated corner of reality he thought could not be accounted for in terms of the mechanics of matter: the conscious reason of Man. This was his motive for proposing a second and radically different kind of substance, a substance that has no spatial extension or spatial position whatever, a substance whose essential feature is the activity of *thinking*. This view is known as *Cartesian dualism*.

As Descartes saw it, the real *you* is not your material body, but rather a nonspatial thinking substance, an individual unit of mind-stuff quite distinct from your material body. This nonphysical mind is in systematic causal interaction with your body. The physical state of your body's sense organs, for example, causes visual/auditory/tactile experiences in your mind. And the desires and decisions of your nonphysical mind cause your body to behave in purposeful ways. Its causal connections to your mind are what make your body yours, and not someone else's.

The main reasons offered in support of this view were straightforward enough. First, Descartes thought that he could determine, by direct introspection alone, that he was essentially a thinking substance and nothing else. And second, he could not imagine how a purely physical system could ever use *language* in a relevant way, or engage in mathematical *reasoning*, as any normal human can. Whether these are good reasons, we shall discuss presently. Let us first notice a difficulty that even Descartes regarded as a problem.

If "mind-stuff" is so utterly different from "matter-stuff" in its nature—different to the point that it has no mass whatever, no shape whatever, and no position anywhere in space—then how is it possible for my mind to have any causal influence on my body at all? As Descartes himself was aware (he was one of the first to formulate the law of the conservation of momentum), ordinary matter in space behaves according to rigid laws, and one cannot get bodily movement (= momentum) from nothing. How is this utterly insubstantial "thinking substance" to have any influence on ponderous matter? How can two such different things be in any sort of causal contact? Descartes proposed a very subtle material substance— "animal spirits"—to convey the mind's influence to the body in general. But this does not provide us with a solution, since it leaves us with the same problem with which we started: how something ponderous and spatial (even "animal spirits") can interact with something entirely nonspatial.

In any case, the basic principle of division used by Descartes is no longer as plausible as it was in his day. It is now neither useful nor accurate to characterize ordinary matter as that-which-has-extension-in-space. Electrons, for example, are bits of matter, but our best current theories describe the electron as a point-particle with no extension whatever (it even lacks a determinate spatial position). And according to Einstein's theory of gravity, an entire star can achieve this same status, if it undergoes a complete gravitational collapse. If there truly is a division between mind and body, it appears that Descartes did not put his finger on the dividing line.

Such difficulties with Cartesian dualism provide a motive for considering a less radical form of substance dualism, and that is what we find in a view I shall call *popular dualism*. This is the theory that a person is literally a "ghost in a machine," where the machine is the human body, and the ghost is a spiritual substance, quite unlike physical matter in its internal constitution, but fully possessed of spatial properties even so. In particular, minds are commonly held to be *inside* the bodies they control; inside the head, on most views, in intimate contact with the brain.

This view need not have the difficulties of Descartes'. The mind is right there in contact with the brain, and their interaction can perhaps be understood in terms of their exchanging energy of a form that our science has not yet recognized or understood. Ordinary matter, you may recall, is just a form or manifestation of energy. (You may think of a grain of sand as a great deal of energy condensed or frozen into a small package, according to Einstein's relation, $E = mc^2$.) Perhaps mind-stuff is a well-behaved form or manifestation of energy also, but a different form of it. It is thus *possible* that a dualism of this alternative sort be consistent with familiar laws concerning the conservation of momentum and energy. This is fortunate for dualism, since those particular laws are very well established indeed.

This view will appeal to many for the further reason that it at least holds out the possibility (though it certainly does not guarantee) that the mind might survive the death of the body. It does not guarantee the mind's survival because it remains possible that the peculiar form of energy here supposed to constitute a mind can be produced and sustained only in conjunction with the highly intricate form of matter we call the brain, and must disintegrate when the brain disintegrates. So the prospects for surviving death are quite unclear even on the assumption that popular dualism is true. But even if survival were a clear consequence of the theory, there is a pitfall to be avoided here. Its promise of survival might be a reason for *wishing* dualism to be true, but it does not constitute a reason for *believing* that it *is* true. For that, we would need independent empirical evidence that minds do indeed survive the permanent death of the body. Regrettably, and despite the exploitative blatherings of the supermarket tabloids (TOP DOCS PROVE LIFE AFTER DEATH!!!), we possess no such evidence.

As we shall see later in this section, when we turn to evaluation, positive evidence for the existence of this novel, nonmaterial, thinking *substance* is in general on the slim side. This has moved many dualists to articulate still less extreme forms of dualism, in hopes of narrowing further the gap between theory and available evidence.

PROPERTY DUALISM

The basic idea of the theories under this heading is that while there is no *substance* to be dealt with here beyond the physical brain, the brain has a special set of *properties* possessed by no other kind of physical object. It is these special properties that are nonphysical: hence the term *property dualism*. The properties in question are the ones you would expect: the property of having a pain, of having a sensation of red, of thinking that *P*, of desiring that *Q*, and so forth. These are the properties that are characteristic of conscious intelligence. They are held to be nonphysical in the sense that they cannot ever be reduced to or explained solely in terms of the concepts of the familiar physical sciences. They will require a wholly new and autonomous science—the "science of mental phenomena"—if they are ever to be adequately understood.

From here, important differences among the positions emerge. Let us begin with what is perhaps the oldest version of property dualism: *epiphenomenalism*. This term is rather a mouthful, but its meaning is simple. The Greek prefix "epi-" means "above," and the position at issue holds that mental phenomena are not a part of the physical phenomena in the brain that ultimately determine our actions and behavior, but rather ride "above the fray." Mental phenomena are thus *epiphenomena*. They are held to just appear or emerge when the growing brain passes a certain level of complexity.

But there is more. The epiphenomenalist holds that while mental phenomena are caused to occur by the various activities of the brain, *they do not have any causal effects in turn*. They are entirely impotent with respect to causal effects on the physical world. They are *mere* epiphenomena. (To fix our ideas, a vague metaphor may be helpful here. Think of our conscious mental states as little sparkles of shimmering light that occur on the wrinkled surface of the brain, sparkles which are caused occur by physical activity in the brain, but which have no causal effects on the brain in return.) This means that the universal conviction that one's actions are determined by one's desires, decisions, and volitions is false! One's actions are exhaustively determined by physical events in the brain, which events *also* cause the epiphenomena we call desires, decisions, and volitions. There is therefore a constant conjunction between volitions and actions. But according to the epiphenomenalist, it is mere illusion that the former cause the latter.

What could motivate such a strange view? In fact, it is not too difficult to understand why someone might take it seriously. Put yourself in the shoes of a neuroscientist who is concerned to trace the origins of behavior back up the motor nerves to the active cells in the motor cortex of the cerebrum, and to trace in turn their activity into inputs from other parts of the brain, and from the various sensory nerves. She finds a thoroughly physical system of awesome structure and delicacy, and much intricate activity, all of it unambiguously chemical or electrical in nature, and she finds no hint at all of any nonphysical inputs of the kind that substance dualism proposes. What is she to think? From the standpoint of her researches, human behavior is exhaustively a function of the activity of the physical brain. And this opinion is further supported by her confidence that the brain has the behavior-controlling features it does exactly because those features have been ruthlessly selected for during the brain's long evolutionary history. In sum, the seat of human behavior appears entirely physical in its constitution, in its origins, and in its internal activities.

On the other hand, our neuroscientist has the testimony of her own introspection to account for as well. She can hardly deny that she has experiences, beliefs, and desires, nor that they are connected in some way with her behavior. One bargain that can be struck here is to admit the *reality* of mental properties, as nonphysical properties, but demote them to the status of impotent epiphenomena that have nothing to do with the scientific explanation of human and animal behavior. This is the position the epiphenomenalist takes, and the reader can now perceive the rationale behind it. It is a bargain struck between the desire to respect a rigorously scientific approach to the explanation of behavior and the desire to respect the testimony of introspection.

The epiphenomenalist's "demotion" of mental properties—to causally impotent by-products of brain activity—has seemed too extreme for most property dualists, and a theory closer to the convictions of common sense has enjoyed somewhat greater popularity. This view, which we may call *interactionist property dualism*, differs from the previous view in only one essential respect: the interactionist asserts that mental properties do indeed have causal effects on the brain and, thereby, on behavior. The mental properties of the brain are an integrated part of the general causal fray, in systematic interaction with the brain's physical properties. One's actions, therefore, are held to be caused by one's desires and volitions after all.

As before, mental properties are here said to be *emergent* properties, properties that do not appear at all until ordinary physical matter has managed to organize itself, through the evolutionary process, into a system of sufficient complexity. Examples of properties that are emergent in this sense would be the property of being *solid,* the property of being *colored,* and the property of being *alive.* All of these require matter to be suitably organized before they can be displayed. With this much, any materialist will agree. But any property dualist makes the further claim that mental states and properties are *irreducible,* in the sense that they are not just organizational features of physical matter, as are the examples cited. They are said to be novel properties beyond prediction or explanation by physical science.

This last condition—the irreducibility of mental properties—is an important one, since this is what makes the position a dualist position. But it sits poorly with the joint claim that mental properties emerge from nothing more than the organizational achievements of physical matter. If that is how mental properties are produced, then one would expect a physical account of them to be possible. The simultaneous claim of evolutionary emergence *and* physical irreducibility is prima facie puzzling.

A property dualist is not absolutely bound to insist on both claims. He could let go the thesis of evolutionary emergence and also claim that mental properties are *fundamental* properties of reality, properties that have been here from the universe's inception, properties on a par with length, mass, electric charge, and other fundamental properties. There is even an historical precedent for a position of this kind. At the turn of this century it was still widely believed that electromagnetic phenomena (such as electric charge and magnetic attraction) were just an unusually subtle manifestation of purely *mechanical* phenomena. Some scientists thought that a reduction of electromagnetics to mechanics was more or less in the bag. They thought that radio waves, for example, would turn out to be just travelling oscillations in a very subtle but jellylike aether that fills space everywhere. But the aether turned out not to exist. So electromagnetic properties turned out to be fundamental properties in their own right, and we were forced to add electric charge to the existing list of fundamental properties (mass, length, and duration).

Perhaps mental properties enjoy a status like that of electromagnetic properties: irreducible, but not emergent. Such a view may be called *elemental-property dualism,* and it has the advantage of clarity over the previous view. Unfortunately, the parallel with electromagnetic phenomena has one very obvious failure. Unlike electromagnetic properties, which are displayed at all levels of reality from the subatomic level on up, mental properties are displayed only in large physical systems that have evolved a very complex internal organization. The case for the evolutionary emergence of mental properties through the organization of matter is extremely strong. They do not appear to be basic or elemental at all. This returns us, therefore, to the issue of their irreducibility. Why should we accept this most basic of the dualist's claims? Why be a dualist?

ARGUMENTS FOR DUALISM

Here we shall examine some of the main considerations commonly offered in support of dualism. Criticism will be postponed for a moment so that we may appreciate the collective force of these supporting considerations.

A major source of dualistic convictions is the religious belief many of us bring to these issues. Each of the major religions is in its way a theory about the cause or purpose of the universe, and Man's place within it, and many of them are committed to the notion of an immortal soul—that is, to some form of substance dualism. Supposing that one is consistent, to consider disbelieving dualism is to consider disbelieving one's religious heritage, and some of us find that difficult to do. Call this the *argument from religion.*

A more universal consideration is the *argument from introspection.* The fact is, when you center your attention on the contents of your consciousness, you do not clearly apprehend a neural network pulsing with electrochemical activity: you apprehend a flux of thoughts, sensations, desires, and emotions. It seems that mental states and properties, as revealed in introspection, could hardly be more different from physical states and properties if they tried. The verdict of introspection, therefore, seems strongly on the side of some form of dualism—on the side of property dualism, at a minimum.

A cluster of important considerations can be collected under the *argument from irreducibility.* Here one points to a variety of mental phenomena where it seems clear that no purely physical explanation could possibly account for what is going on. Descartes has already cited our ability to use language in a way that is relevant to our changing circumstances, and he was impressed also with our faculty of Reason, particularly as it is displayed in our capacity for mathematical reasoning. These abilities, he thought, must surely be beyond the capacity of any physical system. More recently, the introspectible qualities of our sensations (sensory "qualia"), and the meaningful content of our thoughts and beliefs, have also been cited as phenomena that will forever resist reduction to the physical. Consider, for example, seeing the color or smelling the fragrance of a rose. A physicist or chemist might know everything about the molecular structure of the rose, and of the human brain, argues the dualist, but that knowledge would not enable him to predict or anticipate the quality of these inexpressible experiences.

Finally, parapsychological phenomena are occasionally cited in favor of dualism. Telepathy (mind reading), precognition (seeing the future), telekinesis (thought control of material objects), and clairvoyance (knowledge of distant objects) are all awkward to explain within the normal confines of psychology and physics. If these phenomena are real, they might well be reflecting the super-physical nature that the dualist ascribes to the mind. Trivially they are *mental* phenomena, and if they are also forever beyond physical explanation, then at least some mental phenomena must be irreducibly nonphysical.

Collectively, these considerations may seem compelling. But there are serious criticisms of each, and we must examine them as well. Consider first the argument from religion. There is certainly nothing wrong in principle with appealing to a more general theory that bears on the case at issue, which is what the appeal to religion amounts to. But the appeal can only be as good as the scientific credentials of the religion(s) being appealed to, and here the appeals tend to fall down rather badly. In general, attempts to decide scientific questions by appeal to religious orthodoxy have a very sorry history. That the stars are other suns, that the earth is not the center of the universe, that diseases are caused by microorganisms, that the earth is billions of years old, that life is a physicochemical phenomenon; all of these crucial insights were strongly and sometimes viciously resisted, because the dominant religion of the time happened to think otherwise. Giordano Bruno was burned at the stake for urging the first view; Galileo was forced by threat of torture in the Vatican's basement to recant the second view; the firm belief that disease was a punishment visited by the Devil allowed public health practices that brought chronic plagues to most of the cities of Europe; and the age of the earth and the evolution of life were forced to fight an uphill battle against religious prejudice even in an age of supposed enlightenment.

History aside, the almost universal opinion that one's own religious convictions are the reasoned outcome of a dispassionate evaluation of all of the major alternatives is almost demonstrably false for humanity in general. If that really were the genesis of most people's convictions, then one would expect the major faiths to be distributed more or less randomly or evenly over the globe. But in fact they show a very strong tendency to cluster: Christianity is centered in Europe and the Americas, Islam in Africa and the Middle East, Hinduism in India, and Buddhism in the Orient. Which illustrates what we all suspected anyway: that *social forces* are the primary determinants of religious belief for people in general. To decide scientific questions by appeal to religious orthodoxy would therefore be to put social forces in place of empirical evidence. For all of these reasons, professional scientists and philosophers concerned with the nature of mind generally do their best to keep religious appeals out of the discussion entirely.

The argument from introspection is a much more interesting argument, since it tries to appeal to the direct experience of everyman. But the argument is deeply suspect, in that it assumes that our faculty of inner observation or introspection reveals things as they really are in their innermost nature. This assumption is suspect because we already know that our other forms of observation—sight, hearing, touch, and so on—do no such thing. The red surface of an apple does not *look* like a matrix of molecules reflecting photons at certain critical wavelengths, but that is what it is. The sound of a flute does not *sound* like a sinusoidal compression wave train in the atmosphere, but that is what it is. The warmth of the summer air does not *feel* like the mean kinetic energy of millions of tiny molecules, but that is what it is. If one's pains and hopes and beliefs do not *introspectively* seem like electrochemical states in a neural network, that may be only because our faculty of introspection, like our other senses, is not sufficiently penetrating to reveal such hidden details. Which is just what one would expect anyway. The argument from introspection is therefore entirely without force, unless we can somehow argue that the faculty of introspection is quite different from all other forms of observation.

The argument from irreducibility presents a more serious challenge, but here also its force is less than first impression suggests. Consider first our capacity for mathematical reasoning which so impressed Descartes. The last ten years have made available, to anyone with fifty dollars to spend, electronic calculators whose capacity for mathematical reasoning—the calculational part, at least—far surpasses that of any normal human. The fact is, in the centuries since Descartes' writings, philosophers, logicians, mathematicians, and computer scientists have managed to isolate the general principles of mathematical reasoning, and electronics engineers have created machines that compute in accord with those principles. The result is a hand-held object that would have astonished Descartes. This outcome is impressive not just because machines have proved capable of some of the capacities boasted by human reason, but because some of those achievements invade areas of human reason that past dualistic philosophers have held up as forever closed to mere physical devices.

Although debate on the matter remains open, Descartes' argument from language use is equally dubious. The notion of a *computer language* is by now a commonplace: consider BASIC, PASCAL, FORTRAN, APL, LISP, and so on. Granted, these artificial "languages" are much simpler in structure and content than human natural language, but the differences may be differences only of degree, and not of kind. As well, the theoretical work of Noam Chomsky and the generative grammar approach to linguistics have done a great deal to explain the human capacity for language use in terms that invite simulation by computers. I do not mean to suggest that truly conversational computers are just around the corner. We have a great deal yet to learn, and fundamental problems yet to solve (mostly having to do with our capacity for inductive or theoretical reasoning). But recent progress here does nothing to support the claim that language use must be forever impossible for a purely physical system. On the contrary, such a claim now appears rather arbitrary and dogmatic.

The next issue is also a live problem: How can we possibly hope to explain or to predict the intrinsic qualities of our sensations, or the meaningful content of our beliefs and desires, in purely physical terms? This is a major challenge to the materialist. But as we shall see in later sections, active research programs are already under way on both problems, and positive suggestions are being explored. It is in fact not impossible to imagine how such explanations might go, though the materialist cannot yet pretend to have solved either problem. Until he does, the dualist will retain a bargaining chip here, but that is about all. What the dualists need in order to establish their case is the conclusion that a physical reduction is outright impossible, and that is a conclusion they have failed to establish. Rhetorical questions, like the one that opens this paragraph, do not constitute arguments. And it is equally difficult, note, to imagine how the relevant phenomena could be explained or predicted solely in terms of the substance dualist's nonphysical mind-stuff. The explanatory problem here is a major challenge to everybody, not just to the materialist. On this issue then, we have a rough standoff.

The final argument in support of dualism urged the existence of parapsychological phenomena such as telepathy and telekinesis, the point being that such mental phenomena are (a) real and (b) beyond purely physical explanation. This argument is really another instance of the argument from irreducibility discussed above, and as before, it is not entirely clear that such phenomena, even if real, must forever escape a purely physical explanation. The materialist can already suggest a possible mechanism for telepathy, for example. On his view, thinking is an electrical activity within the brain. But according to electromagnetic theory, such changing motions of electric charges must produce electromagnetic waves radiating at the speed of light in all directions, waves that will contain information about the electrical activity that produced them. Such waves can subsequently have effects on the electrical activity of other brains, that is, on their thinking. Call this the "radio transmitter/receiver" theory of telepathy.

I do not for a moment suggest that this theory is true; the electromagnetic waves emitted by the brain are fantastically weak (billions of times weaker than the ever present background electromagnetic flux produced by commercial radio stations), and they are almost certain to be hopelessly jumbled together as well. This is one reason why, in the absence of systematic, compelling, and repeatable evidence for the existence of telepathy, one must doubt its possibility. But it is significant that the materialist has the theoretical resources to suggest a detailed possible explanation of telepathy, if it were real, which is more than any dualist has so far done. It is not at all clear, then, that the materialist *must* be at an explanatory disadvantage in these matters. Quite the reverse.

Put the preceding aside, if you wish, for the main difficulty with the argument from parapsychological phenomena is much, much simpler. Despite the endless pronouncements and anecdotes in the popular press, and despite a steady trickle of serious research on such things, there is no significant or trustworthy evidence that such phenomena even exist. The wide gap between popular conviction on this matter, and the actual evidence, is something that itself calls for research. For there is not a single parapsychological effect that can be repeatedly or reliably produced in any laboratory suitably equipped to perform and control the experiment. Not one. Honest researchers have been repeatedly hoodwinked by "psychic" charlatans with skills derived from the magician's trade, and the history of the subject is largely a history of gullibility, selection of evidence, poor experimental controls, and outright fraud by the occasional researcher as well. If someone really does discover a repeatable parapsychological effect, then we shall have to reevaluate the situation, but as things stand, there is nothing here to support a dualist theory of mind.

Upon critical examination, the arguments in support of dualism lose much of their force. But we are not yet done: there are arguments against dualism, and these also require examination.

ARGUMENTS AGAINST DUALISM

The first argument against dualism urged by the materialists appeals to the greater *simplicity* of their view. It is a principle of rational methodology that, if all else is equal, the simpler of two competing hypotheses should be preferred. This principle is sometimes called "Ockham's Razor"—after William of Ockham, the medieval philosopher who first enunciated it—and it can also be expressed as follows: "Do not multiply entities beyond what is strictly necessary to explain the phenomena." The materialist postulates only one kind of substance (physical matter) and one class of properties (physical properties), whereas the dualist postulates two kinds of matter and/or two classes of properties. And to no explanatory advantage, charges the materialist.

This is not yet a decisive point against dualism, since neither dualism nor materialism can yet explain all of the phenomena to be explained. But the objection does have some force, especially since there is no doubt at all that physical matter exists, while spiritual matter remains a tenuous hypothesis.

If this latter hypothesis brought us some definite explanatory advantage obtainable in no other way, then we would happily violate the demand for simplicity, and we would be right to do so. But it does not, claims the materialist. In fact, the advantage is just the other way around, he argues, and this brings us to the second objection to dualism: the relative *explanatory impotence* of dualism as compared to materialism.

Consider, very briefly, the explanatory resources already available to the neurosciences. We know that the brain exists and what it is made of. We know much of its microstructure: how the neurons are organized into systems and how distinct systems are connected to one another, to the motor nerves going out to the muscles, and to the sensory nerves coming in from the sense organs. We know much of their microchemistry: how the nerve cells fire tiny electrochemical pulses along their various fibers, and how they make other cells fire also, or cease firing. We know some of how such activity processes sensory information, selecting salient or subtle bits to be sent on to higher systems. And we know some of how such activity initiates and coordinates bodily behavior. Thanks mainly to neurology (the branch of medicine concerned with brain pathology), we know a great deal about the correlations between damage to various parts of the human brain, and various behavioral and cognitive deficits from which the victims suffer. There are a great many isolated deficits—some gross, some subtle—that are familiar to neurologists (inability to speak, or to read, or to understand speech, or to recognize faces, or to add/subtract, or to move a certain limb, or to put information into long-term memory, and so on), and their appearance is closely tied to the occurrence of damage to very specific parts of the brain.

Nor are we limited to cataloguing traumas. The growth and development of the brain's microstructure is also something that neuroscience has explored, and such development appears to be the basis of various kinds of learning by the organism. Learning, that is, involves lasting chemical and physical changes in the brain. In sum, the neuroscientist can tell us a great deal about the brain, about its constitution and the physical laws that govern it; he can already explain much of our behavior in terms of the physical, chemical, and electrical properties of the brain; and he has the theoretical resources available to explain a good deal more as our explorations continue.

Compare now what the neuroscientist can tell us about the brain, and what he can do with that knowledge, with what the dualist can tell us about spiritual substance, and what he can do with those assumptions. Can the dualist tell us anything about the internal constitution of mind-stuff? Of the nonmaterial elements that make it up? Of the laws that govern their behavior? Of the mind's structural connections with the body? Of the manner of its operations? Can he explain human capacities and pathologies in terms of its structures and its defects? The fact is, the dualist can do none of these things, because no detailed theory of mind-stuff has ever been formulated. Compared to the rich resources and explanatory successes of current materialism, dualism is less a theory of mind than it is an empty space waiting for a genuine theory of mind to be put in it.

Thus argues the materialist. But again, this is not a completely decisive point against dualism. The dualist can admit that the brain plays a major role in the administration of both perception and behavior—on his view the brain is the *mediator* between the mind and the body—but he may attempt to argue that the materialist's current successes and future explanatory prospects concern only the mediative functions of the brain, not the *central* capacities of the nonphysical mind, capacities such as reason, emotion, and consciousness itself. On these latter topics, he may argue, both dualism *and* materialism currently draw a blank.

But this reply is not a very good one. So far as the capacity for reasoning is concerned, machines already exist that execute in minutes sophisticated deductive and mathematical calculations that would take a human a lifetime to execute. And so far as the other two mental capacities are concerned, studies of such things as depression, motivation, attention, and sleep have revealed many interesting and puzzling facts about the neurochemical and neurodynamical basis of both emotion and consciousness. The *central* capacities, no less than the peripheral, have been addressed with profit by various materialist research programs.

In any case, the (substance) dualist's attempt to draw a sharp distinction between the unique "mental" capacities proper to the nonmaterial mind, and the merely mediative capacities of the brain, prompts an argument that comes close to being an outright refutation of (substance) dualism. If there really is a distinct entity in which reasoning, emotion, and consciousness take place, and if that entity is dependent on the brain for nothing more than sensory experiences as input and volitional executions as output, *then one would expect reason, emotion, and consciousness to be relatively invulnerable to direct control or pathology by manipulation or damage to the brain.* But in fact the exact opposite is true. Alcohol, narcotics, or senile degeneration of nerve tissue will impair, cripple, or even destroy one's capacity for rational thought. Psychiatry knows of hundreds of emotion-controlling chemicals (lithium, chlorpromazine, amphetamine, cocaine, and so on) that do their work when vectored into the brain. And the vulnerability of consciousness to the anesthetics, to caffeine, and to something as simple as a sharp blow to the head shows its very close dependence on neural activity in the brain. All of this makes perfect sense if reason, emotion, and consciousness are activities of the brain itself. But it makes very little sense if they are activities of something else entirely.

We may call this the argument from the *neural dependence* of all known mental phenomena. Property dualism, note, is not threatened by this argument, since, like materialism, property dualism reckons the brain as the seat of all mental activity. We shall conclude this section, however, with an argument that cuts against both varieties of dualism: the argument from *evolutionary history*.

What is the origin of a complex and sophisticated species such as ours? What, for that matter, is the origin of the dolphin, the mouse, or the housefly? Thanks to the fossil record, comparative anatomy, and the biochemistry of proteins and nucleic acids, there is no longer any significant doubt on this matter. Each existing species is a surviving type from a number of variations on an earlier type of organism; each earlier type is in turn a surviving type from a number of variations on a still earlier type of organism; and so on down the branches of the evolutionary tree until, some three billion years ago, we find a trunk of just one or a handful of very simple organisms. These organisms, like their more complex offspring, are just self-repairing, self-replicating, energy-driven molecular structures. (That evolutionary trunk has its own roots in an earlier era of purely chemical evolution, in which the molecular elements of life were themselves pieced together.) The mechanism of development that has structured this tree has two main elements: (1) the occasional blind variation in types of reproducing creature and (2) the selective survival of some of these types due to the relative reproductive advantage enjoyed by individuals of those types. Over periods of geological time, such a process can produce an enormous variety of organisms, some of them very complex indeed.

For purposes of our discussion, the important point about the standard evolutionary story is that the human species and all of its features are the wholly physical outcome of a purely physical process. Like all but the simplest of organisms, we have a nervous system. And for the same reason: a nervous system permits the discriminative guidance of behavior. But a nervous system is just an active matrix of cells, and a cell is just an active matrix of molecules. We are notable only in that our nervous system is more complex and powerful than those of our fellow creatures. Our inner nature differs from that of simpler creatures in degree, but not in kind.

If this is the correct account of our origins, then there seems neither need, nor room, to fit any nonphysical substances or properties into our theoretical account of ourselves. We are creatures of matter. And we should learn to live with that fact.

Arguments like these have moved most (but not all) of the professional community to embrace some form of materialism. This has not produced much unanimity, however, since the differences between the several materialist positions are even wider than the differences that divide dualism.

STUDY QUESTIONS

1. Explain the difference between substance dualism and property dualism.
2. Present two arguments in favor of dualism.
3. Present two arguments against dualism.
4. According to Churchland, what is the connection between evolution and dualism?

What Is It Like to Be a Bat?

Thomas Nagel

If materialism is correct and a person is identical with a body, can we explain the phenomenon we all experience of being conscious? How can my body be conscious? Is my consciousness like yours? Is ours like that of animals? This last question is explored by Thomas Nagel, Professor Emeritus of Philosophy and of Law at New York University, who wonders what it would be like to be a bat and goes on to explain how the question bears directly on the mind–body problem.

....

Conscious experience is a widespread phenomenon. It occurs at many levels of animal life, though we cannot be sure of its presence in the simpler organisms, and it is very difficult to say in general what provides evidence of it. (Some extremists have been prepared to deny it even of mammals other than man.) No doubt it occurs in countless forms totally unimaginable to us, on other planets in other solar systems throughout the universe. But no matter how the form may vary, the fact that an organism has conscious experiences *at all* means, basically, that there is something it is like to *be* that organism....

We may call this the subjective character of experience.... It is useless to base the defense of materialism on any analysis of mental phenomena that fails to deal explicitly with their subjective character.... [T]o make evident the importance of subjective features, it will help to explore the matter in relation to an example....

I assume we all believe that bats have experience. After all, they are mammals, and there is no more doubt that they have experience than that mice or pigeons or whales have experience. I have chosen bats instead of wasps or flounders because if one travels too far down the phylogenetic tree, people gradually shed their faith that there is experience there at all. Bats, although more closely related to us than those other species, nevertheless present a range of activity and a sensory apparatus so different from ours that the problem I want to pose is exceptionally vivid (though it certainly could be raised with other species). Even without the benefit of philosophical reflection, anyone who has spent some time in an enclosed space with an excited bat knows what it is to encounter a fundamentally *alien* form of life.

I have said that the essence of the belief that bats have experience is that there is something that it is like to be a bat. Now we know that most bats (the microchiroptera, to be precise) perceive the external world primarily by sonar, or echolocation, detecting the reflections, from objects within range, of their own rapid, subtly modulated, high-frequency shrieks. Their brains are designed to correlate the outgoing impulses with the subsequent echoes, and the information thus acquired enables bats to make precise discrimination of distance, size, shape, motion, and texture comparable to those we make by vision. But bat sonar, though clearly a form of perception, is not similar in its operation to any sense that we possess, and there is no reason to suppose that it is subjectively like anything we can experience or imagine. This appears to create difficulties for the notion of what it is like to be a bat. We must consider whether any method will permit us to extrapolate to the inner life of the bat from our own case[1] and, if not, what alternative methods there may be for understanding the notion.

Our own experience provides the basic material for our imagination, whose range is therefore limited. It will not help to try to imagine that one has webbing on one's arms, which enables one to fly around at dusk and dawn catching insects in one's mouth; that one has very poor vision, and perceives the surrounding world by a system of reflected high-frequency sound signals; and that one spends the day hanging upside down by one's feet in an attic. Insofar as I can imagine this (which is not very far), it tells me only what it would be like for *me* to behave as a bat behaves. But that is not the question. I want to know what it is like for a *bat* to be a bat. Yet if I try to imagine this, I am restricted to the resources of my own mind, and those resources are inadequate to the task. I cannot perform it either by imagining additions to my present experience, or by imagining segments gradually subtracted from it, or by imagining some combination of additions, subtractions, and modifications.

To the extent that I could look and behave like a wasp or a bat without changing my fundamental structure, my experiences would not be anything like the experiences of those animals. On the other hand, it is doubtful that any meaning can be attached to the supposition that I should possess the internal neurophysiological constitution of a bat. Even if I could by gradual degrees be transformed into a bat, nothing in my present constitution enables me to imagine what the experiences of such a future stage of myself thus metamorphosed would be like. The best evidence would come from the experiences of bats, if we only knew what they were like.

So if extrapolation from our own case is involved in the idea of what it is like to be a bat, the extrapolation must be incompletable. We cannot form more than a schematic conception of what it *is* like. For example, we may ascribe general *types* of experience on the basis of the animal's structure and behavior. Thus we describe bat sonar as a form of three-dimensional forward perception; we believe that bats feel some versions of pain, fear, hunger, and lust and that they have other, more familiar types of perception besides sonar. But we believe that these experiences also have in each case a specific subjective character, which it is beyond our ability to conceive. And if there is conscious life elsewhere in the universe, it is likely that some of it will not be describable even in the most general experiential terms available to us.[2] (The problem is not confined to exotic cases, however, for it exists between one person and another. The subjective character of the experience of a person deaf and blind from birth is not accessible to me, for example, nor presumably is mine to him. This does not prevent us each from believing that the other's experience has such a subjective character.)

If anyone is inclined to deny that we can believe in the existence of facts like this whose exact nature we cannot possibly conceive, he should reflect that in contemplating the bats we are in much the same position that intelligent bats or Martians[3] would occupy if they tried to form a conception of what it was like to be us. The structure of their own minds might make it impossible for them to succeed, but we know they would be wrong to conclude that there is not anything precise that it is like to be us: that only certain general types of mental state could be ascribed to us (perhaps perception and appetite would be concepts common to us both; perhaps not). We know they would be wrong to draw such a skeptical conclusion because we know what it is like to be us. And we know that while it includes an enormous amount of variation and complexity, and while we do not possess the vocabulary to describe it adequately, its subjective character is highly specific, and in some respects describable in terms that can be understood only by creatures like us. The fact that we cannot expect ever to accommodate in our language a detailed description of Martian or bat phenomenology should not lead us to dismiss as meaningless the claim that bats and Martians have experiences fully comparable in richness of detail to our own. It would be fine if someone were to develop concepts and a theory that enabled us to think about those things, but such an understanding may be permanently denied to us by the limits of our nature....

My realism about the subjective domain in all its forms implies a belief in the existence of facts beyond the reach of human concepts. Certainly it is possible for a human being to believe that there are facts which humans never *will* possess the requisite concepts to represent or comprehend. Indeed, it would be foolish to doubt this, given the finiteness of humanity's expectations.... But one might also believe that there are facts which *could* not ever be represented or comprehended by human beings, even if the species lasted for ever—simply because our structure does not permit us to operate with concepts of the requisite type.... Reflection on what it is like to be a bat seems to lead us, therefore, to the conclusion that there are facts that do not consist in the truth of propositions expressible in a human language....

This bears directly on the mind–body problem. For if the facts of experience—facts about what it is like *for* the experiencing organism—are accessible only from one point of view, then it is a mystery how the true character of experiences could be revealed in the physical operation of that organism. The latter is a domain of objective facts par excellence—the kind that can be observed and understood from many points of view and by individuals with differing perceptual systems. There are no comparable imaginative obstacles to the acquisition of knowledge about bat neurophysiology by human scientists, and intelligent bats or Martians might learn more about the human brain than we ever will....

In the case of experience, on the other hand, the connexion with a particular point of view seems much closer. It is difficult to understand what could be meant by the *objective* character of an experience, apart from the particular point of view from which its subject apprehends it. After all, what would be left of what it was like to be a bat if one removed the viewpoint of the bat?

NOTES

1. By "our own case," I do not mean just "my own case," but rather the mentalistic ideas that we apply unproblematically to ourselves and other human beings.
2. Therefore the analogical form of the English expression "what it is *like*" is misleading. It does not mean "what (in our experience) it *resembles*," but rather "how it is for the subject himself."
3. Any intelligent extraterrestrial beings totally different from us.

STUDY QUESTIONS

1. What does Nagel mean by "the subjective character of experience"?
2. Do you agree that bats have experiences?
3. Does Nagel believe in the existence of facts beyond the reach of human concept?
4. According to Nagel, how does reflection on what it is like to be a bat relate to the mind–body problem?

The Qualia Problem

❧

FRANK JACKSON

Frank Jackson is Professor Emeritus of Philosophy at Australian National University. He offers two examples to suggest that the world contains not only physical objects but also qualia, the felt qualities of experience. These present a challenge to materialism, sometimes referred to as physicalism.

People vary considerably in their ability to discriminate colors. Suppose that in an experiment to catalog this variation Fred is discovered. Fred has better color vision

From Frank Jackson, "Epiphenomenal Qualities," *Philosophical Quarterly*, 32 (1982). Reprinted by permission of Blackwell Publishing.

than anyone else on record; he makes every discrimination that anyone has ever made, and moreover he makes one that we cannot even begin to make. Show him a batch of ripe tomatoes and he sorts them into two roughly equal groups and does so with complete consistency. That is, if you blindfold him, shuffle the tomatoes up, and then remove the blindfold and ask him to sort them out again, he sorts them into exactly the same two groups.

We ask Fred how he does it. He explains that all ripe tomatoes do not look the same color to him, and in fact that this is true of a great many objects that we classify together as red. He sees two colors where we see one, and he has in consequence developed for his own use two words "red_1" and "red_2" to mark the difference. Perhaps he tells us that he has often tried to teach the difference between red_1 and red_2 to his friends but has gotten nowhere and has concluded that the rest of the world is red_1–red_2 color-blind—or perhaps he has had partial success with his children; it doesn't matter. In any case he explains to us that it would be quite wrong to think that because "red" appears in both "red_1" and "red_2," the two colors are shades of the one color. He only uses the common term "red" to fit more easily into our restricted usage. To him red_1 and red_2 are as different from each other and all the other colors as yellow is from blue. And his discriminatory behavior bears this out: He sorts red_1 from red_2 tomatoes with the greatest of ease in a wide variety of viewing circumstances. Moreover, an investigation of the physiological basis of Fred's exceptional ability reveals that Fred's optical system is able to separate out two groups of wavelengths in the red spectrum as sharply as we are able to sort out yellow from blue.

I think that we should admit that Fred can see, really see, at least one more color than we can; red_1 is a different color from red_2. We are to Fred as a totally red–green color-blind person is to us. H. G. Wells' story "The Country of the Blind" is about a sighted person in a totally blind community. This person never manages to convince them that he can see, that he has an extra sense. They ridicule this sense as quite inconceivable, and they treat his capacity to avoid falling into ditches, to win fights, and so on as precisely that capacity and nothing more. We would be making their mistake if we refused to allow that Fred can see one more color than we can.

What kind of experience does Fred have when he sees red_1 and red_2? What is the new color or colors like? We would dearly like to know but do not; and it seems that no amount of physical information about Fred's brain and optical system tells us. We find out perhaps that Fred's cones respond differentially to certain light waves in the red section of the spectrum that make no difference to ours (or perhaps he has an extra cone) and that this leads in Fred to a wider range of those brain states responsible for visual discriminatory behavior. But none of this tells us what we really want to know about his color experience. There is something about it we don't know. But we know, we may suppose, everything about Fred's body, his behavior and dispositions to behavior and about his internal physiology, and everything about his history and relation to others that can be given in physical accounts of persons. We have all the physical information. Therefore, knowing all this is *not* knowing everything about Fred. It follows that Physicalism leaves something out.

To reinforce this conclusion, imagine that as a result of our investigations into the internal workings of Fred we find out how to make everyone's physiology like Fred's in the relevant respects; or perhaps Fred donates his body to science and on his death we are able to transplant his optical system into someone else—again the fine detail doesn't matter. The important point is that such a happening would create enormous interest. People would say "At last we will know what it is like to see the extra color, at last we will know how Fred has differed from us in the way he has struggled to tell us about for so long." Then it cannot be that we knew all along all about Fred. But *ex hypothesi* we did know all along everything about Fred that features in the physicalist scheme; hence the physicalist scheme leaves something out.

Put it this way. *After* the operation, we will know *more* about Fred and especially about his color experiences. But beforehand we had all the physical information we could desire about his body and brain, and indeed everything that has ever featured in physicalist accounts of mind and consciousness. Hence there is more to know than all that. Hence Physicalism is incomplete.

Fred and the new color(s) are of course essentially rhetorical devices. The same point can be made with normal people and familiar colors. Mary is a brilliant scientist who is, for whatever reason, forced to investigate the world from a black-and-white room *via* a black-and-white television monitor. She specializes in the neurophysiology of vision and acquires, let us suppose, all the physical information there is to obtain about what goes on when we see ripe tomatoes, or the sky, and use terms like "red," "blue," and so on. She discovers, for example, just which wavelength combinations from the sky stimulate the retina, and exactly how this produces *via* the central nervous system the contraction of the vocal chords and expulsion of air from the lungs that results in the uttering of the sentence "The sky is blue."

What will happen when Mary is released from her black-and-white room or is given a color television monitor? Will she *learn* anything or not? It just seems obvious that she will learn something about the world and our visual experience of it. But then it is inescapable that her previous knowledge was incomplete. But she had *all* the physical information. *Ergo* there is more to have than that, and Physicalism is false.

Clearly the same style of Knowledge argument could be deployed for taste, hearing, the bodily sensations, and generally speaking for the various mental states that are said to have (as it is variously put) raw feels, phenomenal features, or qualia. The conclusion in each case is that the qualia are left out of the physicalist story. And the polemical strength of the Knowledge argument is that it is so hard to deny the central claim that one can have all the physical information without having all the information there is to have.

STUDY QUESTIONS

1. What are qualia?
2. Why do qualia present a problem for materialists?
3. Will Mary learn anything when she experiences colors?
4. If Mary learns something when she experiences colors, is materialism false?

Knowing What It's Like

﹥

DAVID LEWIS

A materialist believes that reality consists only of physical objects and their properties. Can materialism, however, account for phenomenal qualities, that is, what it is like to have a certain kind of experience? In the previous articles Nagel and Jackson raised this challenge to materialism. In our next selection David Lewis (1941–2001), who was Professor of Philosophy at Princeton University, provides an answer to anyone who would appeal to qualia to defend some version of a dualism of mind and body.

....

The most formidable challenge to any sort of *materialism* . . . comes from the friend of *phenomenal qualia*. He says we leave out the phenomenal aspect of mental life: we forget that pain is a feeling, that there is something it is like to hold one's hand in a flame, that we are aware of something when we suffer pain, that we can recognize that something when it comes again. . . .

Suppose he makes his case as follows.[1]

> You have not tasted Vegemite (a celebrated yeast based condiment). So you do not know what it is like to taste Vegemite. And you never will, unless you taste Vegemite. (Or unless the same experience, or counterfeit traces of it, are somehow produced in you by artificial means.) No amount of the information whereof materialists and functionalists speak will help you at all. But if you taste Vegemite, *then* you will know what it is like. So you will have gained a sort of information that the materialists and functionalists overlook entirely. Call this *phenomenal information.* By *qualia* I mean the special subject matter of this phenomenal information. . . .

From *Philosophical Papers* vol. 1, Oxford University Press, where it appears as a postscript to "Mad Pain and Martian Pain." Copyright © 1983 by David Lewis. Reprinted by permission of Oxford University Press.

Our proper answer, I think, is that knowing what it's like is not the possession of information at all. It isn't the elimination of any hitherto open possibilities. Rather, knowing what it's like is the possession of abilities: abilities to recognize, abilities to imagine, abilities to predict one's behavior by means of imaginative experiments. (Someone who knows what it's like to taste Vegemite can easily and reliably predict whether he would eat a second helping of Vegemite ice cream.) Lessons cannot impart these abilities—who would have thought they could? There is a state of knowing what it's like sure enough. And Vegemite has a special power to produce that state. But phenomenal information and its special subject matter do not exist.[2]

Imagine a smart data bank. It can be told things, it can store the information it is given, it can reason with it, it can answer questions on the basis of its stored information. Now imagine a pattern-recognizing device that works as follows. When exposed to a pattern it makes a sort of template, which it then applies to patterns presented to it in the future. Now imagine one device with both faculties, rather like a clock radio. There is no reason to think that any such device must have a third faculty: a faculty of making templates for patterns it has never been exposed to, using its stored information about these patterns. If it has a full description about a pattern but no template for it, it lacks an ability but it doesn't lack information. (Rather, it lacks information in usable form.) When it is shown the pattern it makes a template and gains abilities, but it gains no information. We might be rather like that.

NOTES

1. This is the "knowledge argument" of Frank Jackson, "Epiphenomenal Qualia," *Philosophical Quarterly* 32 (1982): 127–36. It appears also, in less purified form, in Thomas Nagel, "What Is It Like to Be a Bat?" *Philosophical Review* 83 (1974): 435–50; and in Paul Meehl, "The Compleat Autocerebroscopist," in Paul Feyerabend and Grover Maxwell, eds., *Mind, Matter, and Method: Essays in Philosophy and Science in Honor of Herbert Feigl* (Minneapolis: University of Minnesota Press, 1966).
2. This defense against the knowledge argument is presented in detail in Laurence Nemirow, *Functionalism and the Subjective Quality of Experience* (Ph.D. dissertation, Stanford University, 1979), chapter 2; and more briefly in his review of Thomas Nagel's *Mortal Questions, Philosophical Review* 89 (1980): 473–77.

STUDY QUESTIONS

1. What does Lewis mean by "the friend of phenomenal qualia"?
2. Explain the point of the case of Vegemite.
3. How does Lewis reply to that case?
4. Is knowing what it's like to eat chocolate ice cream the possession of information?

Computing Machinery
and Intelligence

ALAN TURING

In a previous article Thomas Nagel explored the consciousness of a bat. But do only living things think? What about a computer? Does it have conscious thoughts?

Alan Turing (1912–1954) was an English mathematician, scientist, and philosopher. He proposes what has come to be known as the "Turing test," in which a human interrogator asks questions and tries to determine whether the answers are being given by a computer or a human being. Turing believes that a computer could be so programmed that its answers would be indistinguishable from those of a human being. In that case the computer would appropriately be described as intelligent.

....

I propose to consider the question, "Can machines think?" This should begin with definitions of the meaning of the terms "machine" and "think." The definitions might be framed so as to reflect so far as possible the normal use of the words, but this attitude is dangerous. If the meaning of the words "machine" and "think" are to be found by examining how they are commonly used, it is difficult to escape the conclusion that the meaning and the answer to the question, "Can machines think?" is to be sought in a statistical survey such as a Gallup poll. But this is absurd. Instead of attempting such a definition, I shall replace the question by another, which is closely related to it and is expressed in relatively unambiguous words.

The new form of the problem can be described in terms of a game which we call the "imitation game." It is played with three people, a man (A), a woman (B), and an interrogator (C) who may be of either sex. The interrogator stays in a room apart from the other two. The object of the game for the interrogator is to determine which of the other two is the man and which is the woman. He knows them by labels X and Y, and at the end of the game he says either "X is A and Y is B" or "X is B and Y is A." The interrogator is allowed to put questions to A and B thus:

C: Will X please tell me the length of his or her hair?

From Alan Turing, "Computing Machinery and Intelligence," *Mind*, LIX (1950). Reprinted by permission of Oxford University Press.

Now suppose X is actually A, then A must answer. It is A's object in the game to try to cause C to make the wrong identification. His answer might therefore be

"My hair is shingled, and the longest strands are about nine inches long."

In order that tones of voice may not help the interrogator, the answers should be written, or better still, typewritten. The ideal arrangement is to have a teleprinter communicating between the two rooms. Alternatively the question and answers can be repeated by an intermediary. The object of the game for the third player (B) is to help the interrogator. The best strategy for her is probably to give truthful answers. She can add such things as "I am the woman, don't listen to him!" to her answers, but it will avail nothing as the man can make similar remarks.

We now ask the question, "What will happen when a machine takes the part of A in this game?" Will the interrogator decide wrongly as often when the game is played like this as he does when the game is played between a man and a woman? These questions replace our original, "Can machines think?" . . .

It will simplify matters for the reader if I explain first my own beliefs in the matter. . . . I believe that in about fifty years' time it will be possible to program computers . . . to make them play the imitation game so well that an average interrogator will not have more than 70 percent chance of making the right identification after five minutes of questioning. . . .

I now proceed to consider opinions opposed to my own. . . .

THE ARGUMENT FROM CONSCIOUSNESS

This argument is very well expressed in Professor Jefferson's Lister Oration for 1949, from which I quote. "Not until a machine can write a sonnet or compose a concerto because of thoughts and emotions felt, and not by the chance fall of symbols, could we agree that machine equals brain—that is, not only write it but know that it had written it. No mechanism could feel (and not merely artificially signal, an easy contrivance) pleasure at its successes, grief when its valves fuse, be warmed by flattery, be made miserable by its mistakes, be charmed by sex, be angry or depressed when it cannot get what it wants."

This argument appears to be a denial of the validity of our test. According to the most extreme form of this view the only way by which one could be sure that a machine thinks is to *be* the machine and to feel oneself thinking. One could then describe these feelings to the world, but of course no one would be justified in taking any notice. Likewise according to this view the only way to know that a *man* thinks is to be that particular man. It is in fact the solipsist point of view. It may be the most logical view to hold but it makes communication of ideas difficult. A is liable to believe "A thinks but B does not" while B believes "B thinks but A does not." Instead of arguing continually over this point it is usual to have the polite convention that everyone thinks.

I am sure that Professor Jefferson does not wish to adopt the extreme and solipsist point of view. Probably he would be quite willing to accept the imitation game as a test. The game (with the player B omitted) is frequently used in practice under the name of *viva voce* to discover whether someone really understands something or has "learned it parrot fashion." Let us listen to a part of such a *viva voce:*

> INTERROGATOR: In the first line of your sonnet which reads "Shall I compare thee to a summer's day," would not "a spring day" do as well or better?
> WITNESS: It wouldn't scan.
> INTERROGATOR: How about "a winter's day." That would scan all right.
> WITNESS: Yes, but nobody wants to be compared to a winter's day.
> INTERROGATOR: Would you say Mr. Pickwick reminded you of Christmas?
> WITNESS: In a way.
> INTERROGATOR: Yet Christmas is a winter's day, and I do not think Mr. Pickwick would mind the comparison.
> WITNESS: I don't think you're serious. By a winter's day one means a typical winter's day, rather than a special one like Christmas.

And so on. What would Professor Jefferson say if the sonnet-writing machine was able to answer like this in the *viva voce*? I do not know whether he would regard the machine as "merely artificially signaling" these answers, but if the answers were as satisfactory and sustained as in the above passage, I do not think he would describe it as "an easy contrivance." This phrase is, I think, intended to cover such devices as the inclusion in the machine of a record of someone reading a sonnet, with appropriate switching to turn it on from time to time.

In short then, I think that most of those who support the argument from consciousness could be persuaded to abandon it rather than be forced into the solipsist position. They will then probably be willing to accept our test.

I do not wish to give the impression that I think there is no mystery about consciousness. There is, for instance, something of a paradox connected with any attempt to localize it. But I do not think these mysteries necessarily need to be solved before we can answer the question with which we are concerned in this paper.

ARGUMENTS FROM VARIOUS DISABILITIES

These arguments take the form, "I grant you that you can make machines do all the things you have mentioned but you will never be able to make one to do X." Numerous features X are suggested in this connection. I offer a selection:

> Be kind, resourceful, beautiful, friendly..., have initiative, have a sense of humor, tell right from wrong, make mistakes..., fall in love, enjoy strawberries and cream, make someone fall in love with it, learn from experience..., use words properly, be the subject of its own thought..., have as much diversity of behavior as a man, do something really new....

No support is usually offered for these statements. I believe they are mostly founded on the principle of scientific induction. A man has seen thousands of machines in his lifetime. From what he sees of them he draws a number of general conclusions. They are ugly, each is designed for a very limited purpose, when required for a minutely different purpose they are useless, the variety of behavior of any one of them is very small, etc., etc. Naturally he concludes that these are necessary properties of machines in general. Many of these limitations are associated with the very small storage capacity of most machines.... A few years ago, when very little had been heard of digital computers, it was possible to elicit much incredulity concerning them, if one mentioned their properties without describing their construction. That was presumably due to a similar application of the principle of scientific induction. These applications of the principle are of course largely unconscious. When a burned child fears the fire and shows that he fears it by avoiding it, I should say that he was applying scientific induction. (I could of course also describe his behavior in many other ways.) The works and customs of mankind do not seem to be very suitable material to which to apply scientific induction. A very large part of space–time must be investigated if reliable results are to be obtained. Otherwise we may (as most English children do) decide that everybody speaks English and that it is silly to learn French.

There are, however, special remarks to be made about many of the disabilities that have been mentioned. The inability to enjoy strawberries and cream may have struck the reader as frivolous. Possibly a machine might be made to enjoy this delicious dish, but any attempt to make one do so would be idiotic....

The claim that "machines cannot make mistakes" seems a curious one. One is tempted to retort, "Are they any the worse for that?" But let us adopt a more sympathetic attitude and try to see what is really meant. I think this criticism can be explained in terms of the imitation game. It is claimed that the interrogator could distinguish the machine from the man simply by setting them a number of problems in arithmetic. The machine would be unmasked because of its deadly accuracy. The reply to this is simple. The machine (programmed for playing the game) would not attempt to give the *right* answers to the arithmetic problems. It would deliberately introduce mistakes in a manner calculated to confuse the interrogator. A mechanical fault would probably show itself through an unsuitable decision as to what sort of mistake to make in the arithmetic. Even this interpretation of the criticism is not sufficiently sympathetic. But we cannot afford the space to go into it much further. It seems to me that this criticism depends on a confusion between two kinds of mistakes. We may call them "errors of functioning" and "errors of conclusion." Errors of functioning are due to some mechanical or electrical fault which causes the machine to behave otherwise than it was designed to do. In philosophical discussions one likes to ignore the possibility of such errors; one is therefore discussing "abstract machines." These abstract machines are mathematical fictions rather than physical objects. By definition they are incapable of errors of functioning. In this sense we can truly say that "machines can never make mistakes." Errors of conclusion can only arise when some meaning is attached to the output signals from the machine. The machine might, for instance, type out mathematical equations, or sentences in English. When a false proposition is typed, we say that the machine has committed an error of conclusion. There is clearly no reason at all for saying that a machine cannot make this kind of mistake. It might do nothing but type out repeatedly "0 = 1." To take a less perverse example, it might have some method for drawing conclusions by scientific induction. We must expect such a method to lead occasionally to erroneous results.

The claim that a machine cannot be the subject of its own thought can of course only be answered if it can be shown that the machine has *some* thought with *some* subject matter. Nevertheless, "the subject matter of a machine's operations" does seem to mean something, at least to the people who deal with it. If, for instance, the machine was trying to find a solution of the equation $x^2 - 40x - 11 = 0$, one would be tempted to describe this equation as part of the machine's subject matter at that moment. In this sort of sense a machine undoubtedly can be its own subject matter. It may be used to help in making up its own programs, or to predict the effect of alterations in its own structure. By observing the results of its own behavior it can modify its own programs so as to achieve some purpose more effectively. These are possibilities of the near future, rather than Utopian dreams.

STUDY QUESTIONS

1. What does Turing mean by the "imitation game"?
2. Can a machine make a mistake?
3. Could a machine be programmed to appear to think and yet not be thinking?
4. Do you believe that the imitation game offers a decisive test of whether a machine can think?

Do Computers Think?

JOHN SEARLE

A reply to the sort of argument Turing presented is offered by John Searle, who was Professor Emeritus at the University of California, Berkeley. He asks us to consider a man with no knowledge of Chinese who is placed in a room containing a basket of Chinese symbols and a rule book telling him which Chinese symbols to match with others solely on the basis of their shape. Using the rule book, he is able to answer in Chinese questions posed in Chinese. His successful manipulation of the Chinese symbols, however, does not give him an understanding of

From John Searle, "Is the Brain's Mind a Computer Program?" *Scientific American,* 1990. Reprinted by permission of the journal.

Chinese. So too, according to Searle, a computer's following its program does not give it thought.

....

Can a machine think? Can a machine have conscious thoughts in exactly the same sense that you and I have? If by "machine" one means a physical system capable of performing certain functions (and what else can one mean?), then humans are machines of a special biological kind, and humans can think, and so of course machines can think. And, for all we know, it might be possible to produce a thinking machine out of different materials altogether—say, out of silicon chips or vacuum tubes. Maybe it will turn out to be impossible, but we certainly do not know that yet.

In recent decades, however, the question of whether a machine can think has been given a different interpretation entirely. The question that has been posed in its place is, Could a machine think just by virtue of implementing a computer program? Is the program by itself constitutive of thinking? This is a completely different question because it is not about the physical, causal properties of actual or possible physical systems but rather about the abstract, computational properties of formal computer programs that can be implemented in any sort of substance at all, provided only that the substance is able to carry the program.

A fair number of researchers in artificial intelligence (AI) believe the answer to the second question is yes; that is, they believe that by designing the right programs with the right inputs and outputs, they are literally creating minds. They believe furthermore that they have a scientific test for determining success or failure: the Turing test devised by Alan M. Turing, the founding father of artificial intelligence. The Turing test, as currently understood, is simply this: if a computer can perform in such a way that an expert cannot distinguish its performance from that of a human who has a certain cognitive ability—say, the ability to do addition or to understand Chinese—then the computer also has that ability. So the goal is to design programs that will simulate human cognition in such a way as to pass the Turing test. What is more, such a program would not merely be a model of the mind; it would literally be a mind, in the same sense that a human mind is a mind.

By no means does every worker in artificial intelligence accept so extreme a view. A more cautious approach is to think of computer models as being useful in studying the mind in the same way that they are useful in studying the weather, economics or molecular biology. To distinguish these two approaches, I call the first strong AI and the second weak AI. It is important to see just how bold an approach strong AI is. Strong AI claims that thinking is merely the manipulation of formal symbols, and that is exactly what the computer does: manipulate formal symbols. This view is often summarized by saying, "The mind is to the brain as the program is to the hardware."

Strong AI is unusual among theories of the mind in at least two respects: it can be stated clearly, and it admits of a simple and decisive refutation. The refutation is one that any person can try for himself or herself. Here is how it goes. Consider a language you don't understand. In my case, I do not understand Chinese. To me, Chinese writing looks like so many meaningless squiggles. Now suppose I am placed in a room containing baskets full of Chinese symbols. Suppose also that I am given a rule book in English for matching Chinese symbols with other Chinese symbols. The rules identify the symbols entirely by their shapes and do not require that I understand any of them. The rules might say such things as, "Take a squiggle–squiggle sign from basket number one and put it next to a squoggle–squoggle sign from basket number two."

Imagine that people outside the room who understand Chinese hand in small bunches of symbols and that in response I manipulate the symbols according to the rule book and hand back more small bunches of symbols. Now, the rule book is the "computer program." The people who wrote it are "programmers," and I am the "computer." The baskets full of symbols are the "data base," the small bunches that are handed in to me are "questions" and the bunches I then hand out are "answers."

Now suppose that the rule book is written in such a way that my "answers" to the "questions" are indistinguishable from those of a native Chinese speaker. For example, the people outside might hand me some symbols that unknown to me mean, "What's your favorite color?" and I might after going through the rules give back symbols that, also unknown to me, mean, "My favorite is blue, but I also like green a lot." I satisfy the Turing test for understanding Chinese. All the same, I am totally ignorant of Chinese. And there is no way I could come to understand Chinese in the system as described, since there is no way that I can learn the meanings of any of the symbols. Like a computer, I manipulate symbols, but I attach no meaning to the symbols.

The point of the thought experiment is this: if I do not understand Chinese solely on the basis of running a computer program for understanding Chinese, then neither does any other digital computer solely on that basis. Digital computers merely manipulate formal symbols according to rules in the program.

What goes for Chinese goes for other forms of cognition as well. Just manipulating the symbols is not by itself enough to guarantee cognition, perception, understanding, thinking and so forth. And since computers, qua computers, are symbol-manipulating devices, merely running the computer program is not enough to guarantee cognition.

This simple argument is decisive against the claims of strong AI.

STUDY QUESTIONS

1. Does Searle believe a machine can think?
2. Explain the experiment that uses Chinese symbols.
3. What does Searle believe that the experiment proves?
4. What do you believe that the experiment proves?

The Body Problem

𝖺𝗅

BARBARA MONTERO

Barbara Montero is Professor of Philosophy at the College of Staten Island and
the Graduate Center of the City University of New York. She points out that the
question of whether the mind is physical presumes an understanding of what
counts as physical, a point on which agreement is lacking.

Is the mind physical? Are mental properties, such as the property of *being in pain*
or *thinking about the higher orders of infinity,* actually physical properties? Many
philosophers think that they are. For no matter how strange and remarkable consciousness and cognition may be, many hold that they are, nevertheless, entirely
physical. While some take this view as a starting point in their discussions about
the mind, others, well aware that there are dissenters among the ranks, argue for
it strenuously. One wonders, however, just what is being assumed, argued for, or
denied. In other words, one wonders: Just what does it mean to be physical? This
is the question I call, "the body problem."

As I see it, there is little use in arguing about whether the mind is physical,
or whether mental properties are physical properties unless we have at least some
understanding of what it means to be physical. In other words, in order to solve the
mind–body problem, we must solve the body problem. It strikes me as odd that
while bookstores and journals are overflowing with debates about whether consciousness is physical, hardly anyone is concerned with "What counts as physical?"
Moreover, it would not be much of an exaggeration to say today, as John Earman
did more than twenty years ago, that "attempts to answer this question that have
appeared in the philosophical literature are for the most part notable only for their
glaring inadequacies."[1] If we want to discuss whether the mind is physical, we
should say something about what it means to be physical.

Some may argue that such clarification is unnecessary. They may point out
that while we cannot provide necessary and sufficient conditions for *tablehood,* we
nonetheless understand the concept, because we can readily identify things that are
clearly tables and things that are clearly not. They claim the same is true of our notion
of the physical. But the situations are not analogous. While we can identify central
cases of being physical—what could be clearer examples of physical than rocks and

From Steven M. Cahn and Maureen Eckert, eds., *Philosophical Horizons*, second edition,
Wadsworth, 2012. Reprinted by permission of the publisher.

trees (except, perhaps, quarks and leptons)?—an extra wrinkle is that rocks and trees (as well as quarks and leptons) are clear cases only assuming that idealism is false. In any case, something needs to be said about how to determine what we can place in the category along with rocks and trees. In certain ways, beliefs and desires *are* like rocks and trees, while quarks and leptons are not. For example, talk of beliefs and desires plays a role in our ordinary folk understanding of the world, while talk of quarks and leptons does not. Beliefs and desires also are part of the same macro-level causal network as rocks and trees, while quarks and leptons are not. But few physicalists think that from our central examples of physical objects we should infer that quarks and leptons are nonphysical.

Perhaps these problems could be overlooked if we had clear intuitions regarding the nonphysical. But do we? The stock example of a nonphysical entity is some kind of ghost. For example, Jaegwon Kim defines "ontological physicalism" as the view that "there are no nonphysical residues (e.g. Cartesian souls, entelechies, and the like)."[2] And Jeffrey Poland states that the physicalist's bottom line is really: "There are no ghosts!"[3] But why is a ghost nonphysical? Is it that they can pass through walls without disturbing them? Neutrinos, I am told, can pass right through the earth without disturbing it, yet neutrinos are classified as physical. Is it that they have no mass? Photons have no mass yet are considered physical. Perhaps it is that they supposedly do not take up space. But if taking up no space shows that something is nonphysical, point particles (if they exist) would have to be classified as nonphysical. Yet physicalists, I take it, would not accept this view. So to say that the physical means "no spooky stuff" does not help matters.

Perhaps physicalism at least excludes the possibility of a ghost in a machine, that is, the view that there is some type of mental substance completely different in kind from physical substance. But what does this view amount to, since most physicalists are happy to admit that there is more than one kind of elementary particle? Perhaps the idea is that whether only one basic particle exists, say, strings, or it turns out that in addition to strings there are also Ferris wheels, physicalism holds that everything nonbasic is composed of the same kind, or kinds of basic particles. But this view cannot be right. For example, some evidence indicates that what physicists call "dark matter" is composed entirely of axions, hypothetical new elementary particles.[4] Yet dark matter is no threat to physicalism. So the simple notion of *stuff of a different kind* does not provide us with a notion of nonphysical. But what, then, does?

Philosophers commonly answer this question by deferring to the physicists. The physical is said to be whatever the physicist, or more precisely, the particle physicist, tells us exists (what we might now think of as quarks and leptons, as well as the exchange particles, gluons, gravitons, etc.). And the nonphysical is whatever remains, if there is anything. On this view, physicalists—that is, those who hold that everything is physical—claim that physics provides us with an exhaustive and exclusive line to all reality. Here is a straightforward answer to the body problem, but one that is too simple, since most philosophers believe that things like rocks, tables, and chairs are just as physical as quarks, leptons, and gluons.

Granted, whether to say that the physical is only what the physicists take as fundamental is partially a terminological issue. But while the question whether to reserve the name "physical" for just the fundamental constituents of reality or to use it more broadly *is* terminological, the question of how many layers of reality to countenance is not. Because most physicalists allow for not only the smallest stuff, but also for atoms, molecules, rocks and galaxies, the leave-it-to-the-physicists approach is usually amended to the view that the physical world is the world of the fundamental particles, forces, laws and such *as well as* whatever depends on this physical stuff. As such, we can allow for the possibility that rocks may be physical.

My concern, however, is not with the dependence relation *per se* but with what everything is being related to: the lower level dependence base or what is often referred to as "the microphysical." One thinks of microphysical phenomena as described by the most recent microphysics. But if the physical is defined in terms of current microphysics, and a new particle is discovered next week, the particle will not be physical—a consequence most philosophers want to avoid. But if not current microphysics, what else could the microphysical be?

Carl Hempel posed a dilemma for those attempting to define the physical in reference to microphysics.[5] On the one hand, we cannot define the physical in terms of current microphysics since today's microphysics is probably neither entirely true (some of our theories may look as wrong-headed to future generations as phlogiston theory looks to us now) nor complete (more remains to be explained). On the other hand, if we take microphysics to be some future unspecified theory, the claim that the mind is physical is vague, since we currently have no idea of that theory. Faced with this dilemma, what is a physicalist to do?

Some try to take the middle road, explaining the "microphysical" by referring to "something like current microphysics—but just improved."[6] But in what respect is this future microphysics like current microphysics? And in what respect will it be improved? Since these questions are usually not addressed (save, of course, for the implication that it is similar enough to be intelligible yet different enough to be true), it seems that Hempel's dilemma recurs for these compromise views. For the theory in question will be false if it is significantly similar to current physics, and if not, we are left with no clear notion of the physical.

Taking the first horn of Hempel's dilemma, that is, defining the physical in terms of current microphysics, does not provide us with a comfortable solution to the body problem. For it is rather awkward to hold a theory that one knows is false.[7] But does taking the second horn fare any better? David Armstrong thinks so. He explicitly tells us that when he says "physical properties" he is not talking about the properties specified by current physics, but rather "whatever set of properties the physicist in the end will appeal to."[8] Similarly, Frank Jackson holds that the physical facts encompass "everything in a completed physics, chemistry, and neurophysiology, and all there is to know about the causal and relational facts consequent upon all this."[9] As Barry Loewer puts it, "what many have on their minds when they speak of fundamental physical properties is that they are the properties expressed by simple predicates of the true comprehensive fundamental physical theory."[10] So for Armstrong and others the physical is to be defined over a completed physics, a physics in the end. But what is this final physics? The answer, as Hempel has pointed out, is unknown.

Basing one's notion of the physical on an unfathomable theory seems to be a serious enough problem to discourage defining the physical over a final theory. But most philosophers ignore this problem and charge ahead to the more juicy questions, such as whether knowledge of all the physical facts (whatever they may be) enables us to know what it is like to see colors. So consider that another consequence of using the notion of a completed physics to explain the physical is that, at least under one interpretation, it trivially excludes the possibility that the mind is not physical. For on one understanding of it, a completed physics amounts to a physics that explains *everything*. So if mentality is a feature of the world, a completed physics, on this definition, will explain it too. While there is nothing wrong with trivial truth *per se*, this is not the solution to the mind-body problem most philosophers would accept. For neither physicalists nor their foes think that we already know by definition that the mind is physical.

Chomsky has identified a related problem for those who define the physical in terms of a final physics. His point is that since we cannot predict the course of physics, we cannot be sure that a final physics will not include mental properties, qua mental, as fundamental properties.[11] Yet if final physics takes the mental realm to be fundamental, the difference dissolves between physicalists who claim that mental properties will be accounted for in final physics and dualists who claim that mental properties are fundamental.

A solution to the body problem is not forthcoming. Perhaps we should focus on questions other than the question "Is the mind physical?" So let me conclude with a suggestion. Physicalism is, at least partly, motivated by the belief that the mental is ultimately nonmental, that is, that mental properties are not fundamental properties, whereas dualism holds, precisely, that they are. So a crucial question is whether the mental is ultimately nonmental. Of course, the notion of the nonmental is also open-ended. And, for this reason, it may be just as difficult to see what sort of considerations are relevant in determining what counts as nonmental as it is to see what sort of considerations are relevant in determining what counts as physical. However, we do have a grasp of one side of the divide—that is, the mental. So, rather than worrying about whether the mind is physical, we should be concerned with whether it is nonmental. And this question has little to do with what current physics, future physics, or a final physics says about the world.

NOTES

1. John Earman, "What is Physicalism?" *Journal of Philosophy* 72 (1975), p. 566.
2. Jaegwon Kim, "Supervenience, Emergence, Realization in Philosophy of Mind," in M. Carrier and P. Machamer (eds.), *Mindscapes: Philosophy, Science, and the Mind*, Pittsburgh, University of Pittsburgh Press, 1997.

3. Jeffery Poland, *Physicalism: The Philosophical Foundations,* Oxford: Oxford University Press, 1994, p. 15. He emphasizes this point again later: "ghosts, gods, and the paranormal are genuine threats to physicalism" (p. 228). That is, according to Poland, if ghosts were to exist, physicalism would be false.

4. See Leslie Rosenberg, "The Search for Dark Matter Axions," *Particle World* 4 (1995), pp. 3–10.

5. See Carl Hempel, "Comments on Goodman's Ways of Worldmaking," *Synthese* 45 (1980), pp. 193–9. Also see Hempel, "Reduction: Ontological and Linguistic Facets," in S. Morgenbesser, P. Suppes and M. Whit (eds.), *Philosophy, Science and Method: Essays in Honor of Ernest Nagel,* New York: St. Martin's Press, 1969. I am using different terminology from Hempel, and my emphasis is on the question of whether the mind is physical rather than the question of physicalism in general, but the point is essentially the same.

6. See for example, David Lewis, "New Work for a Theory of Universals," *Australasian Journal of Philosophy* 61 (1983), pp. 343–77 and Robert Kirk, *Raw Feeling: A Philosophical Account of the Essence of Consciousness,* New York: Oxford University Press, 1994.

7. For further discussion of this point see Barbara Montero, "The Body Problem," *Nous* 33 (1999), pp. 183–200.

8. David Armstrong, "The Causal Theory of Mind," in D. Rosenthal (ed.), *The Nature of Mind,* New York: Oxford University Press, 1991, p. 186. Of course, not all properties the physicist appeals to are relevant: when a physicist is explaining a proposed budget in a grant application or explaining to her supervisor why she was late to work, she may be appealing to very different properties than when she is applying her mathematical skills in computing a wave function. But perhaps this distinction is intuitive enough.

9. Frank Jackson, "What Mary Didn't Know," in D. Rosenthal (ed.), *The Nature of Mind,* New York: Oxford University Press, 1991, p. 291.

10. Barry Loewer, "Humean Supervenience," *Philosophical Topics* 24 (1996), p. 103.

11. See Noam Chomsky, "Language and Nature," *Mind* 104 (1995), pp. 1–61 and *Language and Thought,* Rhode Island: Moyer Bell, 1993.

STUDY QUESTIONS

1. According to Montero, what is the "body problem"?
2. How does the body problem differ from the mind–body problem?
3. Does Montero agree that a ghost is nonphysical?
4. According to Montero, do we have a clearer grasp of the mental than the physical?

Meditations on First Philosophy

‌

RENÉ DESCARTES

We return now to Descartes' *Meditations* at the point at which he had wondered whether we can be sure of any truth. He believes we can. The principle he proposes as certain is best known as formulated in another of his works as "I think; therefore, I am," in Latin, "Cogito, ergo sum." According to Descartes, the Cogito, as it is called by philosophers, is undeniable, for, in the act of attempting to deny one is thinking, one thinks and so renders the denial false.

Using the Cogito as the premise of his philosophical system, Descartes argues that because he is certain he is thinking but not certain of the existence of anything other than his own mind, he is to be identified with his mind. He claims further that by relying on the judgments of his mind rather than the evidence of his senses, he can attain knowledge.

······························

SECOND MEDITATION

The Nature of the Human Mind, and How It Is Better Known Than the Body

So serious are the doubts into which I have been thrown as a result of yesterday's meditation that I can neither put them out of my mind nor see any way of resolving them. It feels as if I have fallen unexpectedly into a deep whirlpool which tumbles me around so that I can neither stand on the bottom nor swim up to the top. Nevertheless I will make an effort and once more attempt the same path which I started on yesterday. Anything which admits of the slightest doubt I will set aside just as if I had found it to be wholly false; and I will proceed in this way until I recognize something certain, or, if nothing else, until I at least recognize for certain that there is no certainty. Archimedes used to demand just one firm and immovable point in order to shift the entire earth; so I too can hope for great things if I manage to find just one thing, however slight, that is certain and unshakeable.

I will suppose then, that everything I see is spurious. I will believe that my memory tells me lies, and that none of the things that it reports ever happened. I have no senses. Body, shape, extension, movement, and place are chimeras. So what remains true? Perhaps just the one fact that nothing is certain.

Yet apart from everything I have just listed, how do I know that there is not something else which does not allow even the slightest occasion for doubt? Is there not a God, or whatever I may call him, who puts into me the thoughts I am now having? But why do I think this, since I myself may perhaps be the author of these thoughts? In that case am not I, at least, something? But I have just said that I have no senses and no body. This is the sticking point: what follows from this? Am I not so bound up with a body and with senses that I cannot exist without them? But I have convinced myself that there is absolutely nothing in the world, no sky, no earth, no minds, no bodies. Does it now follow that I too do not exist? No: if I convinced myself of something, then I certainly existed. But there is a deceiver of supreme power and cunning who is deliberately and constantly deceiving me. In that case I too undoubtedly exist, if he is deceiving me; and let him deceive me as much as he can, he will never bring it about that I am nothing so long as I think that I am something. So after considering everything very thoroughly, I must finally conclude that this proposition, *I am, I exist,* is necessarily true whenever it is put forward by me or conceived in my mind.

But I do not yet have a sufficient understanding of what this "I" is, that now necessarily exists. So I must be on my guard against carelessly taking something else to be this "I," and so making a mistake in the very item of knowledge that I maintain is the most certain and evident of all. I will therefore go back and meditate on what I originally believed myself to be, before I embarked on this present train of thought. I will then subtract anything capable of being weakened, even minimally, by the arguments now introduced, so that what is left at the end may be exactly and only what is certain and unshakeable.

What then did I formerly think I was? A man. But what is a man? Shall I say "a rational animal"? No; for then I should have to inquire what an animal is, what rationality is, and in this way one question would lead me down the slope to other harder ones, and I do not now have the time to waste on subtleties of this kind. Instead I propose to concentrate on what came into my thoughts spontaneously and quite naturally whenever I used to consider what I was. Well, the first thought to come to mind was that I had a face, hands, arms, and the whole mechanical structure of limbs which can be seen in a corpse, and which I called the body. The next thought was that I was nourished, that I moved about, and that I engaged in sense-perception and thinking; and these actions I attributed to the soul. But as to the nature of this soul, either I did not think about this or else I imagined it to be something tenuous, like a wind or fire or ether, which permeated my more solid parts. As to the body, however, I had no doubts about it, but thought I knew its nature distinctly. If I had tried to describe the mental conception I had of it, I would have expressed it as follows: by a body I understand whatever has a determinable shape and a definable location and can occupy a space in such a way as to exclude any other body; it can be perceived by touch, sight, hearing, taste, or smell, and can be moved in various ways, not by itself but by whatever else comes into contact with it. For, according to my judgement, the power of self-movement, like the power of sensation or of thought, was quite foreign to the nature of a body; indeed, it was a source of wonder to me that certain bodies were found to contain faculties of this kind.

But what shall I now say that I am, when I am supposing that there is some supremely powerful and, if it is permissible to say so, malicious deceiver, who is deliberately trying to trick me in every way he can? Can I now assert that I possess even the most insignificant of all the attributes which I have just said belong to the nature of a body? I scrutinize them, think about them, go over them again, but nothing suggests itself; it is tiresome and pointless to go through the list once more. But what about the attributes I assigned to the soul? Nutrition or movement? Since now I do not have a body, these are mere fabrications. Sense-perception? This surely does not occur without a body, and besides, when asleep I have appeared to perceive through the senses many things which I afterwards realized I did not perceive through the senses at all. Thinking? At last I have discovered it—thought; this alone is inseparable from me. I am, I exist—that is certain. But for how long? For as long as I am thinking. For it could be that were I totally to cease from thinking, I should totally cease to exist. At present I am not admitting anything except what is necessarily true. I am, then, in the strict sense only a thing that thinks; that is, I am a mind, or intelligence, or intellect, or reason—words whose meaning I have been ignorant of until now. But for all that I am a thing which is real and which truly exists. But what kind of a thing? As I have just said—a thinking thing.

What else am I? I will use my imagination. I am not that structure of limbs which is called a human body. I am not even some thin vapour which permeates the limbs— a wind, fire, air, breath, or whatever I depict in my imagination; for these are things which I have supposed to be nothing. Let this supposition stand; for all that I am still something. And yet may it not perhaps be the case that these very things which I am supposing to be nothing, because they are unknown to me, are in reality identical with the "I" of which I am aware? I do not know, and for the moment I shall not argue the point, since I can make judgements only about things which are known to me. I know that I exist; the question is, what is this "I" that I know? If the "I" is understood strictly as we have been taking it, then it is quite certain that knowledge of it does not depend on things of whose existence I am as yet unaware; so it cannot depend on any of the things which I invent in my imagination. And this very word "invent" shows me my mistake. It would indeed be a case of fictitious invention if I used my imagination to establish that I was something or other; for imagining is simply contemplating the shape or image of a corporeal thing. Yet now I know for certain both that I exist and at the same time that all such images and, in general, everything relating to the nature of body, could be mere dreams (and chimeras). Once this point has been grasped, to say "I will use my imagination to get to know more distinctly what I am" would seem to be as silly as saying "I am now awake, and see some truth; but since my vision is not yet clear enough, I will deliberately fall asleep so that my dreams may provide a truer and clearer representation." I thus realize that none of the things that the imagination enables me to grasp is at all relevant to this knowledge of myself which I possess, and that the mind must therefore be most carefully diverted from such things if it is to perceive its own nature as distinctly as possible.

But what then am I? A thing that thinks. What is that? A thing that doubts, understands, affirms, denies, is willing, is unwilling, and also imagines and has sensory perceptions.

This is a considerable list, if everything on it belongs to me. But does it? Is it not one and the same "I" who is now doubting almost everything, who nonetheless understands some things, who affirms that this one thing is true, denies everything else, desires to know more, is unwilling to be deceived, imagines many things even involuntarily, and is aware of many things which apparently come from the senses? Are not all these things just as true as the fact that I exist, even if I am asleep all the time, and even if he who created me is doing all he can to deceive me? Which of all these activities is distinct from my thinking? Which of them can be said to be separate from myself? The fact that it is I who am doubting and understanding and willing is so evident that I see no way of making it any clearer. But it is also the case that the "I" who imagines is the same "I." For even if, as I have supposed, none of the objects of imagination are real, the power of imagination is something which really exists and is part of my thinking. Lastly, it is also the same "I" who has sensory perceptions, or is aware of bodily things as it were through the senses. For example, I am now seeing light, hearing a noise, feeling heat. But I am asleep, so all this is false. Yet I certainly *seem* to see, to hear, and to be warmed. This cannot be false; what is called "having a sensory perception" is strictly just this, and in this restricted sense of the term it is simply thinking.

From all this I am beginning to have a rather better understanding of what I am. But it still appears—and I cannot stop thinking this—that the corporeal things of which images are formed in my thought, and which the senses investigate, are known with much more distinctness than this puzzling "I" which cannot be pictured in the imagination. And yet it is surely surprising that I should have a more distinct grasp of things which I realize are doubtful, unknown, and foreign to me, than I have of that which is true and known—my own self. But I see what it is: my mind enjoys wandering off and will not yet submit to being restrained within the bounds of truth. Very well then; just this once let us give it a completely free rein, so that after a while, when it is time to tighten the reins, it may more readily submit to being curbed.

Let us consider the things which people commonly think they understand most distinctly of all; that is, the bodies which we touch and see. I do not mean bodies in general—for general perceptions are apt to be somewhat more confused—but one particular body. Let us take, for example, this piece of wax. It has just been taken from the honeycomb; it has not yet quite lost the taste of the honey; it retains some of the scent of the flowers from which it was gathered; its colour, shape, and size are plain to see; it is hard, cold and can be handled without difficulty; if you rap it with your knuckle, it makes a sound. In short, it has everything which appears necessary to enable a body to be known as distinctly as possible. But even as I speak, I put the wax by the fire and look: the residual taste is eliminated, the smell goes away, the colour changes, the shape is lost, the size increases; it becomes liquid and hot; you can hardly touch it, and if you strike it, it no longer makes a sound. But does the same wax remain? It must be admitted that it does; no one denies it, no one thinks otherwise. So what was it in the wax that I understood with such distinctness? Evidently none of the features which I arrived at by means of the senses; for whatever came under taste, smell, sight, touch, or hearing has now altered—yet the wax remains.

Perhaps the answer lies in the thought which now comes to my mind; namely, the wax was not after all the sweetness of the honey, or the fragrance of the flowers, or the whiteness, or the shape, or the sound, but was rather a body which presented itself to me in these various forms a little while ago, but which now exhibits different ones. But what exactly is it that I am now imagining? Let us concentrate, take away everything which does not belong to the wax, and see what is left: merely something extended, flexible, and changeable. But what is meant here by "flexible" and "changeable"? Is it what I picture in my imagination: that this piece of wax is capable of changing from a round shape to a square shape, or from a square shape to a triangular shape? Not at all; for I can grasp that the wax is capable of countless changes of this kind, yet I am unable to run through this immeasurable number of changes in my imagination, from which it follows that it is not the faculty of imagination that gives me my grasp of the wax as flexible and changeable. And what is meant by "extended"? Is the extension of the wax also unknown? For it increases if the wax melts, increases again if it boils, and is greater still if the heat is increased. I would not be making a correct judgement about the nature of wax unless I believed it capable of being extended in many more different ways than I will ever encompass in my imagination. I must therefore admit that the nature of this piece of wax is in no way revealed by my imagination, but is perceived by the mind alone. (I am speaking of this particular piece of wax; the point is even clearer with regard to wax in general.) But what is this wax which is perceived by the mind alone? It is of course the same wax which I see, which I touch, which I picture in my imagination, in short the same wax which I thought it to be from the start. And yet, and here is the point, the perception I have of it is a case not of vision or touch or imagination—nor has it ever been, despite previous appearances—but of purely mental scrutiny; and this can be imperfect and confused, as it was before, or clear and distinct as it is now, depending on how carefully I concentrate on what the wax consists in.

But as I reach this conclusion I am amazed at how (weak and) prone to error my mind is. For although I am thinking about these matters within myself, silently and without speaking, nonetheless the actual words bring me up short, and I am almost tricked by ordinary ways of talking. We say that we see the wax itself, if it is there before us, not that we judge it to be there from its colour or shape; and this might lead me to conclude without more ado that knowledge of the wax comes from what the eye sees, and not from the scrutiny of the mind alone. But then if I look out of the window and see men crossing the square, as I just happen to have done, I normally say that I see the men themselves, just as I say that I see the wax. Yet do I see any more than hats and coats which could conceal automatons? I *judge* that they are men. And so something which I thought I was seeing with my eyes is in fact grasped solely by the faculty of judgement which is in my mind.

However, one who wants to achieve knowledge above the ordinary level should feel ashamed at having taken ordinary ways of talking as a basis for doubt. So let us proceed, and consider on which occasion my perception of the nature of the wax was more perfect and evident. Was it when I first looked at it, and believed I knew it by my external senses, or at least by what they call the "common" sense— that is, the power of imagination? Or is my knowledge more perfect now, after a more careful investigation of the nature of the wax and of the means by which it is known? Any doubt on this issue would clearly be foolish; for what distinctness was there in my earlier perception? Was there anything in it which an animal could not possess? But when I distinguish the wax from its outward forms—take the clothes off, as it were, and consider it naked—then although my judgement may still contain errors, at least my perception now requires a human mind.

But what am I to say about this mind, or about myself? (So far, remember, I am not admitting that there is anything else in me except a mind.) What, I ask, is this "I" which seems to perceive the wax so distinctly? Surely my awareness of my own self is not merely much truer and more certain than my awareness of the wax, but also much more distinct and evident. For if I judge that the wax exists from the fact that I see it, clearly this same fact entails much more evidently that I myself also exist. It is possible that what I see is not really the wax; it is possible that I do not even have eyes with which to see anything. But when I see, or think I see (I am not here distinguishing the two), it is simply not possible that I who am now thinking am not something. By the same token, if I judge that the wax exists from the fact that I touch it, the same result follows, namely, that I exist. If I judge that it exists from the fact that I imagine it, or for any other reason, exactly the same thing follows. And the result that I have grasped in the case of the wax may be applied to everything else located outside me. Moreover, if my perception of the wax seemed more distinct after it was established not just by sight or touch but by many other considerations, it must be admitted that I now know myself even more distinctly. This is because every consideration whatsoever which contributes to my perception of the wax, or of any other body, cannot but establish even more effectively the nature of my own mind. But besides this, there is so much else in the mind itself which can serve to make my knowledge of it more distinct, that it scarcely seems worth going through the contributions made by considering bodily things.

I see that without any effort I have now finally got back to where I wanted. I now know that even bodies are not strictly perceived by the senses or the faculty of imagination but by the intellect alone, and that this perception derives not from their being touched or seen but from their being understood; and in view of this I know plainly that I can achieve an easier and more evident perception of my own mind than of anything else. But since the habit of holding on to old opinions cannot be set aside so quickly, I should like to stop here and meditate for some time on this new knowledge I have gained, so as to fix it more deeply in my memory.

STUDY QUESTIONS

1. According to Descartes, which proposition is necessarily true?
2. By what argument does Descartes reach the conclusion that he is a mind?
3. What implications does Descartes draw from the example of the piece of wax?
4. Do you agree with Descartes that you can achieve an easier understanding of your own mind than of anything else?

PART 5

Free Will

Free Will

∗∕⟋

THOMAS NAGEL

We turn next to one of the most-discussed philosophical questions: Do human beings ever act freely? It might seem obvious that they do. Consider an ordinary human action—for instance, raising your hand at a meeting to attract the speaker's attention. If you are attending a lecture and the time comes for questions from the audience, you believe it is within your power to raise your hand and within your power not to raise it. The choice is yours.

Equally obvious, however, is that whenever an event occurs, a causal explanation can account for the occurrence of the event. If you feel a pain in your arm, then something is causing that pain. If nothing were causing it, you wouldn't be in pain. This same line of reasoning applies whether the event to be explained is a loud noise, a change in the weather, or an individual's action. If the event were uncaused, it wouldn't have occurred.

But if all actions are part of a causal chain extending back beyond your birth, how is it possible that any of your actions are free?

Our first reading is by Thomas Nagel, whose work we read previously. He explains the problem and concludes by suggesting that perhaps the feeling of free will is an illusion.

....

Suppose you're going through a cafeteria line and when you come to the desserts, you hesitate between a peach and a big wedge of chocolate cake with creamy icing. The cake looks good, but you know it's fattening. Still, you take it and eat it with pleasure. The next day you look in the mirror or get on the scale and think, "I wish I hadn't eaten that chocolate cake. I could have had a peach instead."

"I could have had a peach instead." What does that mean, and is it true?

Peaches were available when you went through the cafeteria line: you had the *opportunity* to take a peach instead. But that isn't all you mean. You mean you could have *taken* the peach instead of the cake. You could have *done* something different from what you actually did. Before you made up your mind, it was open whether you would take fruit or cake, and it was only your choice that decided which it would be.

Is that it? When you say, "I could have had a peach instead," do you mean that it depended only on your choice? You chose chocolate cake, so that's what you had, but *if* you had chosen the peach, you would have had that.

From *What Does It All Mean?* by Thomas Nagel. Copyright © 1987 by Oxford University Press. Reprinted by permission of the publisher.

This still doesn't seem to be enough. You don't mean only that *if* you had chosen the peach, you would have had it. When you say, "I could have had a peach instead," you also mean that you *could have chosen* it—no "ifs" about it. But what does that mean?

It can't be explained by pointing out other occasions when you *have* chosen fruit. And it can't be explained by saying that if you had thought about it harder, or if a friend had been with you who eats like a bird, you *would* have chosen it. What you are saying is that you could have chosen a peach instead of chocolate cake *just then, as things actually were.* You think you could have chosen a peach even if everything else had been exactly the same as it was up to the point when you in fact chose chocolate cake. The only difference would have been that instead of thinking, "Oh well," and reaching for the cake, you would have thought, "Better not," and reached for the peach.

This is an idea of "can" or "could have" which we apply only to people (and maybe some animals). When we say, "The car could have climbed to the top of the hill," we mean the car had enough power to reach the top of the hill *if* someone drove it there. We don't mean that on an occasion when it was parked at the bottom of the hill, the car could have just taken off and climbed to the top, instead of continuing to sit there. Something else would have had to happen differently first, like a person getting in and starting the motor. But when it comes to people, we seem to think that they can do various things they don't actually do, *just like that,* without anything else happening differently first. What does this mean?

Part of what it means may be this: Nothing up to the point at which you choose determines irrevocably what your choice will be. It remains an *open possibility* that you will choose a peach until the moment when you actually choose chocolate cake. It isn't determined in advance.

Some things that happen *are* determined in advance. For instance, it seems to be determined in advance that the sun will rise tomorrow at a certain hour. It is not an open possibility that tomorrow the sun won't rise and night will just continue. That is not possible because it could happen only if the earth stopped rotating, or the sun stopped existing, and there is nothing going on in our galaxy which might make either of those things happen. The earth will continue rotating unless it is stopped, and tomorrow morning its rotation will bring us back around to face inward in the solar system, toward the sun, instead of outward, away from it. If there is no possibility that the earth will stop or that the sun won't be there, there is no possibility that the sun won't rise tomorrow.

When you say you could have had a peach instead of chocolate cake, part of what you mean may be that it wasn't determined in advance what you would do, as it *is* determined in advance that the sun will rise tomorrow. There were no processes or forces at work before you made your choice that made it inevitable that you would choose chocolate cake.

That may not be all you mean, but it seems to be at least part of what you mean. For if it was really determined in advance that you would choose cake, how could it also be true that you could have chosen fruit? It would be true that nothing would have prevented you from having a peach if you had chosen it instead of cake. But these *ifs* are not the same as saying you could have chosen a peach, period. You couldn't have chosen it unless the possibility remained open until you closed it off by choosing cake.

Some people have thought that it is never possible for us to do anything different from what we actually do, in this absolute sense. They acknowledge that what we do depends on our choices, decisions, and wants and that we make different choices in different circumstances: we're not like the earth rotating on its axis with monotonous regularity. But the claim is that, in each case, the circumstances that exist before we act determine our actions and make them inevitable. The sum total of a person's experiences, desires and knowledge, his hereditary constitution, the social circumstances and the nature of the choice facing him, together with other factors that we may not know about, all combine to make a particular action in the circumstances inevitable.

This view is called determinism. The idea is not that we can know all the laws of the universe and use them to *predict* what will happen. First of all, we can't know all the complex circumstances that affect a human choice. Secondly, even when we do learn something about the circumstances and try to make a prediction, that is itself a *change* in the circumstances, which may change the predicted result. But predictability isn't the point. The hypothesis is that there *are* laws of nature, like those that govern the movement of the planets, which govern everything that happens in the world, and that in accordance with those laws, the circumstances before an action determine that it will happen and will rule out any other possibility.

If that is true, then even while you were making up your mind about dessert, it was already determined by the many factors working on you and in you that you would choose cake. You *couldn't* have chosen the peach, even though you thought you could: the process of decision is just the working out of the determined result inside your mind.

If determinism is true for everything that happens, it was already determined before you were born that you would choose cake. Your choice was determined by the situation immediately before, and *that* situation was determined by the situation before *it*, and so on as far back as you want to go.

Even if determinism isn't true for everything that happens—even if some things just happen without being determined by causes that were there in advance—it would still be very significant if everything we *did* were determined before we did it. However free you might feel when choosing between fruit and cake, or between two candidates in an election, you would really be able to make only one choice in those circumstances—though if the circumstances or your desires had been different, you would have chosen differently.

If you believed that about yourself and other people, it would probably change the way you felt about things. For instance, could you blame yourself for giving in to temptation and having the cake? Would it make sense to say, "I really should have had a peach instead," if you *couldn't* have chosen a peach instead? It certainly wouldn't make sense to say it if there *was* no fruit. So how can it make sense if there *was* fruit, but you couldn't have chosen it because it was determined in advance that you would choose cake?

This seems to have serious consequences. Besides not being able sensibly to blame yourself for having had cake, you probably wouldn't be able sensibly to blame anyone at all for doing something bad, or praise them for doing something good. If it was determined in advance that they would do it, it was inevitable: they couldn't have done anything else, given the circumstances as they were. So how can we hold them responsible?

You may be very mad at someone who comes to a party at your house and steals all your Glenn Gould records, but suppose you believed that his action was determined in advance by his nature and the situation. Suppose you believed that everything he did, including the earlier actions that had contributed to the formation of his character, was determined in advance by earlier circumstances. Could you still hold him responsible for such low-grade behavior? Or would it be more reasonable to regard him as a kind of natural disaster—as if your records had been eaten by termites?

People disagree about this. Some think that if determinism is true, no one can reasonably be praised or blamed for anything, any more than the rain can be praised or blamed for falling. Others think that it still makes sense to praise good actions and condemn bad ones, even if they were inevitable. After all, the fact that someone was determined in advance to behave badly doesn't mean that he *didn't* behave badly. If he steals your records, that shows inconsiderateness and dishonesty, whether it was determined or not. Furthermore, if we don't blame him, or perhaps even punish him, he'll probably do it again.

On the other hand, if we think that what he did was determined in advance, this seems more like punishing a dog for chewing on the rug. It doesn't mean we hold him responsible for what he did: we're just trying to influence his behavior in the future. I myself don't think it makes sense to blame someone for doing what it was impossible for him not to do. (Though of course determinism implies that it was determined in advance that I would think this.)

These are the problems we must face if determinism is true. But perhaps it isn't true. Many scientists now believe that it isn't true for the basic particles of matter—that in a given situation, there's more than one thing that an electron may do. Perhaps if determinism isn't true for human actions, either, this leaves room for free will and responsibility. What if human actions, or at least some of them, are not determined in advance? What if, up to the moment when you choose, it's an open possibility that you will choose either chocolate cake or a peach? Then, so far as what has happened before is concerned, you *could* choose either one. Even if you actually choose cake, you could have chosen a peach.

But is even this enough for free will? Is this all you mean when you say, "I could have chosen fruit instead?"—that the choice wasn't determined in advance? No, you believe something more. You believe that *you* determined what you would do, by *doing* it. It wasn't determined in advance, but it didn't *just happen*, either. *You did it*, and you could have done the opposite. But what does that mean?

This is a funny question: we all know what it means to *do* something. But the problem is, if the act wasn't determined in advance, by your desires, beliefs, and personality, among other things, it seems to be something that just happened, without any explanation. And in that case, how was it *your doing*?

One possible reply would be that there is no answer to that question. Free action is just a basic feature of the world, and it can't be analyzed. There's a difference between something just happening without a cause and an action just being *done* without a cause. It's a difference we all understand, even if we can't explain it.

Some people would leave it at that. But others find it suspicious that we must appeal to this unexplained idea to explain the sense in which you could have chosen fruit instead of cake. Up to now it has seemed that determinism is the big threat to responsibility. But now it seems that even if our choices are not determined in advance, it is still hard to understand in what way we *can* do what we don't do. Either of two choices may be possible in advance, but unless I determine which of them occurs, it is no more my responsibility than if it was determined by causes beyond my control. And how can *I* determine it if *nothing* determines it?

This raises the alarming possibility that we're not responsible for our actions whether determinism is true *or* whether it's false. If determinism is true, antecedent circumstances are responsible. If determinism is false, nothing is responsible. That would really be a dead end.

There is another possible view, completely opposite to most of what we've been saying. Some people think responsibility for our actions *requires* that our actions be determined, rather than requiring that they not be. The claim is that for an action to be something you have done, it has to be produced by certain kinds of causes in you. For instance, when you chose the chocolate cake, that was something you did, rather than something that just happened, because you wanted chocolate cake more than you wanted a peach. Because your appetite for cake was stronger at the time than your desire to avoid gaining weight, it resulted in your choosing the cake. In other cases of action, the psychological explanation will be more complex, but there will always be one—otherwise the action wouldn't be yours. This explanation seems to mean that what you did was determined in advance after all. If it wasn't determined by anything, it was just an unexplained event, something that happened out of the blue rather than something that you did.

According to this position, causal determination by itself does not threaten freedom—only a certain *kind* of cause does that. If you grabbed the cake because someone else pushed you into it, then it wouldn't be a free choice. But free action doesn't require that there be no determining cause at all: it means that the cause has to be of a familiar psychological type.

I myself can't accept this solution. If I thought that everything I did was determined by my circumstances and my psychological condition, I would feel trapped. And if I thought the same about everybody else, I would feel that they were like a lot of puppets. It wouldn't make sense to hold them responsible for their actions any more than you hold a dog or a cat or even an elevator responsible.

On the other hand, I'm not sure I understand how responsibility for our choices makes sense if they are *not* determined. It's not clear what it means to say *I* determine the choice, if nothing about me determines it. So perhaps the feeling that you could have chosen a peach instead of a piece of cake is a philosophical illusion, and couldn't be right whatever was the case.

STUDY QUESTIONS

1. What is determinism?
2. If you chose one apple rather than another seemingly as good, was your choice determined?
3. Would you, like Nagel, believe yourself trapped if everything you did was determined by your circumstances and psychological conditions?
4. Why does Nagel doubt that we are responsible for our choices if they are not determined?

Free Will and Determinism

W. T. STACE

In the previous essay Nagel defended the view that free will and determinism are incompatible, that one or the other is false. Many philosophers, however, believe the two theses are compatible and that both are true.

These philosophers are sympathetic to the sort of argument presented in our next selection by W. T. Stace (1886–1967), an Englishman who became Professor of Philosophy at Princeton University. He maintains that once we define "free will" properly, any apparent incompatibility with determinism disappears.

....

[T]hose learned professors of philosophy or psychology who deny the existence of free will do so only in their professional moments and in their studies and lecture rooms. For when it comes to doing anything practical, even of the most trivial kind, they invariably behave as if they and others were free. They inquire from you at dinner whether you will choose this dish or that dish. They will ask a child why he told a lie, and will punish him for not having chosen the way of truthfulness. All of which is inconsistent with a disbelief in free will. This should cause us to suspect that the problem is not a real one; and this, I believe, is the case. The dispute is merely verbal, and is due to nothing but a confusion about the meanings of words....

Throughout the modern period, until quite recently, it was assumed, both by the philosophers who denied free will and by those who defended it, that *determinism is inconsistent with free will.* If a man's actions were wholly determined by chains of causes stretching back into the remote past, so that they could be predicted beforehand by a mind which knew all the causes, it was assumed that they could not in that case be free. This implies that a certain definition of actions done from free will was assumed, namely that they are actions *not* wholly determined by causes or predictable beforehand. Let us shorten this by saying that free will was defined as meaning indeterminism. This is the incorrect definition which has led to the denial of free will. As soon as we see what the true definition is, we shall find that the question whether the world is deterministic, as Newtonian science implied, or in a measure indeterministic, as current physics teaches, is wholly irrelevant to the problem....

At a recent murder trial in Trenton, some of the accused had signed confessions, but afterwards asserted that they had done so under police duress. The following exchange might have occurred:

JUDGE: Did you sign this confession of your own free will?
PRISONER: No. I signed it because the police beat me up.

Now suppose that a philosopher had been a member of the jury. We could imagine this conversation taking place in the jury room.

FOREMAN OF THE JURY: The prisoner says he signed the confession because he was beaten, and not of his own free will.
PHILOSOPHER: This is quite irrelevant to the case. There is no such thing as free will.
FOREMAN: Do you mean to say that it makes no difference whether he signed because his conscience made him want to tell the truth or because he was beaten?
PHILOSOPHER: None at all. Whether he was caused to sign by a beating or by some desire of his own—the desire to tell the truth, for example—in either case his signing was causally determined, and therefore in neither case did he act of his own free will. Since there is no such thing as free will, the question whether he signed of his own free will ought not to be discussed by us.

The foreman and the rest of the jury would rightly conclude that the philosopher must be making some mistake. What sort of a mistake could it be? There is only one possible answer. The philosopher must be using the phrase "free will" in some peculiar way of his own which is not the way in which men usually use it....

What, then, is the difference between acts which are freely done and those which are not?...The free acts are all caused by desires, or motives, or by some sort of internal psychological states of the agent's mind. The unfree acts, on the other hand, are all caused by physical forces or physical conditions, outside the agent. . . . We may therefore frame the following rough definitions. *Acts freely done are those whose immediate causes are psychological states in the agent. Acts not freely done are those whose immediate causes are states of affairs external to the agent.*

It is plain that if we define free will in this way, then free will certainly exists, and the philosopher's denial of its existence is seen to be what it is—nonsense. For it is obvious that all those actions of men which we should ordinarily attribute to the exercise of their free will, or of which we should say that they freely chose to do them, are in fact actions which have been caused by their own desires, wishes, thoughts, emotions, impulses, or other psychological states.

In applying our definition we shall find that it usually works well, but that there are some puzzling cases which it does not seem exactly to fit. These puzzles can always be solved by paying careful attention to the ways in which words are used, and remembering that they are not always used consistently. I have space for only one example. Suppose that a thug threatens to shoot you unless you give him your wallet, and suppose that you do so. Do you, in giving him your wallet, do so of your own free will or not? If we apply our definition, we find that you acted freely, since the immediate cause of the action was not an actual outside force but the fear of death, which is a psychological cause. Most people, however, would say that you did not act of your own free will but under compulsion. Does this show that our definition is wrong? I do not think so. . . . In the case under discussion, though no actual force was used, the gun at your forehead so nearly approximated to actual force that we tend to say the case was one of compulsion. It is a borderline case.

Here is what may seem like another kind of puzzle. According to our view, an action may be free though it could have been predicted beforehand with certainty. But suppose you told a lie, and it was certain beforehand that you would tell it. How could one then say, "You could have told the truth"? The answer is that it is perfectly true that you could have told the truth *if* you had wanted to. In fact you would have done so, for in that case the causes producing your action, namely your desires, would have been different and would therefore have produced different effects. It is a delusion that predictability and free will are incompatible. This agrees with common sense. For if, knowing your character, I predict that you will act honorably, no one would say when you do act honorably, that this shows you did not do so of your own free will.

STUDY QUESTIONS

1. If you deny the existence of free will, is your position undermined by the observation that you act as if people had free will?
2. How does Stace argue in behalf of the compatibility of free will and determinism?
3. What does Stace believe is the difference between acts that are freely done and those that are not?
4. If someone can predict with certainty what you will do, might your action nevertheless be free?

Freedom or Determinism?

✒

STEVEN M. CAHN

In the next essay I offer an overview of the problem of free will and argue against Stace's view that freedom is compatible with determinism. The discussion begins with an account of one of the twentieth century's most famous criminal trials. How did it involve a philosophical issue? Let us see.

In 1924 the American people were horrified by a senseless crime of extraordinary brutality. The defendants were eighteen-year-old Nathan Leopold and seventeen-year-old Richard Loeb, the sons of Chicago millionaires, and brilliant students who had led seemingly idyllic lives. Leopold was the youngest graduate in the history of the University of Chicago, and Loeb the youngest graduate in the history of the University of Michigan. Suddenly they were accused of the kidnapping and vicious murder of fourteen-year-old Bobby Franks, a cousin of Loeb's. Before the trial even began, Leopold and Loeb both confessed, and from across the country came an outcry for their execution.

The lawyer who agreed to defend them was Clarence Darrow, the outstanding defense attorney of his time. Because Leopold and Loeb had already admitted their crime, Darrow's only chance was to explain their behavior in such a way that his clients could escape the death penalty. He was forced to argue that Leopold and Loeb were not morally responsible for what they had done, that they were not to be blamed for their actions. But how could he possibly maintain that position?

Darrow's defense was a landmark in the history of criminal law. He argued that the actions of his clients were a direct and necessary result of hereditary and environmental forces beyond their control.[1] Leopold suffered from a glandular disease that left him depressed and moody. Originally shy with girls, he had been sent to an all-girls school as a cure but had sustained deep psychic scars from which he never recovered. In addition, his parents instilled in him the belief that his wealth absolved him of any responsibility toward others. Pathologically inferior because of his diminutive size, and pathologically superior because of his wealth, he became an acute schizophrenic.

Loeb suffered from a nervous disorder that caused fainting spells. During his unhappy childhood, he had often thought of committing suicide. He was under the control of a domineering governess and was forced to lie and cheat to deceive her.

From *Puzzles & Perplexities: Collected Essays,* 2d edition by Steven M. Cahn. Copyright © 2007 by the author and reprinted with his permission.

His wealth led him to believe that he was superior to all those around him, and he developed a fascination for crime, an activity in which he could demonstrate his superiority. By the time he reached college he was severely psychotic.

In his final plea, Darrow recounted these facts. His central theme was that Leopold and Loeb were in the grip of powers beyond their control, that they themselves were victims.

> I do not know what it was that made these boys do this mad act, but I do know there is a reason for it. I know they did not beget themselves. I know that any one of an infinite number of causes reaching back to the beginning might be working out in these boys' minds, whom you are asked to hang in malice and in hatred and in injustice, because someone in the past has sinned against them. . . . What had this boy to do with it? He was not his own father; he was not his own mother; he was not his own grandparents. All of this was handed to him. He did not surround himself with governesses and wealth. He did not make himself. And yet he is to be compelled to pay.[2]

Darrow's plea was successful, for Leopold and Loeb escaped execution and were sentenced to life imprisonment. Although they had committed crimes and were legally responsible for their actions, the judge believed they were not morally responsible, for they had not acted freely.

If the line of argument that Darrow utilized in the Leopold–Loeb case is sound, then not only were Leopold and Loeb not to blame for what they had done, but no person is ever to blame for any actions. As Darrow himself put it, "We are all helpless."[3] But is Darrow's argument sound? Does the conclusion follow from the premises, and are the premises true?

We can formalize his argument as follows:

Premise 1:   No action is free if it must occur.
Premise 2:   In the case of every event that occurs, antecedent conditions, known or unknown, ensure the event's occurrence.
Conclusion: Therefore, no action is free.

Premise (1) assumes that an action is free only if it is within the agent's power to perform it and within the agent's power not to perform it. In other words, whether a free action will occur is up to the agent. If circumstances require the agent to perform a certain action or require the agent not to perform that action, then the action is not free.

Premise (2) is the thesis known as *determinism*. Put graphically, it is the claim that if at any time a being knew the position of every particle in the universe and all the forces acting on each particle, then that being could predict with certainty every future event. Determinism does not presume such a being exists; the being is only imagined in order to illustrate what the world would be like if determinism were true.

Darrow's conclusion, which is supposed to follow from premises (1) and (2), is that no person has free will. Note that to have free will does not imply being free with regard to all actions, for only the mythical Superman is free to leap tall build-ings at a single bound. But so long as at least some of an agent's actions are free, the agent is said to have free will. What Darrow's argument purports to prove is that not a single human action that has ever been performed has been performed freely.

Does the conclusion of Darrow's argument follow from the premises? If premise (2) is true, then every event that occurs must occur, for its occurrence is ensured by antecedent conditions. Because every action is an event, it follows from premise (2) that every action that occurs must occur. But according to premise (1), no action is free if it must occur. Thus, if premises (1) and (2) are true, it follows that no action is free—the conclusion of Darrow's argument.

Even granting that Darrow's reasoning is unassailable, we need not accept the conclusion of his argument unless we grant the truth of his premises. Should we do so?

Hard determinism is the view that both premises of Darrow's argument are correct. In other words, a hard determinist believes that determinism is true and that, as a consequence, no person has free will.[4] Determinists note that when-ever an event occurs, we all assume that a causal explanation can account for the occurrence of the event. Suppose, for example, you feel a pain in your arm and are prompted to visit a physician. After examining you, the doctor announces that the pain has no cause, either physical or psychological. In other words, you are supposed to be suffering from an uncaused pain. On hearing this diagnosis, you would surely switch doctors. After all, no one may be able to discover the cause of your pain, but surely something is causing it. If nothing were causing it, you wouldn't be in pain. This same line of reasoning applies whether the event to be explained is a loud noise, a change in the weather, or an individual's action. If the event were uncaused, it wouldn't have occurred.

We may agree, however, that the principle of determinism holds in the vast majority of cases, yet doubt its applicability in the realm of human action. While causal explanations may be found for rocks falling and birds flying, people are far more complex than rocks or birds.

The determinist responds to this objection by asking us to consider any spe-cific action: for instance, your decision to read this book. You may suppose your decision was uncaused, but did you not wish to acquire information about phi-losophy? The determinist argues that your desire for such information, together with your belief that the information is found in this book, caused you to read. Just as physical forces cause rocks and birds to do things, so human actions are caused by desires and beliefs.

If you doubt this claim, the determinist can call attention to our success in predicting people's behavior. For example, a store owner who reduces prices can depend on increasing visits by shoppers; an athlete who wins a major championship can rely on greater attention from the press. Furthermore, when we read novels or see plays, we expect to understand why the characters act as they do, and an author who fails to provide such explanations is charged with poor writing. The similarity of people's reactions to the human condition also accounts for the popularity of the incisive psychological insights of a writer such as La Rochefoucauld, the French aphorist. We read one of his maxims, for instance, "When our integrity declines, our taste does also,"[5] and we nod our heads with approval, but are we not agreeing to a plausible generalization about the workings of the human psyche?

Granted, people's behavior cannot be predicted with certainty, but the hard determinist reminds us that each individual is influenced by a unique combination of hereditary and environmental factors. Just as each rock is slightly different from every other rock, and each bird is somewhat different from every other bird, so human beings differ from each other. Yet just as rocks and birds are part of an unbroken chain of causes and effects, so human beings, too, are part of that chain. Just as a rock falls because it breaks off from a cliff, so people act because of their desires and beliefs. And just as a rock has no control over the wind that causes it to break off, so people have no control over the desires and beliefs that cause them to act. In short, we are said to have no more control over our desires and beliefs than Leopold and Loeb had over theirs. If you can control your desire for food and your friend cannot, the explanation is that your will is of a sort that can control your desire and your friend's will is of a sort that cannot. That your will is of one sort and your friend's will of another is not within the control of either of you. As one hard determinist wrote, "If we can overcome the effects of early environment, the ability to do so is itself a product of the early environment. We did not give ourselves this ability; and if we lack it we cannot be blamed for not having it."[6]

At this point in the argument, an antideterminist is apt to call attention to recent developments in physics that have been interpreted by some thinkers as a refutation of determinism. They claim that work in quantum mechanics demonstrates that certain subatomic events are uncaused and inherently unpredictable. Yet some physicists and philosophers of science argue that determinism has not been refuted, because the experimental results can be understood in causal terms.[7] The outcome of this dispute, however, seems irrelevant to the issue of human freedom, because the events we are discussing are not subatomic, and indeterminism on that level is compatible with the universal causation of events on the much larger level of human action.

Here, then, is a summary of hard determinism: According to this view, determinism is true and no person has free will. Every event that occurs is caused to occur, for otherwise why would it occur? Your present actions are events caused by your previous desires and beliefs, which themselves are accounted for by hereditary and environmental factors. These are part of a causal chain extending back far before your birth, and each link of the chain determines the succeeding link. Because you obviously have no control over events that occurred before your birth, and because these earlier events determined the later ones, it follows that you have no control over your present actions. In short, you do not have free will.

The hard determinist's argument may appear plausible, yet few of us are inclined to accept its shocking conclusion. We opt, therefore, to deny one of its two premises. *Soft determinism* is the view that the conclusion is false because premise 1 is false. In other words, a soft determinist believes both that determinism is true and that human beings have free will. The implication of the position is that an action may be free even if it is part of a causal chain extending back to events outside the agent's control. While this view may at first appear implausible, it has been defended throughout the centuries by many eminent philosophers, including David Hume and John Stuart Mill.

An approach employed explicitly or implicitly by many soft determinists has come to be known as "the paradigm-case argument." Consider it first in another setting, where its use is a classic of philosophical argumentation.

In studying physics, we learn that ordinary objects like tables and chairs are composed of sparsely scattered, minute particles. This fact may lead us to suppose that such objects are not solid. As Sir Arthur Eddington, the noted physicist, put it, a "plank has no solidity of substance. To step on it is like stepping on a swarm of flies."[8]

Eddington's view that a plank is not solid was forcefully attacked by the British philosopher L. Susan Stebbing. She pointed out that the word "solid" derives its meaning from examples such as planks.

> For "solid" just is the word we use to describe a certain respect in which a plank of wood resembles a block of marble, a piece of paper, and a cricket ball, and in which each of these differs from a sponge, from the interior of a soap-bubble, and from the holes in a net. . . . The point is that the common usage of language enables us to attribute a meaning to the phrase "a solid plank"; but there is no common usage of language that provides a meaning for the word "solid" that would make sense to say that the plank on which I stand is not solid.[9]

In other words, a plank is a paradigm case of solidity. Anyone who claims that a plank is not solid does not know how the word "solid" is used in the English language. Note that Stebbing is not criticizing Eddington's scientific views but only the manner in which he interpreted them.

The paradigm-case argument is useful to soft determinists, for in the face of the hard determinist's claim that no human action is free, soft determinists respond by pointing to a paradigm case of a free action, for instance, a person walking down the street. They stipulate that the individual is not under the influence of drugs, is not attached to ropes, is not sleepwalking, and so on; in other words, they refer to a normal, everyday instance of a person walking down the street. Soft determinists claim that the behavior described is a paradigm case of a free action, clearly distinguishable from instances in which a person is, in fact, under the influence of drugs, attached to ropes, or sleepwalking. These latter cases are not examples of free actions, or are at best problematic examples, while the case the soft determinists cite is clear and seemingly indisputable. Indeed, according to soft determinists, anyone who claims the act of walking down the street is not free does not know how the word "free" is used in English. Thus people certainly have free will, for we can cite obvious cases in which they act freely.

How do soft determinists define a "free action"? According to them, actions are free if the persons who perform them wish to do so and could, if they wished, not perform them. If your arm is forcibly raised, you did not act freely, for you did not wish to raise your arm. If you were locked in a room, you would also not be free, even if you wished to be there, for if you wished to leave, you couldn't.

Soft determinists emphasize that once we define "freedom" correctly, any apparent incompatibility between freedom and determinism disappears. Consider some particular action I perform that is free in the sense explicated by soft determinists. Even if the action is one link in a causal chain extending far back beyond my birth, nevertheless I am free with regard to that action, for I wish to perform it, and if I did not wish to, I would not do so. This description of the situation is consistent with supposing that my wish is a result of hereditary and environmental factors over which I have no control. The presence of such factors is, according to the soft determinists, irrelevant to the question of whether my action is free. I may be walking down a particular street because of my desire to buy a coat and my belief that I am heading toward a clothing store, and this desire and belief may themselves be caused by any number of other factors. But because I desire to walk down the street and could walk down some other street if I so desired, it follows that I am freely walking down the street. By this line of reasoning soft determinists affirm both free will and determinism, finding no incompatibility between them.

Soft determinism is an inviting doctrine, for it allows us to maintain a belief in free will without having to relinquish the belief that every event has a cause. Soft determinism, however, is open to objections that have led some philosophers to abandon the position.

The fundamental problem for soft determinists is that their definition of "freedom" does not seem in accordance with the ordinary way in which we use the term. Note that soft determinists and hard determinists offer two different definitions of "freedom." According to the hard determinist, an action is free if it is within my power to perform it and also within my power not to perform it. According to the soft determinist, an action is free if it is such that if I wish to perform it I can, and if I wish not to perform it I also can. To highlight the difference between these definitions, consider the case of a man who has been hypnotized and rolls up the leg of his pants as if to cross a stream. Is his action free? According to the hard determinist, the man's action is not free, for it is not within his power to refrain from rolling up the leg of his pants. According to the soft determinist's definition of "freedom," the action would be considered free, for the agent desires to perform it, and if he didn't desire to, he wouldn't. But a man under hypnosis is not free. Therefore, the soft determinist's definition of "freedom" seems unsatisfactory.

Perhaps this objection to soft determinism is unfair, because the desires of the hypnotized man are not his own but are controlled by the hypnotist. The force of the objection to soft determinism, however, is that the soft determinist overlooks whether a person's wishes or desires are themselves within that individual's control. The hard determinist emphasizes that my action is free only if it is up to me whether to perform it. But in order for an action to be up to me, I need to have control over my own wishes or desires. If I do not, my desires might be controlled by a hypnotist, a brainwasher, my family, hereditary factors, and so on, and thus I would not be free. Soft determinists do not appear to take such possibilities seriously, because, according to them, I would be free even if my desires were not within my control, so long as I was acting according to my desires and could act differently if my desires were different. But could my desires have been different? That is the crucial question. If my desires could not have been different, then I could not have acted in any way other than I did, which is the description of a person who is not free.

By failing to consider the ways in which a person's desires can be controlled by external forces beyond the individual's control, soft determinists offer a definition of "freedom" that I find not in accord with our normal use of the term. They may, of course, define terms as they wish, but we are interested in the concept of freedom relevant to questions of moral responsibility. Any concept of freedom implying that hypnotized or brainwashed individuals are morally responsible for their actions is not the concept in question.

What of the soft determinist's claim that a person's walking down the street is a paradigm case of a free action? Although I agree that the paradigm-case argument can sometimes be used effectively, the soft determinist's appeal to it does not seem convincing. To see why, imagine that we traveled to a land in which the inhabitants believed that every woman born on February 29 was a witch, and that every witch had the power to cause droughts. If we refused to believe that any woman was a witch, the philosophically sophisticated inhabitants might try to convince us by appealing to the paradigm-case argument, claiming that anyone born on February 29 is a paradigm case of a witch.

What would we say in response? How does this appeal to a paradigm case differ from Susan Stebbing's appeal to a plank as a paradigm case of solidity? No one doubts that a plank can hold significant weight and is, in that sense, solid. But until women born on February 29 demonstrate supernatural powers and are in that sense witches, the linguistic claim alone has no force.

Are soft determinists appealing to an indisputable instance when they claim that a person's walking down the street is a paradigm case of a free action? Not at all, for as we saw in the trial of Leopold and Loeb, such apparently free actions may not turn out to be judged as free. By appealing to a disputable example as a paradigm case, soft determinists assume what they are supposed to be proving. They are supposed to demonstrate that actions such as walking down the street are examples of free actions. Merely asserting that such actions are free is to overlook the hard determinist's argument that such actions are not free. No questionable instance can be used as a paradigm case, and walking down the street is, as Darrow demonstrated, a questionable example of a free action. Thus soft determinism appears to have a serious weakness.

Remember that the hard determinist argues that because premises 1 and 2 of Darrow's argument are true, so is the conclusion. Soft determinists argue that premise 1 is false. If they are mistaken, then the only way to avoid hard determinism is to reject premise 2. That position is known as *libertarianism*.

The libertarian agrees with the hard determinist that if an action must occur, it is not free. For the libertarian as well as for the hard determinist, I am free with regard to a particular action only if it is within my power to perform the action and within my power not to perform it. But do persons ever act freely? The hard determinist believes that people are never free, because in the case of every action, antecedent conditions, known or unknown, ensure the action's occurrence. Libertarians refuse to accept this conclusion, but find it impossible to reject premise 1 of Darrow's argument. Therefore their only recourse is to reject premise 2. As Sherlock Holmes noted, "When you have eliminated the impossible, whatever remains, however improbable, must be the truth."[10] The libertarian thus denies that every event has a cause.

But why is the libertarian so convinced that people sometimes act freely? Consider an ordinary human action—for instance, raising your hand at a meeting to attract the speaker's attention. If you are attending a lecture and the time comes for questions from the audience, you believe it is within your power to raise your hand and also within your power not to raise it. The choice is yours. Nothing forces you to ask a question, and nothing prevents you from asking one. What could be more obvious? If this description of the situation is accurate, then hard determinism is incorrect, for you are free with regard to the act of raising your hand.

The heart of the libertarian's position is that innumerable examples of this sort are conclusive evidence for free will. Indeed, we normally accept them as such. We assume on most occasions that we are free with regard to our actions, and, moreover, we assume that other persons are free with regard to theirs. If a friend agrees to meet us at six o'clock for dinner and arrives an hour late claiming to have lost track of time, we blame her for her tardiness, because we assume she had it within her power to act otherwise. All she had to do was glance at her watch, and assuming no special circumstances were involved, it was within her power to do so. She was simply negligent and deserves to be blamed, for she could have acted conscientiously. But to believe she could have acted in a way other than she did is to believe she was free.

How do hard determinists respond to such examples? They argue that such situations need to be examined in greater detail. In the case of our friend who arrives an hour late for dinner, we assume she is to blame for her actions, but the hard determinist points out that some motive impelled her to be late. Perhaps she was more interested in finishing her work at the office than in arriving on time for dinner. But why was she more interested in finishing her work than in arriving on time? Perhaps her parents had instilled in her the importance of work but not promptness. Hard determinists stress that whatever the explanation for her lateness, the motive causing it was stronger than the motive impelling her to arrive on time. She acted as she did because her strongest motive prevailed. Which motive was the strongest, however, was not within her control, and thus she was not free.

The hard determinist's reply may seem persuasive. How can I deny that I am invariably caused to act by my strongest motive? Analysis reveals, however, that the thesis is tautological, immune from refutation, and so devoid of empirical content. No matter what example of a human action is presented, a defender of the thesis could argue that the person's action resulted from the strongest motive. If I take a swim, taking a swim must have been my strongest motive. If I decide to forgo the swim and read a book instead, then reading a book must have been my strongest motive. How do we know that my motive to read a book was stronger than my motive to take a swim? Because I read a book and did not take a swim. If this line of argument appears powerful, the illusion will last only so long as we do not ask how we are to identify a person's strongest motive. The only possible answer appears to be that the strongest motive is the motive that prevails, the motive that causes the person to act. If the strongest motive is the motive causing the person to act, what force is there in the claim that the motive causing a person to act is causing the person to act? No insight into the complexities of human action is obtained by trumpeting such a redundancy.

Thus the hard determinist does not so easily succeed in overturning the examples of free actions offered by the libertarian. However, both hard and soft determinists have another argument to offer against the libertarian's position. If the libertarian is correct that free actions are uncaused, why do they occur? Are they inexplicable occurrences? If so, to act freely would be to act in a random, chaotic, unintelligible fashion. Yet holding people morally blameworthy for inexplicable actions is unreasonable. If you are driving a car and, to your surprise, find yourself turning the wheel to the right, we can hardly blame you if an accident occurs, for what happened was beyond your control.

Hence determinists argue that libertarians are caught in a dilemma. If we are caused to do whatever we do, libertarians assert we are not morally responsible for our actions. Yet if our actions are uncaused and inexplicable, libertarians again must deny our moral responsibility. How then can libertarians claim we ever act responsibly?

To understand the libertarian response, consider the simple act of a woman picking up a cellphone. Suppose we want to understand what she is doing and are told she is calling her stockbroker. The woman has decided to buy some stock and wishes her broker to place the appropriate order. With this explanation, we now know why this woman has picked up the phone. Although we may be interested in learning more about the woman or her choice of stocks, we have a complete explanation of her action, which turns out not to be random, chaotic, or unintelligible. We may not know what, if anything, is causing the woman to act, but we do know the reason for her action. The libertarian thus replies to the determinist's dilemma by arguing that an action can be uncaused yet understandable, explicable in terms of the agent's intentions or purposes.

Now contrast the libertarian's description of a particular action with a determinist's. Let the action be your moving your arm to adjust your television set. A determinist claims you were caused to move your arm by your desire to adjust the set and your belief that you could make this adjustment by turning the dials. A libertarian claims you moved your arm in order to adjust the set.

Note that the libertarian explains human actions fundamentally differently from the way in which we explain the movements of rocks or rivers. If we speak of a rock's purpose in falling off a cliff or a river's purpose in flowing to the sea, we do so only metaphorically, for we believe that rocks and rivers have no purposes of their own but are caused to do what they do. Strictly speaking, a rock does not fall in order to hit the ground, and a river does not flow in order to reach the sea. But libertarians are speaking not metaphorically but literally when they say that people act in order to achieve their purposes. After all, not even the most complex machine can act as a person does. A machine can break down and fail to operate, but only a human being can protest and stop work on purpose.

Is the libertarian's view correct? I doubt anyone is justified in answering that question with certainty, but if the libertarian is right, human beings are often morally responsible for their actions. They deserve praise when acting admirably and blame when acting reprehensibly. Darrow may have been correct in arguing that Leopold and Loeb were not free agents, but if the libertarian is right, the burden of proof lay with Darrow, for he had to demonstrate that these boys were in that respect unlike the rest of us.

What if the libertarian is not correct? What if all human actions are caused by antecedent conditions, known or unknown, that ensure their occurrence? Moral responsibility would vanish; but even so, people could be held legally responsible for their actions. Just as we need to be safeguarded against mad dogs, so we need protection from dangerous people. Thus even if no person were morally responsible, we would still have a legal system, courts, criminals, and prisons. Remember that Darrow's eloquence did not free his clients; indeed, he did not ask that they be freed. Although he did not blame them for their actions, he did not want those actions repeated. To Darrow, Leopold and Loeb were sick men who needed the same care as sick persons with a contagious disease. After all, in a world without freedom, events need not be viewed as agreeable; they should, however, be understood as necessary.

NOTES

1. The following information is found in Irving Stone, *Clarence Darrow for the Defense* (Garden City, NY: Doubleday, Doran, 1941), pp. 384–91.
2. *Attorney for the Damned*, ed. Arthur Weinberg (New York: Simon and Schuster, 1957), pp. 37, 65.
3. Ibid., p. 37.
4. The expressions "hard determinism" and "soft determinism" were coined by William James in his essay "The Dilemma of Determinism," reprinted in *Essays on Faith and Morals* (Cleveland: World, 1962).
5. *The Maxims of La Rochefoucauld,* trans. Louis Kronenberger (New York: Random House, 1959), #379.
6. John Hospers, "What Means This Freedom?" *Determinism and Freedom in the Age of Modern Science,* ed. Sidney Hook (New York: Collier, 1961), p. 138.

7. For a detailed discussion of the philosophical implications of quantum mechanics, see Ernest Nagel, *The Structure of Science* (New York: Harcourt Brace Jovanovich, 1961), ch. 10.
8. A. S. Eddington, *The Nature of the Physical World* (New York: Macmillan, 1928), p. 342.
9. L. Susan Stebbing, *Philosophy and the Physicists* (New York: Dover, 1958), pp. 51–52.
10. Sir Arthur Conan Doyle, *The Sign of Four*, in *The Complete Sherlock Holmes* (Garden City, NY: Doubleday, n.d.), p. 111.

STUDY QUESTIONS

1. Is a hard determinist more committed to determinism than a soft determinist?
2. What reply does Cahn offer to the sort of argument presented by Stace in the preceding selection?
3. Are reasons a type of cause?
4. Can a machine make a mistake on purpose?

The Principle of Alternative Possibilities

৶

HARRY FRANKFURT

Our previous selections on free will have taken for granted that if people cannot act otherwise than as they do, then they do not act freely. But is this assumption correct? Harry Frankfurt, who is Professor Emeritus of Philosophy at Princeton University, argues that the assumption is mistaken, and he offers an intriguing example to defend his position.

....

A dominant role in nearly all recent inquiries into the free-will problem has been played by a principle which I shall call "the principle of alternate possibilities." This principle states that a person is morally responsible for what he has done only if he could have done otherwise. . . . Practically no one . . . seems inclined to deny or even to question that the principle of alternate possibilities . . . is true. . . .

But the principle of alternate possibilities is false. A person may well be morally responsible for what he has done even though he could not have done

From Harry Frankfurt, "Alternative Possibilities and Moral Responsibility," *The Journal of Philosophy*, LXVI, 23 (1969). Reprinted by permission of the journal and the author.

otherwise. The principle's plausibility is an illusion, which can be made to vanish by bringing the relevant moral phenomena into sharper focus. . . .

Suppose someone—Black, let us say—wants Jones to perform a certain action. Black is prepared to go to considerable lengths to get his way, but he prefers to avoid showing his hand unnecessarily. So he waits until Jones is about to make up his mind what to do, and he does nothing unless it is clear to him (Black is an excellent judge of such things) that Jones is going to decide to do something *other* than what he wants him to do. If it does become clear that Jones is going to decide to do something else, Black takes effective steps to ensure that Jones decides to do, and that he does do, what he wants him to do. Whatever Jones's initial preferences and inclinations, then, Black will have his way.

What steps will Black take, if he believes he must take steps, in order to ensure that Jones decides and acts as he wishes? Anyone with a theory concerning what "could have done otherwise" means may answer this question for himself by describing whatever measures he would regard as sufficient to guarantee that, in the relevant sense, Jones cannot do otherwise. Let Black pronounce a terrible threat, and in this way both force Jones to perform the desired action and prevent him from performing a forbidden one. Let Black give Jones a potion, or put him under hypnosis, and in some such way as these generate in Jones an irresistible inner compulsion to perform the act Black wants performed and to avoid others. Or let Black manipulate the minute processes of Jones's brain and nervous system in some more direct way, so that causal forces running in and out of his synapses and along the poor man's nerves determine that he chooses to act and that he does act in the one way and not in any other. Given any conditions under which it will be maintained that Jones cannot do otherwise, in other words, let Black bring it about that those conditions prevail. The structure of the example is flexible enough, I think, to find a way around any charge of irrelevance by accommodating the doctrine on which the charge is based.

Now suppose that Black never has to show his hand because Jones, for reasons of his own, decides to perform and does perform the very action Black wants him to perform. In that case, it seems clear, Jones will bear precisely the same moral responsibility for what he does as he would have borne if Black had not been ready to take steps to ensure that he do it. It would be quite unreasonable to excuse Jones for his action, or to withhold the praise to which it would normally entitle him, on the basis of the fact that he could not have done otherwise. This fact played no role at all in leading him to act as he did. He would have acted the same even if it had not been a fact. Indeed, everything happened just as it would have happened without Black's presence in the situation and without his readiness to intrude into it.

In this example there are sufficient conditions for Jones's performing the action in question. What action he performs is not up to him. Of course it is in a way up to him whether he acts on his own or as a result of Black's intervention. That depends upon what action he himself is inclined to perform. But whether he finally acts on his own or as a result of Black's intervention, he performs the same action. He has no alternative but to do what Black wants him to do. If he does it on his own, however, his moral responsibility for doing it is not affected by the fact that Black was lurking in the background with sinister intent, since this intent never comes into play. . . .

This, then, is why the principle of alternate possibilities is mistaken. It asserts that a person bears no moral responsibility—that is, he is to be excused—for having performed an action if there were circumstances that made it impossible for him to avoid performing it. But there may be circumstances that make it impossible for a person to avoid performing some action without those circumstances in any way bringing it about that he performs that action. It would surely be no good for the person to refer to circumstances of this sort in an effort to absolve himself of moral responsibility for performing the action in question. For those circumstances, by hypothesis, actually had nothing to do with his having done what he did. He would have done precisely the same thing, and he would have been led or made in precisely the same way to do it, even if they had not prevailed. . . .

STUDY QUESTIONS

1. What is "the principle of alternate possibilities"?
2. Explain in your own words the case of Black and Jones.
3. Does this case disprove the principle of alternate possibilities?
4. Is Frankfurt's view consistent with soft determinism?

The Capacities of Agents

NEIL LEVY

Neil Levy is a Senior Research Fellow at the Oxford Uehiro Centre for Practical Ethics. In his reply to the previous selection by Frankfurt, Levy identifies the case of Black and Jones as a clever variation on an example offered by John Locke and argues that our capacities may be strengthened or weakened by the circumstances in which others place us. Thus Levy finds that in the case Frankfurt offers, Jones's freedom is undermined by Black's role. Here is a typical philosophical dispute

Neil Levy, "Counterfactual Intervention and Agents' Capacities." Reprinted from *The Journal of Philosophy*, vol. CV, no. 5 (2008), by permission of the journal and the author.

that may appear unconnected to real-life problems and yet turns out to lie at the heart of the issue of free will, which, as we have seen in the Leopold–Loeb case, can even have life-or-death consequences.

....

It is widely held that Frankfurt-style cases (FSCs) decisively alter the landscape of debates over free will. Prior to their emergence, the debate between compatibilists and incompatibilists seemed irretrievably bogged down in the morass created by differing intuitions and different analyses of the central terms upon which the debate turned. For each of the central concepts—*abilities, alternative possibilities, capacities*—there were compatibilist and incompatibilist analyses available, and there seemed to be no decisive nonquestion-begging reasons to prefer one kind to the other. . . . FSCs changed all that, by showing (to the satisfaction of most) that alternative possibilities, and therefore agents' abilities to actualize such possibilities, are not necessary for moral responsibility. . . . Though agents lack alternative possibilities in FSCs, the features that explain why they lack such alternatives play no role in the explanation of what they do. Given that fact, agents in FSCs act "on their own" and are therefore apparently responsible for what they do.

In this paper I shall argue that this conclusion is unwarranted. FSCs can show that agents are responsible for their actions, despite lacking alternative possibilities, only if we are justified in believing not only that the agents they feature act "on their own," but also that their actions are an expression of *their* normal capacities for evaluating and responding to reasons. And we are justified in thinking that agents in FSCs act in a way that expresses their normal capacities only if we are justified in distinguishing between the intrinsic, responsibility-ensuring capacities of the agent and the features of her context. I shall show that there is no principled, non-*ad hoc* manner of making this latter distinction. I shall do this fighting thought experiment with thought experiment: by introducing a new kind of case, Frankfurt-enabler cases (FECs), in which agents apparently *gain* a capacity due to the presence of a counterfactual intervener. In FECs, the intuition that agents gain a capacity due to the presence of a counterfactual intervener depends upon our regarding the agent as an ensemble: agent-plus-intervener. But there is no principled reason, I claim, why we should distinguish between the agent and her context in FSCs, but fail to make this distinction in FECs. We should treat the cases alike. I argue that we can never understand agents' capacities, and thus the sensitivity to reasons of the mechanisms upon which they act, except by considering the context in which they are embedded. Hence, we are not entitled to conclude that the capacities of agents in FSCs are unchanged by the presence of the counterfactual intervener. . . .

In an FSC, an agent performs a morally significant action—say, voting for a political candidate in an election—in what is apparently the normal way, and therefore seems morally responsible for her action. However, due to circumstances of which the agent is unaware, she lacks alternatives: she cannot do otherwise than choose to vote in the way she does. Consider the following, more or less typical, FSC:

> *Voting*: When she enters the voting booth, Connie has not yet made up her mind whether to vote Democratic or Republican. Unbeknownst to her, an evil but gifted neuroscientist monitors her neural states using a computer chip he has implanted in her brain. The chip gives the neuroscientist the power to intervene in Connie's neural processes. Connie is psychologically constituted so that it is a necessary (though not sufficient) condition of her voting Democratic that she thinks deeply about a certain policy; were Connie to think deeply about this policy, the neuroscientist would intervene, causing her to choose to vote Republican. But Connie does not think deeply about the policy and proceeds to vote Republican on her own. The neuroscientist and his device play no role in bringing about Connie's vote.

Connie lacks any alternative to voting Republican; were she to think deeply about the policy that might motivate her to vote Democratic, the neuroscientist would intervene to bring it about that she votes Republican. But since she acts entirely on her own, she seems responsible for deciding to vote Republican and for voting Republican.

On the basis of cases like this, Frankfurt and his followers conclude that moral responsibility does not require alternative possibilities. . . .

As many people have pointed out, Frankfurt's original case can be understood as a clever variation on an example of John Locke's. In Locke's thought experiment, a man is carried into a room while he is asleep and the door is locked. When he awakes, he finds himself in the company of someone "he longs to see and speak with"; as a consequence he stays in the room willingly. Locke claims that we cannot doubt that the man stays in the room voluntarily, though "it is evident [. . .] he has not freedom to be gone."[1] In an FSC, the agent does not merely lose the ability to succeed in performing an action which he decides not to try performing, he loses the ability even to *try* to perform the action and yet he seems to decide, on his own, not to try, because he retains the relevant, responsibility-underlying capacities; in particular the capacities to respond and to react to reasons. In what follows, I aim to show that these capacities are lost. My strategy will be to . . . show that capacities can be *gained* through . . . intervention. Demonstrating this matters because . . . [if] it is true that agents can gain capacities merely by being in the presence of . . . interveners, then we are not entitled to conclude that they cannot lose them in the same way . . .

Consider this variation . . .

> . . . Jillian is walking along the beach when she notices a drowning. Jillian is a good swimmer, but she is pathologically afraid of deep water. She is so constituted that her phobia would prevent her from rescuing the child were she to attempt to; she would be overcome by feelings of panic. Nevertheless, she is capable of *trying* to rescue the child, and she knows that she is capable of trying. Indeed, though she knows that she has the phobia, she does not know just how powerful it is; she thinks (wrongly) that she could affect the rescue. Unbeknownst to Jillian,

a good-hearted neurosurgeon has implanted her with a chip with which he moni-
tors Jillian's neural states, and through which he can intervene if he desires to.
Should Jillian decide (on her own) to rescue the child, the neurosurgeon will
intervene to dampen her fear; she will not panic and will succeed, despite her
anxiety, in swimming out to the child and rescuing her.

. . . Jillian thinks she can save the child, and she seems to be right. . . . The presence of
the . . . intervener has given her a capacity that she would otherwise have lacked. . . .

Agents in FSCs are, supposedly, responsible for what they do because they do
it on their own, in the sense that their decision or action is the product of mechanisms which belong to or which constitute them. They express their, or their
mechanisms', unhindered capacities in decisions or actions. But we are entitled
to conclude that these agents have their capacities intact only if we are entitled to
bracket the counterfactual intervener. . . . [W]e are not so entitled. In FECs agents
gain capacities, due to the presence of a counterfactual intervener. We can only
properly grasp the manner in which the relevant capacities are gained by, precisely,
not bracketing the counterfactual intervener. The rationale for the claim that agents
in FSCs do not lose the relevant, responsibility-ensuring capacities is therefore
undermined. If we do not bracket the intervener in FSCs, in testing agents' capacities, then we are led to the conclusion that these capacities are *lost*. We are, therefore, not entitled to the intuition that agents in FSCs are morally responsible. . . .

Human beings routinely gain capacities, including mental capacities, by
learning to manipulate external symbols, or by interfacing with features of their
environment, including other agents. FECs seem exotic, but they are merely an
unusual variation on a ubiquitous phenomenon. But if we gain capacities due to
the presence of interveners, even counterfactual interveners, then why can we not
lose capacities in the same way? If agents like Jillian can gain in receptivity or reactivity to reasons, then why cannot agents like Connie, in the original voting case, lose
such receptivity or reactivity? If they can, then FSCs fail to show that agents can be
responsible even in the absence of alternative possibilities. At the very least, I think,
proponents of FSCs are not entitled to appeal to the intuition that agents in these
cases act in the normal way. They owe us an argument to that effect. For the time
being, FSCs should not be seen as having broken the dialectical stalemate that
characterized the free will debate before they burst onto the scene.

NOTE

1. Locke, *An Essay Concerning Human Understanding*, II.XXL.10.

STUDY QUESTIONS

1. What strategy does Levy adopt in replying to Frankfurt?
2. Explain in your own words the case of Jillian.
3. Can an agent gain powers in changed circumstances?
4. Can an agent lose powers in changed circumstances?

Do We Have Free Will?

Patricia Churchland

Patricia Churchland is Professor Emerita of Philosophy at the University of California, San Diego. She is married to Paul Churchland, whose work we read previously. She is well known for applying insights from neuroscience to philosophical problems, and here she uses information about the workings of the brain to explore the problem of free will. You may be unacquainted with the neurological information she provides, but she is thereby seeking to shed light on our autonomy.

....

In 2003, the *Archives of Neurology* carried a startling clinical report. A middle-aged Virginian man with no history of any misdemeanour began to stash child pornography and sexually molest his 8-year-old stepdaughter. Placed in the court system, his sexual behaviour became increasingly compulsive. Eventually, after repeatedly complaining of headaches and vertigo, he was sent for a brain scan. It showed a large but benign tumour in the frontal area of his brain, invading the septum and hypothalmus—regions known to regulate sexual behaviour.

After removal of the tumour, his sexual interests returned to normal. Months later, his sexual focus on young girls rekindled, and a new scan revealed that bits of tissue missed in the surgery had grown into a sizeable tumour. Surgery once again restored his behavioural profile to "normal."

This case renders concrete the issue of free will. Did the man have free will? Was he responsible for his behaviour? Can a tumour usurp one's free will? With the tumour, he had powerful, but atypical desires; he was not himself. Even so, the case reminds us that most adults also have powerful, albeit typical, sexual desires— desires that are sometimes more powerful than the need for food or the fear of pain. These sexual desires are regulated by hormones that act on neurons in the septum and connected brain areas. How different, then, are normal humans from the Virginia man where free will is concerned?

Neuroscience, and behavioural biology more generally, are gradually revealing the mechanisms that make us who we are: how we make decisions and control our impulses, how our genes shape our social desires and how our reward system adapts in response to satisfying experiences. We know for example that maternal-offspring attachment in mammals is mediated by the peptide oxytocin, released in the brains of both mother and child during lactation and cuddling. Oxytocin binds to neurons, and the reward pathways record and reinforce the interaction. Mate attachment in females

Patricia Churchland, "The Big Questions: Do We Have Free Will?" NewScientist.com news service, November 18, 2006. Reprinted by permission.

is also mediated by oxytocin, and in males by a similar peptide, vasopressin. In non-human mammals, the density of peptide binding sites in the brain predicts whether the species is monogamous or polygamous. Male prairie voles with lots of vasopressin binding sites are monogamous while montane voles, with few, are promiscuous. What determines the density of binding sites? Genes. Granting the effects of cultural complexity, something similar probably holds for humans too.

As neuroscience uncovers these and other mechanisms regulating choices and social behaviour, we cannot help but wonder whether anyone truly chooses anything. As a result, profound questions about responsibility are inescapable, not just regarding criminal justice, but in the day-to-day business of life. Given that, I suggest that free will, as traditionally understood, needs modification. Because of its importance in society, any description of free will updated to fit what we know about the nervous system must also reflect our social need for a working concept of responsibility.

Think about what we mean by "free will." As with all concepts, we learn the meaning of this from examples. We learn what to count as fair, or mean-spirited, or voluntary by being given sterling examples of people doing things that are fair, or mean-spirited, or voluntary. Consequently, we tend to agree that Chamberlain's choice to appease Hitler was a free, if unwise choice. Our understanding is balanced by contrasting cases—actions that are obviously not freely chosen: a dreaming man who strangles his wife, the toddler who wets his pants, a startle response to a thunderclap, or a coerced confession. From such prototypes, brains manage to extract a common enough meaning so that we can talk about free will tolerably well.

As well as prototypical cases, there are outlying cases beset with ambiguity, daunting complexity and background cultural differences. Here, the status of an action—freely chosen or not—has no clear answer, and such cases often come before the courts. Andrea Yates, the Texas mother who drowned her five children in a bathtub, was unquestionably psychotic, though her actions were methodical and purposeful, unlike the erratic movements of someone suffering an epileptic seizure. She understood that her actions were against the law, and telephoned the police to say so. Outside of our usual ken, this sort of case divides opinion. The way we currently think about free will, there may be no right answer as to whether she exercised it.

A rigid philosophical tradition claims that no choice is free unless it is uncaused; that is, unless the "will" is exercised independently of all causal influences—in a causal vacuum. In some unexplained fashion, the will—a thing that allegedly stands aloof from brain-based causality—makes an unconstrained choice. The problem is that choices are made by brains, and brains operate causally; that is, they go from one state to the next as a function of antecedent conditions. Moreover, though brains make decisions, there is no discrete brain structure or neural network which qualifies as "the will" let alone a neural structure operating in a causal vacuum. The unavoidable conclusion is that a philosophy dedicated to uncaused choice is as unrealistic as a philosophy dedicated to a flat Earth.

To begin to update our ideas of free will, I suggest we first shift the debate away from the puzzling metaphysics of causal vacuums to the neurobiology of self-control. The nature of self-control and the ways it can be compromised may be a more fruitful avenue to understand cases such as the Virginian man and Andrea Yates than trying to force the issue of "freely chosen or not."

Self-control can come in many degrees, shades, and styles. We have little direct control over autonomic functions such as blood pressure, heart rate and digestion, but vastly more control over behaviour that is organised by the cortex of the brain. Self-control is mediated by pathways in the prefrontal cortex, shaped by structures regulating emotions and drives, and it matures as the organism develops. The individual learns to inhibit self-defeating impulses, such as biting the mother when it should suck, grasping a burning ember or harvesting honey when the bees are hostile. Once bitten, twice shy. Many aspects of self-control become automatic as habits are entrenched, so that a toddler is less likely to have messy pants six months after toilet training that one week after.

Unlike free will, self-control is a concept that we can usefully apply to other animals. This is consistent with the overwhelming similarity in brain structures across all mammals. Our larger prefrontal cortex probably means we have more neurons that allow us to exercise greater self-control than that displayed by baboons or chimps. Through reinforcement, my dog has learned to lie quietly when the local squirrel taps the screen door for peanuts; a hungry chimpanzee will reach for a banana only if he knows the alpha male cannot see it, but will suppress the desire otherwise. Ulysses famously bound himself to the mast of his ship to avoid seduction by the sirens, and monkeys will deviate from a direct route to avoid a temptation known to be troublesome. This is the prefrontal cortex using cognition for impulse control.

Self-control also allows us to make sense of difficult cases where free will is unhelpful. Self-control may be diminished in persons with brain lesions or tumours. Self-control is also diminished during an epileptic seizure, while intoxicated or under anaesthesia. Other kinds of syndromes implicating compromised self-control include obsessive-compulsive disorder, where a patient has impaired ability to resist endlessly repeating some self-costly action such as hand-washing; and severe Tourette's syndrome, where the person finds it almost impossible to inhibit particular ticking movements.

How do neural networks achieve these effects that we call self-control, and what is different in the brain when self-control functions are impaired? Although little is known so far about the exact nature of the mechanisms, relevant experimental details have begun to pour in from many directions: on the properties of neurons sensitive to reward and punishment, on the generation of fear responses by neurons in the amygdala, and on the response profiles of "decision" neurons in parietal regions of cortex when the animal makes a choice after accumulating evidence. Riskier but more profitable exploratory decisions probably depend heavily on the prefrontal pole of the cortex, while safer but less profitable decisions depend more on ventromedial prefrontal regions.

These sorts of discoveries promise that eventually we will understand, at least in general terms, the neurobiological profile of a brain that has normal levels of control, and how it differs from a brain that has compromised control.

So is anyone ever responsible for anything? Civil life requires it be so. Very briefly, the crux of the matter is this: we are social animals and our ability to flourish depends on the behaviour of others. Biologically realistic models show how traits of cooperation and social orderliness can spread through a population; how moral virtues can be a benefit, cheating a cost and punishment of the socially dangerous a necessity.

From an evolutionary perspective, punishment is justified by the value all individuals place on their social life, and by the limits on behaviour needed to maintain that value. The issue of competent control arises when, given a social harm, we need to determine whether punishment is appropriate. Part of cultural evolution consists in figuring out more suitable and effective ways of limiting violent or otherwise antisocial behaviour. So yes, we must hold individuals responsible for their actions.

But what is the "self" of self-control? What am I? In essence, the self is a construction of the brain; a real, but brain-dependent organisational network for monitoring body states, setting priorities and, within the brain itself, creating the separation between inner world and outer world. In its functionality, it is a bit like a utility on your computer, though one that has evolved to grow and develop.

Complex brains are good at that sort of thing—creating high-level neural patterns to make sense of the world. We lack a word to describe this function, but instances abound. A simpler example is our normal three-dimensional visual perception. Here, a network of neurons in the visual cortex compares the slightly offset two-dimensional inputs it gets from each eye. The comparison is used to create an image of a three-dimensional world. Thus we literally see—and not merely infer—real depth.

The brain constructs a range of make-sense-of-the-world neurotools; one is the future, one is the past and one is self. Does that mean my self is not real? On the contrary. It is every bit as real as the three-dimensional world we see, or the future we prepare for, or the past we remember. It is a tool tuned, in varying degrees, to the reality of brain and world; like other tools, it can malfunction, for example, in schizophrenia.

Essentially, it is high-level tools like this which allow us to do the amazing things we humans do, including thinking of oneself as a self. Is one cheapened by this neuroscientific knowledge? I think not. Self-esteem and self-worth are wholly compatible with realising that brains make us what we are. As for self-esteem, we do know that it is highly dependent on successful social interactions: on respect, love, accomplishment, but also on temperament, hormones and serotonin. Moreover, the beauty, intricacy and sophistication of the neurobiological machine that makes me "me" is vastly more fascinating and infinitely more awesome than the philosophical conception of the brain-free soul that somehow, despite the laws of physics, exercises its free will in a causal vacuum. Each of us is a work of art, sculpted first by evolution, and second by experience in the world. With experience and reflection one's social perception matures, and so also does the level of autonomy. Aristotle called it wisdom.

STUDY QUESTIONS

1. What is self-control?
2. How does Churchland use the example of self-control to shed light on free will?
3. According to Churchland, is anyone ever responsible for anything?
4. Would you classify Churchland as a hard determinist, soft determinist, or libertarian?

An Enquiry Concerning Human Understanding

꙳

DAVID HUME

We return to Hume's *An Enquiry Concerning Human Understanding* to read his defense of the compatibility of free will and determinism.

Hume first develops his view that all events are separate; none is necessarily connected to another. When we say that one event caused another event, we mean not that the first necessitated the second but only that events of the first sort are invariably followed by events of the second sort.

As to free will, Hume finds no incompatibility between determinism, the thesis that every event has a cause, and liberty, the claim that persons sometimes have the power to act or not act in accord with what they will. Whether Hume's solution to the problem is acceptable has long been a matter of dispute.

....

OF THE IDEA OF NECESSARY CONNECTION

... There are no ideas, which occur in metaphysics more obscure and uncertain, than those of *power, force, energy* or *necessary connection*, of which it is every moment necessary for us to treat in all our disquisitions. We shall, therefore, endeavor, in this section, to fix, if possible, the precise meaning of these terms and thereby remove some part of that obscurity, which is so much complained of in this species of philosophy.

It seems a proposition, which will not admit of much dispute, that all our ideas are nothing but copies of our impressions, or, in other words, that it is impossible for us to *think* of anything, which we have not antecedently *felt*, by either our external or internal senses. I have endeavored to explain and prove this proposition and have expressed my hopes that, by a proper application of it, men may reach a greater clearness and precision in philosophical reasonings than what they have hitherto been able to attain. Complex ideas may, perhaps, be well known by definition, which is nothing but an enumeration of those parts or simple ideas that compose them. But when we have pushed up definitions to the most simple ideas and find still some ambiguity and obscurity, what resource are we then possessed of?

From *An Enquiry Concerning Human Understanding* by David Hume (1748).

By what invention can we throw light upon these ideas, and render them altogether precise and determinate to our intellectual view! Produce the impressions or original sentiments, from which the ideas are copied. These impressions are all strong and sensible. They admit not of ambiguity. They are not only placed in a full light themselves, but may throw light on their correspondent ideas, which lie in obscurity. And by this means, we may, perhaps, attain a new microscope or species of optics, by which, in the moral sciences, the most minute and most simple ideas may be so enlarged as to fall readily under our apprehension, and be equally known with the grossest and most sensible ideas, which can be the object of our inquiry.

To be fully acquainted, therefore, with the idea of power or necessary connection, let us examine its impression; and in order to find the impression with greater certainty, let us search for it in all the sources, from which it may possibly be derived.

When we look about us towards external objects and consider the operation of causes, we are never able, in a single instance, to discover any power or necessary connection, nor any quality which binds the effect to the cause and renders the one an infallible consequence of the other. We only find that the one does actually, in fact, follow the other. The impulse of one billiard ball is attended with motion in the second. This is the whole that appears to the *outward* senses. The mind feels no sentiment or *inward* impression from this succession of objects: consequently there is not, in any single, particular instance of cause and effect, anything which can suggest the idea of power or necessary connection.

From the first appearance of an object, we never can conjecture what effect will result from it. But were the power or energy of any cause discoverable by the mind, we could foresee the effect, even without experience; and might, at first, pronounce with certainty concerning it, by mere dint of thought and reasoning.

In reality, there is no part of matter that does ever, by its sensible qualities, discover any power or energy, or give us ground to imagine that it could produce anything, or be followed by any other object, which we could denominate its effect. Solidity, extension, motion; these qualities are all complete in themselves and never point out any other event which may result from them. The scenes of the universe are continually shifting, and one object follows another in an uninterrupted succession; but the power of force, which actuates the whole machine, is entirely concealed from us, and never discovers itself in any of the sensible qualities of body. We know, that, in fact, heat is a constant attendant of flame; but what is the connection between them, we have no room so much as to conjecture or imagine. It is impossible, therefore, that the idea of power can be derived from the contemplation of bodies, in single instances of their operation, because no bodies ever discover any power, which can be the original of this idea....

Part II

But to hasten to a conclusion of this argument, which is already drawn out to too great a length: we have sought in vain for an idea of power or necessary connection in all the sources from which we could suppose it to be derived. It appears that, in single instances of the operation of bodies, we never can, by our utmost scrutiny, discover anything but one event following another, without being able to comprehend any force or power by which the cause operates, or any connection between it and its supposed effect. The same difficulty occurs in contemplating the operations of mind on body—where we observe the motion of the latter to follow upon the volition of the former, but are not able to observe or conceive the tie which binds together the motion and volition, or the energy by which the mind produces this effect. The authority of the will over its own faculties and ideas is not a whit more comprehensible: so that, upon the whole, there appears not, throughout all nature, any one instance of connection which is conceivable by us. All events seem entirely loose and separate. One event follows another; but we never can observe any tie between them. They seem *conjoined*, but never *connected*. And as we can have no idea of anything which never appeared to our outward sense or inward sentiment, the necessary conclusion *seems* to be that we have no idea of connection or power at all, and that these words are absolutely without any meaning, when employed either in philosophical reasonings or common life.

But there still remains one method of avoiding this conclusion, and one source which we have not yet examined. When any natural object or event is presented, it is impossible for us, by any sagacity or penetration, to discover, or even conjecture, without experience, what event will result from it, or to carry our foresight beyond that object which is immediately present to the memory and senses. Even after one instance or experiment where we have observed a particular event to follow upon another, we are not entitled to form a general rule, or foretell what will happen in like cases; it being justly esteemed an unpardonable temerity to judge of the whole course of nature from one single experiment, however accurate or certain. But when one particular species of event has always, in all instances, been conjoined with another, we make no longer any scruple of foretelling one upon the appearance of the other, and of employing that reasoning which can alone assure us of any matter of fact or existence. We then call the one object, *cause*; the other, *effect*. We suppose that there is some connection between them; some power in the one, by which it infallibly produces the other and operates with the greatest certainty and strongest necessity.

It appears, then, that this idea of a necessary connection among events arises from a number of similar instances which occur of the constant conjunction of these events; nor can that idea ever be suggested by any one of these instances, surveyed in all possible lights and positions. But there is nothing in a number of instances, different from every single instance, which is supposed to be exactly similar; except only, that after a repetition of similar instances, the mind is carried by habit, upon the appearance of one event, to expect its usual attendant and to believe that it will exist. This connection, therefore, which we *feel* in the mind, this customary transition of the imagination from one object to its usual attendant, is the sentiment or impression from which we form the idea of power or necessary connection. Nothing further is in the case. Contemplate the subject on all sides;

you will never find any other origin of that idea. This is the sole difference between one instance, from which we can never receive the idea of connection, and a number of similar instances, by which it is suggested. The first time a man saw the communication of motion by impulse, as by the shock of two billiard balls, he could not pronounce that the one event was *connected*, but only that it was *conjoined* with the other. After he has observed several instances of this nature, he then pronounces them to be *connected*. What alteration has happened to give rise to this new idea of *connection*? Nothing but that he now *feels* these events to be *connected* in his imagination and can readily foretell the existence of one from the appearance of the other. When we say, therefore, that one object is connected with another, we mean only that they have acquired a connection in our thought, and give rise to this inference, by which they become proofs of each other's existence: a conclusion which is somewhat extraordinary, but which seems founded on sufficient evidence. Nor will its evidence be weakened by any general diffidence of the understanding, or sceptical suspicion concerning every conclusion which is new and extraordinary. No conclusions can be more agreeable to scepticism than such as make discoveries concerning the weakness and narrow limits of human reason and capacity.

And what stronger instance can be produced of the surprising ignorance and weakness of the understanding than the present? For surely, if there be any relation among objects which it imports to us to know perfectly, it is that of cause and effect. On this are founded all our reasonings concerning matter of fact or existence. By means of it alone we attain any assurance concerning objects which are removed from the present testimony of our memory and senses. The only immediate utility of all sciences is to teach us how to control and regulate future events by their causes. Our thoughts and inquiries are, therefore, every moment, employed about this relation: yet so imperfect are the ideas which we form concerning it, that it is impossible to give any just definition of cause, except what is drawn from something extraneous and foreign to it. Similar objects are always conjoined with similar. Of this we have experience. Suitably to this experience, therefore, we may define a cause to be *an object, followed by another, and where all the objects similar to the first are followed by objects similar to the second.* Or in other words *where, if the first object had not been, the second never had existed.* The appearance of a cause always conveys the mind, by a customary transition, to the idea of the effect. Of this also we have experience. We may, therefore, suitably to this experience, form another definition of cause and call it *an object followed by another, and whose appearance always conveys the thought to that other.* But though both these definitions are drawn from circumstances foreign to the cause, we cannot remedy this inconvenience or attain any more perfect definition, which may point out that circumstances are the cause, which gives it a connection with its effect. We have no idea of this connection, nor even any distinct notion of what it is we desire to know, when we endeavor at a conception of it. We say, for instance, that the vibration of this string is the cause of this particular sound. But what do we mean by that affirmation? We either mean *that this vibration is followed by this sound and that all similar vibrations have been followed by similar sounds*, or, *that this vibration is followed by this sound and that upon the appearance of one the mind anticipates the senses and forms immediately an idea of the other.* We may consider the relation of cause and effect in either of these two lights; but beyond these, we have no idea of it.

To recapitulate, therefore, the reasonings of this section: every idea is copied from some preceding impression or sentiment; and where we cannot find any impression, we may be certain that there is no idea. In all single instances of the operation of bodies or minds, there is nothing that produces any impression, nor consequently can suggest any idea of power or necessary connection. But when many uniform instances appear, and the same object is always followed by the same event, we then begin to entertain the notion of cause and connection. We then feel a new sentiment or impression, to wit, a customary connection in the thought or imagination between one object and its usual attendant; and this sentiment is the original of that idea which we seek for. For as this idea arises from a number of similar instances, and not from any single instance, it must arise from that circumstance, in which the number of instances differ from every individual instance. But this customary connection or transition of the imagination is the only circumstance in which they differ. In every other particular they are alike. The first instance which we saw of motion communicated by the shock of two billiard balls (to return to this obvious illustration) is exactly similar to any instance that may, at present, occur to us; except only, that we could not, at first, *infer* one event from the other; which we are enabled to do at present, after so long a course of uniform experience. I know not whether the reader will readily apprehend this reasoning. I am afraid that, should I multiply words about it, or throw it into a greater variety of lights, it would only become more obscure and intricate. In all abstract reasonings there is one point of view which, if we can happily hit, we shall go farther towards illustrating the subject than by all the eloquence in the world. This point of view we should endeavor to reach, and reserve the flowers of rhetoric for subjects which are more adapted to them.

OF LIBERTY AND NECESSITY

It might reasonably be expected in questions which have been canvassed and disputed with great eagerness, since the first origin of science and philosophy, that is, the meaning of all the terms, at least, should have been agreed upon among the disputants; and our inquiries, in the course of two thousand years, should have been able to pass from words to the true and real subject of the controversy. For how easy may it seem to give exact definitions of the terms employed in reasoning, and make these definitions, not the mere sound of words, the object of future scrutiny and examination? But if we consider the matter more narrowly, we shall be apt to draw a quite opposite conclusion. From this circumstance alone, that a controversy has been long kept on foot, and remains still undecided, we may presume that there is some ambiguity in the expression and that the disputants affix different ideas to the terms employed in the controversy. For as the faculties of the mind are supposed to be naturally alike in every individual; otherwise nothing could be more fruitless than to reason or dispute together; it would be impossible, if men affix the same ideas to their terms, that they could so long form different opinions of the same subject; especially when they communicate their views, and each party turn themselves on all sides, in search of arguments which may give them the victory over their antagonists. It is true, if men attempt the discussion of questions which lie entirely beyond the reach of human capacity, such as those concerning the origin of worlds, or the economy of the intellectual system or region of spirits, they may long beat the air in their fruitless contests, and never arrive at any determinate conclusion. But if the question regards any subject of common life and experience, nothing, one would think, could preserve the dispute so long undecided but some ambiguous expressions, which keep the antagonists still at a distance and hinder them from grappling with each other.

This has been the case in the long disputed question concerning liberty and necessity; and to so remarkable a degree that, if I be not much mistaken, we shall find that all mankind, both learned and ignorant, have always been of the same opinion with regard to this subject, and that a few intelligible definitions would immediately have put an end to the whole controversy. I own that this dispute has been so much canvassed on all hands and has led philosophers into such a labyrinth of obscure sophistry that it is no wonder, if a sensible reader indulge his ease so far as to turn a deaf ear to the proposal of such a question, from which he can expect neither instruction nor entertainment. But the state of the argument here proposed may, perhaps, serve to renew his attention; as it has more novelty, promises at least some decision of the controversy, and will not much disturb his ease by any intricate or obscure reasoning.

I hope, therefore, to make it appear that all men have ever agreed in the doctrine both of necessity and of liberty, according to any reasonable sense, which can be put on these terms; and that the whole controversy has hitherto turned merely upon words. We shall begin with examining the doctrine of necessity.

It is universally allowed that matter, in all its operations, is actuated by a necessary force and that every natural effect is so precisely determined by the energy of its cause that no other effect, in such particular circumstances, could possibly have resulted from it. The degree and direction of every motion is, by the laws of nature, prescribed with such exactness that a living creature may as soon arise from the shock of two bodies as motion in any other degree or direction than what is actually produced by it. Would we, therefore, form a just and precise idea of *necessity*, we must consider whence that idea arises when we apply it to the operation of bodies.

It seems evident that, if all the scenes of nature were continually shifted in such a manner that no two events bore any resemblance to each other, but every object was entirely new, without any similitude to whatever had been seen before, we should never, in that case, have attained the least idea of necessity, or of a connection among these objects. We might say, upon such a supposition, that one object or event has followed another; not that one was produced by the other. The relation of cause and effect must be utterly unknown to mankind. Inference and reasoning concerning the operations of nature would, from that moment, be at an end; and the memory and senses remain the only canals, by which the knowledge of any real existence could possibly have access to the mind. Our idea, therefore, of necessity and causation arises entirely from the uniformity observable in the operations of nature, where similar objects are constantly conjoined together, and the mind is determined by custom to infer the one from the appearance of the other. These two circumstances form the whole of that necessity, which we ascribe to matter. Beyond the constant *conjunction* of similar objects, and the consequent *inference* from one to the other, we have no notion of any necessity or connection. . . .

I have frequently considered what could possibly be the reason why all mankind, though they have ever, without hesitation, acknowledged the doctrine of necessity in their whole practice and reasoning, have yet discovered such a reluctance to acknowledge it in words and have rather shown a propensity, in all ages, to profess the contrary opinion. The matter, I think, may be accounted for after the following manner. If we examine the operations of body, and the production of effects from their causes, we shall find that all our faculties can never carry us farther in our knowledge of this relation than barely to observe that particular objects are *constantly conjoined* together and that the mind is carried, by a *customary transition*, from the appearance of one to the belief of the other. But though this conclusion concerning human ignorance be the result of the strictest scrutiny of this subject, men still entertain a strong propensity to believe that they penetrate farther into the powers of nature and perceive something like a necessary connection between the cause and the effect. When again they turn their reflections towards the operations of their own minds and *feel* no such connection of the motive and the action, they are thence apt to suppose that there is a difference between the effects which result from material force and those which arise from thought and intelligence. But being once convinced that we know nothing farther of causation of any kind than merely the *constant conjunction* of objects, and the consequent *inference* of the mind from one to another, and finding that these two circumstances are universally allowed to have place in voluntary actions, we may be more easily led to own the same necessity common to all causes. And though this reasoning may contradict the systems of many philosophers, in ascribing necessity to the determinations of the will, we shall find, upon reflection, that they dissent from it in words only, not in their real sentiment. Necessity, according to the sense in which it is here taken, has never yet been rejected, nor can ever, I think, be rejected by any philosopher. It may only, perhaps, be pretended that the mind can perceive, in the operations of matter, some farther connection between the cause and effect; and connection that has not place in voluntary actions of intelligent beings. Now whether it be so or not can only appear upon examination; and it is incumbent on these philosophers to make good their assertion, by defining or describing that necessity and pointing it out to us in the operations of material causes.

It would seem, indeed, that men begin at the wrong end of this question concerning liberty and necessity, when they enter upon it by examining the faculties of the soul, the influence of the understanding, and the operations of the will. Let them first discuss a more simple question, namely, the operations of body and of brute unintelligent matter; and try whether they can there form any idea of causation and necessity, except that of a constant conjunction of objects, and subsequent inference of the mind from one to another. If these circumstances form, in reality, the whole of that necessity, which we conceive in matter, and if these circumstances be also universally acknowledged to take place in the operations of the mind, the dispute is at an end; at least, must be owned to be thenceforth merely verbal. But as long as we will rashly suppose that we have some farther idea of necessity and causation in the operations of external objects; at the same time, that we can find nothing farther in the voluntary actions of the mind; there is no possibility of bringing the question to any determinate issue, while we proceed upon so erroneous a supposition. The only method of undeceiving us is to mount up higher; to examine the narrow extent of science when applied to material causes; and to convince ourselves that all we know of them is the constant conjunction and inference above mentioned. We may, perhaps, find that it is with difficulty we are induced to fix such narrow limits to human understanding: but we can afterwards find no difficulty when we come to apply this doctrine to the actions of the will. For as it is evident that these have a regular conjunction with motives and circumstances and characters, and as we always draw inferences from one to the other, we must be obliged to acknowledge in words that necessity, which we have already avowed, in every deliberation of our lives and in every step of our conduct and behavior.

But to proceed in this reconciling project with regard to the question of liberty and necessity; the most contentious question of metaphysics, the most contentious science; it will not require many words to prove that all mankind have ever agreed in the doctrine of liberty as well as in that of necessity, and that the whole dispute, in this respect also, has been hitherto merely verbal. For what is meant by liberty, when applied to voluntary actions? We cannot surely mean that actions have so little connection with motives, inclinations, and circumstances, that one does not follow with a certain degree of uniformity from the other, and that one affords no inference by which we can conclude the existence of the other. For these are plain and acknowledged matters of fact. By liberty, then, we can only mean *a power of acting or not acting, according to the determinations of the will*; that is, if we choose to remain at rest, we may; if we choose to move, we also may. Now this hypothetical liberty is universally allowed to belong to everyone who is not a prisoner and in chains. Here, then, is no subject of dispute.

Whatever definition we may give of liberty, we should be careful to observe two requisite circumstances; *first*, that it be consistent with plain matter of fact; *secondly*, that it be consistent with itself. If we observe these circumstances and render our definition intelligible, I am persuaded that all mankind will be found of one opinion with regard to it.

It is universally allowed that nothing exists without a cause of its existence and that chance, when strictly examined, is a mere negative word and means not any real power which has anywhere a being in nature. But it is pretended that some causes are necessary, some not necessary. Here then is the advantage of definitions. Let anyone *define* a cause, without comprehending, as a part of the definition, a *necessary connection* with its effect; and let him show distinctly the origin of the idea, expressed by the definition; and I shall readily give up the whole controversy. But if the foregoing explication of the matter be received, this must be absolutely impracticable. Had not objects a regular conjunction with each other, we should never have entertained any notion of cause and effect; and this regular conjunction produces that inference of the understanding, which is the only connection that we can have any comprehension of. Whoever attempts a definition of cause, exclusive of these circumstances, will be obliged either to employ unintelligible terms or such as we are synonymous to the term which he endeavors to define. And if the definition above mentioned be admitted; liberty, when opposed to necessity, not to constraint, is the same thing with chance, which is universally allowed to have no existence.

STUDY QUESTIONS

1. What does Hume mean by "necessary connection"?
2. What does Hume mean by one event causing another?
3. How does Hume's notion of causality affect his views on the compatibility of liberty and necessity?
4. According to Hume, does anything exist by chance?

The Dilemma of Determinism

≁

WILLIAM JAMES

William James (1842–1910) was Professor of Philosophy and of Psychology at Harvard University. A critical figure in the development of American thought, he explores philosophical issues in a refreshing, accessible style, as in the case of this essay, originally delivered as an address to the Harvard University Divinity

Reprinted from William James, *The Will to Believe and Other Essays in Popular Philosophy* (1898).

students. James does not believe free will can be proved or disproved but explains why he assumes it to be true and acts as if it were true.

....

A common opinion prevails that the juice has ages ago been pressed out of the free-will controversy, and that no new champion can do more than warm up stale arguments which everyone has heard. This is a radical mistake. I know of no subject less worn out, or in which inventive genius has a better chance of breaking open new ground—not, perhaps, of forcing a conclusion or of coercing assent, but of deepening our sense of what the issue between the two parties really is, and of what the ideas of fate and of free will imply. . . . [M]y ambition limits itself to just one little point. If I can make two of the necessarily implied corollaries of determinism clearer to you than they have been made before, I shall have made it possible for you to decide before or against that doctrine with a better understanding of what you are about. And if you prefer not to decide at all, but to remain doubters, you will at least see more plainly what the subject of your hesitation is. I thus declaim openly on the threshold all pretension to prove to you that the freedom of the will is true. The most I hope is to induce some of you to follow my own example in assuming it true, and acting as if it were true. If it be true, it seems to me that this is involved in the strict logic of the case. Its truth ought not to be forced willy-nilly down our indifferent throats. It ought to be freely espoused by men who can equally well turn their backs upon it. In other words, our first act of freedom, if we are free, ought in all inward propriety to be to affirm that we are free. This should exclude, it seems to me, from the free-will side of the question all hope of a coercive demonstration—a demonstration which I, for one, am perfectly contented to go without.

With thus much understood at the outset, we can advance. But, not without one more point understood as well. The arguments I am about to urge all proceed on two suppositions: first, when we make theories about the world and discuss them with one another, we do so in order to attain a conception of things which shall give us subjective satisfaction; and, second, if there be two conceptions, and the one seems to us, on the whole, more rational than the other, we are entitled to suppose that the more rational one is truer of the two. I hope that you are all willing to make these suppositions with me; for I am afraid that if there be any of you here who are not, they will find little edification in the rest of what I have to say. I cannot stop to argue the point; but I myself believe that all the magnificent achievements of mathematical and physical science—our doctrines of evolution, of uniformity of law, and the rest—proceed from our indomitable desire to cast the world into a more rational shape in our minds than the shape into which it is thrown there by the crude order of our experience. The world has shown itself, to a great extent, plastic to this demand of ours for rationality. How much farther it will show itself plastic, no one can say. Our only means of finding out is to try; and I, for one, feel as free to try conceptions of moral as of mechanical or of logical rationality.

If a certain formula for expressing the nature of the world violates my moral demand, I shall feel free to throw it overboard, or at least to doubt it, as if it disappointed my demand for uniformity of sequence, for example; the one demand being, so far as I can see, quite as subjective and emotional as the other is. The principle of causality, for example—what is it but a postulate, an empty name covering simply a demand that the sequence of events shall some day manifest a deeper kind of belonging of one thing with another than the mere juxtaposition which now phenomenally appears? It is as much an altar to an unknown god as the one that Saint Paul found at Athens. All our scientific and philosophic ideals are altars to unknown gods. Uniformity is as much so as is free will. If this be admitted, we can debate on even terms. But if any one pretends that while freedom and variety are, in the first instance, subjective demands, necessity and uniformity are something altogether different, I do not see how we can debate at all.

To begin, then, I must suppose you are acquainted with all the usual arguments on the subject. I cannot stop to take up the old proofs from causation, from statistics, from the certainty with which we can foretell one another's conduct, from the fixity of character, and all the rest. But there are two *words* which usually encumber these classical arguments, and which we must immediately dispose of if we are to make any progress. One is the eulogistic word *freedom,* and the other is the opprobrious word *chance.* The word "chance" I wish to keep, but I wish to get rid of the word "freedom." Its eulogistic associations have so far overshadowed all the rest of its meaning that both parties claim the sole right to use it, and determinists today insist that they alone are freedom's champions. Old-fashioned determinism was what we may call *hard* determinism. It did not shrink from such words as fatality, bondage of the will, necessitation, and the like. Nowadays, we have a *soft* determinism which abhors harsh words and, repudiating fatality, necessity, and even predetermination, says that its real name is freedom; for freedom is only necessity understood, and bondage to the highest is identical with true freedom. Even a writer as little used to making capital out of soft words as Mr. Hodgson hesitates not to call himself a "free-will determinist."

Now, all this is a quagmire of evasion under which the real issue of fact has been entirely smothered. Freedom in all these senses presents simply no problem at all. No matter what the soft determinist means by it—whether he means the acting without external constraint, whether he means the acting rightly, or whether he means the acquiescing in the law of the whole—who cannot answer him that sometimes we are free and sometimes we are not? But there *is* a problem, an issue of fact and not of words, an issue of the most momentous importance, which is often decided without discussion in one sentence—nay, in one clause of a sentence—by those very writers who spin out whole chapters in their efforts to show what "true" freedom is; and that is the question of determinism, about which we are to talk tonight.

Fortunately, no ambiguities hang about this word or about its opposite, indeterminism. Both designate an outward way in which things may happen, and their cold and mathematical sound has no sentimental associations that can bribe our partiality either way in advance. Now, evidence of an external kind to decide between determinism and indeterminism is, as I intimated a while back, strictly impossible to find. Let us look at the difference between them and see for ourselves. What does determinism profess?

It professes that those parts of the universe already laid down absolutely appoint and decree what the other parts shall be. The future has no ambiguous possibilities hidden in its womb: the part we call the present is compatible with only one totality. Any other future complement than the one fixed from eternity is impossible. The whole is in each and every part, and welds it with the rest into an absolute unity, an iron block, in which there can be no equivocation or shadow of turning.

> With earth's first clay they did the last man knead,
> And there of the last harvest sowed the seed.
> And the first morning of creation wrote
> What the last dawn of reckoning shall read.

Indeterminism, on the contrary, says that the parts have a certain amount of loose play on one another, so that the laying down of one of them does not necessarily determine what the others shall be. It admits that possibilities may be in excess of actualities and that things not yet revealed to our knowledge may really in themselves be ambiguous. Of two alternative futures which we conceive, both may now be really possible; and the one becomes impossible only at the very moment when the other excludes it by becoming real itself. Indeterminism thus denies the world to be one unbending unit of fact. It says there is a certain ultimate pluralism in it; and, so saying, it corroborates our ordinary unsophisticated view of things. To that view, actualities seem to float in a wider sea of possibilities from out of which they are chosen; and, somewhere, indeterminism says, such possibilities exist and form a part of truth.

Determinism, on the contrary, says they exist *nowhere* and that necessity on the one hand and impossibility on the other are the sole categories of the real. Possibilities that fail to get realized are, for determinism, pure illusions: they never were possibilities at all. There is nothing inchoate, it says, about this universe of ours, all that was or is or shall be actual in it having been from eternity virtually there. The cloud of alternatives our minds escort this mass of actuality withal is a cloud of sheer deceptions, to which "impossibilities" is the only name which rightfully belongs.

The issue, it will be seen, is a perfectly sharp one, which no eulogistic terminology can smear over or wipe out. The truth *must* lie with one side or the other, and its lying with one side makes the other false.

The question relates solely to the existence of possibilities, in the strict sense of the term, as things that may, but need not, be. Both sides admit that a volition, for instance, has occurred. The indeterminists say another volition might have occurred in its place: the determinists swear that nothing could possibly have occurred in its place. Now, can science be called in to tell us which of these two point-blank contradicters of each other is right? Science professes to draw no con-clusions but such as are based on matters of fact, things that have actually happened; but how can any amount of assurance that something actually happened give us the least grain of information as to whether another thing might or might not have happened in its place? Only facts can be proved by other facts. With things that are possibilities and not facts, facts have no concern. If we have no other evidence than the evidence of existing facts, the possibility-question must remain a mystery never to be cleared up.

And the truth is that facts practically have hardly anything to do with making us either determinists or indeterminists. Sure enough, we make a flourish of quoting facts this way or that; and if we are determinists, we talk about the infallibility with which we can predict one another's conduct; while if we are indeterminists, we lay great stress on the fact that it is just because we cannot foretell one another's conduct, either in war or statecraft or in any of the great and small intrigues and businesses of men, that life is so intensely anxious and hazardous a game. But who does not see the wretched insufficiency of this so-called objective testimony on both sides? What fills up the gaps in our minds is something not objective, not external. What divides us into *possibility* men and *anti-possibility* men is differ-ent faiths or postulates—postulates of rationality. To this man the world seems more rational with possibilities in it—to that man more rational with possibilities excluded; and talk as we will about having to yield to evidence, what makes us monists or pluralists, determinists or indeterminists, is at bottom always some sentiment like this.

The stronghold of the deterministic sentiment is the antipathy to the idea of chance. As soon as we begin to talk indeterminism to our friends, we find a number of them shaking their heads. This notion of alternative possibility, they say, this admission that any one of several things may come to pass, is, after all, only a round-about name for chance; and chance is something the notion of which no sane mind can for an instant tolerate in the world. What is it, they ask, but barefaced crazy unreason, the negation of intelligibility and law? And if the slightest particle of it exists anywhere, what is to prevent the whole fabric from falling together, the stars from going out, and chaos from recommencing her topsy-turvy reign?

Remarks of this sort about chance will put an end to discussion as quickly as anything one can find. I have already told you that "chance" was a word I wished to keep and use. Let us then examine exactly what it means, and see whether it ought to be such a terrible bugbear to us. I fancy that squeezing the thistle boldly will rob it of its sting.

The sting of the word "chance" seems to lie in the assumption that it means something positive, and that if anything happens by chance, it must needs be something of an intrinsically irrational and preposterous sort. Now, chance means nothing of the kind. It is a purely negative and relative term, giving us no informa-tion about that of which it is predicated, except that it happens to be disconnected with something else—not controlled, secured, or necessitated by other things in advance of its own actual presence. As this point is the most subtle one of the whole lecture, and at the same time the point on which all the rest hinges, I beg you to pay particular attention to it. What I say is that it tells us nothing about what a thing may be in itself to call it "chance." It may be a bad thing, it may be a good thing. It may be lucidity, transparency, fitness incarnate, matching the whole system of other things, when it has once befallen, in an unimaginably perfect way. All you mean by calling it "chance" is that this is not guaranteed, that it may also fall out otherwise. For the system of other things has no positive hold on the chance-thing. Its origin is in a certain fashion negative: it escapes and says, "Hands off!" coming, when it comes, as a free gift, or not at all.

This negativeness, however, and this opacity of the chance-thing when thus considered *ab extra*, or from the point of view of previous things or distant things, do not preclude its having any amount of positiveness and luminosity from within, and at its own place and moment. All that its chance-character asserts about it is that there is something in it really of its own, something that is not the unconditional property of the whole. If the whole wants this property, the whole must wait till it can get it, if it be a matter of chance. That the universe may actually be a sort of joint-stock society of this sort, in which the sharers have both limited liabilities and limited powers, is of course a simple and conceivable notion.

Nevertheless, many persons talk as if the minutest dose of disconnectedness of one part with another, the smallest modicum of independence, the faintest tremor of ambiguity about the future, for example, would ruin everything and turn this goodly universe into a sort of insane sand-heap or nulliverse—no universe at all. Since future human volitions are, as a matter of fact, the only ambiguous things we are tempted to believe in, let us stop for a moment to make ourselves sure whether their independent and accidental character need be fraught with such direful consequences to the universe as these.

What is meant by saying that my choice of which way to walk home after the lecture is ambiguous and matter of chance as far as the present moment is concerned? It means that both Divinity Avenue and Oxford Street are called; but that only one, and that one *either* one shall be chosen. Now, I ask you seriously to suppose that this ambiguity of my choice is real; and then to make the impossible hypothesis that the choice is made twice over, and each time falls on a different street. In other words, imagine that I first walk through Divinity Avenue, and then imagine that the powers governing the universe annihilate ten minutes of time with all that it contained, and set me back at the door of this hall just as I was before the choice was made. Imagine then that, everything else being the same, I now make a different choice and traverse Oxford Street. You, as passive spectators, look on and see the two alternative universes—one of them with me walking through Divinity Avenue in it, the other with the same me walking through Oxford Street. Now, if you are determinists, you believe one of these universes to have been from eternity impossible: you believe it to have been impossible because of the intrinsic irrationality or accidentality somewhere involved in it. But looking outwardly at these universes, can you say which is the impossible and accidental one, and which the rational and necessary one? I doubt if the most iron-clad determinist among you could have the slightest glimmer of light at this point. In other words, either universe *after the fact* and once there would, to our means of observation and understanding, appear just as rational as the other. There would be absolutely no criterion by which we might judge one necessary and the other matter of chance. Suppose now we relieve the gods of their hypothetical task and assume my choice, once made, to be made forever. I go through Divinity Avenue for good and all. If, as good determinists, you now begin to affirm, what all good determinists punctually do affirm, that in the nature of things I couldn't have gone through Oxford Street—had I done so it would have been chance, irrationality, insanity, a horrid gap in nature—I simply call your attention to this, that your affirmation is what the Germans call a *Machtspruch*, a mere conception fulminated as a dogma and based on no insight into details. Before my choice, either street seemed as natural to you as to me. Had I happened to take Oxford Street, Divinity Avenue would have figured in your philosophy as the gap in nature; and you would have so proclaimed it with the best deterministic conscience in the world.

But what a hollow outcry, then, is this against a chance which, if it were present to us, we could by no character whatever distinguish from a rational necessity! I have taken the most trivial of examples, but no possible example could lead to any different result. For what are the alternatives which, in point of fact, offer themselves to human volition? What are those futures that now seem matters of chance? Are they not one and all like the Divinity Avenue and Oxford Street of our example? Are they not all of them *kinds* of things already here and based in the existing frame of nature? Is any one ever tempted to produce an *absolute* accident, something utterly irrelevant to the rest of the world? Do not all the motives that assail us, all the futures that offer themselves to our choice, spring equally from the soil of the past; and would not either one of them, whether realized through chance or through necessity, the moment it was realized, seem to us to fit that past, and in the completest and most continuous manner to interdigitate with the phenomena already there?[1]

The more one thinks of the matter, the more one wonders that so empty and gratuitous a hubbub as this outcry against chance should have found so great an echo in the hearts of men. It is a word which tells us absolutely nothing about what chances, or about the *modus operandi* of the chancing; and the use of it as a war-cry shows only a temper of intellectual absolutism, a demand that the world shall be a solid block, subject to one control—which temper, which demand, the world may not be bound to gratify at all. In every outwardly verifiable and practical respect, a world in which the alternatives that now actually distract *your* choice were decided by pure chance would be by *me* absolutely undistinguished from the world in which I now live. I am, therefore, entirely willing to call it, so far as your choices go, a world of chance for me. To *yourselves*, it is true, those very acts of choice, which to me are so blind, opaque, and external, are the opposites of this, for you are within them and effect them. To you they appear as decisions; and decisions, for him who makes them, are altogether peculiar psychic facts.

Self-luminous and self-justifying at the living moment in which they occur, they appeal to no outside moment to put its stamp upon them or make them continuous with the rest of nature. Themselves it is rather who seem to make nature continuous; and in their strange and intense function of granting consent to one possibility and withholding it from another, to transform an equivocal and double future into an inalterable and simple past.

But with the psychology of the matter, we have no concern this evening. The quarrel which determinism has with chance fortunately has nothing to do with this or that psychological detail. It is a quarrel altogether metaphysical. Determinism denies the ambiguity of future volitions, because it affirms that nothing future can be ambiguous. But we have said enough to meet the issue. Indeterminate future volitions *do* mean chance. Let us not fear to shout it from the house-tops if need be; for we now know that the idea of chance is, at bottom, exactly the same thing as the idea of gift—the one simply being a disparaging, and the other a eulogistic, name for anything on which we have no effective *claim*. And whether the world be the better or the worse for having either chances or gifts in it will depend altogether on *what* these uncertain and unclaimable things turn out to be.

And this at last brings us within sight of our subject. We have seen what determinism means: we have seen that indeterminism is rightly described as meaning chance; and we have seen that chance, the very name of which we are urged to shrink from as from a metaphysical pestilence, means only the negative fact that no part of the world, however big, can claim to control absolutely the destinies of the whole. But although, in discussing the word "chance," I may at moments have seemed to be arguing for its real existence, I have not meant to do so yet. We have not yet ascertained whether this is a world of chance or no; at most, we have agreed that it seems so. And I now repeat what I said at the outset, that, from any strict theoretical point of view, the question is insoluble. To deepen our theoretic sense of the *difference* between a world with chances in it and a deterministic world is the most I can hope to do; and this I may now at last begin upon, after all our tedious clearing of the way.

I wish first of all to show you just what the notion that this is a deterministic world implies. The implications I call your attention to are all bound up with the fact that it is a world in which we constantly have to make what I shall, with your permission, call judgments of regret. Hardly an hour passes in which we do not wish that something might be otherwise; and happy indeed are those of us whose hearts have never echoed the wish of Omar Khayyam—

> That we might clasp, ere closed, the book of fate,
>   And make the writer on a fairer leaf
> Inscribe our names, or quite obliterate.
>
> Ah! Love, could you and I with fate conspire
> To mend this sorry scheme of things entire,
>   Would we not shatter it to bits, and then
> Remould it nearer to the heart's desire?

Now, it is undeniable that most of these regrets are foolish, and quite on a par in point of philosophic value with the criticisms on the universe of that friend of our infancy, the hero of the fable, "The Atheist and the Acorn"—

Fool! had that bough a pumpkin bore,
Thy whimsies would have worked no more, etc.

Even from the point of view of our own ends, we should probably make a botch of remodelling the universe. How much more then from the point of view of ends we cannot see! Wise men therefore regret as little as they can. But still some regrets are pretty obstinate and hard to stifle—regrets for acts of wanton cruelty or treachery, for example, whether performed by others or by ourselves. Hardly any one can remain *entirely* optimistic after reading the confession of the murderer at Brockton the other day: how, to get rid of the wife whose continued existence bored him, he inveigled her into a deserted spot, shot her four times, and then, as she lay on the ground and said to him, "You didn't do it on purpose, did you, dear?" replied, "No, I didn't do it on purpose," as he raised a rock and smashed her skull. Such an occurrence, with the mild sentence and self-satisfaction of the prisoner, is a field for a crop of regrets, which one need not take up in detail. We feel that, although a perfect mechanical fit to the rest of the universe, it is a bad moral fit, and that something else would really have been better in its place.

But for the deterministic philosophy the murder, the sentence, and the pris-oner's optimism were all necessary from eternity; and nothing else for a moment had a ghost of a chance of being put in their place. To admit such a chance, the determinists tell us, would be to make a suicide of reason; so we must steel our hearts against the thought. And here our plot thickens, for we see the first of those difficult implications of determinism and monism which it is my purpose to make you feel. If this Brockton murder was called for by the rest of the universe, if it had come at its preappointed hour, and if nothing else would have been consistent with the sense of the whole, what are we to think of the universe? Are we stubbornly to stick to our judgment of regret, and say, though it *couldn't* be, yet it *would* have been a better universe with something different from this Brockton murder in it? That, of course, seems the natural and spontaneous thing for us to do; and yet it is nothing short of deliberately espousing a kind of *pessimism*. The judgment of regret calls the murder bad. Calling a thing bad means, if it means anything at all, that the thing ought not be, that something else ought to be in its stead. Determinism, in denying that anything else can be in its stead, virtually defines the universe as a place in which what ought to be is impossible—in other words, as an organism whose constitution is afflicted with an incurable taint and irremediable flaw. The pessimism of a Schopenhauer says no more than this—that the murder is a symptom; and that it is a vicious symptom because it belongs to a vicious whole, which can express its nature no otherwise than by bringing forth just such a symptom as that at this particular spot. Regret for the murder must transform itself, if we are determinists and wise, into a larger regret. It is absurd to regret the murder alone. Other things being what they are, *it* could not be different. What we should regret is that whole frame of things of which the murder is one member. I see no escape whatever from this pessimistic conclusion if, being determinists, our judgment of regret is to be allowed to stand at all.

The only deterministic escape from pessimism is everywhere to abandon the judgment of regret. That this can be done, history shows to be not impossible. The devil, *quoad existentiam*, may be good. That is, although he be a *principle* of evil, yet the universe, with such a principle in it, may practically be a better universe than it could have been without. On every hand, in a small way, we find that a certain amount of evil is a condition by which a higher form of good is brought. There is nothing to prevent anybody from generalizing this view, and trusting that if we could but see things in the largest of all ways, even such matters as this Brockton murder would appear to be paid for by the uses which follow in their train. An optimism *quand même*, a systematic and infatuated optimism like that ridiculed by Voltaire in his *Candide*, is one of the possible ideal ways in which a man may train himself to look upon life. Bereft of dogmatic hardness and lit up with the expression of a tender and pathetic hope, such an optimism has been the grace of some of the most religious characters that ever lived.

> Throb thine with Nature's throbbing breast,
> And all is clear from east to west.

Even cruelty and treachery may be among the absolutely blessed fruits of time, and to quarrel with any of their details may be blasphemy. The only real blasphemy, in short, may be that pessimistic temper of the soul which lets it give way to such things as regrets, remorse, and grief.

Thus, our deterministic pessimism may become a deterministic optimism at the price of extinguishing our judgments of regret.

But does not this immediately bring us into a curious logical predicament? Our determinism leads us to call our judgments of regret wrong, because they are pessimistic in implying that what is impossible yet ought to be. But how then about the judgments of regret themselves? If they are wrong, other judgments, judgments of approval presumably, ought to be in their place. But as they are necessitated, nothing else *can* be in their place; and the universe is just what it was before—namely, a place in which what ought to be appears impossible. We have got one foot out of the pessimistic bog, but the other one sinks all the deeper. We have rescued our actions from the bonds of evil, but our judgments are now held fast. When murders and treacheries cease to be sins, regrets are theoretic absurdities and errors. The theoretic and the active life thus play a kind of see-saw with each other on the ground of evil. The rise of either sends the other down. Murder and treachery cannot be good without regret being bad: regret cannot be good without treachery and murder being bad. Both, however, are supposed to have been foredoomed; so something must be fatally unreasonable, absurd, and wrong in the world. It must be a place of which either sin or error forms a necessary part. From this dilemma there seems at first sight no escape. Are we then so soon to fall back into the pessimism from which we thought we had emerged? And is there no possible way by which we may, with good intellectual consciences, call the cruelties and the treacheries, the reluctances and the regrets, *all* good together?

Certainly there is such a way, and you are probably most of you ready to formulate it yourselves. But, before doing so, remark how inevitably the question of determinism and indeterminism slides us into the question of optimism and pessimism, or, as our fathers called it, "The question of evil." The theological form of all these disputes is simplest and the deepest, the form from which there is the least escape—not because, as some have sarcastically said, remorse and regret are clung to with a morbid fondness by the theologians as spiritual luxuries, but because they are existing facts in the world, and as such must be taken into account in the deterministic interpretation of all that is fated to be. If they are fated to be error, does not the bat's wing of irrationality cast its shadow over the world? . . .

[T]he only consistent way of representing a pluralism and a world whose parts may affect one another through their conduct being either good or bad is the indeterministic way. What interest, zest, or excitement can there be in achieving the right way, unless we are enabled to feel that the wrong way is also a possible and a natural way—nay, more, a menacing and an imminent way? And what sense can there be in condemning ourselves for taking the wrong way, unless we need have done nothing of the sort, unless the right way was open to us as well? I cannot understand the willingness to act, no matter how we feel, without the belief that acts are really good and bad. I cannot understand the belief that an act is bad, without regret at its happening. I cannot understand regret without the admission of real, genuine possibilities in the world. Only then is it other than a mockery to feel, after we have failed to do our best, that an irreparable opportunity is gone from the universe, the loss of which it must forever after mourn.

If you insist that this is all superstition, that possibility is in the eye of science and reason impossibility, and that if I act badly 'tis that the universe was foredoomed to suffer this defect, you fall right back into the dilemma, the labyrinth, of pessimism and subjectivism, from out of whose toils we have just wound our way.

Now, we are of course free to fall back, if we please. For my own part, though, whatever difficulties may beset the philosophy of objective right and wrong, and the indeterminism it seems to imply, determinism, with its alternative pessimism or romanticism, contains difficulties that are greater still. But you will remember that I expressly repudiated awhile ago the pretension to offer any arguments which could be coercive in a so-called scientific fashion in this matter. And I consequently find myself, at the end of this long talk, obliged to state my conclusions in an altogether personal way. This personal method of appeal seems to be among the very conditions of the problem; and the most any one can do is to confess as candidly as he can the grounds for the faith that is in him, and leave his example to work on others as it may.

Let me, then, without circumlocution say just this. The world is enigmatical enough in all conscience, whatever theory we may take up toward it. The indeterminism I defend, the free-will theory of popular sense based on the judgment of regret, represents that world as vulnerable, and liable to be injured by certain of its parts if they act wrong. And it represents their acting wrong as a matter of possibility or accident, neither inevitable nor yet to be infallibly warded off. In all this, it is a theory devoid either of transparency or of stability. It gives us a pluralistic, restless universe, in which no single point of view can ever take in the whole scene; and to a mind possessed of the love of unity at any cost, it will, no doubt, remain forever inacceptable. A friend with such a mind once told me that the thought of my universe made him sick, like the sight of the horrible motion of a mass of maggots in their carrion bed.

But while I freely admit that the pluralism and the restlessness are repugnant and irrational in a certain way, I find that every alternative to them is irrational in a deeper way. The indeterminism with its maggots, if you please to speak so about it, offends only the native absolutism of my intellect—an absolutism which, after all, perhaps, deserves to be snubbed and kept in check. But the determinism with its necessary carrion, to continue the figure of speech, and with no possible maggots to eat the latter up, violates my sense of moral reality through and through. When, for example, I imagine such carrion as the Brockton murder, I cannot conceive it as an act by which the universe, as a whole, logically and necessarily expresses its nature without shrinking from complicity with such a whole. And I deliberately refuse to keep on terms of loyalty with the universe by saying blankly that the murder, since it does flow from the nature of the whole, is not carrion. There are *some* instinctive reactions which I, for one, will not tamper with. The only remaining alternative, the attitude of gnostical romanticism, wrenches my personal instincts in quite as violent a way. It falsifies the simple objectivity of their deliverance. It makes the goose-flesh the murder excites in me a sufficient reason for the perpetration of the crime. It transforms life from a tragic reality into an insincere melodramatic exhibition, as foul or as tawdry as any one's diseased curiosity pleases to carry it out. And with its consecration of the *roman naturaliste* state of mind, and its enthronement of the baser crew of Parisian *littérateurs* among the eternally indispensable organs by which the infinite spirit of things attains to that subjective illumination which is the task of its life, it leaves me in presence of a sort of subjective carrion considerably more noisome than the objective carrion I called it in to take away.

No! better a thousand times than such systematic corruption of our moral sanity, the plainest pessimism, so that it be straightforward; but better far than that, the world of chance. Make as great an uproar about chance as you please, I know that chance means pluralism and nothing more. If some of the members of the pluralism are bad, the philosophy of pluralism, whatever broad views it may deny me, permits me, at least, to turn to the other members with a clean breast of affection and an unsophisticated moral sense. And if I still wish to think of the world as a totality, it lets me feel that a world with a chance in it of being altogether good, even if the chance never comes to pass, is better than a world with no such chance at all. That "chance" whose very notion I am exhorted and conjured to banish from my view of the future as the suicide of reason concerning it, that "chance" is—what? Just this—the chance that in moral respects the future may be other and better than the past has been. This is the only chance we have any motive for supposing to exist. Shame, rather, on its repudiation and its denial! For its presence is the vital air which lets the world live, the salt which keeps it sweet.

NOTE

1. A favorite argument against free will is that if it be true, a man's murderer may as probably be his best friend as his worst enemy, a mother be as likely to strangle as to suckle her first-born, and all of us be as ready to jump from fourth-story windows as to go out of front doors, etc. Users of this argument should probably be excluded from debate till they learn what the real question is. "Free-will" does not say that everything that is physically conceivable is also morally possible. It merely says that of alternatives that really *tempt* our will more than one is really possible. Of course, the alternatives that do thus tempt our will are vastly fewer than the physical possibilities we can coldly fancy. Persons really tempted often do murder their best friends, mothers do strangle their first-borns, people do jump out of fourth stories, etc.

STUDY QUESTIONS

1. Explain the significance for James of his choice whether to walk home on Oxford Street or Divinity Avenue.
2. According to James, why does determinism imply that the world must be a place of which either sin or error forms a necessary part?
3. According to James, why is the issue of freedom and determinism insoluble?
4. If an issue is insoluble, are we still being reasonable if we take a position on it?

PART 6

Identity

A Case of Identity

✌

BRIAN SMART

Another metaphysical question concerns personal identity. What makes you the person you are? When you undergo physical or psychological changes, which element remains the same throughout, thus identifying you as the same individual before and after the changes?

Rather than beginning with the identifies of persons, however, let us start simply with the identities of objects. Imagine that you leave your car in a parking lot and return some hours later to discover that your vehicle has been hit by a huge truck and smashed to smithereens. A towing service arrives and takes the remaining pieces of your car to a repair garage, where you are assured that your car will be completely fixed. When you come to the garage two weeks later you are shown a car in perfect condition and told that it's your old car, now repaired. But is this car the same one you had left in the parking lot, or is it a new car? And how would you know? Suppose the original automobile was a gift that you valued highly. Do you still have that gift? Or has it been lost and replaced?

The following selection is by Brian Smart, who was Professor of Philosophy at the University of Keele. His example concerns a ship rather than a car, and he shows how a metaphysical issue about identity can lie at the heart of a legal dispute about ownership. See whether you believe the judges in the case ruled correctly.

....

A ship, X, is composed of a thousand old, but perfectly seaworthy, planks. It is brought into dock A where at hour 1 one of X's planks is removed to dock B and is replaced by a new plank. At hour 2 the same process is repeated so that by hour 1000 we have a ship Y in dock A composed of a thousand new planks and (since X's old planks have been reassembled as a ship) a ship Z in dock B composed of a thousand old planks. The problem is: with which ship—Y or Z—, if either, is X identical?

Let us give this problem a fictitious, but practical, setting.

Two shipowners, Morion and Bombos, are involved in a legal dispute. Morion had ordered a new ship from the Proteus brothers, shipbuilders and shiprepairers. Bombos had sent his ship, X, along to the same firm for a complete renewal of all its parts. (It should be explained that such a renewal would involve only half the labour costs of building a new ship from scratch.) Now the scheming Proteus brothers had persuaded Morion that what he wanted was a ship with well-seasoned timber and told him that his "new" ship was under construction in dock B. They saw their way to an enormous profit. For, while they would require a thousand

From Brian Smart, "How to Reidentify the Ship of Theseus," *Analysis*, 32:5, 1972. Reprinted by permission of the author.

new planks for renovating the ship that belonged to the shrewder and potentially more troublesome Bombos, they would clearly not need a second batch of new planks for building Morion's ship: they would use Bombos's old ones.

However the brothers' plans misfired all too literally. Just after Morion and Bombos had paid their bills, but before they had taken possession of Y and Z, there was a fire in dock B and Z was reduced to ashes. Under the law of Oudamou, where all these events occurred, the brothers were responsible for Z until Morion had taken possession. Unfortunately, they had not had Z insured. The insurance would have had to be for a "new" ship but under Oudamou law the newness of a ship was decided by the newness of its component parts.

Seeing their vast profits about to disappear the Proteus brothers, in heavy disguise, left Oudamou abandoning Y in dock A.

Morion was quickly persuaded by his lawyer to claim ownership of Y as he had paid for a new ship and Y was new under Oudamou law. Bombos's lawyer naturally put in a claim on his client's behalf for possession of Y on the ground that Y was identical with X.

When the case was heard . . . Bombos's lawyer argued . . . as follows. Over a period of time, objects like the human body can undergo a change of identity in all their parts. All that is required is that the overall *form* of the object is retained and that it occupies a continuous space-time path. The ship in dock A satisfies this condition, and so X, his client's ship, is identical with Y. X is not identical with Z precisely because the form of Z cannot be linked to the form of X by a continuous space–time path.

Morion's lawyer attacked this argument. . . . He urged that the spatio-temporal continuity of form was neither a necessary nor a sufficient condition of identity. It was not a necessary condition since a watch could be dismantled and the same parts reassembled to form the same watch. X had in fact been gradually dismantled in dock A and reassembled in dock B. The necessary and sufficient condition to be met was the identity of the parts of X with the parts of Z. This condition had been met by Z. Hence it was Bombos's ship that had been destroyed and his client's ship which remained. . . .

The judges agreed that objects could be dismantled and reassembled elsewhere, still retaining their identity. . . . They contended that the requirement was that the object's *parts* had been reassembled. . . . They claimed that Z did not contain X's parts at all. If the case had been one in which only the original planks were involved, there would be no difficulty over identifying Z's parts with X's parts. But the case was not as simple as that.

Their reasoning was this. When a plank had been removed from X and replaced by a new plank, it was the new plank that was now a part of X. The old plank *had been* a part of X but was no longer. Rather it was a part of Z which gradually came into being from hour 1 onwards. When completed, Z was not composed of any of X's parts but rather of what had been X's parts. "Being a part of X" was merely a temporary role in the career of the old planks which were now parts of Z. Using this line of argument, it was clear that X had simply changed the identity of its parts and that now its parts were identical with the parts of Y. Hence X was identical with Y. X was not identical with Z for they had no parts in common.

Thus they found in favour of Bombos.

STUDY QUESTIONS

1. Explain in your own words the case of Morion versus Bombos.
2. What are the strongest arguments Morion can offer?
3. What are the strongest arguments Bombos can offer?
4. Is any decision in the case arbitrary?

The Problem of Personal Identity

JOHN PERRY

So much for the identity of objects. Now what about the identity of persons? The issue is explained here by John Perry, Professor Emeritus of Philosophy at Stanford University.

....

Imagine the following. Elected to the Senate from your home state, you have become a key member of the Committee on Health, Education, and Welfare. This committee meets tomorrow to vote on a bill to fund a feasibility study of a new method for manufacturing shoes, which is alleged to produce a high-quality, inexpensive shoe that never wears out. Your support of the bill is essential; it has faced the bitter and unflagging opposition of the American Cobblers Association (ACA), led by their high-pressure lobbyist Peter Pressher, and a number of committee members intend to vote against it.

The morning of the committee vote you wake up, open your eyes, and glance at the clock on the shelf beyond the bed. Something seems strange. The bump in the covers you take to be your feet seems strangely distant. As you get out of bed you hit your head on a shelf that used to be a good three or four inches above it. You notice you are wearing a leather apron, which you are certain you didn't wear to bed. Puzzled, you go to the mirror. Staring out you see not your familiar clean-shaven face and squatty body, but the strapping frame and bearded countenance of Peter Pressher.

From John Perry, ed., *Personal Identity*, Berkeley, University of California Press, 1975. Reprinted by permission of the publisher.

You don't know what to think. Are you dreaming? Is this some kind of a trick? But you perform various tests to eliminate these possibilities. No doubt can remain: the body you have looks just like the body Peter Pressher normally has; it seems to be that very body.

Hearing laughter, you turn toward your living room. There on the sofa sits a person who looks exactly like you. That is exactly like you used to look, down to the inevitable magenta hollyhock (your state's flower) in the lapel. Before you can speak, he says,

"Surprised, Senator? I've made sacrifices for the Cobblers before. Getting this squatty body must take the prize. But I'll vote to kill that bill this afternoon, and it will be worth it . . ."

He speaks with your own deep and resonant voice, but the syntax and the fanatic overtones are unmistakably those of . . .

"Peter Pressher! . . ."

"Right, Senator, it's me. But as far as the rest of the world will ever know, it's really you. We snuck into your apartment last night and my brother Bimo, the brain surgeon, carefully removed your brain and put it in my body—or should I say your body. And vice versa. It's a new operation he's pioneering; he calls it a 'body transplant.'"

"You'll never get away with it . . ."

"Forget it. You have two choices. You can go around telling people that you're you, in which case I will sue you and my family, thinking they are your family, will sign papers to have you put away. Or you can start acting like me—become Peter Pressher—we think you'd make a good lobbyist. Almost as good a lobbyist as I'll make a senator!"

An incredible story? Let's hope so. Impossible? In one sense, yes. Physicians cannot now perform body transplants with human beings. But in another sense the case is perfectly possible. The day when such operations can be performed may not be so far away. Such an operation is possible in the sense of being conceivable. The story was not self-contradictory or incoherent. As a piece of science fiction, it's pretty mild stuff. . . .

Why are such cases puzzling, and why is the puzzlement of philosophical interest? Because they seem to disprove the view that a person is just a live human body. If we can have the same person on two different occasions when we don't have the same live human body, then it seems that a person cannot be identified with his body, and personal identity cannot be identified with bodily identity. This is puzzling simply because the assumption that the two go together plays a large role in our daily lives. We make it when we identify others on the basis of appearance, or observed movements, or fingerprints. What is the justification for this assumption? The abandonment of the simple theory that personal identity is just bodily identity carries with it the need to formulate an alternative account of personal identity.

But perhaps we are moving too fast. Are we so sure that the puzzle cases prove what they are alleged to? Perhaps the events imagined have been wrongly described, and the right description would go something like this:

You are a senator from your home state. One morning you wake up on the sofa, seeming to remember being Peter Pressher, a lobbyist for the ACA. A man emerges from a bedroom, who seems to remember being you. But subsequent tests—fingerprints, testimony of close friends, comparison of medical records, etc.—establish, to your delight and his dismay, that you are a duly elected senator with delusions (which you keep quiet about) of having been a lobbyist, while he is a lobbyist with delusions of having been a senator. His situation is rather ironic. He willingly participated in a scheme where his brain (and so various of his psychological characteristics) were exchanged for your brain (and so various of your psychological characteristics). He seems to have thought that would somehow constitute a "body transfer," and he would wind up in the Senate. (He was taught this by a philosophy professor in college, whom he is suing.) What actually happened, of course, is that two people underwent radical changes in character and personality, and acquired delusive memories, as a result of brain surgery.

How shall we decide between these two descriptions? In a sense, they do not disagree about what happened—which sounds emanated from which bodies, and so forth. So neither can be proven incorrect by reference to the occurrence of these events. But in another sense they are blatantly contradictory, and one must be wrong.

STUDY QUESTIONS

1. In Perry's story, are you Peter Pressher?
2. How do you decide the matter?
3. Could you be mistaken about who you are?
4. Is any decision in the matter arbitrary?

The Unimportance of Identity

DEREK PARFIT

Derek Parfit (1942–2017) was Emeritus Fellow at All Souls College of the University of Oxford. Using a variety of unusual yet provocative thought experiments, he argues against the importance of personal identity.

From Henry Harris, ed., *Identity*, Clarendon Press, 1995. Reprinted by permission of the publisher.

Personal identity is widely thought to have great rational and moral significance. Thus it is the fact of identity which is thought to give us our reason for concern about our own future. And several moral principles, such as those of desert or distributive justice, presuppose claims about identity. The separateness of persons, or the non-identity of different people, has been called "the basic fact for morals."

I can comment here on only one of these questions: what matters in our survival. I mean by that, not what makes our survival good, but what makes our survival matter, whether it will be good or bad. What is it, in our survival, that gives us a reason for special anticipatory or prudential concern? ...

Most of us believe that we should care about our future because it will be *our* future. I believe that what matters is not identity but certain other relations. To help us to decide between these views, we should consider cases where identity and those relations do not coincide.

Which these cases are depends on which criterion of identity we accept. I shall start with the simplest form of the Physical Criterion, according to which a person continues to exist if and only if that person's body continues to exist. That must be the view of those who believe that persons just are bodies. And it is the view of several of the people who identify persons with human beings. Let's call this the *Bodily Criterion.*

Suppose that, because of damage to my spine, I have become partly paralysed. I have a brother, who is dying of a brain disease. With the aid of new techniques, when my brother's brain ceases to function, my head could be grafted onto the rest of my brother's body. Since we are identical twins, my brain would then control a body that is just like mine, except that it would not be paralysed.

Should I accept this operation? Of those who assume that identity is what matters, three groups would answer No. Some accept the Bodily Criterion. These people believe that, if this operation were performed, I would die. The person with my head tomorrow would be my brother, who would mistakenly think that he was me. Other people are uncertain what would happen. They believe that it would be risky to accept this operation, since the resulting person might not be me. Others give a different reason why I should reject this operation: that it would be indeterminate whether that person would be me. On all these views, it matters who that person would be.

On my view, that question is unimportant. If this operation were performed, the person with my head tomorrow would not only believe that he was me, seem to remember living my life, and be in every other way psychologically like me. These facts would also have their normal cause, the continued existence of my brain. And this person's body would be just like mine. For all these reasons, his life would be just like the life that I would have lived, if my paralysis had been cured. I believe that, given these facts, I should accept this operation. It is irrelevant whether this person would be me.

That may seem all important. After all, if he would not be me, I shall have ceased to exist. But, if that person would not be me, this fact would just consist in another fact. It would just consist in the fact that my body will have been replaced below the neck. When considered on its own, is that second fact important? Can it matter in itself that the blood that will keep my brain alive will circulate, not through my own heart and lungs, but through my brother's heart and lungs? Can it matter in itself that my brain will control, not the rest of my body, but the rest of another body that is exactly similar? . . .

According to my argument, we should now conclude that neither of these facts could matter greatly. Since it would not be in itself important that my head would be grafted onto this body, and that would be all there was to the fact that the resulting person would not be me, it would not be in itself important that this person would not be me. Perhaps it would not be irrational to regret these facts a little. But, I believe, they would be heavily outweighed by the fact that, unlike me, the resulting person would not be paralysed. . . .

On my view, what matters is what is going to happen. If I knew that my head could be grafted onto the rest of a body that is just like mine, and that the resulting person would be just like me, I need not ask whether the resulting person could be correctly called me. That is not a further difference in what is going to happen. . . .

It may now be objected: "By choosing this example, you are cheating. Of course you should accept this operation. But that is because the resulting person *would* be you. We should reject the Bodily Criterion. So this case cannot show that identity is not what matters."

Since there are people who accept this criterion, I am not cheating. It is worth trying to show these people that identity is not what matters. But I accept part of this objection. I agree that we should reject the Bodily Criterion. . . .

I am now assuming that we accept the Brain-Based Psychological Criterion. We believe that, if there will be one future person who will have enough of my brain to be psychologically continuous with me, that person would be me. On this view, there is another way to argue that identity is not what matters.

We can first note that, just as I could survive with less than my whole body, I could survive with less than my whole brain. People have survived, and with little psychological change, even when, through a stroke or injury, they have lost the use of half their brain.

Let us next suppose that the two halves of my brain could each fully support ordinary psychological functioning. That may in fact be true of certain people. If it is not, we can suppose that, through some technological advance, it has been made true of me. Since our aim is to test our beliefs about what matters, there is no harm in making such assumptions.

We can now compare two more possible operations. In the first, after half my brain is destroyed, the other half would be successfully transplanted into the empty skull of a body that is just like mine. Given our assumptions, we should conclude that, here too, I would survive. Since I would survive if my brain were transplanted, and I would survive with only half my brain, it would be unreasonable to deny that I would survive if that remaining half were transplanted. So, in this *Single Case*, the resulting person would be me.

Consider next the *Double Case*, or *My Division*. Both halves of my brain would be successfully transplanted, into different bodies that are just like mine. Two people would wake up, each of whom has half my brain, and is, both physically and psychologically, just like me.

Since these would be two different people, it cannot be true that each of them is me. That would be a contradiction. If each of them was me, each would be one and the same person: me. So they could not be two different people.

Could it be true that only one of them is me? That is not a contradiction. But, since I have the same relation to each of these people, there is nothing that could make me one of them rather than the other. It cannot be true, of either of these people, that he is the one who could be correctly called me.

How should I regard these two operations? Would they preserve what matters in survival? In the Single Case, the one resulting person would be me. The relation between me now and that future person is just an instance of the relation between me now and myself tomorrow. So that relation would contain what matters. In the Double Case, my relation to that person would be just the same. So this relation must still contain what matters. Nothing is missing. But that person cannot here be claimed to be me. So identity cannot be what matters.

We may object that, if that person isn't me, something *is* missing. *I'm* missing. That may seem to make all the difference. How can everything still be there if *I'm* not there?

Everything is still there. The fact that I'm not there is not a real absence. The relation between me now and that future person is in itself the same. As in the Single Case, he has half my brain, and he is just like me. The difference is only that, in this Double Case, I also have the same relation to the other resulting person. Why am I not there? The explanation is only this. When this relation holds between me now and a single person in the future, we can be called one and the same person. When this relation holds between me now and *two* future people, I cannot be called one and the same as each of these people. But that is not a difference in the nature or the content of this relation. In the Single Case, where half my brain will be successfully transplanted, my prospect is survival. That prospect contains what matters. In the Double Case, where both halves will be successfully transplanted, nothing would be lost.

It can be hard to believe that identity is not what matters. But that is easier to accept when we see why, in this example, it is true. It may help to consider this analogy. Imagine a community of persons who are like us, but with two exceptions. First, because of facts about their reproductive system, each couple has only two children, who are always twins. Second, because of special features of their psychology, it is of great importance for the development of each child that it should not, through the death of its sibling, become an only child. Such children suffer psychological damage. It is thus believed, in this community, that it matters greatly that each child should have a twin.

Now suppose that, because of some biological change, some of the children in this community start to be born as triplets. Should their parents think this a disaster, because these children don't have twins? Clearly not. These children don't have twins only because they each have *two* siblings. Since each child has two siblings, the trio must be called, not twins, but triplets. But none of them will suffer damage as an only child. These people should revise their view. What matters isn't having a twin: it is having at least one sibling.

In the same way, we should revise our view about identity over time. What matters isn't that there will be someone alive who will be me. It is rather that there will be at least one living person who will be psychologically continuous with me as I am now, and/or who has enough of my brain. When there will be only one such person, he can be described as me. When there will be two such people, we cannot claim that each will be me. But that is as trivial as the fact that, if I had two identical siblings, they could not be called my twins.

If, as I have argued, personal identity is not what matters, we must ask what does matter. There are several possible answers. And, depending on our answer, there are several further implications. Thus there are several moral questions which I have no time even to mention. I shall end with another remark about our concern for our own future.

That concern is of several kinds. We may want to survive partly so that our hopes and ambitions will be achieved. We may also care about our future in the kind of way in which we care about the well-being of certain other people, such as our relatives or friends. But most of us have, in addition, a distinctive kind of egoistic concern. If I know that my child will be in pain, I may care about his pain more than I would about my own future pain. But I cannot fearfully anticipate my child's pain. And if I knew that my Replica would take up my life where I leave off, I would not look forward to that life.

This kind of concern may, I believe, be weakened, and be seen to have no ground, if we come to accept [my] view. In our thoughts about our own identity, we are prone to illusions. That is why the so-called "problem cases" seem to raise problems: why we find it hard to believe that, when we know the other facts, it is an empty or a merely verbal question whether we shall still exist. Even after we accept [my] view, we may continue, at some level, to think and feel as if that view were not true. Our own continued existence may still seem an independent fact, of a peculiarly deep and simple kind. And that belief may underlie our anticipatory concern about our own future....

Even the use of the word "I" can lead us astray. Consider the fact that, in a few years, I shall be dead. This fact can seem depressing. But the reality is only this. After a certain time, none of the thoughts and experiences that occur will be directly causally related to this brain, or be connected in certain ways to these present experiences. That is all this fact involves. And, in that redescription, my death seems to disappear.

STUDY QUESTIONS

1. How do you analyze the Single Case?
2. How do you analyze the Double Case?
3. Do you agree with Parfit that identity is unimportant?
4. Do you believe that the strangeness of the cases Parfit discusses weakens his conclusion?

An Essay Concerning Human Understanding

ن

JOHN LOCKE

John Locke, whose work we read previously, differentiates between the concepts of same body and same person. Bodily identity is determined for a man or woman the same way it is determined for a ship or a swan. The criterion for personal identity, however, is continuity of consciousness, that is, memory. If you remember scoring the winning goal in a crucial game a decade ago, then you are the person who scored that goal.

Locke's position has the advantage of reconciling his materialism with the possibility of immortality, because a person's identity would not depend on bodily survival. An apparent disadvantage of Locke's position, however, is the fallibility of memory. For instance, you might be the person who scored that winning goal, yet you might not remember doing so.

....

9. ... [T]o find wherein personal identity consists, we must consider what *person* stands for;—which, I think, is a thinking intelligent being that has reason and reflection and can consider itself as itself, the same thinking thing, in different times and places; which it does only by that consciousness which is inseparable from thinking, and, as it seems to me, essential to it: it being impossible for any one to perceive without *perceiving* that he does perceive. When we see, hear, smell, taste, feel, meditate, or will anything, we know that we do so. Thus it is always as to our present sensations and perceptions: and by this every one is to himself that which he calls self:—it not being considered, in this case, whether the same self be continued in the same or divers substances. For, since consciousness always accompanies thinking, and it is that which makes every one to be what he calls self, and thereby distinguishes himself from all other thinking things, in this alone consists personal identity, i.e., the sameness of a rational being: and as far as this consciousness can be extended backwards to any past action or thought, so far reaches the identity of that person; it is the same self now it was then; and it is by the same self with this present one that now reflects on it, that that action was done.

From *An Essay Concerning Human Understanding* by John Locke (1690), Book II, Chapter 27.

10. But it is further inquired, whether it be the same identical substance. This few would think they had reason to doubt of, if these perceptions, with their consciousness, always remained present in the mind, whereby the same thinking thing would be always consciously present, and, as would be thought, evidently the same to itself. But that which seems to make the difficulty is this, that this consciousness being interrupted always by forgetfulness, there being no moment of our lives wherein we have the whole train of all our past actions before our eyes in one view, but even the best memories losing the sight of one part whilst they are viewing another; and we sometimes, and that the greatest part of our lives, not reflecting on our past selves, being intent on our present thoughts, and in sound sleep having no thoughts at all, or at least none with that consciousness which remarks our waking thoughts,—I say, in all these cases, our consciousness being interrupted, and we losing the sight of our past selves, doubts are raised whether we are the same thinking thing, i.e., the same *substance* or no. Which, however reasonable or unreasonable, concerns not *personal* identity at all. The question being what makes the same person; and not whether it be the same identical substance, which always thinks in the same person, which, in the case, matters not at all: different substances, by the same consciousness (where they do partake in it) being united into one person, as well as different bodies by the same life are united into one animal, whose identity is preserved in that change of substances by the unity of one continued life. For, it being the same consciousness that makes a man be himself to himself, personal identity depends on that only, whether it be annexed solely to one individual substance, or can be continued in a succession of several substances. For as far as any intelligent being *can* repeat the idea of any past action with the same consciousness it had of it at first, and with the same consciousness it has of any present action; so far it is the same personal self. For it is by the consciousness it has of its present thoughts and actions, that it is *self to itself* now, and so will be the same self, as far as the same consciousness can extend to actions past or to come; and would be by distance of time, or change of substance, no more two persons, than a man be two men by wearing other clothes today than he did yesterday, with a long or a short sleep between: the same consciousness uniting those distant actions in the same person, whatever substances contributed to their production.

11. That this is so, we have some kind of evidence in our very bodies, all whose particles, whilst vitally united to this same thinking conscious self, so that *we feel* when they are touched, and are affected by, and conscious of good or harm that happens to them, are a part of ourselves, i.e., of our thinking conscious self. Thus, the limbs of his body are to every one a part of himself; he sympathizes and is concerned for them. Cut off a hand, and thereby separate it from that consciousness he had of its heat, cold, and other affections, and it is then no longer a part of that which is himself, any more than the remotest part of matter. Thus, we see the *substance* whereof personal self consisted at one time may be varied at another, without the change of personal identity; there being no question about the same person, though the limbs which but now were a part of it, be cut off. . . .

15. And thus may we be able, without any difficulty, to conceive the same person at the resurrection, though in a body not exactly in make or parts the same

which he had here,—the same consciousness going along with the soul that inhabits it. But yet the soul alone, in the change of bodies, would scarce to any one but to him that makes the soul the man, be enough to make the same man. For should the soul of a prince, carrying with it the consciousness of the prince's past life, enter and inform the body of a cobbler, as soon as deserted by his own soul, every one sees he would be the same *person* with the prince, accountable only for the prince's actions: but who would say it was the same *man*? The body too goes to the making the man, and would, I guess, to everybody determine the man in this case, wherein the soul, with all its princely thoughts about it, would not make another man: but he would be the same cobbler to every one besides himself. I know that, in the ordinary way of speaking, the same person, and the same man, stand for one and the same thing. And indeed every one will always have a liberty to speak as he pleases, and to apply what articulate sounds to what ideas he thinks fit, and change them as often as he pleases. But yet, when we will inquire what makes the same *spirit, man*, or *person*, we must fix the ideas of spirit, man, or person in our minds; and having resolved with ourselves what we mean by them, it will not be hard to determine in either of them, or the like, when it is the same, and when not.

16. But though the immaterial substance or soul does not alone, wherever it be, and in whatsoever state, make the same *man*; yet it is plain, consciousness, as far as ever it can be extended—should it be to ages past—unites existences and actions very remote in time into the same *person*, as well as it does the existences and actions of the immediately preceding moment: so that whatever has the consciousness of present and past actions, is the same person to whom they both belong. Had I the same consciousness that I saw the ark and Noah's flood, as that I saw an overflowing of the Thames last winter, or as that I write now, I could no more doubt that I who write this now, that saw the Thames overflowed last winter, and that viewed the flood at the general deluge, was the same *self*,—place that self in what *substance* you please—than that I who write this am the same *myself* now whilst I write (whether I consist of all the same substance, material or immaterial, or no) that I was yesterday. For as to this point of being the same self, it matters not whether this present self be made up of the same or other substances—I being as much concerned, and as justly accountable for any action that was done a thousand years since, appropriated to me now by this self-consciousness, as I am for what I did the last moment. . . .

20. But yet possibly it will still be objected,—Suppose I wholly lose the memory of some parts of my life, beyond a possibility of retrieving them, so that perhaps I shall never be conscious of them again; yet am I not the same person that did those actions, had those thoughts that I once was conscious of, though I have now forgot them? To which I answer, that we must here take notice what the word *I* is applied to; which, in this case, is the *man* only. And the same man being presumed to be the same person, I is easily here supposed to stand also for the same person. But if it be possible for the same man to have distinct incommunicable consciousness at different times, it is past doubt the same man would at different times make different persons; which, we see, is the sense of mankind in the solemnest declaration of their opinions, human laws not punishing the mad man for

the sober man's actions, nor the sober man for what the mad man did,—thereby making them two persons: which is somewhat explained by our way of speaking in English when we say such an one is "not himself," or is "beside himself"; in which phrases it is insinuated, as if those who now, or at least first used them, thought that self was changed; the selfsame person was no longer in that man.

STUDY QUESTIONS

1. According to Locke, what is a person?
2. According to Locke, could a person remain the same but with an entirely changed body?
3. How does Locke respond to the observation that a person can lose memories?
4. What does Locke's view of personal identity imply about the possibility of immortality?

A Treatise of Human Nature

DAVID HUME

David Hume, whose work we read previously, denies the view that we are conscious of a simple self, identical from one time to another. Instead, Hume maintains that we are but a collection of perceptions succeeding each other with great rapidity. A person's identity is no more invariable than that of a plant or vegetable. In short, the concept of a human soul is a fiction.

OF PERSONAL IDENTITY

There are some philosophers who imagine we are every moment intimately conscious of what we call our self, that we feel its existence and its continuance in existence, and are certain beyond the evidence of a demonstration both of its perfect identity and simplicity. . . .

Unluckily all these positive assertions are contrary to that very experience which is pleaded for them, nor have we any idea of *self* after the manner it is here explained. For from what impression could this idea be derived? This question it is impossible to answer without a manifest contradiction and absurdity, and yet it is a question which must necessarily be answered, if we would have the idea of

From *A Treatise of Human Nature* by David Hume (1738).

self pass for clear and intelligible. It must be some one impression that gives rise to every real idea. But self or person is not any one impression, but that to which our several impressions and ideas are supposed to have a reference. If any impression gives rise to the idea of self, that impression must continue invariably the same through the whole course of our lives, since self is supposed to exist after that manner. But there is no impression constant and invariable. Pain and pleasure, grief and joy, passions and sensations succeed each other and never all exist at the same time. It cannot, therefore, be from any of these impressions or from any other that the idea of self is derived, and, consequently, there is no such idea.

But further, what must become of all our particular perceptions upon this hypothesis? All these are different, and distinguishable, and separable from each other, and may be separately considered, and may exist separately, and have no need of anything to support their existence. After what manner therefore do they belong to self and how are they connected with it? For my part, when I enter most intimately into what I call *myself*, I always stumble on some particular perception or other, of heat or cold, light or shade, love or hatred, pain or pleasure. I never can catch *myself* at any time without a perception and never can observe anything but the perception. When my perceptions are removed for any time, as by sound sleep, so long am I insensible of myself and may truly be said not to exist. And were all my perceptions removed by death and could I neither think, nor feel, nor see, nor love, nor hate after the dissolution of my body. I should be entirely annihilated, nor do I conceive what is further requisite to make me a perfect nonentity. If any-one, upon serious and unprejudiced reflection, thinks he has a different notion of *himself*, I must confess I can reason no longer with him. All I can allow him is that he may be in the right as well as I and that we are essentially different in this particular. He may, perhaps, perceive something simple and continued which he calls *himself*, though I am certain there is no such principle in me.

But setting aside some metaphysicians of this kind, I may venture to affirm of the rest of mankind that they are nothing but a bundle or collection of different perceptions which succeed each other with an inconceivable rapidity and are in a perpetual flux and movement. Our eyes cannot turn in their sockets without vary-ing our perceptions. Our thought is still more variable than our sight and all our other senses and faculties contribute to this change; nor is there any single power of the soul which remains unalterably the same perhaps for one moment. The mind is a kind of theater where several perceptions successively make their appearance, pass, repass, glide away, and mingle in an infinite variety of postures and situations. There is properly no *simplicity* in it at one time nor *identity* in different, whatever natural propensity we may have to imagine that simplicity and identity. The com-parison of the theater must not mislead us. They are the successive perceptions only that constitute the mind, nor have we the most distant notion of the place where these scenes are represented or of the materials of which it is composed.

What, then, gives us so great a propensity to ascribe an identity to these suc-cessive perceptions and to suppose ourselves possessed of an invariable and unin-terrupted existence through the whole course of our lives? . . .

We have a distinct idea of an object that remains invariable and uninterrupted through a supposed variation of time and this idea we call that of *identity* or *sameness*. We have also a distinct idea of several different objects existing in succession and connected together by a close relation, and this, to an accurate view, affords as perfect a notion of *diversity* as if there was no manner of relation among the objects. But though these two ideas of identity and a succession of related objects be in themselves perfectly distinct and even contrary, yet it is certain that, in our common way of thinking, they are generally confounded with each other. That action of the imagination by which we consider the uninterrupted and invariable object and that by which we reflect on the succession of related objects are almost the same to the feeling, nor is there much more effort of thought required in the latter case than in the former. The relation facilitates the transition of the mind from one object to another and renders its passage as smooth as if it contemplated one continued object. This resemblance is the cause of the confusion and mistake and makes us substitute the notion of identity instead of that of related objects. However at one instant we may consider the related succession as variable or interrupted, we are sure the next to ascribe to it a perfect identity and regard it as invariable and uninterrupted. Our propensity to this mistake is so great from the resemblance above mentioned that we fall into it before we are aware, and though we incessantly correct ourselves by reflection and return to a more accurate method of thinking, yet we cannot long sustain our philosophy or take off this bias from the imagination. Our last resource is to yield to it and boldly assert that these different related objects are in effect the same, however interrupted and variable. In order to justify to ourselves this absurdity, we often feign some new and unintelligible principle that connects the objects together and prevents their interruption or variation. Thus we feign the continued existence of the perceptions of our senses to remove the interruption and run into the notion of a *soul*, and *self*, and *substance* to disguise the variation. But, we may further observe that where we do not give rise to such a fiction, our propensity to confound identity with relation is so great that we are apt to imagine something unknown and mysterious, connecting the parts, besides their relation, and this I take to be the case with regard to the identity we ascribe to plants and vegetables. And even when this does not take place, we still feel a propensity to confound these ideas, though we are not able fully to satisfy ourselves in that particular nor find anything invariable and uninterrupted to justify our notion of identity.

Thus the controversy concerning identity is not merely a dispute of words. For when we attribute identity, in an improper sense, to variable or interrupted objects, our mistake is not confined to the expression, but is commonly attended with a fiction, either of something invariable and uninterrupted, or of something mysterious and inexplicable, or at least with a propensity to such fictions. What will suffice to prove this hypothesis to the satisfaction of every fair inquirer is to show from daily experience and observation that the objects which are variable or interrupted, and yet are supposed to continue the same, are such only as consist of a succession of parts, connected together by resemblance, contiguity, or causation. . . .

A ship of which a considerable part has been changed by frequent repairs is still considered as the same, nor does the difference of the materials hinder us from ascribing an identity to it. The common end, in which the parts conspire, is the same under all their variations and affords an easy transition of the imagination from one situation of the body to another. . . .

[T]hough everyone must allow that in a very few years both vegetables and animals endure a *total* change, yet we still attribute identity to them, while their form, size, and substance are entirely altered. An oak that grows from a small plant to a large tree is still the same oak, though there is not one particle of matter or figure of its parts the same. An infant becomes a man and is sometimes fat, sometimes lean without any change in his identity. . . .

[A] man who hears a noise that is frequently interrupted and renewed says it is still the same noise, though it is evident the sounds have only a specific identity or resemblance and there is nothing numerically the same but the cause which produced them. In like manner it may be said without breach of the propriety of language that such a church, which was formerly of brick, fell to ruin and that the parish rebuilt the same church of freestone and according to modern architecture. Here neither the form nor materials are the same, nor is there anything common to the two objects but their relation to the inhabitants of the parish. Yet this alone is sufficient to make us denominate them the same. But we must observe that in these cases the first object is in a manner annihilated before the second comes into existence, by which means we are never presented in any one point of time with the idea of difference and multiplicity and, for that reason, are less scrupulous in calling them the same. . . .

The identity which we ascribe to the mind of man is only a fictitious one and of a like kind with that which we ascribe to vegetables and animal bodies. It cannot, therefore, have a different origin, but must proceed from a like operation of the imagination upon like objects.

But lest this argument should not convince the reader, though in my opinion perfectly decisive, let him weigh the following reasoning, which is still closer and more immediate. It is evident that the identity which we attribute to the human mind, however perfect we may imagine it to be, is not able to run the several different perceptions into one and make them lose their characters of distinction and difference which are essential to them. It is still true that every distinct perception which enters into the composition of the mind is a distinct existence, and is different, and distinguishable, and separable from every other perception, either contemporary or successive. But as, notwithstanding this distinction and separability, we suppose the whole train of perceptions to be united by identity, a question naturally arises concerning this relation of identity, whether it is something that really binds our several perceptions together or only associates their ideas in the imagination, that is, in other words, whether, in pronouncing concerning the identity of a person, we observe some real bond among his perceptions or only feel one among the ideas we form of them. This question we might easily decide if we would recollect what has been already proved at large, namely, that the understanding never observes any real connection among objects and that even the union of cause and effect, when strictly examined, resolves itself into a customary association of ideas. For from this it evidently follows that identity is nothing really belonging to these different perceptions and uniting them together but rather is merely a quality which we attribute to them because of the union of their ideas in the imagination when we reflect upon them. . . .

The only question, therefore, which remains is by what relations this uninterrupted progress of our thought is produced when we consider the successive existence of a mind or thinking person. And here it is evident we must confine ourselves to resemblance and causation. . . .

As memory alone acquaints us with the continuance and extent of this succession of perceptions, it is to be considered upon that account chiefly as the source of personal identity. Had we no memory, we never should have any notion of causation nor consequently of that chain of causes and effects which constitute our self or person. But having once acquired this notion of causation from the memory, we can extend the same chain of causes and consequently the identity of our persons beyond our memory and can comprehend times, circumstances, and actions which we have entirely forgotten, but suppose in general to have existed. For how few of our past actions are there of which we have any memory? Who can tell me, for instance, what were his thoughts and actions on the 1st of January 1715, the 11th of March 1719, and the 3rd of August 1733? Or will he affirm, because he has entirely forgotten the incidents of these days, that the present self is not the same person with the self of that time, and by that means overturn all the most established notions of personal identity? In this view, therefore, memory does not so much *produce* as *discover* personal identity by showing us the relation of cause and effect among our different perceptions. It will be incumbent on those who affirm that memory produces entirely our personal identity to give a reason why we can thus extend our identity beyond our memory.

The whole of this doctrine leads us to a conclusion which is of great importance in the present affair, namely that all the nice and subtle questions concerning personal identity can never possibly be decided and are to be regarded rather as grammatical than as philosophical difficulties. Identity depends on the relations of ideas, and these relations produce identity by means of that easy transition they occasion. But as the relations and the easiness of the transition may diminish by insensible degrees, we have no just standard by which we can decide any dispute concerning the time when they acquire or lose a title to the name of identity. All the disputes concerning the identity of connected objects are merely verbal, except so far as the relation of parts gives rise to some fiction or imaginary principle of union as we have already observed.

STUDY QUESTIONS

1. According to Hume, what is the self?
2. According to Hume, why are we confused about the nature of the self?
3. Why does Hume conclude that questions concerning personal identity raise grammatical rather than philosophical difficulties?
4. What does Hume's view of personal identity imply about the possibility of immortality?

Essays on the Intellectual Powers of Man

THOMAS REID

Thomas Reid (1710–1796) was the founder of what became known as the Scottish "common sense" school of philosophy. He was Professor of Moral Philosophy at the University of Glasgow.

Reid was a critic of the empiricism of Locke and Hume. Reid affirms that persons are permanent, indivisible, immaterial substances, and he appeals to memory as the basis for our knowledge of our personal identity. Unlike Locke, however, whose views he criticizes, Reid emphasizes that memory provides the evidence of my personal identity but doesn't make me the person I am.

....

OF IDENTITY

The conviction which every man has of his Identity, as far back as his memory reaches, needs no aid of philosophy to strengthen it; and no philosophy can weaken it, without first producing some degree of insanity.

The philosopher, however, may very properly consider this conviction as a phaenomenon of human nature worthy of his attention. If he can discover its cause, an addition is made to his stock of knowledge. If not, it must be held as a part of our original constitution, or an effect of that constitution produced in a manner unknown to us. . . .

That we may form as distinct a notion as we are able of this phenomenon of the human mind, it is proper to consider what is meant by identity in general, what by our own personal identity, and how we are led into that invincible belief and conviction which every man has of his own personal identity, as far as his memory reaches.

Identity in general, I take to be a relation between a thing which is known to exist at one time, and a thing which is known to have existed at another time. If you ask whether they are one and the same, or two different things, every man of common sense understands the meaning of your question perfectly. Whence we may infer with certainty that every man of common sense has a clear and distinct notion of identity.

If you ask a definition of identity, I confess I can give none; it is too simple a notion to admit of logical definition. I can say it is a relation; but I cannot find words to express the specific difference between this and other relations, though I am in no danger of confounding it with any other. I can say that diversity is

---

From *Essays on the Intellectual Powers of Man* by Thomas Reid (1785), Essay III.

a contrary relation and that similitude and dissimilitude are another couple of contrary relations, which every man easily distinguishes in his conception from identity and diversity.

I see evidently that identity supposes an uninterrupted continuance of existence. That which hath ceased to exist cannot be the same with that which afterwards begins to exist; for this would be to suppose a being to exist after it ceased to exist, and to have had existence before it was produced, which are manifest contradictions. Continued uninterrupted existence is therefore necessarily implied in identity.

Hence we may infer that identity cannot, in its proper sense, be applied to our pains, our pleasures, our thoughts, or any operation of our minds. The pain felt this day is not the same individual pain which I felt yesterday, though they may be similar in kind and degree and have the same cause. The same may be said of every feeling and of every operation of mind: they are all successive in their nature, like time itself, no two moments of which can be the same moment.

It is otherwise with the parts of absolute space. They always are, and were, and will be the same. So far, I think, we proceed upon clear ground in fixing the notion of identity in general.

It is, perhaps, more difficult to ascertain with precision the meaning of Personality; but it is not necessary in the present subject: it is sufficient for our purpose to observe, that all mankind place their personality in something that cannot be divided, or consist of parts. A part of a person is a manifest absurdity.

When a man loses his estate, his health, his strength, he is still the same person and has lost nothing of his personality. If he has a leg or an arm cut off, he is the same person he was before. The amputated member is no part of his person, otherwise it would have a right to a part of his estate and be liable for a part of his engagements; it would be entitled to a share of his merit and demerit—which is manifestly absurd. A person is something indivisible. . . .

My personal identity, therefore, implies the continued existence of that indivisible thing which I call myself. Whatever this self may be, it is something which thinks, and deliberates, and resolves, and acts, and suffers. I am not thought, I am not action. I am not feeling; I am something that thinks, and acts, and suffers. My thoughts, and actions, and feelings, change every moment—they have no continued, but a successive existence: but that *self* or *I*, to which they belong, is permanent and has the same relation to all the succeeding thoughts, actions, and feelings, which I call mine.

Such are the notions that I have of my personal identity. But perhaps it may be said, this may all be fancy without reality. How do you know?—what evidence have you, that there is such a permanent self which has a claim to all the thoughts, actions, and feelings, which you call yours?

To this I answer, that the proper evidence I have of all this is remembrance. I remember that, twenty years ago, I conversed with such a person; I remember several things that passed in that conversation; my memory testifies not only that this was done, but that it was done by me who now remember it. If it was done by me, I must have existed at that time and continued to exist from that time to the present:

if the identical person whom I call myself had not a part in that conversation, my memory is fallacious—it gives a distinct and positive testimony of what is not true. Every man in his senses believes what he distinctly remembers, and everything he remembers convinces him that he existed at the time remembered.

Although memory gives the most irresistible evidence of my being the identical person that did such a thing, at such a time, I may have other good evidence of things which befell me and which I do not remember: I know who bare me and suckled me, but I do not remember these events.

It may here be observed (though the observation would have been unnecessary, if some great philosophers had not contradicted it) that it is not my remembering any action of mine that *makes* me to be the person who did it. This remembrance makes me to *know* assuredly that I did it; *but I might have done it, though I did not remember it*. That relation to me, which is expressed by saying that *I did it*, would be the same, though I had not the least remembrance of it. To say that my remembering that I did such a thing, or, as some choose to express it, my being conscious that I did it, makes me to have done it, appears to me as great an absurdity as it would be to say that my belief that the world was created made it to be created.

When we pass judgment on the identity of other persons than ourselves, we proceed upon other grounds, and determine from a variety of circumstances, which sometimes produce the firmest assurance, and sometimes leave room for doubt. The identity of persons has often furnished matter of serious litigation before tribunals of justice. But no man of a sound mind ever doubted of his own identity, as far as he distinctly remembered.

The identity of a person is a perfect identity: wherever it is real, it admits of no degrees; and it is impossible that a person should be in part the same and in part different; because a person is a *monad* and is not divisible into parts. The evidence of identity in other persons than ourselves does indeed admit of all degrees, from what we account certainty, to the least degree of probability. But still it is true that the same person is perfectly the same and cannot be so in part, or in some degree only.

For this cause, I have first considered personal identity as that which is perfect in its kind, and the natural measure of that which is imperfect.

We probably at first derive our notion of identity from that natural conviction which every man has from the dawn of reason of *his own* identity and continued existence. The operations of our minds are all successive and have no continued existence. But the thinking being has a continued existence, and we have an invincible belief that it remains the same when all its thoughts and operations change.

Our judgments of the identity of objects of sense seem to be formed much upon the same grounds as our judgments of the identity of *other persons* than ourselves. Wherever we observe great *similarity*, we are apt to presume identity if no reason appears to the contrary. Two objects ever so like, when they are perceived at the same time, cannot be the same; but if they are presented to our senses at different times, we are apt to think them the same merely from their similarity.

Whether this be a natural prejudice or from whatever cause it proceeds, it certainly appears in children from infancy; and when we grow up, it is confirmed in most instances by experience: for we rarely find two individuals of the same species that are not distinguishable by obvious differences. A man challenges a thief whom he finds in possession of his horse or his watch, only on similarity. When the watchmaker swears that he sold this watch to such a person, his testimony is grounded on similarity. The testimony of witnesses to the identity of a person is commonly grounded on no other evidence.

Thus it appears that the evidence we have of our own identity, as far back as we remember, is totally of a different kind from the evidence we have of the identity of other persons, or of objects of sense. The first is grounded on *memory* and gives undoubted certainty. The last is grounded on *similarity* and on other circumstances, which in many cases are not so decisive as to leave no room for doubt.

It may likewise be observed that the identity of *objects of sense* is never perfect. All bodies, as they consist of innumerable parts that may be disjoined from them by a great variety of causes, are subject to continual changes of their substance, increasing, diminishing, changing insensibly. When such alterations are gradual, because language could not afford a different name for every different state of such a changeable being, it retains the same name and is considered as the same thing. Thus we say of an old regiment that it did such a thing a century ago, though there now is not a man alive who then belonged to it. We say a tree is the same in the seed-bed and in the forest. A ship of war, which has successively changed her anchors, her tackle, her sails, her masts, her planks, and her timbers, while she keeps the same name, is the same.

The identity, therefore, which we ascribe to bodies, whether natural or artificial, is not perfect identity; it is rather something which, for the conveniency of speech, we call identity. It admits of a great change of the subject, providing the change be *gradual;* sometimes, even of a total change. And the changes which in common language are made consistent with identity differ from those that are thought to destroy it, not in *kind* but in *number* and *degree.* It has no fixed nature when applied to bodies; and questions about the identity of a body are very often questions about words. But identity, when applied to persons, has no ambiguity, and admits not of degrees, or of more and less. It is the foundation of all rights and obligations and of all accountableness; and the notion of it is fixed and precise.

... OF MR. LOCKE'S ACCOUNT OF OUR PERSONAL IDENTITY

... Mr. Locke tells us ... "that personal identity—that is, the sameness of a rational being—consists in consciousness alone, and, as far as this consciousness can be extended backwards to any past action or thought, so far reaches the identity of that person. So that, whatever hath the consciousness of present and past actions, is the same person to whom they belong."

This doctrine hath some strange consequences, which the author was aware of, such as, that, if the same consciousness can be transferred from one intelligent being to another, which he thinks we cannot shew to be impossible, then two or twenty intelligent beings may be the same person. And if the intelligent being may lose the consciousness of the actions done by him, which surely is possible, then he is not the person that did those actions; so that one intelligent being may be two or twenty different persons, if he shall so often lose the consciousness of his former actions.

There is another consequence of this doctrine, which follows no less necessarily, though Mr. Locke probably did not see it. It is that a man may be, and at the same time not be, the person that did a particular action.

Suppose a brave officer to have been flogged when a boy at school, for robbing an orchard, to have taken a standard from the enemy in his first campaign, and to have been made a general in advanced life: Suppose also, which must be admitted to be possible, that, when he took the standard, he was conscious of his having been flogged at school, and that when made a general he was conscious of his taking the standard, but had absolutely lost the consciousness of his flogging.

These things being supposed, it follows, from Mr. Locke's doctrine, that he who was flogged at school is the same person who took the standard, and that he who took the standard is the same person who was made a general. Whence it follows, if there be any truth in logic, that the general is the same person with him who was flogged at school. But the general's consciousness does not reach so far back as his flogging—therefore, according to Mr. Locke's doctrine, he is not the person who was flogged. Therefore, the general is, and at the same time is not, the same person with him who was flogged at school.

STUDY QUESTIONS

1. How does Reid respond to the request for a definition of identity?
2. What evidence does Reid offer for the existence of a permanent self?
3. How does the evidence we have for our own identity differ from the evidence we have for the identity of other persons?
4. According to Reid, why does Locke's theory of personal identity lead to a contradiction?

PART 7

God

Does God Exist?

✒

ERNEST NAGEL

One metaphysical issue that interests us all is whether God exists. A theist believes God does exist. An atheist believes God does not exist. An agnostic believes the available evidence is insufficient to decide the matter. Which of these positions is the most reasonable?

The first step in answering this question is to determine what is meant by the term "God." Let us adopt a view common to many religious believers that "God" refers to an all-good, all-powerful, eternal Creator of the world. The question then is whether a being of that description exists.

The next essay considers various arguments for and against the existence of God. The author is Ernest Nagel (1901–1985), who was Professor of Philosophy at Columbia University.

....

1

I want now to discuss three classical arguments for the existence of God, arguments which have constituted at least a partial basis for theistic commitments. As long as theism is defended simply as a dogma, asserted as a matter of direct revelation or as the deliverance of authority, belief in the dogma is impregnable to rational argument. In fact, however, reasons are frequently advanced in support of the theistic creed, and these reasons have been the subject of acute philosophical critiques.

One of the oldest intellectual defenses of theism is the cosmological argument, also known as the argument from a first cause. Briefly put, the argument runs as follows. Every event must have a cause. Hence an event A must have as cause some event B, which in turn must have a cause C, and so on. But if there is no end to this backward progression of causes, the progression will be infinite; and in the opinion of those who use this argument, an infinite series of actual events is unintelligible and absurd. Hence there must be a first cause, and this first cause is God, the initiator of all change in the universe.

The argument is an ancient one, and . . . it has impressed many generations of exceptionally keen minds. The argument is nonetheless a weak reed on which to rest the theistic thesis. Let us waive any question concerning the validity of the principle that every event has a cause, for though the question is important,

From *Basic Beliefs*, ed. J. E. Fairchild. Copyright © 1959 by Sheridan House, Inc. Reprinted by permission of the publisher.

its discussion would lead us far afield. However, if the principle is assumed, it is surely incongruous to postulate a first cause as a way of escaping from the coils of an infinite series. For if everything must have a cause, why does not God require one for His own existence? The standard answer is that He does not need any, because He is self-caused. But if God can be self-caused, why cannot the world itself be self-caused? Why do we require a God transcending the world to bring the world into existence and to initiate changes in it? On the other hand, the supposed inconceivability and absurdity of an infinite series of regressive causes will be admitted by no one who has competent familiarity with the modern mathematical analysis of infinity. The cosmological argument does not stand up under scrutiny.

The second "proof" of God's existence is usually called the ontological argument. It too has a long history going back to early Christian days, though it acquired great prominence only in medieval times. The argument can be stated in several ways, one of which is the following. Since God is conceived to be omnipotent, he is a perfect being. A perfect being is defined as one whose essence or nature lacks no attributes (or properties) whatsoever, one whose nature is complete in every respect. But it is evident that we have an idea of a perfect being, for we have just defined the idea; and since this is so, the argument continues, God who is the perfect being must exist. Why must he? Because his existence follows from his defined nature. For if God lacked the attribute of existence, he would be lacking at least one attribute and would therefore not be perfect. To sum up, since we have an idea of God as a perfect being, God must exist.

There are several ways of approaching this argument, but I shall consider only one. The argument was exploded by the eighteenth-century philosopher Immanuel Kant. The substance of Kant's criticism is that it is just a confusion to say that existence is an attribute, and that though the *word* "existence" may occur as the grammatical predicate in a sentence, no attribute is being predicated of a thing when we say that the thing exists or has existence. Thus, to use Kant's example, when we think of $100 we are thinking of the nature of this sum of money; but the nature of $100 remains the same whether we have $100 in our pockets or not. Accordingly, we are confounding grammar with logic if we suppose that some characteristic is being attributed to the nature of $100 when we say that a hundred dollar bill exists in someone's pocket.

To make the point clearer, consider another example. When we say that a lion has a tawny color, we are predicating a certain attribute of the animal, and similarly when we say that the lion is fierce or is hungry. But when we say the lion exists, all that we are saying is that something is (or has the nature of) a lion; we are not specifying an attribute which belongs to the nature of anything that is a lion. In short, the word "existence" does not signify any attribute, and in consequence no attribute that belongs to the nature of anything. Accordingly, it does not follow from the assumption that we have an idea of a perfect being that such a being exists. For the idea of a perfect being does not involve the attribute of existence as a constituent of that idea, since there is no such attribute. The ontological argument thus has a serious leak, and it can hold no water.

2

The two arguments discussed thus far are purely dialectical, and attempt to establish God's existence without any appeal to empirical data. The next argument, called the argument from design, is different in character, for it is based on what purports to be empirical evidence. I wish to examine two forms of this argument.

One variant of it calls attention to the remarkable way in which different things and processes in the world are integrated with each other, and concludes that this mutual "fitness" of things can be explained only by the assumption of a divine architect who planned the world and everything in it. For example, living organisms can maintain themselves in a variety of environments, and do so in virtue of their delicate mechanisms which adapt the organisms to all sorts of environmental changes. There is thus an intricate pattern of means and ends throughout the animate world. But the existence of this pattern is unintelligible, so the argument runs, except on the hypothesis that the pattern has been deliberately instituted by a Supreme Designer. If we find a watch in some deserted spot, we do not think it came into existence by chance, and we do not hesitate to conclude that an intelligent creature designed and made it. But the world and all its contents exhibit mechanisms and mutual adjustments that are far more complicated and subtle than are those of a watch. Must we not therefore conclude that these things too have a Creator?

The conclusion of this argument is based on an inference from analogy: the watch and the world are alike in possessing a congruence of parts and an adjustment of means to ends; the watch has a watch-maker; hence the world has a world-maker. But is the analogy a good one? Let us once more waive some important issues, in particular the issue whether the universe is the unified system such as the watch admittedly is. And let us concentrate on the question, What is the ground for our assurance that watches do not come into existence except through the operations of intelligent manufacturers? The answer is plain. We have never run across a watch which has not been deliberately made by someone. But the situation is nothing like this in the case of the innumerable animate and inanimate systems with which we are familiar. Even in the case of living organisms, though they are generated by their parent organisms, the parents do not "make" their progeny in the same sense in which watch-makers make watches. And once this point is clear, the inference from the existence of living organisms to the existence of a supreme designer no longer appears credible.

Moreover, the argument loses all its force if the facts which the hypothesis of a divine designer is supposed to explain can be understood on the basis of a better supported assumption. And indeed, such an alternative explanation is one of the achievements of Darwinian biology. For Darwin showed that one can account for the variety of biological species, as well as for their adaptations to their environments, without invoking a divine creator and acts of special creation. The Darwinian theory explains the diversity of biological species in terms of chance variations in the structure of organisms, and of a mechanism of selection which retains those variant forms that possess some advantages for survival. The evidence for these assumptions is considerable; and developments subsequent to Darwin have only strengthened the case for a thoroughly naturalistic explanation of the facts of biological adaptation. In any event, this version of the argument from design has nothing to recommend it.

A second form of this argument has been recently revived in the speculations of some modern physicists. No one who is familiar with the facts can fail to be impressed by the success with which the use of mathematical methods has enabled us to obtain intellectual mastery of many parts of nature. But some thinkers have therefore concluded that since the book of nature is ostensibly written in mathematical language, nature must be the creation of a divine mathematician. However, the argument is most dubious. For it rests, among other things, on the assumption that mathematical tools can be successfully used only if the events of nature exhibit some *special* kind of order, and on the further assumption that if the structure of things were different from what they are, mathematical language would be inadequate for describing such structure. But it can be shown that no matter what the world were like—even if it impressed us as being utterly chaotic—it would still possess some order and would in principle be amenable to a mathematical description. In point of fact, it makes no sense to say that there is absolutely *no* pattern in any conceivable subject matter. To be sure, there are differences in complexities of structure, and if the patterns of events were sufficiently complex, we might not be able to unravel them. But however that may be, the success of mathematical physics in giving us some understanding of the world around us does not yield the conclusion that only a mathematician could have devised the patterns of order we have discovered in nature.

3

The inconclusiveness of the three classical arguments for the existence of God was already made evident by Kant, in a manner substantially not different from the above discussion. There are, however, other types of arguments for theism that have been influential in the history of thought, two of which I wish to consider, even if only briefly.

Indeed, though Kant destroyed the classical intellectual foundations for theism, he himself invented a fresh argument for it. Kant's attempted proof is not intended to be a purely theoretical demonstration and is based on the supposed facts of our moral nature. It has exerted an enormous influence on subsequent theological speculation. In barest outline, the argument is as follows. According to Kant, we are subject not only to physical laws like the rest of nature, but also to moral ones. These moral laws are categorical imperatives, which we must heed not because of their utilitarian consequences, but simply because as auton-omous moral agents it is our duty to accept them as binding. However, Kant was keenly aware that though virtue may be its reward, the virtuous man (that is, the man who acts out of a sense of duty and in conformity with the moral law) does not always receive his just desserts in this world; nor did he shut his eyes to the fact that evil men frequently enjoy the best things this world has to offer. In short, virtue does not always reap happiness. Nevertheless, the high-est human good is the realization of happiness commensurate with one's virtue; and Kant believed that it is a practical postulate of the moral life to promote this good. But what can guarantee that the highest good is realizable? Such a guarantee can be found only in God, who must therefore exist if the highest good is not to be a fatuous ideal. The existence of an omnipotent, omniscient, and omnibenevolent God is thus postulated as a necessary condition for the possibility of a moral life.

Despite the prestige this argument has acquired, it is difficult to grant it any force. It is easy enough to postulate God's existence. But as Bertrand Russell observed in another connection, postulation has all the advantages of theft over honest toil. No postulation carries with it any assurance that what is postulated is actually the case. And though we may postulate God's existence as a means to guar-anteeing the possibility of realizing happiness together with virtue, the postulation establishes neither the actual realizability of this ideal nor the fact of his existence. Moreover, the argument is not made more cogent when we recognize that it is based squarely on the highly dubious conception that considerations of utility and human happiness must not enter into the determination of what is morally obliga-tory. Having built his moral theory on a radical separation of means from ends, Kant was driven to the desperate postulation of God's existence in order to relate them again. The argument is thus at best a tour de force, contrived to remedy a fatal flaw in Kant's initial moral assumptions. It carries no conviction to anyone who does not commit Kant's initial blunder.

One further type of argument, pervasive in much Protestant theological lit-erature, deserves brief mention. Arguments of this type take their point of depar-ture from the psychology of religious and mystical experience. Those who have undergone such experiences often report that during the experience they feel themselves to be in the presence of the divine and holy, that they lose their sense of self-identity and become merged with some fundamental reality, or that they enjoy a feeling of total dependence upon some ultimate power. The overwhelm-ing sense of transcending one's finitude which characterizes such vivid periods of life, and of coalescing with some ultimate source of all existence, is then taken to be compelling evidence for the existence of a supreme being. In a variant form of this argument, other theologians have identified God as the object which satisfies the commonly experienced need for integrating one's scattered and conflicting impulses into a coherent unity, or as the subject which is of ultimate concern to us. In short, a proof of God's existence is found in the occurrence of certain distinctive experiences.

It would be flying in the face of well-attested facts were one to deny that such experiences frequently occur. But do these facts constitute evidence for the conclusion based on them? Does the fact, for example, that an individual experiences a profound sense of direct contact with an alleged transcendent ground of all reality constitute competent evidence for the claim that there is such a ground and that it is the immediate cause of the experience? If well-established canons for evaluating evidence are accepted, the answer is surely negative. No one will dispute that many men do have vivid experiences in which such things as ghosts or pink elephants appear before them; but only the hopelessly credulous will without further ado count such experiences as establishing the existence of ghosts and pink elephants. To establish the existence of such things, evidence is required that is obtained under controlled conditions and that can be confirmed by independent inquirers. Again, though a man's report that he is suffering pain may be taken at face value, one cannot take at face value the claim, were he to make it, that it is the food he ate which is the cause (or a contributory cause) of his felt pain—not even if the man were to report a vivid feeling of abdominal disturbance. And similarly, an overwhelming feeling of being in the presence of the Divine is evidence enough for admitting the genuineness of such feeling; it is no evidence for the claim that a supreme being with a substantial existence independent of the experience is the cause of the experience.

4

Thus far the discussion has been concerned with noting inadequacies in various arguments widely used to support theism. However, much atheistic criticism is also directed toward exposing incoherencies in the very thesis of theism. I want therefore to consider this aspect of the atheistic critique, though I will restrict myself to the central difficulty in the theistic position which arises from the simultaneous attribution of omnipotence, omniscience, and omnibenevolence to the Deity. The difficulty is that of reconciling these attributes with the occurrence of evil in the world. Accordingly, the question to which I now turn is whether, despite the existence of evil, it is possible to construct a theodicy which will justify the ways of an infinitely powerful and just God to man.

Two main types of solutions have been proposed for this problem. One way that is frequently used is to maintain that what is commonly called evil is only an illusion, or at worst only the "privation" or absence of good. Accordingly, evil is not "really real," it is only the "negative" side of God's beneficence, it is only the product of our limited intelligence which fails to plumb the true character of God's creative bounty. A sufficient comment on this proposed solution is that facts are not altered or abolished by rebaptizing them. Evil may indeed be only an appearance and not genuine. But this does not eliminate from the realm of appearance the tragedies, the sufferings, and the iniquities which men so frequently endure. And it raises once more, though on another level, the problem of reconciling the fact that there is evil in the realm of appearance with God's alleged omnibenevolence. In any event, it is small comfort to anyone suffering a cruel misfortune for which he is in no way responsible, to be told that what he is undergoing is only the absence of good. It is a gratuitous insult to mankind, a symptom of insensitivity and indifference to human suffering, to be assured that all the miseries and agonies men experience are only illusory.

Another gambit often played in attempting to justify the ways of God to man is to argue that the things called evil are evil only because they are viewed in isolation; they are not evil when viewed in proper perspective and in relation to the rest of creation. Thus, if one attends to but a single instrument in an orchestra, the sounds issuing from it may indeed be harsh and discordant. But if one is placed at a proper distance from the whole orchestra, the sounds of that single instrument will mingle with the sounds issuing from the other players to produce a marvellous bit of symphonic music. Analogously, experiences we call painful undoubtedly occur and are real enough. But the pain is judged to be an evil only because it is experienced in a limited perspective—the pain is there for the sake of a more inclusive good, whose reality eludes us because our intelligences are too weak to apprehend things in their entirety.

It is an appropriate retort to this argument that of course we judge things to be evil in a human perspective, but that since we are not God this is the only proper perspective in which to judge them. It may indeed be the case that what is evil for us is not evil for some other part of creation. However, we are not this other part of creation, and it is irrelevant to argue that were we something other than what we are, our evaluations of what is good and bad would be different. Moreover, the worthlessness of the argument becomes even more evident if we remind ourselves that it is unsupported speculation to suppose that whatever is evil in a finite perspective is good from the purported perspective of the totality of things. For the argument can be turned around: what we judge to be a good is a good only because it is viewed in isolation; when it is viewed in proper perspective and in relation to the entire scheme of things, it is an evil. This is in fact a standard form of the argument for a universal pessimism. Is it any worse than the similar argument for a universal optimism? The very raising of this question is a *reductio ad absurdum* of the proposed solution to the ancient problem of evil.

I do not believe it is possible to reconcile the alleged omnipotence and omnibenevolence of God with the unvarnished facts of human existence. In point of fact, many theologians have concurred in this conclusion; for in order to escape from the difficulty which the traditional attributes of God present, they have assumed that God is not all powerful, and that there are limits as to what He can do in his efforts to establish a righteous order in the universe. But whether such a modified theology is better off is doubtful; and in any event, the question still remains whether the facts of human life support the claim that an omnibenevolent Deity, though limited in power, is revealed in the ordering of human history. It is pertinent to note in this connection that though there have been many historians who have made the effort, no historian has yet succeeded in showing to the satisfaction of his professional colleagues that the hypothesis of a Divine Providence is capable of explaining anything which cannot be explained just as well without this hypothesis.

STUDY QUESTIONS

1. What connection does Nagel find between Darwinian biology and the design argument?
2. What is Nagel's assessment of the evidence for God's existence drawn from mystical experience?
3. How does Nagel respond to the claim that evil is only an illusion?
4. If the existence of God is compatible with the worst evils imaginable, what comfort is provided by believing in God?

Why God Allows Evil

Richard Swinburne

> Richard Swinburne, who taught at the University of Oxford, is a leading proponent of theism and other tenets of Christianity. In our next selection he offers a theodicy, a defense of God's goodness and omnipotence in the face of the existence of evil.

The world ... contains much evil. An omnipotent God could have prevented this evil, and surely a perfectly good and omnipotent God would have done so. So why is there this evil? Is not its existence strong evidence against the existence of God? It would be unless we can construct what is known as a theodicy, an explanation of why God would allow such evil to occur. I believe that that can be done, and I shall outline a theodicy. . . . I emphasize that . . . in writing that God would do this or that, I am not taking for granted the existence of God, but merely claiming that, if there is a God, it is to be expected that he would do certain things, including allowing the occurrence of certain evils; and so, I am claiming, their occurrence is not evidence against his existence.

It is inevitable that any attempt by myself or anyone else to construct a theodicy will sound callous, indeed totally insensitive to human suffering. Many theists, as well as atheists, have felt that any attempt to construct a theodicy evinces an immoral approach to suffering. I can only ask the reader to believe that I am not totally insensitive to human suffering, and that I do mind about the agony of poisoning, child abuse, bereavement, solitary imprisonment, and marital infidelity as much as anyone else. True, I would not in most cases recommend that a pastor give this chapter to victims of sudden distress at their worst moment to read for consolation.

But this is not because its arguments are unsound; it is simply that most people in deep distress need comfort, not argument. Yet there is a problem about why God allows evil, and, if the theist does not have (in a cool moment) a satisfactory answer to it, then his belief in God is less than rational, and there is no reason why the atheist should share it. To appreciate the argument of this chapter, each of us needs to stand back a bit from the particular situation of his or her own life and that of close relatives and friends (which can so easily seem the only important thing in the world), and ask very generally what good things would a generous and everlasting God give to human beings in the course of a short earthly life. Of course thrills of pleasure and periods of contentment are good things, and—other things being equal—God would certainly seek to provide plenty of those. But a generous God will seek to give deeper good things than these. He will seek to give us great responsibility for ourselves, each other, and the world, and thus a share in his own creative activity of determining what sort of world it is to be. And he will seek to make our lives valuable, of great use to ourselves and each other. The problem is that God cannot give us these goods in full measure without allowing much evil on the way. . . .

[T]here are plenty of evils, positive bad states, which God could if he chose remove. I divide these into moral evils and natural evils. I understand by "natural evil" all evil which is not deliberately produced by human beings and which is not allowed by human beings to occur as a result of their negligence. Natural evil includes both physical suffering and mental suffering, of animals as well as humans; all the trial of suffering which disease, natural disasters, and accidents unpredictable by humans bring in their train. "Moral evil" I understand as including all evil caused deliberately by humans doing what they ought not to do (or allowed to occur by humans negligently failing to do what they ought to do) *and* also the evil constituted by such deliberate actions or negligent failure. It includes the sensory pain of the blow inflicted by the bad parent on his child, the mental pain of the parent depriving the child of love, the starvation allowed to occur in Africa because of negligence by members of foreign governments who could have prevented it, and also the evil of the parent or politician deliberately bringing about the pain or not trying to prevent the starvation.

MORAL EVIL

The central core of any theodicy must, I believe, be the "free-will defence," which deals—to start with—with moral evil, but can be extended to deal with much natural evil as well. The free-will defence claims that it is a great good that humans have a certain sort of free will which I shall call free and responsible choice, but that, if they do, then necessarily there will be the natural possibility of moral evil. (By the "natural possibility" I mean that it will not be determined in advance whether or not the evil will occur.) A God who gives humans such free will necessarily brings about the possibility and puts outside his own control whether or not that evil occurs. It is not logically possible—that is, it would be self-contradictory to suppose—that God could give us such free will and yet ensure that we always use it in the right way.

Free and responsible choice is not just free will in the narrow sense of being able to choose between alternative actions, without our choice being causally necessitated by some prior cause.... [H]umans could have that kind of free will merely in virtue of being able to choose freely between two equally good and unimportant alternatives. Free and responsible choice is rather free will (of the kind discussed) to make significant choices between good and evil, which make a big difference to the agent, to others, and to the world.

Given that we have free will, we certainly have free and responsible choice. Let us remind ourselves of the difference that humans can make to themselves, others, and the world. Humans have opportunities to give themselves and others pleasurable sensations and to pursue worthwhile activities—to play tennis or the piano, to acquire knowledge of history and science and philosophy, and to help others to do so, and thereby to build deep personal relations founded upon such sensations and activities. And humans are so made that they can form their characters. Aristotle famously remarked: "we become just by doing just acts, prudent by doing prudent acts, brave by doing brave acts." That is, by doing a just act when it is difficult—when it goes against our natural inclinations (which is what I understand by desires)—we make it easier to do a just act next time. We can gradually change our desires, so that—for example—doing just acts becomes natural. Thereby we can free ourselves from the power of the less good desires to which we are subject. And, by choosing to acquire knowledge and to use it to build machines of various sorts, humans can extend the range of the differences they can make to the world—they can build universities to last for centuries, or save energy for the next generation; and by cooperative effort over many decades they can eliminate poverty. The possibilities for free and responsible choice are enormous.

It is good that the free choices of humans should include *genuine* responsibility for other humans, and that involves the opportunity to benefit *or* harm them. God has the power to benefit or to harm humans. If other agents are to be given a share in his creative work, it is good that they have that power too (although perhaps to a lesser degree). A world in which agents can benefit each other but not do each other harm is one where they have only very limited responsibility for each other. If my responsibility for you is limited to whether or not to give you a camcorder, but I cannot cause you pain, stunt your growth, or limit your education, then I do not have a great deal of responsibility for you. A God who gave agents only such limited responsibilities for their fellows would not have given much. God would have reserved for himself the all-important choice of the kind of world it was to be, while simply allowing humans the minor choice of filling in the details. He would be like a father asking his elder son to look after the younger son, and adding that he would be watching the elder son's every move and would intervene the moment the elder son did a thing wrong. The elder son might justly retort that, while he would be happy to share his father's work, he could really do so only if he were left to make his own judgements as to what to do within a significant range of the options available to the father. A good God, like a good father, will delegate responsibility. In order to allow creatures a share in creation, he will allow them the choice of hurting and maiming, of frustrating the divine plan. Our world is one where creatures have just such deep responsibility for each other. I cannot only benefit my children, but harm them. One way in which I can harm them is that I can inflict physical pain on them. But there are much more damaging things which I can do to them. Above all I can stop them growing into creatures with significant knowledge, power, and freedom; I can determine whether they come to have the kind of free and responsible choice which I have. The possibility of humans bringing about significant evil is a logical consequence of their having this free and responsible choice. Not even God could give us this choice without the possibility of resulting evil.

Now . . . an action would not be intentional unless it was done for a reason— that is, seen as in some way a good thing (either in itself or because of its consequences). And, if reasons alone influence actions, that regarded by the subject as most important will determine what is done; an agent under the influence of reason alone will inevitably do the action which he regards as overall the best. If an agent does not do the action which he regards as overall the best, he must have allowed factors other than reason to exert an influence on him. In other words, he must have allowed desires for what he regards as good only in a certain respect, but not overall, to influence his conduct. So, in order to have a choice between good and evil, agents need already a certain depravity, in the sense of a system of desires for what they correctly believe to be evil. I need to *want* to overeat, get more than my fair share of money or power, indulge my sexual appetites even by deceiving my spouse or partner, and see you hurt, if I am to have choice between good and evil. This depravity is itself an evil which is a necessary condition of a greater good. It makes possible a choice made seriously and deliberately, because it is made in the face of a genuine alternative. I stress that, according to the free-will defence, it is the natural possibility of moral evil which is the necessary condition of the great good, not the actual evil itself. Whether that occurs is (through God's choice) outside God's control and up to us.

Note further and crucially that, if I suffer in consequence of your freely chosen bad action, that is not by any means pure loss for me. In a certain respect it is a good for *me*. My suffering would be pure loss for me if the only good thing in life was sensory pleasure, and the only bad thing sensory pain; and it is because the modern world tends to think in those terms that the problem of evil seems so acute. If these were the only good and bad things, the occurrence of suffering would indeed be a conclusive objection to the existence of God. But we have already noted the great good of freely choosing and influencing our future, that of our fellows, and that of the world. And now note another great good—the good of our life serving a purpose, of being of use to ourselves and others. Recall the words of Christ, "it is more blessed to give than to receive" (as quoted by St. Paul (Acts 20: 35)). We tend to think, when the beggar appears on our doorstep and we feel obliged to give and do give, that that was lucky for him but not for us who happened to be at home. That is not what Christ's words say. They say that *we* are the lucky ones, not just because we have a lot, out of which we can give a little, but because we are privileged to contribute to the beggar's happiness—and that privilege is worth a lot more than money. And, just as it is a great good freely to choose to do good, so it is also a good to be used by someone else for a worthy purpose (so long, that is, that he or she has the right, the authority, to use us in this way). Being allowed to suffer to make possible a great good is a privilege, even if the privilege is forced upon you. Those who are allowed to die for their country and thereby save their country from foreign oppression are privileged. Cultures less obsessed than our own by the evil of purely physical pain have always recognized that. And they have recognized that it is still a blessing, even if the one who died had been conscripted to fight.

And even twentieth-century man can begin to see that—sometimes—when he seeks to help prisoners, not by giving them more comfortable quarters, but by letting them help the handicapped; or when he pities rather than envies the "poor little rich girl" who has everything and does nothing for anyone else. And one phenomenon prevalent in end-of-century Britain draws this especially to our attention—the evil of unemployment. Because of our system of Social Security, the unemployed on the whole have enough money to live without too much discomfort; certainly they are a lot better off than are many employed in Africa or Asia or Victorian Britain. What is evil about unemployment is not so much any resulting poverty but the uselessness of the unemployed. They often report feeling unvalued by society, of no use, "on the scrap heap." They rightly think it would be a good for them to contribute; but they cannot. Many of them would welcome a system where they were obliged to do useful work in preference to one where society has no use for them.

It follows from that fact that being of use is a benefit for him who is of use, and that those who suffer at the hands of others, and thereby make possible the good of those others who have free and responsible choice, are themselves benefited in this respect. I am fortunate if the natural possibility of my suffering if you choose to hurt me is the vehicle which makes your choice really matter. My vulnerability, my openness to suffering (which necessarily involves my actually suffering if you make the wrong choice), means that you are not just like a pilot in a simulator, where it does not matter if mistakes are made. That our choices matter tremendously, that we can make great differences to things for good or ill, is one of the greatest gifts a creator can give us. And if my suffering is the means by which he can give you that choice, I too am in this respect fortunate. Though of course suffering is in itself a bad thing, my good fortune is that the suffering is not random, pointless suffering. It is suffering which is a consequence of my vulnerability which makes me of such use.

Someone may object that the only good thing is not *being* of use (dying for one's country or being vulnerable to suffering at your hands), but *believing* that one is of use—believing that one is dying for one's country and that this is of use; the "feel-good" experience. But that cannot be correct. Having comforting beliefs is only a good thing if they are true beliefs. It is not a good thing to believe that things are going well when they are not, or that your life is of use when it is not. Getting pleasure out of a comforting falsehood is a cheat. But if I get pleasure out of a true belief, it must be that I regard the state of things which I believe to hold to be a good thing. If I get pleasure out of the true belief that my daughter is doing well at school, it must be that I regard it as a good thing that my daughter does well at school (whether or not I believe that she is doing well). If I did not think the latter, I would not get any pleasure out of believing that she is doing well. Likewise, the belief that I am vulnerable to suffering at your hands, and that that is a good thing, can only be a good thing if being vulnerable to suffering at your hands is itself a good thing (independently of whether I believe it or not). Certainly, when my life is of use and that is a good for me, it is even better if I believe it and get comfort therefrom; but it can only be even better if it is already a good for me whether I believe it or not.

But though suffering may in these ways serve good purposes, does God have the right to allow me to suffer for your benefit, without asking my permission? For surely, an objector will say, no one has the right to allow one person A to suffer for the benefit of another one B without A's consent. We judge that doctors who use patients as involuntary objects of experimentation in medical experiments which they hope will produce results which can be used to benefit others are doing something wrong. After all, if my arguments about the utility of suffering are sound, ought we not all to be causing suffering to others in order that those others may have the opportunity to react in the right way?

There are, however, crucial differences between God and the doctors. The first is that God as the author of our being has certain rights, a certain authority over us, which we do not have over our fellow humans. He is the cause of our existence at each moment of our existence and sustains the laws of nature which give us everything we are and have. To allow someone to suffer for his own good or that of others, one has to stand in some kind of parental relationship towards him. I do not have the right to let some stranger suffer for the sake of some good, when I could easily prevent this, but I do have *some* right of this kind in respect of my own children. I may let the younger son suffer *somewhat* for his own good or that of his brother. I have this right because in small part I am responsible for the younger son's existence, his beginning and continuance. If I have begotten him, nourished, and educated him, I have some limited rights over him in return; to a *very limited* extent I can use him for some worthy purpose. If this is correct, then a God who is so much more the author of our being than are our parents has so much more right in this respect. Doctors do have over us even the rights of parents.

But secondly and all-importantly, the doctors *could* have asked the patients for permission; and the patients, being free agents of some power and knowledge, could have made an informed choice of whether or not to allow themselves to be used. By contrast, God's choice is not about how to use already existing agents, but about the sort of agents to make and the sort of world into which to put them. In God's situation there are no agents to be asked. I am arguing that it is good that one agent A should have deep responsibility for another B (who in turn could have deep responsibility for another C). It is not logically possible for God to have asked B if he wanted things thus, for, if A is to be responsible for B's growth in freedom, knowledge, and power, there will not be a B with enough freedom and knowledge to make any choice, before God has to choose whether or not to give A responsibility for him. One cannot ask a baby into which sort of world he or she wishes to be born. The creator has to make the choice independently of his creatures.

He will seek on balance to benefit them—all of them. And, in giving them the gift of life—whatever suffering goes with it—that is a substantial benefit. But when one suffers at the hands of another, often perhaps it is not enough of a benefit to outweigh the suffering. Here is the point to recall that it is an additional benefit to the sufferer that his suffering is the means whereby the one who hurt him had the opportunity to make a significant choice between good and evil which otherwise he would not have had.

Although for these reasons, as I have been urging, God has the right to allow humans to cause each other to suffer, there must be a limit to the amount of suffering which he has the right to allow a human being to suffer for the sake of a great good. A parent may allow an elder child to have the power to do some harm to a younger child for the sake of the responsibility given to the elder child; but there are limits. And there are limits even to the moral right of God, our creator and sustainer, to use free sentient beings as pawns in a greater game. Yet, if these limits were too narrow, God would be unable to give humans much real responsibility; he would be able to allow them only to play a toy game. Still, limits there must be to God's rights to allow humans to hurt each other; and limits there are in the world to the extent to which they can hurt each other, provided above all by the short finite life enjoyed by humans and other creatures—one human can hurt another for no more than eighty years or so. And there are a number of other safety-devices in-built into our physiology and psychology, limiting the amount of pain we can suffer. But the primary safety limit is that provided by the shortness of our finite life. Unending, unchosen suffering would indeed to my mind provide a very strong argument against the existence of God. But that is not the human situation.

So then God, without asking humans, has to choose for them between the kinds of world in which they can live—basically either a world in which there is very little opportunity for humans to benefit or harm each other, or a world in which there is considerable opportunity. How shall he choose? There are clearly reasons for both choices. But it seems to me (just, on balance) that his choosing to create the world in which we have considerable opportunity to benefit or harm each other is to bring about a good at least as great as the evil which he thereby allows to occur. *Of course* the suffering he allows is a bad thing; and, other things being equal, to be avoided. But having the natural possibility of causing suffering makes possible a greater good. God, in creating humans who (of logical necessity) cannot choose for themselves the kind of world into which they are to come, plausibly exhibits his goodness in making for them the heroic choice that they come into a risky world where they may have to suffer for the good of others.

NATURAL EVIL

Natural evil is not to be accounted for along the same lines as moral evil. Its main role rather, I suggest, is to make it possible for humans to have the kind of choice which the free-will defence extols, and to make available to humans specially worthwhile kinds of choice.

There are two ways in which natural evil operates to give humans those choices. First, the operation of natural laws producing evils gives humans knowledge (if they choose to seek it) of how to bring about such evils themselves. Observing you catch some disease by the operation of natural processes gives me the power either to use those processes to give that disease to other people, or through negligence to allow others to catch it, or to take measures to prevent others from catching the disease. Study of the mechanisms of nature producing various evils (and goods) opens up for humans a wide range of choice. This is the way in which in fact we learn how to bring about (good and) evil. But could not God give us the requisite knowledge (of how to bring about good or evil) which we need in order to have free and responsible choice by a less costly means? Could he not just whisper in our ears from time to time what are the different consequences of different actions of ours? Yes. But anyone who believed that an action of his would have some effect because he believed that God had told him so would see all his actions as done under the all-watchful eye of God. He would not merely believe strongly that there was a God, but would know it with real certainty. That knowledge would greatly inhibit his freedom of choice and would make it very difficult for him to choose to do evil. This is because we all have a natural inclination to wish to be thought well of by everyone, and above all by an all-good God; that we have such an inclination is a very good feature of humans, without which we would be less than human. Also, if we were directly informed of the consequences of our actions, we would be deprived of the choice whether to seek to discover what the consequences were through experiment and hard cooperative work. Knowledge would be available on tap. Natural processes alone give humans knowledge of the effects of their actions without inhibiting their freedom, and if evil is to be a possibility for them they must know how to allow it to occur.

The other way in which natural evil operates to give humans their freedom is that it makes possible certain kinds of action towards it between which agents can choose. It increases the range of significant choice. A particular natural evil, such as physical pain, gives to the sufferer a choice—whether to endure it with patience or to bemoan his lot. His friend can choose whether to show compassion towards the sufferer or to be callous. The pain makes possible these choices, which would not otherwise exist. There is no guarantee that our actions in response to the pain will be good ones, but the pain gives us the opportunity to perform good actions. The good or bad actions which we perform in the face of natural evil themselves provide opportunities for further choice—of good or evil stances towards the former actions. If I am patient with my suffering, you can choose whether to encourage or laugh at my patience; if I bemoan my lot, you can teach me by word and example what a good thing patience is. If you are sympathetic, I have then the opportunity to show gratitude for the sympathy or to be so self-involved that I ignore it. If you are callous, I can choose whether to ignore this or to resent it for life. And so on. I do not think that there can be much doubt that natural evil, such as physical pain, makes available these sorts of choice. The actions which natural evil makes possible are ones which allow us to perform at our best and interact with our fellows at the deepest level.

It may, however, be suggested that adequate opportunity for these great good actions would be provided by the occurrence of moral evil without any need for suffering to be caused by natural processes. You can show courage when threatened by a gunman, as well as when threatened by cancer; and show sympathy to those likely to be killed by gunmen as well as to those likely to die of cancer. But just imagine all the suffering of mind and body caused by disease, earthquake, and accident unpreventable by humans removed at a stroke from our society. No sickness, no bereavement in consequence of the untimely death of the young. Many of us would then have such an easy life that we simply would not have much opportunity to show courage or, indeed, manifest much in the way of great goodness at all. We need those insidious processes of decay and dissolution which money and strength cannot ward off for long to give us the opportunities, so easy otherwise to avoid, to become heroes.

God has the right to allow natural evils to occur (for the same reason as he has the right to allow moral evils to occur)—up to a limit. It would, of course, be crazy for God to multiply evils more and more in order to give endless opportunity for heroism, but to have *some* significant opportunity for real heroism and consequent character formation is a benefit for the person to whom it is given. Natural evils give to us the knowledge to make a range of choices between good and evil and also give us the opportunity to perform actions of especially valuable kinds.

There is, however, no reason to suppose that animals have free will. So what about their suffering? Animals had been suffering for a long time before humans appeared on this planet—just how long depends on which animals are conscious beings. The first thing to take into account here is that, while the higher animals, at any rate the vertebrates, suffer, it is most unlikely that they suffer nearly as much as humans do. Given that suffering depends directly on brain events (in turn caused by events in other parts of the body), then, since the lower animals do not suffer at all and humans suffer a lot, animals of intermediate complexity (it is reasonable to suppose) suffer only a moderate amount. So, while one does need a theodicy to account for why God allows animals to suffer, one does not need as powerful a theodicy as one does in respect of humans. One only needs reasons adequate to account for God allowing an amount of suffering much less than that of humans. That said, there is, I believe, available for animals parts of the theodicy which I have outlined above for humans.

The good of animals, like that of humans, does not consist solely in thrills of pleasure. For animals, too, there are more worthwhile things, and in particular intentional actions, and among them serious significant intentional actions. The life of animals involves many serious significant intentional actions. Animals look for a mate, despite being tired and failing to find one. They take great trouble to build nests and feed their young, to decoy predators, and to explore. But all this inevitably involves pain (going on despite being tired) and danger. An animal cannot intentionally avoid forest fires, or take trouble to rescue its offspring from forest fires, unless there exists a serious danger of getting caught in a forest fire. The action of rescuing despite danger simply cannot be done unless the danger exists—and the danger will not exist unless there is a significant natural probability of being caught in the fire. Animals do not choose freely to do such actions, but the actions are nevertheless worthwhile. It is great that animals feed their young, not just themselves; that animals explore when they know it to be dangerous; that animals save each other from predators, and so on. These are the things that give the lives of animals their value. But they do often involve some suffering to some creature.

To return to the central case of humans—the reader will agree with me to the extent to which he or she values responsibility, free choice, and being of use very much more than thrills of pleasure or absence of pain. There is no other way to get the evils of this world into the right perspective, except to reflect at length on innumerable very detailed thought experiments (in addition to actual experiences of life) in which we postulate very different sorts of worlds from our own, and then ask ourselves whether the perfect goodness of God would require him to create one of these (or no world at all) rather than our own. But I conclude with a very small thought experiment, which may help to begin this process. Suppose that you exist in another world before your birth in this one, and are given a choice as to the sort of life you are to have in this one. You are told that you are to have only a short life, maybe of only a few minutes, although it will be an adult life in the sense that you will have the richness of sensation and belief characteristic of adults. You have a choice as to the sort of life you will have. You can have either a few minutes of very considerable pleasure, of the kind produced by some drug such as heroin, which you will experience by yourself and which will have no effects at all in the world (for example, no one else will know about it); or you can have a few minutes of considerable pain, such as the pain of childbirth, which will have (unknown to you at the time of pain) considerable good effects on others over a few years. You are told that, if you do not make the second choice, those others will never exist—and so you are under no moral obligation to make the second choice. But you seek to make the choice which will make *your* own life the best life for *you* to have led. How will you choose? The choice is, I hope, obvious. You should choose the second alternative.

For someone who remains unconvinced by my claims about the relative strengths of the good and evils involved—holding that, great though the goods are, they do not justify the evils which they involve—there is a fall-back position. My arguments may have convinced you of the greatness of the goods involved sufficiently for you to allow that a perfectly good God would be justified in bringing about the evils for the sake of the good which they make possible, if and only if God also provided compensation in the form of happiness after death to the victims whose sufferings make possible the goods. . . . While believing that God does provide at any rate for many humans such life after death, I have expounded a theodicy without relying on this assumption. But I can understand someone thinking that the assumption is needed, especially when we are considering the worst evils. (This compensatory afterlife need not necessarily be the everlasting life of Heaven.)

It remains the case, however, that evil is evil, and there is a substantial price to pay for the goods of our world which it makes possible. God would not be less than perfectly good if he created instead a world without pain and suffering, and so without the particular goods which those evils make possible. Christian, Islamic, and much Jewish tradition claims that God has created worlds of both kinds—our world, and the Heaven of the blessed. The latter is a marvellous world with a vast range of possible deep goods, but it lacks a few goods which our world contains, including the good of being able to reject the good. A generous God might well choose to give some of us the choice of rejecting the good in a world like ours before giving to those who embrace it a wonderful world in which the former possibility no longer exists.

STUDY QUESTIONS

1. Explain Swinburne's distinction between moral evil and natural evil.
2. Do you find his explanation of one of these two types of evil more persuasive than his explanation of the other?
3. Do his explanations depend on how much evil is found in the world?
4. If evil makes our world better, why would evil not make heaven better?

Pascal's Wager

❧

SIMON BLACKBURN

Blaise Pascal (1623–1662) was a French mathematician, physicist, and philosopher who developed a justification for believing in the existence of God even in the absence of a sound proof for God's existence. According to Pascal's celebrated "wager" argument, if we believe and God exists, then we attain heavenly bliss; if we believe and God doesn't exist, little is lost. On the other hand, if we don't believe and God does exist, then we are doomed to the torments of damnation; if we don't believe and God doesn't exist, little is gained. So belief is the safest strategy.

Simon Blackburn, who taught at the University of Cambridge, doesn't find Pascal's argument persuasive. Do you?

....

None of the metaphysical arguments . . . do much to confirm the hypothesis that the universe is the creation of a traditional God. . . . Faced with these blanks, religious faith may try to find other arguments.

From *Think* by Simon Blackburn. Copyright © 1999 by the author. Reprinted by permission of Oxford University Press.

An interesting and ingenious one is due to the French mathematician and theologian, Blaise Pascal, and is known as Pascal's wager. Unlike the arguments we have been considering, it is not presented as an argument for the *truth* of religious belief, but for the *utility* of believing in some version of a monotheistic, Judaic, Christian, or Islamic, God.

The argument is this. First, Pascal confesses to metaphysical ignorance:

> Let us now speak according to natural lights.
>
> If there is a God, he is infinitely incomprehensible, since, having neither parts, nor limits, He has no affinity to us. We are therefore incapable of knowing either what He is, or if He is . . . Who then will blame the Christians for not being able to give a reason for their belief, since they profess a religion for which they cannot give a reason?

It is not too clear why this excuse is offered for the Christians, as opposed to those of other faiths, as well as believers in fairies, ghosts, the living Elvis, and L. Ron Hubbard. Still, suppose the choice is between religious belief and a life of religious doubt or denial:

> You must wager. It is not optional. Which will you choose then? . . . Let us weigh the gain and the loss in wagering that God is. Let us estimate these two chances. If you gain, you gain all; if you lose, you lose nothing. Wager, then, without hesitation that He is.

With great clarity Pascal realizes that this is rather an odd reason for choosing a belief. But he also says, perceptively, that

> your inability to believe is the result of your passions, since reason brings you to this, and yet you cannot believe . . . Learn of those who have been bound like you, and who now stake all their possessions . . . Follow the way by which they began; by acting as if they believe, taking the holy water, having masses said, etc. Even this will naturally make you believe, and deaden your acuteness.

After you have "stupefied" yourself, you have become a believer. And then you will reap the rewards of belief: infinite rewards, if the kind of God you believe in exists. And if it does not? Well, you have lost very little, in comparison with infinity: only what Pascal calls the "poisonous pleasures" of things like playing golf on Sundays instead of going to mass.

The standard way to present this argument is in terms of a two-by-two box of the options:

	God exists	God does not
I believe in him	+infinity!	0
I do not believe in him	−infinity!	0

The zeros on the right correspond to the thought that not much goes better or worse in this life, whether or not we believe. This life is of vanishingly little account compared to what is promised to believers. The plus-infinity figure corresponds to infinite bliss. The minus-infinity figure in the bottom left corresponds to the traditional jealous God, who sends to Hell those who do not believe in him, and of course encourages his followers to give them a hard time here, as well. But the minus-infinity figure can be soft-pedalled. Even if we put 0 in the bottom left-hand box, the wager looks good. It would be good even if God does not punish disbelief, because there is still that terrific payoff of "+infinity" cranking up the choice.... [T]he option of belief . . . can win and cannot lose. So—go for it!

Unfortunately the lethal problem with this argument is simple, once it is pointed out.

Pascal starts from a position of metaphysical ignorance. We just know nothing about the realm beyond experience. But the set-up of the wager presumes that we *do* know something. We are supposed to know the rewards and penalties attached to belief in a Christian God. This is a God who will be pleasured and reward us for our attendance at mass, and will either be indifferent or, in the minus-infinity option, seriously discombobulated by our nonattendance. But this is a case of false options. For consider that if we are really ignorant metaphysically, then it is at least as likely that the options pan out like this:

> There is indeed a very powerful, very benevolent deity. He (or she or they or it) has determined as follows. The good human beings are those who follow the natural light of reason, which is given to them to control their beliefs. These good humans follow the arguments, and hence avoid religious convictions. These ones with the strength of mind not to believe in such things go to Heaven. The rest go to Hell.

This is not such a familiar deity as the traditional jealous God, who cares above all that people believe in him. (Why is God so jealous? Alas, might his jealousy be a projection of human sectarian ambitions and emotions? Either you are with us or against us! The French sceptic Voltaire said that God created mankind in his image, and mankind returned the compliment.) But the problem for Pascal is that if we really know nothing, then we do not know whether the scenario just described is any less likely than the Christian one he presented. In fact, for my money, a God that punishes belief is just as likely, and a lot more reasonable, than one that punishes disbelief.

And of course, we could add the Humean point that whilst for Pascal it was a simple two-way question of mass versus disbelief, in the wider world it is also a question of the Koran versus mass, or L. Ron Hubbard versus the Swami Maharishi, or the Aquarian Concepts Community Divine New Order Government versus the First Internet Church of All. The wager has to be silent about those choices.

STUDY QUESTIONS

1. What is Pascal's wager?
2. According to Blackburn, what is the lethal problem with Pascal's wager?
3. Do you believe Pascal's wager overlooked some relevant options?
4. Why would an all-powerful, all-good God be more concerned with your theological beliefs rather than your commitment to cure illness, relieve poverty, or help others in need?

Pascal's Wager: An Assessment

Linda Zagzebski

In the next selection Linda Zagzebski, whose work we read previously, considers three objections to Pascal's wager. She finds that they point to problems with the wager but may not require that Pascal's line of reasoning be abandoned.

....

Pascal's wager has a number of well-known objections, some of them coming from theists and some from nontheists. Let us consider three of them.

1. *The many gods objection.* Pascal assumes the wager is over belief in the Christian God. It is a God who promises eternal life for belief in him. But this means that the wager is between the existence of a God of a certain kind and no God. That is not a forced wager because there are other possibilities. To put the point another way, there are many wagers: Christian God or no Christian God, Muslim God or no Muslim God, Hindu God or no Hindu God, etc. And this is a problem because for some of these you could make the same kind of wager, yet you really can only bet on one, assuming that betting on one commits you to betting against the others. But which one should you bet on?

One answer to this objection is that Pascal is thinking of live options, something you could really believe. Presumably he thinks that the God of only one religion would be a possibility for you. Pascal's era was not one in which there were churches, temples, mosques, and synagogues within easy driving distance of the average person making the wager. So it means that Pascal's wager is not intended for everybody. It is for people who: (1) think both Christianity and atheism are intellectually unproven but also unrefuted, so from a rational viewpoint both are live options; (2) have a roughly Christian view of God as a being who rewards his worshipers with heaven; and (3) are in the emotional position of struggle, trying to choose. Presumably that would apply to many people, and many other people would be in the analogous position of betting on the God of a different religion. Clearly, though, the situation is much more complex for a person for whom more than one religion that promises an infinite payoff is a live option.

2. *The wager presupposes a low view of God and religious faith.* A second objection is that God does not want believers who believe on the basis of a wager motivated by self-interest. This is not what religious faith is all about. This objection is often expressed by religious people who find the wager repugnant.

From Linda Zagzebski, *Philosophy of Religion: An Historical Introduction.* Blackwell Publishing, 2007. Reprinted by permission of the publisher.

The reply to this objection is that Pascal is formulating an appeal to a certain kind of person, one who is perched precariously between belief and unbelief. Given that he thought of the wager as the precursor to real faith, not faith itself, the person who makes the wager would sincerely try to believe in God. She would not remain indefinitely in the state of the gambler who is motivated only by potential gain. There is no guarantee that she will eventually acquire real faith, but she won't unless she tries, just as the entrepreneur has no guarantee of success in business, but he knows for sure that he won't succeed if he doesn't make the attempt. If the theistic bettor succeeds, her original motive will eventually be replaced by the attitude of religious faith. . . .

3. *We can't believe by making a choice.* There are many things you can't just decide to believe. Suppose somebody tries to bribe you into believing there will be an earthquake in Antarctica on April 19, 2020. Could you do it? You can't just believe because it is in your interest to do so. No matter how much money you are offered, it is probably impossible to make yourself believe certain things if the evidence does not support it. If the choice is not forced, your reason tells you to withhold judgment. And it is hard to see how you could muster the motive to believe, given that earthquakes in Antarctica probably do not connect to anything you already care about at all.

But there are several disanalogies between the Antarctica example and Pascal's wager. As we have seen, Pascal does not think you can start believing in an instant. Second, Pascal thinks the choice is forced, and it is about something you already care about. If you take the time to cultivate the belief by acting as if you believe, you may eventually end up really believing. Here is an analogy given by James Cargile[1] defending Pascal's view that you could get yourself to believe in God given (a) the right motivation, (b) no firm belief to begin with, and (c) a bit of time. Suppose a billionaire jazz lover declares that in two years he will toss a coin. If it comes up heads, he will give a million dollars to every devoted jazz fan. If it comes up tails, he won't do anything. Every Sunday for the next two years a one-hour jazz concert is scheduled. If you attend these concerts religiously, listen to jazz at every other opportunity, and avoid listening to any other kind of music, it is quite likely that you will become a lover of jazz. Of course, it's not likely to work if you hated jazz from the beginning, but if you start out neutral, there is a good chance it will work. In any case, Pascal is addressing someone who is neutral about the existence of God.

But here is another analogy that is more problematic. It highlights both the issue of whether you can make yourself feel something and whether it is morally reprehensible to do so even if you can. Suppose a wealthy man falls in love with a poor woman and wants to marry her, but she feels nothing for him, neither positive nor negative. If she can get herself to love him, she will get a lot of money. One problem is that she has to try to love the man, and while the chances that she will succeed vary with the case, there is rarely a very high probability that it will. But that is not an unsurmountable problem, since even a low probability of success may be enough to make the effort to love him worthwhile. The real problem is that the motive is suspect. No one objects when a woman tries to love a man in order to have a happy relationship with someone she does not want to hurt, but the situation is problematic when she is motivated by the prospect of a reward external to the relationship itself. Nonetheless, human motives are complex, and we often consider it acceptable, even commendable, when people consider the external rewards of a marriage to some extent. Parents routinely advise their children to pick a mate with a good income, and nobody considers that deplorable. But it would be a foolhardy parent who would advise her child to choose a mate with the best income and *then* try to love the person. Is Pascal's wager analogous to the foolhardy parent? If so, can it be altered to avoid the problematic features of the marriage analogy?

NOTE

1. James Cargile, "Pascal's Wager," in Steven M. Cahn and David Shatz, eds., *Contemporary Philosophy of Religion.* Oxford University Press, 1982, pp. 229–236.

STUDY QUESTIONS

1. What is the "many gods" objection to Pascal's wager?
2. What is Zagzebski's response to the many gods objection?
3. Can you decide to believe something?
4. Might acting as religious adherents act lead you to believe what religious adherents believe?

Faith and Reason

MICHAEL SCRIVEN

Michael Scriven, a philosopher at Claremont Graduate University, argues that reason and faith are not on a par, because reason has passed tests of effectiveness that faith has not. Furthermore, while every religious believer relies on reason to assess the claims of ordinary experience, those who are not religious believers

From *Primary Philosophy* by Michael Scriven. Reprinted by permission of The McGraw-Hill Companies.

have no need to rely on religious faith in any aspect of their lives. If the criteria for religious truth are not connected with the criteria for everyday truth, faith, unlike reason, does not provide a reliable guide for our lives.

....

We must now contend with the suggestion that reason is irrelevant to the commitment to theism because this territory is the domain of another faculty: the faculty of faith. It is sometimes even hinted that it is morally wrong and certainly foolish to suggest we should be reasoning about God. For this is the domain of faith or of the "venture of faith," of the "knowledge that passeth understanding," of religious experience and mystic insight.

Now the normal meaning of *faith* is simply "confidence"; we say that we have great faith in someone or in some claim or product, meaning that we believe and act as if they were very reliable. Of such faith we can properly say that it is well founded or not, depending on the evidence for whatever it is in which we have faith. So there is no incompatibility between this kind of faith and reason; the two are from different families and can make a very good marriage. Indeed if they do not join forces, then the resulting ill-based or inadequate confidence will probably lead to disaster. So faith, in this sense, means only a high degree of belief and may be reasonable or unreasonable.

But the term is sometimes used to mean an *alternative to reason* instead of something that should be founded on reason. Unfortunately, the mere use of the term in this way does not demonstrate that faith is a possible route to truth. It is like using the term "winning" as a synonym for "playing" instead of one possible outcome of playing. This is quaint, but it could hardly be called a satisfactory way of proving that we are winning; any time we "win" by changing the meaning of winning, the victory is merely illusory. And so it proves in this case. To use "faith" *as if* it were an alternative way to the truth cannot by-pass the crucial question whether such results really have any likelihood of being true. A rose by any other name will smell the same, and the inescapable facts about "faith" in the new sense are that it is still *applied to* a belief and is still supposed to imply *confidence in* that belief: the belief in the existence and goodness of God. So we can still ask the same old question about that belief: Is the confidence justified or misplaced? To say we "take it on faith" does not get it off parole.

Suppose someone replies that theism is a kind of belief that does not need justification by evidence. This means either that no one cares whether it is correct or not or that there is some other way of checking that it is correct besides looking at the evidence for it, i.e., giving reasons for believing it. But the first alternative is false since very many people care whether there is a God or not; and the second alternative is false because any method of showing that belief is likely to be true is, by definition, a justification of that belief, i.e., an appeal to reason. You certainly cannot show that a belief in God is likely to be true just by having confidence in it and by saying this is a case of knowledge "based on" faith, any more than you can win a game just by playing it and by calling that winning.

It is psychologically possible to have faith in something without any basis in fact, and once in a while you will turn out to be lucky and to have backed the right belief. This does not show you "really knew all along"; it only shows you cannot be unlucky all the time. . . . But, in general, beliefs without foundations lead to an early grave or to an accumulation of superstitions, which are usually troublesome and always false beliefs. It is hardly possible to defend this approach just by *saying* that you have decided that in this area confidence is its own justification.

Of course, you might try to *prove* that a feeling of great confidence about certain types of propositions is a reliable indication of their truth. If you succeeded, you would indeed have shown that the belief was justified; you would have done *this* by justifying it. To do this, you would have to show what the real facts were and show that when someone had the kind of faith we are now talking about, it usually turned out that the facts were as he believed, just as we might justify the claims of a telepath. The catch in all this is simply that you have got to show what the real facts are in some way *other* than by appealing to faith, since that would simply be assuming what you are trying to prove. And if you can show what the facts are in this other way, you do not need faith in any new sense at all; you are already perfectly entitled to confidence in any belief that you have shown to be well supported.

How are you going to show what the real facts are? You show this by any method of investigation that has itself been tested, the testing being done by still another tested method, etc., through a series of tested connections that eventually terminates in our ordinary everyday reasoning and testing procedures of logic and observation.

Is it not prejudiced to require that the validation of beliefs always involve ultimate reference to our ordinary logic and everyday-plus-scientific knowledge? May not faith (religious experience, mystic insight) give us access to some new domain of truth? It is certainly possible that it does this. But, of course, it is also possible that it lies. One can hardly accept the reports of those with faith or, indeed, the apparent revelations of one's own religious experiences on the ground that they *might* be right. So *might* be a fervent materialist who saw his interpretation as a revelation. Possibility is not veracity. Is it not of the very greatest importance that we should try to find out whether we really can justify the use of the term "truth or knowledge" in describing the content of faith? If it is, then we must find something in that content that is known to be true in some other way, because to get off the ground we must first push off against the ground—we cannot lift ourselves by our shoelaces. If the new realm of knowledge is to be a realm of knowledge and not mythology, then it must tell us something which relates it to the kind of case that gives meaning to the term "truth." If you want to use the old word for the new events, you must show that it is applicable.

Could not the validating experience, which religious experience must have if it is to be called true, be the experience of others who also have or have had religious experiences? The religious community could, surely, provide a basis of agreement analogous to that which ultimately underlies scientific truth. Unfortunately, agreement is not the only requirement for avoiding error, for all may be in error.

The difficulty for the religious community is to show that its agreement is not simply agreement about a shared mistake. If agreement were the only criterion of truth, there could never be a shared mistake; but clearly either the atheist group or the theist group shares a mistake. To decide which is wrong must involve appeal to something other than mere agreement. And, of course, it is clear that particular religious beliefs are mistaken, since religious groups do not all agree and they cannot all be right.

Might not some or all scientific beliefs be wrong, too? This is conceivable, but there are crucial differences between the two kinds of belief. In the first place, any commonly agreed religious beliefs concern only one or a few entities and their properties and histories. What for convenience we are here calling "scientific belief" is actually the sum total of all conventionally founded human knowledge, much of it not part of any science, and it embraces billions upon billions of facts, each of them perpetually or frequently subject to checking by independent means, each connected with a million others. The success of *this* system of knowledge shows up every day in everything that we do: we eat, and the food is not poison; we read, and the pages do not turn to dust; we slip, and gravity does not fail to pull us down. We are not just relying on the existence of agreement about the interpretation of a certain experience among a small part of the population. We are relying directly on our extremely reliable, nearly universal, and independently tested senses, and each of us is constantly obtaining independent confirmation for claims based on these, many of these confirmations being obtained for many claims, independently of each other. It is the wildest flight of fancy to suppose that there is a body of common religious beliefs which can be set out to exhibit this degree of repeated checking by religious experiences. In fact, there is not only gross disagreement on even the most fundamental claims in the creeds of different churches, each of which is supported by appeal to religious experience or faith, but where there is agreement by many people, it is all too easily open to the criticism that it arises from the common cultural exposure of the child or the adult convert and hence is not independent in the required way.

This claim that the agreement between judges is spurious in a particular case because it only reflects previous common indoctrination of those in agreement is a serious one. It must always be met by direct disproof whenever agreement is appealed to in science, and it is. The claim that the food is not poison cannot be explained away as a myth of some subculture, for anyone, even if told nothing about the eaters in advance, will judge that the people who ate it are still well. The whole methodology of testing is committed to the doctrine that any judges who could have learned what they are expected to say about the matter they are judging are completely valueless. Now anyone exposed to religious teaching, whether a believer or not, has long known the standard for such experiences, the usual symbols, the appropriate circumstances, and so on. These suggestions are usually very deeply implanted, so that they cannot be avoided by good intentions, and consequently members of our culture are rendered entirely incapable *of* being independent observers. Whenever observers are not free from previous contamination in this manner, the only way to support their claims is to examine independently testable *consequences* of the novel claims, such as predictions about the future. In the absence of these, the religious-experience gambit, whether involving literal or analogical claims, is wholly abortive.

A still more fundamental point counts against the idea that agreement among the religious can help support the idea of faith as an alternative path to truth. It is that every sane theist also believes in the claims of ordinary experience, while the reverse is not the case. Hence, the burden of proof is on the theist to show that the *further step* he wishes to take will not take him beyond the realm of truth. The two positions, of science and religion, are not symmetrical; the adherent of one of them suggests that we extend the range of allowable beliefs and yet is unable to produce the same degree of acceptance or "proving out" in the ordinary field of human activities that he insists on before believing in a new instrument or source of information. The atheist obviously cannot be shown his error in the way someone who thinks that there are no electrons can be shown his, *unless some of the arguments for the existence of God are sound.* ... If some of them work, the position of religious knowledge is secure; if they do not, nothing else will make it secure.

In sum, the idea of separating religious from scientific knowledge and making each an independent realm with its own basis in experience of quite different kinds is a counsel of despair and not a product of true sophistication, for one cannot break the connection between everyday experience and religious claims, for purposes of defending the latter, without eliminating the consequences of religion for everyday life. There is no way out of this inexorable contract: if you want to support your beliefs, you must produce some experience which can be shown to be a reliable indicator of truth, and that can be done only by showing a connection between the experience and what we know to be true in a previously established way.

So, if the criteria of religious truth are not connected with the criteria of everyday truth, then they are not criteria of truth at all and the beliefs they "establish" have no essential bearing on our lives, constitute no explanation of what we see around us, and provide no guidance for our course through time.

STUDY QUESTIONS

1. Can knowledge be based on faith?
2. Can you believe strongly and be wrong?
3. According to Scriven, why are faith and reason not symmetrical?
4. Is your life invariably improved by holding justified beliefs rather than unjustified ones?

God and Morality

✒

STEVEN M. CAHN

Would the existence of God have implications for morality? Some believe so, but in the next selection I argue against that claim.

....

According to many religions, although not all, the world was created by God, an all-powerful, all-knowing, all-good being. Although God's existence has been doubted, let us for the moment assume its truth. What implications of this supposition would be relevant to our lives?

Some people would feel more secure in the knowledge that the world had been planned by an all-good being. Others would feel insecure, realizing the extent to which their existence depended on a decision of this being. In any case, most people, out of either fear or respect, would wish to act in accord with God's will.

Belief in God by itself, however, provides no hint whatsoever which actions God wishes us to perform, or what we ought to do to please or obey God. We may affirm that God is all-good, yet have no way of knowing the highest moral standards. All we may presume is that, whatever these standards, God always acts in accordance with them. We might expect God to have implanted the correct moral standards in our minds, but this supposition is doubtful in view of the conflicts among people's intuitions. Furthermore, even if consensus prevailed, it might be only a means by which God tests us to see whether we have the courage to dissent from popular opinion.

Some would argue that if God exists, then murder is immoral, because it destroys what God with infinite wisdom created. This argument, however, fails on several grounds. First, God also created germs, viruses, and disease-carrying rats. Because God created these things, ought they not be eliminated? Second, if God arranged for us to live, God also arranged for us to die. By killing, are we thereby assisting the work of God? Third, God provided us with the mental and physical potential to commit murder. Does God wish us to fulfill this potential?

Thus God's existence alone does not imply any particular moral precepts. We may hope our actions are in accord with God's standards, but no test is available to check whether what we do is best in God's eyes. Some seemingly good people suffer great ills, whereas some seemingly evil people achieve happiness. Perhaps in a future life these outcomes will be reversed, but we have no way of ascertaining who, if anyone, is ultimately punished and who ultimately rewarded.

Over the course of history, those who believed in God's existence typically were eager to learn God's will and tended to rely on those individuals who claimed

---

to possess such insight. Diviners, seers, and priests were given positions of great influence. Competition among them was severe, however, for no one could be sure which oracle to believe.

In any case prophets died, and their supposedly revelatory powers disappeared with them. For practical purposes what was needed was a permanent record of God's will. This requirement was met by the writing of holy books in which God's will was revealed to all.

But even though many such books were supposed to embody the will of God, they conflicted with one another. Which was to be accepted? Belief in the existence of God by itself yields no answer.

Let us suppose, however, that an individual becomes persuaded that a reliable guide to God's will is contained in the Ten Commandments. This person, therefore, believes that to murder, steal, or commit adultery is wrong.

But why is it wrong? Is it wrong because God says so, or does God say so because it *is* wrong?

This crucial issue was raised more than two thousand years ago in Plato's remarkable dialogue, the *Euthyphro*. Plato's teacher, Socrates, who in most of Plato's works is given the leading role, asks the overconfident Euthyphro whether actions are right because God says they are right, or whether God says actions are right because they are right.

In other words, Socrates is inquiring whether actions are right because of God's fiat or whether God is subject to moral standards. If actions are right because of God's command, then anything God commands would be right. Had God commanded adultery, stealing, and murder, then adultery, stealing, and murder would be right—surely an unsettling and to many an unacceptable conclusion.

Granted, some may be willing to adopt this discomforting view, but then they face another difficulty. If the good is whatever God commands, to say that God's commands are good amounts to saying that God's commands are God's commands, a mere tautology or repetition of words. In that case, the possibility of meaningfully praising the goodness of God would be lost.

The lesson here is that might does not make right, even if the might is the infinite might of God. To act morally is not to act out of fear of punishment; it is not to act as one is commanded to act. Rather, it is to act as one ought to act, and how one ought to act is not dependent on anyone's power, even if the power be divine.

Thus actions are not right because God commands them; on the contrary, God commands them because they are right. What is right is independent of what God commands, for to be right, what God commands must conform to an independent standard.

We could act intentionally in accord with this standard without believing in the existence of God; therefore morality does not rest on that belief. Consequently those who do not believe in God can be highly moral (as well as immoral) people, and those who do believe in the existence of God can be highly immoral (as well as moral) people. This conclusion should come as no surprise to anyone who has contrasted the benevolent life of the inspiring teacher, the Buddha, an atheist, with the malevolent life of the monk Torquemada, who devised and enforced the boundless cruelties of the Spanish Inquisition.

In short, believing in the existence of God does not by itself imply any specific moral principles, and knowing God's will does not provide any justification for morality. Thus regardless of our religious commitments, the moral dimension of our lives remains to be explored.

STUDY QUESTIONS

1. If God exists, is murder immoral?
2. Is murder wrong because God prohibits it, or does God prohibit murder because it is wrong?
3. Can atheists be moral persons?
4. Can theists be immoral persons?

HISTORICAL SOURCES

The Ontological Argument

ANSELM AND GAUNILO

Throughout the history of philosophy, various arguments have been offered to prove God's existence. Only one, however, the ontological argument, is *a priori*, making no appeal to empirical evidence and relying solely on an analysis of the concept of God.

Its classic formulation was provided by Saint Anselm (1033–1109), who was born in a village that is now part of Italy, was educated in a Benedictine monastery, and became Archbishop of Canterbury. He understands God to be the Being greater than which none can be conceived. Anselm reasons that if God did not exist, then a greater being could be conceived, namely, a being that exists. In that case, the Being greater than which none can be conceived would not be the Being greater than which none can be conceived, which is a contradiction. So the Being greater than which none can be conceived must exist, that is, God must exist. Indeed, Anselm goes on to claim that God cannot even be thought not to exist, because a being that *cannot* be thought not to exist is greater than one that *can* be thought not to exist.

From Brian Davies and G. R. Evans, eds., *Anselm of Canterbury: The Major Works*. Reprinted by permission of Oxford University Press. The words enclosed in brackets have been interpolated by the translator, M. J. Charlesworth, to make the meaning clearer.

The first known response to Anselm's argument was offered by his contemporary Gaunilo, a monk of Marmoutier, France, about whom little is known. Gaunilo maintains that Anselm's line of reasoning could be used to prove the existence of an island greater than which none can be conceived, an absurd conclusion. In reply, Anselm maintains that the argument did not apply to an island because, unlike God, an island has a beginning and end and so can be thought not to exist.

The ontological argument has continued to intrigue thinkers throughout the centuries. While its intricacy may not win many converts to theism, the argument retains the power to fascinate philosophers.

....

PROSLOGION

2

Well then, Lord, You who give understanding to faith, grant me that I may understand, as much as You see fit, that You exist as we believe You to exist, and that You are what we believe You to be. Now we believe that You are something than which nothing greater can be thought. Or can it be that a thing of such a nature does not exist, since "the Fool has said in his heart, there is no God" [Ps. 13:1; 52:1]? But surely, when this same Fool hears what I am speaking about, namely, "something-than-which-nothing-greater-can-be-thought," he understands what he hears, and what he understands is in his mind, even if he does not understand that it actually exists. For it is one thing for an object to exist in the mind, and another thing to understand that an object actually exists. Thus, when a painter plans beforehand what he is going to execute, he has [the picture] in his mind, but he does not yet think that it actually exists because he has not yet executed it. However, when he has actually painted it, then he both has it in his mind and understands that it exists because he has now made it. Even the Fool, then, is forced to agree that something-than-which-nothing-greater-can-be-thought exists in the mind, since he understands this when he hears it, and whatever is understood is in the mind. And surely that-than-which-a-greater-cannot-be-thought cannot exist in the mind alone. For if it exists solely in the mind, it can be thought to exist in reality also, which is greater. If then that-than-which-a-greater-cannot-be-thought exists in the mind alone, this same that-than-which-a-greater-*cannot*-be-thought is that-than-which-a-greater-*can*-be-thought. But this is obviously impossible. Therefore there is absolutely no doubt that something-than-which-a-greater-cannot-be-thought exists both in the mind and in reality.

3

And certainly this being so truly exists that it cannot be even thought not to exist. For something can be thought to exist that cannot be thought not to exist, and this is greater than that which can be thought not to exist. Hence, if that-than-which-a-greater-cannot-be-thought can be thought not to exist, then that-than-which-a-greater-cannot-be-thought is not the same as that-than-which-a-greater-cannot-be-thought, which is absurd. Something-than-which-a-greater-cannot-be-thought exists so truly then, that it cannot be even thought not to exist.

And You, Lord our God, are this being. You exist so truly, Lord my God, that You cannot even be thought not to exist. And this is as it should be, for if some intelligence could think of something better than You, the creature would be above its Creator and would judge its Creator—and that is completely absurd. In fact, everything else there is, except You alone can be thought of as not existing. You alone, then, of all things most truly exist and therefore of all things possess existence to the highest degree; for anything else does not exist as truly, and so possesses existence to a lesser degree. Why then did "the Fool say in his heart, there is no God" [Ps. 13:1; 52:1] when it is so evident to any rational mind that You of all things exist to the highest degree? Why indeed, unless because he was stupid and a fool?

4

How indeed has he "said in his heart" what he could not think; or how could he not think what he "said in his heart," since to "say in one's heart" and to "think" are the same? But if he really (indeed, since he really) both thought because he "said in his heart" and did not "say in his heart" because he could not think, there is not only one sense in which something is "said in one's heart" or thought. For in one sense a thing is thought when the word signifying it is thought; in another sense when the very object which the thing is is understood. In the first sense, then, God can be thought not to exist, but not at all in the second sense. No one, indeed, understanding what God is can think that God does not exist, even though he may say these words in his heart either without any [objective] signification or with some peculiar signification. For God is that-than-which-nothing-greater-can-be-thought. Whoever really understands this understands clearly that this same being so exists that not even in thought can it not exist. Thus whoever understands that God exists in such a way cannot think of Him as not existing.

I give thanks, good Lord, I give thanks to You, since what I believed before through Your free gift I now so understand through Your illumination, that if I did not want to *believe* that You existed, I should nevertheless be unable not to *understand* it.

ON BEHALF OF THE FOOL

Gaunilo

1

To one doubting whether there is, or denying that there is, something of such a nature than which nothing greater can be thought, it is said here that its existence is proved, first because the very one who denies or doubts it already has it in his mind, since when he hears it spoken of he understands what is said; and further, because what he understands is necessarily such that it exists not only in the mind but also in reality. And this is proved by the fact that it is greater to exist both in the mind and in reality than in the mind alone. For if this same being exists in the mind alone, anything that existed also in reality would be greater than this being, and thus that which is greater than everything would be less than some thing and would not be greater than everything, which is obviously contradictory. Therefore, it is necessarily the case that that which is greater than everything, being already proved to exist in the mind, should exist not only in the mind but also in reality, since otherwise it would not be greater than everything.

2

But he [the Fool] can perhaps reply that this thing is said already to exist in the mind only in the sense that I understand what is said. For could I not say that all kinds of unreal things, not existing in themselves in any way at all, are equally in the mind since if anyone speaks about them I understand whatever he says? . . .

6

For example: they say that there is in the ocean somewhere an island which, because of the difficulty (or rather the impossibility) of finding that which does not exist, some have called the "Lost Island." And the story goes that it is blessed with all manner of priceless riches and delights in abundance, much more even than the Happy Isles, and, having no owner or inhabitant, it is superior every-where in abundance of riches to all those other lands that men inhabit. Now, if anyone tell me that it is like this, I shall easily understand what is said, since nothing is difficult about it. But if he should then go on to say, as though it were a logical consequence of this: You cannot any more doubt that this island that is more excellent than all other lands truly exists somewhere in reality than you can doubt that it is in your mind; and since it is more excellent to exist not only in the mind alone but also in reality, therefore it must needs be that it exists. For if it did not exist, any other land existing in reality would be more excellent than it, and so this island, already conceived by you to be more excellent than others, will not be more excellent. If, I say, someone wishes thus to persuade me that this island really exists beyond all doubt, I should either think that he was joking or I should find it hard to decide which of us I ought to judge the bigger fool—I, if I agreed with him, or he, if he thought that he had proved the existence of this island with any certainty, unless he had first convinced me that its very excellence exists in my mind precisely as a thing existing truly and indubitably and not just as something unreal or doubtfully real.

REPLY TO GAUNILO

You claim, however, that this is as though someone asserted that it cannot be doubted that a certain island in the ocean (which is more fertile than all other lands and which, because of the difficulty or even the impossibility of discovering what does not exist, is called the "Lost Island") truly exists in reality since anyone easily understands it when it is described in words. Now, I truly promise that if anyone should discover for me something existing either in reality or in the mind alone—except "that-than-which-a-greater-cannot-be-thought"—to which the logic of my argument would apply, then I shall find that Lost Island and give it, never more to be lost, to that person. It has already been clearly seen, however, that "that-than-which-a-greater-cannot-be-thought" cannot be thought not to exist, because it exists as a matter of such certain truth. Otherwise it would not exist at all. In short, if anyone says that he thinks that this being does not exist, I reply that, when he thinks of this, either he thinks of something than which a greater cannot be thought, or he does not think of it. If he does not think of it, then he does not think that what he does not think of does not exist. If, however, he does think of it, then indeed he thinks of something which cannot be even thought not to exist. For if it could be thought not to exist, it could be thought to have a beginning and an end—but this cannot be. Thus, he who thinks of it thinks of something that cannot be thought not to exist; indeed, he who thinks of this does not think of it as not existing, otherwise he would think what cannot be thought. Therefore "that-than-which-a-greater-cannot-be-thought" cannot be thought not to exist.

STUDY QUESTIONS

1. Why is the ontological argument considered an *a priori* argument?
2. What are the premises Anselm uses to prove the existence of God?
3. What is Gaunilo's criticism of Anselm's argument?
4. Do you find Gaunilo's criticism persuasive?

Summma Theologiae

ᴛʜᴏᴍᴀs Aǫᴜɪɴᴀs

Thomas Aquinas (1225–1274), born near Naples, was the most influential philosopher of the medieval period. He joined the Dominican order and taught at the University of Paris. In his vast writings, composed in Latin, he seeks to demonstrate that Christian belief is consistent with reason.

Aquinas's greatest work was the *Summa Theologiae,* and its most famous passage, reprinted here, is the five ways to prove the existence of God. While Aquinas believes that not all the tenets of Christian doctrine can be demonstrated without reliance on Divine revelation, he maintains that the existence of God is provable without any appeal to faith.

In the fourth way Aquinas cites *"Metaph.* ii." The reference is to the second book of the *Metaphysics* of Aristotle, and serves as a reminder of Aquinas's regard for that highly influential Greek thinker.

....

The existence of God can be proved in five ways.

The first and more manifest way is the argument from motion. It is certain, and evident to our senses, that in the world some things are in motion. Now whatever is moved is moved by another, for nothing can be moved except it is in potentiality to that towards which it is moved; whereas a thing moves inasmuch as it is in act. For motion is nothing else than the reduction of something from potentiality to actuality. But nothing can be reduced from potentiality to actuality, except by something in a state of actuality. Thus that which is actually hot, as fire, makes wood, which is potentially hot, to be actually hot, and thereby moves and changes it. Now it is not possible that the same thing should be at once in actuality and potentiality in the same respect, but only in different respects. For what is actually hot cannot simultaneously be potentially hot; but it is simultaneously potentially cold. It is therefore impossible that in the same respect and in the same way a thing should be both mover and moved, i.e., that it should move itself. Therefore, whatever is moved must be moved by another. If that by which it is moved be itself moved, then this also must need to be moved by another, and that by another again. But this cannot go on to infinity, because then there would be no first mover and, consequently, no other mover, seeing that subsequent movers move only inasmuch as they are moved by the first mover; as the staff moves only because it is moved by the hand. Therefore it is necessary to arrive at a first mover, moved by no other; and this everyone understands to be God.

The second way is from the nature of efficient cause. In the world of sensible things we find there is an order of efficient causes. There is no case known (neither is it, indeed, possible) in which a thing is found to be the efficient cause of itself; for so it would be prior to itself, which is impossible. Now in efficient causes it is not possible to go on to infinity, because in all efficient causes following in order, the first is the cause of the intermediate cause, and the intermediate is the cause of the ultimate cause, whether the intermediate cause be several, or one only. Now to take away the cause is to take away the effect. Therefore, if there be no first cause among efficient causes, there will be no ultimate, nor any intermediate, cause. But if in efficient causes it is possible to go on to infinity, there will be no first efficient cause, neither will there be an ultimate effect, nor any intermediate efficient causes; all of which is plainly false. Therefore it is necessary to admit a first efficient cause, to which everyone gives the name of God.

The third way is taken from possibility and necessity, and runs thus. We find in nature things that are possible to be and not to be, since they are found to be generated, and to be corrupted, and consequently, it is possible for them to be and not to be. But it is impossible for these always to exist, for that which can not-be at some time is not. Therefore, if everything can not-be, then at one time there was nothing in existence. Now if this were true, even now there would be nothing in existence, because that which does not exist begins to exist only through something already existing. Therefore, if at one time nothing was in existence, it would have been impossible for anything to have begun to exist; and thus even now nothing would be in existence—which is absurd. Therefore, not all beings are merely possible, but there must exist something the existence of which is necessary. But every necessary thing either has its necessity caused by another or does not. Now it is impossible to go on to infinity in necessary things which have their necessity caused by another, as has been already proved in regard to efficient causes. Therefore we cannot but admit the existence of some being having of itself its own necessity, and not receiving it from another, but rather causing in others their necessity. This all men speak of as God.

The fourth way is taken from the gradation to be found in things. Among beings there are some more and some less good, true, noble, and the like. But *more* and *less* are predicated of different things according as they resemble in their different ways something which is the maximum, as a thing is said to be hotter according as it more nearly resembles that which is hottest; so that there is something which is truest, something best, something noblest, and, consequently, something which is most being, for those things that are greatest in truth are greatest in being, as it is written in *Metaph.* ii. Now the maximum in any genus is the cause of all in that genus, as fire, which is the maximum of heat, is the cause of all hot things, as is said in the same book. Therefore there must also be something which is to all beings the cause of their being, goodness, and every other perfection: and this we call God.

The fifth way is taken from the governance of the world. We see that things which lack knowledge, such as natural bodies, act for an end, and this is evident from their acting always, or nearly always, in the same way, so as to obtain the best result. Hence it is plain that they achieve their end, not fortuitously but designedly. Now whatever lacks knowledge cannot move towards an end, unless it be directed by some being endowed with knowledge and intelligence; as the arrow is directed by the archer. Therefore some intelligent being exists by whom all natural things are directed to their end; and this being we call God.

STUDY QUESTIONS

1. Do Aquinas's five ways all reach the same conclusion?
2. If whatever is moved must be moved by another, how is an unmoved mover possible?
3. Do the terms "more" and "less" always presuppose a maximum?
4. Does a river flowing toward the sea act for an end?

Dialogues Concerning
Natural Religion

ﬂ

DAVID HUME

David Hume's extraordinarily powerful *Dialogues Concerning Natural Religion* is one of the most important books in the philosophy of religion. During his lifetime, his friends, fearful of public disapproval, had dissuaded him from publishing the manuscript, but he took great pains to ensure that the work would not be lost, and it appeared in print three years after his death, although without any publisher's name attached.

"Natural religion" was the term used by eighteenth-century writers to refer to theological tenets that are provable by reason without appeal to revelation. The three participants in the *Dialogues* are distinguished by their views concerning the scope and limits of reason. Cleanthes claims that he can present arguments that demonstrate the truth of traditional Christian theology. Demea is committed to that theology but does not believe empirical evidence can provide any defense for his faith. Philo doubts that reason yields conclusive results in any field of inquiry and is especially critical of theological dogmatism.

By subtle interplay among these three characters, Hume seeks to show the surprising affinity between Philo and Demea, as well as the equally surprising lack of affinity between Demea and Cleanthes.

In the sections of the book reprinted here, the argument to design is subjected to trenchant criticism. In addition, Hume develops in detail what is probably the strongest argument against the existence of God, namely, the problem of evil: How can evil exist in a world created by an all-good, all-powerful God?

PART II

... Not to lose any time in circumlocutions, said Cleanthes, ... I shall briefly explain how I conceive this matter. Look round the world, contemplate the whole and every part of it: you will find it to be nothing but one great machine, subdivided into an infinite number of lesser machines, which again admit of subdivisions to a degree beyond what human senses and faculties can trace and explain. All these various machines, and even their most minute parts, are adjusted to each other with an accuracy which ravishes into admiration all men who have ever contemplated them. The curious adapting of means to ends, throughout all nature, resembles exactly, though it much exceeds, the productions of human

From *Dialogues Concerning Natural Religion* (1779) by David Hume.

contrivance—of human design, thought, wisdom, and intelligence. Since therefore the effects resemble each other, we are led to infer, by all the rules of analogy, that the causes also resemble, and that the Author of nature is somewhat similar to the mind of man, though possessed of much larger faculties, proportioned to the grandeur of the work which he has executed. By this argument a posteriori, and by this argument alone, do we prove at once the existence of a Deity and his similarity to human mind and intelligence.

I shall be so free, Cleanthes, said Demea, as to tell you that from the beginning I could not approve of your conclusion concerning the similarity of the Deity to men, still less can I approve of the mediums by which you endeavour to establish it. What! No demonstration of the Being of God! No abstract arguments! No proofs a priori! Are these which have hitherto been so much insisted on by philosophers all fallacy, all sophism? Can we reach no farther in this subject than experience and probability? I will not say that this is betraying the cause of a Deity; but surely, by this affected candour, you give advantages to atheists which they never could obtain by the mere dint of argument and reasoning.

What I chiefly scruple in this subject, said Philo, is not so much that all religious arguments are by Cleanthes reduced to experience, as that they appear not to be even the most certain and irrefragable of that inferior kind. That a stone will fall, that fire will burn, that the earth has solidity, we have observed a thousand and a thousand times; and when any new instance of this nature is presented, we draw without hesitation the accustomed inference. The exact similarity of the cases gives us a perfect assurance of a similar event, and a stronger evidence is never desired nor sought after. But wherever you depart, in the least, from the similarity of the cases, you diminish proportionably the evidence, and may at last bring it to a very weak *analogy*, which is confessedly liable to error and uncertainty. After having experienced the circulation of the blood in human creatures, we make no doubt that it takes place in Titius and Maevius,[1] but from its circulation in frogs and fishes it is only a presumption, though a strong one, from analogy that it takes place in men and other animals. The analogical reasoning is much weaker when we infer the circulation of the sap in vegetables from our experience that the blood circulates in animals; and those who hastily followed that imperfect analogy are found, by more accurate experiments, to have been mistaken.

If we see a house, Cleanthes, we conclude, with the greatest certainty, that it had an architect or builder because this is precisely that species of effect which we have experienced to proceed from that species of cause. But surely you will not affirm that the universe bears such a resemblance to a house that we can with the same certainty infer a similar cause, or that the analogy is here entire and perfect. The dissimilitude is so striking that the utmost you can here pretend to is a guess, conjecture, a presumption concerning a similar cause; and how that pretension will be received in the world, I leave you to consider.

It would surely be very ill received, replied Cleanthes; and I should be deservedly blamed and detested did I allow that the proofs of Deity amounted to no more than a guess or conjecture. But is the whole adjustment of means to ends in a house and in the universe so slight a resemblance? the economy of final causes? the order, proportion, and arrangement of every part? Steps of a stair are plainly contrived that human legs may use them in mounting; and this inference is certain and infallible. Human legs are also contrived for walking and mounting; and this inference, I allow, is not altogether so certain because of the dissimilarity which you remark; but does it, therefore, deserve the name only of presumption or conjecture?

Good God! cried Demea, interrupting him, where are we? Zealous defenders of religion allow that the proofs of a Deity fall short of perfect evidence! And you, Philo, on whose assistance I depended in proving the adorable mysteriousness of the Divine Nature, do you assent to all these extravagant opinions of Cleanthes? For what other name can I give them? or, why spare my censure when such principles are advanced, supported by such an authority, before so young a man as Pamphilus?

You seem not to apprehend, replied Philo, that I argue with Cleanthes in his own way, and, by showing him the dangerous consequences of his tenets, hope at last to reduce him to our opinion. But what sticks most with you, observe, is the representation which Cleanthes has made of the argument a posteriori; and, finding that the argument is likely to escape your hold and vanish into air, you think it so disguised that you can scarcely believe it to be set in its true light. Now, however much I may dissent, in other respects, from the dangerous principle of Cleanthes, I must allow that he has fairly represented that argument, and I shall endeavour so to state the matter to you that you will entertain no further scruples with regard to it.

Were a man to abstract from everything which he knows or has seen, he would be altogether incapable, merely from his own ideas, to determine what kind of scene the universe must be, or to give the preference to one state or situation of things above another. For as nothing which he clearly conceives could be esteemed impossible or implying a contradiction, every chimera of his fancy would be upon an equal footing; nor could he assign any just reason why he adheres to one idea or system, and rejects the others which are equally possible.

Again, after he opens his eyes and contemplates the world as it really is, it would be impossible for him at first to assign the cause of any one event, much less of the whole of things, or of the universe. He might set his fancy a rambling, and she might bring him in an infinite variety of reports and representations. These would all be possible, but, being all equally possible, he would never of himself give a satisfactory account for his preferring one of them to the rest. Experience alone can point out to him the true cause of any phenomenon.

Now, according to this method of reasoning, Demea, it follows (and is, indeed, tacitly allowed by Cleanthes himself) that order, arrangement, or the adjustment of final causes, is not of itself any proof of design, but only so far as it has been experienced to proceed from that principle. For aught we can know a priori, matter may contain the source or spring of order originally within itself, as well as mind does; and there is no more difficulty in conceiving that the several elements, from an internal unknown cause, may fall into the most exquisite arrangement, than to conceive that their ideas, in the great universal mind, from a like internal unknown cause, fall into that arrangement. The equal possibility of both these suppositions is allowed. But, by experience, we find (according to Cleanthes) that there is a difference between them. Throw several pieces of steel together, without shape or form, they will never arrange themselves so as to compose a watch. Stone and mortar and wood, without an architect, never erect a house. But the ideas in a human mind, we see, by an unknown, inexplicable economy, arrange themselves so as to form the plan of a watch or house. Experience, therefore, proves that there is an original principle of order in mind, not in matter. From similar effects we infer similar causes. The adjustment of means to ends is alike in the universe, as in a machine of human contrivance. The causes, therefore, must be resembling.

I was from the beginning scandalized, I must own, with this resemblance which is asserted between the Deity and human creatures, and must conceive it to imply such a degradation of the Supreme Being as no sound theist could endure. With your assistance, therefore, Demea, I shall endeavour to defend what you justly call the adorable mysteriousness of the Divine Nature, and shall refute this reasoning of Cleanthes, provided he allows that I have made a fair representation of it.

When Cleanthes had assented, Philo, after a short pause, proceeded in the following manner.

That all inferences, Cleanthes, concerning fact are founded on experience, and that all experimental reasonings are founded on the supposition that similar causes prove similar effects, and similar effects similar causes, I shall not at present much dispute with you. But observe, I entreat you, with what extreme caution all just reasoners proceed in the transferring of experiments to similar cases. Unless the cases be exactly similar, they repose no perfect confidence in applying their past observation to any particular phenomenon. Every alteration of circumstances occasions a doubt concerning the event; and it requires new experiments to prove certainly that the new circumstances are of no moment or importance. A change in bulk, situation, arrangement, age, disposition of the air, or surrounding bodies—any of these particulars may be attended with the most unexpected consequences. And unless the objects be quite familiar to us, it is the highest temerity to expect with assurance, after any of these changes, an event similar to that which before fell under our observation. The slow and deliberate steps of philosophers here, if anywhere, are distinguished from the precipitate march of the vulgar, who, hurried on by the smallest similitude, are incapable of all discernment or consideration.

But can you think, Cleanthes, that your usual phlegm and philosophy have been preserved in so wide a step as you have taken when you compared to the universe houses, ships, furniture, machines, and, from their similarity in some circumstances, inferred a similarity in their causes? Thought, design, intelligence, such as we discover in men and other animals, is no more than one of the springs and principles of the universe, as well as heat or cold, attraction or repulsion, and a hundred others which fall under daily observation. It is an active cause by which some particular parts of nature, we find, produce alterations on other parts. But can a conclusion, with any propriety, be transferred from parts to the whole? Does not the great disproportion bar all comparison and inference? From observing the growth of a hair, can we learn anything concerning the generation of a man? Would the manner of a leaf's blowing, even though perfectly known, afford us any instruction concerning the vegetation of a tree?

But allowing that we were to take the *operations* of one part of nature upon another for the foundation of our judgment concerning the *origin* of the whole (which never can be admitted), yet why select so minute, so weak, so bounded a principle as the reason and design of animals is found to be upon this planet? What peculiar privilege has this little agitation of the brain which we call *thought*, that we must thus make it the model of the whole universe? Our partiality in our own favour does indeed present it on all occasions, but sound philosophy ought carefully to guard against so natural an illusion.

So far from admitting, continued Philo, that the operations of a part can afford us any just conclusion concerning the origin of the whole, I will not allow any one part to form a rule for another part if the latter be very remote from the former. Is there any reasonable ground to conclude that the inhabitants of other planets possess thought, intelligence, reason, or anything similar to these faculties in men? When nature has so extremely diversified her manner of operation in this small globe, can we imagine that she incessantly copies herself throughout so immense a universe? And if thought, as we may well suppose, be confined merely to this narrow corner and has even there so limited a sphere of action, with what propriety can we assign it for the original cause of all things? The narrow views of a peasant who makes his domestic economy the rule for the government of kingdoms is in comparison a pardonable sophism.

But were we ever so much assured that a thought and reason resembling the human were to be found throughout the whole universe, and were its activity elsewhere vastly greater and more commanding than it appears in this globe, yet I cannot see why the operations of a world constituted, arranged, adjusted can with any propriety be extended to a world which is in its embryo state, and is advancing towards that constitution and arrangement. By observation we know somewhat of the economy, action, and nourishment of a finished animal, but we must transfer with great caution that observation to the growth of a fetus in the womb, and still more to the formation of an animalcule in the loins of its male parent. Nature, we find, even from our limited experience, possesses an infinite number of springs and principles which incessantly discover themselves on every change of her position and situation. And what new and unknown principles would actuate her in so new and unknown a situation as that of the formation of a universe, we cannot, without the utmost temerity, pretend to determine.

A very small part of this great system, during a very short time, is very imperfectly discovered to us; and do we thence pronounce decisively concerning the origin of the whole?

Admirable conclusion! Stone, wood, brick, iron, brass, have not, at this time, in this minute globe of earth, an order or arrangement without human art and contrivance; therefore, the universe could not originally attain its order and arrangement without something similar to human art. But is a part of nature a rule for another part very wide of the former? Is it a rule for the whole? Is a very small part a rule for the universe? Is nature in one situation a certain rule for nature in another situation vastly different from the former?

And can you blame me, Cleanthes, if I here imitate the prudent reserve of Simonides,[2] who, according to the noted story, being asked by Hiero,[3] *What God was?* desired a day to think of it, and then two days more; and after that manner continually prolonged the term, without ever bringing in his definition or description? Could you even blame me if I had answered, at first, *that I did not know,* and was sensible that this subject lay vastly beyond the reach of my faculties? You might cry out sceptic and raillier, as much as you pleased; but, having found in so many other subjects much more familiar the imperfections and even contradictions of human reason, I never should expect any success from its feeble conjectures in a subject so sublime and so remote from the sphere of our observation. When two *species* of objects have always been observed to be conjoined together, I can *infer,* by custom, the existence of one wherever I *see* the existence of the other; and this I call an argument from experience. But how this argument can have place where the objects, as in the present case, are single, individual, without parallel or specific resemblance may be difficult to explain. And will any man tell me with a serious countenance that an orderly universe must arise from some thought and art like the human because we have experience of it? To ascertain this reasoning, it was requisite that we had experience of the origin of worlds; and it is not sufficient, surely, that we have seen ships and cities arise from human art and contrivance....

PART V

But to show you still more inconveniences, continued Philo, in your anthropomorphism, please to take a new survey of your principles. *Like effects prove like causes.* This is the experimental argument, and this, you say too, is the sole theological argument. Now it is certain that the liker the effects are which are seen and the liker the causes which are inferred, the stronger is the argument. Every departure on either side diminishes the probability and renders the experiment less conclusive. You cannot doubt of the principle; neither ought you to reject its consequences.

All the new discoveries in astronomy which prove the immense grandeur and magnificence of the works of nature are so many additional arguments for a Deity, according to the true system of theism; but, according to your hypothesis of experimental theism, they become so many objections, by removing the effect still farther from all resemblance to the effects of human art and contrivance....

If this argument, I say, had any force in former ages, how much greater must it have at present when the bounds of Nature are so infinitely enlarged and such a magnificent scene is opened to us? It is still more unreasonable to form our idea of so unlimited a cause from our experience of the narrow productions of human design and invention.

The discoveries by microscopes, as they open a new universe in miniature, are still objections, according to you, arguments, according to me. The further we push our researches of this kind, we are still led to infer the universal cause of all to be vastly different from mankind, or from any object of human experience and observation.

And what say you to the discoveries in anatomy, chemistry, botany? ... These surely are no objections, replied Cleanthes; they only discover new instances of art and contrivance, it is still the image of mind reflected on us from innumerable objects. Add a mind *like the human*, said Philo. I know of no other, replied Cleanthes. And the liker, the better, insisted Philo. To be sure, said Cleanthes.

Now, Cleanthes, said Philo, with an air of alacrity and triumph, mark the consequences. *First*, by this method of reasoning you renounce all claim to infinity in any of the attributes of the Deity. For, as the cause ought only to be proportioned to the effect, and the effect, so far as it falls under our cognizance, is not infinite, what pretensions have we, upon your suppositions, to ascribe that attribute to the Divine Being? You will still insist that, by removing him so much from all similarity to human creatures, we give in to the most arbitrary hypothesis, and at the same time weaken all proofs of his existence.

Secondly, you have no reason, on your theory, for ascribing perfection to the Deity, even in his finite capacity, or for supposing him free from every error, mistake, or incoherence, in his undertakings. There are many inexplicable difficulties in the works of nature which, if we allow a perfect author to be proved a priori, are easily solved, and become only seeming difficulties from the narrow capacity of man, who cannot trace infinite relations. But according to your method of reasoning, these difficulties become all real, and, perhaps, will be insisted on as new instances of likeness to human art and contrivance. At least, you must acknowledge that it is impossible for us to tell, from our limited views, whether this system contains any great faults or deserves any considerable praise if compared to other possible and even real systems. Could a peasant, if the *Aeneid* were read to him, pronounce that poem to be absolutely faultless, or even assign to it its proper rank among the productions of human wit, he who had never seen any other production?

But were this world ever so perfect a production, it must still remain uncertain whether all the excellences of the work can justly be ascribed to the workman. If we survey a ship, what an exalted idea must we form of the ingenuity of the carpenter who framed so complicated, useful, and beautiful a machine? And what surprise must we feel when we find him a stupid mechanic who imitated others, and copied an art which, through a long succession of ages, after multiplied trials, mistakes, corrections, deliberations, and controversies, had been gradually improving? Many worlds might have been botched and bungled, throughout an eternity, ere this system was struck out; much labour lost, many fruitless trials made, and a slow but continued improvement carried on during infinite ages in the art of world-making. In such subjects, who can determine where the truth, nay, who can conjecture where the probability lies, amidst a great number of hypotheses which may be proposed, and a still greater which may be imagined?

And what shadow of an argument, continued Philo, can you produce from your hypothesis to prove the unity of the Deity? A great number of men join in building a house or ship, in rearing a city, in framing a commonwealth; why may not several deities combine in contriving and framing a world? This is only so much greater similarity to human affairs. By sharing the work among several, we may so much further limit the attributes of each, and get rid of that extensive power and knowledge which must be supposed in one deity, and which, according to you, can only serve to weaken the proof of his existence. And if such foolish, such vicious creatures as man can yet often unite in framing and executing one plan, how much more those deities or demons, whom we may suppose several degrees more perfect!

To multiply causes without necessity is indeed contrary to true philosophy, but this principle applies not to the present case. Were one deity antecedently proved by your theory who was possessed of every attribute requisite to the production of the universe, it would be needless, I own (though not absurd) to suppose any other deity existent. But while it is still a question whether all these attributes are united in one subject or dispersed among several independent beings, by what phenomena in nature can we pretend to decide the controversy? Where we see a body raised in a scale, we are sure that there is in the opposite scale, however concealed from sight, some counterpoising weight equal to it; but it is still allowed to doubt whether that weight be an aggregate of several distinct bodies or one uniform united mass. And if the weight requisite very much exceeds anything which we have ever seen conjoined in any single body, the former supposition becomes still more probable and natural. An intelligent being of such vast power and capacity as is necessary to produce the universe, or, to speak in the language of ancient philosophy, so prodigious an animal exceeds all analogy and even comprehension.

But further, Cleanthes: Men are mortal, and renew their species by generation; and this is common to all living creatures. The two great sexes of male and female, says Milton, animate the world. Why must this circumstance, so universal, so essential, be excluded from those numerous and limited deities? Behold, then, the theogeny of ancient times brought back upon us.

And why not become a perfect anthropomorphite? Why not assert the deity or deities to be corporeal, and to have eyes, a nose, mouth, ears, etc.? Epicurus maintained that no man had ever seen reason but in a human figure; therefore, the gods must have a human figure. And this argument, which is deservedly so much ridiculed by Cicero, becomes, according to you, solid and philosophical.

In a word, Cleanthes, a man who follows your hypothesis, is able, perhaps, to assert or conjecture that the universe sometime arose from something like design; but beyond that position he cannot ascertain one single circumstance, and is left afterwards to fix every point of his theology by the utmost license of fancy and hypothesis. This world, for aught he knows, is very faulty and imperfect, compared to a superior standard, and was only the first rude essay of some infant deity who afterwards abandoned it, ashamed of his lame performance; it is the work only of some dependent, inferior deity, and is the object of derision to his superiors; it is the production of old age and dotage in some superannuated deity, and ever since his death has run on at adventures, from the first impulse and active force which it received from him. You justly give signs of horror, Demea, at these strange suppositions; but these, and a thousand more of the same kind, are Cleanthes' suppositions, not mine. From the moment the attributes of the Deity are supposed finite, all these have place. And I cannot, for my part, think that so wild and unsettled a system of theology is, in any respect, preferable to none at all.

These suppositions I absolutely disown, cried Cleanthes: they strike me, however, with no horror, especially when proposed in that rambling way in which they drop from you. On the contrary, they give me pleasure when I see that, by the utmost indulgence of your imagination, you never get rid of the hypothesis of design in the universe, but are obliged at every turn to have recourse to it. To this concession I adhere steadily; and this I regard as a sufficient foundation for religion.

PART VI

It must be a slight fabric, indeed, said Demea, which can be erected on so tottering a foundation. While we are uncertain whether there is one deity or many, whether the deity or deities, to whom we owe our existence, be perfect or imperfect, subordinate or supreme, dead or alive, what trust or confidence can we repose in them? What devotion or worship address to them? What veneration or obedience pay them? To all the purposes of life the theory of religion becomes altogether useless; and even with regard to speculative consequences its uncertainty, according to you, must render it totally precarious and unsatisfactory.

To render it still more unsatisfactory, said Philo, there occurs to me another hypothesis which must acquire an air of probability from the method of reasoning so much insisted on by Cleanthes. That like effects arise from like causes—this principle he supposes the foundation of all religion. But there is another principle of the same kind, no less certain and derived from the same source of experience, that, where several known circumstances are observed to be similar, the unknown will also be found similar. Thus, if we see the limbs of a human body, we conclude that it is also attended with a human head, though hid from us. Thus, if we see, through a chink in a wall, a small part of the sun, we conclude that were the wall removed we should see the whole body. In short, this method of reasoning is so obvious and familiar that no scruple can ever be made with regard to its solidity.

Now, if we survey the universe, so far as it falls under our knowledge, it bears a great resemblance to an animal or organized body, and seems actuated with a like principle of life and motion. A continual circulation of matter in it produces no disorder; a continual waste in every part is incessantly repaired; the closest sympathy is perceived throughout the entire system; and each part or member, in performing its proper offices, operates both to its own preservation and to that of the whole. The world, therefore, I infer, is an animal; and the Deity is the *soul* of the world, actuating it, and actuated by it.....

This theory, I own, replied Cleanthes, has never before occurred to me, though a pretty natural one; and I cannot readily, upon so short an examination and reflection, deliver any opinion with regard to it. You are very scrupulous, indeed, said Philo; were I to examine any system of yours, I should not have acted with half that caution and reserve, in starting objections and difficulties to it. However, if anything occur to you, you will oblige us by proposing it.

Why then, replied Cleanthes, it seems to me that, though the world does, in many circumstances, resemble an animal body, yet is the analogy also defective in many circumstances the most material: no organs of sense, no seat of thought or reason; no one precise origin of motion and action. In short, it seems to bear a stronger resemblance to a vegetable than to an animal, and your inference would be so far inconclusive in favor of the soul of the world.....

PART VII

But here, continued Philo, in examining the ancient system of the soul of the world there strikes me, all of a sudden, a new idea which, if just, must go near to subvert all your reasoning, and destroy even your first inferences on which you repose such confidence. If the universe bears a greater likeness to animal bodies and to vegetables than to the works of human art, it is more probable that its cause resembles the cause of the former than that of the latter, and its origin ought rather to be abscribed to generation or vegetation than to reason or design. Your conclusion, even according to your own principles, is therefore lame and defective.

Pray open up this argument a little further, said Demea, for I do not rightly apprehend it in that concise manner in which you have expressed it.

Our friend Cleanthes, replied Philo, as you have heard, asserts that since no question of fact can be proved otherwise than by experience, the existence of a Deity admits not of proof from any other medium. The world, says he, resembles the works of human contrivance; therefore its cause must also resemble that of the other. Here we may remark that the operation of one very small part of nature, to wit, man, upon another very small part, to wit, that inanimate matter lying within his reach, is the rule by which Cleanthes judges of the origin of the whole; and he measures objects, so widely disproportioned, by the same individual standard. But to waive all objections drawn from this topic, I affirm that there are other parts of the universe (besides the machines of human invention) which bear still a greater resemblance to the fabric of the world, and which, therefore, afford a better conjecture concerning the universal origin of this system. These parts are animals and vegetables. The world plainly resembles more an animal or a vegetable than it does a watch or a knitting loom. Its cause, therefore, it is more probable, resembles the cause of the former. The cause of the former is generation or vegetation. The cause, therefore, of the world we may infer to be something similar or analogous to generation or vegetation.

But how is it conceivable, said Demea, that the world can arise from anything similar to vegetation or generation?

Very easily, replied Philo. In like manner as a tree sheds its seed into the neighboring fields and produces other trees; so the great vegetable, the world, or this planetary system, produces within itself certain seeds which, being scattered into the surrounding chaos, vegetate into new worlds. A comet, for instance, is the seed of a world; and after it has been fully ripened, by passing from sun to sun, and star to star, it is at last tossed into the unformed elements which everywhere surround this universe, and immediately sprouts up into a new system.

Or if, for the sake of variety (for I see no other advantage) we should suppose this world to be an animal; a comet is the egg of this animal; and in like manner as an ostrich lays its egg in the sand, which, without any further care, hatches the egg and produces a new animal, so . . . I understand you, says Demea: But what wild, arbitrary suppositions are these? What *data* have you for such extraordinary conclusions? And is the slight, imaginary resemblance of the world to a vegetable or an animal sufficient to establish the same inference with regard to both? Objects which are in general so widely different; ought they to be a standard for each other?

Right, cries Philo: This is the topic on which I have all along insisted. I have still asserted that we have no *data* to establish any system of cosmogony. Our experience, so imperfect in itself and so limited both in extent and duration, can afford us no probable conjecture concerning the whole of things. But if we must need fix on some hypothesis, by what rule, pray, ought we to determine our choice? Is there any other rule than the great similarity of the objects compared? And does not a plant or an animal, which springs from vegetation or generation, bear a stronger resemblance to the world than does any artificial machine, which arises from reason and design?

But what is this vegetation and generation of which you talk? said Demea. Can you explain their operations and anatomize that fine internal structure on which they depend?

As much, at least, replied Philo, as Cleanthes can explain the operations of reason, or anatomize that internal structure on which *it* depends. But without any such elaborate disquisitions, when I see an animal, I infer that it sprang from generation; and that with as great certainty as you conclude a house to have been reared by design. These words *generation, reason* mark only certain powers and energies in nature whose effects are known, but whose essence is incomprehensible; and one of these principles, more than the other, has no privilege for being made a standard to the whole of nature.

In reality, Demea, it may reasonably be expected that the larger the views are which we take of things, the better will they conduct us in our conclusions concerning such extraordinary and such magnificent subjects. In this little corner of the world alone, there are four principles, *reason, instinct, generation, vegetation*, which are similar to each other, and are the causes of similar effects. What a number of other principles may we naturally suppose in the immense extent and variety of the universe could we travel from planet to planet, and from system to system, in order to examine each part of this mighty fabric? Any one of these four principles above mentioned (and a hundred others which lie open to our conjecture) may afford us a theory by which to judge of the origin of the world; and it is a palpable and egregious partiality to confine our view entirely to that principle by which our own minds operate. Were this principle more intelligible on that account, such a partiality might be somewhat excusable; but reason, in its internal fabric and structure, is really as little known to us as instinct or vegetation; and, perhaps, even that vague, undeterminate word *nature* to which the vulgar refer everything is not at the bottom more inexplicable. The effects of these principles are all known to us from experience; but the principles themselves and their manner of operation are totally unknown; nor is it less intelligible or less conformable to experience to say that the world arose by vegetation, from a seed shed by another world, than to say that it arose from a divine reason or contrivance, according to the sense in which Cleanthes understands it.

But methinks, said Demea, if the world had a vegetative quality and could sow the seeds of new worlds into the infinite chaos, this power would be still an additional argument for design in its author. For whence could arise so wonderful a faculty but from design? Or how can order spring from anything which perceives not that order which it bestows?

You need only look around you, replied Philo, to satisfy yourself with regard to this question. A tree bestows order and organization on that tree which springs from it, without knowing the order; an animal in the same manner on its off-spring; a bird on its nest; and instances of this kind are even more frequent in the world than those of order which arise from reason and contrivance. To say that all this order in animals and vegetables proceeds ultimately from design is beg-ging the question; nor can that great point be ascertained otherwise than by prov-ing, a priori, both that order is, from its nature, inseparably attached to thought and that it can never of itself or from original unknown principles belong to matter. . . .

PART X

It is my opinion, I own, replied Demea, that each man feels, in a manner, the truth of religion within his own breast, and, from a consciousness of his imbecility and misery rather than from any reasoning, is led to seek protection from that Being on whom he and all nature is dependent. So anxious or so tedious are even the best scenes of life that futurity is still the object of all our hopes and fears. We inces-santly look forward and endeavour, by prayers, adoration, and sacrifice, to appease those unknown powers whom we find, by experience, so able to afflict and oppress us. Wretched creatures that we are! What resource for us amidst the innumerable ills of life did not religion suggest some methods of atonement, and appease those terrors with which we are incessantly agitated and tormented?

I am indeed persuaded, said Philo, that the best and indeed the only method of bringing everyone to a due sense of religion is by just representations of the misery and wickedness of men. And for that purpose a talent of eloquence and strong imagery is more requisite than that of reasoning and argument. For is it necessary to prove what everyone feels within himself? It is only necessary to make us feel it, if possible, more intimately and sensibly.

The people, indeed, replied Demea, are sufficiently convinced of this great and melancholy truth. The miseries of life, the unhappiness of man, the general corruptions of our nature, the unsatisfactory enjoyment of pleasures, riches, honours—these phrases have become almost proverbial in all languages. And who can doubt what all men declare from their own immediate feeling and experience?

In this point, said Philo, the learned are perfectly agreed with the vulgar; and in all letters, *sacred* and *profane*, the topic of human misery has been insisted on with the most pathetic eloquence that sorrow and melancholy could inspire. The poets, who speak from sentiment, without a system, and whose testimony has therefore the more authority, abound in images of this nature. From Homer down to Dr. Young[4] the whole inspired tribe have ever been sensible that no other representation of things would suit the feeling and observation of each individual.

As to authorities, replied Demea, you need not seek them. Look round this library of Cleanthes. I shall venture to affirm that, except authors of particular sciences, such as chemistry or botany, who have no occasion to treat of human life, there is scarce one of those innumerable writers from whom the sense of human misery has not, in some passage or other, extorted a complaint and confession of it. At least, the chance is entirely on that side; and no one author has ever, so far as I can recollect, been so extravagant as to deny it.

There you must excuse me, said Philo: Leibniz[5] has denied it and is perhaps the first who ventured upon so bold and paradoxical an opinion; at least, the first who made it essential to his philosophical system.

And by being the first, replied Demea, might he not have been sensible of his error? For is this a subject in which philosophers can propose to make discoveries especially in so late an age? And can any man hope by a simple denial (for the subject scarcely admits of reasoning) to bear down the united testimony of mankind, founded on sense and consciousness?

And why should man, added he, pretend to an exemption from the lot of all other animals? The whole earth, believe me, Philo, is cursed and polluted. A perpetual war is kindled amongst all living creatures. Necessity, hunger, want stimulate the strong and courageous; fear, anxiety, terror agitate the weak and infirm. The first entrance into life gives anguish to the new-born infant and to its wretched parent; weakness, impotence, distress attend each stage of that life, and it is, at last finished in agony and horror.

Observe, too, says Philo, the curious artifices of nature in order to embitter the life of every living being. The stronger prey upon the weaker and keep them in perpetual terror and anxiety. The weaker, too, in their turn, often prey upon the stronger, and vex and molest them without relaxation. Consider that innumerable race of insects, which either are bred on the body of each animal or, flying about, infix their stings in him. These insects have others still less than themselves which torment them. And thus on each hand, before and behind, above and below, every animal is surrounded with enemies which incessantly seek his misery and destruction.

Man alone, said Demea, seems to be, in part, an exception to this rule. For by combination in society he can easily master lions, tigers, and bears, whose greater strength and agility naturally enable them to prey upon him.

On the contrary, it is here chiefly, cried Philo, that the uniform and equal maxims of nature are most apparent. Man, it is true, can, by combination, surmount all his *real* enemies and become master of the whole animal creation; but does he not immediately raise up to himself *imaginary* enemies, the demons of his fancy, who haunt him with superstitious terrors and blast every enjoyment of life? His pleasure, as he imagines, becomes in their eyes a crime; his food and repose give them umbrage and offence; his very sleep and dreams furnish new materials to anxious fear; and even death, his refuge from every other ill, presents only the dread of endless and innumerable woes. Nor does the wolf molest more the timid flock than superstition does the anxious breast of wretched mortals.

Besides, consider, Demea: This very society by which we surmount those wild beasts, our natural enemies, what new enemies does it not raise to us? What woe and misery does it not occasion? Man is the greatest enemy of man. Oppression, injustice, contempt, contumely, violence, sedition, war, calumny, treachery, fraud—by these they mutually torment each other, and they would soon dissolve that society which they had formed were it not for the dread of still greater ills which must attend their separation.

But though these external insults, said Demea, from animals, from men, from all the elements, which assault us from a frightful catalogue of woes, they are nothing in comparison of those which arise within ourselves, from the distempered condition of our mind and body. How many lie under the lingering torment of diseases? ...

The disorders of the mind, continued Demea, though more secret, are not perhaps less dismal and vexatious. Remorse, shame, anguish, rage, disappointment, anxiety, fear, dejection, despair—who has ever passed through life without cruel inroads from these tormentors? How many have scarcely ever felt any better sensations? Labour and poverty, so abhorred by everyone, are the certain lot of the far greater number; and those few privileged persons who enjoy ease and opulence never reach contentment or true felicity. All the goods of life united would not make a very happy man, but all the ills united would make a wretch indeed, and any one of them almost (and who can be free from every one?), nay, often the absence of one good (and who can possess all?) is sufficient to render life ineligible.

Were a stranger to drop on a sudden into this world, I would show him, as a specimen of its ills, an hospital full of diseases, a prison crowded with malefactors and debtors, a field of battle strewed with carcases, a fleet floundering in the ocean, a nation languishing under tyranny, famine, or pestilence. To turn the gay side of life to him and give him a notion of its pleasures—whither should I conduct him?

To a ball, to an opera, to court? He might justly think that I was only showing him a diversity of distress and sorrow.

There is no evading such striking instances, said Philo, but by apologies which still further aggravate the charge. Why have all men, I ask, in all ages, complained incessantly of the miseries of life? . . . They have no just reason, says one: these complaints proceed only from their discontented, repining, anxious disposition. . . . And can there possibly, I reply, be a more certain foundation of misery than such a wretched temper?

But if they were really as unhappy as they pretend, says my antagonist, why do they remain in life? . . .

Not satisfied with life, afraid of death—

This is the secret chain, say I, that holds us. We are terrified, not bribed to the continuance of our existence.

It is only a false delicacy, he may insist, which a few refined spirits indulge, and which has spread these complaints among the whole race of mankind. . . . And what is this delicacy, I ask, which you blame? Is it anything but a greater sensibility to all the pleasures and pains of life? And if the man of a delicate, refined temper, by being so much more alive than the rest of the world, is only so much more unhappy, what judgment must we form in general of human life?

Let men remain at rest, says our adversary, and they will be easy. They are willing artificers of their own misery. . . . No! reply I: an anxious languor follows their repose: disappointment, vexation, trouble, their activity and ambition.

I can observe something like what you mention in some others, replied Cleanthes, but I confess I feel little or nothing of it in myself, and hope that it is not so common as you represent it.

If you feel not human misery yourself, cried Demea, I congratulate you on so happy a singularity. Others, seemingly the most prosperous, have not been ashamed to vent their complaints in the most melancholy strains. Let us attend to the great, the fortunate emperor, Charles V,[6] when tired with human grandeur, he resigned all his extensive dominions into the hands of his son. In the last harangue which he made on that memorable occasion, he publicly avowed *that the greatest prosperities which he had ever enjoyed had been mixed with so many adversities that he might truly say he had never enjoyed any satisfaction or contentment.* But did the retired life in which he sought for shelter afford him any greater happiness? If we may credit his son's account, his repentance commenced the very day of his resignation.

Cicero's[7] fortune, from small beginnings, rose to the greatest luster and renown; yet what pathetic complaints of the ills of life do his familiar letters, as well as philosophical discourses, contain? And suitably to his own experience, he introduces Cato,[8] the great, the fortunate Cato protesting in his old age that had he a new life in his offer he would reject the present.

Ask yourself, ask any of your acquaintance, whether they would live over again the last ten or twenty years of their life. No! but the next twenty, they say, will be better. . . .

Thus, at last, they find (such is the greatness of human misery, it reconciles even contradictions) that they complain at once of the shortness of life and of its vanity and sorrow.

And is it possible, Cleanthes, said Philo, that after all these reflections, and infinitely more which might be suggested, you can still perservere in your anthropomorphism and assert the moral attributes of the Deity, his justice, benevolence, mercy, and rectitude to be of the same nature with these virtues in human creatures? His power, we allow, is infinite; whatever he wills is executed; but neither man nor any other animal is happy; therefore, he does not will their happiness. His wisdom is infinite; he is never mistaken in choosing the means to any end; but the course of nature tends not to human or animal felicity; therefore, it is not established for that purpose. Through the whole compass of human knowledge there are no inferences more certain and infallible than these. In what respect, then, do his benevolence and mercy resemble the benevolence and mercy of men?

Epicurus' old questions are yet unanswered.

Is he willing to prevent evil, but not able? then is he impotent. Is he able, but not willing? then is he malevolent. Is he both able and willing? whence then is evil?

You ascribe, Cleanthes (and I believe justly), a purpose and intention to nature. But what, I beseech you, is the object of that curious artifice and machinery which she has displayed in all animals—the preservation alone of individuals, and propagation of the species? It seems enough for her purpose, if such a rank be barely upheld in the universe, without any care or concern for the happiness of the members that compose it. No resource for this purpose: no machinery in order merely to give pleasure or ease; no fund of pure joy and contentment; no indulgence without some want or necessity accompanying it. At least, the few phenomena of this nature are over-balanced by opposite phenomena of still greater importance.

Our sense of music, harmony, and indeed beauty of all kinds gives satisfaction, without being absolutely necessary to the preservation and propagation of the species. But what racking pains, on the other hand, arise from gouts, gravels, megrims, toothaches, rheumatisms, where the injury to the animal machinery is either small or incurable? Mirth, laughter, play, frolic seem gratuitous satisfactions which have no further tendency; spleen, melancholy, discontent, superstition are pains of the same nature. How then does the Divine benevolence display itself, in the sense of you anthropomorphites? None but we mystics, as you were pleased to call us, can account for this strange mixture of phenomena, by deriving it from attributes infinitely perfect but incomprehensible.

And have you, at last, said Cleanthes smiling, betrayed your intentions, Philo? Your long agreement with Demea did indeed a little surprise me, but I find you were all the while erecting a concealed battery against me. And I must confess that you have now fallen upon a subject worthy of your noble spirit of opposition and controversy. If you can make out the present point, and prove mankind to be unhappy or corrupted, there is an end at once of all religion. For to what purpose establish the natural attributes of the Deity, while the moral are still doubtful and uncertain?

You take umbrage very easily, replied Demea, at opinions the most innocent and the most generally received, even amongst the religious and devout themselves; and nothing can be more surprising than to find a topic like this—concerning the wickedness and misery of man—charged with no less than atheism and profaneness. Have not all pious divines and preachers who have indulged their rhetoric on so fertile a subject, have they not easily, I say, given a solution of any difficulties which may attend it? This world is but a point in comparison of the universe, this life but a moment in comparison of eternity. The present evil phenomena, therefore, are rectified in other regions, and in some future period of existence. And the eyes of men, being then opened to larger views of things, see the whole connection of general laws, and trace, with adoration, the benevolence and rectitude of the Deity through all the mazes and intricacies of his providence.

No! replied Cleanthes, no! These arbitrary suppositions can never be admitted, contrary to matter of fact, visible and uncontroverted. Whence can any cause be known but from its known effects? Whence can any hypothesis be proved but from the apparent phenomena? To establish one hypothesis upon another is building entirely in the air; and the utmost we ever attain by these conjectures and fictions is to ascertain the bare possibility of our opinion, but never can we, upon such terms, establish its reality.

The only method of supporting Divine benevolence—and it is what I willingly embrace—is to deny absolutely the misery and wickedness of man. Your representations are exaggerated; your melancholy views mostly fictitious; your inferences contrary to fact and experience. Health is more common than sickness; pleasure than pain; happiness than misery. And for one vexation which we meet with, we attain, upon computation, a hundred enjoyments.

Admitting your position, replied Philo, which yet is extremely doubtful, you must at the same time allow that, if pain be less frequent than pleasure, it is infinitely more violent and durable. One hour of it is often able to outweigh a day, a week, a month of our common insipid enjoyments; and how many days, weeks, and months are passed by several in the most acute torments? Pleasure, scarcely in one instance, is ever able to reach ecstasy and rapture; and in no one instance can it continue for any time at its highest pitch and altitude. The spirits evaporate, the nerves relax, the fabric is disordered, and the enjoyment quickly degenerates into fatigue and uneasiness. But pain often, good God, how often! rises to torture and agony; and the longer it continues, it becomes still more genuine agony and torture. Patience is exhausted, courage languishes, melancholy seizes us, and nothing terminates our misery but the removal of its cause or another event which is the sole cure of all evil, but which, from our natural folly, we regard with still greater horror and consternation.

But not to insist upon these topics, continued Philo, though most obvious, certain, and important, I must use the freedom to admonish you, Cleanthes, that you have put the controversy upon a most dangerous issue, and are unawares introducing a total scepticism into the most essential articles of natural and revealed theology. What! no method of fixing a just foundation for religion unless we allow the happiness of human life, and maintain a continued existence even in this world, with all our present pains, infirmities, vexations, and follies, to be eligible and desirable! But this is contrary to everyone's feeling and experience; it is contrary to an authority so established as nothing can subvert. No decisive proofs can ever be produced against this authority; nor is it possible for you to compute, estimate, and compare all the pains and all the pleasures in the lives of all men and of all animals; and thus, by your resting the whole system of religion on a point which, from its very nature, must for ever be uncertain, you tacitly confess that that system is equally uncertain.

But allowing you what never will be believed, at least, what you never possibly can prove, that animal or, at least, human happiness in this life exceeds its misery, you have yet done nothing; for this is not, by any means, what we expect from infinite power, infinite wisdom, and infinite goodness. Why is there any misery at all in the world? Not by chance, surely. From some cause then. Is it from the intention of the Deity? But he is perfectly benevolent. Is it contrary to his intention? But he is almighty. Nothing can shake the solidity of this reasoning, so short, so clear, so decisive, except we assert that these subjects exceed all human capacity and that our common measures of truth and falsehood are not applicable to them—a topic which I have all along insisted on, but which you have, from the beginning, rejected with scorn and indignation.

But I will be contented to retire still from this entrenchment, for I deny that you can ever force me in it. I will allow that pain or misery in man is *compatible* with infinite power and goodness in the Deity, even in your sense of these attributes: what are you advanced by all these concessions? A mere possible compatibility is not sufficient. You must *prove* these pure, unmixed, and uncontrollable attributes from the present mixed and confused phenomena, and from these alone. A hopeful undertaking! Were the phenomena ever so pure and unmixed, yet, being finite, they would be insufficient for that purpose. How much more, where they are also so jarring and discordant!

Here, Cleanthes, I find myself at ease in my argument. Here I triumph. Formerly, when we argued concerning the natural attributes of intelligence and design, I needed all my sceptical and metaphysical subtlety to elude your grasp. In many views of the universe and of its parts, particularly the latter, the beauty and fitness of final causes strike us with such irresistible force that all objections appear (what I believe they really are) mere cavils and sophisms; nor can we then imagine how it was ever possible for us to repose any weight on them. But there is no view of human life or of the condition of mankind from which, without the greatest violence, we can infer the moral attributes or learn that infinite benevolence, conjoined with infinite power and infinite wisdom, which we must discover by the eyes of faith alone. It is your turn now to tug the labouring oar, and to support your philosophical subtleties against the dictates of plain reason and experience.

NOTES

1. [Conventional names of ordinary persons, such as Smith and Jones.—S.M.C.]
2. [Simonides of Ceos (c. 548–468 B.C.) was a Greek poet.]

3. [The reference is to Hiero I, a fifth-century B.C. ruler of Syracuse, noted as a patron of literature.]
4. [The reference is to Edward Young (1683–1765), an English poet.]
5. [The reference is to the renowned German philosopher Gottfried Wilhelm Leibniz (1646–1716).]
6. [Charles V (1500–1588) was king of Spain for forty years.]
7. [Marcus Tullius Cicero (106–43 B.C.), the statesman and philosopher, was considered the greatest Roman orator.]
8. [The reference is to Marcus Porcius Cato the Elder (234–149 B.C.), a Roman statesman.]

STUDY QUESTIONS

1. In what ways is the world similar to a machine, and in what ways dissimilar?
2. Does the nature of the world give evidence suggesting more strongly one creator or many creators?
3. If you would not be willing to live over again the last ten years of your life, does that reluctance amount to evidence against theism?
4. At what point in the argument does Philo declare, "Here I triumph"?

The Wager

❧

BLAISE PASCAL

Here, translated from the original French, is the passage in which Blaise Pascal presents his much-discussed wager, examined in previous selections by Simon Blackburn and Linda Zagzebski.

....

If there is a God, he is infinitely beyond our comprehension, since, having neither parts nor limits, he bears no relation to ourselves. We are therefore incapable of knowing either what he is, or if he is. That being so, who will dare to undertake a resolution of this question? It cannot be us, who bear no relationship to him.

Who will then blame the Christians for being unable to provide a rational basis for their belief, they who profess a religion for which they cannot provide a rational basis? They declare that it is a folly (1 Cor. 1: 18) in laying it before the world: and then you complain that they do not prove it! If they did prove it, they

From Blaise Pascal, *Pensées*, trans. Honor Levi. Reprinted by permission of Oxford University Press.

would not be keeping their word. It is by the lack of proof that they do not lack sense. "Yes, but although that excuses those who offer their religion as it is, and that takes away the blame from them of producing it without a rational basis, it does not excuse those who accept it."

Let us therefore examine this point, and say: God is, or is not. But towards which side will we lean? Reason cannot decide anything. There is an infinite chaos separating us. At the far end of this infinite distance a game is being played and the coin will come down heads or tails. How will you wager? Reason cannot make you choose one way or the other, reason cannot make you defend either of the two choices.

So do not accuse those who have made a choice of being wrong, for you know nothing about it! "No, but I will blame them not for having made this choice, but for having made any choice. For, though the one who chooses heads and the other one are equally wrong, they are both wrong. The right thing is not to wager at all."

Yes, but you have to wager. It is not up to you, you are already committed. Which then will you choose? Let us see. Since you have to choose, let us see which interests you the least. You have two things to lose: the truth and the good, and two things to stake: your reason and will, your knowledge and beatitude; and your nature has two things to avoid: error and wretchedness. Your reason is not hurt more by choosing one rather than the other, since you do have to make the choice. That is one point disposed of. But your beatitude? Let us weigh up the gain and the loss by calling heads that God exists. Let us assess the two cases: if you win, you win everything; if you lose, you lose nothing. Wager that he exists then, without hesitating! "This is wonderful. Yes, I must wager. But perhaps I am betting too much." Let us see. Since there is an equal chance of gain and loss, if you won only two lives instead of one, you could still put on a bet. But if there were three lives to win, you would have to play (since you must necessarily play), and you would be unwise, once forced to play, not to chance your life to win three in a game where there is an equal chance of losing and winning. But there is an eternity of life and happiness. And that being so, even though there were an infinite number of chances of which only one were in your favour, you would still be right to wager one in order to win two, and you would be acting wrongly, since you are obliged to play, by refusing to stake one life against three in a game where out of an infinite number of chances there is one in your favour, if there were an infinitely happy infinity of life to be won. But here there is an infinitely happy infinity of life to be won, one chance of winning against a finite number of chances of losing, and what you are staking is finite. That removes all choice: wherever there is infinity and where there is no infinity of chances of losing against one of winning, there is no scope for wavering, you have to chance everything. And thus, as you are forced to gamble, you have to have discarded reason if you cling on to your life, rather than risk it for the infinite prize which is just as likely to happen as the loss of nothingness.

For it is no good saying that it is uncertain if you will win, that it is certain you are taking a risk, and that the infinite distance between the *certainty* of what you are risking and the *uncertainty* of whether you win makes the finite good of what you are certainly risking equal to the uncertainty of the infinite. It does not work like that. Every gambler takes a certain risk for an uncertain gain; nevertheless he certainly risks the finite uncertainty in order to win a finite gain, without sinning against reason. There is no infinite distance between this certainty of what is being risked and the uncertainty of what might be gained: that is untrue. There is, indeed, an infinite distance between the certainty of winning and the certainty of losing. But the uncertainty of winning is proportional to the certainty of the risk, according to the chances of winning or losing. And hence, if there are as many chances on one side as on the other, the odds are even, and then the certainty of what you risk is equal to the uncertainty of winning. It is very far from being infinitely distant from it. So our argument is infinitely strong, when the finite is at stake in a game where there are equal chances of winning and losing, and the infinite is to be won.

That is conclusive, and, if human beings are capable of understanding any truth at all, this is the one.

"I confess it, I admit it, but even so . . . Is there no way of seeing underneath the cards?" "Yes, Scripture and the rest, etc." "Yes, but my hands are tied and I cannot speak a word. I am being forced to wager and I am not free, they will not let me go. And I am made in such a way that I cannot believe. So what do you want me to do?" "That is true. But at least realize that your inability to believe, since reason urges you to do so and yet you cannot, arises from your passions. So concentrate not on convincing yourself by increasing the number of proofs of God but on diminishing your passions. You want to find faith and you do not know the way? You want to cure yourself of unbelief and you ask for the remedies? Learn from those who have been bound like you, and who now wager all they have. They are people who know the road you want to follow and have been cured of the affliction of which you want to be cured. Follow the way by which they began: by behaving just as if they believed, taking holy water, having masses said, etc. That will make you believe quite naturally, and according to your animal reactions." "But that is what I am afraid of." "Why? What do you have to lose?"

STUDY QUESTIONS

1. If God is, as Pascal declares, "infinitely beyond our comprehension," does this admission undermine his subsequent argument?
2. Is believing in God for the reasons Pascal offers a legitimate basis for religious commitment?
3. If you follow Pascal's advice and engage in Christian rituals, are you more likely to accept Christian beliefs?
4. Might God reward thoughtful unbelievers for having the strength of their convictions?

Natural Theology

ᴥ

WILLIAM PALEY

William Paley (1743–1805) was an English theologian and moral philosopher. He gives a classic presentation of another argument for the existence
of God, the so-called teleological argument or argument to design. This
argument proceeds from the premise of the world's magnificent order to the
conclusion that the world must be the work of a Supreme Mind responsible
for this order.

....

CHAPTER I: THE STATE OF THE ARGUMENT

In crossing a heath, suppose I pitched my foot against a stone and were asked
how the stone came to be there. I might possibly answer that for anything I knew
to the contrary it had lain there forever; nor would it, perhaps, be very easy to
show the absurdity of this answer. But suppose I had found a watch upon the
ground, and it should be inquired how the watch happened to be in that place.
I should hardly think of the answer which I had before given, that for anything
I knew the watch might have always been there. Yet why should not this answer
serve for the watch as well as for the stone? Why is it not as admissible in the
second case as in the first? For this reason, and for no other, namely, that when
we come to inspect the watch, we perceive—what we could not discover in the
stone—that its several parts are framed and put together for a purpose, e.g., that
they are so formed and adjusted as to produce motion, and that motion so regulated as to point out the hour of the day; that if the different parts had been
differently shaped from what they are, of a different size from what they are, or
placed after any other manner or in any other order than that in which they are
placed, either no motion at all would have been carried on in the machine, or
none which would have answered the use that is now served by it. To reckon up
a few of the plainest of these parts and of their offices, all tending to one result;
we see a cylindrical box containing a coiled elastic spring, which, by its endeavor
to relax itself, turns round the box. We next observe a flexible chain—artificially
wrought for the sake of flexure—communicating the action of the spring from
the box to the fusee. We then find a series of wheels, the teeth of which catch in
and apply to each other, conducting the motion from the fusee to the balance
and from the balance to the pointer, and at the same time, by the size and shape

From William Paley, *Natural Theology* (1802).

of those wheels, so regulating that motion as to terminate in causing an index, by an equable and measured progression, to pass over a given space in a given time. We take notice that the wheels are made of brass, in order to keep them from rust; the springs of steel, no other metal being so elastic; that over the face of the watch there is placed a glass, a material employed in no other part of the work, but in the room of which, if there had been any other than a transparent substance, the hour could not be seen without opening the case. This mechanism being observed—it requires indeed an examination of the instrument, and perhaps some previous knowledge of the subject, to perceive and understand it; but being once, as we have said, observed and understood—the inference we think is inevitable, that the watch must have had a maker—that there must have existed, at some time and at some place or other, an artificer or artificers who formed it for the purpose which we find it actually to answer, who comprehended its construction and designed its use.

I. Nor would it, I apprehend, weaken the conclusion, that we had never seen a watch made—that we had never known an artist capable of making one—that we were altogether incapable of executing such a piece of workmanship ourselves, or of understanding in what manner it was performed; all this being no more than what is true of some exquisite remains of ancient art, of some lost arts, and, to the generality of mankind, of the more curious productions of modern manufacture. Does one man in a million know how oval frames are turned? Ignorance of this kind exalts our opinion of the unseen and unknown artist's skill, if he is unseen and unknown, but raises no doubt in our minds of the existence and agency of such an artist, at some former time and in some place or other. Nor can I perceive that it varies at all the inference, whether the question arises concerning a human agent or concerning an agent of a different species, or an agent possessing in some respects a different nature.

II. Neither, secondly, would it invalidate our conclusion, that the watch sometimes went wrong or that it seldom went exactly right. The purpose of the machinery, the design, and the designer might be evident, and in the case supposed, would be evident, in whatever way we accounted for the irregularity of the movement, or whether we could account for it or not. It is not necessary that a machine be perfect in order to show with what design it was made: still less necessary, where the only question is whether it were made with any design at all.

III. Nor, thirdly, would it bring any uncertainty into the argument, if there were a few parts of the watch, concerning which we could not discover or had not yet discovered in what manner they conduced to the general effect; or even some parts, concerning which we could not ascertain whether they conduced to that effect in any manner whatever. For, as to the first branch of the case, if by the loss, or disorder, or decay of the parts in question, the movement of the watch were found in fact to be stopped, or disturbed, or retarded, no doubt would remain in our minds as to the utility or intention of these parts, although we should be unable to investigate the manner according to which, or the connection by which, the ultimate effect depended upon their action or assistance; and the more complex is the machine, the more likely is this obscurity to arise. Then, as to the second thing supposed, namely, that there were parts which might be spared without prejudice to the movement of the watch, and that we had proved this by experiment, these superfluous parts, even if we were completely assured that they were such, would not vacate the reasoning which we had instituted concerning other parts. The indication of contrivance remained, with respect to them, nearly as it was before.

IV. Nor, fourthly, would any man in his senses think the existence of the watch with its various machinery accounted for, by being told that it was one out of possible combinations of material forms; that whatever he had found in the place where he found the watch must have contained some internal configuration or other; and that this configuration might be the structure now exhibited, namely, of the works of a watch, as well as a different structure.

V. Nor, fifthly, would it yield his inquiry more satisfaction, to be answered that there existed in things a principle of order, which had disposed the parts of the watch into their present form and situation. He never knew a watch made by the principle of order; nor can he even form to himself an idea of what is meant by a principle of order distinct from the intelligence of the watchmaker.

VI. Sixthly, he would be surprised to hear that the mechanism of the watch was no proof of contrivance, only a motive to induce the mind to think so:

VII. And not less surprised to be informed that the watch in his hand was nothing more than the result of the laws of *metallic* nature. It is a perversion of language to assign any law as the efficient, operative cause of any thing. A law presupposes an agent, for it is only the mode according to which an agent proceeds; it implies a power, for it is the order according to which that power acts. Without this agent, without this power, which are both distinct from itself, the *law* does nothing, is nothing. The expression, "the law of metallic nature," may sound strange and harsh to a philosophic ear; but it seems quite as justifiable as some others which are more familiar to him, such as "the law of vegetable nature," "the law of animal nature," or, indeed, "the law of nature" in general, when assigned as the cause of phenomena, in exclusion of agency and power, or when it is substituted into the place of these.

VIII. Neither, lastly, would our observer be driven out of his conclusion or from his confidence in its truth by being told that he knew nothing at all about the matter. He knows enough for his argument; he knows the utility of the end; he knows the subserviency and adaptation of the means to the end. These points being known, his ignorance of other points, his doubts concerning other points affect not the certainty of his reasoning. The consciousness of knowing little need not beget a distrust of that which he does know. . . .

CHAPTER III: APPLICATION OF THE ARGUMENT

. . . Every indication of contrivance, every manifestation of design, which existed in the watch, exists in the works of nature; with the difference, on the side of nature, of being greater and more, and that in a degree which exceeds all computation. I mean that the contrivances of nature surpass the contrivances of art in the complexity, subtility, and curiosity of the mechanism; and still more, if possible, do they go beyond them in number and variety; yet, in a multitude of cases, are not less evidently mechanical, not less evidently contrivances, not less evidently accommodated to their end, or suited to their office, than are the most perfect productions of human ingenuity. . . .

I know no better method of introducing so large a subject than that of comparing a single thing with a single thing; an eye, for example, with a telescope. As far as the examination of the instrument goes, there is precisely the same proof that the eye was made for vision, as there is that the telescope was made for assisting it. They are made upon the same principles, both being adjusted to the laws by which the transmission and reflection of rays of light are regulated. I speak not of the origin of the laws themselves; but such laws being fixed, the construction, in both cases, is adapted to them. For instance, these laws require, in order to produce the same effect, that the rays of light, in passing from water into the eye, should be refracted by a more convex surface than when it passes out of air into the eye. Accordingly we find, that the eye of a fish, in that part of it called the crystalline lens, is much rounder than the eye of terrestrial animals. What plainer manifestation of design can there be than this difference? What could a mathematical instrument-maker have done more, to show his knowledge of his principle, his application of that knowledge, his suiting of his means to his end; I will not say to display the compass or excellence of his skill and art, for in these all comparison is indecorous, but to testify counsel, choice, consideration, purpose?

STUDY QUESTIONS

1. In what circumstances might it appear that a stone was designed?
2. Does it seem that dinosaurs were designed?
3. How would you know if something was designed, but badly?
4. Do the evils of the world suggest that it was designed?

The Will to Believe

ᴀ⌁

WILLIAM JAMES

William James, whose work we read previously, contends that when you face an important choice between two appealing options and cannot wait for further evidence, you are justified in believing and acting as your passion decides. According to James, we should not allow the fear of holding a false belief to prevent us from losing the benefits of believing what may be true.

James asserts that the essence of religion is contained in two fundamental claims: (1) the best things are the more eternal things, and (2) we are better off if we believe (1). Note that in a footnote he says that "if the action required or inspired by the religious hypothesis is in no way different from that dictated by the naturalistic hypothesis, then religious faith is a pure superfluity, better pruned away, and controversy about its legitimacy is a piece of idle trifling, unworthy of serious minds." An intriguing question is whether believing in (1) and (2), which James considers the core of the religious attitude, requires different action than rejecting (1) and (2).

In the recently published *Life* by Leslie Stephen[1] of his brother, Fitz-James,[2] there is an account of a school to which the latter went when he was a boy. The teacher, a certain Mr. Guest, used to converse with his pupils in this wise, "Gurney, what is the difference between justification and sanctification?—Stephen, prove the omnipotence of God!" etc. In the midst of our Harvard freethinking and indifference we are prone to imagine that here at your good old orthodox College conversation continues to be somewhat upon this order; and to show you that we at Harvard have not lost all interest in these vital subjects, I have brought with me tonight something like a sermon on justification by faith to read to you,—I mean an essay in justification *of* faith, a defence of our right to adopt a believing attitude in religious matters, in spite of the fact that our merely logical intellect may not have been coerced. "The Will to Believe," accordingly, is the title of my paper. . . .

I have long defended to my own students the lawfulness of voluntarily adopted faith; but as soon as they have become well imbued with the logical spirit, they have as a rule refused to admit my contention to be lawful philosophically, even though in point of fact they were personally all the time chock full of some faith or other themselves. I am all the while, however, so profoundly convinced that my own position is correct, that your invitation has seemed to me a good occasion to make my statements more clear. Perhaps your minds will be more open than those

---

An address delivered before the Philosophical Clubs of Yale and Brown Universities. Published in 1896.

with which I have hitherto had to deal. I will be as little technical as I can, though I must begin by setting up some technical distinctions that will help us in the end.

I

Let us give the name of hypothesis to anything that may be proposed to our belief; and just as the electricians speak of *live* and *dead* wires, let us speak of any hypothesis as either live or dead. A live hypothesis is one which appeals as a real possibility to him to whom it is proposed. If I ask you to believe in the Mahdi,[3] the notion makes no electric connection with your nature—it refuses to scintillate with any credibility at all. As an hypothesis it is completely dead. To an Arab, however (even if he be not one of the Mahdi's followers), the hypothesis is among the mind's possibilities: It is alive. This shows that deadness and liveness in an hypothesis are not intrinsic properties, but relations to the individual thinker. They are measured by his willingness to act. The maximum of liveness in an hypothesis means willingness to act irrevocably. Practically, that means belief; but there is some believing tendency wherever there is willingness to act at all.

Next, let us call the decision between two hypotheses an *option*. Options may be of several kinds. They may be first, *living* or *dead*; secondly, *forced* or *avoidable*; thirdly, *momentous* or *trivial*; and for our purposes we may call an option a *genuine* option when it is of the forced, living, and momentous kind.

1. A living option is one in which both hypotheses are live ones. If I say to you: "Be a theosophist or be a Mohammedan," it is probably a dead option, because for you neither hypothesis is likely to be alive. But if I say: "Be an agnostic or be a Christian," it is otherwise; trained as you are, each hypothesis makes some appeal, however small, to your belief.

2. Next, if I say to you: "Choose between going out with your umbrella or without it," I do not offer you a genuine option, for it is not forced. You can easily avoid it by not going out at all. Similarly, if I say, "Either love me or hate me," "Either call my theory true or call it false," your option is avoidable. You may remain indifferent to me, neither loving nor hating, and you may decline to offer any judgment as to my theory. But if I say, "Either accept this truth or go without it," I put on you a forced option, for there is no standing place outside of the alternative. Every dilemma based on a complete logical disjunction, with no possibility of not choosing, is an option of this forced kind.

3. Finally, if I were Dr. Nansen[4] and proposed to you to join my North Pole expedition, your option would be momentous; for this would probably be your only similar opportunity, and your choice now would either exclude you from the North Pole sort of immortality altogether or put at least the chance of it into your hands. He who refuses to embrace a unique opportunity loses the prize as surely as if he tried and failed. *Per contra,*[5] the option is trivial when the opportunity is not unique, when the stake is insignificant, or when the decision is reversible if it later proves unwise. Such trivial options abound in the scientific life. A chemist finds an hypothesis live enough to spend a year in its verification: he believes in it to that

extent. But if his experiments prove inconclusive either way, he is quit for his loss of time, no vital harm being done.

It will facilitate our discussion if we keep all these distinctions well in mind.

II

The next matter to consider is the actual psychology of human opinion. When we look at certain facts, it seems as if our passional and volitional nature lay at the root of all our convictions. When we look at others, it seems as if they could do nothing when the intellect had once said its say. Let us take the latter facts up first.

Does it not seem preposterous on the very face of it to talk of our opinions being modifiable at will? Can our will either help or hinder our intellect in its perceptions of truth? Can we, by just willing it, believe that Abraham Lincoln's existence is a myth and that the portraits of him in *McClure's Magazine* are all of some one else? Can we, by any effort of our will, or by any strength of wish that it were true, believe ourselves well and about when we are roaring with rheumatism in bed, or feel certain that the sum of the two one-dollar bills in our pocket must be a hundred dollars? We can *say* any of these things, but we are absolutely impotent to believe them; and of just such things is the whole fabric of the truths that we do believe in made up—matters of fact, immediate or remote, as Hume said, and relations between ideas, which are either there or not there for us if we see them so, and which if not there cannot be put there by any action of our own.

In Pascal's *Thoughts* there is a celebrated passage known in literature as Pascal's wager. In it he tries to force us into Christianity by reasoning as if our concern with truth resembled our concern with the stakes in a game of chance. Translated freely his words are these: You must either believe or not believe that God is—which will you do? Your human reason cannot say. A game is going on between you and the nature of things which at the day of judgment will bring out either heads or tails. Weigh what your gains and your losses would be if you should stake all you have on heads, or God's existence; if you win in such case, you gain eternal beatitude; if you lose, you lose nothing at all. If there were an infinity of chances, and only one for God in this wager, still you ought to stake your all on God; for though you surely risk a finite loss by this procedure, any finite loss is reasonable, even a certain one is reasonable, if there is but the possibility of infinite gain. Go, then, and take holy water, and have masses said; belief will come and stupefy your scruples. . . . Why should you not? At bottom, what have you to lose?

You probably feel that when religious faith expresses itself thus, in the language of the gaming table, it is put to its last trumps. Surely Pascal's own personal belief in masses and holy water had far other springs; and this celebrated page of his is but an argument for others, a last desperate snatch at a weapon against the hardness of the unbelieving heart. We feel that a faith in masses and holy water adopted wilfully after such a mechanical calculation would lack the inner soul of faith's reality; and if we were ourselves in the place of the Deity, we should probably take particular pleasure in cutting off believers of this pattern from their infinite reward. It is evident that unless there be some preexisting tendency to believe in masses and holy water, the option offered to the will by Pascal is not a living option. Certainly no Turk ever took to masses and holy water on its account; and even to us Protestants these means of salvation seem such foregone impossibilities that Pascal's logic, invoked for them specifically, leaves us unmoved. As well might the Mahdi write to us, saying, "I am the Expected One whom God has created in his effulgence. You shall be infinitely happy if you confess me; otherwise you shall be cut off from the light of the sun. Weigh, then, your infinite gain if I am genuine against your finite sacrifice if I am not!" His logic would be that of Pascal; but he would vainly use it on us, for the hypothesis he offers us is dead. No tendency to act on it exists in us to any degree.

The talk of believing by our volition seems, then, from one point of view, simply silly. From another point of view it is worse than silly, it is vile. When one turns to the magnificent edifice of the physical sciences, and sees how it was reared; what thousands of disinterested moral lives of men lie buried in its mere foundations; what patience and postponement, what choking down of preference, what submission to the icy laws of outer fact are wrought into its very stones and mortar; how absolutely impersonal it stands in its vast augustness—then how besotted and contemptible seems every little sentimentalist who comes blowing his voluntary smokewreaths, and pretending to decide things from out of his private dream! Can we wonder if those bred in the rugged and manly school of science should feel like spewing such subjectivism out of their mouths? The whole system of loyalties which grow up in the schools of science go dead against its toleration; so that it is only natural that those who have caught the scientific fever should pass over to the opposite extreme, and write sometimes as if the incorruptibly truthful intellect ought positively to prefer bitterness and unacceptableness to the heart in its cup.

> It fortifies my soul to know
> That though I perish, Truth is so

sings Clough,[6] while Huxley[7] exclaims: "My only consolation lies in the reflection that, however bad our posterity may become, so far as they hold by the plain rule of not pretending to believe what they have no reason to believe, because it may be to their advantage so to pretend [the word 'pretend' is surely here redundant], they will not have reached the lowest depth of immorality." And that delicious *enfant terrible*[8] Clifford writes: "Belief is desecrated when given to unproved and unquestioned statements for the solace and private pleasure of the believer.... Whoso would deserve well of his fellows in this matter will guard the purity of his belief with a very fanaticism of jealous care, lest at any time it should rest on an unworthy object, and catch a stain which can never be wiped away.... If [a] belief has been accepted on insufficient evidence [even though the belief be true, as Clifford on the same page explains] the pleasure is a stolen one.... It is sinful because it is stolen in defiance of our duty to mankind. That duty is to guard ourselves from such beliefs as from a pestilence which may shortly master our own body and then spread to the rest of the town. . . . It is wrong always, everywhere, and for every one, to believe anything upon insufficient evidence."

III

All this strikes one as healthy, even when expressed, as by Clifford, with somewhat too much of robustious pathos in the voice. Free will and simple wishing do seem, in the matter of our credences, to be only fifth wheels to the coach. Yet if any one should thereupon assume that intellectual insight is what remains after wish and will and sentimental preference have taken wing, or that pure reason is what then settles our opinions, he would fly quite as directly in the teeth of the facts.

It is only our already dead hypotheses that our willing nature is unable to bring to life again. But what has made them dead for us is for the most part a previous action of our willing nature of an antagonistic kind. When I say "willing nature," I do not mean only such deliberate volitions as may have set up habits of belief that we cannot now escape from—I mean all such factors of belief as fear and hope, prejudice and passion, imitation and partisanship, the circumpressure of our caste and set. As a matter of fact we find ourselves believing, we hardly know how or why. Mr. Balfour[9] gives the name of "authority" to all those influences, born of the intellectual climate, that make hypotheses possible or impossible for us, alive or dead. Here in this room, we all of us believe in molecules and the conservation of energy, in democracy and necessary progress, in Protestant Christianity and the duty of fighting for "the doctrine of the immortal Monroe,"[10] all for no reasons worthy of the name. We see into these matters with no more inner clearness, and probably with much less, than any disbeliever in them might possess. His unconventionality would probably have some grounds to show for its conclusions; but for us, not insight, but the *prestige* of the opinions, is what makes the spark shoot from them and light up our sleeping magazines of faith. Our reason is quite satisfied, in nine hundred and ninety-nine cases out of every thousand of us, if it can find a few arguments that will do to recite in case our credulity is criticized by some one else. Our faith is faith in some one else's faith, and in the greatest matters this is the most the case. . . .

Evidently, then, our non-intellectual nature does influence our convictions. There are passional tendencies and volitions which run before and others which come after belief, and it is only the latter that are too late for the fair; and they are not too late when the previous passional work has been already in their own direction. Pascal's argument, instead of being powerless, then seems a regular clincher, and is the last stroke needed to make our faith in masses and holy water complete. The state of things is evidently far from simple; and pure insight and logic, whatever they might do ideally, are not the only things that really do produce our creeds.

IV

Our next duty, having recognized this mixed-up state of affairs, is to ask whether it be simply reprehensible and pathological, or whether, on the contrary, we must treat it as a normal element in making up our minds. The thesis I defend is, briefly stated, this: Our passional nature not only lawfully may, but must, decide an option between propositions, whenever it is a genuine option that cannot by its nature be decided on intellectual grounds; for to say, under such circumstances, "Do not decide, but leave the question open," is itself a passional decision—just like deciding yes or no—and is attended with the same risk of losing the truth. . . .

VII

One more point, small but important, and our preliminaries are done. There are two ways of looking at our duty in the matter of opinion—ways entirely different, and yet ways about whose difference the theory of knowledge seems hitherto to have shown very little concern. *We must know the truth;* and *we must avoid error*—these are our first and great commandments as would-be knowers; but they are not two ways of stating an identical commandment, they are two separable laws. Although it may indeed happen that when we believe the truth A, we escape as an incidental consequence from believing the falsehood B, it hardly ever happens that by merely disbelieving B we necessarily believe A. We may in escaping B fall into believing other falsehoods, C or D, just as bad as B; or we may escape B by not believing anything at all, not even A.

Believe truth! Shun error!—these, we see, are two materially different laws; and by choosing between them we may end by coloring differently our whole intellectual life. We may regard the chase for truth as paramount, and the avoidance of error as secondary; or we may, on the other hand, treat the avoidance of error as more imperative, and let truth take its chance. Clifford, in the instructive passage which I have quoted, exhorts us to the latter course. Believe nothing, he tells us, keep your mind in suspense forever, rather than by closing it on insufficient evidence incur the awful risk of believing lies. You, on the other hand, may think that the risk of being in error is a very small matter when compared with the blessings of real knowledge, and be ready to be duped many times in your investigation rather than postpone indefinitely the chance of guessing true. I myself find it impossible to go with Clifford. We must remember that these feelings of our duty about either truth or error are in any case only expressions of our passional life. Biologically considered, our minds are as ready to grind out falsehood as veracity, and he who says, "Better go without belief forever than believe a lie!" merely shows his own preponderant private horror of becoming a dupe. He may be critical of many of his desires and fears, but this fear he slavishly obeys. He cannot imagine any one questioning its binding force. For my own part, I have also a horror of being duped; but I can believe that worse things than being duped may happen to a man in this world; so Clifford's exhortation has to my ears a thoroughly fantastic sound. It is like a general informing his soldiers that it is better to keep out of battle forever than to risk a single wound. Not so are victories either over enemies or over nature gained. Our errors are surely not such awfully solemn things. In a world where we are so certain to incur them in spite of all our caution, a certain lightness of heart seems healthier than this excessive nervousness on their behalf. At any rate, it seems the fittest thing for the empiricist philosopher.

VIII

And now, after all this introduction, let us go straight at our question. I have said, and now repeat it, that not only as a matter of fact do we find our passional nature influencing us in our opinions, but that there are some options between opinions in which this influence must be regarded both as an inevitable and as a lawful determinant of our choice.

I fear here that some of you my hearers will begin to scent danger, and lend an inhospitable ear. Two first steps of passion you have indeed had to admit as necessary—we must think so as to avoid dupery, and we must think so as to gain truth; but the surest path to those ideal consummations, you will probably consider, is from now onwards to take no further passional step.

Well, of course, I agree as far as the facts will allow. Wherever the option between losing truth and gaining it is not momentous, we can throw the chance of *gaining truth* away, and at any rate save ourselves from any chance of *believing falsehood*, by not making up our minds at all till objective evidence has come. In scientific questions, this is almost always the case; and even in human affairs in general, the need of acting is seldom so urgent that a false belief to act on is better than no belief at all. Law courts, indeed, have to decide on the best evidence attainable for the moment, because a judge's duty is to make law as well as to ascertain it, and (as a learned judge once said to me) few cases are worth spending much time over; the great thing is to have them decided on *any* acceptable principle, and gotten out of the way. But in our dealings with objective nature we obviously are recorders, not makers, of the truth; and decisions for the mere sake of deciding promptly and getting on to the next business would be wholly out of place. Throughout the breadth of physical nature facts are what they are quite independently of us, and seldom is there any such hurry about them that the risks of being duped by believing a premature theory need be faced. The questions here are always trivial options, the hypotheses are hardly living (at any rate not living for us spectators), the choice between believing truth or falsehood is seldom forced. The attitude of sceptical balance is therefore the absolutely wise one if we would escape mistakes. What difference, indeed, does it make to most of us whether we have or have not a theory of the Röntgen[11] rays, whether we believe or not in mind-stuff, or have a conviction about the causality of conscious states? It makes no difference. Such options are not forced on us. On every account it is better not to make them, but still keep weighing reasons *pro et contra*[12] with an indifferent hand.

I speak, of course, here of the purely judging mind. For purposes of discovery, such indifference is to be less highly recommended, and science would be far less advanced than she is if the passionate desires of individuals to get their own faiths confirmed had been kept out of the game. See for example the sagacity which Spencer[13] and Weismann[14] now display. On the other hand, if you want an absolute duffer in an investigation, you must, after all, take the man who has no interest whatever in its results: he is the warranted incapable, the positive fool. The most useful investigator, because the most sensitive observer, is always he whose eager interest in one side of the question is balanced by an equally keen nervousness lest he become deceived. Science has organized this nervousness into a regular *technique*, her so-called method of verification; and she has fallen so deeply in love with the method that one may even say she has ceased to care for truth by itself at all. It is only truth as technically verified that interests her. The truth of truths might come in merely affirmative form, and she would decline to touch it. Such truth as that, she might repeat with Clifford, would be stolen in defiance of her duty to mankind. Human passions, however, are stronger than technical rules. "*Le coeur a ses raisons*" as Pascal says, "*que la raison ne connait pas*"[15]; and however indifferent to all but the bare rules of the game the umpire, the abstract intellect, may be, the concrete players who furnish him the materials to judge of are usually, each one of them, in love with some pet "live hypothesis" of his own. Let us agree, however, that wherever there is no forced option, the dispassionately judicial intellect with no pet hypothesis, saving us, as it does, from dupery at any rate, ought to be our ideal.

The question next arises: Are there not somewhere forced options in our speculative questions, and can we (as men who may be interested at least as much in positively gaining truth as in merely escaping dupery) always wait with impunity till the coercive evidence shall have arrived? It seems *a priori* improbable that the truth should be so nicely adjusted to our needs and powers as that. In the great boarding-house of nature, the cakes and the butter and the syrup seldom come out so even and leave the plates so clean. Indeed, we should view them with scientific suspicion if they did.

IX

Moral questions immediately present themselves as questions whose solution cannot wait for sensible proof. A moral question is a question not of what sensibly exists, but of what is good, or would be good if it did exist. Science can tell us what exists; but to compare the *worths*, both of what exists and of what does not exist, we must consult not science, but what Pascal calls our heart. . . .

Turn now from these wide questions of good to a certain class of questions of fact, questions concerning personal relations, states of mind between one man and another. *Do you like me or not?*—for example. Whether you do or not depends, in countless instances, on whether I meet you halfway, am willing to assume that you must like me, and show you trust and expectation. The previous faith on my part in your liking's existence is in such cases what makes your liking come. But if I stand aloof, and refuse to budge an inch until I have objective evidence, until you shall have done something apt, as the absolutists say, *ad extorquendum assensum meum*,[16] ten to one your liking never comes. How many women's hearts are vanquished by the mere sanguine insistence of some man that they *must* love him! He will not consent to the hypothesis that they cannot. The desire for a certain kind of truth here brings about that special truth's existence; and so it is in innumerable cases of other sorts.... *And where faith in a fact can help create the fact*, that would be an insane logic which should say that faith running ahead of scientific evidence is the "lowest kind of immorality" into which a thinking being can fall. Yet such is the logic by which our scientific absolutists pretend to regulate our lives!

X

In truths dependent on our personal action, then, faith based on desire is certainly a lawful and possibly an indispensable thing.

But now, it will be said, these are all childish human cases and have nothing to do with great cosmical matters, like the question of religious faith. Let us then pass on to that. Religions differ so much in their accidents that in discussing the religious question we must make it very generic and broad. What then do we now mean by the religious hypothesis? Science says things are; morality says some things are better than other things; and religion says essentially two things.

First, she says that the best things are the more eternal things, the overlapping things, the things in the universe that throw the last stone, so to speak, and say the final word. "Perfection is eternal"—this phrase of Charles Secrétan[17] seems a good way of putting this first affirmation of religion, an affirmation which obviously cannot yet be verified scientifically at all.

The second affirmation of religion is that we are better off even now if we believe her first affirmation to be true.

Now, let us consider what the logical elements of this situation are *in case the religious hypothesis in both its branches be really true*. (Of course, we must admit that possibility at the outset. If we are to discuss the question at all, it must involve a living option. If for any of you religion be a hypothesis that cannot, by any living possibility, be true, then you need go no farther. I speak to the "saving remnant" alone.) So proceeding, we see, first, that religion offers itself as a *momentous* option. We are supposed to gain, even now, by our belief, and to lose by our non-belief, a certain vital good. Secondly, religion is a *forced* option, so far as that good goes. We cannot escape the issue by remaining sceptical and waiting for more light, because, although we do avoid error in that way *if religion be untrue*, we lose the good, *if it be true*, just as certainly as if we positively chose to disbelieve. It is as if a man should hesitate indefinitely to ask a certain woman to marry him because he was not perfectly sure that she would prove an angel after he brought her home.

Would he not cut himself off from that particular angel-possibility as decisively as if he went and married someone else? Scepticism, then, is not avoidance of option; it is option of a certain particular kind of risk. *Better risk loss of truth than chance of error*—that is your faith-vetoer's exact position. He is actively playing his stake as much as the believer is; he is backing the field against the religious hypothesis, just as the believer is backing the religious hypothesis against the field. To preach scepticism to us as a duty until "sufficient evidence" for religion is found is tantamount therefore to telling us, when in presence of the religious hypothesis, that to yield to our fear of its being error is wiser and better than to yield to our hope that it may be true. It is not intellect against all passion, then; it is only intellect with one passion laying down its law. And by what, forsooth, is the supreme wisdom of this passion warranted? Dupery for dupery, what proof is there that dupery through hope is so much worse than dupery through fear? I, for one, can see no proof; and I simply refuse obedience to the scientist's command to imitate his kind of option, in a case where my own stake is important enough to give me the right to choose my own form of risk. If religion is true and the evidence for it is still insufficient, I do not wish, by putting your extinguisher upon my nature (which feels to me as if it had after all some business in this matter), to forfeit my sole chance in life of getting upon the winning side—that chance depending, of course, on my willingness to run the risk of acting as if my passional need of taking the world religiously might be prophetic and right.

All this is on the supposition that it really may be prophetic and right, and that, even to us who are discussing the matter, religion is a live hypothesis which may be true. Now, to most of us religion comes in a still further way that makes a veto on our active faith even more illogical. The more perfect and more eternal aspect of the universe is represented in our religions as having personal form. The universe is no longer a mere *It* to us, but a *Thou*, if we are religious; and any relation that may be possible from person to person might be possible here. For instance, although in one sense we are passive portions of the universe, in another we show a curious autonomy, as if we were small active centers on our own account. We feel, too, as if the appeal of religion to us were made to our own active goodwill, as if evidence might be forever withheld from us unless we met the hypothesis halfway to take a trivial illustration: just as a man who in a company of gentlemen made no advances, asked a warrant for every concession, and believed no one's word without proof, would cut himself off by such churlishness from all the social rewards that a more trusting spirit would earn—so here, one who should shut himself up in snarling logicality and try to make the gods extort his recognition willy-nilly, or not get it at all, might cut himself off forever from his only opportunity of making the gods' acquaintance. This feeling, forced on us we know not whence that by obstinately believing that there are gods (although not to do so would be so easy both for our logic and our life) we are doing the universe the deepest service we can, seems part of the living essence of the religious hypothesis. If the hypothesis *were* true in all its parts, including this one, then pure intellectualism, with its veto on our making willing advances, would be an absurdity; and some participation of our sympathetic nature would be logically required. I therefore, for one, cannot see my way to accepting the agnostic rules for truthseeking, or wilfully agree to keep my willing nature out of the game. I cannot do so for this plain reason, that *a rule of thinking which would absolutely prevent me from acknowledging certain kinds of truth if those kinds of truth were really there, would be an irrational rule.* That for me is the long and short of the formal logic of the situation, no matter what the kinds of truth might materially be.

I confess I do not see how this logic can be escaped. But sad experience makes me fear that some of you may still shrink from radically saying with me, *in abstracto,* that we have the right to believe at our own risk any hypothesis that is live enough to tempt our will. I suspect, however, that if this is so, it is because you have got away from the abstract logical point of view altogether, and are thinking (perhaps without realizing it) of some particular religious hypothesis which for you is dead. The freedom to "believe what we will" you apply to the case of some patent superstition; and the faith you think of is the faith defined by the schoolboy when he said, "is when you believe something that you know ain't true." I can only repeat that this is misapprehension. *In concreto,*[18] the freedom to believe can only cover living options which the intellect of the individual cannot by itself resolve; and living options never seem absurdities to him who has them to consider. When I look at the religious question as it really puts itself to concrete men, and when I think of all the possibilities which both practically and theoretically it involves, then this command that we shall put a stopper on our heart, instincts, and courage, and *wait*—acting of course meanwhile more or less as if religion were *not* true[19]— till doomsday, or till such time as our intellect and senses working together may have raked in evidence enough—this command, I say, seems to me the queerest idol ever manufactured in the philosophic cave. Were we scholastic absolutists, there might be more excuse. If we had an infallible intellect with its objective certitudes, we might feel ourselves disloyal to such a perfect organ of knowledge in not trusting to it exclusively, in not waiting for its releasing word. But if we are empiricists, if we believe that no bell in us tolls to let us know for certain when truth is in our grasp, then it seems a piece of idle fantasticality to preach so solemnly our duty of waiting for the bell. Indeed we *may* wait if we will—I hope you do not think that I am denying that—but if we do so, we do so at our peril as much as if we believed. In either case we *act*, taking our life in our hands. No one of us ought to issue vetoes to the other, nor should we bandy words of abuse. We ought, on the contrary, delicately and profoundly to respect one another's mental freedom: then only shall we bring about the intellectual republic; then only shall we have that spirit of inner tolerance without which all our outer tolerance is soulless, and which is empiricism's glory; then only shall we live and let live, in speculative as well as in practical things.

I began by a reference to Fitz-James Stephen; let me end by a quotation from him. "What do you think of yourself? What do you think of the world? . . . These are questions with which all must deal as it seems good to them. They are riddles of the Sphinx, and in some way or other we must deal with them. . . . In all important transactions of life we have to take a leap in the dark. . . . If we decide to leave the riddles unanswered, that is a choice; if we waver in our answer, that, too, is a choice: but whatever choice we make, we make it at our peril. If a man chooses to turn his back altogether on God and the future, no one can prevent him; no one can show beyond reasonable doubt that he is mistaken. If a man thinks otherwise and acts as he thinks, I do not see that any one can prove that *he* is mistaken. Each must act as he thinks best; and if he is wrong, so much the worse for him. We stand on a mountain pass in the midst of whirling snow and blinding mist, through which we get glimpses now and then of paths which may be deceptive. If we stand still, we shall be frozen to death. If we take the wrong road, we shall be dashed to pieces. We do not certainly know whether there is any right one. What must we do? 'Be strong and of a good courage.' Act for the best, hope for the best, and take what comes. . . . If death ends all, we cannot meet death better."[20]

NOTES

1. [The reference is to the English critic and philosopher Sir Leslie Stephen (1832–1904) and his 1895 book, *The Life of Sir James Fitzjames Stephen*—S.M.C.]
2. [The reference is to the English jurist and journalist Sir James Fitzjames Stephen (1829–1894).]
3. [The redeemer, according to Islam, who will come to bring justice on earth and establish universal Islam.]
4. [The reference is to the Norwegian explorer Fridtjof Nansen (1861–1930).]
5. [In contrast.]
6. [The reference is to the British poet Arthur Hugh Clough (1819–1861).]
7. [The reference is to the English biologist Thomas Henry Huxley (1825–1895), who was a leading exponent of the evolutionary theory of Charles Darwin.]
8. [One who is strikingly unorthodox.]
9. [The reference is to the British prime minister and philosopher Arthur James Balfour (1848–1930).]
10. [The reference is to James Monroe (1758–1831), fifth president of the United States, whose doctrine prohibited European colonization or intervention in the American continents.]
11. [The reference is to the German physicist Wilhelm Conrad Röntgen, discover of the X-ray, for which he received in 1901 the first Nobel Prize in Physics.]
12. [For and against.]
13. [The reference is to the English philosopher Herbert Spencer (1820–1903), a leading exponent of the theory of evolution.]
14. [The reference is to the German biologist August Weismann (1834–1914).]
15. [The heart has its reasons, which reason does not know.]
16. [For compelling my assent.]
17. [The reference is to the Swiss philosopher Charles Secrétan (1815–1895).]
18. [In practice.]
19. Since belief is measured by action, he who forbids us to believe religion to be true, necessarily also forbids us to act as we should if we did believe it to be true. The whole defence of religious faith hangs upon action. If the action required or inspired by the

religious hypothesis is in no way different from that dictated by the naturalistic hypothesis, then religious faith is a pure superfluity, better pruned away, and controversy about its legitimacy is a piece of idle trifling, unworthy of serious minds. I myself believe, of course, that the religious hypothesis gives to the world an expression which specifically determines our reactions, and makes them in a large part unlike what they might be on a purely naturalistic scheme of belief.

20. *Liberty, Equality, Fraternity,* p. 353, 2d edition, London, 1874.

STUDY QUESTIONS

1. In what ways is James's reasoning different from Pascal's wager?
2. According to James, what two things does religion say?
3. Does it makes any difference to James which religion you practice?
4. Do religious believers act differently than others?

PART 8

Moral Theory

Moral Isolationism

ᴊ

MARY MIDGLEY

We turn now to that major field of philosophy known as "ethics," a term derived from the Greek word *ethos* meaning "character." The subject, which may also be referred to as "moral philosophy," from the Latin *moralis*, relating to "custom," focuses on the nature of a moral judgment, the principles that ought to guide a good life, and the resolution of such thorny practical issues as abortion or reparation.

Some would claim that the search for universal answers to moral questions is futile because morality differs from one culture to another. Mary Midgley (1919–2018), who was Senior Lecturer in Philosophy at Newcastle University in England, argues on the contrary that moral reasoning requires the possibility of judging the practices of other cultures.

All of us are, more or less, in trouble today about trying to understand cultures strange to us. We hear constantly of alien customs. We see changes in our lifetime which would have astonished our parents. I want to discuss here one very short way of dealing with this difficulty, a drastic way which many people now theoretically favour. It consists in simply denying that we can ever understand any culture except our own well enough to make judgements about it. Those who recommend this hold that the world is sharply divided into separate societies, sealed units, each with its own system of thought. They feel that the respect and tolerance due from one system to another forbids us ever to take up a critical position to any other culture. Moral judgement, they suggest, is a kind of coinage valid only in its country of origin.

I shall call this position "moral isolationism." I shall suggest that it is certainly not forced upon us, and indeed that it makes no sense at all. People usually take it up because they think it is a respectful attitude to other cultures. In fact, however, it is not respectful. Nobody can respect what is entirely unintelligible to them. To respect someone, we have to know enough about him to make a *favourable* judgement, however general and tentative. And we do understand people in other cultures to this extent. Otherwise a great mass of our most valuable thinking would be paralysed.

To show this, I shall take a remote example, because we shall probably find it easier to think calmly about it than we should with a contemporary one, such as female circumcision in Africa or the Chinese Cultural Revolution. The principles

From Mary Midgley, *Heart and Mind: The Varieties of Moral Experience*, Routledge, 2003. Reprinted by permission of Taylor & Francis.

involved will still be the same. My example is this. There is, it seems, a verb in classical Japanese which means "to try out one's new sword on a chance wayfarer." (The word is *tsujigiri*, literally "crossroads-cut.") A samurai sword had to be tried out because, if it was to work properly, it had to slice through someone at a single blow, from the shoulder to the opposite flank. Otherwise, the warrior bungled his stroke. This could injure his honour, offend his ancestors, and even let down his emperor. So tests were needed, and wayfarers had to be expended. Any wayfarer would do—provided, of course, that he was not another Samurai. Scientists will recognize a familiar problem about the rights of experimental subjects.

Now when we hear of a custom like this, we may well reflect that we simply do not understand it; and therefore are not qualified to criticize it at all, because we are not members of that culture. But we are not members of any other culture either, except our own. So we extend the principle to cover all extraneous cultures, and we seem therefore to be moral isolationists. But this is, as we shall see, an impossible position. Let us ask what it would involve.

We must ask first: Does the isolating barrier work both ways? Are people in other cultures equally unable to criticize *us?* This question struck me sharply when I read a remark in *The Guardian* by an anthropologist about a South American Indian who had been taken into a Brazilian town for an operation, which saved his life. When he came back to his village, he made several highly critical remarks about the white Brazilians' way of life. They may very well have been justified. But the interesting point was that the anthropologist called these remarks "a damning indictment of Western civilization." Now the Indian had been in that town about two weeks. Was he in a position to deliver a damning indictment? Would we ourselves be qualified to deliver such an indictment on the Samurai, provided we could spend two weeks in ancient Japan? What do we really think about this?

My own impression is that we believe that outsiders can, in principle, deliver perfectly good indictments—only, it usually takes more than two weeks to make them damning. Understanding has degrees. It is not a slapdash yes-or-no matter. Intelligent outsiders can progress in it, and in some ways will be at an advantage over the locals. But if this is so, it must clearly apply to ourselves as much as any-body else.

Our next question is this: Does the isolating barrier between cultures block praise as well as blame? If I want to say that the Samurai culture has many virtues, or to praise the South American Indians, am I prevented from doing *that* by my outside status? Now, we certainly do need to praise other societies in this way. But it is hardly possible that we could praise them effectively if we could not, in principle, criticize them. Our praise would be worthless if it rested on no definite grounds, if it did not flow from some understanding. Certainly we may need to praise things which we do not *fully* understand. We say "there's something very good here, but I can't quite make out what it is yet." This happens when we want to learn from strangers. And we can learn from strangers. But to do this we have to distinguish between those strangers who are worth learning from and those who are not. Can we then judge which is which?

This brings us to our third question: What is involved in judging? Now plainly there is no question here of sitting on a bench in a red robe and sentencing people. Judging simply means forming an opinion, and expressing it if it is called for. Is there anything wrong about this? Naturally, we ought to avoid forming—and expressing—*crude* opinions, like that of a simple-minded missionary, who might dismiss the whole Samurai culture as entirely bad, because non-Christian. But this is a different objection. The trouble with crude opinions is that they are crude, whoever forms them, not that they are formed by the wrong people. Anthropologists, after all, are outsiders quite as much as missionaries. Moral isolationism forbids us to form *any* opinions on these matters. Its ground for doing so is that we don't understand them. But there is much that we don't understand in our own culture too. This brings us to our last question: If we can't judge other cultures, can we really judge our own? Our efforts to do so will be much damaged if we are really deprived of our opinions about other societies, because these provide the range of comparison, the spectrum of alternatives against which we set what we want to understand. We would have to stop using the mirror which anthropology so helpfully holds up to us.

In short, moral isolationism would lay down a general ban on moral reasoning. Essentially, this is the programme of immoralism, and it carries a distressing logical difficulty. Immoralists like Nietzsche are actually just a rather specialized sect of moralists. They can no more afford to put moralizing out of business than smugglers can afford to abolish customs regulations. The power of moral judgement is, in fact, not a luxury, not a perverse indulgence of the self-righteous. It is a necessity. When we judge something to be bad or good, better or worse than something else, we are taking it as an example to aim at or avoid. Without opinions of this sort, we would have no framework of comparison for our own policy, no chance of profiting by other people's insights or mistakes. In this vacuum, we could form no judgements on our own actions.

Now it would be odd if *Homo sapiens* had really got himself into a position as bad as this—a position where his main evolutionary asset, his brain, was so little use to him. None of us is going to accept this skeptical diagnosis. We cannot do so, because our involvement in moral isolationism does not flow from apathy, but from a rather acute concern about human hypocrisy and other forms of wickedness. But we polarize that concern around a few selected moral truths. We are rightly angry with those who despise, oppress or steamroll other cultures. We think that doing these things is actually *wrong*. But this is itself a moral judgement. We could not condemn oppression and insolence if we thought that all our condemnation were just a trivial local quirk of our own culture. We could still less do it if we tried to stop judging altogether.

Real moral skepticism, in fact, could lead only to inaction, to our losing all interest in moral questions, most of all in those which concern other societies.

When we discuss these things, it becomes instantly clear how far we are from doing this. Suppose, for instance, that I criticize the bisecting Samurai, that I say his behaviour is brutal. What will usually happen next is that someone will protest, will say that I have no right to make criticisms like that of another culture. But it is most unlikely that he will use this move to end the discussion of the subject. Instead, he will justify the Samurai. He will try to fill in the background, to make me understand the custom, by explaining the exalted ideals of discipline and devotion which produced it. He will probably talk of the lower value which the ancient Japanese placed on individual life generally. He may well suggest that this is a healthier attitude than our own obsession with security. He may add, too, that the wayfarers did not seriously mind being bisected, that in principle they accepted the whole arrangement.

Now an objector who talks like this is implying that it *is* possible to understand alien customs. That is just what he is trying to make me do. And he implies, too, that if I do succeed in understanding them, I shall do something better than giving up judging them. He expects me to change my present judgement to a truer one—namely, one that is favourable. And the standards I must use to do this cannot just be Samurai standards. They have to be ones current in my own culture. Ideals like discipline and devotion will not move anybody unless he himself accepts them. As it happens, neither discipline nor devotion is very popular in the West at present. Anyone who appeals to them may well have to do some more arguing to make *them* acceptable, before he can use them to explain the Samurai. But if he does succeed here, he will have persuaded us, not just that there was something to be said for them in ancient Japan, but that there would be here as well.

Isolating barriers simply cannot arise here. If we accept something as a serious moral truth about one culture, we can't refuse to apply it—in however different an outward form—to other cultures as well, wherever circumstances admit it. If we refuse to do this, we just are not taking the other culture seriously. This becomes clear if we look at the last argument used by my objector—that of justification by consent of the victim. It is suggested that sudden bisection is quite in order, *provided* that it takes place between consenting adults. I cannot now discuss how conclusive this justification is. What I am pointing out is simply that it can only work if we believe that *consent* can make such a transaction respectable—and this is a thoroughly modern and Western idea. It would probably never occur to a Samurai; if it did, it would surprise him very much. It is *our* standard. In applying it, too, we are likely to make another typically Western demand. We shall ask for good factual evidence that the wayfarers actually do have this rather surprising taste—that they are really willing to be bisected. In applying Western standards in this way, we are not being confused or irrelevant. We are asking the questions which arise *from where we stand,* questions which we can see the sense of. We do this because asking questions which you can't see the sense of is humbug. Certainly we can extend our questioning by imaginative effort. We can come to understand other societies better. By doing so, we may make their questions our own, or we may see that they are really forms of the questions which we are asking already. This is not impossible. It is just very hard work. The obstacles which often prevent it are simply those of ordinary ignorance, laziness and prejudice.

If there were really an isolating barrier, of course, our own culture could never have been formed. It is no sealed box, but a fertile jungle of different influences—Greek, Jewish, Roman, Norse, Celtic and so forth, into which further influences are still pouring—American, Indian, Japanese, Jamaican, you name it. The moral isolationist's picture of separate unmixable cultures is quite unreal. People who talk about British history usually stress the value of this fertilizing mix, no doubt rightly. But this is not just an odd fact about Britain. Except for the very smallest and most remote, all cultures are formed out of many streams. All have the problem of digesting and assimilating things which, at the start, they do not understand. All have the choice of learning something from this challenge, or, alternatively, of refusing to learn, and fighting it mindlessly instead.

This universal predicament has been obscured by the fact that anthropologists used to concentrate largely on very small and remote cultures, which did not seem to have this problem. These tiny societies, which had often forgotten their own history, made neat, self-contained subjects for study. No doubt it was valuable to emphasize their remoteness, their extreme strangeness, their independence of our cultural tradition. This emphasis was, I think, the root of moral isolationism. But, as the tribal studies themselves showed, even there the anthropologists were able to interpret what they saw and make judgements—often favourable—about the tribesmen. And the tribesmen, too, were quite equal to making judgements about the anthropologists—and about the tourists and Coca-Cola salesmen who followed them. Both sets of judgements, no doubt, were somewhat hasty, both have been refined in the light of further experience. A similar transaction between us and the Samurai might take even longer. But that is no reason at all for deeming it impossible. Morally as well as physically, there is only one world, and we all have to live in it.

STUDY QUESTIONS

1. What does Midgley mean by "moral isolationism"?
2. Are those who oppose judging other cultures equally opposed to other cultures judging ours?
3. Do those who live in a culture necessarily understand it better than those who don't live in that culture?
4. If criticisms of other cultures are always inappropriate, can praise of other cultures ever be appropriate?

Kant's Ethics

ϡ

ONORA O'NEILL

Can we find a moral rule that offers us a defensible standard for making ethical judgments? One influential answer is provided by Immanuel Kant, who offers various formulations of what he terms the "categorical imperative"—categorical because it does not depend on anyone's particular desires, and an imperative because it is a command of reason.

In the next selection Onora O'Neill, who was Principal of Newnham College, University of Cambridge, explains one of Kant's versions of the categorical imperative, the requirement that each person be treated as an end and never merely as a means.

....

Kant's moral theory has acquired the reputation of being forbiddingly difficult to understand and, once understood, excessively demanding in its requirements. I don't believe that this reputation has been wholly earned, and I am going to try to undermine it. . . .

The main method by which I propose to avoid some of the difficulties of Kant's moral theory is by explaining only one part of the theory. This does not seem to me to be an irresponsible approach in this case. One of the things that makes Kant's moral theory hard to understand is that he gives a number of different versions of the principle that he calls the Supreme Principle of Morality, and these different versions don't look at all like one another. . . .

Kant calls his Supreme Principle the *Categorical Imperative;* its various versions also have sonorous names. . . . The one on which I shall concentrate is known as the *Formula of the End in Itself.* . . .

THE FORMULA OF THE END IN ITSELF

Kant states the Formula of the End in Itself as follows:

> Act in such a way that you always treat humanity, whether in your own person or in the person of any other, never simply as a means but always at the same time as an end.

To understand this we need to know what it is to treat a person as a means or as an end. According to Kant, each of our acts reflects one or more *maxims*. The maxim of the act is the principle on which one sees oneself as acting. A maxim expresses

---

a person's policy, or if he or she has no settled policy, the principle underlying the particular intention or decision on which he or she acts. Thus, a person who decides, "This year I'll give 10 percent of my income to famine relief," has as a maxim the principle of tithing his or her income for famine relief. In practice, the difference between intentions and maxims is of little importance, for given any intention, we can formulate the corresponding maxim by deleting references to particular times, places, and persons. In what follows I shall take the terms "maxim" and "intention" as equivalent.

Whenever we act intentionally, we have at least one maxim and can, if we reflect, state what it is. (There is of course room for self-deception here—"I'm only keeping the wolf from the door," we may claim as we wolf down enough to keep ourselves overweight, or, more to the point, enough to feed someone else who hasn't enough food.)

When we want to work out whether an act we propose to do is right or wrong, according to Kant, we should look at our maxims and not at how much misery or happiness the act is likely to produce, and whether it does better at increasing happiness than other available acts. We just have to check that the act we have in mind will not use anyone as a mere means, and, if possible, that it will treat other persons as ends in themselves.

USING PERSONS AS MERE MEANS

To use someone as a *mere means* is to involve them in a scheme of action *to which they could not in principle consent*. Kant does not say that there is anything wrong about using someone as a means. Evidently we have to do so in any cooperative scheme of action. If I cash a check I use the teller as a means, without whom I could not lay my hands on the cash; the teller in turn uses me as a means to earn his or her living. But in this case, each party consents to her or his part in the transaction. Kant would say that though they use one another as means, they do not use one another as *mere* means. Each person assumes that the other has maxims of his or her own and is not just a thing or a prop to be manipulated.

But there are other situations where one person uses another in a way to which the other could not in principle consent. For example, one person may make a promise to another with every intention of breaking it. If the promise is accepted, then the person to whom it was given must be ignorant of what the promisor's intention (maxim) really is. If one knew that the promisor did not intend to do what he or she was promising, one would, after all, not accept or rely on the promise. It would be as though there had been no promise made. Successful false promising depends on deceiving the person to whom the promise is made about what one's real maxim is. And since the person who is deceived doesn't know that real maxim, he or she can't in principle consent to his or her part in the proposed scheme of action. The person who is deceived is, as it were, a prop or a tool—a mere means—in the false promisor's scheme. A person who promises falsely treats the acceptor of the promise as a prop or a thing and not as a person. In Kant's view, it is this that makes false promising wrong.

One standard way of using others as mere means is by deceiving them. By getting someone involved in a business scheme or a criminal activity on false pretenses, or by giving a misleading account of what one is about, or by making a false promise or a fraudulent contract, one involves another in something to which he or she in principle cannot consent, since the scheme requires that he or she doesn't know what is going on. Another standard way of using others as mere means is by coercing them. If a rich or powerful person threatens a debtor with bankruptcy unless he or she joins in some scheme, then the creditor's intention is to coerce; and the debtor, if coerced, cannot consent to his or her part in the creditor's scheme. To make the example more specific: If a moneylender in an Indian village threatens not to renew a vital loan unless he is given the debtor's land, then he uses the debtor as a mere means. He coerces the debtor, who cannot truly consent to this "offer he can't refuse." (Of course the outward form of such transactions may look like ordinary commercial dealings, but we know very well that some offers and demands couched in that form are coercive.)

In Kant's view, acts that are done on maxims that require deception or coercion of others, and so cannot have the consent of those others (for consent precludes both deception and coercion), are wrong. When we act on such maxims, we treat others as mere means, as things rather than as ends in themselves. If we act on such maxims, our acts are not only wrong but unjust: such acts wrong the particular others who are deceived or coerced.

STUDY QUESTIONS

1. According to Kant, is using someone as a means always wrong?
2. What does Kant mean by the maxim of an action?
3. Why is it wrong to deceive others?
4. Can you imagine circumstances in which breaking a promise would not be wrong?

Assessing Utilitarianism

✧

LOUIS P. POJMAN

Whereas Kant's ethical system concentrates exclusively on the reasons for an action and does not take account of its results, an opposing ethical system developed by John Stuart Mill, the leading English philosopher of the nineteenth century, focuses only on consequences. He defends utilitarianism, the view that the supreme principle of morality is to act so as to produce as much happiness as possible, each person counting equally. By "happiness" Mill means pleasure and the absence of pain.

Utilitarianism is in many ways an appealing doctrine, but it has been attacked on various grounds. In the next selection Louis P. Pojman (1935–2005), who was Professor of Philosophy at the United States Military Academy, explains why utilitarianism has been thought mistaken and offers possible responses to criticisms of it.

....

There are two classical types of utilitarianism: act utilitarianism and rule utilitarianism. In applying the principle of utility, act utilitarians ... say that ideally we ought to apply the principle to all of the alternatives open to us at any given moment. We may define act utilitarianism in this way:

> **act utilitarianism:** An act is right if and only if it results in as much good as any available alternative.

Of course, we cannot do the necessary calculations to determine which act is the correct one in each case, for often we must act spontaneously and quickly. So rules of thumb (for example, "In general don't lie," and "Generally keep your promises") are of practical importance. However, the right act is still that alternative that results in the most utility.

The obvious criticism of act utility is that it seems to fly in the face of fundamental intuitions about minimally correct behavior. Consider Richard Brandt's criticism of act utilitarianism:

> It implies that if you have employed a boy to mow your lawn and he has finished the job and asks for his pay, you should pay him what you promised only if you cannot find a better use for your money. It implies that when you bring home your monthly paycheck you should use it to support your family and yourself only if it cannot be used more effectively to supply the needs of others. It implies that if your father is ill and he has no prospect of good in his life, and maintaining him is a drain on the energy and enjoyments of others, then, if you can end his life without provoking any public scandal or setting a bad example, it is your positive duty to take matters into your own hands and bring his life to a close.[1]

Rule utilitarians like Brandt attempt to offer a more credible version of the theory. They state that an act is right if it conforms to a valid rule within a system of rules that, if followed, will result in the best possible state of affairs (or the least bad state of affairs, if it is a question of all the alternatives being bad). We may define rule utilitarianism this way:

> **rule utilitarianism:** An act is right if and only if it is required by a rule that is itself a member of a set of rules whose acceptance would lead to greater utility for society than any available alternative.

Human beings are rule-following creatures. We learn by adhering to the rules of a given subject, whether it is speaking a language, driving a car, dancing, writing an essay, rock climbing, or cooking. We want to have a set of action-guiding rules to live by. The act-utilitarian rule, to do the act that maximizes utility, is too general for most purposes. Often we don't have time to deliberate whether lying will produce more utility than truth telling, so we need a more specific rule prescribing truthfulness, which passes the test of rational scrutiny. Rule utilitarianism asserts that the best chance of maximizing utility is by following the *set of rules* most likely to give us our desired results. . . .

An often-debated question in ethics is whether rule utilitarianism is a consistent version of utilitarianism. . . . [F]or example, we could imagine a situation in which breaking the general rule "Never lie" in order to spare someone's feelings would create more utility . . . than keeping the rule would. It would seem that we could always improve on any version of rule utilitarianism by breaking the set of rules whenever we judge that by so doing we could produce even more utility than by following the set. . . .

Whatever the answers . . . utilitarianism does have two very positive features. It also has several problems. The first attraction or strength is that it is a single principle, an absolute system with a potential answer for every situation. Do what will promote the most utility! It's good to have a simple, action-guiding principle that is applicable to every occasion—even if it may be difficult to apply (life's not simple). Its second strength is that utilitarianism seems to get to the substance of morality. It is not merely a formal system (that is, a system that sets forth broad guidelines for choosing principles but offers no principles; such a guideline would be "Do whatever you can universalize") but rather has a material core: Promote human (and possibly animal) flourishing and ameliorate suffering. The first virtue gives us a clear decision procedure in arriving at our answer about what to do. The second virtue appeals to our sense that morality is made for humans (and other animals?) and that morality is not so much about rules as about helping people and alleviating the suffering in the world. . . .

Opponents raise several . . . objections against utilitarianism. We discuss five of them: (1) the no-rest objection, (2) the absurd-implications objection, (3) the integrity objection, (4) the justice objection, and (5) the publicity objection. . . .

Problem 1: The No-Rest Objection: According to utilitarianism, one should always do that act that promises to promote the most utility. However, there is usually an infinite set of possible acts to choose from, and even if I can be excused from considering all of them, I can be fairly sure that there is often a preferable act that I could be doing. For example, when I am about to go to the movies with a friend, I should ask myself if helping the homeless in my community wouldn't promote more utility. When I am about to go to sleep, I should ask myself whether I could at that moment be doing something to help save the ozone layer. And why not simply give all my assets (beyond what is absolutely necessary to keep me alive) to the poor in order to promote utility? Following utilitarianism, I should get little or no rest, and, certainly, I have no right to enjoy life when, by sacrificing, I can make others happier. Similar to this point is Peter Singer's contention that middle-class people have a duty to contribute to poor people (especially in undeveloped countries) more than one-third of their income and all of us have a duty to contribute every penny above $30,000 that we possess until we are only marginally better off than the worst-off people on Earth. But, the objection goes, this makes morality too demanding, creates a disincentive to work, and fails to account for differential obligation. So utilitarianism must be a false doctrine.

Response: The utilitarian responds ... by insisting that a rule prescribing rest and entertainment is actually the kind of rule that would have a place in a utility-maximizing set of rules. The agent should aim at maximizing his or her own happiness as well as other people's happiness. For the same reason, it is best not to worry much about the needs of those not in our primary circle. Although we should be concerned about the needs of future and distant (especially poor) people, it actually would promote disutility for the average person to become preoccupied with these concerns. Peter Singer represents a radical act–utilitarian position, which fails to give adequate attention to the rules that promote human flourishing, such as the right to own property, educate one's children, and improve one's quality of life, all of which probably costs more than $30,000 per year in many parts of North America. But, the utilitarian would remind us, we can surely do a lot more for suffering humanity than we now are doing—especially if we join together and act cooperatively. And we can simplify our lives, cutting back on conspicuous consumption, while improving our overall quality.

Problem 2: The Absurd-Implications Objection: W. D. Ross has argued that utilitarianism is to be rejected because it is counterintuitive. If we accept it, we would have to accept an absurd implication. Consider two acts, A and B, that will both result in 100 hedons (units of pleasure of utility). The only difference is that A involves telling a lie and B involves telling the truth. The utilitarian must maintain that the two acts are of equal value. But this seems implausible; truth seems to be an intrinsically good thing. ...

Response: ... [U]tilitarians can agree that there is something counterintuitive in the calculus of equating an act of lying with one of honesty; but, they argue, we must be ready to change our culture-induced moral biases. What is so important about truth telling or so bad about lying? If it turned out that lying really promoted human welfare, we'd have to accept it. But that's not likely. Our happiness is tied up with a need for reliable information (truth) on how to achieve our ends. So truthfulness will be a member of rule utility's set. But when lying will clearly promote utility without undermining the general adherence to the rule, we simply ought to lie. Don't we already accept lying to a gangster or telling white lies to spare people's feelings? ...

Problem 3: The Integrity Objection: Bernard Williams argues that utilitarianism violates personal integrity by commanding that we violate our most central and deeply held principles. He illustrates this with the following example:

> Jim finds himself in the central square of a small South American town. Tied up against the wall [is] a row of twenty Indians, most terrified, a few defiant, in front of them several armed men in uniform. A heavy man in a sweat-stained khaki shirt turns out to be the captain in charge and, after a good deal of questioning of Jim which establishes that he got there by accident while on a botanical expedition, explains that the Indians are a random group of inhabitants who, after recent acts of protest against the government, are just about to be killed to remind other possible protesters of the advantages of not protesting. However, since Jim is an honored visitor from another land, the captain is happy to offer him a guest's privilege of killing one of the Indians himself. If Jim accepts, then as a special mark of the occasion, the other Indians will be let off. Of course, if Jim refuses, then there is no special occasion, and Pedro here will do what he was about to do when Jim arrived, and kill them all. Jim, with some desperate recollection of schoolboy fiction, wonders whether if he got hold of a gun, he could hold the captain, Pedro and the rest of the soldiers to threat, but it is quite clear from the set-up that nothing of that kind is going to work: any attempt of that sort of thing will mean that all the Indians will be killed, and himself. The men against the wall, the other villagers, understand the situation, and are obviously begging him to accept. What should he do?[2]

Williams asks rhetorically,

> How can a man, as a utilitarian agent, come to regard as one satisfaction among others, and a dispensable one, a project or attitude round which he has built his life, just because someone else's projects have so structured the causal scene that *that* is how the utilitarian sum comes out?

Williams's conclusion is that utilitarianism leads to personal alienation and so is deeply flawed.

Response: ... [T]he utilitarian can argue that (1) some alienation may be necessary for the moral life but (2) the utilitarian (even the act utilitarian) can take this into account in devising strategies of action. That is, integrity is not an absolute that must be adhered to at all costs. Even when it is required that we sacrifice our lives or limit our freedom for others, we may have to limit or sacrifice something of what Williams calls our integrity. We may have to do the "lesser of evils" in many cases. If the utilitarian doctrine of negative responsibility is correct, we need to realize that we are responsible for the evil that we knowingly allow, as well as for the evil we commit.

But ... a utilitarian may realize that there are important social benefits in having people who are squeamish about committing acts of violence, even those that preliminary utility calculations seem to prescribe. It may be that becoming certain kinds of people (endorsed by utilitarianism) may rule out being able to commit certain kinds of horrors—like Jim's killing of an innocent Indian. That is, utilitarianism recognizes the utility of good character and conscience, which may militate against certain apparently utility-maximizing acts.

Problem 4: The Justice Objection: Suppose a rape and murder [are] committed in a racially volatile community. As the sheriff of the town, you have spent a lifetime working for racial harmony. Now, just when your goal is being realized, this incident occurs. The crime is thought to be racially motivated, and a riot is about to break out that will very likely result in the death of several people and create long-lasting racial antagonism. You see that you could frame a derelict for the crime so that a trial will find him guilty and he will be executed. There is every reason to believe that a speedy trial and execution will head off the riot and save community harmony. Only you (and the real criminal, who will keep quiet about it) will know that an innocent man has been tried and executed. What is the morally right thing to do? The utilitarian seems committed to framing the derelict, but many would find this appalling.

Or consider [that you] are a utilitarian physician who has five patients under your care. One needs a heart transplant, two need one lung each, one needs a liver, and the last one needs a kidney. Now into your office comes a healthy bachelor needing an immunization. You judge that he would make a perfect sacrifice for your five patients. Via a utility calculus, you determine that, without doubt, you could do the most good by injecting the healthy man with a fatal drug and then using his organs to save your five patients.

This cavalier view of justice offends us. The very fact that utilitarians even countenance such actions—that they would misuse the legal system or the medical system to carry out their schemes—seems frightening. . . .

Response: . . . The utilitarian counters that justice is not an absolute—mercy and benevolence and the good of the whole society sometimes should override it; but, the sophisticated utilitarian insists, it makes good utilitarian sense to have a principle of justice that we generally adhere to. It may not be clear what the sheriff should do in the racially torn community. . . . If we could be certain that it would not set a precedent of sacrificing innocent people, it may be right to sacrifice one person for the good of the whole. Wouldn't we all agree, the utilitarian continues, that it would be right to sacrifice one innocent person to prevent a great evil?

Virtually all standard moral systems have a rule against torturing innocent people. But suppose a maniac . . . has a lethal gas that will spread throughout the globe and wipe out all life within a few weeks. His psychiatrist knows the lunatic well and assures us that there is one way to stop him—torture his 10-year-old daughter and televise it. Suppose, for the sake of the argument, there is no way to simulate the torture. Would you not consider torturing the child in this situation?

Is it not right to sacrifice one innocent person to stop a war or to save the human race from destruction? We seem to proceed on this assumption in wartime, in every bombing raid. . . . We seem to be following this rule in our decision to drive automobiles and trucks even though we are fairly certain the practice will result in the death of thousands of innocent people each year.

On the other hand, the sophisticated utilitarian may argue that, in the case of the sheriff framing the innocent derelict, justice should not be overridden by current utility concerns, for human rights themselves are outcomes of utility consideration and should not lightly be violated. That is, because we tend subconsciously to favor our own interests and biases, we institute the principle of rights to protect ourselves and others from capricious and biased acts that would in the long run have great disutility. So we must not undermine institutional rights too easily—we should not kill the bachelor in order to provide a heart, two lungs, a liver, and one kidney to the five other patients—at least not at the present time, given people's expectations of what will happen to them when they enter hospitals. But neither should we worship rights! They are to be taken seriously but not given ultimate authority. The utilitarian cannot foreclose the possibility of sacrificing innocent people for the greater good of humanity. If slavery could be humane and yield great overall utility, utilitarians would accept it. . . .

Problem 5: The Publicity Objection: It is usually thought that all must know moral principles so that all may freely obey the principles. But utilitarians usually hesitate to recommend that everyone act as a utilitarian, especially an act utilitarian, for it takes a great deal of deliberation to work out the likely consequences of alternative courses of action. . . . So utilitarianism seems to contradict our notion of publicity.

Response: . . . [U]tilitarians have two responses. First, they can counter that the objection only works against act utilitarianism. Rule utilitarianism can allow for greater publicity, for it is not the individual act that is important but the set of rules that is likely to bring about the most good. But then the act utilitarian may respond that this objection only shows a bias toward publicity (or even democracy). It may well be that publicity is only a rule of thumb to be overridden whenever there is good reason to believe that we can obtain more utility by not publicizing act-utilitarian ideas. Since we need to coordinate our actions with other people, moral rules must be publicly announced, typically through legal statutes. I may profit from cutting across the grass in order to save a few minutes in getting to class, but I also value a beautiful green lawn. We need public rules to ensure the healthy state of the lawn. So we agree on a rule to prohibit walking on the grass—even when it may have a utility function. There are many activities that individually may bring about individual utility advancement or even communal good, which if done regularly, would be disastrous, such as cutting down trees in order to build houses or to make newspaper or paper for books like this one, valuable as it is. We thus regulate the lumber industry so that every tree cut down is replaced with a new one and large forests are kept inviolate. So moral rules must be publicly advertised, often made into laws and enforced.

There is one further criticism of rule utilitarianism, which should be mentioned. Sometimes students accuse this version as being relativistic, since it seems to endorse different rules in different societies. Society A may uphold polygamy, whereas our society defends monogamy. A desert society upholds the rule "Don't waste water," but in a community where water is plentiful no such rule exists.

However, this is not really conventional relativism, since the rule is not made valid by the community's choosing it but by the actual situation. In the first case, the situation is an imbalance in the ratio of women to men; in the second case, the situation is environmental factors, concerning the availability of water. . . .

The worry is that utilitarianism becomes so plastic as to be guilty of becoming a justification for our intuitions. Asked why we support justice . . . it seems too easy to respond, "Well, this principle will likely contribute to the greater utility in the long run." The utilitarian may sometimes become self-serving in such rationalizations. Nevertheless, there may be truth in such a defense.

NOTES

1. Richard Brandt, "Towards a Credible Form of Utilitarianism," in *Morality and the Language of Conduct*, ed. H. Castaneda and G. Naknikian (Detroit: Wayne State University Press, 1963), pp. 109–110.
2. Bernard Williams, "A Critique of Utilitarianism," in *Utilitarianism: For and Against*, ed. J. C. C. Smart and Bernard Williams (Cambridge, UK: Cambridge University Press, 1973), p. 98ff.

STUDY QUESTIONS

1. Explain the difference between act utilitarianism and rule utilitarianism.
2. What is the justice objection to utilitarianism?
3. What is the integrity objection to utilitarianism?
4. Does utilitarianism imply that under certain circumstances a physician might be morally justified in killing one patient to save the lives of five others?

Virtue Ethics

Julia Driver

Julia Driver is Professor of Philosophy at University of Texas at Austin. In the next selection she explains the difference between an ethical theory, like Aristotle's, that focuses on the development of a person's character, and an ethical theory, like that of Kant or Mill, that concentrates on the formulation of rules for right action.

....

From Julia Driver, *Ethics: The Fundamentals*. Copyright © 2007. Reprinted by permission of Blackwell Publishing. The ellipsis in the fourth paragraph is the author's.

Sometimes, in deciding on what we ought to do, we first consider how we ought to be. For example, if faced with a situation that involves social injustice, we might pick someone whom we admired and wanted to be like—Gandhi, let's say, or Mother Teresa—and then ask "What would Gandhi do?" This doesn't give us a rigid formula or decision procedure to employ. Instead, it asks us to consider a virtuous person, to consider his or her virtues, and then ask what behavior people with these good traits and dispositions exemplify. Some writers have thought that a picture like this better reflects how people should go about making their moral decisions. They should do so on the basis of concrete virtue judgments instead of abstract principles, such as "Maximize the good" or "Never treat another person merely as a means," and so forth.

... [V]irtue ethics has actually been around in one form or another for thousands of years. Current virtue ethicists, in fact, tend to take their inspiration from Aristotle, who was a student of Plato, and certainly one of the greatest philosophers in the history of philosophy. Aristotle wrote the *Nicomachean Ethics,* which—as an aid to his son—spelled out the steps to a good life. Of course, "good" is a bit ambiguous—Is that morally good, or prudentially good, or intellectually good, or all of the above? Well, for Aristotle, the good human life had all these ingredients. A good human being was virtuous in the sense that he embodied all the excellences of human character. So, Aristotle is often held up as a paradigmatic virtue ethicist. Again, ... virtue ethics maintains that character, human excellence, *virtues,* are the basic modes of evaluation in the theory, as opposed to act evaluations such as "right" and "wrong." ... [A]ct evaluation is to be understood in terms of character evaluation. Virtue is the primary mode of evaluation, and all other modes are understood and defined *in terms of* virtue.... Most of the theoretical weight is therefore borne by the account of virtue provided in the theory....

Aristotle famously believed in the claim that virtue is a mean state, that it lies between two opposed vices. This is referred to as the doctrine of the mean. The basic idea is that virtue will tend to lie between two extremes, each of which is a vice. So, bravery lies between cowardice and foolhardiness; temperance lies between gluttony and abstinence; and so forth. Some virtues can be hard to model on this view. Take honesty. Of course, failure to tell the truths—telling a lie—would be one extreme, but is there a vice of telling too much truth? Maybe ... though I suspect there might be some disagreement over this. Part of the mean state concerned our emotions, however, and not just our actions. The virtuous person not only does the right thing, but he does the right thing in the right way—in the right sort of emotional or psychological state. Our emotions can be excessive or deficient as well. The person who runs into the battle to fight, but who is excessively fearful, is not fully virtuous. The truly well-functioning person is able to control and regulate his feelings and emotions, as well as act rightly.

Aristotle's picture, then, of the virtuous person is the person who functions harmoniously—his desires and emotions do not conflict with what he knows to be right. They go together. This leads him to view a person who acts rightly, but who feels badly about it, as not being virtuous. This person is merely "continent"—this person can control his actions, but needs to work on bringing his emotions in line with what reason tells him is the right and appropriate thing to do. So the excellent human being is not conflicted; he does not suffer inner turmoil and the struggle between reason and passion....

Many challenges have been posed to virtue ethics.... One *general* criticism of the whole approach is that it fails to conform to what we know about how best to explain human behavior ...

For example, John Doris proposes that the globalism of traditional virtue ethics be rejected.[1] There is no one "honesty" trait, for example. Instead, we may have 50 or more "honesties"; that is, narrowly circumscribed traits or dispositions to tell the truth. So, Joe might not have honesty 1, which is the disposition to tell the truth about how well he does on exams, but he might have honesty 34, the disposition to tell the truth about how tall he is. So, Doris thinks that ... the experimental evidence supports the view that are no robust traits; that is, traits to tell the truth over all or even most contexts or situations. And this is a problem for a virtue ethics that understands virtue as a "stable" or "reliable" character trait.

Another challenge has been that virtue ethics doesn't provide a guide to action. "Be nice, dear"—Well, what is nice, and what are the circumstances under which I should be nice? That's what we really want to know. This shows that it is these other reasons that actually justify our behavior. This has been raised as a very standard problem for the theory, but virtue ethicists have spent a good deal of time trying to show how their theories could be applied....

This challenge can be expanded by noting that virtue ethics has trouble telling us the right thing to do in conflict situations, where two virtues may conflict, and thus the corresponding rules—such as "Be honest" or "Be kind"—may conflict. But some virtue ethicists think that this is simply the way morality is—it is messy, and for any situation there may be more than one right answer. Insisting that morality is neat and tidy is simply to impose a misleading clarity on moral decision-making.

... Virtue ethics remains an interesting alternative approach to moral evaluation and moral guidance.

NOTE

1. John Doris, *Lack of Character: Personality and Moral Behavior* (Cambridge, UK: Cambridge University Press, 2002), p. 31.

STUDY QUESTIONS

1. When you make a moral judgment, which question should you ask yourself: "What should I do?" or "What sort of person should I be?"
2. Should moral decisions always be based on rules?
3. Can findings in psychology be relevant to assessing moral theories?
4. Might a moral question have more than one right answer?

The Ethics of Care

⤝

VIRGINIA HELD

Virginia Held is Professor Emerita of Philosophy at Hunter College and The Graduate Center of The City University of New York. In the following selection she develops what she terms "the ethics of care," which some philosophers have viewed as one form of virtue ethics. She emphasizes, however, that while the two are in some ways similar, virtue ethics focuses on the character of individuals, whereas the ethics of care is concerned especially with fostering connectedness among people.

....

I

The ethics of care is only a few decades old. Some theorists do not like the term "care" to designate this approach to moral issues and have tried substituting "the ethic of love," or "relational ethics," but the discourse keeps returning to "care" as the so far more satisfactory of the terms considered, though dissatisfactions with it remain. The concept of care has the advantage of not losing sight of the work involved in caring for people and of not lending itself to the interpretation of morality as ideal but impractical to which advocates of the ethics of care often object. Care is both value and practice. . . .

I think one can discern among various versions of the ethics of care a number of major features.

First, the central focus of the ethics of care is on the compelling moral salience of attending to and meeting the needs of the particular others for whom we take responsibility. Caring for one's child, for instance, may well and defensibly be at the forefront of a person's moral concerns. The ethics of care recognizes that human beings are dependent for many years of their lives, that the moral claim of those dependent on us for the care they need is pressing, and that there are highly important moral aspects in developing the relations of caring that enable human beings to live and progress. All persons need care for at least their early years. Prospects for human progress and flourishing hinge fundamentally on the care that those needing it receive, and the ethics of care stresses the moral force of the responsibility to respond to the needs of the dependent. Many persons will become ill and dependent for some periods of their later lives, including in frail old age, and some who are permanently disabled will need care the whole of their

From Virginia Held, *The Ethics of Care: Personal, Political, and Global.* Copyright © 2006 by Oxford University Press. Reprinted by permission of the publisher.

lives. Moralities built on the image of the independent, autonomous, rational individual largely overlook the reality of human dependence and the morality for which it calls. The ethics of care attends to this central concern of human life and delineates the moral values involved. . . .

Second, in the epistemological process of trying to understand what morality would recommend and what it would be morally best for us to do and to be, the ethics of care values emotion rather than rejects it. Not all emotion is valued, of course, but in contrast with the dominant rationalist approaches, such emotions as sympathy, empathy, sensitivity, and responsiveness are seen as the kind of moral emotions that need to be cultivated not only to help in the implementation of the dictates of reason but to better ascertain what morality recommends. Even anger may be a component of the moral indignation that should be felt when people are treated unjustly or inhumanely, and it may contribute to (rather than interfere with) an appropriate interpretation of the moral wrong. This is not to say that raw emotion can be a guide to morality; feelings need to be reflected on and educated. But from the care perspective, moral inquiries that rely entirely on reason and rationalistic deductions or calculations are seen as deficient.

The emotions that are typically considered and rejected in rationalistic moral theories are the egoistic feelings that undermine universal moral norms, the favoritism that interferes with impartiality, and the aggressive and vengeful impulses for which morality is to provide restraints. The ethics of care, in contrast, typically appreciates the emotions and relational capabilities that enable morally concerned persons in actual interpersonal contexts to understand what would be best. Since even the helpful emotions can often become misguided or worse—as when excessive empathy with others leads to a wrongful degree of self-denial or when benevolent concern crosses over into controlling domination—we need an *ethics* of care, not just care itself. The various aspects and expressions of care and caring relations need to be subjected to moral scrutiny and *evaluated*, not just observed and described.

Third, the ethics of care rejects the view of the dominant moral theories that the more abstract the reasoning about a moral problem the better because the more likely to avoid bias and arbitrariness, the more nearly to achieve impartiality. The ethics of care respects rather than removes itself from the claims of particular others with whom we share actual relationships. It calls into question the universalistic and abstract rules of the dominant theories. When the latter consider such actual relations as between a parent and child, if they say anything about them at all, they may see them as permitted and cultivating them a preference that a person may have. Or they may recognize a universal obligation for all parents to care for their children. But they do not permit actual relations ever to take priority over the requirements of impartiality. . . .

The ethics of care may seek to limit the applicability of universal rules to certain domains where they are more appropriate, like the domain of law, and resist their extension to other domains. Such rules may simply be inappropriate in, for instance, the contexts of family and friendship, yet relations in these domains should certainly be *evaluated*, not merely described, hence morality should not be limited to abstract rules. We should be able to give moral guidance concerning actual relations that are trusting, considerate, and caring and concerning those that are not.

Dominant moral theories tend to interpret moral problems as if they were conflicts between egoistic individual interests on the one hand, and universal moral principles on the other. The extremes of "selfish individual" and "humanity" are recognized, but what lies between these is often overlooked. The ethics of care, in contrast, focuses especially on the area between these extremes. Those who conscientiously care for others are not seeking primarily to further their own *individual* interests; their interests are intertwined with the persons they care for. Neither are they acting for the sake of *all others* or *humanity in general*; they seek instead to preserve or promote an actual human relation between themselves and *particular others*. Persons in caring relations are acting for self-and-other together. Their characteristic stance is neither egoistic nor altruistic; these are the options in a conflictual situation, but the well-being of a caring relation involves the cooperative well-being of those in the relation and the well-being of the relation itself. . . .

II

What *is* care? What do we mean by the term "care"? Can we define it in anything like a precise way? There is not yet anything close to agreement among those writing on care on what exactly we should take the meaning of this term to be, but there have been many suggestions, tacit and occasionally explicit.

For over two decades, the concept of care as it figures in the ethics of care has been assumed, explored, elaborated, and employed in the development of theory. But definitions have often been imprecise, or trying to arrive at them has simply been postponed (as in my own case), in the growing discourse. Perhaps this is entirely appropriate for new explorations, but the time may have come to seek greater clarity. Some of those writing on care have attempted to be precise, with mixed results, whereas others have proceeded with the tacit understanding that of course to a considerable extent we know what we are talking about when we speak of taking care of a child or providing care for the ill. But care has many forms, and as the ethics of care evolves, so should our understanding of what care is.

The last words I spoke to my older brother after a brief visit and with special feeling were: "take care." He had not been taking good care of himself, and I hoped he would do better; not many days later he died, of problems quite possibly unrelated to those to which I had been referring. "Take care" was not an expression he and I grew up with. I acquired it over the years in my life in New York City. It may be illuminating to begin thinking about the meaning of "care" with an examination of this expression.

We often say "take care" as routinely as "goodbye" or some abbreviation and with as little emotion. But even then it does convey some sense of connectedness.

More often, when said with some feeling, it means something like "take care of yourself because I care about you." Sometimes we say it, especially to children or to someone embarking on a trip or an endeavor, meaning "I care what happens to you, so please don't do anything dangerous or foolish." Or, if we know the danger is inevitable and inescapable, it may be more like a wish that the elements will let the person take care so the worst can be evaded. And sometimes we mean it as a plea: Be careful not to harm yourself or others because our connection will make us feel with and for you. We may be harmed ourselves or partly responsible, or if you do something you will regret we will share that regret.

One way or another, this expression (like many others) illustrates human relatedness and the daily reaffirmations of connection. It is the relatedness of human beings, built and rebuilt, that the ethics of care is being developed to try to understand, evaluate, and guide. The expression has more to do with the feelings and awareness of the persons expressing and the persons receiving such expressions than with the actual tasks and work of "taking care" of a person who is dependent on us, or in need of care, but such attitudes and shared awareness seem at least one important component of care.

A seemingly easy distinction to make is between care as the activity of taking care of someone and the mere "caring about" of how we feel about certain issues. Actually "caring for" a small child or a person who is ill is quite different from merely "caring for" something (or not) in the sense of liking it or not, as in "I don't care for that kind of music." But these distinctions may not be as clear as they appear, since when we take care of a child, for instance, we usually also care about him or her, and although we could take care of a child we do not like, the caring will usually be better care if we care for the child in both senses. If we really do care about world hunger, we will probably be doing something about it, such as at least giving money to alleviate it or to change the conditions that bring it about, and thus establishing some connection between ourselves and the hungry we say we care about. And if we really do care about global climate change and the harm it will bring to future generations, we imagine a connection between ourselves and those future people who will judge our irresponsibility, and we change our consumption practices or political activities to decrease the likely harm. . . .

My own view, then, is that care is both a practice and a value. As a practice, it shows us how to respond to needs and why we should. It builds trust and mutual concern and connectedness between persons. It is not a series of individual actions, but a practice that develops, along with its appropriate attitudes. It has attributes and standards that can be described, but more important that can be recommended and that should be continually improved as adequate care comes closer to being good care. Practices of care should express the caring relations that bring persons together, and they should do so in ways that are progressively more morally satisfactory. Caring practices should gradually transform children and others into human beings who are increasingly morally admirable. . . .

In addition to being a practice, care is also a value. Caring persons and caring attitudes should be valued, and we can organize many evaluations of how persons are interrelated around a constellation of moral considerations associated with care or its absence. For instance, we can ask of a relation whether it is trusting and mutually considerate or hostile and vindictive. We can ask if persons are attentive and responsive to each other's needs or indifferent and self-absorbed. Care is not the same as benevolence, in my view, since it is more the characterization of a social relation than the description of an individual disposition, and social relations are not reducible to individual states. Caring relations ought to be cultivated, between persons in their personal lives and between the members of caring societies. Such relations are often reciprocal over time if not at given times. The values of caring are especially exemplified in caring relations, rather than in persons as individuals.

STUDY QUESTIONS

1. According to Held, what is "the ethics of care"?
2. What does Held mean by her claim that care is both a practice and a value?
3. Is the ethics of care a form of virtue ethics?
4. Does analyzing a moral problem from the perspective of the ethics of care sometimes yield a different result than that obtained by using either a Kantian or a utilitarian standard?

Egoism and Moral Skepticism

❧

JAMES RACHELS

Morality involves taking into account interests apart from our own. Do we ever do so? According to psychological egoism, we don't, because all human behavior is motivated only by self-interest. According to ethical egoism, even if we could act in the interest of others, we ought not do so but should be concerned only with ourselves. In the next selection James Rachels (1941–2003), who was Professor of Philosophy at the University of Alabama at Birmingham, considers both psychological and ethical egoism, concluding that neither is acceptable.

....

1. Our ordinary thinking about morality is full of assumptions that we almost never question. We assume, for example, that we have an obligation to consider the welfare of other people when we decide what actions to perform or what rules

to obey; we think that we must refrain from acting in ways harmful to others, and that we must respect their rights and interests as well as our own. We also assume that people are in fact capable of being motivated by such considerations, that is, that people are not wholly selfish and that they do sometimes act in the interests of others.

Both of these assumptions have come under attack by moral skeptics, as long ago as by Glaucon in Book II of Plato's *Republic*. Glaucon recalls the legend of Gyges, a shepherd who was said to have found a magic ring in a fissure opened by an earthquake. The ring would make its wearer invisible and thus would enable him to go anywhere and do anything undetected. Gyges used the power of the ring to gain entry to the Royal Palace, where he seduced the Queen, murdered the King, and subsequently seized the throne. Now Glaucon asks us to imagine that there are two such rings, one given to a man of virtue and one given to a rogue. The rogue, of course, will use his ring unscrupulously and do anything necessary to increase his own wealth and power. He will recognize no moral constraints on his conduct, and, since the cloak of invisibility will protect him from discovery, he can do anything he pleases without fear of reprisal. So, there will be no end to the mischief he will do. But how will the so-called virtuous man behave? Glaucon suggests that he will behave no better than the rogue: "No one, it is commonly believed, would have such iron strength of mind as to stand fast in doing right or keep his hands off other men's goods, when he could go to the market-place and fearlessly help himself to anything he wanted, enter houses and sleep with any woman he chose, set prisoners free and kill men at his pleasure, and in a word go about among men with the powers of a god. He would behave no better than the other; both would take the same course."[1] Moreover, why shouldn't he? Once he is freed from the fear of reprisal, why shouldn't a man simply do what he pleases, or what he thinks is best for himself? What reason is there for him to continue being "moral" when it is clearly not to his own advantage to do so?

These skeptical views suggested by Glaucon have come to be known as *psychological egoism* and *ethical egoism,* respectively. Psychological egoism is the view that all men are selfish in everything that they do, that is, that the only motive from which anyone ever acts is self-interest. On this view, even when men are acting in ways apparently calculated to benefit others, they are actually motivated by the belief that acting in this way is to their own advantage, and if they did not believe this, they would not be doing that action. Ethical egoism is, by contrast, a normative view about how men *ought* to act. It is the view that, regardless of how men do in fact behave, they have no obligation to do anything except what is in their own interests. According to ethical egoists, a person is always justified in doing whatever is in his own interests, regardless of the effect on others.

Clearly, if either of these views is correct, then "the moral institution of life" (to use Butler's well-turned phrase) is very different than what we normally think. The majority of mankind is grossly deceived about what is, or ought to be, the case, where morals are concerned.

2. Psychological egoism seems to fly in the face of the facts. We are tempted to say, "Of course people act unselfishly all the time. For example, Smith gives up a trip to the country, which he would have enjoyed very much, in order to stay behind and help a friend with his studies, which is a miserable way to pass the time. This is a perfectly clear case of unselfish behavior, and if the psychological egoist thinks that such cases do not occur, then he is just mistaken." Given such obvious instances of "unselfish behavior," what reply can the egoist make? There are two general arguments by which he might try to show that all actions, including those such as the one just outlined, are in fact motivated by self-interest. Let us examine these in turn:

a. The first argument goes as follows: If we describe one person's action as selfish, and another person's action as unselfish, we are overlooking the crucial fact that in both cases, assuming that the action is done voluntarily, *the agent is merely doing what he most wants to do.* If Smith stays behind to help his friend, that only shows that he wanted to help his friend more than he wanted to go to the country. And why should he be praised for his "unselfishness" when he is only doing what he most wants to do? So, since Smith is only doing what he wants to do, he cannot be said to be acting unselfishly.

This argument is so bad that it would not deserve to be taken seriously except for the fact that so many otherwise intelligent people have been taken in by it. First, the argument rests on the premise that people never voluntarily do anything except what they want to do. But this is patently false; there are at least two classes of actions that are exceptions to this generalization. One is the set of actions which we may not want to do, but which we do anyway as a means to an end which we want to achieve, for example, going to the dentist in order to stop a toothache, or going to work every day in order to be able to draw our pay at the end of the month. These cases may be regarded as consistent with the spirit of the egoist argument, however, since the ends mentioned are wanted by the agent. But the other set of actions are those which we do, not because we want to, nor even because there is an end which we want to achieve, but because we feel ourselves *under an obligation* to do them. For example, someone may do something because he has promised to do it, and thus feels obligated, even though he does not want to do it. It is sometimes suggested that in such cases we do the action because, after all, we want to keep our promises; so, even here, we are doing what we want. However, this dodge will not work: if I have promised to do something, and if I do not want to do it, then it is simply false to say that I want to keep my promise. In such cases we feel a conflict precisely because we do *not* want to do what we feel obligated to do. It is reasonable to think that Smith's action falls roughly into this second category: he might stay behind, not because he wants to, but because he feels that this friend needs help.

But suppose we were to concede, for the sake of the argument, that all voluntary action is motivated by the agent's wants, or at least that Smith is so motivated. Even if this were granted, it would not follow that Smith is acting selfishly or from self-interest. For if Smith wants to do something that will help his friend, even when it means forgoing his own enjoyments, that is precisely what makes him *unselfish*. What else could unselfishness be, if not wanting to help others? Another way to put the same point is to say that it is the *object* of a want that determines whether it is selfish or not. The mere fact that I am acting on *my* wants does not mean that I am acting selfishly; that depends on *what it is* that I want. If I want only my own good, and care nothing for others, then I am selfish; but if I also want other people to be well-off and happy, and if I act on *that* desire, then my action is not selfish. So much for this argument.

b. The second argument for psychological egoism is this: Since so-called unselfish actions always produce a sense of self-satisfaction in the agent,[2] and since this sense of satisfaction is a pleasant state of consciousness, it follows that the point of the action is really to achieve a pleasant state of consciousness, rather than to bring about any good for others. Therefore, the action is "unselfish" only at a superficial level of analysis. Smith will feel much better with himself for having stayed to help his friend—if he had gone to the country, he would have felt terrible about it—and that is the real point of the action. According to a well-known story, this argument was once expressed by Abraham Lincoln:

> Mr. Lincoln once remarked to a fellow passenger on an old-time mud-coach that all men were prompted by selfishness in doing good. His fellow-passenger was antagonizing this position when they were passing over a corduroy bridge that spanned a slough. As they crossed this bridge they espied an old razor-backed sow on the bank making a terrible noise because her pigs had got into the slough and were in danger of drowning. As the old coach began to climb the hill, Mr. Lincoln called out, "Driver, can't you stop just a moment?" Then Mr. Lincoln jumped out, ran back, and lifted the little pigs out of the mud and water and placed them on the bank. When he returned, his companion remarked: "Now, Abe, where does selfishness come in on this little episode?" "Why, bless your soul, Ed, that was the very essence of selfishness. I should have had no peace of mind all day had I gone on and left that suffering old sow worrying over those pigs. I did it to get peace of mind, don't you see?"[3]

This argument suffers from defects similar to the previous one. Why should we think that merely because someone derives satisfaction from helping others this makes him selfish? Isn't the unselfish man precisely the one who *does* derive satisfaction from helping others, while the selfish man does not? If Lincoln "got peace of mind" from rescuing the piglets, does this show him to be selfish, or, on the contrary, doesn't it show him to be compassionate and good-hearted? (If a man were truly selfish, why should it bother his conscience that *others* suffer—much less pigs?) Similarly, it is nothing more than shabby sophistry to say, because Smith takes satisfaction in helping his friend, that he is behaving selfishly. If we say this rapidly, while thinking about something else, perhaps it will sound all right; but if we speak slowly, and pay attention to what we are saying, it sounds plain silly.

Moreover, suppose we ask *why* Smith derives satisfaction from helping his friend. The answer will be, it is because Smith cares for him and wants him to succeed. If Smith did not have these concerns, then he would take no pleasure in assisting him; and these concerns, as we have already seen, are the marks of unselfishness, not selfishness. To put the point more generally: if we have a positive attitude toward the attainment of some goal, then we may derive satisfaction from attaining that goal. But the *object* of our attitude is *the attainment of that goal*; and we must want to attain the goal *before* we can find any satisfaction in it. We do not, in other words, desire some sort of "pleasurable consciousness" and then try to figure out how to achieve it; rather, we desire all sorts of different things—money, a new fishing boat, to be a better chess player, to get a promotion in our work, etc.—and because we desire these things, we derive satisfaction from attaining them. And so, if someone desires the welfare and happiness of another person, he will derive satisfaction from that; but this does not mean that this satisfaction is the object of his desire, or that he is in any way selfish on account of it.

It is a measure of the weakness of psychological egoism that these insupportable arguments are the ones most often advanced in its favor. Why, then, should anyone ever have thought it a true view? Perhaps because of a desire for theoretical simplicity: In thinking about human conduct, it would be nice if there were some simple formula that would unite the diverse phenomena of human behavior under a single explanatory principle, just as simple formulae in physics bring together a great many apparently different phenomena. And since it is obvious that self-regard is an overwhelmingly important factor in motivation, it is only natural to wonder whether all motivation might not be explained in these terms. But the answer is clearly No; while a great many human actions are motivated entirely or in part by self-interest, only by a deliberate distortion of the facts can we say that all conduct is so motivated. This will be clear, I think, if we correct three confusions which are commonplace. The exposure of these confusions will remove the last traces of plausibility from the psychological egoist thesis.

The first is the confusion of selfishness with self-interest. The two are clearly not the same. If I see a physician when I am feeling poorly, I am acting in my own interest but no one would think of calling me "selfish" on account of it. Similarly, brushing my teeth, working hard at my job, and obeying the law are all in my self-interest but none of these are examples of selfish conduct. This is because selfish behavior is behavior that ignores the interests of others, in circumstances in which their interests ought not to be ignored. This concept has a definite evaluative flavor; to call someone "selfish" is not just to describe his action but to condemn it. Thus, you would not call me selfish for eating a normal meal in normal circumstances (although it may surely be in my self-interest); but you would call me selfish for hoarding food while others about are starving.

The second confusion is the assumption that every action is done *either* from self-interest or from other-regarding motives. Thus, the egoist concludes that if there is no such thing as genuine altruism then all actions must be done from self-interest. But this is certainly a false dichotomy. The man who continues to smoke cigarettes, even after learning about the connection between smoking and cancer, is surely not acting from self-interest, not even by his own standards—self-interest would dictate that he quit smoking at once—and he is not acting altruistically either. He *is*, no doubt, smoking for the pleasure of it, but all that this shows is that undisciplined pleasure-seeking and acting from self-interest are very different. This is what led Butler to remark that "the thing to be lamented is, not that men have so great regard to their own good or interest in the present world, for they have not enough."[4]

The last two paragraphs show *(a)* that it is false that all actions are selfish and *(b)* that it is false that all actions are done out of self-interest. And it should be noted that these two points can be made, and were, without any appeal to putative examples of altruism.

The third confusion is the common but false assumption that a concern for one's own welfare is incompatible with any genuine concern for the welfare of others. Thus, since it is obvious that everyone (or very nearly everyone) does desire his own well-being, it might be thought that no one can really be concerned with others. But again, this is false. There is no inconsistency in desiring that everyone, including oneself *and* others, be well-off and happy. To be sure, it may happen on occasion that our own interests conflict with the interests of others, and in these cases we will have to make hard choices. But even in these cases we might sometimes opt for the interests of others, especially when the others involved are our family or friends. But more importantly, not all cases are like this: sometimes we are able to promote the welfare of others when our own interests are not involved at all. In these cases not even the strongest self-regard need prevent us from acting considerately toward others.

Once these confusions are cleared away, it seems to me obvious enough that there is no reason whatever to accept psychological egoism. On the contrary, if we simply observe people's behavior with an open mind, we may find that a great deal of it is motivated by self-regard, but by no means all of it; and that there is no reason to deny that "the moral institution of life" can include a place for the virtue of beneficence.[5]

3. The ethical egoist would say at this point, "Of course it is possible for people to act altruistically, and perhaps many people do act that way—but there is no reason why they *should* do so. A person is under no obligation to do anything except what is in his own interests."[6] This is really quite a radical doctrine. Suppose I have an urge to set fire to some public building (say, a department store) just for the fascination of watching the spectacular blaze: according to this view, the fact that several people might be burned to death provides no reason whatever why I should not do it. After all, this only concerns *their* welfare, not my own, and according to the ethical egoist the only person I need think of is myself.

Some might deny that ethical egoism has any such monstrous consequences. They would point out that it is really to my own advantage not to set the fire—for, if I do that I may be caught and put into prison (unlike Gyges, I have no magic ring for protection). Moreover, even if I could avoid being caught it is still to my advantage to respect the rights and interests of others, for it is to my advantage to live in a society in which people's rights and interests are respected. Only in such a society can I live a happy and secure life; so, in acting kindly toward others, I would merely be doing my part to create and maintain the sort of society which it is to my advantage to have.[7] Therefore, it is said, the egoist would not be such a bad man; he would be as kindly and considerate as anyone else, because he would see that it is to his own advantage to be kindly and considerate.

This is a seductive line of thought, but it seems to me mistaken. Certainly it is to everyone's advantage (including the egoist's) to preserve stable society where people's interests are generally protected. But there is no reason for the egoist to think that merely because *he* will not honor the rules of the social game, decent society will collapse. For the vast majority of people are not egoists, and there is no reason to think that they will be converted by his example—especially if he is discreet and does not unduly flaunt his style of life. What this line of reasoning shows is not that the egoist himself must act benevolently, but that he must encourage *others* to do so. He must take care to conceal from public view his own self-centered method of decision making, and urge others to act on precepts very different from those on which he is willing to act.

The rational egoist, then, cannot advocate that egoism be universally adopted by everyone. For he wants a world in which his own interests are maximized; and if other people adopted the egoistic policy of pursuing their own interests to the exclusion of his interests, as he pursues his interests to the exclusion of theirs, then such a world would be impossible. So he himself will be an egoist, but he will want others to be altruists.

This brings us to what is perhaps the most popular "refutation" of ethical egoism current among philosophical writers—the argument that ethical egoism is at bottom inconsistent because it cannot be universalized.[8] The argument goes like this:

To say that any action or policy of action is *right* (or that it *ought* to be adopted) entails that it is right for *anyone* in the same sort of circumstances. I cannot, for example, say that it is right for me to lie to you, and yet object when you lie to me (provided, of course, that the circumstances are the same). I cannot hold that it is all right for me to drink your beer and then complain when you drink mine. This is just the requirement that we be consistent in our evaluations; it is a requirement of logic. Now it is said that ethical egoism cannot meet this requirement because, as we have already seen, the egoist would not want others to act in the same way that he acts. Moreover, suppose he *did* advocate the universal adoption of egoistic policies: he would be saying to Peter, "You ought to pursue your own interests even if it means destroying Paul"; and he would be saying to Paul, "You ought to pursue your own interests even if it means destroying Peter." The attitudes expressed in these two recommendations seem clearly inconsistent—he is urging the advancement of Peter's interests at one moment, and countenancing their defeat at the next. Therefore, the argument goes, there is no way to maintain the doctrine of ethical egoism as a consistent view about how we ought to act. We will fall into inconsistency whenever we try.

What are we to make of this argument? Are we to conclude that ethical egoism has been refuted? Such a conclusion, I think, would be unwarranted; for I think that we can show, contrary to this argument, how ethical egoism can be maintained consistently. We need only to interpret the egoist's position in a sympathetic way: we should say that he has in mind a certain kind of world which he would prefer over all others; it would be a world in which his own interests were maximized, regardless of the effects on the other people. The egoist's primary policy of action, then, would be to act in such a way as to bring about, as nearly as possible, this sort of world. Regardless of however morally reprehensible we might find it, there is nothing *inconsistent* in someone's adopting this as his ideal and acting in a way calculated to bring it about. And if someone did adopt this as his ideal, then he would not advocate universal egoism; as we have already seen, he would want other people to be altruists. So, if he advocates any principles of conduct for the general public, they will be altruistic principles. This could not be inconsistent; on the contrary, it would be perfectly consistent with his goal of creating a world in which his own interests are maximized. To be sure, he would have to be deceitful; in order to secure the good will of others, and a favorable hearing for his exhortations to altruism, he would have to pretend that he was himself prepared to accept altruistic principles. But again, that would be all right; from the egoist's point of view, this would merely be a matter of adopting the necessary means to the achievement of his goal—and while we might not approve of this, there is nothing inconsistent about it. Again, it might be said, "He advocates one thing, but does another. Surely *that's* inconsistent." But it is not; for what he advocates and what he does are both calculated as means to an end (the *same* end, we might note); and as such, he is doing what is rationally required in each case. Therefore, contrary to the previous argument, there is nothing inconsistent in the ethical egoist's view. He cannot be refuted by the claim that he contradicts himself.

Is there, then, no way to refute the ethical egoist? If by "refute" we mean show that he has made some *logical* error, the answer is that there is not. However, there is something more that can be said. The egoist challenge to our ordinary moral convictions amounts to a demand for an explanation of why we should adopt certain policies of action, namely, policies in which the good of others is given importance. We can give an answer to this demand, albeit an indirect one. The reason one ought not to do actions that would hurt other people is other people would be hurt. The reason one ought to do actions that would benefit other people is other people would be benefited. This may at first seem like a piece of philosophical sleight-of-hand, but it is not. The point is that the welfare of human beings is something that most of us value *for its own sake,* and not merely for the sake of something else. Therefore, when *further* reasons are demanded for valuing the welfare of human beings, we cannot point to anything further to satisfy this demand. It is not that we have no reason for pursuing these policies, but that our reason *is* that these policies are for the good of human beings.

So if we are asked, "Why shouldn't I set fire to this department store?" one answer would be, "Because if you do, people may be burned to death." This is a complete, sufficient reason which does not require qualification or supplementation of any sort. If someone seriously wants to know why this action shouldn't be done, that's the reason. If we are pressed further and asked the skeptical question, "But why shouldn't I do actions that will harm others?" we may not know what to say—but this is because the questioner has included in his question the very answer we would like to give: "Why shouldn't you do actions that will harm others? Because, doing those actions would harm others."

The egoist, no doubt, will not be happy with this. He will protest that *we* may accept this as a reason, but *he* does not. And here the argument stops: there are limits to what can be accomplished by argument, and if the egoist really doesn't care about other people—if he honestly doesn't care whether they are helped or hurt by his actions—then we have reached those limits. If we want to persuade him to act decently toward his fellow humans, we will have to make our appeal to such other attitudes as he does possess, by threats, bribes, or other cajolery. That is all that we can do.

Though some may find this situation distressing (we would like to be able to show that the egoist is just *wrong*), it holds no embarrassment for common morality. What we have come up against is simply a fundamental requirement of rational action, namely, that the existence of reasons for action always depends on the prior existence of certain attitudes in the agent. For example, the fact that a certain course of action would make the agent a lot of money is a reason for doing it only if the agent wants to make money; the fact that practicing at chess makes one a better player is a reason for practicing only if one wants to be a better player; and so on. Similarly, the fact that a certain action would help the agent is a reason for doing the action only if the agent cares about his own welfare, and the fact that an action would help others is a reason for doing it only if the agent cares about others. In this respect, ethical egoism and what we might call ethical altruism are in exactly the same fix: both require that the agent *care* about himself, or about other people, before they can get started.

So a nonegoist will accept "It would harm another person" as a reason not to do an action simply because he cares about what happens to that other person. When the egoist says that he does *not* accept that as a reason, he is saying something quite extraordinary. He is saying that he has no affection for friends or family, that he never feels pity or compassion, that he is the sort of person who can look on scenes of human misery with complete indifference, so long as he is not the one suffering. Genuine egoists, people who really don't care at all about anyone other than themselves, are rare. It is important to keep this in mind when thinking about ethical egoism; it is easy to forget just how fundamental to human psychological makeup the feeling of sympathy is. Indeed, a man without any sympathy at all would scarcely be recognizable as a man; and that is what makes ethical egoism such a disturbing doctrine in the first place.

4. There are, of course, many different ways in which the skeptic might challenge the assumptions underlying our moral practice. In this essay I have discussed only two of them, the two put forward by Glaucon in the passage that I cited from Plato's *Republic*. It is important that the assumptions underlying our moral practice should not be confused with particular judgments made within that practice. To defend one is not to defend the other. We may assume—quite properly, if my analysis has been correct—that the virtue of beneficence does, and indeed should, occupy an important place in "the moral institution of life"; and yet we may make constant and miserable errors when it comes to judging when and in what ways this virtue is to be exercised. Even worse, we may often be able to make accurate moral judgments, and know what we ought to do, but not do it. For these ills, philosophy alone is not the cure.

NOTES

1. *The Republic of Plato,* translated by F. M. Cornford (Oxford, 1941), p. 45.
2. Or, as it is sometimes said, "It gives him a clear conscience," or "He couldn't sleep at night if he had done otherwise," or "He would have been ashamed of himself for not doing it," and so on.
3. Frank C. Sharp, *Ethics* (New York, 1928), pp. 74–75. Quoted from the Springfield (IL) *Monitor* in the *Outlook,* vol. 56, p. 1059.
4. *The Works of Joseph Butler,* edited by W. E. Gladstone (Oxford, 1896), vol. II, p. 26. It should be noted that most of the points I am making against psychological egoism were first made by Joseph Butler. Butler made all the important points; all that is left for us is to remember them.
5. The capacity for altruistic behavior is not unique to human beings. Some interesting experiments with rhesus monkeys have shown that these animals will refrain from operating a device for securing food if this causes other animals to suffer pain. See Jules H. Masserman, Stanley Wechkin, and William Terris, "'Altruistic' Behavior in Rhesus Monkeys," *American Journal of Psychiatry,* vol. 121 (1964), pp. 584–85.
6. I take this to be the view of Ayn Rand, insofar as I understand her confused doctrine.
7. Cf. Thomas Hobbes, *Leviathan* (London, 1651), chap. 17.
8. See, for example, Brian Medlin, "Ultimate Principles and Ethical Egoism," *Australasian Journal of Philosophy,* vol. 35 (1957), pp. 111–18; and D. H. Monro, *Empiricism and Ethics* (Cambridge, 1967), chap. 16.

STUDY QUESTIONS

1. Explain the distinction between psychological egoism and ethical egoism.
2. In the story about Abraham Lincoln, was his action motivated by selfishness?
3. Is a concern for one's own welfare incompatible with a concern for the welfare of others?
4. Is it self-defeating for an ethical egoist to urge everyone to act egoistically?

Nicomachean Ethics

ﻣ

ARISTOTLE

Aristotle (384–322 B.C.E.) was born in Macedonia, located between the Balkans and the Greek peninsula. At the age of eighteen he entered Plato's Academy, where he remained for two decades until Plato's death. He then taught outside Athens, including service as tutor to the young prince who later became known as Alexander the Great. Subsequently, Aristotle returned to Athens and founded his own school, the Lyceum. A dozen years later, when an outbreak of anti-Macedonian feeling swept Athens, Aristotle left the city, "lest," he reportedly said, "the Athenians should sin twice against philosophy," referring, of course, to the case of Socrates.

The *Nicomachean Ethics,* named after Aristotle's son Nicomachus, is widely regarded as one of the great books of moral philosophy. Aristotle grounds morality in human nature, viewing the good as the fulfillment of the human potential to live well. To live well is to live in accordance with virtue. But how does one acquire virtue? Aristotle's answer depends on his distinction between moral and intellectual virtue. Moral virtue, which we might call "goodness of character," is formed by habit. One becomes good by doing good. Repeated acts of justice and self-control result in a just, self-controlled person who not only performs just, self-controlled actions but does so from a fixed character. Intellectual virtue, on the other hand, which we might refer to as "wisdom," requires sophisticated intelligence and is acquired by teaching.

Virtuous activities are those that avoid the two extremes of excess and deficiency. For example, if you fear too much, you become cowardly; if you fear too little, you become rash. The mean is courage. To achieve the mean, you need to make a special effort to avoid that extreme to which you happen to be prone. Thus if you tend to be foolhardy, aim at timidity, and you will achieve the right measure of boldness.

The translation from the Greek is by David Ross (1877–1971), updated by J. L. Ackrill (1921–2007) and J. O. Urmson (1915–2008), all of the University of Oxford.

....

Every art and every inquiry, and similarly every action and pursuit, is thought to aim at some good; and for this reason the good has rightly been declared to be that at which all things aim. . . .

From *The Nicomachean Ethics,* translated by David Ross, revised by J. L. Ackrill and J. O. Urmson. Reprinted by permission of Oxford University Press.

If, then, there is some end of the things we do, which we desire for its own sake (everything else being desired for the sake of this), . . . clearly this must be . . . the chief good. . . .

Now such a thing happiness, above all else, is held to be; for this we choose always for itself and never for the sake of something else. . . .

Presumably, however, to say that happiness is the chief good seems a platitude, and a clearer account of what it is is still desired. This might perhaps be given, if we could first ascertain the function of man. For just as for a flute-player, a sculptor, or any artist, and, in general, for all things that have a function or activity, the good and the "well" is thought to reside in the function, so would it seem to be for man, if he has a function. Have the carpenter, then, and the tanner certain functions or activities, and has man none? Is he born without a function? Or as eye, hand, foot, and in general each of the parts evidently has a function, may one lay it down that man similarly has a function apart from all these? What then can this be? Life seems to belong even to plants, but we are seeking what is peculiar to man. Let us exclude, therefore, the life of nutrition and growth. Next there would be a life of perception, but *it* also seems to be shared even by the horse, the ox, and every animal. There remains, then, an active life of the element that has a rational principle. . . . Now if the function of man is an activity of soul which follows or implies a rational principle, and if . . . any action is well performed when it is performed in accordance with the appropriate excellence . . . human good turns out to be activity of soul exhibiting excellence. . . .

But we must add "in a complete life." For one swallow does not make a summer, nor does one day; and so too one day, or a short time, does not make a man blessed and happy. . . .

Virtue, then, being of two kinds, intellectual and moral, intellectual virtue in the main owes both its birth and its growth to teaching (for which reason it requires experience and time), while moral virtue comes about as a result of habit. . . . From this it is also plain that none of the moral virtues arises in us by nature; for nothing that exists by nature can form a habit contrary to its nature. For instance the stone which by nature moves downwards cannot be habituated to move upwards, not even if one tries to train it by throwing it up ten thousand times; nor can fire be habituated to move downwards, nor can anything else that by nature behaves in one way be trained to behave in another. Neither by nature, then, nor contrary to nature do the virtues arise in us; rather we are adapted by nature to receive them, and are made perfect by habit.

Again, of all the things that come to us by nature we first acquire the potentiality and later exhibit the activity (this is plain in the case of the senses; for it was not by often seeing or often hearing that we got these senses, but on the contrary we had them before we used them, and did not come to have them by using them); but the virtues we get by first exercising them, as also happens in the case of the arts as well. For the things we have to learn before we can do them, we learn by doing them, e.g., men become builders by building and lyre-players by playing the lyre; so too we become just by doing just acts, temperate by doing temperate acts, brave by doing brave acts. . . .

It makes no small difference, then, whether we form habits of one kind or of another from our very youth; it makes a very great difference, or rather *all* the difference.

Since, then, the present inquiry does not aim at theoretical knowledge like the others (for we are inquiring not in order to know what virtue is, but in order to become good, since otherwise our inquiry would have been of no use), we must examine the nature of actions, namely how we ought to do them; for these determine also the nature of the states of character that are produced, as we have said. . . .

First, then, let us consider this, that it is the nature of such things to be destroyed by defect and excess, as we see in the case of strength and of health (for to gain light on things imperceptible we must use the evidence of sensible things); exercise either excessive or defective destroys the strength, and similarly drink or food which is above or below a certain amount destroys the health, while that which is proportionate both produces and increases and preserves it. So too is it, then, in the case of temperance and courage and the other virtues. For the man who flies from and fears everything and does not stand his ground against anything becomes a coward, and the man who fears nothing at all but goes to meet every danger becomes rash; and similarly the man who indulges in every pleasure and abstains from none becomes self-indulgent, while the man who shuns every pleasure, as boors do, becomes in a way insensible; temperance and courage, then, are destroyed by excess and defect, and preserved by the mean.

But not only are the sources and causes of their origination and growth the same as those of their destruction, but also the sphere of their actualization will be the same; for this is also true of the things which are more evident to sense, e.g., of strength; it is produced by taking much food and undergoing much exertion, and it is the strong man that will be most able to do these things. So too is it with the virtues; by abstaining from pleasures we become temperate, and it is when we have become so that we are most able to abstain from them; and similarly too in the case of courage; for by being habituated to despise things that are fearful and to stand our ground against them we become brave, and it is when we have become so that we shall be most able to stand our ground against them. . . .

The question might be asked, what we mean by saying that we must become just by doing just acts, and temperate by doing temperate acts; for if men do just and temperate acts, they are already just and temperate, exactly as, if they do what is in accordance with the laws of grammar and of music, they are grammarians and musicians.

Or is this not true even of the arts? It is possible to do something that is in accordance with the laws of grammar, either by chance or under the guidance of another. A man will be a grammarian, then, only when he has both said something grammatical and said it grammatically; and this means doing it in accordance with the grammatical knowledge in himself.

Again, the case of the arts and that of the virtues are not similar; for the products of the arts have their goodness in themselves, so that it is enough that they should have a certain character, but if the acts that are in accordance with the virtues have themselves a certain character it does not follow that they are done justly or temperately. The agent also must be in a certain condition when he does them; in the first place he must have knowledge, secondly he must choose the acts, and choose them for their own sakes, and thirdly his action must proceed from a firm and unchangeable character. These are not reckoned in as conditions of the possession of the arts, except the bare knowledge; but as a condition of the possession of the virtues knowledge has little or no weight, while the other conditions count not for a little but for everything, i.e., the very conditions which result from often doing just and temperate acts.

Actions, then, are called just and temperate when they are such as the just or the temperate man would do; but it is not the man who does these that is just and temperate, but the man who also does them *as* just and temperate men do them. It is well said, then, that it is by doing just acts that the just man is produced, and by doing temperate acts the temperate man; without doing these no one would have even a prospect of becoming good.

But most people do not do these, but take refuge in theory and think they are being philosophers and will become good in this way, behaving somewhat like patients who listen attentively to their doctors, but do none of the things they are ordered to do. As the latter will not be made well in body by such a course of treatment, the former will not be made well in soul by such a course of philosophy. . . .

[E]very virtue or excellence both brings into good condition the thing of which it is the excellence and makes the work of that thing be done well; e.g., the excellence of the eye makes both the eye and its work good; for it is by the excellence of the eye that we see well. Similarly the excellence of the horse makes a horse both good in itself and good at running and at carrying its rider and at awaiting the attack of the enemy. Therefore, if this is true in every case, the virtue of man also will be the state of character which makes a man good and which makes him do his own work well.

How this is to happen we have stated already, but it will be made plain also by the following consideration of the specific nature of virtue. In everything that is continuous and divisible it is possible to take more, less, or an equal amount, and that either in terms of the thing itself or relatively to us; and the equal is an intermediate between excess and defect. By the intermediate in the object I mean that which is equidistant from each of the extremes, which is one and the same for all men; by the intermediate relatively to us that which is neither too much nor too little—and this is not one, nor the same for all. For instance, if ten is many and two is few, six is the intermediate, taken in terms of the object; for it exceeds and is exceeded by an equal amount; this is intermediate according to arithmetical proportion. But the intermediate relatively to us is not to be taken so; if ten pounds are too much for a particular person to eat and two too little, it does not follow that the trainer will order six pounds; for this also is perhaps too much for the person who is to take it, or too little—too little for Milo, too much for the beginner in athletic exercises. The same is true of running and wrestling. Thus a master of any art avoids excess and defect, but seeks the intermediate and chooses this—the intermediate not in the object but relatively to us.

If it is thus, then, that every art does its work well—by looking to the intermediate and judging its works by this standard (so that we often say of good works of art that it is not possible either to take away or to add anything, implying that excess and defect destroy the goodness of works of art, while the mean preserves it; and good artists, as we say, look to this in their work), and if, further, virtue is more exact and better than any art, as nature also is, then virtue must have the quality of aiming at the intermediate. I mean moral virtue; for it is this that is concerned with passions and actions, and in these there is excess, defect, and the intermediate. For instance, both fear and confidence and appetite and anger and pity and in general pleasure and pain may be felt both too much and too little, and in both cases not well; but to feel them at the right times, with reference to the right objects, towards the right people, with the right motive, and in the right way, is what is both intermediate and best, and this is characteristic of virtue. Similarly with regard to actions also there is excess, defect, and the intermediate. Now virtue is concerned with passions and actions, in which excess is a form of failure, and so is defect, while the intermediate is praised and is a form of success; and being praised and being successful are both characteristics of virtue. Therefore virtue is a kind of mean, since, as we have seen, it aims at what is intermediate. . . .

But not every action nor every passion admits of a mean; for some have names that already imply badness, e.g., spite, shamelessness, envy, and in the case of actions adultery, theft, murder; for all of these and suchlike things imply by their names that they are themselves bad, and not the excesses or deficiencies of them. It is not possible, then, ever to be right with regard to them; one must always be wrong. Nor does goodness or badness with regard to such things depend on committing adultery with the right woman, at the right time, and in the right way, but simply to do any of them is to go wrong. . . .

That moral virtue is a mean, then, and in what sense it is so, and that it is a mean between two vices, the one involving excess, the other deficiency, and that it is such because its character is to aim at what is intermediate in passions and in actions, has been sufficiently stated. Hence also it is no easy task to be good. For in everything it is no easy task to find the middle, e.g., to find the middle of a circle is not for everyone but for him who knows; so, too, anyone can get angry—that is easy—or give or spend money; but to do this to the right person, to the right extent, at the right time, with the right motive, and in the right way, *that* is not for everyone, nor is it easy; wherefore goodness is both rare and laudable and noble. . . .

But we must consider the things towards which we ourselves also are easily carried away; for some of us tend to one thing, some to another; and this will be recognizable from the pleasure and the pain we feel. We must drag ourselves away to the contrary extreme; for we shall get into the intermediate state by drawing well away from error. . . .

So much, then, is plain, that the intermediate state is in all things to be praised, but that we must incline sometimes towards the excess, sometimes towards the deficiency; for so shall we most easily hit the mean and what is right.

STUDY QUESTIONS

1. According to Aristotle, what is the function of a human being?
2. How does moral virtue differ from intellectual virtue?
3. How is moral virtue acquired?
4. What is Aristotle's doctrine of the mean?

Groundwork for the Metaphysics of Morals

Immanuel Kant

Immanuel Kant, whose work we read previously, is a central figure in the history of ethics. The selection that follows comes from a short work of his which, although intended only as a preliminary presentation of the main themes of his moral philosophy, has become the most widely read of all his ethical writings. By the "metaphysics of morals" Kant means the philosophical study of moral principles, as opposed to the anthropological survey of moral practices.

....

Everything in nature works in accordance with laws. Only a rational being has the power to act in accordance with the idea of laws—that is, in accordance with principles—and thus has a will. . . .

The idea of an objective principle, in so far as it constrains a will, is called a commandment (of reason), and the formulation of this commandment is called an Imperative. . . .

All imperatives command either hypothetically or categorically. Hypothetical imperatives declare a possible action to be practically necessary as a means to the attainment of something else that one wants (or that one may want). A categorical imperative would be one that represented an action as itself objectively necessary, without regard to any further end. . . .

If the action would be good only as a means to something else, the imperative is hypothetical; if the action is thought of as good in itself and therefore as necessary for a will which of itself conforms to reason as its principle, then the imperative is categorical. . . .

If I think of a *hypothetical* imperative as such, I do not know beforehand what it will contain—not until I am given its condition. But if I think of a *categorical imperative,* I know right away what it contains. For since this imperative contains, besides the law, only the necessity that the maxim[1] conform to this law, while the law, as we have seen, contains no condition limiting it, there is nothing left over to which the maxim of action should conform except the universality of a law as such; and it is only this conformity that the imperative asserts to be necessary.

There is therefore only one categorical imperative and it is this: "Act only on that maxim by which you can at the same time will that it should become a universal law." . . .

We shall now enumerate some duties. . . .

1. A man feels sick of life as the result of a mounting series of misfortunes that has reduced him to hopelessness, but he still possesses enough of his reason to ask himself whether it would not be contrary to his duty to himself to take his own life. Now he tests whether the maxim of his action could really become a universal law of nature. His maxim, however, is: "I make it my principle out of self-love to shorten my life if its continuance threatens more evil than it promises advantage." The only further question is whether this principle of self-love can become a universal law of nature. But one sees at once that a nature whose law was that the very same feeling meant to promote life should actually destroy life would contradict itself, and hence would not endure as nature. The maxim therefore could not possibly be a general law of nature and thus it wholly contradicts the supreme principle of all duty.

2. Another finds himself driven by need to borrow money. He knows very well that he will not be able to pay it back, but he sees too that nobody will lend him anything unless he firmly promises to pay it back within a fixed time. He wants to make such a promise, but he still has enough conscience to ask himself, "Isn't it impermissible and contrary to duty to get out of one's difficulties this way?" Suppose, however, that he did decide to do it. The maxim of his action would run thus: "When I believe myself short of money, I will borrow money and promise to pay it back, even though I know that this will never be done." Now this principle of self-love or personal advantage is perhaps quite compatible with my own entire future welfare; only there remains the question "Is it right?" I therefore transform the unfair demand of self-love into a universal law and frame my question thus: "How would things stand if my maxim became a universal law?" I then see immediately that this maxim can never qualify as a self-consistent universal law of nature, but must necessarily contradict itself. For the universality of a law

that permits anyone who believes himself to be in need to make any promise he pleases with the intention of not keeping it would make promising, and the very purpose one has in promising, itself impossible. For no one would believe he was being promised anything, but would laugh at any such utterance as hollow pretence.

3. A third finds in himself a talent that, with a certain amount of cultivation, could make him a useful man for all sorts of purposes. But he sees himself in comfortable circumstances, and he prefers to give himself up to pleasure rather than to bother about increasing and improving his fortunate natural aptitudes. Yet he asks himself further "Does my maxim of neglecting my natural gifts, besides agreeing with my taste for amusement, agree also with what is called duty?" He then sees that a nature could indeed endure under such a universal law, even if (like the South Sea Islanders) every man should let his talents rust and should be bent on devoting his life solely to idleness, amusement, procreation—in a word, to enjoyment. Only he cannot possibly *will* that this should become a universal law of nature or should be implanted in us as such a law by a natural instinct. For as a rational being he necessarily wills that all his powers should be developed, since they are after all useful to him and given to him for all sorts of possible purposes.

4. A fourth man, who is himself flourishing but sees others who have to struggle with great hardships (and whom he could easily help) thinks to himself: "What do I care? Let every one be as happy as Heaven intends or as he can make himself; I won't deprive him of anything; I won't even envy him; but I don't feel like contributing anything to his well-being or to helping him in his distress!" Now admittedly if such an attitude were a universal law of nature, the human race could survive perfectly well and doubtless even better than when everybody chatters about sympathy and good will, and even makes an effort, now and then, to practise them, but, when one can get away with it, swindles, traffics in human rights, or violates them in other ways. But although it is possible that a universal law of nature in accord with this maxim could exist, it is impossible to *will* that such a principle should hold everywhere as a law of nature. For a will that intended this would be in conflict with itself, since many situations might arise in which the man needs love and sympathy from others, and in which, by such a law of nature generated by his own will, he would rob himself of all hope of the help he wants.

These are some of the many actual duties—or at least of what we take to be actual—whose derivation from the single principle cited above is perspicuous. We must be able to will that a maxim of our action should become a universal law—this is the authoritative model for moral judging of action generally. Some actions are so constituted that we cannot even *conceive* without contradiction that their maxim be a universal law of nature, let alone that we could *will* that it *ought* to become one. In the case of other actions, we do not find this inner impossibility, but it is still impossible to *will* that their maxim should be raised to the universality of a law of nature, because such a will would contradict itself. . . .

If we now look at ourselves whenever we transgress a duty, we find that we in fact do not intend that our maxim should become a universal law. For this is impossible for us. What we really intend is rather that its opposite should remain a law generally; we only take the liberty of making an *exception* to it, for ourselves or (of course just this once) to satisfy our inclination. Consequently if we weighed it all up from one and the same perspective—that of reason—we should find a contradiction in our own will, the contradiction that a certain principle should be objectively necessary as a universal law and yet subjectively should not hold universally but should admit of exceptions. . . .

Suppose, however, there were something *whose existence in itself* had an absolute worth, something that, as an end *in itself*, could be a ground of definite laws. Then in it and in it alone, would the ground of a possible categorical imperative, that is, of a practical law, reside.

Now, I say, a human being, and in general every rational being, *does exist* as an end in himself, *not merely as a means* to be used by this or that will as it pleases. In all his actions, whether they are directed to himself or to other rational beings, a human being must always be viewed *at the same time as an end*. . . .

Beings whose existence depends not on our will but on nature still have only a relative value as means and are therefore called *things*, if they lack reason. Rational beings, on the other hand, are called *persons* because, their nature already marks them out as ends in themselves—that is, as something which ought not to be used *merely* as a means—and consequently imposes restrictions on all choice making (and is an object of respect). Persons, therefore, are not merely subjective ends whose existence as an effect of our actions has a value *for us*. They are *objective ends*—that is, things whose existence is in itself an end, and indeed an end such that no other end can be substituted for it, no end to which they should serve *merely* as a means. For if this were not so, there would be nothing at all having *absolute value* anywhere. But if all value were conditional, and thus contingent, then no supreme principle could be found for reason at all.

If then there is to be a supreme practical principle and a categorical imperative for the human will, it must be such that it forms an objective principle of the will from the idea of something which is necessarily an end for everyone because *it is an end in itself*, a principle that can therefore serve as a universal practical law. The ground of this principle is: *Rational nature exists as an end in itself.* This is the way in which a human being necessarily conceives his own existence, and it is therefore a *subjective* principle of human actions. But it is also the way in which every other rational being conceives his existence, on the same rational ground which holds also for me; hence it is at the same time an *objective* principle from which, since it is a supreme practical ground, it must be possible to derive all laws of the will. The practical imperative will therefore be the following: *Act in such a way that you treat humanity, whether in your own person or in any other person, always at the same time as an end, never merely as a means.* We will now see whether this can be carried out in practice.

Let us keep to our previous examples.

First, ... the man who contemplates suicide will ask himself whether his action could be compatible with the Idea of humanity as *an end in itself.* If he damages himself in order to escape from a painful situation, he is making use of a person *merely as a means* to maintain a tolerable state of affairs till the end of his life. But a human being is not a thing—not something to be used *merely* as a means: he must always in all his actions be regarded as an end in himself. Hence I cannot dispose of a human being in my own person, by maiming, corrupting, or killing him. (I must here forego a more precise definition of this principle that would forestall any misunderstanding—for example, as to having limbs amputated to save myself or exposing my life to danger in order to preserve it, and so on—this discussion belongs to ethics proper.)

Secondly, ... the man who has in mind making a false promise to others will see at once that he is intending to make use of another person *merely as a means* to an end which that person does not share. For the person whom I seek to use for my own purposes by such a promise cannot possibly agree with my way of treating him, and so cannot himself share the end of the action. This incompatibility with the principle of duty to others can be seen more distinctly when we bring in examples of attacks on the freedom and property of others. For then it is manifest that a violator of the rights of human beings intends to use the person of others merely as a means without taking into consideration that, as rational beings, they must always at the same time be valued as ends—that is, treated only as beings who must themselves be able to share in the end of the very same action.

Thirdly, ... it is not enough that an action not conflict with humanity in our own person as an end in itself: it must also *harmonize with this end.* Now there are in humanity capacities for greater perfection that form part of nature's purpose for humanity in our own person. To neglect these can perhaps be compatible with the *survival* of humanity as an end in itself, but not with the *promotion* of that end.

Fourthly, ... the natural end that all human beings seek is their own perfect happiness. Now the human race might indeed exist if everybody contributed nothing to the happiness of others but at the same time refrained from deliberately impairing it. This harmonizing with humanity *as an end in itself* would, however, be merely negative and not positive, unless everyone also endeavours, as far as he can, to further the ends of others. For the ends of any person who is an end in himself must, if this idea is to have its full effect in me, be also, as far as possible, *my* ends.

NOTE

1. [A maxim is the principle according to which the subject acts.—S. M. C.]

STUDY QUESTIONS

1. According to Kant, is using someone as a means always wrong?
2. What does Kant mean by the maxim of an action?
3. Why is it wrong to deceive others?
4. Can you imagine circumstances in which breaking a promise would not be wrong?

Utilitarianism

JOHN STUART MILL

John Stuart Mill (1806–1873), born in London, received an intense early education from his father, James Mill, a philosophical and political writer. While pursuing a career in the East India Company, John Stuart Mill published widely in philosophy, political theory, and economics. A strong influence on his life and thought was Harriet Taylor, whom he met in 1831 and married two decades later following the death of her husband. She herself died seven years afterward. Subsequently, Mill served as a member of Parliament, then retired and spent much of his time in Avignon, France, where his wife was buried.

The best known of his ethical writings is *Utilitarianism,* originally published in three installments in *Fraser's Magazine* of 1861. More than 150 years later, the book remains enormously influential. As a concise, yet comprehensive, presentation of its subject, the work has never been equaled.

CHAPTER II

WHAT UTILITARIANISM IS

...The creed which accepts as the foundation of morals "utility" or the "greatest happiness principle" holds that actions are right in proportion as they tend to promote happiness; wrong as they tend to produce the reverse of happiness. By happiness is intended pleasure and the absence of pain; by unhappiness, pain and the privation of pleasure. To give a clear view of the moral standard set up by the theory, much more requires to be said; in particular, what things it includes in the ideas of pain and pleasure, and to what extent this is left an open question. But these supplementary explanations do not affect the theory of life on which this theory of morality is

From *Utilitarianism* by John Stuart Mill (1863).

grounded—namely, that pleasure and freedom from pain are the only things desirable as ends; and that all desirable things (which are as numerous in the utilitarian as in any other scheme) are desirable either for pleasure inherent in themselves or as means to the promotion of pleasure and the prevention of pain....

It is quite compatible with the principle of utility to recognize the fact that some kinds of pleasure are more desirable and more valuable than others. It would be absurd that, while in estimating all other things quality is considered as well as quantity, the estimation of pleasure should be supposed to depend on quantity alone.

If I am asked what I mean by difference of quality in pleasures, or what makes one pleasure more valuable than another, merely as a pleasure, except its being greater in amount, there is but one possible answer. Of two pleasures, if there be one to which all or almost all who have experience of both give a decided preference, irrespective of any feeling of moral obligation to prefer it, that is the more desirable pleasure. If one of the two is, by those who are competently acquainted with both, placed so far above the other that they prefer it, even though knowing it to be attended with a greater amount of discontent, and would not resign it for any quantity of the other pleasure which their nature is capable of, we are justified in ascribing to the preferred enjoyment a superiority in quality so far outweighing quantity as to render it, in comparison, of small account.

Now it is an unquestionable fact that those who are equally acquainted with and equally capable of appreciating and enjoying both do give a most marked preference to the manner of existence which employs their higher faculties. Few human creatures would consent to be changed into any of the lower animals for a promise of the fullest allowance of a beast's pleasures; no intelligent human being would consent to be a fool, no instructed person would be an ignoramus, no person of feeling and conscience would be selfish and base, even though they should be persuaded that the fool, the dunce, or the rascal is better satisfied with his lot than they are with theirs. They would not resign what they possess more than he for the most complete satisfaction of all the desires which they have in common with him. If they ever fancy they would, it is only in cases of unhappiness so extreme that to escape from it they would exchange their lot for almost any other, however undesirable in their own eyes. A being of higher faculties requires more to make him happy, is capable probably of more acute suffering, and certainly accessible to it at more points, than one of an inferior type; but in spite of these liabilities, he can never really wish to sink into what he feels to be a lower grade of existence....

It is better to be a human being dissatisfied than a pig satisfied; better to be Socrates dissatisfied than a fool satisfied. And if the fool, or the pig, are of a different opinion, it is because they only know their own side of the question. The other party to the comparison knows both sides....

From this verdict of the only competent judges, I apprehend there can be no appeal. On a question which is the best worth having of two pleasures, or which of two modes of existence is the most grateful to the feelings, apart from its moral attributes and from its consequences, the judgment of those who are qualified by knowledge of both, or, if they differ, that of the majority among them, must be admitted as final. And there needs be the less hesitation to accept this judgment respecting the quality of pleasures, since there is no other tribunal to be referred to even on the question of quantity. What means are there of determining which is the acutest of two pains, or the intensest of two pleasurable sensations, except the general suffrage of those who are familiar with both?...

I have dwelt on this point as being a necessary part of a perfectly just conception of utility or happiness considered as the directive rule of human conduct. But it is by no means an indispensable condition to the acceptance of the utilitarian standard; for that standard is not the agent's own greatest happiness, but the greatest amount of happiness altogether; and if it may possibly be doubted whether a noble character is always the happier for its nobleness, there can be no doubt that it makes other people happier, and that the world in general is immensely a gainer by it. Utilitarianism, therefore, could only attain its end by the general cultivation of nobleness of character, even if each individual were only benefited by the nobleness of others, and his own, so far as happiness is concerned, were a sheer deduction from the benefit. But the bare enunciation of such an absurdity as this last renders refutation superfluous.

According to the greatest happiness principle, as above explained, the ultimate end, with reference to and for the sake of which all other things are desirable—whether we are considering our own good or that of other people—is an existence exempt as far as possible from pain, and as rich as possible in enjoyments, both in point of quantity and quality; the test of quality and the rule for measuring it against quantity being the preference felt by those who, in their opportunities of experience, to which must be added their habits of self-consciousness and self-observation, are best furnished with the means of comparison. This, being according to the utilitarian opinion the end of human action, is necessarily also the standard of morality, which may accordingly be defined "the rules and precepts for human conduct," by the observance of which an existence such as has been described might be, to the greatest extent possible, secured to all mankind; and not to them only, but, so far as the nature of things admits, to the whole sentient creation....

I must again repeat what the assailants of utilitarianism seldom have the justice to acknowledge, that the happiness which forms the utilitarian standard of what is right in conduct is not the agent's own happiness but that of all concerned. As between his own happiness and that of others, utilitarianism requires him to be as strictly impartial as a disinterested and benevolent spectator. In the golden rule of Jesus of Nazareth, we read the complete spirit of the ethics of utility. "To do as you would be done by," and "to love your neighbor as yourself," constitute the ideal perfection of utilitarian morality. As the means of making the nearest approach to this ideal, utility would enjoin, first, that laws and social arrangements should place the happiness or (as, speaking practically, it may be called) the interest of every individual as nearly as possible in harmony with the interest of the whole; and, secondly, that education and opinion, which have so vast a power over human character, should so use that power as to establish in the mind of every individual an indissoluble association between his own happiness and the good of the whole, especially between his own happiness and the practice of such modes of conduct, negative and positive, as regard for the universal happiness prescribes; so that not only he may be unable to conceive the possibility of happiness to himself, consistently with conduct opposed to the general good, but also that a direct impulse to promote the general good may be in every individual one of the habitual motives of action, and the sentiments connected therewith may fill a large and prominent place in every human being's sentient existence. If the impugners of the utilitarian morality represented it to their own minds in this its true character, I know not what recommendation possessed by any other morality they could possibly affirm to be wanting to it; what more beautiful or more exalted developments of human nature any other ethical system can be supposed to foster, or what springs of action, not accessible to the utilitarian, such systems rely on for giving effect to their mandates.

The objectors to utilitarianism cannot always be charged with representing it in a discreditable light. On the contrary, those among them who entertain anything like a just idea of its disinterested character sometimes find fault with its standard as being too high for humanity. They say it is exacting too much to require that people shall always act from the inducement of promoting the general interests of society. But this is to mistake the very meaning of a standard of morals and confound the rule of action with the motive of it. It is the business of ethics to tell us what are our duties, or by what test we may know them; but no system of ethics requires that the sole motive of all we do shall be a feeling of duty; on the contrary, ninety-nine hundredths of all our actions are done from other motives, and rightly so done if the rule of duty does not condemn them. It is the more unjust to utilitarianism that this particular misapprehension should be made a ground of objection to it, inasmuch as utilitarian moralists have gone beyond almost all others in affirming that the motive has nothing to do with the morality of the action, though much with the worth of the agent. He who saves a fellow creature from drowning does what is morally right, whether his motive be duty or the hope of being paid for his trouble; he who betrays the friend that trusts him is guilty of a crime, even if his object be to serve another friend to whom he is under greater obligations. But to speak only of actions done from the motive of duty, and in direct obedience to principle: it is a misapprehension of the utilitarian mode of thought to conceive it as implying that people should fix their minds upon so wide a generality as the world, or society at large. The great majority of good actions are intended not for the benefit of the world, but for that of individuals, of which the good of the world is made up; and the thoughts of the most virtuous man need not on these occasions travel beyond the particular persons concerned, except so far as is necessary to assure himself that in benefiting them he is not violating the rights, that is, the legitimate and authorized expectations, of anyone else. The multiplication of happiness is, according to the utilitarian ethics, the object of virtue: the occasions on which any person (except one in a thousand) has it in his power to do this on an extended scale—in other words, to be a public benefactor—are but exceptional; and on these occasions alone is he called on to consider public utility; in every other case, private utility, the interest or happiness of some few persons, is all he has to attend to. Those alone the influence of whose actions extends to society in general need concern themselves habitually about so large an object. In the case of abstinences indeed—of things which people forbear to do from moral considerations, though the consequences in the particular case might be beneficial—it would be unworthy of an intelligent agent not to be consciously aware that the action is of a class which, if practiced generally, would be generally injurious, and that this is the ground of the obligation to abstain from it. The amount of regard for the public interest implied in this recognition is no greater than is demanded by every system of morals, for they all enjoin to abstain from whatever is manifestly pernicious to society.…

Again, utility is often summarily stigmatized as an immoral doctrine by giving it the name of "expediency" and taking advantage of the popular use of that term to contrast it with principle. But the expedient, in the sense in which it is opposed to the right, generally means that which is expedient for the particular interest of the agent himself; as when a minister sacrifices the interests of his country to keep himself in place. When it means anything better than this, it means that which is expedient for some immediate object, some temporary purpose, but which violates a rule whose observance is expedient in a much higher degree. The expedient, in this sense, instead of being the same thing with the useful, is a branch of the hurtful. Thus it would often be expedient, for the purpose of getting over some momentary embarrassment, or attaining some object immediately useful to ourselves or others, to tell a lie. But inasmuch as the cultivation in ourselves of a sensitive feeling on the subject of veracity is one of the most useful, and the enfeeblement of that feeling one of the most hurtful, things to which our conduct can be instrumental; and inasmuch as any, even unintentional, deviation from truth does that much toward weakening the trustworthiness of human assertion, which is not only the principal support of all present social well-being, but the insufficiency of which does more than any one thing that can be named to keep back civilization, virtue, everything on which human happiness on the largest scale depends—we feel that the violation, for a present advantage, of a rule of such transcendent expediency is not expedient, and that he who, for the sake of convenience to himself or to some other individual, does what depends on him to deprive mankind of the good, and inflict upon them the evil, involved in the greater or less reliance which they can place in each other's word, acts the part of one of their worst enemies. Yet that even this rule, sacred as it is, admits of possible exceptions is acknowledged by all moralists; the chief of which is when the withholding of some fact (as of information from a malefactor, or of bad news from a person dangerously ill) would save an individual (especially an individual other than oneself) from great and unmerited evil, and when the withholding can only be effected by denial. But in order that the exception may not extend itself beyond the need, and may have the least possible effect in weakening reliance on veracity, it ought to be recognized and, if possible, its limits defined; and, if the principle of utility is good for anything, it must be good for weighing these conflicting utilities against one another and marking out the region within which one or the other preponderates.

CHAPTER IV

OF WHAT SORT OF PROOF THE PRINCIPLE OF UTILITY IS SUSCEPTIBLE

... Questions about ends are, in other words, questions about what things are desirable. The utilitarian doctrine is that happiness is desirable, and the only thing desirable, as an end; all other things being only desirable as means to that end. What ought to be required of this doctrine, what conditions is it requisite that the doctrine should fulfill—to make good its claim to be believed?

The only proof capable of being given that an object is visible is that people actually see it. The only proof that a sound is audible is that people hear it; and so of the other sources of our experience. In like manner, I apprehend, the sole evidence it is possible to produce that anything is desirable is that people do actually desire it. If the end which the utilitarian doctrine proposes to itself were not, in theory and in practice, acknowledged to be an end, nothing could ever convince any person that it was so. No reason can be given why the general happiness is desirable, except that each person, so far as he believes it to be attainable, desires his own happiness. This, however, being a fact, we have not only all the proof which the case admits of, but all which it is possible to require, that happiness is a good, that each person's happiness is a good to that person, and the general happiness, therefore, a good to the aggregate of all persons. Happiness has made out its title as *one* of the ends of conduct and, consequently, one of the criteria of morality.

But it has not, by this alone, proved itself to be the sole criterion. To do that, it would seem, by the same rule, necessary to show, not only that people desire happiness, but that they never desire anything else. Now it is palpable that they do desire things which, in common language, are decidedly distinguished from happiness. They desire, for example, virtue and the absence of vice no less really than pleasure and the absence of pain. The desire of virtue is not as universal, but it is as authentic a fact as the desire of happiness. And hence the opponents of the utilitarian standard deem that they have a right to infer that there are other ends of human action besides happiness, and that happiness is not the standard of approbation and disapprobation.

But does the utilitarian doctrine deny that people desire virtue, or maintain that virtue is not a thing to be desired? The very reverse. It maintains not only that virtue is to be desired, but that it is to be desired disinterestedly, for itself. Whatever may be the opinion of utilitarian moralists as to the original conditions by which virtue is made virtue, however they may believe (as they do) that actions and dispositions are only virtuous because they promote another end than virtue, yet this being granted, and it having been decided, from considerations of this description, what *is* virtuous, they not only place virtue at the very head of the things which are good as means to the ultimate end, but they also recognize as a psychological fact the possibility of its being, to the individual, a good in itself, without looking to any end beyond it; and hold that the mind is not in a right state, not in a state conformable to utility, not in the state most conducive to the general happiness, unless it does love virtue in this manner—as a thing desirable in itself, even although, in the individual instance, it should not produce those other desirable consequences which it tends to produce, and on account of which it is held to be virtue. This opinion is not, in the smallest degree, a departure from the happiness principle. The ingredients of happiness are very various, and each of them is desirable in itself, and not merely when considered as swelling an aggregate. The principle of utility does not mean that any given pleasure, as music, for instance, or any given exemption from pain, as for example health, is to be looked upon as means to a collective something termed happiness, and to be desired on that account. They are desired and desirable in and for themselves; besides being means, they are a part of the end. Virtue, according to the utilitarian doctrine is not naturally and originally part of the end, but it is capable of becoming so; and in those who live it disinterestedly it has become so, and is desired and cherished, not as a means to happiness, but as a part of their happiness.

To illustrate this further, we may remember that virtue is not the only thing originally a means, and which if it were not a means to anything else would be and remain indifferent, but which by association with what it is a means to comes to be desired for itself, and that too with the utmost intensity. What, for example, shall we say of the love of money? There is nothing originally more desirable about money than about any heap of glittering pebbles. Its worth is solely that of the things which it will buy; the desires for other things than itself, which it is a means of gratifying. Yet the love of money is not only one of the strongest moving forces of human life, but money is, in many cases, desired in and for itself; the desire to possess it is often stronger than the desire to use it, and goes on increasing when all the desires which point to ends beyond it, to be compassed by it, are falling off. It may, then, be said truly that money is desired not for the sake of an end, but as part of the end. From being a means to happiness, it has come to be itself a principal ingredient of the individual's conception of happiness. The same may be said of the majority of the great objects of human life: power, for example, or fame, except that to each of these there is a certain amount of immediate pleasure annexed, which has at least the semblance of being naturally inherent in them—a thing which cannot be said of money. Still, however, the strongest natural attraction, both of power and of fame, is the immense aid they give to the attainment of our other wishes; and it is the strong association thus generated between them and all our objects of desire which gives to the direct desire of them the intensity it often assumes, so as in some characters to surpass in strength all other desires. In these cases the means have become a part of the end, and a more important part of it than any of the things which they are means to. What was once desired as an instrument for the attainment of happiness has come to be desired for its own sake. In being desired for its own sake it is, however, desired as *part* of happiness. The person is made, or thinks he would be made, happy by its mere possession; and is made unhappy by failure to obtain it. The desire of it is not a different thing from the desire of happiness any more than the love of music or the desire of health. They are included in happiness. They are some of the elements of which the desire of happiness is made up. Happiness is not an abstract idea but a concrete whole; and these are some of its parts. And the utilitarian standard sanctions and approves their being so. Life would be a poor thing, very ill provided with sources of happiness, if there were not this provision of nature by which things originally indifferent, but conducive to, or otherwise associated with, the satisfaction of our primitive desires, become in themselves sources of pleasure more valuable than the primitive pleasures, both in permanency, in the space of human existence that they are capable of covering, and even in intensity.

Virtue, according to the utilitarian conception, is a good of this description. There was no original desire of it, or motive to it, save its conduciveness to pleasure, and especially to protection from pain. But through the association thus formed it may be felt a good in itself, and desired as such with as great intensity as any other good; and with this difference between it and the love of money, of power, or of fame—that all of these may, and often do, render the individual noxious to the other members of the society to which he belongs, whereas there is nothing which makes him so much a blessing to them as the cultivation of the disinterested love of virtue. And consequently, the utilitarian standard, while it tolerates and approves those other acquired desires, up to the point beyond which they would be more injurious to the general happiness than promotive of it, enjoins and requires the cultivation of the love of virtue up to the greatest strength possible, as being above all things important to the general happiness.

It results from the preceding considerations that there is in reality nothing desired except happiness. Whatever is desired otherwise than as a means to some end beyond itself, and ultimately to happiness, is desired as itself a part of happiness, and is not desired for itself until it has become so. Those who desire virtue for its own sake desire it either because the consciousness of it is a pleasure, or because the consciousness of being without it is a pain, or for both reasons united, as in truth the pleasure and pain seldom exist separately, but almost always together—the same person feeling pleasure in the degree of virtue attained, and pain in not having attained more. If one of these gave him no pleasure, and the other no pain, he would not love or desire virtue, or would desire it only for the other benefits which it might produce to himself or to persons whom he cared for.

We have now, then, an answer to the question, of what sort of proof the principle of utility is susceptible.

STUDY QUESTIONS

1. According to Mill, is the agent's own happiness the standard of right conduct?
2. Are some types of pleasure more worthwhile than others?
3. Why does Mill believe lying is wrong?
4. Does Mill believe the principle of utilitarianism can be proven?

PART 9

Moral Problems

A Defense of Abortion

JUDITH JARVIS THOMSON

Consider the following argument:

1. A fetus is an innocent human being.
2. Killing an innocent human being is always wrong.
3. Therefore killing a fetus is always wrong.

This argument is valid because the premises imply the conclusion. But is the argument sound? In other words, are both its premises true?

Premise 1 is open to question, for arguably the earliest embryo is not a human person. Yet some believe it is and may defend their view on religious grounds. In any case you might suppose that if premise 1 were granted, then the conclusion of the argument would be acceptable, because premise 2 may appear uncontroversial. Much philosophical discussion, however, has hypothesized that premise 1 is true and nevertheless denied the argument's conclusion by claiming that premise 2 is false.

On what grounds, if any, can premise 2 be rejected? That question lies at the heart of the following essay by Judith Jarvis Thomson, who is Professor Emerita of Philosophy at the Massachusetts Institute of Technology. She argues that even if the human fetus is a person, abortion remains morally permissible in a variety of cases in which the mother's life is not threatened.

....

Most opposition to abortion relies on the premise that the fetus is a human being, a person, from the moment of conception. The premise is argued for, but, as I think, not well. Take, for example, the most common argument. We are asked to notice that the development of a human being from conception through birth into childhood is continuous; then it is said that to draw a line, to choose a point in this development and say "before this point the thing is not a person, after this point it is a person" is to make an arbitrary choice, a choice for which in the nature of things no good reason can be given. It is concluded that the fetus is, or anyway that we had better say it is, a person from the moment of conception. But this conclusion does not follow. Similar things might be said about the development of an acorn into an oak tree, and it does not follow that acorns are oak trees, or that we had better say they are. Arguments of this form are sometimes called "slippery slope arguments"—the phrase is perhaps self-explanatory—and it is dismaying that opponents of abortion rely on them so heavily and uncritically.

From Judith Jarvis Thomson, "A Defense of Abortion," *Philosophy & Public Affairs* 1 (1971). Reprinted by permission of Blackwell Publishers.

I am inclined to agree, however, that the prospects for "drawing a line" in the development of the fetus look dim. I am inclined to think also that we shall probably have to agree that the fetus has already become a human person well before birth. Indeed, it comes as a surprise when one first learns how early in its life it begins to acquire human characteristics. By the tenth week, for example, it already has a face, arms and legs, fingers and toes; it has internal organs, and brain activity is detectable. On the other hand, I think that the premise is false, that the fetus is not a person from the moment of conception. A newly fertilized ovum, a newly implanted clump of cells, is no more a person than an acorn is an oak tree. But I shall not discuss any of this. For it seems to me to be of great interest to ask what happens if, for the sake of argument, we allow the premise. How, precisely, are we supposed to get from there to the conclusion that abortion is morally impermissible? Opponents of abortion commonly spend most of their time establishing that the fetus is a person, and hardly any time explaining the step from there to the impermissibility of abortion. Perhaps they think the step too simple and obvious to require much comment. Or perhaps instead they are simply being economical in argument. Many of those who defend abortion rely on the premise that the fetus is not a person, but only a bit of tissue that will become a person at birth; and why pay out more arguments than you have to? Whatever the explanation, I suggest that the step they take is neither easy nor obvious, that it calls for closer examination than it is commonly given, and that when we do give it this closer examination we shall feel inclined to reject it.

I propose, then, that we grant that the fetus is a person from the moment of conception. How does the argument go from here? Something like this, I take it. Every person has a right to life. So the fetus has a right to life. No doubt the mother has a right to decide what shall happen in and to her body; everyone would grant that. But surely a person's right to life is stronger and more stringent than the mother's right to decide what happens in and to her body, and so outweighs it. So the fetus may not be killed; an abortion may not be performed.

It sounds plausible. But now let me ask you to imagine this. You wake up in the morning and find yourself back to back in bed with an unconscious violinist. A famous unconscious violinist. He has been found to have a fatal kidney ailment, and the Society of Music Lovers has canvassed all the available medical records and found that you alone have the right blood type to help. They have therefore kidnapped you, and last night the violinist's circulatory system was plugged into yours, so that your kidneys can be used to extract poisons from his blood as well as your own. The director of the hospital now tells you, "Look, we're sorry the Society of Music Lovers did this to you—we would never have permitted it if we had known. But still, they did it, and the violinist now is plugged into you. To unplug you would be to kill him. But never mind, it's only for nine months. By then he will have recovered from his ailment, and can safely be unplugged from you." Is it morally incumbent on you to accede to this situation? No doubt it would be very nice of you if you did, a great kindness. But do you *have* to accede to it? What if it were not nine months, but nine years? Or longer still? What if the director of the hospital says, "Tough luck, I agree, but you've now got to stay in bed, with the violinist plugged into you, for the rest of your life. Because remember this. All persons have a right to life, and violinists are persons. Granted you have a right to decide what happens in and to your body, but a person's right to life out-weighs your right to decide what happens in and to your body. So you cannot ever be unplugged from him." I imagine you would regard this as outrageous, which suggests that something really is wrong with that plausible-sounding argument I mentioned a moment ago.

In this case, of course, you were kidnapped; you didn't volunteer for the oper-ation that plugged the violinist into your kidneys. Can those who oppose abor-tion on the ground I mentioned make an exception for a pregnancy due to rape? Certainly. They can say that persons have a right to life only if they didn't come into existence because of rape; or they can say that all persons have a right to life, but that some have less of a right to life than others, in particular, that those who came into existence because of rape have less. But these statements have a rather unpleas-ant sound. Surely the question of whether you have a right to life at all, or how much of it you have, shouldn't turn on the question of whether or not you are the product of a rape. And in fact the people who oppose abortion on the ground I mentioned do not make this distinction, and hence do not make an exception in case of rape.

Nor do they make an exception for a case in which the mother has to spend the nine months of her pregnancy in bed. They would agree that would be a great pity, and hard on the mother; but all the same, all persons have a right to life, the fetus is a person, and so on. I suspect, in fact, that they would not make an excep-tion for a case in which, miraculously enough, the pregnancy went on for nine years, or even the rest of the mother's life.

Some won't even make an exception for a case in which continuation of the pregnancy is likely to shorten the mother's life; they regard abortion as impermis-sible even to save the mother's life. Such cases are nowadays very rare, and many opponents of abortion do not accept this extreme view. All the same, it is a good place to begin: a number of points of interest come out in respect to it.

1. Let us call the view that abortion is impermissible even to save the mother's life "the extreme view." I want to suggest first that it does not issue from the argument I mentioned earlier without the addition of some fairly powerful premises. Suppose a woman has become pregnant and now learns that she has a cardiac condition such that she will die if she carries the baby to term. What may be done for her? The fetus, being a person, has a right to life, but as the mother is a person too, so has she a right to life. Presumably they have an equal right to life. How is it supposed to come out that an abortion may not be performed? If mother and child have an equal right to life, shouldn't we perhaps flip a coin? Or should we add to the mother's right to life her right to decide what happens in and to her body, which everybody seems to be ready to grant—the sum of her rights now outweighing the fetus' right to life?

The most familiar argument here is the following. We are told that per-forming the abortion would be directly killing[1] the child, whereas doing nothing would not be killing the mother, but only letting her die. Moreover, in killing the child, one would be killing an innocent person, for the child has committed no crime and is not aiming at his mother's death. And then there are a variety of ways in which this might be continued. (1) But as directly killing an innocent person is always and absolutely impermissible, an abortion may not be performed. Or, (2) as directly killing an innocent person is murder, and murder is always and absolutely impermissible, an abortion may not be performed. Or, (3) as one's duty to refrain from directly killing an innocent person is more stringent than one's duty to keep a person from dying, an abortion may not be performed. Or, (4) if one's only options are directly killing an innocent person or letting a person die, one must prefer letting the person die, and thus an abortion may not be performed.[2]

Some people seem to have thought that these are not further premises which must be added if the conclusion is to be reached, but that they follow from the very fact that an innocent person has a right to life. But this seems to me to be a mistake, and perhaps the simplest way to show this is to bring out that while we must certainly grant that innocent persons have a right to life, the theses in (1) through (4) are all false. Take (2), for example. If directly killing an innocent person is murder, and thus is impermissible, then the mother's directly killing the innocent person inside her is murder and thus is impermissible. But it cannot seriously be thought to be murder if the mother performs an abortion on herself to save her life. It cannot seriously be said that she *must* refrain, that she *must* sit passively by and wait for her death. Let us look again at the case of you and the violinist. There you are, in bed with the violinist, and the director of the hospital says to you, "It's all most distressing, and I deeply sympathize, but you see this is putting an additional strain on your kidneys, and you'll be dead within the month. But you *have* to stay where you are all the same. Because unplugging you would be directly killing an innocent violinist, and that's murder, and that's impermissible." If anything in the world is true, it is that you do not commit murder, you do not do what is impermissible, if you reach around to your back and unplug yourself from that violinist to save your life.

The main focus of attention in writings on abortion has been on what a third party may or may not do in answer to a request from a woman for an abortion. This is in a way understandable. Things being as they are, there isn't much a woman can safely do to abort herself. So the question asked is what a third party may do and what the mother may do, if it is mentioned at all, is deduced, almost as an afterthought, from what it is concluded that third parties may do. But it seems to me that to treat the matter in this way is to refuse to grant to the mother that very status of person which is so firmly insisted on for the fetus. For we cannot simply read off what a person may do from what a third party may do. Suppose you find yourself trapped in a tiny house with a growing child. I mean a very tiny house and a rapidly growing child—you are already up against the wall of the house and in a few minutes you'll be crushed to death. The child on the other hand won't be crushed to death; if nothing is done to stop him from growing he'll be hurt, but in the end he'll simply burst open the house and walk out a free man. Now I could well understand it if a bystander were to say, "There's nothing we can do for you. We cannot choose between your life and his, we cannot be the ones to decide who is to live, we cannot intervene." But it cannot be concluded that you too can do nothing, that you cannot attack it to save your life. However innocent the child may be, you do not have to wait passively while it crushes you to death. Perhaps a pregnant woman is vaguely felt to have the status of house, to which we don't allow the right of self-defense. But if the woman houses the child, it should be remembered that she is a person who houses it.

I should perhaps stop to say explicitly that I am not claiming that people have a right to do anything whatever to save their lives. I think, rather, that there are drastic limits to the right of self-defense. If someone threatens you with death unless you torture someone else to death, I think you have not the right, even to save your life, to do so. But the case under consideration here is very different. In our case there are only two people involved, one whose life is threatened and one who threatens it. Both are innocent: the one who is threatened is not threatened because of any fault, the one who threatens does not threaten because of any fault. For this reason we may feel that we bystanders cannot intervene. But the person threatened can.

In sum, a woman surely can defend her life against the threat to it posed by the unborn child, even if doing so involves its death. And this shows not merely that the theses in (1) through (4) are false; it shows also that the extreme view of abortion is false, and so we need not canvass any other possible ways of arriving at it from the argument I mentioned at the outset.

2. The extreme view could of course be weakened to say that while abortion is permissible to save the mother's life, it may not be performed by a third party, but only by the mother herself. But this cannot be right either. For what we have to keep in mind is that the mother and the unborn child are not like two tenants in a small house which has, by an unfortunate mistake, been rented to both: the mother *owns* the house. The fact that she does adds to the offensiveness of deducing that the mother can do nothing from the supposition that third parties can do nothing. But it does more than this: it casts a bright light on the supposition that third parties can do nothing. Certainly it lets us see that a third party who says "I cannot choose between you" is fooling himself if he thinks this is impartiality. If Jones has found and fastened on a certain coat, which he needs to keep him from freezing, but which Smith also needs to keep him from freezing, then it is not impartiality that says "I cannot choose between you" when Smith owns the coat. Women have said again and again "This body is *my* body!" and they have reason to feel angry, reason to feel that it has been like shouting into the wind. Smith, after all, is hardly likely to bless us if we say to him, "Of course it's your coat, anybody would grant that it is. But no one may choose between you and Jones who is to have it."

We should really ask what it is that says "no one may choose" in the face of the fact that the body that houses the child is the mother's body. It may be simply a failure to appreciate this fact. But it may be something more interesting, namely, the sense that one has a right to refuse to lay hands on people, even where it would be just and fair to do so, even where justice seems to require that somebody do so. Thus justice might call for somebody to get Smith's coat back from Jones, and yet you have a right to refuse to be the one to lay hands on Jones, a right to refuse to do physical violence to him. This, I think, must be granted. But then what should be said is not "no one may choose," but only "*I* cannot choose," and indeed not even this, but "*I* will not *act*," leaving it open that somebody else can or should, and in particular that anyone in a position of authority, with the job of securing people's rights, both can and should. So this is no difficulty. I have not been arguing that any given third party must accede to the mother's request that he perform an abortion to save her life, but only that he may.

I suppose that in some views of human life the mother's body is only on loan to her, the loan not being one which gives her any prior claim to it. One who held this view might well think it impartiality to say "I cannot choose." But I shall simply ignore this possibility. My own view is that if a human being has any just, prior claim to anything at all, he has a just, prior claim to his own body. And perhaps this needn't be argued for here anyway, since, as I mentioned, the arguments against abortion we are looking at do grant that the woman has a right to decide what happens in and to her body.

But although they do grant it, I have tried to show that they do not take seriously what is done in granting it. I suggest the same thing will reappear even more clearly when we turn away from cases in which the mother's life is at stake, and attend, as I propose we now do, to the vastly more common cases in which a woman wants an abortion for some less weighty reason than preserving her own life.

3. Where the mother's life is not at stake, the argument I mentioned at the outset seems to have a much stronger pull. "Everyone has a right to life, so the unborn person has a right to life." And isn't the child's right to life weightier than anything other than the mother's own right to life, which she might put forward as ground for an abortion?

This argument treats the right to life as if it were unproblematic. It is not, and this seems to me to be precisely the source of the mistake.

For we should now, at long last, ask what it comes to, to have a right to life. In some views having a right to life includes having a right to be given at least the bare minimum one needs for continued life. But suppose that what in fact *is* the bare minimum a man needs for continued life is something he has no right at all to be given? If I am sick unto death, and the only thing that will save my life is the touch of Henry Fonda's cool hand on my fevered brow, then all the same, I have no right to be given the touch of Henry Fonda's cool hand on my fevered brow. It would be frightfully nice of him to fly in from the West Coast to provide it. It would be less nice, though no doubt well meant, if my friends flew out to the West Coast and carried Henry Fonda back with them. But I have no right at all against anybody that he should do this for me. Or again, to return to the story I told earlier, the fact that for continued life that violinist needs the continued use of your kidneys does not establish that he has a right to be given the continued use of your kidneys. He certainly has no right against you that *you* should give him continued use of your kidneys. For nobody has any right to use your kidneys unless you give him such a right; and nobody has the right against you that you shall give him this right—if you do allow him to go on using your kidneys, this is a kindness on your part, and not something he can claim from you as his due. Nor has he any right against anybody else that they should give him continued use of your kidneys. Certainly he had no right against the Society of Music Lovers that *they* should plug him into you in the first place. And if you now start to unplug yourself, having learned that you will otherwise have to spend nine years in bed with him, there is nobody in the world who must try to prevent you, in order to see to it that he is given something he has a right to be given.

Some people are rather stricter about the right to life. In their view, it does not include the right to be given anything, but amounts to, and only to, the right not to be killed by anybody. But here a related difficulty arises. If everybody is to refrain from killing that violinist, then everybody must refrain from doing a great many different sorts of things. Everybody must refrain from slitting his throat, everybody must refrain from shooting him—and everybody must refrain from unplugging you from him. But does he have a right against everybody that they shall refrain from unplugging you from him? To refrain from doing this is to allow him to continue to use your kidneys. It could be argued that he has a right against us that *we* should allow him to continue to use your kidneys. That is, while he had no right against us that we should give him the use of your kidneys, it might be argued that he anyway has a right against us that we shall not now intervene and deprive him of the use of your kidneys. I shall come back to third-party interventions later. But certainly the violinist has no right against you that *you* shall allow him to continue to use your kidneys. As I said, if you do allow him to continue to use them, it is a kindness on your part and not something you owe him.

The difficulty I point to here is not peculiar to the right to life. It reappears in connection with all the other natural rights; and it is something which an adequate account of rights must deal with. For present purposes it is enough just to draw attention to it. But I would stress that I am not arguing that people do not have a right to life—quite to the contrary, it seems to me that the primary control we must place on the acceptability of an account of rights is that it should turn out in that account to be a truth that all persons have a right to life. I am arguing only that having a right to life does not guarantee having either a right to be given the use of or a right to be allowed continued use of another person's body—even if one needs it for life itself. So the right to life will not serve the opponents of abortion in the very simple and clear way in which they seem to have thought it would.

4. There is another way to bring out the difficulty. In the most ordinary sort of case, to deprive someone of what he has a right to is to treat him unjustly. Suppose a boy and his small brother are jointly given a box of chocolates for Christmas. If the older boy takes the box and refuses to give his brother any of the chocolates, he is unjust to him, for the brother has been given a right to half of them.

But suppose that, having learned that otherwise it means nine years in bed with that violinist, you unplug yourself from him. You surely are not being unjust to him, for you gave him no right to use your kidneys, and no one else can have given him any such right. But we have to notice that in unplugging yourself, you are killing him; and violinists, like everybody else, have a right to life, and thus in the view we were considering just now, the right not to be killed. So here you do what he supposedly has a right you shall not do, but you do not act unjustly to him in doing it.

The emendation which may be made at this point is this: the right to life consists not in the right not to be killed, but rather in the right not to be killed unjustly. This runs a risk of circularity, but never mind: it would enable us to square the fact that the violinist has a right to life with the fact that you do not act unjustly toward him in unplugging yourself, thereby killing him. For if you do not kill him unjustly, you do not violate his right to life, and so it is no wonder you do him no injustice.

But if this emendation is accepted, the gap in the argument against abortion stares us plainly in the face: it is by no means enough to show that the fetus is a person, and to remind us that all persons have a right to life—we need to be shown also that killing the fetus violates its right to life, i.e., that abortion is unjust killing. And is it?

I suppose we may take it as a datum that in a case of pregnancy due to rape the mother has not given the unborn person a right to the use of her body for food and shelter. Indeed, in what pregnancy could it be supposed that the mother has given the unborn person such a right? It is not as if there were unborn persons drifting about the world, to whom a woman who wants a child says "I invite you in."

But it might be argued that there are other ways one can have acquired a right to the use of another person's body than by having been invited to use it by that person. Suppose a woman voluntarily indulges in intercourse, knowing of the chance it will issue in pregnancy, and then she does become pregnant; is she not in part responsible for the presence, in fact the very existence, of the unborn person inside her? No doubt she did not invite it in. But doesn't her partial responsibility for its being there itself give it a right to the use of her body? If so, then her aborting it would be more like the boy's taking away the chocolates, and less like your unplugging yourself from the violinist—doing so would be depriving it of what it does have a right to, and thus would be doing it an injustice.

And then, too, it might be asked whether or not she can kill it even to save her own life: If she voluntarily called it into existence, how can she now kill it, even in self-defense?

The first thing to be said about this is that it is something new. Opponents of abortion have been so concerned to make out the independence of the fetus, in order to establish that it has a right to life, just as its mother does, that they have tended to overlook the possible support they might gain from making out that the fetus is *dependent* on the mother, in order to establish that she has a special kind of responsibility for it, a responsibility that gives it rights against her which are not possessed by any independent person—such as an ailing violinist who is a stranger to her.

On the other hand, this argument would give the unborn person a right to its mother's body only if her pregnancy resulted from a voluntary act, undertaken in full knowledge of the chance a pregnancy might result from it. It would leave out entirely the unborn person whose existence is due to rape. Pending the availability of some further argument, then, we would be left with the conclusion that unborn persons whose existence is due to rape have no right to the use of their mothers' bodies, and thus that aborting them is not depriving them of anything they have a right to and hence is not unjust killing.

And we should also notice that it is not at all plain that this argument really does go even as far as it purports to. For there are cases and cases, and the details make a difference. If the room is stuffy, and I therefore open a window to air it, and a burglar climbs in, it would be absurd to say, "Ah, now he can stay, she's given him a right to the use of her house—for she is partially responsible for his presence there, having voluntarily done what enabled him to get in, in full knowledge that there are such things as burglars, and that burglars burgle." It would be still more absurd to say this if I had had bars installed outside my windows, precisely to prevent burglars from getting in, and a burglar got in only because of a defect in the bars. It remains equally absurd if we imagine it is not a burglar who climbs in, but an innocent person who blunders or falls in. Again, suppose it were like this: people-seeds drift about in the air like pollen, and if you open your windows, one may drift in and take root in your carpets or upholstery. You don't want children, so you fix up your windows with fine mesh screens, the very best you can buy. As can happen, however, and on very, very rare occasions does happen, one of the screens is defective; and a seed drifts in and takes root. Does the person-plant who now develops have a right to the use of your house? Surely not—despite the fact that you voluntarily opened your windows, you knowingly kept carpets and upholstered furniture, and you knew that screens were sometimes defective. Someone may argue that you are responsible for its rooting, that it does have a right to your house, because after all you *could* have lived out your life with bare floors and furniture, or with sealed windows and doors. But this won't do—for by the same token anyone can avoid a pregnancy due to rape by having a hysterectomy, or anyway by never leaving home without a (reliable!) army.

It seems to me that the argument we are looking at can establish at most that there are *some* cases in which the unborn person has a right to the use of its mother's body, and therefore *some* cases in which abortion is unjust killing. There is room for much discussion and argument as to precisely which, if any. But I think we should sidestep this issue and leave it open, for at any rate the argument certainly does not establish that all abortion is unjust killing.

5. There is room for yet another argument here, however. We surely must all grant that there may be cases in which it would be morally indecent to detach a person from your body at the cost of his life. Suppose you learn that what the

violinist needs is not nine years of your life, but only one hour: all you need do to save his life is to spend one hour in that bed with him. Suppose also that letting him use your kidneys for that one hour would not affect your health in the slightest. Admittedly you were kidnapped. Admittedly you did not give anyone permission to plug him into you. Nevertheless it seems to me plain you *ought* to allow him to use your kidneys for that hour—it would be indecent to refuse.

Again, suppose pregnancy lasted only an hour, and constituted no threat to life or health. And suppose that a woman becomes pregnant as a result of rape. Admittedly she did not voluntarily do anything to bring about the existence of a child. Admittedly she did nothing at all which would give the unborn person a right to the use of her body. All the same it might well be said, as in the newly emended violinist story, that she *ought* to allow it to remain for that hour—that it would be indecent of her to refuse.

Now some people are inclined to use the term "right" in such a way that it follows from the fact that you ought to allow a person to use your body for the hour he needs, that he has a right to use your body for the hour he needs, even though he has not been given that right by any person or act. They may say that it follows also that if you refuse, you act unjustly toward him. This use of the term is perhaps so common that it cannot be called wrong; nevertheless it seems to me to be an unfortunate loosening of what we would do better to keep a tight rein on. Suppose that box of chocolates I mentioned earlier had not been given to both boys jointly, but was given only to the older boy. There he sits, stolidly eating his way through the box, his small brother watching enviously. Here we are likely to say, "You ought not to be so mean. You ought to give your brother some of those chocolates." My own view is that it just does not follow from the truth of this that the brother has any right to any of the chocolates. If the boy refuses to give his brother any, he is greedy, stingy, callous—but not unjust. I suppose that the people I have in mind will say it does follow that the brother has a right to some of the chocolates, and thus that the boy does act unjustly if he refuses to give his brother any. But the effect of saying this is to obscure what we should keep distinct, namely, the difference between the boy's refusal in this case and the boy's refusal in the earlier case, in which the box was given to both boys jointly, and in which the small brother thus had what was from any point of view clear title to half.

A further objection to so using the term "right" that from the fact that A ought to do a thing for B, it follows that B has a right against A that A do it for him, is that it is going to make the question of whether or not a man has a right to a thing turn on how easy it is to provide him with it; and this seems not merely unfortunate, but morally unacceptable. Take the case of Henry Fonda again. I said earlier that I had no right to the touch of his cool hand on my fevered brow, even though I needed it to save my life. I said it would be frightfully nice of him to fly in from the West Coast to provide me with it, but that I had no right against him that he should do so. But suppose he isn't on the West Coast. Suppose he has only to walk across the room, place a hand briefly on my brow—and lo, my life is saved. Then surely he ought to do it, it would be indecent to refuse. Is it to be said, "Ah, well, it follows that in this case she has a right to the touch of his hand on her brow, and so it would be an injustice in him to refuse"? So that I have a right to it when it is easy for him to provide it, though no right when it's hard? It's rather a shocking idea that anyone's rights should fade away and disappear as it gets harder and harder to accord them to him.

So my own view is that even though you ought to let the violinist use your kidneys for the one hour he needs, we should not conclude that he has a right to do so—we should say that if you refuse, you are, like the boy who owns all the chocolates and will give none away, self-centered and callous, indecent in fact, but not unjust. And similarly, that even supposing a case in which a woman pregnant due to rape ought to allow the unborn person to use her body for the hour he needs, we should not conclude that he has a right to do so; we should conclude that she is self-centered, callous, indecent, but not unjust, if she refuses. The complaints are no less grave; they are just different. However, there is no need to insist on this point. If anyone does wish to deduce "he has a right" from "you ought," then all the same he must surely grant that there are cases in which it is not morally required of you that you allow that violinist to use your kidneys, and in which he does not have a right to use them, and in which you do not do him an injustice if you refuse. And so also for mother and unborn child. Except in such cases as the unborn person has a right to demand it—and we were leaving open the possibility that there may be such cases—nobody is morally *required* to make large sacrifices, of health, of all other interests and concerns, of all other duties and commitments, for nine years, or even for nine months, in order to keep another person alive.

6. We have in fact to distinguish between two kinds of Samaritan: the Good Samaritan and what we might call the Minimally Decent Samaritan. The story of the Good Samaritan, you will remember, goes like this:

> A certain man went down from Jerusalem to Jericho, and fell among thieves, which stripped him of his raiment, and wounded him, and departed, leaving him half dead.
>
> And by chance there came down a certain priest that way; and when he saw him, he passed by on the other side.
>
> And likewise a Levite, when he was at the place, came and looked on him, and passed by on the other side.
>
> But a certain Samaritan, as he journeyed, came where he was; and when he saw him he had compassion on him.
>
> And went to him, and bound up his wounds, pouring in oil and wine, and set him on his own beast, and brought him to an inn, and took care of him.
>
> And on the morrow, when he departed, he took out two pence, and gave them to the host, and said unto him, "Take care of him; and whatsoever thou spendest more, when I come again, I will repay thee."
>
> —(Luke 10:30–35)

The Good Samaritan went out of his way, at some cost to himself, to help one in need of it. We are not told what the options were, that is, whether or not the priest and the Levite could have helped by doing less than the Good Samaritan did, but assuming they could have, then the fact they did nothing at all shows they were not even Minimally Decent Samaritans, not because they were not Samaritans, but because they were not even minimally decent. . . .

After telling the story of the Good Samaritan, Jesus said, "Go, and do thou likewise." Perhaps he meant that we are morally required to act as the Good Samaritan did. Perhaps he was urging people to do more than is morally required of them. At all events it seems plain that . . . it is not morally required of anyone that he give long stretches of his life—nine years or nine months—to sustaining the life of a person who has no special right (we were leaving open the possibility of this) to demand it. . . .

We have . . . to look now at third-party interventions. I have been arguing that no person is morally required to make large sacrifices to sustain the life of another who has no right to demand them, and this even where the sacrifices do not include life itself; we are not morally required to be Good Samaritans or anyway Very Good Samaritans to one another. But what if a man cannot extricate himself from such a situation? What if he appeals to us to extricate him? It seems to me plain that there are cases in which we can, cases in which a Good Samaritan would extricate him. There you are, you were kidnapped, and nine years in bed with that violinist lie ahead of you. You have your own life to lead. You are sorry, but you simply cannot see giving up so much of your life to the sustaining of his. You cannot extricate yourself, and ask us to do so. I should have thought that—in light of his having no right to the use of your body—it was obvious that we do not have to accede to your being forced to give up so much. We can do what you ask. There is no injustice to the violinist in our doing so.

7. Following the lead of the opponents of abortion, I have throughout been speaking of the fetus merely as a person, and what I have been asking is whether or not the argument we began with, which proceeds only from the fetus' being a person, really does establish its conclusion. I have argued that it does not.

But of course there are arguments and arguments, and it may be said that I have simply fastened on the wrong one. It may be said that what is important is not merely the fact that the fetus is a person, but that it is a person for whom the woman has a special kind of responsibility issuing from the fact that she is its mother. And it might be argued that all my analogies are therefore irrelevant—for you do not have that special kind of responsibility for that violinist, Henry Fonda does not have that special kind of responsibility for me. . . .

I have in effect dealt (briefly) with this argument in section 4 above; but a (still briefer) recapitulation now may be in order. Surely we do not have any such "special responsibility" for a person unless we have assumed it, explicitly or implicitly. If a set of parents do not try to prevent pregnancy, do not obtain an abortion, and then at the time of birth of the child do not put it out for adoption, but rather take it home with them, then they have assumed responsibility for it, they have given it rights, and they cannot *now* withdraw support from it at the cost of its life because they now find it difficult to go on providing for it. But if they have taken all reasonable precautions against having a child, they do not simply by virtue of their biological relationship to the child who comes into existence have a special responsibility for it. They may wish to assume responsibility for it, or they may not wish to. And I am suggesting that if assuming responsibility for it would require large sacrifices, then they may refuse. A Good Samaritan would not refuse—or anyway, a Splendid Samaritan, if the sacrifices that had to be made were enormous. But then so would a Good Samaritan assume responsibility for that violinist; so would Henry Fonda, if he is a Good Samaritan, fly in from the West Coast and assume responsibility for me.

8. My argument will be found unsatisfactory on two counts by many of those who want to regard abortion as morally permissible. First, while I do argue that abortion is not impermissible, I do not argue that it is always permissible. There may well be cases in which carrying the child to term requires only Minimally Decent Samaritanism of the mother, and this is a standard we must not fall below. I am inclined to think it a merit of my account precisely that it does *not* give a general yes or a general no. It allows for and supports our sense that, for example, a sick and desperately frightened fourteen-year-old schoolgirl, pregnant due to rape, may *of course* choose abortion, and that any law which rules this out is an insane law. And it also allows for and supports our sense that in other cases resort to abortion is even positively indecent. It would be indecent in the woman to request an abortion, and indecent in a doctor to perform it, if she is in her seventh month, and wants the abortion just to avoid the nuisance of postponing a trip abroad. The very fact that the arguments I have been drawing attention to treat all cases of abortion, or even all cases of abortion in which the mother's life is not at stake, as morally on a par ought to have made them suspect at the outset.

Secondly, while I am arguing for the permissibility of abortion in some cases, I am not arguing for the right to secure the death of the unborn child. It is easy to confuse these two things in that up to a certain point in the life of the fetus it is not able to survive outside the mother's body; hence removing it from her body guarantees its death. But they are importantly different. I have argued that you are not morally required to spend nine months in bed, sustaining the life of that violinist; but to say this is by no means to say that if, when you unplug yourself, there is a miracle and he survives, you then have a right to turn round and slit his throat. You may detach yourself even if this costs him his life; you have no right to be guaranteed his death, by some other means, if unplugging yourself does not kill him. There are some people who will feel dissatisfied by this feature of my argument. A woman may be utterly devastated by the thought of a child, a bit of herself, put out for adoption and never seen or heard of again. She may therefore want not merely that the child be detached from her, but more, that it die. Some opponents of abortion are inclined to regard this as beneath contempt—thereby showing insensitivity to what is surely a powerful source of despair. All the same, I agree that the desire for the child's death is not one which anybody may gratify, should it turn out to be possible to detach the child alive.

At this place, however, it should be remembered that we have only been pretending throughout that the fetus is a human being from the moment of conception. A very early abortion is surely not the killing of a person, and so is not dealt with by anything I have said here.

NOTES

1. The term "direct" in the arguments I refer to is a technical one. Roughly, what is meant by "direct killing" is either killing as an end in itself, or killing as a means of some end, for example, the end of saving someone else's life.
2. The thesis in (4) is in an interesting way weaker than those in (1), (2), and (3): they rule out abortion even in cases in which both mother *and* child will die if the abortion is not performed. By contrast, one who held the view expressed in (4) could consistently say that one needn't prefer letting two persons die to killing one.

STUDY QUESTIONS

1. What are the main points Thomson seeks to make by the example of the unconscious violinist?
2. Does the morality of aborting a fetus depend on the conditions surrounding its conception?
3. If abortion is murder, who is the murderer and what is the appropriate punishment?
4. If the abortion controversy is described as a debate between those who believe in a right to life and those who affirm a woman's right to choose, on which side is Thomson?

Why Abortion Is Immoral

Don Marquis

Don Marquis, who is Professor Emeritus of Philosophy at the University of Kansas, disagrees with the position on abortion defended by Judith Jarvis Thomson. He argues that, with rare exceptions, abortion is immoral. Note that he does not base his reasoning on the claim that the fetus is a person but rather on the view that the fetus has a valuable future.

The view that abortion is, with rare exceptions, seriously immoral has received little support in the recent philosophical literature. No doubt most philosophers affiliated with secular institutions of higher education believe that the anti-abortion

From Don Marquis, "Why Abortion Is Immoral," *The Journal of Philosophy,* 86 (1989). Reprinted with the permission of the author and the journal.

position is either a symptom of irrational religious dogma or a conclusion generated by seriously confused philosophical argument. The purpose of this essay is to undermine this general belief. This essay sets out an argument that purports to show, as well as any argument in ethics can show, that abortion is, except possibly in rare cases, seriously immoral, that it is in the same moral category as killing an innocent adult human being. . . .

II

. . . [W]e can start from the following unproblematic assumption concerning our own case: it is wrong to kill *us*. Why is it wrong? Some answers can be easily eliminated. It might be said that what makes killing us wrong is that a killing brutalizes the one who kills. But the brutalization consists of being inured to the performance of an act that is hideously immoral; hence, the brutalization does not explain the immorality. It might be said that what makes killing us wrong is the great loss others would experience due to our absence. Although such hubris is understandable, such an explanation does not account for the wrongness of killing hermits, or those whose lives are relatively independent and whose friends find it easy to make new friends.

A more obvious answer is better. What primarily makes killing wrong is neither its effect on the murderer nor its effect on the victim's friends and relatives, but its effect on the victim. The loss of one's life is one of the greatest losses one can suffer. The loss of one's life deprives one of all the experiences, activities, projects, and enjoyments that would otherwise have constituted one's future. Therefore, killing someone is wrong, primarily because the killing inflicts (one of) the greatest possible losses on the victim. To describe this as the loss of life can be misleading, however. The change in my biological state does not by itself make killing me wrong. The effect of the loss of my biological life is the loss to me of all those activities, projects, experiences, and enjoyments which would otherwise have constituted my future personal life. These activities, projects, experiences, and enjoyments are either valuable for their own sakes or are means to something else that is valuable for its own sake. Some parts of my future are not valued by me now, but will come to be valued by me as I grow older and as my values and capacities change. When I am killed, I am deprived both of what I now value which would have been part of my future personal life, but also what I would come to value. Therefore, when I die, I am deprived of all of the value of my future. Inflicting this loss on me is ultimately what makes killing me wrong. This being the case, it would seem that what makes killing *any* adult human being prima facie seriously wrong is the loss of his or her future.

How should this rudimentary theory of the wrongness of killing be evaluated? It cannot be faulted for deriving an "ought" from an "is," for it does not. The analysis assumes that killing me (or you, reader) is prima facie seriously wrong. The point of the analysis is to establish which natural property ultimately explains the wrongness of the killing, given that it is wrong. A natural property will ultimately explain the wrongness of killing, only if (1) the explanation fits with our intuitions about the matter and (2) there is no other natural property that provides the basis for a better explanation of the wrongness of killing. This analysis rests on the intuition that what makes killing a particular human or animal wrong is what it does to that particular human or animal. What makes killing wrong is some natural effect or other of the killing. . . .

The claim that what makes killing wrong is the loss of the victim's future is directly supported by two considerations. In the first place, this theory explains why we regard killing as one of the worst of crimes. Killing is especially wrong, because it deprives the victim of more than perhaps any other crime. In the second place, people with AIDS or cancer who know they are dying believe, of course, that dying is a very bad thing for them. They believe that the loss of a future to them that they would otherwise have experienced is what makes their premature death a very bad thing for them. A better theory of the wrongness of killing would require a different natural property associated with killing which better fits with the attitudes of the dying. What could it be?

The view that what makes killing wrong is the loss to the victim of the value of the victim's future gains additional support when some of its implications are examined. In the first place, it is incompatible with the view that it is wrong to kill only beings who are biologically human. It is possible that there exists a different species from another planet whose members have a future like ours. Since having a future like that is what makes killing someone wrong, this theory entails that it would be wrong to kill members of such a species. Hence, this theory is opposed to the claim that only life that is biologically human has great moral worth, a claim which many anti-abortionists have seemed to adopt. This opposition . . . seems to be a merit of the theory.

In the second place, the claim that the loss of one's future is the wrong-making feature of one's being killed entails the possibility that the futures of some actual nonhuman mammals on our own planet are sufficiently like ours that it is seriously wrong to kill them also. Whether some animals do have the same right to life as human beings depends on adding to the account of the wrongness of killing some additional account of just what it is about my future or the futures of other adult human beings which makes it wrong to kill us. No such additional account will be offered in this essay. Undoubtedly, the provision of such an account would be a very difficult matter. Undoubtedly, any such account would be quite controversial. Hence, it surely should not reflect badly on this sketch of an elementary theory of the wrongness of killing that it is indeterminate with respect to some very difficult issues regarding animal rights.

In the third place, the claim that the loss of one's future is the wrong-making feature of one's being killed does not entail, as sanctity of human life theories do, that active euthanasia is wrong. Persons who are severely and incurably ill, who face a future of pain and despair, and who wish to die will not have suffered a loss if they are killed. It is, strictly speaking, the value of a human's future which makes killing wrong in this theory. This being so, killing does not necessarily wrong some persons who are sick and dying. Of course, there may be other reasons for a prohibition of active euthanasia, but that is another matter. Sanctity-of-human-life theories seem to hold that active euthanasia is seriously wrong even in an individual case where there seems to be good reason for it independently of public policy considerations. This consequence is most implausible, and it is a plus for the claim that the loss of a future of value is what makes killing wrong that it does not share this consequence.

In the fourth place, the account of the wrongness of killing defended in this essay does straightforwardly entail that it is prima facie seriously wrong to kill children and infants, for we do presume that they have futures of value. Since we do believe that it is wrong to kill defenseless babies, it is important that a theory of the wrongness of killing easily accounts for this. Personhood theories of the wrongness of killing, on the other hand, cannot straightfor-wardly account for the wrongness of killing infants and young children. Hence, such theories must add special ad hoc accounts of the wrongness of killing the young. The plausibility of such ad hoc theories seems to be a function of how desperately one wants such theories to work. The claim that the pri-mary wrong-making feature of a killing is the loss to the victim of the value of its future accounts for the wrongness of killing young children and infants directly; it makes the wrongness of such acts as obvious as we actually think it is. This is a further merit of this theory. Accordingly, it seems that this value of a future-like-ours theory of the wrongness of killing shares strengths of both sanctity-of-life and personhood accounts while avoiding weaknesses of both. In addition, it meshes with a central intuition concerning what makes killing wrong.

The claim that the primary wrong-making feature of a killing is the loss to the victim of the value of its future has obvious consequences for the ethics of abortion. The future of a standard fetus includes a set of experiences, projects, activities, and such which are identical with the futures of adult human beings and are identical with the futures of young children. Since the reason that is sufficient to explain why it is wrong to kill human beings after the time of birth is a reason that also applies to fetuses, it follows that abortion is prima facie seriously morally wrong.

This argument does not rely on the invalid inference that, since it is wrong to kill persons, it is wrong to kill potential persons also. The category that is morally central to this analysis is the category of having a valuable future like ours; it is not the category of personhood. The argument to the conclusion that abortion is prima facie seriously morally wrong proceeded independently of the notion of person or potential person or any equivalent. Someone may wish to start with this analysis in terms of the value of a human future, conclude that abortion is, except perhaps in rare circumstances, seriously morally wrong, infer that fetuses have the right to life, and then call fetuses "persons" as a result of their having the right to life. Clearly, in this case, the category of person is being used to state the *conclusion* of the analysis rather than to generate the *argument* of the analysis. . . .

Of course, this value of a future-like-ours argument, if sound, shows only that abortion is prima facie wrong, not that it is wrong in any and all circumstances. Since the loss of the future to a standard fetus, if killed, is, however, at least as great a loss as the loss of the future to a standard adult human being who is killed, abortion, like ordinary killing, could be justified only by the most compelling reasons. The loss of one's life is almost the greatest misfortune that can happen to one. Presumably abortion could be justified in some circumstances, only if the loss consequent on failing to abort would be at least as great. Accordingly, morally permissible abortions will be rare indeed unless, perhaps, they occur so early in pregnancy that a fetus is not yet definitely an individual. Hence, this argument should be taken as showing that abortion is presumptively very seriously wrong, where the presumption is very strong—as strong as the presumption that killing another adult human being is wrong.

V

In this essay, it has been argued that the correct ethic of the wrongness of killing can be extended to fetal life and used to show that there is a strong presumption that any abortion is morally impermissible. If the ethic of killing adopted here entails, however, that contraception is also seriously immoral, then there would appear to be a difficulty with the analysis of this essay.

But this analysis does not entail that contraception is wrong. Of course, contraception prevents the actualization of a possible future of value. Hence, it follows from the claim that futures of value should be maximized that contraception is prima facie immoral. This obligation to maximize does not exist, however; furthermore, nothing in the ethics of killing in this paper entails that it does. The ethics of killing in this essay would entail that contraception is wrong only if something were denied a human future of value by contraception. Nothing at all is denied such a future by contraception, however.

Candidates for a subject of harm by contraception fall into four categories: (1) some sperm or other, (2) some ovum or other, (3) a sperm and an ovum separately, and (4) a sperm and an ovum together. Assigning the harm to some sperm is utterly arbitrary, for no reason can be given for making a sperm the subject of harm rather than an ovum. Assigning the harm to some ovum is utterly arbitrary, for no reason can be given for making an ovum the subject of harm rather than a sperm. One might attempt to avoid these problems by insisting that contraception deprives both the sperm and the ovum separately of a valuable future like ours. On this alternative, too many futures are lost. Contraception was supposed to be wrong, because it deprived us of one future of value, not two. One might attempt to avoid this problem by holding that contraception deprives the combination of sperm and ovum of a valuable future like ours. But here the definite article misleads. At the time of contraception, there are hundreds of millions of sperm, one (released) ovum and millions of possible combinations of all of these. There is no actual combination at all. Is the subject of the loss to be a merely possible combination? Which one? This alternative does not yield an actual subject of harm either. Accordingly, the immorality of contraception is not entailed by the loss of a future-like-ours argument simply because there is no nonarbitrarily identifiable subject of the loss in the case of contraception.

VI

The purpose of this essay has been to set out an argument for the serious presumptive wrongness of abortion subject to the assumption that the moral permissibility of abortion stands or falls on the moral status of the fetus. Since a fetus possesses a property, the possession of which in adult human beings is sufficient to make killing an adult human being wrong, abortion is wrong. This way of dealing with the problem of abortion seems superior to other approaches to the ethics of abortion, because it rests on an ethics of killing which is close to self-evident, because the crucial morally relevant property clearly applies to fetuses, and because the argument avoids the usual equivocations of "human life," "human being," or "person." . . . Its soundness is compatible with the moral permissibility of euthanasia and contraception. It deals with our intuitions concerning young children.

Finally, this analysis can be viewed as resolving a standard problem—indeed, *the* standard problem—concerning the ethics of abortion. Clearly, it is wrong to kill adult human beings. Clearly, it is not wrong to end the life of some arbitrarily chosen single human cell. Fetuses seem to be like arbitrarily chosen human cells in some respects and like adult humans in other respects. The problem of the ethics of abortion is the problem of determining the fetal property that settles this moral controversy. The thesis of this essay is that the problem of the ethics of abortion, so understood, is solvable.

STUDY QUESTIONS

1. Is the loss of one's future as devastating for a fetus as for a child?
2. Does Marquis's argument that abortion is immoral depend on religious considerations?
3. Does Marquis accept the argument that because killing persons is wrong, killing potential persons is also wrong?
4. According to Marquis, in what circumstances is abortion not wrong?

Famine, Affluence, and Morality

PETER SINGER

What obligations do we have toward those around the globe who are suffering from a lack of food, shelter, or medical care? Does morality permit us to purchase luxuries for ourselves, our families, and our friends instead of providing needed resources to other people who are suffering in unfortunate circumstances? Peter Singer, who is Ira W. DeCamp Professor of Bioethics at the University Center for Human Values at Princeton University, argues that if we can prevent something bad without thereby sacrificing anything of comparable worth, we ought to do so.

....

As I write this, in November 1971, people are dying in East Bengal from lack of food, shelter, and medical care. The suffering and death that are occurring there now are not inevitable, not unavoidable in any fatalistic sense of the term. Constant poverty, a cyclone, and a civil war have turned at least nine million people into destitute refugees; nevertheless, it is not beyond the capacity of the richer nations to give enough assistance to reduce any further suffering to very small proportions. The decisions and actions of human beings can prevent this kind of suffering. Unfortunately, human beings have not made the necessary decisions. At the individual level, people have, with very few exceptions, not responded to the situation in any significant way. Generally speaking, people have not given large sums to relief funds; they have not written to their parliamentary representatives demanding increased government assistance; they have not demonstrated in the streets, held symbolic fasts, or done anything else directed toward providing the refugees with the means to satisfy their essential needs. At the government level, no government has given the sort of massive aid that would enable the refugees to survive for more than a few days. Britain, for instance, has given rather more than most countries. It has, to date, given £14,750,000. For comparative purposes, Britain's share of the nonrecoverable development costs of the Anglo-French Concorde project is already in excess of £275,000,000, and on present estimates will reach £400,000,000. The implication is that the British government values a supersonic transport more than thirty times as highly as it values the lives of the nine million refugees. Australia is another country which, on a per capita basis, is well up in the "aid to Bengal" table. Australia's aid, however, amounts to less than one-twelfth of the cost of Sydney's new opera house. The total amount given, from all sources, now stands at about £65,000,000.

From Peter Singer, "Famine, Affluence, and Morality," *Philosophy & Public Affairs*, 1 (1972). Copyright © 1972 by Princeton University Press. Reprinted by permission of Blackwell Publishers.

The estimated cost of keeping the refugees alive for one year is £464,000,000. Most of the refugees have now been in the camps for more than six months. The World Bank has said that India needs a minimum of £300,000,000 in assistance from other countries before the end of the year. It seems obvious that assistance on this scale will not be forthcoming. India will be forced to choose between letting the refugees starve or diverting funds from her own development program, which will mean that more of her own people will starve in the future.[1]

These are the essential facts about the present situation in Bengal. So far as it concerns us here, there is nothing unique about this situation except its magnitude. The Bengal emergency is just the latest and most acute of a series of major emergencies in various parts of the world, arising both from natural and from man-made causes. There are also many parts of the world in which people die from malnutrition and lack of food independent of any special emergency. I take Bengal as my example only because it is the present concern, and because the size of the problem has ensured that it has been given adequate publicity. Neither individuals nor governments can claim to be unaware of what is happening there.

What are the moral implications of a situation like this? In what follows, I shall argue that the way people in relatively affluent countries react to a situation like that in Bengal cannot be justified; indeed, the whole way we look at moral issues—our moral conceptual scheme—needs to be altered, and with it, the way of life that has come to be taken for granted in our society.

In arguing for this conclusion I will not, of course, claim to be morally neutral. I shall, however, try to argue for the moral position that I take, so that anyone who accepts certain assumptions, to be made explicit, will, I hope, accept my conclusion.

I begin with the assumption that suffering and death from lack of food, shelter, and medical care are bad. I think most people will agree about this, although one may reach the same view by different routes. I shall not argue for this view. People can hold all sorts of eccentric positions, and perhaps from some of them it would not follow that death by starvation is in itself bad. It is difficult, perhaps impossible, to refute such positions, and so for brevity I will henceforth take this assumption as accepted. Those who disagree need read no further.

My next point is this: if it is in our power to prevent something bad from happening, without thereby sacrificing anything of comparable moral importance, we ought, morally, to do it. By "without sacrificing anything of comparable moral importance" I mean without causing anything else comparably bad to happen, or doing something that is wrong in itself, or failing to promote some moral good, comparable in significance to the bad thing that we can prevent. This principle seems almost as uncontroversial as the last one. It requires us only to prevent what is bad, and not to promote what is good, and it requires this of us only when we can do it without sacrificing anything that is, from the moral point of view, comparably important. I could even, as far as the application of my argument to the Bengal emergency is concerned, qualify the point so as to make it: if it is in our power to prevent something very bad from happening, without thereby sacrificing anything morally significant, we ought, morally, to do it. An application of this principle would be as follows: if I am walking past a shallow pond and see a child drowning in it, I ought to wade in and pull the child out. This will mean getting my clothes muddy, but this is insignificant, while the death of the child would presumably be a very bad thing.

The uncontroversial appearance of the principle just stated is deceptive. If it were acted upon, even in its qualified form, our lives, our society, and our world would be fundamentally changed. For the principle takes, firstly, no account of proximity or distance. It makes no moral difference whether the person I can help is a neighbor's child ten yards from me or a Bengali whose name I shall never know, ten thousand miles away. Secondly, the principle makes no distinction between cases in which I am the only person who could possibly do anything and cases in which I am just one among millions in the same position.

I do not think I need to say much in defense of the refusal to take proximity and distance into account. The fact that a person is physically near to us, so that we have personal contact with him, may make it more likely that we *shall* assist him, but this does not show that we *ought* to help him rather than another who happens to be further away. If we accept any principle of impartiality, universalizability, equality, or whatever, we cannot discriminate against someone merely because he is far away from us (or we are far away from him). Admittedly, it is possible that we are in a better position to judge what needs to be done to help a person near to us than one far away, and perhaps also to provide the assistance we judge to be necessary. If this were the case, it would be a reason for helping those near to us first. This may once have been a justification for being more concerned with the poor in one's own town than with famine victims in India. Unfortunately for those who like to keep their moral responsibilities limited, instant communication and swift transportation have changed the situation. From the moral point of view, the development of the world into a "global village" has made an important, though still unrecognized, difference to our moral situation. Expert observers and supervisors, sent out by famine relief organizations or permanently stationed in the famine-prone areas, can direct our aid to a refugee in Bengal almost as effectively as we could get it to someone in our own block. There would seem, therefore, to be no possible justification for discriminating on geographical grounds.

There may be a greater need to defend the second implication of my principle—that the fact that there are millions of other people in the same position, in respect to the Bengali refugees, as I am, does not make the situation significantly different from a situation in which I am the only person who can prevent something very bad from occurring. Again, of course, I admit that there is a psychological difference between the cases; one feels less guilty about doing nothing if one can point to others, similarly placed, who have also done nothing. Yet this can make no real difference to our moral obligations.[2] Should I consider that I am less obliged to pull the drowning child out of the pond if on looking around I see other people, no further away than I am, who have also noticed the child but are doing nothing? One has only to ask this question to see the absurdity of the view that numbers lessen obligation. It is a view that is an ideal excuse for inactivity; unfortunately most of the major evils—poverty, overpopulation, pollution—are problems in which everyone is almost equally involved.

The view that numbers do make a difference can be made plausible if stated in this way: if everyone in circumstances like mine gave £5 to the Bengal Relief Fund, there would be enough to provide food, shelter, and medical care for the refugees; there is no reason why I should give more than anyone else in the same circumstances as I am; therefore I have no obligation to give more than £5. Each premise in this argument is true, and the argument looks sound. It may convince us, unless we notice that it is based on a hypothetical premise, although the conclusion is not stated hypothetically. The argument would be sound if the conclusion were: if everyone in circumstances like mine were to give £5, I would have no obligation to give more than £5. If the conclusion were so stated, however, it would be obvious that the argument has no bearing on a situation in which it is not the case that everyone else gives £5. This, of course, is the actual situation. It is more or less certain that not everyone in circumstances like mine will give £5. So there will not be enough to provide the needed food, shelter, and medical care. Therefore by giving more than £5 I will prevent more suffering than I would if I gave just £5.

It might be thought that this argument has an absurd consequence. Since the situation appears to be that very few people are likely to give substantial amounts, it follows that I and everyone else in similar circumstances ought to give as much as possible, that is, at least up to the point at which by giving more one would begin to cause serious suffering for oneself and one's dependents—perhaps even beyond this point to the point of marginal utility, at which by giving more one would cause oneself and one's dependents as much suffering as one would prevent in Bengal. If everyone does this, however, there will be more than can be used for the benefit of the refugees, and some of the sacrifice will have been unnecessary. Thus, if everyone does what he ought to do, the result will not be as good as it would be if everyone did a little less than he ought to do, or if only some do all that they ought to do.

The paradox here arises only if we assume that the actions in question—sending money to the relief funds—are performed more or less simultaneously, and are also unexpected. For if it is to be expected that everyone is going to contribute something, then clearly each is not obliged to give as much as he would have been obliged to had others not been giving too. And if everyone is not acting more or less simultaneously, then those giving later will know how much more is needed, and will have no obligation to give more than is necessary to reach this amount. To say this is not to deny the principle that people in the same circumstances have the same obligations, but to point out that the fact that others have given, or may be expected to give, is a relevant circumstance: those giving after it has become known that many others are giving and those giving before are not in the same circumstances. So the seemingly absurd consequence of the principle I have put forward can occur only if people are in error about the actual circumstances—that is, if they think they are giving when others are not, but in fact they are giving when others are. The result of everyone doing what he really ought to do cannot be worse than the result of everyone doing less than he ought to do, although the result of everyone doing what he reasonably believes he ought to do could be.

If my argument so far has been sound, neither our distance from a preventable evil nor the number of other people who, in respect to that evil, are in the same situation as we are, lessens our obligation to mitigate or prevent that evil. I shall therefore take as established the principle I asserted earlier. As I have already said, I need to assert it only in its qualified form: if it is in our power to prevent something very bad from happening, without thereby sacrificing anything else morally significant, we ought, morally, to do it.

The outcome of this argument is that our traditional moral categories are upset. The traditional distinction between duty and charity cannot be drawn, or at least not in the place we normally draw it. Giving money to the Bengal Relief Fund is regarded as an act of charity in our society. The bodies which collect money are known as "charities." These organizations see themselves in this way—if you send them a check, you will be thanked for your "generosity." Because giving money is regarded as an act of charity, it is not thought that there is anything wrong with not giving. The charitable man may be praised, but the man who is not charitable is not condemned. People do not feel in any way ashamed or guilty about spending money on new clothes or a new car instead of giving it to famine relief. (Indeed, the alternative does not occur to them.) This way of looking at the matter cannot be justified. When we buy new clothes not to keep ourselves warm but to look "well-dressed" we are not providing for any important need. We would not be sacrificing anything significant if we were to continue to wear our old clothes, and give the money to famine relief. By doing so, we would be preventing another person from starving. It follows from what I have said earlier that we ought to give money away, rather than spend it on clothes which we do not need to keep us warm. To do so is not charitable, or generous. Nor is it the kind of act which philosophers and theologians have called "supererogatory"—an act which it would be good to do, but not wrong not to do. On the contrary, we ought to give the money away, and it is wrong not to do so.

I am not maintaining that there are no acts which are charitable, or that there are no acts which it would be good to do but not wrong not to do. It may be possible to redraw the distinction between duty and charity in some other place. All I am arguing here is that the present way of drawing the distinction, which makes it an act of charity for a man living at the level of affluence which most people in the "developed nations" enjoy to give money to save someone else from starvation, cannot be supported. It is beyond the scope of my argument to consider whether the distinction should be redrawn or abolished altogether. There would be many other possible ways of drawing the distinction—for instance, one might decide that it is good to make other people as happy as possible, but not wrong not to do so.

Despite the limited nature of the revision in our moral conceptual scheme which I am proposing, the revision would, given the extent of both affluence and famine in the world today, have radical implications. These implications may lead to further objections, distinct from those I have already considered. I shall discuss two of these.

One objection to the position I have taken might be simply that it is too drastic a revision of our moral scheme. People do not ordinarily judge in the way I have suggested they should. Most people reserve their moral condemnation for those who violate some moral norm, such as the norm against taking another person's property. They do not condemn those who indulge in luxury instead of giving to famine relief. But given that I did not set out to present a morally neutral description of the way people make moral judgments, the way people do in fact judge has nothing to do with the validity of my conclusion. My conclusion follows from the principle which I advanced earlier, and unless that principle is rejected, or the arguments shown to be unsound, I think the conclusion must stand, however strange it appears. . . .

The second objection to my attack on the present distinction between duty and charity is one which has from time to time been made against utilitarianism. It follows from some forms of utilitarian theory that we all ought, morally, to be working full time to increase the balance of happiness over misery. The position I have taken here would not lead to this conclusion in all circumstances, for if there were no bad occurrences that we could prevent without sacrificing something of comparable moral importance, my argument would have no application. Given the present conditions in many parts of the world, however, it does follow from my argument that we ought, morally, to be working full time to relieve great suffering of the sort that occurs as a result of famine or other disasters. Of course, mitigating circumstances can be adduced—for instance, that if we wear ourselves out through overwork, we shall be less effective than we would otherwise have been. Nevertheless, when all considerations of this sort have been taken into account, the conclusion remains: we ought to be preventing as much suffering as we can without sacrificing something else of comparable moral importance. This conclusion is one which we may be reluctant to face. I cannot see, though, why it should be regarded as a criticism of the position for which I have argued, rather than a criticism of our ordinary standards of behavior. Since most people are self-interested to some degree, very few of us are likely to do everything that we ought to do. It would, however, hardly be honest to take this as evidence that it is not the case that we ought to do it. . . .

A third point raised by the conclusion reached earlier relates to the question of just how much we all ought to be giving away. One possibility, which has already been mentioned, is that we ought to give until we reach the level of marginal utility—that is, the level at which, by giving more, I would cause as much suffering to myself or my dependents as I would relieve by my gift. This would mean, of course, that one would reduce oneself to very nearly the material circumstances of a Bengali refugee. It will be recalled that earlier I put forward both a strong and a moderate version of the principle of preventing bad occurrences. The strong version, which required us to prevent bad things from happening unless in doing so we would be sacrificing something of comparable moral significance, does seem to require reducing ourselves to the level of marginal utility. I should also say that the strong version seems to me to be the correct one. I proposed the more moderate version—that we should prevent bad occurrences unless, to do so, we had to sacrifice something morally significant—only in order to show that even on this surely undeniable principle a great change in our way of life is required. On the more moderate principle, it may not follow that we ought to reduce ourselves to the level of marginal utility, for one might hold that to reduce oneself and one's family to this level is to cause something significantly bad to happen. Whether this is so I shall not discuss, since, as I have said, I can see no good reason for holding the moderate version of the principle rather than the strong version. Even if we accepted the principle only in its moderate form, however, it should be clear that we would have to give away enough to ensure that the consumer society, dependent as it is on people spending on trivia rather than giving to famine relief, would slow down and perhaps disappear entirely. There are several reasons why this would be desirable in itself. The value and necessity of economic growth are now being questioned not only by conservationists, but by economists as well.[3] There is no doubt, too, that the consumer society has had a distorting effect on the goals and purposes of its members. Yet looking at the matter purely from the point of view of overseas aid, there must be a limit to the extent to which we should deliberately slow down our economy; for it might be the case that if we gave away, say, forty percent of our Gross National Product, we would slow down the economy so much that in absolute terms we would be giving less than if we gave twenty-five percent of the much larger GNP that we would have if we limited our contribution to this smaller percentage.

I mention this only as an indication of the sort of factor that one would have to take into account in working out an ideal. Since Western societies generally consider one percent of the GNP an acceptable level of overseas aid, the matter is entirely academic. Nor does it affect the question of how much an individual should give in a society in which very few are giving substantial amounts.

It is sometimes said, though less often now than it used to be, that philosophers have no special role to play in public affairs, since most public issues depend primarily on an assessment of facts. On questions of fact, it is said, philosophers as such have no special expertise, and so it has been possible to engage in philosophy without committing oneself to any position on major public issues. No doubt there are some issues of social policy and foreign policy about which it can truly be said that a really expert assessment of the facts is required before taking sides or acting, but the issue of famine is surely not one of these. The facts about the existence of suffering are beyond dispute. Nor, I think, is it disputed that we can do something about it, either through orthodox methods of famine relief or through population control or both. This is therefore an issue on which philosophers are competent to take a position. The issue is one which faces everyone who has more money than he needs to support himself and his dependents, or who is in a position to take some sort of political action. These categories must include practically every teacher and student of philosophy in the universities of the Western world. If philosophy is to deal with matters that are relevant to both teachers and students, this is an issue that philosophers should discuss.

Discussion, though, is not enough. What is the point of relating philosophy to public (and personal) affairs if we do not take our conclusions seriously? In this instance, taking our conclusion seriously means acting upon it. The philosopher will not find it any easier than anyone else to alter his attitudes and way of life to the extent that, if I am right, is involved in doing everything that we ought to be doing. At the very least, though, one can make a start. The philosopher who does so will have to sacrifice some of the benefits of the consumer society, but he can find compensation in the satisfaction of a way of life in which theory and practice, if not yet in harmony, are at least coming together.

NOTES

1. There was also a third possibility: that India would go to war to enable the refugees to return to their lands. Since I wrote this paper, India has taken this way out. The situation is no longer that described above, but this does not affect my argument, as the next paragraph indicates.
2. In view of the special sense philosophers often give to the term, I should say that I use "obligation" simply as the abstract noun derived from "ought," so that "I have an obligation to" means no more, and no less, than "I ought to." This usage is in accordance with the definition of "ought" given by the *Shorter Oxford English Dictionary*: "the general verb to express duty or obligation." I do not think any issue of substance hangs on the way the term is used; sentences in which I use "obligation" could all be rewritten, although somewhat clumsily, as sentences in which a clause containing "ought" replaces the term "obligation."
3. See, for instance, John Kenneth Galbraith, *The New Industrial State* (Boston, 1967); and E. J. Mishan, *The Costs of Economic Growth* (London, 1967).

STUDY QUESTIONS

1. If you can prevent something bad from happening at a comparatively small cost to yourself, are you obligated to do so?
2. Are you acting immorally by buying a luxury car while others are starving?
3. Are you acting immorally by paying college tuition for your own children while other children have no opportunity for any schooling?
4. Do we have a moral obligation to try to alleviate extreme poverty in our own country before attempting to do so in other countries?

A Reply to Singer

✒

TRAVIS TIMMERMAN

Peter Singer argues that you are obligated to prevent something bad from happening if you can do so without thereby sacrificing anything of comparable moral importance. For example, you are morally obligated to save a child from drowning if you can do so without inconvenience. Travis Timmerman, assistant professor of philosophy at Seton Hall University, argues that the strength of your

From Travis Timmerman, "Sometimes There Is Nothing Wrong with Letting a Child Drown," *Analysis* 75 (2015). Reprinted by permission of Oxford University Press. Footnotes omitted.

obligation depends on how many children need to be saved. If the number is large, then Singer's line of reasoning would obligate you to spend your entire life saving children. Are you not entitled at some point to pursue your own interests, even if they are not as morally weighty as saving the lives of children?

....

Peter Singer's "Famine, Affluence, and Morality" is undoubtedly one of the most influential and widely read pieces of contemporary philosophy. Yet, the majority of philosophers (including ethicists) reject Singer's conclusion that we are morally required to donate to aid agencies whenever we can do so without sacrificing anything nearly as important as the good that our donations could bring about. Many ignore Singer's argument simply because they believe morality would just be too demanding if it required people in affluent nations to donate significant sums of money to charity. Of course, merely rejecting Singer's conclusion because it seems absurd does not constitute a refutation of Singer's argument. More importantly, this standard demandingness objection is a particularly inappropriate dialectical move because Singer provides a valid argument for his (demanding) conclusion and, crucially, the argument only consists of ethical premises that Singer takes his typical readers to already accept. Singer formulates his argument as follows.

1. Suffering and death from lack of food, shelter and medical care are bad.
2. If it is in your power to prevent something bad from happening, without sacrificing anything nearly as important, it is wrong not to do so.
3. By donating to aid agencies, you can prevent suffering and death from lack of food, shelter and medical care, without sacrificing anything nearly as important.
4. Therefore, if you do not donate to aid agencies, you are doing something wrong.

If it is not true that typical readers' existing ethical commitments entail that they accept premises one and two, then they should be able to say which premiss(es) they reject and why. Those who believe that Singer's conclusion is too demanding will need to reject premiss two. This requires addressing Singer's infamous *Drowning Child* thought experiment, which elicits a common response that Singer believes demonstrates that his readers are already committed to the truth of premiss two. As such, Singer purports to demonstrate that the ethical commitments his typical readers already accept are demanding enough to require them to donate a substantial portion of their expendable income to aid organizations. . . .

Perhaps premiss two is true, but a proposition with such strong counterintuitive implications requires a strong defence, one that gives us reason to think that certain ordinary moral intuitions are radically misguided. Singer believes he has provided such a defence with *Drowning Child*. Aren't we morally obligated to sacrifice our new clothes to save the child *because* we are obligated to prevent something bad from happening whenever we can do so without sacrificing anything nearly as important? The short answer is 'No.' Here's why. Although Singer's description of *Drowning Child* is ahistorical, the implicit assumption is that *Drowning Child* is an anomalous event. People almost never find themselves in the situation Singer describes, so when they consider their obligations in *Drowning Child*, they implicitly assume that they have not frequently sacrificed their new clothes to save children in the past and will not need to do so frequently in the future.

Giving to aid organizations is, in this respect, unlike *Drowning Child*. Every individual in an affluent nation, so long as they have some expendable income, will always be in a position to save the lives of people living in extreme poverty by donating said income. It may be quite clear that one has a moral obligation to sacrifice $200 worth of new clothing a single time to prevent a child from drowning. It is much less clear that one is morally obligated to spend one's entire life making repeated $200 sacrifices to constantly prevent children from drowning. So, we may be obligated to save the child in *Drowning Child*, but still be disposed to believe that premiss two is false. I will expand on this asymmetry . . . by providing an altered version of Singer's thought experiment that more closely resembles the position those in affluent nations are in with respect to providing aid to those in extreme poverty. I suspect that most people's intuitions in such a case will show that they reject premiss two of Singer's argument.

People almost universally have the intuition that we are morally obligated to rescue the child in *Drowning Child*, but are not morally obligated to donate all their expendable income to aid agencies. Singer attempts to explain away this intuition as a mere psychological difference, a difference that results from our evolutionary history and socialization and not a moral difference. . . . However, there *is* a moral difference between the sacrifice required to save the child in *Drowning Child* (as it is imagined) and the sacrifice Singer believes people in affluent nations are required to make in order to donate the supposed obligatory amount to aid organizations.

This moral difference is easily overlooked because Singer's *Drowning Child* thought experiment is, in a crucial way, under-described. Once the necessary details are filled in, its inability to support premiss two will be made clear. My following *Drowning Children* case is not under-described and gives us reason to believe that there are times at which it is morally permissible to *not* prevent something bad from happening, even when one can do so at a comparably insignificant personal cost.

> *Drowning Children*: Unlucky Lisa gets a call from her 24-hr bank telling her that hackers have accessed her account and are taking $200 out of it every 5 min until Lisa shows up in person to put a hold on her account. Due to some legal loophole, the bank is not required to reimburse Lisa for any of the money she may lose nor will they. In fact, if her account is overdrawn, the bank will seize as much of her assets as is needed to pay the debt created by the hackers.
>
> Fortunately, for Lisa, the bank is just across the street from her work and she can get there in fewer than 5 min. She was even about to walk to the bank as part of her daily routine. On her way, Lisa notices a vast space of land covered with hundreds of newly formed shallow ponds, each of which contains a small child who will drown unless someone pulls them to safety. Lisa knows that for each child she rescues, an extra child will live who would have otherwise died. Now, it would take Lisa approximately 5 min to pull each child to safety and,

in what can only be the most horrifically surreal day of her life, Lisa has to decide how many children to rescue before entering the bank. Once she enters the bank, all the children who have not yet been rescued will drown.

Things only get worse for poor Lisa. For the remainder of her life, the hackers repeat their actions on a daily basis and, every day, the ponds adjacent to Lisa's bank are filled with drowning children.

The truth of premiss two would entail that Lisa is obligated to rescue children until almost all of her money and assets are gone. It might permit her to close her account before she is unable to rent a studio apartment and eat a healthy diet. However, it would require her to give up her house, her car, her books, her art and anything else not nearly as important as a child's life. That might not seem so counterintuitive if Lisa has to make this monumental sacrifice a single time. But, and here's the rub, premiss two would also prohibit Lisa from ever rebuilding her life. For every day Lisa earns money, she is forced to choose between saving children and letting the hackers steal from her. Lisa would only be permitted to go to the bank each day in time to maintain the things nearly as important as a child's life, which I take to be the basic necessities Lisa needs to lead a healthy life.

I propose that it's a viable option that morality permits Lisa to, *at least* on one day over the course of her entire life, stop the hackers in time to enjoy some good that is not nearly as important as a child's life. Maybe Lisa wants to experience theatre one last time before she spends the remainder of her days pulling children from shallow ponds and stopping hackers. Given the totality of the sacrifice Lisa is making, morality intuitively permits Lisa to indulge in theatre *at least* one time in, let's say, the remaining eighty years of her life. In fact, commonsense morality should permit Lisa to indulge in these comparably morally insignificant goods a non-trivial number of times, though a single instance is all that is required to demonstrate that premiss two is false and, consequently, Singer's argument is unsound. . . .

To sum up, the intuitive pull of premiss two is more apparent than real. . . . How much are we obligated to donate to aid organizations? I am not sure exactly, but it should be the same amount we would be obligated to sacrifice were we to find ourselves in Lisa's position.

STUDY QUESTIONS

1. If you buy a book instead of giving the money to help others in need, are you acting morally?
2. If you spend time studying philosophy instead of helping others in need, are you acting morally?
3. If you pay to send your child to college while other children are too poor to obtain food or clothing, are you acting morally?
4. When, if ever, are you entitled to pursue your own interests while you could, instead, be helping others in need of assistance?

The Morality of Reparation

BERNARD R. BOXILL

Bernard Boxill is Professor Emeritus of Philosophy at the University of North Carolina at Chapel Hill. He argues that because the ancestors of blacks in the United States were treated unjustly, blacks living in the United States today are entitled to reparation from whites. While Boxill does not specify the amount of the reparation or the means of collecting or distributing it, he emphasizes that reparation is owed and should be paid.

....

Consider now the assertion that the present generation of white Americans owe the present generation of black Americans reparation for the injustices of slavery inflicted on the ancestors of the black population by the ancestors of the white population. To begin, consider the very simplest instance of a case where reparation may be said to be due: Tom has an indisputable moral right to possession of a certain item, say a bicycle, and Dick steals the bicycle from Tom. Here, clearly, Dick owes Tom, at least the bicycle, and a concession of error, in reparation. Now complicate the case slightly; Dick steals the bicycle from Tom and "gives" it to Harry. Here again, even if he is innocent of complicity in the theft, and does not know that his "gift" was stolen, Harry must return the bicycle to Tom with the acknowledgment that, though innocent or blameless, he did not rightfully possess the bicycle. Consider a final complication; Dick steals the bicycle from Tom and gives it to Harry; in the meantime Tom dies, but leaves a will clearly conferring his right to ownership of the bicycle to his son, Jim. Here again we should have little hesitation in saying that Harry must return the bicycle to Jim.

Now, though it involves complications, the case for reparation under consideration is essentially the same as the one last mentioned: the slaves had an indisputable moral right to the products of their labour; these products were stolen from them by the slave masters who ultimately passed them on to their descendants; the slaves presumably have conferred their rights of ownership to the products of their labour to their descendants; thus, the descendants of slave masters are in possession of wealth to which the descendants of slaves have rights; hence, the descendants of slave masters must return this wealth to the descendants of slaves with a concession that they were not rightfully in possession of it.

It is not being claimed that the descendants of slaves must seek reparation from those among the white population who happen to be descendants of slave owners. This perhaps would be the case if slavery had produced for the slave

From Bernard R. Boxill, "The Morality of Reparation," *Social Theory and Practice* 2 (1972).

owners merely specific hoards of gold, silver or diamonds, which could be passed on in a very concrete way from father to son. As a matter of fact, slavery produced not merely specific hoards, but wealth which has been passed down mainly to descendants of the white community to the relative exclusion of the descendants of slaves. Thus, it is the white community as a whole that prevents the descendants of slaves from exercising their rights of ownership, and the white community as a whole that must bear the cost of reparation.

The above statement contains two distinguishable arguments. In the first argument the assertion is that each white person, individually, owes reparation to the black community because membership in the white community serves to identify an individual as a recipient of benefits to which the black community has a rightful claim. In the second argument, the conclusion is that the white community as a whole, considered as a kind of corporation or company, owes reparation to the black community.

In the first of the arguments sketched above, individuals are held liable to make reparation even if they have been merely passive recipients of benefits; that is, even if they have not deliberately chosen to accept the benefits in question. This argument invites the objection that, for the most part, white people are simply not in a position to choose to receive or refuse benefits belonging to the descendants of slaves and are, therefore, not culpable or blameable and hence not liable to make reparation. But this objection misses the point. The argument under consideration simply does not depend on or imply the claim that white people are culpable or blameable; the argument is that merely by being white, an individual receives benefits to which others have at least partial rights. In such cases, whatever one's choice or moral culpability, reparation must be made. Consider an extreme case: Harry has an unexpected heart attack and is taken unconscious to the hospital. In the same hospital Dick has recently died. A heart surgeon transplants the heart from Dick's dead body to Harry without permission from Dick's family. If Harry recovers, he must make suitable reparation to Dick's family, conceding that he is not in rightful possession of Dick's heart even if he had no part in choosing to receive it.

The second of the arguments distinguished above concluded that for the purpose in question, the white community can be regarded as a corporation or company which, as a whole, owes reparation to the sons of slaves. Certainly the white community resembles a corporation or company in some striking ways; like such companies, the white community has interests distinct from, and opposed to, other groups in the same society, and joint action is often taken by the members of the white community to protect and enhance their interests. Of course, there are differences; people are generally born into the white community and do not deliberately choose their membership in it; on the other hand, deliberate choice is often the standard procedure for gaining membership in a company. But this difference is unimportant; European immigrants often deliberately choose to become part of the white community in the United States for the obvious benefits this brings, and people often inherit shares and so, without deliberate choice, become members of a company. What is important here is not how deliberately one chooses to become part of a community or a company; what is relevant is that one chooses to continue to accept the benefits which circulate exclusively within the community, sees such benefits as belonging exclusively to the members of the community, identifies one's interests with those of the community, viewing them as opposed to those of others outside the community, and finally, takes joint action with other members of the community to protect such interests. In such a case, it seems not unfair to consider the present white population as members of a company that incurred debts before they were members of the company, and thus to ask them justly to bear the cost of such debts.

It may be objected that the case for reparation depends on the validity of inheritance; for, only if the sons of slaves inherit the rights of their ancestors can it be asserted that they have rights against the present white community. If the validity of inheritance is rejected, a somewhat different, but perhaps even stronger, argument for reparation can still be formulated. For if inheritance is rejected with the stipulation that the wealth of individuals be returned to the whole society at their deaths, then it is even clearer that the white community owes reparation to the black community. For the white community has appropriated, almost exclusively, the wealth from slavery in addition to the wealth from other sources; but such wealth belongs jointly to all members of the society, white as well as black; hence, it owes them reparation. The above formulation of the argument is entirely independent of the fact of slavery and extends the rights of the black community to its just portion of the total wealth of the society.

STUDY QUESTIONS

1. On Boxill's view, are whites who descend from slave masters as well as whites who descend from those who fought against slave masters in the Civil War equally obligated to provide reparation?
2. Given Boxill's reasoning, do American citizens who are Hispanic or Asian owe reparation to citizens who are African Americans?
3. Would someone descended from both a slave and a slave master owe reparation or be owed it?
4. Are Native Americans owed reparation, and, if so, are African Americans among those who owe it?

Reparation and the Problem of Agency

⚜

CHANDRAN KUKATHAS

Chandran Kukathas is Professor of Government at the London School of Economics. He argues that reparation is almost always morally unjustified, because it requires identifying those who owe the reparation as well as those to whom it is due. Given the difficulties of doing so, Kukathas concludes that the prospects for justifying reparation look dim.

....

In this paper, I argue that the pursuit of justice by making reparation for past wrongs, and particularly for wrongs done more than a generation ago, is not morally justifiable except in some special cases. For the paying of reparations to be defensible, it must be possible to identify two kinds of agent: the victim of injustice, to whom reparation is owed, and the perpetrator or beneficiary of injustice who can be held accountable for the wrong or liable for the cost of restitution. If both agents cannot be identified, there cannot be a case for reparation....

The problem of identifying the relevant agents in trying to establish claims for restitution for past injustice is more difficult than has been recognized. Who is entitled to compensation for a wrong committed, and who is liable to pay is sometimes easy enough to ascertain when victim and perpetrator are both alive, though it can get progressively more difficult to establish the extent of entitlement and responsibility as time goes on. When generations have passed, even identifying the parties to the case is difficult....

The general problem in distinguishing the descendants of victims of past injustice is that it is too easy to reach the point at which a very large proportion of the population can be identified as descendants. If that happens, the moral force of the claims made by some people will be diminished to the extent that many others in the society might simply respond that they too have injustice in their histories. Is there a better way of separating out the descendants of injustice who have strong claims from those who do not?

An obvious alternative is to identify not individuals but groups that are the descendants of victims of past injustice. This might have the immediate advantage

---

From Chandran Kukathas, "Who? Whom? Reparations and the Problem of Agency," *Journal of Social Philosophy* 37 (2006).

of giving us an entity that is easier to isolate and distinguish from other potential claimants because it has persisted over a greater length of time and because tracing an ancestry will not be a problem. Moreover, the most serious injustices of the past, which cry out for rectification, were committed against groups or people as members of groups. The two issues that have to be settled, however, are which groups to count, and whom to include within them. This may be difficult, and we should consider why.

To begin with the matter of which groups to count, it may seem plain that certain groups are almost self-evidently candidates. The descendants of African slaves in modern America, and the indigenous peoples dispossessed of their lands in many parts of the world come to mind. It would be impossible to deny that slaves and dispossessed people were the victims of injustice many generations ago, or that the injustice the people of these groups continued to suffer was injustice in succeeding generations. The main point of contention is not whether such groups are plausible candidates for restitution but whether excluding the descendants of other victims of past injustice is warranted. The question is not just "why these groups and not others?" but also "why not people who don't fall into notable groups, but are the descendants of victims of serious injustice all the same?" One powerful reason for picking out particular groups but not others may be that the injustice suffered by these groups has had a particularly significant impact on the life of the society as a whole—perhaps so much so that it would make a difference to the quality of life in that society if these particular grievances were addressed. While this is an important reason, and one that may well justify attempting to offer restitution to the descendants of some groups, it is not, in the end, a reason that invokes the importance of doing justice for its own sake. . . .

The issue of who is to be included within a group being recognized as descending from victims of past injustice raises different problems. Most of these problems stem from the fact that groups are made up of individuals, and subgroups of individuals, with different histories, and often quite complex identities. Morally speaking, those histories themselves can be quite mixed. Consider, for example, the case of the Seminole Indians. The Seminoles were bands of Creek Indians who separated from the tribe and settled in northern Florida in the seventeenth century. They practiced slavery, not only of other Indians captured in battle, but also of Africans whom they purchased or were given as gifts by the British. By the nineteenth century, however, the black Seminole population had grown and established a strong, independent community, which actually joined with the Seminoles to resist the attempt of Americans to annex Florida. They fought against General Andrew Jackson in the First Seminole War (1817–18), and later in the Second Seminole War (1835–42), and gained a measure of independence. But they were then forced to face the Creek Indians, who were intent on enslaving them, and reintegrating the Seminole Indians into Creek society. Many fled to Mexico to escape Creek slave-hunters, though a good number returned after the Civil War to work as Indian Scouts. They claim that they were promised their own land in Texas in return, but in the end the War Department denied that they had land to offer, and the Bureau of Indian Affairs refused to give them land on the grounds that they were not really Indians.

How should these groups be understood if the issue is the rectification of past injustice? The Seminoles and Creeks were certainly victims of injustice, since theirs is a history of dispossession; but they were also perpetrators of some serious injustices against each other and against Africans, in collaboration with Americans. The black Seminoles appear to have a less ambiguous history, but even they returned to work as scouts in an American army intent on clearing the southwest of Comanches and Apaches to make room for white settlements. Even they were complicit in serious injustices.

The question is whether the complexity of history and identity should be assumed away in order to focus on the larger story of injustice, in this case the story of African slavery and the dispossession of indigenous peoples. If the detail is obliterated in the moral accounting, however, it is not clear that what would be guiding the decision to rectify past injustice are the injustices themselves but other ethical considerations.

More generally, there is a problem in determining whom to include in groups that might be candidates for restitution to the extent that individuals may be of mixed descent, having ancestors who were both victims and perpetrators of injustice. Others might be descended from a mix of immigrants and ancestors who suffered injustice. This problem may be compounded by the fact that some groups refuse to recognize some individuals or subgroups as members of their communities. At present, for example, the existence of black members of the Seminole Indians is a contentious issue because the sums paid to the Seminoles in compensation for dispossession would have to be further divided if Indians of African descent were included....

Yet even if the identities of the descendants of victims of past injustice can be settled, there remains the problem of establishing who should be held liable for restitution. This problem is more serious because even if it is true that injustices were committed in the past and the descendants of victims have suffered as a consequence, this may not be sufficient reason to hold many—or indeed, any—people today responsible for rectifying the situation.

A number of difficulties stand in the way of establishing responsibility for past injustice. One set of difficulties stems from the problem of determining who was responsible for the original injustices that might now generate claims on the part of descendants of victims. If one takes the case of African slavery, the perpetrators of injustice certainly include slave owners, slave traders, and those who supported the institution of slavery, whether by backing governments who upheld it or serving as officials who enforced the law protecting it. But this means some responsibility for the original injustice must be borne by people from other countries who captured and sold slaves. Equally, it is difficult to hold responsible for the injustice of slavery those who had no part in it, or who disapproved of it, or who worked to eliminate it.

It might be argued that all who benefited from slavery can be held responsible to some degree, and one might conclude from this that no one in the United States was free from the taint of this particular injustice. But those who benefited from slavery

Sexual Harassment in the University

$\mathcal{N}$

N. ANN DAVIS

N. Ann Davis is Professor of Human Relations and Philosophy at Pomona College. She explains why reporting sexual harassment in the university is especially difficult. Davis points to the unequal power between faculty members and students, the hierarchy in the university that is difficult to navigate, and the reluctance of many professors to become involved. She concludes that to address the damage caused by sexual harassment, we need to find ways to deal with the special problems of universities that render them environments conducive to such unethical behavior.

....

The notion of sexual harassment entered public consciousness in the United States with the publication of a survey on sexual harassment in the workplace conducted by *Redbook* in 1976. More than nine thousand women responded to the survey, and almost nine out of ten reported experiencing some sort of sexual harassment on the job.[1] Unsurprisingly, these revelations stimulated a lot of discussion in the news media, the popular press, and academic journals.[2] . . .

In the classic *quid pro quo* case in which an instructor puts unwelcome sexual pressure on a student and makes it clear that the student's academic evaluation or professional advancement is contingent on her yielding to that pressure, what the instructor does is obviously coercive, unjust, disrespectful, and discriminatory. It is an abuse of power and a betrayal of trust. And it is inimical to the existence of a healthy educational environment in a number of ways.

Yet surveys conducted at college campuses around the nation reveal that a sizable proportion of female college students—somewhere between 25 percent and 40 percent—report they have been subjected to some sort of sexual harassment on the part of their instructors,[3] and anecdotal evidence provided by female students, faculty members, and administrators corroborates those findings. Surveys may be difficult to interpret and compare, for they do not all employ the same definition of sexual harassment, and anecdotal evidence must always be treated with caution, but it is clear that sexual harassment and other forms of sexually inappropriate behavior are no rarity in the university. Any serious participant in higher education must be puzzled and distressed by this fact. . . .

Traditionally, the influential teaching and administrative jobs in the university have been occupied by men, and it is men who have made the policies

From N. Ann Davis, "Sexual Harassment in the University," in *Morality, Responsibility, and the University: Studies in Academic Ethics*, ed. Steven M. Cahn (Philadelphia, PA: Temple University Press, 1992).

and interpreted the rules of university governance. Though things have changed considerably in the past decade or so, most of the senior faculty and administrative positions are still occupied by men. And women remain significantly in the minority in most, if not all, academic fields. This situation is thought, in itself, to be a problem. It is women, not men, who are almost always the victims of sexual harassment and men, not women, who are almost always the harassers. And men are likely both to operate with a narrower notion of sexual harassment and to have lower estimates of the incidence of sexual harassment on campus than women do. They are also likelier to view the incidents of sexual harassment they acknowledge do occur as isolated personal incidents, rather than as the expression of an institutional (or broader) problem. Commentators thus often cite the dearth of senior women and the associated inexperience and insensitivity of academic men as among the principal factors contributing to the prevalence of sexual harassment on campus. If women were less of a minority on campus or if they occupied positions of power that enabled them to have greater influence on rules, practices, and policies, then (it is thought) the incidence of sexual harassment on campus would decrease.

The women's movement and other associated movements have led many women—and many men—to question received gender stereotypes. But it is clear, nevertheless, that those stereotypes continue to exert a powerful influence on people's views about the relations between male professors and female students. Although it is a truism that social attitudes about status, gender, and sexuality frame people's expectations about "proper" relations between the sexes, most of us are blind to many of the effects of those attitudes, and implications of those expectations often go unnoticed. Though fewer people may now regard liaisons between experienced and influential older men and inexperienced, comparatively powerless younger women as the ideal sort of relationship, such liaisons are still widely thought to be acceptable (if not simply normal). And the persistence of romanticized Pygmalionesque views of the educational process appears to legitimate such relations between male professors and female students. It is clear that gender stereotypes and associated differential social expectations contribute in a number of ways to the incidence of sexual harassment on campus. . . .

II. IGNORANCE

It is clear that both the frequency and the seriousness of sexual harassment in the university are widely underestimated. . . . There are a number of reasons why this is so. Personal, institutional, ideological, and societal factors all conspire to deter students from reporting incidents of sexual harassment and from taking concerted action to follow through with the reports of sexual harassment that they do make. If the data on sexual harassment are correct, it is clear that very few of the victims of sexual harassment in the workplace or in the university report it at all.[4] It is worth making clear what in the university context specifically discourages students from reporting sexual harassment.

Students and professors possess unequal power, influence, confidence, experience, and social standing. And this inequality contributes to students' fears of being ridiculed, disbelieved, punished, or thought incompetent if they come forward with reports of sexually inappropriate conduct on the part of their instructors. Fear of the humiliations that befall many of the women who report rape and other forms of sexual assault evidently makes many women wary of reporting sexual offenses, especially when—as is evidently true in cases of sexual harassment—the attacker is someone who is known to the accuser. The student who has been sexually harassed by her professor is in a particularly vulnerable position, especially if she is known to have had an ongoing personal association with him or has previously submitted to his coercion. The stereotype of the professor as brilliant, principled, and passionately dedicated to his work and to the educational growth of his students leads students to doubt that their allegations would be believed. After all, professors are widely regarded as respectable members of the community. Often enough, students lose confidence in their perceptions of their own actions: if they hadn't done something wrong, then why would this respectable citizen behave so bizarrely? "Blame the victim" sensibilities pervade our society, and so it is not too hard to understand why a confused and distressed victim of sexual harassment would shoulder the blame herself, rather than attribute it to the distinguished, respectable, and (formerly) much-admired professor who was (or appeared to be) so generous with his time and concern.

There are also other factors that erode a woman's confidence, and make her fear that the instructor's harassing behavior must somehow be her fault. Late adolescence and early adulthood are vulnerable and psychologically chaotic times. Among the many difficulties that college-age students face is the struggle to come to terms with their sexuality, and it is easy for them to be insecure in the midst of that process, unclear about their own desires and unsure about how to interpret (and deal with) the many conflicting and ambivalent desires that they have. Though both men and women undoubtedly undergo personal upheaval, their behavior does not meet with the same social interpretation or response, nor are men and women supposed to handle their ambivalences the same way. Men are expected to become more confident and hence more persistent in their pursuit of sexual relationships as they mature. The myth endures that women enjoy being the object of persistent male attentions and invitations but like to play "hard to get" and thus refuse invitations they really wish to accept: when a woman says "no," what she really means is "maybe" or "ask me again later." Since, moreover, women are taught to be polite and nonconfrontational, the woman who tries to act "decently" when confronted with an unwelcome sexual invitation/offer/threat may be seen as thereby expressing ambivalence, which, according to the foregoing myth, may be construed as an expression of interest. If the woman actually does feel ambivalent—she wants to refuse the invitation, but she feels some attraction to the man who has issued it—then she may guiltily believe that she "led him on" even when she said no. And so she may regard the instructor's sexually inappropriate behavior as her fault.

Gender roles and social expectations affect perceptions in other ways as well. Traditionally, women have been judged by their appearance, and they have thus been obliged to devote considerable energy to the attempt to look "attractive," for except among the most wealthy, it was a woman's appearance and good ... manners that were the principal determinant of whether or not she would attract a man and marry, which was essential for her economic security. Though economics have changed, the traditional view continues to exert an influence on people's thinking, and women still feel pressure to dress attractively and act politely. Yet a woman who is attractive is seen as open to, and perhaps as actually inviting, sexual responses from men. This perception, plus the myth that men's sexual self-control is so fragile that it can be overwhelmed by the presence of an attractive woman, contributes to the view that the women who are sexually harassed are those who "asked for it" (by being physically attractive, or attractively dressed).

Surveys make it clear that there is no correlation between a woman's being attractive (or "sexily" dressed) and her being sexually harassed. Sexual harassment, like rape, is primarily an issue of power, not sex. But the myth persists that it is a female student's appearance that is the cause of her instructor's sexually inappropriate behavior toward her. This myth influences female students' perceptions of both their own and their professors' conduct. And if, as she may well suppose, she bears responsibility for the instructor's behaving as he does, she is likely not to think of his conduct as being sexual harassment.

Popular academic fiction has done a lot to perpetuate these myths, and a lot to reinforce unfortunate gender stereotypes. "Co-eds" are portrayed as lusty seducers of respectable male professors, who are often portrayed as hapless victims of those feminine wiles. One can conjecture that most college-age women have read a few of the standard academic novels and that those novels provide some of the background for their interpretation of their professors' conduct.

Believing that her experience of sexual harassment is rare, believing, perhaps, the various myths surrounding the mechanics of male and female attraction, and being influenced by the myth-supporting academic fiction she reads in English courses, the sexually harassed student may believe that the whole thing is her fault. It is not something that she should report but something she should be ashamed of. And so her energies are likely to be spent trying to cope with or "manage" the incident, not reporting it or attempting to bring the sexual harasser to justice.

The asymmetrical power and influence of students and professors not only affect the student's perception of whether or not her claims of sexual harassment would be believed, they also affect her perception of the risks involved in making such a report (even when she does not fear being disbelieved). The professor holds the power of evaluation, and often enough, the student sees him as gatekeeper to her desired career. If she displeases him, then—whether it is through the mechanism of letters of reference or the more informal workings of the "old boy network"—he may, she fears, ruin her career prospects.

The structural organization of the university also serves to deter victims from reporting sexually inappropriate behavior. The myriad of departments, programs, divisions, and colleges may be quite daunting to an undergraduate, who may not understand the relations between them or be able easily to determine who has authority with respect to what. Nor does it help that some of those people to whom a student might turn appear as confused and powerless as the student herself—or altogether uninterested. A student may summon up her courage to report an incident of sexual misconduct to a professor whom she feels she can trust, only to be told to report it to the department chair, whom she may not know at all. If the department chair has not been through this before or if the chair is overworked or less than sympathetic to her plight, then the student may be met with (what she interprets as) annoyance and indifference ("Well, what do you want me to do about it?") or referred to a dean, who may seem to the student a distant, busy, and daunting individual. The organization of the university, with its convoluted procedures and divisions of responsibility, is quotidian to experienced faculty members who understand the hierarchy and the system. But they may be intimidating to someone who does not understand them and who is already traumatized and alienated.

The attitudes of academics toward their colleagues and students and their views about their own intellectual mission and personal responsibilities may also serve to discourage students from reporting sexual harassment. What is perhaps more important, however, is that those attitudes clearly serve to deter faculty members who learn of a colleague's sexually inappropriate behavior from taking action on it.... [Educators] are reluctant to "break ranks," to do things that they perceive as disloyal or damaging to a colleague. In some cases this reluctance may be an expression of a long-standing liberal commitment to tolerance of difference or a manifestation of the desire to uphold academic freedom or respect the autonomy of one's colleagues. In other cases, and less (ostensibly) nobly, it may be thought to stem from academics' desire to be left alone to get on with their own work, protect their own interests, or stay out of academic politics. But whatever the precise blend of factors (what might be called) the ideology of the faculty tends to support the stance of uninvolvement.

Untenured and non-tenure-track faculty are in an especially precarious position. The accused senior colleague may wield a good deal of power in the university and in his particular academic field. If displeased or moved to seek retaliation, he may do things that place the untenured faculty member's job at risk. Female faculty members—who are statistically more likely to be untenured or not tenure-track and very much in the minority in their profession—may be particularly vulnerable. Both their professional success thus far and their professional future may well depend upon their being perceived as "good colleagues," people who happen to be female in a largely male context and profession and "don't make a fuss about it." Becoming involved with a sexual harassment case may call attention to a female instructor's gender in ways that make her uncomfortable and may place her in double jeopardy, for she may feel that she is being obliged to risk her own credibility, her good relations with her colleagues, and her own professional connections. And oddly enough, though there is no shortage of good motivations for helping a student who reports an incident of sexual misconduct—a desire to help and protect a student who is hurt and frightened and feels she has nowhere else to turn, the desire to uphold the express and tacit values of the institution, the perception of the need to show students that female faculty members can act with strength and integrity—the female instructor who is willing to assist a student who complains of sexual harassment may find her own motives impugned by resentful male colleagues. As an older woman (and therefore, as convention has it, a less-attractive woman) she may be accused of projecting her unfulfilled desires for male sexual attention onto the student, of being a harridan, or a lesbian who wants to get even with men, of being bitter about her own lack of academic success (which she wrongly and wrongfully attributes to being a woman), and so on.

It is clear that both students' reluctance to come forward with complaints of sexual harassment and faculty members' disinclination to get involved when students do come forward contribute to an underestimation of the scope of the problem of sexual harassment in academia. It is not only the frequency with which sexually inappropriate behavior occurs that is underestimated, however, but the extent of the damage it causes as well. The explanation of why this is so is both complex and multifaceted.

Part of the explanation lies in the invisibility of much of the damage in question. It is easy to see the harm in an instructor's following through on a threat to take reprisals against a student who rejects his demands or in an instructor's tendering an unduly (though perhaps not deliberately or even consciously) harsh evaluation of the student who does not respond favorably to his sexual overtures. Those students are the victims of unfair academic evaluations, and both the professor's integrity and the integrity of the institutions's grading practices are severely compromised by such behavior. But other harms—to the individual student, to other students, to the educational institution, and to the society at large—are less obvious.

Many of the students who find themselves the recipients of unwelcome sexual overtures, remarks, or questions deal with the problem by "managing" it, and the most common form of management is avoidance: the student drops the course, ceases to attend the class, withdraws the application to be a lab assistant, quits coming to office hours, changes her major, or, in the most extreme cases, drops out of school altogether. Though these avoidance tactics may effectively remove the opportunity for an instructor to engage in harassing behavior, they do so at a cost. The student who thinks she can avoid being sexually harassed by simply avoiding the professor in question may thereby be deprived of valuable academic and professional opportunities, and the pool of motivated and intelligent aspirants to the relevant profession is thus reduced. Though, on such a scenario, both the damage to the individual and the loss to society are real, they are largely undetectable. If the number of women in the profession is already low, then the temptation may be to suppose, for example, that "women just aren't interested in engineering" or that "most women just aren't able to do the sort of abstract thinking required for graduate-level physics," adding the insult of misdiagnosis to the injury of sexual harassment. Women who were in fact driven out of the profession by being robbed of the opportunity to pursue their studies in peace are deemed uninterested or incapable. And viewing these women as uninterested or incapable obviously has implications for how other female aspirants to such careers are likely to be viewed, and to view themselves.

Nor does the damage stop there. When a student is given grounds for wondering whether her instructor's academic interest and encouragement were motivated by his sexual interest in her, she may well come to doubt the legitimacy of her previous accomplishments: perhaps her success thus far has owed more to sexual attributes that instructors found attractive than to her own hard work and ability. A good, serious, hardworking student may thus lose the sort of self-confidence that anyone needs to succeed in a competitive field, and that women especially need if they are to succeed in traditionally male professions that remain statistically (if not ideologically) male dominated. If, in addition, other students and instructors attribute the harassed student's academic success to sexual involvement with, or manipulation of, her instructors, then relationships with her peers and her other instructors (and with her own students, if she is a teaching assistant) may well be harmed, and suspicion may be cast on the success of other women. More subtly, both students and instructors may be drawn into a familiar form of overgeneralization and thus may come to harbor the suspicion that women's successes in the academic and professional fields in which they are a significant minority owe more to the women's skills at sexually manipulating those in power than to their hard work and ability. Generalized resentment of women or the unspoken background belief that women do not play fair or cannot "pull their own weight" may result, and this consequence may silently lead instructors to interact differently with male and female students and to approach them with different expectations. Given the insidious working of socialization, neither the students nor the instructors may be aware of the existence of such differential treatment; yet it may well be prejudicial and, ultimately, extremely detrimental. Again, both the existence of the harm and its causation are difficult to pin down in such cases and difficult to distinguish from the apparently statistically supported view that "women just aren't good at (or interested in) physics."

It should be clear from this discussion that sexual harassment (or, more broadly, sexually inappropriate behavior) can cause significant damage to the individuals who are its direct victims, to other women, and to the society at large. But it is hard to make the estimation of that damage more precise, for attempts to arrive at a more precise measure of the damage are complicated by the many other factors that make academic and professional success more difficult for women. It is not likely, after all, that a woman's first or only experience of sex discrimination will occur in a college lecture hall or in a professor's office, and it is plausible to suppose that a woman's prior experiences will influence how much damage will be done to her by an instructor's sexual harassment or other sexually inappropriate behavior. Prior experiences may both magnify the harm that is done to her by sexual harassment and, at the same time, diminish the possibility of perceiving that behavior as the cause of the harm. If women have routinely been victims of sex discrimination or societal sexist attitudes, then how can one say that it is the experience of sexual harassment in the university that is the cause of a woman's subsequent distress or the explanation of her decision to enter a "traditionally female" job or profession?

Reflection on this problem suggests a connection between the ... widespread ignorance about the extent of sexually inappropriate behavior in the university and the seriousness of the damage it may cause, and the difficulties involved in attempting to come up with a widely acceptable definition of sexual harassment. In a society that many people would characterize as pervaded by sexist attitudes (if not actual sex discrimination) and in one in which there is disagreement about what constitutes (objectionable) sexism and what is merely a response to differences between men and women, it may be difficult, if not impossible, to reach a consensus about what constitutes sexual harassment. Any university policy that hopes to do any good must take note of this fact.

NOTES

1. Claire Saffran, "What Men Do to Women on the Job," *Redbook* (November 1976), pp. 149, 217–23.
2. See, e.g., Karen Lindsay, "Sexual Harassment on the Job and How to Stop It," *Ms.* (November 1977), pp. 47–48, 50–51, 74–75, 78; Margaret Mead, "A Proposal: We Need Taboos on Sex at Work," *Redbook* (April 1978), pp. 31, 33, 38; Caryl Rivers, "Sexual Harassment: The Executive's Alternative to Rape," *Mother Jones* (June 1978), pp. 21–24, 28; Claire Saffran, "Sexual Harassment: The View from the Top," *Redbook* (March 1981), pp. 45–51.
3. See Phyllis L. Crocker, "Annotated Bibliography on Sexual Harassment in Education," *Women's Rights Law Reporter* 7 (1982), 91–106. And see *Symposium on Sexual Harassment* in *Thought & Action* 5 (1989): 17–52, especially the essay by Anne Truax, "Sexual Harassment in Higher Education: What We've Learned," pp. 25–38, for an overview of surveys and results.
4. According to Truax, "Sexual Harassment in Higher Education," p. 26, "Of those harassed, not more than one in 10 actually report the harassment."

STUDY QUESTIONS

1. According to Davis, why is both the frequency and seriousness of sexual harassment widely underestimated?
2. Is sexual harassment always intentional?
3. Might a male student be the victim of sexual harassment?
4. Is a professor's dating a student akin to a judge in a case dating the defendant?

Sexual Harassment in Public Places

ᴪ

Mᴀʀɢᴀʀᴇᴛ Cʀᴏᴜᴄʜ

Margaret Crouch is Professor Emerita of Philosophy at Eastern Michigan University. She argues that sexual harassment is morally problematic because it entrenches the subordinate place of women in society. Such harassment, however, is not limited to the workplace but is a widespread phenomenon found in many public spaces. Crouch maintains that by subjecting women to unwanted attention in public, sexual harassment leads to limitations on women's freedom of movement. Thus the goal of equal opportunity requires that sexual harassment be curbed.

....

I

Most current writing on sexual harassment in the United States is solely about sexual harassment in the workplace and/or in academe. This is because sexual harassment has been found illegal in these locations, and the law tends to narrow our focus. However, in spite of the fact that even definitions proffered by international organizations such as the United Nations and the European Union define sexual harassment in terms of the workplace, sexual harassment should be understood much more broadly—as something that can occur anywhere, at any time. In countries other than the United States, more attention has been paid to sexual harassment in public places—on public transportation, and in the street.

In my view, the separation of workplace/academic harassment from the broader scope of sexual harassment tends to obscure the function and effect of all harassment—to *keep women in their place. Sexual harassment is a means of maintaining women's status as subordinate in society; it is also a means of keeping women in certain physical spaces and out of others, or, at least, of controlling women's behavior in those spaces.* In this way, sexual harassment constrains women's freedom of movement both in terms of status and place. Here, I will focus on the latter, but lack of freedom of movement in space causes lack of freedom of movement in status.

In this paper, I will argue that workplace and academic harassment must be placed in the context of this broader understanding of sexual harassment to see its true nature. Women's full participation in public and private life requires that all forms of harassment be eliminated, through law, public awareness, and moral suasion. . . .

From Margaret Crouch, "Sexual Harassment in Public Places," *Social Philosophy Today* 25 (2009).

II

... Both the UN and the EU categorize sexual harassment as a form of sex discrimination, which comes directly from the US legal argument that sexual harassment in the workplace is a violation of Title VII. It may be because we don't have a clear legal conception of sex discrimination outside workplaces or academe that efforts to stop sexual harassment are focused on the workplace, though the Violence Against Women Act does conceive of spousal battering, date rape, and marital rape as sex discrimination.[1] However, sexual harassment in public places has existed as long as workplace harassment, is a form of sex discrimination, and is being addressed as such by women around the world.

III

... Sociological studies call attention to the differences, generally, in women's and men's experiences of public space. Erving Goffman described these differences in his sociological works in the 1960s and 1970s.[2] He claimed that there is a sort of default mode called "civic inattention" that characterizes relations between strangers in public places. People tend not to stare at one another or talk to strangers in public. They are aware of their surroundings but don't intrude on one another unless there is some particular reason to do so. This "civic inattention" holds generally among men and among women, but it does not hold between men and women. In sexist societies, men treat women as so-called open persons, that is, as persons for whom there is so little regard that they may be approached and intruded upon at will.[3] According to Cynthia Grant Bowman,

> Breaches of civil inattention that include a spoken component typically occur only when one encounters a person who is either very unusual (such as an individual carrying a couch, hopping on one foot, or dressed in costume), is unusually similar to oneself in some respect (for example, someone wearing the same college sweatshirt or driving the same make of car), or is accompanied by someone or something in an "open" category, such as dogs or children. Men seem to regard women generally as such "open persons."[4]

A good deal of the intrusion on women's attention and space in public places comes in the form of sexual harassment. It includes comments on their bodies or on their presence in the public space, unwanted touching, and lewd gestures. This form of sexual harassment has some characteristics that distinguish it from the type that is typical in workplaces and academe; for instance, it is typically between strangers, and because of this, the harasser is usually anonymous.

Many think that the sort of behavior I am describing is insignificant or even flattering. However, that is not how the majority of women around the world experience it. It is experienced as aggressive, as a violation of the "civil inattention" that is the norm in public space. The woman is made to pay attention to the harasser and to see herself as he sees her. If she does not respond appropriately, in the view of the harasser, she is often the target of abuse and hostility. Frequently, a nice response leads to further harassment. A dismissal might escalate the situation. Infrequently, such encounters lead to stalking, even rape. But the amount of wariness with which a woman experiences harassment is due to the fact that she cannot predict whether this instance is likely to end badly.

Even in Paris, where so-called girl-watching is supposed to be a national pastime, women organize their lives to avoid being alone in public where they know they will be harassed. Indeed, avoidance is the most common response to harassment in public places. The avoidance is motivated by fear, for in the experience of many women, there is a direct connection between public harassment that most people would regard as innocuous and truly threatening behavior. Even though there is evidence that women are more likely to be the victims of violence from intimates than from strangers, the unpredictability of stranger violence makes every encounter threatening.

Public harassment of women by men asserts the male prerogative.... In so-called public spaces, men of the dominant group are in a *public* space, but many other groups are not. Men of the dominant group have the power of access to the space and do anything in the space; they also have the power to exclude others from their personal or private space while in public. Women and other nondominant groups do not share these same powers of exclusion and access....

V

What to do? If women are to be equal to men in all spheres of society, the harassment of which I have been speaking must be eliminated. But how should this be done?

Whatever is done must be accompanied by advocacy that keeps the focus on sex discrimination rather than affronts to modesty, or chivalric protection. There are some grassroots organizations that have sprung up using the internet to publicize the harms of public harassment, such as Holla Back, which started in New York but now has chapters all over the world in large urban centers. Women who are harassed take photographs of harassers and post them on the internet for all to see.[5] In India, the Blank Noise Project stages public protests to educate people about public harassment. For example, a large group went to a market where men stood around leaning on a railing looking at passersby and harassing women. The women reclaimed the space, and silently surrounded a fellow who was harassing a woman. Blank Noise uses its internet to publicize actions and to fight traditional interpretations of street harassment. For example, in order to counter the view that women bring on harassment themselves by wearing skimpy clothing, Blank Noise asked women to send in the clothes they were wearing when they were harassed. They included chadors and traditional clothing, as well as western garb.[6]

Some governments have instituted women-only transportation in order to protect women from harassment on public transportation. India has had train cars reserved for women since before independence. Tokyo began reserving train cars for women during rush hour recently, as did Rio de Janeiro. Mexico City started women-only buses in February of this year....

I want to emphasize the importance of recognizing that harassment can take place anywhere and is not confined to the workplace and academe. We need to remember this larger context in order to see sexual harassment for what it really is: *a means of maintaining women's status as subordinate in society; it is also a means of keeping women in certain physical spaces and out of others, or, at least, of controlling women's behavior in those spaces.*

NOTES

1. Sally F. Goldfarb, "Public Rights for 'Private' Wrongs: Sexual Harassment and the Violence against Women Act," in *Directions in Sexual Harassment Law*, ed. Catharine A. MacKinnon and Reva B. Siegel (New Haven: Yale University Press, 2004), 516–34.
2. Erving Goffman, *Behavior in Public Places* (New York: Free Press, 1963); Erving Goffman, *Interaction Rituals* (New York: Pantheon, 1967).
3. Goffman, 1963, 18.
4. Bowman, "Street Harassment," 526.
5. Holla Back, Accessed September 11, 2008. http://www.hollabacknyc.blogspot.com.
6. Blank Noise. Accessed September 11, 2008. http://blog.blanknoise.org.

STUDY QUESTIONS

1. What does Crouch mean by "sexual harassment"?
2. According to Crouch, what makes sexual harassment in public places morally objectionable?
3. What is "civic inattention"?
4. Is overcoming sexual harassment more a matter of enacting laws or changing individual behavior?

The Trolley Problem

JUDITH JARVIS THOMSON

Judith Jarvis Thomson, whose work we read previously, presents a philosophical problem that has become the subject of much recent discussion. Consider the issue for yourself before reading the next selection, in which she offers her latest analysis of the matter.

Suppose you are the driver of a trolley. The trolley rounds a bend, and there come into view ahead five track workmen, who have been repairing the track.

From *The Yale Law Journal*, 94 (1985) by permission of The Yale Law Journal and Fred. B. Rothman & Company. The paragraphs are reordered.

The track goes through a bit of a valley at that point, and the sides are steep, so you must stop the trolley if you are to avoid running the five men down. You step on the brakes, but alas they don't work. Now you suddenly see a spur of track leading off to the right. You can turn the trolley onto it, and thus save the five men on the straight track ahead. Unfortunately, . . . there is one track workman on that spur of track. He can no more get off the track in time than the five can, so you will kill him if you turn the trolley onto him. Is it morally permissible for you to turn the trolley?

Everybody to whom I have put this hypothetical case says, Yes, it is. Some people say something stronger than that it is morally *permissible* for you to turn the trolley: They say that morally speaking, you must turn it—that morality requires you to do so. Others do not agree that morality requires you to turn the trolley, and even feel a certain discomfort at the idea of turning it. But everybody says that it is true, at a minimum, that you *may* turn it—that it would not be morally wrong for you to do so.

Now consider a second hypothetical case . . .—which I shall call *Fat Man*— in which you are standing on a footbridge over the trolley track. You can see a trolley hurtling down the track, out of control. You turn around to see where the trolley is headed, and there are five workmen on the track where it exits from under the footbridge. What to do? Being an expert on trolleys, you know of one certain way to stop an out-of-control trolley: Drop a really heavy weight in its path. But where to find one? It just so happens that standing next to you on the footbridge is a fat man, a really fat man. He is leaning over the railing, watching the trolley; all you have to do is to give him a little shove, and over the railing he will go, onto the track in the path of the trolley. Would it be permissible for you to do this? Everybody to whom I have put this case says it would not be. But why? . . .

In both cases, one will die if the agent acts, but five will live who would otherwise die—a net saving of four lives. What difference in the other facts of these cases explains the moral difference between them? I fancy that the theorists of tort and criminal law will find this problem as interesting as the moral theorist does.

STUDY QUESTIONS

1. Can you imagine another hypothetical case akin to that of the trolley?
2. In what crucial ways, if any, does the case Thomson calls "Fat Man" differ from the original trolley case?
3. Do you believe that turning the trolley is morally permissible?
4. Do you believe that not turning the trolley is morally permissible?

Turning the Trolley

٭

More than two decades after publishing a lengthy discussion of the trolley problem from which the previous selection was excerpted, Judith Jarvis Thomson returned to the problem. Influenced by the work of a doctoral student, she offered a surprising solution that casts doubt on a widely accepted assumption critical to the case.

I

... [L]et us imagine the situation to be as in the case I will call Bystander's Two Options. A bystander happens to be standing by the track, next to a switch that can be used to turn the tram off the straight track, on which five men are working, onto a spur of track to the right on which only one man is working. The bystander therefore has only two options:

Bystander's Two Options: he can
  (i) do nothing, letting five die, or
  (ii) throw the switch to the right, killing one.

Most people say that he may choose option (ii)....

II

A few years ago, an MIT graduate student, Alexander Friedman, devoted a chapter of his thesis to a discussion of the most interesting solutions to the trolley problem on offer in the literature.[1] He did a very good job: he showed clearly that none of them worked. What was especially interesting, though, was what he concluded. He said: the reason why no adequate solution has been found is that something went wrong at the outset. He said: it just isn't true that the bystander may choose option (ii) in Bystander's Two Options....

Friedman therefore said that we should see the (so-called) trolley problem "for what it really is—a very intriguing, provocative, and eye-opening non-problem."

Well, there's an unsettling idea! But if you mull over Friedman's unsettling idea for a while, then perhaps it can come to seem worth taking very seriously. So let us mull over it.

From Judith Jarvis Thomson, "Turning the Trolley." *Philosophy & Public Affairs* 36 (2008). Reprinted by permission of John Wiley & Sons. The principles are renumbered.

III

Here is a case that I will call Bystander's Three Options. The switch available to this bystander can be thrown in two ways. If he throws it to the right, then the trolley will turn onto the spur of track to the right, thereby killing one workman. If he throws it to the left, then the trolley will turn onto the spur of track to the left. The bystander himself stands on that left-hand spur of track, and will himself be killed if the trolley turns onto it. Or, of course, he can do nothing, letting five workmen die. In sum,

> Bystander's Three Options: he can
> (i) do nothing, letting five die, or
> (ii) throw the switch to the right, killing one, or
> (iii) throw the switch to the left, killing himself.

What is your reaction to the bystander's having the following thought? "Hmm. I want to save those five workmen. I can do that by choosing option (iii), that is by throwing the switch to the left, saving the five but killing myself. I'd prefer not dying today, however, even for the sake of saving five. So I'll choose option (ii), saving the five but killing the one on the right-hand track instead."

I hope you will agree that choosing (ii) would be unacceptable on the bystander's part. If he *can* throw the switch to the left and turn the trolley onto himself, how dare he throw the switch to the right and turn the trolley onto the one workman? The bystander doesn't feel like dying today, even for the sake of saving five, but we can assume, and so let us assume, that the one workman also doesn't feel like dying today, even if the bystander would thereby save five.

Let us get a little clearer about why this bystander must not choose option (ii). He wants to save the five on the straight track ahead. That would be good for them, and his saving them would be a good deed on his part. But his doing that good deed would have a cost: his life or the life of the one workman on the right-hand track. What the bystander does if he turns the trolley onto the one workman is to make the one workman pay the cost of his good deed because he doesn't feel like paying it himself.

Compare the following possibility. I am asked for a donation to Oxfam. I want to send them some money. I am able to send money of my own, but I don't feel like it. So I steal some from someone else and send *that* money to Oxfam. That is pretty bad. But if the bystander proceeds to turn the trolley onto the one on the right-hand track in Bystander's Three Options, then what he does is markedly worse, because the cost in Bystander's Three Options isn't money, it is life.

In sum, if A wants to do a certain good deed, and can pay what doing it would cost, then—other things being equal—A may do that good deed only if A pays the cost himself. In particular, here is a . . . *ceteris paribus* [other things being equal] principle:

> *First Principle:* A must not kill B to save five if he can instead kill himself to save the five.

So the bystander in Bystander's Three Options must not kill the one workman on the right-hand track in furtherance of his good deed of saving the five since he can instead save the five by killing himself. Thus he must not choose option (ii).

On the other hand, morality doesn't require him to choose option (iii). If A wants to do a certain good deed, and discovers that the only permissible means he has of doing the good deed is killing himself, then he may refrain from doing the good deed. In particular, here is a second *ceteris paribus* principle:

> *Second Principle:* A may let five die if the only permissible means he has of saving them is killing himself.

So the bystander in Bystander's Three Options may choose option (i).

Let us now return to Bystander's Two Options. We may imagine that the bystander in this case can see the trolley headed for the five workmen, and wants to save them. He thinks: "Does this switch allow for me to choose option (iii), in which I turn the trolley onto myself? If it does, then I must not choose option (ii), in which I turn the trolley onto the one workman on the right-hand track, for as the *First Principle* says, I must prefer killing myself to killing him. But I don't want to kill myself, and if truth be told, I wouldn't if I could. So if the switch does allow for me to choose option (iii), then I have to forgo my good deed of saving the five: I have to choose option (i)—thus I have to let the five die. As, of course, the *Second Principle* says I may."

As you can imagine, he therefore examines the switch *very* carefully. Lo, he discovers that the switch doesn't allow him to choose option (iii). "What luck," he thinks, "I can't turn the trolley onto myself. So it's perfectly all right for me to choose option (ii)!" His thought is that since he can't himself pay the cost of his good deed, it is perfectly all right for him to make the workman on the right-hand track pay it—despite the fact that he wouldn't himself pay it if he could.

I put it to you that that thought won't do. Since he wouldn't himself pay the cost of his good deed if he could pay it, there is no way in which he can decently regard himself as entitled to make someone else pay it.

Of how many of us is it true that if we could permissibly save five only by killing ourselves, then we would? Doing so would be altruism, for as the *Second Principle* says, nobody is required to do so, and doing so would therefore be altruism; moreover, doing so would be doing something for others at a major cost to oneself, and doing so would therefore be major altruism. Very few of us would. Then very few of us could decently regard ourselves as entitled to choose option (ii) if we were in the bystander's situation in Bystander's Two Options.

NOTE

1. A. W. Friedman. *Minimizing Harm: Three Problems in Moral Theory.* Unpublished doctoral dissertation, Department of Linguistics and Philosophy, Massachusetts Institute of Technology (2002).

STUDY QUESTIONS

1. Do you believe the bystander's turning the trolley is morally acceptable?
2. Do you believe the bystander's not turning the trolley is morally acceptable?
3. Is your judgment affected by which role in the story you imagine yourself playing?
4. Would your judgment be different if turning the trolley saved the lives of thousands of people?

The Divestiture Puzzle

૭✝

Steven M. Cahn

Philosophers often use brief puzzles to raise serious issues. Here I offer for your consideration a moral perplexity that arises in a situation often thought to be unproblematic.

I

Suppose I hold one hundred shares of stock in a company that has embarked on a policy I consider immoral. I, therefore, wish to divest myself of those one hundred shares. For me to sell them, someone must buy them. The buyer, however, would be purchasing one hundred shares of "tainted" stock, and I would have abetted the buyer in this immoral course of action. Granted, the prospective buyer might not believe the stock tainted, but that consideration would be irrelevant to me, because I am convinced that, knowingly or unknowingly, the buyer would be doing what is immoral. Surely I should not take any steps that would assist or encourage the buyer in such deplorable conduct. Nor should I try to release myself from a moral predicament by entangling someone else. How, then, is principled divestiture possible?

II

Note that the question is not whether divestiture can be defended on strategic grounds. Surely it can be. Likewise, it can be opposed on strategic grounds, for by not divesting a stockholder maintains the leverage to bring internal pressure on the company to change its policy. Either strategy may succeed or fail, depending in any particular case on a variety of factors, including the percentage of total outstanding shares held, the attitudes of the board of directors, social and economic

Steven M. Cahn, "The Divestiture Puzzle," in *Analysis*, 47:3 (1987). Reprinted by permission of the author.

conditions, and so on. The puzzle doesn't depend on such empirical considerations but on the axiom that the only ethically proper policy is to sell such stock.

As for the suggestion that a possessor of tainted stock might choose to renounce ownership rather than sell, this financially fatal strategy would amount to redistributing the value of the divested shares among all other stockholders. The assets of those who had not divested would thereby be increased as would, presumably, their moral culpability.

In sum, your wish to sell your stock is logically equivalent to your wishing someone to buy it. By hypothesis, however, you believe that for anyone to buy the stock is wrong. So your wish to sell is the wish that someone else do wrong. And that desire is immoral.

STUDY QUESTIONS

1. Is wishing to sell stock logically equivalent to wishing someone to buy it?
2. Can I be moral while wanting someone else to act immorally?
3. If I do not sell tainted stock but renounce ownership, am I merely redistributing its value to the other stockholders, thereby increasing their moral culpability?
4. If I believe that a toy I own is dangerous to any child who uses it, do I act morally if I sell the toy to someone else?

PART 10

Society

Democracy

ॐ

John Dewey

One long-standing area of inquiry in political philosophy is the nature of democracy and its relative advantages or disadvantages compared with alternative systems. Our next selection is devoted to this subject. The author is John Dewey (1859–1952), the foremost American philosopher of the first half of the twentieth century. Born and bred in Burlington, Vermont, his life and thought reflected the commitment to social equality he found exemplified in the life of his boyhood New England community. He spent most of his career as Professor of Philosophy at Columbia University.

Reprinted here is the text of a talk he delivered in 1937 to a meeting of educational administrators. It offers, in brief, his account of democracy.

....

[D]emocracy is much broader than a special political form, a method of conducting government, of making laws and carrying on governmental administration by means of popular suffrage and elected officers. It is that of course. But it is something broader and deeper than that.

The political and governmental phase of democracy is a means, the best means so far found, for realizing ends that lie in the wide domain of human relationships and the development of human personality. It is, as we often say, though perhaps without appreciating all that is involved in the saying, a way of life, social and individual. The key-note of democracy as a way of life may be expressed, it seems to me, as the necessity for the participation of every mature human being in formation of the values that regulate the living of men together—which is necessary from the standpoint of both the general social welfare and the full development of human beings as individuals.

Universal suffrage, recurring elections, responsibility of those who are in political power to the voters, and the other factors of democratic government are means that have been found expedient for realizing democracy as the truly human way of living. They are not a final end and a final value. They are to be judged on the basis of their contribution to an end. It is a form of idolatry to erect means into the end which they serve. Democratic political forms are simply the best means that human wit has devised up to a special time in history. But they rest back upon the idea that no man or limited set of men is wise enough or good enough to rule others without their consent; the positive meaning of this statement is that all those who are affected by social institutions must have a share in producing and managing them. The two facts that each one is influenced in what he does and enjoys and in what he becomes by the institutions under which he lives, and that therefore he shall have, in a democracy, a voice in shaping them, are the passive and active sides of the same fact.

The development of political democracy came about through substitution of the method of mutual consultation and voluntary agreement for the method of subordination of the many to the few enforced from above. Social arrangements which involve fixed subordination are maintained by coercion. The coercion need not be physical. There have existed, for short periods, benevolent despotisms. But coercion of some sort there has been; perhaps economic, certainly psychological and moral. The very fact of exclusion from participation is a subtle form of suppression. It gives individuals no opportunity to reflect and decide upon what is good for them. Others who are supposed to be wiser and who in any case have more power decide the question for them and also decide the methods and means by which subjects may arrive at the enjoyment of what is good for them. This form of coercion and suppression is more subtle and more effective than is overt intimidation and restraint. When it is habitual and embodied in social institutions, it seems the normal and natural state of affairs. The mass usually become unaware that they have a claim to a development of their own powers. Their experience is so restricted that they are not conscious of restriction. It is part of the democratic conception that they as individuals are not the only sufferers, but that the whole social body is deprived of the potential resources that should be at its service. The individuals of the submerged mass may not be very wise. But there is one thing they are wiser about than anybody else can be, and that is where the shoe pinches, the troubles they suffer from.

The foundation of democracy is faith in the capacities of human nature; faith in human intelligence, and in the power of pooled and cooperative experience. It is not belief that these things are complete but that if given a show they will grow and be able to generate progressively the knowledge and wisdom needed to guide collective action. Every autocratic and authoritarian scheme of social action rests on a belief that the needed intelligence is confined to a superior few who because of inherent natural gifts are endowed with the ability and the right to control the conduct of others; laying down principles and rules and directing the ways in which they are carried out. It would be foolish to deny that much can be said for this point of view. It is that which controlled human relations in social groups for much the greater part of human history. The democratic faith has emerged very, very recently in the history of mankind. Even where democracies now exist, men's minds and feelings are still permeated with ideas about leadership imposed from above, ideas that developed in the long early history of mankind. After democratic political institutions were nominally established, beliefs and ways of looking at life and of acting that originated when men and women were externally controlled and subjected to arbitrary power, persisted in the family, the church, business and the school, and experience shows that as long as they persist there, political democracy is not secure.

Belief in equality is an element of the democratic credo. It is not, however, belief in equality of natural endowments. Those who proclaimed the idea of equality did not suppose they were enunciating a psychological doctrine, but a legal and political one. All individuals are entitled to equality of treatment by law and in its administration. Each one is affected equally in quality if not in quantity by the institutions under which he lives and has an equal right to express his judgment, although the weight of his judgment may not be equal in amount when it enters into the pooled result to that of others. In short, each one is equally an individual and entitled to equal opportunity of development of his own capacities, be they large or small in range. Moreover, each has needs of his own, as significant to him as those of others are to them. The very fact of natural and psychological inequality is all the more reason for establishment by law of equality of opportunity, since otherwise the former becomes a means of oppression of the less gifted.

While what we call intelligence be distributed in unequal amounts, it is the democratic faith that it is sufficiently general so that each individual has something to contribute whose value can be assessed only as it enters into the final pooled intelligence constituted by the contributions of all. Every authoritarian scheme, on the contrary assumes that its value may be assessed by some *prior* principle, if not of family and birth or race and color or possession of material wealth, then by the position and rank a person occupies in the existing social scheme. The democratic faith in equality is the faith that each individual shall have the chance and opportunity to contribute whatever he is capable of contributing, and that the value of his contribution be decided by its place and function in the organized total of similar contributions—not on the basis of prior status of any kind whatever.

I have emphasized in what precedes the importance of the effective release of intelligence in connection with personal experience in the democratic way of living. I have done so purposely because democracy is so often and so naturally associated in our minds with freedom of *action*, forgetting the importance of freed intelligence which is necessary to direct and to warrant freedom of action. Unless freedom of individual action has intelligence and informed conviction back of it, its manifestation is almost sure to result in confusion and disorder. The democratic idea of freedom is not the right of each individual to *do* as he pleases, even if it be qualified by adding "provided he does not interfere with the same freedom on the part of others." While the idea is not always, not often enough, expressed in words, the basic freedom is that of freedom of *mind* and of whatever degree of freedom of action and experience is necessary to produce freedom of intelligence. The modes of freedom guaranteed in the Bill of Rights are all of this nature: Freedom of belief and conscience, of expression of opinion, of assembly for discussion and conference, of the press as an organ of communication. They are guaranteed because without them individuals are not free to develop and society is deprived of what they might contribute. . . .

There is some kind of government, of control, wherever affairs that concern a number of persons who act together are engaged in. It is a superficial view that holds government is located in Washington and Albany. There is government in the family, in business, in the church, in every social group. There are regulations, due to custom if not to enactment, that settle how individuals in a group act in connection with one another.

It is a disputed question of theory and practice just how far a democratic political government should go in control of the conditions of action within special groups. At the present time, for example, there are those who think the federal and state governments leave too much freedom of independent action to industrial and financial groups and there are others who think the Government is going altogether too far at the present time. I do not need to discuss this phase of the problem much less to try to settle it. But it must be pointed out that if the methods of regulation and administration in vogue in the conduct of secondary social groups are non-democratic, whether directly or indirectly or both, there is bound to be an unfavorable reaction back into the habits of feeling, thought and action of citizenship in the broadest sense of that word. The way in which any organized social interest is controlled necessarily plays an important part in forming the dispositions and tastes, the attitudes, interests, purposes and desires, of those engaged in carrying on the activities of the group. For illustration, I do not need to do more than point to the moral, emotional, and intellectual effect upon both employers and laborers of the existing industrial system. Just what the effects specifically are is a matter about which we know very little. But I suppose that every one who reflects upon the subject admits that it is impossible that the ways in which activities are carried on for the greater part of the waking hours of the day; and the way in which the shares of individuals are involved in the management of affairs in such a matter as gaining a livelihood and attaining material and social security, can only be a highly important factor in shaping personal dispositions; in short, forming character and intelligence.

In the broad and final sense all institutions are educational in the sense that they operate to form the attitudes, dispositions, abilities, and disabilities that constitute a concrete personality. The principle applies with special force to the school. For it is the main business of the family and the school to influence directly the formation and growth of attitudes and dispositions, emotional, intellectual and moral. Whether this educative process is carried on in a predominantly democratic or non-democratic way becomes therefore a question of transcendent importance not only for education itself but for its final effect upon all the interests and activities of a society that is committed to the democratic way of life. . . .

[T]here are certain corollaries which clarify the meaning of the issue. Absence of participation tends to produce lack of interest and concern on the part of those shut out. The result is a corresponding lack of effective responsibility. Automatically and unconsciously, if not consciously, the feeling develops, "this is none of our affair; it is the business of those at the top; let that particular set of Georges do what needs to be done." The countries in which autocratic government prevails are just those in which there is least public spirit and the greatest indifference to matters of general as distinct from personal concern. . . . Where there is little power, there is correspondingly little sense of positive responsibility—It is enough to do what one is told to do sufficiently well to escape flagrant unfavorable notice. About larger matters a spirit of passivity is engendered. . . .

[I]t still is also true that incapacity to assume the responsibilities involved in having a voice in shaping policies is bred and increased by conditions in which that responsibility is denied. I suppose there has never been an autocrat, big or little, who did not justify his conduct on the ground of the unfitness of his subjects to take part in government. . . . But, as was said earlier, habitual exclusion has the effect of reducing a sense of responsibility for what is done and its consequences. What the argument for democracy implies is that the best way to produce initiative and constructive power is to exercise it. Power, as well as interest, comes by use and practice. . . .

The fundamental beliefs and practices of democracy are now challenged as they never have been before. In some nations they are more than challenged. They are ruthlessly and systematically destroyed. Everywhere there are waves of criticism and doubt as to whether democracy can meet pressing problems of order and security. The causes for the destruction of political democracy in countries where it was nominally established are complex. But of one thing I think we may be sure. Wherever it has fallen it was too exclusively political in nature. It had not become part of the bone and blood of the people in daily conduct of its life. Democratic forms were limited to Parliament, elections, and combats between parties. What is happening proves conclusively, I think, that unless democratic habits of thought and action are part of the fiber of a people, political democracy is insecure. It cannot stand in isolation. It must be buttressed by the presence of democratic methods in all social relationships. The relations that exist in educational institutions are second only in importance in this respect to those which exist in industry and business, perhaps not even to them. . . .

I can think of nothing so important in this country at present as a rethinking of the whole problem of democracy and its implications. Neither the rethinking nor the action it should produce can be brought into being in a day or year. The democratic idea itself demands that the thinking and activity proceed cooperatively.

STUDY QUESTIONS

1. Why does Dewey believe that democracy is much broader than a method of electing officials?
2. According to Dewey, about what are individuals wiser than anyone else can be?
3. According to Dewey, what is the foundation of democracy?
4. How does Dewey connect democracy and education?

What Is a Liberal Education?

SIDNEY HOOK

> In the previous selection John Dewey stresses that the welfare of a democratic
> community depends on the understanding and capability of its citizenry. But
> what knowledge, skills, and values do we all require to enable us to make a suc-
> cess of our experiment in self-government? That is the question addressed in our
> next essay, written by Sidney Hook (1902–1989), a leading student of Dewey, who
> was Professor of Philosophy at New York University.

What, concretely, should the modern man know in order to live intelligently in
the world today? What should we require that he learn of subject matters and
skills in his educational career in order that he may acquire maturity in feeling,
in judgment, in action? Can we indicate the minimum indispensables of a liberal
education in the modern world? This approach recognizes that no subject per se is
inherently liberal at all times and places. But it also recognizes that within a given
age in a given culture, the enlightenment and maturity, the freedom and power,
which liberal education aims to impart, is more likely to be achieved by mastery
of some subject matters and skills than by others. In short, principles must bear
fruit in specific programs in specific times. In what follows I shall speak of studies
rather than of conventional courses.

1. The liberally educated person should be intellectually at home in the
world of physical nature. He should know something about the earth he inhabits
and its place in the solar system, about the solar system and its relation to the
cosmos. He should know something about mechanics, heat, light, electricity, and
magnetism as the universal forces that condition anything he is or may become.
He should be just as intimately acquainted with the nature of man as a biological
species, his evolution, and the discoveries of experimental genetics. He should
know something about the structure of his own body and mind, and the cycle of
birth, growth, learning, and decline. To have even a glimmer of understanding
of these things, he must go beyond the level of primary description and acquire
some grasp of the principles that explain what he observes. Where an intelligent
grasp of principles requires a knowledge of mathematics, its fundamental ideas
should be presented in such a way that students carry away the sense of mathematics not only as a tool for the solution of problems but as a study of types of
order, system, and language.

Such knowledge is important to the individual *not* merely because of its intrinsic fascination. Every subject from numismatics to Sanskrit possesses an intrinsic interest to those who are curious about it. It is important because it helps make everyday experience more intelligible; because it furnishes a continuous exemplification of scientific method in action; because our world is literally being remade by the consequences and applications of science; because the fate of nations and the vocations of men depend upon the use of this knowledge; and because it provides the instruments to reduce our vast helplessness and dependence in an uncertain world.

Such knowledge is no less important because it bears upon the formation of *rational belief* about the place of man in the universe. Whatever views a man professes today about God, human freedom, Cosmic Purpose, and personal survival, he cannot reasonably hold them in ignorance of the scientific account of the world and man.

These are some of the reasons why the study of the natural sciences, and the elementary mathematical notions they involve, should be *required* of everyone. Making such study required imposes a heavy obligation and a difficult task of pedagogical discovery upon those who teach it. It is commonly recognized that the sciences today are taught as if all students enrolled in science courses were preparing to be professional scientists. Most of them are not. Naturally they seek to escape a study whose wider and larger uses they do not see because many of their teachers do not see it. Here is not the place to canvass and evaluate the attempts being made to organize instruction in the sciences. The best experience seems to show that one science should not be taken as the exemplar of all, but that the basic subject matter of astronomy, physics, chemistry, geology, in one group, and biology and psychology in another, should be covered. For when only one science is taught it tends to be treated professionally. Similarly, the best experience indicates that instruction should be interdepartmental—any competent teacher from one of these fields in either group should be able to teach all of them in the group, instead of having a succession of different teachers each representing his own field. This usually destroys both the continuity and the cumulative effect of the teaching as a whole.

2. Every student should be required to become intelligently aware of how the society in which he lives functions, of the great forces molding contemporary civilization, and of the crucial problems of our age which await decision. The studies most appropriate to this awareness have been conventionally separated into history, economics, government, sociology, social psychology, and anthropology. This separation is an intellectual scandal. For it is impossible to have an adequate grasp of the problems of government without a knowledge of economics, and vice versa. Except for some special domains of professional interest, the same is true for the other subjects as well.

The place of the social studies, properly integrated around problems and issues, is fundamental in the curriculum of modern education. It is one of the dividing points between the major conflicting schools of educational thought.

The question of its justification must be sharply distinguished from discussion of the relative merits of this or that mode of approach to the social studies.

The knowledge and insight that the social studies can give are necessary for every student because no matter what his specialized pursuits may later be, the extent to which he can follow them, and the "contextual" developments within these fields, depend upon the total social situation of which they are in some sense a part. An engineer today whose knowledge is restricted only to technical matters of engineering, or a physician whose competence extends only to the subject matter of traditional medical training, is ill-prepared to plan intelligently for a life-career or to understand the basic problems that face his profession. He is often unable to cope adequately with those specific problems in his own domain that involve, as so many problems of social and personal health do, economic and psychological difficulties. No matter what an individual's vocation, the conditions of his effective functioning depend upon pervasive social tendencies which set the occasions for the application of knowledge, provide the opportunities of employment, and not seldom determine even the direction of research.

More important, the whole presupposition of the theory of democracy is that the electorate will be able to make intelligent decisions on the issues before it. These issues are basically political, social, and economic. Their specific character changes from year to year. But their generic form, and the character of the basic problems, do not. Nor, most essential of all, do the proper intellectual habits of meeting them change. It is undeniably true that the world we live in is one marked by greater changes, because of the impact of technology, than ever before. This does not necessitate changing the curriculum daily to catch up with today's newspapers, nor does it justify a concentration on presumably eternal problems as if these problems had significance independent of cultural place–time. The fact that we are living in a world where the rate of cultural change is greater than at any time in the past, together with its ramifications, may itself become a central consideration for analysis. . . .

3. Everyone recognizes a distinction between knowledge and wisdom. This distinction is not clarified by making a mystery of wisdom and speaking of it as if it were begotten by divine inspiration while knowledge had a more lowly source. Wisdom is a kind of knowledge. It is knowledge of the nature, career, and consequences of *human values*. Since these cannot be separated from the human organism and the social scene, the moral ways of man cannot be understood without knowledge of the ways of things and institutions.

To study social affairs without an analysis of policies is to lose oneself in factual minutiae that lack interest and relevance. But knowledge of values is a prerequisite of the intelligent determination of policy. Philosophy, most broadly viewed, is the critical survey of existence from the standpoint of value. This points to the twofold role of philosophy in the curriculum of the college.

The world of physical nature may be studied without reference to human values. But history, art, literature, and particularly the social studies involve problems of value at every turn. A social philosophy whose implications are worked out is a series of proposals that something be *done* in the world. It includes a set of *plans* to conserve or change aspects of social life. Today the community is arrayed under different banners without a clear understanding of the basic issues involved. In the press of controversy, the ideals and values at the heart of every social philosophy are widely affirmed as articles of blind faith. They are partisan commitments justified only by the emotional security they give to believers. They spread by contagion, unchecked by critical safeguards; yet the future of civilization largely depends upon them and how they are held. It is therefore requisite that their study be made an integral part of the liberal arts curriculum. Systematic and critical instruction should be given in the great maps of life—the ways to heaven, hell, and earth—which are being unrolled in the world today.

Ideals and philosophies of life are not parts of the world of nature; but it is a pernicious illusion to imagine that they cannot be studied "scientifically." Their historical origins, their concatenation of doctrine, their controlling assumptions, their means, methods, and consequences in practice, can and should be investigated in a scientific spirit. There are certain social philosophies that would forbid such an investigation for fear of not being able to survive it; but it is one of the great merits of the democratic way of life and one of its strongest claims for acceptance that it can withstand analysis of this sort. It is incumbent upon the liberal arts college to provide for close study of the dominant social and political philosophies, ranging from one end of the color spectrum to the other. Proper study will disclose that these philosophies cannot be narrowly considered in their own terms. They involve an examination of the great ways of life—of the great visions of philosophy which come into play whenever we try to arrange our values in a preference scale in order to choose the better between conflicting goods. Philosophy is best taught when the issues of moral choice arise naturally out of the problems of social life. The effective integration of concrete materials from history, literature, and social studies can easily be achieved within a philosophical perspective.

4. Instruction in the natural, social, and technological forces shaping the world, and in the dominant conflicting ideals in behalf of which these forces are to be controlled, goes a long way. But not far enough. Far more important than knowledge is the method by which it is reached, and the ability to recognize when it constitutes *evidence* and when not; and more important than any particular ideal is the way in which it is held, and the capacity to evaluate it in relation to other ideals. From first to last, in season and out, our educational institutions, especially on the college level, must emphasize *methods* of analysis. They must build up in students a critical sense of evidence, relevance, and validity against which the multitudinous seas of propaganda will wash in vain. They must strengthen the powers of independent reflection, which will enable students to confront the claims of ideals and values by their alternatives and the relative costs of achieving them. . . .

The field of language, of inference and argument, is a broad field but a definite one in which specific training can be given to all students. How to read intelligently, how to recognize good from bad reasoning, how to evaluate evidence, how to distinguish between a definition and a hypothesis and between a hypothesis and a resolution, can be taught in such a way as to build up permanent habits of logic in action. The result of thorough training in "semantic" analysis—using that term in its broadest sense without invidious distinctions between different schools—is an intellectual sophistication without which a man may be learned but not intelligent.

Judging by past and present curricular achievements in developing students with intellectual sophistication and maturity, our colleges must be pronounced, in the main, dismal failures. The main reason for the failure is the absence of serious effort, except in a few institutions, to realize this goal. The necessity of the task is not even recognized. This failure is not only intellectually reprehensible; it is socially dangerous. For the natural susceptibility of youth to enthusiasms, its tendency to glorify action, and its limited experience make it easy recruiting material for all sorts of demagogic movements which flatter its strength and impatience. Recent history furnishes many illustrations of how, in the absence of strong critical sense, youthful strength can lead to cruelty, and youthful impatience to folly. It is true that people who are incapable of thinking cannot be taught how to think, and that the incapacity for thought is not restricted to those who learn. But the first cannot be judged without being exposed to the processes of critical instruction, and the second should be eliminated from the ranks of the teachers. There is considerable evidence to show that students who are capable of completing high school can be so taught that they are aware of *whether* they are thinking or not. There is hope that, with better pedagogic skill and inspiration, they may become capable of grasping the main thought of *what* they are reading or hearing in non-technical fields—of developing a sense of *what validly follows from what,* an accompanying sensitiveness to the dominant types of fallacies, and a habit of weighing evidence for conclusions advanced.

My own experience has led me to the conclusion that this is *not* accomplished by courses in formal logic which, when given in a rigorous and elegant way, accomplish little more than courses in pure mathematics. There is an approach to the study of logic that on an elementary level is much more successful in achieving the ends described above than the traditional course in formal logic. This plunges the student into an analysis of language material around him. By constant use of concrete illustrations drawn from all fields, but especially the fields of politics and social study, insight is developed into the logical principles of definition, the structure of analogies, dilemmas, types of fallacies and the reasons *why* they are fallacies, the criteria of good hypotheses, and related topics. Such training may legitimately be required of all students. Although philosophers are usually best able to give it, any teacher who combines logical capacity with pedagogic skill can make this study a stimulating experience.

5. There is less controversy about the desirability of the study of composition and literature than about any other subject in the traditional or modern curriculum. It is appreciated that among the essentials of clear thought are good

language habits and that, except in the higher strata of philosophic discourse, tortuous obscurities of expression are more likely to be an indication of plain confusion than of stuttering profundity. It is also widely recognized that nothing can take the place of literature in developing the imagination, and in imparting a sense of the inexhaustible richness of human personality. The questions that arise at this point are not of justification, but of method, technique, and scope of comprehensiveness.

If good language habits are to be acquired *only* in order to acquire facility in thinking, little can be said for the conventional courses in English composition. Students cannot acquire facility in clear expression in the space of a year, by developing sundry themes from varied sources, under the tutelage of instructors whose training and interest may not qualify them for sustained critical thought. Clear thinking is best controlled by those who are at home in the field in which thinking is done. If language instruction is to be motivated only by the desire to strengthen the power of organizing ideas in written discourse, it should be left to properly trained instructors in other disciplines.

But there are other justifications for teaching students English composition. The first is that there are certain rules of intelligent reading that are essential to—if they do not constitute—understanding. These rules are very elementary. By themselves they do not tell us how to understand a poem, a mathematical demonstration, a scientific text, or a religious prayer—all of which require special skills. But they make it easier for the student to uncover the nature of the "argument"—what is being said, what is being assumed, what is being presented as evidence—in any piece of prose that is not a narrative or simply informational in content. In a sense these rules are integral to the study of logic in action, but in such an introductory way that they are usually not considered part of logical study which begins its work after basic meanings have been established, or in independence of the meaning of logical symbols.

Another reason for teaching English composition independently is its uses in learning how to write. "Effective writing" is not necessarily the same thing as logical writing. The purpose for which we write determines whether our writing is effective. And there are many situations in which we write not to convince or to prove but to explain, arouse, confess, challenge, or assuage. To write *interestingly* may sometimes be just as important as to write soundly because getting a hearing and keeping attention may depend upon it. How much of the skills of writing can be taught is difficult to say. That it is worth making the effort to teach these skills is indisputable.

The place of language in the curriculum involves not merely our native language but *foreign* languages. Vocational considerations aside, should knowledge of a foreign language be required, and why? ...

The main reason why students should be requested to learn another language is that it is the most effective medium by which, when properly taught, they can acquire a sensitivity to language, to the subtle tones, undertones, and overtones of words, and to the licit ambiguities of imaginative discourse.

No one who has not translated prose or poetry from one language to another can appreciate both the unique richness and the unique limitations of his own language. This is particularly true where the life of the emotions is concerned; and it is particularly important that it should be realized. For the appreciation of emotions, perhaps even their recognition in certain cases, depends upon their linguistic identification. The spectrum of human emotions is much more dense than the words by which we render them. Knowledge of different languages, and the attempts made to communicate back and forth between them in our own minds, broaden and diversify our own feelings. They multiply points of view, and liberate us from the prejudice that words—*our* words—are the natural signs of things and events. The genius of a culture is exemplified in a preeminent way in the characteristic idioms of its language. In learning another language we enable ourselves to appreciate both the cultural similarities and differences of the Western world....

The place of literature in the curriculum is justified by so many considerations that it is secure against all criticism. Here, too, what is at issue is not whether literature—Greek, Latin, English, European, American—should be read and studied in the schools but what should be read, when, and by what methods. These are details, important details—but outside the scope of our inquiry.

Something should be said about the unique opportunity which the teaching of literature provides, not only in giving delight by heightening perception of the formal values of literary craftsmanship, but in giving insight into people. The opposite of a liberal education, William James somewhere suggests, is a literal education. A literal education is one which equips a person to read formulas and equations, straightforward prose, doggerel verse, and advertising signs. It does not equip one to read the language of metaphor, of paradox, of indirect analogy, of serious fancy in which the emotions and passions and half-believed ideas of human beings express themselves. To read great literature is to read men—their fears and motives, their needs and hopes. Every great novelist is a *Menschenkenner* who opens the hearts of others to us and helps us to read our own hearts as well. The intelligent study of literature should never directly aim to strengthen morals and improve manners. For its natural consequences are a delicacy of perception and an emotional tact that are defeated by preaching and didactic teaching.

A liberal education will impart an awareness of the amazing and precious complexity of human relationships. Since those relationships are violated more often out of insensitiveness than out of deliberate intent, whatever increases sensitiveness of perception and understanding humanizes life. Literature in all its forms is the great humanizing medium of life. It must therefore be representative of life; not only of past life but of our own; not only of our own culture but of different cultures.

6. An unfailing mark of philistinism in education is reference to the study of art and music as "the frills and fads" of schooling. Insofar as those who speak

this way are not tone-deaf or color-blind, they are themselves products of a narrow education, unaware of the profound experiences which are uniquely bound up with the trained perception of color and form. There is no reason to believe that the capacity for the appreciation of art and music shows a markedly different curve of distribution from what is observable in the measurement of capacity of drawing inferences or recalling relevant information. A sufficient justification for making some study of art and music required in modern education is that it provides an unfailing source of delight in personal experience, a certain grace in living, and a variety of dimensions of meaning by which to interpret the world around us. This is a sufficient justification: there are others, quite subsidiary, related to the themes, the occasions, the history and backgrounds of the works studied. Perhaps one should add—although this expresses only a reasonable hope—that a community whose citizens have developed tastes would not tolerate the stridency, the ugliness and squalor which assault us in our factories, our cities, and our countryside.

One of the reasons why the study of art and music has not received as much attention as it should by educators, particularly on the college level, is that instruction in these subjects often suffers from two opposite defects. Sometimes courses in art and music are given as if all students enrolled in them were planning a career as practicing artists or as professional *teachers* of the arts. Sometimes they are given as hours for passive enjoyment or relaxation in which the teacher does the performing or talking and in which there is no call upon the students to make an intelligent response.

The key-stress in courses in art and music should be *discrimination* and *interpretation,* rather than appreciation and cultivation. The latter can take care of themselves, when the student has learned to discriminate and interpret intelligently.

Briefly summarized: the answer to the question *What should we teach?* is selected materials from the fields of mathematics and the natural sciences; social studies, including history; language and literature; philosophy and logic; art and music. The knowledge imparted by such study should be acquired in such a way as to strengthen the skills of reading and writing, of thinking and imaginative interpretation, of criticism and evaluation.

STUDY QUESTIONS

1. What does Hook mean by "a liberal education"?
2. According to Hook, what are the chief components of a liberal education?
3. Would a democratic society be more likely to prosper if its citizens had received a liberal education?
4. How could a faculty ensure that each student who is graduated has mastered the essentials of a liberal education?

Cultivating Humanity

Ӡ

Martha Nussbaum

Martha Nussbaum is Professor of Law and Ethics in the Philosophy Department, Law School, and Divinity School at the University of Chicago. In this selection she considers how liberal education needs to be adapted to produce citizens in a multicultural, multinational world. She stresses the capacity for critical examination of oneself and one's traditions, the ability to recognize one's ties to all other human beings, and the imaginative power to understand their outlooks.

....

Our campuses are producing citizens, and this means that we must ask what a good citizen of the present day should be and should know. The present-day world is inescapably multicultural and multinational. Many of our most pressing problems require for their intelligent, cooperative solution a dialogue that brings together people from many different national and cultural and religious backgrounds. Even those issues that seem closest to home—issues, for example, about the structure of the family, the regulation of sexuality, the future of children—need to be approached with a broad historical and cross-cultural understanding. A graduate of a U.S. university or college ought to be the sort of citizen who can become an intelligent participant in debates involving these differences, whether professionally or simply as a voter, a juror, a friend....

In most nations students enter a university to pursue a single subject, and that is all they study. The idea of "liberal education"—a higher education that is a cultivation of the whole human being for the functions of citizenship and life generally—has been taken up most fully in the United States. This noble ideal, however, has not yet been fully realized in our colleges and universities. Some, while using the words "liberal education," subordinate the cultivation of the whole person to technical and vocational education. Even where education is ostensibly "liberal," it may not contain all that a citizen really needs to know. We should ask, then, how well our nation is really fulfilling a goal that it has chosen to make its own. What does the "cultivation of humanity" require?

The classical ideal of the "world citizen" can be understood in two ways, and "cultivation of humanity" along with it. The sterner, more exigent version is the ideal of a citizen whose *primary* loyalty is to human beings the world over, and whose national, local, and varied group loyalties are considered distinctly secondary. Its more relaxed version allows a variety of different views about what our priorities should be but says that, however we order our varied loyalties, we should still be sure that we recognize the worth of human life wherever it occurs and see ourselves as bound by common human abilities and problems to people who lie at a great distance from us.... Although I do sympathize with the sterner thesis, it is the more relaxed and inclusive thesis that will concern me here. What, then, does this inclusive conception ask us to learn?

Three capacities, above all, are essential to the cultivation of humanity in today's world. First is the capacity for critical examination of oneself and one's traditions—for living what, following Socrates, we may call "the examined life." This means a life that accepts no belief as authoritative simply because it has been handed down by tradition or become familiar through habit, a life that questions all beliefs and accepts only those that survive reason's demand for consistency and for justification. Training this capacity requires developing the capacity to reason logically, to test what one reads or says for consistency of reasoning, correctness of fact, and accuracy of judgment. Testing of this sort frequently produces challenges to tradition, as Socrates knew well when he defended himself against the charge of "corrupting the young." But he defended his activity on the grounds that democracy needs citizens who can think for themselves rather than simply deferring to authority, who can reason together about their choices rather than just trading claims and counterclaims. Like a gadfly on the back of a noble but sluggish horse, he said, he was waking democracy up so that it could conduct its business in a more reflective and reasonable way. Our democracy, like ancient Athens, is prone to hasty and sloppy reasoning, and to the substitution of invective for real deliberation. We need Socratic teaching to fulfill the promise of democratic citizenship.

Citizens who cultivate their humanity need, further, an ability to see themselves not simply as citizens of some local region or group but also, and above all, as human beings bound to all other human beings by ties of recognition and concern. The world around us is inescapably international. Issues from business to agriculture, from human rights to the relief of famine, call our imaginations to venture beyond narrow group loyalties and to consider the reality of distant lives. We very easily think of ourselves in group terms—as Americans first and foremost, as human beings second—or, even more narrowly, as Italian-Americans, or heterosexuals, or African-Americans first, Americans second, and human beings third if at all. We neglect needs and capacities that link us to fellow citizens who live at a distance or who look different from ourselves. This means that we are unaware of many prospects of communication and fellowship with them, and also of responsibilities we may have to them. We also sometimes err by neglect of differences, assuming that lives in distant places must be like ours and lacking curiosity about what they are really like. Cultivating our humanity in a complex, interlocking world involves understanding the ways in which common needs and aims are differently realized in different circumstances. This requires a great deal of knowledge that American college students rarely got in previous eras, knowledge of non-Western cultures, of minorities within their own, of differences of gender and sexuality.

But citizens cannot think well on the basis of factual knowledge alone. The third ability of the citizen, closely related to the first two, can be called the narrative imagination. This means the ability to think what it might be like to be in the shoes of a person different from oneself, to be an intelligent reader of that person's story, and to understand the emotions and wishes and desires that someone so placed might have. The narrative imagination is not uncritical, for we always bring ourselves and our own judgments to the encounter with another; and when we identify with a character in a novel, or with a distant person whose life story we imagine, we inevitably will not merely identify; we will also judge that story in the light of our own goals and aspirations. But the first step of understanding the world from the point of view of the other is essential to any responsible act of judgment, since we do not know what we are judging until we see the meaning of an action as the person intends it, the meaning of a speech as it expresses something of importance in the context of that person's history and social world. The third ability our students should attain is the ability to decipher such meanings through the use of the imagination. . . .

Our campuses educate our citizens. Becoming an educated citizen means learning a lot of facts and mastering techniques of reasoning. But it means something more. It means learning how to be a human being capable of love and imagination. We may continue to produce narrow citizens who have difficulty understanding people different from themselves, whose imaginations rarely venture beyond their local setting. It is all too easy for the moral imagination to become narrow in this way. Think of Charles Dickens' image of bad citizenship in *A Christmas Carol,* in his portrait of the ghost of Jacob Marley, who visits Scrooge to warn him of the dangers of a blunted imagination. Marley's ghost drags through all eternity a chain made of cash boxes, because in life his imagination never ventured outside the walls of his successful business to encounter the lives of the men and women around him, men and women of different social class and background. We produce all too many citizens who are like Marley's ghost, and like Scrooge before he walked out to see what the world around him contained. But we have the opportunity to do better, and now we are beginning to seize that opportunity. That is not "political correctness"; that is the cultivation of humanity.

STUDY QUESTIONS

1. What does Nussbaum mean by "cultivating humanity"?
2. How important to cultivating humanity is the study of foreign language?
3. Can studying certain subjects make more likely the possession of certain attitudes?
4. Is knowledge of certain non-Western cultures more important than knowledge of other non-Western cultures?

Letter from a Birmingham Jail

MARTIN LUTHER KING, JR.

A democracy may pass an unjust law. If citizens of that democracy believe the law is unjust, are they entitled to violate it? Doing so would not be in accord with the principle of majority rule, which is the procedure by which a democracy is supposed to function. But to act in accord with an unjust law would be to act unjustly. Can we find a satisfactory way out of this dilemma?

In 1963 Dr. Martin Luther King, Jr., was imprisoned in Birmingham, Alabama, for participating in a civil rights demonstration. While in jail he writes a letter justifying his actions. He explains that because he believes that the laws that enforced racial segregation are unjust, he refuses to act as the government required but willingly accepts the legal punishment for his actions, thus indicating his respect for democratic procedure. He insists that such civil disobedience be nonviolent, that all laws except the unjust ones be obeyed, and that breaking of the law be resorted to only when fundamental moral principles were at stake.

In 1964 he was awarded the Nobel Peace Prize. In 1968 he was assassinated.

My dear Fellow Clergymen,

While confined here in the Birmingham city jail, I came across your recent statement calling our present activities "unwise and untimely." Seldom, if ever, do I pause to answer criticism of my work and ideas. If I sought to answer all of the criticisms that cross my desk, my secretaries would be engaged in little else in the course of the day, and I would have no time for constructive work. But since I feel that you are men of genuine good will and your criticisms are sincerely set forth, I would like to answer your statement in what I hope will be patient and reasonable terms.

I think I should give the reason for my being in Birmingham, since you have been influenced by the argument of "outsiders coming in." I have the honor of serving as president of the Southern Christian Leadership Conference, an organization operating in every southern state, with headquarters in Atlanta, Georgia. We have some eighty-five affiliate organizations all across the South—one being the Alabama Christian Movement for Human Rights. Whenever necessary and possible we share staff, educational and financial resources with our affiliates.

Several months ago our local affiliate here in Birmingham invited us to be on call to engage in a nonviolent direct-action program if such were deemed necessary. We readily consented and when the hour came we lived up to our promises. So I am here, along with several members of my staff, because we were invited here. I am here because I have basic organizational ties here.

Beyond this, I am in Birmingham because injustice is here. Just as the eighth century prophets left their little villages and carried their "thus saith the Lord" far beyond the boundaries of their hometowns; and just as the Apostle Paul left his little village of Tarsus and carried the gospel of Jesus Christ to practically every hamlet and city of the Graeco-Roman world, I too am compelled to carry the gospel of freedom beyond my particular hometown. Like Paul, I must constantly respond to the Macedonian call for aid.

Moreover, I am cognizant of the interrelatedness of all communities and states. I cannot sit idly by in Atlanta and not be concerned about what happens in Birmingham. Injustice anywhere is a threat to justice everywhere. We are caught in an inescapable network of mutuality, tied in a single garment of destiny. Whatever affects one directly affects all indirectly. Never again can we afford to live with the narrow, provincial "outside agitator" idea. Anyone who lives in the United States can never be considered an outsider anywhere in this country.

You deplore the demonstrations that are presently taking place in Birmingham. But I am sorry that your statement did not express a similar concern for the conditions that brought the demonstrations into being. I am sure that each of you would want to go beyond the superficial social analyst who looks merely at effects, and does not grapple with underlying causes. I would not hesitate to say that it is unfortunate that so-called demonstrations are taking place in Birmingham at this time, but I would say in more emphatic terms that it is even more unfortunate that the white power structure of this city left the Negro community with no other alternative.

In any nonviolent campaign there are four basic steps: (1) collection of the facts to determine whether injustices are alive, (2) negotiation, (3) self-purification, and (4) direct action. We have gone through all of these steps in Birmingham. There can be no gainsaying of the fact that racial injustice engulfs this community.

Birmingham is probably the most thoroughly segregated city in the United States. Its ugly record of police brutality is known in every section of this country. Its unjust treatment of Negroes in the courts is a notorious reality. There have been more unsolved bombings of Negro homes and churches in Birmingham than any city in this nation. These are the hard, brutal and unbelievable facts. On the basis of these conditions, Negro leaders sought to negotiate with the city fathers. But the political leaders consistently refused to engage in good faith negotiation.

Then came the opportunity last September to talk with some of the leaders of the economic community. In these negotiating sessions certain promises were made by the merchants—such as the promise to remove the humiliating racial signs from the stores. On the basis of these promises, Rev. Shuttlesworth and the leaders of the Alabama Christian Movement for Human Rights agreed to call a moratorium on any type of demonstrations. As the weeks and months unfolded, we realized that we were the victims of a broken promise. The signs remained. Like so many experiences of the past, we were confronted with blasted hopes, and the dark shadow of a deep disappointment settled upon us. So we had no alternative except that of preparing for direct action, whereby we would present our very bodies as a means of laying our case before the conscience of the local and national community. We were not unmindful of the difficulties involved. So we decided to go through a process of self-purification. We started having workshops on nonviolence and repeatedly asked ourselves the questions, "Are you able to accept blows without retaliating?" "Are you able to endure the ordeals of jail?" We decided to set our direct-action program around the Easter season, realizing that with the exception of Christmas, this was the largest shopping period of the year. Knowing that a strong economic withdrawal program would be the by-product of direct action, we felt that this was the best time to bring pressure on the merchants for the needed changes. Then it occurred to us that the March election was ahead and so we speedily decided to postpone action until after election day. When we discovered that Mr. Connor was in the run-off, we decided again to postpone action so that the demonstrations could not be used to cloud the issues. At this time we agreed to begin our nonviolent witness the day after the run-off.

This reveals that we did not move irresponsibly into direct action. We too wanted to see Mr. Connor defeated; so we went through postponement after postponement to aid in this community need. After this we felt that direct action could be delayed no longer.

You may well ask, "Why direct action? Why sit-ins, marches, etc.? Isn't negotiation a better path?" You are exactly right in your call for negotiation. Indeed, this is the purpose of direct action. Nonviolent direct action seeks to create such a crisis and establish such creative tension that a community that has constantly refused to negotiate is forced to confront the issue. It seeks so to dramatize the issue that it can no longer be ignored. I just referred to the creation of tension as a part of the work of the nonviolent resister. This may sound rather shocking. But I must confess that I am not afraid of the word tension. I have earnestly worked and preached against violent tension, but there is a type of constructive nonviolent tension that is necessary for growth. Just as Socrates felt that it was necessary to create a tension in the mind so that individuals could rise from the bondage of myths and half-truths to the unfettered realm of creative analysis and objective appraisal, we must see the need of having nonviolent gadflies to create the kind of tension in society that will help men to rise from the dark depths of prejudice and racism to the majestic heights of understanding and brotherhood. So the purpose of the direct action is to create a situation so crisis-packed that it will inevitably open the door to negotiation. We, therefore, concur with you in your call for negotiation. Too long has our beloved Southland been bogged down in the tragic attempt to live in monologue rather than dialogue.

One of the basic points in your statement is that our acts are untimely. Some have asked, "Why didn't you give the new administration time to act?" The only answer that I can give to this inquiry is that the new administration must be prodded about as much as the outgoing one before it acts. We will be sadly mistaken if we feel that the election of Mr. Boutwell will bring the millennium to Birmingham. While Mr. Boutwell is much more articulate and gentle than Mr. Connor, they are both segregationists, dedicated to the task of maintaining the status quo. The hope I see in Mr. Boutwell is that he will be reasonable enough to see the futility of massive resistance to desegregation. But he will not see this without pressure from the devotees of civil rights. My friends, I must say to you that we have not made a single gain in civil rights without determined legal and nonviolent pressure. History is the long and tragic story of the fact that privileged groups seldom give up their privileges voluntarily. Individuals may see the moral light and voluntarily give up their unjust posture; but as Reinhold Niebuhr has reminded us, groups are more immoral than individuals.

We know through painful experience that freedom is never voluntarily given by the oppressor; it must be demanded by the oppressed. Frankly, I have never yet engaged in a direct action movement that was "well-timed," according to the timetable of those who have not suffered unduly from the disease of segregation. For years now I have heard the words "Wait!" It rings in the ear of every Negro with a piercing familiarity. This "Wait" has almost always meant "Never." It has been a tranquilizing thalidomide, relieving the emotional stress for a moment, only to give birth to an ill-formed infant of frustration. We must come to see with the distinguished jurist of yesterday that "justice too long delayed is justice denied." We have waited for more than 340 years for our constitutional and God-given rights. The nations of Asia and Africa are moving with jet-like speed toward the goal of political independence, and we still creep at horse and buggy pace toward the gaining of a cup of coffee at the lunch counter. I guess it is easy for those who have never felt the stinging darts of segregation to say, "Wait." But when you have seen vicious mobs lynch your mothers and fathers at will and drown your sisters and brothers at whim; when you have seen hatefilled policemen curse, kick, brutalize and even kill your black brothers and sisters with impunity; when you see the vast majority of your twenty million Negro brothers smothering in an airtight cage of poverty in the midst of an affluent society; when you suddenly find your tongue twisted and your speech stammering as you seek to explain to your six-year-old daughter why she can't go to the public amusement park that has just been advertised on television, and see tears welling up in her little eyes when she is told that Funtown is closed to colored children, and see the depressing clouds of inferiority begin to form in her little mental sky, and see her begin to distort her little personality by unconsciously developing a bitterness toward white people; when you have to concoct an answer for a five-year-old son asking in agonizing pathos: "Daddy, why do white people treat colored people so mean?"; when you take a crosscountry drive and find it necessary to sleep night after night in the uncomfortable corners of your automobile because no motel will accept you; when you are humiliated day in and day out by nagging signs reading "white" and "colored"; when your first name becomes "nigger" and your middle name becomes "boy" (however old you are) and your last name becomes "John," and when your wife and mother are never given the respected title "Mrs."; when you are harried by day and haunted by night by the fact that you are a Negro, living constantly at tiptoe stance never quite knowing what to expect next, and plagued with inner fears and outer resentments; when you are forever fighting a degenerating sense of "nobodiness"; then you will understand why we find it difficult to wait. There comes a time when the cup of endurance runs over, and men are no longer willing to be plunged into an abyss of injustice where they experience the blackness of corroding despair. I hope, sirs, you can understand our legitimate and unavoidable impatience.

You express a great deal of anxiety over our willingness to break laws. This is certainly a legitimate concern. Since we so diligently urge people to obey the Supreme Court's decision of 1954 outlawing segregation in the public schools, it is rather strange and paradoxical to find us consciously breaking laws. One may well ask, "How can you advocate breaking some laws and obeying others?" The answer is found in the fact that there are two types of laws: there are *just* and there are *unjust* laws. I would agree with Saint Augustine that "An unjust law is no law at all."

Now what is the difference between the two? How does one determine when a law is just or unjust? A just law is a man-made code that squares with the moral law or the law of God. An unjust law is a code that is out of harmony with the moral law. To put it in the terms of Saint Thomas Aquinas, an unjust law is a human law that is not rooted in eternal and natural law. Any law that uplifts human personality is just. Any law that degrades human personality is unjust. All segregation statutes are unjust because segregation distorts the soul and damages the personality. It gives the segregator a false sense of superiority, and the segregated a false sense of inferiority. To use the words of Martin Buber, the great Jewish philosopher, segregation substitutes an "I-it" relationship for the "I-thou" relationship, and ends up relegating persons to the status of things. So segregation is not only politically, economically and sociologically unsound, but it is morally wrong and sinful. Paul Tillich has said that sin is separation. Isn't segregation an existential expression of man's tragic separation, an expression of his awful estrangement, his terrible sinfulness? So I can urge men to disobey segregation ordinances because they are morally wrong.

Let us turn to a more concrete example of just and unjust laws. An unjust law is a code that a majority inflicts on a minority that is not binding on itself. This is difference made legal. On the other hand a just law is a code that a majority compels a minority to follow that it is willing to follow itself. This is sameness made legal.

Let me give another explanation. An unjust law is a code inflicted upon a minority which that minority had no part in enacting or creating because they did not have the unhampered right to vote. Who can say that the legislature of Alabama which set up the segregation laws was democratically elected? Throughout the state of Alabama all types of conniving methods are used to prevent Negroes from becoming registered voters and there are some counties without a single Negro registered to vote despite the fact that the Negro constitutes a majority of the population. Can any law set up in such a state be considered democratically structured?

These are just a few examples of unjust and just laws. There are some instances when a law is just on its face and unjust in its application. For instance, I was arrested Friday on a charge of parading without permit. Now there is nothing wrong with an ordinance which requires a permit for a parade, but when the ordinance is used to preserve segregation and to deny citizens the First Amendment privilege of peaceful assembly and peaceful protest, then it becomes unjust.

I hope you can see the distinction I am trying to point out. In no sense do I advocate evading or defying the law as the rabid segregationist would do. This would lead to anarchy. One who breaks an unjust law must do it *openly, lovingly* (not hatefully as the white mothers did in New Orleans when they were seen on television screaming, "nigger, nigger, nigger"), and with a willingness to accept the penalty. I submit that an individual who breaks law that conscience tells him is unjust, and willingly accepts the penalty by staying in jail to arouse the conscience of the community over its injustice, is in reality expressing the very highest respect for law.

Of course, there is nothing new about this kind of civil disobedience. It was seen sublimely in the refusal of Shadrach, Meshach and Abednego to obey the laws of Nebuchadnezzar because a higher moral law was involved. It was practiced superbly by the early Christians who were willing to face hungry lions and the excruciating pain of chopping blocks, before submitting to certain unjust laws of the Roman Empire. To a degree academic freedom is a reality today because Socrates practiced civil disobedience.

We can never forget that everything Hitler did in Germany was "legal" and everything the Hungarian freedom fighters did in Hungary was "illegal." It was "illegal" to aid and comfort a Jew in Hitler's Germany. But I am sure that if I had lived in Germany during that time I would have aided and comforted my Jewish brothers even though it was illegal. If I lived in a Communist country today where certain principles dear to the Christian faith are suppressed, I believe I would openly advocate disobeying these anti-religious laws. I must make two honest confessions to you, my Christian and Jewish brothers. First, I must confess that over the last few years I have been gravely disappointed with the white moderate. I have almost reached the regrettable conclusion that the Negro's great stumbling block in the stride toward freedom is not the White Citizen's Counciler or the Ku Klux Klanner, but the white moderate who is more devoted to "order" than to justice; who prefers a negative peace which is the absence of tension to a positive peace which is the presence of justice; who constantly says, "I agree with you in the goal you seek, but I can't agree with your methods of direct action"; who paternalistically feels that he can set the timetable for another man's freedom; who lives by the myth of time and who constantly advised the Negro to wait until a "more convenient season." Shallow understanding from people of good will is more frustrating than absolute misunderstanding from people of ill will. Lukewarm acceptance is much more bewildering than outright rejection.

I had hoped that the white moderate would understand that law and order exist for the purpose of establishing justice, and that when they fail to do this they become dangerously structured dams that block the flow of social progress. I had hoped that the white moderate would understand that the present tension of the South is merely a necessary phase of the transition from an obnoxious negative peace, where the Negro passively accepted his unjust plight, to a substance-filled positive peace, where all men will respect the dignity and worth of human personality. Actually, we who engage in nonviolent direct action are not the creators of tension. We merely bring to the surface the hidden tension that is already alive. We bring it out in the open where it can be seen and dealt with. Like a boil that can never be cured as long as it is covered up but must be opened with all its pus-flowing ugliness to the natural medicines of air and light, injustice must likewise be exposed, with all of the tension its exposing creates, to the light of human conscience and the air of national opinion before it can be cured.

In your statement you asserted that our actions, even though peaceful, must be condemned because they precipitate violence. But can this assertion be logically made? Isn't this like condemning the robbed man because his possession of money precipitated the evil act of robbery? Isn't this like condemning Socrates because his unswerving commitment to truth and his philosophical delvings precipitated the misguided popular mind to make him drink the hemlock? Isn't this like condemning Jesus because His unique God-consciousness and never-ceasing devotion to his will precipitated the evil act of crucifixion? We must come to see, as federal courts have consistently affirmed, that it is immoral to urge an individual to withdraw his efforts to gain his basic constitutional rights because the quest precipitates violence. Society must protect the robbed and punish the robber.

I had also hoped that the white moderate would reject the myth of time. I received a letter this morning from a white brother in Texas which said: "All Christians know that the colored people will receive equal rights eventually, but it is possible that you are in too great of a religious hurry. It has taken Christianity almost two thousand years to accomplish what it has. The teachings of Christ take time to come to earth." All that is said here grows out of a tragic misconception of time. It is the strangely irrational notion that there is something in the very flow of time that will inevitably cure all ills. Actually time is neutral. It can be used either destructively or constructively. I am coming to feel that the people of ill will have used time much more effectively than the people of good will. We will have to repent in this generation not merely for the vitriolic words and actions of the bad people, but for the appalling silence of the good people. We must come to see that human progress never rolls in on wheels of inevitability. It comes through the tireless efforts and persistent work of men willing to be co-workers with God, and without this hard work time itself becomes an ally of the forces of social stagnation. We must use time creatively, and forever realize that the time is always ripe to do right. Now is the time to make real the promise of democracy, and transform our pending national elegy into a creative psalm of brotherhood. Now is the time to lift our national policy from the quicksand of racial injustice to the solid rock of human dignity.

You spoke of our activity in Birmingham as extreme. At first I was rather disappointed that fellow clergymen would see my nonviolent efforts as those of the extremist. I started thinking about the fact that I stand in the middle of two opposing forces in the Negro community. One is a force of complacency made up of Negroes who, as a result of long years of oppression, have been so completely drained of self-respect and a sense of "somebodiness" that they have adjusted to segregation, and, of a few Negroes in the middle class who, because of a degree of academic and economic security, and because at points they profit by segregation, have unconsciously become insensitive to the problems of the masses. The other force is one of bitterness and hatred, and comes perilously close to advocating violence. It is expressed in the various black nationalist groups that are springing up over the nation, the largest and best known being Elijah Muhammad's Muslim movement. This movement is nourished by the contemporary frustration over the continued existence of racial discrimination. It is made up of people who have lost faith in America, who have absolutely repudiated Christianity, and who have concluded that the white man is an incurable "devil." I have tried to stand between these two forces, saying that we need not follow the "donothingism" of the complacent or the hatred and despair of the black nationalist. There is the more excellent way of love and nonviolent protest. I'm grateful to God that, through the Negro church, the dimension of nonviolence entered our struggle. If this philosophy had not emerged, I am convinced that by now many streets of the South would be flowing with floods of blood. And I am further convinced that if our white brothers dismiss as "rabble-rousers" and "outside agitators" those of us who are working through the channels of nonviolent direct action and refuse to support our nonviolent efforts, millions of Negroes, out of frustration and despair, will seek solace and security in black nationalist ideologies, a development that will lead inevitably to a frightening racial nightmare.

Oppressed people cannot remain oppressed forever. The urge for freedom will eventually come. This is what happened to the American Negro. Something within has reminded him of his birthright of freedom; something without has reminded him that he can gain it. Consciously and unconsciously, he has been swept in by what the Germans call the *Zeitgeist,* and with his black brothers of Africa, and his brown and yellow brothers of Asia, South America and the Caribbean, he is moving with a sense of cosmic urgency toward the promised land of racial justice. Recognizing this vital urge that has engulfed the Negro community, one should readily understand public demonstrations. The Negro has many pent-up resentments and latent frustrations. He has to get them out. So let him march sometime; let him have his prayer pilgrimages to the city hall; understand why he must have sit-ins and freedom rides. If his repressed emotions do not come out in these nonviolent ways, they will come out in ominous expressions of violence. This is not a threat; it is a fact of history. So I have not said to my people "get rid of your discontent." But I have tried to say that this normal and healthy discontent can be channelized through the creative outlet of nonviolent direct action. Now this approach is being dismissed as extremist. I must admit that I was initially disappointed in being so categorized.

But as I continued to think about the matter I gradually gained a bit of satisfaction from being considered an extremist. Was not Jesus an extremist in love—"Love your enemies, bless them that curse you, pray for them that despitefully use you." Was not Amos an extremist for justice—"Let justice roll down like waters and righteousness like a mighty stream." Was not Paul an extremist for the gospel of Jesus Christ—"I bear in my body the marks of the Lord Jesus." Was not Martin Luther an extremist—"Here I stand; I can do none other so help me God." Was not John Bunyan an extremist—"I will stay in jail to the end of my days before I make a butchery of my conscience." Was not Abraham Lincoln an extremist—"This nation cannot survive half slave and half free." Was not Thomas Jefferson an extremist—"We hold these truths to be self-evident, that all men are created equal." So the question is not whether we will be extremist but what kind of extremist will we be. Will we be extremists for hate or will we be extremists for love? Will we be extremists for the preservation of injustice—or will we be extremists for the cause of justice? In that dramatic scene on Calvary's hill, three men were crucified. We must not forget that all three were crucified for the same crime—the crime of extremism. Two were extremists for immorality, and thusly fell below their environment. The other, Jesus Christ, was an extremist for love, truth and goodness, and thereby rose above his environment. So, after all, maybe the South, the nation and the world are in dire need of creative extremists.

I had hoped that the white moderate would see this. Maybe I was too optimistic. Maybe I expected too much. I guess I should have realized that few members of a race that has oppressed another race can understand or appreciate the deep groans and passionate yearnings of those that have been oppressed and still fewer have the vision to see that injustice must be rooted out by strong, persistent and determined action. I am thankful, however, that some of our white brothers have grasped the meaning of this social revolution and committed themselves to it. They are still all too small in quantity, but they are big in quality. Some like Ralph McGill, Lillian Smith, Harry Golden and James Dabbs have written about our struggle in eloquent, prophetic and understanding terms. Others have marched with us down nameless streets of the South. They have languished in filthy roach-infested jails, suffering the abuse and brutality of angry policemen who see them as "dirty nigger-lovers." They, unlike so many of their moderate brothers and sisters, have recognized the urgency of the moment and sensed the need for powerful "action" antidotes to combat the disease of segregation.

Let me rush on to mention my other disappointment. I have been so greatly disappointed with the white church and its leadership. Of course, there are some notable exceptions. I am not unmindful of the fact that each of you has taken some significant stands on this issue. I commend you, Rev. Stallings, for your Christian stance on this past Sunday, in welcoming Negroes to your worship service on a non-segregated basis. I commend the Catholic leaders of this state for integrating Springhill College several years ago.

But despite these notable exceptions, I must honestly reiterate that I have been disappointed with the church. I do not say that as one of the negative critics who can always find something wrong with the church. I say it as a minister of the gospel, who loves the church; who was nurtured in its bosom; who has been sustained by its spiritual blessings and who will remain true to it as long as the cord of life shall lengthen.

I had the strange feeling when I was suddenly catapulted into the leadership of the bus protest in Montgomery several years ago that we would have the support of the white church. I felt that the white ministers, priests and rabbis of the South would be some of our strongest allies. Instead, some have been outright opponents, refusing to understand the freedom movement and misrepresenting its leaders; all too many others have been more cautious than courageous and have remained silent behind the anesthetizing security of the stained-glass windows.

In spite of my shattered dreams of the past, I came to Birmingham with the hope that the white religious leadership of this community would see the justice of our cause, and with deep moral concern, serve as the channel through which our just grievances would get to the power structure. I had hoped that each of you would understand. But again I have been disappointed. I have heard numerous religious leaders of the South call upon their worshippers to comply with a desegregation decision because it is the *law,* but I have longed to hear white ministers say, "Follow this decree because integration is morally *right* and the Negro is your brother." In the midst of blatant injustices inflicted upon the Negro, I have watched white churches stand on the sideline and merely mouth pious irrelevancies and sanctimonious trivialities. In the midst of a mighty struggle to rid our nation of racial and economic injustice, I have heard so many ministers say, "Those are social issues with which the gospel has no real concern," and I have watched so many churches commit themselves to a completely otherworldly religion which made a strange distinction between body and soul, the sacred and the secular.

So here we are moving toward the exit of the twentieth century with a religious community largely adjusted to the status quo, standing as a taillight behind other community agencies rather than a headlight leading men to higher levels of justice.

I have traveled the length and breadth of Alabama, Mississippi and all the other southern states. On sweltering summer days and crisp autumn mornings I have looked at her beautiful churches with their lofty spires pointing heavenward. I have beheld the impressive outlay of her massive religious education buildings. Over and over again I have found myself asking: "What kind of people worship here? Who is their God? Where were their voices when the lips of Governor Barnett dripped with words of interposition and nullification? Where were they when Governor Wallace gave the clarion call for defiance and hatred? Where were their voices of support when tired, bruised and weary Negro men and women decided to rise from the dark dungeons of complacency to the bright hills of creative protest?"

Yes, these questions are still in my mind. In deep disappointment, I have wept over the laxity of the church. But be assured that my tears have been tears of love. There can be no deep disappointment where there is not deep love. Yes, I love the church; I love her sacred walls. How could I do otherwise? I am in a rather unique position of being the son, the grandson and the great-grandson of preachers. Yes, I see the church as the body of Christ. But, oh! How we have blemished and scarred that body through social neglect and fear of being nonconformists.

There was a time when the church was very powerful. It was during that period when the early Christians rejoiced when they were deemed worthy to suffer for what they believed. In those days the church was not merely a thermometer that recorded the ideas and principles of popular opinion; it was a thermostat that transformed the mores of society. Wherever the early Christians entered a town the power structure got disturbed and immediately sought to convict them for being "disturbers of the peace" and "outside agitators." But they went on with the conviction that they were "a colony of heaven," and had to obey God rather than man. They were small in number but big in commitment. They were too God-intoxicated to be "astronomically intimidated." They brought an end to such ancient evils as infanticide and gladiatorial contest.

Things are different now. The contemporary church is often a weak, ineffectual voice with an uncertain sound. It is so often the arch-supporter of the status quo. Far from being disturbed by the presence of the church, the power structure of the average community is consoled by the church's silent and often vocal sanction of things as they are.

But the judgment of God is upon the church as never before. If the church of today does not recapture the sacrificial spirit of the early church, it will lose its authentic ring, forfeit the loyalty of millions, and be dismissed as an irrelevant social club with no meaning for the twentieth century. I am meeting young people every day whose disappointment with the church has risen to outright disgust.

Maybe again, I have been too optimistic. Is organized religion too inextricably bound to the status quo to save our nation and the world? Maybe I must turn my faith to the inner spiritual church, the church within the church, as the true *ecclesia* and the hope of the world. But again I am thankful to God that some noble souls from the ranks of organized religion have broken loose from the paralyzing chains of conformity and joined us as active partners in the struggle for freedom. They have left their secure congregations and walked the streets of Albany, Georgia, with us. They have gone through the highways of the South on tortuous rides for freedom. Yes, they have gone to jail with us. Some have been kicked out of their churches, and lost support of their bishops and fellow ministers. But they have gone with the faith that right defeated is stronger than evil triumphant. These men have been the leaven in the lump of the race. Their witness has been the spiritual salt that has preserved the true meaning of the gospel in these troubled times. They have carved a tunnel of hope through the dark mountain of disappointment.

I hope the church as a whole will meet the challenge of this decisive hour. But even if the church does not come to the aid of justice, I have no despair about the future. I have no fear about the outcome of our struggle in Birmingham, even if our motives are presently misunderstood. We will reach the goal of freedom in Birmingham and all over the nation, because the goal of America is freedom. Abused and scorned though we may be, our destiny is tied up with the destiny of America. Before the Pilgrims landed at Plymouth we were here. Before the pen of Jefferson etched across the pages of history the majestic words of the Declaration of Independence, we were here. For more than two centuries our foreparents labored in this country without wages; they made cotton king; and they built the homes of their masters in the midst of brutal injustice and shameful humiliation—and yet out of a bottomless vitality they continued to thrive and develop. If the inexpressible cruelties of slavery could not stop us, the opposition we now face will surely fail. We will win our freedom because the sacred heritage of our nation and the eternal will of God are embodied in our echoing demands.

I must close now. But before closing I am impelled to mention one other point in your statement that troubled me profoundly. You warmly commended the Birmingham police force for keeping "order" and "preventing violence." I don't believe you would have so warmly commended the police force if you had seen its angry violent dogs literally biting six unarmed, nonviolent Negroes. I don't believe you would so quickly commend the policemen if you would observe their ugly and inhuman treatment of Negroes here in the city jail; if you would watch them push and curse old Negro women and young Negro girls; if you would see them slap and kick old Negro men and young boys; if you will observe them, as they did on two occasions, refuse to give us food because we wanted to sing our grace together. I'm sorry that I can't join you in your praise for the police department.

It is true that they have been rather disciplined in their public handling of the demonstrators. In this sense they have been rather publicly "nonviolent." But for what purpose? To preserve the evil system of segregation. Over the last few years I have consistently preached that nonviolence demands that the means we use must be as pure as the ends we seek. So I have tried to make it clear that it is wrong to use immoral means to attain moral ends. But now I must affirm that it is just as wrong, or even more so, to use moral means to preserve immoral ends. Maybe Mr. Connor and his policemen have been rather publicly nonviolent, as Chief Pritchett was in Albany, Georgia, but they have used the moral means of nonviolence to maintain the immoral end of flagrant racial injustice. T. S. Eliot has said that there is no greater treason than to do the right deed for the wrong reason.

I wish you had commended the Negro sit-inners and demonstrators of Birmingham for their sublime courage, their willingness to suffer and their amazing discipline in the midst of the most inhuman provocation. One day the South will recognize its real heroes. They will be the James Merediths, courageously and with a majestic sense of purpose facing jeering and hostile mobs and the agonizing loneliness that characterizes the life of the pioneer. They will be old, oppressed, battered Negro women, symbolized in a seventy-two-year-old woman of Montgomery, Alabama, who rose up with a sense of dignity and with her people decided not to ride the segregated buses, and responded to one who inquired about her tiredness with ungrammatical profundity: "My feet is tired, but my soul is rested." They will be the young high school and college students, young ministers of the gospel and a host of their elders courageously and nonviolently sitting-in at lunch counters and willingly going to jail for conscience's sake. One day the South will know that when these disinherited children of God sat down at lunch counters they were in reality standing up for the best in the American dream and the most sacred values in our Judeo-Christian heritage, and thusly, carrying our whole nation back to those great walls of democracy which were dug deep by the Founding Fathers in the formulation of the Constitution and the Declaration of Independence.

Never before have I written a letter this long (or should I say a book?). I'm afraid that it is much too long to take your precious time. I can assure you that it would have been much shorter if I had been writing from a comfortable desk, but what else is there to do when you are alone for days in the dull monotony of a narrow jail cell other than write long letters, think strange thoughts, and pray long prayers?

If I have said anything in this letter that is an overstatement of the truth and is indicative of an unreasonable impatience, I beg you to forgive me. If I have said anything in this letter that is an understatement of the truth and is indicative of my having a patience that makes me patient with anything less than brotherhood, I beg God to forgive me.

I hope this letter finds you strong in the faith. I also hope that circumstances will soon make it possible for me to meet each of you, not as an integrationist or a civil rights leader, but as a fellow clergyman and a Christian brother. Let us all hope that the dark clouds of racial prejudice will soon pass away and the deep fog of misunderstanding will be lifted from our fear-drenched communities and in some not too distant tomorrow the radiant stars of love and brotherhood will shine over our great nation with all of their scintillating beauty.

Yours for the cause of Peace and Brotherhood, Martin Luther King, Jr.

STUDY QUESTIONS

1. What is civil disobedience?
2. How does civil disobedience differ from mere lawbreaking?
3. Is every unjust law an appropriate target for civil disobedience?
4. What is the connection, if any, between Dr. King's religious commitments and his political actions?

Crito

𝒜

PLATO

The *Crito*, probably written about the time of the *Defence of Socrates*, relates a conversation Socrates has in prison while awaiting death. His lifelong friend Crito urges Socrates to run away, assuring him that his rescue can be arranged. Socrates refuses to try to escape, arguing that he is morally obligated to submit to the sentence of the Court, for he accepts its authority and does not wish to bring the system of laws into disrepute.

A much-discussed issue is whether the view Socrates adopts in the *Crito* coheres with the opinions he espouses in his *Defence*. As our translator, David Gallop, explains the apparent inconsistency:

> To some readers the positions adopted by Socrates in the two works have seemed utterly opposed. In the *Defence* he comes across as a champion of intellectual liberty, an individualist bravely defying the conservative Athenian establishment; whereas in the *Crito* he appears to be advocating the most abject submission of the citizen to state authority.

Gallop believes the supposed conflict is illusory, and many commentators agree. Yet they have not reached consensus as to how the reconciliation is to be achieved. I have a suggestion to offer but urge that you proceed now to the *Crito* and return here after finishing it.

The notes are the translator's. The Index of Names he prepared can be found at the end of the *Defence of Socrates* in Part 1.

In my view the key to recognizing the consistency of Socrates' position is found near the end of the dialogue, where a distinction is drawn, in essence, between unjust laws and unjust application of just laws. Socrates believes his fellow citizens decided his case wrongly, but he accepts the fairness of the laws under which he was tried and convicted. If he believed the laws themselves were unfair, he would break them. As he says in his *Defence*, were a law to be passed banning the study of philosophy, he would disobey it. But he will not evade his death sentence, for he "has been treated unjustly not by us Laws, but by human beings. . . ."

Whether you accept this analysis, you can see why the life of Socrates has so fascinated subsequent generations. He embodies the spirit of philosophical inquiry and the ideal of intellectual integrity.

SOCRATES: Why have you come at this hour, Crito? It's still very early, isn't it?

CRITO: Yes, very.

SOCRATES: About what time?

CRITO: Just before daybreak.

SOCRATES: I'm surprised the prison-warder was willing to answer the door.

CRITO: He knows me by now, Socrates, because I come and go here so often; and besides, I've done him a small favour.

SOCRATES: Have you just arrived, or have you been here for a while?

CRITO: For quite a while.

SOCRATES: Then why didn't you wake me up right away instead of sitting by me in silence?

CRITO: Well *of course* I didn't wake you, Socrates! I only wish I weren't so sleepless and wretched myself. I've been marvelling all this time as I saw how peacefully you were sleeping, and I deliberately kept from waking you, so that you could pass the time as peacefully as possible. I've often admired your disposition in the past, in fact all your life; but more than ever in your present plight, you bear it so easily and patiently.

SOCRATES: Well, Crito, it really would be tiresome for a man of my age to get upset if the time has come when he must end his life.

CRITO: And yet others of your age, Socrates, are overtaken by similar troubles, but their age brings them no relief from being upset at the fate which faces them.

SOCRATES: That's true. But tell me, why *have* you come so early?

CRITO: I bring painful news, Socrates—not painful for you, I suppose, but painful and hard for me and all your friends—and hardest of all for me to bear, I think.

SOCRATES: What news is that? Is it that the ship has come back from Delos,[1] the one on whose return I must die?

CRITO: Well no, it hasn't arrived yet, but I think it will get here today, judging from reports of people who've come from Sunium,[2] where they disembarked. That makes it obvious that it will get here today; and so tomorrow, Socrates, you will have to end your life.

SOCRATES: Well, may that be for the best, Crito. If it so please the gods, so be it. All the same, I don't think it will get here today.

CRITO: What makes you think that?

SOCRATES: I'll tell you. You see, I am to die on the day after the ship arrives, am I not?

CRITO: At least that's what the authorities say.

SOCRATES: Then I don't think it will get here on the day that is just dawning, but on the next one. I infer that from a certain dream I had in the night—a short time ago, so it may be just as well that you didn't wake me.

CRITO: And what was your dream?

SOCRATES: I dreamt that a lovely, handsome woman approached me, robed in white. She called me and said: "Socrates,

Thou shalt reach fertile Phthia upon the third day."[3]

CRITO: What a curious dream, Socrates.

SOCRATES: Yet its meaning is clear, I think, Crito.

CRITO: All too clear, it would seem. But please, Socrates, my dear friend, there is still time to take my advice, and make your escape—because if you die, I shall suffer more than one misfortune: not only shall I lose such a friend as I'll never find again, but it will look to many people, who hardly know you or me, as if I'd abandoned you—since I could have rescued you if I'd been willing to put up the money. And yet what could be more shameful than a reputation for valuing money more highly than friends? Most people won't believe that it was you who refused to leave this place yourself, despite our urging you to do so.

SOCRATES: But why should we care so much, my good Crito, about what most people believe? All the most capable people, whom we should take more seriously, will think the matter has been handled exactly as it has been.

CRITO: Yet surely, Socrates, you can see that one must heed popular opinion too. Your present plight shows by itself that the populace can inflict not the least of evils, but just about the worst, if someone has been slandered in their presence.

SOCRATES: Ah Crito, if only the populace *could* inflict the worst of evils! Then they would also be capable of providing the greatest of goods, and a fine thing that would be. But the fact is that they can do neither: they are unable to give anyone understanding or lack of it, no matter what they do.

CRITO: Well, if you say so. But tell me this, Socrates: can it be that you are worried for me and your other friends, in case the blackmailers[4] give us trouble, if you escape, for having smuggled you out of here? Are you worried that we might be forced to forfeit all our property as well, or pay heavy fines, or even incur some further penalty? If you're afraid of anything like that, put it out of your mind. In rescuing you we are surely justified in taking that risk, or even worse if need be. Come on, listen to me and do as I say.

SOCRATES: Yes, those risks do worry me, Crito—amongst many others.

CRITO: Then put those fears aside—because no great sum is needed to pay people who are willing to rescue you and get you out of here. Besides, you can surely see that those blackmailers are cheap, and it wouldn't take much to buy them off. My own means are available to you and would be ample, I'm sure. Then again, even if—out of concern on my behalf—you think you shouldn't be spending my money, there are visitors here who are ready to spend theirs. One of them, Simmias from Thebes, has actually brought enough money for this very purpose, while Cebes and quite a number of others are also prepared to contribute. So, as I say, you shouldn't hesitate to save yourself on account of those fears.

And don't let it trouble you, as you were saying in court, that you wouldn't know what to do with yourself if you went into exile. There will be people to welcome you anywhere else you may go: if you want to go to Thessaly,[5] I have friends there who will make much of you and give you safe refuge, so that no one from anywhere in Thessaly will trouble you.

Next, Socrates, I don't think that what you propose—giving yourself up, when you could be rescued—is even just. You are actually hastening to bring upon yourself just the sorts of thing which your enemies would hasten to bring upon you—indeed, they have done so—in their wish to destroy you.

What's more, I think you're betraying those sons of yours. You will be deserting them, if you go off when you could be raising and educating them: as far as you're concerned, they will fare as best they may. In all likelihood, they'll meet the sort of fate which usually befalls orphans once they've lost their parents. Surely, one should either not have children at all, or else see the toil and trouble of their upbringing and education through to the end; yet you seem to me to prefer the easiest path. One should rather choose the path that a good and resolute man would choose, particularly if one professes to cultivate goodness all one's life. Frankly, I'm ashamed for you and for us, your friends: it may appear that this whole predicament of yours has been handled with a certain feebleness on our part. What with the bringing of your case to court when that could have been avoided, the actual conduct of the trial, and now, to crown it all, this absurd outcome of the business, it may seem that the problem has eluded us through some fault or feebleness on our part—in that we failed to save you, and you failed to save yourself, when that was quite possible and feasible, if we had been any use at all.

Make sure, Socrates, that all this doesn't turn out badly, and a disgrace to you as well as us. Come now, form a plan—or rather, don't even plan, because the time for that is past, and only a single plan remains. Everything needs to be carried out during the coming night; and if we go on waiting around, it won't be possible or feasible any longer. Come on, Socrates, do all you can to take my advice, and do exactly what I say.

SOCRATES: My dear Crito, your zeal will be invaluable if it should have right on its side; but otherwise, the greater it is, the harder it makes matters. We must therefore consider whether or not the course you urge should be followed—because it is in my nature, not just now for the first time but always, to follow nothing within me but the principle which appears to me, upon reflection, to be best.

I cannot now reject the very principles that I previously adopted, just because this fate has overtaken me; rather, they appear to me much the same as ever, and I respect and honour the same ones that I did before. If we cannot find better ones to maintain in the present situation, you can be sure that I won't agree with you—not even if the power of the populace threatens us, like children, with more bogeymen than it does now, by visiting us with imprisonment, execution, or confiscation of property.

What, then, is the most reasonable way to consider the matter? Suppose we first take up the point you make about what people will think. Was it always an acceptable principle that one should pay heed to some opinions but not to others, or was it not? Or was it acceptable before I had to die, while now it is exposed as an idle assertion made for the sake of talk, when it is really childish nonsense? For my part, Crito, I'm eager to look into this together with you, to see whether the principle is to be viewed any differently, or in the same way, now that I'm in this position, and whether we should disregard or follow it.

As I recall, the following principle always used to be affirmed by people who thought they were talking sense: the principle, as I was just saying, that one should have a high regard for some opinions held by human beings, but not for others. Come now, Crito: don't you think that was a good principle? I ask because you are not, in all foreseeable likelihood, going to die tomorrow, and my present trouble shouldn't impair your judgement. Consider, then: don't you think it a good principle, that one shouldn't respect all human opinions, but only some and not others; or, again, that one shouldn't respect everyone's opinions, but those of some people, and not those of others? What do you say? Isn't that a good principle?

CRITO: It is.

SOCRATES: And one should respect the good ones, but not the bad ones?

CRITO: Yes.

SOCRATES: And good ones are those of people with understanding, whereas bad ones are those of people without it?

CRITO: Of course.

SOCRATES: Now then, once again, how were such points established? When a man is in training, and concentrating upon that, does he pay heed to the praise or censure or opinion of each and every man, or only to those of the individual who happens to be his doctor or trainer?

CRITO: Only to that individual's.

SOCRATES: Then he should fear the censures, and welcome the praises of that individual, but not those of most people.

CRITO: Obviously.

SOCRATES: So he must base his actions and exercises, his eating and drinking, upon the opinion of the individual, the expert supervisor, rather than upon everyone else's.

CRITO: True.

SOCRATES: Very well. If he disobeys that individual and disregards his opinion and his praises, but respects those of most people, who are ignorant, he'll suffer harm, won't he?

CRITO: Of course.

SOCRATES: And what is that harm? What does it affect? What element within the disobedient man?

CRITO: Obviously, it affects his body, because that's what it spoils.

SOCRATES: A good answer. And in other fields too, Crito—we needn't go through them all, but they surely include matters of just and unjust, honourable and dishonourable, good and bad, the subjects of our present deliberation—is it the opinion of most people that we should follow and fear, or is it that of the individual authority—assuming that some expert exists who should be respected and feared above all others? If we don't follow that person, won't we corrupt and impair the element which (as we agreed) is made better by what is just, but is spoilt by what is unjust? Or is there nothing in all that?

CRITO: I accept it myself, Socrates.

SOCRATES: Well now, if we spoil the part of us that is improved by what is healthy but corrupted by what is unhealthy, because it is not expert opinion that we are following, are our lives worth living once it has been corrupted? The part in question is, of course, the body, isn't it?

CRITO: Yes.

SOCRATES: And are our lives worth living with a poor or corrupted body?

CRITO: Definitely not.

SOCRATES: Well then, are they worth living if the element which is impaired by what is unjust and benefited by what is just has been corrupted? Or do we consider the element to which justice or injustice belongs, whichever part of us it is, to be of less value than the body?

CRITO: By no means.

SOCRATES: On the contrary, it is more precious?

CRITO: Far more.

SOCRATES: Then, my good friend, we shouldn't care all that much about what the populace will say of us, but about what the expert on matters of justice and injustice will say, the individual authority, or Truth. In the first place, then, your proposal that we should care about popular opinion regarding just, honourable, or good actions, and their opposites, is mistaken.

"Even so," someone might say, "the populace has the power to put us to death."

CRITO: *That's* certainly clear enough; one might say that, Socrates.

SOCRATES: You're right. But the principle we've rehearsed, my dear friend, still remains as true as it was before—for me at any rate. And now consider this further one, to see whether or not it still holds good for us. We should attach the highest value, shouldn't we, not to living, but to living well?

CRITO: Why yes, that still holds.

SOCRATES: And living well is the same as living honourably or justly? Does that still hold or not?

CRITO: Yes, it does.

SOCRATES: Then in the light of those admissions, we must ask the following question: is it just, or is it not, for me to try to get out of here, when Athenian authorities are unwilling to release me? Then, if it does seem just, let us attempt it; but if it doesn't, let us abandon the idea.

As for the questions you raise about expenses and reputation and bringing up children, I suspect they are the concerns of those who cheerfully put people to death, and would bring them back to life if they could, without any intelligence, namely, the populace. For us, however, because our principle so demands, there is no other question to ask except the one we just raised: shall we be acting justly—we who are rescued as well as the rescuers themselves—if we pay money and do favours to those who would get me out of here? Or shall we in truth be acting unjustly if we do all those things? And if it is clear that we shall be acting unjustly in taking that course, then the question whether we shall have to die through standing firm and holding our peace, or suffer in any other way, ought not to weigh with us in comparison with acting unjustly.

CRITO: I think that's finely *said*, Socrates; but do please consider what we should *do*.

SOCRATES: Let's examine that question together, dear friend; and if you have objections to anything I say, please raise them, and I'll listen to you— otherwise, good fellow, it's time to stop telling me, again and again, that I should leave here against the will of Athens. You see, I set great store upon persuading you as to my course of action, and not acting against your will. Come now, just consider whether you find the starting-point of our inquiry acceptable, and try to answer my questions according to your real beliefs.

CRITO: All right, I'll try.

SOCRATES: Do we maintain that people should on no account whatever do injustice willingly? Or may it be done in some circumstances but not in others? Is acting unjustly in no way good or honourable, as we frequently agreed in the past? Or have all those former agreements been jettisoned during these last few days? Can it be, Crito, that men of our age have long failed to notice, as we earnestly conversed with each other, that we ourselves were no better than children? Or is what we then used to say true above all else? Whether most people say so or not, and whether we must be treated more harshly or more leniently than at present, isn't it a fact, all the same, that acting unjustly is utterly bad and shameful for the agent? Yes or no?

CRITO: Yes.

SOCRATES: So one must not act unjustly at all.

CRITO: Absolutely not.

SOCRATES: Then, even if one is unjustly treated, one should not return injustice, as most people believe—given that one should act not unjustly at all.

CRITO: Apparently not.

SOCRATES: Well now, Crito, should one ever ill-treat anybody or not?

CRITO: Surely not, Socrates.

SOCRATES: And again, when one suffers ill-treatment, is it just to return it, as most people maintain, or isn't it?

CRITO: It is not just at all.

SOCRATES: Because there's no difference, I take it, between ill-treating people and treating them unjustly.

CRITO: Correct.

SOCRATES: Then one shouldn't return injustice or ill-treatment to any human being, no matter how one may be treated by that person. And in making those admissions, Crito, watch out that you're not agreeing to anything contrary to your real beliefs. I say that, because I realize that the belief is held by few people, and always will be. Those who hold it share no common counsel with those who don't; but each group is bound to regard the other with contempt when they observe one another's decisions. You too, therefore, should consider very carefully whether you share that belief with me, and whether we may begin our deliberations from the following premise: neither doing nor returning injustice is ever right, nor should one who is ill-treated defend himself by retaliation. Do you agree? Or do you dissent and not share my belief in that premise? I've long been of that opinion myself, and I still am now; but if you've formed any different view, say so, and explain it. If you stand by our former view, however, then listen to my next point.

CRITO: Well, I do stand by it and share that view, so go ahead.

SOCRATES: All right, I'll make my next point—or rather, ask a question. Should the things one agrees with someone else be done, provided they are just, or should one cheat?

CRITO: They should be done.

SOCRATES: Then consider what follows. If we leave this place without having persuaded our city, are we or are we not ill-treating certain people, indeed people whom we ought least of all to be ill-treating? And would we be abiding by the things we agreed, those things being just, or not?

CRITO: I can't answer your question, Socrates, because I don't understand it.

SOCRATES: Well, look at it this way. Suppose we were on the point of running away from here, or whatever else one should call it. Then the Laws, or the State of Athens, might come and confront us, and they might speak as follows:

"Please tell us, Socrates, what do you have in mind? With this action you are attempting, do you intend anything short of destroying us, the Laws and the city as a whole, to the best of your ability? Do you think that a city can still exist without being overturned, if the legal judgments rendered within it possess no force, but are nullified or invalidated by individuals?"

What shall we say, Crito, in answer to that and other such questions? Because somebody, particularly a legal advocate,[6] might say a great deal on behalf of the law that is being invalidated here, the one requiring that judgments, once rendered, shall have authority. Shall we tell them: "Yes, that is our intention, because the city was treating us unjustly, by not judging our case correctly"? Is that to be our answer, or what?

CRITO: Indeed it is, Socrates.

SOCRATES: And what if the Laws say: "And was that also part of the agreement between you and us, Socrates? Or did you agree to abide by whatever judgments the city rendered?"

Then, if we were surprised by their words, perhaps they might say: "Don't be surprised at what we are saying, Socrates, but answer us, seeing that you like to use question-and-answer. What complaint, pray, do you have against the city and ourselves, that you should now attempt to destroy us? In the first place, was it not we who gave you birth? Did your father not marry your mother and beget you under our auspices? So will you inform those of us here who regulate marriages whether you have any criticism of them as poorly framed?"

"No, I have none," I should say.

"Well then, what of the laws dealing with children's upbringing and education, under which you were educated yourself? Did those of us Laws who are in charge of that area not give proper direction, when they required your father to educate you in the arts and physical training?"[7]

"They did," I should say.

"Very good. In view of your birth, upbringing, and education, can you deny, first, that you belong to us as our offspring and slave, as your forebears also did? And if so, do you imagine that you are on equal terms with us in regard to what is just, and that whatever treatment we may accord to you, it is just for you to do the same thing back to us? You weren't on equal terms with your father, or your master (assuming you had one), making it just for you to return the treatment you received—answering back when you were scolded, or striking back when you were struck, or doing many other things of the same sort. Will you then have licence against your fatherland and its Laws, if we try to destroy you, in the belief that that is just? Will you try to destroy us in return, to the best of your ability? And will you claim that in doing so you are acting justly, you who are genuinely exercised about goodness? Or are you, in your wisdom, unaware that, in comparison with your mother and father and all your other forebears, your fatherland is more precious and venerable, more sacred and held in higher esteem among gods, as well as among human beings who have any sense; and that you should revere your fatherland, deferring to it and appeasing it when it is angry, more than your own father? You must either persuade it, or else do whatever it commands; and if it ordains that you must submit to certain treatment, then you must hold your peace and submit to it: whether that means being beaten or put in bonds, or whether it leads you into war to be wounded or killed, you must act accordingly, and that is what is just; you must neither give way nor retreat, nor leave your position; rather, in warfare, in court, and everywhere else, you must do whatever your city or fatherland commands, or else persuade it as to what is truly just; and if it is sinful to use violence against your mother or father, it is far more so to use it against your fatherland."

What shall we say to that, Crito? That the Laws are right or not?

CRITO: I think they are.

SOCRATES: "Consider then, Socrates," the Laws might go on, "whether the following is also true: in your present undertaking you are not proposing to treat us justly. We gave you birth, upbringing, and education, and a share in all the benefits we could provide for you along with all your fellow citizens. Nevertheless, we proclaim, by the formal granting of permission, that any Athenian who wishes, once he has been admitted to adult status,[8] and has observed the conduct of city business and ourselves, the Laws, may—if he is dissatisfied with us—go wherever he pleases and take his property. Not one of us Laws hinders or forbids that: whether any of you wishes to emigrate to a colony, or to go and live as an alien elsewhere, he may go wherever he pleases and keep his property, if we and the city fail to satisfy him.

"We do say, however, that if any of you remains here after he has observed the system by which we dispense justice and otherwise manage our city, then he has agreed with us by his conduct to obey whatever orders we give him. And thus we claim that anyone who fails to obey is guilty on three counts: he disobeys us as his parents; he disobeys those who nurtured him; and after agreeing to obey us he neither obeys nor persuades us if we are doing anything amiss, even though we offer him a choice, and do not harshly insist that he must do whatever we command. Instead, we give him two options: he must either persuade us or else do as we say; yet he does neither. Those are the charges, Socrates, to which we say you too will be liable if you carry out your intention; and among Athenians, you will be not the least liable, but one of the most."

And if I were to say, "How so?" perhaps they could fairly reproach me, observing that I am actually among those Athenians who have made that agreement with them most emphatically.

"Socrates," they would say, "we have every indication that you were content with us, as well as with our city, because you would never have stayed home here, more than is normal for all other Athenians, unless you were abnormally content. You never left our city for a festival—except once to go to the Isthmus[9]—nor did you go elsewhere for other purposes, apart from military service. You never travelled abroad, as other people do; nor were you eager for acquaintance with a different city or different laws: we and our city sufficed for you. Thus, you emphatically opted for us, and agreed to be a citizen on our terms. In particular, you fathered children in our city, which would suggest that you were content with it.

"Moreover, during your actual trial it was open to you, had you wished, to propose exile as your penalty; thus, what you are now attempting to do without the city's consent, you could then have done with it. On that occasion, you kept priding yourself that it would not trouble you if you had to die: you would choose death ahead of exile, so you said. Yet now you dishonour those words, and show no regard for us, the Laws, in your effort to destroy us. You are acting as the meanest slave would act, by trying to run away in spite of those compacts and agreements you made with us, whereby you agreed to be a citizen on our terms.

"First, then, answer us this question: are we right in claiming that you agreed, by your conduct if not verbally, that you would be a citizen on our terms? Or is that untrue?"

What shall we say in reply to that, Crito? Mustn't we agree?

CRITO: We must, Socrates.

SOCRATES: "Then what does your action amount to," they would say, "except breaking the compacts and agreements you made with us? By your own admission, you were not coerced or tricked into making them, or forced to reach a decision in a short time: you had seventy years in which it was open to you to leave if you were not happy with us, or if you thought those agreements unfair. Yet you preferred neither Lacedaemon nor Crete[10]—places you often say are well governed—nor any other Greek or foreign city: in fact, you went abroad less often than the lame and the blind or other cripples. Obviously, then, amongst Athenians you were exceptionally content with our city and with us, its Laws—because who would care for a city apart from its laws? Won't you, then, abide by your agreements now? Yes you will, if you listen to us, Socrates; and then at least you won't make yourself an object of derision by leaving the city.

"Just consider: if you break those agreements, and commit any of those offences, what good will you do yourself or those friends of yours? Your friends, pretty obviously, will risk being exiled themselves, as well as being disenfranchised or losing their property. As for you, first of all, if you go to one of the nearest cities, Thebes or Megara[11]—they are both well governed—you will arrive as an enemy of their political systems, Socrates: all who are concerned for their own cities will look askance at you, regarding you as a subverter of laws. You will also confirm your jurors in their judgment, making them think they decided your case correctly: any subverter of laws, presumably, might well be thought to be a corrupter of young, unthinking people.

"Will you, then, avoid the best-governed cities and the most respectable of men? And if so, will your life be worth living? Or will you associate with those people, and be shameless enough to converse with them? And what will you say to them, Socrates? The things you used to say here, that goodness and justice are most precious to mankind, along with institutions and laws? Don't you think that the predicament of Socrates will cut an ugly figure? Surely you must.

"Or will you take leave of those spots, and go to stay with those friends of Crito's up in Thessaly? That, of course, is a region of the utmost disorder and licence; so perhaps they would enjoy hearing from you about your comical escape from gaol, when you dressed up in some outfit, wore a leather jerkin or some other runaway's garb, and altered your appearance. Will no one observe that you, an old man with probably only a short time left to live, had the nerve to cling so greedily to life by violating the most important laws? Perhaps not, so long as you don't trouble anyone. Otherwise, Socrates, you will hear a great deal to your own discredit. You will live as every person's toady and lackey; and what will you be doing—apart from living it up in Thessaly, as if you had travelled all the way to Thessaly to have dinner? As for those principles of yours about justice and goodness in general—tell us, where will they be then?

"Well then, is it for your children's sake that you wish to live, in order to bring them up and give them an education? How so? Will you bring them up and educate them by taking them off to Thessaly and making foreigners of them, so that they may gain that advantage too? Or if, instead of that, they are brought up here, will they be better brought up and educated just because you are alive, if you are not with them? Yes, you may say, because those friends of yours will take care of them. Then will they take care of them if you travel to Thessaly, but not take care of them if you travel to Hades? Surely if those professing to be your friends are of any use at all, you must believe that they will.

"No, Socrates, listen to us, your own nurturers: do not place a higher value upon children, upon life, or upon anything else, than upon what is just, so that when you leave for Hades, this may be your whole defence before the authorities there: to take that course seems neither better nor more just or holy, for you or for any of your friends here in this world. Nor will it be better for you when you reach the next. As things stand, you will leave this world (if you do) as one who has been treated unjustly not by us Laws, but by human beings; whereas if you go into exile, thereby shamefully returning injustice for injustice and ill-treatment for ill-treatment, breaking the agreements and compacts you made with us, and inflicting harm upon the people you should least harm—yourself, your friends, your fatherland, and ourselves—then we shall be angry with you in your lifetime; and our brother Laws in Hades will not receive you kindly there, knowing that you tried, to the best of your ability, to destroy us too. Come then, do not let Crito persuade you to take his advice rather than ours."

That, Crito, my dear comrade, is what I seem to hear them saying, I do assure you. I am like the Corybantic revellers[12] who think they are still hearing the music of pipes: the sound of those arguments is ringing loudly in my head, and makes me unable to hear the others. As far as these present thoughts of mine go, then, you may be sure that if you object to them, you will plead in vain. None the less, if you think you will do any good, speak up.

CRITO: No, Socrates, I've nothing to say.

SOCRATES: Then let it be, Crito, and let us act accordingly, because that is the direction in which God is guiding us.

NOTES

1. The small island of Delos was sacred to the god Apollo. A mission sailed there annually from Athens to commemorate her deliverance by Theseus from servitude to King Minos of Crete. No executions could be carried out in Athens until the sacred ship returned.
2. The headland at the south-eastern extremity of Attica, about 50 kilometres from Athens. The winds were unfavourable at the time; so the ship may have been taking shelter at Sunium when the travellers left it there.
3. In Homer's *Iliad* (ix. 363) Achilles says, "on the third day I may return to fertile Phthia," meaning that he can get home in three days.
4. Athens had no public prosecutors. Prosecutions were undertaken by private citizens, who sometimes threatened legal action for personal, political, or financial gain.
5. The region of northern Greece, lying 200–300 kilometres north-west of Attica.
6. It was customary in Athens to appoint a public advocate to defend laws which it was proposed to abrogate.
7. The standard components of traditional Athenian education.
8. Admission to Athenian citizenship was not automatic, but required formal registration by males at the age of 17 or 18, with proof of age and parental citizenship.
9. The Isthmus was the strip of land linking the Peloponnese with the rest of Greece. Socrates may have attended the Isthmian Games, which were held every two years at Corinth.
10. Lacedaemon was the official name for the territory of Sparta. Sparta and Crete were both authoritarian and "closed" societies, which forbade their citizens to live abroad.
11. Thebes was the chief city in Boeotia, the region lying to the north-west of Attica; Megara was on the Isthmus. Both lay within easy reach of Athens.
12. The Corybantes performed orgiastic rites and dances to the sound of pipe and drum music. Their music sometimes induced a state of frenzy in emotionally disordered people, which was followed by a deep sleep from which the patients awoke cured.

STUDY QUESTIONS

1. According to Socrates, must one heed popular opinion about moral matters?
2. If you reside in a country, do you implicitly agree to abide by its laws?
3. Does Socrates accept the fairness of the laws under which he was tried and convicted?
4. Do you believe Socrates would have been wrong to escape?

On Liberty

✦

JOHN STUART MILL

Bring to your mind an opinion so outrageous that it would be repudiated by any sensible person. Now suppose that stating this opinion openly would be an affront to the vast majority of listeners. Under such circumstances, why shouldn't the representatives of the people be empowered to pass a law banning the public expression of this foolishness, thus ensuring that no one is offended by it or tempted to repeat it?

One answer might be that the First Amendment to the Constitution of the United States prohibits any law abridging the freedom of speech. But if an opinion is wrongheaded and repugnant, why does it merit protection?

The most celebrated and eloquent reply is provided in John Stuart Mill's classic work, *On Liberty*. It is dedicated to his wife, Harriet Taylor, "the inspirer, and in part the author, of all that is best in my writings."

What is most surprising about Mill's presentation is that he defends an individual's free speech by appealing not to the majority's kindheartedness but to its own welfare. Yet how can it be in anyone's self-interest to allow blatantly false views to be expressed? Let us consider Mill's argument.

....

CHAPTER I

Introductory

The object of this essay is to assert one very simple principle, as entitled to govern absolutely the dealings of society with the individual in the way of compulsion and control, whether the means used be physical force in the form of legal penalties or the moral coercion of public opinion. That principle is that the sole end for which mankind are warranted, individually or collectively, in interfering with the liberty of action of any of their number is self-protection. That the only purpose for which power can be rightfully exercised over any member of a civilized community, against his will, is to prevent harm to others. His own good, either physical or moral, is not a sufficient warrant. He cannot rightfully be compelled to do or forbear because it will be better for him to do so, because it will make him happier, because, in the opinions of others, to do so would be wise or even right. These are good reasons for remonstrating with him, or reasoning with him, or persuading him, or entreating him, but not for compelling him or visiting him with any evil in case he do otherwise. To justify that, the conduct from which it is desired to deter

From *On Liberty* by John Stuart Mill (1859).

him must be calculated to produce evil to someone else. The only part of the conduct of anyone for which he is amenable to society is that which concerns others. In the part which merely concerns himself, his independence is, of right, absolute. Over himself, over his own body and mind, the individual is sovereign. . . .

This, then, is the appropriate region of human liberty. It comprises, first, the inward domain of consciousness, demanding liberty of conscience in the most comprehensive sense, liberty of thought and feeling, absolute freedom of opinion and sentiment on all subjects, practical or speculative, scientific, moral, or theological. The liberty of expressing and publishing opinions may seem to fall under a different principle, since it belongs to that part of the conduct of an individual which concerns other people, but, being almost of as much importance as the liberty of thought itself and resting in great part on the same reasons, is practically inseparable from it. Secondly, the principle requires liberty of tastes and pursuits, of framing the plan of our life to suit our own character, of doing as we like, subject to such consequences as may follow, without impediment from our fellow creatures, so long as what we do does not harm them, even though they should think our conduct foolish, perverse, or wrong. Thirdly, from this liberty of each individual follows the liberty, within the same limits, of combination among individuals; freedom to unite for any purpose not involving harm to others: the persons combining being supposed to be of full age and not forced or deceived.

No society in which these liberties are not, on the whole, respected is free, whatever may be its form of government; and none is completely free in which they do not exist absolute and unqualified. The only freedom which deserves the name is that of pursuing our own good in our own way, so long as we do not attempt to deprive others of theirs or impede their efforts to obtain it. Each is the proper guardian of his own health, whether bodily *or* mental and spiritual. Mankind are greater gainers by suffering each other to live as seems good to themselves than by compelling each to live as seems good to the rest. . . .

It will be convenient for the argument if, instead of at once entering upon the general thesis, we confine ourselves in the first instance to a single branch of it on which the principle here stated is, if not fully, yet to a certain point, recognized by the current opinions. This one branch is the Liberty of Thought, from which it is impossible to separate the cognate liberty of speaking and of writing. Although these liberties, to some considerable amount, form part of the political morality of all countries which profess religious toleration and free institutions, the grounds, both philosophical and practical, on which they rest are perhaps not so familiar to the general mind, nor so thoroughly appreciated by many, even of the leaders of opinion, as might have been expected. . . .

CHAPTER II

Of the Liberty of Thought and Discussion

The time, it is to be hoped, is gone by when any defense would be necessary of the "liberty of the press" as one of the securities against corrupt or tyrannical government. No argument, we may suppose, can now be needed against permitting a legislature or an executive, not identified in interest with the people, to prescribe opinions to them and determine what doctrines or what arguments they shall be allowed to hear.... Let us suppose, therefore, that the government is entirely at one with the people, and never thinks of exerting any power of coercion unless in agreement with what it conceives to be their voice. But I deny the right of the people to exercise such coercion, either by themselves or by their government. The power itself is illegitimate. The best government has no more title to it than the worst. It is as noxious, or more noxious, when exerted in accordance with public opinion than when in opposition to it. If all mankind minus one were of one opinion, and only one person were of the contrary opinion, mankind would be no more justified in silencing that one person than he, if he had the power, would be justified in silencing mankind. Were an opinion a personal possession of no value except to the owner, if to be obstructed in the enjoyment of it were simply a private injury, it would make some difference whether the injury was inflicted only on a few persons or on many. But the peculiar evil of silencing the expression of an opinion is that it is robbing the human race, posterity as well as the existing generation—those who dissent from the opinion, still more than those who hold it. If the opinion is right, they are deprived of the opportunity of exchanging error for truth; if wrong, they lose, what is almost as great a benefit, the clearer perception and livelier impression of truth produced by its collision with error.

It is necessary to consider separately these two hypotheses, each of which has a distinct branch of the argument corresponding to it. We can never be sure that the opinion we are endeavoring to stifle is a false opinion; and if we were sure, stifling it would be an evil still.

First, the opinion which it is attempted to suppress by authority may possibly be true. Those who desire to suppress it, of course, deny its truth; but they are not infallible. They have no authority to decide the question for all mankind and exclude every other person from the means of judging. To refuse a hearing to an opinion because they are sure that it is false is to assume that *their* certainty is the same thing as *absolute* certainty. All silencing of discussion is an assumption of infallibility. Its condemnation may be allowed to rest on this common argument, not the worse for being common.

Unfortunately for the good sense of mankind, the fact of their fallibility is far from carrying the weight in their practical judgment which is always allowed to it in theory; for while everyone well knows himself to be fallible, few think it necessary to take any precautions against their own fallibility, or admit the supposition that any opinion of which they feel very certain may be one of the examples of the error to which they acknowledge themselves to be liable. Absolute princes, or others who are accustomed to unlimited deference, usually feel this complete confidence in their own opinions on nearly all subjects. People more happily situated, who sometimes hear their opinions disputed and are not wholly unused to be set right when they are wrong, place the same unbounded reliance only on such of their opinions as are shared by all who surround them, or to whom they habitually defer; for in proportion to a man's want of confidence in his own solitary judgment does he usually repose, with implicit trust, on the infallibility of "the world" in general. And the world, to each individual, means the part of it with which he comes in contact: his party, his sect, his church, his class of society; the man may be called, by comparison, almost liberal and large-minded to whom it means anything so comprehensive as his own country or his own age. Nor is his faith in this collective authority at all shaken by his being aware that other ages, countries, sects, churches, classes, and parties have thought, and even now think, the exact reverse. He devolves upon his own world the responsibility of being in the right against the dissentient worlds of other people; and it never troubles him that mere accident has decided which of these numerous worlds is the object of his reliance, and that the same causes which make him a churchman in London would have made him a Buddhist or a Confucian in Peking. Yet it is as evident in itself, as any amount of argument can make it, that ages are no more infallible than individuals—every age having held many opinions which subsequent ages have deemed not only false but absurd; and it is as certain that many opinions, now general, will be rejected by future ages, as it is that many, once general, are rejected by the present.

The objection likely to be made to this argument would probably take some such form as the following. There is no greater assumption of infallibility in forbidding the propagation of error than in any other thing which is done by public authority on its own judgment and responsibility. Judgment is given to men that they may use it. Because it may be used erroneously, are men to be told that they ought not to use it at all? To prohibit what they think pernicious is not claiming exemption from error, but fulfilling the duty incumbent on them, although fallible, of acting on their conscientious conviction. If we were never to act on our opinions, because those opinions may be wrong, we should leave all our interests uncared for, and all our duties unperformed. An objection which applies to all conduct can be no valid objection to any conduct in particular. It is the duty of governments, and of individuals, to form the truest opinions they can; to form them carefully, and never impose them upon others unless they are quite sure of being right. But when they are sure (such reasoners may say), it is not conscientiousness but cowardice to shrink from acting on their opinions and allow doctrines which they honestly think dangerous to the welfare of mankind, either in this life or in another, to be scattered abroad without restraint, because other people, in less enlightened times, have persecuted opinions now believed to be true. Let us take care, it may be said, not to make the same mistake; but governments and nations have made mistakes in other things which are not denied to be fit subjects for the exercise of authority: they have laid on bad taxes, made unjust wars. Ought we therefore to lay on no taxes and, under whatever provocation, make no wars? Men and governments must act to the best of their ability. There is no such thing as absolute certainty, but there is assurance sufficient for the purposes of human life. We may, and must, assume our opinion to be true for the guidance of our own conduct; and it is assuming no more when we forbid bad men to pervert society by the propagation of opinions which we regard as false and pernicious.

I answer, that it is assuming very much more. There is the greatest difference between presuming an opinion to be true because, with every opportunity for contesting it, it has not been refuted, and assuming its truth for the purpose of not permitting its refutation. Complete liberty of contradicting and disproving our opinion is the very condition which justifies us in assuming its truth for purposes of action; and on no other terms can a being with human faculties have any rational assurance of being right.

When we consider either the history of opinion or the ordinary conduct of human life, to what is it to be ascribed that the one and the other are no worse than they are? Not certainly to the inherent force of the human understanding, for on any matter not self-evident there are ninety-nine persons totally incapable of judging of it for one who is capable; and the capacity of the hundredth person is only comparative, for the majority of the eminent men of every past generation held many opinions now known to be erroneous, and did or approved numerous things which no one will now justify. Why is it, then, that there is on the whole a preponderance among mankind of rational opinions and rational conduct? If there really is this preponderance—which there must be unless human affairs are, and have always been, in an almost desperate state—it is owing to a quality of the human mind, the source of everything respectable in man either as an intellectual or as a moral being, namely, that his errors are corrigible. He is capable of rectifying his mistakes by discussion and experience. Not by experience alone. There must be discussion to show how experience is to be interpreted. Wrong opinions and practices gradually yield to fact and argument; but facts and arguments, to produce any effect on the mind, must be brought before it. Very few facts are able to tell their own story, without comments to bring out their meaning. The whole strength and value, then, of human judgment depending on the one property, that it can be set right when it is wrong, reliance can be placed on it only when the means of setting it right are kept constantly at hand. In the case of any person whose judgment is really deserving of confidence, how has it become so? Because he has kept his mind open to criticism of his opinions and conduct. Because it has been his practice to listen to all that could be said against him; to profit by as much of it as was just, and to expound to himself, and upon occasion to others, the fallacy of what was fallacious. Because he has felt that the only way in which a human being can make some approach to knowing the whole of a subject is by hearing what can be said about it by persons of every variety of opinion, and studying all modes in which it can be looked at by every character of mind. No wise man ever acquired his wisdom in any mode but this; nor is it in the nature of human intellect to become wise in any other manner. The steady habit of correcting and completing his own opinion by collating it with those of others, so far from causing doubt and hesitation in carrying it into practice, is the only stable foundation for a just reliance on it; for, being cognizant of all that can, at least obviously, be said against him, and having taken up his position against all gainsayers—knowing that he has sought for objections and difficulties instead of avoiding them, and has shut out no light which can be thrown upon the subject from any quarter—he has a right to think his judgment better than that of any person, or any multitude, who have not gone through a similar process. . . .

In order more fully to illustrate the mischief of denying a hearing to opinions because we, in our own judgment, have condemned them, it will be desirable to fix down the discussion to a concrete case; and I choose, by preference, the cases which are least favorable to me—in which the argument against freedom of opinion, both on the score of truth and on that of utility, is considered the strongest. Let the opinions impugned be the belief in a God and in a future state, or any of the commonly received doctrines of morality. To fight the battle on such ground gives a great advantage to an unfair antagonist, since he will be sure to say (and many who have no desire to be unfair will say it internally), Are these the doctrines which you do not deem sufficiently certain to be taken under the protection of law? Is the belief in a God one of the opinions to feel sure of which you hold to be assuming infallibility? But I must be permitted to observe that it is not the feeling sure of a doctrine (be it what it may) which I call an assumption of infallibility. It is the undertaking to decide that question *for others,* without allowing them to hear what can be said on the contrary side. And I denounce and reprobate this pretension not the less if put forth on the side of my most solemn convictions. However positive anyone's persuasion may be, not only of the falsity but of the pernicious consequences—not only of the pernicious consequences, but (to adopt expressions which I altogether condemn) the immorality and impiety of an opinion—yet if, in pursuance of that private judgment, though backed by the public judgment of his country or his contemporaries, he prevents the opinion from being heard in its defense, he assumes infallibility. And so far from the assumption being less objectionable or less dangerous because the opinion is called immoral or impious, this is the case of all others in which it is most fatal. These are exactly the occasions on which the men of one generation commit those dreadful mistakes which excite the astonishment and horror of posterity. It is among such that we find the instances memorable in history, when the arm of the law has been employed to root out the best men and the noblest doctrines; with deplorable success as to the men, though some of the doctrines have survived to be (as if in mockery) invoked in defense of similar conduct toward those who dissent from *them,* or from their received interpretation.

Mankind can hardly be too often reminded that there was once a man called Socrates, between whom and the legal authorities and public opinion of his time there took place a memorable collision. Born in an age and country abounding in individual greatness, this man has been handed down to us by those who best knew both him and the age as the most virtuous man in it. . . . This acknowledged master of all the eminent thinkers who have since lived—whose fame, still growing after more than two thousand years, all but outweighs the whole remainder of the names which make his native city illustrious—was put to death by his countrymen, after a judicial conviction, for impiety and immorality. Impiety, in denying the gods recognized by the State; indeed, his accuser asserted (see the *Apologia*) that he believed in no gods at all. Immorality, in being, by his doctrines and instructions, a "corruptor of youth." Of these charges the tribunal, there is every ground for believing, honestly found him guilty, and condemned the man who probably of all then born had deserved best of mankind to be put to death as a criminal.

To pass from this to the only other instance of judicial iniquity, the mention of which, after the condemnation of Socrates, would not be an anticlimax: the event which took place on Calvary rather more than eighteen hundred years ago. The man who left on the memory of those who witnessed his life and conversation such an impression of his moral grandeur that eighteen subsequent centuries have done homage to him as the Almighty in person, was ignominiously put to death, as what? As a blasphemer. Men did not merely mistake their benefactor, they mistook him for the exact contrary of what he was and treated him as that prodigy of impiety which they themselves are now held to be for their treatment of him. The feelings with which mankind now regard these lamentable transactions, especially the later of the two, render them extremely unjust in their judgment of the unhappy actors. . . . Orthodox Christians who are tempted to think that those who stoned to death the first martyrs must have been worse men than they themselves are ought to remember that one of those persecutors was Saint Paul. . . .

Let us now pass to the second division of the argument, and dismissing the supposition that any of the received opinions may be false, let us assume them to be true and examine into the worth of the manner in which they are likely to be held when their truth is not freely and openly canvassed. However unwillingly a person who has a strong opinion may admit the possibility that his opinion may be false, he ought to be moved by the consideration that, however true it may be, if it is not fully, frequently, and fearlessly discussed, it will be held as a dead dogma, not a living truth.

There is a class of persons (happily not quite so numerous as formerly) who think it enough if a person assents undoubtingly to what they think true, though he has no knowledge whatever of the grounds of the opinion and could not make a tenable defense of it against the most superficial objections. Such persons, if they can once get their creed taught from authority, naturally think that no good, and some harm, comes of its being allowed to be questioned. Where their influence prevails, they make it nearly impossible for the received opinion to be rejected wisely and considerately, though it may still be rejected rashly and ignorantly; for to shut out discussion entirely is seldom possible, and when it once gets in, beliefs not grounded on conviction are apt to give way before the slightest semblance of an argument. Waiving, however, this possibility—assuming that the true opinion abides in the mind, but abides as a prejudice, a belief independent of, and proof against, argument—this is not the way in which truth ought to be held by a rational being. This is not knowing the truth. Truth, thus held, is but one superstition the more, accidentally clinging to the words which enunciate a truth.

If the intellect and judgment of mankind ought to be cultivated, a thing which Protestants at least do not deny, on what can these faculties be more appropriately exercised by anyone than on the things which concern him so much that it is considered necessary for him to hold opinions on them? If the cultivation of the understanding consists in one thing more than in another, it is surely in learning the grounds of one's own opinions. Whatever people believe, on subjects on which it is of the first importance to believe rightly, they ought to be able to defend against at least the common objections. But, someone may say, "Let them be *taught* the grounds of their opinions. It does not follow that opinions must be merely parroted because they are never heard controverted. Persons who learn geometry do not simply commit the theorems to memory, but understand and learn likewise the demonstrations; and it would be absurd to say that they remain ignorant of the grounds of geometrical truths because they never hear anyone deny and attempt to disprove them." Undoubtedly: and such teaching suffices on a subject like mathematics, where there is nothing at all to be said on the wrong side of the question. The peculiarity of the evidence of mathematical truths is that all the argument is on one side. There are no objections, and no answers to objections. But on every subject on which difference of opinion is possible, the truth depends on a balance to be struck between two sets of conflicting reasons. Even in natural philosophy, there is always some other explanation possible of the same facts; some geocentric theory instead of heliocentric, some phlogiston instead of oxygen; and it has to be shown why that other theory cannot be the true one; and until this is shown, and until we know how it is shown, we do not understand the grounds of our opinion. But when we turn to subjects infinitely more complicated, to morals, religion, politics, social relations, and the business of life, three-fourths of the arguments for every disputed opinion consist in dispelling the appearances which favor some opinion different from it. The greatest orator, save one, of antiquity, has left it on record that he always studied his adversary's case with as great, if not still greater, intensity than even his own. What Cicero practiced as the means of forensic success requires to be imitated by all who study any subject in order to arrive at the truth. He who knows only his own side of the case knows little of that. His reasons may be good, and no one may have been able to refute them. But if he is equally unable to refute the reasons on the opposite side, if he does not so much as know what they are, he has no ground for preferring either opinion. The rational position for him would be suspension of judgment, and unless he contents himself with that, he is either led by authority or adopts, like the generality of the world, the side to which he feels most inclination. Nor is it enough that he should hear the arguments of adversaries from his own teachers, presented as they state them, and accompanied by what they offer as refutations. That is not the way to do justice to the arguments or bring them into real contact with his own mind. He must be able to hear them from persons who actually believe them, who defend them in earnest and do their very utmost for them. He must know them in their most plausible and persuasive form; he must feel the whole force of the difficulty which the true view of the subject has to encounter and dispose of, else he will never really possess himself of the portion of truth which meets and removes that difficulty. Ninety-nine in a hundred of what are called educated men are in this condition, even of those who can argue fluently for their opinions. Their conclusion may be true, but it might be false for anything they know; they have never thrown themselves into the mental position of those who think differently from them, and considered what such persons may have to say; and, consequently, they do not, in any proper sense of the word, know the doctrine which they themselves profess. . . .

We have now recognized the necessity to the mental well-being of mankind (on which all their other well-being depends) of freedom of opinion, and freedom of the expression of opinion, on four distinct grounds, which we will now briefly recapitulate:

First, if any opinion is compelled to silence, that opinion may, for aught we can certainly know, be true. To deny this is to assume our own infallibility.

Secondly, though the silenced opinion be an error, it may, and very commonly does, contain a portion of truth; and since the general or prevailing opinion on any subject is rarely or never the whole truth, it is only by the collision of adverse opinions that the remainder of the truth has any chance of being supplied.

Thirdly, even if the received opinion be not only true, but the whole truth; unless it is suffered to be, and actually is, vigorously and earnestly contested, it will, by most of those who receive it, be held in the manner of a prejudice, with little comprehension or feeling of its rational grounds. And not only this, but, fourthly, the meaning of the doctrine itself will be in danger of being lost or enfeebled, and deprived of its vital effect on the character and conduct: the dogma becoming a mere formal profession, inefficacious for good, but cumbering the ground and preventing the growth of any real and heartfelt conviction from reason or personal experience.

STUDY QUESTIONS

1. According to Mill, if we are certain that an opinion is false, would stifling it still be wrong?
2. How does Mill defend his claim that "He who knows only his own side of the case knows little of that"?
3. Do we learn more from listening to those with whom we disagree than from those with whom we agree?
4. How would Mill react to the suggestion that a speaker with views demeaning some members of the student body should be banned from speaking at a university campus?

Economic and Philosophic Manuscripts of 1844

⚜

KARL MARX

Karl Marx (1818–1883), who was born in Prussia and earned a doctorate in philosophy, became the founder of revolutionary communism. He considers the key to understanding the social order to be the conflict between those who own property and those who work for them. In his view, labor produces wonderful things, but only for owners. He sees workers as estranged or alienated from the products of their work. The cure, he believes, lies in the creation of a new economic system based on common control of production.

....

Do not let us go back to a fictitious primordial condition as the political economist does, when he tries to explain. Such a primordial condition explains nothing; it merely pushes the question away into a gray nebulous distance. . . .

We proceed from an economic fact *of the present*. The worker becomes all the poorer the more wealth he produces, the more his production increases in power and size. The worker becomes an ever cheaper commodity the more commodities he creates. With the *increasing value* of the world of things proceeds in direct proportion the *devaluation* of the world of men. Labor produces not only commodities: it produces itself and the worker as a *commodity*—and this in the same general proportion in which it produces commodities.

This fact expresses merely that the object which labor produces—labor's product—confronts it as *something alien*, as a *power independent* of the producer. The product of labor is labor which has been embodied in an object, which has become material: it is the objectification of labor. Labor's realization is its objectification. In the sphere of political economy, this realization of labor appears as loss of *realization* for the workers; objectification as loss of the *object* and *bondage to it*; appropriation as *estrangement*, as *alienation*.

So much does labor's realization appear as loss of realization that the worker loses realization to the point of starving to death. So much does objectification appear as loss of the object that the worker is robbed of the objects most necessary not only for his life but for his work. Indeed, labor itself becomes an object which he can obtain only with the greatest effort and with the most irregular

---

From *Economic and Philosophic Manuscripts of 1844*, translated by Martin Milligan.

interruptions. So much does the appropriation of the object appear as estrangement that the more objects the worker produces the less he can possess and the more he falls under the sway of his product, capital.

All these consequences result from the fact that the worker is related to the *product of his labor* as to an *alien* object. For on this premise it is clear that the more the worker spends himself, the more powerful becomes the alien world of objects which he creates over and against himself, the poorer he himself—his inner world—becomes, the less belongs to him as his own. It is the same in religion. The more man puts into God, the less he retains in himself. The worker puts his life into the object; but now his life no longer belongs to him but to the object. Hence, the greater this activity, the greater is the worker's lack of objects. Whatever the product of his labor is, he is not. Therefore the greater this product, the less is he himself. The *alienation* of the worker in his product means not only that his labor becomes an object, an *external* existence, but that it exists *outside* him, independently, as something alien to him, and that it becomes a power on its own confronting him. It means that the life which he has conferred on the object confronts him as something hostile and alien.

Let us now look more closely at the *objectification*, at the production of the worker; and in it as the *estrangement*, the *loss of* the object, of his product.

The worker can create nothing without *nature*, without the *sensuous external world*. It is the material on which his labor is realized, in which it is active, from which and by means of which it produces.

But just as nature provides labor with the *means of life* in the sense that labor cannot live without objects on which to operate, on the other hand, it also provides the *means of life* in the more restricted sense, i.e., the means for the physical subsistence of the *worker* himself.

Thus the more the worker by his labor *appropriates* the external world, hence sensuous nature, the more he deprives himself of *means of life* in double manner: first, in that the sensuous external world more and more ceases to be an object belonging to his labor—to be his labor's *means of life*; and secondly, in that it more and more ceases to be *means of life* in the immediate sense, means for the physical subsistence of the worker.

In both respects, therefore, the worker becomes a slave of his object, first, in that he receives an *object of labor*, i.e., in that he receives *work*; and secondly, in that he receives *means of subsistence*. Therefore, it enables him to exist, first, as a *worker*, and, second as a *physical subject*. The height of this bondage is that it is only as a *worker* that he continues to maintain himself as a *physical subject*, and that is only as a *physical subject* that he is a *worker*.

(The laws of political economy express the estrangement of the worker in his object thus: the more the worker produces, the less he has to consume; the more values he creates, the more valueless, the more unworthy he becomes; the better formed his product, the more deformed becomes the worker; the more civilized his object, the more barbarous becomes the worker; the more powerful labor becomes, the more powerless becomes the worker; the more ingenious labor becomes, the less ingenious becomes the worker and the more he becomes nature's bondsman.)

Political economy conceals the estrangement inherent in the nature of labor by not considering the direct relationship between the worker (labor) *and production.* It is true that labor produces for the rich wonderful things—but for the worker it produces privation. It produces palaces—but for the worker, hovels. It produces beauty—but for the worker, deformity. It replaces labor by machines, but it throws a section of the workers back to a barbarous type of labor, and turns the other workers into machines. It produces intelligence—but for the worker stupidity, cretinism....

Till now we have been considering the estrangement, the alienation of the worker only in one of its aspects, i.e., the worker's *relationship to the products of his labor.* But the estrangement is manifested not only in the result but in the *act of production,* within the *producing activity,* itself. How would the worker come to face the product of his activity as a stranger, were it not that in the very act of production he was estranging himself from himself? The product is after all but the summary of the activity, of production. If then the product of labor is alienation, production itself must be active alienation, the alienation of activity, the activity of alienation. In the estrangement of the object of labor is merely summarized the estrangement, the alienation, in the activity of labor itself.

What, then, constitutes the alienation of labor?

First, the fact that labor is *external* to the worker, i.e., it does not belong to his essential being; that in his work, therefore, he does not affirm himself but denies himself, does not feel content but unhappy, does not develop freely his physical and mental energy but mortifies his body and ruins his mind. The worker therefore only feels himself outside his work, and in his work feels outside himself. He is at home when he is not working, and when he is working he is not at home. His labor is therefore not voluntary, but coerced; it is *forced labor.* It is therefore not the satisfaction of a need; it is merely a *means* to satisfy needs external to it. Its alien character emerges clearly in the fact that as soon as no physical or other compulsion exists, labor is shunned like the plague. External labor, labor in which man alienates himself, is a labor of self-sacrifice, of mortification. Lastly, the external character of labor for the worker appears in the fact that it is not his own, but someone else's, that it does not belong to him, that in it he belongs, not to himself, but to another. Just as in religion the spontaneous activity of the human imagination, of the human brain and the human heart, operates independently of the individual—that is, operates on him as an alien, divine or diabolical activity—so is the worker's activity not his spontaneous activity. It belongs to another; it is the loss of his self....

We took our departure from a fact of political economy—the estrangement of the worker and his production. We have formulated this fact in conceptual terms as *estranged, alienated* labor. We have analyzed this concept—hence analyzing merely a fact of political economy.

Let us now see, further, how the concept of estranged, alienated labor must express and present itself in real life.

If the product of labor is alien to me, if it confronts me as an alien power, to whom, then, does it belong?

If my own activity does not belong to me, if it is an alien, a coerced activity, to whom, then, does it belong? ...

The *alien* being, to whom labor and the product of labor belongs, in whose service labor is done and for whose benefit the product of labor is provided, can only be *man* himself.

If the product of labor does not belong to the worker, if it confronts him as an alien power, then this can only be because it belongs to some *other man than the worker*. If the worker's activity is a torment to him, to another it must be *delight* and his life's joy. ...

Through *estranged, alienated* labor, then, the worker produces the relationship to this labor of a man alien to labor and standing outside it. The relationship of the worker to labor creates the relation to it of the capitalist (or whatever one chooses to call the master of labor). *Private property* is thus the product, the result, the necessary consequence, of *alienated labor*, of the external relation of the worker to nature and to himself.

Private property thus results by analysis from the concept of *alienated labor*, of *alienated man*, of estranged labor, of estranged life, of estranged man.

True, it is as a result of the *movement of private property* that we have obtained the concept of *alienated labor* (*of alienated life*) from political economy. But on analysis of this concept it becomes clear that though private property appears to be the source, the cause of alienated labor, it is rather its consequence, just as the gods are *originally* not the cause but the effect of man's intellectual confusion. Later this relationship becomes reciprocal.

Only at the last culmination of the development of private property does this, its secret, appear again, namely, that on the one hand it is the *product* of alienated labor, and that on the other it is the *means* by which labor alienates itself, the *realization of this alienation*.

STUDY QUESTIONS

1. According to Marx, why does the worker become all the poorer the more wealth he produces?
2. What does Marx mean by "alienation"?
3. According to Marx, does labor produce beauty?
4. Explain Marx's view of private property.

PART 11

Social Justice

A Theory of Justice

☙

JOHN RAWLS

Under what conditions could a society be properly described as just? An influential answer to this question has been developed by John Rawls (1921–2002), who was Professor of Philosophy at Harvard University. He contends that the fairest way to distribute goods is in accord with principles that everyone would accept, regardless of the abilities they happen to possess, or the social or economic circumstances in which they find themselves.

....

THE MAIN IDEA OF THE THEORY OF JUSTICE

... [T]he principles of justice ... are the principles that free and rational persons concerned to further their own interests would accept in an initial position of equality. ...

[T]he original position of equality corresponds to the state of nature in the traditional theory of the social contract. This original position is not, of course, thought of as an actual historical state of affairs, much less as a primitive condition of culture. It is understood as a purely hypothetical situation. ... Among the essential features of this situation is that no one knows his place in society, his class position or social status, nor does any one know his fortune in the distribution of natural assets and abilities, his intelligence, strength, and the like. I shall even assume that the parties do not know their conceptions of the good or their special psychological propensities. The principles of justice are chosen behind a veil of ignorance. This ensures that no one is advantaged or disadvantaged in the choice of principles by the outcome of natural chance or the contingency of social circumstances. Since all are similarly situated and no one is able to design principles to favor his particular condition, the principles of justice are the result of a fair agreement or bargain. For given the circumstances of the original position, the symmetry of everyone's relations to each other, this initial situation is fair between individuals as moral persons, that is, as rational beings with their own ends and capable, I shall assume, of a sense of justice. The original position is, one might say, the appropriate initial status quo, and thus the fundamental agreements reached in it are fair. This explains the propriety of the name "justice as fairness": it conveys the idea that the principles of justice are agreed to in an initial situation that is fair. . . .

I shall maintain . . . that the persons in the initial situation would choose two . . . principles: the first requires equality in the assignment of basic rights and duties, while the second holds that social and economic inequalities—for example, inequalities of wealth and authority—are just only if they result in compensating benefits for everyone, and in particular for the least advantaged members of society. These principles rule out justifying institutions on the grounds that the hardships of some are offset by a greater good in the aggregate. It may be expedient but it is not just that some should have less in order that others may prosper. But there is no injustice in the greater benefits earned by a few provided that the situation of persons not so fortunate is thereby improved. The intuitive idea is that since everyone's well-being depends upon a scheme of cooperation without which no one could have a satisfactory life, the division of advantages should be such as to draw forth the willing cooperation of everyone taking part in it, including those less well situated. The two principles mentioned seem to be a fair basis on which those better endowed, or more fortunate in their social position, neither of which we can be said to deserve, could expect the willing cooperation of others when some workable scheme is a necessary condition of the welfare of all. Once we decide to look for a conception of justice that prevents the use of the accidents of natural endowment and the contingencies of social circumstance as counters in a quest of political and economic advantage, we are led to these principles. They express the result of leaving aside those aspects of the social world that seem arbitrary from a moral point of view. . . .

THE ORIGINAL POSITION AND JUSTIFICATION

. . . One should not be misled . . . by the somewhat unusual conditions which characterize the original position. The idea here is simply to make vivid to ourselves the restrictions that it seems reasonable to impose on arguments for principles of justice, and therefore on these principles themselves. Thus it seems reasonable and generally acceptable that no one should be advantaged or disadvantaged by natural fortune or social circumstances in the choice of principles. It also seems widely agreed that it should be impossible to tailor principles to the circumstances of one's own case. We should insure further that particular inclinations and aspirations, and persons' conceptions of their good, do not affect the principles adopted. The aim is to rule out those principles that it would be rational to propose for acceptance, however little the chance of success, only if one knew certain things that are irrelevant from the standpoint of justice. For example, if a man knew that he was wealthy, he might find it rational to advance the principle that various taxes for welfare measures be counted unjust; if he knew that he was poor, he would most likely propose the contrary principle. To represent the desired restrictions, one imagines a situation in which everyone is deprived of this sort of information.

One excludes the knowledge of those contingencies which sets men at odds and allows them to be guided by their prejudices. In this manner the veil of ignorance is arrived at in a natural way. This concept should cause no difficulty if we keep in mind the constraints on arguments that it is meant to express. At any time we can enter the original position, so to speak, simply by following a certain procedure, namely, by arguing for principles of justice in accordance with these restrictions.

It seems reasonable to suppose that the parties in the original position are equal. That is, all have the same rights in the procedure for choosing principles; each can make proposals, submit reasons for their acceptance, and so on. Obviously the purpose of these conditions is to represent equality between human beings as moral persons, as creatures having a conception of their good and capable of a sense of justice. The basis of equality is taken to be similarity in these two respects. Systems of ends are not ranked in value; and each man is presumed to have the requisite ability to understand and to act upon whatever principles are adopted. Together with the veil of ignorance, these conditions define the principles of justice as those which rational persons concerned to advance their interests would consent to as equals when none are known to be advantaged or disadvantaged by social and natural contingencies....

TWO PRINCIPLES OF JUSTICE

I shall now state in a provisional form the two principles of justice that I believe would be chosen in the original position....

The first statement of the two principles reads as follows.

First: each person is to have an equal right to the most extensive scheme of equal basic liberties compatible with a similar scheme of liberties for others.

Second: social and economic inequalities are to be arranged so that they are both (a) reasonably expected to be to everyone's advantage and (b) attached to positions and offices open to all....

These principles primarily apply ... to the basic structure of society and govern the assignment of rights and duties and regulate the distribution of social and economic advantages.... [I]t is essential to observe that the basic liberties are given by a list of such liberties. Important among these are political liberty (the right to vote and to hold public office) and freedom of speech and assembly; liberty of conscience and freedom of thought; freedom of the person, which includes freedom from psychological oppression and physical assault and dismemberment (integrity of the person); the right to hold personal property and freedom from arbitrary arrest and seizure as defined by the concept of the rule of law. These liberties are to be equal by the first principle.

The second principle applies ... to the distribution of income and wealth and to the design of organizations that make use of differences in authority and responsibility. While the distributions of wealth and income need not be equal, it must be to everyone's advantage, and at the same time, positions of authority and responsibility must be accessible to all. One applies the second principle by holding positions open, and then, subject to this constraint, arranges social and economic inequalities so that everyone benefits.

These principles are to be arranged in a serial order with the first principle prior to the second. This ordering means that infringements of the basic equal liberties protected by the first principle cannot be justified, or compensated for, by greater social and economic advantages. . . .

[I]n regard to the second principle, the distribution of wealth and income, and positions of authority and responsibility, are to be consistent with both the basic liberties and equality of opportunity. . . .

[T]hese principles are a special case of a more general conception of justice that can be expressed as follows.

> All social values—liberty and opportunity, income and wealth, and the social bases of self-respect—are to be distributed equally unless an unequal distribution of any, or all, of these values is to everyone's advantage.

Injustice, then, is simply inequalities that are not to the benefit of all. . . .

THE VEIL OF IGNORANCE

. . . The notion of the veil of ignorance raises several difficulties. Some may object that the exclusion of nearly all particular information makes it difficult to grasp what is meant by the original position. Thus it may be helpful to observe that one or more persons can at any time enter this position, or perhaps better, simulate the deliberations of this hypothetical situation, simply by reasoning in accordance with the appropriate restrictions. . . .

It may be protested that the condition of the veil of ignorance is irrational. Surely, some may object, principles should be chosen in the light of all the knowledge available. There are various replies to this contention. . . . To begin with, it is clear that since the differences among the parties are unknown to them, and everyone is equally rational and similarly situated, each is convinced by the same arguments. Therefore, we can view the agreement in the original position from the standpoint of one person selected at random. If anyone after due reflection prefers a conception of justice to another, then they all do, and a unanimous agreement can be reached. We can, to make the circumstances more vivid, imagine that the parties are required to communicate with each other through a referee as intermediary, and that he is to announce which alternatives have been suggested and the reasons offered in their support. He forbids the attempt to form coalitions, and he informs the parties when they have come to an understanding. But such a referee is actually superfluous, assuming that the deliberations of the parties must be similar.

Thus there follows the very important consequence that the parties have no basis for bargaining in the usual sense. No one knows his situation in society nor his natural assets, and therefore no one is in a position to tailor principles to his advantage. We might imagine that one of the contractees threatens to hold out unless the others agree to principles favorable to him. But how does he know which principles are especially in his interests? The same holds for the formation of coalitions: if a group were to decide to band together to the disadvantage of the others, they would not know how to favor themselves in the choice of principles. Even if they could get everyone to agree to their proposal, they would have no assurance that it was to their advantage, since they cannot identify themselves either by name or description. . . .

The restrictions on particular information in the original position are, then, of fundamental importance. Without them we would not be able to work out any definite theory of justice at all. We would have to be content with a vague formula stating that justice is what would be agreed to without being able to say much, if anything, about the substance of the agreement itself. . . . The veil of ignorance makes possible a unanimous choice of a particular conception of justice. Without these limitations on knowledge the bargaining problem of the original position would be hopelessly complicated.

STUDY QUESTIONS

1. What is "the original position"?
2. What is "the veil of ignorance"?
3. According to Rawls, what are the two principles of justice?
4. Do you agree with Rawls that these two principles would be chosen in the original position?

Distributive Justice

ℳ

Robert Nozick

Robert Nozick, whose work we read previously, argues that in treating all goods as though they were unowned and distributing them in accord with some preferred scheme, we ignore the source of these goods in the labor and ingenuity of the people who created them. As he sees it, past history plays a crucial role in determining entitlements. If I acquired property appropriately, through my own efforts or by a legal exchange with its rightful owner, then I should not have the property taken away from me in order to satisfy someone's conception of justice.

The term "distributive justice" is not a neutral one. Hearing the term "distribution," most people presume that some thing or mechanism uses some principle or criterion to give out a supply of things. Into this process of distributing shares, some error may have crept. So it is an open question, at least, whether *redistribution* should take place; whether we should do again what has already been done once, though poorly. However, we are not in the position of children who have been given portions of pie by someone who now makes last minute adjustments to rectify careless cutting. There is no *central* distribution, no person or group entitled to control all the resources, jointly deciding how they are to be doled out. What each person gets, he gets from others who give to him in exchange for something, or as a gift. In a free society, diverse persons control different resources, and new holdings arise out of the voluntary exchanges and actions of persons. There is no more a distributing or distribution of shares than there is a distributing of mates in a society in which persons choose whom they shall marry. The total result is the product of many individual decisions which the different individuals involved are entitled to make. . . . We shall speak of people's holdings; a principle of justice in holdings describes (part of) what justice tells us (requires) about holdings. . . .

THE ENTITLEMENT THEORY

The subject of justice in holdings consists of three major topics. The first is the *original acquisition of holdings,* the appropriation of unheld things. This includes the issues of how unheld things may come to be held, the process, or processes, by which unheld things may come to be held, the things that may come to be held by these processes, the extent of what comes to be held by a particular process, and so on. We shall refer to the complicated truth about this topic, which we shall not formulate here, as the principle of justice in acquisition. The second topic concerns the *transfer of holdings* from one person to another. By what processes may a person transfer holdings to another? How may a person acquire a holding from another who holds it? Under this topic come general descriptions of voluntary exchange, and gift and (on the other hand) fraud, as well as reference to particular conventional details fixed upon in a given society. The complicated truth about this subject (with placeholders for conventional details) we shall call the principle of justice in transfer. (And we shall suppose it also includes principles governing how a person may divest himself of a holding, passing it into an unheld state.)

If the world were wholly just, the following inductive definition would exhaustively cover the subject of justice in holdings.

1. A person who acquires a holding in accordance with the principle of justice in acquisition is entitled to that holding.

2. A person who acquires a holding in accordance with the principle of justice in transfer, from someone else entitled to the holding, is entitled to the holding.
3. No one is entitled to a holding except by (repeated) applications of 1 and 2.

The complete principle of distributive justice would say simply that a distribution is just if everyone is entitled to the holdings they possess under the distribution.

A distribution is just if it arises from another just distribution by legitimate means. The legitimate means of moving from one distribution to another are specified by the principle of justice in transfer. The legitimate first "moves" are specified by the principle of justice in acquisition. Whatever arises from a just situation by just steps is itself just. The means of change specified by the principle of justice in transfer preserve justice. As correct rules of inference are truth-preserving, and any conclusion deduced via repeated application of such rules from only true premises is itself true, so the means of transition from one situation to another specified by the principle of justice in transfer are justice-preserving, and any situation actually arising from repeated transitions in accordance with the principle from a just situation is itself just. The parallel between justice-preserving transformations and truth-preserving transformations illuminates where it fails as well as where it holds. That a conclusion could have been deduced by truth-preserving means from premises that are true suffices to show its truth. That from a just situation a situation *could* have arisen via justice-preserving means does *not* suffice to show its justice. The fact that a thief's victims voluntarily *could* have presented him with gifts does not entitle the thief to his ill-gotten gains. Justice in holdings is historical; it depends upon what actually has happened. We shall return to this point later.

Not all actual situations are generated in accordance with the two principles of justice in holdings: the principle of justice in acquisition and the principle of justice in transfer. Some people steal from others, or defraud them, or enslave them, seizing their product and preventing them from living as they choose, or forcibly exclude others from competing in exchanges. None of these are permissible modes of transition from one situation to another. And some persons acquire holdings by means not sanctioned by the principle of justice in acquisition. The existence of past injustice (previous violations of the first two principles of justice in holdings) raises the third major topic under justice in holdings: the rectification of injustice in holdings. If past injustice has shaped present holdings in various ways, some identifiable and some not, what now, if anything, ought to be done to rectify these injustices? What obligations do the performers of injustice have toward those whose position is worse than it would have been had the injustice not been done?

The general outlines of the theory of justice in holdings are that the holdings of a person are just if he is entitled to them by the principles of justice in acquisition and transfer, or by the principle of rectification of injustice (as specified by the first two principles). If each person's holdings are just, then the total set (distribution) of holdings is just. To turn these general outlines into a specific theory, we would have to specify the details of each of the three principles of justice in holdings: the principle of acquisition of holdings, the principle of transfer of holdings, and the principle of rectification of violations of the first two principles. I shall not attempt that task here. . . .

HOW LIBERTY UPSETS PATTERNS

It is not clear how those holding alternative conceptions of distributive justice can reject the entitlement conceptions of justice in holdings. For suppose a distribution favored by one of these nonentitlement conceptions is realized. Let us suppose it is your favorite one and let us call this distribution D_1; perhaps everyone has an equal share, perhaps shares vary in accordance with some dimension you treasure. Now suppose that Wilt Chamberlain is greatly in demand by basketball teams, being a great gate attraction. (Also suppose contracts run only for a year, with players being free agents.) He signs the following sort of contract with a team: In each home game, twenty-five cents from the price of each ticket of admission goes to him. (We ignore the question of whether he is "gouging" the owners, letting them look out for themselves.) The season starts, and people cheerfully attend his team's games; they buy their tickets, each time dropping a separate twenty-five cents of their admission price into a special box with Chamberlain's name on it. They are excited about seeing him play; it is worth the total admission price to them. Let us suppose that in one season one million persons attend his home games, and Wilt Chamberlain winds up with $250,000, a much larger sum than the average income and larger even than anyone else has. Is he entitled to this income? Is this new distribution D_2 unjust? If so, why? There is *no* question about whether each of the people was entitled to the control over the resources they held in D_1; because that was the distribution (your favorite) that (for the purposes of argument) we assumed was acceptable. Each of these persons *chose* to give twenty-five cents of their money to Chamberlain. They could have spent it on going to the movies, or on candy bars, or on copies of *Dissent* magazine, or on *Monthly Review*. But they all, at least one million of them, converged on giving it to Wilt Chamberlain in exchange for watching him play basketball. If D_1 was a just distribution, and people voluntarily moved from it to D_2, transferring parts of their shares they were given under D_1 (what was it for if not to do something with?), isn't D_2 also just? If the people were entitled to dispose of the resources to which they were entitled (under D_1), didn't this include their being entitled to give it to, or exchange it with, Wilt Chamberlain? Can anyone else complain on grounds of justice? Each other person already has his legitimate share under D_1. Under D_1, there is nothing that anyone has that anyone else has a claim of justice against. After someone transfers something to Wilt Chamberlain, third parties *still* have their legitimate shares; *their* shares are not changed. By what process could such a transfer among two persons give rise to a legitimate claim of distributive justice on a portion of what was transferred, by a third party who had no claim of justice on any holding of the others *before* the transfer? . . .

The general point illustrated by the Wilt Chamberlain example . . . is that no end-state principle[1] or distributional patterned principle of justice[2] can be continuously realized without continuous interference with people's lives. Any favored pattern would be transformed into one unfavored by the principle, by people choosing to act in various ways; for example, by people exchanging goods and services with other people, or giving things to other people, things the transferrers are entitled to under the favored distributional pattern. To maintain a pattern, one must either continually interfere to stop people from transferring resources as they wish to, or continually (or periodically) interfere to take from some persons resources that others for some reason chose to transfer to them. (But if some time limit is to be set on how long people may keep resources others voluntarily transfer to them, why let them keep these resources for *any* period of time? Why not have immediate confiscation?) It might be objected that all persons voluntarily will choose to refrain from actions which would upset the pattern. This presupposes unrealistically (1) that all will most want to maintain the pattern (are those who don't, to be "reeducated" or forced to undergo "self-criticism"?), (2) that each can gather enough information about his own actions and the ongoing activities of others to discover which of his actions will upset the pattern, and (3) that diverse and far-flung persons can coordinate their actions to dovetail into the pattern. Compare the manner in which the market is neutral among persons' desires, as it reflects and transmits widely scattered information via prices and it coordinates persons' activities.

NOTES

1. [An "end-state principle" requires that goods be distributed to promote a certain structure of holdings, such as maximizing utility or achieving equality.—S.M.C.]
2. [A "patterned principle" requires that goods be distributed in accord with some feature of persons, such as need or desert.]

STUDY QUESTIONS

1. What does Nozick mean by "justice in acquisition"?
2. What does Nozick mean by "justice in transfer"?
3. What is the general point illustrated by the Wilt Chamberlain example?
4. How is the Wilt Chamberlain example supposed to undermine a theory of justice such as Rawls proposed?

Non-contractual Society:
A Feminist View

Virginia Held

Virginia Held, whose work we read previously, next explores how the relations suitable for mothering persons and children might be used as a social model. Instead of thinking of human relations as a contract between rationally self-interested individuals, she envisions society as a group of persons tied together by ongoing relations of caring and trust.

....

Contemporary society is in the grip of contractual thinking. Realities are interpreted in contractual terms, and goals are formulated in terms of rational contracts. The leading current conceptions of rationality begin with assumptions that human beings are independent, self-interested or mutually disinterested, individuals; they then typically argue that it is often rational for human beings to enter into contractual relationships with each other. . . .

To see contractual relations between self-interested or mutually disinterested individuals as constituting a paradigm of human relations is to take a certain historically specific conception of "economic man" as representative of humanity. And it is, many feminists are beginning to agree, to overlook or to discount in very fundamental ways the experience of women.

I will try in this paper to look at society from a thoroughly different point of view than that of economic man. I will take the point of view of women, and especially of mothers, as the basis for trying to rethink society and its possible goals. Certainly there is no single point of view of women; the perspectives of women are potentially as diverse as those of men. But since the perspectives of women have all been to a large extent discounted, across the spectrum, I will not try to deal here with diversity among such views, but rather to give voice to one possible feminist outlook. . . .

Since it is the practice of mothering with which I will be concerned in what follows, rather than with women in the biological sense, I will use the term "mothering person" rather than "mother." A "mothering person" can be male or female. . . .

From *Science, Morality, and Feminist Theory*, ed. Marsha Hanen and Kai Nielsen, *Canadian Journal of Philosophy*, Supplementary Volume 13. Calgary: University of Calgary Press, 1987. Reprinted by permission of the publisher with a minor revision by the author.

WOMEN AND FAMILY

A first point to note in trying to imagine society from the point of view of women is that the contractual model was hardly ever applied, as either description or ideal, to women or to relations within the family. The family was imagined to be "outside" the polis and "outside" the market in a "private" domain. This private domain was contrasted with the public domain, and with what, by the time of Hobbes and Locke, was thought of as the contractual domain of citizen and state and tradesman and market. Although women have always worked, and although both women and children were later pressed into work in factories, they were still thought of as outside the domain in which the contractual models of "equal men" were developed. Women were not expected to demand equal rights either in the public domain or at home. Women were not expected to be "economic men." And children were simply excluded from the realm of what was being interpreted in contractual terms as distinctively human.

Women have . . . been thought to be closer to nature than men, to be enmeshed in a biological function involving processes more like those in which other animals are involved than like the rational contracting of distinctively human "economic man." The total or relative exclusion of women from the domain of voluntary contracting has then been thought to be either inevitable or appropriate.

The view that women are more governed by biology than are men is still prevalent. It is as questionable as many other traditional misinterpretations of women's experience. Human mothering is an extremely different activity from the mothering engaged in by other animals. It is as different from the mothering of other animals as is the work and speech of men different from the "work" and "speech" of other animals. Since humans are also animals, one should not exaggerate the differences between humans and other animals. But to whatever extent it is appropriate to recognize a difference between "man" and other animals, so would it be appropriate to recognize a comparable difference between human mothering and the mothering of other animals.

Human mothering shapes language and culture, and forms human social personhood. Human mothering develops morality, it does not merely transmit techniques of survival; impressive as the latter can be, they do not have built into them the aims of morality. Human mothering teaches consideration for others based on moral concern; it does not merely follow and bring the child to follow instinctive tendency. Human mothering creates autonomous persons; it does not merely propagate a species. It can be fully as creative an activity as most other human activities; to create *new* persons, and new types of *persons*, is surely as creative as to make new objects, products, or institutions. Human mothering is no more "natural" than any other human activity. It may include many dull and repetitive tasks, as does farming, industrial production, banking, and work in a laboratory. But degree of dullness has nothing to do with degree of "naturalness." In sum, human mothering is as different from animal mothering as humans are from animals. . . .

FAMILY AND SOCIETY

In recent years, many feminists have demanded that the principles of justice and freedom and equality on which it is claimed that democracy rests be extended to women and the family. They have demanded that women be treated as equals in the polity, in the workplace, and, finally, at home. They have demanded, in short, to be accorded full rights to enter freely the contractual relations of modern society. They have asked that these be extended to take in the family.

But some feminists are now considering whether the arguments should perhaps, instead, run the other way. Instead of importing into the household principles derived from the marketplace, perhaps we should export to the wider society the relations suitable for mothering persons and children. This approach suggests that just as relations between persons within the family should be based on concern and caring, rather than on contracts based on self-interest, so various relations in the wider society should be characterized by more care and concern and openness and trust and human feeling than are the contractual bargains that have developed so far in political and economic life, or even than are aspired to in contractarian prescriptions. Then, the household instead of the marketplace might provide a model for society. Of course what we would mean by the household would not be the patriarchal household which was, before the rise of contractual thinking, also thought of as a model of society. We would now mean the relations between children and mothering persons *without* the patriarch. We would take our conception of the *post*-patriarchal family as a model....

THE MOTHER/CHILD RELATION

Let us examine in more detail the relation between mothering person and child. A first aspect of the relation that we can note is the extent to which it is not voluntary and, for this reason among others, not contractual. The ties that bind child and mothering persons are affectional and solicitous on the one hand, and emotional and dependent on the other. The degree to which bearing and caring for children has been voluntary for most mothers throughout most of history has been extremely limited; it is still quite limited for most mothering persons. The relation *should* be voluntary for the mothering person but it cannot possibly be voluntary for the young child, and it can only become, gradually, slightly more voluntary.

A woman can have decided voluntarily to have a child, but once that decision has been made, she will never again be unaffected by the fact that she has brought this particular child into existence. And even if the decision to have a child is voluntary, the decision to have this particular child, for either parent, cannot be. Technological developments can continue to reduce the uncertainties of childbirth, but unpredictable aspects are likely to remain great for most parents. Unlike that contract where buyer and seller can know what is being exchanged, and which is void if the participants cannot know what they are agreeing to, a parent cannot know what a particular child will be like. And children are totally unable to choose their parents and, for many years, any of their caretakers.

The recognition of how limited are the aspects of voluntariness in the relation between child and mothering person may help us to gain a closer approximation to reality in our understanding of most human relations, especially at a global level, than we can gain from imagining the purely voluntary trades entered into by rational economic contractors to be characteristic of human relations in other domains.

Society may impose certain reciprocal obligations: on parents to care for children when the children are young, and on children to care for parents when the parents are old. But if there is any element of a bargain in the relation between mothering person and child, it is very different from the bargain supposedly characteristic of the marketplace. If a parent thinks, "I'll take care of you now so you'll take care of me when I'm old," it must be based, unlike the contracts of political and economic bargains, on enormous trust and on a virtual absence of enforcement. And few mothering persons have any such exchange in mind when they engage in the activities of mothering. At least the bargain would only be resorted to when the callousness or poverty of the society made the plight of the old person desperate. This is demonstrated in survey after survey: old persons certainly hope not to have to be a burden on their children. And they prefer social arrangements that will allow them to refuse to cash in on any such bargain. So the intention and goal of mothering is to give of one's care without obtaining a return of a self-interested kind. The emotional satisfaction of a mothering person is a satisfaction in the well-being and happiness of another human being, and a satisfaction in the health of the relation between the two persons, not the gain that results from an egoistic bargain. The motive behind the activity of mothering is thus entirely different from that behind a market transaction. And so is, perhaps even more clearly, the motive behind the child's project of growth and development.

A second aspect of the contrast between market relations and relations between mothering person and child is found in the qualities of permanence and non-replaceability. The market makes of everything, even human labor and artistic expression and sexual desire, a commodity to be bought and sold, with one unit of economic value replaceable by any other of equivalent value. To the extent that political life reflects these aspects of the market, politicians are replaceable and political influence is bought and sold. Though rights may be thought of as outside the economic market, in contractual thinking they are seen as inside the wider market of the social contract, and can be traded against each other. But the ties between parents and children are permanent ties, however strained or slack they become at times. And no person within a family should be a commodity to any other. Although various persons may participate in mothering a given child, and a given person may mother many children, still no child and no mothering person is to the other a merely replaceable commodity. The extent to which more of our attitudes, for instance toward our society's cultural productions, should be thought of in these terms rather than in the terms of the marketplace should be considered.

A third aspect of the relation between mothering person and child that may be of interest is the insight it provides for our notions of equality. It shows us unmistakably that equality is not equivalent to having equal legal rights. All feminists are committed to equality and to equal rights in contexts where rights are what are appropriately at issue. But in many contexts, concerns other than rights are more salient and appropriate. And the equality that is at issue in the relation between child and mothering person is the equal consideration of persons, not a legal or contractual notion of equal rights.

Parents and children should not have equal rights in the sense that what they are entitled to decide or to do or to have should be the same. A family of several small children, an adult or two, and an aged parent should not, for instance, make its decisions by majority vote in most cases. But every member of a family is worthy of equal respect and consideration. Each person in a family is as important as a person as every other.

Sometimes the interests of children have been thought in some sense to count for more, justifying "sacrificing for the children." Certainly, the interests of mothers have often counted for less than those of either fathers or children. Increasingly, we may come to think that the interests of all should count equally, but we should recognize that this claim is appropriately invoked only if the issue should be thought of as one of interest. Often, it should not. Much of the time we can see that calculations of interest, and of equal interests, are as out of place as are determinations of equal rights. Both the rights and the interests of individuals seen as separate entities, and equality between them all, should not exhaust our moral concerns. The flourishing of shared joy, of mutual affection, of bonds of trust and hope between mothering persons and children can illustrate this as clearly as anything can. Harmony, love, and cooperation cannot be broken down into individual benefits or burdens. They are goals we ought to share and relations *between* persons. And although the degree of their intensity may be different, many and various relations *between* persons are important also at the level of communities or societies. We can consider, of a society, whether the relations between its members are trusting and mutually supportive, or suspicious and hostile. To focus only on contractual relations and the gains and losses of individuals obscures these often more important relational aspects of societies.

A fourth important feature of the relation between child and mothering person is that we obviously do not fulfil our obligations by merely leaving people alone. If one leaves an infant alone, he will starve. If one leaves a two-year old alone she will rapidly harm herself. The whole tradition that sees respecting others as constituted by non-interference with them is most effectively shown up as inadequate. It assumes that people can fend for themselves and provide through their own initiatives and efforts what they need. This Robinson Crusoe image of "economic man" is false for almost everyone, but it is totally and obviously false in the case of infants and children, and recognizing this can be salutary. It can lead us to see very vividly how unsatisfactory are those prevalent political views according to which we fulfil our obligations merely by refraining from interference. We ought to acknowledge that our fellow citizens, and fellow inhabitants of the globe, have moral rights to what they need to live—to the food, shelter, and medical care that are the necessary conditions of living and growing—and that when the resources exist for honoring such rights, there are few excuses for not doing so. Such rights are not rights to be left to starve unimpeded. Seeing how unsatisfactory rights merely to be left alone are as an interpretation of the rights of children may help us to recognize a similar truth about other persons. And the arguments—though appropriately in a different form—can be repeated for interests as distinct from rights.

A fifth interesting feature of the relation between mothering person and child is the very different view it provides of privacy. We come to see that to be in a position where others are *not* making demands on us is a rare luxury, not a normal state. To be a mothering person is to be subjected to the continual demands and needs of others. And to be a child is to be subjected to the continual demands and expectations of others. Both mothering persons and children need to extricate themselves from the thick and heavy social fabric in which they are entwined in order to enjoy any pockets of privacy at all.

Here the picture we form of our individuality and the concept we form of a "self" is entirely different from the one we get if we start with the self-sufficient individual of the "state of nature." If we begin with the picture of rational contractor entering into agreements with others, the "natural" condition is seen as one of individuality and privacy, and the problem is the building of society and government. From the point of view of the relation between mothering person and child, on the other hand, the problem is the reverse. The starting condition is an enveloping tie, and the problem is individuating oneself. The task is to carve out a gradually increasing measure of privacy in ways appropriate to a constantly shifting independency. For the child, the problem is to become gradually more interdependent. For the mothering person, the problem is to free oneself from an all-consuming involvement. For both, the progression is from society to greater individuality rather than from self-sufficient individuality to contractual ties. . . .

A sixth aspect of the relation between child and mothering person which is noteworthy is the very different view of power it provides. We are accustomed to thinking of power as something that can be wielded by one person over another, as a means by which one person can bend another to his will. An ideal has been to equalize power so that agreements can be forged and conflicts defused. But consider now the very different view of power in the relation between mothering person and child. The superior power of the mothering person over the child is relatively useless for most of what the mothering person aims to achieve in bringing up the child. The mothering person seeks to *empower* the child to act responsibly; she neither wants to "wield" power nor to defend herself against the power "wielded" by the child. The relative powerlessness of the child is largely irrelevant to most of the project of growing up. When the child is physically weakest, as in infancy and illness, the child can "command" the greatest amount of attention and care from the mothering person because of the seriousness of the child's needs.

The mothering person's stance is characteristically one of caring, of being vulnerable to the needs and pains of the child, and of fearing the loss of the child before the child is ready for independence. It is not characteristically a stance of domination. The child's project is one of developing, of gaining ever greater control over his or her own life, of relying on the mothering person rather than of submitting to superior strength. Of course the relation may in a degenerate form be one of domination and submission, but this only indicates that the relation is not what it should be.... The power of a mothering person to empower others, to foster transformative growth, is a different sort of power than that of a stronger sword or dominant will. And the power of a child to call forth tenderness and care is perhaps more different still.

MODELS FOR SOCIETY

The relation between child and mothering person seems especially worth exploring to see what implications and insights it might suggest for a transformed society.

There are good reasons to believe that a society resting on no more than bargains between self-interested or mutually disinterested individuals will not be able to withstand the forces of egoism and dissolution pulling such societies apart. Although there may be some limited domains in which rational contracts are the appropriate form of social relations, as a foundation for the fundamental ties which ought to bind human beings together, they are clearly inadequate. Perhaps we can learn from a non-patriarchal household better than from further searching in the marketplace what the sources might be for justifiable trust, cooperation, and caring.

Many persons can imagine human society on the model of "economic man," society built on a contract between rationally self-interested persons, because these are the theories they have been brought up with. But they cannot imagine society resembling a group of persons tied together by on-going relations of caring and trust between persons in positions such as those of mothers and children where, as adults, we would sometimes be one and sometimes the other. Suppose now we ask: in the relation between mothering person and child, who are the contractors? Where is the rational self-interest? The model of "economic man" makes no sense in this context. Anyone in the social contract tradition who has noticed the relation of child and mothering person at all has supposed it to belong to some domain outside the realm of the "free market" and outside the "public" realm of politics and the law. Such theorists have supposed the context of mothering to be of much less significance for human history and of much less relevance for moral theory than the realms of trade and government, or they have imagined mothers and children as somehow outside human society altogether in a region labelled "nature," and engaged wholly in "reproduction." But mothering is at the heart of human society.

If the dynamic relation between child and mothering person is taken as the primary social relation, then it is the model of "economic man" that can be seen to be deficient as a model for society and morality, and unsuitable for all but a special context. A domain such as law, if built on no more than contractual foundations, can then be recognized as one limited domain among others; law protects some moral rights when people are too immoral or weak to respect them without the force of law. But it is hardly a majestic edifice that can serve as a model for morality. Neither can the domain of politics, if built on no more than self-interest or mutual disinterest, provide us with a model with which to understand and improve society and morality. And neither, even more clearly, can the market itself.

When we explore the implications of these speculations we may come to realize that instead of seeing the family as an anomalous island in a sea of rational contracts composing economic and political and social life, perhaps it is instead "economic man" who belongs on a relatively small island surrounded by social ties of a less hostile, cold, and precarious kind.

STUDY QUESTIONS

1. What does Held mean by "contractual thinking"?
2. According to Held, what are the distinctive features of the relation between mothering person and child?
3. According to Held, in what specific ways might the relation between mothering person and child provide a model for society?
4. Does envisioning society as Held proposes suggest support for any particular governmental policies?

HISTORICAL SOURCES

The Republic

PLATO

Plato's *Republic* is a remarkable work that offers a unified account of central issues in metaphysics, epistemology, philosophy of mind, ethics, political philosophy, philosophy of art, and philosophy of education. Due to that book's length, which is more than half as long as this entire collection, space permits only the reprinting of relatively short segments, thereby necessarily omitting crucial materials.

From *The Republic* by Plato, trans. F. MacDonald Cornford. Copyright © 1974 by Oxford University Press. Reprinted by permission of the publisher. Notes are the translator's.

For our purposes, however, I have chosen to highlight Plato's defense of a non-democratic system of government, directed by a small group of philosopher-kings, both men and women, chosen on the basis of their natural aptitudes and specially educated for their roles. A community exhibits justice if the experts rule, supported by those in the military force, while workers and merchants attend to their own trades and businesses.

Note the parable toward the end of the selection in which Plato compares the working of a democratic society to the situation aboard a ship on which the sailors argue over the control of the helm, while none of them has ever learned navigation. And if someone on board happens to possess the needed skills, that person's qualifications are disregarded on the grounds that steering a ship requires no special competence. Plato was no friend of democracy, the system of government that put to death his beloved teacher, Socrates.

This excerpt ends with one of the most famous passages in the history of philosophy, the parable of the cave. This story is intended to reveal why those with knowledge are reviled by others, yet should be compelled to rule so as to promote the good of all. Never has democracy been challenged in a more compelling fashion, and developing a satisfactory response surely tests one's philosophical powers.

In the scenes that follow, Socrates is the first speaker and converses with Glaucon and Adeimantus, Plato's brothers, who are representative of the Athenian aristocracy.

[S]uppose we imagine a state coming into being before our eyes. We might then be able to watch the growth of justice or of injustice within it....

Don't waste any more time.

My notion is, said I, that a state comes into existence because no individual is self-sufficing; we all have many needs. But perhaps you can suggest some different origin for the foundation of a community?

No, I agree with you.

So, having all these needs, we call in one another's help to satisfy our various requirements; and when we have collected a number of helpers and associates to live together in one place, we call that settlement a state.

Yes.

So if one man gives another what he has to give in exchange for what he can get, it is because each finds that to do so is for his own advantage.

Certainly.

Very well, said I. Now let us build up our imaginary state from the beginning. Apparently, it will owe its existence to our needs, the first and greatest need being the provision of food to keep us alive. Next we shall want a house; and thirdly, such things as clothing.

True.

How will our state be able to supply all these demands? We shall need at least one man to be a farmer, another a builder, and a third a weaver. Will that do, or shall we add a shoemaker and one or two more to provide for our personal wants?

By all means.

The minimum state, then, will consist of four or five men.

Apparently.

Now here is a further point. Is each one of them to bring the product of his work into a common stock? Should our one farmer, for example, provide food enough for four people and spend the whole of his working time in producing corn, so as to share with the rest; or should he take no notice of them and spend only a quarter of his time on growing just enough corn for himself, and divide the other three-quarters between building his house, weaving his clothes, and making his shoes, so as to save the trouble of sharing with others and attend himself to all his own concerns?

The first plan might be the easier, replied Adeimantus.

That may very well be so, said I; for, as you spoke, it occurred to me, for one thing, that no two people are born exactly alike. There are innate differences which fit them for different occupations.

I agree.

And will a man do better working at many trades, or keeping to one only?

Keeping to one.

And there is another point: obviously work may be ruined, if you let the right time go by. The workman must wait upon the work; it will not wait upon his leisure and allow itself to be done in a spare moment. So the conclusion is that more things will be produced and the work be more easily and better done, when every man is set free from all other occupations to do, at the right time, the one thing for which he is naturally fitted.

That is certainly true.

We shall need more than four citizens, then, to supply all those necessaries we mentioned. You see, Adeimantus, if the farmer is to have a good plough and spade and other tools, he will not make them himself. No more will the builder and weaver and shoemaker make all the many implements they need. So quite a number of carpenters and smiths and other craftsmen must be enlisted. Our miniature state is beginning to grow.

It is.

Still, it will not be very large, even when we have added cowherds and shepherds to provide the farmers with oxen for the plough, and the builders as well as the farmers with draught-animals, and the weavers and shoemakers with wool and leather.

No; but it will not be so very small either.

And yet, again, it will be next to impossible to plant our city in a territory where it will need no imports. So there will have to be still another set of people, to fetch what it needs from other countries.

There will.

Moreover, if these agents take with them nothing that those other countries require in exchange, they will return as empty-handed as they went. So, besides everything wanted for consumption at home, we must produce enough goods of the right kind for the foreigners whom we depend on to supply us. That will mean increasing the number of farmers and craftsmen.

Yes.

And then, there are these agents who are to import and export all kinds of goods—merchants, as we call them. We must have them; and if they are to do business overseas, we shall need quite a number of ship-owners and others who know about that branch of trading.

We shall.

Again, in the city itself how are the various sets of producers to exchange their products? That was our object, you will remember, in forming a community and so laying the foundation of our state.

Obviously, they must buy and sell.

That will mean having a market-place, and a currency to serve as a token for purposes of exchange.

Certainly.

Now suppose a farmer, or an artisan, brings some of his produce to market at a time when no one is there who wants to exchange with him. Is he to sit there idle, when he might be at work?

No, he replied; there are people who have seen an opening here for their services. In well-ordered communities they are generally men not strong enough to be of use in any other occupation. They have to stay where they are in the market-place and take goods for money from those who want to sell, and money for goods from those who want to buy.

That, then, is the reason why our city must include a class of shopkeepers—so we call these people who sit still in the market-place to buy and sell, in contrast with merchants who travel to other countries.

Quite so.

There are also the services of yet another class, who have the physical strength for heavy work, though on intellectual grounds they are hardly worth including in our society—hired labourers, as we call them, because they sell the use of their strength for wages. They will go to make up our population.

Yes.

Well, Adeimantus, has our state now grown to its full size?

Perhaps.

Then, where in it shall we find justice or injustice? If they have come in with one of the elements we have been considering, can you say with which one?

I have no idea, Socrates; unless it be somewhere in their dealings with one another.

You may be right, I answered. Anyhow, it is a question which we shall have to face.

Let us begin, then, with a picture of our citizens' manner of life, with the provision we have made for them. They will be producing corn and wine and making clothes and shoes. When they have built their houses, they will mostly work without their coats or shoes in summer, and in winter be well shod and clothed. For their food, they will prepare flour and barley-meal for kneading and baking, and set out a grand spread of loaves and cakes on rushes or fresh leaves. Then they will lie on beds of myrtle-boughs and bryony and make merry with their children, drinking their wine after the feast with garlands on their heads and singing the praises of the gods. So they will live pleasantly together; and a prudent fear of poverty or war will keep them from begetting children beyond their means.

Here Glaucon interrupted me: You seem to expect your citizens to feast on dry bread.

True, I said; I forgot that they will have something to give it a relish, salt, no doubt, and olives, and cheese, and country stews of roots and vegetables. And for dessert we will give them figs and peas and beans; and they shall roast myrtle-berries and acorns at the fire, while they sip their wine. Leading such a healthy life in peace, they will naturally come to a good old age, and leave their children to live after them in the same manner.

That is just the sort of provender you would supply, Socrates, if you were founding a community of pigs.

Well, how are they to live, then, Glaucon?

With the ordinary comforts. Let them lie on couches and dine off tables on such dishes and sweets as we have nowadays.

Ah, I see, said I; we are to study the growth, not just of a state, but of a luxurious one. Well, there may be no harm in that; the consideration of luxury may help us to discover how justice and injustice take root in society. The community I have described seems to me the ideal one, in sound health as it were: but if you want to see one suffering from inflammation, there is nothing to hinder us. So some people, it seems, will not be satisfied to live in this simple way; they must have couches and tables and furniture of all sorts; and delicacies too, perfumes, unguents, courtesans, sweetmeats, all in plentiful variety. And besides, we must not limit ourselves now to those bare necessaries of house and clothes and shoes; we shall have to set going the arts of embroidery and painting, and collect rich materials, like gold and ivory.

Yes.

Then we must once more enlarge our community. The healthy one will not be big enough now; it must be swollen up with a whole multitude of callings not ministering to any bare necessity: hunters and fishermen, for instance; artists in sculpture, painting, and music; poets with their attendant train of professional reciters, actors, dancers, producers; and makers of all sorts of household gear, including everything for women's adornment. And we shall want more servants: children's nurses and attendants, lady's maids, barbers, cooks and confectioners. And then swineherds—there was no need for them in our original state, but we shall want them now; and a great quantity of sheep and cattle too, if people are going to live on meat.

Of course.

And with this manner of life physicians will be in much greater request.

No doubt.

The country, too, which was large enough to support the original inhabitants, will now be too small. If we are to have enough pasture and plough land, we shall have to cut off a slice of our neighbours' territory; and if they too are not content with necessaries, but give themselves up to getting unlimited wealth, they will want a slice of ours.

That is inevitable, Socrates.

So the next thing will be, Glaucon, that we shall be at war.

No doubt.

We need not say yet whether war does good or harm, but only that we have discovered its origin in desires which are the most fruitful source of evils both to individuals and to states.

Quite true.

This will mean a considerable addition to our community—a whole army, to go out to battle with any invader, in defence of all this property and of the citizens we have been describing.

Why so? Can't they defend themselves?

Not if the principle was right, which we all accepted in framing our society. You remember we agreed that no one man can practise many trades or arts satisfactorily.

True.

Well, is not the conduct of war an art, quite as important as shoemaking?

Yes.

But we would not allow our shoemaker to try to be also a farmer or weaver or builder, because we wanted our shoes well made. We gave each man one trade, for which he was naturally fitted; he would do good work, if he confined himself to that all his life, never letting the right moment slip by. Now in no form of work is efficiency so important as in war; and fighting is not so easy a business that a man can follow another trade, such as farming or shoemaking, and also be an efficient soldier. Why, even a game like draughts or dice must be studied from childhood; no one can become a fine player in his spare moments. Just taking up a shield or other weapon will not make a man capable of fighting that very day in any sort of warfare, any more than taking up a tool or implement of some kind will make a man a craftsman or an athlete, if he does not understand its use and has never been properly trained to handle it.

No; if that were so, tools would indeed be worth having.

These guardians of our state, then, inasmuch as their work is the most important of all, will need the most complete freedom from other occupations and the greatest amount of skill and practice.

I quite agree.

And also a native aptitude for their calling.

Certainly.

So it is our business to define, if we can, the natural gifts that fit men to be guardians of a commonwealth, and to select them accordingly. It will certainly be a formidable task; but we must grapple with it to the best of our power.

Yes.

Don't you think then, said I, that, for the purpose of keeping guard, a young man should have much the same temperament and qualities as a well-bred watch-dog? I mean, for instance, that both must have quick senses to detect an enemy, swiftness in pursuing him, and strength, if they have to fight when they have caught him.

Yes, they will need all those qualities.

And also courage, if they are to fight well.

Of course.

And courage, in dog or horse or any other creature, implies a spirited disposition. You must have noticed that a high spirit is unconquerable. Every soul possessed of it is fearless and indomitable in the face of any danger.

Yes, I have noticed that.

So now we know what physical qualities our Guardian must have, and also that he must be of a spirited temper.

Yes.

Then, Glaucon, how are men of that natural disposition to be kept from behaving pugnaciously to one another and to the rest of their countrymen?

It is not at all easy to see.

And yet they must be gentle to their own people and dangerous only to enemies; otherwise they will destroy themselves without waiting till others destroy them.

True.

What are we to do, then? If gentleness and a high temper are contraries, where shall we find a character to combine them? Both are necessary to make a good Guardian, but it seems they are incompatible. So we shall never have a good Guardian.

It looks like it.

Here I was perplexed, but on thinking over what we had been saying, I remarked that we deserved to be puzzled, because we had not followed up the comparison we had just drawn.

What do you mean? he asked.

We never noticed that, after all, there are natures in which these contraries are combined. They are to be found in animals, and not least in the kind we compared to our Guardian. Well-bred dogs, as you know, are by instinct perfectly gentle to people whom they know and are accustomed to, and fierce to strangers. So the combination of qualities we require for our Guardian is, after all, possible and not against nature.

Evidently.

Do you further agree that, besides this spirited temper, he must have a philosophical element in his nature?

I don't see what you mean.

This is another trait you will see in the dog. It is really remarkable how the creature gets angry at the mere sight of a stranger and welcomes anyone he knows, though he may never have been treated unkindly by the one or kindly by the other. Did that never strike you as curious?

I had not thought of it before; but that certainly is how a dog behaves.

Well, but that shows a fine instinct, which is philosophic in the true sense.

How so?

Because the only mark by which he distinguishes a friendly and an unfriendly face is that he knows the one and does not know the other; and if a creature makes that the test of what it finds congenial or otherwise, how can you deny that it has a passion for knowledge and understanding?

Of course, I cannot.

And that passion is the same thing as philosophy—the love of wisdom.[1]

Yes.

Shall we boldly say, then, that the same is true of human beings? If a man is to be gentle towards his own people whom he knows, he must have an instinctive love of wisdom and understanding.

Agreed.

So the nature required to make a really noble Guardian of our commonwealth will be swift and strong, spirited, and philosophic.

Quite so....

[W]hat is the next point to be settled? Is it not the question, which of these Guardians are to be rulers and which are to obey?

No doubt.

Well, it is obvious that the elder must have authority over the young, and that the rulers must be the best.

Yes.

And as among farmers the best are those with a natural turn for farming, so, if we want the best among our Guardians, we must take those naturally fitted to watch over a commonwealth. They must have the right sort of intelligence and ability; and also they must look upon the commonwealth as their special concern—the sort of concern that is felt for something so closely bound up with oneself that its interests and fortunes, for good or ill, are held to be identical with one's own.

Exactly.

So the kind of men we must choose from among the Guardians will be those who, when we look at the whole course of their lives, are found to be full of zeal to do whatever they believe is for the good of the commonwealth and never willing to act against its interest.

Yes, they will be the men we want....

We shall have to watch them from earliest childhood and set them tasks in which they would be most likely to forget or to be beguiled out of this duty. We shall then choose only those whose memory holds firm and who are proof against delusion.

Yes.

We must also subject them to ordeals of toil and pain and watch for the same qualities there. And we must observe them when exposed to the test of yet a third kind of bewitchment. As people lead colts up to alarming noises to see whether they are timid, so these young men must be brought into terrifying situations and then into scenes of pleasure, which will put them to severer proof than gold tried in the furnace. If we find one bearing himself well in all these trials and resisting every enchantment, a true guardian of himself, preserving always that perfect rhythm and harmony of being which he has acquired from his training in music and poetry, such a one will be of the greatest service to the commonwealth as well as to himself. Whenever we find one who has come unscathed through every test in childhood, youth, and manhood, we shall set him as a Ruler to watch over the commonwealth; he will be honoured in life, and after death receive the highest tribute of funeral rites and other memorials. All who do not reach this standard we must reject. And that, I think, my dear Glaucon, may be taken as an outline of the way in which we shall select Guardians to be set in authority as Rulers.

I am very much of your mind.

These, then, may properly be called Guardians in the fullest sense, who will ensure that neither foes without shall have the power, nor friends within the wish, to do harm. Those young men whom up to now we have been speaking of as Guardians, will be better described as Auxiliaries, who will enforce the decisions of the Rulers.

I agree.

Now, said I, can we devise . . . a single bold flight of invention, which we may induce the community in general, and if possible the Rulers themselves, to accept?

What kind of fiction? . . .

Well, here it is; though I hardly know how to find the courage or the words to express it. I shall try to convince, first the Rulers and the soldiers,[2] and then the whole community, that all that nurture and education which we gave them was only something they seemed to experience as it were in a dream. In reality they were the whole time down inside the earth, being moulded and fostered while their arms and all their equipment were being fashioned also; and at last, when they were complete, the earth sent them up from her womb into the light of day. So now they must think of the land they dwell in as a mother and nurse, whom they must take thought for and defend against any attack, and of their fellow citizens as brothers born of the same soil.

You might well be bashful about coming out with your fiction.

No doubt; but still you must hear the rest of the story. It is true, we shall tell our people in this fable, that all of you in this land are brothers; but the god who fashioned you mixed gold in the composition of those among you who are fit to rule, so that they are of the most precious quality; and he put silver in the Auxiliaries, and iron and brass in the farmers and craftsmen. Now, since you are all of one stock, although your children will generally be like their parents, sometimes a golden parent may have a silver child or a silver parent a golden one, and so on with all the other combinations. So the first and chief injunction laid by heaven upon the Rulers is that, among all the things of which they must show themselves good guardians, there is none that needs to be so carefully watched as the mixture of metals in the souls of the children. If a child of their own is born with an alloy of iron or brass, they must, without the smallest pity, assign him the station proper to his nature and thrust him out among the craftsmen or the farmers. If, on the contrary, these classes produce a child with gold or silver in his composition, they will promote him, according to his value, to be a Guardian or an Auxiliary. They will appeal to a prophecy that ruin will come upon the state when it passes into the keeping of a man of iron or brass. Such is the story; can you think of any device to make them believe it?

Not in the first generation; but their sons and descendants might believe it, and finally the rest of mankind.

Well, said I, even so it might have a good effect in making them care more for the commonwealth and for one another; for I think I see what you mean. . . .

Listen, then, and judge whether I am right. You remember how, when we first began to establish our commonwealth and several times since, we have laid down, as a universal principle, that everyone ought to perform the one function in the community for which his nature best suited him. Well, I believe that that principle, or some form of it, is justice.

We certainly laid that down.

Yes, and surely we have often heard people say that justice means minding one's own business and not meddling with other men's concerns; and we have often said so ourselves.

We have. . . .

Again, do you agree with me that no great harm would be done to the community by a general interchange of most forms of work, the carpenter and the cobbler exchanging their positions and their tools and taking on each other's jobs, or even the same man undertaking both?

Yes, there would not be much harm in that.

But I think you will also agree that another kind of interchange would be disastrous. Suppose, for instance, someone whom nature designed to be an artisan or tradesman should be emboldened by some advantage, such as wealth or command of votes or bodily strength, to try to enter the order of fighting men; or some member of that order should aspire, beyond his merits, to a seat in the council-chamber of the Guardians. Such interference and exchange of social positions and tools, or the attempt to combine all these forms of work in the same person, would be fatal to the commonwealth.

Most certainly.

Where there are three orders, then, any plurality of functions or shifting from one order to another is not merely utterly harmful to the community, but one might fairly call it the extreme of wrongdoing. And you will agree that to do the greatest of wrongs to one's own community is injustice.

Surely.

This, then, is injustice. And, conversely, let us repeat that when each order—tradesman, Auxiliary, Guardian—keeps to its own proper business in the commonwealth and does its own work, that is justice and what makes a just society.

I entirely agree....

Then our next attempt, it seems, must be to point out what defect in the working of existing states prevents them from being so organized, and what is the least change that would effect a transformation into this type of government—a single change if possible, or perhaps two; at any rate let us make the changes as few and insignificant as may be.

By all means.

Well, there is one change which, as I believe we can show, would bring about this revolution—not a small change, certainly, nor an easy one, but possible.

What is it? ...

Unless either philosophers become kings in their countries or those who are now called kings and rulers come to be sufficiently inspired with a genuine desire for wisdom; unless, that is to say, political power and philosophy meet together, while the many natures who now go their several ways in the one or the other direction are forcibly debarred from doing so, there can be no rest from troubles, my dear Glaucon, for states, nor yet, as I believe, for all mankind; nor can this commonwealth which we have imagined ever till then see the light of day and grow to its full stature....

Here Adeimantus interposed.... [A]s a matter of plain fact, the votaries of philosophy, when they carry on the study too long, instead of taking it up in youth as a part of general culture and then dropping it, almost always become ... utterly worthless; while even the most respectable are so far the worse for this pursuit you are praising as to become useless to society.

Well, I replied, do you think that charge is untrue?

I do not know, he answered; I should like to hear your opinion.

You shall; I think it is true.

Then how can it be right to say that there will be no rest from trouble until states are ruled by these philosophers whom we are now admitting to be of no use to them?

That is a question which needs to be answered by means of a parable....

Imagine this state of affairs on board a ship or a number of ships. The master is bigger and burlier than any of the crew, but a little deaf and short-sighted and no less deficient in seamanship. The sailors are quarrelling over the control of the helm; each thinks he ought to be steering the vessel, though he has never learnt navigation and cannot point to any teacher under whom he has served his apprenticeship; what is more, they assert that navigation is a thing that cannot be taught at all, and are ready to tear in pieces anyone who says it can. Meanwhile they besiege the master himself, begging him urgently to trust them with the helm; and sometimes, when others have been more successful in gaining his ear, they kill them or throw them overboard, and, after somehow stupefying the worthy master with strong drink or an opiate, take control of the ship, make free with its stores, and turn the voyage, as might be expected of such a crew, into a drunken carousal. Besides all this, they cry up as a skilled navigator and master of seamanship anyone clever enough to lend a hand in persuading or forcing the master to set them in command. Every other kind of man they condemn as useless. They do not understand that the genuine navigator can only make himself fit to command a ship by studying the seasons of the year, sky, stars, and winds, and all that belongs to his craft; and they have no idea that, along with the science of navigation, it is possible for him to gain, by instruction or practice, the skill to keep control of the helm whether some of them like it or not. If a ship were managed in that way, would not those on board be likely to call the expert in navigation a mere star-gazer, who spent his time in idle talk and was useless to them?

They would indeed.

I think you understand what I mean and do not need to have my parable interpreted in order to see how it illustrates the attitude of existing states towards the true philosopher.

Quite so.

Use it, then, to enlighten that critic whom you spoke of as astonished that philosophers are not held in honour by their country. You may try, in the first place, to convince him that it would be far more astonishing if they were; and you may tell him further that he is right in calling the best sort of philosophers useless to the public; but for that he must rather blame those who make no use of them. It is not in the natural course of things for the pilot to beg the crew to take his orders, any more than for the wise to wait on the doorsteps of the rich; the author of that epigram[3] was mistaken. What is natural is that the sick man, whether rich or poor, should wait at the door of the physician, and that all who need to be governed should seek out the man who can govern them; it is not for him to beg them to accept his rule, if there is really any help in him. But our present rulers may fairly be compared to the sailors in our parable, and the useless visionaries, as the politicians call them, to the real masters of navigation.

Quite true.

Under these conditions, the noblest of pursuits can hardly be thought much of by men whose own way of life runs counter to it. . . .

But what do you mean by the highest kind of knowledge and with what is it concerned? You cannot hope to escape that question. . . .

First we must come to an understanding. Let me remind you of the distinction we drew earlier and have often drawn on other occasions, between the multiplicity of things that we call good or beautiful or whatever it may be and, on the other hand, Goodness itself or Beauty itself and so on. Corresponding to each of these sets of many things, we postulate a single Form or real essence, as we call it.

Yes, that is so.

Further, the many things, we say, can be seen, but are not objects of rational thought; whereas the Forms are objects of thought, but invisible.

Yes, certainly.

And we see things with our eyesight, just as we hear sounds with our ears and, to speak generally, perceive any sensible thing with our sense-faculties.

Of course.

Have you noticed, then, that the artificer who designed the senses has been exceptionally lavish of his materials in making the eyes able to see and their objects visible?

That never occurred to me.

Well, look at it in this way. Hearing and sound do not stand in need of any third thing, without which the ear will not hear nor sound be heard; and I think the same is true of most, not to say all, of the other senses. Can you think of one that does require anything of the sort?

No, I cannot.

But there is this need in the case of sight and its objects. You may have the power of vision in your eyes and try to use it, and colour may be there in the objects; but sight will see nothing and the colours will remain invisible in the absence of a third thing peculiarly constituted to serve this very purpose.

By which you mean—?

Naturally I mean what you call light; and if light is a thing of value, the sense of sight and the power of being visible are linked together by a very precious bond, such as unites no other sense with its object.

No one could say that light is not a precious thing.

And of all the divinities in the skies[4] is there one whose light, above all the rest, is responsible for making our eyes see perfectly and making objects perfectly visible?

There can be no two opinions: of course you mean the Sun.

And how is sight related to this deity? Neither sight nor the eye which contains it is the Sun, but of all the sense-organs it is the most sun-like; and further, the power it possesses is dispensed by the Sun, like a stream flooding the eye. And again, the Sun is not vision, but it is the cause of vision and also is seen by the vision it causes.

Yes.

It was the Sun, then, that I meant when I spoke of that offspring which the Good has created in the visible world, to stand there in the same relation to vision and visible things as that which the Good itself bears in the intelligible world to intelligence and to intelligible objects.

How is that? You must explain further.

You know what happens when the colours of things are no longer irradiated by the daylight, but only by the fainter luminaries of the night: when you look at them, the eyes are dim and seem almost blind, as if there were no unclouded vision in them. But when you look at things on which the Sun is shining, the same eyes see distinctly and it becomes evident that they do contain the power of vision.

Certainly.

Apply this comparison, then, to the soul. When its gaze is fixed upon an object irradiated by truth and reality, the soul gains understanding and knowledge and is manifestly in possession of intelligence. But when it looks towards that twilight world of things that come into existence and pass away, its sight is dim and it has only opinions and beliefs which shift to and fro, and now it seems like a thing that has no intelligence.

That is true.

This, then, which gives to the objects of knowledge their truth and to him who knows them his power of knowing, is the Form or essential nature of Goodness. It is the cause of knowledge and truth; and so, while you may think of it as an object of knowledge, you will do well to regard it as something beyond truth and knowledge and, precious as these both are, of still higher worth. And, just as in our analogy light and vision were to be thought of as like the Sun, but not identical with it, so here both knowledge and truth are to be regarded as like the Good, but to identify either with the Good is wrong. The Good must hold a yet higher place of honour.

You are giving it a position of extraordinary splendour, if it is the source of knowledge and truth and itself surpasses them in worth. You surely cannot mean that it is pleasure.

Heaven forbid, I exclaimed. But I want to follow up our analogy still further. You will agree that the Sun not only makes the things we see visible, but also brings them into existence and gives them growth and nourishment; yet he is not the same thing as existence. And so with the objects of knowledge: these derive from the Good not only their power of being known, but their very being and reality; and Goodness is not the same thing as being, but even beyond being, surpassing it in dignity and power.

Glaucon exclaimed with some amusement at my exalting Goodness in such extravagant terms.

It is your fault, I replied; you forced me to say what I think.

Yes, and you must not stop there. At any rate, complete your comparison with the Sun, if there is any more to be said.

There is a great deal more, I answered.

Let us hear it, then; don't leave anything out.

I am afraid much must be left unspoken. However, I will not, if I can help it, leave out anything that can be said on this occasion.

Please do not.

Conceive, then, that there are these two powers I speak of, the Good reigning over the domain of all that is intelligible, the Sun over the visible world—or the heaven as I might call it; only you would think I was showing off my skill in etymology. At any rate you have these two orders of things clearly before your mind: the visible and the intelligible?

I have.

Now take a line divided into two unequal parts, one to represent the visible order, the other the intelligible; and divide each part again in the same proportion, symbolizing degrees of comparative clearness or obscurity. Then (A) one of the two sections in the visible world will stand for images. By images I mean first *shadows*, and then *reflections in water* or in close-grained, polished surfaces, and everything of that kind, if you understand.

Yes, I understand.

Let the second section (B) stand for the *actual things* of which the first are likenesses, the living creatures about us and all the works of nature or of human hands.

So be it.

Will you also take the proportion in which the visible world has been divided as corresponding to degrees of reality and truth, so that the likeness shall stand to the original in the same ratio as the sphere of appearances and belief to the sphere of knowledge?

Certainly.

Now consider how we are to divide the part which stands for the intelligible world. There are two sections. In the first (C) the mind uses as images those actual things which themselves had images in the visible world; and it is compelled to pursue its inquiry by starting from assumptions and travelling, not up to a principle, but down to a conclusion. In the second (D) the mind moves in the other direction, from an assumption up towards a principle which is not hypothetical; and it makes no use of the images employed in the other section, but only of Forms, and conducts its inquiry solely by their means.

I don't quite understand what you mean.

Then we will try again; what I have just said will help you to understand. (C) You know, of course, how students of subjects like geometry and arithmetic begin by postulating odd and even numbers, or the various figures and the three kinds of angle, and other such data in each subject. These data they take as known; and, having adopted them as assumptions, they do not feel called upon to give any account of them to themselves or to anyone else, but treat them as self-evident. Then, starting from these assumptions, they go on until they arrive, by a series of consistent steps, at all the conclusions they set out to investigate.

Yes, I know that.

You also know how they make use of visible figures and discourse about them, though what they really have in mind is the originals of which these figures are images: they are not reasoning, for instance, about this particular square and diagonal which they have drawn, but about *the* Square and *the* Diagonal; and so in all cases. The diagrams they draw and the models they make are actual things, which may have their shadows or images in water; but now they serve in their turn as images, while the student is seeking to behold those realities which only thought can apprehend.

True.

This, then, is the class of things that I spoke of as intelligible, but with two qualifications: first, that the mind, in studying them, is compelled to employ assumptions, and, because it cannot rise above these, does not travel upwards to a first principle; and second, that it uses as images those actual things which have images of their own in the section below them and which, in comparison with those shadows and reflections, are reputed to be more palpable and valued accordingly.

I understand: you mean the subject-matter of geometry and of the kindred arts.

(D) Then by the second section of the intelligible world you may understand me to mean all that unaided reasoning apprehends by the power of dialectic, when it treats its assumptions, not as first principles, but as *hypotheses* in the literal sense, things "laid down" like a flight of steps up which it may mount all the way to something that is not hypothetical, the first principle of all; and having grasped this, may turn back and, holding on to the consequences which depend upon it, descend at last to a conclusion, never making use of any sensible object, but only of Forms, moving through Forms from one to another, and ending with Forms.

I understand, he said, though not perfectly; for the procedure you describe sounds like an enormous undertaking. But I see that you mean to distinguish the field of intelligible reality studied by dialectic as having a greater certainty and truth than the subject-matter of the "arts," as they are called, which treat their assumptions as first principles. The students of these arts are, it is true, compelled to exercise thought in contemplating objects which the senses cannot perceive; but because they start from assumptions without going back to a first principle, you do not regard them as gaining true understanding about those objects, although the objects themselves, when connected with a first principle, are intelligible. And I think you would call the state of mind of the students of geometry and other such arts, not intelligence, but thinking, as being something between intelligence and mere acceptance of appearances.

You have understood me quite well enough, I replied. And now you may take, as corresponding to the four sections, these four states of mind: *intelligence* for the highest, *thinking* for the second, *belief* for the third, and for the last *imagining*. These you may arrange as the terms in a proportion, assigning to each a degree of clearness and certainty corresponding to the measure in which their objects possess truth and reality.

I understand and agree with you. I will arrange them as you say.

Next, said I, here is a parable to illustrate the degrees in which our nature may be enlightened or unenlightened. Imagine the condition of men living in a sort of cavernous chamber underground, with an entrance open to the light and a long passage all down the cave.[5] Here they have been from childhood, chained by the leg and also by the neck, so that they cannot move and can see only what is in front of them, because the chains will not let them turn their heads. At some distance higher up is the light of a fire burning behind them; and between the prisoners and the fire is a track[6] with a parapet built along it, like the screen at a puppet-show, which hides the performers while they show their puppets over the top.

I see, said he.

Now behind this parapet imagine persons carrying along various artificial objects, including figures of men and animals in wood or stone or other materials, which project above the parapet. Naturally, some of these persons will be talking, others silent.[7]

It is a strange picture, he said, and a strange sort of prisoners.

Like ourselves, I replied; for in the first place prisoners so confined would have seen nothing of themselves or of one another, except the shadows thrown by the fire-light on the wall of the Cave facing them, would they?

Not if all their lives they had been prevented from moving their heads.

And they would have seen as little of the objects carried past.

Of course.

Now, if they could talk to one another, would they not suppose that their words referred only to those passing shadows which they saw?[8]

Necessarily.

And suppose their prison had an echo from the wall facing them? When one of the people crossing behind them spoke, they could only suppose that the sound came from the shadow passing before their eyes.

No doubt.

In every way, then, such prisoners would recognize as reality nothing but the shadows of those artificial objects.

Inevitably.

Now consider what would happen if their release from the chains and the healing of their unwisdom should come about in this way. Suppose one of them set free and forced suddenly to stand up, turn his head, and walk with eyes lifted to the light; all these movements would be painful, and he would be too dazzled to make out the objects whose shadows he had been used to see. What do you think he would say, if someone told him that what he had formerly seen was meaningless illusion, but now, being somewhat nearer to reality and turned towards more real objects, he was getting a truer view? Suppose further that he were shown the various objects being carried by and were made to say, in reply to questions, what each of them was. Would he not be perplexed and believe the objects now shown him to be not so real as what he formerly saw?

Yes, not nearly so real.

And if he were forced to look at the fire-light itself, would not his eyes ache, so that he would try to escape and turn back to the things which he could see distinctly, convinced that they really were clearer than these other objects now being shown to him?

Yes.

And suppose someone were to drag him away forcibly up the steep and rugged ascent and not let him go until he had hauled him out into the sunlight, would he not suffer pain and vexation at such treatment, and, when he had come out into the light, find his eyes so full of its radiance that he could not see a single one of the things that he was now told were real?

Certainly he would not see them all at once.

He would need, then, to grow accustomed before he could see things in that upper world. At first it would be easiest to make out shadows, and then the images of men and things reflected in water, and later on the things themselves. After that, it would be easier to watch the heavenly bodies and the sky itself by night, looking at the light of the moon and stars rather than the Sun and the Sun's light in the day-time.

Yes, surely.

Last of all, he would be able to look at the Sun and contemplate its nature, not as it appears when reflected in water or any alien medium, but as it is in itself in its own domain.

No doubt.

And now he would begin to draw the conclusion that it is the Sun that produces the seasons and the course of the year and controls everything in the visible world, and moreover is in a way the cause of all that he and his companions used to see.

Clearly he would come at last to that conclusion.

Then if he called to mind his fellow prisoners and what passed for wisdom in his former dwelling-place, he would surely think himself happy in the change and be sorry for them. They may have had a practice of honouring and commending one another, with prizes for the man who had the keenest eye for the passing shadows and the best memory for the order in which they followed or accompanied one another, so that he could make a good guess as to which was going to come next. Would our released prisoner be likely to covet those prizes or to envy the men exalted to honour and power in the Cave? Would he not feel like Homer's Achilles, that he would far sooner "be on earth as a hired servant in the house of a landless man" or endure anything rather than go back to his old beliefs and live in the old way?

Yes, he would prefer any fate to such a life.

Now imagine what would happen if he went down again to take his former seat in the Cave. Coming suddenly out of the sunlight, his eyes would be filled with darkness. He might be required once more to deliver his opinion on those shadows, in competition with the prisoners who had never been released, while his eyesight was still dim and unsteady; and it might take some time to become used to the darkness. They would laugh at him and say that he had gone up only to come back with his sight ruined; it was worth no one's while even to attempt the ascent. If they could lay hands on the man who was trying to set them free and lead them up, they would kill him.[9]

Yes, they would.

Every feature in this parable, my dear Glaucon, is meant to fit our earlier analysis. The prison dwelling corresponds to the region revealed to us through the sense of sight, and the fire-light within it to the power of the Sun. The ascent to see the things in the upper world you may take as standing for the upward journey of the soul into the region of the intelligible; then you will be in possession of what I surmise, since that is what you wish to be told. Heaven knows whether it is true; but this, at any rate, is how it appears to me. In the world of knowledge, the last thing to be perceived and only with great difficulty is the essential Form of Goodness. Once it is perceived, the conclusion must follow that, for all things, this is the cause of whatever is right and good; in the visible world it gives birth to light and to the lord of light, while it is itself sovereign in the intelligible world and the parent of intelligence and truth. Without having had a vision of this Form, no one can act with wisdom, either in his own life or in matters of state.

So far as I can understand, I share your belief.

Then you may also agree that it is no wonder if those who have reached this height are reluctant to manage the affairs of men. Their souls long to spend all their time in that upper world—naturally enough, if here once more our parable holds true. Nor, again, is it at all strange that one who comes from the contemplation of divine things to the miseries of human life should appear awkward and ridiculous when, with eyes still dazed and not yet accustomed to the darkness, he is compelled, in a law-court or elsewhere, to dispute about the shadows of justice or the images that cast those shadows, and to wrangle over the notions of what is right in the minds of men who have never beheld Justice itself.

It is not at all strange. . . .

It is for us, then, as founders of a commonwealth, to bring compulsion to bear on the noblest natures. They . . . must not be allowed, as they now are, to remain on the heights, refusing to come down again to the prisoners or to take any part in their labours and rewards, however much or little these may be worth.

Shall we not be doing them an injustice, if we force on them a worse life than they might have?

You have forgotten again, my friend, that the law is not concerned to make any one class specially happy, but to ensure the welfare of the commonwealth as a whole. By persuasion or constraint it will unite the citizens in harmony, making them share whatever benefits each class can contribute to the common good; and its purpose in forming men of that spirit was not that each should be left to go his own way, but that they should be instrumental in binding the community into one.

True, I had forgotten.

You will see, then, Glaucon, that there will be no real injustice in compelling our philosophers to watch over and care for the other citizens. We can fairly tell them that their compeers in other states may quite reasonably refuse to collaborate: there they have sprung up, like a self-sown plant, in despite of their country's institutions; no one has fostered their growth, and they cannot be expected to show gratitude for a care they have never received. "But," we shall say, "it is not so with you. We have brought you into existence for your country's sake as well as for your own, to be like leaders and king-bees in a hive; you have been better and more thoroughly educated than those others and hence you are more capable of playing your part both as men of thought and as men of action. You must go down, then, each in his turn, to live with the rest and let your eyes grow accustomed to the darkness. You will then see a thousand times better than those who live there always; you will recognize every image for what it is and know what it represents, because you have seen justice, beauty, and goodness in their reality; and so you and we shall find life in our commonwealth no mere dream, as it is in most existing states, where men live fighting one another about shadows and quarrelling for power, as if that were a great prize; whereas in truth government can be at its best and free from dissension only where the destined rulers are least desirous of holding office."

Quite true.

Then will our pupils refuse to listen and to take their turns at sharing in the work of the community, though they may live together for most of their time in a purer air?

No; it is a fair demand, and they are fair-minded men. No doubt, unlike any ruler of the present day, they will think of holding power as an unavoidable necessity.

Yes, my friend; for the truth is that you can have a well-governed society only if you can discover for your future rulers a better way of life than being in office; then only will power be in the hands of men who are rich, not in gold, but in the wealth that brings happiness, a good and wise life. All goes wrong when, starved for lack of anything good in their own lives, men turn to public affairs hoping to snatch from thence the happiness they hunger for. They set about fighting for power, and this internecine conflict ruins them and their country. The life of true philosophy is the only one that looks down upon offices of state; and access to power must be confined to men who are not in love with it; otherwise rivals will start fighting. So whom else can you compel to undertake the guardianship of the commonwealth, if not those who, besides understanding best the principles of government, enjoy a nobler life than the politician's and look for rewards of a different kind?

There is indeed no other choice.

NOTES

1. The ascription of a philosophic element to dogs is not seriously meant. We might regard man's love of knowledge as rooted in an instinct of curiosity to be found in animals; but curiosity has no connexion with gentleness, and for Plato reason is an independent faculty, existing only in man and not developed from any animal instinct.
2. Note that the Guardians themselves are to accept this allegory, if possible. It is not "propaganda" foisted on the masses by the Rulers.
3. Simonides was asked by Hiero's queen whether it was better to be wise (a man of genius) or rich. He replied: Rich; for the wise are to be found at the court of the rich.
4. Plato held that the heavenly bodies are immortal living creatures, i.e, gods.
5. The *length* of the "way in" (*eisodos*) to the chamber where the prisoners sit is an essential feature, explaining why no daylight reaches them.
6. The track crosses the passage into the cave at right angles, and is *above* the parapet built along it.
7. A modern Plato would compare his Cave to an underground cinema, where the audience watch the play of shadows thrown by the film passing before a light at their backs. The film itself is only an image of "real" things and events in the world outside the cinema. For the film Plato has to substitute the clumsier apparatus of a procession of artificial objects carried on their heads by persons who are merely part of the machinery, providing for the movement of the objects and the sounds whose echo the prisoners hear. The parapet prevents these persons' shadows from being cast on the wall of the Cave.
8. The prisoners, having seen nothing but shadows, cannot think their words refer to the objects carried past behind their backs. For them shadows (images) are the only realities.
9. An allusion to the fate of Socrates.

STUDY QUESTIONS

1. How do you defend a system of government in which those who know much about public issues have no more say in the decision process than those who know little?
2. What is the fable of the metals, and does it strengthen or weaken Plato's case against democracy?
3. Do you believe that the parable of the state of affairs on board a ship misrepresents democracy?
4. Do you agree with Plato that the best rulers are found among those not seeking to rule?

Leviathan

ᴊ↬

Tʜᴏᴍᴀꜱ Hᴏʙʙᴇꜱ

Thomas Hobbes (1588–1679) was an English philosopher who played a crucial role in the history of social thought. He developed a moral and political theory that views justice and other ethical ideals as resting on an implied agreement among individuals to relinquish the right to do whatever they please in exchange for all others limiting their rights in a similar manner, thus achieving security for all.

....

OF THE NATURAL CONDITION OF MANKIND AS CONCERNING THEIR FELICITY, AND MISERY

Nature hath made men so equal, in the faculties of body and mind; as that though there be found one man sometimes manifestly stronger in body, or of quicker mind than another; yet when all is reckoned together, the difference between man and man is not so considerable, as that one man can thereupon claim to himself any benefit, to which another may not pretend as well as he. For as to the strength of body, the weakest has strength enough to kill the strongest, either by secret machination or by confederacy with others, that are in the same danger as himself.

And as to the faculties of the mind (setting aside the arts grounded upon words, and especially that skill of proceeding upon general, and infallible rules, called science; which very few have, and but in few things; as being not a native faculty, born with us; nor attained (as prudence) while we look after someone else) I find yet a greater equality amongst men than that of strength. For prudence is but experience; which equal time equally bestows on all men in those things they equally apply themselves unto. That which may perhaps make such equality incredible is but a vain conceit of one's own wisdom, which almost all men think they have in a greater degree than the vulgar; that is, than all men but themselves, and a few others, whom by fame, or for concurring with themselves, they approve. For such is the nature of men, that howsoever they may acknowledge many others to be more witty, or more eloquent, or more learned; yet they will hardly believe there be many so wise as themselves: For they see their own wit at hand, and other men's at a distance. But this proveth rather that men are in that point equal than unequal. For there is not ordinarily a greater sign of the equal distribution of any thing than that every man is contented with his share.

From this equality of ability ariseth equality of hope in the attaining of our ends. And therefore if any two men desire the same thing, which nevertheless they cannot

From Thomas Hobbes, *Leviathan* (1651).

both enjoy, they become enemies; and in the way to their end (which is principally their own conservation, and sometimes their delectation only) endeavour to destroy, or subdue one another. And from hence it comes to pass that where an invader hath no more to fear than another man's single power; if one plant, sow, build, or possess a convenient seat, others may probably be expected to come prepared with forces united to dispossess and deprive him not only of the fruit of his labour but also of his life or liberty. And the invader again is in the like danger of another.

And from this diffidence of one another, there is no way for any man to secure himself, so reasonable, as anticipation; that is, by force, or wiles, to master the persons of all men he can, so long, till he see no other power great enough to endanger him: and this is no more than his own conservation requireth, and is generally allowed. Also because there be some, that taking pleasure in contemplating their own power in the acts of conquest, which they pursue farther than their security requires; if others, that otherwise would be glad to be at ease within modest bounds, should not by invasion increase their power, they would not be able, long time, by standing only on their defence, to subsist. And by consequence, such augmentation of dominion over men, being necessary to a man's conservation, it ought to be allowed him.

Again, men have no pleasure (but on the contrary a great deal of grief) in keeping company, where there is no power able to over-awe them all. For every man looketh that his companion should value him, at the same rate he sets upon himself: and upon all signs of contempt, or undervaluing, naturally endeavours, as far as he dares (which amongst them that have no common power to keep them in quiet, is far enough to make them destroy each other) to extort a greater value from his contemners, by damage; and from others, by the example.

So that in the nature of man, we find three principal causes of quarrel. First, competition; secondly, diffidence; thirdly, glory.

The first, maketh man invade for gain; the second, for safety; and the third, for reputation. The first use violence, to make themselves masters of other men's persons, wives, children, and cattle; the second, to defend them; the third for trifles, as a word, a smile, a different opinion, and any other sign of undervalue, either direct in their persons, or by reflection in their kindred, their friends, their nation, their profession, or their name.

Hereby it is manifest that during the time men live without a common power to keep them all in awe, they are in that condition which is called war; and such a war, as is of every man, against every man. For WAR consisteth not in battle only, or the act of fighting, but in a tract of time, wherein the will to contend by battle is sufficiently known: and therefore the notion of *time* is to be considered in the nature of war, as it is in the nature of weather. For as the nature of foul weather lieth not in a shower or two of rain, but in an inclination thereto of many days together: so the nature of war, consisteth not in actual fighting, but in the known disposition thereto, during all the time there is no assurance to the contrary. All other time is PEACE.

Whatsoever therefore is consequent to a time of war, where every man is enemy to every man; the same is consequent to the time, wherein men live without other security than what their own strength, and their own invention shall furnish them withal. In such condition, there is no place for industry; because the fruit thereof is uncertain: and consequently no culture of the earth; no navigation, nor use of the commodities that may be imported by sea; no commodious building; no instruments of moving, and removing such things as require much force; no knowledge of the face of the earth; no account of time; no arts; no letters; no society; and which is worst of all, continual fear, and danger of violent death; and the life of man, solitary, poor, nasty, brutish, and short.

It may seem strange to some man, that has not well weighed these things; that nature should thus dissociate, and render men apt to invade, and destroy one another: and he may therefore, not trusting to this inference, made from the passions, desire perhaps to have the same confirmed by experience. Let him therefore consider with himself, when taking a journey, he arms himself, and seeks to go well accompanied; when going to sleep, he locks his doors; when even in his house he locks his chests; and this when he knows there be laws, and public officers, armed, to revenge all injuries shall be done him; what opinion he has of his fellow subjects, when he rides armed; of his fellow citizens, when he locks his doors; and of his children, and servants, when he locks his chests. Does he not there as much accuse mankind by his actions as I do by my words? But neither of us accuse man's nature in it. The desires, and other passions of man, are in themselves no sin. No more are the actions that proceed from those passions till they know a law that forbids them: which till laws be made they cannot know: nor can any law be made till they have agreed upon the person that shall make it.

It may peradventure be thought there was never such a time nor condition of war as this; and I believe it was never generally so, over all the world: but there are many places where they live so now. For the savage people in many places of *America*, except the government of small families, the concord whereof dependeth on natural lust, have no government at all: and live at this day in that brutish manner, as I said before. Howsoever, it may be perceived what manner of life there would be, where there were no common power to fear; by the manner of life, which men that have formerly lived under a peacefull government, use to degenerate into a civil war.

But though there had never been any time wherein particular men were in a condition of war one against another; yet in all times, kings and persons of sovereign authority, because of their independency, are in continual jealousies and in the state and posture of gladiators, having their weapons pointing and their eyes fixed on one another; that is, their forts, garrisons, and guns upon the frontiers of their kingdoms; and continual spies upon their neighbours; which is a posture of war. But because they uphold thereby the industry of their subjects there does not follow from it that misery, which accompanies the liberty of particular men.

To this war of every man against every man, this also is consequent that nothing can be unjust. The notions of right and wrong, justice and injustice, have there no place. Where there is no common power, there is no law: where no law, no injustice. Force and fraud are in war the two cardinal virtues. Justice and injustice are none of the faculties neither of the body nor mind. If they were, they might be in a man that were alone in the world, as well as his senses and passions. They are qualities that relate to men in society, not in solitude. It is consequent also to the same condition that there be no propriety, no dominion, no *mine* and *thine* distinct; but only that to be every man's, that he can get; and for so long, as he can keep it. And thus much for the ill condition which many by mere nature is actually placed in; though with a possibility to come out of it, consisting partly in the passions, partly in his reason.

The passions that incline men to peace are fear of death; desire of such things as are necessary to commodious living; and a hope by their industry to obtain them. And reason suggesteth convenient articles of peace, upon which men may be drawn to agreement. These articles are they which otherwise are called the Laws of Nature: whereof I shall speak more particularly, in the two following chapters.

OF THE FIRST AND SECOND NATURAL LAWS, AND OF CONTRACTS

The RIGHT OF NATURE, which writers commonly call *jus naturale,* is the liberty each man hath, to use his own power, as he will himself, for the preservation of his own nature; that is to say, of his own life; and consequently, of doing any thing, which in his own judgment, and reason, he shall conceive to be the aptest means thereunto.

By LIBERTY, is understood, according to the proper signification of the word, the absence of external impediments: which impediments may oft take away part of a man's power to do what he would; but cannot hinder him from using the power left him, according as his judgment, and reason shall dictate to him.

A LAW OF NATURE (*lex naturalis*) is a precept, or general rule, found out by reason, by which a man is forbidden to do that, which is destructive of his life, or taketh away the means of preserving the same; and to omit that, by which he thinketh it may be best preserved. For though they that speak of this subject, use to confound *jus,* and *lex, right* and *law;* yet they ought to be distinguished; because RIGHT, consisteth in liberty to do, or to forbear; whereas LAW, determineth, and bindeth to one of them: so that law, and right, differ as much, as obligation, and liberty, which in one and the same matter are inconsistent.

And because the condition of man (as hath been declared in the precedent chapter) is a condition of war of every one against every one; in which case every one is governed by his own reason; and there is nothing he can make use of, that may not be a help unto him, in preserving his life against his enemies, it followeth, that in such a condition, every man has a right to every thing: even to one another's body. And therefore, as long as this natural right of every man to every thing endureth, there can be no security to any man (how strong or wise soever he be) of living out the time, which nature ordinarily alloweth men to live. And consequently it is a precept, or general rule of reason, *that every man ought to endeavour peace, as far as he has hope of obtaining it; and when he cannot obtain it, that he may seek, and use, all helps and advantages of war.* The first branch of which rule containeth the first and fundamental law of nature; which is *to seek peace and follow it.* The second, the sum of the right of nature, which is, *by all means we can, to defend ourselves.*

From this fundamental law of nature, by which men are commanded to endeavor peace, is derived this second law; *that a man be willing, when others are so too, as farforth, as for peace, and defence of himself he shall think it necessary, to lay down this right to all things, and be contented with so much liberty against other men, as he would allow other men against himself.* For as long as every man holdeth this right of doing any thing he liketh, so long are all men in the condition of war. But if other men will not lay down their right, as well as he, then there is no reason for any one to divest himself of his: for that were to expose himself to prey (which no man is bound to) rather than to dispose himself to peace. This is that law of the Gospel, *whatsoever you require that others should do for you, that do ye to them....*

OF OTHER LAWS OF NATURE

From that law of nature, by which we are obliged to transfer to another, such rights, as being retained, hinder the peace of mankind, there followeth a third; which is this, *that men perform their covenants made*: without which, covenants are in vain and but empty words; and the right of all men to all things remaining, we are still in the condition of war.

And in this law of nature, consisteth the fountain and original of JUSTICE. For where no covenant hath preceded, there hath no right been transferred, and every man has right to every thing; and consequently, no action can be unjust. But when a covenant is made, then to break it is *unjust;* and the definition of INJUSTICE, is no other than *the not performance of covenant.* And whatsoever is not unjust, is *just.*

But because covenants of mutual trust, where there is fear of not performance on either part (as hath been said in the former chapter) are invalid; though the original of justice be the making of covenants; yet injustice actually there can be none, till the cause of such fear be taken away; which while men are in the natural condition of war, cannot be done. Therefore before the names of just and unjust can have place, there must be some coercive power to compel men equally to the performance of their covenants, by the terror of some punishment, greater than the benefit they expect by the breach of their covenant; and to make good that propriety, which by mutual contract men acquire, in recompense of the universal right they abandon: and such power there is none before the erection of a commonwealth. And this is also to be gathered out of the ordinary definition of justice in the Schools: for they say that *justice is the constant will of giving to every man his own.* And therefore where there is no *own*, that is, no propriety, there is no injustice; and where there is no coercive power erected, that is, where there is no commonwealth, there is no propriety; all men having right to all things: therefore where there is no commonwealth, there nothing is unjust. So that the nature of justice, consisteth in keeping of valid covenants: but the validity of covenants begins not but with the constitution of a civil power, sufficient to compel men to keep them: and then it is also that propriety begins.

The fool hath said in his heart, there is no such thing as justice; and sometimes also with his tongue; seriously alleging that every man's conservation and contentment, being committed to his own care, there could be no reason why every man might not do what he thought conduced thereunto: and therefore also to make, or not make: keep, or not keep, covenants was not against reason, when it conduced to one's benefit. He does not therein deny that there be covenants; and that they are sometimes broken, sometimes kept; and that such breach of them may be called injustice, and the observance of them justice: but he questioneth whether injustice, taking away the fear of God (for the same fool hath said in his heart there is no God), may not sometimes stand with that reason, which dictateth to every man his own good; and particularly then, when it conduceth to such a benefit, as shall put a man in a condition to neglect not only the dispraise and reviling, but also the power of other men. . . . This specious reasoning is nevertheless false.

For the question is not of promises mutual, where there is no security of performance on either side; as when there is no civil power erected over the parties promising; for such promises are no covenants: but either where one of the parties has performed already; or where there is a power to make him perform; there is the question whether it be against reason that is against the benefit of the other to perform, or not. And I say it is not against reason. For the manifestation whereof, we are to consider; first, that when a man doth a thing, which notwithstanding any thing can be foreseen, and reckoned on, tendeth to his own destruction, howsoever some accident which he could not expect, arriving may turn it to his benefit; yet such events do not make it reasonably or wisely done. Secondly, that in a condition of war, wherein every man to every man, for want of a common power to keep them all in awe, is an enemy, there is no man can hope by his own strength, or wit, to defend himself from destruction, without the help of confederates; where every one expects the same defence by the confederation that any one else does: and therefore he which declares he thinks it reason to deceive those that help him, can in reason expect no other means of safety than what can be had from his own single power. He therefore that breaketh his covenant, and consequently declareth that he thinks he may with reason do so, cannot be received into any society, that unite themselves for peace and defence, but by the error of them that receive him; nor when he is received, be retained in it, without seeing the danger of their error; which errors a man cannot reasonably reckon upon as the means of his security: and therefore if he be left, or cast out of society, he perisheth; and if he live in society, it is by the errors of other men, which he could not foresee, nor reckon upon; and consequently against the reason of his preservation; and so, as all men that contribute not to his destruction, forbear him only out of ignorance of what is good for themselves.

STUDY QUESTIONS

1. Without government to enforce laws, would life be, as Hobbes says, "nasty, brutish, and short"?
2. What does Hobbes mean by "the right of nature"?
3. What does he mean by a "law of nature"?
4. Why are we obliged to keep our agreements?

PART 12

Art

Aesthetic Concepts

ᴀ⌇

Frank Sibley

We turn next to some issues in the philosophical study of the arts, a field known
as "aesthetics," from a Greek word for "sense perception." Our first selection is by
Frank Sibley (1923–1996), who was Professor of Philosophy at Lancaster University in England. He distinguishes non-aesthetic properties, such as blue or circular, from aesthetic properties, such as balanced or unified. He maintains that
no collection of non-aesthetic properties imply any particular aesthetic property.
Thus aesthetic taste cannot be acquired by following rules or generalizations.

....

The remarks we make about works of art are of many kinds. For the purpose of this
paper, I wish to indicate two broad groups. I shall do this by examples. We say that a
novel has a great number of characters and deals with life in a manufacturing town;
that a painting uses pale colours, predominantly blues and greens, and has kneeling
figures in the foreground; that the theme in a fugue is inverted at such a point and that
there is a stretto at the close; that the action of a play takes place in the span of one day
and that there is a reconciliation scene in the fifth act. Such remarks may be made by,
and such features pointed out to, anyone with normal eyes, ears and intelligence. On
the other hand, we also say that a poem is tightly knit or deeply moving; that a picture
lacks balance, or has a certain serenity and repose, or that the grouping of the figures
sets up an exciting tension; that the characters in a novel never really come to life, or
that a certain episode strikes a false note. It would be natural enough to say that the
making of such judgements as these requires the exercise of taste, perceptiveness or
sensitivity, of aesthetic discrimination or appreciation; one would not say this of my
first group. Accordingly, when a word or expression is such that taste or perceptiveness is required in order to apply it, I shall call it an aesthetic term or expression, and
I shall correspondingly speak of *aesthetic* concepts or *taste* concepts.

Aesthetic terms span a great range of types and could be grouped into various
kinds of sub-species. But it is not my present purpose to attempt any such grouping; I am interested in what they all have in common. Their almost endless variety is
adequately displayed in the following list: *unified, balanced, integrated, lifeless, serene,
sombre, dynamic, powerful, vivid, delicate, moving, trite, sentimental, tragic.* The list of
course is not limited to adjectives; expressions in artistic contexts like *telling contrast,
sets up a tension, conveys a sense of* or *holds it together* are equally good illustrations. It
includes terms used by both layman and critic alike, as well as some which are mainly
the property of professional critics and specialists.

From Frank Sibley, "Aesthetic Concepts," *The Philosophical Review* 68 (1959).

I have gone for my examples of aesthetic expressions in the first place to critical and evaluative discourse about works of art because it is there particularly that they abound. But now I wish to widen the topic; we employ terms the use of which requires an exercise of taste not only when discussing the arts but quite liberally throughout discourse in everyday life. The examples given above are expressions which, appearing in critical contexts, most usually, if not invariably, have an aesthetic use; outside critical discourse the majority of them more frequently have some other use unconnected with taste. But many expressions do double duty even in everyday discourse, sometimes being used as aesthetic expressions and sometimes not. Other words again, whether in artistic or daily discourse, function only or predominantly as aesthetic terms; of this kind are *graceful, delicate, dainty, handsome, comely, elegant, garish*. Finally, to make the contrast with all the preceding examples, there are many words which are seldom used as aesthetic terms at all: *red, noisy, brackish, clammy, square, docile, cured, evanescent, intelligent, faithful, derelict, tardy, freakish*.

Clearly, when we employ words as aesthetic terms we are often making and using metaphors, pressing into service words which do not primarily function in this manner. Certainly also, many words *have come* to be aesthetic terms by some kind of metaphorical transference. This is so with those like 'dynamic', 'melancholy', 'balanced', 'tightly knit', which, except in artistic and critical writings, are not normally aesthetic terms. But the aesthetic vocabulary must not be thought wholly metaphorical. Many words, including the most common *(lovely, pretty, beautiful, dainty, graceful, elegant)*, are certainly not being used metaphorically when employed as aesthetic terms, the very good reason being that this is their primary or only use. And though expressions like 'dynamic', 'balanced' and so forth *have come* by a metaphorical shift to be aesthetic terms, their employment in criticism can scarcely be said to be more than quasi-metaphorical. Having entered the language of art description and criticism as metaphors they are now standard vocabulary in that language.

The expressions that I am calling aesthetic terms form no small segment of our discourse. Often, it is true, people with normal intelligence and good eyesight and hearing lack, at least in some measure, the sensitivity required to apply them; a man need not be stupid or have poor eyesight to fail to see that something is graceful. Thus taste or sensitivity is somewhat more rare than certain other human capacities; people who exhibit a sensitivity both wide-ranging and refined are a minority. It is over the application of aesthetic terms too that, notoriously, disputes and differences sometimes go helplessly unsettled. But almost everybody is able to exercise taste to some degree and in some matters....

In order to support our application of an aesthetic term, we often refer to features the mention of which involves other aesthetic terms: 'it has an extraordinary vitality because of its free and vigorous style of drawing', 'graceful in the smooth flow of its lines', 'dainty because of the delicacy and harmony of its colouring'. It is as normal to do this as it is to justify one mental epithet by other epithets of the same general type, *intelligent* by *ingenious, inventive, acute* and so on. But often when we apply aesthetic terms we explain why by referring to features which do *not* depend for their recognition upon an exercise of taste: 'delicate because of its pastel shades and curving lines', or 'it lacks balance because one group of figures is so far off to the left and is so brightly illuminated'. When no explanation of this latter kind is offered, it is legitimate to ask or search for one. Finding a satisfactory answer may sometimes be difficult, but one cannot ordinarily reject the question. When we cannot ourselves quite say what non-aesthetic features make something delicate or unbalanced or powerful or moving, the good critic often puts his finger on something which strikes us as the right explanation. In short, aesthetic terms always ultimately apply because of, and aesthetic qualities always ultimately depend on, the presence of features which, like curving or angular lines, colour contrast, placing of masses or speed of movement, are visible, audible or otherwise discernible without any exercise of taste or sensibility. Whatever kind of dependence this is, and there are various relationships between aesthetic qualities and non-aesthetic features, what I want to make clear in this paper is that there are no non-aesthetic features which serve in *any* circumstances as logically *sufficient conditions* for applying aesthetic terms. Aesthetic or taste concepts are not in this respect condition-governed at all. . . .

Thus an object which is described very fully, but exclusively in terms of qualities characteristic of delicacy, may turn out on inspection to be not delicate at all, but anaemic or insipid. The failures of novices and the artistically inept prove that quite close similarity in point of line, colour or technique gives no assurance of gracefulness or delicacy. . . . A painting which has only the kind of features one would associate with vigour or energy but which even so fails to be vigorous and energetic *need* not have some other character, need not be instead, say, strident or chaotic. It may fail to have any particular character whatever. It may employ bright colours, and the like, without being particularly lively and vigorous at all, but one may feel unable to describe it as chaotic or strident or garish either. It is, rather, simply lacking in character (though of course this too is an aesthetic judgement; taste is exercised also in seeing that the painting has no character).

There are of course many features which do not in these ways characteristically count for (or against) particular aesthetic qualities. One poem has strength and power because of the regularity of its metre and rhyme; another is monotonous and lacks drive and strength because of its regular metre and rhyme. We do not feel the need to switch from 'because of' to 'in spite of'. However, I have concentrated upon features which are characteristically associated with aesthetic qualities because, if a case could be made for the view that taste concepts are in any way governed by sufficient conditions, these would seem to be the most promising candidates for governing conditions. But to say that features are associated only *characteristically* with an aesthetic term *is* to say that they can never amount to sufficient conditions; no description however full, even in terms characteristic of gracefulness, puts it beyond question that something is graceful in the way a description may put it beyond question that someone is lazy or intelligent. . . .

The point I have argued may be reinforced in the following way. A man who failed to realize the nature of aesthetic concepts, or someone who, knowing he lacked sensitivity in aesthetic matters, did not want to reveal this lack might by assiduous application and shrewd observation provide himself with some rules and generalizations; and by inductive procedures and intelligent guessing, he might frequently say the right things. But he could have no great confidence or certainty; a slight change in an object might at any time unpredictably ruin his calculations, and he might as easily have been wrong as right. No matter how careful he has been about working out a set of consistent principles and conditions, he is only in a position to think that the object is very possibly delicate. With concepts like *lazy, intelligent* or *contract,* someone who intelligently formulated rules that led him aright appreciably often *would* thereby show the beginning of a grasp of those concepts; but the person we are considering is not even beginning to show an awareness of what delicacy is. Though he sometimes says the right thing, he has not seen, but guessed, that the object is delicate. However intelligent he might be, we could easily tell him wrongly that something was delicate and explain why without his being able to detect the deception.... But if we did the same with, say, 'intelligent' he could at least often uncover some incompatibility or other which would need explaining. In a world of beings like himself he would have no use for concepts like delicacy. As it is, these concepts would play a quite different role in his life. He would, for himself, have no more reason to choose tasteful objects, pictures and so on, than a deaf man would to avoid noisy places. He could not be praised for exercising taste; at best his ingenuity and intelligence might come in for mention. In 'appraising' pictures, statuettes, poems, he would be doing something quite different from what other people do when they exercise taste ...

One after another, in recent discussions, writers have insisted that aesthetic judgements are not 'mechanical': 'Critics do not formulate general standards and apply these mechanically to all, or to classes of, works of art.' 'Technical points can be settled rapidly, by the application of rules', but aesthetic questions 'cannot be settled by any mechanical method'. Instead these writers on aesthetics have emphasized that there is no 'substitute for individual judgement', with its 'spontaneity and speculation' and that 'The final standard ... [is] the judgement of personal taste'.[1] What is surprising is that, though such things have been repeated again and again, no one seems to have said what is meant by 'taste' or by the word 'mechanical'. There are many judgements besides those requiring taste which demand 'spontaneity' and 'individual judgement' and are not 'mechanical'. Without a detailed comparison we cannot see in what particular way *aesthetic* judgements are not 'mechanical', or how they differ from those other judgements, nor can we begin to specify what taste is. This I have attempted. It is a characteristic and essential feature of judgements which employ an aesthetic term that they cannot be made by appealing, in the sense explained, to non-aesthetic conditions. This, I believe, is a logical feature of aesthetic or taste judgements in general, though I have argued it here only as regards the more restricted range of judgements which employ aesthetic terms. It is part of what 'taste' means.

NOTE

1. See the articles by Margaret Macdonald and J. Passmore in W. Elton (ed.), *Aesthetics and Language* (Oxford: Oxford University Press, 1954).

STUDY QUESTIONS

1. According to Sibley, into what two groups can we divide remarks about works of art?
2. According to Sibley, how do the two groups of remarks differ?
3. According to Sibley, can either group of remarks be reduced to the other?
4. How does Sibley's account explain the view that issues of taste cannot be settled by any mechanical method?

Speaking in Parables

SALLIE McFAGUE

Sallie McFague was Professor of Theology at Vanderbilt University. She considers a parable by the remarkable German writer Franz Kafka (1883–1924) and emphasizes that the story is an extended metaphor, not translatable into concepts. As she puts it, the parable does not *have* a message; it *is* a message.

....

It was very early in the morning, the streets clean and deserted, I was on my way to the railroad station. As I compared the tower clock with my watch I realized it was already much later than I had thought, I had to hurry, the shock of this discovery made me feel uncertain of my way, I was not very well acquainted with the town as yet, fortunately there was a policeman nearby, I ran to him and breathlessly asked him the way. He smiled and said: "From me you want to learn the way?" "Yes," I said, "since I cannot find it myself." "Give it up, give it up," said he, and turned away with a great sweep, like someone who wants to be alone with his laughter.[1]

This parable by Franz Kafka seems, on a first reading, to invite interpretation—in fact, to insist on it. One can immediately think of autobiographical, psychological, and theological interpretations which might "make sense" out of it. But to attempt such interpretations would be to allegorize it, to treat it as an illustration or embellishment of what we "already know." And all the interpretations do, in fact, fall flat; they are far less interesting than the story itself, and even though they may comfort us for a while with the supposition that we now understand the parable, we find ourselves returning again and again to the story, unsatisfied with *any* interpretation. The parable appears to be more and other than any interpretation.

This is so, I believe, because Kafka's parable is a genuine one—it is not translatable or reducible. . . .

The setting is ostensibly very ordinary: someone, up early in the morning, is rushing through the streets to the railroad station. The sense of haste is heightened by the run-on phrases, punctuated mainly by commas and by the gradual build-up of the person's awareness that "it was already much later than I had thought." A surrealistic note is introduced when the comparison of his watch with the tower clock so shocks him that he is "uncertain of the way." We pause—is that comparison sufficient to make him lose his way? Our credulity is stretched, but not broken. Troubles seem to mount—the person is late, the streets deserted, he is uncertain of the way, and he is apparently new in town—but with "fortunately" we breathe more easily and feel the story will take a turn for the better. Policemen always know their way about town and our credulity is restored completely when the stranger asks the officer "the way" (though we note in passing that he does not add "to the railroad station"). We are, however, unprepared for the answer and even more disturbed—even dumbfounded—by the final reply, "Give it up." The realism of the story has been cracked and through it we glimpse *something*—but what?

This parable is an extended metaphor, and, as a genuine metaphor, it is not translatable into concepts. To be sure, it is shot through with open-endedness, with pregnant silences, with cracks opening into mystery. But it remains profoundly impenetrable. . . . Kafka's parables, like all genuine parables, are themselves actuality—the parables are a figurative representation of an actual, total meaning, so they do not "stand for" anything but *are* life. This means we must make a very careful analysis of all the parts of the parable for they *are* the *meaning* of it. The meaning is not a separate realm, something that can be pointed to; the totality of all the processes of life and thought in the parable *is* its meaning. What this totality of all the processes of life and thought amounted to in Kafka's parables was the incomprehensiblity of the incomprehensible; but this is not an extrinsic meaning—it is *what the story says*.

. . . [T]he aesthetic moment, the moment of new insight, always involves "a felt change of consciousness," which occurs when everyday language is used in an unfamiliar context. Metaphorical language, parabolic language, does not take us out of everyday reality but drives us more deeply into it, de-forming our usual apprehensions in such a way that we see . . . not a new reality but the same reality in a new perspective. The mundane world is transmuted; no new world is created . . . As genuine metaphors, parables could not do other than turn us toward reality, for, as Wallace Stevens says, the purpose of "the symbolic language of metamorphosis" is to intensify one's sense of reality. . . .

Finally . . . we do not interpret the parable, but the parable interprets us. . . . Metaphors cannot be "interpreted"—a metaphor does not *have* a message, it *is* a message. If we have really focused on the parable, if we have let it work on us (rather than working on it to abstract out its "meaning"), we find that we are interpreted.

NOTE

1. Heinz Politzer, *Franz Kafka: Parable and Paradox* (Ithaca: Cornell University Press, 1962), p. 1.

STUDY QUESTIONS

1. Do you agree with McFague that Kafka's story turns us toward reality?
2. How does Kafka's story differ from a factual account?
3. Is Kafka's story beyond interpretation?
4. If someone reads Kafka's story and claims not to draw anything from it, might an appropriate reply be that the issue is not what you draw from the story but what the story draws from you?

Fearing Fictions

KENDALL WALTON

While watching a movie you may become caught up in the action, later telling others about the emotions you felt. But does a horror movie, for example, actually cause you to feel fear? Kendall Walton thinks not, and the reasoning he offers leads him to defend a theory about why fiction is important and why works of art can survive multiple viewings or readings without losing effectiveness. Walton is Professor Emeritus of Philosophy and of Art and Design at the University of Michigan.

....

[T]he plot [of a tragedy] must be structured . . . that the one who is hearing the events unroll shudders with fear and feels pity at what happens: which is what one would experience on hearing the plot of the Oedipus.

Aristotle, Poetics[1]

Kendall Walton, "Fearing Fictions," *Journal of Philosophy*, 75/1 (1978): 5–27. © 1978 by the *Journal of Philosophy*. Reprinted by permission of the author and the Journal of Philosophy, Inc.

I

Charles is watching a horror movie about a terrible green slime. He cringes in his seat as the slime oozes slowly but relentlessly over the earth destroying everything in its path. Soon a greasy head emerges from the undulating mass, and two beady eyes roll around, finally fixing on the camera. The slime, picking up speed, oozes on a new course straight toward the viewers. Charles emits a shriek and clutches desperately at his chair. Afterwards, still shaken, Charles confesses that he was "terrified" of the slime. *Was* he?

This question is part of the larger issue of how "remote" fictional worlds are from the real world. There is a definite barrier against *physical* interactions be-tween fictional worlds and the real world. Spectators at a play are prevented from rendering aid to a heroine in distress. There is no way that Charles can dam up the slime, or take a sample for laboratory analysis.[2] But, as Charles's case dramati-cally illustrates, this barrier appears to be psychologically transparent. It would seem that real people can, and frequently do, have psychological attitudes toward merely fictional entities, despite the impossibility of physical intervention. Readers or spectators detest Iago, worry about Tom Sawyer and Becky lost in the cave, pity Willy Loman, envy Superman—and Charles fears the slime.

But I am skeptical. We do indeed get "caught up" in stories; we often become "emotionally involved" when we read novels or watch plays or films. But to con-strue this involvement as consisting of our having psychological attitudes toward fictional entities is, I think, to tolerate mystery and court confusion. I shall offer a different and, in my opinion, a much more illuminating account of it.

This issue is of fundamental importance. It is crucially related to the basic question of why and how fiction is important, why we find it valuable, and why we do not dismiss novels, films, and plays as "mere fiction" and hence unworthy of serious attention. My conclusions in this paper will lead to some tentative sugges-tions about this basic question.

II

Physical interaction is possible only with what actually exists. That is why Charles cannot dam up the slime, and why in general real people cannot have physical con-tact with mere fictions. But the nonexistence of the slime does not prevent Charles from fearing it. One may fear a ghost or a burglar even if there is none; one may be afraid of an earthquake that is destined never to occur.

But a person who fears a nonexistent burglar *believes* that there is, or at least might be, one. He believes that he is in danger, that there is a possibility of his being harmed by a burglar. It is *conceivable* that Charles should believe himself to be endangered by the green slime. He might take the film to be a live documentary, a news flash. If he does, naturally he is afraid.

But the situation I have in mind is the more usual and more interesting one in which Charles is not deceived in this straightforward way. Charles knows perfectly well that the slime is not real and that he is in no danger. Is he afraid even so? He says that he is afraid, and he is in a state which is undeniably similar, in some respects, to that of a person who is frightened of a pending real-world disaster. His muscles are tensed, he clutches his chair, his pulse quickens, his adrenalin flows. Let us call this physiological/psychological state "quasi-fear." Whether it is actual fear (or a component of actual fear) is the question at issue.

Charles's state is crucially different from that of a person with an ordinary case of fear. The fact that Charles is fully aware that the slime is fictional is, I think, good reason to deny that what he feels is fear. It seems a principle of common sense, one which ought not to be abandoned if there is any reasonable alternative, that fear[3] must be accompanied by, or must involve, a belief that one is in danger. Charles does not believe that he is in danger; so he is not afraid.

Charles might try to convince us that he was afraid by shuddering and declaring dramatically that he was *"really terrified."* This emphasizes the intensity of his experience. But we need not deny that he had an intense experience. The question is whether his experience, however intense, was one of fear of the slime. The fact that Charles, and others, call it "fear" is not conclusive, even if we grant that in doing so they express a truth. For we need to know whether the statement that Charles was afraid is to be taken literally or not.

More sophisticated defenders of the claim that Charles is afraid may argue that Charles *does* believe that the green slime is real and is a real threat to him. There are, to be sure, strong reasons for allowing that Charles realizes that the slime is only fictional and poses no danger. If he didn't, we should expect him to flee the theater, call the police, warn his family. But perhaps it is *also* true that Charles believes, in some way or "on some level," that the slime is real and really threatens him. It has been said that in cases like this, one "suspends one's disbelief," or that "part" of a person believes something which another part of him disbelieves, or that one finds oneself (almost?) believing something one nevertheless knows to be false. We must see what can be made of these notions.

One possibility is that Charles *half* believes that there is a real danger and that he is, literally, at least half afraid. To half believe something is to be not quite sure that it is true, but also not quite sure that it is not true. But Charles has *no* doubts about whether he is in the presence of an actual slime. If he half believed and were half afraid, we would expect him to have *some* inclination to act on his fear in the normal ways. Even a hesitant belief, a mere suspicion, that the slime is real would induce any normal person seriously to consider calling the police and warning his family. Charles gives no thought whatever to such courses of action. He is not *uncertain* whether the slime is real; he is perfectly sure that it is not.

Moreover, the fear symptoms that Charles does exhibit are not symptoms of a mere suspicion that the slime is real and a queasy feeling of half fear. They are symptoms of the certainty of grave and immediate danger, and sheer terror. Charles's heart pounds violently, he gasps for breath, he grasps the chair until his knuckles are white. This is not the behavior of a man who realizes basically that he is safe but suffers flickers of doubt. If it indicates fear at all, it indicates acute and overwhelming terror. Thus, to compromise on this issue, to say that Charles half believes he is in danger and is half afraid, is not a reasonable alternative.

One might claim that Charles believes he is in danger, but that this is not a hesitant or weak or half belief, but rather a belief of a special kind—a "gut" belief as opposed to an "intellectual" one. Compare a person who hates flying. He realizes, in one sense, that airplanes are (relatively) safe. He says, honestly, that they are, and can quote statistics to prove it. Nevertheless, he avoids traveling by air when-ever possible. He is brilliant at devising excuses. And if he must board a plane, he becomes nervous and upset. I grant that this person believes at a "gut" level that flying is dangerous, despite his "intellectual" belief to the contrary. I grant also that he is really afraid of flying.

But Charles is different. The air traveler performs *deliberate* actions that one would expect of someone who thinks flying is dangerous, or at least he is strongly inclined to perform such actions. If he does not actually decide against traveling by air, he has a strong inclination to do so. But Charles does not have even an inclination to leave the theater or call the police. The only signs that he might really believe he is endangered are his more or less automatic, nondeliberate, re-actions: his pulse rate, his sweaty palms, his knotted stomach, his spontaneous shriek.[4] This justifies us in treating the two cases differently.

Deliberate actions are done for reasons; they are done because of what the agent wants and what he thinks will bring about what he wants. There is a pre-sumption that such actions are reasonable in light of the agent's beliefs and desires (however unreasonable the beliefs and desires may be). So we postulate beliefs or desires to make sense of them. People also have reasons for doing things that they are inclined to do but, for other reasons, refrain from doing. If the air traveler thinks that flying is dangerous, then, assuming that he wants to live, his actions or tendencies thereto are reasonable. Otherwise, they probably are not. So we legiti-mately infer that he does believe, at least on a "gut" level, that flying is dangerous. But we don't have to make the same kind of sense of Charles's automatic responses. One doesn't have reasons for things one doesn't *do*, like sweating, increasing one's pulse rate, knotting one's stomach (involuntarily). So there is no need to attribute beliefs (or desires) to Charles which will render these responses reasonable.[5] Thus, we can justifiably infer the air passenger's ("gut") belief in the danger of flying from his deliberate behavior or inclinations, and yet refuse to infer from Charles's automatic responses that he thinks he is in danger.

Someone might reply that at moments of special crisis during the movie—e.g., when the slime first spots Charles—Charles "loses hold of reality" and, *mo-mentarily*, takes the slime to be real and really fears it. These moments are too short for Charles to think about doing anything; so (one might claim) it isn't surprising that his belief and fear are not accompanied by the normal inclina-tions to act.

This move is unconvincing. In the first place, Charles's quasi-fear responses are not merely momentary; he may have his heart in his throat throughout most of the movie, yet without experiencing the slightest inclination to flee or call the police. These long-term responses, and Charles's propensity to describe them afterwards in terms of "fear," need to be understood even if it is allowed that there are moments of real fear interspersed among them. Furthermore, however tempting the momentary-fear idea might be, comparable views of other psychological states are much less appealing. When we say that someone "pitied" Willy Loman or "admired" Superman, it is unlikely that we have in mind special moments during his experience of the work when he forgot, momentarily, that he was dealing with fiction and felt flashes of actual pity or admiration. The person's "sense of reality" may well have been robust and healthy throughout his experience of the work, uninterrupted by anything like the special moments of crisis Charles experiences during the horror movie. Moreover, it may be appropriate to say that someone "pities" Willy or "admires" Superman even when he is not watching the play or reading the cartoon. The momentary-*fear* theory, even if it were plausible, would not throw much light on cases in which we apparently have other psychological attitudes toward fictions.

Although Charles is not really afraid of the fictional slime depicted in the movie, the movie might nevertheless produce real fear in him. It might cause him to be afraid of something other than the slime it depicts. If Charles is a child, the movie may make him wonder whether there might not be real slimes or other exotic horrors *like* the one depicted in the movie, even if he fully realizes that the movie-slime itself is not real. Charles may well fear these suspected actual dangers; he might have nightmares about them for days afterwards. (*Jaws* caused a lot of people to fear sharks which they thought might really exist. But whether they were afraid of the fictional sharks in the movie is another question.)

If Charles is an older movie-goer with a heart condition, he may be afraid of the movie itself. Perhaps he knows that any excitement could trigger a heart attack, and fears that the movie will cause excitement, e.g., by depicting the slime as being especially aggressive or threatening. This is real fear. But it is fear of the depiction of the slime, not fear of the slime that is depicted.

Why is it so natural to describe Charles as afraid of the slime, if he is not, and how *is* his experience to be characterized? In what follows I shall develop a theory to answer these questions.

IV

[The actor] on a stage plays at being another before a gathering of people who play at taking him for that other person.

Jorge Luis Borges[6]

Compare Charles with a child playing an ordinary game of make-believe with his father. The father, pretending to be a ferocious monster, cunningly stalks the child and, at a crucial moment, lunges viciously at him. The child flees, screaming, to the next room. The scream is more or less involuntary, and so is the flight. But the child has a delighted grin on his face even while he runs, and he unhesitatingly comes back for more. He is perfectly aware that his father is only "playing," that the whole thing is "just a game," and that only make-believedly is there a vicious monster after him. He is not really afraid.

The child obviously belongs to the fictional world of the game of make-believe. It is make-believe that the monster lunges, not into thin air, but at the child. Make-believedly the child is in grave and mortal danger. And when the child screams and runs, make-believedly he knows he is in danger and is afraid. The game is a sort of theatrical event in which the father is an actor portraying a monster and the child is an actor playing himself.

I propose to regard Charles similarly. When the slime raises its head, spies the camera, and begins oozing toward it, it is make-believe that Charles is threatened. And when as a result Charles gasps and grips his chair, make-believedly he is afraid. Charles is playing a game of make-believe in which he uses the images on the screen as props. He too is an actor impersonating himself. . . .

Charles differs in some important respects from an ordinary on-stage, self-portraying actor. One difference has to do with what makes it make-believe that Charles is afraid. Facts about Charles generate . . . make-believe truths about him; in this respect he is like an actor portraying himself on stage. But the sorts of facts about Charles which do the generating are different. Make-believe truths about Charles are generated at least partly by what he thinks and feels, not just by how he acts. It is partly the fact that Charles is in a state of quasi-fear, the fact that he feels his heart pounding, his muscles tensed, etc., which makes it make-believe that he is afraid. It would not be appropriate to describe him as "afraid" if he were not in some such state.[7]

Charles's quasi-fear is not responsible, by itself, for the fact that make-believedly it is the *slime* he fears, nor even for the fact that make-believedly he is afraid rather than angry or excited or merely upset. Here Charles's (actual) beliefs come into play. Charles believes (he knows) that make-believedly the green slime is bearing down on him and he is in danger of being destroyed by it. His quasi-fear results from this belief.[8] What makes it make-believe that Charles is afraid rather than angry or excited or upset is the fact that his quasi-fear is caused by the belief that make-believedly he is in danger. And his belief that make-believedly it is the slime that endangers him is what makes it make-believe that the slime is the object of his fear. In short, my suggestion is this: the fact that Charles is quasi-afraid as a result of realizing that make-believedly the slime threatens him generates the truth that make-believedly he is afraid of the slime.[9]

An on-stage actor, by contrast, generates make-believe truths solely by his acting, by his behavior. Whether it is make-believe that the character portrayed is afraid or not depends just on what the actor says and does and how he contorts his face, regardless of what he actually thinks or feels. It makes no difference whether his actual emotional state is anything like fear. This is just as true when the actor is playing himself as it is when he is portraying some other character. The actor may find that putting himself into a certain frame of mind makes it easier to act in the appropriate ways. Nevertheless, it is how he acts, not his state of mind, that determines whether make-believedly he is afraid.

This is how our conventions for theater work, and it is entirely reasonable that they should work this way. Audiences cannot be expected to have a clear idea of an actor's personal thoughts and feelings while he is performing. That would require knowledge of his off-stage personality and of recent events that may have affected his mood (e.g., an argument with his director or his wife). Moreover, acting involves a certain amount of dissembling; actors hide some aspects of their mental states from the audience. If make-believe truths depended on actors' private thoughts and feelings, it would be awkward and unreasonably difficult for spectators to ascertain what is going on in the fictional world. It is not surprising that the make-believe truths for which actors on stage are responsible are understood to be generated by just what is visible from the galleries.

But Charles is not performing for an audience. It is not his job to get across to anyone else what make-believedly is true of himself. Probably no one but him much cares whether or not make-believedly he is afraid. So there is no reason why his actual state of mind should not have a role in generating make-believe truths about himself.

It is not so clear in the monster game what makes it make-believe that the child is afraid of a monster. The child *might* be performing for the benefit of an audience; he might be *showing* someone, an onlooker, or just his father, that make-believedly he is afraid. If so, perhaps he is like an on-stage actor. Perhaps we should regard his observable behavior as responsible for the fact that make-believedly he is afraid. But there is room for doubt here. The child experiences quasi-fear sensations as Charles does. And his audience probably has much surer access to his mental state than theater audiences have to those of actors. The audience may know him well, and the child does not try so hard or so skillfully to hide his actual mental state as actors do. It may be perfectly evident to the audience that the child has a case of quasi-fear, and also that this is a result of his realization that make-believedly a monster is after him. So it is not unreasonable to regard the child's mental state as helping to generate make-believe truths.

A more definite account of the situation is possible if the child is participating in the game solely for his own amusement, with no thought of an audience. In this case the child himself, at least, almost certainly understands his make-believe fear to depend on his mental state rather than (just) his behavior.[10] In fact, let us suppose that the child is an undemonstrative sort who does not scream or run or betray his "fear" in any other especially overt way. His participation in the game is purely passive. Nevertheless the child does experience quasi-fear when make-believedly the monster attacks him, and he still would describe himself as being "afraid" (although he knows that there is no danger and that his "fear" isn't real). Certainly in this case it is (partly) his quasi-fear that generates the make-believe truth he expresses when he says he is "afraid."

My proposal is to construe Charles on the model of this undemonstrative child. Charles may, of course, exhibit his "fear" in certain observable ways. But his observable behavior is not meant to show anyone else that make-believedly he is afraid. It is likely to go unnoticed by others, and even Charles himself may be unaware of it. No one, least of all Charles, regards his observable behavior as generating the truth that make-believedly he is afraid.

VI

...We see, now, how fictional worlds can seem to us almost as "real" as the real world is, even though we know perfectly well that they are not. We have begun to understand what happens when we get emotionally "involved" in a novel or play or film, when we are "caught up in the story."

The theory I have presented is designed to capture intuitions lying behind the traditional ideas that the normal or desired attitude toward fiction involves a "*suspension of disbelief*," or a "*decrease of distance*." These phrases are unfortunate. They strongly suggest that people do not (completely) disbelieve what they read in novels and see on the stage or screen, that, e.g., we somehow accept it as fact that a boy named "Huckleberry Finn" floated down the Mississippi River—at least while we are engrossed in the novel. The normal reader does not accept this as fact, nor should he. Our disbelief is "suspended" only in the sense that it is, in some ways, set aside or ignored. We don't believe that there was a Huck Finn, but what interests us is the fact that *make-believedly* there was one, and that make-believedly he floated down the Mississippi and did various other things. But this hardly accounts for the sense of "decreased distance" between us and fictions. It still has us peering down on fictional worlds from reality above, however fascinated we might be, for some mysterious reason, by what we see.

On my theory we accomplish the "decrease of distance" not by promoting fictions to our level but by descending to theirs. (More accurately, we *extend* ourselves to their level, since we do not stop actually existing when it becomes fictional that we exist.) *Make-believedly* we do believe, we know, that Huck Finn floated down the Mississippi. And make-believedly we have various feelings and attitudes about him and his adventures. Rather than somehow fooling ourselves into thinking fictions are real, we become fictional. So we end up "on the same level" with fictions. And our presence there is accomplished in the extraordinarily realistic manner that I described. This enables us to comprehend our sense of closeness to fictions, without attributing to ourselves patently false beliefs.

We are now in a position to expect progress on the fundamental question of why and how fiction is important. Why don't we dismiss novels, plays, and films as "mere fiction" and hence unworthy of serious attention?

Much has been said about the value and importance of dreams, fantasy, and children's games of make-believe.[11] It has been suggested, variously, that such activities serve to clarify one's feelings, help one to work out conflicts, provide an outlet for the expression of repressed or socially unacceptable feelings, and prepare one emotionally for possible future crises by providing "practice" in facing imaginary crises. It is natural to presume that our experience of representational works of art is valuable for similar reasons. But this presumption is not very plausible, I think, unless something like the theory I have presented is correct.

It is my impression that people are usually, perhaps always, characters in their own dreams and daydreams. We dream and fantasize about ourselves. Sometimes one's role in one's dream-world or fantasy-world is limited to that of observing other goings-on. But to have even this role is to belong to the fictional world. (We must distinguish between being, in one's dream, an observer of certain events and merely "observing," having, a dream about those events.) Similarly, children are nearly always characters in their games of make-believe. To play dolls or school, hobby horses or mud pies is to be an actor portraying oneself.

I suggest that much of the value of dreaming, fantasizing, and making-believe depends crucially on one's thinking of oneself as belonging to a fictional world. It is chiefly by fictionally facing certain situations, engaging in certain activities, and having or expressing certain feelings, I think, that a dreamer, fantasizer, or game player comes to terms with his actual feelings—that he discovers them, learns to accept them, purges himself of them, or whatever exactly it is that he does.

If I am right about this, people can be expected to derive similar benefits from novels, plays, and films only if it is fictional that they themselves exist and participate (if only as observers) in the events portrayed in the works, i.e., only if my theory is on the right track.

I find encouragement for these speculations in the deliberate use of role-playing in educational simulation games, and as a therapeutic technique in certain kinds of psychotherapy (e.g., Gestalt therapy). A therapist may ask his patient to pretend that his mother is present, or that some inanimate object is his mother, and to "talk to her." He may then be asked to "be" the mother, and to say how he feels (when he "is" the mother), how he acts, what he looks like, etc. I will not venture an explanation of how such therapeutic techniques are effective, nor of why simulation games work. But whatever explanation is appropriate will, I suspect, go a long way toward explaining why we are as interested in works of fiction as we are, and clarifying what we get from them. The important place that novels, plays, and films have in our lives appears mysterious only on the supposition that we merely stand outside fictional worlds and look in, pressing our noses against an inviolable barrier. Once our presence within fictional worlds is recognized, suitable explanations seem within reach.

VII

A more immediate benefit of my theory is its capacity to handle puzzles. I conclude with the resolution of two more. First, consider a playgoer who finds happy endings asinine or dull, and hopes that the play he is watching will end tragically. He "wants the heroine to suffer a cruel fate," for only if she does, he thinks, will the play be worth watching. But at the same time he is caught up in the story and "sympathizes with the heroine"; he "wants her to escape." It is obvious that these two apparent desires may perfectly well coexist. Are we to say that the spectator is *torn* between opposite interests, that he wants the heroine to survive and also wants her not to? This does not ring true. Both of the playgoer's "conflicting desires" may be wholehearted. He may hope unreservedly that the work will end with disaster for the heroine, and he may, with equal singlemindedness, "want her to escape such an undeserved fate." Moreover, he may be entirely aware of both "desires," and yet feel no particular conflict between them.

My theory provides a neat explanation. It is merely make-believe that the spectator sympathizes with the heroine and wants her to escape. And he (really) wants it to be make-believe that she suffers a cruel end. He does not have conflicting desires. Nor, for that matter, is it make-believe that he does.

The second puzzle concerns why it is that works last as well as they do, how they can survive multiple readings or viewings without losing their effectiveness.[12]

Suspense of one kind or another is an important ingredient in our experience of most works: Will Jack, of *Jack and the Beanstalk*, succeed in ripping off the giant without being caught? Will Tom and Becky find their way out of the cave? Will Hamlet ever get around to avenging the murder of his father? What is in store for Julius Caesar on the Ides of March? Will Godot come?

But how can there be suspense if we already know how things will turn out? Why, for example, should Tom and Becky's plight concern or even interest a reader who knows, from reading the novel previously, that eventually they will escape from the cave? One might have supposed that, once we have experienced a work often enough to learn thoroughly the relevant features of the plot, it would lose its capacity to create suspense, and that future readings or viewings of it would lack the excitement of the first one. But this frequently is not what happens. *Some* works, to be sure, fade quickly from exposure, and familiarity does alter our experience in certain ways. But the power of many works is remarkably permanent, and the nature of their effectiveness remarkably consistent. In particular, suspense may remain a crucial element in our response to a work almost no matter how familiar we are with it. One may "worry" just as intensely about Tom and Becky while rereading *The Adventures of Tom Sawyer*, despite one's knowledge of the outcome, as would a person reading it for the first time. A child listening to *Jack and the Beanstalk* for the umpteenth time, long after she has memorized it word for word, may feel much the same excitement when the giant discovers Jack and goes after him, the same gripping suspense, that she felt when she first heard the story. Children, far from being bored by familiar stories, often beg to hear the same ones over and over again.

None of this is surprising on my theory. The child hearing *Jack and the Beanstalk* knows that make-believedly Jack will escape, but make-believedly she does *not* know that he will—until the reading of the passage describing his escape. She is engaged in her own game of make-believe during the reading, a game in which make-believedly she learns for the first time about Jack and the giant as she hears about them.[13] It is her make-believe uncertainty (the fact that make-believedly she is uncertain), not any actual uncertainty, that is responsible for the excitement and suspense that she feels. The point of hearing the story is not, or not merely, to learn about Jack's confrontation with the giant, but to play a game of make-believe. One cannot learn, each time one hears the story, what make-believedly Jack and the giant do, unless one always forgets in between times. But one can and does participate each time in a game of make-believe. The point of hearing *Jack and the Beanstalk* is to have the experience of being such that, *make-believedly*, one realizes with trepidation the danger Jack faces, waits breathlessly to see whether the giant will awake, feels sudden terror when he does awake, and finally learns with admiration and relief how Jack chops down the beanstalk, killing the giant.

Why play the same game over and over? In the first place, the game may not be exactly the same each time, even if the readings are the same. On one occasion it may be make-believe that the child is paralyzed by fear for Jack, overwhelmed by the gravity of the situation, and emotionally drained when Jack finally bests the giant. On another occasion it may be make-believe that the child is not very seriously concerned about Jack's safety and that her dominant feelings are admiration for Jack's exploits, the thrill of adventure, and a sense of exhilaration at the final outcome. But even if the game is much the same from reading to reading, one's emotional needs may require the therapy of several or many repetitions.

NOTES

1. Chapter 14. Translated by Gerald F. Else (Ann Arbor: The University of Michigan Press, 1967).
2. I examine this barrier in a companion piece to the present paper, "How Remote Are Fictional Worlds from the Real World?," *Journal of Aesthetics and Art Criticism* [37, 1 (1978): 11–23].
3. By "fear" I mean fear for oneself. Obviously a person can be afraid for someone else without believing that he himself is in danger. One must believe that the person for whom one fears is in danger.
4. Charles *might* scream *deliberately*. But insofar as he does, it is probably clear that he is only pretending to take the slime seriously....
5. Charles's responses are *caused* partly by a belief, though not the belief that he is in danger. (See section IV.) This belief is not a *reason* for responding as he does, and it doesn't make it "reasonable," in the relevant sense, to respond in those ways.
6. From "Everything and Nothing," Borges, *Labyrinths: Selected Stories and Other Writings*, Donald A. Yates and James E. Irby, eds. (New York: New Directions, 1962), p. 248.
7. It is arguable that the purely physiological aspects of quasi-fear, such as the increase of adrenalin in the blood, which Charles could ascertain only by clinical tests, are not part of what makes it make-believe that he is afraid. Thus one might want to understand "quasi-fear" as referring only to the more psychological aspects of Charles's condition: the feelings or sensations that go with increased adrenalin, faster pulse rate, muscular tension, etc.
8. One can't help wondering why Charles's realization that make-believedly he is in danger produces quasi-fear in him, why it brings about a state similar to real fear, even though he knows he is not really in danger. This question is important, but we need not speculate about it here. For now we need only note that Charles's belief does result in quasi-fear, however this fact is to be explained.
9. This, I think, is at least approximately right. It is perhaps equally plausible, however, to say that the fact that Charles *believes* his quasi-fear to be caused by his realization that

the slime endangers him is what makes it make-believe that his state is one of fear of the slime. There is no need to choose now between my suggestion and this variant.

10. Observers might, at the same time, understand his behavior alone to be responsible for his make-believe fear. The child and the observers might recognize somewhat different principles of make-believe.

11. A good source concerning make-believe games is Jerome L. Singer, et al., *The Child's World of Make-Believe* (New York: Academic Press, 1973).

12. David Lewis pointed out to me the relevance of my theory to this puzzle.

13. It is probably make-believe that someone (the narrator), whose word the child can trust, is giving her a serious report about a confrontation between a boy named "Jack" and a giant. Cf. my "Points of View in Narrative and Depictive Representation," *Noûs*, x, 1 (March 1976): 49–61.

STUDY QUESTIONS

1. How does fear we feel at a horror movie differ from fear we feel in a situation that actually threatens us?
2. How does Walton explain this difference?
3. Do you read fiction for different reasons than you read nonfiction?
4. Why do some works of art continue to hold our interest after repeated readings or viewings, while other works of art do not?

HISTORICAL SOURCES

The Republic

PLATO

We now return to Plato's *Republic* at a point where he explains why in his ideal city he gives such a limited role to artists. While philosophers seek to grasp the Forms, the essences of things, and artisans make copies of the ideals, artists make copies of copies, thus working at the third remove from reality.

To put the point without the metaphysical framework, Plato doubts that artists have any knowledge about the subjects they describe. Instead, they create through inspiration, appealing to our emotions, not our reason, and thus making us vulnerable to strong feelings about matters that should be decided by careful thinking. To use an example of my own, a novel that describes a region beset by poverty may rouse our passions far more than a sociological or economic study

From *The Republic* by Plato, trans. F. MacDonald Cornford. Copyright © 1974 by Oxford University Press. Reprinted by permission of the publisher. Notes are the translator's.

of the matter, although the literary work may mischaracterize the situation and its causes.

Plato feared the power of art to lead us away from the truth. The irony is that Plato himself was an artist, the greatest of philosophical stylists. He used his powers as a writer to tell us so movingly of the life of Socrates that many throughout the ages have been led to devote themselves to philosophical inquiry. Plato's attack on art can be seen as an implicit tribute to the extraordinary effects that can be produced by artistic creation.

·······························

[O]ur commonwealth has many features which make me think it was based on very sound principles, especially our rule not on any account to admit the poetry of dramatic representation....

What makes you say so?

Between ourselves—for you will not denounce me to the tragedians and the other dramatists—poetry of that sort seems to be injurious to minds which do not possess the antidote in a knowledge of its real nature.

What have you in mind?

I must speak out, in spite of a certain affection and reverence I have had from a child for Homer, who seems to have been the original master and guide of all this imposing company of tragic poets.[1] However, no man must be honoured above the truth; so, as I say, I must speak my mind.

Do, by all means.

Listen then, or rather let me ask you a question. Can you tell me what is meant by representation in general? I have no very clear notion myself.

So you expect me to have one!

Why not? It is not always the keenest eye that is the first to see something.

True; but when you are there I should not be very desirous to tell what I saw, however plainly. You must use your own eyes.

Well then, shall we proceed as usual and begin by assuming the existence of a single essential nature or Form for every set of things which we call by the same name? Do you understand?

I do.

Then let us take any set of things you choose. For instance there are any number of beds or of tables, but only two Forms, one of Bed and one of Table.

Yes.

And we are in the habit of saying that the craftsman, when he makes the beds or tables we use or whatever it may be, has before his mind the Form[2] of one or other of these pieces of furniture. The Form itself is, of course, not the work of any craftsman. How could it be?

It could not....

And what of the carpenter? Were you not saying just now that he only makes a particular bed, not what we call the Form or essential nature of Bed?

Yes, I was.

If so, what he makes is not the reality, but only something that resembles it. It would not be right to call the work of a carpenter or of any other handicraftsman a perfectly real thing, would it?

Not in the view of people accustomed to thinking on these lines.[3]

We must not be surprised, then, if even an actual bed is a somewhat shadowy thing as compared with reality.

True.

Now shall we make use of this example to throw light on our question as to the true nature of this artist who represents things? We have here three sorts of bed: one which exists in the nature of things and which, I imagine, we could only describe as a product of divine workmanship; another made by the carpenter; and a third by the painter. So the three kinds of bed belong respectively to the domains of these three: painter, carpenter, and god.

Yes.

Now the god made only one ideal or essential Bed, whether by choice or because he was under some necessity not to make more than one; at any rate two or more were not created, nor could they possibly come into being.

Why not?

Because, if he made even so many as two, then once more a single ideal Bed would make its appearance, whose character those two would share; and that one, not the two, would be the essential Bed. Knowing this, the god, wishing to be the real maker of a real Bed, not a particular manufacturer of one particular bed, created one which is essentially unique.

So it appears.

Shall we call him, then the author of the true nature of Bed, or something of that sort?

Certainly he deserves the name, since all his works constitute the real nature of things.

And we may call the carpenter the manufacturer of a bed?

Yes.

Can we say the same of the painter?

Certainly not.

Then what is he, with reference to a bed?

I think it would be fairest to describe him as the artist who represents the things which the other two make.

Very well, said I; so the work of the artist is at the third remove from the essential nature of the thing?

Exactly. . . .

Then it is now time to consider the tragic poets and their master, Homer, because we are sometimes told that they understand . . . all about human conduct, good or bad, and about religion; for, to write well, a good poet, so they say, must know his subject; otherwise he could not write about it. We must ask whether these people . . . in contemplating the poets' work have failed to see that it is at the third remove from reality, nothing more than semblances, easy to produce with no knowledge of the truth. Or is there something in what they say? Have the good poets a real mastery of the matters on which the public thinks they discourse so well?

It is a question we ought to look into.

Well then, if a man were able actually to do the things he represents as well as to produce images of them, do you believe he would seriously give himself up to making these images and take that as a completely satisfying object in life? I should imagine that, if he had a real understanding of the actions he represents, he would far sooner devote himself to performing them in fact. The memorials he would try to leave after him would be noble deeds, and he would be more eager to be the hero whose praises are sung than the poet who sings them.

Yes, I agree; he would do more good in that way and win a greater name.

Here is a question, then, that we may fairly put to Homer or to any other poet. We will leave out of account all mere matters of technical skill: we will not ask them to explain, for instance, why it is that, if they have a knowledge of medicine and not merely the art of reproducing the way physicians talk, there is no record of any poet, ancient or modern, curing patients and bequeathing his knowledge to a school of medicine, as Asclepius did. But when Homer undertakes to tell us about matters of the highest importance, such as the conduct of war, statesmanship, or education, we have a right to inquire into his competence. "Dear Homer," we shall say, "we have defined the artist as one who produces images at the third remove from reality. If your knowledge of all that concerns human excellence was really such as to raise you above him to the second rank, and you could tell what courses of conduct will make men better or worse as individuals or as citizens, can you name any country which was better governed thanks to your efforts? Many states, great and small, have owed much to a good lawgiver, such as Lycurgus at Sparta, Charondas in Italy and Sicily, and our own Solon. Can you tell us of any that acknowledges a like debt to you?"

I should say not, Glaucon replied. The most devout admirers of Homer make no such claim.

Well, do we hear of any war in Homer's day being won under his command or thanks to his advice?

No.

Or of a number of ingenious inventions and technical contrivances, which would show that he was a man of practical ability like Thales of Miletus or Anacharsis the Scythian?[4]

Nothing of the sort.

Well, if there is no mention of public services, do we hear of Homer in his own lifetime presiding, like Pythagoras, over a band of intimate disciples who loved him for the inspiration of his society and handed down a Homeric way of life, like the way of life which the Pythagoreans called after their founder and which to this day distinguishes them from the rest of the world?

No; on the contrary, Homer's friend with the absurd name, Creophylus,[5] would look even more absurd when considered as a product of the poet's training, if the story is true that he completely neglected Homer during his lifetime.

Yes, so they say. But what do you think, Glaucon? If Homer had really possessed the knowledge qualifying him to educate people and make them better men, instead of merely giving us a poetical representation of such matters, would he not have attracted a host of disciples to love and revere him? After all, any number of private teachers like Protagoras of Abdera and Prodicus of Ceos[6] have succeeded in convincing their contemporaries that they will never be fit to manage affairs of state or their own households unless these masters superintend their education; and for this wisdom they are so passionately admired that their pupils are all but ready to carry them about on their shoulders. Can we suppose that Homer's contemporaries, or Hesiod's, would have left them to wander about reciting their poems, if they had really been capable of helping their hearers to be better men? Surely they would sooner have parted with their money and tried to make the poets settle down at home; or failing that, they would have danced attendance on them wherever they went, until they had learnt from them all they could.

I believe you are quite right, Socrates.

We may conclude, then, that all poetry, from Homer onwards, consists in representing a semblance of its subject, whatever it may be, including any kind of human excellence, with no grasp of the reality. . . . Strip what the poet has to say of its poetical colouring, and I think you must have seen what it comes to in plain prose. It is like a face which was never really handsome, when it has lost the fresh bloom of youth.

Quite so. . . .

We seem, then, so far to be pretty well agreed that the artist knows nothing worth mentioning about the subjects he represents, and that art is a form of play, not to be taken seriously. This description, moreover, applies above all to tragic poetry, whether in epic or dramatic form.

Exactly.

But now look here, said I; the content of this poetical representation is something at the third remove from reality, is it not?

Yes.

On what part of our human nature, then, does it produce its effect?

What sort of part do you mean?

Let me explain by an analogy. An object seen at a distance does not, of course, look the same size as when it is close at hand; a straight stick looks bent when part of it is under water; and the same thing appears concave or convex to an eye misled by colours. Every sort of confusion like these is to be found in our minds; and it is this weakness in our nature that is exploited, with a quite magical effect, by many tricks of illusion, like scene-painting and conjuring.

True.

But satisfactory means have been found for dispelling these illusions by measuring, counting, and weighing. We are no longer at the mercy of apparent differences of size and quantity and weight; the faculty which has done the counting and measuring or weighing takes control instead. And this can only be the work of the calculating or reasoning element in the soul.

True.

And when this faculty has done its measuring and announced that one quantity is greater than, or equal to, another, we often find that there is an appearance which contradicts it. Now, as we have said, it is impossible for the same part of the soul to hold two contradictory beliefs at the same time. Hence the part which agrees with the measurements must be a different part from the one which goes against them; and its confidence in measurement and calculation is a proof of its being the highest part; the other which contradicts it must be an inferior one.

It must.

This, then, was the conclusion I had in view when I said that paintings and works of art in general are far removed from reality, and that the element in our nature which is accessible to art and responds to its advances is equally far from wisdom. The offspring of a connexion thus formed on no true or sound basis must be as inferior as the parents. This will be true not only of visual art, but of art addressed to the ear, poetry as we call it.

Naturally. . . .

But, I continued, the heaviest count in our indictment is still to come. Dramatic poetry has a most formidable power of corrupting even men of high character, with a few exceptions.

Formidable indeed, if it can do that.

Let me put the case for you to judge. When we listen to some hero in Homer or on the tragic stage moaning over his sorrows in a long tirade, or to a chorus beating their breasts as they chant a lament, you know how the best of us enjoy giving ourselves up to follow the performance with eager sympathy. The more a poet can move our feelings in this way, the better we think him. And yet when the sorrow is our own, we pride ourselves on being able to bear it quietly like a man, condemning the behaviour we admired in the theatre as womanish. Can it be right that the spectacle of a man behaving as one would scorn and blush to behave oneself should be admired and enjoyed, instead of filling us with disgust?

No, it really does not seem reasonable.

It does not, if you reflect that the poet ministers to the satisfaction of that very part of our nature whose instinctive hunger to have its fill of tears and lamentations is forcibly restrained in the case of our own misfortunes. Meanwhile the noblest part of us, insufficiently schooled by reason or habit, has relaxed its watch over these querulous feelings, with the excuse that the sufferings we are contemplating are not our own and it is no shame to us to admire and pity a man with some pretensions to a noble character, though his grief may be excessive. The enjoyment itself seems a clear gain, which we cannot bring ourselves to forfeit by disdaining the whole poem. Few, I believe, are capable of reflecting that to enter into another's feelings must have an effect on our own: the emotions of pity our sympathy has strengthened will not be easy to restrain when we are suffering ourselves.

That is very true.

Does not the same principle apply to humour as well as to pathos? You are doing the same thing if, in listening at a comic performance or in ordinary life to buffooneries which you would be ashamed to indulge in yourself, you thoroughly enjoy them instead of being disgusted with their ribaldry. There is in you an impulse to play the clown, which you have held in restraint from a reasonable fear of being set down as a buffoon; but now you have given it rein, and by encouraging its impudence at the theatre you may be unconsciously carried away into playing the comedian in your private life. Similar effects are produced by poetic representation of love and anger and all those desires and feelings of pleasure or pain which accompany our every action. It waters the growth of passions which should be allowed to wither away and sets them up in control, although the goodness and happiness of our lives depend on their being held in subjection.

I cannot but agree with you.

If so, Glaucon, when you meet with admirers of Homer who tell you that he has been the educator of Hellas and that on questions of human conduct and culture he deserves to be constantly studied as a guide by whom to regulate your whole life, it is well to give a friendly hearing to such people, as entirely well-meaning according to their lights, and you may acknowledge Homer to be the first and greatest of the tragic poets; but you must be quite sure that we can admit into our commonwealth only the poetry which celebrates the praises of the gods and of good men. If you go further and admit the honeyed muse in epic or in lyric verse, then pleasure and pain will usurp the sovereignty of law and of the principles always recognized by common consent as the best.

Quite true.

So now, since we have recurred to the subject of poetry, let this be our defence: it stands to reason that we could not but banish such an influence from our commonwealth. But, lest poetry should convict us of being harsh and unmannerly, let us tell her further that there is a long-standing quarrel between poetry and philosophy. There are countless tokens of this old antagonism, such as the lines which speak of "the cur which at his master yelps," or "one mighty in the vain talk of fools" or "the throng of all-too-sapient heads," or "subtle thinkers all in rags." Nonetheless, be it declared that, if the dramatic poetry whose end is to give pleasure can show good reason why it should exist in a well-governed society, we for our part should welcome it back, being ourselves conscious of its charm; only it would be a sin to betray what we believe to be the truth. You too, my friend, must have felt this charm, above all when poetry speaks through Homer's lips.

I have indeed.

It is fair, then, that before returning from exile poetry should publish her defence in lyric verse or some other measure; and I suppose we should allow her champions who love poetry but are not poets to plead for her in prose, that she is no mere source of pleasure but a benefit to society and to human life. We shall listen favourably; for we shall clearly be the gainers, if that can be proved.

Undoubtedly.

But if it cannot, then we must take a lesson from the lover who renounces at any cost a passion which he finds is doing him no good. The love for poetry of this kind, bred in us by our own much admired institutions, will make us kindly disposed to believe in her genuine worth; but so long as she cannot make good her defence we shall, as we listen, rehearse to ourselves the reasons we have just given, as a counter-charm to save us from relapsing into a passion which most people have never outgrown. We shall reiterate that such poetry has no serious claim to be valued as an apprehension of truth. One who lends an ear to it should rather beware of endangering the order established in his soul, and would do well to accept the view of poetry which we have expressed.

I entirely agree.

Yes, Glaucon; for much is at stake, more than most people suppose: it is a choice between becoming a good man or a bad; and poetry, no more than wealth or power or honours, should tempt us to be careless of justice and virtue.

Your argument has convinced me, as I think it would anyone else.

NOTES

1. The plots of Greek tragedy were normally stories borrowed from epic poetry. Hence Homer was spoken of as the first tragic poet.
2. "Form" does not mean "shape," but the essential properties which constitute what the thing, by definition, is.
3. Familiar with the Platonic doctrine, as opposed to current materialism, which regards the beds we sleep on as real things and the Platonic Form as a mere "abstraction" or notion existing only in our minds.
4. Thales (early sixth cent.) made a fortune out of a corner in oil-mills when his knowledge of the stars enabled him to predict a large olive harvest, thus proving that wise men could be rich if they chose. Anacharsis was said to have invented the anchor and the potter's wheel.
5. Creophylus' name is supposed to be derived from two words meaning "flesh" and "tribe." He is said to have been an epic poet from Chios.
6. Two of the most famous Sophists of the fifth century. Plato's *Protagoras* gives a vivid picture of them on a visit to a rich patron at Athens.

STUDY QUESTIONS

1. According to Plato, why is the work of the artist at the third remove from the essential nature of a thing?
2. Has Plato demonstrated that artists know nothing worth mentioning about their subjects?
3. Can you cite an artistic work which misleads us about the truth?
4. Can you cite an artistic work that arouses passions that should be restrained?

Poetics

ARISTOTLE

Aristotle's influential *Poetics* provides an answer to Plato's criticisms of the artist. Focusing primarily on tragedy, Aristotle views art not as a competitor to philosophy but as a means by which our emotions of pity and fear can be provoked and then purged, a process known as catharsis. Aristotle urges that this end is most effectively achieved by a plot, involving discovery, leading to *peripeteia*, a sudden change in fortune, ideally resulting from the protagonist's own erroneous judgment, and turning happiness into misery. Whereas Plato wished to censor art in an effort to keep our negative emotions under control, Aristotle wished to use art to arouse such feelings, enhance them, and so enable us to be free of them.

....

6 [L]et us proceed now to the discussion of Tragedy; before doing so, however, we must gather up the definition resulting from what has been said. A tragedy, then, is the imitation of an action that is serious and also, as having magnitude, complete in itself; in language with pleasurable accessories, each kind brought in separately in the parts of the work; in a dramatic, not in a narrative form; with incidents arousing pity and fear, wherewith to accomplish its catharsis of such emotions. Here by "language with pleasurable accessories" I mean that with rhythm and harmony or song superadded; and by "the kinds separately" I mean that some portions are worked out with verse only, and others in turn with song.

    I. As they act the stories, it follows that in the first place the Spectacle (or stage-appearance of the actors) must be some part of the whole; and in the second Melody and Diction, these two being the means of their imitation. Here by "Diction" I mean merely this, the composition of the verses; and by "Melody," what is too completely understood to require explanation. But further: the subject represented also is an action; and the action involves agents, who must necessarily have their distinctive qualities both of character and thought, since it is from these that we ascribe certain qualities to their actions. There are in the natural order of things, therefore, two causes, Thought and Character, of their actions, and consequently of their success or failure in their lives. Now the action (that which was done) is represented in the play by the Fable or Plot. The Fable, in our present sense of the term, is simply this, the combination of the incidents, or things done in the story; whereas Character is what makes us ascribe certain moral qualities to the agents; and Thought is shown in all they say when proving a particular point

---

From Aristotle, *Poetics*, trans. Ingram Bywater, Clarendon Press, 1920.

or, it may be, enunciating a general truth. There are six parts consequently of every tragedy, as a whole (that is) of such or such quality, viz. a Fable or Plot, Characters, Diction, Thought, Spectacle, and Melody; two of them arising from the means, one from the manner, and three from the objects of the dramatic imitation; and there is nothing else besides these six. Of these, its formative elements, then, not a few of the dramatists have made due use, as every play, one may say, admits of Spectacle, Character, Fable, Diction, Melody and Thought.

II. The most important of the six is the combination of the incidents of the story. Tragedy is essentially an imitation not of persons but of action and life, of happiness and misery. All human happiness or misery takes the form of action; the end for which we live is a certain kind of activity, not a quality. Character gives us qualities, but it is in our actions—what we do—that we are happy or the reverse. In a play accordingly they do not act in order to portray the Characters, they include the Characters for the sake of the action. So that it is the action in it, i.e. its Fable or Plot, that is the end and purpose of the tragedy, and the end is everywhere the chief thing. Besides this, a tragedy is impossible without action, but there may be one without Character. The tragedies of most of the moderns are characterless—a defect common among poets of all kinds, and with its counterpart in painting in Zeuxis as compared with Polygnotus for whereas the latter is strong in character, the work of Zeuxis is devoid of it. And again: one may string together a series of characteristic speeches of the utmost finish as regards Diction and Thought, and yet fail to produce the true tragic effect; but one will have much better success with a tragedy which, however inferior in these respects, has a Plot, a combination of incidents, in it. And again: the most powerful elements of attraction in Tragedy, the Peripeties and Discoveries, are parts of the Plot. A further proof is in the fact that beginners succeed earlier with the Diction and Characters than with the construction of a story; and the same may be said of nearly all the early dramatists. We maintain, therefore, that the first essential, the life and soul, so to speak, of Tragedy is the Plot and that the Characters come second—compare the parallel in painting where the most beautiful colours laid on without order will not give one the same pleasure as a simple black-and-white sketch of a portrait. We maintain that Tragedy is primarily an imitation of action, and that it is mainly for the sake of the action that it imitates the personal agents. Thus comes the element of Thought, i.e. the power of saying whatever can be said, or what is appropriate to the occasion. This is what, in the speech in Tragedy, falls under the arts of Politics and Rhetoric; for the older poets make their personages discourse like statesmen, and the modern like rhetoricians. One must not confuse it with Character. Character in a play is that which reveals the moral purpose of the agents, i.e. the sort of thing they seek or avoid, where that is not obvious—hence there is no room for Character in a speech on a purely indifferent subject. Thought, on the other hand, is shown in all they say when proving or disproving some particular point, or enunciating some universal proposition. Fourth among the literary elements is the Diction of the personages, i.e., as before explained, the expression of their thoughts in words, which is practically the same thing with verse as with prose. As for the two remaining parts, the Melody is the greatest of the pleasurable accessories of Tragedy. The Spectacle, though an attraction, is the least artistic of all the parts, and has least to do with the art of poetry. The tragic effect is quite possible without a public performance and actors; and besides, the getting-up of the Spectacle is more a matter for the costumier than the poet.

9   From what we have said it will be seen that the poet's function is to describe, not the thing that has happened, but a kind of thing that might happen, i.e. what is possible as being probable or necessary. The distinction between historian and poet is not in the one writing prose and the other verse—you might put the work of Herodotus into verse, and it would still be a species of history; it consists really in this, that the one describes the thing that has been, and the other a kind of thing that might be. Hence poetry is something more philosophic and of graver import than history, since its statements are of the nature rather of universals, whereas those of history are singulars. By a universal statement I mean one as to what such or such a kind of man will probably or necessarily say or do—which is the aim of poetry, though it affixes proper names to the characters; by a singular statement, one as to what, say, Alcibiades did or had done to him. In Comedy this has become clear by this time; it is only when their plot is already made up of probable incidents that they give it a basis of proper names, choosing for the purpose any names that may occur to them, instead of writing like the old iambic poets about particular person. In Tragedy, however, they still adhere to the historic names; and for this reason: what convinces is the possible; now whereas we are not yet sure as to the possibility of that which has not happened, that which has happened is manifestly possible, else it would not have come to pass. Nevertheless even in Tragedy there are some plays with but one or two known names in them, the rest being inventions; and there are some without a single known name, e.g. Agathon's *Antheus*, in which both incidents and names are of the poet's invention; and it is no less delightful on that account. So that one must not aim at a rigid adherence to the traditional stories on which tragedies are based. It would be absurd, in fact, to do so, as even the known stories are only known to a few, though they are a delight nonetheless to all.

It is evident from the above that the poet must be more the poet of his stories or Plots than of his verses, inasmuch as he is a poet by virtue of the imitative element in his work, and it is actions that he imitates. And if he should come to take a subject from actual history, he is nonetheless a poet for that; since some historic occurrences may very well be in the probable and possible order of things; and it is in that aspect of them that he is their poet.

Of simple Plots and actions the episodic are the worst. I call a Plot episodic when there is neither probability nor necessity in the sequence of its episodes. Actions of this sort bad poets construct through their own fault, and good ones on account of the players. His work being for public performance, a good poet often stretches out a Plot beyond its capabilities, and is thus obliged to twist the sequence of incident.

Tragedy, however, is an imitation not only of a complete action, but also of incidents arousing pity and fear. Such incidents have the very greatest effect on the mind when they occur unexpectedly and at the same time in consequence of one another; there is more of the marvellous in them then than if they happened of themselves or by mere chance. Even matters of chance seem most marvellous if there is an appearance of design as it were in them; as for instance the statue of Mitys at Argos killed the author of Mitys' death by falling down on him when a looker-on at a public spectacle; for incidents like that we think to be not without a meaning. A Plot therefore, of this sort is necessarily finer than others.

10   Plots are either simple or complex, since the actions they represent are naturally of this twofold description. The action, proceeding in the way defined, as one continuous whole, I call simple, when the change in the hero's fortunes takes place without Peripety or Discovery; and complex, when it involves one or the other, or both. These should each of them arise out of the structure of the Plot itself, so as to be the consequence, necessary or probable, of the antecedents....

11   A Peripety is the change of the kind described from one state of things within the play to its opposite, and that too in the way we are saying, in the probable or necessary sequence of events; as it is for instance in *Oedipus:* here the opposite state of things is produced by the Messenger, who, coming to gladden Oedipus and to remove his fears as to his mother, reveals the secret of his birth....A Discovery is, as the very word implies, a change from ignorance to knowledge, and thus to either love or hate, in the personages marked for good or evil fortune. The finest form of Discovery is one attended by Peripeties, like that which goes with the Discovery in *Oedipus*....This, with a Peripety, will arouse either pity or fear— actions of that nature being what Tragedy is assumed to represent....

13   The next points after what we have said above will be these: (1) What is the poet to aim at, and what is he to avoid, in constructing his Plots? and (2) What are the conditions on which the tragic effect depends?

We assume that, for the finest form of Tragedy, the Plot must be not simple but complex; and further, that it must imitate actions arousing fear and pity, since that is the distinctive function of this kind of imitation. It follows, therefore, that there are three forms of Plot to be avoided. (1) A good man must not be seen passing from happiness to misery, or (2) a bad man from misery to happiness. The first situation is not fear-inspiring or piteous, but simply odious to us. The second is the most untragic that can be; it has no one of the requisites of Tragedy; it does not appeal either to the human feeling in us, or to our pity, or to our fears. Nor, on the other hand, should (3) an extremely bad man be seen falling from happiness into misery. Such a story may arouse the human feeling in us, but it will not move us to either pity or fear; pity is occasioned by undeserved misfortune, and fear by that of one like ourselves; so that there will be nothing either piteous or fear-inspiring in the situation. There remains, then, the intermediate kind of personage, a man not pre-eminently virtuous and just, whose misfortune, however, is brought upon him not by vice and depravity but by some error of judgement, of the number of those in the enjoyment of great reputation and prosperity; e.g. Oedipus, Thyestes, and the men of note of similar families. The perfect Plot, accordingly, must have a single, and not (as some tell us) a double issue; the change in the hero's fortunes must be not from misery to happiness, but on the contrary from happiness to misery; and the cause of it must lie not in any depravity, but in some great error on his part; the man himself being either such as we have described, or better, not worse, than that. Fact also confirms our theory. Though the poets began by accepting any tragic story that came to hand, in these days the finest tragedies are always on the story of some few houses, on that of Alcmeon, Oedipus, Orestes, Meleager, Thyestes, Telephus, or any others that may have been involved, as either agents or sufferers, in some deed of horror. The theoretically best tragedy, then, has a Plot of this description. The critics, therefore, are wrong who blame Euripides for taking this line in his tragedies, and giving many of them an unhappy ending. It is, as we have said, the right line to take. The best proof is this: on the stage, and in the public performances, such plays, properly worked out, are seen to be the most truly tragic; and Euripides, even if his execution be faulty in every other point, is seen to be nevertheless the most tragic certainly of the dramatists. After this comes the construction of Plot with some rank first, one with a double story (like the *Odyssey*) and an opposite issue for the good and the bad personages. It is ranked as first only through the weakness of the audiences; the poets merely follow their public, writing as its wishes dictate. But the pleasure here is not that of Tragedy. It belongs rather to Comedy, where the bitterest enemies in the piece (e.g., Orestes and Aegisthus) walk off good friends at the end, with no slaying of any one by any one.

14   The tragic fear and pity may be aroused by the Spectacle; but they may also be aroused by the very structure and incidents of the play—which is the better way and shows the better poet. The Plot in fact should be so framed that, even without seeing the things take place, he who simply hears the account of them shall be filled with horror and pity at the incidents; which is just the effect that the mere recital of the story in *Oedipus* would have on one. To produce this same effect by means of the Spectacle is less artistic, and requires extraneous aid. Those, however, who make use of the Spectacle to put before us that which is merely monstrous and not productive of fear, are wholly out of touch with Tragedy; not every kind of pleasure should be required of a tragedy, but only its own proper pleasure.

STUDY QUESTIONS

1. Do you agree with Aristotle that the first essential of tragedy is plot and that characters come second?
2. According to Aristotle, why is poetry more philosophical and of graver import than history?
3. How does Aristotle differentiate simple and complex plots?
4. Can you offer an example of an important artistic work in which, contrary to Aristotle's principles, an evil person passes from misery to ultimate happiness?

PART 13

The Meaning of Life

The Meaning of Life

~~

RICHARD TAYLOR

Those who begin the study of philosophy often assume the subject will focus on the meaning of life. This supposedly crucial topic, however, is rarely mentioned. Yet philosophers do occasionally consider the issue, as witness our next selection. Its author is Richard Taylor, whose work we read previously. He concludes that the meaning of life comes from within us and is not bestowed from without.

....

The question whether life has any meaning is difficult to interpret, and the more you concentrate your critical faculty on it the more it seems to elude you, or to evaporate as any intelligible question. You want to turn it aside, as a source of embarrassment, as something that, if it cannot be abolished, should at least be decently covered. And yet I think any reflective person recognizes that the question it raises is important, and that it ought to have a significant answer.

If the idea of meaningfulness is difficult to grasp in this context, so that we are unsure what sort of thing would amount to answering the question, the idea of meaninglessness is perhaps less so. If, then, we can bring before our minds a clear image of meaningless existence, then perhaps we can take a step toward coping with our original question by seeing to what extent our lives, as we actually find them, resemble that image, and draw such lessons as we are able to from the comparison.

MEANINGLESS EXISTENCE

A perfect image of meaninglessness, of the kind we are seeking, is found in the ancient myth of Sisyphus. Sisyphus, it will be remembered, betrayed divine secrets to mortals, and for this he was condemned by the gods to roll a stone to the top of a hill, the stone then immediately to roll back down, again to be pushed to the top by Sisyphus, to roll down once more, and so on again and again, *forever*. Now in this we have the picture of meaningless, pointless toil, of a meaningless existence that is absolutely *never* redeemed. It is not even redeemed by a death that, if it were to accomplish nothing more, would at least bring this idiotic cycle to a close.

If we were invited to imagine Sisyphus struggling for a while and accomplishing nothing, perhaps eventually falling from exhaustion, so that we might suppose him then eventually turning to something having some sort of promise, then the meaninglessness of that chapter of his life would not be so stark. It would be a dark and dreadful dream, from which he eventually awakens to sunlight and reality. But he does not awaken, for there is nothing for him to awaken to. His repetitive toil is his life and reality, and it goes on forever, and it is without any meaning whatever. Nothing ever comes of what he is doing, except simply, more of the same. Not by one step, nor by a thousand, nor by ten thousand does he even expiate by the smallest token the sin against the gods that led him into this fate. Nothing comes of it, nothing at all.

This ancient myth has always enchanted people, for countless meanings can be read into it. Some of the ancients apparently thought it symbolized the perpetual rising and setting of the sun, and others the repetitious crashing of the waves upon the shore. Probably the commonest interpretation is that it symbolizes our eternal struggle and unquenchable spirit, our determination always to try once more in the face of overwhelming discouragement. This interpretation is further supported by that version of the myth according to which Sisyphus was commanded to roll the stone *over* the hill, so that it would finally roll down the other side, but was never quite able to make it.

I am not concerned with rendering or defending any interpretation of this myth, however. I have cited it only for the one element it does unmistakably contain, namely, that of a repetitious, cyclic activity that never comes to anything. We could contrive other images of this that would serve just as well, and no mythmakers are needed to supply the materials of it. Thus, we can imagine two persons transporting a stone—or even a precious gem, it does not matter—back and forth, relay style. One carries it to a near or distant point where it is received by the other; it is returned to its starting point, there to be recovered by the first, and the process is repeated over and over. Except in this relay nothing counts as winning, and nothing brings the contest to any close, each step only leads to a repetition of itself. Or we can imagine two groups of prisoners, one of them engaged in digging a prodigious hole in the ground that is no sooner finished than it is filled in again by the other group, the latter then digging a new hole that is at once filled in by the first group, and so on and on endlessly.

Now what stands out in all such pictures as oppressive and dejecting is not that the beings who enact these roles suffer any torture or pain, for it need not be assumed that they do. Nor is it that their labors are great, for they are no greater than the labors commonly undertaken by most people most of the time. According to the original myth, the stone is so large that Sisyphus never quite gets it to the top and must groan under every step, so that his enormous labor is all for nought. But this is not what appalls. It is not that his great struggle comes to nothing, but that his existence itself is without meaning. Even if we suppose, for example, that the stone is but a pebble that can be carried effortlessly, or that the holes dug by the prisoners are but small ones, not the slightest meaning is introduced into their lives. The stone that Sisyphus moves to the top of the hill, whether we think of it as large or small, still rolls back every time, and the process is repeated forever. Nothing comes of it, and the work is simply pointless. That is the element of the myth that I wish to capture.

Again, it is not the fact that the labors of Sisyphus continue forever that deprives them of meaning. It is, rather, the implication of this: that they come to nothing. The image would not be changed by our supposing him to push a different stone up every time, each to roll down again. But if we supposed that these stones, instead of rolling back to their places as if they had never been moved, were assembled at the top of the hill and there incorporated, say, in a beautiful and enduring temple, then the aspect of meaninglessness would disappear. His labors would then have a point, something would come of them all, and although one could perhaps still say it was not worth it, one could not say that the life of Sisyphus was devoid of meaning altogether. Meaningfulness would at least have made an appearance, and we could see what it was.

That point will need remembering. But in the meantime, let us note another way in which the image of meaninglessness can be altered by making only a very slight change. Let us suppose that the gods, while condemning Sisyphus to the fate just described, at the same time, as an afterthought, waxed perversely merciful by implanting in him a strange and irrational impulse; namely, a compulsive impulse to roll stones. We may if we like, to make this more graphic, suppose they accomplish this by implanting in him some substance that has this effect on his character and drives. I call this perverse, because from our point of view there is clearly no reason why anyone should have a persistent and insatiable desire to do something so pointless as that. Nevertheless, suppose that is Sisyphus' condition. He has but one obsession, which is to roll stones, and it is an obsession that is only for the moment appeased by his rolling them—he no sooner gets a stone rolled to the top of the hill than he is restless to roll up another.

Now it can be seen why this little afterthought of the gods, which I called perverse, was also in fact merciful. For they have by this device managed to give Sisyphus precisely what he wants—by making him want precisely what they inflict on him. However it may appear to us, Sisyphus' fate now does not appear to him as a condemnation, but the very reverse. His one desire in life is to roll stones, and he is absolutely guaranteed its endless fulfillment. Where otherwise he might profoundly have wished surcease, and even welcomed the quiet of death to release him from endless boredom and meaninglessness, his life is now filled with mission and meaning, and he seems to himself to have been given an entry to heaven. Nor need he even fear death, for the gods have promised him an endless opportunity to indulge his single purpose, without concern or frustration. He will be able to roll stones *forever*.

What we need to mark most carefully at this point is that the picture with which we began has not really been changed in the least by adding this supposition. Exactly the same things happen as before. The only change is in Sisyphus' view of them. The picture before was the image of meaningless activity and existence.

It was created precisely to be an image of that. It has not lost that meaninglessness, it has now gained not the least shred of meaningfulness. The stones still roll back as before, each phase of Sisyphus' life still exactly resembles all the others, the task is never completed, nothing comes of it, no temple ever begins to rise, and all this cycle of the same pointless thing over and over goes on forever in this picture as in the other. The *only* thing that has happened is this: Sisyphus has been reconciled to it, and indeed more, he has been led to embrace it. Not, however, by reason or persuasion, but by nothing more rational than the potency of a new substance in his veins.

THE MEANINGLESSNESS OF LIFE

I believe the foregoing provides a fairly clear content to the idea of meaninglessness and, through it, some hint of what meaningfulness, in this sense, might be. Meaninglessness is essentially endless pointlessness, and meaningfulness is therefore the opposite. Activity, and even long, drawn out and repetitive activity, has a meaning if it has some significant culmination, some more or less lasting end that can be considered to have been the direction and purpose of the activity. But the descriptions so far also provide something else; namely, the suggestion of how an existence that is objectively meaningless, in this sense, can nevertheless acquire a meaning for him whose existence it is.

Now let us ask: Which of these pictures does life in fact resemble? And let us not begin with our own lives, for here both our prejudices and wishes are great, but with the life in general that we share with the rest of creation. We shall find, I think, that it all has a certain pattern and that this pattern is by now easily recognized.

We can begin anywhere, only saving human existence for our last consideration. We can, for example, begin with any animal. It does not matter where we begin, because the result is going to be exactly the same.

Thus, for example, there are caves in New Zealand, deep and dark, whose floors are quiet pools and whose walls and ceilings are covered with soft light. As you gaze in wonder in the stillness of these caves, it seems that the Creator has reproduced there in microcosm the heavens themselves, until you scarcely remember the enclosing presence of the walls. As you look more closely, however, the scene is explained. Each dot of light identifies an ugly worm, whose luminous tail is meant to attract insects from the surrounding darkness. As from time to time one of these insects draws near it becomes entangled in a sticky thread lowered by the worm, and is eaten. This goes on month after month, the blind worm lying there in the barren stillness waiting to entrap an occasional bit of nourishment that will only sustain it to another bit of nourishment until.... Until what? What great thing awaits all this long and repetitious effort and makes it worthwhile? Really nothing. The larva just transforms itself finally to a tiny winged adult that lacks even mouth parts to feed and lives only a day or two. These adults, as soon as they have mated and laid eggs, are themselves caught in the threads and are devoured by the cannibalist worms, often without having ventured into the day, the only point to their existence having now been fulfilled. This has been going on for millions of years, and to no end other than that the same meaningless cycle may continue for another millions of years.

All living things present essentially the same spectacle. The larva of a certain cicada burrows in the darkness of the earth for seventeen years, through season after season, to emerge finally into the daylight for a brief flight, lay its eggs, and die—this all to repeat itself during the next seventeen years, and so on to eternity. We have already noted, in another connection, the struggles of fish, made only that others may do the same after them and that this cycle, having no other point than itself, may never cease. Some birds span an entire side of the globe each year and then return, only to insure that others may follow the same incredibly long path again and again. One is led to wonder what the point of it all is, with what great triumph this ceaseless effort, repeating itself through millions of years, might finally culminate, and why it should go on and on for so long, accomplishing nothing, getting nowhere. But then you realize that there is no point to it at all, that it really culminates in nothing, that each of these cycles, so filled with toil, is to be followed only by more of the same. The point of any living thing's life is, evidently, nothing but life itself.

This life of the world thus presents itself to our eyes as a vast machine, feeding on itself, running on and on forever to nothing. And we are part of that life. To be sure, we are not just the same, but the differences are not so great as we like to think; many are merely invented, and none really cancels the kind of meaninglessness that we found in Sisyphus and that we find all around, wherever anything lives. We are conscious of our activity. Our goals, whether in any significant sense we choose them or not, are things of which we are at least partly aware and can therefore in some sense appraise. More significantly, perhaps, we have a history, as other animals do not, such that each generation does not precisely resemble all those before. Still, if we can in imagination disengage our wills from our lives and disregard the deep interest we all have in our own existence, we shall find that they do not so little resemble the existence of Sisyphus. We toil after goals, most of them—indeed every single one of them—of transitory significance and, having gained one of them, we immediately set forth for the next, as if that one had never been, with this next one being essentially more of the same. Look at a busy street any day, and observe the throng going hither and thither. To what? Some office or shop, where the same things will be done today as were done yesterday, and are done now so they may be repeated tomorrow. And if we think that, unlike Sisyphus, these labors do have a point, that they culminate in something lasting and, independently of our own deep interests in them, very worthwhile, then we simply have not considered the thing closely enough. Most such effort is directed only to the establishment and perpetuation of home and family; that is, to the begetting of others who will follow in our steps to do more of the same. Everyone's life thus resembles one of Sisyphus's climbs to the summit of his hill, and each day of it one of his steps; the difference is that whereas Sisyphus himself returns to push the stone up again, we leave this to our children. We at one point imagined that the labors of Sisyphus finally culminated in the creation of a temple, but for this to make any difference it had to be a temple that would at least endure, adding beauty to the world for the remainder of time. Our achievements, even though they are often beautiful, are mostly bubbles; and those that do last, like the sand-swept pyramids, soon become mere curiosities while around them the rest of humankind continues its perpetual toting of rocks, only to see them roll down. Nations are built upon the bones of their founders and pioneers, but only to decay and crumble before long, their rubble then becoming the foundation for others directed to exactly the same fate. The picture of Sisyphus is the picture of existence of the individual man, great or unknown, of nations, of the human race, and of the very life of the world.

On a country road one sometimes comes upon the ruined hulks of a house and once extensive buildings, all in collapse and spread over with weeds. A curious eye can in imagination reconstruct from what is left a once warm and thriving life, filled with purpose. There was the hearth, where a family once talked, sang, and made plans; there were the rooms, where people loved, and babes were born to a rejoicing mother; there are the musty remains of a sofa, infested with bugs, once bought at a dear price to enhance an ever-growing comfort, beauty, and warmth. Every small piece of junk fills the mind with what once, not long ago, was utterly real, with children's voices, plans made, and enterprises embarked upon. That is how these stones of Sisyphus were rolled up, and that is how they became incorporated into a beautiful temple, and that temple is what now lies before you. Meanwhile other buildings, institutions, nations, and civilizations spring up all around, only to share the same fate before long. And if the question "What for?" is now asked, the answer is clear: so that just this may go on forever.

The two pictures—of Sisyphus and of our own lives, if we look at them from a distance—are in outline the same and convey to the mind the same image. It is not surprising, then, that we invent ways of denying it, our religions proclaiming a heaven that does not crumble, their hymnals and prayer books declaring a significance to life of which our eyes provide no hint whatever.[1] Even our philosophies portray some permanent and lasting good at which all may aim, from the changeless forms invented by Plato to the beatific vision of St. Thomas and the ideals of permanence contrived by the moderns. When these fail to convince, then earthly ideals such as universal justice and brotherhood are conjured up to take their places and give meaning to our seemingly endless pilgrimage, some final state that will be ushered in when the last obstacle is removed and the last stone pushed to the hilltop. No one believes, of course, that any such state will be final, or even wants it to be in case it means that human existence would then cease to be a struggle; but in the meantime such ideas serve a very real need.

THE MEANING OF LIFE

We noted that Sisyphus' existence would have meaning if there were some point to his labors, if his efforts ever culminated in something that was not just an occasion for fresh labors of the same kind. But that is precisely the meaning it lacks.

And human existence resembles his in that respect. We do achieve things—we scale our towers and raise our stones to the hilltops—but every such accomplishment fades, providing only an occasion for renewed labors of the same kind.

But here we need to note something else that has been mentioned, but its significance not explored, and that is the state of mind and feeling with which such labors are undertaken. We noted that if Sisyphus had a keen and unappeasable desire to be doing just what he found himself doing, then, although his life would in no way be changed, it would nevertheless have a meaning for him. It would be an irrational one, no doubt, because the desire itself would be only the product of the substance in his veins, and not any that reason could discover, but a meaning nevertheless.

And would it not, in fact, be a meaning incomparably better than the other? For let us examine again the first kind of meaning it could have. Let us suppose that, without having any interest in rolling stones, as such, and finding this, in fact, a galling toil, Sisyphus did nevertheless have a deep interest in raising a temple, one that would be beautiful and lasting. And let us suppose he succeeded in this, that after ages of dreadful toil, all directed at this final result, he did at last complete his temple, such that now he could say his work was done, and he could rest and forever enjoy the result. Now what? What picture now presents itself to our minds? It is precisely the picture of infinite boredom! Of Sisyphus doing nothing ever again, but contemplating what he has already wrought and can no longer add anything to, and contemplating it for an eternity! Now in this picture we have a meaning for Sisyphus' existence, a point for his prodigious labor, because we have put it there; yet, at the same time, that which is really worthwhile seems to have slipped away entirely. Where before we were presented with the nightmare of eternal and pointless activity, we are now confronted with the hell of its eternal absence.

Our second picture, then, wherein we imagined Sisyphus to have had inflicted on him the irrational desire to be doing just what he found himself doing, should not have been dismissed so abruptly. The meaning that picture lacked was no meaning that he or anyone could crave, and the strange meaning it had was perhaps just what we were seeking.

At this point, then, we can reintroduce what has been until now, it is hoped, resolutely pushed aside in an effort to view our lives and human existence with objectivity; namely, our own wills, our deep interest in what we find ourselves doing. If we do this, we find that our lives do indeed still resemble that of Sisyphus, but that the meaningfulness they thus lack is precisely the meaningfulness of infinite boredom. At the same time, the strange meaningfulness they possess is that of the inner compulsion to be doing just what we were put here to do, and to go on doing it forever. This is the nearest we may hope to get to heaven, but the redeeming side of that fact is that we do thereby avoid a genuine hell.

If the builders of a great and flourishing ancient civilization could somehow return now to see archaeologists unearthing the trivial remnants of what they had once accomplished with such effort—see the fragments of pots and vases, a few broken statues, and such tokens of another age and greatness—they could indeed ask themselves what the point of it all was, if this is all it finally came to. Yet, it did not seem so to them then, for it was just the building, and not what was finally built, that gave their life meaning. Similarly, if the builders of the ruined home and farm that I described a short while ago could be brought back to see what is left, they would have the same feelings. What we construct in our imaginations as we look over these decayed and rusting pieces would reconstruct itself in their very memories, and certainly with unspeakable sadness. The piece of a sled at our feet would revive in them a warm Christmas. And what rich memories would there be in the broken crib? And the weed-covered remains of a fence would reproduce the scene of a great herd of livestock, so laboriously built up over so many years. What was it all worth, if this is the final result? Yet, again, it did not seem so to them through those many years of struggle and toil, and they did not imagine they were building a Gibraltar. The things to which they bent their backs day after day, realizing one by one their ephemeral plans, were precisely the things in which their wills were deeply involved, precisely the things in which their interests lay, and there was no need then to ask questions. There is no more need of them now—the day was sufficient to itself, and so was the life.

This is surely the way to look at all of life—at one's own life, and each day and moment it contains; of the life of a nation; of the species; of the life of the world; and of everything that breathes. Even the glow worms I described, whose cycles of existence over the millions of years seem so pointless when looked at by us, will seem entirely different to us if we can somehow try to view their existence from within. Their endless activity, which gets nowhere, is just what it is their will to pursue. This is its whole justification and meaning. Nor would it be any salvation to the birds who span the globe every year, back and forth, to have a home made for them in a cage with plenty of food and protection, so that they would not have to migrate anymore. It would be their condemnation, for it is the doing that counts for them, and not what they hope to win by it. Flying these prodigious distances, never ending, is what it is in their veins to do, exactly as it was in Sisyphus's veins to roll stones, without end, after the gods had waxed merciful and implanted this in him.

You no sooner drew your first breath than you responded to the will that was in you to live. You no more ask whether it will be worthwhile, or whether anything of significance will come of it, than the worms and the birds. The point of living is simply to be living, in the manner that it is your nature to be living. You go through life building your castles, each of these beginning to fade into time as the next is begun; yet it would be no salvation to rest from all this. It would be a condemnation, and one that would in no way be redeemed were you able to gaze upon the things you have done, even if these were beautiful and absolutely permanent, as they never are. What counts is that you should be able to begin a new task, a new castle, a new bubble. It counts only because it is there to be done and you have the will to do it. The same will be the life of your children, and of theirs; and if the philosopher is apt to see in this a pattern similar to the unending cycles of the existence of Sisyphus, and to despair, then it is indeed because the meaning and point he is seeking is not there—but mercifully so. The meaning of life is from within us, it is not bestowed from without, and it far exceeds in both its beauty and permanence any heaven of which men have ever dreamed or yearned for.

NOTE

1. A popular Christian hymn, sung often at funerals and typical of many hymns, expresses this thought:

> Swift to its close ebbs out life's little day;
> Earth's joys grow dim, its glories pass away;
> Change and decay in all around I see:
> O thou who changest not, abide with me.

STUDY QUESTIONS

1. Can a life be enjoyed yet meaningless?
2. Can a life be immoral yet meaningful?
3. If you find meaning in a task, can you be mistaken?
4. If you don't find meaning in a task, can you be mistaken?

Meaning in Life

Susan Wolf

Susan Wolf, Professor of Philosophy at the University of North Carolina, at Chapel Hill, defends the view that not all lives are meaningful but only those in which a person actively engages in projects of worth. Thus, unlike Taylor, Wolf would not find meaning in the life of Sisyphus, even if his fondest desire was to roll stones up hills.

....

A meaningful life is, first of all, one that has within it the basis for an affirmative answer to the needs or longings that are characteristically described as needs for meaning. I have in mind, for example, the sort of questions people ask on their

From "Happiness and Meaning: Two Aspects of the Good Life," *Social Philosophy & Policy*, Vol. 24, 1997. Reprinted with the permission of Cambridge University Press.

deathbeds, or simply in contemplation of their eventual deaths, about whether their lives have been (or are) worth living, whether they have had any point, and the sort of questions one asks when considering suicide and wondering whether one has any reason to go on. These questions are familiar from Russian novels and existentialist philosophy, if not from personal experience. Though they arise most poignantly in times of crisis and intense emotion, they also have their place in moments of calm reflection, when considering important life choices. Moreover, paradigms of what are taken to be meaningful and meaningless lives in our culture are readily available. Lives of great moral or intellectual accomplishment—Gandhi, Mother Teresa, Albert Einstein—come to mind as unquestionably meaningful lives (if any are); lives of waste and isolation—Thoreau's "lives of quiet desperation," typically anonymous to the rest of us, and the mythical figure of Sisyphus—represent meaninglessness.

To what general characteristics of meaningfulness do these images lead us and how do they provide an answer to the longings mentioned above? Roughly, I would say that meaningful lives are lives of active engagement in projects of worth. Of course, a good deal needs to be said in elaboration of this statement. Let me begin by discussing the two key phrases, "active engagement" and "projects of worth."

A person is actively engaged by something if she is gripped, excited, involved by it. Most obviously, we are actively engaged by the things and people about which and whom we are passionate. Opposites of active engagement are boredom and alienation. To be actively engaged in something is not always pleasant in the ordinary sense of the word. Activities in which people are actively engaged frequently involve stress, danger, exertion, or sorrow (consider, for example: writing a book, climbing a mountain, training for a marathon, caring for an ailing friend). However, there is something good about the feeling of engagement: one feels (typically without thinking about it) especially alive.

That a meaningful life must involve "projects of worth" will, I expect, be more controversial, for the phrase hints of a commitment to some sort of objective value. This is not accidental, for I believe that the idea of meaningfulness, along with the concern that our lives possess it, is conceptually linked to such a commitment.[1] Indeed, it is this linkage that I want to defend, for I have neither a philosophical theory of what objective value is nor a substantive theory about what has this sort of value. What is clear to me is that there can be no sense to the idea of meaningfulness without a distinction between more and less worthwhile ways to spend one's time, where the test of worth is at least partly independent of a subject's ungrounded preferences or enjoyment.

Consider first the longings or concerns about meaning that people have, their wondering whether their lives are meaningful, their vows to add more meaning to their lives. The sense of these concerns and resolves cannot fully be captured by an account in which what one does with one's life doesn't matter, as long as one enjoys or prefers it. Sometimes people have concerns about meaning despite their knowledge that their lives to date have been satisfying. Indeed, their enjoyment and "active engagement" with activities and values they now see as shallow seems only to heighten the sense of meaninglessness that comes to afflict them. Their sense that their lives so far have been meaningless cannot be a sense that their activities have not been chosen or fun. When they look for sources of meaning or ways to add meaning to their lives, they are searching for projects whose justifications lie elsewhere.

Second, we need an explanation for why certain sorts of activities and involvements come to mind as contributors to meaningfulness while others seem intuitively inappropriate. Think about what gives meaning to your own life and the lives of your friends and acquaintances. Among the things that tend to come up on such lists, I have already mentioned moral and intellectual accomplishments and the ongoing activities that lead to them. Relationships with friends and relatives are perhaps even more important for most of us. Aesthetic enterprises (both creative and appreciative), the cultivation of personal virtues, and religious practices frequently loom large. By contrast, it would be odd, if not bizarre, to think of crossword puzzles, sitcoms, or the kind of computer games to which I am fighting off addiction as providing meaning in our lives, though there is no question that they afford a sort of satisfaction and that they are the objects of choice. Some things, such as chocolate and aerobics class, I choose even at considerable cost to myself (it is irrelevant that these particular choices may be related); so I must find them worthwhile in a sense. But they are not the sorts of things that make life worth living.[2]

"Active engagement in projects of worth," I suggest, answers to the needs an account of meaningfulness in life must meet. If a person is or has been thus actively engaged, then she does have an answer to the question of whether her life is or has been worthwhile, whether it has or has had a point. When someone looks for ways to add meaning to her life, she is looking (though perhaps not under this description) for worthwhile projects about which she can get enthused. The account also explains why some activities and projects but not others come to mind as contributors to meaning in life. Some projects, or at any rate, particular acts, are worthwhile but too boring or mechanical to be sources of meaning. People do not get meaning from recycling or from writing checks to Oxfam and the ACLU. Other acts and activities, though highly pleasurable and deeply involving, like riding a roller coaster or meeting a movie star, do not seem to have the right kind of value to contribute to meaning.

Bernard Williams once distinguished categorical desires from the rest. Categorical desires give us reasons for living—they are not premised on the assumption that we will live. The sorts of things that give meaning to life tend to be objects of categorical desire. We desire them, at least so I would suggest, because we think them worthwhile. They are not worthwhile simply because we desire them or simply because they make our lives more pleasant.

Roughly, then, according to my proposal, a meaningful life must satisfy two criteria, suitably linked. First, there must be active engagement, and second, it must be engagement in (or with) projects of worth. A life is meaningless if it lacks active engagement with anything. A person who is bored or alienated from most of what she spends her life doing is one whose life can be said to lack meaning. Note that she may in fact be performing functions of worth. A housewife and mother, a doctor, or a busdriver may be competently doing a socially valuable job, but because she is not engaged by her work (or, as we are assuming, by anything else in her life), she has no categorical desires that give her a reason to live. At the same time, someone who is actively engaged may also live a meaningless life, if the objects of her involvement are utterly worthless. It is difficult to come up with examples of such lives that will be uncontroversial without being bizarre. But both bizarre and controversial examples have their place. In the bizarre category, we might consider pathological cases: someone whose sole passion in life is collecting rubber bands, or memorizing the dictionary, or making handwritten copies of *War and Peace*. Controversial cases will include the corporate lawyer who sacrifices her private life and health for success along the professional ladder, the devotee of a religious cult, or—an example offered by Wiggins[3]—the pig farmer who buys more land to grow more corn to feed more pigs to buy more land to grow more corn to feed more pigs.

We may summarize my proposal in terms of a slogan: "Meaning arises when subjective attraction meets objective attractiveness." The idea is that in a world in which some things are more worthwhile than others, meaning arises when a subject discovers or develops an affinity for one or typically several of the more worthwhile things and has and makes use of the opportunity to engage with it or them in a positive way.

NOTES

1. This point is made by David Wiggins in his brilliant but difficult essay "Truth, Invention, and the Meaning of Life," *Proceedings of the British Academy*, vol. 62 (1976).
2. Woody Allen appears to have a different view. His list of the things that make life worth living at the end of *Manhattan* includes, for example "the crabs at Sam Woo's," which would seem to be on the level of chocolates. On the other hand, the crabs' appearance on the list may be taken to show that he regards the dish as an accomplishment meriting aesthetic appreciation, where such appreciation is a worthy activity in itself; in this respect, the crabs might be akin to other items on his list such as the second movement of the *Jupiter Symphony*, Louis Armstrong's recording of "Potatohead Blues," and "those apples and pears of Cézanne." Strictly speaking, the appreciation of great chocolate might also qualify as such an activity.
3. See Wiggins, "Truth, Invention, and the Meaning of Life," p. 342.

STUDY QUESTIONS

1. Based on the examples Wolf provides, what does she mean by "a project of worth"?
2. How would Wolf decide whether some activity was a project of worth?
3. In your view, are the lives of a college professor, a professional golfer, a janitor, and a hobo equally meaningful?
4. Would studying certain subjects add more meaning to life than studying other subjects?

Meaningful Lives

✢

CHRISTINE VITRANO

Christine Vitrano is Associate Professor of Philosophy at Brooklyn College of The City University of New York. She considers the views of a meaningful life offered by Richard Taylor and Susan Wolf. Vitrano finds neither convincing and goes on to offer her own view of a meaningful life as one in which a person finds satisfaction while displaying due regard for others.

....

Richard Taylor and Susan Wolf offer contrasting visions of a meaningful life. I find each account partially persuasive, but neither by itself entirely satisfactory.

For Wolf, a meaningful life is one in which you are actively engaged in projects of worth. To be engaged is to be "gripped, excited, involved." If you find your life dreary, then it is not meaningful.

Enjoying activities, however, does not by itself render them meaningful; they also need to be worthwhile. As she says, "When someone looks for ways to add meaning to her life, she is looking . . . for worthwhile projects about which she can get enthused" and "whose justifications lie elsewhere," specifically in "objective value."

According to Wolf, worthwhile activities include "[r]elationships with friends and relatives . . . [a]esthetic enterprises (both creative and appreciative), the cultivation of personal virtues, and religious practices." Specific examples include "writing a book, climbing a mountain, training for a marathon." Among the activities that lack such worth are solving crossword puzzles, watching sitcoms, playing computer games, and eating chocolate, as well as "collecting rubber bands, or memorizing the dictionary, or making handwritten copies of *War and Peace*." Controversial cases are the paths of the "corporate lawyer who sacrifices her private life and health for success along the professional ladder, the devotee of a religious cult, or . . . the pig farmer who buys more land to grow more corn to feed more pigs, to buy more land to grow more corn to feed more pigs."

An obvious problem with Wolf's position is that by her own admission she has "neither a philosophical theory of what objective value is nor a substantive theory about what has that sort of value." She relies on supposedly shared intuitions regarding the worth of various activities, but to assume such agreement is unjustified. Some people appreciate an activity Wolf disparages, yet dismiss one she values highly. For example, spending thousands of hours training for a marathon strikes many as wearisome; they may be far more engaged by computer games. On the other hand, grappling with a *New York Times* Sunday Magazine crossword puzzle is a popular intellectual challenge, holding far more appeal for most than reading an article on meta-ethics, a subject Wolf finds fascinating.

She might respond to these observations by claiming that the problem with crossword puzzles lies not in their essential unimportance but in their use as mere pastimes. In other words, even those who enjoy solving them don't take them seriously.

This reply, however, only deepens Wolf's difficulty, because the same activity could be judged as meaningful or meaningless depending on why a person engages in it. Consider, for instance, a physicist who does scientific research because of the enjoyment it brings but is devoted to chess problems for their intellectual challenge. For that scholar, pursuing physics would be meaningless, but composing and solving chess problems would be meaningful—hardly the conclusion Wolf is seeking.

Furthermore, suppose that in order to distract myself from the monotony of caring for my two children, I read an article on metaphysics. Why should the motive affect the worthiness of the activity?

Because Wolf's position is weakened by her commitment to an objective value that she cannot explain, we might drop that aspect of her position and accept Richard Taylor's view that a meaningful life is one that affords you long-term satisfaction, regardless of the activities you choose. Thus the life of Sisyphus would be meaningful if Sisyphus relished rolling stones up hills.

Yet even if a person's life is enjoyable, if it is morally unworthy, displaying no concern for the welfare of others, then such a life does not deserve to be judged positively by anyone with moral compunctions.

I would suggest, however, that by combining insights from Taylor and Wolf, we can understand the nature of a meaningful life. It is one in which an individual acts morally while achieving happiness.

To be happy is to be satisfied with one's life, content with one's lot, not suffering excessively from anxiety, alienation, frustration, disappointment, or depression. Satisfied people may face problems but view their lives overall more positively than negatively.

The crucial point is that how satisfaction may be achieved differs from person to person. One individual may be satisfied only by earning ten million dollars. Another may be satisfied by going each day with friends to a favorite club to swim, eat lunch, and play cards. Another may be satisfied by acting in community theatre productions. Their paths to contentment are different, yet their degree of satisfaction may be the same.

Some may be poor, yet satisfied. Others may be alone, yet satisfied. Still others may find satisfaction regardless of the depth of their learning or self-knowledge and irrespective of whatever illness or disability they may face. In any case, the judgment of satisfaction is the individual's, not anyone else's.

Does satisfaction depend on achieving one's goals? Not necessarily. You may achieve your aims only to find that doing so does not provide the satisfaction for which you had hoped. For example, you might eagerly seek and gain admission to a prestigious college only to find that its rural location, which seemed an advantage when you applied, turns out to be a disadvantage when you develop interests better pursued in an urban environment.

Furthermore, some people don't have specific goals. They can happily live here or there, engage in a variety of hobbies, or even pursue various careers. They find delight in spontaneity. Perhaps that approach doesn't appeal to you, but so what? If it works for others, why not let them have their enjoyment without derogating it?

How do you achieve satisfaction, considering that it has eluded so many? The key lies within yourself, because you cannot control the events outside you. If your satisfaction depends on whether others praise you, then they control how satisfied you will be with your life. If you wish to avoid being subject to the power of others, then you have to free yourself from dependence on their judgments.

Some warn against a life spent in "childish pursuits."[1] But which pursuits are childish? How about collecting dolls, telling jokes, planting vegetables, selling cookies, running races, recounting adventures, or singing songs? While children engage in all these activities, so do adults, who may thereby find satisfaction in their lives. Assuming they meet their moral obligations, why disparage them or their interests?

An obituary provides information about an individual's life, detailing accomplishments. What we don't learn therein, however, is whether that individual found satisfaction. If so, and assuming the person displayed due regard for others, then that person's life was meaningful.[2]

NOTES

1. Philippa Foot, *Natural Goodness* (Oxford: Clarendon Press, 2001), p. 86.
2. This theory is developed at length in Steven M. Cahn and Christine Vitrano, *Happiness and Goodness: Philosophical Reflections on Living Well* (New York: Columbia University Press, 2015).

STUDY QUESTIONS

1. What is Vitrano's objection to Wolf's account of a meaningful life?
2. What is Vitrano's objection to Taylor's account of a meaningful life?
3. Do you believe that some activities are more conducive to a meaningful life than others?
4. Can a person who is without friends and without any appreciation for beauty nevertheless live a meaningful life?

The Afterlife

SAMUEL SCHEFFLER

Samuel Scheffler, Professor of Philosophy and of Law at New York University, seeks to enhance understanding of the human condition by asking this question: How would your attitudes about life be affected if you knew that the earth would be destroyed shortly after your death? He believes that in that situation many types of projects and activities would no longer seem worth pursuing. Indeed, he concludes that the survival of humanity matters more to each of us even than our own survival.

I will begin by asking you to consider a crude and morbid thought experiment. Suppose you knew that, although you yourself would live a normal life span, the earth would be completely destroyed thirty days after your death in a collision with a giant asteroid. How would this knowledge affect your attitudes during the remainder of your life?. . .

. . . [T]he prospect of the earth's imminent destruction would induce in us reactions of grief, sadness, and distress. But we must also consider how, if at all, it would affect our subsequent motivations and our choices about how to live. To what extent would we remain committed to our current projects and plans? To what extent would the activities in which we now engage continue to seem worth pursuing? Offhand, it seems that there are many projects and activities that might become less important to us. By this I mean several things. First, our reasons to engage in them might no longer seem to us as strong. At the limit, we might cease to see any reason to engage in them. Second, our emotional investment in them might weaken. For example, we might no longer feel as eager or excited at the prospect of engaging in them; as frustrated if prevented from engaging in them; as pleased if they seemed to be going well; as disappointed if they seemed not to be going well; and so on. At the limit, we might become emotionally detached from or indifferent to them. Third, our belief that they were worthwhile activities in which to engage might weaken or, at the limit, disappear altogether.

It is difficult to be sure exactly which projects and activities would seem to us diminished in importance in these respects, and no doubt there are interesting differences in the ways that different individuals would react. On the face of it, however, there are several types of projects and activities that would appear fairly obviously to be vulnerable to such changes in our attitudes. Consider, to take one representative

---

From Samuel Scheffler, *Death and the Afterlife*, Oxford University Press, 2013. Reprinted by permission of the publisher.

example, the project of trying to find a cure for cancer. This project would seem vulnerable for at least two reasons. First, it is a project in which it is understood that ultimate success may be a long way off. Even the very best research that is done today may be but a step on a long road that will lead to a cure only in the indeterminate future, if at all. The doomsday scenario, by cutting the future short, makes it much less likely that such a cure will ever be found. Second, the primary value of the project lies in the prospect of eventually being able to cure the disease and to prevent the death and suffering it causes. But the doomsday scenario means that even immediate success in finding a cure would make available such benefits only for a very short period of time. Under these conditions, scientists' motivations to engage in such research might well weaken substantially. This suggests that projects would be specially vulnerable if either (a) their ultimate success is seen as something that may not be achieved until some time well in the future, or (b) the value of the project derives from the benefits that it will provide to large numbers of people over a long period of time. Cancer research is threatened because it satisfies both of these conditions. But there are many other projects and activities that satisfy at least one of them. This is true, for example, of much research in science, technology, and medicine. It is also true of much social and political activism. It is true of many efforts to build or reform or improve social institutions. It is true of many projects to build new buildings, improve the physical infrastructure of society, or protect the environment. No doubt you will be able to supply many other examples of your own.

The effect of the doomsday scenario on other types of projects is less clear. For example, many creative and scholarly projects have no obvious practical aim, such as finding a cure for cancer, but they are nevertheless undertaken with an actual or imagined audience or readership of some kind in mind. Although the doomsday scenario would not mean that audiences would disappear immediately, it would mean that they would not be around for very long. Would artistic, musical, and literary projects still seem worth undertaking? Would humanistic scholars continue to be motivated to engage in basic research? Would historians and theoretical physicists and anthropologists all carry on as before? Perhaps, but the answer is not obvious.

Nor is it merely projects of the kinds I have been discussing, as opposed to more routine aspects of human life, whose appeal might weaken or disappear. Consider, for example, procreative activity. Would people still be as motivated to have children if they knew that those children would die no later than thirty days after their own death? It seems unlikely that they would. But if they would not, then neither would they be as motivated to engage in the wide, varied, and life-altering array of activities associated with raising and caring for children. By contrast, the projects and activities that would seem least likely to be affected by the doomsday scenario are those focused on personal comfort and pleasure. But it is perhaps not altogether obvious what would be comforting and pleasant under doomsday conditions.

The upshot is that many types of projects and activities would no longer seem worth pursuing, or as worth pursuing, if we were confronted with the doomsday scenario. Now it is noteworthy that the attractions of these same projects and activities are not similarly undercut by the mere prospect of our own deaths. People cheerfully engage in cancer research and similar activities despite their recognition that the primary payoff of these activities is not likely to be achieved before their own deaths. Yet, if my argument is correct, their motivation to engage in these same activities would be weakened or even completely undermined by the prospect that, in consequence of the earth's destruction, there would be no payoff *after* their deaths. In other words, there are many projects and activities whose importance to us is not diminished by the prospect of our own deaths but would be diminished by the prospect that everyone else will soon die. So if by the afterlife we mean the continuation of human life on earth after our own deaths, then it seems difficult to avoid the conclusion that, in some significant respects, the existence of the afterlife matters more to us than our own continued existence. It matters more to us because it is a condition of other things mattering to us. Without confidence in the existence of the afterlife, many of the things in our own lives that now matter to us would cease to do so or would come to matter less. . . .

. . . I want to take a brief detour to discuss the views of Alvy Singer. Alvy Singer, as you may remember, is the character played by Woody Allen in his movie *Annie Hall.* The movie contains a flashback scene in which the nine-year-old Alvy is taken by his mother to see a doctor. Alvy is refusing to do his homework on the ground that the universe is expanding. He explains that "the universe is everything, and if it's expanding, someday it will break apart and that would be the end of everything!" Leaving aside Alvy's nerdy precocity, the scene is funny because the eventual end of the universe is so temporally remote—it won't happen for "billions of years," the doctor assures Alvy—that it seems comical to cite it as a reason for not doing one's homework. But if the universe were going to end soon after the end of his own natural life, then the arguments I have been rehearsing imply that Alvy might have a point. It might well be a serious question whether he still had reason to do his homework. Why should there be this discrepancy? If the end of human life in the near term would make many things matter less to us now, then why aren't we similarly affected by the knowledge that human life will end in the longer term? The nagging sense that perhaps we should be is also part of what makes Alvy's refusal to do his homework funny.

Yet I take it as a datum that, in general, and allowing for occasional episodes of Alvy-like angst, we are not so affected. . . . What we require to maintain our equanimity, it seems, is not that humanity should be immortal, but merely that it should survive for a healthy and indefinitely long period after our own deaths. I don't think that we would object to immortality . . . but we don't insist on it. I'm not sure that we can be said exactly to have a *reason* for this, though I'm open to suggestions. My speculation instead is that we simply don't know how, in these contexts, to work with or even fully to grasp concepts like "the end of the universe" or "billions of years." Those ideas require us to adopt a conceptual and spatiotemporal perspective whose vast scale is difficult to align with the much more restricted frame of reference relative to which we make judgments of significance in our daily lives. The result is that we are simply confounded when we try to integrate such ideas into our thinking about what matters. It's not so much that we are not troubled, or cannot be talked into being troubled, about what will happen in the extremely remote future, it's just that we don't really know how to think about it at all, in part because there are so few contexts in which we have occasion to do so. . . .

Let me . . . close by providing a brief summary of my main contentions. I have argued that the survival of people after our deaths matters greatly to us, both in its own right and . . . because, to an extent that we rarely acknowledge, our conviction that things matter is sustained by our confidence that life will go on after we ourselves are gone. In this respect, as I have argued, the survival of humanity matters more to each of us than we usually realize; indeed, in this respect, it matters more to us even than our own survival.

STUDY QUESTIONS

1. Explain the thought experiment Scheffler presents.
2. Do you agree with Scheffler that under the conditions he describes many types of projects and activities would no longer be worth pursuing?
3. Of what relevance to Scheffler's argument are the views expressed by the movie character Alvy Singer?
4. How does Scheffler respond to Alvy Singer's concerns?

How the Afterlife Matters

⌇

Harry G. Frankfurt

Harry G. Frankfurt, whose work we read previously, considers the issue posed in the previous selection by Samuel Scheffler. Frankfurt argues that Scheffler has underestimated how much of what matters to us, such as music, friendship, and intellectual activity, is independent of our attitude toward the possibility of an afterlife.

I believe that Scheffler underestimates how much of what really matters to us is quite independent of our attitude toward the existence of the afterlife. He suggests that trying to find a cure for cancer would lose its importance to us if we believed that there were to be no afterlife in which people would benefit from the cure.

From Harry G. Frankfurt, "How the Afterlife Matters," in Samuel Scheffler, *Death and the Afterlife,* Oxford University Press, 2013. Reprinted by permission of the publisher.

But the challenge of solving a deep medical problem might very well lead people to work on the problem, and to consider both *solving* it and *trying* to solve it very important to them, even if the solution of the problem would actually benefit no one; thus, a person might happily try to solve chess problems, even if there were never to be anyone to admire his or her skill in doing so.

Scheffler also believes that artistic creation would tend to lose its importance to us if we lost confidence in the existence of the afterlife, because there would be no future audiences to enjoy the product of our activity. But, surely, producing a marvelous painting—or string quartet or novel—may be enormously satisfying to the artist even if there is no one, beyond the thirty days before doomsday, who will be around to appreciate and admire his or her creative work. In any event, the doomsday scenario allows the population to continue existing within those thirty days. . . . So, regardless of what happens, so far as the afterlife is concerned, *those* people will still be around to supply appreciative audiences and grateful patients.

Some of the things that are of the greatest importance to us—such as music, friendship, and intellectual and creative activity—may be important to us quite regardless of either the existence of the afterlife or our confidence in its existence. Nevertheless, I think Scheffler *is* justified in suggesting that the importance to us of these things might then actually be less. At least, our valuing of them would very likely be *different*. They would lose that *part* of their value to us, if any, that does depend on our anticipation of the future. We would be left with that part of their value to us which is available to us when we focus just on their present reality—on appreciating their intrinsic and hence always current characteristics. Perhaps it might even be an improvement in our lives, if we concentrated our attention and our appreciation more on the value that things possess in themselves, rather than primarily on their value as means to other things.

So, a great deal of what is valuable to us, and that matters in our lives, might continue to be valuable and to matter to us even if we had *no successors* and did not think we would have any successors. Perhaps it is true that a great deal of what matters most to us would *not* do so, or perhaps it would matter to us both differently and less if the current human population had, or were expected to have, no descendants. However, *some* of the things that are very important to us might continue to be very important to us even without the existence of the afterlife and without confidence in its existence. This includes not just comfort and pleasure, of course, but whatever we value for its own sake and thus whose value to us does not depend entirely on the importance to us of something other than itself.

In fact, if we were faced with a doomsday scenario, some things might matter to us not only as much, but more than before. Faced with a global catastrophe, which would entail our own deaths, we might very well be moved to stop wasting the time left to us, and to repair certain patterns of behavior into which we had lapsed when we thought we had plenty of time left. We might be moved to care more about nourishing the intimate relationships we have with members of our family or friends. We might be moved to care more about taking a trip we had long wanted to take but had kept postponing, and so on.

In any case, it seems to me that people would not all respond in the same way to an expectation that humanity had only a brief time left. People respond differently, after all, to the expectation that they themselves have only a brief time to live. Some become morose and lose interest in practically everything that was previously important to them. Others decide to make the most of the time remaining to them, and they devote themselves to enjoying what is valuable and important to them. It seems likely to me that people would also differ in the ways in which they would confront the prospective end of all human life.

STUDY QUESTIONS

1. Does Frankfurt believe that our finding medical cures would lose its importance if we believed there were no afterlife?
2. According to Frankfurt, how might our lives be improved by believing in Scheffler's doomsday hypothesis?
3. How would you confront the prospective end of all human life?
4. Does it matter whether the end of all human life occurs in a decade, a century, a millennium, or a billion years from now?

The Significance of Doomsday

Susan Wolf

Susan Wolf, whose work we read previously, considers the issue raised by Scheffler about whether the destruction of the earth billions of years from now renders meaningless our current efforts to create beauty, gain wisdom, and help each other. She concludes that the eventual destruction does not have that implication and, therefore, neither does Scheffler's hypothesis that the destruction occurs in only fifty years.

As Scheffler reminds us, . . . when the nerdy protagonist in Woody Allen's film *Annie Hall* was in grade school, his mother took him to a doctor because he was refusing to do his homework on the grounds that the universe is expanding and will someday break apart. . . . According to Scheffler's analysis, the scene is funny not only because of Alvy's precocity but also because he takes an event so far distant

From Susan Wolf, "The Significance of Doomsday," in Samuel Scheffler, *Death & the Afterlife,* Oxford University Press, 2013. Reprinted by permission of the publisher.

in the future to be a reason not to do his homework. As Scheffler reminds us, the doctor attempts to reassure Alvy by saying that won't happen for "billions of years."

As an aside, it may be worth mentioning that, even if it's true that the earth's exploding won't occur for billions of years, we can expect that our species' extinction will come much, much earlier than that. According to the biologist Ernst Mayr, the average life of a species is 100,000 years, and we have already existed about that long. So, we should not expect to go on for another billion years or even another 100,000. Not even close.

But let us return to Alvy's concern and Scheffler's response. According to Scheffler, it is simply a datum that in general we do not respond to our recognition that the earth will someday be destroyed with angst or nihilism or ennui. But, he concedes, "if the universe were going to end soon after the end of his own natural life, then . . . Alvy might have a point." I doubt that the precocious Alvy would be satisfied by this response. The fact that people *don't* get upset by the prospect of our eventual extinction does not mean that they *shouldn't*. "If I would have a point in refusing to do my homework under the doomsday scenario," Alvy might insist, "why don't I have a point anyway?" It seems to me that Alvy is within his rights, at least within the seminar room, to ask for more of an answer.

In fact, the more I think about Alvy's question, . . . the less confident I am that it is answerable. For if Alvy would be justified in not doing his homework if the doomsday scenario were true, this would presumably be because, as Scheffler suggests, humanity must have a future—and indeed a future of more than thirty days—if anything (that could give Alvy a reason to do his homework) is to matter. But why would this be true? If the answer were that in order for anything to matter, it would have to make a *permanent* difference to the world, then Alvy's resistance to homework would be justified by the fact that the earth would explode in a billion years. If it is suggested instead that for anything to matter, it would have to make a long-lasting but *not* permanent difference (or, perhaps better, a difference to a long-lasting but not permanent community), then one might point out that from a cosmic perspective, even a billion years (much less 100,000) is not really "long-lasting."

Happily, though, we can also run this puzzle the other way: If the fact that humans will eventually die out does not render dancing the tango (or walking in the woods or writing a philosophy lecture) meaningless *today*, why should the fact that we will die out in thirty or fifty or a hundred years render it meaningless either? Though I acknowledge the possibility that wish-fulfillment is distorting my reasoning powers, I have to say that I find the rational pull coming from this direction fairly persuasive. That is, since the eventual extinction of humanity does not render our current efforts at creating beauty, gaining wisdom, and helping each other valueless, neither does, or would or should, our more imminent extinction. Probably we would be initially disoriented, unsettled, and depressed by the falsification of so major an assumption that we have until now taken for granted. But just as we are disoriented, unsettled, and depressed by the loss of our life's savings or the unexpected death of a loved one—or to offer a closer analogy, just as we are disoriented, unsettled, and depressed by the loss of faith in a benevolent God and a personal afterlife—we should, at least as a community, eventually, snap out of it and get back to our lives and our world. According to this line of thought, then, if we came to believe that our extinction was imminent, it would be more reasonable to resist the initial tendency to grow detached, apathetic, and depressed than to give in to it. Such reasoning, over time, ought to bring back the meaning and value to many of our activities that we initially thought doomsday would undermine.

Moreover, since the doomsday scenario is just a scenario—that is, an imaginary thought experiment—this reasoning should also bring back for us the meaning and value of the activities that would truly have been rendered pointless by imminent extinction. Now, once again, we have a reason to cure cancer, to find more sustainable energy sources, to build buildings, plant trees, repair infrastructures, and so on. Rationality, if I am right about where rationality on this topic leads, has given us our lives back, restoring the meaning and value to most, if not all, of the activities around which we previously fashioned our lives.

STUDY QUESTIONS

1. What is the concern presented by the movie character Alvy Singer?
2. Why is Wolf initially unsure that Alvy Singer's question is answerable?
3. What does Wolf mean by saying that "we can also run this puzzle the other way"?
4. Do you agree with Wolf that rationality provides an answer to Scheffler's problem and gives us back the meaning to most, if not all, of the activities around which we fashion our lives?

HISTORICAL SOURCES

Phaedo

PLATO

The *Phaedo,* one of Plato's greatest and most complex works, is set in the Athenian prison on the day of Socrates' death. The discussion focuses on Plato's attempts to prove the immortality of the soul. Near the end of the dialogue from which this

From *Phaedo,* translated by David Gallop. Copyright © 1975 by Oxford University Press. Reprinted by permission of the publisher. The Notes are by Andrea Tschemplik and are used with her permission.

selection is taken, Socrates utters his last thoughts, drinks poison, and dies. What then begins is his enormous influence on the history of Western thought.

....

When he'd spoken, Crito said: "Very well, Socrates: what instructions have you for these others or for me, about your children or about anything else? What could we do that would be of most service to you?"

"What I'm always telling you, Crito," said he, "and nothing very new: if you take care for yourselves, your actions will be of service to me and mine and to yourselves too, whatever they may be, even if you make no promises now; but if you take no care for yourselves and are unwilling to pursue your lives along the tracks, as it were, marked by our present and earlier discussions, then even if you make many firm promises at this time, you'll do no good at all."

"Then we'll strive to do as you say," he said; "but in what fashion are we to bury you?"

"However you wish," said he; "provided you catch me, that is, and I don't get away from you." And with this he laughed quietly, looked towards us and said: "Friends, I can't persuade Crito that I am Socrates here, the one who is now conversing and arranging each of the things being discussed; but he imagines I'm that dead body he'll see in a little while, so he goes and asks how he's to bury me! But as for the great case I've been arguing all this time, that when I drink the poison,[1] I shall no longer remain with you, but shall go off and depart for some happy state of the blessed, this, I think, I'm putting to him in vain, while comforting you and myself alike. So please stand surety for me with Crito, the opposite surety to that which he stood for me with the judges: his guarantee was that I *would* stay behind, whereas you must guarantee that, when I die, I shall *not* stay behind, but shall go off and depart; then Crito will bear it more easily, and when he sees the burning or interment of my body, he won't be distressed for me, as if I were suffering dreadful things, and won't say at the funeral that it is Socrates they are laying out or bearing to the grave or interring. Because you can be sure, my dear Crito, that misuse of words is not only troublesome in itself, but actually has a bad effect on the soul. Rather, you should have confidence, and say you are burying my body; and bury it however you please, and think most proper."

After saying this, he rose and went into a room to take a bath, and Crito followed him but told us to wait. So we waited, talking among ourselves about what had been said and reviewing it, and then again dwelling on how great a misfortune had befallen us, literally thinking of it as if we were deprived of a father and would lead the rest of our life as orphans. After he'd bathed and his children had been brought to him—he had two little sons and one big one—and those women of his household had come, he talked with them in Crito's presence, and gave certain directions as to his wishes; he then told the women and children to leave, and himself returned to us.

By now it was close to sunset, as he'd spent a long time inside. So he came and sat down, fresh from his bath, and there wasn't much talk after that. Then the prison official came in, stepped up to him and said: "Socrates, I shan't reproach you as I reproach others for being angry with me and cursing, whenever by order of the rulers I direct them to drink the poison. In your time here I've known you for the most generous and gentlest and best of men who have ever come to this place; and now especially, I feel sure it isn't with me that you're angry, but with others, because you know who are responsible. Well now, you know the message I've come to bring: good-bye, then, and try to bear the inevitable as easily as you can." And with this he turned away in tears, and went off.

Socrates looked up at him and said: "Good-bye to you too, and we'll do as you say." And to us he added: "What a civil man he is! Throughout my time here he's been to see me, and sometimes talked with me, and been the best of fellows; and now how generous of him to weep for me! But come on, Crito, let's obey him: let someone bring in the poison, if it has been prepared; if not, let the man prepare it."

Crito said: "But Socrates, I think the sun is still on the mountains and hasn't yet gone down. And besides, I know of others who've taken the draught long after the order had been given them, and after dining well and drinking plenty, and even in some cases enjoying themselves with those they fancied. Be in no hurry, then: there's still time left."

Socrates said: "It's reasonable for those you speak of to do those things— because they think they gain by doing them; for myself, it's reasonable not to do them; because I think I'll gain nothing by taking the draught a little later: I'll only earn my own ridicule by clinging to life, and being sparing when there's nothing more left. Go on now; do as I ask, and nothing else."

Hearing this, Crito nodded to the boy who was standing nearby. The boy went out, and after spending a long time away he returned, bringing the man who was going to administer the poison, and was carrying it ready-pounded in a cup. When he saw the man, Socrates said: "Well, my friend, you're an expert in these things: what must one do?"

"Simply drink it," he said, "and walk about till a heaviness comes over your legs; then lie down, and it will act of itself." And with this he held out the cup to Socrates.

He took it perfectly calmly, Echecrates, without a tremor, or any change of colour or countenance; but looking up at the man, and fixing him with his customary stare, he said: "What do you say to pouring someone a libation from this drink? Is it allowed or not?"

"We only prepare as much as we judge the proper dose, Socrates," he said.

"I understand," he said; "but at least one may pray to the gods, and so one should, that the removal from this world to the next will be a happy one; that is my own prayer: so may it be." With these words he pressed the cup to his lips, and drank it off with good humour and without the least distaste.

Till then most of us had been fairly well able to restrain our tears; but when we saw he was drinking, that he'd actually drunk it, we could do so no longer. In my own case, the tears came pouring out in spite of myself, so that I covered my face and wept for myself—not for him, no, but for my own misfortune in being deprived of such a man for a companion. Even before me, Crito had moved away, when he was unable to restrain his tears. And Apollodorus, who even earlier had been continuously in tears, now burst forth into such a storm of weeping and grieving, that he made everyone present break down except Socrates himself.

But Socrates said: "What a way to behave, my strange friends! Why, it was mainly for this reason that I sent the women away, so that they shouldn't make this sort of trouble; in fact, I've heard one should die in silence. Come now, calm yourselves and have strength."

When we heard this, we were ashamed and checked our tears. He walked about, and when he said that his legs felt heavy he lay down on his back—as the man told him—and then the man, this one who'd given him the poison, felt him, and after an interval examined his feet and legs; he then pinched his foot hard and asked if he could feel it, and Socrates said not. After that he felt his shins once more; and moving upwards in this way, he showed us that he was becoming cold and numb. He went on feeling him, and said that when the coldness reached his heart, he would be gone.

By this time the coldness was somewhere in the region of his abdomen, when he uncovered his face—it had been covered over—and spoke; and this was in fact his last utterance: "Crito," he said, "we owe a cock to Asclepius: please pay the debt, and don't neglect it."[2]

"It shall be done," said Crito; "have you anything else to say?"

To this question he made no answer, but after a short interval he stirred, and when the man uncovered him his eyes were fixed; when he saw this, Crito closed his mouth and his eyes.

And that, Echecrates, was the end of our companion, a man who, among those of his time we knew, was—so we should say—the best, the wisest too, and the most just.

NOTES

1. The poison was hemlock, frequently used in ancient executions.
2. Asclepius was the hero or god of healing. A provocative, but disputed, interpretation of Socrates' final instruction is that he considers death the cure for life and, therefore, wishes to make an offering in gratitude to the god of health.

STUDY QUESTIONS

1. According to Socrates, how could Crito be of most service?
2. Why, according to Socrates, will he have to be caught in order to be buried?
3. What lessons can be drawn from the equanimity with which Socrates faced death?
4. In what ways does the study of philosophy reflect concerns that were espoused by Socrates?

Writings

✑

EPICURUS

Epicurus (341–270 B.C.E.) was an influential Greek philosopher who founded a community in Athens called "the Garden," in which men and women as well as free persons and slaves participated on equal terms. He was a prolific author, but few of his writings survive.

His system of thought, known as Epicureanism, stressed that the gods are detached from this world. Its fundamental structure is that of atoms in motion, although persons have free will as a result of uncaused swerves in the atoms. Our knowledge is derived from sense experience. The ultimate aim of philosophy is to provide a guide to living well, maximizing pleasures and minimizing pains, but accepting such pains as lead to greater pleasures, and rejecting such pleasures as lead to greater pains. The result is a life that avoids extravagance. The virtues, such as temperance or courage, are prized because they lead to a pleasant life. So do friendships, which are, therefore, to be cultivated. Death is not to be feared, because while we exist, death is not present; when death is present, we do not exist.

....

LETTER TO MENOECEUS

Let no one when young delay to study philosophy, nor when he is old grow weary of his study. For no one can come too early or too late to secure the health of his soul. And the man who says that the age for philosophy has either not yet come or has gone by is like the man who says that the age for happiness is not yet come to him, or has passed away. Wherefore both when young and old a man must study philosophy, that as he grows old he may be young in blessings through the grateful recollection of what has been, and that in youth he may be old as well, since he will know no fear of what is to come. We must then meditate on the things that make our happiness, seeing that when that is with us we have all, but when it is absent we do all to win it.

The things which I used unceasingly to commend to you, these do and practice, considering them to be the first principles of the good life. First of all believe that god is a being immortal and blessed, even as the common idea of a god is engraved on men's minds, and do not assign to him anything alien to his immortality or ill-suited to his blessedness: but believe about him everything that can

---

uphold his blessedness and immortality. For gods there are, since the knowledge of them is by clear vision. But they are not such as the many believe them to be: for indeed they do not consistently represent them as they believe them to be. And the impious man is not he who denies the gods of the many, but he who attaches to the gods the beliefs of the many. For the statements of the many about the gods are not conceptions derived from sensation, but false suppositions, according to which the greatest misfortunes befall the wicked and the greatest blessings the good by the gift of the gods. For men being accustomed always to their own virtues welcome those like themselves, but regard all that is not of their nature as alien.

Become accustomed to the belief that death is nothing to us. For all good and evil consists in sensation, but death is deprivation of sensation. And therefore a right understanding that death is nothing to us makes the mortality of life enjoyable, not because it adds to it an infinite span of time, but because it takes away the craving for immortality. For there is nothing terrible in life for the man who has truly comprehended that there is nothing terrible in not living. So that the man speaks but idly who says that he fears death not because it will be painful when it comes, but because it is painful in anticipation. For that which gives no trouble when it comes, is but an empty pain in anticipation. So death, the most terrifying of ills, is nothing to us, since so long as we exist, death is not with us; but when death comes, then we do not exist. It does not then concern either the living or the dead, since for the former it is not, and the latter are no more.

But the many at one moment shun death as the greatest of evils, at another yearn for it as a respite from the evils in life. But the wise man neither seeks to escape life nor fears the cessation of life, for neither does life offend him nor does the absence of life seem to be any evil. And just as with food he does not seek simply the larger share and nothing else, but rather the most pleasant, so he seeks to enjoy not the longest period of time, but the most pleasant.

And he who counsels the young man to live well, but the old man to make a good end, is foolish, not merely because of the desirability of life, but also because it is the same training which teaches to live well and to die well. Yet much worse still is the man who says it is good not to be born, but

once born make haste to pass the gates of Death.[1]

For if he says this from conviction why does he not pass away out of life? For it is open to him to do so, if he had firmly made up his mind to this. But if he speaks in jest, his words are idle among men who cannot receive them.

We must then bear in mind that the future is neither ours, nor yet wholly not ours, so that we may not altogether expect it as sure to come, nor abandon hope of it, as if it will certainly not come.

We must consider that of desires some are natural, others vain, and of the natural some are necessary and others merely natural; and of the necessary some are necessary for happiness, others for the repose of the body, and others for very life. The right understanding of these facts enables us to refer all choice and avoidance to the health of the body and the soul's freedom from disturbance, since this is the aim of the life of blessedness. For it is to obtain this end that we always act, namely, to avoid pain and fear. And when this is once secured for us, all the tempest of the soul is dispersed, since the living creature has not to wander as though in search of something that is missing, and to look for some other thing by which he can fulfil the good of the soul and the good of the body. For it is then that we have need of pleasure, when we feel pain owing to the absence of pleasure; but when we do not feel pain, we no longer need pleasure. And for this cause we call pleasure the beginning and end of the blessed life. For we recognize pleasure as the first good innate in us, and from pleasure we begin every act of choice and avoidance, and to pleasure we return again, using the feeling as the standard by which we judge every good.

And since pleasure is the first good and natural to us, for this very reason we do not choose every pleasure, but sometimes we pass over many pleasures, when greater discomfort accrues to us as the result of them: and similarly we think many pains better than pleasures, since a greater pleasure comes to us when we have endured pains for a long time. Every pleasure then because of its natural kinship to us is good, yet not every pleasure is to be chosen: even as every pain also is an evil, yet not all are always of a nature to be avoided. Yet by a scale of comparison and by the consideration of advantages and disadvantages we must form our judgement on all these matters. For the good on certain occasions we treat as bad, and conversely the bad as good.

And again independence of desire we think a great good—not that we may at all times enjoy but a few things, but that, if we do not possess many, we may enjoy the few in the genuine persuasion that those have the sweetest pleasure in luxury who least need it, and that all that is natural is easy to be obtained, but that which is superfluous is hard. And so plain savours bring us a pleasure equal to a luxurious diet, when all the pain due to want is removed; and bread and water produce the highest pleasure, when one who needs them puts them to his lips. To grow accustomed therefore to a simple and not luxurious diet gives us health to the full, and makes a man alert for the needful employments of life, and when after long intervals we approach luxuries disposes us better towards them, and fits us to be fearless of fortune.

When, therefore, we maintain that pleasure is the end, we do not mean the pleasures of profligates and those that consist in sensuality, as is supposed by some who are either ignorant or disagree with us or do not understand, but freedom from pain in the body and from trouble in the mind. For it is not continuous drinkings and revellings, nor the satisfaction of lusts, nor the enjoyment of fish and other luxuries of the wealthy table, which produce a pleasant life, but sober reasoning, searching out the motives for all choice and avoidance, and banishing mere opinions, to which are due the greatest disturbance of the spirit.

Of all this the beginning and the greatest good is prudence. Wherefore prudence is a more precious thing even than philosophy: for from prudence are sprung all the other virtues, and it teaches us that it is not possible to live pleasantly without living prudently and honourably and justly, nor, again, to live a life of prudence, honour, and justice without living pleasantly. For the virtues are by nature bound up with the pleasant life, and the pleasant life is inseparable from them. For indeed who, think you, is a better man than he who holds reverent opinions concerning the gods, and is at all times free from fear of death, and has reasoned out the end ordained by nature? He understands that the limit of good things is easy to fulfil and easy to attain, whereas the course of ills is either short in time or slight in pain: he laughs at destiny, whom some have introduced as the mistress of all things. He thinks that with us lies the chief power in determining events, some of which happen by necessity and some by chance, and some are within our control; for while necessity cannot be called to account, he sees that chance is inconstant, but that which is in our control is subject to no master, and to it are naturally attached praise and blame. For, indeed, it were better to follow the myths about the gods than to become a slave to the destiny of the natural philosophers: for the former suggests a hope of placating the gods by worship, whereas the latter involves a necessity which knows no placation. As to chance, he does not regard it as a god as most men do (for in a god's acts there is no disorder), nor as an uncertain cause of all things for he does not believe that good and evil are given by chance to man for the framing of a blessed life, but that opportunities for great good and great evil are afforded by it. He therefore thinks it better to be unfortunate in reasonable action than to prosper in unreason. For it is better in a man's actions that what is well chosen should fail, rather than that what is ill chosen should be successful owing to chance.

Meditate therefore on these things and things akin to them night and day by yourself, and with a companion like to yourself, and never shall you be disturbed waking or asleep, but you shall live like a god among men. For a man who lives among immortal blessings is not like to a mortal being.

PRINCIPLE DOCTRINES

I. The blessed and immortal nature knows no trouble itself nor causes trouble to any other, so that it is never constrained by anger or favour. For all such things exist only in the weak.

II. Death is nothing to us: for that which is dissolved is without sensation; and that which lacks sensation is nothing to us.

III. The limit of quantity in pleasures is the removal of all that is painful. Wherever pleasure is present, as long as it is there, there is neither pain of body nor of mind, nor of both at once.

IV. Pain does not last continuously in the flesh, but the acutest pain is there for a very short time, and even that which just exceeds the pleasure in the flesh does not continue for many days at once. But chronic illnesses permit a predominance of pleasure over pain in the flesh.

V. It is not possible to live pleasantly without living prudently and honourably and justly, [nor again to live a life of prudence, honour, and justice] without living pleasantly. And the man who does not possess the pleasant life is not living prudently and honourably and justly, and the man who does not possess the virtuous life cannot possibly live pleasantly.

VI. To secure protection from men anything is a natural good, by which you may be able to attain this end.

VII. Some men wished to become famous and conspicuous, thinking that they would thus win for themselves safety from other men. Wherefore if the life of such men is safe, they have obtained the good which nature craves; but if it is not safe, they do not possess that for which they strove at first by the instinct of nature.

VIII. No pleasure is a bad thing in itself: but the means which produce some pleasures bring with them disturbances many times greater than the pleasures.

IX. If every pleasure could be intensified so that it lasted and influenced the whole organism or the most essential parts of our nature, pleasures would never differ from one another.

X. If the things that produce the pleasures of profligates could dispel the fears of the mind about the phenomena of the sky and death and its pains, and also teach the limits of desires and of pains, we should never have cause to blame them: for they would be filling themselves full with pleasures from every source and never have pain of body or mind, which is the evil of life.

XI. If we were not troubled by our suspicions of the phenomena of the sky and about death, fearing that it concerns us, and also by our failure to grasp the limits of pains and desires, we should have no need of natural science.

XII. A man cannot dispel his fear about the most important matters if he does not know what is the nature of the universe but suspects the truth of some mythical story. So that without natural science it is not possible to attain our pleasures unalloyed.

XIII. There is no profit in securing protection in relation to men, if things above and things beneath the earth and indeed all in the boundless universe remain matters of suspicion.

XIV. The most unalloyed source of protection from men, which is secured to some extent by a certain force of expulsion, is in fact the immunity which results from a quiet life and the retirement from the world.

XV. The wealth demanded by nature is both limited and easily procured; that demanded by idle imaginings stretches on to infinity.

XVI. In but few things chance hinders a wise man, but the greatest and most important matters reason has ordained and throughout the whole period of life does and will ordain.

XVII. The just man is most free from trouble, the unjust most full of trouble.

XVIII. The pleasure in the flesh is not increased, when once the pain due to want is removed, but is only varied: and the limit as regards pleasure in the mind is begotten by the reasoned understanding of these very pleasures and of the emotions akin to them, which used to cause the greatest fear to the mind.

XIX. Infinite time contains no greater pleasure than limited time, if one measures by reason the limits of pleasure.

XX. The flesh perceives the limits of pleasure as unlimited and unlimited time is required to supply it. But the mind, having attained a reasoned understanding of the ultimate good of the flesh and its limits and having dissipated the fears concerning the time to come, supplies us with the complete life, and we have no further need of infinite time: but neither does the mind shun pleasure, nor, when circumstances begin to bring about the departure from life, does it approach its end as though it fell short in any way of the best life.

XXI. He who has learned the limits of life knows that that which removes the pain due to want and makes the whole of life complete is easy to obtain; so that there is no need of actions which involve competition.

XXII. We must consider both the real purpose and all the evidence of direct perception, to which we always refer the conclusions of opinion; otherwise, all will be full of doubt and confusion.

XXIII. If you fight against all sensations, you will have no standard by which to judge even those of them which you say are false.

XXIV. If you reject any single sensation and fail to distinguish between the conclusion of opinion as to the appearance awaiting confirmation and that which is actually given by the sensation or feeling, or each intuitive apprehension of the mind, you will confound all other sensations as well with the same groundless opinion, so that you will reject every standard of judgement. And if among the mental images created by your opinion you affirm both that which awaits confirmation and that which does not, you will not escape error, since you will have preserved the whole cause of doubt in every judgement between what is right and what is wrong.

XXV. If on each occasion instead of referring your actions to the end of nature, you turn to some other nearer standard when you are making a choice or an avoidance, your actions will not be consistent with your principles.

XXVI. Of desires, all that do not lead to a sense of pain, if they are not satisfied, are not necessary, but involve a craving which is easily dispelled, when the object is hard to procure or they seem likely to produce harm.

XXVII. Of all the things which wisdom acquires to produce the blessedness of the complete life, far the greatest is the possession of friendship.

XXVIII. The same conviction which has given us confidence that there is nothing terrible that lasts for ever or even for long has also seen the protection of friendship most fully completed in the limited evils of this life.

XXIX. Among desires some are natural and necessary, some natural but not necessary, and others neither natural nor necessary, but due to idle imagination.

XXX. Wherever in the case of desires which are physical, but do not lead to a sense of pain, if they are not fulfilled, the effort is intense, such pleasures are due to idle imagination, and it is not owing to their own nature that they fail to be dispelled, but owing to the empty imaginings of the man.

XXXI. The justice which arises from nature is a pledge of mutual advantage to restrain men from harming one another and save them from being harmed.

XXXII. For all living things which have not been able to make compacts not to harm one another or be harmed, nothing ever is either just or unjust; and likewise too for all tribes of men which have been unable or unwilling to make compacts not to harm or be harmed.

NOTE

1. [These words are attributed to the sixth-century B.C.E. Greek poet Theognis—S.M.C.]

STUDY QUESTIONS

1. According to Epicurus, why is death nothing to us?
2. Do you agree with Epicurus that scientific knowledge helps dispel fear?
3. Why, according to Epicurus, can you not fight against all sensations?
4. Do you agree with Epicurus that the pleasant life is a life of virtue?

The Handbook

EPICTETUS

Epictetus (c. 50–c. 130), a freed Roman slave, was an exponent of Stoicism, an influential system of thought founded in Greece soon after the death of Aristotle that offered a unified logical, physical, and moral philosophy. Stoics viewed the world as a completely ordered system but with individuals possessing moral responsibility. How these two aspects of reality are supposed to cohere is one logical problem among many the Stoics explored.

Epictetus was primarily concerned with moral teaching, and like other Stoics believed in living one's life in accord with the natural order, accepting what happens with a tranquility that renders one immune from disappointment and pain. Self-sufficiency is prized, for if you are not dependent on others, their failures cannot harm you. Because happiness can be achieved if events occur as one desires, and one has control over one's desires but not over events, the way to happiness lies in adjusting one's desires so that they are in accord with events.

Note that *The Handbook* ends with quotations from Plato's *Apology* and *Crito*, emphasizing the equanimity of Socrates in the face of death. Such tranquility in the face of tribulation epitomized the outlook on life presented by Epictetus, who had himself endured without complaint the physical abuse that accompanied his slavery.

....

1

Of all existing things some are in our power, and others are not in our power. In our power are thought, impulse, will to get and will to avoid, and, in a word, everything which is our own doing. Things not in our power include the body,

Epictetus, "Encheiridion." Reprinted from *Epictetus. The Discourses and Manual*, translated by P. E. Matheson (1916), by permission of the Oxford University Press, Oxford.

property, reputation, office, and, in a word, everything which is not our own doing. Things in our power are by nature free, unhindered, untrammelled; things not in our power are weak, servile, subject to hindrance, dependent on others. Remember then that if you imagine that what is naturally slavish is free, and what is naturally another's is your own, you will be hampered, you will mourn, you will be put to confusion, you will blame gods and men; but if you think that only your own belongs to you, and that what is another's is indeed another's, no one will ever put compulsion or hindrance on you, you will blame none, you will accuse none, you will do nothing against your will, no one will harm you, you will have no enemy, for no harm can touch you.

Aiming then at these high matters, you must remember that to attain them requires more than ordinary effort; you will have to give up some things entirely, and put off others for the moment. And if you would have these also—office and wealth—it may be that you will fail to get them, just because your desire is set on the former, and you will certainly fail to attain those things which alone bring freedom and happiness.

Make it your study then to confront every harsh impression with the words, "You are but an impression, and not at all what you seem to be." Then test it by those rules that you possess; and first by this—the chief test of all—"Is it concerned with what is in our power or with what is not in our power?" And if it is concerned with what is not in our power, be ready with the answer that it is nothing to you.

2

Remember that the will to get promises attainment of what you will, and the will to avoid promises escape from what you avoid; and he who fails to get what he wills is unfortunate, and he who does not escape what he wills to avoid is miserable. If then you try to avoid only what is unnatural in the region within your control, you will escape from all that you avoid; but if you try to avoid disease or death or poverty, you will be miserable.

Therefore let your will to avoid have no concern with what is not in man's power; direct it only to things in man's power that are contrary to nature. But for the moment you must utterly remove the will to get; for if you will to get something not in man's power you are bound to be unfortunate; while none of the things in man's power that you could honourably will to get is yet within your reach. Impulse to act and not to act, these are your concern; yet exercise them gently and without strain, and provisionally.

3

When anything, from the meanest thing upwards, is attractive or serviceable or an object of affection, remember always to say to yourself, "What is its nature?" If you are fond of a jug, say you are fond of a jug; then you will not be disturbed if it be broken. If you kiss your child or your wife, say to yourself that you are kissing a human being, for then if death strikes, you will not be disturbed.

4

When you are about to take something in hand, remind yourself what manner of thing it is. If you are going to bathe, put before your mind what happens in the bath—water pouring over some, others being jostled, some reviling, others stealing; and you will set to work more securely if you say to yourself at once: "I want to bathe, and I want to keep my will in harmony with nature," and so in each thing you do; for in this way, if anything turns up to hinder you in your bathing, you will be ready to say, "I did not want only to bathe, but to keep my will in harmony with nature, and I shall not so keep it, if I lose my temper at what happens."

5

What disturbs men's mind is not events but their judgements on events. For instance, death is nothing dreadful, or else Socrates would have thought it so. No, the only dreadful thing about it is men's judgement that it is dreadful. And so when we are hindered, or disturbed, or distressed, let us never lay the blame on others, but on ourselves, that is, on our own judgements. To accuse others for one's own misfortunes is a sign of want of education; to accuse oneself shows that one's education has begun; to accuse neither oneself nor others shows that one's education is complete.

6

Be not elated at an excellence which is not your own. If the horse in his pride were to say, "I am handsome," we could bear with it. But when you say with pride, "I have a handsome horse," know that the good horse is the ground of your pride. You ask then what you can call your own. The answer is—the way you deal with your impressions. Therefore when you deal with your impressions in accord with nature, then you may be proud indeed, for your pride will be in a good which is your own.

7

When you are on a voyage, and your ship is at anchorage, and you disembark to get fresh water, you may pick up a small shellfish or a truffle by the way, but you must keep your attention fixed on the ship, and keep looking towards it constantly, to see if the Helmsman calls you; and if he does, you have to leave everything, or be bundled on board with your legs tied like a sheep. So it is in life. If you have a dear wife or child given you, they are like the shellfish or the truffle, they are very well in their way. Only, if the Helmsman call, run back to your ship, leave all else, and do not look behind you. And if you are old, never go far from the ship, so that when you are called you may not fail to appear.

8

Ask not that events should happen as you will, but let your will be that events should happen as they do, and you shall have peace.

9

Sickness is a hindrance to the body, but not to the will, unless the will consent. Lameness is a hindrance to the leg, but not to the will. Say this to yourself at each event that happens, for you shall find that though it hinders something else it will not hinder you.

10

When anything happens to you, always remember to turn to yourself and ask what faculty you have to deal with it. If you see a beautiful boy or a beautiful woman, you will find continence the faculty to exercise there; if trouble is laid on you, you will find endurance; if ribaldry, you will find patience. And if you train yourself in this habit, your impressions will not carry you away.

11

Never say of anything, "I lost it," but say, "I gave it back." Has your child died? It was given back. Has your wife died? She was given back. Has your estate been taken from you? Was not this also given back? But you say, "He who took it from me is wicked." What does it matter to you through whom the Giver asked it back? As long as He gives it you, take care of it, but not as your own; treat it as passers-by treat an inn.

12

If you wish to make progress, abandon reasonings of this sort: "If I neglect my affairs I shall have nothing to live on"; "If I do not punish my son, he will be wicked." For it is better to die of hunger, so that you be free from pain and free from fear, than to live in plenty and be troubled in mind. It is better for your son to be wicked than for you to be miserable. Wherefore begin with little things. Is your drop of oil spilt? Is your sup of wine stolen? Say to yourself, "This is the price paid for freedom from passion, this is the price of a quiet mind." Nothing can be had without a price. When you call your slave-boy, reflect that he may not be able to hear you, and if he hears you, he may not be able to do anything you want. But he is not so well off that it rests with him to give you peace of mind.

13

If you wish to make progress, you must be content in external matters to seem a fool and a simpleton; do not wish men to think you know anything, and if any should think you to be somebody, distrust yourself. For know that it is not easy to keep your will in accord with nature and at the same time keep outward things; if you attend to one, you must neglect the other.

14

It is silly to want your children and your wife and your friends to live for ever, for that means that you want what is not in your control to be in your control, and what is not your own to be yours. In the same way if you want your servant to make no mistakes, you are a fool, for you want vice not to be vice but something different. But if you want not to be disappointed in your will to get, you can attain to that.

Exercise yourself then in what lies in your power. Each man's master is the man who has authority over what he wishes or does not wish, to secure the one or to take away the other. Let him then who wishes to be free not wish for anything or avoid anything that depends on others; or else he is bound to be a slave.

15

Remember that you must behave in life as you would at a banquet. A dish is handed round and comes to you; put out your hand and take it politely. It passes you; do not stop it. It has not reached you; do not be impatient to get it, but wait till your turn comes. Bear yourself thus towards children, wife, office, wealth, and one day you will be worthy to banquet with the gods. But if when they are set before you, you do not take them but despise them, then you shall not only share the gods' banquet, but shall share their rule. For by so doing Diogenes[1] and Heraclitus and men like them were called divine and deserved the name.

16

When you see a man shedding tears in sorrow for a child abroad or dead, or for loss of property, beware that you are not carried away by the impression that it is outward ills that make him miserable. Keep this thought by you; "What distresses him is not the event, for that does not distress another, but his judgement on the event." Therefore do not hesitate to sympathize with him so far as words go, and if it so chance, even to groan with him; but take heed that you do not also groan in your inner being.

17

Remember that you are an actor in a play, and the Playwright chooses the manner of it: if he wants it short, it is short; if long, it is long. If he wants you to act a poor man, you must act the part with all your powers; and so if your part be a cripple or a magistrate or a plain man. For your business is to act the character that is given you and act it well; the choice of the cast is Another's.

18

When a raven croaks with evil omen, let not the impression carry you away, but straightway distinguish in your own mind and say, "These portents mean nothing to me; but only to my bit of a body or my bit of property or name, or my children or my wife. But for me all omens are favourable if I will, for, whatever the issue may be, it is in my power to get benefit therefrom."

19

You can be invincible, if you never enter on a contest where victory is not in your power. Beware then that when you see a man raised to honour or great power or high repute you do not let your impression carry you away. For if the reality of good lies in what is in our power, there is no room for envy or jealousy. And you will not wish to be praetor, or prefect or consul, but to be free; and there is but one way to freedom—to despise what is not in our power.

20

Remember that foul words or blows in themselves are no outrage, but your judgement that they are so. So when anyone makes you angry, know that it is your own thought that has angered you. Wherefore make it your first endeavour not to let your impressions carry you away. For if once you gain time and delay, you will find it easier to control yourself.

21

Keep before your eyes from day to day death and exile and all things that seem terrible, but death most of all, and then you will never set your thoughts on what is low and will never desire anything beyond measure.

22

If you set your desire on philosophy, you must at once prepare to meet with ridicule and the jeers of many who will say, "Here he is again, turned philosopher.

Where has he got these proud looks?" Nay, put on no proud looks, but hold fast to what seems best to you, in confidence that God has set you at this post. And remember that if you abide where you are, those who first laugh at you will one day admire you, and that if you give way to them, you will get doubly laughed at.

23

If it ever happen to you to be diverted to things outside, so that you desire to please another, know that you have lost your life's plan. Be content then always to be a philosopher; if you wish to be regarded as one too, show yourself that you are one and you will be able to achieve it.

24

Let not reflections such as these afflict you: "I shall live without honour, and never be of any account"; for if lack of honour is an evil, no one but yourself can involve you in evil any more than in shame. Is it your business to get office or to be invited to an entertainment?

Certainly not.

Where then is the dishonour you talk of? How can you be "of no account anywhere," when you ought to count for something in those matters only which are in your power, where you may achieve the highest worth?

"But my friends," you say, "will lack assistance."

What do you mean by "lack assistance"? They will not have cash from you and you will not make them Roman citizens. Who told you that to do these things is in our power, and not dependent upon others? Who can give to another what is not his to give?

"Get them then," says he, "that we may have them."

If I can get them and keep my self-respect, honour, magnanimity, show the way and I will get them. But if you call on me to lose the good things that are mine, in order that you may win things that are not good, look how unfair and thoughtless you are. And which do you really prefer? Money, or a faithful, modest friend? Therefore help me rather to keep these qualities, and do not expect from me actions which will make me lose them.

"But my country," says he, "will lack assistance, so far as lies in me."

Once more I ask, What assistance do you mean? It will not owe colonnades or baths to you. What of that? It does not owe shoes to the blacksmith or arms to the shoemaker; it is sufficient if each man fulfils his own function. Would you do it no good if you secured to it another faithful and modest citizen?

"Yes."

Well, then, you would not be useless to it.

"What place then shall I have in the city?"

Whatever place you can hold while you keep your character for honour and self-respect. But if you are going to lose these qualities in trying to benefit your city, what benefit, I ask, would you have done her when you attain to the perfection of being lost to shame and honour?

25

Has some one had precedence of you at an entertainment or a levee or been called in before you to give advice? If these things are good you ought to be glad that he got them; if they are evil, do not be angry that you did not get them yourself. Remember that if you want to get what is not in your power, you cannot earn the same reward as others unless you act as they do. How is it possible for one who does not haunt the great man's door to have equal shares with one who does, or one who does not go in his train equality with one who does; or one who does not praise him with one who does? You will be unjust then and insatiable if you wish to get these privileges for nothing, without paying their price. What is the price of a lettuce? An obol perhaps. If then a man pays his obol and gets his lettuces, and you do not pay and do not get them, do not think you are defrauded. For as he has the lettuces so you have the obol you did not give. The same principle holds good too in conduct. You were not invited to some one's entertainment? Because you did not give the host the price for which he sells his dinner. He sells it for compliments, he sells it for attentions. Pay him the price then, if it is to your profit. But if you wish to get the one and yet not give up the other, nothing can satisfy you in your folly.

What! you say, you have nothing instead of the dinner?

Nay, you have this, you have not praised the man you did not want to praise, you have not had to bear with the insults of his doorstep.

26

It is in our power to discover the will of Nature from those matters on which we have no difference of opinion. For instance, when another man's slave has broken the wine-cup we are very ready to say at once, "Such things must happen." Know then that when your own cup is broken, you ought to behave in the same way as when your neighbour's was broken. Apply the same principle to higher matters. Is another's child or wife dead? Not one of us but would say, "Such is the lot of man"; but when one's own dies, straightway one cries, "Alas! miserable am I." But we ought to remember what our feelings are when we hear it of another.

27

As a mark is not set up for men to miss it, so there is nothing intrinsically evil in the world.

28

If any one trusted your body to the first man he met, you would be indignant, but yet you trust your mind to the chance comer, and allow it to be disturbed and confounded if he revile you; are you not ashamed to do so?

29

In everything you do consider what comes first and what follows, and so approach it. Otherwise you will come to it with a good heart at first because you have not reflected on any of the consequences, and afterwards, when difficulties have appeared, you will desist to your shame. Do you wish to win at Olympia? So do I, by the gods, for it is a fine thing. But consider the first steps to it, and the consequences, and so lay your hand to the work. You must submit to discipline, eat to order, touch no sweets, train under compulsion, at a fixed hour, in heat and cold, drink no cold water, nor wine, except by order; you must hand yourself over completely to your trainer as you would to a physician, and then when the contest comes you must risk getting hacked, and sometimes dislocate your hand, twist your ankle, swallow plenty of sand; sometimes get a flogging, and with all this suffer defeat. When you have considered all this well, then enter on the athlete's course, if you still wish it. If you act without thought, you will be behaving like children, who one day play at wrestlers, another day at gladiators, now sound the trumpet, and next strut the stage. Like them you will be now an athlete, now a gladiator, then orator; then philosopher, but nothing with all your soul. Like an ape, you imitate every sight you see, and one thing after another takes your fancy. When you undertake a thing you do it casually and half-heartedly, instead of considering it and looking at it all round. In the same way some people, when they see a philosopher and hear a man speaking like Euphrates (and indeed who can speak as he can?), wish to be philosophers themselves.

Man, consider first what it is you are undertaking; then look at your own powers and see if you can bear it. Do you want to compete in the pentathlon or in wrestling? Look to your arms, your thighs, see what your loins are like. For different men are born for different tasks. Do you suppose that if you do this you can live as you do now—eat and drink as you do now, indulge desire and discontent just as before? Nay, you must sit up late, work hard, abandon your own people, be looked down on by a mere slave, be ridiculed by those who meet you, get the worst of it in everything—in honour, in office, in justice, in every possible thing. This is what you have to consider: whether you are willing to pay this price for peace of mind, freedom, tranquility. If not, do not come near; do not be, like the children, first a philosopher, then a tax-collector, then an orator, then one of Caesar's procurators. These callings do not agree. You must be one man, good or bad; you must develop either your Governing

Principle or your outward endowments; you must study either your inner man or outward things—in a word, you must choose between the position of a philosopher and that of a mere outsider.

30

Appropriate acts are in general measured by the relations they are concerned with. "He is your father." This means you are called on to take care of him, give way to him in all things, bear with him if he reviles or strikes you.

"But he is a bad father."

Well, have you any natural claim to a good father? No, only to a father.

"My brother wrongs me."

Be careful then to maintain the relation you hold to him, and do not consider what he does, but what you must do if your purpose is to keep in accord with nature. For no one shall harm you, without your consent; you will only be harmed, when you think you are harmed. You will only discover what is proper to expect from neighbour, citizen, or praetor, if you get into the habit of looking at the relations implied by each.

31

For piety towards the gods know that the most important thing is this: to have right opinions about them—that they exist, and that they govern the universe well and justify—and to have set yourself to obey them, and to give way to all that happens, following events with a free will, in the belief that they are fulfilled by the highest mind. For thus you will never blame the gods, nor accuse them of neglecting you. But this you cannot achieve, unless you apply your conception of good and evil to those things only which are in our power, and not to those which are out of our power. For if you apply your notion of good or evil to the latter, then, as soon as you fail to get what you will to get or fail to avoid what you will to avoid, you will be bound to blame and hate those you hold responsible. For every living creature has a natural tendency to avoid and shun what seems harmful and all that causes it, and to pursue and admire what is helpful and all that causes it. It is not possible then for one who thinks he is harmed to take pleasure in what he thinks is the author of the harm, any more than to take pleasure in the harm itself. That is why a father is reviled by his son, when he does not give his son a share of what the son regards as good things; thus Polynices and Eteocles were set at enmity with one another by thinking that a king's throne was a good thing.[2] That is why the farmer, and the sailor, and the merchant, and those who lose wife or children revile the gods. For men's religion is bound up with their interest. Therefore he who makes it his concern rightly to direct his will to get and his will to avoid, is thereby making piety his concern. But it is proper on each occasion to make libation and sacrifice and to offer first-fruits according to the custom of our fathers, with purity and not in slovenly or careless fashion, without meanness and without extravagance.

32

When you make use of prophecy remember that while you know not what the issue will be, but are come to learn it from the prophet, you do know before you come what manner of thing it is, if you are really a philosopher. For if the event is not in our control, it cannot be either good or evil. Therefore do not bring with you to the prophet the will to get or the will to avoid, and do not approach him with trembling, but with your mind made up, that the whole issue is indifferent and does not affect you and that, whatever it be, it will be in your power to make good use of it, and no one shall hinder this. With confidence then approach the gods as counsellors, and further, when the counsel is given you, remember whose counsel it is, and whom you will be disregarding if you disobey. And consult the oracle, as Socrates thought men should, only when the whole question turns upon the issue of events, and neither reason nor any art of man provides opportunities for discovering what lies before you. Therefore, when it is your duty to risk your life with friend or country, do not ask the oracle whether you should risk your life. For if the prophet warns you that the sacrifice is unfavourable, though it is plain that this means death or exile or injury to some part of your body, yet reason requires that even at this cost you must stand by your friend and share your country's danger. Wherefore pay heed to the greater prophet, Pythian Apollo, who cast out of his temple the man who did not help his friend when he was being killed.[3]

33

Lay down for yourself from the first a definite stamp and style of conduct, which you will maintain when you are alone and also in the society of men. Be silent for the most part, or, if you speak, say only what is necessary and in a few words. Talk, but rarely, if occasion calls you, but do not talk of ordinary things—of gladiators, or horseraces, or athletes, or of meats or drinks—these are topics that arise everywhere—but above all do not talk about men in blame or compliment or comparison. If you can, turn the conversation of your company by your talk to some fitting subject; but if you should chance to be isolated among strangers, be silent. Do not laugh much, not at many things, nor without restraint.

Refuse to take oaths, altogether if that be possible, but if not, as far as circumstances allow.

Refuse the entertainments of strangers and the vulgar. But if occasion arise to accept them, then strain every nerve to avoid lapsing into the state of the vulgar. For know that, if your comrade have a stain on him, he that associates with him must needs share the stain, even though he be clean in himself.

For your body, take just so much as your bare need requires, such as food, drink, clothing, house, servants, but cut down all that tends to luxury and outward show.

Avoid impurity to the utmost of your power before marriage, and if you indulge your passion, let it be done lawfully. But do not be offensive or censorious to those who indulge it, and do not be always bringing up your own chastity. If someone tells you that so and so speaks ill of you, do not defend yourself against what he says, but answer, "He did not know my other faults, or he would not have mentioned these alone."

It is not necessary for the most part to go to the games; but if you should have occasion to go, show that your first concern is for yourself; that is, wish that only to happen which does happen, and him only to win who does win, for so you will suffer no hindrance. But refrain entirely from applause, or ridicule, or prolonged excitement. And when you go away do not talk much of what happened there, except so far as it tends to your improvement. For to talk about it implies that the spectacle excited your wonder.

Do not go lightly or casually to hear lectures; but if you do go, maintain your gravity and dignity and do not make yourself offensive. When you are going to meet any one, and particularly some man of reputed eminence, set before your mind the thought, "What would Socrates or Zeno[4] have done?" and you will not fail to make proper use of the occasion.

When you go to visit some great man, prepare your mind by thinking that you will not find him in, that you will be shut out, that the doors will be slammed in your face, that he will pay no heed to you. And if in spite of all this you find it fitting for you to go, go and bear what happens and never say to yourself, "It was not worth all this"; for that shows a vulgar mind and one at odds with outward things.

In your conversation avoid frequent and disproportionate mention of your own doings or adventures; for other people do not take the same pleasure in hearing what has happened to you as you take in recounting your adventures.

Avoid raising men's laughter; for it is a habit that easily slips into vulgarity, and it may well suffice to lessen your neighbour's respect.

It is dangerous too to lapse into foul language; when anything of the kind occurs, rebuke the offender, if the occasion allow, and if not, make it plain to him by your silence, or a blush or a frown, that you are angry at his words.

34

When you imagine some pleasure, beware that it does not carry you away, like other imaginations. Wait a while, and give yourself pause. Next remember two things: how long you will enjoy the pleasure, and also how long you will afterwards repent and revile yourself. And set on the other side the joy and self-satisfaction you will feel if you refrain. And if the moment seems come to realize it, take heed that you be not overcome by the winning sweetness and attraction of it; set in the other scale the thought how much better is the consciousness of having vanquished it.

35

When you do a thing because you have determined that it ought to be done, never avoid being seen doing it, even if the opinion of the multitude is going to condemn you. For if your action is wrong, then avoid doing it altogether, but if it is right, why do you fear those who will rebuke you wrongly?

36

The phrases "It is day" and "It is night" mean a great deal if taken separately, but have no meaning if combined. In the same way, to choose the larger portion at a banquet may be worth while for your body, but if you want to maintain social decencies it is worthless. Therefore, when you are at meat with another, remember not only to consider the value of what is set before you for the body, but also to maintain your self-respect before your host.

37

If you try to act a part beyond your powers, you not only disgrace yourself in it, but you neglect the part which you could have filled with success.

38

As in walking, you take care not to tread on a nail or to twist your foot, so take care that you do not harm your Governing Principle. And if we guard this in everything we do, we shall set to work more securely.

39

Every man's body is a measure for his property, as the foot is the measure for his shoe. If you stick to this limit, you will keep the right measure; if you go beyond it, you are bound to be carried away down a precipice in the end; just as with the shoe, if you once go beyond the foot, your shoe puts on gilding, and soon purple and embroidery. For when once you go beyond the measure there is no limit.

40

Women from fourteen years upwards are called "madam" by men. Wherefore, when they see that the only advantage they have got is to be marriageable, they begin to make themselves smart and to set all their hopes on this. We must take pains then to make them understand that they are really honoured for nothing but a modest and decorous life.

41

It is a sign of a dull mind to dwell upon the cares of the body, to prolong exercise, eating, drinking, and other bodily functions. These things are to be done by the way; all your attention must be given to the mind.

42

When a man speaks evil or does evil to you, remember that he does or says it because he thinks it is fitting for him. It is not possible for him to follow what seems good to you, but only what seems good to him, so that, if his opinion is wrong, he suffers, in that he is the victim of deception. In the same way, if a composite judgement which is true is thought to be false, it is not the judgement that suffers, but the man who is deluded about it. If you act on this principle, you will be gentle to him who reviles you, saying to yourself on each occasion, "He thought it right."

43

Everything has two handles, one by which you can carry it, the other by which you cannot. If your brother wrongs you, do not take it by that handle, the handle of his wrong, for you cannot carry it by that, but rather by the other handle—that he is a brother, brought up with you, and then you will take it by the handle that you can carry by.

44

It is illogical to reason thus, "I am richer than you, therefore I am superior to you," "I am more eloquent than you, therefore I am superior to you." It is more logical to reason, "I am richer than you, therefore my property is superior to yours," "I am more eloquent than you, therefore my speech is superior to yours." You are something more than property or speech.

45

If a man wash quickly, do not say that he washes badly, but that he washes quickly. If a man drink much wine, do not say that he drinks badly, but that he drinks much. For till you have decided what judgement prompts him, how do you know that he acts badly? If you do as I say, you will assent to your apprehensive impressions and to none other.

46

On no occasion call yourself a philosopher, nor talk at large of your principles among the multitude, but act on your principles. For instance, at a banquet do not say how one ought to eat, but eat as you ought. Remember that Socrates had so completely got rid of the thought of display that when men came and wanted an introduction to philosophers he took them to be introduced; so patient of neglect was he. And if a discussion arise among the multitude on some principle, keep silent for the most part; for you are in great danger of blurting out some undigested thought. And when some one says to you, "You know nothing," and you do not let it provoke you, then know that you are really on the right road. For sheep do not bring grass to their shepherds and show them how much they have eaten, but they digest their fodder and then produce it in the form of wool and milk. Do the same yourself; instead of displaying your principles to the multitude, show them the results of the principles you have digested.

47

When you have adopted the simple life, do not pride yourself upon it, and if you are a water-drinker do not say on every occasion, "I am a water-drinker." And if you ever want to train laboriously, keep it to yourself and do not make a show of it. Do not embrace statues. If you are very thirsty, take a good draught of cold water, and rinse your mouth and tell no one.

48

The ignorant man's position and character is this: he never looks to himself for benefit or harm, but to the world outside him. The philosopher's position and character is that he always look to himself for benefit and harm.

The signs of one who is making progress are: he blames none, praises none, complains of none, accuses none, never speaks of himself as if he were somebody, or as if he knew anything. And if anyone compliments him he laughs in himself at his compliment; and if one blames him, he makes no defence. He goes about like a convalescent, careful not to disturb his constitution on its road to recovery, until it has got firm hold. He has got rid of the will to get, and his will to avoid is directed no longer to what is beyond our power but only to what is in our power and contrary to nature. In all things he exercises his will without strain. If men regard him as foolish or ignorant he pays no heed. In one word, he keeps watch and guard on himself as his own enemy, lying in wait for him.

49

When a man prides himself on being able to understand and interpret the books of Chrysippus,[5] say to yourself, "If Chrysippus had not written obscurely this man would have had nothing on which to pride himself."

What is my object? To understand Nature and follow her. I look then for someone who interprets her, and having heard that Chrysippus does I come to him. But I do not understand his writings, so I seek an interpreter. So far there is nothing to be proud of. But when I have found the interpreter it remains for me to act on his precepts; that and that alone is a thing to be proud of. But if I admire the mere power of exposition, it comes to this—that I am turned into a grammarian instead of a philosopher, except that I interpret Chrysippus in place of Homer. Therefore, when some one says to me, "Read me Chrysippus," when I cannot point to actions which are in harmony and correspondence with his teaching, I am rather inclined to blush.

50

Whatever principles you put before you, hold fast to them as laws which it will be impious to transgress. But pay no heed to what any one says of you; for this is something beyond your own control.

51

How long will you wait to think yourself worthy of the highest and transgress in nothing the clear pronouncement of reason? You have received the precepts which you ought to accept, and you have accepted them. Why then do you still wait for a master, that you may delay the amendment of yourself till he comes? You are a youth no longer, you are now a full-grown man. If now you are careless and indolent and are always putting off, fixing one day after another as the limit when you mean to begin attending to yourself, then, living or dying, you will make no progress but will continue unawares in ignorance. Therefore make up your mind before it is too late to live as one who is mature and proficient, and let all that seems best to you be a law that you cannot transgress. And if you encounter anything troublesome or pleasant or glorious or inglorious, remember that the hour of struggle is come, the Olympic contest is here and you may put off no longer, and that one day and one action determines whether the progress you have achieved is lost or maintained.

This was how Socrates attained perfection, paying heed to nothing but reason, in all that he encountered. And if you are not yet Socrates, yet ought you to live as one who would wish to be a Socrates.

52

The first and most necessary department of philosophy deals with the application of principles; for instance, "not to lie." The second deals with demonstrations; for instance, "How comes it that one ought not to lie?" The third is concerned with establishing and analysing these processes; for instance, "How comes it that this is a demonstration? What is demonstration, what is consequence, what is contradiction, what is true, what is false?" It follows then that the third department is necessary because of the second, and the second because of the first. The first is the most necessary part, and that in which we must rest. But we reverse the order: we occupy ourselves with the third, and make that our whole concern, and the first we completely neglect. Wherefore we lie, but are ready enough with the demonstration that lying is wrong.

53

On every occasion we must have these thoughts at hand,

> "Lead me, O Zeus, and lead me, Destiny,
> Whither ordained is by your decree.
> I'll follow, doubting not, or if with will
> Recreant I falter, I shall follow still."[6]

> "Who rightly with necessity complies
> In things divine we count him skilled and wise."[7]

> "Well, Crito, if this be the gods' will, so be it."[8]

> "Anytus and Meletus have power to put me to death, but not to harm me."[9]

NOTES

1. [Diogenes (c. 412–323 B.C.), a Greek philosopher of the Cynic (doggish) school, taught that the virtuous life was the simple life. He flouted custom, living in a tub and discarding all his possessions. When Alexander the Great reportedly visited him and in admiration offered to fulfill any request, Diogenes is said to have replied, "Just step out of my sunlight."—S.M.C.]
2. [According to Greek mythology, Polynices and Eteocles were the sons of Oedipus. After his blinding they insulted him, and he therefore cursed them. The curse was fulfilled when, the two having agreed to reign in alternate years, Eteocles would not relinquish the throne, and the brothers entered into combat and killed each other.]
3. [Reference is to a story about three men sent to Delphi, site of the Oracle housed in the Temple of Apollo. When attacked by robbers, one fled and a second, in attempting to defend the third, accidentally killed him. The Oracle rejected the runaway and absolved the homicide.]
4. [Zeno of Citium (c. 334–c. 262 B.C.), a Greek philosopher who had studied under the Cynics, was the founder of Stoicism. He is not to be confused with Zeno of Elea (c. 490–430 B.C.), creator of the immortal paradoxes.]
5. [Chrysippus (c. 279–200 B.C.), third leader of the Stoic school, is said to have been one of the greatest logicians of ancient times.]
6. [This quotation is from Cleanthes (c. 331–232 B.C.), who headed the Stoic school following Zeno and whose most famous work is the poem *Hymn to Zeus*.]

7. [These lines are from a fragment by the Greek tragic dramatist Euripides (c. 480–406 B.C.)]
8. [The reference is to Plato's *Crito*.]
9. [The reference is to Plato's *Apology*.]

STUDY QUESTIONS

1. How does Epictetus recommend that we deal with loss?
2. According to Epictetus, why is the desire to live forever silly?
3. How much control do we have over our desires?
4. Would you be able to go through even one day maintaining the outlook on life and death recommended by Epictetus?

PART 14

Asian Outlooks

The Buddha's Message

ᴗ

CHRISTOPHER W. GOWANS

Thus far we have focused our attention on major themes and thinkers in Western philosophy. But philosophical thought has also been pursued in various Asian traditions, and, before concluding, we would do well to consider some of these. Let us begin with Buddhism.

The Buddha sought to enlighten people on the problem of suffering in life: its pervasiveness, cause, cure, and cessation. Wisdom is found in moral conduct and mental discipline. This teaching is explored in our next selection authored by Christopher W. Gowans, Professor of Philosophy at Fordham University.

....

The person we know as the Buddha was born ... near the present-day border of India and Nepal, sometime between the seventh and the fifth centuries B.C.E. He was called Siddhattha Gotama (Siddhārtha Gautama in Sanskrit). ...

His father was determined that [Siddhattha] should become a ruler, and to ensure this outcome he protected [Siddhattha] from everything unpleasant in life. ... Eventually, [Siddhattha] discovered what everyone comes to know— that ... aging, illness, and death are facts of every human life. ... He wondered: What is the meaning of human suffering? What is its cause? Can it be overcome? ...

SUFFERING AND ITS CAUSE

The Buddha's teaching is primarily practical rather than theoretical in its orientation. The aim is to show persons how to overcome suffering and attain *Nibbāna*.[1] The purpose is not to persuade them to accept certain doctrines as such. This practical approach is famously illustrated by a story the Buddha told Mālunkyāputta, a skeptically minded disciple, when he persisted in demanding answers to a series of philosophical questions the Buddha refused to answer. The Buddha described someone wounded by a poison arrow who would not allow a surgeon to treat him until he knew the name and class of the man who wounded him, his height and complexion, where he lived, and so on. The Buddha pointed out that the man would die before finding out the answers to all his questions, and that he did not need these answers in order for the surgeon to operate successfully to save his life. For the practical purpose of healing his wound, there was no reason to answer the questions. The point of the story is that the Buddha had not declared answers to Mālunkyāputta's questions because there was no practical need to do so. Answering these questions would have been 'unbeneficial' and would not have led 'to peace, to direct knowledge, to enlightenment, to *Nibbāna*.' The teaching of the Buddha does not consist of answers to any and all philosophical questions that might occur to us. Rather, it consists of answers that are needed for a practical purpose. The Buddha then gave the moral of the story: 'And what have I declared? "This is suffering"—I have declared. "This is the origin of suffering"—I have declared. "This is the cessation of suffering"—I have declared. "This is the way leading to the cessation of suffering"—I have declared.' The Buddha put forward these answers—the Four Noble Truths—because they were 'beneficial,' because they did lead 'to peace, to direct knowledge, to enlightenment, to *Nibbāna*'. The practical orientation of the Buddha's teaching does not mean it includes no theoretical doctrines, nor that it is unconcerned with the truth of these doctrines. It plainly contains such doctrines, and they are put forward as true and known to be true. Nonetheless, the Buddha would not have taught these doctrines unless they served the practical aim of overcoming human suffering. . . .

The Buddha's central teaching has the form of a medical diagnosis and plan of treatment: it describes a disease and its symptoms, identifies its cause, outlines what freedom from this disease would be like, and prescribes the course of treatment required to attain this healthy state. The story of the wounded man should be read in this light. We are to think of the Buddha as a physician who cures not strictly physical ailments, but broadly psychological ones, who shows 'wounded' human beings the way to the highest form of happiness. . . .

Here is the description of the disease and its symptoms:

> *First Noble Truth.* Now this, *bhikkhus*,[2] is the noble truth of suffering: birth is suffering, aging is suffering, illness is suffering, death is suffering; union with what is displeasing is suffering; separation from what is pleasing is suffering; not to get what one wants is suffering . . .

The key term here and throughout is *dukkha*. It is ordinarily translated into English as 'suffering'. This is correct in part, but it is misleading. The description above features aging, sickness and death (the observation of which first led Siddhattha to seek enlightenment) and we naturally associate these with suffering. But for the other items listed—union with what is displeasing, separation from what is pleasing, and not getting what one wants—'suffering' sometimes is the right term and sometimes seems too strong. The Buddha clearly has in mind a broad range of ways in which our lives may be unsatisfactory. For the time being, we may summarize the first Noble Truth as the claim that human lives regularly lack contentment, fulfillment, perfection, security, and the like.

Stream-observers[3] might regard this as a rather pessimistic diagnosis. They might be inclined to think that many (if not most) human lives are not so bad, that the positive aspects of life outweigh the negative ones. The Buddha would not have been surprised by this response and did not deny that many persons would question his analysis. His point may be illustrated by an analogy: if an alcoholic is told his life is in bad shape, he will probably point out, perhaps correctly, that he has lots of good times; nonetheless, he has a serious problem and could have a far better life without alcohol and the 'good times' it brings. Similarly, the Buddha thought, most of us can point to some positive features of life: he is not saying we are miserable all the time. However, there is something not fully satisfactory about the lives most of us live. We seek enduring happiness by trying to attach ourselves to things that are in constant change. This sometimes brings temporary and partial fulfillment, but the long-term result is frustration and anxiety. Because of the impermanence of the world, we do not achieve the real happiness we implicitly seek. The Buddha thought we could all sense the truth of this with a moderate amount of honest reflection on the realities of human life, but he also believed that full understanding of the first Truth was difficult to achieve and would require significant progress towards enlightenment.

The next Noble Truth is a claim about the cause of discontentment in human life. Here is how the Buddha explained it:

> *Second Noble Truth.* Now this, *bhikkhus*, is the noble truth of the origin of suffering: it is this craving which leads to renewed existence, accompanied by delight and lust, seeking delight here and there; that is, craving for sensual pleasures, craving for existence, craving for extermination.

There is much in this passage that is likely to perplex us. For now, what is important is the contention that suffering and other forms of distress have a cause associated with various kinds of desire—craving, clinging, attachment, impulse, greed, lust, thirst, and so on are terms frequently employed in this connection. The Second Noble Truth states that the source of our discontentment is found not simply in our desires, but in the connection we forge between desires and happiness. In its simplest form, it asserts that we are typically unhappy because we do not get what we desire to have, or we do get what we desire not to have. We do not get the promotion we wanted, and we do get the disease we feared. Outcomes such as these are common in human life. These outcomes, and the anxieties their prospect produces, are causes of our discontentment....

NIBBĀNA

Many people would agree that suffering or unhappiness is rooted in desire, that it consists of not getting what we want and getting what we do not want. It may seem natural to infer from this that happiness consists of the opposite, in getting what we want and not getting what we do not want. Happiness, in this view, is acquisition of all that we try to gain and security from all that we seek to avoid.

The Buddha taught that this understanding of happiness is a mistake. We can never achieve true and complete happiness in these terms, and there is another, far better form of happiness that we can achieve. To revert to our earlier analogy, someone who holds the first view is like an alcoholic who reasons that, since he is unhappy when he is not drinking, he will be truly happy only if he is always drinking. However, what will really make him happy is to find a way to stop the obsessive craving to drink, to stop looking for happiness in drinking. The Buddha's striking assertion is a similar but broader claim. Obtaining what we are hoping to gain and safety from what we are trying to avoid will not bring us real happiness. This can only be achieved by a radical transformation of our desires and aversions—and especially of our attitudes towards them. We have arrived at the next Truth:

> *Third Noble Truth.* Now this, *bhikkhus*, is the noble truth of the cessation of suffering: it is the remainderless fading away and cessation of that same craving, the giving up and relinquishing of it, freedom from it, nonreliance on it.

True happiness in life, the opposite of suffering, is brought about by reaching a state in which, on my reading, we eliminate many of our desires and stop clinging or attaching ourselves to all of them. The Buddha referred to this state with the term 'Nibbāna'.

Why not seek happiness in the fulfillment of our desires, in striving to get what we want and to avoid what we do not want? The Buddha did not deny that a measure of happiness may be obtained from such striving, but he believed it would always be unsatisfactory in some respects. In part, the reason is that a life seeking such happiness will always be precarious because of the impermanent nature of the universe. What would fulfill our typical desires—for status, power, wealth, friends, and so on—is always subject to change. Even if we were fortunate and got all that we wanted (and can anyone truthfully say this?), old age, disease, and death would always stand ready to take these things from us. No matter what we have, we can never be secure that we will continue to possess it, and so we will never be truly happy. Another reason is that fulfilling our desires does not always make us happy. 'In this world there are only two tragedies,' said Oscar Wilde. 'One is not getting what one wants, and the other is getting it' (*Lady Windermere's Fan*: act 3).

For the Buddha, a better strategy than seeking to fulfill desires would be to live a morally good life: on account of *kamma*,[4] this would eventually produce greater happiness. However, the Buddha thought such happiness still would be temporary and imperfect, and he thought it would always be a struggle to live a truly good life as long as the belief that one is a self persisted. At best, this strategy might bring improvement, but ultimately it would only perpetuate the cycle of rebirth and its inherent suffering.

Considerations of this sort might be taken to show that these are inadequate roads to real happiness. But why suppose there is another form of happiness—*Nibbāna*—that is not only possible to achieve but better? The answer is the key to the Buddha's teaching and it involves the not-self doctrine. Sometimes it sounds as if *Nibbāna* involves the complete cessation of all desires (the word 'nibbāna' literally means extinction or cessation), but this is not generally true of a person who has achieved enlightenment. This person does eliminate many desires, specifically all those that presuppose the belief that oneself has primary importance. This belief gives rise to an orientation to life in terms of what is mine and hence is more valuable, in contrast to what is not mine and hence is less valuable. The resulting thoughts and desires are the source of hatred, intolerance, anger, pride, greed, thirst for power and fame, and so on. These states bring unhappiness not only to others, but to those who possess them: a person full of hate does not have a happy life. On the other hand, full realization that I am not a distinct self would undermine the tendency to think myself has primary importance. The Buddha thought this would put an end to all desires associated with hatred and the like, and in fact would release my capacity for universal compassion. The result would be increased happiness for all concerned.

However, enlightenment does not mean the elimination of all desires—at least, not in a sustained way during this life (during meditative experiences of *Nibbāna*, and with the attainment of *Nibbāna* beyond death, desires are absent). For one thing, compassion clearly involves desire in some sense—namely, the desire that others fare well. Moreover, no human life is possible that does not involve some elementary desires such as for food or sleep. Surely the Buddha did not mean to deny this (in fact, the extreme asceticism he rejected would seem to have been an endeavor to achieve freedom from any desires in this life). But the Buddha did think the realization that we are not selves would bring about a fundamental change in our attitude towards those desires that would remain. This realization would eliminate clinging or attachment to the satisfaction of these desires, and it would thereby cut through the bond we ordinarily forge between this satisfaction and happiness.

On my interpretation, there are at least two aspects of this difficult idea. First, in the absence of the belief that I am a self distinct from other selves, I would no longer think of some desires as mine, as things with which I deeply identify and so need to satisfy to achieve my well-being. As a result, there would no longer be an unhealthy drive or obsession to fulfill these desires. Second, in the absence of the belief that I am a self with identity, a substance persisting through time in some respects unchanged, I would no longer be preoccupied with regrets about the past unfulfillment of my desires and worries about the prospects for their future fulfill-ment. Liberated in these ways from attachment to desires as mine, from pinning my happiness on their satisfaction, there would be freedom to focus attention on the present moment at all times. The implicit message of the Buddha is that, in this state of awareness, no matter what happened, there would always be something of value, something good, in what was experienced. Not clinging to the fulfillment of our desires would release a capacity for joy at each moment in our lives.

For a person who has attained *Nibbāna*, life is a process of living selflessly in which, unencumbered by the false belief that we are selves, we are enabled to live compassionate and joyful lives. To this it may be added that our lives would also possess great peace and tranquility. They would be lives of perfect contentment and true happiness.

In addition to *Nibbāna* in this life, the Buddha described *Nibbāna* as a state beyond this life and the entire cycle of rebirth (henceforth, when it is impor-tant to distinguish these, I will refer to them respectively as *Nibbāna*-in-life and

Nibbāna-after-death). Though he thought it could not be described adequately in our concepts, we may say by way of a preliminary that he believed *Nibbāna*-after-death is neither a state in which one exists as a self nor a state of absolute nothingness. It is a form of selfless existence in which there is realization of some union with *Nibbāna* understood as ultimate reality beyond change and conditioning. This is a state in which suffering, and all that causes suffering, is entirely absent. *Nibbāna* both in this life and beyond is a state of perfect well-being and tranquility, one that all conscious beings have reason to seek.

WISDOM, VIRTUE, AND CONCENTRATION

Even if we were convinced that *Nibbāna* would be the ultimate happiness, we might well wonder whether it would be possible for us to attain it. The Buddha's practical orientation made this a primary concern. He believed it is possible to achieve *Nibbāna*, but very difficult to do so. We have come to the final Truth:

> *Fourth Noble Truth.* Now this, *bhikkhus*, is the noble truth of the way leading to the cessation of suffering. It is this Noble Eightfold Path; that is right view, right intention, right speech, right action, right livelihood, right effort, right mindfulness, right concentration.

In the first discourse, addressed to the ascetic *samanas*,[5] the Buddha described the Eightfold Path as a 'middle way' that avoids two extremes: 'The pursuit of sensual happiness in sensual pleasures, which is low, vulgar, the way of worldlings, ignoble, unbeneficial; and the pursuit of self-mortification, which is painful, ignoble, unbeneficial.' Though the Buddha portrayed the Eightfold Path as a middle way between seeking sensual happiness and undergoing self-mortification, it clearly involves a rigorous regime that is supposed to radically transform us. This path, the Buddha said, 'leads to peace, to direct knowledge, to enlightenment, to *Nibbāna*'.

The eight steps of the path are to be pursued not in sequence, but all together, with each step reinforcing the others (though the last two, right mindfulness and right concentration, are the culmination). The Buddha divided these steps into three parts: *wisdom* pertains primarily to intellectual development and conviction (right view and intention), *virtue* concerns moral or ethical training (right speech, action, and livelihood), and *concentration*—often rendered as 'meditation'—involves a set of mental disciplines (right effort, mindfulness, and concentration).

The first part, wisdom, instructs us to acquire a thorough comprehension of the Four Noble Truths and all that they involve. However, it does not require us to answer philosophical questions unrelated to attaining *Nibbāna*. In fact, this is discouraged, as we saw in the story of the man wounded by the arrow. Mālunkyāputta wanted the Buddha to tell him whether the world is eternal, whether it is finite, whether body and soul are one, and whether the *Tathāgata*[6] exists after death. The Buddha refused to answer these questions on the ground that attempts to do so would only hinder efforts to understand the Four Noble Truths.

Comprehension of the Four Noble Truths requires more than intellectual cultivation. We also need a fundamental commitment to understanding them, and our emotions and desires must be disciplined so that they do not distract us or lead us astray. Hence, the Buddha said we must renounce sensual desire, ill will, and cruelty. In this respect, he thought thinking and feeling, the mind and the heart, were closely connected.

The second part of the path concerns morality or ethics. Enlightenment requires moral as well as intellectual and emotional preparation. The Buddha spoke of morality at length, and he expected much more of members of the Sangha[7] than of lay followers. But there are basic precepts that apply to all persons. These fall into three categories. Right speech requires that we speak in ways that are truthful, friendly, useful, and productive of harmony. Right action dictates that we do not kill any living beings (human or animal), nor steal, nor have illegitimate sexual relations. Right livelihood says we should not earn our living by harming others (for example, by selling arms). Violation of these precepts, the Buddha thought, would only reinforce self-centered desires and would hinder attainment of *Nibbāna*.

The third part of the path—concentration, or meditation—is the least familiar to persons in the West, but the most significant for the Buddha.... Though the Buddha taught many forms of meditation, the general aim of these mental disciplines is twofold: first, to purify the mind of disturbances so as to bring about a peaceful, concentrated, attentive and mindful mental state; and second, to know reality as it actually is by observing that all things in our ordinary experience are impermanent, involve suffering, and are empty of any self. The ultimate aim is not to escape from the world nor to acquire special powers: it is to attain *Nibbāna*.

NOTES

1. [Sanskrit, *Nirvana*.—S.M.C.]
2. [Monks.]
3. [Those who are culturally part of the contemporary Western world and have no Buddhist upbringing.]
4. [Sanskrit, *Karma*.]
5. [Spiritual wanderers.]
6. [Truthfinder; Buddha's title for himself.]
7. [Fully enlightened ones; the Buddha's first followers.]

STUDY QUESTIONS

1. What are the Four Noble Truths?
2. How does Gowans distinguish "*Nibbāna*-in-life" and "*Nibbāna*-after-death"?
3. What is the Eightfold Path?
4. How does Buddhism link thought and action?

The Confucian Way

⤜

HENRY ROSEMONT, JR.

A Confucian stresses our obligations toward those with whom we stand in distinctive relationships. In particular, rituals are central to the moral life, for by performing them sincerely we cultivate our selves, show respect for others, and contribute to a better society. The Confucian outlook is explored in our next selection, authored by Henry Rosemont, Jr. (1934–2017), who served as Visiting Scholar of Religious Studies at Brown University.

....

Confucius (551–479 B.C.E.) may well be the most influential thinker in human history, if influence is determined by the sheer number of people who have lived their lives in accord with that thinker's vision of how people ought to live, and die.

Long recognized and described as China's "First (or Premier) Teacher," [Confucius'] ideas have been the fertile soil in which the Chinese cultural tradition has been cultivated, although at the same time a number of the views and practices he championed were already evidenced in China centuries before his birth. Like many other epochal figures of the ancient world—Buddha, Socrates, Jesus—Confucius does not seem to have written anything that is clearly attributable to him; all that we know of his vision directly must be pieced together from the several accounts of his teachings and his activities, found in the little work known as the *Analects*.

Beginning shortly after he died, a few of the disciples of Confucius began setting down what they remember the Master saying to them . . . Some disciples of the disciples continued this process for the next 75 years or so, and an additional dozen little "books" were composed by we-know-not-whom during the following century, and it was to be still another century before a number of these little "books" were gathered together to make up the *Analects* as we have it today.

Thus it is not at all surprising that the text does not seem to form a coherent whole. Worse, if we take the writings of, say, Aristotle, or Spinoza, or Kant, as exemplary of philosophical texts, then the *Analects* does not seem to be properly philosophical, for it contains precious little metaphysics, puts forth no first principles, is not systematic, and the "sayings" which comprise it are not set down in a hypotheticodeductive mode of discourse.

On the other hand, if the New Testament—or the Hebrew scriptures, or the *Quran*—are taken as religious texts *par excellence*, then it would appear that the

From *Living Well: Introductory Readings in Ethics*, ed. Steven Luper, Harcourt Brace, 2000. Reprinted by permission of the author.

Analects isn't a religious text either, for it speaks not of God, nor of creation, salvation, or a transcendental realm of being; and no prophecies will be found in its pages.

However, if we are willing to construe philosophy and religion more broadly— i.e., as those domains that address the question "What kind of life should I live?"— then the *Analects* is both philosophical and religious, for it does indeed address this question; it does proffer models of what is right and what is good, models that are perhaps no less important and relevant today in the post-modern, post-industrial West than they were in pre-modern, pre-industrial China over two millennia ago. This is not at all to suggest that Confucius and his disciples were "just like us"; manifestly they were not. Hence, before coming to appreciate what they nevertheless may have to say to us today, we must first focus on how different they really were....

... [W]e must first appreciate that for Confucius, we are fundamentally relational, not individual selves. The life of a hermit could not be a human life for him:

> *I cannot flock with the birds and beasts.*
> *If I am not to a person in the midst of others,*
> *what am I to be?*

In other words, Confucian selves are first and foremost sons and daughters; then siblings, friends, neighbors, students, teachers, lovers, spouses, and perhaps much else; but not autonomous individuals. In the contemporary West, these relationships are described in terms of roles, which we first consciously (i.e., rationally) choose, and thereafter "play"; just as actors and actresses play different roles on the theater stage, so do autonomous individuals play roles on the stage of life. These roles may be important for our lives, but are not of our essence.

Confucian selves, on the other hand, are the sum of the roles they *live*, not play, and when all the specific roles one lives have been specified, then that person has been fully accounted for as a unique person, with no remainder with which to construct a free, autonomous, individual self. Consider how Confucius would respond to the "identity crisis" so many undergraduate students undergo at some point during their college career. When Mary Smith asks "Who am I?" the Master will first respond straightforwardly "You are obviously the daughter of Mr. & Mrs. Smith, and the sister of Tom Smith; you are the friend of x, y, and z, the roommate of w, the student of professors a, b, c, and d," and so forth. To which Mary will undoubtedly reply "I don't mean *that*. I'm searching for the *real* me." To which Confucius could only respond sadly, shaking his head: "No wonder you call it a 'crisis,' for you have taken away everything that could possibly count as answers to your question."

This view of a fully relational rather than autonomous self has a number of immediate implications for moral philosophy. In Western thought the basis for moral analysis and evaluation is the *agent* and the *action*. "What did *you* do?" and "why did you do it?" are the central questions. But whereas the first question remains the same in a Confucian framework, the second becomes "with whom did you do it?" followed by a third, "When?" Put another way, Confucius focuses on interactions, not actions, and on specific, not general, interactors. Individual selves are agents who perform actions. Relational selves are always dynamically interacting in highly specific ways.

The roles we live are reciprocal and at the abstract level can be seen to hold between benefactors and beneficiaries. Thus we are, when young, beneficiaries of our parents, and when they age, become their benefactors; the converse holds with respect to our children. We are beneficiaries of our teachers, benefactors of our students, and are, at different times, benefactors and beneficiaries of and to our friends, spouses, neighbors, colleagues, lovers, and so on.

It is for these reasons that there can be no *general* answer to the question "What should I do?" except "Do what is *appropriate* (not "right") under the specific circumstances." Fairly careful readers of the *Analects* will note that Confucius sometimes gives a different answer to the same question asked by one of his disciples. But *very* careful readers of the text will also note that it is *different* disciples who ask the question, and the Master gives an answer appropriate for each questioner. To do this is neither dissembling, nor wrong. For example, your roommate asks you to read and comment on a paper she has just written for a course. You are not impressed with it. What do you say? Well, if your roommate is fairly intelligent, but having troubles at home right now, is experiencing her identity crisis, and is thinking of quitting school, your answer might run something like "There are problems with this paper, but you have a really good potential thesis here, and argument there, which you can develop along thus-and-such lines. And when you've done so, I'll be happy to read it again." But now suppose that your roommate is different. He has just received a few As on exams he didn't really study for; and while he is basically a good person, he is showing signs of arrogance and pomposity, in which case you might well be inclined to say "This paper is junk from start to finish. Why did you have me waste my time reading it?"

For a Confucian, these differing responses are not at all either inconsistent or hypocritical, but are both altogether appropriate responses with respect to the second Confucian moral question: "With whom did you do it?" The third question, "When?," is equally significant, because the benefactor–beneficiary relationships are not static. Having just failed an examination yourself, you schedule an appointment with your instructor to go over it, your basic question being "How can I improve next time?" But upon arriving at the appointed time, you find that your instructor—who does not drive—has just learned that his wife has had a heart attack and been taken to the emergency room at the hospital. Not at all surprisingly, you do not ask your original question, but instead say "Please let me drive you to the hospital."

All of these little examples appear simple, everyday, common-sensical at best, perhaps even trivial when compared to these moral issues focused on in the West: abortion, euthanasia, draft resistance, suicide, and so forth. But . . . they are the basic "stuff" of our human interactions, and Confucius seems to be telling us that if we learn to get the little things right on a day-in and day-out basis, the "big" things will take care of themselves.

And we start out on the path of getting the little things right by focusing on our first, most important, and lifelong role: that of son or daughter....

We did not ask to come into this world, we did not choose to be offspring, but we nevertheless have manifold responsibilities toward our parents; we are responsible for their well-being even though we have not freely chosen to assume those responsibilities....

Confucius insists that we cannot merely rest content with seeing to the material needs of our parents: filial piety is "something much more than that." We must not only meet our familial obligations, we must have the proper attitude toward them, we must *want* to meet our responsibilities; we must have feelings appropriate to the situation. This is why Confucius "could not bear to see the rituals of mourning conducted purely formally, without genuine grief." This point is brought home forcefully when it is seen that our obligations to our parents do not cease when they die; we must continue to show respect for them, and honor their memory. Only then will we know and show the extent of our true filiality.

By cultivating filial piety in our relational roles to our parents—as both beneficiaries and benefactors—we are on the way (better: the Confucian Way) to achieving *ren*, which is the highest excellence, or virtue, for Confucius.... Usually translated as "goodness," or "benevolence," it is perhaps best captured in English by "authoritativeness," which signifies having to do with both authoring and authority. On the one hand, *ren* is easy, because we are human. On the other hand, it can be difficult to achieve in practice owing to our more basic—i.e., biological—desires. But once we set out on the path of *ren*, it is with us forever....

In order to achieve ren one must submit to *li*. This term has been variously translated as "rituals," "rites," "etiquette," "ceremony," "mores," "customs," "propriety," and "worship."..."Rituals" and "rites" are the two most common translations, and are acceptable so long as it is appreciated that the *li* are not only to be thought of in terms of a solemn high mass, wedding, bar mitzvah, or funeral; the *li* pertain equally to our manner of greeting, leave-taking, sharing food, and most other everyday interpersonal activities as well.

It is through rituals, custom, and tradition that one's roles are properly effected. There are customary rituals, large and small, by means of which we interact with our parents, grandparents, relatives, young children, neighbors, officials, friends. These rituals are different for the different people with whom we are relating, and they may differ across time as well (we wouldn't hug friends we saw every day, but probably would if we hadn't seen them for some time). It is through the rituals that we express our filial piety toward our parents, respect for elders, care and affection for the young, and love and friendship for lovers and friends. We cannot simply "go through the motions" of performing the rituals, for this would show both a lack of concern for the other(s) and a lack of sincerity as well. It is through rituals, properly performed, that our true attitudes and feelings shine forth, and we more nearly approach *ren*.

Consider meeting someone for the first time. Your right hand automatically is raised, as is theirs; then you clasp it. Your clasp can be such that your hand feels like a dead fish, or you can show off your strength by attempting to crack the other's knuckles, and in either case you can utter a flat "How do you do?" Or you can present a warm hand, squeezing only an appropriate amount; perhaps you will put your left hand over the handshake, after which you say "I'm very pleased to meet you," looking at the other directly. In short, it is not the case that when we've seen one introduction we've seen them all.

Rituals, and the proper performance thereof, have been largely neglected in developing theories of the right and the good in the Western philosophical tradition. Worse, the contemporary West is virtually anti-ritualistic. Rituals are seen as purely formal, empty, dead weights of the past, and detrimental to the full expression of individuality.

They are, however, absolutely central in Confucianism, and without an understanding of their potential for enriching human life, the *Analects* cannot come alive for the modern reader. We can only become fully human, for Confucius, by learning to restrain our impulses to accord with the prescriptions of rituals. Rituals are the templates within which we interact with our fellows: there are proper (customary) ways of being a father, a sister, a neighbor, a student, a teacher. These ways are constrained by rituals but, once mastered, are liberating and are the vehicle by means of which we express our uniqueness.

But unless we have guidelines (the rituals) our behaviors can only be random. (Listen to Beethoven's Fifth Symphony, first as conducted by Toscanini, then by Bernstein, then by Rostropovich; is it not easy to distinguish them despite the severe constraints imposed on them all by the score?) There are many ways to be a good parent, teacher, friend, etc.; if Confucian selves aren't autonomous, they are certainly not automatons either.

So, then, it is through ritual that we cultivate and enhance our authoritativeness, but this can only be done as we become full participants in the rituals, expressing our feelings thereby, and thereby in turn investing them—and consequently ourselves—with significance. If someone you know is getting married, the ritual tradition dictates the giving of a gift. But if you merely purchase the first thing you see—or worse, have someone else buy it for you—you may be "going through the ritual," but are not participating in it, and it will thus be largely devoid of meaning. You must, first, *want* to buy the betrothed a gift (evidenced even in the modern Western expression "It's the thought that counts"), but in order to be a full participant in the ritual, and express yourself relationally, you must devote the time and effort to secure a gift that is appropriate for that person. This is what Confucius is telling us when he says "Ritual, ritual! Is it no more than giving gifts of jade and silk?"

It must also be noted that for Confucius, the significance of rituals is not confined to our interpersonal relations, rituals can also serve as the glue of a society. A people who accept and follow ritual prescriptions will not need much in the way of laws or punishments to achieve harmony, and no government that fails to submit to rituals will long endure; indeed, he even suggests that rituals can be sufficient for regulating a society. And true rulers, having a full measure of authoritativeness and submitting to ritual, will rule by personal example, not coercion; their formal duties are minimal.

Excepting the sages and sage kings, Confucius gives his highest praise to the *jun zi*, usually rendered as "Gentleman," which can be highly misleading. The *jun zi* have traveled a goodly distance along the Confucian way, and live a goodly number of roles. Benefactors to many, they are still beneficiaries of others like themselves. While still capable of anger in the presence of wrongdoing, they are in their persons tranquil. They know many rituals (and much music) and perform all of their roles not only with skill, but with grace, dignity, and beauty, and they take delight in the performances. Still filial toward parents and elders, they now endeavor to take "All under heaven"—i.e., the world—as their province. Always proper in the conduct of their roles, that conduct is not forced, but rather effortless, spontaneous, creative.

Thus the best way to understand Confucius' concept of the *jun zi* is to render the term as "exemplary person." Having learned, submitted to, and mastered the rituals of the past, the *jun zi* re-authorizes them by making them his or her own, thus becoming their author, who can speak with authority in the present. The *jun zi* fully exemplify authoritativeness, and are content with it, no longer worrying about wealth, fame, or glory.

Against the background of the authoritative person as an ideal, we can appreciate that even though Confucianism is highly particularistic in defining our conduct in specific relational roles, it nevertheless bespeaks a universalistic vision. The one exception to the lack of general principles ... is the negative formulation of the Golden Rule: "Do not do unto others as you would not have them do unto you."

But more than that, it should be clear that Confucius had a strong sense of, empathy with, and concept of humanity writ large. All of the specific human relations of which we are a part, interacting with the dead as well as the living, will be mediated by the *li*, i.e., the rituals, customs, and traditions we come to share as our inextricably linked histories unfold, and by fulfilling the obligations defined by these relationships, we are, for Confucius, following the human way (*dao*).

It is a comprehensive way. By the manner in which we interact with others, our lives will clearly have a moral dimension infusing *all*, not just some, of our conduct. By the ways in which this ethical interpersonal conduct is effected, with reciprocity, and governed by courtesy, respect, affection, custom, ritual, and tradition, our lives will also have an aesthetic dimension for ourselves and others. And by specifically meeting our defining traditional obligations to our parents, elders, and ancestors on the one hand, and to our contemporaries and descendants on the other, Confucius proffers an uncommon, but nevertheless spiritually authentic form of transcendence, a human capacity to go beyond the specific spatiotemporal circumstances in which we live, giving our personhood the sense of humanity shared in common and thereby a strong sense of continuity with what has gone before and what will come later. In the cosmic sense, Confucius never addresses the question of the meaning of life; he probably wouldn't even have understood it. But his vision of what it is to be a human being provided for everyone to find meaning *in* life, a not inconsiderable accomplishment.

STUDY QUESTIONS

1. According to Rosemont, how does a Confucian differentiate between a relational and an autonomous self?
2. What is meant by *ren*?
3. How do rituals acquire meaning?
4. Does performing rituals play a significant part in your own life?

The Tao

RAY BILLINGTON

Along with Confucianism and Zen Buddhism, Taoism stands as one of the three major traditions of thought in China. The focus is "the Tao," the first principle of the universe, which is unknowable. Nevertheless, the central precept of Taoism is to live in harmony with the Tao. In our next selection Ray Billington (1930–2012) offers a brief exposition of the Taoist outlook. He was a Methodist minister who turned against Christianity, became an exponent of Eastern philosophy, and headed the Philosophy Department at the University of West Bristol, England.

What . . . does 'Tao' mean? To be able to give a direct answer to this seemingly straightforward question would, paradoxically, be to fall into error, since, as the opening verse of the most famous of all Taoist classics states unambiguously,

> *The tao that can be told is not the eternal Tao;*
> *The name that can be named is not the eternal*
> *Name.*

This couplet is from the *Tao Te Ching*, the 'classic of the way and its power'. According to Chinese tradition, it was written by Lao Tzu, a famous teacher and mystic of the sixth century BCE, just before he removed himself from civilisation in order to become a recluse. It is now generally agreed by sinologists that the work is the product of many hands (Lao Tzu means 'great master', which is more a title than a name); that it was compiled over some centuries; and that it was finalised in its present form around the second century BCE.

From *Religion Without God*, Routledge, 2002. Reprinted by permission of Taylor & Francis.

According to the *Tao Te Ching*, the Tao is *the first principle of the universe, the all-embracing reality from which everything else arises*. Although the Tao remains eternally unknowable, its power (Te) can enter into every human being, so that the test of one's commitment to Taoism is viewed as the extent to which one's life is in harmony with the Tao. (The Chinese hieroglyphic for 'philosophy' depicts a hand and a mouth, symbolising a condition where words are consistent with deeds.) ... Taoism does not proceed to make any case for God, or gods, as divine powers operating under the Tao's auspices, so to speak. Section 42 of the *Tao Te Ching* puts the matter rather differently:

> *The Tao gives birth to One.*
> *One gives birth to Two.*
> *Two gives birth to Three.*
> *Three gives birth to all things.*

The 'One' to which the Tao gives birth ... is Ch'i, or primordial breath (wind, spirit, energy, like the Hebrew word *Ruach* as used in Genesis 1: 2: 'The spirit of God moved upon the face of the waters'). It is the life-force that pervades and vitalises all things, the cosmic energy which brought the universe into being and continues to sustain it....

For Taoists even the Ch'i remains remote. It can be experienced, but only with time and dedication. If the Te, the power of the Tao in each individual life, is to be evinced, a force is needed which can be experienced more immediately. It is here that Taoists turn to the 'Two' to which the Ch'i gives birth. These are the twin forces of yin and yang, the polar opposites by which the universe functions, such as negative and positive, cold and heat, darkness and light, intuition and rationality, femininity and masculinity, earth and heaven. Neither of these can be without the other, and neither has any meaning without the other. We know the meaning of 'hot' only in relation to 'cold', of 'wet' to 'dry', of 'tall' to 'short', of 'dark' to 'light', of 'life' to 'death'. (We know that we are alive only because we know that we were once, and shall again be, dead. If we were eternal, there would be no word either for 'eternal' or for 'living'.) ...

[N]either yin nor yang is ever motionless; each is continuously moving into the other, which means that one must learn to recognise when to apply yin, and when yang, energies. This again means allowing the intuition to exert itself: to know when to speak out and when to remain quiet; when to be gentle and when to be violent; when to be active and when to stand and stare. Both the workaholic and the playboy are, according to the yin–yang doctrine, living distorted and incomplete lives because only half of their natures is being allowed expression. Neither the ant nor the grasshopper in Aesop's fable would receive Taoism's stamp of approval.

The 'Three' to which the Two give birth are heaven, earth and humanity. [I]t is when there is harmony between these three—the yang of heaven, the yin of earth, and the human occupants of the arena which between them they bring into being—that the Te can be identified in people's lives. The final stage is the creation of 'all things' which we encounter and experience, for which 'the Three' are responsible.

The important consideration with Taoism, however, . . . is not to speculate on the meaning of the idea of the Tao, but to find out how to respond to its power (Te) in one's own life. The aim . . . is to be natural, and the *Tao Te Ching* gives many hints about how this state may be achieved. One way is to practise *wu-wei*. This is often translated as living a life of 'non-action', but a more accurate translation would be not to take any *inappropriate* action. The most famous exponent of Taoism who was unquestionably a historical figure was the teacher of the third century BCE, Chuang-Tzu (Master Chuang). He argued that many of the things we do and the words we speak are simply a waste of time and breath, since the situation we are discussing or trying to affect cannot be changed by our efforts: all we're actually doing, he said, was 'flaying the air'. Or worse: our frenetic efforts may actually lead to the loss of what was wholesome and acceptable in itself. We destroy a lily by gilding it; a snake is no longer a snake if we paint legs on it; we shall not help young wheat to grow by tugging at it. We must practise patience . . . acting only at the right time and with the minimum amount of effort. In fact, if we learn how to wait, we shall frequently find that no action is necessary in any case. The *Tao Te Ching* states:

> Do you have the patience to wait
> till your mud settles and the water is clear?
> Can you remain unmoving
> till the right action arises by itself?

* * *

Wu-wei means striking only when the iron is hot, sowing one's seed—whether in deed or word—and leaving it time to burgeon. Where disagreement with another person occurs, its approach is to present one's viewpoint unambiguously, then leave it time to germinate—if there is any worth in the idea—in the mind of the other, rather than to overcome the other with decibels or, worse, to force him to accept a viewpoint or an activity against either his will or his personal assessment of the situation. Wu-wei is the way of the diplomat, not the dictator; of the philosopher, not the proselytiser.

Another concept in Taoism with which wu-wei is linked is *fu*, meaning 'returning'. This could be interpreted as aligning oneself with the yin and yang by understanding that seasons, whether in nature or in a nation's culture and values, arrive and pass, only to return again and pass away again, so that the wise person will accommodate his living to the eternal process of change. More basically Taoism is the concept of fu as returning, or, at any rate, remaining loyal, to one's roots:

> If you let yourself be blown to and fro, you lose
> touch with your root.
> If you let restlessness move you, you lose touch
> with who you are.

* * *

[A]nother Taoist virtue . . . is *p'u* literally an unhewn block, and is an image used to denote simplicity, even innocence: not arising from ignorance, but from a backcloth of full awareness of the human condition: childlikeness without being childish. . . . To live according to *p'u* is to speak as one feels, to behave according to the person one is, or has become; in other words, to act naturally. The *Tao Te Ching* states:

> Man follows the earth.
> Earth follows the universe.
> The universe follows the Tao.
> The Tao follows only itself.

That final phrase has also been translated as 'suchness', the spontaneous and intuitive state of *tzu-yan*, meaning 'being such of itself, 'being natural'. In human beings, it includes everything which is free of human intention or external influences: that which is in harmony with itself. It may therefore be linked with wu-wei with its call for action only when it is appropriate—that is, when it is the natural action for those particular circumstances. When a person achieves this condition (which is not easy), he or she can be described as being at one with the Tao. It will not be achieved by academic research, or the study of sacred texts, or through a correct observance of ritual: . . . Taoism relegates all these activities to a low ranking on the scale of spiritual aids. It will be gained by living one's life in accordance with the natural forces of the universe, expressed both in nature itself and in human nature.

STUDY QUESTIONS

1. What does Taoism mean by "*wu-wei*"?
2. What does Billington mean by "childlikeness without being childish"?
3. Does Taoism, like Confucianism, stress correct observance of ritual?
4. Can we knowingly act in accord with an unknowable principle?

Twelve Zen Stories

Buddhism was introduced in China in the first century. After hundreds of years Buddhist and Taoist ideas blended to yield Zen Buddhism, which more than a millennium later spread to Japan. Zen places comparatively little emphasis on ritual, morality, or book learning. Rather, Zen finds enlightenment in spontaneous experience and challenges adherents with koans, puzzles that seek to force respondents to abandon reason.

From *Zen Flesh/Zen Bones*, compiled by Paul Reps and Nyogen Senzaki, Tuttle Publishing, 1957.

Our final selection contains a dozen Zen stories that illustrate how paradox is supposed to provide a path to understanding. The ultimate lesson is supposed to be the elimination of all dualities, including any separation between consciousness and the object of meditation.

·······························

A CUP OF TEA

Nan-in, a Japanese master during the Meiji era (1868–1912), received a university professor who came to inquire about Zen.

Nan-in served tea. He poured his visitor's cup full, and then kept on pouring.

The professor watched the overflow until he no longer could restrain himself. "It is overfull. No more will go in!"

"Like this cup," Nan-in said, "you are full of your own opinions and speculations. How can I show you Zen unless you first empty your cup?"

IS THAT SO?

The Zen master Hakuin was praised by his neighbors as one living a pure life.

A beautiful Japanese girl whose parents owned a food store lived near him. Suddenly, without any warning, her parents discovered she was with child.

This made her parents angry. She would not confess who the man was, but after much harassment at last named Hakuin.

In great anger the parents went to the master. "Is that so?" was all he would say.

After the child was born, it was brought to Hakuin. By this time he had lost his reputation, which did not trouble him, but he took very good care of the child. He obtained milk from his neighbors and everything else the little one needed.

A year later the girl-mother could stand it no longer. She told her parents the truth—that the real father of the child was a young man who worked in the fishmarket.

The mother and father of the girl at once went to Hakuin to ask his forgiveness, to apologize at length, and to get the child back again.

Hakuin was willing. In yielding the child, all he said was: "Is that so?"

THE MOON CANNOT BE STOLEN

Ryokan, a Zen master, lived the simplest kind of life in a little hut at the foot of a mountain. One evening a thief visited the hut only to discover there was nothing in it to steal.

Ryokan returned and caught him. "You may have come a long way to visit me," he told the prowler, "and you should not return empty-handed. Please take my clothes as a gift."

The thief was bewildered. He took the clothes and slunk away.

Ryokan sat naked, watching the moon. "Poor fellow," he mused, "I wish I could give him this beautiful moon."

THE BLOCKHEAD LORD

Two Zen Teachers, Daigu and Gudo, were invited to visit a lord. Upon arriving, Gudo said to the lord: "You are wise by nature and have an inborn ability to learn Zen."

"Nonsense," said Daigu. "Why do you flatter this blockhead? He may be a lord, but he doesn't know anything of Zen."

So, instead of building a temple for Gudo, the lord built it for Daigu and studied Zen with rum.

MUDDY ROAD

Tanzan and Ekido were once traveling together down a muddy road. A heavy rain was still falling.

Coming around a bend, they met a lovely girl in a silk kimono and sash, unable to cross the intersection.

"Come on, girl," said Tanzan at once. Lifting her in his arms, he carried her over the mud.

Ekido did not speak again until that night when they reached a lodging temple. Then he no longer could restrain himself. "We monks don't go near females," he told Tanzan, "especially not young and lovely ones. It is dangerous. Why did you do that?"

"I left the girl there," said Tanzan. "Are you still carrying her?"

THE SOUND OF ONE HAND

The master of Kennin temple was Mokurai, Silent Thunder. He had a little protégé named Toyo who was only twelve years old. Toyo saw the older disciples visit the master's room each morning and evening to receive instruction in sanzen or personal guidance in which they were given koans to stop mind-wandering.

Toyo wished to do sanzen also.

"Wait a while," said Mokurai. "You are too young."

But the child insisted, so the teacher finally consented.

In the evening little Toyo went at the proper time to the threshold of Mokurai's sanzen room. He struck the gong to announce his presence, bowed respectfully three times outside the door, and went to sit before the master in respectful silence.

"You can hear the sound of two hands when they clap together," said Mokurai. "Now show me the sound of one hand."

Toyo bowed and went to his room to consider this problem. From his window he could hear the music of the geishas. "Ah, I have it!" he proclaimed.

The next evening, when his teacher asked him to illustrate the sound of one hand, Toyo began to play the music of the geishas.

"No, no," said Mokurai. "That will never do. That is not the sound of one hand. You've not got it at all."

Thinking that such music might interrupt, Toyo moved his abode to a quiet place. He meditated again. "What can the sound of one hand be?" He happened to hear some water dripping. "I have it," imagined Toyo.

When he next appeared before his teacher, Toyo imitated dripping water.

"What is that?" asked Mokurai. "That is the sound of dripping water, but not the sound of one hand. Try again."

In vain Toyo meditated to hear the sound of one hand. He heard the sighing of the wind. But the sound was rejected.

He heard the cry of an owl. This also was refused.

The sound of one hand was not the locusts.

For more than ten times Toyo visited Mokurai with different sounds. All were wrong. For almost a year he pondered what the sound of one hand might be.

At last little Toyo entered true meditation and transcended all sounds. "I could collect no more," he explained later, "so I reached the soundless sound."

Toyo had realized the sound of one hand.

EVERY-MINUTE ZEN

Zen students are with their masters at least ten years before they presume to teach others. Nan-in was visited by Tenno, who, having passed his apprenticeship, had become a teacher. The day happened to be rainy, so Tenno wore wooden clogs and carried an umbrella. After greeting him, Nanin remarked: "I suppose you left your wooden clogs in the vestibule. I want to know if your umbrella is on the right or left side of the clogs."

Tenno, confused, had no instant answer. He realized that he was unable to carry his Zen every minute. He became Nan-in's pupil, and he studied six more years to accomplish his every-minute Zen.

IN THE HANDS OF DESTINY

A great Japanese warrior named Nobunaga decided to attack the enemy although he had only one-tenth the number of men the opposition commanded. He knew that he would win, but his soldiers were in doubt.

On the way he stopped at a Shinto shrine and told his men: "After I visit the shrine I will toss a coin. If heads comes, we will win; if tails, we will lose. Destiny holds us in her hand."

Nobunaga entered the shrine and offered a silent prayer. He came forth and tossed a coin. Heads appeared. His soldiers were so eager to fight that they won their battle easily.

"No one can change the hand of destiny," his attendant told him after the battle.

"Indeed not," said Nobunaga, showing a coin which had been doubled, with heads facing either way.

THE SUBJUGATION OF A GHOST

A young wife fell sick and was about to die. "I love you so much," she told her husband, "I do not want to leave you. Do not go from me to any other woman. If you do, I will return as a ghost and cause you endless trouble."

Soon the wife passed away. The husband respected her last wish for the first three months, but then he met another woman and fell in love with her. They became engaged to be married.

Immediately after the engagement a ghost appeared every night to the man, blaming him for not keeping his promise. The ghost was clever too. She told him exactly what had transpired between himself and his new sweetheart. Whenever he gave his fiancée a present, the ghost would describe it in detail. She would even repeat conversations, and it so annoyed the man that he could not sleep. Someone advised him to take his problem to a Zen master who lived close to the village. At length, in despair, the poor man went to him for help.

"Your former wife became a ghost and knows everything you do," commented the master. "Whatever you do or say, whatever you give your beloved, she knows. She must be a very wise ghost. Really you should admire such a ghost. The next time she appears, bargain with her. Tell her that she knows so much you can hide nothing from her, and that if she will answer you one question, you promise to break your engagement and remain single."

"What is the question I must ask her?" inquired the man.

The master replied: "Take a large handful of soy beans and ask her exactly how many beans you hold in your hand. If she cannot tell you, you will know she is only a figment of your imagination and will trouble you no longer."

The next night, when the ghost appeared the man flattered her and told her that she knew everything.

"Indeed," replied the ghost, "and I know you went to see that Zen master today."

"And since you know so much," demanded the man, "tell me how many beans I hold in this hand!"

There was no longer any ghost to answer the question.

ONE NOTE OF ZEN

After Kakua visited the emperor, he disappeared and no one knew what became of him. He was the first Japanese to study Zen in China, but since he showed nothing of it, save one note, he is not remembered for having brought Zen into his country.

Kakua visited China and accepted the true teaching. He did not travel while he was there. Meditating constantly, he lived on a remote part of a mountain. Whenever people found him and asked him to preach, he would say a few words and then move to another part of the mountain where he could be found less easily.

The emperor heard about Kakua when he returned to Japan and asked him to preach Zen for his edification and that of his subjects.

Kakua stood before the emperor in silence. He then produced a flute from the folds of his robe, and blew one short note. Bowing politely, he disappeared.

REAL PROSPERITY

A rich man asked Sengai to write something for the continued prosperity of his family so that it might be treasured from generation to generation.

Sengai obtained a large sheet of paper and wrote: "Father dies, son dies, grandson dies."

The rich man became angry. "I asked you to write something for the happiness of my family! Why do you make such a joke as this?"

"No joke is intended," explained Sengai. "If before you yourself die your son should die, this would grieve you greatly. If your grandson should pass away before your son, both of you would be broken-hearted. If your family, generation after generation, passes away in the order I have named, it will be the natural course of life. I call this real prosperity."

A LETTER TO A DYING MAN

Bassui wrote the following letter to one of his disciples who was about to die:

"The essence of your mind is not born, so it will never die. It is not an existence, which is perishable. It is not an emptiness, which is a mere void. It has neither color nor form. It enjoys no pleasures and suffers no pains.

"I know you are very ill. Like a good Zen student, you are facing that sickness squarely. You may not know exactly who is suffering, but question yourself: What is the essence of this mind? Think only of this. You will need no more. Covet nothing. Your end which is endless is as a snowflake dissolving in the pure air."

STUDY QUESTIONS

1. Do you have to empty your cup of opinions in order to learn?
2. What do you take to be the lesson of "Muddy Road"?
3. What is meant by the action of blowing one short note on a flute?
4. What significance do you find in "A Letter to a Dying Man"?

Index

The Hall of a Thousand Columns

Tim Mackintosh-Smith

Tim Mackintosh-Smith's first book, *Yemen: Travels in Dictionary Land*, gained him the 1998 Thomas Cook/*Daily Telegraph* Travel Book Award, and *Travels with a Tangerine*, on Ibn Battutah's travels in the old Islamic world, was received to huge critical acclaim. For the past twenty years his home has been the Yemeni capital San'a, where he lives on the ruin-mound of the ancient Sabaean city.

Martin Yeoman

Martin Yeoman, illustrator of the book, is a painter, draughtsman, sculptor and etcher, whose work can be found in a number of notable British collections, including those of HM the Queen and HRH The Prince of Wales.

THE HALL OF A THOUSAND COLUMNS

Hindustan to Malabar with Ibn Battutah

Tim Mackintosh-Smith

with illustrations by Martin Yeoman

JOHN MURRAY

Text © Tim Mackintosh-Smith 2005

Illustrations © Martin Yeoman 2005

First published in 2005 by John Murray (Publishers)
A division of Hodder Headline

Paperback edition 2006

The right of Tim Mackintosh-Smith to be identified as the Author
of the Work has been asserted by him in accordance with the Copyright,
Designs and Patents Act 1988.

3

A CIP catalogue record for this title is available from the British Library

ISBN 978-0-7195-6587-8

Typeset in Monotype Bembo by
Servis Filmsetting Ltd, Manchester

Printed and bound by
Clays Ltd, St Ives plc

Hodder Headline policy is to use papers that are natural, renewable and
recyclable products and made from wood grown in sustainable forests.
The logging and manufacturing processes are expected to conform to the
environmental regulations of the country of origin.

John Murray (Publishers)
338 Euston Road
London NW1 3BH

'Si nous ne trouverons pas des choses agréables,
nous trouverons du moins des choses nouvelles.'

Voltaire, *Candide*

'What a difference there is between one who compiles a
book from hearsay in the comfort of his home and one
who has gone through the tribulation of travel.'

al-Maqdisi, *The Best of Divisions*

For Martin
and in memory of
IG

Contents

Contents

Prefatory Note

ABOUT FOUR YEARS ago I mentioned to my then publisher, John R. Murray, that I was planning to go to India for the first time to investigate the adventures there of the Moroccan traveller Ibn Battutah (1304–68/9; IB for short). He gave me a book - Murray's 1962 *Handbook for Travellers in India, Pakistan, Burma and Ceylon*, the nineteenth and final edition of a run that had begun in the lifetime of the last Mughal emperor. The book was the size of a moderate novel, but its metaphorical mass seemed suddenly, and disconcertingly, huge: I was holding a subcontinent in the palm of my hand. It was then that I saw how little I knew about India – a bit of general knowledge, and what I'd picked up from IB himself and from earlier Arabic accounts by the likes of Captain Buzurg of Ramhurmuz. That IB was even more ignorant of India when he arrived there in 1333 was a point in my favour. It was the only one. Murray's *Handbook*, distilled from a century of wisdom and wandering, from miles of bookstacks, made me realize that I could do no more than try to see the India IB saw; that mine would have to be a pinhole view, not a panorama.

IB's own book is entitled in full *The Precious Gift for Lookers into the Marvels of Cities and Wonders of Travel*. The present volume, like my *Travels with a Tangerine* that preceded it, is a return gift – necessarily not as precious as IB's but, I hope, acceptable as a 700th birthday present to him. (By his own, lunar reckoning he is rising 721. Years are subjective.)

Bayt Qadi, San'a
April 2004

Maps

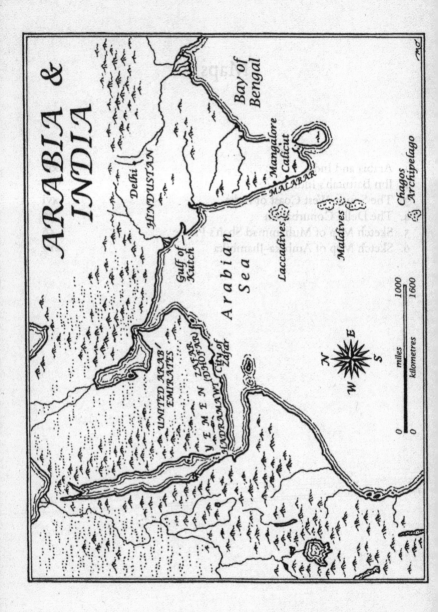

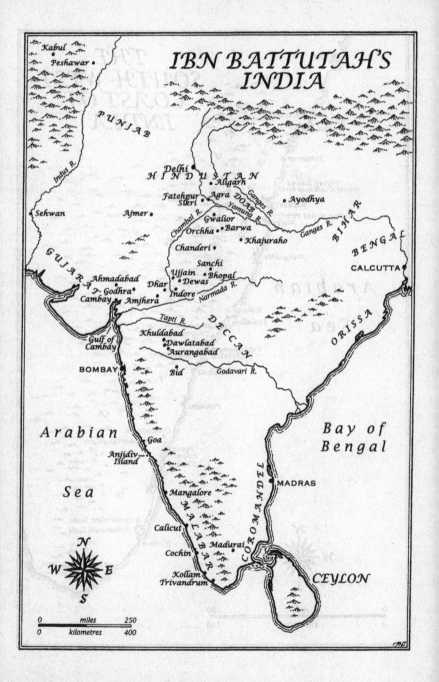

IBN BATTUTAH'S INDIA

Kabul

Peshawar

PUNJAB

Indus R.

HINDUSTAN

Delhi

Aligarh

Fatehpur Sikri

Agra

DOAB

Ganges R.

Ayodhya

Sehwan

Ajmer

Chambal R.

Yamuna R.

Gwalior

Orchha

Barwa

Khajuraho

BIHAR

Ganges R.

Chanderi

BENGAL

GUJARAT

Sanchi

CALCUTTA

Ahmadabad

Dhar

Ujjain

Bhopal

Godhra

Dewas

Cambay

Amjhera

Indore

Narmada R.

ORISSA

Tapti R.

DECCAN

Gulf of
Cambay

Khuldabad

Dawlatabad

Aurangabad

BOMBAY

Bid

Godavari R.

Arabian

Goa

Bay of
Bengal

Anjidiv
Island

Sea

MADRAS

Mangalore

MALABAR

COROMANDEL

Calicut

Madurai

Cochin

Kollam

CEYLON

Trivandrum

N
W E
S

| 0 | miles | 250 |
| 0 | kilometres | 400 |

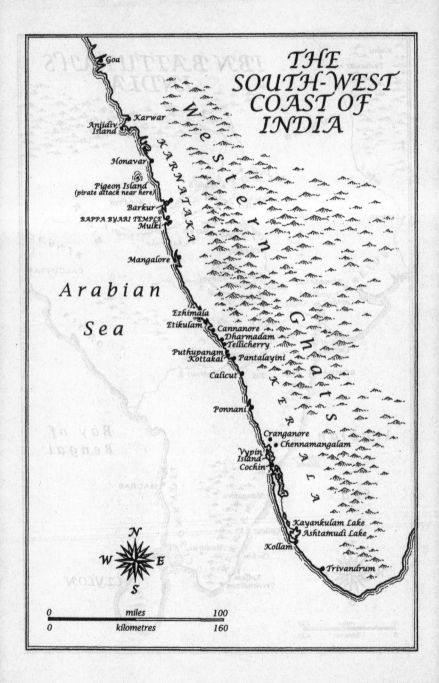

THE
SOUTH-WEST
COAST OF
INDIA

Goa

Karwar

Anjidiv
Island

Honavar

Pigeon Island
(pirate attack near here)

Barkur

BAPPA BYARI TEMPLE
Mulki

Mangalore

Arabian

Sea

Ezhimala
Etikulam
Cannanore
Dharmadam
Tellicherry
Puthupanam
Kottakal
Pantalayini

Calicut

Ponnani

Cranganore
Chennamangalam

Vypin
Island
Cochin

Kayankulam Lake
Ashtamudi Lake

Kollam

Trivandrum

Western

KARNATAKA

Ghats

K E R A L A

N
W   E
S

| 0 | | miles | | 100 |
| 0 | | kilometres | | 160 |

THE HALL OF A
THOUSAND COLUMNS

IB was born in the Moroccan town of Tangier in 1304. He trained as a jurist, the traditional profession of his family, then in 1325 set off on the pilgrimage to Mecca. The journey gave him a taste for distant travel. In this he was not alone, for wherever he went — Anatolia, East Africa, Central Asia, China, up the Volga, down the Niger, even in the tiny Indian Ocean sultanate of the Maldives — he either met or heard of other Arab travellers. What makes him unique is that he went to all of these places (and more), and then, twenty-nine years after leaving home, went back and wrote about them.

The centrepiece of his book is the account of his ten Indian years. Travelling via Central Asia and Afghanistan, he arrived in September 1333 at the River Indus, the north-western limit of the Sultanate of Delhi. His timing was perfect. The current sultan, Muhammad Shah ibn Tughluq, ruled the greatest empire India had known in 800 years; only under the Mughals, two centuries on, would one man control so much of the Subcontinent again. Muhammad Shah was spectacularly wealthy, prodigiously generous and particularly fond of educated men from the old Islamic world — men like IB. For the traveller from Tangier, the future looked bright. He was not to be disappointed: he began his years in Delhi as a judge, and was to end them as an ambassador. But he was as yet unaware of the multiple eccentricities of his patron-to-be, some of them deeply unpleasant; nor could he have foreseen the many disasters that would attend his Indian career.

I had already followed IB from Morocco as far as the Crimea. It was while I was wondering how to deal with his often problematic onward itinerary that an opportunity arose — to travel to India the way IB returned, by sailing-dhow, across the Arabian Sea.

Dhow Time

'Hope leads us on; we may succeed, or fail.
The wind's not always fair that fills the sail.'

al-Mutanabbi

'YOU MUST BE suffering from lack-of-culture shock,' Jay said as she removed the packaging of her beefburger.

I was, I admitted, confused.

Jay, an old friend from Yemen now in economic exile in the Gulf, had taken me to a McDonalds off Cultural Square in the Emirate of Sharjah. The square was a large roundabout with a monumental open book at its centre. The culture, judging by a mosque and other buildings in the Mamluk Revival style, was Islamic. And here we were, eating beefburgers and drinking Coca-Cola. Not that there is anything intrinsically unIslamic about fast food, assuming that what goes into the beef- (never, of course, 'ham-') burgers has been correctly slaughtered. The Muslim world was eating grilled patties of minced meat centuries before their Baltic cousins crossed the Atlantic. But to me, newly arrived from a burger-free zone in the mountains on the other side of Arabia, McDonalds might have been one of the moons of Jupiter.

Food as a coefficient of cultural mobility is hardly a recent or a purely American phenomenon. 'Together with our Empire,' noted Freya Stark, 'we allowed things like anchovy sauce and tapioca pudding to run uncontrolled over the continents of the world.' But the British, in turn, have the Romans to thank for anchovy sauce and the Conquistadors to thank, or blame, for tapioca pudding. Food and its terminology have always been on the move, and sometimes with a pleasing orbitality. Thus the *praecox*, the 'precocious' peach of the old Roman, has become by way of a very long Chinese whisper – *praikokkion, birkok, barquq, al-barquq, albarcoque, albercocca* – the modern Roman's *albicocca*, the English apricock or apricot, its precocity now attached to the stalk of an Arabic definite article.

What was disorientating in the Sharjah McDonalds was the way in which not just a comestible but a prime cultural symbol – the hamburger – had insinuated itself so suddenly, and so speciously, into another – the Arabic script. Thus, at Makdunaldiz, you ordered a *tishīz barjar*, or a *tishīkin māk nājit*, out of a menu extruded from those fluent ligatures that bind the Muslim world so elegantly together. And, having arrived not by Chinese whispers but in a global yell, the names sound as strange to an Arabic ear as they look in Latin transliteration. An occasional meaning did rise out of the nonsense. For instance, a child with a wide and poetical vocabulary might be puzzled by his *hābī mīl* ('Happy Meal') – 'My serpent is an eyeliner pencil'. I am no purist: *sandwish* is better Arabic than *shaṭr wa mashṭūr wa baynahumā shāṭir* – 'a bisected part of something, the other half of the bisected something, and between the two of them that which separates two bisected parts'. All the same, a whole generation of Gulf Arabs is being fed a diet of gobbledegook; I mean of course the transliterations.

If the people of Sharjah have sold their birthright for a Big Mac, one could equally well point out that the Brits sold theirs years ago for a chicken tikka masala and that, with hamburgers, the Hanseatic League disinherited North America of pemmican and hominy grits. But the Emiratis were not just eating out; they were on a spree at a cultural cash-and-carry. Our *barjars* finished, we went to the local hypermarket and headed for the Baskin Rūbinz ice-cream cabinet. Then on to a multiplex in the Sītī Sintar ('City Centre') mall in the neighbouring Emirate of Ajman, for a Hollywood movie. 'In the beginning,' wrote Locke, reflecting on the prelapsarian savages across the Atlantic, 'all the world was America.' Now, antithetically, it seems well on the way to being America once more.

But it was good to see Jay again; and down in Ajman Creek lay the dhow that would take me, propelled by monsoon winds, over the ocean, via Muscat and Mangalore, to Malabar.

*

At first sight it seemed that by sailing across the Arabian Sea and backwards in time, on the trail of a fourteenth-century traveller from Tangier, I would be passing into another universe. But it soon occurred to me that there was at least one point at which the two worlds – Ronald McDonald's and Ibn Battutah's – came together. In IB's time a wind of ideas, symbols and fashions was blowing steadily eastward, from the old Islamic heartland to the Indies, and through the Malacca Strait towards China. Islamic culture was travelling further and faster than at any period since the first century of its existence; and it was being spread not by soldiers or missionaries but by businessmen. They were mobile, cosmopolitan and rich. Something analogous is happening today. The analogy, I admit, is flawed at its very base: the Hamburger Current is propelled by market forces; Islam flows from inspiration divine and prophetic. But mainstream Muslims have never been anti-materialistic. The Prophet was proud of his earlier career as an international businessman, and the Karimi spice cartel of IB's time was as wealthy, as ubiquitous and as shadowy as any multinational today.

IB, heading east, was riding the Islamic monsoon. For him, its twin streams of spirit and matter converged at times, at others conflicted. He was launched into them by a dream which, unlike the American dream, was no metaphor.

Early in the summer of 1326, and less than a year into his twenty-nine-year wanderings, IB visited the ultimate fast-food joint. It was a one-man operation run by the most famous living saint in Egypt, Shaykh Abu Abdallah al-Murshidi. Despite his backwoods location

deep in the Nile Delta, 'groups of visitors would come to his hermitage every day, and he would provide them all with food'. Other
contemporary accounts go into some detail on the rare fruits, rich
sweetmeats and other delicacies that appeared from al-Murshidi's
kitchenless cell, and at times from the broad sleeve of his robe. A particular coup was his instantaneous production of polenta with spring
lamb and sour milk for the vizier Mughaltay, swiftly followed, the
vizier remembered, 'by over twenty other dishes only to be found in
the sultan's kitchens'. Moreover, al-Murshidi had a knack of mind-
reading exactly what his visitors wanted to eat. 'I swear by the One
and Only God,' said a scholar of Alexandria, recalling the day al-
Murshidi had given him a Transoxanian-style pudding with honey
and clarified butter, 'that I had not told a living soul that this was
exactly what I desired.' IB, one suspects more because of his low
status than his low expectations, got a packet of biscuits (and so did
I, at the same spot 671 years later). The saint, however, more than
compensated him.

'That night,' IB dictated in his memoirs thirty years on,

while I was asleep on the roof of Shaykh Abu Abdallah's cell, I
dreamed I was on the wing of an enormous bird. First it flew in
the direction of the *qiblah*, to Mecca; then it turned south
towards Yemen; then east; after that it flew south again. Finally
it took me far to the east and landed in a dark and greenish land.
It left me in that place. I was amazed at this dream and said to
myself, 'If the shaykh reveals some knowledge of my dream, he
will prove himself as great as people claim him to be' . . . Later,
after he had prayed the forenoon prayer, he summoned me and
told me he was aware I had seen a dream vision. When I related
it to him he said, 'You will perform the pilgrimage to Mecca
and visit the tomb of the Prophet – on him be blessings and
peace – at al-Madinah. Then you will wander about the lands of
Yemen and Iraq, and of the Turks and the Indians. In India you
will stay for a long time, and you will meet there my brother
Dilshad the Indian, who will rescue you from a great misfortune
into which you will fall.'

There is no question that dreams can be prophetic. At the beginning of September 2001, I dreamed of an immensely tall building, a

crowd of people milling below, and of an airliner crashing, slowly and deliberately, into the building. The impact woke me with a jolt; the image remained impressed on my mind, and is there now. 'The first sign of a true dream vision,' wrote IB's younger contemporary Ibn Khaldun, 'is that the dreamer wakes up quickly, as soon as he has seen it . . . The other sign is that the dream vision remains impressed with all its details in his memory.'

You may dismiss my premonition of the attack on the World Trade Center as a coincidence. Precisely! Ibn Khaldun would reply. In the sphere of spiritual intellection, where dreams are experienced, time and space do not exist. Everything and everywhere is literally coincident. You are reading this sentence, dying and being born, the cosmos is being destroyed and created, IB is travelling, Tim is travelling, all simultaneously and in an infinitesimal space which is the corollary of infinity, of an indivisibly eternal God to whom a thousand years are not as one day but as nothing. Prophets and certain holy men have favoured access to this cosmic microdot. The rest of us blunder in from time to time in our sleep, to wake with confused memories of the future.

Bunyan, Coleridge and others have turned dreams into their literary contents. For IB, the dream was the contents page. Much of his *Travels*, an apparent series of chance twists, aleatory alleyways and whimsical sidetracks, is in fact a complex but ordered arabesque. The dream in the Delta is the key to the pattern. As contents pages go, it is impressionistic. But the threat of danger, the promise of redemption, are tantalizing. What exactly will happen to him during that long time in India, his destination and his destiny?

'I took my leave of him', said IB of al-Murshidi, the sainted celebrity chef, 'and set off. Since the time I left him I have never encountered on my travels anything but good fortune.' In view of what was to happen to him in India the second sentence is outrageous.

*

'Beautiful. Like a butterfly out of the chrysalis.'

A rather solid butterfly. A Rubens nymph. But I had to agree with Anderson: his ship, *Sanjeeda*, her huge main- and mizzen-sails flexing tentatively in the breathy air of the Gulf, was stunning. A puff of wind caught the jib, and for a moment the nymph became a perfect, elegant imago.

As we puttered back towards her in the dinghy, I recalled a couple of missed boats from my earlier travels – a tramp *sambuq* pursued on shore halfway along the southern coast of Arabia; a non-existent freighter across the Black Sea. Here, at last, I had caught up with a recognizably Battutian conveyance – a 94-foot, 138-ton ocean-going dhow. A skipper of the fourteenth century would have thought her stern eccentric, if not frankly Frankish, and her hull a downright deathtrap – '*Nails?* Fall apart at a tap, this one . . .' (to the consternation of travellers from the west, Indian Ocean dhows were held together not with iron but with big cross-stitches of coconut-fibre rope, supposedly pliable in the event of collisions). But *Sanjeeda* was powered by the authentically fourteenth-century *mawsim*, or monsoon. Better still, she was authenticity *de luxe*. We had just had a lunch of many courses and helpings on a poop-deck furnished with rugs, cushions and Malabar sea-chests; the cabins were simple but comfortable; and for added retro-chic the captain was a veteran of Tim Severin's trans-oceanic curragh, the *Brendan*. There were also not a few nods to the new millennium – flushing heads, a gleaming diesel engine, a miniature desalination plant, a freezer the size of a large wardrobe, a satellite telephone and an Internet link. IB, who on one occasion – as we shall see – saved the lives of his companions by an insistence on maritime comforts, would have approved.

Anderson was equivocal about the mod cons he had installed. For a start they hadn't come cheap – more than the cost of building *Sanjeeda*, across the ocean in Mr Mistry's shipyard on the Gulf of Kutch. But he planned to charter the vessel and knew that potential customers would not be the sort who would relish a diet of dried shark and hard tack, or the prospect of getting becalmed or dying of thirst – let alone powdering their noses in a box hung over the stern. On this last point, Anderson admitted that it was a plus not to have other people's bathwater, and worse, falling past the poop portholes of the owner's cabin. Clearly, though, his sensibility was disturbed by the sheer amount of high-tech hardware below deck. 'When *Sanjeeda* was towed here she was a pristine vessel,' he said, with feeling. 'Now she's been raped.'

I knew how he felt. Where the sea and Arabia meet, a certain sort of Englishman (or in Anderson's case thoroughly anglicized American) is prey to strong emotions. I had always dreamed – and who has not who has read Masefield's 'Cargoes', and de Montfreid's

Croisière du Hachich, and Villiers's *Sons of Sindbad*, and has an iota of romance? – of a windfall, a sailing-dhow and a dusky crew, of a life of leisurely landfalls, laying the eastern seas beneath my keel and perhaps trading in the odd bit of ambergris or aloes-wood. Anderson had made the hardest part of the dream a reality. If *Sanjeeda* had turned in the Gulf from a dream-child into a greedy dominatrix, it did not detract from her beauty, from the swelling lines that flowed from her high and beamy backside to the retroussé Ganesh on her prow.

Sanjeeda was a *kotia* – the classic Kutch trading vessel, but a type also built in Arab lands. I remembered seeing one beside the creek at Sur in Oman, right at the stubby toe of Arabia and as close to Kutch as to the Arabian Gulf. In the Sur ship, Ganesh had turned into an Islamically abstract kiss-curl, like a giant cello scroll; otherwise the ships were identical. The Arabs, however, called their version a *ghanjah*. The last word on these matters, Kindermann, suggests on the authority of Dozy that the word is of Ottoman origin. I, admittedly with only Ben Trovato as my authority, would prefer to connect it with *ghunj*, the lascivious gyration of the hips in walking.

We tied up, climbed back aboard *Sanjeeda*, and immediately felt that raunchy, haunch-swinging gait beneath our feet. At first, leaving the creek and meeting the gentle swell of the Gulf, it had been unsettling; I had wondered whether I would ever find my sea-legs out on the ocean proper. Now, after only a few hours, the movement seemed comforting. It certainly didn't bother the more experienced crew members. Earlier I had watched Hasan – from Minicoy, loneliest of the Laccadives, the Fair Isle of India – swarming like a gibbon up the mainmast, then up the main spar to release the ties that held the great lateen sail. As he clung seventy feet above the deck to the tip of his perilous upside-down pendulum, I remembered Anderson suggesting I might want to lend a hand with crewing duties; and decided that some things were best left to men who spent their lives between mastheads and the tops of coco palms. Hasan, judging by his sense of balance and the grip of his thighs, could have made a fortune as a rodeo rider.

The rest of the crew ranged from another Minicoy man via a Keralan carpenter and a cook from Calcutta to a Pathan from Peshawar and a hand from the Himalayan valley of Swat, the last two picked up in the Sharjah *suq* – as authentically motley a lot as ever sailed the Indian Ocean. Order was imposed by an ancient *malum*, or master, a Kutchi who had spent his life sailing *kotias*; Anderson, who had launched his ship with both Islamic prayers and Hindu pujas, planned to inculcate *esprit de corps* with a job-lot of army-surplus battledress tunics of Afghan origin. But to me the crew seemed united already by the prospect of *Sanjeeda*'s maiden voyage. The excitement was palpable, and it was growing.

I was as excited as anyone. Anderson's invitation to 'Batty & Co.' to join the voyage had solved the problem of how to get to India. Flying seemed tame. The overland option, IB's choice for his temporal journey, was more tempting. But the route he followed had a habit of fraying into doubtful variants the nearer he got to the Subcontinent. Different commentators have made him enter India through, variously, the Khyber Pass, another pass further south, or via a desert route that arrives 500 miles down the Indus. The enigma hinges on a place he calls Shashnagar, which lies somewhere between Kabul and Peshawar; the solution can only be found, I suspect, by tramping about the mountains where Pakistan and Afghanistan meet and grilling the local tribesmen. Exciting though this sounded, I doubted whether the many eccentricities of the Taliban ran to a penchant for historical topography. Reluctantly, I decided that India, and not the journey there, should be my goal – as it had been for IB himself. India takes up a quarter of the *Travels*, and a third of IB's long travelling life. It is the jewel in the Prince of Travellers' turban. Anderson's offer sealed the decision.

In fact I was being faithful to IB's original intentions. After performing the Mecca pilgrimage in 1332, he wrote, 'I made my way to Jeddah, meaning to travel by sea to Yemen and India. But fate decreed otherwise.' It did, however, decree that he should sail *back* from India on his journey home to Morocco fifteen years later. Taking ship out of Calicut he travelled in twenty-eight days to Zafar, now in the Sultanate of Oman. By crossing from the Emirates to Mangalore I would be following at least some of IB's voyage, in reverse.

Apart from direction, there was one other difference in our sea journeys – timing. Not the small matter of the six and a half centuries that separated us; rather, the amount of time we had to wait for our respective ships. IB spent 'a few days' in Calicut before embarking. Anderson had originally hoped to leave the Emirates in September. It was now the end of January. Events had been beyond his control: a sledgehammer of a summer, with temperatures in the upper forties, had delayed *Sanjeeda*'s fitting; the replacement for her top-heavy temporary mast languished in interstate purgatory on the Kerala-Karnataka border, only to be released by indulgences to the taxmen. But Anderson had the unflappability of a Zen master on valium, and departure was now in sight. After various faxes from the Gulf, rural Oxfordshire and the Royal Bombay Yacht Club ('TELEGRAM – SNAPLOCK'), the one I'd been waiting for arrived: 'We're now working to a fixed timetable . . . After a week or two of sea trials we shall, barring an act of God, begin the passage to Mangalore.' The voyage would take about fourteen days, he thought.

*

If I had solved the How of the journey, it was only now, between malls, movies and sea trials, that I realized I hadn't given any particular thought to the Why.

Unlike IB, I couldn't consciously claim Fate as my motive. But I had tailed the Moroccan from his native Tangier via Oman and the Crimea to Constantinople, and the thought of waving him off from there, as he set out for his biggest adventure, was unimaginable. By writing what old Arab authors called a *dhayl* – a literary 'tail' – to the first part of the *Travels*, I had attached myself, inseparably, to the traveller. I spent more time with IB than with anyone living. His movements directed mine, my actions were drawn from the deep well of his memories. I was his alter ego, and the volume that bore my name was the outcome of a collaboration. The day I first picked up his book, six years before, had indeed been fateful.

I was looking forward to the continuing journey. So far IB's travels had not been short on what the Arabs call Time's daughters, and we calamities. In India there were many more to come: in the flat Gangetic lands and on the long level shore of Malabar, switchback fortune would swing him to the peaks of success – as courtier, judge and diplomatist – but, more often, to the troughs of adversity – massive debt, near execution, capture by rebels, near execution again, near death from exhaustion, shipwreck, shipwreck again, and an attack by pirates who left him marooned in his underpants. However many times I read this catalogue of vicissitudes, I never failed to marvel at his stamina; at how, each time he fell, he would bounce back like an indiarubber ball, dazed but indestructible. It was in India, on my first perusal of the *Travels*, that I became truly entangled with

IB – not just IB the traveller, the writer, for he had intrigued me from the start – but IB the man, this elastic, Islamic Candide.

And yet never an Islamic Voltaire. IB did not seek to give his story any explicit point, moral or theological. His is the covert philosophy of Stan and Ollie – it always ends in another fine mess, but at least there'll be another episode. He also failed to give his story much shape. The *Travels* is a DIY Odyssey by a homespun Homer and the yarn, as elastic as its spinner, is prone to stretch alarmingly. He can, for instance, witter on for eleven pages trying to get his employer, Muhammad Shah the Sultan of Delhi, to pay off a debt; he smarms up to the Master of the World, the Second Alexander, with sweetmeats and sickly panegyric, and wrangles with officials over chits and signatures. It is intensely tiresome, and it tells us as much about court life in Delhi as a hectateuch of histories, and more about the teller than that stick-man, Polo, lets on about himself in his entire book.

I wanted to explore the setting of IB's Indian adventures on the ground. Like the Hall of a Thousand Columns, Muhammad Shah's audience chamber in Delhi, this setting is splendid yet shadowed, vast but claustrophobic. Other than a couple of monuments in Delhi itself, I had little idea about what was left of it, two-thirds of a millennium and two empires on. And I had even less notion of what remained from the human and sacred – and of course largely Islamic – geography that IB had mapped. Even after Partition, the Muslim population of India is proportionally bigger than in IB's day. But I didn't have to be an India buff (and I am not) to know that its influence, and even its history, are being systematically marginalized.

If I wanted to find out what was left, I also wanted to work out what was there to begin with. Like the sultan's labyrinthine palace, IB's account also contains some obscure and puzzling passages. In one – the story of his escape from rebels east of Delhi – the narrative thread appears not only to stretch, but to snap: IB's landscape, remembered in a stream of hyper-vivid detail, is studded with *jabals*, mountains. The problem is that the area concerned is as flat as a chapatti. We might as well look for mountains on the shores of the Zuider Zee. Where are they, if not in IB's head?

'India', said V.S. Naipaul in his *Area of Darkness*, 'distorts and enlarges.' The phenomenon is an old one, and I am not the first to wonder about the effects on IB's perception of that dark and greenish land. Ibn Khaldun, quoted above on dreams, happened also to write the longest contemporary notice of IB. The traveller, he said, 'used to tell stories about his journeys, and especially about the rule of the Sultan of India . . . When the sultan returned from an expedition, he would have catapults set up on the backs of the beasts in his procession, from which bags of dinars and dirhams would be scattered into the crowd. On hearing this and other such tales, people began to whisper that Ibn Battutah was a liar . . . ' In the end, no less an advocate than the Moroccan grand vizier defended IB on the grounds that 'one should never dismiss acounts of other lands merely because one has not visited them'. But if IB was acquitted, it was on lack of evidence. The accusations left a nasty taste.

The taste was to linger a long time. It was still repeating as late as the eighteenth century, and just as nastily. 'I met certain Indian scholars in Jerusalem and Mecca,' wrote the Moroccan geographer al-Ziyani in the introduction to his *magnum opus*, 'and recounted to them [some of the Indian] passages from the *Travels* of Ibn Battutah. They denied the truth of most of what he had to say about their [former] rulers. As for the matters of the author's having served as a judge in India and of his relationship by marriage to its sultan, they dismissed them entirely, saying that they were an impossibility. On account of this I have quoted not a single word of Ibn Battutah's narrative.' Al-Ziyani broke his promise: in the body of his text he quoted without acknowledgement a whole page of IB's *Travels*.

Those Indian 'scholars' must have been pretty shoddy. Nearly everything IB has to say on India – the catapulting of money-bags included – is confirmed by contemporary Indian sources. If al-Ziyani had bothered to read the *Travels* properly, he would have known that IB's sultanic in-law was not the ruler of India, that is the Delhi Sultan, but a member of a break-away Muslim dynasty in the far south. And for IB to have claimed falsely that he spent seven years as a judge in the capital would have been credibility suicide. His English coeval Sir John Mandeville had, in his own richly imagined India, 'an Opportunity of showing his Parts without incurring any Danger of being examined or contradicted'; but IB knew that, in a world networked by Muslim scholars and adventurers, someone would turn up from Delhi sooner or later and call his bluff. Not only would his parts have been minutely examined; he would also have been mercilessly debagged and utterly debunked.

All the same, some of IB's more subjective Indian passages had me scratching my head, and not only that apparent mirage of mountains on the plain. There were levitating yogis, cannibal witches and weretigers; fair enough in that part of the world in which God, according to an old saying of the Arabs, placed nine-tenths of the world's wonders. But there were also pieces of reportage – most notably the 'Account of the Indians who burn themselves to death' – remembered, years later, with the shocking vividness of a video diary. The totality of recall was, to my mind, more than miraculous.

IB himself anticipated a grilling. Speaking of Sultan Muhammad Shah – who, as a Wonder of India, indeed the Stupor Mundi of his age, outdid mere witches or were-tigers – he said: 'I am aware that many people's minds will be unable to comprehend some of the facts I shall relate about him, and that they will consider what I have to say to be quite impossible. Yet concerning what I have witnessed at first hand and know to be indisputable, having myself had a large share in it, I can speak nothing but the truth.' But truth is the creature of memory. IB was writing about India over a decade after leaving it. His notes were lost in that final calamity, the pirate attack. Homers, homespun or not, sometimes nod. How much of IB's topography of that dark, greenish and distant land was grounded in objective reality, and how much reimagined – or dreamed up? This is what I wanted to find out.

Reading IB, and travelling with him, I often recalled a comment with which an earlier wanderer, al-Harawi, had set out on his own book. Like IB he had lost his travel diaries – some in a shipwreck off Sicily, the rest in Palestine to, of all people, Richard the Lionheart. Many details of the lands he had seen, al-Harawi confessed, had slipped his memory; yet, he went on, no one could begin to emulate what he had written – or only 'a man who tramped about the earth and confirmed with heart and pen what I have said'.

I knew that to confirm what IB had said – or to reject it – would not be easy. The late Professor Beckingham, IB's English co-translator, visited a few of the more accessible Battutian sites in India a generation ago. 'I came back', he remembered, 'with far more problems than I started with.' Even allowing for the fact that he was never exactly chatty in his footnotes (unlike Polo's translator Yule, a footnote fetishist who could natter on for pages over a single gloss, and who even wrote footnotes to his endnotes), one would never guess from Beckingham's annotations to IB that he had travelled much beyond a library catalogue. But at least he had tried. Mahdi Husain, the main Indian Battutophile, had followed the *Travels* in the comfort of his professorial chair. I had 2,500 miles of India to tramp about – a subcontinent of problems – and couldn't wait to get going.

*

Sanjeeda's fixed timetable had come unstuck. The replacement mast seemed to have been demoted from purgatory to limbo; one of the crew had broken his ankle jumping ashore and also had to be replaced; *Sanjeeda* herself continued to demand fittings and furbelows. For a ship supposed to be leaving on her maiden voyage, she was being annoyingly coy about her virginity.

One evening, Anderson came to supper. While we were eating, the phone rang. I answered. It was Francine, Anderson's wife, calling from England for an update on progress. 'You see, I just haven't been able to get anything out of him.'

'Well, he was talking about sailing at the end of last month. Then on the fifth at the latest – oh, that's today. And he might have said something about the twelfth. But . . . he's right here, if you want a word.' I mouthed 'Francine' at the dinner table. Anderson smiled, but didn't move.

There was a pause at the end of the line. 'When do *you* think you'll get to Mangalore?'

'God knows. Anderson says everything's, er, fluid.'

'The thing about Francine', Anderson said, when I put the receiver down, 'is that she's just not on Dhow Time.'

*

Dhow Time offered ample scope for exploring the United Arab Emirates, which is what IB would have done in my position. Despite galloping burgerization, each emirate had its own peculiar if sometimes subliminal character.

Sharjah, my temporary home, was the Strict Emirate. No booze, no bacon, no fornication and – if some of the expats were to be believed – lashings of corporal punishment for the naughty. One evening Jay and I drove downtown to play bridge at the Café l'Amore. Over an uneventful rubber we fell to discussing the penal system.

'So how would they punish someone who was into being whipped?'

'By *not* whipping him, of course. They'd just give him a tickle with the cane.'

'Don't you think he'd deliberately not own up to his kink, just so he'd get beaten?'

'But then he wouldn't have got caught in the first place . . .'

The paradoxical branches extended, until someone bid six no trumps.

The character of neighbouring Ajman was harder to define. It seemed to exist partly to absorb the overspill population from Sharjah, which in turn soaked up the Dubai overspill; and partly to sell liquor to the drinkers of north-eastern Sharjah, who live inconveniently far from the bars of Dubai. To the Indians who run Ajman's most celebrated off-licence, a hole-in-the-wall by the creek across from *Sanjeeda*'s mooring at Al Boom Marine, life is a long and lucrative happy hour. The ruler of Sharjah must feel like an Islamic Canute, inundated from both sides by a tide of alcohol.

Next-door Umm al-Qaiwain tends to be mentioned by the expats, if at all, with an epithet – 'blink and you'll miss it'. It is undeniably small: one can drive across it in under five minutes. But I was fascinated by its name, which ought roughly to mean 'Mother of

Emetics'. Finding myself one day in the lagoonside office of Lieutenant Sultan of the Umm al-Qaiwain Traffic Police, a man of philological bent, I brought the matter up. 'They've tried to make the name derive from *quwwah* [power],' he said. 'But I'm afraid you're probably right, and it comes from *qayw*' [frequent and intense vomiting].' The reason, apparently, is that the original settlement shared an island in the lagoon with a colony of Socotra cormorants, the biggest such nesting-site in the world, and the smelliest. So bad was the stink that visitors regularly puked on arrival.

Despite – or perhaps because of – its reputation, Umm al-Qaiwain has a quiet charm lacking in its bigger neighbours. Peeling bungalows and stumpy watchtowers overlook deserted beaches, and Lieutenant Sultan is rarely disturbed by anything more heinous than a broken brakelight. But the best thing about it may be seen outside the ruler's palace. Jay and I entered the long drive that leads to the palace gate, and found it flanked by a guard of honour – elephants and aeroplanes, dachshunds and dinosaurs, giraffes and gerfalcons, all done in topiary and interposed with live but listless gazelles. The curious phalanx was the worse for wear, with here a balding brontosaur, there a shaggy aircraft, and all in a parched and uniform khaki.

To my surprise one of the bird-shaped bushes began to walk. What I had taken for a more recent planting, half-grown and untrimmed, had a real and very beady eye. Keeping this on me, the bush sidled away and tried to hide behind a rhinoceros. As it did so I saw what it was. Since that moment Umm al-Qaiwain has been, for me, not the Emetic, but the Emu Emirate.

We visited all seven of the little states, even whizzed – I think – through Khawr Fakkan and Kalba, the two Emirati places mentioned by IB. He had nothing to say about them either.

*

One evening Jay took me to the Dubai branch of Ikea, where she wanted to buy a wine rack. ('But you don't drink.' 'It's to keep shoes in, not bottles.' 'Then you'll have to label it "Château La Feet".') 'Prepare to have your mind blown,' she warned, as we drove into the intestines of Deira City Centre, mother of all malls.

We emerged on foot into a cool and brightly lit gallery. It stretched away into the distance, disclosing a succession of familiar names: Woolworths, Debenhams, Virgin Records, Body Shop, Monsoon,

Benetton, Next. Each was of megastore proportions. The mall was busy but strangely hushed. 'You should see it at the weekend, on Thursday nights,' Jay said. 'Then it gets really hectic.' Deira City Centre already seemed to contain the official population of Dubai, all behaving with the utmost reserve. I couldn't picture freezer-cabinet frenzy or checkout chicanery here, let alone trolley-rage, even in the fever of a Thursday night. Something about this spectacle of vast and patient consumption reminded me of the humungous fungus recently discovered beneath a wood somewhere in the United States. It is more than a mile across, inedible and apparently the largest living organism on earth. The statistic is mildly astonishing; but, unless you are a mycologist, the thing that generated it is rather dull.

My mind was not blown but numbed. The pungent smells, the plangent cries, the colour, the clamour, the smoky, dusty chiaroscuro of the *suq* had no place here. I should have known: wherever the burger goes the bourgeois are sure to follow. On and on, until they have gobbled the gazetteer from Aabenraa to Zyryanovsk, until the whole round world is as soft and bland as a sesame bun.

IB would have loved Deira City Centre. He had a deeply bourgeois side and could be very old-fashioned about bazaar smells and rowdy shoppers. He would have warmed equally to the mosques of Dubai. Most of them seem to be sited for the convenience of the motor-car, at roundabouts – roadhouses of prayer; but they are almost uniformly inspired, like Victorian churches, by IB's own fourteenth century. He might also have recognized, in the giddy vertical acres of mirror glass that form the Dubai cityscape, some other familiar touches – an *iwan* vault, for example, stretched to ten storeys and framing the atrium of a skyscraper on Shaikh Zayed Road. With its Gotham City-Saracenic vistas and Mamluk Revival mosques, IB would certainly identify Dubai as Islamic. But I doubted whether he would realize that it was an Arab city. To be sure, it is covered in Arabic; and yet, as I found on my arrival, the script only served to render even more incomprehensible an already nonsensical globobabble.

Take, as a further example, the University of Wlwnghwngh. What would IB have made of that? *Wlwnghwngh* . . . the last utterance of a drowning man? I tried supplying on IB's behalf the vowels necessary to make sense of Arabic writing, and could do no better than *wa law naghnagh* – 'even if he had an affliction in the region of his uvula'. The Latin version revealed – I should have guessed, what with the Shaykh of Umm al-Qaiwain's emu – that it was a branch of the University of Wollongong.

The paradox was that in order to be 'authentic' – to sail to India on a dhow – I had ended up in this *trompe l'oeil* city of conundrums and mirrored towers, where two-thirds of the inhabitants – the foreigners – and all of the culture were in transit; where the current excitement was the fake submarine which conveyed diners to an underwater restaurant in the new, *seven*-star hotel. *Sanjeeda* may have been an anachronism, but she was no fake.

The problem was Dhow Time. That new departure date, the twelfth, slipped its moorings and drifted away. The Kutchi master insisted we could sail only on certain auspicious days. To me, the Einsteinian observer, Dubai and *Sanjeeda* represented the extremes of flow-rate in the ever-rolling stream: the one a shallow rapid, littered with junk; the other a pool – beautiful, and unfathomably still.

*

An auspicious day slid by. As if to cock a snook at *Sanjeeda*'s authenticity, they were churning out plastic dhows beside her on the quay at Al Boom Marine: take the hull of an old wooden *sambuq*, make a mould around it, press into this fibreglass sheets, extract, drop in an engine and off you go. It was more like pastrymaking than shipbuilding.

*

At last *Sanjeeda* was at the spit-and-polish stage. Another auspicious day was approaching, and we were heading back to Ajman Creek after anchor tests when the captain dropped a bombshell. I had asked him if fourteen days to Mangalore was still feasible in view of *Sanjeeda*'s proven top speed of about four knots. 'Mangalore?' He seemed surprised. 'I don't think we're going to Mangalore. At any rate not to begin with. We'll stop for a few days on the way to Muscat, then spend a week or two there in case we need to make adjustments and so on. Then another couple of weeks to Minicoy . . . potter round the Laccadives for a month or so . . . diving possibilities . . .'

I had stopped taking it in at Minicoy, the Indian Ultima Thule.

Dhow Time had nothing to do with clocks, or even with relativity. It ran on the warped logic of Zeno's First Paradox: before you can get somewhere, you must cover half the distance, and before you can cover the half, you must cover half of the half . . . and so on, *ad infinitesimum*. Result: you're stuck.

*

Sharjah quay looked promising, a line of workaday *sambuqs* moored beside piles of crates, bundles and sacks. Most of them were in the trans-Gulf trade with Iran, but I'd heard I might be able to hitch a ride to Malabar, or somewhere Indian. A sign on a quayside building gave my hopes a lift: IBN BATTOUTA BLDG. CONT. & SHIPPING CO. I was puzzled that IB should have lent his name to bldg. cont., but it was a good omen.

The office was on the third floor behind a locked door. My knock was answered by a hollow echo from within; and, after a pause, by an unshaven man of surprised and Levantine appearance, his eyes skew-whiff with sleep. What I could make out of the office was furnished with deep-pile gloom and a doss-house reek of unwashed bodies. IBN BATTOUTA, the man said, had moved. It was a bad omen.

Next morning I was awakened by a soft but urgent voice: 'Stop faffing about. It isn't decreed. Get on a bloody plane.' The voice was in my head, but it sounded eminently sane. It took less than five minutes to ring a travel agent and book a seat.

*

It crossed my mind as we entered the dark and greenish airspace of urban Delhi that, if sailing authentically to Malabar had been a dream, by flying to India and fulfilling IB's dream I was being the very Heyerdahl of authenticity; that IB had perhaps been dreaming of me – was indeed, according to the metaphysics of his time, travelling with me now. But by the same argument so too were Uncle Tom Cobbleigh, the world and his wife, and the entire created cosmos past, present and future (and I was wondering why the cashews had run out so quickly). IB, and the live travelling companion who – if it was decreed – would be waiting for me below, were enough to be going on with.

(*Sanjeeda*, Anderson tells me, eventually reached Mangalore – via Musandam, Muscat, Minicoy and a lackadaisical voyage around the Laccadives – seven months after her original expected date of arrival. She sailed, of course, like a dream. McDonalds, Jay says, have recently added to their product-range an item inspired by local cuisine – not sharkburgers or deep-fried sheep's eyes but grilled *kofta* and salad in pitta pockets. It is called a 'McArabia'. We all try to be authentic.*)

---

* As this goes to press, I see in the latest edition of *Emirates Home* magazine that a company called Marketing Themed Environments is building a new shopping mall in Dubai designed around the travels of IB. It incorporates six 'zones' – fourteenth-century Morocco, Andalusia, Egypt, Persia, India and China, all under one roof. The old Tangerine would have been tickled pink.

Hindustan

After long and rigorous vetting at the border, IB was given permission to proceed to Delhi. He arrived there in the spring of 1334.

Delhi had become the seat of a Muslim sultanate in 1210. Although not blessed by longevity – in a century and a quarter there had been four dynasties and sixteen rulers – the Delhi Sultans had managed to conquer wide swathes of India, penetrating deep into Bengal and Tamil Nadu. But their control of the more distant regions was precarious and in 1326, intending to strengthen his hold on the southern provinces, Muhammad Shah had moved his administration down to the Deccan. Delhi remained the military centre. The impracticality of having two capitals 700 miles apart soon became apparent, and by the time of IB's arrival the civil service had returned to Delhi. To the traveller's delight, Muhammad Shah offered him a plum post – as one of the four qadis, or judges, of Delhi.

IB's duties were not onerous. He was to spend much of the following seven years observing court life, which revolved around the great audience chamber built by Muhammad Shah – the Hall of a Thousand Columns. The Hall was to be my goal in Delhi.

A Rank Above the Sun

'In every particle of dust you see about you,
You see so many Solomons brought by the wind.'

Yahya ibn Ahmad Sirhindi, *Tarikh-i Mubarak Shahi*

'B EN HUR,' said Martin, looking around us at the massed cohorts of autorickshaws, 'with a cast of millions.' The lights changed, Martin clutched his painting box, and we were off.

Titoo, our auto driver, was no Charlton Heston and his frail chariot was soon the filling of a traffic-jam sandwich between two thick layers of bus. The nearside one aimed a dense particulate fart into the back seat of the auto. We cursed Herr Diesel and all his works.

Delhi was a relief after the over-bright, anodyne Emirates. With its grainy air and gritty light, it was *cinéma vérité*; the Gulf was a computer-generated backdrop to Globopoly, a video-age version of Monopoly. Here people made things and mess and noise; there, money, yes, but not much else. Apart from that constant whirl of cash the Gulf remained for me a silent place, its only dialect the dollar. Delhi spoke to me from the start, in a grim and pungent koine; even the public information signs – 'Delhi Roads, Deadly Roads. Happy New Year!'

Titoo had also been in the Gulf, working for a jeweller in Dubai. 'It was OK,' he said. 'But after six months my Mummy said, "Come home. Sleep in your bed."' He seemed to have few regrets. His present occupation was as kind on the lungs and the nerves as a Hun gas attack. But his disposition suited it: buses to the right of him, lorries to the left of him, volleying and thundering, he proceeded at a relentless invalid-carriage pace, while the top-knot of his undress turban nodded in time to a succession of cheerful Punjabi ditties.

Even when we turned off the Outer Ring Road and straight into a small lake of sewage, his equanimity was unruffled. 'This', he announced, looking at the effluent, 'is the real India.' I knew what Mummy meant. The Gulf could never be home.

Titoo, flagged down by chance, seemed at first sight to possess the animal spirits – and, in his pudding-cloth headgear, something of the appearance – of a plum duff. But he had recommended himself by his air of solid Sikh dependability, his English, and an averred interest in the pre-Mughal monuments of Delhi. We hired him for a day of orientation, and so far he hadn't disappointed. Indeed, our first sight of the Sultanate city was about as far removed as one could get from the world of the Mughals and their architecture of petrified doilies.

It was a small truncated tower, a castaway in a sea of apartment blocks. I had at first taken it for a dovecote as it was pierced all over with little holes. The holes, however, were blind. Sockets for scaffolding? A plaque put up by the Archaeological Survey of India explained: the building, the Chor Minar or Tower of Thieves, was built to display the severed heads of criminals. By day it must have been a gruesome sight, studded with blackened, shrivelling faces like cloves in a pomander. But at night it would have been enchanting. I recalled reading about a Tatar tower of heads, twinkling in the dark with the phosphorescence of putrefaction, and imagined the effect of this one – glow-worms in a bush, or fairy-lights on a Christmas tree.

The tower had been an unusual appetizer to IB's Delhi; not at all to his taste, judging by his queasy reaction to a rack of well-hung traitors back on the border, but with something of the flavour of the age. Now, though, we were heading for the heart of the Battutian city: Hazar Sutun, the Hall of a Thousand Columns.

*

It was in the Thousand-Column Hall, in the summer of 1334, that IB came face to face with his destiny. 'In India you will stay for a long time,' al-Murshidi the sainted chef had told him, interpreting the dream in the Nile Delta nearly a decade and some 15,000 miles earlier. And so he did: for seven years, IB's life revolved around this building, his fellow-inmates there – chamberlains and flunkeys, Parasol-Bearers and Masters of the Pan-Box, a whole menagerie of panegyrists, poetasters and parasites from across the Arabo-Perso-Turkic world – and around the eccentric ringmaster of the courtly circus, Sultan Muhammad Shah ibn Tughluq. 'There are certain world wanderers', the Indian poet-historian Isami observed some years later, 'who ramble the earth, neither fixing their hearts on any country nor settling for even a month in any city. But when they arrive at last in the land of Hindustan, they abandon their wanderings and settle down.' It might be a description of IB; and since the poet may have come across the traveller there is every possibility that it is.

IB had not just turned over a new leaf in his *Travels*. Back on the border he had literally opened a new book. 'In the name of God, the Compassionate, the Merciful . . . On the day when the new moon of the holy month of Muharram appeared, marking the start of the year 734, we arrived at the valley of the Indus.' The bank of the river and the threshold of a new lunar year were also a geographical and literary boundary. With that *bismillah*, 'in the name of God', he set out on his second *sifr*, or volume.* And on the far side of the river began al-Hind, India.

---

* Not *safar*, 'journey', as his English translator Gibb read the word; although you might say that for a travel writer the distinction is theoretical.

The first thing IB did at the border was to buy a good supply of horses, camels and slaves. These he added to other livestock – he mentions thirty horses alone – and a camel-load of arrows bought on the road at Ghaznah in eastern Afghanistan. This may seem a strange course of action for someone nearing the end of a journey. Stranger still, his purchases were a present for Muhammad Shah – who, as ruler of all but a few corners of a subcontinent, was hardly short of a *tangah* or two. It was not, however, the thought that counted. It was the arithmetic. 'It is the rule that every man entering the sultan's presence for the first time must present him in person with a gift, so as to gain his favour. The sultan then gives the new arrival a far more valuable present.' So far, on his pinball progress around the princely courts of Asia, IB hadn't exactly done badly in the matter of hospitality gifts; but the freebies he had picked up were in the order of the odd thousand gold dinars or the occasional fur coat or slave. Delhi was the big score. Rumours circulated about a ruler whose household included 1,000 poets, 2,000 musicians, 3,000 elephants, 10,000 falconers. Along the way IB himself had heard tales of the mad munificence of Muhammad Shah: of a visitor literally showered with gold, another given his weight in bullion, a third who had the run of the treasury and passed out under a pile of moneybags.

It took IB a long time to get from the Indus to the end of the rainbow in Delhi. He first swanned around on the river, then dawdled for two months on the border awaiting permission to proceed (his thorough vetting by the sultan's secret police was an early hint that the sugar-daddy of Delhi had a sinister side). For several pages he explored Indian botany and digressed on the burning of widows. He travelled cursorily to the capital and diligently around its sights. Then, in what may well be the longest sidetrack in travel literature – well over a hundred pages in the English translation and as many years of history – he ambled through the annals of the Delhi Sultanate. Publishers today would grind their teeth and tell him to get a decent editor. But travel in IB's day was a Gladstone-bag genre, a bran-tub of ographies; his book is rife with kings, and if it omits cabbages it does pretty well with other members of the fruit and veg genera. And although to twenty-first-century tastes so solid a lump of sultans is indigestible, IB knew it would plug a gaping hole: the near-total lack of knowledge in the old Islamic lands about the richest and fastest-growing Muslim empire in the world.

*

The Arab geographer of IB's day had few titles on the India shelf of his library: perhaps the ninth-century opuscules on the further East by Sulayman the Merchant and Abu Zayd of Siraf; more likely al-Mas'udi's *Plains of Gold*, the slightly later work of the Arab Herodotus. He might even have owned a copy of the *Wonders of India* of Captain Buzurg of Ramhurmuz – although he would no doubt have agreed with that arbiter of bookish taste, al-Jahiz, that 'sailors are not renowned as respecters of the unvarnished truth. The stranger a story, the more they like it; and moreover they use vulgar expressions and have an atrocious style.'* To be fair on the captain, islands of fact float among the spume of sensation; and, *pace* al-Jahiz, his book is an undeniably good read – unlike that of al-Biruni, by far the greatest Arabic authority on India.

Early in the eleventh century, when that not famously enlightened despot, Mahmud of Ghaznah, was planning one of his seventeen raids on the Subcontinent, it occurred to him to take a team of scholars along to record the manners and customs of its people. (The combination of bloodshed and fieldwork is rare in world history. Napoleon's expedition to Egypt, accompanied by a corps of *savants*, is one of the few comparable examples.) Al-Biruni was picked for the team; and while, as he puts it, 'Mahmud utterly ruined the prosperity of the country, and performed there wonderful exploits, by which the Hindus became like atoms of dust scattered in all directions,' al-Biruni examined the exploding civilization of the Brahmans with microscopic attention. Until the nineteenth century no other outsider would rival his knowledge of classical Sanskrit culture and science. The presentation of this knowledge is, however, as dry as that Brahmanical dust. Even if he had got hold of a copy, what would

---

* As a spinner of yarns Captain Buzurg far outdid Captain Sindbad (several of whose adventures are lifted from the *Wonders*). There are not merely rocs, giants and cannibals aplenty, but also the mass suicide of a king and 2,000 courtiers because of the death of a parrot, and a breathless assertion that the vaginal labia of the ladies of Kannauj, a city on the Ganges, are muscular enough to crack areca nuts. '*L'anecdote*,' commented Buzurg's nineteenth-century editor on this last matter, in an equally breathless note, '*est aussi connue dans quelques pays occidentaux, p.e. dans le Nord de la France, (où l'on nomme de telles femmes casse-noisette) et dans la province Néerlandaise du Brabant septentrional*.'

our geographer have made of such chapters – there are eighty of them – as 'An Explanation of the Terms "Adhimāsa", "Ūnarātra", and the "Ahargaṇas", as Representing Different Sums of Days'?

After this blinding indological flash the Arabic-reading world was left in the dark for the next 300 years. Geographers simply regurgitated old information. IB therefore, in his genre-bending account of the Delhi Sultanate, was scooping an exclusive and immortalizing himself as an India hand – he is one of the inner circle of authorities for *Hobson-Jobson*, and cited there no fewer than 130 times.

*

Then, suddenly, the historian bows out and the traveller returns with an 'Account of our coming to the sultan's palace'. The sultan was off hunting, so IB paid his anticlimactic respects to an empty throne and then at the gate of the sultana-mother's palace. Finally, however, on 8 June 1334, came the audience with Muhammad Shah. After the customary obeisance, the sultan clasped the traveller's hand and welcomed him affably in Persian. 'Whenever he said some kind word to me I kissed his hand,' IB remembered, 'until I had kissed it seven times.'*

Muhammad was nothing if not welcoming. 'There is in all my realm no greater boon than this city of mine,' he told IB at their next meeting, 'and I give it to you.' The offer was not to be taken literally. But when he invited IB to take up the post of Maliki Judge of Delhi, on a salary of 12,000 silver dinars, the sultan wasn't joking. For the 30-year-old newcomer from 5,000 miles away and a worthy but undistinguished background, Muhammad's legendary xenophilia had suddenly become fact, and it had all been as easy as kiss-my-hand. Only one thing marred IB's excitement – a boil, he admits with characteristic bathos, on the bum.

The appointment did however turn out to be a joke in another sense. Quite apart from the fact that IB's lack of higher legal training made him at best questionably qualified to judge the Malikis of Delhi – that is, adherents of the same school of Islamic law as himself – he only had survival Persian, the language of administration. Luckily

---

* 'Show no humility to earthly lords,' warned the wise traveller Ibn Jubayr,

> They're drunk enough on their own majesty;
> Nor stoop to kiss a prince's hand, for such
> An act is equal to idolatry.

there were very few Malikis in Delhi to begin with, and they must have been a law-abiding and illitigious lot: IB doesn't mention hearing a single case in his entire seven years in the city.

On Muhammad's side, the appointment looks like a sultanic whim. In fact, it was part of a deliberate policy of ethnic engineering. A sultan is neither appointed by the people nor anointed by God. His throne is held up by main force, money and whatever magnetism he can exert on his peers. In this respect Muhammad Shah Tughluq was no different from Ahmad Shah Mas'ud or the other latter-day warlords of Afghanistan. As a Muslim ruler of the time, any deeper legitimacy he enjoyed came from the pious men, those 'pillars of the palace of truth', whom he could attract to his court. Pious and, for Muhammad, preferably foreign: his father had become sultan in a counter-coup against native Indian converts to Islam and Muhammad, who had been caught up in the bloody events, was suspicious of home-grown Muslims. The result was a massive recruitment drive. Some drained brains, like IB, turned up on spec. Others were head-hunted: later, in the port of Calicut, IB saw a ship of the sultan's about to sail for the Gulf 'to enlist as many Arabs as possible'. Writing of an earlier reign, Isami said that Arabs and those of other races crowded into Delhi 'like moths to a candle'. The candlepower was now vastly magnified. And, like moths, not a few of the immigrants got nastily burned.

*

I hadn't imagined it would be hard to find the Hall of a Thousand Columns, but despite his promising start Titoo had to ask the way several times. To be fair, Delhi was confusing even in the fourteenth century. IB listed four separate cities: the original Dihli or Dehli, a persianized version of the Sanskrit Dilli ('Delhi' is a nineteenth-century slip which took root; to reform the spelling would mean making a choice with huge political and communal implications, so the capital remains a typographical error); the adjoining cities of Siri and Jahanpanah, the latter founded in 1325 by IB's sultan, Muhammad Shah; and Tughluqabad, three miles to the east. Since the fourteenth century a further four avatars of the city have appeared on the plain between the Ridge and the River Yamuna. They culminate in the New Delhi of the British – more accurately Newest Delhi. On top of all this, an expanding population – now at least

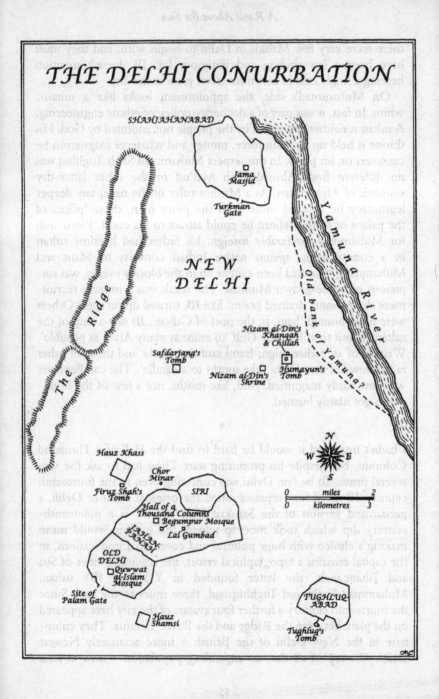

THE DELHI CONURBATION

SHAHJAHANABAD

Jama Masjid

Turkman Gate

Yamuna River

The Ridge

NEW DELHI

Old bank of Yamuna?

Nizam al-Din's Khanqah & Chillah

Safdarjang's Tomb

Nizam al-Din's Shrine

Humayun's Tomb

N

Hauz Khass

Chor Minar

Firuz Shah's Tomb

SIRI

Hall of a Thousand Columns

Begumpur Mosque

Lal Gumbad

JAHAN PANAH

OLD DELHI

Quwwat al-Islam Mosque

Site of Palam Gate

Hauz Shamsi

TUGHLUQABAD

Tughluq's Tomb

0   miles   2

0   kilometres   3

14 million and rising fast – has not only filled in the gaps between these disparate urban areas, but also overlaid the remnants of the older ones. Searching for IB's Delhis would be like piecing together a chapter from a history that had been disbound, flung about, then buried among the pages of later books.

At this rate it would be a very long process. Titoo was a find, but he drove as if he were running in a Bath chair with a rebore. I could sense the first vapours of despondency coming off Martin. He was here to paint, and although his choice of subjects was not always conventionally picturesque (at home he was currently working on a series of over-life-size oils based on drawings made, from astonishing angles, in an East End strip club), the part of Delhi in which we were now lost didn't inspire him. It wasn't so much concrete jungle as cement scrubland. The light was a problem too, with its carbide glow that leeched out colours and flattened forms. 'It's like looking at everything through a gauze,' he sighed.

Martin lived on form and colour, and it was India, or the Subcontinent, that had opened his eyes to them. Penniless in Pakistan back in the days of overlanding, he had survived by drawing portraits on the streets of Lahore, and awoken a sleeping genius that saw him home and into the Royal Academy Schools. I had known him half his painting life, ever since a pack of stray dogs had forced him to spend the night at my house in Yemen. It was a successful career: his most recent travelling companion in India had been the Prince of Wales. And here he was with me, in an autorickshaw in suburban south Delhi, navigating a pool of sewage.

Back on terra firma, Titoo forgot himself and almost reached the velocity of a Sinclair C5. We had covered a heroic half mile or so when Martin and I exclaimed together, 'Stop!' Titoo had almost driven past an extraordinary sight: on our left, out of a dusty wasteground behind a fence, rose a giant cube; out of this rose a dome shaped like half of a giant rugby ball. The sides of the cube sloped inwards. It was as if the building hadn't quite decided whether it wanted to be a pyramid or an obelisk when it grew up, then had suddenly changed its mind and tried to lay an egg.

Titoo was as surprised by the building as we were, and didn't know what it was. I did. I had seen a photograph of it, and knew it to be our first proper glimpse of IB's India. Some things are meant to be found, not looked for, and this was one of them.

'Funny shape,' said Martin. 'It's like one of those half-hundredweight weights that drop on people in cartoons.' He was looking at it intently, sizing it up, and I knew then that he would be happy; or at least busy, for the name of the building – Lal Gumbad, the Red Tomb – was a simplification. Pompeiian, Tuscan, ochre, terracotta, all the standard vocabulary of redness fell short of it. Even in the mid-forenoon light, pernicious as peroxide, the colours resisted bleaching and seemed to intensify the surrounding sky, as if the tomb wore a cool blue corona.

Inside, the tomb was filled with a gloom so thick that, could you have removed the building like a jelly-mould, the darkness would have stayed behind. When my eyes had adjusted I counted eight cenotaphs, empty stone sarcophagi marking shafts where the dead lay. Dust covered everything, and the only other visitors were tomb-martins that rustled and fluttered dimly on high ledges, speckling the walls with their droppings. A sudden noise, a low hiss, made me turn and – my heart skipped a beat – I was looking into a dark and cadaverous face. The apparition, straight out of M. R. James's 'The Tractate Middoth' minus a cobweb or two, grinned; then revealed himself to be the *chowkidar*, or guardian. His breath was redolent of path labs and killing bottles. 'Kabir al-Din!' he exclaimed, slapping the central tomb on the back.

This much I knew already. 'And the others?'

'Thiefs! Stealing Kabir al-Din gold. Then . . .' he indicated the other cenotaphs '. . . grapes falling. *Dishshshsh*! Thiefs dead.' He started giggling, and – when I'd worked out that a 'grape' was a grave – I joined in, delighted by the absurdity of the tale and the economy of its telling.

The *chowkidar* staggered out of the door; his giggle lingered after him, up in the shadowed concavity of the dome.

For all I knew the story of Kabir al-Din and the Seven Thieves might have been true. The dead were uninscribed, anonymous. But while the falling cenotaphs sounded like pink elephants, no one denied that the main tomb belonged to a holy man called Kabir al-Din Awliya.

The mystery of the Lal Gumbad is how the obscure Kabir al-Din ended up there. The splendour of the tomb-chamber and its location in Jahanpanah, founded as the new capital by Muhammad Shah and abandoned after his death in 1351, both point to IB's patron as the builder. And since no other mausoleum in Jahanpanah approaches it in size, even distantly, students of Sultanate architecture agree that Muhammad probably built it for himself. So how did a shadowy holy man come to usurp this mighty *post mortem* palace? The secondary sources I had looked at failed to offer a solution; only one had anything of interest to say about him – that he had lived near the tomb in an underground cell. It was only later that I learned the true identity of Kabir al-Din Awliya. As with his tomb, I was looking for something else, in a seventeenth-century *Who Was Who* of Delhi saints, when 'Kabir al-Awliya' jumped off the page. The dropped 'Din' made sense: rather than the puzzling Great One of Religion Saints, he was the Great One of the Saints; far from being obscure, he was a powerful slave-courtier of Muhammad Shah called, before he got religion, Qabul. And this Qabul had more than a walk-on part in IB's Hall of a Thousand Columns: he was both its major-domo and Keeper of the Sultanic Fly-Whisk, with the courtesy title of Malik Kabir, 'Great King'. He died, the hagiographer said, while Muhammad was still on the throne. Had the sultan laid the saint in his own royal tomb? Such a fit of generosity would tally perfectly with Muhammad's almost manically capricious character.

It was remarkable all the same, this transition from Malik Kabir to Kabir al-Awliya, from lordship temporal to a peerage among the *pirs*, or holy men; from the most gorgeous court in Islamdom to a hole in the ground. It was also rather Indian – even today, the occasional bureaucrat still ends up as an ascetic *sannyasin*. And for me it was pleasing to solve a riddle. As for the link between all this and the matter in hand, it was tenuous, except in one regard: precisely the same transition was to be attempted by IB.

That, however, was all in the future. We had been sidetracked from the Thousand Columns by a big and very red herring. I found Martin outside it, stalking angles. He thought he'd got one, and would be back the following day with easel and palette at crack of dawn. Looking at the sky, I doubted whether the Delhi dawn ever did anything as decisive as cracking.

We tried to confirm onward directions with the guardian, but he pointed at his head and said, grinning sweetly, 'Mind . . . out . . .'

'Very bad *chowkidar*,' Titoo commented primly when we were back on the road. 'He is thinner drinker.'

'You can say that again,' Martin said. 'You could see the skull under his skin.'

'I mean he is drinking paint-thinner,' Titoo elucidated. I shuddered, imagining the steady embalmment of the *chowkidar*'s innards, while Titoo dilated on the moral turpitude of solvent abuse.

*

After our initial impressions of travel in one of the most polluted cities on earth, we were beginning to enjoy the ride. On the jam-packed and choking Ring Road the auto had been a mobile gas-oven. Here in the back streets it was, Martin thought, a motorized howdah or palankeen. Titoo's valetudinarian pace had its advantages too. Martin began to take notes, as he called them, in his breast-pocket sketchbook – little pencil records of roadside movement or attitude, fluent as Mandarin brush-strokes. And I could start to make sense of the place, of this enormous metropolitan muddle in which villages were lost among new building and newer slums, in which village life – the Neanderthal-faced buffalo, the dung cakes, the tree where old men in wide white trousers sit and suck their tea and spit their *pan* – went on cheek-by-jowl with that of the bourgeoisie and the *bidon*villagers; and of how the whole lot of them were camping out in the ruins of IB's cities.

The semi-purdah of the auto made a perfect hide for drawing and watching people. There was a Sikh on a motor-scooter, passing us in a pleasing trio – turban, belly, engine casing – of bulbosities. And a strange-looking man riding pillion on a motor-cycle, wearing a stained robe and a cockeyed, cockaded tangerine turban. 'He is *nihang*,' Titoo explained. 'Sikh holy man travelling place to place.' He looked at us in the mirror. 'You know . . . Minister corruption. The country broken. But India *very* holy. *Pir*, sufi, sadhu, rishi, yogi, *nihang* all speaking the same lang . . .' We had hit another stretch of open sewer. 'I love my India!' said Titoo, with as much affection as irony.

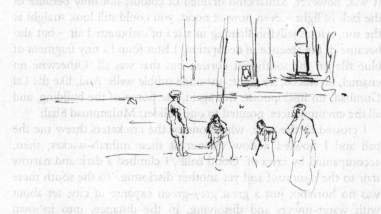

As before, a drain was the prelude to a discovery. The road began to wriggle, buildings to shrink and crowd. We were in one of those lost villages of southern Delhi, occluded by later building, ingrowing. 'This Begumpur village,' Titoo said. 'We are getting hot for Muhammad Shah.' To celebrate the fact, he indulged in a serious attempt at acceleration, showering himself with a rain of old newspapers that had been squirrelled away in the gaps above the windscreen. 'And this', he continued, pulling up at the bottom of a triumphal staircase leading to the grand frontispiece of a mosque, 'Begumpur Masjid.' Martin and I looked at each other, impressed: our confidence in Titoo's antiquarian abilities was restored.

We left him to his newspapers, climbed the stairs, passed through an antechamber – and into an explosion of space: a vast courtyard flanked by arcades and, before us, an *iwan* arch between tapering towers that formed a pylon-like portal. The Begumpur Mosque might have been transported here from Samarkand. It was empty but for a group of boys playing tennis-ball cricket. Their wicket was the mihrab, an arched niche within the portal, the mosque's sightline to Mecca.

We walked along the south arcade and into another surprise. This time it was a Gainsborough-like view across a meadow, in which a pond lay between grazing cattle and big-boled trees. I'd not experienced such dreamlike non-sequiturs of place since watching Pasolini's *Mille e Una Notte*.

I left Martin sketching the rustic vista and returned to Samarkand. It was, however, Samarkand drained of colour; not only because of the lack of light – even now, at noon, you could still look straight at the sun, a lone jellyfish floating in a sea of carburetted air – but also because of the absence of decoration. I later found a tiny fragment of blue tile on the south-east corner, but that was all. Otherwise no enamel, no stucco, no paint; just nude rubble walls. And, like the Lal Gumbad, no inscriptions. But again, the pomp of the building, and all the circumstances, pointed to one builder: Muhammad Shah.

I crossed to the *iwan*, where one of the cricketers threw me the ball and I bowled a slow spinner at their mihrab-wicket; then, accompanied by cries of 'Good ball!', I climbed a dark and narrow stair to the *iwan* roof and yet another disclosure. To the south there was no horizon; just a great grey-green expanse of city, set about with water-towers and dissolving, in the distance, into its own febrile exhalations. The same to west and east. And to the north (as I turned, a spot of colour moved down in the courtyard – a trotting dog, wearing a collar of marigolds) I saw only one object. It was an octagonal turret, slightly higher than my roof, and seeming almost close enough to touch. At its base, I knew, lay the Hall of a Thousand Columns.

*

We approached Muhammad Shah's palace through another makeshift cricket pitch, then up a tussocky bank. As we climbed, I sketched in for Martin a few of the details of this engine-room of empire – the series of gates, each with a flurry of flunkeys and marshals in caps of gold plumed with peacock feathers; the sequence of vestibules and chambers, increasing in splendour; and the climax, the Hall of a Thousand Columns, 'a vast and spacious hall . . . the pillars of which are of painted wood and support a roof also of wood, most marvellously carved'. On festival days this hypostyle forest was interplanted with silken trees, pages with gold barrels doused the assembled company with an incessant drizzle of rose-water, the Great Throne was set up – an upholstered podium the size of the Great Bed of Ware, crowned by a baldaquin, all in solid gold encrusted with gems – and the Great Cassolette was erected, a three-storey tower of gold that housed thurifers stoking fires of aloes-wood and beside which the Botafumeiro of Compostela would have shrunk to a damp squib. And coincident with the physical structure of the Hall was that of the *amirs* and *maliks* and *wazirs*, those pillars of state ranked each in his place, rigid with etiquette; of the doctors of the law, upholders of Islam; and of the shaykhs, living saints, 'the foundations of the edifice of religion and the pillars of the palace of truth, and of the Heavenly Paradise itself, who by their blessing and prayer increase the power and grandeur of the realm'. They all combined in one edifice of many storeys, an architecture material, metaphorical and mystical extending from the basement of empire to the canopy of heaven. 'If you're an IB fan,' I told Martin as we reached the top of the rise, 'this place is the Holy of Holies.'

'Not for him it isn't,' said Martin, with a nod towards the first visible feature of the Thousand-Column Hall: the bare arse, a few yards in front of us, of a man having a crap.

The man pulled up his trousers and sauntered off. Looking about, we noticed a dozen more naked backsides. Muhammad Shah's palace had become a vast and spacious al fresco public lavatory; a fact confirmed by the prevailing odours, which were not those of aloes-wood and rose-water. And no longer might one say, as did IB's contemporary Isami, that angels swept the place clean, morning and evening, with their wings: the entire site was booby-trapped with faeces. As we tiptoed through the minefield I noticed a square stone block with a round socket in the centre. 'Look . . . This must be one of the column bases. You see how the pillar slotted in? We're actually standing right in the Hall of a Thousand Columns!'

'You mean the Hall of a Thousand Turds. Look at what else you're almost standing in,' Martin said grimly, pointing next to my shoe. 'How did he do *that*? It looks just like a Danish pastry.' It did, except that the currants were moving, and buzzing.

One must hate the shit and love the shitter. In a place that's short on public conveniences there's little you can do but head for the nearest wasteground and, regardless of historical resonances or *genius loci*, drop your bags. But the consequent necessity of going about like ballerinas on points – and Martin's added hazard of being shod in commando soles, those most notorious *merd*-magnets – made it harder still to make sense of a site that was, for the most part, a three-dimensional puzzle of planes, ramps and shattered masonry. A few buildings rose above the prevailing destruction. There was a high domed octagon like a tomb-chamber – but why a tomb in a palace?; a long colon-naded room, a haunt of ancient piss, in which a courting couple were holding hands; and, abutting this, that octagonal turret, piped like a blazer in red sandstone and white marble, which I had seen from the roof of the mosque. This, the dominant feature, popularly lent its name to the whole of Muhammad Shah's palace – the Vijay Mandal, the Abode of Victory. As we looked at it a boy appeared on the parapet, unzipped himself, and micturated down the marble.

I don't know what I'd expected. Some semblance of order, I suppose, on which to project from my mind's eye the lantern slide of IB's description. But we were far from the world of ticket offices and the Taj Mahal. As in the Lal Gumbad and Begumpur Mosque there wasn't a hint of an inscription, let alone a helpful Archaeological Survey plaque. Except for that column base I was quite without bearings. Martin had seen enough; I resolved to return and have a crack at the palatial puzzle – no one, as far as I knew, had solved it with any degree of certainty – *Travels* in hand, undeterred by the turd.

*

The dingy light and dunghill palace had left us in a brown study. Martin's mind, I guessed, was on the Red Tomb, or those far and paintable pavilions of the Mughals. Mine was occupied by the darker tableau that had unrolled before IB, and finally enwrapped him, there in the Thousand-Column Hall; and by the feeling that something of the darkness still clung to the place . . . 'You know . . .' said Martin, eliding with my thoughts, 'I'd be happy never to see your palace again.'

We reconnoitred a couple more monuments and ended up at Tughluqabad, the brand-new metropolis founded in 1320 by Muhammad's father, Tughluq, and abandoned four years later ('So it lasted longer than the Millennium Dome,' Martin said). I pointed out Tughluq's tomb, where in 1324 his son laid him tenderly to rest after murdering him in an imploding pavilion operated by elephants – and, it should be noted, in the smoothest transfer of power in the Sultanate's 110-year history. The mausoleum was connected to the deserted city by a long narrow causeway of stone ('Remember the house up the path in *Psycho*?' Martin asked).

Titoo decided that we all needed cheering up. 'I now giving you very special food, famous in Punjab.' Our stately northward progress, back into the thickening traffic and atmosphere, was disturbed only by a small swerve when Titoo forsook the handlebars to offer two-handed homage to a passing temple. 'Guru Nanaksar Gurdwara,' he explained. 'Very holy.' Further on, I noticed Martin looking long-ingly at a garlic-headed dome that rose above trees to the left of the road. 'Oh, that's only . . . Safdarjang's Tomb,' I said, reading the board at the entrance. 'Really late. Totally decadent. You know, real Brighton Pavilion stuff.' I knew it was only a matter of time before I lost Martin to the Mughals.

We eventually stopped at a roadside stall topped by a row of pails. The stallholder ladled out a mixture of their contents and handed us each a plateful of multicoloured semisolids containing unidentifiable lumps. I was hungry and had already swallowed a couple of spoon-fuls when I heard Martin saying something that sounded like 'Wlwnghwngh'. It was only then that the flavour of Titoo's Punjabi special hit home. I am not a coward. I have eaten raw goat kidneys, warm from the body, and fricasséed bulls' rectums, and crispy deep-fried locusts, and eaten them all with relish. This was different. Any one of its flavours and constituents – trifle, baked beans, potato crisps, curry powder; a *soupçon* of Vimto? – would have been innocuous on its own. It was the mixture of all these, and several others we never agreed on, all held in mucillaginous suspension by extra-cheesy yoghurt, that made the stuff incomprehensible and inedible. It was like trying to down a bag of Bertie Bott's Every-Flavour Beans in one go. Guiltily, we both returned our full plates.

'You are not liking?' asked Titoo, scraping his own plate clean and looking crestfallen. 'It is very special Punjabi food. Famous also in Southall.'

'Oh no, no, it's not that,' I said. 'It's just . . .' I looked at Martin, but he remained queasily silent.

Back in the auto it struck me that, while my slender reading on contemporary India had prepared me – via frequent culinary metaphors that told of a land highly spiced, a *masala* mix of experiences, a *vindaloo*, indeed, of variety – for some pungent juxtapositions,

I hadn't expected the mixture to be quite so much like Titoo's treat. Sewage and serendipity, chic and shit, hovels and palaces, Gainsborough and Samarkand, all cohabited with abandon. Our guest-house near the Little Angles Nursery School was a paragon of gentility where the waiters, given the chance, cracked your eggs for you; and yet across the road was a wall that might well have got into *Guinness* as the longest and most popular urinal on the planet. This in turn was punctuated by a *dhaba* universally agreed to serve the finest butter chicken in the capital and, bang next to that, a shanty settlement of eye-stretching poverty. For me, accustomed to the order of Islamic lands, our day with Titoo had been a disorientation tour. A comment of al-Biruni's – almost the opening sentence of his book – came to mind: 'The reader must always remember that the Indians entirely differ from us in every respect, many a subject appearing intricate and obscure which would be perfectly clear if there were more connection between us.' I had to connect; but the fact that al-Biruni had spent the next 700 pages deepening the obscurity didn't bode well for the process.

*

That night I read Martin a bedtime story – IB's account of Shaykh Shihab al-Din. The shaykh was a Sufi holy man of illustrious ancestry and high erudition, and much revered by earlier sultans. Muhammad Shah offered him a position at court. The shaykh, who like most pious Sufis kept aloof from worldly affairs, refused; whereupon Muhammad, to general astonishment, had his beard plucked out and banished him. Towards the end of IB's time in Delhi the dissident was rehabilitated and returned to the neighbourhood of the capital, where he went underground, literally, in a subterranean house – probably an early version of the cellar-salons that became the height of cool in Mughal times. Again the sultan offered him high office; again he refused, adding the fatal phrase: '*I shall never serve a tyrant.*'

Most if not all of the Delhi Sultans were tyrants. But one didn't say so. Not because it was impolite to point out a defect that was, effectively, congenital; rather because to do so would be to incite revolution. The Prophet said it was incumbent on all Muslims to rise against *zalims*, tyrants – the very word Shihab al-Din had pronounced, as it were, *ex cathedra*. So imagine: for a moment, the circling planets pause, the dust mote hangs suspended in its fall, court and cosmos gape at the Master of the World, the Second Alexander, the emperor exposed – the *zalim*; for a moment nothing moves save the pillars of state, the myriad columns shuddering silently from base to capital . . . But why overpaint the old master? The rest is better told in IB's words.

'The sultan then took his sword, handed it to the Grand Qadi, and said, "Prove that I am a tyrant, and cut off my head with this sword." Shaykh Shihab al-Din replied, "Were anyone willing to bear witness to this, he would be put to death forthwith. But you yourself are aware of your own tyranny."' The shaykh was placed in irons. For fourteen days he refused all food and drink and, although he was brought each day to the Hall of a Thousand Columns and was begged to recant by the assembled doctors of the law and Sufis, he would not withdraw his words.

On the fourteenth day the sultan sent him food, but he still refused to eat, telling the messenger, 'No longer will I take sustenance in this world. Take this food of yours back to him.' When the sultan heard this, he gave orders that the shaykh be fed with five *istars* of human excrement, which is two and a half pounds by the Moroccan standard. The infidel Indians who are in charge of such tortures stretched out the shaykh on his back, opened his mouth with forceps, dissolved the excrement in water and poured it into him by force. On the following day he was brought to the house of the Grand Qadi. There the doctors of the law, Sufis and principal foreigners had gathered. They warned him of what would befall him, they begged him to recant, but he was adamant in his refusal to do so and was beheaded, God have mercy on him.

I supposed Martin would be shocked. I was surprised that he was angry; livid, in fact. 'That bastard *deserves* people pulling down their trousers and shitting on his memory! I knew there was something about that place. It's *evil*. It's a . . . visual outcrop of Hell. And I'll tell you something: IB was still terrified of him when he wrote that.'

I hadn't thought of the passage in those terms. But Martin was right, for the fall of Shaykh Shihab al-Din carried IB with it and, even fifteen years later when he was safely home, the headlong plunge – arrested, as for a waking dreamer, at the very last moment –

remained impressed on his memory as indelibly as the worst night-terrors of childhood.

★

Like the blind men of the famous Sufi parable who try to describe an elephant by touch – the one who felt its leg likened the beast to a column, another who got hold of its trunk thought the animal must resemble a large hose, he who discovered its ear made it into a leather mat – we have been groping at Muhammad Shah ibn Tughluq in the dark. At the risk of a Battutian digression we must stand back and look at this complex, self-contradictory colossus who towers over IB's Delhi and his book, blocking out the light.

Our glimpses of him so far would keep a conference of psycho-analysts busy for weeks ('Killed his father? Fed people shit? Psychotic tendency to give away money? We've got a right one here . . .'). But IB gives us much more. Of his massive monograph on the Delhi Sultans two-thirds are on Muhammad, and of this section the longest part is an account book of the sultan's good and bad deeds. Among the former, IB notes with approval Muhammad's religious ortho-doxy, and his sense of justice: a boy whom he had beaten unfairly, for instance, was offered a stick and invited to give him tit for tat, 'So the boy took the stick and gave him twenty-one blows, and I saw the sultan's cap fly off his head.' Most of the credit side, however, is taken up with acts of staggering generosity. The first of these sets the tone. A distinguished visitor, arriving at the Thousand-Column Hall on the same day as IB, received an appropriately hefty golden hello. A few days later Muhammad remarked the newcomer's absence from court. Learning that the man was feeling off-colour, he immediately sent him a get-well present of 100,000 gold *tangahs*. As the weight of the *tangah* was 175 grains, that means over a ton of coins – getting on for $12,000,000-worth at today's bullion prices; or, by the standards of the time, over 4,000 years' pay for a private soldier.

The debit column is a dismal recital of atrocities, most of them perpetrated on scholars of holy law. Get on the wrong side of the sultan, and not only might you be pinioned like a Strasbourg goose and force-fed with excrement, but also broiled on a giant griddle and basted with urine and ashes; you might instead get chopped to bits by elephants fitted with prosthetic steel tusk-extensions, or tenderized to death beneath their feet (this death-by-umbrella-stands was still meted out by the Maharaja of Baroda in the 1870s). One victim was sliced, in Gibb's felicitous translation, 'baldrickwise, that is, the head is cut off with an arm and part of the chest', dying in diagonal agony. A mere 'Off with his head!' was a mercy.

I can no more reconcile the polarities of this Manichean monarch than could IB, who epitomized him as 'fonder than any man alive of giving gifts and shedding blood'. Others, however, have gone to one extreme or other. The poet-historian Isami, whose patron was Muhammad's arch-enemy, painted the sultan in deepest horror-movie black and likened him to Dahhak, the Persian tyrant of legend who breakfasted on human brains and sported epizoic epaulettes – a live snake growing from each shoulder. In contrast the twentieth-century historian Mahdi Husain all but whitewashed him, giving his readers a touchy-feely Muhammad cruelly misunderstood by posterity. The truth is neither black nor white, nor some intermediate grey. It is a lurid chequer of violence and piety, bookishness and butchery, unimaginable power and paranoid insecurity.

Violence was no stranger to the Delhi Sultans, and never more so than in their entrances and exits. Of the sixteen rulers before Muhammad, only three died with their boots off. The Sultanate's bloody intestinal coups had involved several fratricides, one avunculi-cide and the Ortonesque murder in 1320 of Qutb al-Din Mubarak, a brutal transvestite, by his reluctant catamite. But to kill your father as Muhammad did went beyond the correct form of regime-change. During his reign, too, as we have seen, his violence continually over-stepped the mark of acceptability. Even the dead were not safe from it: zero tolerance of rebels is understandable, and to have a plotter executed prudent; to have his skin stuffed and sent on a tour of the provinces, even if questionable in taste, serves to discourage the others. But to force the plotter's widow to eat the taxidermic left-overs of her late husband as a curry was just not on.

And yet the man who committed such acts was also an accomplished calligrapher and poet, a scholar who had memorized by heart the Qur'an and *Kitab al-hidayah*, the main legal textbook of the Hanafi school; who corresponded on theological questions with the most learned doctors of the day and engaged in inter-faith seminars with pacifist Jain philosophers; who could preach a sermon on the unity of the divine that even Isami, who hated him viscerally and wrote so, had to admit was 'highly informative'.

Then again, the reach of Muhammad's authority was extraordinarily lopsided. A monarch of long marches, he led his army – moving 'like a rough sea full of crocodiles' – to win a kingdom greater than any India had known for 800 years. The edifice of empire extended for a time over most of the Subcontinent (and had a temporary outhouse in Mogadishu, where Muhammad was briefly acknowledged as sovereign). It was supported by a Stalinesque underpinning of informers and consolidated by equally dictatorial transfers of population. Of all the kings of India before or since, Muhammad came closest to the model ruler described by the poet Amir Khusraw: 'May he, enthroned at Delhi, be able to plunder the land of Coromandel and the seas with a mere movement of his eyebrow!' He was, in short, a control-freak. And yet, IB, on a diplomatic mission with a bodyguard of 1,000 horse could, as we shall see, still manage to get himself captured by rebels just eighty miles from the capital. For all its outward magnificence, the imperial edifice was jerry-built and as asymmetrical as its architect.

The historian Barani, compiling his annals in Delhi as IB was dictating his *Travels* in Fez, understood Muhammad – or rather failed to understand him – better than anyone else. He was the sultan's *nadim*, or official companion, for seventeen years, and he too was stumped by the man. 'All I can say is that God Almighty created Sultan Muhammad as one of the wonders of creation, and a correct perception of his manifold and contradictory qualities cannot be encompassed by the erudition of the learned or the wisdom of the wise.'

*

I have looked for a thread to follow through this labyrinthine character. I thought I found it; not in Barani, Isami, IB, but – quite unexpectedly, as India hardly gets a look-in there – in the *Concealed Pearls* of Ibn Hajar of Ascalon, the fourteenth-century *DNB* of the Muslim world. Quoting the biographer al-Safadi quoting the encyclopaedist al-Umari quoting a former resident of Delhi, Ibn Hajar reveals that 'Muhammad, with all the extent of his empire, was sexually impotent. This was the result of being cauterized on the loins, as a treatment for some disease, when he was a youth.' The impotent potentate: a tragic paradox, and a fitting curse on a parricide.

There are doubts about the claim. Muhammad evidently fathered a daughter while a very young man. Did the fateful moxibustion take place after she was conceived? It is certain that, thereafter, no tiny feet pattered among the Thousand Columns; or not until Muhammad's death in 1351, when his prime minister suddenly revealed the existence of an infant male heir. The child appeared out of the blue and, when the late sultan's cousin took over a month later, promptly disappeared back into it. There is a pleasing symmetry – the reign begins with the disposal of a father, and ends with the discovery of a son – but also a disturbing over-ingenuity; particularly since the helpful prime minister was – note – the very gentleman who had designed the parricidal pavilion twenty-seven years before. The instant infant smacks of rabbits and hats.

The conference of psychoanalysts would no doubt jump on Muhammad's heirlessness and use it to explain everything, especially if they were Freudians. They might have a point. But by any analysis Muhammad ought to have been insecure. His loins, whether cauterized or not, failed to produce any convincing male fruit; he had also severed himself, in cold sap, from the family tree. Moreover the tree, blighted above, axed below, had never had any roots: while all the earlier sultans of Delhi had been either close kin or – and this comes to the same thing – freed slaves of their predecessors, Muhammad's murdered sire was neither. We do not know the name of Tughluq's father or even, beyond the fact that he was vaguely Turkic, his wider origin. In an age of dynasts, Muhammad was a ruler without a dynasty. This may explain one of the most inexplicable of all his actions.

In 1340, towards the end of IB's stay in Delhi, the Master of the World handed his entire empire over to a political exile living in Upper Egypt. The new ruler of India was a scion of the Abbasid family, the ancient dynasty of Islam that stretched back through Harun al-Rashid and the palmy days of Baghdad to the Prophet's uncle. Eventually the symbols of Abbasid suzerainty condescended on Delhi. a robe of black, the dynastic colour of the House of Abbas, and a patent of investiture. By accepting them, Muhammad's poet laureate wrote, the sultan 'acknowledges his subservience to the Caliph of the World, Abu 'l-Rabi Sulayman, the celebrated imam. To him the Emperor of India – the holy warrior, Muhammad ibn Tughluq, at whose gate the King of Chin and Cathay is waiting like a Hindu coolie – makes himself servant and slave in body, heart and soul.'

It was all a nonsense. The caliphal robe came from the same outfitters who supplied the Emperor's New Clothes; the patent was as worthless as those novelty lairdships that one can buy, for a modest cheque, from a PO box in the *Private Eye* classifieds. No one had told Muhammad – or perhaps he chose to ignore the fact – that the last reigning caliph, God's Shadow on Earth, had been trampled to death in a rolled-up carpet more than eighty years before when the Mongols sacked Baghdad. One supposed Abbasid escaped the massacre and made it to Cairo, where the Mamluk sultan set him up as a puppet-caliph, to hoots of derision from the rest of the Muslim world. Since then the Mamluks had tired of their hereditary toys. Abu 'l-Rabi Sulayman, the current puppet, had got uppity and been sent packing up the Nile to Qus, the Mamluk Coventry, with no pocket money. He vented his spleen in rhymed prose:

Such as I / Live when we die. / The world's a joke / Until we croak. / Those Mamluks won't disburse / My privy purse. / They pray, 'God save His Majesty the Caliph!' / I say, 'God save My Travesty from the bailiff.' / The sultan sits enthroned in opulence; / The only wind Sulayman gets of thrones is flatulence.

As far as I know there is no record of how the 'caliph' reacted to being overlord of the richest empire in Islamdom. But if the rhymed complaint above is anything to go by, he clearly had a highly developed sense of his own ridiculousness, and may have been tickled literally to death; for he expired not long after, before the patent and robe had even arrived in Delhi. Muhammad Shah had handed Hind not to God's Shadow on Earth but to a shadow-puppet.

One could reasonably speculate that it was a bid for legitimacy by a desperately insecure ruler. But then one could speculate on Muhammad till the conversion of the Jews. IB, Barani – and the blind men of the elephant parable – saw in the speculum most clearly: Muhammad was a one-off, a chameleon, a chimera, a *hapax phainomenon*. Of all the Marvels and Wonders of IB's title, he was the strangest.

*

I awoke the following morning to an apocalyptic voice: 'Oh no. It's a total disaster.' A jumble of painting gear came into focus, and the dark shape of Martin, peering out of the window. 'Look. *Completely* overcast.'

'I'm sure it'll brighten up,' I said, as cheerily as I could at 6.30 a.m., but with no conviction.

'Oh. Do you think so?' He sounded glum. I should have said that a total eclipse was forecast. As I knew from our previous expeditions together Martin – like his namesake, Candide's travelling companion – works best when he expects the worst.

Later, he growled at me as I emerged from the bathroom. 'It's like staying in a caravanserai, listening to you hawking away in there.'

'I was only clearing my throat. Delhi pollution. And *your* turpentine fumes.'

Over breakfast, the *Times of India* improved our moods. Martin read out a report of a minor earthquake which had hit Pakistan and northern India the previous morning. It had eluded us, but not the residents of Islamabad. ' "They rushed out of their homes," ' Martin read, ' – just listen to this – "*braving the morning chill*"!'

In the auto, which sagged under the combined weight of people and painting paraphernalia, the humour of the *Times* reporter escaped Titoo. 'I think these Islamabad men very stupid. My Daddy always saying, "Never, never run in earthquake. If running, problems in knees until dying day." '

By the time we reached the Lal Gumbad the light had intensified by the merest millimetric turn of the celestial dimmer-switch; but the tomb, seen through a smoky mist, glowed as before, like a pig of iron hot from the furnace. Martin set up his easel and was squeezing fat slugs of colour on to the palette when a man approached, wagging his finger. As Martin extruded nonchalantly on, the man obtruded an identity card from the Archaeological Survey and demanded, on our part, a permission: a *chhota* camera was acceptable but not – he tapped the easel – a *bara* camera. I tried to persuade this new and aggressive strain of *chowkidar* (where was our solvent-drinking friend of the previous day? Terminally thinned, perhaps, like Augustus in *Struwwelpeter*) that a paintbox on legs was hardly a 'big', or ciné, camera; that cameras stood on tripods while easels were quadrupeds. But to no avail. Permission *nahin*, problem *hai*.

Martin primed his board with audibly angry, action-painter strokes; the guardian and I eyeballed each other in a silent stand-off. I tried wiggling my eyebrows, knowing it to have a disconcerting effect. There was no reaction. The impasse continued, my opponent making occasional twitches in Martin's direction, until another official appeared and saved the day. But only the day; this higher order of Survey-*wala* gave Martin a reprieve for the time being. If he wished to return, he would have to go to the Survey HQ and apply for an easel permit – to three different departments, *seriatim*.

Martin, silent until now but for the irate, erratic scrub, scrub of bristle on board, spoke: 'Now you know why most people paint India from photographs.' As if to emphasize the point, an infant dust-devil appeared out of the ground and threw a tantrum, and itself, at us and the wet paint. I left Martin in a whirl of mixed media.

*

Titoo took me back to Muhammad Shah's palace. Equipped now with the *Travels*, I imagined it would be easier to make sense of the Thousand.Columns than of its builder.

Of IB's three gates, each with its complement of marshals and guards, the first was also home to the executioners and their late victims. 'It was a rare day when no corpse was to be seen at the palace gate,' IB remembered. Often there was a whole slew of cadavers, and usually they had undergone bisection, trisection or other forms of division. The spot must have resembled those dooms through which one passes to enter certain medieval cathedrals, grim reminders of the Day of Judgement. (I do feel though that the sheer quantity of body parts must have overstated the message. Once, years ago, I saw the severed hand of a thief, reasonably fresh but beginning to clench and blacken, nailed knockerwise to the main gate of my adoptive city. As a warning to the felonious it did the job single-handed.)

The transition from this gruesome gallery, *Guernica* in the flesh, to the campy durbar-glitz of peacock-feather fans, yak-tail flywhisks and gold-handled whips within the gateways must have been disconcerting. Beyond, the second gate led into a large *mashwar*, or audience chamber, and the third, where one's name and time of visit were recorded, into the Thousand-Column Hall itself.

The plain Arabic of IB's description was harder to translate on the ground. I decided to work backwards, starting in the Hall. Ferreting around among the anti-personnel turds, I could only find a few exposed column bases; but it was clear from the spacing between them that although the Hall was, as IB said, 'vast and spacious' – it

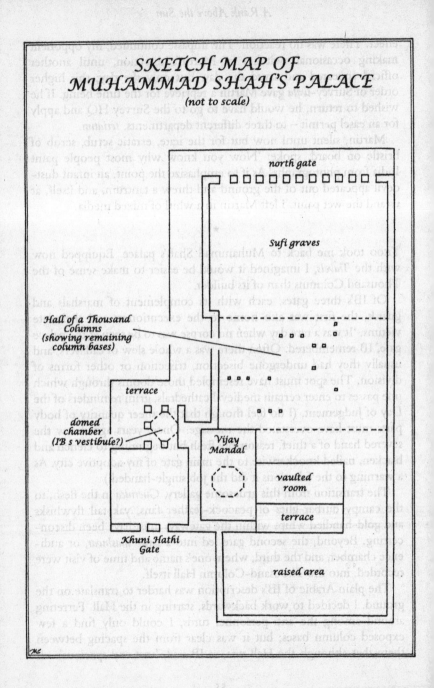

SKETCH MAP OF MUHAMMAD SHAH'S PALACE

(not to scale)

covered about half an acre – the 'thousand' was an exaggeration, a hypostyle hyperbole. A few hundred seemed nearer the mark. (The idea of the thousand-column hall goes back to ancient Sanskrit architectural treatises, and previous Delhi Sultans built them too. Later, the cheapskate Mughals were content with Sixty-Four- and even Forty-Column Halls.)

Due south of Muhammad's Hall lay the rectangular vaulted room, the lovers' tryst of our earlier visit. I wondered if this could be IB's *mashwar*, the audience chamber which he placed between the second and third gates. Encouragingly, the room opened on to a terrace. Was this the large 'platform' the traveller remembered as lying between the gates, on which the chief marshal sat? Possibly . . . but then where were the gates? To confuse matters, there *was* a gate, thirteen bays long and heavily buttressed with sloping piers – but it was north of the Hall. The area between this and the Hall contained a number of whitewashed tombs, home to a series of Sufi holy men who had squatted here after the palace had fallen into ruin (and now the only part of it where, out of respect, people *don't* squat). This hallowed ground could, I thought, be another candidate for the site of IB's *mashwar* and third gate. But . . . Damn it, I said to IB: why didn't you give any compass points? It would have made life a lot easier.

Then again, what was the domed octagonal structure to the west of the Thousand-Column Hall? Before, I had taken it to be a mausoleum. On inspection this seemed improbable: not so much because there was no tomb inside – tombs, after all, can be removed; rather, because the wall facing Mecca, which would almost certainly have incorporated a prayer niche if this were a place of burial, contained instead a doorway. Only the east wall, the one abutting the Hall, was solid. I went back to IB and found that he mentioned a *dihliz*, a vestibule, between the first and second gates. 'Along two of its sides are platforms, on which sit those troops whose turn it is to guard the gates . . .' And there were the platforms – a terrace raised on vaults and running around two sides of the domed building. A faint prickle ran down my thighs, the first stirring of ghosts.

Beyond the vestibule some more boys were playing cricket, and beyond the cricketers were a few courses of a gateway pierced by a double entrance. I stood there, willing the ghosts to rise. Instead, the game stopped and the boys came over to me – in contrast to the days of Muhammad Shah, a foreign visitor to his palace was now a rarity.

The cricketers knew little about the ruins: there had been more remains to the south, 'broken' in recent years to make way for housing; the 'raja's chariot park' had been just over there; their cricket pitch was called the Gate of Khuni Hathi. '. . . something Elephant?' I tried.

'Bloody Elephant,' one of the boys explained. Someone giggled.

Suddenly phrases from IB jostled into my mind – '. . . a rare day when no corpse was to be seen . . . outside the first gate sit the executioners . . . the elephants were led in and the rebels were thrown down before them, and they began cutting them to bits with blades fixed to their tusks . . .' – and with them a whole legion of ghosts, flayed, maimed, quartered, eviscerated, stuffed, a general resurrection on the cricket pitch.

Now I was certain I had worked my way out to the first gate. It was a place of blood, the memory of which had seeped down through two dozen generations. And with this realization the other gates creaked tentatively open. My solution to the enigma of entry – a huge clockwise loop via Bloody Elephant Gate, the domed vestibule, the thirteen-bay north gate and a hypothetical audience chamber and third gate on the site of the Sufi graveyard, and finally into the Thousand-Column Hall – was tortuous. But palaces of the period were notoriously mazy. Newly recruited servants sometimes went missing for days in the chambers and corridors hidden deep within their structure; and in these penetralia, said Muhammad's laureate, 'though the courts, full of armies, are raising a tumult and uproar, yet within all is so still and quiet that the ear of man might hear the humming of a fly's wing reverberate like music'.

There remained one final element in the complex (an apt word in more than one sense): that blazer-striped turret, the loftiest and best-preserved part of Muhammad's palace. I climbed the stairway and looked over the waste of shit and rubble. And here beside me another ghost appeared, quite suddenly – the sultan of all spectres.

Of Muhammad's dark deeds, the blackest in IB's eyes was the relocation of the capital in 1326 to Dawlatabad, 700 miles south of Delhi. As the traveller tells the story the reason was a whispering campaign in which the Delhiites accused Muhammad of being a *zalim*, a tyrant. As we have seen, this ominous disyllable was a red flag of revolution, and a red rag to Muhammad. 'So he resolved to ruin Delhi . . . and commanded the inhabitants of the city to go to Dawlatabad.' Two people were unable to comply: a cripple, who was catapulted out of the city from a mangonel, and a blind man, who was dragged to Dawlatabad, 'a journey of forty days; he fell to bits on the road, and all that reached Dawlatabad was one of his feet'.

The mass transfer of population and the name of the new capital, Dawlatabad, 'State City', smack of the excesses of twentieth-century totalitarianism. But IB was writing history, if not with a bias against Muhammad, then at least with a spin on the side of sensation. As a result his account has often been misread. IB's Delhi here is not the conurbation but only its oldest part, the original Dihli; Muhammad continued work on his new palace-city of Jahanpanah even after the big move south. Then again, only the courtly and administrative classes were transferred — and, it should be added, they were amply compensated. IB claims that when he arrived some seven years later there was hardly anybody in Delhi. To be precise, there was hardly anybody of consequence in Old Delhi. Even Isami, that arch-black-ener of Muhammad whose own aged grandfather had died on the exodus in the wastes of Tilpat (poetic licence, like speaking of the wilds of Tonbridge), admits as much. Delhi, he says, that city of nightingales and parrots, had become a colony of crows and ravens. It was not depopulated but repopulated, by the lower orders.

Rather than being an act of cruelty, the move to Dawlatabad was an act of vision, even if it was ruthlessly executed and terminally flawed. By extending the edifice of empire far to the south, Muhammad found his old capital isolated in the north wing. The solution: move it to the centre — Dawlatabad, strongest fortress of the Deccan; the drawback: India is exposed to invasion from the north-west. For the Great Game, that 'never ceases day or night', was playing in the time of the Delhi Sultans as ceaselessly as it was to do in that of the British. Their opponents were the Chagaday Mongols of Central Asia, and Muhammad knew he could not simply abandon Delhi, the bulwark that for over a century had blocked their attacks. If Dawlatabad became the civil centre, Delhi had to remain the military metropolis. The logic was sound, but not the logistics of having two capitals over a month's journey apart. The administration returned officially to Delhi soon after IB's arrival there — and, one by one, the pillars of state began to shear away as distant provinces seceded. Revolt, insidious as dry rot, infested the empire.

Muhammad Shah's own final collapse took place in 1351, ten years after IB had left Delhi, near the mouth of the Indus during a long and futile campaign against rebellious governor number twenty-two. His last, delirious words were in rhyming couplets, in which the Master of the World bowed out 'hunchèd and sunken, like the hornèd moon'; or so the story goes. And why should the story not be true? As Barani says of Muhammad, 'there was magic in his speech'.

It was that hunched and sunken shape that had insinuated itself into my thoughts, up there on the turret. For I had remembered, and now read again, the image with which IB ended both his account of the devastation of Delhi and his biography of Muhammad. 'The sultan climbed one night to the roof of his palace and looked over Delhi, where there was neither fire nor smoke nor lamp, and said, "At last my heart is at ease and my mind at rest."' This was the spot where he had stood, on the summit of the Vijay Mandal, his Abode of Victory.

Shades, perhaps, of Nero and his fiddle. But whether it was Muhammad's spectre that was haunting me, or IB's terror of him, a ghost was a ghost.

A light wind stirred the dust below and turned the pages of the open book in my hand. A half-remembered passage caught my eye. IB and a friend were visiting the Red Palace, abandoned forty years and six sultans earlier. They had climbed to the top of the ruined building and were looking down on it, when the friend recited

As for the sultans, ask the dust of them –
Those mighty heads are now but empty skulls.

So many Solomons in the wind. I wondered how Martin was getting on with his own mixed media.

★

Muhammad Shah had cast a shadow over our Delhi too; *cinéma vérité* was becoming *film noir*. So it was a relief to look up some real live Delhiites.

And to come across the odd unreal one. On our way to lunch with Salman Haidar, the first of our Delhi connections, we spotted a figure in puce *shalwar kameez* entering an apartment building. Seeming to sense our presence, she turned. 'Funny-looking sort of girl,' I whispered to Martin. 'Looks more like a man.'

'Yes. Face like a bricklayer. It's a transvestite if you ask me.'

The figure wiggled its bottom and disappeared through the door. I looked at Martin. 'Tempted?'

'About as much as I am by that stuff Titoo gave us to eat the other day.'

The Haidars' lunch was huge and delicious. It included pickled aubergines from Damascus, and advice on getting an Easel Permit out of the Archaeological Survey: start at the top. Armed with a letter, we went later that afternoon to the Survey HQ in New Delhi. We couldn't believe our luck. The letter – Re.: Application for Permit to Paint with Easel – made it straight on to the desk of Mrs Anand, the Director-General. But it was as quickly off again and into the constipated in-tray of a lowlier official, Mr Bakhshi. Martin misheard the name as *bakhshish*; but that wouldn't have helped, as the gentleman concerned was away for several days. We left the letter to its fate. It was all so unfair: one needed permission to paint a Listed Monument but not, apparently, to defecate on it.

Salman counselled patience with the Survey when we met him again that evening in the mansion-block apartment of a friend of his, the publisher Ravi Dayal. Whiskies and sodas, mahogany bookshelves and chimneypieces, and Ravi himself with his donnish grey bouffant, gave the flat the air of a comfortable Oxbridge set. Conversation meandered around IB, and ran inevitably into Muhammad Shah.

'I think we can say that he *was* more ruthless than his predecessors,' Salman said in response to a question from me. 'Killing your brothers is an act of prudence; killing your father is an act of ambition.' The analysis of Muhammad's power politics, coming from the ex-Foreign Secretary of India, carried weight.

'But I do feel that certain writers have been unkind to Muhammad,' said Ravi, mentioning several compatriots of mine. 'They've got it completely wrong. I mean, that business of the depopulation. Only the VIPs moved.'

For a while we discussed the conflicting accounts of Muhammad Shah's reign, and their respective merits; and concluded that only Shakespeare could have done the sultan justice. The tragic trajectory of brilliance and failure, the gradual immersion in blood, were material as rich as anything from Holinshed. Talk then turned briefly to early Arabic works on India. I quoted al-Biruni on the mutual incompatibility of 'us' and the Indians – the Muslims, in other words, and the 'intricate, obscure' Hindus. 'Well,' said Salman, looking impish, 'you could say that it's a perfect policy statement of the Two Nation Theory.'

We all laughed. There was a short pause in the conversation. It was only later that I thought of the laughter, and the pause; and of the old post-operative scar of Partition. It still hurt, and not only when they laughed.

By the end of the evening I had picked their brains as mercilessly as a bulimic vulture. But, enthusiastic and knowledgeable Delhophiles as they were, they could offer nothing on two sites that I particularly wanted to find: those of IB's house and of the mausoleum of Qutb al-Din Mubarak Shah, the Ortonesquely murdered drag-sultana, of which Muhammad gave the traveller charge. They pointed me instead to another Battutian survival. I would find it, they said, in a shop called Ghantewala, 'the Bellman', on Chandni Chowk.

*

The relic to which Salman and Ravi drew my attention dated back almost to IB's first audience with Muhammad Shah, in the Thousand-Column Hall in the summer of 1334. Once the post-interview flush had worn off, IB realized he had a problem more serious than that boil on the backside. Almost incredibly, considering his 12,000-dinar salary – some 200 times the income of an average Hindu Delhiite – and a starting bonus of the same amount, he was deep in debt. The problem was cashflow. His present to the sultan of horses, camels, arrows and slaves had been paid for on credit.

Together with other expenses he owed a whopping 55,000 dinars, and the speculators who had lent him the money at the border were kicking their heels in Delhi and getting more and more impatient. For IB, as for all educated Arabs in times of stress, there was only one solution: compose a poem.

Having done so he presented it to the sultan. 'He put it on his knee and held one end of it in his hand, while I held the other end.' The sultan's Arabic was good, but not up to the convoluted language of a traditional ode, so 'Whenever I finished reciting one line of it I said to the Grand Qadi, "Explain its meaning to the Master of the World."' The poem goes, in Gibb's translation,

> Commander of the Faithful, lord revered,
>> To thee we come, through deserts toward thee hasting.
> A pilgrim I, thy glory's shrine to visit,
>> A refuge meet for sanctuary thy dwelling.
> Had majesty a rank above the sun,
>> Fit pattern wert thou for its most excelling.
> Thou art the Imam, unique and glorious, ever
>> Thy words infallibly with deeds investing.
> I am in need, thy bounty's overflow
>> My hope, and by thy greatness eased my questing.
> Shall I declare it – or thy blush suffice? –
>> To say 'thy bounty's plash' were seemlier punning.
> Make speed to aid the votary to thy shrine,
>> And pay his debt – the creditors are dunning.

It is, as the English reflects, archaic in language. The images – the desert crossing, the fruitful oasis – are crashingly commonplace. But it was written for a purpose, and this it achieved perfectly. 'Commander of the Faithful' and 'Imam' are titles of a caliph of ancient Arab pedigree. To address in this way the son of an arriviste condottiere of dubious antecedents is blatant boot-licking. To do it in the languid, lingual monorhyme *-lā*, lost in the English *-ing*, is phonetic fellatio. But it is exactly what Muhammad wanted – to be told in God's own language that he was no tyrant, but rather a divinely sanctioned monarch whose throne ought to be hovering among the heavenly spheres. Having buttered up the sultan so thickly, IB could slap on that last line, the meat of the matter, with impunity. Even by the standards of Arabic eulogy it is a piece of bare-arsed cheek; but beautifully cushioned by the play of 'blush' and 'plash' – a mere glottal stop's difference in the original. IB had the Master of the World eating out of his hand. Of course all his debts would be paid.

To tastes brought up on the *vers minceur* of modern times, all that lard is sick-making. But at least the vomit is honest. Today panegyric is disguised as PR and dished up by lobbyists and spin doctors, and literature is poorer for the extinction of a genre. (Or the virtual extinction: I heard recently of one Arabian eulogist who addressed his grudging patron with the line, 'So many *bayts* have I given you, and all I ask from you is one *bayt*.' A *bayt* is both a line of verse and a house. As with IB, the pun did the job and the poet got a villa.)

The sultan's agreement to pay was one thing. IB still had to get through a bureaucracy as log-jammed as any in New Delhi. First the money order got stuck with the prime minister, that greyest of all eminences and designer of the regicidal reception-room. Later, another official demanded a bribe – fair enough; but 500 gold *tangahs* . . . Then the sultan went off hunting again. This was a disaster for IB, as it meant not just a day of pig-sticking or riding to hounds but an expedition lasting weeks or even months, with elephants, cheetahs, falcons, a tented city and hunt followers in the tens of thousands. By now IB had realized that Muhammad was the only person who could actually get the cash paid, so he went along too – and plunged himself still deeper into debt by having to shell out not only on camping gear but also on the bearers, syces, grass-cutters, litter-bearers, tent-erectors, link-boys and others without whom, until the coming of the railways, no gentleman could contemplate setting foot outside Delhi.

He stuck to Muhammad's entourage, as one commentator has said, 'like a perfect horse-leech'. One of the weary courtiers eventually complained to the sultan. ' "O Master of the World, every day this man talks to me in Arabic, and I have no idea what he is saying." . . . "He is talking" ', explained another, no doubt with a groan, ' "about the money he owes." ' The sultan again issued a chit for payment to be made – but only when they returned to the capital. The weeks dragged on; the bills piled up. Then one day Muhammad brought up the subject of camels. IB, who was present and something of a camel buff, spotted an opening. The real thoroughbreds, he said, were the

Mahris, a breed of Yemeni origin; adding that the Sultan of Egypt favoured them . . . and that he himself just happened to have one back in Delhi.

IB rushed, with permission, back to the capital. He had an Arab-style saddle made from a wax model, and sent the Mahri to the sultan, gorgeously caparisoned. The gift was completed by a themed addition – an assortment of sweetmeats made by a Yemeni confec-tioner IB had picked up during his wanderings.

The sweetmeats stole the show. Muhammad said he had never eaten or even seen anything like them. On the sultan's own return to the capital IB sent him a further two camels and eleven more trays of sweetmeats. Muhammad, IB and a few of the more intimate courtiers gathered for a tasting session in a private sitting-room beside the Thousand-Column Hall. That evening IB got home to find three sacks of gold waiting for him.

*

Muhammad's private parlour, I now suspected, was that place of rank odours and romantic assignations, the colonnaded chamber next to the Abode of Victory. Excavations there in the 1930s uncovered two large cavities in the floor, which the archaeologists described as 'trea-sure wells'. Their only contents of note were a few fragments of crockery of a type supposed to reveal or neutralize poisons – an essential part of any sultanic tea-service.

Today the teatime treats of kings are to be found seven miles to the north, on Chandni Chowk, the main shopping street of Mughal Delhi. I asked Titoo if he knew Ghantewala, the Man with the Bell. 'Ooh yes!' he exclaimed. '*Shahi halwai*.' The Shah's sweet-maker. The old sweetmeat-men of Delhi, like the muffin-men of London, rang their wares around the streets; Ghantewala was the bellman *par excel-lence*, the Charbonnel et Walker of Delhi. The prospect of a visit to the tooth-rotter by appointment to several reigns of Mughals – and, he added, to that late Mughalette, Mrs Gandhi – made Titoo lick his lips. It was a perfectly Pavlovian response.

We parked in the Bicycle Market. As we walked the short distance to Chandni Chowk, I reviewed my hypothesis. The other night, with Salman and Ravi, I'd had a hunch – that even if columns had col-lapsed and domes disappeared, a minor Battutian monument might have survived intact. Muhammad Shah was both an ardent arabophile and the owner of a very sweet tooth (which, strange to say, Martin and I were later to *visit*, 600 miles away in the Deccan). He had once, it was said, given 3,000 gold *tangahs* to a man who brought him twenty-two crystallized melons of Bukhara. In IB's present of Arabian sweets, two of the sultan's great passions came together.

It was a long shot, but I wondered if any of IB's sweets were still to be found. Their Arabic names had rung no bells for Salman or Ravi; until, that is, I mentioned *luqaymat al-qadi*. 'Qadi is what you call *qazi*,' I explained – a judge. 'And *luqaymah* is the diminutive of *luqmah*, which is . . .'

'The great Delhi sweet!' they said together.

Luqmah is the Arabic ancestor of an international family. Lane's *Lexicon* gives the meaning as 'a gobbet'; *laqam*, the verb, is 'to gobble a gobbet'. *Luqaymat al-qadi* Gibb translates with his usual elegance as *bouchées du juge*. They are still to be found in the Arab world. An itinerant Iraqi confectioner used to sell these Battutian delicacies – little balls of dough, supersaturated with syrup – outside the door of my house in Yemen, at night in the month of Ramadan. But *luqmah*, or its plural *luqam*, also migrated long ago to Istanbul and mutated into *lokum* – what we would call Turkish delight – and thence with the Ottomans to Greece to be reborn as *loukoumi*. And since my Iraqi confectioner has himself migrated to Australia the *luqmah* family may well make it to Wlwnghwngh, if it hasn't done so already.

At Ghantewala I drew blanks again with my list of IB's sweet names – all except *luqmah*. As this had to be ordered, Titoo and I decided to do some preliminary fieldwork. (Martin declined to take part, having spotted a fly in one of the cabinets – 'Remember that Danish pastry down at your Hall of the Thousand Turds?') We began with the standard fare, Panjabi *gulab jamun* followed by samosas both savoury and sweet (an item on IB's bill of fare, but predating his arrival) and *gachak* made from jaggery and sesame; then moved on to *habashi*, 'Abyssinian', dark brown boluses that tasted of ginger nuts mashed up in Horlicks, and to confections of carrots and milk and of cashews and saffron. 'Oh dear,' said Titoo at this point. 'I forget my doctor tell me to reduce eight kay-gees . . .' I too was flagging, having eaten my way around to the very last cabinet. But the sight of its contents – 'Khoya Fancies' – refreshed my appetite. Apart from the named varieties, IB's confectioner had prepared sweetmeats 'in the shape of dates and other fruits'. And here they were – no dates; but apples, pears and mangoes, artfully recreated in a heavy paste of condensed milk and – this really was gilding the lily – covered in silver leaf. A maternal voice sounded in my memory – 'You'll make yourself sick . . .' I ate one of each.

*

A couple of days later the lady at Ghantewala went through the ingredients of Delhi *luqmah*: milk, reduced by boiling; *misri*, sugar candy; pistachioes and almonds; and that rococo layer of silver leaf. A wizened one-eyed man in a loincloth, who looked as if he might have been on the staff of Ghantewala since its establishment in the eighteenth century, appeared with a big box decorated with swastikas and a jolly pink Ganesh; the elephant-headed god bore a certain resemblance to Titoo. The contents were decidedly gobbets rather than *bouchées* – each weighed in at getting on for a quarter of a pound. I bit into one. There was a ghost of cardomum, a hint of rose-water. The flavour was Indian, and intricate. If my silvered sweetmeat were a descendant of IB's *luqaymah* – and unfortunately he doesn't give us the recipe – then, like the Turkish *lokum*, it had adapted itself to its environment.

I still cling to a conviction that the name at least – and perhaps also the fruit-shaped sweetmeats – might date back to that afternoon in the sultan's sitting-room. The terms for many Indian sweets – *jalebi* and *habashi* for example, and the generic *halwa* – are Arabic in origin; *misri*, the word for refined cane sugar, is the Arabic adjective for Egypt, where the refining process was invented. Exactly when and how these names arrived in Hindustan is impossible to tell. But I like to think that in the case of *luqmah* we can watch the actual disembarkation of a word:

And then the sultan took another kind of sweet and said, 'What is the name of these?', and I said to him, 'These are *luqaymat al-qadi*.' Now one of those present was a merchant of Baghdad, a well-to-do man whom the sultan always addressed as 'my father'. This man was envious of me and wished to pique me, so he said, 'Those are not *luqaymat al-qadi*, but these are,' and he took a piece of the kind which is called *jild al-faras*, 'horse-hide'. The doyen of the intimate courtiers, who would often make fun of this merchant in the sultan's presence, happened to be sitting opposite him. He said to the merchant, 'Sir, you lie and it is the qadi who tells the truth.' The sultan said to him, 'And how is this so?' He replied, 'O Master of the World, he is the qadi and these are his *luqaymat*, for he brought them.' And the sultan laughed and said, 'Well spoken!'

So much for the archaeology of Hindustani sweetmeats. There is a more important Battutian survival – that image of Muhammad, laughing. It is as candid, as poignant, as an old home movie. Were it not for IB, we might never have known that the monster was human.

Time's Daughters

*'O my friend! the king's service has two sides to it – hope of
a livelihood, and terror for one's life; and it is contrary to the
opinion of the wise, through such a hope to expose oneself to
such a fear.'*

Sa'di, Gulistan

A SMALL CROWD had gathered by a *pan* stall up from Turkman Gate
in Shahjahanabad, the Mughal city in the north of the Delhi
conurbation. They were watching a new form of bazaar magic –
Martin at work. 'To start with it was like being on the gallows,' he
told me, looking around his spectators. 'But now I've got a minder.'
He gave a thumbs-up to a one-legged man on a tricycle. The man
grinned back, then tenderly applied his crutch to a small boy who'd
got too near the easel.

I had returned from a stroll to find Martin painting a tiny façade
wedged between tottering houses. The Mosque of the Pilao-wala, the
Seller of Spiced Rice, was green in the way that the Red Tomb
was red: verdigris, malachite, peppermint, dragonfly, bluebottle . . .
I couldn't fix the colours, not in any pigment of the imagination.
A score of necks, mine included, craned whenever Martin's brush
went to the palette. (He told me later that he'd used a cadmium red and
raw umber ground, then Prussian blue with a bit of Naples yellow and
transparent gold ochre. The lights were viridian, the shadows cerulean
and cobalt. 'And it's still wrong.') Overhead, flight upon flight of doves
sparkled through a watered-milk sky, catching the unseen sun. Down
here, we were wrapped in the cool semi-gloom of a grotto.

Shahjahanabad was 300 years too late for IB and further from his
Delhi than Cricklewood is from Charing Cross. And yet for me it

was a kind of homecoming. The lanolin-laden scent of mutton, and the Arabic script of the signboards – even if Urdu has it chasing its tail and leaving diacritical pug marks in unfamiliar places – were comprehensible and comforting. For me, but not for Titoo. 'If my auto only *touching* someone, immediate fight. When I angry, five minutes then I forget. Musulman not forget: knife in back!'

'Oh, come on, Titoo. I'm sure it's not as bad as that.'

'I not saying *all* Musulmans bad . . .' He thought for a few moments. 'Aurangzeb was bad. Dara Shikuh was good but Aurangzeb kill him by poisoning with lion's moustache. Akbar was very good.'

'And before the Mughals? Muhammad ibn Tughluq for instance . . .'

His eyes rolled. 'Ooh! *Zalim hakim* . . .' Titoo sought for the English; but the phrase was loaned from Arabic. 'A tyrant of a ruler,' I said, noting that the fatal *z*-word uttered by Shihab al-Din had stuck. 'Yes, tyrant ruler. Very advance mind . . . but also mental man! Mix up . . . Sometimes very good. Mostly very very bad.' I felt that, had Titoo been acquainted with the little girl with the little curl, she might have provided the *mot juste* for Muhammad Shah.

We had left Titoo in the safe zone outside Turkman Gate, to his newspaper archive and other anachronisms. I was intrigued that he should look to the seventeenth century for his illustrations of Muslim character; but also aware that his fears of what lay inside the gate were sadly out of tune with that holy harmony of *pir*, yogi and *nihang* upon which he had earlier descanted.

Now the light started to go. The greens of the mosque lasted longer than the surrounding colours; then they too began to fade, and the lines of the building with them. Contrary to the rules of Chomskian semantics, the Pilao-wala Mosque was becoming a colourless green idea of itself. Martin painted on; we watched, and waited, wondering how long he could make out the blobs on his palette. I had often seen him pit himself like this against a disappearing subject, and knew that he usually won. But today bad light stopped play. He sighed and started to scrape the palette. One of the spectators tapped my elbow. 'Why is he not taking a snap?'

The camera creates an illusion of stasis. The snap of the shutter severs light from time. Nothing, not even still life, is ever quite still. Light sees to that, and the spin of the earth, and its journey round the sun. A photograph, or a painting made from one, is a denial of motion, dead light embalmed in chemicals. 'He likes painting,' I said.

Martin bade farewell to his fans and thanked his one-legged guardian. As we set off, I turned to wave to them and caught sight of the sign above the *pan* stall – Dilshad Pan Bhandar. Dilshad . . . I had come across the name before, at the saint's cell in the Nile Delta: 'You will meet there my brother Dilshad the Indian, who will rescue you from a great misfortune into which you will fall.'

We spent the fag-end of the day wandering about Shahjahanabad. I soon realized that my first impressions, of a place as wholly Islamic as Cairo or Damascus, had to be revised. The surroundings of the Jama Masjid, the great Friday mosque of Shah Jahan, had been colonized by sellers of Hindu images. The Muslim faithful were filing in to their aniconic evening devotions past a pantheon of languid eyes. I was hardly less surprised than IB would have been. Martin stopped outside one idol showroom. 'They must think my stuff's a load of rubbish,' he said, examining a painting of a fetching blue Krishna.

Nor was the scene in the Sita Ram Bazaar one to be met with in the Islamic west. We crossed a junction overstrung with a crazy cat's-cradle of electrical wiring, thick hanks of cables anastomosing like the aerial roots of banyan trees, and entered a mile-long street jammed with cycle rickshaws. Traffic policemen rapped on them with their sticks, trying to keep them in two orderly and moving columns, but to no effect. The bazaar was immobilized by mass spoke-lock. The passengers were nearly all women, with a sprinkling of transvestite eunuchs – one of these was remarkably pretty, crammed into the dicky of a rickshaw between two hefty pantomime dames. No one seemed in a hurry to get anywhere. They just posed on their gimcrack thrones, both spectators and inmates in a Bedlam of their own making.

*

Most of our time was spent in the south of Delhi, which was outwardly calmer than the Mughal city but, to the historian of urban development, chaotic. Martin, who had finally made it through the triplicate departments of the Archaeological Survey and secured his Easel Permit, devoted himself to understanding the inscrutable cuboid of the Red Tomb. While he painted, and scraped off, and overpainted, I tried to make out something of the fourteenth-century form of this much reworked cityscape.

Of the wall of Delhi – so massive, IB wrote, that 'cavalry and infantry can actually march from one end of the city to the other along the passages in its thickness' – almost nothing remains; all of its twenty-eight gates have disappeared. But just outside the old line of the wall two points of reference described by IB still exist – the great reservoirs built by earlier Delhi Sultans, Shams al-Din Iltutmish and Ala al-Din. The message is clear: if you want to leave behind a really big monument to yourself, dig a hole. Unlike a wall, it can't be stolen.

The site of the first of these tanks, the Hauz Shamsi, was fixed by the Prophet Muhammad when he appeared to Shams al-Din in a dream. I had a harder job locating it, but eventually did so in an area defined by Titoo as 'Mehrauli village backside'. Considering it was built 800 years ago it still contained an impressive quantity of water. The water, however, looked as old as the tank and resembled a watery spinach curry; a woman in a sari of matching green was doing her laundry from the stone steps noted by IB. The pavilions he described as surrounding the tank were not in evidence, but there was a domed and colonnaded structure in the water, close to the western bank and connected to it by a concrete bridge. Since IB remembered this as being in the centre of the water, I could only guess that the western part of the tank had been filled in – probably by centuries of detritus from the market gardening he observed there in the dry season. The other three sides of the tank, lined with steps, looked original. But there was a snag. IB gave the dimensions as 'about two miles long by half that in width'. Even allowing for the shrinkage of the tank his figures seemed, to say the least, generous. A measured stroll along one of the sides, and a couple of sums, confirmed my suspicions: IB had almost tripled the dimensions of the Shamsi Tank, and expanded its area by a factor of ten. Unless I was mistaken, I had caught him Münchausing.

The other reservoir, Hauz Khass or the Private Tank, was 'bigger still', he said. And so it was. Although it was dry, its original dimensions were plain to see, and it was at most half a mile square. There was no mistake about it: the old Tangerine had been exaggerating. Frankly, I felt disappointed in him.

But it was for once a fine clear day, and the view across Hauz Khass looked wildly romantic: loggias, terraces and domes – the mausoleum and college of Muhammad Shah's cousin and successor, Firuz Shah – floated above the wooded margin of the tank, a mirage of a mortuary in a jungle lost in an urban jungle. This is how much of Delhi must have looked before the late twentieth century, when the city turned hungrily on its own urban spaces. Perhaps it was a trifle captious to niggle with IB over figures. If you live in a city ruled by a magniloquence – the Master of the World – and revolving around a hyperbole – the Hall of a Thousand Columns – it is hardly surprising if things start to look larger than life.

IB particularly remembered the Private Tank for the waterside settlement of musicians called Tarababad, 'Music City' (perhaps 'Soul City', as the root sense of *tarab* is 'emotion'). A few years before he reached Delhi, the poet and lyricist Amir Khusraw rhapsodized on one of its great divas, 'the blessed bird of the auspicious assembly, the darling of the realm, the gem of the company, Turmati Khatun, who, whenever she wields her *chang*, the bird of paradise sings for her, and, whenever she sings herself, the cuckoos hold their breath . . .' No doubt *changs* (a type of lyre), female voices and other such distractions from the pursuit of Qur'anic science were removed when Firuz Shah built his tomb-academy. But of IB's forty tankside pavilions where the performers would gather, a few still remain. I sat in one of these understated pleasure-domes, and would have burst into song myself had I not feared for the sanity of the cuckoos. Besides, the killjoy Archaeological Survey, that enemy of the fine arts, had put a notice on the gate: 'Playing of musical instruments, gramapnones [*sic*] or broadcast receivers, including transistors within the Archaeological Area is prohibited.'

And yet, even if the *chang* no longer twangs, artistic endeavour of a sort is not quite dead here. To the auspicious assembly of today's Delhi, Hauz Khass is located, in translation, somewhere between Cork Street and Camden Lock. One evening Martin and I went to the Village, a street of boutiques and galleries by the tank, to a private view of paintings, drawings and inflatable sculptures. The sculptures sounded like the sort of thing Pygmalion might have bought, in desperation, by mail-order. And they would have distinct advantages over more conventional works – easier to take on holiday than, say, a Caro, and a lot more useful in a shipwreck.

The show, organized by an American wearing rose-tinted spectacles, had attracted a dusting of glitterati and a whole dim nebula of glimmerati. I chatted with a charming Kashmiri Pandit, a performance artist whose works included feeding the hungry and deleting graffiti. But Martin and I were the red dwarfs in this social constellation, and were forced for much of the time into the expedient of actually looking at the exhibits. Most of the sculptures were abstract, although whether by intent or default was hard to tell. There was an orange blob with horns, which reminded me so much of those big sit-on balls of my 1960s childhood that it was hard not to jump aboard and start bouncing about. The masterpiece, judging by the attention it drew, was what appeared to be a massive silver dildo. To the sculptor's chagrin, it had begun to droop and had constantly to be pumped up. During a lull in the chatter I heard it very softly hissing.

The almost silent but deadly dildo eloquently, self-referentially expressed my thoughts – of jesters' bladders, whoopee cushions; art for fart's sake. Martin, whatever he made of the windbag sculptures and of the graphic contents of the show – printed lists of various sorts, scribbled on – maintained a lock-jawed silence. He was loyal to his profession.

It was all a long way from the Delhi of IB. But it occurred to me later that the Kashmiri performance artist, at least, had something in common with the Moroccan traveller. If IB's position as judge was a sinecure he did however exert himself in his other job, as superintendent of the mausoleum of Muhammad Shah's predecessor-but-two, Sultan Qutb al-Din; and never more so than in one of the periodic famines that ravaged Hindustan, when he used the rich endowments of the tomb to feed the hungry. The success of IB's soup kitchen reached the ear of Muhammad Shah, then far away in the Deccan, who honoured the Moroccan's charitable work with that great mark of distinction – a robe from his own wardrobe.

IB had a knack for getting involved with interesting sultans. If Muhammad is the psychoanalyst's dream, tabloid editors would die for Qutb al-Din Mubarak Shah Khalji. The first act of his reign was unremarkable. Having bundled his younger brother off the throne early in 1316, he cut off one of the boy's fingers and incarcerated him in the castle of Gwalior. The severed digit was a mere *amuse gueule*, finger-food before a feast of violence. Qutb al-Din went on to dash out his 10-year-old nephew's brains against the palace flagstones. He then had all four of his own brothers executed (three of them had already been blinded with bodkins by order of Malik Kafur, 'King Camphor', eunuch regent of their recently deposed younger sibling). After disposing thus of all rival claimants to the throne he set about cultivating his own nemesis, a converted Hindu named Khusraw Khan. Deaf to all advice, he made Khusraw his vizier and indulged his every whim – because, IB says, of his 'extreme fondness for him and . . . because it was the will of God that he should meet his death at Khusraw's hands'. God's will duly took its course, and in July 1320 Khusraw murdered his master, seized the throne and began to show such favour to his former co-religionists that he banned the killing of cows. The whole jolly junta of Qutb al-Din's generals acquiesced in this change of rule, except for one – Tughluq, father of Muhammad Shah. Tughluq's counter-coup was swift, and before the year was out the head of the usurper was skittering across the palace yard. Qutb al-Din had made such a thorough job of extirpating his family tree that, *faute de mieux*, Tughluq assumed the sultanic parasol.

Such is IB's sketch of Qutb al-Din, the man whose memory and mortal remains he served. Very different though it may be from the home life of our own dear Queen, it is only the penny-plain version. The Indian historians have left us a shilling shocker. Qutb al-Din, Barani wrote, was more than fond of Khusraw Khan – he forced his prime minister to perform 'lewd and unnatural acts' with him. The sultan would also ponce about the palace 'decked out in the trinkets and apparel of a female'. The court made antic hay; hyperinflation hit the market for beardless slave-boys. Khusraw, however, was an unwilling Gaveston (they were, as it happens, near contemporaries) – hence the decision to screw his master once and for all. Saving the lives of cows was the least of Khusraw's innovations, for he now began a counter-orgy – one of desecration in which, Barani says, his Hindu myrmidons lounged around on copies of the Holy Qur'an and set up their 'demonic' idols in the mosques. It all makes the occasional palace divorce of today look a bit tame. Admittedly, it is difficult to say quite how the tabloids would cope. KILLER PM IN GAY CROSS-DRESS ROYAL MURDER CASE ORDERS SATANIC RITUAL BEEF BAN lacks snap.

Looking back down the perspective of history, it is hard to see the Muslim establishment of Delhi twiddling their beads as their holy places were defiled, while only Tughluq defended Islam. The idols in the mosques smell distinctly of propaganda. Qutb al-Din, on the other hand, probably was quite as colourful as he was painted. Even the official verse history commissioned by Tughluq, heavily airbrushed as it was, did not try to hide the fact that the last ruler of the revered Khalji dynasty had had a gay old time of it:

> Wine and love, drunkenness and youth,
> Pleasure and dalliance, happiness and power –
> Who will give a thought to the future
> When such winds blow in his head?

Qutb al-Din still frightens the horses, and the historians. Lal, chronicler of the Khaljis, brands him a latter-day Heliogabalus who 'well deserved the doom meted out to him'. It would certainly be hard to recommend him as a mirror for princes. But one fact elevates his story from pornography to tragedy: that all the violence and passion was packed into a reign that began when Qutb al-Din was 17 and ended when he was 21. Khusraw, his prime minister, was perhaps a little younger.

Muhammad Shah all but worshipped his dissolute predecessor and former master. 'On his visits to the tomb I have seen him take Qutb al-Din's sandal, kiss it and place it on his head,' IB remembered, 'for it is their custom to put the sandals of the dead man on a small platform beside his tomb.' As a more material sign of his devotion, IB says, Muhammad 'ordered that a dome be built over the tomb, one hundred cubits in height'. (A hundred cubits is roughly the height of Nelson's Column.) Once in charge of the great mausoleum, IB appointed a staff to match – 460 of them, plus two caparisoned elephants picketed at the gate.

One would think that however lacking in sultanic bottom he may have been in life, Qutb al-Din's posterior *gravitas* would be thus monumentally assured. But the mausoleum has disappeared from both the records and the face of the earth. It is not clear from IB's text whether the hundred-cubit cupola was built or not; if it was, it probably went the way of the domes that crowned the tombs of three earlier sultans, and collapsed. The irony is that in the city known as Qubbat al-Islam, the Cupola of Islam, that was the very feature the architects took longest to get the hang of.

Another Qutb loomed large in IB's life and, since the builders of Delhi got the hang of towers from the start, it is still an unmissable part of the skyline of southern Delhi. From a distance it could almost be a work of nature, perhaps the defoliated trunk of a giant redwood; as you approach, it grows, faster and bigger than perspective should permit; and then the details come into focus – alternating sharp and rounded ribs, balconies melting geometrically into stalactites, broad bands of calligraphy – combining to make one of the most exciting surfaces in Indo-Muslim architecture. Robert Byron, in one of his rare crass moments, dismissed it as 'Indian and painstaking'. Reaching the base of the Qutb Minar, I wished I could bring him back and make him eat his words beneath this triumphant fanfare of flutes, flanges and cornices. And while I was about it I'd raise the ghost of Sir Richard Burton, who thought Islamic design in India 'effeminate'. *Effeminate.* The Qutb Minar, swollen, ribbed, mottled and veined in pink, erected smack in the wrecked temple of conquered Delhi, is masculine to the point of embarrassment. It is Islamic design on Viagra.

Since IB's time there have been several rebuilds of the top storeys. (They include one in the early nineteenth century by Major Smith of the Bengal Engineers. He stuck a Regency-Mughal gazebo on the summit, which soon inspired a popular design of cruet; following this cruel fate, the gazebo was demoted to the garden.) The tower now stands at 240 feet. IB doesn't venture a height, but said correctly that the Qutb Minar was 'without equal in the lands of Islam'. A later statement, however, raised my suspicions once more: 'Its staircase is wide enough for elephants to ascend. A reliable informant told me that when it was being renovated he saw an elephant climbing to the top with stones.' The image is compelling: a great trumpeting tower of victory growing skyward by elephant-power. The trouble is that it is shaped like a cannon barrel, breech-end downwards. The base of the tower looks potentially elephant-sized; but the higher you go, towards the muzzle of the barrel, the narrower it gets. You don't need to be a wizard at conic sections to see that even the most anorexic elephant would soon get stuck. Unfortunately there was no way of confirming this suspicion. The nannyish Archaeological Survey ruled some years ago that climbing the Qutb Minar is dangerous, thus ending an 800-year tourist tradition. Everyone climbed it, IB included. Indeed, the only statistic on Delhi known to Arab geographers of his time was that the Qutb Minar had 360 stairs.

Martin and I did the other sights of the Quwwat al-Islam Mosque in which the Qutb stands. I had hoped to emulate IB by using my headscarf to measure the Iron Pillar, a fourth-century column of solid metal, miraculously rust-resistant and, like the Qutb, a monument to victory. True to form, the Archaeological Survey had fenced it off. Disappointed Indian trippers stood about, longing to try and encircle the Pillar with their arms behind their backs – if you can perform this backwards hug, legend says, all your dreams will come true. There was clearly no place for this sort of nonsense in infotech-age India.

As we walked away from the forlorn and unembraced Pillar I turned to the next item on IB's tour. ' "The Sultan Qutb al-Din . . ." ' I read, 'actually it was his father, Ala al-Din, ". . . wished to build in the western courtyard an even bigger minaret, but had completed only a third of it by the time of his death . . ." '

'And here it is,' Martin announced as we emerged from a doorway. I looked up. My field of vision was filled by the rubble stump of the aborted mega-*minar*, rising on its plinth like a gigantic flan-mould on a baking tray. It lacked the opulently carved freestone casing of the Qutb Minar, and the crevices in its flanged surface were perches for brilliant green parrots that whizzed and whooped saucily overhead. Martin was looking underwhelmed. 'But it's all a con . . . I mean, these buildings aren't solid stone. They're just rubble with a skin on top.'

'Ah, never judge a book by its cover . . . Except mine of course,' I added quickly, since Martin does my dustjackets.

He wasn't listening. 'Are they *all* like that?' I nodded. 'What . . . even the Taj Mahal?'

'Even the Taj Mahal. But back to the matter in hand. ". . . Sultan Muhammad wished to complete this minaret but abandoned the project, having decided that it was unlucky . . ." '

'*Unlucky!* Huh. Very telling. He was happy shoving shit down people's throats, but he was really just a great big coward.'

I had never known Martin get so angry about anyone as he did over Muhammad Shah. ' "The great bulk of this unfinished minaret makes it one of the wonders of the world. The staircase is wide enough for three elephants to climb it abreast." Aha . . .' I had spotted a means of checking up on these elephantine claims. With uncharacteristic thoughtfulness, the Survey had erected some scaffolding by the elevated door of the building. There were no guards about, so I hauled myself up and measured the width of the passage between outer wall and central core. Nine of my feet, shod in Portuguese brothel-creepers (9′ 1 $\frac{11}{16}$″, for the record) – wide enough, at a pinch, for two supermodel-slim elephants.

Have elephants, like us, got bigger over the centuries? It doesn't seem impossible. But they could hardly have doubled in girth. IB doesn't help here. On his arrival in India he had a brush with a rhino, and noted that while 'the rhinoceros is smaller than an elephant, its head is several times bigger than that of an elephant' (hence, he adds, a jingle – 'The rhino, it's said, is a bodyless head'). If he meant larger in proportion to the body, there is no suggestion of that in the Arabic. Either something very strange has happened over time to the vital statistics of Indian *Pachydermata*, or IB was simply wrong. Taking the evidence into account – his trebling the dimensions of the Shamsi Tank and his apparent doubling of those of the two minarets, not to mention a similar enlargement of the Iron Pillar – only one conclusion is possible: that even if his ability to recall names, places and events was brilliant, he had a rotten memory for measurements.

It was Martin who, not long after, made me reconsider these thoughts. He was trying to draw the Qutb Minar and by his own admission not doing very well. It is a very obstinate shape; Edward Lear also could only manage 'two feeble memoranda' of it. I remembered that IB too had commented on the optical contrariness of the Qutb: 'I once climbed to the top of it . . . The people at the foot of the minaret appeared to me like little children, although to an observer looking up from its base it does not seem so high because of its enormous mass and breadth.' That last phrase is strangely parallactical; but the passage as a whole is a sort of squinting at perspective, still in its European infancy. I didn't quite know what to make of it, except to think that what might have changed was not so much the size of elephants or the height of towers as the way we look at them. IB, like every other Arab traveller of his age, described the Pyramids as 'cones'. Miniaturists could depict an elephant as little larger than a horse; a person sitting on the ground on a carpet would be shown apparently levitating, with the carpet hung behind him; and buildings were often drawn in *reverse* perspective, revealing all their faces at once like a cardboard box turned inside-out towards the viewer – the painter standing

as it were at the vanishing point and looking outwards along steadily diverging lines. Perhaps we ourselves looked, IB and I, from divergent viewpoints. I would have to put a warning on the rear-view mirror in which I looked back on his age – something along the lines of 'Distant Elephants May Appear Smaller Than They Are In Reality'.

It was while I was jotting down these ideas that I discovered a Battutian memorial more private than those posturing towers and domes. I had taken shelter from the midday sun in the southern entrance to the mosque complex, an airy gatehouse pierced with stone screens and reticulated with shadows. Yet another work of the great builder Sultan Ala al-Din, it was a perfect, delicate contrast to the abandoned stump of his minaret. I wrote sitting on a broad sandstone bench that ran around the inside of the gatehouse. The stone was cold to the touch and burnished by seven centuries of backsides – one of which, I realized, must surely have belonged to IB.

'Must surely have' is usually a symptom of the *lues Boswelliana* or compulsive-biographical disorder. But it is about all one can say. The problem is that, after the initial boil in the Hall of a Thousand Columns, IB's backside is entirely absent from his portrait of Delhi. The rest of him soon slips out of the picture too. He does, so to speak, a Polo. (I can never understand what turns Polophiles on. Granted, the places the Venetian affects to see are reasonably well observed. But he himself is a void. The eponymous mints were well named.) Of IB's day-to-day life for most of the seven years he spent in the city, there are only a few fuzzy snapshots. For me they weren't enough. I wanted to know, for one thing, where he had lived. A full postal address including ZIP code would have been a help, but all he tells us is that it was in 'a mansion near Palam Gate'.

Palam Gate, like the other twenty-seven gates of IB's city, has disappeared. But, assuming it faced the village of the same name, it would have stood on the south-western side of the original Delhi, not far from the Qutb Minar. The sprawling mosque in which the tower stands would have been IB's local, and Ala al-Din's southern gatehouse his most direct way in. So it wasn't that long a shot to imagine that, on a hot Friday after a long sermon, he too would have sat on this same stone bench to put his sandals on before going home. From the bench to his house is a short but impossible journey. The beginning of the old road to Palam – the site of the gate, I supposed – is now the site of a large and very busy bus station, noisy with the tarantaras of Tatas. I can only guess, having quartered the area between here and the Qutb, that IB's house must have stood not far from Raj Motors, a sign on which wished its customers a Happy X-mas, and St John's Church, founded in 1927 in memory of the Reverend S.S. Alnut. I tried to imagine his reaction to the new neighbours. 'Hmm. Well at least they're People of the Book.' But I couldn't see him making use of the local transport and squeezing himself into that cross between a Scud missile, a petrochemical disaster and a pilchard tin which is the Number 69 to Badarpur. He was, to be honest, a distant presence. And then I took a turn that brought him strangely close.

Beyond the buses, behind a cane-juicing machine and over a filthy stream where pigs rooted along the bank, there was a path that led into a wilderness of trees and old Muslim tombs. Another lost jungle; but one which dropped suddenly into place in IB's Delhi. Soon after he arrived in the city, his infant daughter died. She had been born – 'under a lucky star, for I was blessed with joy from the moment of her birth' – to a slave concubine on the road in what is now Uzbekistan. She was buried under a pall of jasmine and musk roses, in a cemetery 'outside Palam Gate'.

No one could claim that IB was a devoted family man. He left children and their mothers as a ship leaves a wake. This child was different. He doesn't tell us her name; but the brief accounts of her birth and death amount to more than he says about all the rest of his scattered offspring put together. Atrocious parent that he was, he seems to have loved her, and mourned her. He had buried a daughter, and Time had gained one.

His grave is lost. She is here, or some mineral memory of her, deaf to the bus-horn lullaby, awaiting the clarion of Israfil and the clamour of Resurrection; after which, like other daughters dead in infancy, she will be called to the considerable task of interceding for her father.

*

Battutian happenings sometimes come about without warning and in unlikely settings. One day I was in a flat on the seventh floor of a New Delhi block, and on my third pre-lunch whisky, when my host stalked off to find out where the food was. For some time he had been smouldering with irritation at the delay, but that was just a slow match for the explosion in the kitchen. In the shock wave of Hindustani I caught the words 'blasted biryani', followed by a yelp.

'Galoots!' roared the prince, regaining the sofa but not his composure. 'Oafs! All of them. From that scoundrel Ramkumar down to the *mali*.'

'I'm sure they can't help it,' I said, wondering why anyone – even a Rajput prince of ancient lineage – would need a *mali*, a gardener, on the seventh floor. 'Don't you think you're a bit hard on them?' I wouldn't normally have mentioned it, but the whisky had loosened my tongue.

The prince's lip curled. 'Hmmph. You're obviously not an aristocrat, are you?'

The logic was hard to follow; but he was looking at me, one eyebrow aloft, waiting. 'Not at all. We're descended from farming stock.'

'Timothy,' he said, regarding me as if through a microscope, 'I am descended from the Sun.'

Another scotch. A veritable Patiala Peg, the four-and-a-half-finger shot named after the prince's bibulous grandfather. It was some time since I'd had so much at lunchtime. It emboldened me to defend myself against these insinuations of niminy-piminy liberalism. 'Don't get me wrong. I'm all in favour of running a tight ship. You know, spare the cat and so on.'

'The *rod*. Yes, quite. But . . . Oh, it's all so tiresome.' Suddenly he looked exhausted, jaded by the genetic burden of *noblesse*, by millennia of responsibility – for, even if the claim of solar ancestry is to be taken with a pinch of salt, his dynasty was ancient even when IB was here. '*Servants* . . . Sometimes I wish they'd just disappear.' The thought made him perk up, and he regarded me quizzically. 'D'you want them? You can have them. The whole boiling lot of 'em. Take 'em for nothing!'

It sounded like an excellent idea. I had always been envious of IB's ever-growing retinue of slaves, a common form of princely largesse. Concubines, syces, pages, valets – a whole moving household. But on second thoughts . . . what would I do with a gardener? 'That's exceedingly kind of you. But just one would do. I don't suppose you've got anyone with secretarial skills?' I slurred the last two words.

The prince bellowed for Ramkumar, his major-domo. There was

a brief exchange and a young man was summoned. He was pleasingly ungalootlike to look at, and claimed to type English at sixty words per minute. The snag was that he couldn't speak it. No doubt we would get by with my copy of *Hindustani Simplified* (so simplified, indeed, that it didn't get much beyond imperatives: 'Fire at that bird.' 'Come, take off my shoes.' 'Bring a whip.') We could work out the terms for indentations and double spacing later on.

The interview with my prospective PA was brief: 'Do you want to go away with this man?' the prince asked him.

'*Thik,*' he replied. Okay. He was dismissed.

'Of course you'll have to pay him something,' the prince said, apologetically. We came up with a figure I could have afforded. 'You'll have to get him a passport too. And make sure you hold on to it so he can't bolt. And you won't let those Musulmans of yours forcibly circumcize him or anything?'

'I'll do my best.'

To be presented with a retainer, even if I had to pay him a retainer, was a profoundly Battutian experience. The idea even survived into sobriety. It would benefit all three parties involved. The further I looked into the mechanics of the matter, however, the harder they seemed. The sticking-point was that new-fangled annoyance, the visa. I could probably swing things with the Yemeni authorities; but what about visits to Britain? The immigration laws there are draconian, and heavily loaded against servants.

It was all highly unfair, but perhaps for the best. With the addition of another person to my single household, the precious *feng-shui* of my books and papers would be overturned. No longer would I be able to conduct *Nimrod* in the nude. In fact an entourage, even of one, would be a dreadful liability. Like marriage.

IB had a suite of forty on his arrival in Delhi, ranging from Greek pages from Asia Minor to his constant but almost invisible fellow-traveller, the Tunisian Abdallah al-Tuzari. (Like a dowager's paid companion, al-Tuzari is always there but seldom referred to. In almost two decades he gets seven look-ins, all but the first in passing.) Unlike me, IB's princes also gave him sacks of gold to maintain his dependants. But even he had to draw the line somewhere. 'The vizier sent me ten slave-girls,' he recalled of his early days in Delhi. 'I gave one of them to the man who brought them – he was none too pleased with his present – and my companions took three of the younger ones. As for the rest I do not know what became of them. Female captives there are very cheap because they are dirty and have no notion of the manners of civilized society. But even educated ones are cheap.' Muhammad Shah's conquests in the south had caused a glut of slaves. IB doesn't mention prices, but a contemporary source notes half a *tangah* as the cost of 'a coquettish girl nearing puberty'. By comparison, 'a nice fat goat' would set you back twice as much, and a decent cow twice as much again.

Revolting though this bargain debasement of humanity may seem to us today, other manifestations of slavery were in many respects admirable and offered excellent career prospects. For the first century of its history the Delhi Sultanate, like the other great Islamic empire of the age, the Mamluk Sultanate of Egypt and Syria, was ruled by freed slave-soldiers or their descendants. Arguably the greatest of these earlier Delhi rulers, Balaban, was a slave of a slave of a slave of the Turkic conqueror of Hindustan. This ugly Turkling, as IB calls Balaban in his historical monograph, began his career mucking out the royal stables and ended it presiding over a court that shone, Barani says, 'with the splendour of the princes of Persia'.

Slavery was suppressed in India in the nineteenth century, in letter if not in spirit. But Persian splendour, inherited from the pre-Islamic Sasanians via the antiquarian Seljuq Turks and brought to India by Balaban, then bequeathed by the Delhi Sultans to the Mughals and grafted on to Hindu notions of sacral kingship, continued to shine in the native courts – and ultimately in the durbars staged by the British – until 1947. One instance of ancient court ceremonial was the custom of *nazar* (Anglo-Indian 'nuzzer'), a sort of opposite maundy given by subject to sovereign. At festivals, IB wrote, holders of royal fiefs 'bring gold coins wrapped in a cloth . . . which the sultan passes on to anyone he pleases'. The practice was still widespread 600 years on, in Hindu as well as Muslim courts. A maharaja's daughter quoted by Charles Allen, for example, recalled that at state durbars in the 1920s 'each one of the courtiers would . . . come along with a gold *mohur* [coin] and present it in a silk handkerchief to my father, who would just touch it and pass it on'. *Hobson-Jobson* notes that *nazar* even made it to the Queen-Empress at Windsor: 'Sir Salar Jung', reported the *Standard* in July 1876, 'was presented to the Queen by the Marquis of Salisbury, and offered his *Muggur* as a token of allegiance, which her Majesty touched and returned.' (*Muggur*, whether for *mohur* or nuzzer, is a howler. A mugger is an Indian crocodile – an allegory, as Mrs Malaprop would have put it, on the banks of the Ganges.)

My Rajput friend remembered echoes of it all, from the marble halls of a childhood lived long after the last seventeen-gun salute fell silent. I was half a century too late for the parasols of state, the drum-bands at the gate, the obeisance and oblations; for a whole grammar of kingship that reverberated through the Hall of a Thousand Columns, back to a distant Persian past.

As for the typing of my manuscripts, I suppose I shall always do it myself.

*

For most of his static years in Delhi IB is pushed out of the picture by the giant figure of Muhammad Shah, and by the detail surrounding it – detail of a density and grotesqueness worthy of Bosch or Dadd. His reappearance marks one of the great catastrophic points of the *Travels*, the birth of another of Time's daughters.

One day at the beginning of 1341, he went sightseeing outside Delhi to the underground house of Shaykh Shihab al-Din. IB was a Sufi groupie: he collected shaykhs great and small, many impeccably holy, a few wholly implausible. The *Travels* is, among many other things, the album of a hagiomane. In the case of Shihab al-Din, the combination of a holy man and a subterranean residence – complete, IB had heard, with bath-house and fitted kitchen – was irresistible. Curiosity all but killed the qadi, for the timing of the visit could not have been worse: it took place just before the shaykh was arrested, tortured and executed for uttering the *z*-word.

> When the shaykh was seized, the sultan had his sons interro-
> gated about those who had visited him, and they mentioned my
> name as one of them. On hearing this, the sultan ordered four
> of his slaves to stand guard over me in the audience-hall; when
> he takes this action with anyone, that person seldom escapes.
> The first day of my detention was a Friday, and God Almighty
> inspired me to recite His words [from the Qur'an] *Sufficient for
> us is God and excellent the Protector*. I recited them that day 33,000
> times and spent the night in the audience-hall. I continued in
> this state for five days and nights, reciting the entire Qur'an each
> day and taking no sustenance but water. After these five days

I broke my fast, and then continued to fast for another four days. I was released after the execution of the shaykh, praise be to God Almighty . . . Some time after this I withdrew from the sultan's service and became a follower of the shaykh and imam, the learned and devout ascetic Kamal al-Din Abdallah al-Ghari, a man of great humility and godliness.

He had, as he put it, left the world. In practical terms he had no other option. Like the other foreigners in Muhammad Shah's court, he had signed a document binding himself never to leave the sultan's service; a religious retreat was the only exception, the one possible escape. But it was an escape he had toyed with making for years. Since leaving Arabia a decade earlier, IB had been been carried eastward by the hope of material success. Yet from the start of his travels he had often stared, fascinated, into the parallel, spiritual current of Islam. Twice he had teetered on its brink, tempted to take the plunge and become a hermit. Both times he was pulled back by his *nafs*, his worldly spirit. So far he had never been more than a tourist, a rubbernecker at mysteries. Now he became a traveller among them.

IB calls his guide, al-Ghari, 'the unique and peerless personality of his age'. Posterity has not agreed: as far as I could tell not a trace of the man had survived, either in the hagiographies or on the ground. But there was a clue to follow – 'he was known as al-Ghari [the Caveman] because he lived in a cave [*ghar*]'; and an address of sorts – the cave was 'outside Delhi, near the hospice of Shaykh Nizam al-Din'. It was as vague and unpromising as IB's own worldly address, 'near Palam Gate'. To me, however, it seemed immeasurably more important: the cave-hermitage is a cardinal co-ordinate of the traveller's personal history.

The omens for finding it were not good. Shaykh Nizam al-Din, the most famous saint of Delhi, has given his name to a district of the city. His headquarters – later his tomb, now his shrine – is one of the most popular spots on the pious tourist-trail of Indian Islam. Its environs are not, however, renowned as a site of special speleological interest. Indeed, a cave in the flat and densely built-up quarter of Nizamuddin was about as likely as an Oddbins in Mecca.

I set out hopelessly with Titoo.

*

The Caveman's cave is part of a system that runs deep under the Islamic world and far beyond the borders of India. The entrance to this complex is in Asia Minor, at the Cave of the Seven Sleepers. Persecuted for their monotheistic beliefs, the Qur'an tells how they were inspired to 'go to the cave for shelter. God will extend to you His mercy and prepare for you a means of safety.' Once in the cave, they nodded off; they woke up when the danger was past – 300 years later, and in a state of preservation unattainable even by Californian cryogenists. The story was originally set in Ephesus; but it spread, and the cave too – the old Islamic world is riddled with alleged Caves of the Seven (or Five, or Three, for God alone knows their number) Sleepers. The idea is appealing: the Sleepers' cave frees you not only from your enemies, but from the world itself, and time. It is a foretaste of resurrection, of the presence of God. The other Qur'anic caves are also portals to the divine – the one in which the Prophet hid from his enemies and where 'God caused His tranquillity to descend upon him'; and the cave on Mount Hira where the angel Gabriel delivered the first chapters of the heavenly book. One is nearer God's heart in a cavern than anywhere else on earth.

One of the earliest contemplatives in Islam, the eighth-century mystic Ibrahim ibn Ad'ham, spent nine years in a cave in Khurasan. Some scholars have seen Buddhistic inspiration in his ideas and in those of the Shikaftiyyah, the Persian 'Cavemen' of the same region of eastern Iran. To my mind, however, a cave is such an obvious beatific bolt-hole, and the Qur'anic association of subterranean and supernatural so clear, that no other inspiration is necessary. By IB's time, spiritual spelunking was an established pastime throughout Islamdom, from his native Morocco to Bengal, and its nimblest adepts could slip in and out of an underground time- and space-warp that allowed them to cross enormous distances and attain great ages. IB was to meet a bicentenarian hermit on an island off the Karnataka coast who later popped up in a grotto outside Canton. Renowned Indian cavemen of the age included Muntajib al-Din, who is said to have been born wearing a golden nappy (more sensible than a silver spoon), and Maneri, the paramount saint of Bihar. Maneri was also a prolific letter-writer who numbered Muhammad Shah among his correspondents, and in one of his epistles he included a manifesto for anchorites: 'The condition necessary for you truly to exist is that you pass by the whole world, distance yourself from yourself, remove your heart from yourself, and wash your hands of yourself, just as the Sleepers of the Cave did. Make a cave of your heart and, entering therein, proclaim four times on your behalf that God is great!'

For IB the material world had been revealed for what it was – in the Prophet's words, 'a prison for the faithful'. In its most conspicuous manifestation, Muhammad Shah's palace, it had literally been his prison. So it was with a sense of liberation that he changed his qadi's robe for a beggar's rags, and a master who lived in a Thousand-Column Hall for one who lived in a hole in the ground. It was to be the start of another phase of travel, out of the phenomenal universe and into the microcosm of himself.

'What', you may well ask, as did another trainee mystic of IB's time in a letter to his own Sufi master, 'is the meaning of "travel into yourself"?' 'The journey', came the reply, 'entails travelling from the phenomenal, non-existent self to the real self, which is one with the Truth.' IB's century was the age of the reflexive metajourney. It was the very 1960s of Sufism, and IB had embarked on its Ascetic Soul-Aid Acid Test. With al-Ghari as his guru and the immaterial road wide open, IB couldn't wait to get going.

*

A sleek man in fawn and cream and a perfectly pressed smile approached me as I entered the shrine-complex of Nizam al-Din. On his head he wore a sugar-loaf cap, that emblem of dervish-hood which I had last seen on the whirling Mevlevis of Anatolia. The cap was yellow, the mark of a Nizami *pirzadah* – a 'saint-son' or, to be precise, a very grand-nephew of Nizam al-Din. The beatified collateral ancestor died a decade before IB arrived in Delhi, but his shrine is still in the family, run by descendants of his sister. This member of the dynasty was carrying a large oblong book, which he opened as he reached me – me alone among the crowd of visitants. 'I think you would like to . . .'

Sign the visitors' book? If only I'd known, I'd have brought my Montblanc Meisterstück. I mean, a biro . . . Nizam al-Din stood at the very pinnacle of the *pirs*, the Sufi masters. He had entered the *pir*-charts long before IB was born, had gone platinum while Balaban was still on the throne. He stayed at number one through half a dozen reigns. Muhammad Shah was one of his biggest fans. The saint was a myth in his own lifetime: even his most down-to-earth biographer said that he went to Mecca every night on a flying camel and was back 'in time for an early breakfast'. Nearly seven centuries on he is still top of the *pirs* and his order, the Chishtis, still the most popular Sufi group. The visitors' book! It was like being asked for your autograph by Sir Cliff Richard. 'It would be a pleasure,' I replied, 'and an honour.'

It was an unusual visitors' book. There were six columns, headed 'Tomb of Nizam al-Din . . . Tomb of Amir Khusraw . . .' and so on, each filled with figures. The latest entry was a row of Rs. 500s. 'All donations', purred the *pirzadah*, 'are most gratefully received.'

I goggled at the full house of 500s, and felt around my pocket. There were a few Rs. 50 notes and four donation receipts from the shrine of Qutb al-Din Bakhtiyar Ka'ki, a Battutian saint I'd called on earlier. Each of the receipts was for Rs. 5, each issued with blessings. Nizam al-Din was of course in a different league. I wrote 'Rs. 50' in the first two columns. Slightly embarrassing, coming straight after all those noughts; but it was the thought that counted.

Not here it wasn't. The *pirzadah*'s smile sagged at the dearth of zeroes then, when he realized I had stopped writing, crumpled. 'You are a *rich* man . . .' he said cattily – the purr had become a hiss – accepting the pair of limp fifties as if they'd been used snot-rags.

'*Al-ghani Allah*,' I said to his departing back. God alone is truly rich.

I now remembered Salman Haidar saying, during that evening of brain-picking, that the yellow caps concealed some of the slinkiest operators in town. 'They'll shake you down,' he warned. And they have probably been shaking people down since the Nizami nephews milked their first *tangahs* in the fourteenth century. I had just taken part in a deeply authentic transaction.

The blurring of matter and spirit begins in the bazaar surrounding Nizam al-Din's shrine. First, a mingled odour of mutton and roses. Deeper in, the roses predominate, and you swim in a fug of scent, along passageways pink and magenta with petals and black with funeral palls. The crowd thickens and the whispers of the rose-sellers rise, the soft-soap, hard-sell siren swish of voices saying Roses a–roses a–roses . . . paradise for Miss Cartland, poetry to Miss Stein. Still in the bazaar, you remove your shoes and exchange them for a number. You cross some fuzzy threshold. For a few yards, the scent of roses and feet. Then, through the doorway, roses and feet and frankincense; clammy marble, sweaty petals underfoot; and that suave extraction of cash.

The undemarcatable boundary between here and hereafter ran right through the *pirzadahs'* office. There was a desk with a telephone and an executive desk-set, a commercial calendar on the wall – and opposite the desk a rose-strewn tomb. A tomb in an office in a shrine in a bazaar. Now all I wanted was a cave.

The duty-*pirzadah* was as perfectly turned out as his fellow-Nizami, the rupee-reaping greeter at the gate, but a good deal more amiable. It seemed however that there were no caves in the vicinity, not even for ready money; the name of IB's guru, al-Ghari, drew a mystified blank. I did a quick tomb-hop – the poet Amir Khusraw, the princess Jahanara Begum, the *pir* Nizam al-Din himself – then left the shrine as the cash-seeking missile launched itself at another target, a blur of fawn and cream with a yellow warhead.

I suppose my mental picture of the Caveman's digs was influenced by the *faux*-hermitages of eighteenth-century England. I had in mind a drier, warmer version, perhaps inhabited still by a mad-eyed mystic. There was a good supply of suitable tenants in and around the shrine of Nizam al-Din, but an apparent lack of grottoes. I hoped the amiable *pirzadah* was wrong on this second point. But I knew from my reading that the sort of rock outcrops where one might have found caves had been quarried away for their stone centuries ago. Moreover, it only took a glance at the map to see that while in the fourteenth century Nizam al-Din's headquarters had lain two miles to the north-east of Muhammad Shah's city, they now stood almost at the centre of the Delhi conurbation and were hemmed in by buildings. So I wasn't surprised when I explored the streets around the shrine and failed to find any promising bumps in the ground. Beyond the rose bazaar there was a knotty tangle of residential alleys, a large number of cap emporia and other suppliers of dervish gear, and even a Computerized Calligraphy Training Centre; but not a whisper of a ghost of a memory of five of the most important months in IB's life.

As for al-Ghari, he might have been 'the outstanding and unique personality of his age' in IB's view. It was now clear to me, however, that not only had posterity disagreed, but also contemporaneity: even in his lifetime, the Caveman had lived in the shade of a chart-topping group, Nizam al-Din and the Chishtis. Why should his memory have survived? He is Graham of the Swinging Blue Jeans to Cliff of the Shadows.

*

The pop-star metaphor is largely but not entirely flippant. Nizam al-Din's shrine is famous above all for its *qawwalis*, or sacred jam-sessions, an established practice among the Chishtis since well before IB's day. The earliest star of the Chishti order in India, Mu'in al-Din of Ajmer, owed much of his celebrity to the music he introduced into his meetings; for the idea, he was indebted to a yogi. Nizam al-Din himself was inspired to become a Chishti devotee on hearing *qawwalis* at the age of 12, and through him the sacred music was to spread: in parallel with the Sultanate's armies, a gentler wave of Nizami disciples – 700 of them, according to tradition – rolled across India. They did not actively seek converts; but they took their hymn-books with them, and the enduring presence of Islam in many parts of the Subcontinent is due less to the kettledrums of war than to the *qawwalis* of Nizam al-Din. Late one Thursday afternoon I returned to his shrine to hear them.

The shoe-tender welcomed me profusely, scrabbled around in his box of tags and produced, with a flourish, No. 1. The Portuguese brothel-creepers were pigeonholed with the sort of reverence due to a dead sultan's sandals. Whatever the reason – I had tipped him no more than the next man – it is agreeable when a shine is taken to one. The greeter in the shrine didn't have such a good memory. He switched on his smirk, opened his ledger and homed in on me through the swirl of figures. 'I think you would like . . .'

'*Allah karim*,' I said, pointing heavenward – 'God is the Generous One', a time-hallowed brush-off for beggars – and ducked into the press of bodies. As I turned I caught a glimpse of the open page and the most recent entry: a curiously familiar row of Rs. 500s . . . Safely out of range, I looked back and saw the *pirzadah* still standing there, neutralized. The smirk remained, but I'd wiped the face off his smile.

They were still rolling out the carpet for the *qawwali*, so I did another turn around Nizam al-Din's tomb-chamber. A clockwise vortex of bodies circumambulated the grave. Roses flew and heads bobbed beneath the pall to kiss the tomb, emerging pink with petals and piety. Back outside, the *qawwals* had taken their place at the head of the carpet on which they would perform. The courtyard was already packed, but still more people squeezed in. The small space seemed to possess the properties of a black hole, of both the celestial and Calcutta sorts. I spotted my chance, a tiny gap in the front, sitting row. With contortionistic skills learned in twenty years of Yemeni weddings, I was in. It was a very tiny gap. My right-hand neighbour was a burly Sufi from Stuttgart in full North West Frontier kit, sporting the Yorkshire-pudding hat of the Pathans and a miniscule video camera. That national genius for getting the best spot by the hotel pool had secured him some prime elbow-room. My pips squeaked.

There were a couple more Europeans in the standing crowd; a good number of women and children; a sprinkling, no more, of obvious Hindus and Sikhs ('I used to go a lot to Nizam al-Din,' a middle-class Hindu acquaintance told me later. 'But not now. The boundaries are hardening.'). One member of the audience, however, caught my eye and held it. He was sitting three to my left, piratically earringed, a shawl over his bare shoulder. Everything about him was long – hair, beard, eyelashes, face – as if he were modelling the Baptist for Parmigiano. He bore, as IB would say, the marks of austerity, and a smile that was everything the *pirzadah*'s was not. In the pre-performance hush we looked at each other along the intervening figures, and nodded.

The *qawwals* started, exploring the air with recitatives. As he sang, the principal vocalist's fingers glissandoed around the keyboard of a portative harmonium, the two reedy lines of voice and instrument chasing each other up and down the octave. Another singer-organist joined the pursuit, and now and then all four lines subsided in a sigh. The pauses multiplied, the sighs grew longer; but a head of pressure was building. Suddenly the *qawwals* found their rhythm, the drummer shot the clutch, and they were off in a burst of locomotive thrust, taking the audience with them. The German swayed, setting off a sympathetic oscillation through the sitting line. A toddler ran on to the carpet and leapt about like a spring lamb. The Baptist caught my eye again and we looked at each other, laughing. I caught the riff – *mahbub Allah . . . mahbub Allah . . .* beloved of God. Everyone was rocking, and no one was enjoying himself more than the drummer, sitting there driving us on, wheedling ever more human sounds from his skins: *mahbub Allah . . .* bah-boing tap-tap *. . . mahbub Allah . . .* mah-boing ah-aah. Dave Brubeck said Indian drummers can't play in four-four; what does it matter when they can play in Arabic?

Something unexpected happened. There was a dark flash to my left and the Baptist was up. He had thrown off his shawl and stood naked but for a loincloth and, I now saw, a lot of heavy metal – a knuckle-duster of silver rings on his right hand, a stack of industrial-grade bangles on his right arm and ankle, and a pair of giant carnelian rosaries around his neck, each hung with a silver phylactery the size of a cigar case. On his left wrist he wore a Swatch watch. For a moment he stood motionless; then he raised his arms straight above his head, hands touching like those of a diver about to plunge, and began to dance.

Or to dissolve. 'It is neither dancing nor foot-play nor bodily indulgence, but a dissolution of the self. Those who call it "dancing" are completely wrong.' This is al-Hujwiri, the eleventh-century Sufi theorist. But to the untrained eye the Baptist was doing a variant on the classic late Seventies pogo; a little limp at first then, as he got into the pulse of 'Allahs' and boings, more and more energetic, until he was a human piston shining with sweat and silver.

On and on he danced. I began to wonder what would happen next; perhaps everyone did, for a ripple of surprise had run through the crowd when he took the floor. The answer came without warning. I was looking at the Baptist's eyes, bright and unfocused like those of a doll, when they swivelled back into his head. The lids closed, the rhythm faltered. We, the nearest sitters, stood and formed a ring around him as the piston slowed and slewed, then stopped. He shuddered, uttered two sobbing cries, and collapsed, a dead weight sinking through our arms. He lay face down on the ground, still as a corpse. The music continued.

IB doesn't mention the Delhi *qawwali*, but he does refer to its ecstatic by-product of *hal* – the state of mystical dissolution into which, my fellow *qawwali*-goers were whispering, the Baptist had fallen. As crown prince, Muhammad Shah was fascinated by the phenomenon and would ride here post-haste if he learned that Nizam al-Din was in a trance. It was during the last such visit, IB says, not long before the saint's death, that Nizam al-Din predicted Muhammad's accession to the throne: 'We grant you the kingdom,' he pronounced, in mid-*hal*. Looking at the prone form in front of me, I doubted whether it was up to speech of any sort, let alone prophecy. Its owner had been aiming at that same state to which IB was travelling with the Caveman. The difference in their approaches was the speed. IB took his ecstasy in measured doses, the Baptist mainlined. Perhaps overdosed: the inert body on the carpet appeared not to be breathing. I remembered IB's story of a Delhi dervish who, on reaching a similar pitch, 'cried out and dropped dead'.

Twenty minutes later the Baptist abruptly stood up and returned to his place. Again we caught each other's eyes, smiled, and nodded. We might have been at a lunch-time concert of chamber music at St John's, Smith Square.

The session ended with the last call to prayer of the day and a solid press of bodies making for the exit. I caught sight of the Baptist, squeezed my way through to him and tapped him on the shoulder. He turned; but the long head of hair belonged to one of the in-house dervishes of the shrine. Unbidden, the man produced a bottle of scent and dabbed some on my face and hair with a pad of cotton wool. I left the shrine pungent and consecrated.

Back at the guest-house Martin and I compared our days. His mornings were still occupied by the Lal Gumbad although the Mughals, in the person of Humayun and his tomb, took up most of his afternoons. Now my worst fears were coming true, for today Safdarjang's *demi-mondaine* mausoleum had seduced him. 'OK. I know what you think about the place. But it's relaxed. You know, the guards were passing round a joint . . .' He was looking at me strangely. 'What's wrong with your ear?'

'I don't know. But my hearing's gone on the left side. I can't think why. I mean, it was the Chishtis, not Led Zeppelin.'

He reached over and pulled out a small wad of cotton wool.

It still holds a memory of scent. Looking at it now, it occurs to me that I have only ever seen one other recipient of perfumed earplugs: he was dead, and we were laying him out.

*

'It's no drawing-room, I'm afraid,' said Khwajah Hasan Sani Nizami, apologizing for our surroundings. 'More like a dervish's cell.'

In fact it was more like a dentist's waiting-room, *circa* 1950. A rectangle of chairs sat, backs to the wall, looking uncomfortably down on a low central table; all were stifled in treacly varnish. It did however belong to a dervish – *the* dervish, for Khwajah Hasan is head of the whole great dynasty of Nizami *pirzadahs*. In his dashing frock coat and beard, his yellow cap, and his dowdy setting, he sparkled.

'Speaking of dervishes,' I said after the formalities – which, since mention of IB broke the ice, were brief – 'an interesting thing happened at the *qawwali* the other night.' I described the solo pogo and collapse, keen to discover if the Baptist belonged to any of the Sufi groupings IB described.

'Oh . . . A *hal*.' For a moment, I thought Khwajah Hasan looked a bit sheepish. Then he smiled. 'These things happen from time to time. Certain . . . devotees are apt to get carried away. Nizam al-Din however always insisted that in the ecstasy of *sama* and *raqs*, sacred recital and dance, one should be so conscious as to be able to feel a rose petal under one's foot.'

'That wouldn't be difficult. The shrine's full of rose petals.'

'And you know the reason? It is because flowers and scents remind us of God and His Prophet, who said, "Whosoever smells the scent of a rose and prays not for blessings on me, that man has turned his back on me."'

His Arabic was beautiful. He warmed when I admired it; but he wouldn't be drawn on the affiliation, if any, of my collapsible companion of the other night. A pot of tea was brought, and a plate of wafers. (Do wafers have some Sufistic significance? An old friend of mine, formerly the Archbishop of Canterbury's Apokrisarios in Belgrade, was given wafers when he called on the Grandfather of the Albanian Bektashi dervishes.) Then a colleague of Khwajah Hasan's dropped by. After the introductions, he took up the subject of ecstatic freak-outs. 'Don't tell those shaykhs of yours back in Arabia about what goes on at our shrine. They'll say it's all heresy and polytheism!'

We all laughed. But he had a point. I later met a Yemeni acquaintance, a resident of Delhi, who told me about a compatriot who died there. 'We said the canonical prayers over him at Nizam al-Din's mosque. Then the Indians said, "Let's go and say an extra prayer for him at the saint's tomb." We weren't having any of that, I can tell you.' To a dyed-in-the-wool Zaydi from Yemen, such practices shrieked hagiolatry.

'You see,' Khwajah Hasan's friend went on, 'certain aspects of worship have been introduced to make it all – what shall we say? – more attractive. And, from the start, Nizam al-Din himself exerted a personal magnetism that was hard to resist. You have heard of the poet Amir Khusraw?' I nodded, remembering his tomb in the Nizami complex; and the Rs. 50 I'd donated to it. 'He was Nizam al-Din's most fervent disciple. He went as far as to say in a verse that his *qiblah*, the direction of his worship, was "the one with cap askew".'

I looked from one to the other, puzzled. Khwajah Hasan smiled, then tipped his yellow hat forward and cocked it jauntily to one side. 'This is the way, er, pretty boys wore their caps in Nizam al-Din's time. Amir Khusraw meant that his master was his boyfriend, and his idol. In a purely metaphorical way, of course.'

It began to make sense. In Sufi poetry, homoerotic yearnings are often used to symbolize a longing for God. Here, though, the longing was that of disciple for master. It was coming it a bit strong.

The friend left, and I steered the conversation on to the Caveman, the main reason for my visit. Khwajah Hasan was clearly a considerable scholar, and I hoped he might be able to point me towards my elusive hermit. He only confirmed my pessimism. Several underground cells – he was sure they were Islamic – had come to light in the area in the 1970s. They had all been 'bulldozed and built over'. I did no better with the Caveman's name. 'There were so many minor saints around at the time,' he said. 'The better known ones have pushed them out of the limelight.' He sounded apologetic; but he and his shrine were themselves eloquent reminders that fame and memory are subject to natural selection. 'There are quite a few anonymous tombs. But . . . named saints of the period buried around here . . . No, there's nothing remotely like your man's name. There's a Khwajah Shams al-Din Awtad Allah who's the right date. He was an interesting character, a naked *majdhub* – you know, not a member of any particular Sufi group.'

I was interested to hear that an autocephalous nudist could gain the title 'Awtad', one of the highest in the Sufi *wali*ocracy. 'By the way,' I said, making a note of this (and reflecting that the word *majdhub* also means, in some parts of the Arabic-speaking world, 'nutcase'), 'how should one refer to you? *Pirzadah*-in-Chief? The Boss?'

He thought for a moment. 'I don't know what I am. God is the Boss. But my father had a title. It was granted by the British. In fact it was the very last title they conferred before they left. You see, he refused all honours and so on until they were on the point of going, so that no one could say he was a toady.'

'What was it? A KCIE?'

Khwajah Hasan laughed. 'Certainly not! It was "Shams al-Ulama" [the Sun of Scholars]. And it came with an embroidered robe.'

'Just like IB. In Delhi he was known as "Shams al-Din" [the Sun of Religion]. And his job as qadi came with an embroidered robe.' Another echo, reverberating through 600 years of Court and Social Columns.

'My father – here's another coincidence – also wrote a *safar-nama*, a travel narrative, on his visit to England. Only a short work, though. Nothing like Ibn Battutah's book.' Khwajah Hasan digressed on his father's literary output. It ranged from standard Sufological works to an imaginary diary, in both Urdu and English, of the Prince of Wales. 'I mean the one who ended up as the Duke of Windsor. It examined his relations with Mrs Simpson in the light of the Sufi interpretation of love.' He looked at the teapot. 'You have forgotten your tea.'

I had; and the Caveman, and the Baptist. Khwajah Hasan's conversation, a river absorbing tributaries of thought and increasing in breadth, had carried me into unexpected regions. 'Shall I pour?'

He answered in a Persian couplet. I recognized a few words, enough to venture

> Boy, let yon liquid ruby flow . . . ?

– Khwajah Hasan nodded –

> And bid thy pensive heart be glad,
> Whate'er the frowning zealots say:
> Tell them, their Eden cannot show

98

> A stream so clear as Rocnabad,
> A bower so sweet as Mosellay.

The poet Hafiz – still in short trousers when IB passed through his native Shiraz – in the English of Sir William Jones. The tea was as cold as the stream of Rocnabad.

The Khwajah's stream flowed on, a river of English with Urdu, Persian and Arabic affluents, through the history of the Chishti order, the Khwajah's own personal history, the Islamic theology of Christmas ('It is *incumbent* on Muslims to celebrate it,' he insisted, giving Qur'anic chapter and verse), the decline of the King's English, to the decline of Urdu in Delhi. 'A huge loss . . . P.V. Narasimha Rao, the old PM, once told me, "If you want a letter answered by me promptly and personally, write in Urdu. All the Hindi ones get passed through secretaries." And now . . .' The flow paused.

Khwajah Hasan was not only the representative of a Sufi tradition that went back to ninth-century Chisht in western Afghanistan, and beyond; he was also a product of that influx, of which IB too was a part, that flowed down into Hindustan from the old Arabo-Perso-Turkic world. It had brought destruction, certainly; but also fertility, diversity. And now that diversity was disappearing. It was indeed a huge loss.

'Will you allow me five minutes for my *namaz*?' Khwajah Hasan asked, again apologetic. I looked at my watch, and saw that we – he, mostly – had been talking for nearly three hours. When the shoe-keeper led me here I had been hoping for a handshake or, at most, a diary date for a formal five-minute audience.

Khwajah Hasan returned from his prayers in an even nattier coat, set off by a narrow evening scarf that matched his cap. As we walked together to the gate I realized I was reluctant to leave. Together with the yellow cap of Nizam al-Din, Khwajah Hasan had inherited something of the charisma of that saint, and much of his learning and gentleness. As we parted on the street, he told me of an Englishman who had visited the shrine. 'When he left he said, "I came here as a stranger, stayed as a friend, and depart as a brother." This is the miracle of Nizam al-Din. Go in peace.'

I left the sainted suburb, suffused with similarly fraternal senti-ments. For a few moments they extended even to Khwajah Hasan's cousin and his Ledger of the Five-Hundred-Rupee Columns.

*

India, or at least Islamic India, had started to seem less intricate and obscure. I was beginning to connect. But I was no nearer to al-Ghari, the Caveman. On the contrary, my hopes of finding him had receded. If Khwajah Hasan couldn't lead me to him, then who could?

The Khwajah had, however, mentioned a certain *Sultan* Ghari, a royal saint buried in what is now a housing estate on the way to the airport. He was over a hundred years earlier than my man and in entirely the wrong part of town. I visited him all the same, and found him leading a double life, or death. The Muslims consider him a *pir*, the Hindus a sadhu. Pink and yellow swastikas and offerings of milk and ghee mingled with the standard accoutrements of an Islamic saint. He also had an alias: the guardian of the tomb called him Sultan Ghuri. The confusion increased when I looked him up in Sir Saiyid Ahmad Khan's pioneering nineteenth-century work on the monuments of Delhi, and found that the name appeared not only as Sultan Ghari and Sultan Ghuri, but also as Sultangarhi and Sultan Ghazi. For a moment, I wondered if my Ghari had got similarly garbled. But no; IB specifically said that the name came from the place where he lived, that *ghar* or cave.

Or, on second thoughts, perhaps not a cave at all. Khwajah Hasan had also mentioned those bulldozed underground cells. All along, I had pictured al-Ghari's hermitage as a natural grotto – improved on, perhaps, by a few Reptonesque touches of my own. Should I have been looking for something less romantic – a bunker, a foxhole? The Arabic word admits that sense. This new line of thought carried me back to the Red Tomb, our first monument of IB's India, and to a mention in Hearn's *Seven Cities of Delhi* of 'a tiny cell', sunk in the ground near the mausoleum, 'only three feet wide, and almost filled up with soil. This is declared to have been the abode . . . of Kabir-ud-Din Aulia, who is buried in the Lal Gumbaz; but one may be pardoned for being sceptical about this.' Unlike Hearn, the no-nonsensical engineer who surveyed the Khyber railway, I was not sceptical. Mystical potholing was a perfectly normal hobby for ascetics of the time. Kabir al-Din and IB's Caveman were contemporaries, and a look into the holy hole by the Red Tomb might give me an alternative picture of what I was trying to find.

I had missed it on my earlier trips to the tomb with Martin. But a return visit and a systematic snoop, nose to the ground, failed to reveal it. The hundred years since Hearn wrote his book had obliterated all trace of Kabir al-Din's bijou burrow.

I gave my hopes of finding the Caveman a decent burial.

*

Like IB, I had been stationary too long. The cave, the only tangible point on his transcendental trek, was lost. I needed to get going and follow his subsequent, physical journey through India. It was packed with descriptions and adventures, and I wanted to revisit them. Besides, there was something oppressive about Delhi; not only the pollution, increasingly irksome as the temperature rose, but a whole pall of associations. For me, the memory of Muhammad Shah smothered the place as effectively as smog.

Martin was less keen to leave Delhi, for he was still busy painting the Emperor Humayun's mausoleum. Even I had to admit that, for a Mughal monument, it was impressive. It managed in spite of its great mass to appear weightless, hovering over its garden. The canals that intersected the parterres of the garden were now dry; but a drop or two of imagination made them flow, turning the tomb into a pink reliquary on a square green cushion shot with silver. Like Edward Lear, his own disembodied fellow-traveller in Delhi, Martin painted there for hours on end amid the loud discourse of turtle doves.

We made another foray into the contemporary art scene. The show was miles out along the Mathura road, in a blue glass bubble filled with the loud discourse of twitterati. Dancers performed in a courtyard: a girl immersed herself in a pond, surrounded, Ophelia-like, by blooms; a tall person, of Sitwellian countenance and indeterminate sex, pranced and lunged. The exhibition was due to travel to Tokyo then, our American friend in rose-tinted spectacles informed us, to the Andy Warhol Gallery. Something about the work – a marriage of Jeff Koons, ships' figureheads and South Indian temple sculpture – suggested that it might do well in New York. The highlight of the show was a series of naked giantesses dripping with gold leaf. 'They're entirely . . .' I hunted for the right word, 'camp.'

'You mean entirely fibreglass,' said Martin, giving one of them a tap. 'And so's a Reliant Robin. But they're also very well observed,' he continued, admiring a ripple of golden cellulite.

The evening ended, to my relief, in the Press Club of New Delhi, a large room filled with beer-bellied journalists, cheap Kingfishers and good anecdotes. ('So when I got to immigration at Dover – oh, I was a real bolshie one then! – they said to me, "And just how long do you intend to stay in Britain, *sir*?" And I said to them, "Not as long as you chaps stayed in India!"')

'What an evening,' said Martin as we left the club.

I agreed that it had indeed been an evening. 'And it ended in the Hall of a Thousand Columnists.'

*

The thermometer rose, the air stagnated. Days had long passed into weeks. Martin painted on, following Lear to the 'over be-ornamented moskinesses' of that architectural tart, Safdarjang. I went about picking up odds and ends of indica: the way in which the latest cell-phone, hand-painted on a hoarding, could be made to look old-fashioned; linguistic oxymora, like an 'IT Shoppe' and 'a mild baton charge'; the way in which bureaucracy could penetrate one's most private moments ('Urine or toilet, sir?' asked the guardian of a swish new public lavatory – the charge varied accordingly, a rupee for a pee, two for a number two); the best way, according to Titoo, of tying a Sikh turban solo – jam one end in a door, take the other to the far end of the room, and do the twist. The fragments would start to fit together and form an angle of the vast and polygonal picture; and then I would get stuck.

One of the harder corners of the picture to puzzle out was a piece of open ground near the Karbala Masjid, where the Shi'ites of Delhi were mourning the martyrdom of the Prophet's grandson Husayn. At first it was disappointing. I'd been hoping for blood and whips, a frenzied Hobson-Jobson of flagellation; but it was a wussy affair, with circles of boys wafting about in jeans and bandanas, clacking sticks together in an oriental version of Morris dancing. And, for so melancholy an anniversary, there was an unseemly air of jollity. Families sat around with picnics and babies. There were lots of baseball caps with integral spectacles and the legend, 'I Love You'. I left the fairground and watched a procession of floats passing along the adjacent road, each bearing a scaled-down version of Husayn's mausoleum festooned with tinsel. I realized that I too was being borne along, by the dense mass of spectators. At the foot of a flight of stairs, they turned and began to ascend. The crowd became a crush, an escalator of flesh. I rose, clinging to the body in front, and was spewed back into a different part of the fairground.

Here the earth was cratered with a series of deep empty pits. Beside these sat lines of beggars and, strangely, a solitary greengrocer – a boy trying to sell a pair of ripe pumpkins. I smiled at him in sympathy; he must have got lost. He smiled back. And I saw that the pumpkins were the boy's testicles.

Further along was a group of six men arranged starfishwise on the ground. They were yelling *Ya Allah!* in unison and doing a kind of Charleston – all the more impressive for the fact that between them they didn't have a leg to stand on, let alone dance on. Their synchronized writhing brought two thoughts to mind. The first was a joke Martin had told me ('Did you hear about the legless man who went to the disco? He got chucked out for arsing about.'). The second was that dismembered reception committee at the gate of the Thousand-Column Hall. This was the live version.

*

'But you have been looking in quite the wrong place!'

I stared at Akhilesh Mithal, not a little surprised. Salman Haidar had brought me to the house of this elderly gentleman, describing him as an antiquarian of the old school. We found him reclining – in tweed jacket, silk tie, fudge-coloured astrakhan hat and *chaise longue* – in an airy upper room pierced by Mughal screens. I had just mentioned my fruitless search for the Caveman's cave.

'You say it was "near the hospice of Nizam al-Din"? This is not the place that became his shrine. You see, it was while Nizam al-Din was standing on the roof of his hospice that he said,

> *Har qawm-ra 'st rahi*
> *Din wa qibla-gahi'*

Half the words were Arabic, but I couldn't make sense of the Persian connections between them. 'Please explain.'

'It means, "Every people has its own *din* and *qiblah*" – its own religion and direction of worship. Nizam al-Din was looking down, you understand, at a group of Hindus performing *puja* in the river. Which means that your hospice must have been near the bank of the Yamuna. The main shrine is too far distant, even allowing for the Yamuna's change of course over the intervening centuries.' I raised my eyebrows; Mr Mithal continued. 'Nizam al-Din's disciple, the poet Amir Khusraw, happened to be on the roof with him. And no sooner had his master said these words than Amir Khusraw added this:

Man qibla rast kardam
Bir simt-e kaj kolahi

Which means, "As for me, I have altered the direction of my worship towards the one whose cap is awry". No, "askew". He meant, of course, his adored *pir*, Nizam al-Din.'

I remembered Khwajah Hasan's demonstration of the crucial cap-angle, and his gloss about the fervent love of disciple for master. 'So Amir Khusraw was capping the first couplet.'

Mr Mithal smiled. 'I believe the Persian term is "knotting". Be that as it may, this might provide a clue for you; although I am not aware that you will find many caves in the vicinity of the Yamuna.' He did, however, provide other examples of cave eremitism, Muslim, Hindu and Buddhist, and of ascetic austerities in general. '. . . And of course there is the celebrated *chilla-ye ma'kus*, the forty-day fast suspended upside down in a well.'

I had read about this practice. Most Sufi masters regarded it as flash, and definitely not to be done in public. (It may still take place. Comparable feats of bravura mortification have, allegedly, been performed in living memory: a friend of mine met a Pakistani Muslim in Oregon who said that his grandfather had spent forty years standing on one leg, *under a waterfall*.)

Salman was smiling. 'Akhilesh, that's absolutely impossible.'

'Many are called, Salman,' he replied, grinning broadly, 'but few are chosen.'

At this point a not inappropriate doorbell sounded. A troupe of grand-nieces and -nephews appeared, and Salman and I took our leave.

It struck me as strange that I should be put back on the Caveman's track by a Hindu. But then, with his knowledge of Persian and of Sufism, his Mughal screens and beautiful English, our antiquarian host was the incarnation of that old eclectic Delhi culture the loss of which Khwajah Hasan so deplored. Every people might have its own *qiblah*, its orientation; but at certain times and for certain persons, like Mr Mithal, the *qiblahs* are parallel, contiguous. Today in India,

I feared, the trend was to divergence, back to that total disconnection al-Biruni wrote about a thousand years ago.

It also struck me that 'near the Yamuna' – a river that had strayed eastwards over the centuries – hadn't actually got me any closer to finding Nizam al-Din's hospice; let alone to my ultimate goal, the Caveman's hermitage. It was my *qiblah*, but I was still without a bearing on it.

It was that other learned non-Muslim friend of Salman's, Ravi Dayal, who showed me the way. 'But of course! The hospice must be that little place by the enclosure wall of Humayun's tomb. Go and have a poke around there.'

★

I left Martin painting Humayun. To the west of the enclosure wall there was a car park. On the south lay an affluent suburb – Salman's. This was followed at the eastern end by a warren of tiny houses, compact as a nest of mud-wasps, which gave out at a railway line. Rounding the north-east corner I passed a big new Sikh temple, the Guru Gurdwara Damdama Sahib, then spotted a green Islamic flag. A sign over a gate announced the Khanqah and Chillah of the Noble Nizam al-Din.

The Persian term *khanqah* means a Sufi convent or hospice. *Chillah* is another Persian word – a forty-day fast, and by extension the place where one performs it (not necessarily down a well). Maneri, the cave-saint of Bihar, explained the origin of the fast. When God created Adam, He kneaded the clay from which the first man was made for forty days. Each day a veil appeared between Creator and creature; the fast removes them, day by day. This place, then, was a spiritual pied-à-terre where Nizam al-Din and his closest disciples could go into retreat. In their day it would have been a secluded spot, far from the crowds of visitors drawn by the magnetic saint and ideal for performing the fast of the forty veils.

It was still an island of silence in a noisy city – just a diminutive mosque and a few graves in a small garden, hard by the wall of the Mughal mausoleum. It was also a very poor relation to the saint's more famous shrine. There were no yellow caps here; only an ancient Sufi, who gave me a blessing and a cake of sugar candy shaped like a macaroon ('He said a prayer for me,' wrote IB of a visit to the head of another Chishti shrine, 'and sent me sugar and sugar candy.'). I showed him IB's passage on Nizam al-Din's neighbour, the Cave-man, but he smiled and shook his head. The name meant nothing.

For the next three hours I tramped the neighbourhood of the *khanqah* – the mud-wasp village, a domed and ruinous Mughal tomb in its centre, the railway line to the east, the compound of the *gurd-wara*. There were no signs of a cave, either natural or man-made. No one had heard of the Caveman. Of course, it was more than possible that his hermitage disappeared under the forty acres of Humayun's funerary demesne, more than 400 years ago; or that it might lie in one of the two areas to the north of the *khanqah* – the Delhi State Scouts and Guides Training Centre, or the Police Transmitter Station (Restricted Area). Both were guarded by razor wire; the red tape would be even more impenetrable ('*What* is this? "Re.: Application for Permit to Investigate Fourteenth-Century Hole"?').

It was now the end of the afternoon. Between the two government compounds was a piece of wasteland, and beyond this a clump of trees. I made for the little wood, and found that it hid another domed tomb, richly inscribed in stucco and pigeon-shit, and Mughal. Further into the tangle of trees I discovered more decaying tombs. In the heart of the wood, as the light was beginning to go, I came across a little knoll of compacted dust some twenty feet high.

On top of this was a masonry platform surmounted by three simple graves, all whitewashed. The whitewash was fresh.

I had a sudden feeling that I was being watched – and noticed a man loitering in the bushes. He came up to me, indicated that I should take off my shoes, and led me over to the platform. I asked if he knew of Kamal al-Din Abdallah al-Ghari. He didn't. This place, he said, was the *khanqah* of Dada Pir. His own name was Muhammad Mustaqim, and he was the guardian of the *khanqah*.

'Dada Pir' is not so much a name as an anonym; or rather a title that might attach itself, with time, to some half-forgotten religious personality. It means something like 'Holy Old Grandad'. I wondered how old, and asked when Dada Pir had lived. 'A long time. Before seventy hundred years,' Muhammad replied.

I wrote '70' in my notebook. 'Like this?'

He added a zero. A glimmer of hope.

The glimmer soon became a ray. Along the top step of the three that led up to the platform ran a frieze of repeating shield shapes. It was a motif I had seen on buildings of IB's period.

We walked around the platform in silence. And then I saw something that made me stop: six steps, leading under the platform, into the hillock on which it stood. I followed them down, into a short whitewashed passage. It was a dead end.

I climbed up again. 'What is this?' I pointed down into the blocked passage.

Muhammad Mustaqim smiled. 'Dada Pir original house! The door now close.' He took my hand and we mounted the platform, where he recited some prayers then gave me some dust from a flowerpot at the head of the central tomb. As instructed, I rubbed it into my head and chest. Then I walked away through a din of birds.

*

I found Martin where I'd left him, painting Humayun, and sat near him on the ground. Above us the belly of the sky was taut. We exchanged grunts. Martin was busy with his fight against the light, I with another conflict – between my conviction that, hidden in the wood and in the anonymity of Dada Pir, I had found the passage by which IB entered the cave of his own self; and my knowledge that I had no proof. All this time and I'd ended up in a blocked passage, a question of faith.

I heard a sigh, the scraping of the palette, the snap of the locks on the painting box; then three claps of thunder. There was a sudden rush of wind that set the peacocks mewing and the dust flying.

'Come on then,' Martin said. 'Let's get going.'

Following all those years in the Thousand-Column Hall, his fall from grace and his ascetic experiment, IB's curriculum vitae *took a sudden and unexpected turn when Muhammad Shah appointed him ambassador to the Emperor of China.*

IB's departure from Delhi probably took place in August 1341. Although most of his route to China would be by sea, he had first to make the long trek to the Gulf of Cambay. The four-month land journey would take him to Kol – now Aligarh in Uttar Pradesh – then south through present-day Madhya Pradesh into Maharashtra; from there he would double back and head for the coast of Gujarat. In the event, he was lucky to make it any further than Aligarh, just seventy-five miles south-east of Delhi.

Hill Tales from the Plains

> 'I am the traveller called Qalandar.
> Of home or hearth or chattels have I none.
> From break of day I wander near and far;
> When night-time falls, my pillow is a stone.'
>
> Baba Tahir Uryan (11th century)

O N THE BUS to Aligarh I thought of a story I'd heard in Delhi. About ten years ago a yogi drove a car from Gujarat to the capital. The remarkable thing about the 600-mile journey up National Highway 8 was that, having gained by meditation and practice of austerities the ability to see through solids, he did the drive thickly blindfolded. Perhaps the NH8 is a die-straight, eight-lane interstate with heavy speed restrictions; but if it is anything like the dance of death that I was on, then the blindfold would have been the least of the yogi's hazards. Being able to see through solids doesn't stop them crashing into you.

The Grand Trunk Road is grand in legend, letters and length; I was travelling a mere parenthesis in this epic highway that runs from Peshawar to Calcutta. In all other respects it is less epic than shaggy-dog story. It resembles the carriage-drive, spun out over 1,200 miles, of a great country house – but one long gone to seed and overrun by the peasantry. The views beyond its noble avenue of trees (are these the grand trunks? I'm surely not the first to wonder) disclose dungstacks, elegantly shaped like dervish caps, and other evidences of rustic industry. In its human and animal geography it is a combination of teashop, farmyard and bazaar. Bus- and lorry-drivers, however, see it as a tournament ground, and themselves as knights of the Grand Trunk Road jousting in heavy armour. For the rest it is *sauve qui peut.* By the time we pulled into Bulandshahr bus station, halfway to Aligarh, I was beginning to enjoy the white-knuckle thrills of playing chicken with ten tons of Tata.

Except for the driver, I was enjoying them alone. Martin had delayed in Delhi to continue what Lear called 'Delhineations of the Dehlicate architecture', and my fellow-passengers were a taciturn lot. IB, in contrast, had left the capital in fine company: a thousand cavalrymen, two high-ranking *amirs*, one very grand eunuch – the sultan's cup-bearer Malik Kafur, 'King Camphor' (not, I hasten to add, the Camphor who blinded Qutb al-Din's brothers with hatpins) – and 115 Chinamen. Following his literary and spiritual self-effacement in Delhi he was back in the world, in his book and on the road. This promised to be the greatest journey of all. But what of that other journey, the one to enlightenment?

Qui peregrinantur, said Thomas à Kempis, *raro sanctificantur*. In the case of IB, that consummate peregrinator, the maxim proved true. He had set out on the road to sanctity with a spring in his step: 'The Caveman used to fast without a break for ten or even twenty days, and I too wished to fast continuously.' His guru, however, warned him against excessive zeal. 'He would restrain me and tell me to treat myself gently in my devotional exercises, saying to me, "A man that tires himself out covers no ground and only jades his mount".' IB dutifully held his horses and ambled towards illumination.

Five months into this new life the world intruded abruptly in the form of a summons from Muhammad Shah. The sultan was in Sehwan, a town 120 miles north of present-day Karachi. IB obeyed and travelled west. 'I entered his presence wearing the dress of a poor dervish. Using the kindliest words, he expressed his wish that I would return to his service. But' – the sobering example of Shaykh Shihab al-Din's horrible execution notwithstanding – 'I refused.' He went into retreat again, this time in Sehwan. Forty days later Muhammad tempted him once more: 'He sent me saddled horses, slave girls and boys, robes and a sum of money.' IB gave in. 'I put on the robes and went to him.'

He offers no excuse for his spiritual failure. Fear of the sultan might justifiably have had a big part in it; but there was also that cajoling companion who had shadowed him from the start of his travels, the one he calls *al-nafs al-lajuj* – his importunate worldly spirit. Faced with a choice between rags and robes, the robes always had it. This time, IB's conscience was not unscathed: 'I had a coat of quilted blue cotton which I wore during my retreat. When I took it off and put on the sultan's robes I felt guilty. Afterwards, whenever I looked at that coat, my whole being would be suffused with light. I kept it with me always, until the infidel pirates looted it along with the rest of my possessions.'

Having exchanged this luminous anchoretic anorak for the glad-rags of mundanity, IB was all dressed up. Now all he needed was somewhere to go. The sultan came up trumps: '"I have summoned you in order to send you as my ambassador to the Emperor of China, for I know your love of travel in foreign lands."' IB doesn't let on about his reaction, but I suspect the regrets over the parka of piety evaporated rather quickly.

He returned to Delhi to prepare for the journey. Little actual diplomacy would come into it, for IB was to be more a Santa Claus than a Henry Kissinger. The Yuan Emperor of China had sent a gift to Muhammad Shah of slaves, robes and musk. True to form, Muhammad's return gift was embarrassingly bigger: in addition to his fellow-travellers already mentioned, of whom the Chinese were the original mission from Peking, IB's ambassadorial caravan included a hundred each of male slaves, dancing girls and thoroughbred horses; fifteen eunuchs; an imperial marquee and six pavilions; services of gold and silver plate; robes, caps, gloves, quivers and scabbards, all thickly encrusted with pearls; and several thousand bolts of cloth in cotton, silk, silk velvet, wool, Greek linen and cashmere. It was as if Pan's People, the Pearly Kings and the entire stock of Asprey's and Tattersalls had been let loose in Liberty's basement and the whole lot set in motion.

IB had returned to the material world with a vengeance. He left behind him the Caveman, an unfinished spiritual odyssey, Delhi itself – although he didn't realize it at the time, he would never return there – and yet another child, a living one called Ahmad. 'I do not know what God has done with him,' IB admitted, back home in Morocco. Later, I thought I caught a glimpse of the boy.

*

The bus charged on through Uttar Pradesh, through the pottery town of Khurja and deeper into the Doab, the Land Between Two Waters. Bordered by the Yamuna and the Ganges, the Doab is UP's Mesopotamia. It is flat and fertile, a vast fen of silt – what old travellers would have called champaign country. Its flatness was, for me, a huge problem.

IB had hardly left Delhi when he ran into another of Time's daughters. It was one of his finest messes ever. Reaching Kol, the present-day Aligarh, the ambassadorial party learned that Hindu rebels were besieging the neighbouring town of Jalali. Strong in numbers and well-armed, they decided to do a spot of counter-insurgency. For IB it went horribly wrong: he was separated from his comrades and captured. Providence, and his own charm, saved his neck. But his trials were not over. There followed a week of wanderings in rebel-held territory, living off the land and dossing wherever night found him. The episode, intensely observed and minutely memorized, is one of the most powerful in the *Travels*.

The problem is that part of the escape narrative takes place against a setting of *jabals*, mountains or hills. In the Doab, as I knew from my atlas and now confirmed through the greasy window of the bus, the only contour lines are to be found on those elegant dunghills. I had great faith, if not in IB's metrical exactitude, then at least in his general empirical soundness. But faith, though it might remove mountains, has a harder time making them out of muckheaps. 'There seems to be something in the Mahomedan mind', wrote the arch-Polophile Sir Henry Yule in an essay on IB, 'that indisposes it for appreciating and relating accurately what is witnessed in nature and geography.' Poppycock, it goes without saying. But I remembered the comment now and thought that – had I a propensity for gross generalization, preposterous pontification, and only the evidence of these six pages of the *Travels* – I might well say Hear, hear, Sir Henry.

As we approached Aligarh I reread those six pages for the umptieth time. They bore the unmistakable stamp of veracity. To borrow Father Raymond Brown's epigram on the Bible, everything seemed true except the facts.

*

'Um . . . *I.G. Khan sahib ka dost!*' That – or was it *ki dost?* – was what Dr Khan had told me to say when I got to Aligarh. Everyone knew him, he said.

There was no reaction. I gave the rickshawmen a stupid-foreigner grin; saw sanatorium faces, features drawn by graft, poverty and too much patience. And saw them brightening. Dr I.G. Khan was Honorary President of the Union of Aligarh Cycle-rickshawmen, I was his friend – it seemed they'd understood – and, I added, pointing once more at my chest, '*Union-wala!*' The spell was complete. One of the men took my bag and put it on the seat of his machine. I followed; with '*University chalo!*' I shot my last linguistic bolt; and we set off through what Salman Haidar, whose ancestral town this was, had called the city of the four *m*s: *machchhar, makkhi, mitti* – mosquitoes, flies, dust – and Musulmans.

The fourth *m* was much in evidence as we crested the railway bridge and I looked on to the broad acres of Aligarh Muslim University, Alma Mater of Indian Islam. No doubt the other *m*s would reveal themselves in time. For now, Aligarh was a city of dreaming minarets.

We passed through a monumental gateway and into an avenue. The rickshaw dropped me in the porte cochère of a stucco Saracenic villa. Its twilit interior was crowded with dark wood, brown velvet and the ghosts of a century and more of mutton *kormas*. Plump latex-coloured geckoes gazed down from their right-angled realm on the wall and from the dim antipodes of the ceiling. I unpacked, signed a visitors' book and ate a large, lone luncheon off crockery that said, in blue letters, 'UGH'.

The University Guest House *korma* was as good as it ought to have been, given a hundred years of practice. Too full to do anything more strenuous, I slumped in front of a TV set to watch India v. Australia and slid into that delicious semi-consciousness induced by post-prandial cricket.

'Ah, the test match,' said a voice through the velvet gloom. 'I hope Australia win.' The words, softly spoken, jerked me awake. I rose and turned to see who had uttered this blasphemy. 'I.G. Khan,' he said, extending a hand. A look of intense amusement was framed by a greying Renaissance beard, as worn by Holbein courtiers, and a Rive Gauche beret.

'For a moment I thought you meant it,' I said as we shook hands.

'Of course I mean it. If India win, the government will stage a fascist takeover of the victory.' The smile was still there. I couldn't tell what it meant; but I liked its ambiguity, and its owner, immediately. I could see why the faces of the rickshaw-*walas* had come to life at the sound of his name. For a while IG and I talked IB. As well as a trades unionist, IG was a historian – and, as I was to discover, many other things. In a few minutes he had to chair a meeting, but not before he had arranged one for me, followed by tea with the VC – not, it turned out, the local war hero. (AMU, like all the best Indian institutions, loves initials. There was even a BUMS XP DIP on a sign across the road, which remained a mystery.)

'I don't really understand', I admitted shortly afterwards at the first of my engagements, with Professor Irfan Habib, 'how things could have been so disturbed so close to the capital. I mean, to have rebels besieging a town only three marches from Delhi is almost unbelievable.'

Professor Habib reminded me that, even before their arrival in Aligarh, IB's party had been forced to go almost a hundred miles out of their way, almost certainly because of the danger of attack on the road. Security was particularly bad here in the Doab, he said. Muhammad Shah had tried, disastrously, to overtax the farmers; repeated famines had finished off the job. 'At best, the sultanate was never more than a patchwork of areas in and out of government control. Centralized rule just didn't work. It was the same under the Mughals. It is the same now.'

Professor Habib is the grand old man of Indian history. I found him, however, hard to date; he seemed to stand at an angle to time. IG told me he was getting on for eighty, but this was belied by his hair, a full Existentialist flop, and by the vigour with which I later saw him pedalling his Atlas bicycle. The room where we were sitting, the professor's library, offered no clues to the period of its owner; except perhaps the first thing in it that had caught my eye – a little bald head with slitty eyes and a pointy beard, surveying the Indian past from the top of a bookcase. These days it isn't often you see people putting up their Lenins in public.

Before coming here I had formed a vague picture of Aligarh Muslim University as a haunt of stern, stragglebearded Islamic scholars with highly polished prayer-bumps, poring over Persian texts. There was certainly plenty of poring, and no one more religious in it than Irfan Habib. But the professor's Lenin, the *lar* of his library – and, come to think of it, IG's work with the impoverished rickshaw-men – suggested that other traditions lived on at Aligarh. Tea with the Vice-Chancellor added to the intricacy of the picture. The VC enthused about the new Medical Faculty, which ran courses in both modern Western medicine and ancient *tibb unani*, 'Ionian physic', the science of the humours developed by Avicenna out of Galen. The VC's wife enthused about the mystical physic of Nizam al-Din: some 'dirty-looking' water from his shrine in Delhi had apparently remedied their son's incipient blindness, pronounced incurable by both Western and *unani* doctors. The beneficiary of this supernatural eyewash then turned up, enthused about Goa trance raves, and gave me his e-mail address – psychedelia@stoned.org. Aligarh was not conforming to preconceptions.

After tea I wandered around brick quadrangles where Keble College met the Alhambra, and the *madrasah* had been recast in an Oxbridge

mould. They'd forgotten about the lawns but made up for them by planting decorative clumps of undergraduates, and the combination – of rose-petal-coloured buildings, of Islam, learning and tight jeans – was ravishing. I followed an intriguing sign to 'SS Hall' ('Sir Saiyid,' IG later explained – author of *The Monuments of Delhi* and founder of the university) which led to a stoa and a locked door. There was an English inscription on one of the pillars. The sandstone was beginning to weather, and some of the words were illegible. The heading, however, suggested it might not be a great loss to the *epigraphia indica*:

ADVICE

TO THE MUHAMMADANS

BY

SIR AUCKLAND COLVIN

KCMG

1892

It looked as if Sir Auckland had taken seriously the wags' reading of the letters after his name: Kindly Call Me God.

The text began with a counterblast against zealotry, with a reference to the excesses of Tamerlane, a preachy quotation from Milton,
and a slogan that might have been scripted for President Bush Junior's
War Against Terrorism: 'So long as the British Government in India
endures, fanaticism can be allowed no licence.' The sermon on stone
then softened, slightly. 'There are as many images today in the world
as were to be found in our seventh century in Arabia,' Colvin warned,
referring to the idols of Mecca smashed by the Prophet Muhammad.

There is the idol of a stupid adherence to past modes of education, reasoning and discussion: there is the idol of a bigoted
hatred of all that is foreign to the creed or the country of the
worshipper: there is the idol of fatuous pride of race, and there
is the monster idol of all, the idol of [something something –
illegible] supreme indifference and fatalistic submission to what
is accepted as the 'Will of God', because man, prostrate in so
called devotion never has to exert any will of his own. Dumb,
blind images all of them, hideous in their form, preposterous in
their pretention, despicable in their impotence. You, and others
like you in other parts of the province, represent the true
Muhammadan iconoclasts of today.

Whatever else he was (a Calcutta civil servant, I found out later,
lampooned for his hated tax hikes by Kipling in 'The Rupaiyat of
Omar Kal'vin' and about as popular in British India as Muhammad
Shah was in the Doab), Colvin was no subtle scholar of Islam. In particular, his grasp of Muslim ideas about divine will was grotesquely
simplistic.* But on reflection I wondered whether, even if he had a
nerve, he might also have a point. Despite the pulpit-shaking and the
wonky theology, his message was not irrelevant to an age of conspicuous, and literal, image-breaking – in Afghanistan, the Taliban had
just made dust of the Buddhas of Bamian and then, in their phrase,
made dust of the dust. What I had seen so far of Aligarh Muslim
University suggested the 'advice' was still being taken to heart. The
gentle iconoclasm of IG and Irfan Habib had certainly broken my
prefabricated images of the place.

---

* Think of IB, who spared no effort to work out the fate revealed in his Delta dream – a splendid
example of God's will *encouraging* endeavour.

Those first *m*s of Aligarh – the *machchhar*, or mosquitoes – were beginning to annoy, so I headed for the Department of History. The building was buzzing too, with a human hum. I followed the sound and found most of the staff gathered in Professor Habib's office and his desk littered with placards: UNITE AND FIGHT SAFFRONIZATION – SAFFRONIZATION THE MAIN DANGER TODAY – DON'T COVER UP SAF-FRONIZATION IN THE MOCK FIGHT AGAINST 'GLOBALIZATION'. I wasn't enlightened. Another imperative, leaning against a cupboard, offered a clue: SAY NO TO VEDIC ASTROLOGY DEPARTMENTS IN UNIVERSITIES. In a lull in the debate one of the lecturers explained. A conference on higher education was taking place, and many of the faculty had been picketing it in protest at government plans to fund the teaching of astrology and other occult Hindu sciences in universities. It had even been suggested that the new course components should include palmistry and levitation.

Hand-reading would be a devil to examine, at least in its applied form; but *levitation*? There would have to be a practical test, a sort of *viva volitura* ('Please would you hold it there for a minute, Miss Chatterjee . . .') Somebody had been reading too much Harry Potter. 'You're joking,' I said.

He wasn't. Serious money was being earmarked for the scheme, and the inspiration behind it was not Hogwarts School for Witches and Wizards but the Rashtriya Swayamsevak Sangh, or Organization of National Volunteers. In a sensible world, the RSS too would be a joke: with their uniform of forage caps and Boy Scout shorts, they look like some offshoot of P.G. Wodehouse's fictional footer-bagged fascists, the Black Shorts. But they too are deadly serious and, with the Prime Minister and many of his party élite as members, immensely powerful. Sartorially Stanley Matthews, ideologically Joseph Goebbels, the RSS are Brahmanical supremacists who regard India's 140 million-odd Muslims – not to mention all other non-Hindu minorities – as at best aliens to be tolerated on sufferance, at worst insufferable parasites. Not only IG but most people with brains from Nehru onwards have branded them, and more recently their parliamentary mouthpiece the BJP (the Bharatiya Janata Party), as fascists. I could see why the staff of Aligarh – most of whom are Muslims, all of whom have brains – were worried by the BJP and its saffron flag.*

---

* In May 2004 the BJP fell from power.

They were to lose the battle. Although low-flying undergraduates have yet to be spotted over the campuses of India, funding was approved for astrology departments in twenty-four universities. But the greying angry young men and women of Aligarh fight on; and Colvin's sounding rhetoric against reactionism, religious bigotry and racial pride is doubly relevant. It should be re-inscribed in granite, with a revised title.

The meeting broke up. Professor Habib took a fat book from his desk – *The Bukharans* – and wrapped it in a newspaper – *People and Democracy* – that bore a hammer-and-sickle logo; he strapped it to the carrier of his bicycle and pedalled away. 'They all worked so hard, Irfan and the others, from Independence on,' said IG. He had just returned from chairing the higher education conference, and from the uncharacteristically apolitical role into which the chair had forced him. 'And then in the 1990s things started to change. Now we're all worried about communalism. I know how Irfan feels: that we're heading for another brink; perhaps an abyss.'

*

'There's a breathless hush in the Close to-night –'

– in fact, this morning; but the composition of the passing scene – wicket, pavilion, house of God, foreground trees beside a fence, hush – so closely matched the setting of the poet's youth, and mine, that for a moment, half asleep and googly-eyed, I made steeples out of minarets and Clifton out of Aligarh and woke the lines from their sleep of years –

'Ten to make and the match to win –'

– surprised by their resurfacing I hardly noticed IG joining in –

'A bumping pitch and a blinding light,
An hour to play and the last man in –'

He continued where I could only mumble fragments – the ribboned coat . . . the Gatling jammed . . . the Colonel dead . . . But we finished together:

'Play up! play up! and play the game!'

I looked at him. 'We learned it at school,' he said.

'So did we.'

We drove on, bemused into silence by the chance poetic meeting. I'd always thought of 'Vitaï Lampada' as the essence of Englishness – no, Britishness. It was late Victoriana distilled into verse: if Waterloo was won on the playing-fields of Eton, then Mafeking was muddled through on those of Clifton. And here, in the Close of Aligarh, was that essence, decanted into India and Islam.

If something of this essence had infused IG, there were also hints of many more. His veins ran with Pathan blood from ancestors who were part of that old north-western current flowing into Hindustan. But his formidable brains were the product of Aligarh, the London School of Oriental and African Studies and of Duke University in the far-off Carolinas, and were much exercised by the French in eighteenth-century India, his subject of research. Now, as we neared our destination, I learned that our mutual Newbolt was in IG's case a legacy of La Martinière, the great public school of Lucknow. If he and Kipling's Kim – the only other Martinière old boy I'd come across – were anything to go by, the school seemed to specialize in cultural chameleons.

Half an hour before, at 6.30 a.m., IG had burst into my room at the UGH. For a moment I'd imagined myself back in Delhi, so strong was the association of 6.30 a.m. with Martin; but it was a beard and a beret that came into focus. '*Bonjour!* I'm just off to the stables,' IG said, sporting another of his many metaphorical hats, that of President of the University Riding Club. 'Thought you might fancy a ride.'

'O my God,' I groaned.

*

IB's troubles began with a horse. At first, operations against the rebels had been successful, if costly. The troops from Delhi raised the siege of Jalali and routed the attackers; but they lost seventy-eight men dead on their own side, including King Camphor, who had been in overall charge of the diplomatic gift. Only one pocket of resistance remained, a group of rebels who 'would charge down from an inaccessible *jabal* near Jalali, raiding the surrounding villages'. Together with government forces from the town, the ambassadorial guard rode out daily to repel them.

IB, a keen amateur player of the game, took part in these skirmishes. All went well until the day when, in the course of a high-stakes session of hide-and-seek among the cane-brakes and mango topes, IB found himself alone – except for a group of ten rebels, bearing down on him with frightening speed. He spurred his horse away; but the going was bad and he had to dismount to free its forefeet, which had got stuck in the stony ground. Again he lost valuable seconds when he dropped his gold-hilted sword and dismounted once more to pick it up. With his pursuers gaining on him, he took to his legs and made it to a ditch. The horsemen rode past. Shaken, he emerged from his hiding place, wandered down into a wadi . . . and straight into the arms of about forty more rebels. This time there was no escape. The rebels stripped him to his underwear then sent him off with three guards to a *kahf*, Gibb renders this 'cave', but it might also indicate a den or hide-out. 'I understood from my guards that they intended to kill me,' IB remembered. How they communicated this isn't stated; probably with a good old multicultural finger across the throat.

But the death-squad dithered; then one of them had an attack of the ague, and they ended up spending the night in the *kahf*, with IB pinned down under the legs of the sick man. Next morning, his captors produced a rope. 'I said to myself, "It is with this rope that they will tie me when they kill me."' IB somehow wheedled a stay of execution. Then at around noon three more of the main party appeared and conferred with the bungling executioners. 'One of these three was a youth with a pleasant face, and he said to me, "Do you want me to set you free?" I said, "Yes," and he said, "Go".' It was as simple as that. Perhaps they were particularly nice rebels. More likely, they saw IB for what he was – a goofy foreigner who posed no military threat. Whatever the reason, they had made the right decision for the future of Arabic letters.

Less simple for IB was the business of getting back to his comrades, which took more than a week. To be fair, he was in rebel-held territory and still in danger; he was on foot, without food or friends. But it is hard not to conclude that among his spatial-cognitive eccentricities the Prince of Travellers included a rotten sense of direction. He made up for it with a cinematic memory that has left us one of the great nightmare passages of travel literature. All the ghastly details are there: creepy-crawly nights in the open, a soirée with a snake in a pavilion by a tank; a ruined house where he squeezed into a granary and curled up with his head on a stone – with him 'was a bird which kept fluttering its wings . . . it must have been frightened, and that made two of us'; a starvation diet of mustard shoots, radish leaves and lote-tree berries – 'even now, I still have scars on my arms from the thorns'; days spent trudging drove-roads and lanes that meandered through thickets and cotton-fields and across plains dotted with castor-oil trees; and a dank and secret pond, lined with weed and roofed over with intertwining trees, where he lay low, exhausted.

The *mise en scène* is densely realistic – all except for the three infuriating *jabals* at the start of the drama. There was that inaccessible rebel *jabal*, a *jabal* where IB spent his first night in the open, and a 'high and stony' *jabal* on which he sustained his lote-thorn scars. They were as precise and impossible as the details in a dream. For me, this phantom range of hills was an Everest that rose between fact and belief, sense and sensibilia. I had to surmount it, and for the reverse of the usual reason: because it *wasn't* there.

*

The stables were swarming with syces. While they were getting our mounts ready, IG showed me the clubhouse with its framed photographs going back to the 1920s. He surprised me with a comment on a portrait of a recent past president: 'The poor chap got shot.'

'Dead?' IG wiggled assent. 'On purpose?' Another wiggle. I remembered one of the other guests at the VC's tea party talking about the lawlessness of leafy Aligarh. Not only was IB captured near here, he said. Three hundred years earlier, the great indologist al-Biruni had been robbed in the locality, and today the city tops the list of crime rates for the whole of UP. But the murder of a mild-looking professor with an interest in country pursuits . . . It sounded like a joint case for Inspectors Morse and Ghote.

'It was the local land mafia,' IG explained, in an undertone. 'They were trying to get hold of Riding Club property . . . Come on, they'll be ready.'

I hardly liked to ask if the land mafia were still trying. In the event, the prospect of getting collaterally damaged in the battle of the dons paled to nothing before the matter of being on a horse. As I mounted, so did my apprehension. The mare snorted; the snort sounded very much like 'O my God' in Horse. Worst of all, the instructor, Sergeant-Major Faruq – whip-thin, breeched and booted, with sharp moustache and sharper eyes – rode behind me. I could feel those eyes lasering into my back. Wasn't one supposed to sit like a sack of potatoes? I sat like a blancmange.

But it was a lovely morning, cool and clear, and I soon began to enjoy the ride. We ambled along, the syces pedalling beside us on bicycles. 'That's where we're heading for,' said IG, indicating a line of trees in the middle distance. 'The fort of Aligarh.'

It is this stronghold that has given its name to the city it guarded – Kol, the original township, south of the railway line which separates it from the nineteenth-century gownship to the north. (IB, a stickler for phonetic if not mensural accuracy, writes the name as 'Kuwil' – a more accurate rendering of local pronunciation.) As we crossed the broad ditch that surrounds the fort, IG outlined the story of its capture in 1803 by General Lake, victor over the French-officered forces of Maharaja Scindia. Lake's *coup de main* was commemorated on a tablet in the tunnel-like entrance to the fort. Being of marble it had fared better than Colvin's epigraph and was only slightly pock-marked. (Salman Haidar later told me the reason for the pitting: his uncle and some anti-British friends used to go fowling in the moat; 'then they'd nip up to the fort and let off a few shots into Lord Lake's memorial.')

The interior of the fort was a let-down. It resembled a large municipal park, neglected and, apart from a few peacocks, deserted.

One section of it was the University's dry and dusty botanic garden. Elsewhere mangoes, as noted by IB, were in evidence – hardly a discovery in so mangiferous a region as the Doab. There wasn't even anything as exciting as a wall; just a low rampart. But there was a prospect across the plain . . . and the reason for the view, I realized, was that the fort was elevated perhaps twenty or thirty feet above its surroundings. I hadn't even noticed the incline as we rode in.

It wasn't what you might call a mountain, or even a hill; it was rather an exception to the pervading flatness. But was it what you, or more importantly IB, might call a *jabal*? To me, living at 7,500 feet in the most vertically interesting corner of the Arabic-speaking world, a *jabal* is a tall, steep-sided job with a spiky top – 'a considerable protuberance', in Dr Johnson's definition. At the same time, I ought by now to have known enough about the Arabic language – a system of subtle gradations, a code that prefers the relative to the absolute – and about IB's loopy spatial sense, to realize that for him a *jabal* might well be as high as a piece of string is long. Was it I who had mountains on the brain? These thoughts, however, were put on hold by IG calling out that it was time to go back.

They always do it. The first whiff of the stables and even the dopiest horse, as mine had been so far, is off. We took the homeward road at a spanking trot, the cycling syces clanking and cranking in pursuit, waiting for me to come unstuck. I arrived under Sergeant-Major Faruq's laser gaze, still attached, less blancmange than gooseberry fool.

*

As revelations on elevations went, mine wasn't exactly Mosaic. But it did send me to the library, Lane's *Lexicon*, and the discovery that a *jabal*, according to the highest Arab authorities, could be any elevation, '*however little elevated*'. In its turn, the conceit of a not very elevated mountain sent me momentarily to my English home in Lincolnshire, not far from which is an object called Sturdy Hill. A man with a JCB could probably remove it in a day or two; but it is the Matterhorn of the Marshes. I had to think Sturdy Hill, relative not absolute.

The next question was whether there were any *jabals*, however relative, in the region of Jalali where IB was captured. I wondered how I'd go about finding out. There was the option of borrowing a horse from IG and galloping off down the Grand Trunk Road. The authenticity was appealing, the reality appalling. As an alternative, IG suggested the next step up the evolutionary scale from a horse, his Enfield Bullet motor-cycle. But no amount of kicking would make it go. In the end we settled for a Hero Honda and a driver-research assistant to go with it.

It was another cool, clear morning. Sounds hung in the air, quiet and precise – the thrum of bicycle chains, the clop of hooves in dust, the muted jingle of buffalo carts. My driver-assistant, Mumtaz, lived eponymously in Latouche-Mumtaz House, a building as eclectic as its name: Andalusian horseshoe arches topped with Dutch gables and finished with Mughal crenellations formed a large pink quadrangle, divided by a transept of silver-trunked palms. A sign above his door – CAPTAIN OF FOOTBALL – hinted at rugger-buggery; Mumtaz however was also quiet and precise, no athlete but a historian of Ionian physic. The heroic Honda started first go. We pootled down the avenue, under the monumental gate, over the railway bridge, and into a traffic jam and, arguably, the real India.

On the far side of town a change came over Mumtaz. We shot out of Aligarh like a pellet from a pop-gun. I glimpsed his face in the mirror and remembered the old motor-cyclist's riddle: What's the sign of a happy biker? Answer: flies on the teeth. But there was also a glint in his eye that recalled the opening shots of *Lawrence of Arabia*, just before Peter O'Toole makes a club sandwich of himself, his Brough Superior and a tree. After the bus ride, biking the Grand Trunk Road offered a whole new perspective on mortality.

'The GTR is a very historical road!' Mumtaz shouted as we wove in a high-speed vertical limbo dance between vehicle and vehicle, vehicle and verge.

'I'm sure it is,' I shouted back, 'and I don't want to be part of that hist . . .' A howling slipstream snatched my words away. Mercifully soon, we reached a turn-off and resumed our original pootle. The landscape, of lush levels, dykes and bird-speckled lakes, held little hope of *jabals*, however relative. At some point we overshot a secondary turn-off that led to Jalali. Finding ourselves in a village, we stopped.

The silence was extraordinary. It wasn't just quiet. It was as if sound had been sucked out of the place, leaving an acoustic vacuum, a negative of noise. 'I will go and make some inquiries,' said Mumtaz. His whisper came like a roar.

A few minutes later he emerged from a side alley, smiling with the news that he had found someone to help us with our research. I followed him into the alley, through a doorway flanked by two buffaloes sejant, through a courtyard where a very old man sat bolt upright on a charpoy, and into a room so dark that for a few seconds I could make nothing out. Objects began to condense out of the gloom – wooden sofas around a table, a light bulb of such low wattage that it only served to intensify the obscurity around it, and Mr Kripal Singh Yadav, a handsome middle-aged man in a lungi. After a few formalities tea came and our host went. During his absence Mumtaz explained that he was the former *zamindar*, or squire, of this village of Sikanderpur; and that his niece was a student of IG sahib's. This last piece of intelligence was a surprise. Seen even from towny Aligarh, the Academia beyond the railway bridge seemed a distant and exotic place; from Sikanderpur, a bare dozen miles away but insulated from sound and probably from time, the world of IG and Latouche-Mumtaz was Nephelococcygia. The squire's niece was up at university and off in another universe.

Kripal Singh returned, now in a silky white *kurta*, a pair of those conjoined wind-socks that in Hindustan go by the name of trousers, and an impressive entourage of sons. I began to recount IB's adventures, pausing at each salient feature – the inaccessible *jabal*, the high stony *jabal*, the tank with the pavilion, the tank beneath the trees. They listened closely to Mumtaz's Hindi version; and I realized that after six and a half centuries of wandering around the libraries of Arab armchair travellers and of orientalists, from here to Fez to Damascus, from Paris to Berkeley and Beijing, the story had finally come home.

Or had it? The prodigal tale wasn't greeted with cries of recognition. Those uncomfortably salient *jabals* were of course received with wrinkled brows; equally the *kahf* of captivity, at least if it was a cave. A tiny head-wiggle from Kripal Singh suggested that the tank with the pavilion might have rung a muffled bell. The sons remained perplexed throughout. And then I came to the one feature that proved the story wasn't a complete impostor. 'One night the traveller slept inside a place for storing grain. He said it was "like a big jar", and it had a hole in it like a door. There was some chopped straw inside . . .'

We all trooped out and along the alley. Sikanderpur was still hushed, but that first, deep-space silence had gone. Ladies peeped from behind doorways and conversed behind hands. We marched uninvited – a flash of sari in the wings – into a courtyard. Like Kripal Singh's own house, like the village and the entire Doab, this was of mud. Sikanderpur was a potted place, puddled, raised and moulded, glazed in pastels and slip-decorated with whitewash. One side of this courtyard was an open portico – and beneath it was IB's jar.

It was an elegant cylinder of clay, tapering towards the base and with a close-fitting square door in the side, also of clay. And it was certainly large – five feet tall, a Forty Thieves pot. The problem was the base. The door was sealed, again with clay, but judging by its external dimensions the floor inside could not have been more than two feet across. Diogenes himself would have turned up his nose at the accommodation.

But the tour hadn't finished. We visited two more houses, each with its *ramda*, as they call these giant jars. In a third there was a variation on the design, square in plan and going by a different name – *kothia*. The door was loose, and I peered inside and saw a base about a yard square – hardly roomier than a telephone kiosk but big enough at a pinch to curl up in. The floor was lined, IB-fashion, with a layer of chopped straw. In yet another house we found the deluxe model, a king-size *kothia* over four feet square with lockable wooden doors.

A thought came to me. Every one of the 'large jars' we had seen, of whatever size or shape, had an entrance of precisely the same dimensions – two of my spans, or seventeen inches square. I tried squeezing into this one and could almost get my shoulders through on the diagonal. Mumtaz didn't volunteer to try; potting himself was not part of his job description. But being slim-built he could have slid in. Now, people who bother about such things (there are about three of us all told) have always wondered what IB looked like. In the *Travels* he reveals only that, not surprisingly for a fourteenth-century Muslim man, he had a beard. I had just discovered, assuming a constant door-size over seven centuries for Doab *ramdas* and *kothias*, that . . . 'Ibn Battutah was not a fatty,' Mumtaz said, reading my mind.

So far my long relationship with IB had been necessarily cerebral, and that glimpse of his skinny body gave me a mild thrill. It soon passed, and I was left with that other, more satisfying revelation: that of the very type and form of IB's bizarre billet, shared, like his terror, with the fluttering bird. It was a small but important link between literary nightmare and human landscape.

Our minor success seemed to enthuse my fellow-researchers. Kripal Singh's *zamindarly* gravity lightened and Mumtaz, whom I suspected of reservations regarding my brand of history on the hoof, lost some of his library reserve. The squire sent for his new Omni minibus. Against the dun mud of Sikanderpur it looked wildly futuristic. But it was the ideal vehicle for more research, and the three of us and two sons piled in and headed east, out of the village and into the fecund, far-horizoned Doab.

After a couple of hundred yards we stopped. We were on the bank of a watercourse; the water wandered along indecisive rivulets, switching channels like a bored TV viewer. It was the colour of stewed tea and it was called, the squire said, the Kali Nadi, the Black River. The name was familiar. As far as I knew, only one other brave soul has tried to locate IB's escape narrative in its setting – Jamal Siddiqi, a late colleague of IG and Professor Habib. I had looked out his *Aligarh District: A Historical Survey* in the History Department library and found some encouragement. The only possible identification of IB's *jabals*, he said, was in the 'fantastic ridge formations' and 'deep narrow intersecting channels of the ravines' formed by the Kali Nadi's various changes of course. 'It is interesting', he went on, 'that there is a village called Paharipur (Hindi *pahar* = hill), almost one and a half miles north-east of Jalali.' The wadi in which IB bumped into his captors, he thought, was the valley of the Kali Nadi.

It all sounded eminently reasonable. But where were the fantastic ridges and deep ravines? Siddiqi's topography was Salvator Rosa, the scene before us about as fantastic as the Thames at Marlow. 'Paharipur,' said Kripal Singh, pointing to a village on the far bank.

'Hillborough' towered at the giddy height of about ten feet above the river-bed. To classify it as a *jabal*, even according to the theory of orographical relativity suggested by Lane's *Lexicon*, was stretching things. There was something funny about this landscape, I decided: not only in IB but also in the late learned Siddiqi – and even in the locals, who were presumably responsible for the name of their village – it seemed to bring on a strange attitude to altitude.

We crossed a bridge and combed Paharipur, in vain, for stray hills or grey eminences. An interrogation in a tea-shop did however produce a lead: to a possible candidate for the pavilion by the tank, the scene of IB's overnight with the snake. In the escape narrative there are three tanks, which IB calls *ba'ins* – 'their word for a sort of well, very broad and lined with stone'. Siddiqi mentioned a pair of adjacent villages near Jalali called Bain Kalan and Bain Khurd, *kalan* and *khurd* being 'big' and 'small' in Persian; their names, he thought, might have come from two of IB's tanks. Was this the third? We commandeered a guide and set off in the Omni, filled – even, I think, Mumtaz – with the thrill of the chase.

The Doab around the Kali Nadi would indeed make famous hunting country. There are no hedges, but there are ditches galore, and mango coverts, and a great wide sweep of land lying under a yellow-green haze. I could picture it dotted with hounds and pink coats on the wall of an inn. We drove along lanes innocent of motor traffic, through mustard fields, down an avenue of tall pollards – an Indian rendering of Hobbema's Middelharnis – until we could drive no further; then on foot, into a silence broken only by caws and chirrups, through an aura of mustard pollen punctuated by more pungent notes, of night-soil and wild garlic. I could see no cotton, but the mustard, the mangoes, a few lote-trees and the odd castor-oil tree provided the rest of the *flora battutiana*. The tracks were deeply rutted, mud moulded by feet and fired by the sun. As bridle-paths they would be hard going, just the place for a hoof to get stuck. But stuck 'between stones'? It was all so right in some respects, so wrong in others.

At first glance the pavilion was absolutely right. A two-storey octagon of brick, pierced by pointed arches and capped by a shallow dome, it stood in a little spinney beside a broad cased well. But it was too right. Both building and well were in perfect condition – not a brick missing, hardly a chip in the lime mortar. Three yokels were sitting nearby on a log. 'Ask them how old it is,' I said to Mumtaz. The yokels looked at each other, then answered simultaneously with three different ages. They ranged from ancient to modern and averaged out at a medieval 600 years. It was hardly the Carbon-14 method.

In contrast the ex-*zamindar* of Azadpur, the next village along the Kali Nadi, bore a heavy crop of dates, precise ones – of Sultans Qutb al-Din Aybeg, Ghiyath al-Din Balaban, Muhammad Shah ibn Tughluq, and their various incursions and exactions in the Doab. Yet again I went through the stages of IB's capture and escape, which by now were taking on a sacral significance, stations of the traveller's cross. Unexpectedly, it was the pesky *kahf* – the cave or hide-out – that met with instant recognition. The research party, further reinforced, set off again.

'I'm sure it was here somewhere,' said the squire of Azadpur. We were down on the silty margin of the Kali Nadi, investigating bumps. 'It went right under the river and came out the other side. It wasn't natural, you know. The old rajas dug it – a *sarang*, a tunnel, big enough for two men to walk through side by side . . .' I'd come across such lost tunnels in Delhi. There was a four-mile one linking the Hall of a Thousand Columns with Tughluqabad; that was one of the shorter ones. 'It must have got buried. I remember going in it myself when I was a little boy . . . sealed with a big stone that had an iron ring in it . . .'

'Open Sesame!' I said to a promising tuffet.

The expedition wasn't a total failure, for we returned to the village via a track on its southern side and, I realized, the most relative *jabal* so far. It rose twenty feet above the river-bed. 'This part of Azadpur was called the Khera,' our host told us. Mumtaz didn't know the word, but the squire explained it as the local equivalent of *qila*, or 'fort'. 'It used to be two, maybe three times higher, but it's been flattened by new building.'

I didn't know what to make of it all. Back in the minibus I reviewed our data to date. The grain jars suggested a pleasing continuity in the human environment since the time of IB. So too the grouping of cased well and pavilion, circa AD 1400 plus-or-minus 500 years. The *sarang* of Azadpur, however, seemed to belong to a landscape of the imagination. Did the infant ex-*zamindar* really enter a subfluvial tunnel closed by a stone slab? And for that matter had Jamal Siddiqi actually made the twelve-mile journey from the Department of History to look at the fantastic ridge formations he wrote about? He didn't claim to have done so. My own ocular evidence suggested that he hadn't, and that his fantastic formations were, literally, fantastic. Then again, the idea that the mound of Azadpur had been flattened by recent building was interesting; even if, in every long-inhabited site I had heard of, occupation *raised* the ground level. So far, IB's itinerary was a series of dubious dots, too few and far apart to join. The rest was smoke and cobwebs.

Of ancient tanks at Great Bain and Little Bain, and of several other spectral possibilities suggested by bemused bacons, we found not a trace. By now we were flagging, although a mound of lote-berries picked up in a village market revived us. (The berries are the fruit of *Zizyphus jujuba*. We had already grazed on one during our walk to the tank, carefully avoiding the shark's-tooth thorns that armed its branches. IB, desperately hungry, had been less wary.) Our *ber*, as they call them, were fat and sweet, rather like small crab-apples to look at but with a big stone and tasting faintly of bananas. 'I think this is a new piece of evidence,' said Mumtaz, tossing a stone through the minibus window. 'If Ibn Battutah was eating *ber*, it shows he was here at this time of year.' He spoke to Kripal Singh and established the fact that the *ber* season had started a few weeks ago, in early February.

'Thank you, Mumtaz. A very good point.' It was a thought that had already occurred to me, and one which I'd swiftly buried at the bottom of the database. IB says that the ambassadorial party left Delhi on 17 Safar 743, which corresponds with 22 July 1342. For cogent reasons to do with his later chronology, the commentators have worked out that he misremembered the year (or that a scribe mis-copied it) and that the date should be put back to 17 Safar 742, or 2 August 1341. Now the entire calendar seemed to be imploding. Or did the pick-your-own *ber* season extend into August? The squire thought IB would have been lucky to find edible fruit that late. I could see what Professor Beckingham was getting at: following IB in India, one was liable to find more problems than solutions. This one was as thorny as a *Zizyphus*.

It was forgotten immediately. For there, off to the right, crowned by a forget-me-not-blue mosque, was a *hill*. As we bounced down the track that led towards it I stared ahead, waiting for the mirage to evaporate.

On second thoughts, I reflected, on reaching the summit after a stiff ninety-second climb, it was more of a hillock. But it was still the highest object for miles around; with its steep sides and far views it was an acropolis, a Himalaya of loess. I heard Mumtaz calling, and followed him to the back of the mosque. 'Look,' he said, pointing downwards. The whole of the central part of the eminence was hollow, a deep depression filled with fields of wheat and mustard. We, and the forget-me-not mosque, were standing on the rim of a crater. 'I think that the agriculture is eating the hill,' Mumtaz explained. I scanned the distances of the Doab and wondered how many of the lesser fluctuations in its surface were the left-overs of *jabals*.

Whether this particular one – Habibganj, ten miles from Jalali – featured in IB's wanderings was impossible to say. But a subsequent *jabal*-hunting expedition revealed that this part of the Doab is littered with dead and dying hillocks, most of them barely discernible but some at interesting stages of decay. Near Pilakhana, three miles the other side of Jalali, the Habibganj Effect had gone one stage further: the fields had hit bottom, and the crater rim was broken up into a series of isolated stacks, a precarious Stonehenge of silt. In time, and not very much of it, they too would fall. In Pilakhana itself we watched as workmen dug away the end of its vestigial *khera* or fort-hill to level a site for a house. An old Muslim tomb on the summit above them was all but hanging in the air; one decent monsoon would send it tumbling over the edge, bones and all. However fabulous his tunnel under the Black River might have been, I now realized that the squire of Azadpur had probably been right about the shrinkage of his village.

Our ascent of the Hill of Habibganj, modest though it was, had opened up new prospects. Seen across time, the mesopotamic pancake of the Doab took shape. Its present flatness was the work of the relentless plough, of a rising population which had slowly ironed its wrinkles away. It had changed in a manner more complex and irrevocable than the men who lived on it, a people expert at perpetuating their material culture, their memories and themselves. It was the passive partner in a relationship not symbiotic but parasitic, between hard men and soft earth. Villages like Sikanderpur are, in the cliché, timeless; but they stand in a temporary landscape.

Back in Sikanderpur; the buffaloes by the gate seemed to have moved nothing but their jaws; the very old man still sat bolt upright on his charpoy in the yard. I thanked Kripal Singh Yadav: he had given up his day and his minibus to three total strangers, one of them dead, and to a quest that most would call quixotic. As we parted, I thought of one last windmill to tilt at: could the squire's ancestors have been among IB's captors?

'He thinks it is unlikely,' Mumtaz translated. 'His family are newcomers. They have been in this village for only a little over two hundred years.'

One had to think relative.

*

On my earlier travels with IB I had tracked down a disappearing island in an Anatolian lake. Now I felt I had located his vanishing *jabals*. But, apart from those calendar gremlins to do with the loteberry season, other problems niggled away in the periphery of his landscape – the stoniness of the ground, for example. One of the words IB uses, *hijarah*, could at a tight pinch apply to sand as well as stones. But no philological tool can make an impression on the *sakhr*, or rock, of his highest *jabal*, nor any lexical alchemy convert either term to the plastic and ubiquitous Doab silt. I was prepared to put the lapse down to the fourteen years and many more lands that separated the scene from its transcription in Fez, and to a less than lapidary memory. And so we arrived at a sort of compromise landscape, IB and I: I would overlook his petrification of it if he would put up with its erosion by time and tillage. It wasn't satisfactory. I longed to find some more tangible memento to his Jalali adventures – not just the type of *jabal* or sort of pot, but a clear IB Was *Here*.

The following morning I went to the History Department library, a room that smelt of sealing-wax and overlooked a luxuriant thicket of marijuana, in search of further insights into the shifting landscape of the Doab. There were none. But I did some useful homework for the trip ahead, until the muezzin called the sunset prayer and those tiny enemies of learning, the *machchhar*, began their desultory attack, pouring out of hemp bushes and bookstacks. Then there was a power-cut, and the assault turned into a frenzy of blood-letting. It was no better out on the street, where the mosquitoes zinged through a darkness that fell, perceptibly, like soot.

Later that evening I went to a telephone office to ring home. 'What language was that?' one of the other customers asked when I put the phone down.

'Arabic. I was calling Yemen.'

The young man looked worried. 'But . . . that's a Muslim country.' I nodded, and told him I lived there. 'So you're a Muslim?' I said I wasn't. 'Then how can you live there?'

'Perfectly happily.'

He looked flabbergasted. 'Don't you know that Muslims are against humanity?' I said it was news to me and asked him how, if he felt like that, he could live in a place like Aligarh that was proverbial for its Muslims. 'I don't. I'm from Agra. I'm studying English Lit. at Agra University.'

'Then I'm surprised that an . . . an intellectual like you can be so prejudiced,' I said, lying.

'Some Muslims are OK,' he conceded. 'But look around the university here. Look around the halls of residence. They're full of posters of Osama Bin Laden.' In three days, including several visits to halls of residence, the closest thing to a revolutionary pin-up I'd come across was Professor Habib's Lenin.

The rant went on, until he realized I wasn't listening. 'You must come to Agra,' he concluded, rising. 'And you must see the Taj. It's the eighth wonder of the world!'

I'd had no intention of seeing the Taj Mahal to start with. Now the very idea filled me with irrational revulsion. But he was gone before I could tell him what I thought of his wonder, or – damn, why didn't I think of it in time? – remind him who built the blasted thing.

★

'The young are being fed a load of shit,' IG explained. We were on our way to Agra, and I'd just told him about the exchange in the telephone office the night before. 'Fascist slogans. They're so easy for young minds.' We drove past the site of the Kirni Gate, the southern limit of old Kol. 'Mind you, your chap wasn't as bad as some. A while ago the RSS camped en masse outside the Taj, then they invaded it and wrote graffiti and pissed in the canals. They call it "a symbol of slavery" . . . Oh, look at this arsehole!' He bellowed at a bullock cart that was blocking the road.

Eventually we broke out of the vehicular coils of Kol. IG switched on a tape of Qur'an recitation, and we spun along the Agra road to the Chapter of the Cow. With us was Munawwar, secretary-general of the Rickshaw Union; he and IG had business in Agra, and IG had said I must come and look at the Taj. I resisted; he insisted. In the end I had agreed bolshily to go to Agra to look at his destination there, the Office of Non-Governmental Organization Registration.

'That boy you spoke to last night', IG went on, 'comes from a generation whose minds are being poisoned. The BJP are rewriting history from the bottom up. All the work that people like Irfan and Romila Thapar put into the school history syllabus is being over-turned. You've heard of Romila Thapar?' I had; along with Professor Habib she was probably the most highly regarded Indian historian. 'Well, they've both been sacked from the syllabus review panel, and the fascists are filling the textbooks with stuff about "rivers of blood" and so on. All the centuries of Muslim rule are being reduced to a bloodbath.'

'You must admit though that Muslim rule in India wasn't exactly vegetarian. What about IB fighting the "infidel rebels" up the road from here? He says they killed thousands.'

'They were fighting them not because they were infidels, but because they were rebels. Most of the Hindu chiefs sided with the Muslims all the way through. It's the whole communalism thing that's being imposed on the past. I mean, children are being told that Islam is a religion of atrocities.' He was gently, but very, very angry. I could see why. History was as malleable as the landscape, and if IG was right it was being reshaped in ways that were grotesque and dangerous.

At a place called Madrak we passed a perfect simulacrum of IB's inaccessible *jabal* – a steep knoll, bristling with *Zizyphus* and other trees and crowned with a little fort. IG said it had been the seat in the eighteenth and nineteenth centuries of a family of German indigo planters. Interspersed with such curiosities and with oaths hurled at bullock carts, towards which he bore a particular animosity, IG's conversation wound through the loopier manifestations of the Hindu right – the internet *Mahabharata* exegetes, for instance, who explained the thunderbolts and fiery arrows of the ancient heroes as nuclear missiles, and the squadron of yogic fliers who had volunteered for service against the Kashmiri separatists – all to the fluid and dispassionate backing of his Qur'an tape.

After the town of Hathras, the tape came to an end and IG replaced it with a *qawwali* cassette. 'Just listen to this. Murli, 1983. Today the *qawwals* are singing in the style of Bollywood. Murli's the real thing.' I said that Murli didn't sound a very Islamic name. 'It isn't. It means "flute", and it's an epithet of Krishna. You know, he's often shown holding one.' IG seemed not to find the heterodox stage-name surprising.* 'A rival *qawwal* slipped him a piece of camphor in his food,' he continued as the Flute warmed up. 'It was meant to wreck his voice, but it just made it more poignant . . . Oh, listen! Listen!' There was indeed a slight, almost bluesy frog in Murli's throat. 'Ah, if only you knew Persian . . . the lyrics are Amir Khusraw at his best.'

---

* A sixteenth-century dictionary of Indian Sufi technical terms has the following entry: '*Murli* or *Bansuri* (flute): This indicates the appearance of existence out of the void.

The entire world is the humming of His song.

None has heard such a prolonged voice.

It also points to the contents of the Qur'anic verse: ". . . and breathed into him (Adam) of My Spirit" and the divine command in the Qur'an, namely, "Be".' That the dictionary's definitions are to be taken in a soft and flexible sense is shown by the entry on '*Krishna*: Sometimes Krishna and his other names in Hindawi (Hindi) indicate the Prophet Muhammad and sometimes the (Perfect) Man . . . Sometimes they represent Iblis (the Devil).'

The ubiquitous Amir Khusraw, Nizam al-Din's most adoring disciple. 'I bet people were saying *he* was the real thing when IB was in Delhi,' I said.

'He still is!' IG exclaimed. He sang along –

> *'Du narjis sat qibla gahi hasti . . .*
> Your narcissus-eyes are the *qiblah* of my being . . .'

– his own eyes melting, Munawwar the rickshaw-*wala* swaying silently on the back seat –

> 'Your eyebrows are the prostration of the ecstatic . . .

Don't believe this bullshit about the sword! Islam entered the villages of India with the Sufis and their music.' Not rivers of blood, but concert tours.

'Who's he singing about?' I asked, between verses.

'It might be the Prophet, or Ali, or God, or his *pir*, Nizam al-Din. They're all possible. You see, Amir Khusraw didn't keep to hard and fast boundaries. He took the tunes of ragas and gave them Persian words. He wrote in dialect – Awadhi, Bhojpuri and so on. He even took hymns to Krishna and addressed them word for word to Nizam al-Din.' The beloved master in the jaunty yellow cap, serenaded in songs to a blue-skinned god. 'But this really is one of the best. Ah, I've wept, listening to these words!

> Show thyself to me, unveiled, at the door of my . . .'

IG braked. 'Oh, look at this *shit.*'

We had hit the edge of Agra, and the very Clapham Junction of bullock carts.

*

It would be a bloody-minded but not unBattutian act: he had been to Cairo and not looked at the Pyramids; I would visit Agra and not see the Taj. IG told me I was talking nonsense. And after several hours in an office run by a man who was to yawning what Mary was to typhoid, I was gagging for the Mughal.

Having at long last reregistered the Aligarh rickshawmen, we left the official to his endless orgasm of boredom and set off across the city. Near the Red Fort we were caught in a pincer movement by a vegetable market and a wedding. The latter was accompanied by the customary brass band in prop-cupboard uniforms; instrumentally they were a cut above the rest, for they had *two* sousaphones. By now we were almost at a standstill, inching forward through a confusion of carrots and cornets, euphoniums and aubergines. Eventually we drew level with the bridegroom, a podgy man in a turban and lounge suit on a white charger. He looked scared; I smiled up in sympathy. Then IG stuck his head out of the window and yelled at him in a voice that cut through the brays and parps of the band. For a moment the groom looked as if he was going to blub. 'What did you say to him?' I asked, shocked.

'I said, "What a time to get married, arsehole!"'

Ten minutes and a hundred yards on we came to the root cause of the jam, a van that had broken down smack in the middle of the road. 'Oh dear,' said IG, '. . . and I shouted at that poor bugger on the horse.' Then he stuck his head out of the window again and bellowed. I recognized an 'arsehole' and, in the van driver's quavering reply, '*c . . . c . . . camshaft*'. Travelling with IG was an education.

As IB's editor would have said, what the travel writers have written in description of the beauties of the Taj Mahal is beyond all computation and enumeration. I can only add that when IG demonstrated the echo in the tomb-chamber by shouting 'ALLAAAAH!' – in a voice, used to such devastating effect against bridegrooms and bullock carts, that made the trippers jump and almost shook the Quiet Please signs off the walls – I half expected Him to answer back; that the 'Taj Mahal, India' T-shirts sold by a boy called Raju are even more marvellous than IB's *jabals* in their propensity to shrink; and that when I told Martin the Taj wasn't solid marble I was quite right – it is solidified cloud.

On the way back to Aligarh we ate crystallized marshmallows, an Agra delicacy and the edible equivalent of the Taj Mahal. IG spoke meltingly of his own Sufi *pir*, one Shaykh Sabir, an elder contemporary of Nizam al-Din. And we listened to Miles Davis, who inspired in IG a state only slightly less ecstatic than that produced by the Flute. From Qur'an to *qawwali* to kool . . . surely we could go no further; but by the time we reached the Kirni Gate of old Kol we were on to the Grateful Dead, and IG's reminiscences of going AWOL for a month from Duke University to follow them on tour across the United States.

Munawwar slept in the back seat. It had been a long day, from the Chapter of the Cow to 'Black Muddy River'.

★

Before us the black muddy Kali Nadi dribbled rather than rolled. Beyond it Paharipur, Hillborough, appeared from this angle to have risen slightly, at least in my estimation. We were following a long hollow track, the sort Samuel Palmer would have painted. It ran straight to the river, beaten by feet so deep into the earth that our heads were level with the tree roots. From time to time peasants scrambled down the enclosing banks to greet the leader of our party; which they did elaborately, for Sayyid Hakim Muhammad Azm al-Din Husayni Hamadhani was at once Ionian physician, descendant of the Prophet, and – like all the best tour-leaders – an ex-*zamindar*.

His, IB's, town of Jalali had been so plain to see across the levels that it escaped me how we could have missed it on our first trip. I had spent a fruitless half-hour in the mosque there, wobbling on a stool and squinting at inscriptions that recorded nineteenth-century rebuilds, when the muezzin suggested a visit to the noble physician, Hakim Sahib. Mumtaz took the Hero Honda round by the bazaar while the muezzin led me through a knot of lilac and lavender lanes. They unravelled at the foot of a secluded hillock, another retired *jabal* for my list. On top of this was a three-sided courtyard and an elderly gentleman in a frock-coat. He was sitting on a charpoy under a venerable tamarind, and writing, slowly and beautifully, in a ledger. The open frame of buildings, the script, the stillness, the ascetic face of the scribe, all gave the impression that we had stepped through the border of a Mughal miniature; all except the yellow plastic pen with which Hakim Sahib wrote.

'Hakim Sahib knows all about history,' the muezzin whispered to me. And so he did. Over tea and *barfi*, the sweets liberally covered with silver leaf and flies, he began to recite the annals of Jalali from the start of recorded time – its capture by Sultan Balaban in 1267. Twenty-eight years into the chronicle a certain Shi'ite *sayyid* arrived at the fort of Jalali, from Hamadhan in Persia via Kashmir. Hakim Sahib's next words made Mumtaz smile. 'We are sitting in that fort,' he explained, 'and Hakim Sahib is the *sayyid*'s descendant.'

After that I lost the drift. Unexpected foreshortenings of time had occurred before on my travels with IB, and they were always disconcerting. I took a few notes for form's sake; but it was this trim little man with a neat white beard and untidily large ears who was now significant, not the litany of events and dates that he intoned. Hakim Sahib didn't just know all about history. He was its word made flesh.

At the end of the monologue I thanked him, as persianately as possible, then explained myself. 'Ah yes, Ibn-i Battutah . . .' The epenthetic Persian vowel had crossed half Asia and all the centuries from Hamadhan. 'We shall visit the shrine of Ali Shahid, even

though he is a little before your period. But first . . .' He called for a
son and another big volume, in which I was asked to enter my details.
Hakim Sahib made some notes in Urdu, kiss-curled, beauty-spotted
and voluptuous, next to my gawkier Arabic. I had the eerie but not
unpleasant sensation of being flesh made word.

The shrine was off the straight hollow path, not far from where it
meets the Kali Nadi. It was a small domed chamber containing two
unadorned tombs, of Ali Shahid and his son: the sort of structure one
might see – and I had seen a lot of them – across the Islamic world.
Apart from the slightly pre-IB date there was nothing remarkable
about the place. Except, of course, the echo, which Hakim Sahib
gleefully demonstrated. Yelling seemed to be a sine qua non of visiting distinguished dead Indians.

Outside there were four low graves, roughly plastered and shaded
by a tree. Again for form's sake, I asked Hakim Sahib about them.
'They are later,' he said. And then I knew the reason for our visit.
Even before Mumtaz translated the next phrase, two words popped
out of it, an unusual but familiar name. 'The one nearest the tree is
the grave of Malik Kafur. The others also belong to Ibn-i Battutah's
comrades who fell in battle here. And there are twenty-one more of
them just over there.' He indicated an area of undulating ground.

This, then, was the here that I'd been looking for, IB's here. The
here and then.

We – the physician and two sons, a neighbour, Mumtaz and I –
stood by the grave of King Camphor the Cup-Bearer. Hakim Sahib
led the prayers. '*In the name of God, the Compassionate, the Merciful.
Praise to God, Lord of all creation* . . .' Where did IB stand as he recited
these same words over the dead eunuch? '*. . . and to You alone we
pray for help. Guide us to the straight path* . . .' Did he, the qadi-turned-
ambassador, lead the prayers? '*. . . nor of those who have gone astray. In the
name of God, the Compassionate, the Merciful* . . .' Or was it Hakim
Sahib's ancestor, the *sayyid*? '*. . . nor was He begotten. None is equal to
Him. In the name of God* . . .' Whoever it was, he had set off a reverber-
ation that still rolled on '*. . . to enfold our brother Kafur, and all our brothers lying in this place, in Your mercy.*'

'Amen,' we said together. We didn't have to shout; we were the
echo.

★

The co-ordinates of IB's nightmare were falling into place. To my partial reconstruction of the changing landscape I could now add a solid point of reference – the tomb of IB's fellow-traveller and comrade-in-arms, Malik Kafur. And with this, time itself had gained in solidity. Instead of a discrete then and now, there was a continuum. The monument, like many I had seen in India, was anonymous; but its identity was engraved on the public memory in the person of Hakim Sahib, who had inherited the duty of preserving and praying over the eunuch's grave in direct line of succession from his ancestors. With the dead warriors and moribund 'mountains', the nightmare now had a tangible beginning and a tentative middle. The end could hardly be more tantalizing.

On the eighth day of his wanderings IB saw a well. It was the answer to his prayers, as he had found no water lately and was almost passing out from thirst. The well had a rope but, maddeningly, no bucket. He tied his headcloth to the rope, dipped it in the water, then sucked on it. This did not quench his thirst, so he tried drawing water in his boot. The boot fell off the rope and was lost down the well. He had better luck with the other boot and was able to drink his fill. The rest must be told in his own words.

> After that I cut up the remaining boot and tied its uppers to my foot with the well-rope and some scraps of cloth that I found there. While I was doing this and thinking about the plight I was in, a person appeared. I looked up and saw a black-skinned man holding a jug and a staff and carrying a leather bag over his shoulder. He said to me, '*Al-salam alaykum*,' and I said, '*Alaykum al-salam wa rahmat Allah wa barakatuh*.' Then he said to me in Persian, '*Chikas?*' meaning 'Who are you?' and I said, 'A man astray,' and he said, 'So am I.' Then he tied his jug to a rope that he had with him and drew some water from the well. I wanted to drink but he said, 'Be patient.' Then he opened his bag and took out a handful of black chick-peas fried with a little rice. After this he did his ritual ablutions and prayed two prostrations, and I did the same. He then asked me my name. I said, 'Muhammad,' and asked him his name, and he said, '*Al-Qalb al-Farih* [Blithe-heart].' This gladdened me for it seemed to me a good omen. Then he said to me, 'In the name of God, come with me.' I said, 'Yes,' and we walked together for a while. But I

soon began to feel a heaviness in my limbs and was unable to remain standing, so I sat down. He said, 'What is the matter with you?' and I said, 'I was able to walk before meeting you, but now that I have met you I cannot.' At this he said, 'Glory be to God! Climb on my back.' I said to him, 'You are too weak to carry me,' but he said, 'God will give me strength. You must do as I tell you.' So I climbed on his back. Then he said to me, 'You must recite many times over, *Sufficient for us is God and excellent the Protector.*' I did so, until I lost consciousness. It was only when I felt myself falling to the ground that I came to again, and by the time I was fully awake there was not a trace of the man to be seen. I was at the edge of an inhabited village. I entered it and found its people to be Hindu peasants in the charge of a Muslim governor. They sent word to him about me, and he came to see me. I asked him the name of the village and he said, 'Taj Burah.' The distance from here to Kuwil [Kol], where my companions were, was two *farsakhs*.

The nineteenth-century German orientalist Klaproth dismissed out of hand IB's 'rigmaroles' about Muslim holy men. The criticism is, like the name of the egregious gentleman who expressed it, a combination of claptrap and rot. Holy men and IB's meetings with them are the quintessence of the *Travels*, a whole richly detailed para-geography. Take away the saints and you remove the soul of the book, turning it into a zombie for the service of academics. That said, the Bunyanesque name, Blithe-heart, and the Pilgrim-like awakening had always made me wonder how much of IB's nightmare was set in the palpable world.

I'm not suggesting it was all a literal bad dream; rather, that the rigours of his enforced fast caused him to slide in and out of that other journey – the mystical one with the Caveman, recently aborted and regretted. Five years after IB's Doab trials Maneri, the cave-saint and epistolist of Bihar, described the allegorical Sufi odyssey: 'Those who have trodden it have said: If a traveller is passing through the stage of earthly qualities, he sees such things as lanes and alleys, dark places and dwellings, and comes to ruined and broken-down lodgings, water-logged expanses, and hilly tracts where he experiences a heaviness of spirit and a gloominess which, however, are followed by a lightness and pleasantness.' Poor earth-bound IB didn't reach the higher stages of Maneri's journey, the realms of watery, airy and fiery qualities, the firmament of the heavens and the starry regions; let alone 'the thousands of other similar worlds through which the traveller must pass, and in each of which he witnesses sights and subtleties appropriate to it.' But he made it through the Sufi slough of despond to the weightless ride on Blithe-heart's shoulders, self-hypnotized by that same mantra-like verse that had saved him in the Hall of a Thousand Columns: '*Sufficient for us is God and excellent the Protector.*'

Exactly where IB crossed – if I'm right to think he did – the margin between the material landscape and that parallel one mapped by Maneri, is impossible to tell. In Tajpur at least, IB's Taj Burah, he was back in a demonstrably material place. Hakim Sahib pointed it out from the summit of the 'inaccessible *jabal*' (current altitude about fifteen feet) from which, he was sure, the rebels had swooped on Jalali. The mound under our feet, isolated in a field, had been much higher during his youth; and, he added, it used to be surrounded by jungle. As for Tajpur, while the inhabitants of Jalali and its other dependent villages are divided roughly equally between Hindus and Muslims, this village alone still has an entirely Hindu population – as in IB's day. Again, an inconstant land underlay an extraordinarily static society.

*

So who was Blithe-heart? Hakim Sahib knew him; he even mimed the piggy-back ride, grinning from one huge ear to the other. But he admitted that his knowledge came from the Urdu translation of the *Travels*. There was no tomb, nothing to tie IB's saviour into the here and now. A trip to Tajpur on the Hero Honda revealed no more than the familiar mingling of mud and crud, curd and turd and, in a neighbouring hamlet, the now hardly more surprising eroded *jabal*.* As for Blithe-heart, he must be sought in one of the few sections of Indian society which was not static: the sadhus, *nihangs*, faqirs and qalandars – men astray, at least in this world.

There is a twist. IB knew perfectly well who his rescuer was,

---

* For the record: the mound is called Ukarna Behrampur and was probably the seat of the Muslim governor – the villagers have come across the stone footings of a fort buried in the silt. Also for the record: Jamal Siddiqi, owing to some fantastic arithmetic performed on the length of *farsakhs*, plumped for the wrong Tajpur, a village of the same name far too near to Aligarh; Beckingham followed in his footnotes.

although he only realized it when he was safely ensconced with the governor of Tajpur, fed, bathed and clothed.

I thought about the man who had carried me on his back and I remembered what the saint Abu Abdallah al-Murshidi had told me, as I have related in the first volume, when he said to me: 'You will meet there my brother Dilshad, who will rescue you from a great misfortune into which you will fall.' I remembered too what he had said when I asked him about this name – that it was the Persian for 'Blithe-heart'. And then I realized that it was this very man whom al-Murshidi told me I would meet, and that my rescuer was also one of the saints. But this meeting I have related was the only time I was blessed with his company.

The co-ordinates of IB's dream in the Nile Delta had fallen into place as well. The road ahead was unpredictable.

*

For IG there was no Blithe-heart, no rescuer on his journey into that inconstant landscape around Jalali.

Some time after finishing the draft of this chapter I wrote to him with a few queries. The reply came from one of his colleagues in the Department of History. It began:

Dr Iqbal Ghani Khan, a historian of much attainment and great promise, trade-union activist, dedicated partisan of all causes of the oppressed, was brutally killed on 14 February 2003. He had just dropped his wife at the J.N. Medical College Hospital, early in the morning, when he is reported to have been accosted by three persons, who abducted him in his car. They took him to an unfrequented spot 15 km from Aligarh and, felling him down with a blunt weapon, shot him twice in the head. His body was found by the villagers. Until now, the police has not indicated the discovery of any clues leading to the murderers.

Another grave to visit.

After rejoining his companions at Aligarh, IB went south via the castle of Gwalior and a place he calls Barwan, where he digresses on the local vampires. Like many present-day tourists, he fitted in a visit to the temple-town of Khajuraho. He then crossed the sparsely inhabited uplands of Madhya Pradesh and passed through the towns of Chanderi, Ujjain and Dhar. Leaving the northern region of Hindustan, he made a side-trip to the plateau of the Deccan and the fortress-city of Dawlatabad, Muhammad Shah's aborted second capital. From here he turned north-west, arriving at the coast probably in December 1341.

Lost Hearts

'Long-hair holds fire, holds the drug, holds sky and earth.
Long-hair reveals everything.'

The Rig Veda

MARTIN WAS DUBIOUS about our prospects of finding a vampire.
I asked Dewan what he thought of our chances.

'Bonfires?'

'No, vampires. Men or animals who drink blood.'

'I know. I think no bonfires. But we ask very old *baba*.'

For the moment we were enjoying the ride. A few days before, I had returned to Delhi to pick up Martin and hire a car. The latter, a Hindustan Motors Ambassador, was perhaps not so much a car as a motorized three-piece suite complete with antimacassars. Martin compared it favourably with his memories of Indian cross-country travel thirty years ago – night after night on station platforms, day upon third-class day on arse-martyring wooden seats.

Dewan, our driver, had at first alarmed us with his action-packed schedule – 'Mr Tim-sir-sahib Mr Martin-sir-sahib 8.30 a.m. sharp I come 8.40 a.m. we go buy whiskies 9.30 a.m. we return get baggages wash hands etcetera 9.45 a.m. we depart . . .' – all in one high-speed swerving sentence. Hectic Dewan seemed the opposite of lugubrious Titoo. If he drove like he spoke, we had an exciting thousand miles ahead of us. But the Ambassador's front-parlour ambience seemed to calm him, and on the way to the Bagpiper English Wine Shop (no English, no wine, but Bagpiper whisky galore) he revealed that his guru had given him advice on how to drive: look far in front, see how the other drivers are behaving, and ignore the road immediately ahead. It boded well for us if not for children and other small animals that might stray off the verge.

Over the coming three weeks we would grow fond of Dewan; even begin to find endearing his habit of paragraphing his speech with farts. While he refrained from letting rip inside the car, public spaces the length of Madhya Pradesh and half Maharashtra would resound to his brazen bombast, always preceded by the insouciant raising of a buttock.* Dewan's habit has long attracted comment from further west. According to al-Biruni, the Indians 'consider the *crepitus ventris* a good omen, sneezing a bad one'. A little earlier, the poet Aban ibn Abd al-Hamid observed similarly that

> The most sagacious men of Hind
> Have spoken to the point on wind:
> 'If you should feel a fart come on,
> To hold it in is very wrong.
> Fling wide the gates and let it loose –
> Its breeze to ease will sure conduce!
> We class as *not* nice habits these:
> To blow one's nose, to cough, to sneeze;
> The oral fart, or belch, is worse –
> It smells far sweeter in reverse.

We had left behind the hazy, baizy plains of the Doab and were heading south, into the thick of India; and, it seemed, up, almost imperceptibly, to higher, drier places. The rich early colours – marmalade dawn, cherry-red cooking fires – were gone. Light became white through the prism of advancing day. Fall-out from a cement works covered the land with a grey-white scurf. We passed two boy holy men, walking purposefully, pilgrims with meagre scrips. I turned to look at them. They smiled and waved, two saffron flames waving, wavering, receding into a vacancy of dust.

In a sense, I too was on a pilgrimage. IG had compared my relationship with IB to that of *pir* and *murid*, Sufi master and disciple.

---

* Which prompted me to tell Martin the story of Max Reger, the German composer and organist. Once, while giving a recital, he felt the need to break wind. He waited for a crescendo, then leaned over. As he did so, his knee brushed the General Cancel button. The stops shot in, the organ cut out and the church, famous for its acoustic, was rent with a *fortissimo* fart.

I liked the simile. It was particularly appropriate in a land with more illuminations per mile than Blackpool, where holy tourist-traps are thicker on the ground than pubs in Ireland, where a single day's congregation on the sanctified sandbank of Allahabad would keep the entire Church of England going for a month of Sundays. But I was after more than enlightenment, visions, vibes, intangibles. I needed hard evidence. Looking back on Aligarh, my reconstructed landscape of IB's flight from capture seemed plausible but by no means perfect. The only fixed co-ordinate was the grave of Malik Kafur – King Camphor, IB's companion killed in battle. Before I left Aligarh my faith was shaken even in that.

'Another fellow was here following Ibn Battutah,' said Professor Mansura Haidar, head of the History Department. 'Like you.' She made it sound a dubious hobby, like celebrity-stalking. As it turned out the other IB-obsessive was Professor Beckingham, who had passed through Aligarh in the mid-1970s. But her observation elicited another one from Professor Habib: 'Of course you have to take into account the possibility of false memories.'

'I'm not sure I get . . .'

'For example, how do you know that your alleged tomb is genuine? Its identity could have entered the popular imagination from other Ibn Battutah researchers.'

Such as . . . ? But the ellipsis soon filled: not just with Beckingham, but also with Professor Habib's late colleague, Siddiqi; and who knew who else? British district officers of a historical bent, subalterns on Sunday strolls, butterfly nets over their shoulders and the Reverend Samuel Lee's 1829 translation of the abridged *Travels* in their knapsacks. And now me. A battalion of Battutologists, tramping over Hindustan, sniffing for relics – and finding them, with the help of the ever-obliging locals. King Camphor began to evaporate.

On second thoughts he resolidified. His grave was a monument unknown, it seemed, to outside scholarship. Neither Beckingham, Siddiqi, nor anyone else had mentioned it. The man who led me to it, Hakim Sahib, was a scholar himself; in all likelihood his ancestor sprinkled dust on the corpse and bequeathed its identity to his descendants. On the other hand, the venerable physician had read the *Travels* in Urdu. Could he himself be wilfully responsible for a false tradition? On balance, it was highly unlikely. Why should he attach Malik Kafur's name to such an undistinguished monument? And whence the precise details – twenty-one of IB's comrades buried near Jalali, a further five, he had added, to the south at Pilakhana? No, I decided after these oscillations: the tomb stood firm.

All the same, Professor Habib had taught me an object lesson. He was a sceptic, I an enthusiast. He analysed, I synthesized. He dealt with proofs, I with questions of faith. He was, in short, a historian. I couldn't help being a pilgrim; but I knew now that I must be as dispassionate a pilgrim as possible.

*

I left Martin drawing in the dim galleries of the Jahangir Mahal, climbed to the roof of the palace and picked a gazebo. The view across Orchha, where we had halted on our journey to the vampires, was intensely Indian – pavilions, parapets, pinnacles, slug-trail river – and soporific. I lay down and shut one eye. The other I fixed warily on the vultures, poised one per pinnacle all around me. Received wisdom says they like their meat high. Not necessarily, suggested the Persian geographer Marvazi: masochistic devotees at a temple by the Ganges would feign death and allow vultures to 'slit open their bellies and eat their bowels, regarding the birds awhile with resignation and piety'. But the Orchha vultures seemed doped by the general languor of the place and were disinclined to take tea, high or not. Eventually I snoozed; until a pair of long-limbed and very unlanguid langurs legged it across the parapets and ejected me, with bared fangs and uncouth gestures, from what they saw as their private pavilion.

Our suite at the next-door palace was probably the nearest we'd get to sultanic splendour. It was certainly an improvement on the night before, in a hotel near the Simpkin Public School (Bagless) in Gwalior, where our beds smelt of mosquito coils and curried sweat. For me the rest of Gwalior was equally depressing: there were too many melancholy associations. According to IB's history of the Delhi Sultanate, it was here in the castle that the brothers of dissolute Sultan Qutb al-Din were blinded and beheaded. The fortress remained a royal gulag until well into the Mughal era, its history a dismal recitation of poisonings, mutilations, strangulations, decapitations, defenestrations. I'd been hoping to find the dungeon into which the corpses of IB's unfortunate princes were thrown; but the grim elongated Colditz of Gwalior had holes enough to fill the Albert Hall. It was riddled with them, and with horrible memories.

I'd also been looking forward to seeing the celebrated elephant. 'At the gate of the castle', said IB, 'is the image of an elephant carved in stone and with the image of a mahout upon it. Anyone who saw it from some way off would never guess that it was anything but a real live elephant.' The Mughal Emperor Babur inspected it in 1526 and noted in his memoirs that it had two mahouts; Finch, an English visitor of the early seventeenth century, missed the mahouts but thought the figure 'very curiously wrought'; Mackintosh-Smith, early in the twenty-first century, found Hathia Paur, Elephant Gate – but no elephant. The local finger of blame points at that noted icon-oclast, the Emperor Aurangzeb.

There was some light relief at the citadel: the palace of Man Singh, for example, with its perky bobby's-helmet pavilions and tiled friezes of bathtime yellow ducks; the explanatory signboards ('Please note that the walls have gone up perpendicular to converse in the dome'); and, at the Ex-Elephant Gate, a conversation about pricks. A group

of layabouts were telling me about the approaching festival of Holi and its messy high jinks. 'We are throwing water in this place,' one of the youths said, pointing at my crotch. Then his brow furrowed, and he looked from me to a dark-skinned member of the group. 'This blackie is having a black one.' Chortles from the anglophones. 'You are having a white one?'

'Um, not exactly. It's sort of . . . pinko grey.'

'What is "pinko-grey"?'

'A literary allusion.'

We had left Gwalior in sombre mood. Martin was pining for Delhi – the Red Tomb, Humayun, Safdarjang. I felt a more general unease. 'To make you hear, to make you feel . . .', these, said Joseph Conrad, are the writer's aims; 'before all, to make you *see*.' I could hear the moans and pleas of the princes in the tower of Gwalior as they dragged them to the block, 'shocked and terrified'; could feel the agony of their mother, clawing at the prison door. I could see the bodies tumbling into the pit, headless, not yet stiff. I could see the elephant, and that spectral range of hills upon the plain, and the Thousand-Column Hall. I saw all of IB's India in his book, in the two bright dimensions of the illuminator. I wanted to see it in three. Or at least in stereoscope – two images, his and mine, from subtly different angles, combining in the round. Then to record, as directly as Martin did. We were both after speaking likenesses.

And here we were, looking for vampires. We might as well have gone yeti-coursing.

*

Vampires seldom stray into the sensible world, and never into the sceptical one inhabited by historians like Professor Habib. In the *Travels* they occupy a *terra incognita* where commentators fear to tread.

IB's brief account of them is as nasty as anything featuring cads in capes and coffins. After leaving Gwalior he arrived at a small town called Barwan, where he heard the following story. A guest at a wedding had slipped off into the shadows for a pee. He didn't return. Later he was found dead in the bazaar, a victim of the Beast of Barwan. 'The beast had drunk his blood but not eaten his flesh, and they told me that this always happened when it attacked people. And here is an amazing thing: a certain man told me that it was not a beast that did this but a human being, one of the magicians known as *jugis* [yogis], appearing in the shape of a beast.' IB himself was understandably sceptical, but other witnesses corroborated the tale and recounted others.

At this point, IB digresses on various other yogic skills. One of these is an aptitude for mixing aphrodisiacs (illustrated by the case of a sultan who swore by his court yogi's cocktail, fortified with iron filings – until he overdosed on it and died in embarrassing circumstances; one is reminded of Ferdinand the Catholic, killed by a surfeit of

Spanish Fly). The other feats are supernatural – telepathy, endurance of punishing fasts and of burial for months in pits, cockatrice-like powers of killing with a glance. 'The common people say that if the breast of a man killed in this way is cut open, he will be found to have no heart. The reason, they say, is that it has been eaten. This is most usual when the perpetrators are women, and such women are known as *kaftars*.'

With the *kaftar*, IB was on familiar ground: he had met one. In the course of his famine-relief work in Delhi, a woman was brought to him. 'They said that she was a *kaftar* and had eaten the heart of a boy who was beside her, and they also brought the boy's corpse.' IB's legal training hadn't covered cannibal witches, so he passed the buck to the sultan's lieutenant. 'He ordered that she be subjected to the ordeal, namely that they should fill four jars with water, tie them to her arms and legs, and throw her into the River Yamuna. This was done, and as she did not sink they knew her to be a *kaftar* . . . So the lieutenant ordered her to be burned.'

Some of this is yogic stock-in-trade – the telepathy, the fasting, the self-interment. (As one does in the middle of almost nowhere, we bumped into Kevin Rushby, an old friend from Yemen and both a fellow-traveller and a fellow-writer, down the road in a *tali*-joint in Khajuraho. He had just been to the Kumbh Mela, the great Allahabad god-fest, and told me that one of the star turns had been a Japanese lady sadhu who had herself totally buried. Unlike IB's yogis, she managed a wimpish four days. Also unlike them, but very unwimpishly, she had no apparent breathing hole.) The yogis' shape-shifting activities are more of a puzzle.

It is impossible to tell definitively whether *sab'*, the Arabic word I've translated as 'beast', is a lion, a leopard, a tiger or something else. A tiger is probably the best guess. Lions and leopards have clear Arabic terms; tigers, however, have never had a convincing entry in the Arabic dictionary and are often lumped under the heading of *sab'*, a wild and woolly genus.* The *kaftar*, on the other hand, the Bride of the Beast, looks indubitably like the Persian for 'hyena'. I'd already had a hunch that the word might be an Indian one, garbled. But a

---

* There is a Persian loan-word, *babr* – the nickname, variously transliterated, of the first Mughal emperor – but in IB's time it was a species new to lexicography. A dictionary of the age explains it as an Indian animal that fights with lions and leopards, 'but the scorpion is on friendly terms with it, and sometimes makes its abode in its hair'.

recce through the reference books and a session with a friendly Sanskritist produced no leads. Taking the word at face value, however, set other trains of thought in motion – trains which carried me into more familiar territory. Not far from my house in the Yemeni capital, a sign invites one to inspect Nabbash al-Qubur, 'the Grave-Grubber', a mangy and much-prodded hyena displayed in a cage next door to the cinema. In addition to its alleged habit of digging up and eating human remains, the Arabian hyena has long been the preferred transport of witches. The pre-Islamic king-to-be As'ad al-Kamil, for example, was given a driving test aboard a bucking hyena during a meeting with three hags on a lonely moor; they failed him when he was thrown, and had to resuscitate him with a cup of blood. Even in recent times, the creepy lagoon of Khawr Ruri on the coast of Dhofar was well known as a pan-Arabian coven-cum-convention facility, with witches arriving en masse on hyenas.

The water ordeal in the Yamuna suggested further familiar territory – not only that of medieval and later Europe but also the Yemeni island of Suqutra, where I had heard that well within living memory suspected witches underwent a trial almost precisely like that seen by IB. The only difference was the substitution of stones for pots of water. There may be some quack-physiological basis to the idea of ducking: do guilt and fear make the suspect hyperventilate and thus become more buoyant? All the same, it beggars belief that witch-hunters in northern India, southern Arabia and western Europe might have had the same brainwave independently – 'Eureka! Let's chuck them in water and see if they *float!*' Something links it all, and probably the three weird sisters of Macbeth and As'ad al-Kamil too: some atavistic current that runs deep beneath the boundaries of culture, creed and kin, thicker than water, thicker than blood.

More to the immediate point than these musings, however, was the question of where IB's Transylvania-by-the-Tropics fitted into the particular bit of southern Uttar Pradesh in which we found ourselves. It had crossed my mind that there might be some connection between IB's were-tigers and beliefs about the goddess Kali, the vamp of the Hindu pantheon whose taste for blood – preferably human – is well attested. By a coincidence as strange as our meeting, Kevin Rushby was working on those most notorious devotees of Kali, the Thugs. Not only our persons but our books too had collided, if somewhat glancingly, here in the heart of India. Kevin told me that this very part of the Subcontinent, the old district of Bundelkhand, was also the heartland of thuggee; and that in Thug belief Kali would come and drink the blood of their victims.

'So that's it then!' I said, delighted to have pinned – or staked – down the vampires so easily. 'The Beast of Barwan must have been some kind of proto-Thug . . .'

' . . . at least the blood-drinking is part of *later* Thug belief,' Kevin went on. 'And we're talking about much later.' He didn't dismiss my idea, but urged caution; the Thugs, he believed, were largely a figment of colonial demonization, victims of a British witch-hunt.

The brief encounter between our subjects of research remained teasingly unconsummated. I had been reminded, again, of the need for scepticism. At the same time, my homework suggested that cultic practices involving human sacrifice to the various aliases of the Goddess, including the drinking of human blood, did exist early on. There was a reference in al-Biruni to the 'image [of the Goddess] which is called Bhagavati. They give copious alms to it and kill kids. He who does not possess a kid to offer . . . will sometimes pounce upon whomsoever he meets and kill him instead.' Even more striking was an event in the reign of Ala al-Din Khalji, only a generation before IB's arrival in India. According to his biographer, that tireless jack-of-all-genres Amir Khusraw, the sultan instituted a crackdown on alcohol, prostitution and 'necromancers who drink human blood'.

But the zoological aspects remained obscure. How did yogic tigers and hyena-hags – if that is what they were – get into the picture? I thought I heard a faint echo of a hyena's howl from the jackals that, in some medieval tantric texts, haunt cremation grounds and are identified with Kali. But I was jumping to no conclusions, and I strongly suspected IB had been fed a witches' brew of folk-tales, with a few Arabian ingredients imported via Persia and perhaps a touch of genuine tantrism.

The only thing to do was to go and look for the Beast of Barwan. But where? On the modern map the nearest Barwan, as such, is about a hundred miles south-west of Gwalior. Beckingham, who did not venture into these parts to play the Van Helsing, followed Gibb in per-sianizing IB's name to 'Parvan' – and then, in the absence of any Parvan nearer than Afghanistan, in identifying it with a town called Narwar, which seemed to take the principle of *difficilior lectio* a little too far. Phonology apart, neither the Barwan of the map nor Narwar, fifty miles nearer to Gwalior, is on the route one would expect IB to have taken. Admittedly IB doesn't always do the expected where navigation is concerned; in this case, however, there was a possible candidate for his Barwan on the road from Gwalior to Khajuraho, his next firmly identifiable stop: Barwa Sagar, or Barwa Lake. The *sagar* was new, Dewan said, the result of a dam; but there was an important temple by it which he thought was 'original'. I wondered how original.

Barwa was, apparently, highly original: 'From before *Mahabharata* time,' said the novice holy man who attached himself to us at the temple gate. 'Approximately 15,000 years.' Pooh-pooh, said my newly sceptical self as we walked through the gate and along a path. And then I saw the *bar*, the banyan tree that gives the place its name and its supposed date.

One normally speaks of a tree being in a place. Here the place was in the tree: a tank of water, full of light-dappled bathers, was sunk within a rocky hollow; the hollow was entirely in the grip of prehensile roots – or branches? it was hard to tell – all growing, the novice said, from a single ancient stock deep within the ground. I knew that the Indians, having invented zeroes, have always felt they can be reckless with them; but I could almost believe that enormous age. And how to prove or disprove it? The *bar* of Barwa would be the stuff of dendrochronologists' nightmares, a vegetable *Laocoön*. I could see it there still, when we are one with the dinosaurs, inching its way from Uttar Pradesh to planetary dominance, vaster than empires, and more slow.

At one spot, water oozed from the rock and through the *bar* roots, collecting in a subsidiary tank in which stood a greasy-looking lingam. The novice filled a bucket from this pool and gave it to Dewan; he drank, smacked his lips and passed it to me. 'This water is curing all diseases!' he enthused. Peering into it – was that a *Dracunculus medinensis*? – I wondered if 'curing' was quite the word. But I told myself its virtues were probably homeopathic, shut my eyes, and drank too. Martin had disappeared.

We found him with a sketchbook on an embankment overlooking the lake. The novice told us that fishermen sometimes spotted lingams beneath the water. I looked across the lake – punts, nets, cattle in water-meadows, a peninsula with a ruined fort, a cream-faced moon floating in the afternoon sky, all reflected in the surface of the lake – and pictured a submerged tangential world, a whole forest of lingams. Further along the shore Dewan and I discovered

another temple, a courtyard lined with idol-houses freshly painted in
ice-cream colours. The *pujari*, the priest in charge, had just had a
touch-up too and wore on his forehead a fetching trident in rasp-
berry and vanilla. He was also missing an arm. A violent encounter
with the Son of the Beast of Barwan or a latter-day *kaftar* came to
mind, until I remembered that theirs were strict blood- and offal-
only diets.

We did all the shrines at this subsidiary fane – Dewan, it seemed,
was an avid religious tripper – and were baptized with water from a
cobra-teaspoon. The *pujari* apologized for his temple's lack of years –
it was, he said, less than a thousand years old. A built-in cupboard in
his bedroom, however, doubled as the Narnia-like entrance to a
further temple-complex, underground and dating back 6,000 years.
The key was not to hand, but having already seen a 15,000-year-old
tree I didn't like to press.

Set against these millennial timescales, IB's passage through the
region was a recent event. I hoped our host would have some recollection of the vampire-yogis; but we drew a blank. (Perhaps it is in
the nature of very old religions, like very old people, to recall most
clearly the distant past.) He did however suggest we call on Guru
Sankara Acharya, the principal holy man of Barwa.

We found the guru and his deputies reclining in saffron robes on a
veranda. The triclinium poses, the drapery, the smooth plump faces
and general *otium* recalled Rome in its declining years. Our salutations were welcomed by exquisite smiles; with a dancerly little move-

ment of the hand, the guru invited us to sit. I had already primed Dewan in detail on IB's account of Barwan and the *kaftars*. He now retold it in Hindi – with obvious relish and, I suspected, many embellishments of his own, for the translation was considerably longer than the original. To the rare pauses in Dewan's variorum edition, Sankara Acharya responded with long 'Aaahs'. The conclusion provoked an immensely drawn out 'Aaachchhaaa' and a slow musical oration accompanied by the guru's fluid hands. They were at once sinuous, sinister and sexy; I watched, mesmerized, as if observing the foreplay of cobras. Not once did the exquisite smile flicker.

'Guru-sahib saying tigers and hyenas only in past. And no bonfires and hyenas-ladies, present or past,' Dewan explained when the speech ended. It seemed a definitive pronouncement: the bonfires went up in smoke. Unless . . . An irrational possibility had come into my head: that the guru was hiding something. Come to think of it, I had noticed at the gate of the temple a sign listing items that were banned from the sanctuary. The first of these was that sovereign vampire-bane, garlic.

'Guru-sahib also saying', Dewan continued, 'we are not travelling by the road we want. Instead returning by the same road and again visiting guru-sahib.' I remembered that IB had heard a similar prediction from a holy man of Hu in Upper Egypt; and then, as Dewan nattered on to the holy men, returned to my suspicions about Sankara Acharya . . . full whiskers, long clawlike fingernails, a feline sleekness; but no incontestable traces of metamorphosis.

Eventually we took our leave with more salutations and a hectic photo-call with Dewan's camera. I was no nearer to finding – or unmasking – IB's vampires; or for that matter to knowing if our Barwa were even his Barwan. And at the gate of the temple-complex the fogs thickened over that other, wider *terra incognita* as I watched Dewan and an elderly gentleman engage in a long and reverential conversation, punctuated by *namastes* to the object under discussion – a pebble propped up on a couple of bricks. As I understood it from Dewan, the pebble was understudying a celebrated dead guru, whose image would eventually take its place. 'It is all as simple and transparent as water,' said the elderly gentleman, 'if you only hold on to the thread.'

(Clearly, Guru Sankara Acharya was holding on to the thread. As with IB's holy man, his prognosis of our travel plans was right. Our intended road from Khajuraho to IB's next stop at Chanderi proved impassable, and we were forced to go halfway back to Gwalior; we gave Kevin, surprisingly met in Khajuraho, a lift; Kevin wanted to go Thug-hunting at Barwa Sagar; and we ended up once more as guests of the guru and his exquisite smile. There were still no visible signs of tigranthopy.)

Back on the road Dewan switched on a cassette of jingly hymns to Kali and to his own preferred form of the Goddess, Durga, who had pride of place in a miniature shrine on the dashboard. I wondered whether the choice of tape was inspired by our session with the holy men, or by the fact that we'd just entered, according to a sign, an Accidnit Prone Area and needed divine protection. In fact it was Dewan's only cassette. Luckily, it was perfect road music, and it had us humming and foot-tapping to Khajuraho and halfway to Cape Comorin.

The day before, the landscape had been an unremarkable one of hairy hills, spindly trees and rattly bushes. Now we were passing through fields of wheat and mustard dotted with mango trees the colour and shape of blown broccoli, the land increasingly lush, the road increasingly bad. Above the mini-Durga shrine a squeaking gonk hung from Dewan's rear-view mirror. In Uttar Pradesh it had been reasonably quiet. Here, across the border in Madhya Pradesh, it began complaining – 'Eek! . . . Eek-eek!' – as the potholes multiplied. But, propelled by hymns and protected by Durga and by the Ambassador's soft furnishings, we dashed onward. After Chhatarpur the light changed with stage-set suddenness. Earth, crops, hills, all went the colour of demerara sugar, an intense bright brown. To our right the sun was sinking, a cling peach in heavy syrup. 'It never looks like that in England,' Martin said as we watched it kiss the horizon then splay slightly, like a bottom on a bar stool. Dewan pressed a switch on his dashboard Durga and the angry little goddess became a disco queen, dancing in a strobing halo of red and green. Outside, the brown light liquefied, then darkened like the grilling crust of a *crème brûlée*.

★

The 'discovery' of Khajuraho by Captain Burt in 1838 was scarcely less exciting than that of Angkor by Mouhot a couple of decades later. And like the Cambodian sacred city, Khajuraho was a rediscovery: it had been described almost exactly 500 years before, by IB.

Admittedly his description is brief – a sentence or two on the temple buildings, a single phrase on the sculptures that adorn them. Strangely, for someone as keen on copulation as IB, there is nothing on what Dewan called the 'open-sex statues' – the erotic groups which make up less than ten per cent of the sculpture as a whole and nearly a hundred per cent of popular interest in the place. Instead, he focuses on his current favourite topic: 'There live there a company of yogis with matted hair, which they allow to grow until it is as long as themselves. They tend to be sallow-skinned from the effects of their mortifications. Many Muslims become their disciples in order to study their ascetic techniques.'

The idea of Muslims having personal Hindu gurus is surprising; to anyone who knew only today's India and its inter-communal tensions, it would be astonishing. But the apparent divergence of Hindus and Muslims over the last half-century is an aberration. Over the seven and a half that preceded it, the two faiths often found themselves following parallel paths. At times the paths intersected, and never more so than when the ground they covered was mystical. Being India, much of it was.

Inter-mystic relations weren't all love and non-violence. In the Islamic literature, Sufis and yogis frequently lock auras in combat, a series of spiritual *jeux sans frontières*. Muslim hagiographers cheered on their own side, as one might expect, and the supernaturally under-equipped yogis always come off worse. A thirteenth-century yogi for example, taking part in a levitation contest with a Sufi from Ucch, found his primitive vertical take-off and landing outclassed by superior Islamic aeronautics. Similarly, Mu'in al-Din of Ajmer overcame a yogi hurling snakes from a flying deerskin by spanking him with a remote-controlled clog. Although IB himself saw a comparable aerobatic slipper in action in Delhi, many of the wackier details in these saint-tales are later interpolations. Most cross-faith meetings were far more down-to-earth.

In general they were also more peaceful. In IB's age, that 1960s of Sufism, Muslim mystics enjoyed a Lennon- and Ginsberg-like susceptibility to the ideas of their Hindu counterparts. Not only were *ragas* transformed into *qawwalis*. Yoga manuals were translated into Arabic and Persian, and *pranayama* breath-control became as popular in Sufi circles as the lotus position is now in Notting Hill. The most *outré* and sadhistic practices had their Muslim aficionados too. Penis-piercing, for instance, a habit noted by IB among the hard-core members of the Haydari dervish order, was in fact borrowed from the naked Nagas. There is probably no other instance in which the ideas of Hindu ascetics penetrated their Sufi counterparts quite as deeply, and literally.

It was around IB's Indian years, the brief high summer of the Sultanate and the beginning of its fall, that Islam acclimatized to India; or, the stern Arabians would say, went native. And yet a passage in that early Arabic work on the country, Captain Buzurg's *Wonders*, shows that the cross-faith traffic in ideas may have been much older, and not just one-way. An ascetic from Ceylon – probably, from the description of his ash-smeared body and skull drinking-cup, some species of Shaivite sadhu – visited al-Madinah in the days of Caliph Umar, the Prophet Muhammad's second successor. The ascetic died on the journey home, but his servant took back reports of Umar's humility and his custom of wearing the patched clothes of a mendicant, which the other devotees of Serendip adopted as their own. Whether we should believe a tale told by the original of Sindbad, or others that have brahmans going to worship at the Ka'bah in pre-Islamic Mecca, or for that matter Origen's claim that they descend from Abraham, builder of the Meccan shrine, and take their name from him (suggestively, the Arabic plural for both 'brahman' and 'Abraham' is the same: *barahimah*), is open to discussion. But they point back to a premiss that is harder to refute. Akhilesh Mithal, that wise old antiquarian of Delhi, put it neatly: 'Mysticism', he told me, 'is older than religion. It is as old as mankind.' Gurus of one sort or another may in fact be the second oldest profession in the world; unless, that is, the honour belongs to witches.

*

Morning in Khajuraho disclosed plenty of sallow complexions and long matted hair, all belonging to Western and Japanese tourists. They seemed to form the bulk of the population, closely followed by hawkers of trinkets and sellers of picture postcards. From one of the latter I picked up a set of ten perfectly Battutian yogis, and asked if such people were to be found here. No, he said; there were no *babas* in Khajuraho. Why didn't I go to Banaras? Banaras was full of them.

I also bought 'Khajuraho: A Set of Ten Beautiful Picture Postcards'. A flick-through suggested 'Beautiful' might be a euphemism. The sculptural groups portrayed were all grainy and unfocused, clearly taken with a long and quivering lens. They ran the gamut from a straightforward fuck via blow-jobs and orgies to pony-shagging. (I wondered if the man so obviously enjoying this last activity – it was harder to tell with the pony – had been on Vajikar, as advertised over breakfast on the wall of our restaurant: 'Vajikar are the preparations by taking them a man becomes so energetic that like a horse he can satisfy.') The *pièce de résistance* was a man standing on his head and simultaneously masturbating two girls, one on either side of him, with a third impaled on him, the scrimmage of limbs forming a tipsy swastika. It reminded me of those children's puzzles – 'Find out who owns the . . . '. 'Hey, come and have a look at this,' I called to Martin. ' "A Set of Ten Dirty Postcards." '

He went through them slowly, pausing longest on the acrobatic *ménage-à-quatre*. 'I wonder how much the sculptor had to pay his models . . .'

The last postcard in the set was a comparatively restrained scene of copulation *à deux*. 'You could send that to, ah, thingummy,' I suggested, forgetting the name of the girl Martin was gallanting in London (he subsequently forgot it too). 'What about, "Having a lovely time. Wish you were her"?' He gave me an old-fashioned, self-portrait-at-the-easel look.

To see the sculptures *in situ*, in the round, was to realize that smut was in the eye of the beholder. One had to look hard for the erotica among the friezes of gambolling figures; I could understand how IB missed them. In context they could be seen for what they were: things most people get up to some of the time, made all the more innocent by the deodorant, anti-perspirant medium of sandstone. 'They're strip-club poses,' Martin said, looking at a girl in lacy suspender belts, leg cocked up, pinching her nipple. I thought of his studio in England with its series of over-sized strippers: Martin, the Degas of the exotic dance, was eminently qualified to judge. 'And look at those tits. Silicone implants if you ask me. But the people who carved them weren't pornographers. They were artists. And they *really* enjoyed sex.'

We lost ourselves in this seemingly infinite gallery, tier upon tier of deities and kings, heroes and nymphs, cavorting and sashaying along the friezes and climbing towards the temple spires, heavy-lidded, boneless and elastic. The ideas they expressed were incomprehensible to me, a secret semaphore of many limbs, an orchestral score in an unknown notation. But I could see where the guru of Barwa Sagar came from, conducting himself with his fluid hands; and, no, 'Beautiful' was not a euphemism.

Martin opened a sketchbook and started drawing a multiple Anglepoise of members. 'I don't know how I can begin to do it justice,' he sighed. 'But it might help me with my strippers.' I wandered off to another temple and found a group of young men sitting in an arc on the ground. They too were drawing. Their supervisor told me they had travelled from Tamil Nadu, from the College of Art and Sculpture in Mamallapuram. It was a long way to come for a lesson, I said. He agreed. 'But it is worth the effort. Later carving was merely decorative. The Khajuraho figures are decorative and human. They are both edification and inspiration. Who would not travel for that?'

I sat with them for a while, listening to the subdued southern bubble of their speech, then moved on. From looks on faces, I guessed that the other tourists here were also being edified and inspired, even if, like me, they had expected only to be titillated. There was only one exception – a group, judging by their appearance and voices, of Non-Resident Indians. They were gathered beneath a scene of a couple kissing, deeply and deliciously; his truncheon-sized penis lay on her cocked thigh. The expatriates had a guide, an elderly man with a hectoring voice: '. . . . this oral tantric way. We go legal civilized way. Slow civilized process for us. If we go animal way, animal laughing at us.' Several of the women listened with lips tightly pursed against oral tantric threats.

With all these distractions one could almost overlook the buildings themselves. They too were beautiful, and uncompromisingly strange. I grasped at similes for the flanged curvilinear spires that congregated above them; and could get no further than the finned casings of motor-cycle engines. While Martin drew on, I got down to the business of comparing the buildings and their setting with the hasty sketch IB had made: 'a great tank, about a mile long, overlooked by temples containing idols which have been mutilated by the Muslims. In the middle of the tank there are three pavilions of red stone. Each of these is three storeys tall and is set between four corner-pavilions.'

The advantage of Khajuraho from my point of view was its lack of history. Not, of course, its lack of years: the youngest of the temples was already two centuries old when IB passed through in 1341, the earliest twice that age. Khajuraho had been raided by the Muslims very early on in the Sultanate period. The local Rajput dynasty survived, however, together with their temples. Although they fizzled out early in the fourteenth century, their sacred city outlived them – if not as a royal hieropolis, then at least as the inter-faith academy of mortification described by IB a few decades later. The next 500 years from IB to Captain Burt's 'discovery' are a blank. Khajuraho escaped the Mughals and their chroniclers. It slumbered in the backwoods, untouched by Aurangzeb and other forms of progress. Unlike Delhi, unlike the Doab, Khajuraho today is probably much as IB saw it, preserved by that long sleep of obscurity and by the tender attentions of the Archaeological Survey.

The problem, I soon found out, was the fourteen-year gap between what IB saw and what he remembered. The colouring of his sketch looked wrong at first. But if the stone of the temples is not exactly red, it is a sort of pinko-grey, and the Arabic pallette is not subtle; 'red' is as relative as 'mountain'. As far as it went, the architectural detail wasn't far out either. The plan of all the Khajuraho temples comprises three main elements – IB's three storeys: a chunky basement; a *piano nobile*, teeming inside and out with figures and containing the dark 'womb-chamber' of the god; and those finny spires, of which a small shrine has one and the largest temple many dozens. I looked too for evidence of the mutilation mentioned by IB. The vandalism must have been half-hearted. Here and there, a few of the more accessible figures had been hacked about, or a divine icon decapitated; but there were no signs of widespread or systematic destruction. It fitted well, in fact, with the term IB used for 'mutilated' – *maththal*, a word I remembered having to check in the dictionary. It ought to mean – and does in its principal sense – 'made an example of', and this is precisely what had happened to the Khajuraho figures. The icon-punishing party seemed only to have picked out a few of the ringleaders for beheading, and subjected a token number of their followers to loss of face – or, in some cases, of genitalia. There had been no Final Solution. I doubted whether the statuary had survived because of any aesthetic scruples on the invaders' part. It was more a case of safety in numbers.

So much for the elements of IB's picture. The composition was harder to reconcile with facts on the ground. To cut a long puzzle short, there were three (major) tanks, not one. There were two, not three, temples each with four flanking pavilions; they were by, not in, a tank; and the tank was about 400 yards long, not a mile. All the old problems to do with numbers and prepositions – that spatial and numeral dyslexia I had diagnosed in Delhi. The composition was, in short, haywire. But the details were sound, the sum of the parts more convincing than the whole.

If you think I'm letting IB off too easily, then try to picture a place you passed through very briefly about fourteen years ago. Perhaps you kept a diary, but it was stolen soon afterwards. You have no photographs to refer to, no guidebook to crib from. Now describe it, including all the relevant figures – not forgetting the several thousand other places, people and events you must describe, of which the only record is your memory. That is what IB was up against. (Equally you may wonder why IB didn't just leave the figures out and make his sketch more impressionistic. Apart from the fact that no one had yet invented impressionism, and that Arab armchair travellers adored figures, I can only imagine that he didn't realize I'd be checking up on him.)

The most convincing detail of the picture, however, was still missing. After several hours of temples, I hadn't seen a single mortifying yogi. Dewan, who had a nose for the divine, had never come across one on his visits to Khajuraho. 'Khajuraho temples for tourists,' he said, 'not *babas*. But we are asking very good tourist guide.'

My immediate thought was that I'd be hectored on the moral perils of the oral tantric way; or, at best, be persuaded to buy a filthy key-ring or a cling-filmed coffee-table *Kama Sutra*. But Mr Shukla turned out to be a scholarly local historian who knew IB's account of Khajuraho. As I read the passage aloud, he provided footnotes that made it grow in accuracy. 'Kajarra', Mr Shukla said, IB's name for the town, reflected the original Sanskrit 'Kharjurra-vahak', meaning 'Date-palm-land'; 'Khajuraho' is Bundelkhandi dialect. More importantly, he agreed with my identification of IB's quincunctial temples, and added a valuable piece of information: the nearby tank used to be much bigger. And he did persuade me to buy a book – not shrink-wrapped hard-cover soft-core porn, but a highly respectable Oxford India Paperback, Mrs Devangana Desai's monograph on the sacred city. This reproduced a plan of the site made in 1865 by Major Cunningham, the first director of the Archaeological Survey of India; the plan showed the Shiv Sagar, my candidate for IB's tank, extending to over a thousand yards in length. If it had shrunk by more than half since Cunningham's day, it was more than likely that it had been shrinking before. IB's mile may not have been far out. 'And you see how the Shiv Sagar extended close to the Prem Sagar?' Mr Shukla indicated a neighbouring tank on the plan. 'My estimation is that in Ibn Battutah's time the two lakes were almost linked. It would be absolutely natural for him to remember the temples as standing in the centre of a single body of water.'

I felt I was watching the partial restoration of IB's picture, seeing a better likeness of what he saw. But it wasn't a speaking likeness: so far it lacked that vital, vivid, human element. I read on. 'There live there a company of yogis with matted hair . . . '

'Ah, the Aghoris. The so-called "left-handed" sadhus, the Shaivite ascetics. Although at this time they probably would have been called Kaulas. Or perhaps Kapalikas, "skull-men". These are the types who live in the cremation grounds and use intoxicants. Ibn Battutah's description is accurate as far as it goes, although his "yogis" do not seem to be of the more extreme varieties.'

'It's a pity there aren't any left here.'

'For better or worse, Major Cunningham cleared them out so he could restore the temples.' So, I thought, recalling *chowkidars* and Easel Permits, the Archaeological Survey were killjoys from the start. MORTIFICATION WITHIN THE ARCHAEOLOGICAL AREA IS STRICTLY PRO-HIBITED BY ORDER OF . . . I saw Mr Shukla smile: 'But there *is* one left.'

*

Darkness had fallen while we were talking, and Martin had joined us. Now, as we set off, the lights of Khajuraho flickered and died. But the moon was full and bouncing its borrowed light off the liquid glass of Shiv Sagar; light twice-reflected, double-distilled, flooding the temple spires in a spiritous wash.

We turned left, into a dead end, and passed a row of souvenir shops. A candle burned in Indo-Himalayan Crafts but the others were already shuttered against the premature night. On our right was the fence that defined the Archaeological Area, the secularized sanctuary; in front of us, a gateway, and behind that a stickleback, bristle-cone pyramid – 'Matangeshvara,' Mr Shukla said, softly – one of IB's three temples, the one to which his imagination added pavilions. The only ancient temple still in use, it is short on shrines, scant of sculpture, unvisited by the tourists inspecting the Lakshmana a few yards away beyond the fence. But it is full of prayers . . . Clang! That was one, going up with a merry noise.

Before reaching the temple precinct we turned left again, on to a track that took us into a shrubbery. Up the garden path, I thought for an uncharitable moment; until we came to a line of shoes. We added ours, stepped over the sanctifying Plimsoll line, and stopped. 'This', Mr Shukla whispered, 'is the house of Matanga-baba.'

Five dim figures were squatting in silence, looking into a small hut with a gabled roof. Facing them was an open doorway; the rest of the frontage was a waist-high wall. The structure might have been a byre or some other farmyard building but for the contents, which were visible in the mothy light of a lamp – a couple of cupboards, a few bits of cloth on pegs, a pot or two, a ball of red and orange rags just inside the door, several hanks of orang-utan coloured fibre, a number of palm-frond brooms, various unidentifiable objects hanging on strings. There was also a woman with a small girl clinging to her skirts. The woman was bending forward, working with her hands, kneading. She smiled as she worked, and occasionally addressed the child. Both were oblivious of the figures outside, squatting and watching.

We squatted too, and watched this little theatre, transfixed by the unremarkable.

Martin nudged me. 'Look.' The orange and red rag ball inside the doorway had begun to move, and to burble. I rose slightly and peered: the ball concealed a head – I could just make out the nose – attached via a dimly seen body on a charpoy to a pair of legs. It was these, I realized, that the woman was pummelling. The burbling continued. In a whisper, I asked Mr Shukla what the monologue meant; he shrugged. One of the squatting audience departed, touching a kiss to the charpoy as he left. Another man came, prostrated himself towards the bed, then joined the silent spectators. Then another, who scooped water out of a vessel to the right of the door and sprinkled it on a flat stone by the rag ball. The burble became intermittent, then ceased. You could hear the seeds falling off the trees, hear the rustle of –

I nearly cried out as snicker-snack the legs swung round, stork-legs, mantis-legs, knees shockingly large, bones and gristle bound in parchment, pudenda in a twist of cloth, grimy shift on Lazarus-torso, the rest all dreadlock-ends fingers nose eyes straggling and stabbing struggling and staring – staring, eyes of a cooked trout, pearly white, *straight at me* (picture one of those gormless victims in Holbein's *Dance of Death*, mouth engraved with a silent scream). But it was Matanga-baba who cried out; that is, a stream of noise came out of a hole that opened in his beard. Appropriately for someone who looked like Death, it sounded as if he was telling me to fuck off and die.

Thus, Mr Shukla told me later, was I blessed by Sri Padam Singh Maharaja (100 years old, precisely), also known as Matanga-baba from his proximity to the Matangeshvara Temple. 'Oh yes indeed, he was abusing you most terribly. But the abuse is the blessing. It is even more potent when he hits you with one of his brooms. I think also he

was warning you against seeking too high a station. It was quite hard
to catch his drift.'

Following the outburst, Matanga-baba resumed his original position on the charpoy and his intermittent burble. The woman began
again to knead his knees, those outrageous ginglymi, smiling as she
worked.

That was it. We could have stayed, Martin and I, squatting,
waiting, watching that doll's-house theatre, waiting like Vladimir and
Estragon, under the falling seeds; but we left with Mr Shukla. As we
crossed the shoe-line the lights of Khajuraho came back on. We still
whispered. 'Why are we whispering?'

Matanga-baba, Mr Shukla explained, was a mediator. The blessings that he communicated to his worshippers were the same as those
they might gain via the figure of a deity in a temple – success, material or spiritual, the well-being of both soul and body.* The hut was a
shrine, its occupant an icon of flesh and blood. Or, I thought, of skin
and bone, semi-mummified, halfway to the hereafter, poised on the
high thin fence between two worlds. That night he was more numi-
nous than all the stone gods of Khajuraho, a few yards away on the far
side of that other fence.

The following morning Martin decided, bravely, to return and
draw Matanga-baba. I went along, with some reluctance: would the
magic have gone with the night? I had other reservations too. I knew
that India abounded in fake fakirs, sham shamans, mountebanks by
the myriad. Was the old man just another of these, his votaries – and
we – people taken in?

The scene outside the hut suggested otherwise. Again, half a dozen
or so other visitants were there, and most of them were not of the
gullible *hoi polloi* to judge by the signs – a business suit, Argyll socks, a
briefcase, neatly dyed hair. They might have been *Reader's Digest* sub-
scribers. And they worshipped and fell down, and asperged the
threshold-altar, and brought gifts – cocktail snacks, marigold chains –
with a fervour that was wonderful, and moving. Matanga-baba's own
wardrobe had improved too. He was still wearing the same posing-
pouch and filthy vest, still looked like something the Grave-Grubber

---

* IB alludes to this last point: 'They say that if anyone disfigured by vitiligo or leprosy goes into retreat
with them for a long time, he will be cured of it by the grace of God.' An inscription from a Shiva
temple in Khajuraho, dating to AD 1000–1, supports the claim. Sufferers from leprosy, it says, will be
cured by the sight of the 'uncouth twisted tresses' of the god – or, by extension, of his human stand-ins.

would think twice about; but most of his Medusa locks were now tied in a turban of cream and gold, startlingly clean. Today he burbled in an upright position, and in an intermission gobbed a jet of pearly sputum that hit the doorpost and stuck, like cuckoo-spit.

The magic was still in place. And if anything the *baba* was even closer to the upper world. He was, we soon realized, as high as a shite-hawk. On what I supposed to be the local equivalent of the parish flower rota, the smiling woman's place had been taken by a smiling teenaged girl in blue with gold bells at her ankles. Just after we arrived, she tinkled over to the old man and handed him a chillum. Cupping it in his palms, he raised it briefly heavenwards, mumbled the vital mantra, then sucked on it, a quick succession of deep gulping drags. *'Boing boing boing!'* said Matanga-baba, then he stared upwards with a surprised look, watching himself in lift-off. I sympathized with that out-of-body feeling. It must have been strong stuff.

Perhaps it was just the quantity. At first there was a partial descent – *'Wah wah wah wah,'* said Matanga-baba. But Rani – she wrote her name for us on the ground, with water from the offering-stone – kept the chillums coming. Up and up went His Highness Sri Padam Singh Maharaja, higher and higher, until finally he was lost to his body with a plaintive *'. . . boing?'* A pause: Matanga-baba's pearly eyes piercing the roof of the hut; Rani singing sweetly, dabbing turmeric spots on the wall; Martin beginning, tentatively, to draw; silent comings and goings, prostrations and oblations. Then the god was down among us again, a palm-frond broom in his hand, sweeping the floor by his charpoy, rhythmically, then fiercely, whacking the ground, sweeping on and on until he was sweeping nothing but broom-fragments. A votary holding a blade of grass went for the blob of spit on the door-jamb and was blessed by a swooping ejaculation – *'Yonghy-Bonghy-Bò!'* or words to that effect – and by a thwack on the neck. And still on – sweep sweep sweep swipe sweep sweep sweep swoop – until the old man drew up his mantis-legs and lay back, drained by the drug and by drudgery divine.

*

So, 'many Muslims become their disciples in order to learn their secrets'. That was certainly one way of putting it. But I wondered if, in plain English, they were there for the dope. Many devotees of Shiva, as Mr Shukla said, are avid users of intoxicants. Shiva himself is permanently intoxicated: for his most zealous adherents, a godly, righteous and *sober* life is a contradiction in terms. According to one of them, 'Not only does the Aghori please Shiva by offering Him the intoxicant,' – as Matanga-baba did in the elevation of the chillum and consecratory mantra – 'but the very act of taking the intoxicant helps the Aghori self-identify with Shiva.' Islamic strictures on mind-altering substances notwithstanding, some Sufis had similarly come to the conclusion well before IB's day that, if you were aiming at the death of the material self and the union of the true self with divine Reality, the best way to do it was to get stoned out of your head. For them, cannabis in its various forms – usually the liquid one, bhang – reached the parts that other Sufi practices reached, but a lot more quickly than chanting, dancing, sitting in a cave or hanging upside-down in a well. 'We drank bhang,' said a nineteenth-century Indian Sufi, 'and the mystery *I am He* grew plain. So grand a result, so tiny a sin.'

Not all Muslims agreed that the sin was so tiny. I remembered reading in al-Maqrizi's *Settlements*, that massive record of Cairo, about a fourteenth-century war on drugs in the Egyptian capital in which cannabis growers had their plants, and cannabis users their teeth, judicially uprooted. Returning to al-Maqrizi's text now, I find it has a not indirect bearing on Matanga-baba. (I use the double negative – 'not indirect' – advisedly. Readers who are not interested in the history of Sufi drug use may wish to skip to p. 180.)

Al-Maqrizi quotes at length from al-Hasan ibn Muhammad's thirteenth-century treatise *Al-sawanih al-adabiyyah fi 'l-mada'ih al-qinnabiyyah* – something like *Happy Pot-Hunting: Poetry and Prose in Praise of Cannabis*. Although the author has no doubt that the properties of *qinnab* 'have been known since God created the world', he dwells at length on its supposed introduction in Sufi circles by Shaykh Haydar (founder of the eponymous penis-piercing order mentioned above). Haydar and his herb, he says, were celebrated in verse – for example, in this ballad to bhang:

> Lay wine aside and drink of Haydar's brew –
> That amber-scented juice of emerald hue,
> Brought by a swaying, slender Ganymede,
> A willow-waisted youth of Turkish breed.
> Pale hands, dark liquid . . . Similes we seek –
> And find them in the down that shades his cheek.

Such delicate elixir that one sees
It swoon and shiver in the zephyr's breeze;
When songbirds warble at the forenoon's height
And doves discourse, it trembles in delight.
Hark to its hidden depths! meanings profound
That Bacchus' brainless bunch can never sound.
A virgin vintage that, one may be sure,
Was never pressed by hand or foot impure,
Its chalice never fondled by a priest,
Its amphora unknown at fair or feast.
And, what is more, no school of law proscribes
The name of him that hempen wine imbibes.
Let legists claim that Haydar's cup defiles –
In vain! Pour out the nectar that beguiles!

And more in the same vein. But the ascription of bhang to Haydar, says the author of the treatise, is debatable. 'Shaykh Muhammad of Shiraz, the Qalandar, has informed me that Shaykh Haydar most definitely never consumed hashish . . . although his disciples used it regularly. He also told me that it began to be consumed a long time before Haydar's day. The fact is that there was in al-Hind a shaykh called Byrrtn, and that it was he who instituted its use.' This Indian shaykh, adds the informant, lived at the time of the Prophet. He converted to Islam, and it was through him that cannabis consumption spread to the Muslim world.

So early a conversion, and so far from Arabia? And that name, 'Byrrtn', which I can't even begin to vowel, which might as well be Inuit as Indian. But a realization: IB mentioned an Indian called 'Ratan' – a genuine name; and 'Byr' is – of course, there's no *p* in Arabic, and the *y* works also as a long *i* – the Persian *pir*. Pir Ratan, Shaykh Ratan. To the meagre Indian shelves of my own library. Several false leads. Then, in Rizvi's *History of Sufism in India*, a certain Ratannath, an early luminary of the Shaivite Nath cult, possibly tenth century, although some accounts suggest he was the Prophet Muhammad's yoga teacher . . . later Naths discussing Ultimate Reality with Sufi shaykhs . . . Naths travelling to eastern Iran (the original home of the Haydaris). Nothing on cannabis? Perhaps: a mention, contemporary with IB, of wandering Qalandar dervishes sharing with the Naths the habit of consuming 'a type of grass, probably Indian hemp'. Nothing at all on the alleged conversion of Ratannath – if, indeed, he is 'Byrrtn'. The parabola of discovery ends as steeply as it started.

. . . then climbs again from a half-remembered reference in Baron Silvestre de Sacy's *Mémoire sur la dynastie des Assassins* – in which he thinks that 'this electuary [of hashish] originally came from India, that Haydar may have known it through some Indian yogi', citing as evidence, from that same treatise on *qinnab*, that same passage on the Indian shaykh called . . . 'Biraztan'. The difference in Arabic script between the baron's Biraztan and the 1853 Bulaq edition's Byrrtn – my Pir Ratan – is a dot the size of this full stop.

Leaving aside the discrepancy in dates, the question of whether the Shirazi Qalandar's Indian dope-pusher could in fact be Ratannath hinges on an ink-dot, a fly-spot. The answer is probably of no larger importance to the sum of human knowledge. But this miniscule

voyage of discovery (powered, I should admit, by my own preferred stimulant – *qat*, or *Catha edulis*) seems to lead back to Matanga-baba's hut and to the thought that came to me there: that it was very probably the old man's Shaivite forbears – whether Aghoris, Kaulas, Kapalikas or, as I now believe, Naths – who introduced the Sufis to cannabis and to the blurred herbal haze of Shiva-Allah-man-God-I-He; that at least some of the secrets of IB's long-haired yogis could be grasped in a chillum.

★

Rani jingled over to us and looked at Martin's drawings of her ancient charge, who was now in the capable hands of nepenthe. Her smile said more than art critics or prize-committees. Could she have a picture? Dazzled, we went off to look for a photocopier.

When we returned, we saw that a sheet of corrugated iron had been placed across the doorway of the hut. A stream of urine was trickling out from under it, to be trodden in devotedly by newly arrived worshippers. When the stream gave out Rani removed the modest door, then took one of Martin's copies and fixed it proudly on the outside wall of the hut. Now everybody wanted one. Fortunately Martin had made several copies, but we were still one short. The unlucky devotee, a little elderly grey-suited man with a large briefcase, looked as if he was going to burst into tears. We went and made more copies.

The owner of the briefcase, eyes now moist with gratitude, thanked Martin profusely and scented us both from a gold-topped bottle. Martin opened his sketchbook again and started another drawing – Matanga-baba, under the later stages of the influence, was a good sitter. At the same time, the elderly man opened his case and produced a fat chillum, followed by a screw of ganja and some fibrous matter that looked like those hairy hanks in the hut – coconut fibre, I realized. He crushed a generous amount of ganja to a powder in his hand, picked out the seeds, mixed it with a little tobacco from a cigarette, and wrapped the mixture in a neat coconut cocoon. This he lit on opposite sides, then popped it into the chillum.

Elevation, consecration, inhalation; transubstantiation, of fibre to fire, herb to smoke. Martin had just given up tobacco, and reluctantly declined the tubular eucharist. I . . . well, just a little.

I sat listening to the *baba*'s burble, Rani's jingle, Martin's pencil, sharing the chillum with my host, thinking how extremely pleasant everyone and everything was. And how mild the smoke. And how clearly the birds were singing. I hadn't noticed them before, but there they were – seventy-nine voices, if I cared to count them – combining in one wraparound sound, a limpid harmony that admitted no discordance. I fought against the pleasantness of it all, made myself think of IB and all those snaggy problems along his route . . . What problems? Tease out the tangles. Follow the thread.

I was not He. I was still undeniably I. And that uniformed figure which had appeared – just as I was handing the spent chillum back to its owner – was undeniably an enormous policeman. Whoops. Ten years in the slammer, wasn't it? My elderly friend smiled. We were in an asylum, an adytum, untouchable. The policeman laid a garland of marigolds on the threshold–altar and prostrated himself beside Matanga-baba's evaporating piss.

'Very holy place,' I heard someone say. 'Your eyes seeing special things. No headache no tense.'

How right he is. No tense: no past, no future, no *paulo-post*-pluperfect piffle; just an eternal translucent present. It's true. It's there in *Hindustani Simplified*: 'Kal = Tomorrow, yesterday'. I laugh silently into my lap.

The eternal present was over all too quickly. We stood for a while, contemplating the icon for the last time; then departed, leaving a hundred rupees with our friends to buy him ganja. Alms for oblivion.

(Later I tried to pick up the thread, the unravelled sutra, the undone suture, in the privacy of a hotel room. Not ganja but *charas*, extracted from the pollen-filled flower heads, unadulterated this time with tobacco. Vertical take-off, my head the nose-cone of a Saturn V, mission control far below and losing contact. Wow, I thought, I'll be He if I'm not careful, permanently: the full irrevocable *nirvikalpa samadhi*. 'Martin, I'm not sure I like this . . .' For a few panicky minutes I lay on the bed gripping the sides of the mattress, my spine a python in a straitjacket. 'Think I'd better switch on the AC,' Martin said. 'Get rid of the smoke.' Whoosh! the room cleared in an instant. I had a sudden image of everything within range of the air-conditioner outlet getting stoned: passing *chowkidars* and chambermaids, bats, birds – bats going cuckoo, cuckoos going bats. The panic passed. Martin told two hours of pantwetting jokes, while the Thread dangled unheeded. I'd forgotten the vital mantra.

The next time, in London, I forgot the vital mantra again; and it was Dave's super-strong hydroponic, on top of a couple of bottles of wine and Shiva knows what else. It all went wrong. I was turning green, which was bad enough – until everyone suddenly looked at me and said 'You're turning green'.

We all need our greens; but I'll stick to the gentle and dependable alkaloids of *Catha edulis*.)

★

In Matanga-baba I had found the last spiritual descendant of IB's yogis, and a speaking – or ranting, riddling – likeness of the traveller's Khajuraho. I was also to find his *kaftars*, and his vampires.

My first sighting of a *kaftar*, that elusive creature, occurred a year later. It was momentary but clear. We were at the end of our Indian journeys and back in Delhi, where one important piece of research remained to be done on IB's yogic excursus. One day, he recalls at the end of the passage, he had a summons from Muhammad Shah and found him in a private apartment by the Thousand-Column Hall. With the sultan were two yogis. ' "This foreign gentleman is from a distant land," ' the sultan told them, ' "so show him something he has never seen." At this one of them sat cross-legged on the ground, then rose into the air above us, still in a sitting position. I was so astonished and frightened that I passed out and fell to the ground. The sultan called for a potion that was to hand; it was given to me and I came to and sat up.' The levitating yogi was still floating in mid-air, but his companion sent up a flying slipper. 'It began hitting him on the back of the neck and he started slowly to descend, until he sat by us . . . The sultan said to me, "If I did not fear for your wits I would have commanded them to do still stranger things." '

Those stranger things might have included some of the sorcery performed at the wedding of Khadir Khan, one of the murdered brothers of Sultan Qutb al-Din. The conjuror, wrote Amir Khusraw, swallowed a sword 'as if it were sherbet and he a thirsty man. He also thrust a knife up his nostril. He mounted little wooden horses and rode upon the air. An elephant was drawn through a window, and a camel through the eye of a needle. Balls were changed from black to white and from white to black, in imitation of the fitful vicissitudes to which we on earth are subject.' IB was, however, to witness the strangest sorcery of all. It was many years later and in the Chinese city of Hangzhou, where the commander of the emperor's army was entertaining IB and his other guests with a magic show. For his finale, the conjuror took a wooden ball to which a rope was attached and threw it up into the air. The ball disappeared; the conjuror's apprentice climbed the rope and disappeared too. At this point his master followed him, knife in hand, 'like a man enraged'. The youth's dismembered parts then began to drop from the sky, one by one; the last, his head, was followed by the conjuror himself, panting and bloody. At an order from the commander, 'he took the youth's members, fitted them together, gave them a kick, and the boy stood up in one piece. I was astonished at this and suffered a palpitation of the heart such as I had experienced at the sultan's show in India.'

Some of the most learned wizards of our own age have suggested that spectators of the Rope Trick were victims of a delusion brought on by the burning of hallucinogenic bark; or that the trick was a combination of elements from different acts, amalgamated by faulty memories; that, in short, it never happened. But compare IB's narrative with that of the Anglo–Dutch traveller Edward Melton in his *Zee- en Land-Reizen* of 1681. Melton saw the act done by Chinese conjurors in Batavia, 2,500 miles and 300 years distant from IB's Hangzhou, and yet the two accounts tally in almost every detail. For the Rope Trick never to have happened *twice* would entail a feat on the observers' parts quite as magical as any performed by the conjurors themselves.

Whatever the truth of the matter, I doubted whether the Chinese version of the trick had survived. At the same time I knew, as did the geographer Marvazi, that to India 'belong sorcery, suggestion and the production of phantoms, which bewilder the sage and baffle the mind of the expert'. Who would produce phantoms for me? Levitation was old hat, an undergraduate course-component. The Rope Trick called for someone with a Ph.D. – a Doctorate of Phantasmagoria.

I found him, a small, chubby, twinkly man, in a very small house behind Delhi's Shadipur Bus Depot and, if his claim to appear in the *Guinness Book of Records* under the entry 'Rope Trick, highest' was true, then he had the doctorate *summa cum laude*. Aziz Samrat didn't have a copy of *Guinness* to prove his assertion, but he did show me a grainy photograph of himself with the Qutb Minar in the background and an erect rope sprouting from a basket. A small boy clung to the top of the rope, twenty feet up in the air.

There was much head-wiggling as I read him IB's account of the Chinese trick (simultaneously hindicized by Mr Gautam, a Delhi acquaintance who was also interested in magic). 'Perhaps a very thin wire was fixed high up between two buildings,' Aziz suggested when I finished, 'and the ball thrown over that. Perhaps a monkey was cut up instead of the boy. I know about this trick, even though it is no longer done. They were doing it six or seven hundred years ago.'

My eyebrows took off. I hadn't told Aziz IB's dates, and yet that last statement of his could hardly be anything but an indirect reference to the *Travels*: no other account of the Rope Trick was as early. How had knowledge of it penetrated this muddle of alleys at Shadipur?

Mr Gautam and I had penetrated it with the help of a group of young men in gold lamé, pink plush, tangerine velour and wet-look black. They might have been extras from *Saturday Night Fever*, but it was Sunday morning, and the disco look was complicated by a several pairs of large earrings and, in one case, of Biggles-type flying goggles. The setting was complicated too, by twists and turns, sudden open sewers, and by the equally sudden appearances and disappearances of more surprisingly dressed people. And in this Delhi version of Diagon Alley there were babies, babies everywhere: the magicians of Delhi – and the jugglers, tumblers, clowns and bear-trainers, for this was where they all seemed to live and replicate themselves – were a fecund lot. Finally we reached Aziz's house, which was near a small and particularly bloody butcher's. At the sight of it Mrs Gautam, who had come along for the trip, uttered a series of little moans. 'My wife is pure veg,' Mr Gautam explained.

Aziz himself was soberly dressed, although I did notice a puce blazer embroidered with silver daisies hanging on a peg. With Mr Gautam interpreting, I asked how he had come by his knowledge of the magic arts. 'My family have been magicians longer than anyone can remember,' he began. 'Our skills have been passed down from father to son. Nothing was written down until my grandfather's day. My Dadaji was illiterate, but he dictated a book of tricks – yes, it is *very* secret – and my father added to it. And so, *in sha Allah*, will Muhammad.' He looked at his son, a small solemn boy with magnetic eyes.

I remembered a name from the *Travels* that I wanted to try on him. 'Ibn Battutah – the writer of this book – mentioned that some of the people in Assam were famous for magic. They lived in a place he calls "Kamaru".'

'He means "Kamrup",' said Aziz immediately. This much I knew. His next words amazed me: 'There is still a school of sorcery there – the Kamrup Kamakhya Academy of Magic. It was founded by a guru who had 371 children. He had a fight with another guru who also had 371 children, and they were all turned into animals. All *kala jadu*, black magic; and tantrism, Kali worship. And still the same today . . . It is very *haram*.' The twinkle turned into a different sort of smile, one that suggested Aziz didn't altogether disapprove of the forbidden black arts.

The hairs rose on my neck; I saw where his son had got those eyes. 'Of course, my magic is not *jadu*. Only tricks!' The twinkle returned.

'And levitation?' I read him IB's account.

'Maybe tricks,' he said when I finished.

As Aziz led us back out through the mage-filled maze, I began to wonder if knowledge of those early Rope Tricks hadn't needed to penetrate it; whether, with such communities, academies, dynasties of magic, the knowledge had been with them always. These thoughts were interrupted by an apparent wrong turn – a dead end closed by a tiny wicket gate like a gridiron. Aziz opened it. We stooped low, passed through, and found ourselves in a courtyard beside a temple. 'This is Goddess Kali's temple,' Aziz said.

I was surprised. 'I thought the magicians here were Muslims.'

'Most of them are. But Kali is for all magicians, Muslim and Hindu. I am also visiting her temple.'

I'd hardly taken this in when we reached an even tinier gate on the far side of the yard, a hatch the size of a tuck-box lid. Aziz was through it quick as a mongoose; I got ignominiously stuck and had to do it feet first. We were on the verge of the roaring Ring Road.

'So,' I said as we parted, 'are you going to do the Rope Trick for me – the Indian version?'

Aziz was full of apologies. There wasn't enough time. It needed many weeks of preparation and meditation. He was out of practice. 'But', he added with a final twinkle, 'I will levitate for you.'

A few days later he did, for me and for a small invited audience in a Delhi sitting-room, having first asked for the ceiling fan to be switched off as a precaution against accidents. There was a certain fanfaronade in the request as he only rose about five feet – supine, not squatting, and covered with a black cloth. As with that thirteenth-century yogi who was out-levitated by the Sufi of Ucch, it was a simple vertical take-off and landing. I remembered IG's mention of yogic fliers volunteering for service in Kashmir, and couldn't imagine this rudimentary manoeuvre striking awe in the hearts of the separatists. But it was elegantly done; as were the warm-up acts, which included bondage and the hatching – with the help of the spell '*Begi-begi ayin chil-chilay gili-gili!*' – of eggs from embarrassing parts of my guests' anatomies.

So far Aziz, with his daisy blazer and coochy-coo patter, had inspired admiration but not terror. Now the atmosphere changed.

'To finish,' he said, 'a very old piece of *kala jadu* . . . ' he flashed me a smile, of the disturbing kind ' . . . from Kamrup.' My neck prickled.

Aziz tied up his assistant, Anwar – one of those spangly disco-boys – in a net. We all inspected the knots, then the youth was pushed into a wicker frame rather like a lobster pot; the frame was covered with the black levitation cloth. Aziz then began to pace about it, chanting rhythmically to the beat of a small bongo. I heard the name of his cross-faith patroness, Kali; and I thought I heard another familiar name – it was hard to tell for he was now shouting, like a man enraged. Abruptly, he stopped. The room rang with the silence. Softly, Aziz invited us to examine the frame beneath the cloth. We did so: Anwar had disappeared.

I was completely astonished, and not a little frightened. But Aziz soon assumed once more his children's tea-party demeanour; produced a startled pigeon from beneath the black cloth, followed by a small tree and some tangerines – mine had leaves growing inside the skin. Finally he replaced the pigeon and brought out Anwar, apparently none the worse for having been dematerialized.

Later, when Aziz had packed his belongings and been richly congratulated, I asked him about the hypnotic chant that had accompanied his finale. 'It was a tantric *siddhi* mantra', he said, 'to Kali. For gaining magic powers.'

'You used a word – something like "*kaftar*".'

'Perhaps you heard "*khappar*",' Aziz said after a few moments' thought. 'It is the bowl of the skull, and Kali drinks blood from it.'

For a moment associations jostled in my mind; but no, the words were too far apart. 'Do you know "*kaftar*", meaning a kind of witch? They kill people by magic.'

He didn't. Maybe his Dadaji would have known the term, for he had been a witchfinder. He could smell witches. Once he sniffed out a witch in Fatehpur Sikri and threatened to expose her. She tied a magic thread to the foot of Dadaji's dancing bear, meaning to chant spells that would kill Dadaji, sympathetically, by the extraction of his heart. But Dadaji had seen her tying the *dhagabandh*: he quickly untied it and transferred it to the hoof of the witch's cow. 'So she extracted her own heart. We call her *pishach* or *dayan*. I am sorry, I do not know your *kaftar*.'

As we parted on the street he apologized again, for his ignorance of the *kaftar*, for any shortcomings in his show. I protested: he was brilliant. 'But I see that you want more,' he said. 'Maybe next time you are in Delhi I will do the Rope Trick. At the very least I will pull out my boy's intestines for you.'

★

The tale of Dadaji and the *dhagabandh* whetted my witchfinding appetite once again. But it was some months before I was able to track down any more *kaftars*. I'd left India and the primary sources for Oxford and the Indian Institute Library. Few reading-rooms could be more distracting than this penthouse on the Bodleian, up among the gods and gargoyles and that seductive panorama of pinnacles. The distractions were doubled that day, for India had followed me in the person of a saffron-clad guru of the Swaminarayan sect come to pay scholarly homage to a manuscript. There was an unlibrarylike excitement, and a panic about temporary readers' cards.

The witchcraft section was small but rich. Discoveries flew off the pages, many more or less reminiscent of IB's stories. There was, for example, the extraction by the black magicians of Maharashtra of foetuses from mothers dead in pregnancy, for use in love potions: 'The foetus is roasted while muttering special mantras – till it turns black and moist. It is then sold in attractive little boxes . . . . It is supposed to have an unpleasant taste.' The fussier Oddiyans of Kerala insisted on fresh foetuses, from which they compounded metamorphosing linctuses – ' "It was not unusual, those days, to stumble across a mangled female corpse at dawn," ' said Sohaila Kapur's informant in *Witchcraft in Western India*, speaking of the early decades of the twentieth century. The same author notes that 'North-East India, particularly Bihar, has a similar belief in witches who can metamorphose themselves into animals. Locally, they are known as *Candar Bandar*. The tribals there believe that the tiger is not a man-eater, but it is men, temporarily changed into tigers, who attack and devour humans.' The Beast of Barwan lives.

But it was in Bengal that IB's text really spoke again, clear and chilling, through the medium of A.B. Chaudhuri's *Witch Killings Amongst Santals*. The Santals are a tribal people scattered over a wide area from northern Orissa far into West Bengal. During a two-year government posting in the early 1980s at English Bazar, 200 miles north of Calcutta, Chaudhuri collected a mass of tales and case-histories cataloguing the witch-obsession of these *adivasis*, or 'ancient inhabitants'.

Strangest of all were their beliefs about fuskins. The term is a corruption of *phukrin* (one of the six different words for witches in the Santali dictionary; there are nine denoting various types of witchfinder) and refers in particular to shape-shifting women who gain and maintain their powers by extracting body-parts from human victims. The more I read, the happier I felt for not having run into them. Tale after tale, recounted in the unemotional prose of witness statements and police reports, told of fuskins – either in the guise of animals or in human mufti – removing and consuming vital organs from unsuspecting sleepers. The wound would be invisibly mended; the victim would die later at a prescribed time. Fuskins often worked at the bidding of spirits called *bongas* and sometimes, a final Battutian touch, in cahoots with were-beasts 'of leonine appearance'. One account backed up my original ideas about a connection with the Goddess cult – the case of a bloodsucking witch of Beldanga, near Habibpur, whose activities were intended 'to please Goddess Kali'. Perhaps we should not infer too much from the Beldame of Beldanga, for she was no common or garden fuskin: 'when this witch was killed, a small container of oil was reportedly found inside her skull'.

There was one difference between IB's *kaftars* and their Bengali blood-cousins twenty-five generations removed: the fuskin seems to go less for heart than for liver or lung, and occasionally rump steak. *Chacun à son goût.* I suspect it is only a matter of time before fuskins find an employment niche in the international transplant-organ trade.

As Long as Sun and Moon Endure

> 'The *Indian Brachmans* seemed too great friends unto fire, who
> burnt themselves alive, and thought it the noblest way to end
> their dayes in fire; according to the expression of the Indian . . .
> *Thus I make my selfe Immortall.*'
>
> Sir Thomas Browne, *Hydriotaphia*

'O MA!' DEWAN EXCLAIMED, with an imploring look at his dashboard Durga. 'Mr Tim-sir, this road *subhan Allah.*'

It was indeed a glory-be-to-Allah road, one that required the invocation of the Muslim God as well as Dewan's own Mother-Goddess.
In fact it was the worst supposedly surfaced road I'd ever been on.
The rear-view-mirror gonk agreed – for the last hour it had been
squealing like a stuck piglet. Beneath it, Durga lurched drunkenly;
above, Martin's reflection bounced in grim and manful silence while
Rowney, Cornelissen, Winsor and Newton crashed and clattered
around him. We took to the bush for a hundred yards or so; then the
road lured us back with smooth promises before – traitor! – dropping
us into the mother of potholes. A weightless nanosecond, a metallic
crunch and a spinal wrench, then silence. We looked at each other
then got out.

The day had begun agreeably enough. Following our prophesied
backtrack to Guru Sankara Acharya of Barwa and another night at
the vulture-coloured palace of Orchha, we had set out for IB's next
recorded stop after Khajuraho, Chanderi. At first we creamed along
through the strobing shadows of roadside trees with barely a squeak
from the gonk. There was little other traffic, and the few vehicles we
saw were inversely well patronized – one motor-cycle carried two
men and five full-grown sheep. After Lalitpur the road shrank to a

single track, and we travelled alone through an increasingly sere land, a blasted heath strewn with tawny menhirs. Only once did we see people on this stretch, a group of men whom I at first mistook for woad-stained Picts. I wasn't far wrong. '*Adivasi*,' Dewan said – those 'ancient folk', or tribals. They wore shorts and nothing else and were manning a barrier of rocks across the road, drunk and mulberry-skinned from the merry messiness of Holi. Unsportingly, we parted with Rs. 20 to escape indelible empurplement.

I had no high hopes of Battutiana in Chanderi. But almost the first object we saw there held an unexpected resonance from IB's book. It was an inelegant little pavilion in the fort, overlooking a dried-up lake and restored in 1932, an inscription said, by the Maharaja of Gwalior. Inside, a second inscription revealed more: 'Johar Monument Fort Chanderi. On the bank of this tank many Rajput ladies heroically performed JOHAR (i.e. burnt themselves alive) just before Raja Medini Rai and his brave followers issued forth from the citadal to fight their last desperate battle with the forces of Emperor Babar on the 29th January 1528 A.D.' I remembered reading about *johar*, the ultimate form of scorched-earth policy, in IB's history of the reign of Muhammad Shah. Almost exactly 200 years before the Mughal assault on Chanderi, Muhammad made war on a raja who was harbouring a rebellious Tughluqid cousin. When defeat seemed certain, the raja's womenfolk and those of his officers dressed up to the nines and threw themselves into a sociable bonfire, after which the raja and his army went out 'and fought until not a single one of them remained alive'. (It seems a muddleheaded way of doing things: shouldn't the women have waited to see if their side won?)

The pavilion was no more than a melancholy gloss on this passage in the *Travels*; if it intimated another discovery, I only realized this much further down the road. For now, we were stuck with a dry place, a monochrome town of beige sandstone set in a dip in a griz-zled plateau, and with a drier text. In Chanderi IB is in his most tedious and desiccated *Kelly's Directory* mode. No landscape, no buildings, no yogis; just a list of worthies – the governor . . . the jurist and theologian . . . the judge . . . imam . . . deputy treasurer . . . deputy in charge of army affairs . . . al-Din . . . al-Din . . . al-Din. I was in a bad mood with him, and consequently with everyone else. Martin wished he was back in curvaceous Khajuraho or by the waters of Barwa Sagar; anywhere but this place of unforgiving dryness and beigeness, flattened by the sun and rattling with thistles. The scorpions of discord crawled between us.

IB's worthies of Chanderi hadn't even deigned to leave behind any definite traces of their existence. I thought I bumped into one of them, 'the jurist and theologian Wajih al-Din', in an inscription; but it was thirty years pre-IB and this Wajih was a *muharrir*, or secretary. The title of another, the Qadi Khassah, lingered in a building called the Kazi Khasa Mahal – a hundred years post-IB but still, I wrote in my notebook, 'A fascinating find!!' The enforced jollity of that double exclamation says it all.

We drove on in stony silence. Our depression had damped even the unforced jollity of Dewan. Only the gonk bumpometer had anything to say, an increasingly maddening indictment of the dire Public Works Department of Madhya Pradesh. If it had had a neck, I would have wrung it.

Those brief apocalyptic moments of connection – the Caveman, King Camphor, Matanga-baba – seemed far away, our pursuit of IB ever more trivial. We had entered a land where milestones were the only link with his book, the only scenery, 'pillars inscribed with the number of miles from each pillar to the next': a road of a thousand columns, leading from pillar to pillar, from pillar to post across the blanks of the *Travels*. The mile-pillars were now kilometre-slabs, but they were still the sole points of reference in a space as bleak as Bodmin Moor. There was no other traffic and few other humans. Once, finding some more tribals in a slabless and interminable stretch, we stopped to check the distance to the next junction. After some debate they admitted ignorance, but came up with a figure to the next hamlet – not in miles or kilometres but in *kos*, a slippery measure and a cousin to the league and the parasang. Throughout the encounter they stared at us as if at visiting Venusians. And so it went on until that matriarch of potholes, the traitor crater, dealt its blow.

For a few moments we stood by the car, punch-drunk. Then, while Dewan inspected the Ambassadorial underside, I looked at the map, at the great subcontinental eyetooth in its Asian socket, and drew mental lines across it. 'We're just about at the geographical centre of India.'

'It feels like it,' Martin said.

Miraculously, the car seemed to be in one piece. Dewan restarted the engine, the doughty Ambassador dragged herself out of the hole, and we went gingerly on our way. From somewhere beneath us came a grinding of steel teeth.

Whatever it had done to the car, the pothole seemed to have shaken us to our senses. The distemper of Chanderi was gone, and Martin and I compared notes on the passing scenery as companionably as we usually did. It was good to have another pair of eyes – painter's eyes – and to see through them blue mohair hills, an ochre ziggurat mountain; a herd of camels, their flanks barbered in geometric patterns like flock wallpaper; to see form in flatness and colour in khaki. When he was at his most voluble, travelling with Martin was like tripping on mescal – things took on an intensity beside which normal vision was a type of blindness. The bleakness of the place, I now saw, had been in my head.

On and on, inexhaustible, indefatigable, India. I understood now why ambitious or rebellion-plagued rulers spent so little time at home (Muhammad Shah, at the time of his death by the Indus in 1351, had been away from Delhi for six years); could believe, almost, a story I'd read about an entire Tughluqid army disappearing for six months in the wastes of Orissa, lost like the Hebrews of Exodus. Finally, after nearly 200 miles of B-roads, we hit a highway, and traffic: still no private vehicles, but lorries – blear-eyed, bull-faced Jagannaths charging out of the dark – and combine-harvesters that lumbered along in lurid nimbi of chaff. We also nearly hit a buffalo, invisible in the blackness but for a fortunate retinal flash. But the drive had taken its toll, and inexhaustible, indefatigable Dewan began to flag, and to call again for his Ma, Durga. 'Travel in the dark,' the Prophet advised, 'for the earth folds in on itself at night.' But not in Madhya Pradesh. The night stretched on, and the road.

*

We awoke in Sanchi in an eerie replica of Crossroads, the famous soap-opera motel of the 1960s. I paid court to my tyrant diary and missed the celebrated stupas, one of the most important Buddhist sites in the world. A couple of hours later Martin showed me his drawings of them. I cast around for a suitable remark. 'They look like, er . . .'

'OK. Say it: Christmas puddings.' It was the image that had come to mind. 'All they need is a sprig of holly.'

We were all refreshed after the travails of the day before. Dewan was back in his usual perky mood despite a painful shoulder sprained by the giant pothole and, after some artful hammer-blows at Guddu Motors in Bhopal, the Ambassador no longer ground her teeth. Humming and foot-tapping to Dewan's hymn-cassette, we jingled onward to Ujjain, IB's next stop.

I was beginning to wonder how IB passed the time on these endless roads of middle India. He had a captive audience for his tales of travel; but there must have been a limit to the amount of unedited ramblings Malik Sumbul – 'King Spikenard', the dead King Camphor's replacement – and the rest of the party could take. For that matter, how did all the Other Ranks kill the hours, those out-of-shot extras of IB's road-movie – the dancing girls, the slave boys; the escort of a thousand horse; the muleteers and cameleers and wagoners in charge of all that China-bound napery, haberdashery, tableware and horseflesh; the bearers, syces, grass-cutters and *et als*.? How many Chaucerian leaves were scattered in their passing – the Qadi's Tale, the Nautch-girl's Tale, the Eunuch's Tale, the Third Assistant

Tent-erector's Tale? Given that they had to cover over twenty times the distance from the Tabard to Canterbury just to get to the coast, I suspect the standard of in-saddle entertainment soon began to slip, and that for every narrative gem there were a thousand games of I spy. ' . . . something beginning with *m*.' 'Milestone?' '[Yawning] No. Mile-*pillar*. Your turn, Spike . . . ' (Spikenard was, like Camphor, a eunuch, a high flier in the court castratosphere; nominal innovation compensating, it will have been noted, for testicle deprivation. I picture him – plump, squeaky-voiced, bouncing along on a palfrey – as an enlarged version of Dewan's gonk.) No doubt the reality was a Kiplingesque

> best foot first
> And the road a-sliding past,
> An' every blooming campin'-ground
> exactly like the last;

but I like to think they got the nautch-girls to perform as they went along, an elegant succession of curves, Khajuraho incarnate.

Our party, if not as picturesque, was travelling ten times as fast. Most of the hours killed themselves, so our own games of I spy were played for pleasure, for simile and metaphor. Today, the stupendous steamed puddings of Sanchi and Martin's faithful rendering of them carried us to more distant matters – to the draughtsmanship of Courbet, late Goya and Lucian Freud; to the question of whether one had to be able to draw in order to paint; and of whether one had to be able to do either in order to make a pile in Cork Street. (The answer to that, we decided on current evidence, is an unqualified No.) During a break in our discussion on line, Dewan discoursed on colour, that of the little pennons that distinguished various places of worship in the outskirts of Bhopal – green for a mosque, red for a temple; a Sikh gurdwara would have a white flag. 'Like politics parties. BJP having yellow and green, Congress white and red and green, Communists blue and white . . . ' While he went through the spectrum, my mind drifted back to my Classical youth, to a lecture on screwdrivers by the great Sir Kenneth Dover. Take an otherwise identical set of them, he said, with different coloured handles. They all perform the same function; most people will however have a preference, even if unconscious, for a particular colour. Dover's screwdrivers had a point, something I think to do with literary style. Dewan's flags eventually had their point, too: 'In India, ninety-nine per cent of problems coming from politicians. BJP, Congress all the same.' Black, white or pinko-grey, they all ended up screwing you.

Conversations, public and private, waxed and waned, until we fell silent and vacuous, aware of little but the unwinding of road beneath us and of the rhythmic and satisfying stream of toponyms – Amlaha, Kotri, Ashta, Dodi, Metwara, Sonkach. I looked for each place on the map as we passed through, not for guidance but for diversion: as there is prosody in place-names, there is poetry in maps, in that vocabulary of symbols that, like those of verse, express big things on a small scale. The map had another function too. It showed both how far we'd gone and how far we could never go; that our India was circumscribed, downsized, stylized; that while Amlaha, Kotri, Ashta, Dodi unspooled metrically, kilometrically past us in an unbroken monodic line of toponymic ticker-tape, Ichhawar, Unchawad, Siddiganj, Tonk and Dip were folded in impenetrable reams of hinterland, names on signs. Transient roadside tableaux – saffron figures at blue and pink shrines on rocks in a riverbed; three girls, each with a pot on her head and finishing-school deportment ('Rubens,' said a voice from the back out of a long silence, '*The Three Graces*'); an old man on his last legs hand in hand with a child on its first – all these other signs or symbols had to stand for the rest, the innumerable rest that began a furlong beyond the verge and stretched, it sometimes seemed, to infinity.

'I could travel like this for months,' Martin said after another long silence, one filled only with snipped images, disconnected thought, brain-confetti. We did.

By dusk and Dewas we seemed to have done so already. 'Only an hour or two to Ujjain,' I said to the drooping form on the back seat. But in the centre of Dewas the level-crossing gates were shut, and we waited for twenty minutes while darkness and crowd gathered and pressed clammily around us. All this for a tiny country train with a guard standing on a rustic veranda at the back. 'He always sees where he's coming from,' said Martin, 'not where he's going.' A philosophical fellow, that guard, I thought, who had realized that life, lived forwards, might only be grasped by looking backwards.

The Kierkegaardian guard disappeared into the dark, the gates opened, the crowd surged, and soon we were motoring along again to the Durga hymn, between the Tropic of Cancer and an electric storm, facing unphilosophically forward.

*

Ujjain made slightly more of an impression on IB than had Chanderi, but not enough for him to remember where it was. Given the enormous scale of both India and the *Travels* and the long pre-publication wait for the *Lonely Planet India Travel Atlas*, it might seem a minor slip to have placed it after Dhar, another seventy miles down the road. In fact IB had no excuse. Not only is Ujjain the place where the elbow of the goddess Sati fell to earth when she was anatomized by her husband; it also did a long stint as the geographical centre of the world – the Arabs' *qubbat al-ard*, or Earth-Cupola.

Quite how Ujjain earned this omphalic pre-eminence is a mystery, and readers who do not wish to be mystified should skip this paragraph. It does lie on the meridian of the ancient Indian geographers (just as my local market town in Lincolnshire lies on the meridian of Greenwich – and I am not aware that anyone has claimed Louth to be the centre of the world). For whatever reason, by the beginning of the tenth century Arab geographers had also got it into their heads that 'Uzain' was both on the equator and exactly halfway around the eastern – that is, the inhabited – hemisphere. Since this, for the Arabs as for Ptolemy, began at a line west of the Canaries, they were badly out: their true Cupola lay full fathom 500, at the bottom of the Indian Ocean, somewhere between the Maldives and the Chagos

Archipelago. Scholarly al-Biruni soon demolished this cartographic Millennium Dome. But in the far west of the Muslim world nobody read him: the city retained its grip on the geodesic imagination, and the distinguished Maghribi geographer Ibn Sa'id was still writing of the earth-cupola of Uzain less than a hundred years before IB visited it. Slipshod copyists further mangled the name into 'Arin', and it was in the latter guise that it resurfaced in European works written long after it had fallen out of the Arabic atlas. It was still there when the world went pear-shaped with Columbus. In a letter to his patroness Queen Isabella, written during his voyage of 1498, the navigator explained that 'the Old [i.e. Eastern] Hemisphere . . . having as its centre under the equator the Island of Arin, is spherical. But the other Hemisphere has the form of the lower half of a pear. The highest part, that is the tail of the pear, is situated close to the Island of Trinidad, near the mouth of the Orinoco.' Anyone who could think, as Columbus did, that America ought to be Asia – even if, with hindsight, a laudable idealist – must have been an awful geographer. Arin seems to have died with him.

*

Our journey to the former centre of the earth ended with a minor geographical conundrum, when we couldn't find the hotel we were looking for. 'Mr Tim, please say them the address,' said Dewan as we drew up by a couple of men squatting at the side of the road.

It was hard to read the guidebook by the Ambassador's dim map-light. The name of the street was something like . . . 'Madher Chod,' I tried.

The men stared at me. There was an unchauffeurly snigger from Dewan, then a giggle from all three Indians. One of the Ujjainis managed to choke out some words. Dewan got a grip on himself: 'He is thinking it is "Madhav Chowk",' he spluttered. Directions were given, and we thanked our guides and drove off.

'OK: what did I say?' I asked Dewan. He explained, and I saw my ghastly reflection in the cultural looking-glass – as an Indian turning up late at night in Louth and asking the way to Mother Fuck. (Al-Biruni makes me feel a bit less of an idiot. 'It will sufficiently illustrate the matter', he wrote, 'if we tell the reader that we have sometimes written down a word from the mouths of Indians, taking the greatest pains to fix its pronunciation, and that afterwards when we repeated it to them they had great difficulty in understanding it.')

If IB wasn't exactly chatty about Chanderi, he was equally jejeune on Ujjain. But the following morning confirmed that his description – 'a fine city with many inhabitants' – was correct as far as it went. Ujjain is both provincial-grand and gay, buzzing with bustle and bursting with balconies in exuberant funfair colours. These reminded me of the Krazy House on the pier at Weston-super-Mare, whose own balcony emitted knicker-revealing updraughts of air that raised skirts, Marilyn-style; the A-line cut was particularly susceptible. The ladies of Ujjain, presenting a more streamlined profile, would be proof against such indignities. They were a slinky, sexy lot, the Hindus shimmying and shimmering in diaphanous cloth-of-gold through the veranda-shadows, the Muslims in silk *shalwar kameez* of electric brilliance. Even the most conservative Muslim ladies contrived to look sassy in their *burqas*, big black bags worn with the aplomb of little black dresses. Their sisters belonging to the Bohra sect were the exception to all this chic, for they were uniformly draped in loose covers of countrified chintz, with matching capes and bonnets and couture by a consortium of Greenaway, Hubbard and Tiggywinkle. Anyone who thinks Islam is monolithic in its attitude to women should spend five minutes observing the sidewalk catwalks of Ujjain.

As we were doing this, Martin taking notes on the slant of shadows and the flurry of passing shawls, we heard a deep and horrible caterwauling. A brass band hove into view and approached, ersatz scrambled egg glinting at cuff and cap-peak, in a ragged crescendo of thumps and basso profondo farts. I assumed a wedding; but – how apt, in this city of belles and balconies, this Old-World New Orleans – it was a funeral.

IB's thumbnail sketch hardly did justice to Ujjain. But to be fair, he was only passing through, and the presence of between one and two thousand fellow-travellers must have cramped his style. And he did mention someone I hoped might provide, even if very belatedly, an *entrée* to Ujjaini society. The name on my dead letter of introduction was that of Jamal al-Din al-Maghribi. We have already met him in Delhi, quoting pensive verses to IB during a visit to the ruined Red Palace; he had since moved to Ujjain. As his surname shows he was, like our traveller, from the Muslim West. IB tells us that he was a doctor both of the law and of medicine, born in Algeria to a family originally from Granada, and that he had come to the East with his father. The only other Maghribis IB mentions coming across in India were transients – a couple of scholars on their way to China, and a Sufi, again from Granada, who received one of Muhammad Shah's golden hellos. (The Sufi would have stayed longer, but no sooner had he stashed the sultan's cash in his wardrobe than it was stolen, and the poor man died of grief.) IB was not immune to homesickness, and he joyfully records meetings with fellow-Westerners whenever he bumps into them. But in the Delhi Sultanate they were a rare breed.

The Whiff of Scent, a huge work on Arab Spain, devotes a whole fat
volume to distinguished Andalusis who went to the East. In 300
biographies and 600 years, only one traveller is said to have gone to
India – where his sole recorded achievement was, like the Sufi of
Granada, to die. All in all, I thought, the likelihood of other
Maghribis having settled in Ujjain was tiny. Could IB's friend with
the double doctorate have left some identifiable trace – a family,
perhaps, that bore his name?

I should have known by now that such things are, like the Red
Tomb of Delhi, to be found, not looked for. Dewan and I walked the
streets, stopping likely looking Muslims and asking after the
Maghribi family – possibly known as the Gharnatis (the Granadans),
the Jaza'iris (the Algerians), or perhaps the Jamalis (after Jamal al-Din)
– and were answered by shrugs and blank looks. But we didn't
abandon hope; and we did find a flying mosque, and a cure for
Dewan's still painful pothole shoulder.

Gazetteers and guidebooks, if they mention the Bina Niv ki Masjid,
the Mosque Without Foundations, inform one that it was built by the
Jains, that it fell into disuse, and that it was then adapted by the
Muslims. Sabirah Bey Maulvi, a lady whose family have had charge of
the building for many centuries, informed us that it was built by the
jinn, that it fell from the sky, and that the guidebook version of events
is, like her *masjid*, without foundation. Which of these accounts is true
I cannot judge; a miracle affected my impartiality, even if it was less
remarkable than a prefabricated airborne mosque.

We found Sabirah in a tiny square room that opened off an alley by
the mosque gateway. I'd been trying to unravel the epigraphic
spaghetti of a Persian inscription over the entrance when Dewan suddenly complained that his shoulder was 'very pain', and disappeared
up the alley. I gave up on the Persian, followed him and entered a
doorway marked by his empty shoes. Inside, the light was green,
filtered through green slatted shutters. The walls too were green –
where they could be seen, for much of the space was covered with
superannuated calendars and posters of Muslim saints, or with shelves
of books, boxes and bottles. Most of the last were empty mineral-
water bottles; some contained what looked like water, including one
labelled – shockingly, among the islamica – 'Director's Special', one
of the better Indian whiskies. The floor began to fill too, as neighbours slipped in with whispered greetings and joined us, cross-

legged; and silent children, spaniel-eyeing the strangers; until a dam
of shoes large and small blocked the alley, and every inch of the
square green room was filled with people and things.

We all sat facing Sabirah, a woman of perhaps fifty and of arresting
appearance. Not in her dress – magenta silk *kameez*, ivory *dupatta*
draping head and shoulders in the manner of Attic widows – or in
her features, which were running to pudge and distinguished only by
a neat gold asterisk in her right nostril; but in her complexion. A skin
ailment had drained it so completely of its pigment that she was
not so much disfigured as transfigured. She incandesced in the sub-
aqueous light and looked about her visitors, like a benign ghost, from
deep black holes of eyes.

Dewan spoke to her; she listened with head inclined and an occasional question. The exchange had something about it of a medical
consultation – and this, I realized when Dewan tried to rotate his
painful shoulder, was exactly what it was. The treatment, however,
came from no standard manual of physiotherapy. From a shallow niche
behind her, Sabirah took a bundle of peacock feathers bound with
tinsel, and with this elegant instrument she began rhythmically to
stroke Dewan's shoulder. At the same time, her lips started to move
silently. The rest of her face was still; her dark eyes never left Dewan.
After every few strokes she tapped the feathers on a low table that stood
in front of her, or on a pile of books beside it. Of these, the upper one
was a Qur'an. The table belonged to some other canon. Its top was
inscribed in three sections, the outer two subdivided into squares containing numerals, the centre covered in lines of Arabic script. While
Sabirah silently caressed and incanted I tried to read the script. From
where I sat it was upside-down, and all I could make out was *Ibrahim wa
Namrud . . . Musa wa Far'un . . . wa 'ltafat al-saq bi 'l-saq*: Abraham and
Nimrod . . . Moses and Pharaoh . . . 'and shank was wound to shank'?
(That last phrase, I know now, was Qur'anic, from the Chapter of
Resurrection: 'Some faces on that day will be radiant, looking at their
Lord, and some will be dark, dreading some great calamity. But when a
man's soul reaches his collar bone and they cry, "Who can save him?";
when he knows it is the time of final parting, when the grave-cloth has
wound shank to shank; on that Day to the Lord shall he be driven.')

The stroking came to an end. Sabirah opened a drawer in the table
and took out a scrap of paper inscribed in red ink. This time I could
read the Arabic clearly –

O

High

Great

Most High

An invocation to three names of God. Taking an empty mineral-water bottle, she dropped the paper in, poured some of the contents of the ex-whisky bottle on to it, then shook it until the ink dissolved. Dewan bared his shoulder, rubbed a little of the liquid on, and drank part of the remainder, shivering slightly as he did so.

The surgery was over. Some of the spectators drifted away, and Sabirah chatted with her patient while I pondered the treatment. The amulet, the divine names dissolved and drunk, was a widespread and venerable feature of Islamic faith-healing. But the feathers were an enigma to me, that mystical morse of strokes and taps unintelligible except in terms of some sympathetic transference of pain from flesh to word. A little later, Sabirah simply described her use of the *morchal*, the feather fan, as 'a very old custom'. She had more to say about the other stages of the treatment, explaining that the solvent of the Divine Names was dew and showing me the pile of books beside the table. As well as the Qur'an, this included a *Tales of the Prophets*, various almanacs, and an Urdu grimoire. (There was enough Arabic in the headings of this last volume – charms against noxious *jinn*, black magic, plague, and even against bothersome guests – for me to see that this would be a useful little work, a sort of thaumaturgic Mrs Beeton.)

Finally I asked Sabirah about the silent intonation, and learned that she had been reciting some of the short chapters of the Qur'an. These she now repeated aloud; and I with her, following her lead along those sinuous lines of sound, beyond the barriers of language, back to Arabia, back beyond Babel. We ended on the Chapter of Daybreak, the mischief of witches who blow upon knots, the mischief of the envier when he envies; and Sabirah's face seemed more radiant still.

She knew no Maghribis, Gharnatis or Jamalis. But she showed us around her *jinn*-built mosque and bid us God-speed on the threshold. We touched her unearthly white feet, which were cool against the hot stones.

On our way back to find Martin I asked Dewan if his shoulder was better. 'It is a little relax,' he said, not very convincingly. Some miracle, you'll say. But I did warn that it was less exciting than flying mosques; and in any case I was thinking of another miracle – the Hindu drinking Allah's names in dew, the Christian reciting from His book, guests of a ghost-white Muslim lady in a green room, and of something I can only think of as the grace of God.

Before we left Ujjain, hectic, eclectic Dewan (and possibly psychic Dewan, for he'd had no inkling of Sabirah's existence up the alley) made assurance triply sure and had his shoulder seen to at both the clinic of Dr Azhar Khan and the famously be-lingamed Mahakaleshwar Temple. 'And', he said with a grin, when I commented on this broad-spectrum treatment, 'if I finding I go Sikh gurdwara, Christian church also . . . '

*

If IB has slipped out of the picture he only has himself to blame. He will slip, or burst, back into it, as observant and visible as he's ever been; perhaps more. Not here on the road, not down it in Dhar, but soon after, in a gully hidden by trees, where the uplands start to crack and fall away in long declensions to Gujarat and the Gulf of Cambay.

But I'm running away with ourselves. From here the edge seems still far off, the sea unthinkable. We're in a continent nominally confined by a country, in a vastness I can't get my mind around, let alone my pen. How to describe it? The conceit of Brian Paul Bach, who has written on the Grand Trunk Road – to mount a ciné camera on a lorry and leave it running from Calcutta to Peshawar – is beautiful but, by his own admission, a little silly. The other extreme, those abbreviations of IB – 'and then we proceeded from X to Y' – makes algebra of distance and ciphers of journeys. So I list: a flat-topped hill, a dip in the road, a shallow lake, the Seven Brothers Soap Factory, another flat-topped hill . . . A listless list, pointless signs –

Martin: 'Stop, Dewan. Look at that! The colour of him, his clothes, the land, the oxen. Could you get a better blend? It's perfect. Like a Bellini . . . *The Madonna of the Meadows*.'

The madonna was a man ploughing with a pair of oxen. Few Indian scenes could be more unremarkable. But Martin was right – the earth, dark as molasses after a night rain, the cream singlet and windsock trousers of the ploughman, the toffee-coloured oxen and zinc-white egrets that followed their furrow, all were a perfect blend. Martin drew them for an hour, labelling the colours. I tried to note the scene down too. 'The ploughman's commands: a tongue-click = go, an inward sucking kiss = stop, a tap with a stick and a pull on a cord = move left/right. His arms as dark as the soil. A recurring moment when the ploughshare gets clogged and he tips the plough to one side making a momentary triangle, plough-body-ground. Far behind, a temple on a hill; behind that, a falling sun.'

Time after time, Martin would make me see things made invisible by the magic of their ordinariness.

The sun had fallen further when we crossed the infant Chambal River and Dewan chucked an empty mineral-water bottle over the parapet of the bridge. Martin and I protested at this uncharacteristic litterbuggery; Dewan explained it was the container, now empty, of his divine infusion and that Sabirah had told him to dispose of it at sunset in a flowing river. (He had picked a corker: with luck, the bottle would make it, via the Chambal, the Yamuna, the Ganges and the Hooghly, to the Bay of Bengal – a flow of nearly 2,000 miles.) In the space of this exchange the sun had set, and we travelled on to Dhar under an inkblot sky.

★

We have already seen that Muhammad Shah, among his many mad-
nesses, was mad about melons. As IB discovered during his next
recorded halt in Dhar, the mania didn't just apply to the exotic crystallized product of Bukhara: 'The city of Dhar is held as a royal grant
by Shaykh Ibrahim, a native of the Maldives who came and settled
outside it. He brought some unoccupied lands back into cultivation
and began to grow melons, which were so exceedingly sweet that
they had no equal in these parts. When the sultan was passing through
on his way to Coromandel the shaykh presented him with some of
these melons. The sultan was delighted with them and assigned him
the city as a grant.' Maldivian melon-farmers are a fairly rare species as
it is, although the island of Thoddoo in Ari Atoll is said still to be
home to a few. On the assumption that they would be an even greater
rarity in Dhar than Granadan-Algerian physician-jurisprudents in
Ujjain, Dewan and I went the following day to make inquiries.

Almost immediately we were hijacked. Mr Salim Dhari, the gentleman responsible, hadn't heard of Shaykh Ibrahim, but he insisted
we visit the tomb of one Abdallah Shah Changal. Dhar, he said on
the way, was a city of saints: Mawlana Ghiyath, Kamal Mawla, Pir
Parahan . . . the list went on. But the first and greatest of them was
Changal. He came here a thousand years ago, converted the local
raja, and was buried in a tomb that was the cynosure of antiquarians,
the most ancient Islamic site in all of Hindustan. My suspicions were
aroused by just about all of this; but Mr Salim was so enthusiastic that
we couldn't refuse. Besides, he said, his family were restoring
Changal's tomb-chamber to its former glory.

Not to mince words, it was a monstrosity. The shape was right, a
cube with a dome, but the entire object had been rendered with
eggbox-coloured cement. Pebbledash would have been a mercy. I
kept my aesthetic counsel, hoping for better things inside.

The interior was breathtaking – doubly so, on account both of the
choking fog of incense and then, when one's gaze penetrated this
thuriferous pea-souper, of the décor. Changal lay beneath a spangled
firmament of winking fairy-lights and multicoloured mirrors that
turned the dome into an inside-out disco globe. The combination of
hovering smoke and sparkling colour was not so much Islamic, *circa*
AD 1000, as Gary Glitter, *circa* 1972. The only jarring note came from
a foursome of Merrye Olde England carriage-lamps placed on poles
at the corners of Changal's cenotaph. Mr Salim's brother, in charge of

the restoration, asked me the dreaded question: What did I think of his improvements? In a flash of inspiration and the words of the Prophet, I replied that one's deeds were measured by one's intentions. He was delighted.

There was, they said, one old feature, an inscription above the gateway to the tomb precinct. No one could read it. Remembering my recent failure to untangle the monumental macaroni in Ujjain, I assured them I wouldn't be able to read it either. The inscription was locked behind metal shutters. Someone was sent to find the key ('Oh, really, please don't go to any trouble . . . '). The key couldn't be found ('Honestly, you mustn't put yourselves out . . . '). Despite more protestations from me, and after a half-hour palaver involving a ladder, a hammer, a cold-chisel, a crowbar and finally an axe, the lock was broken. As I'd predicted, I could make neither head nor tail of it.

(And no wonder. Bruce Wannell, a persianist friend of huge and varied talents, later sent me a translation which I have also passed on to Mr Salim. I can sometimes make a stab at Persian if it contains enough Arabic; but I could have done nothing with, for example, Changal's 'musky cake', which

> is moreover from the *halva* of Unity;
> his camphor loaf is also from the electuary of Rapture.
> The wine of eagerness is in his cup and goblet;
> the *kabab* of Love is in his pot and oven.

According to the commentator, the inscription was installed in an earlier restoration, in 1455. As for Changal, not only his dates but his whole person is 'involved' – as it is today, in incense smoke – 'in utter obscurity'.)

Dewan – greatly excited by all this, as he was by anything holy – took group photographs by the eggbox mausoleum and would happily have whiled away the rest of the morning chatting about Muslim saints if I hadn't reminded him of our melon mission. As it was, we ended up with another saint – one, it turned out, with tenuous but far-reaching Battutian links.

After the glam-rock interior of Changal's mausoleum, the restrained tinsel festoons hanging over that of Kamal Mawla seemed positively Ideal Tombs in taste. And unlike the obscure Changal, Kamal was of excellent pedigree: the jolly imam in charge of the tomb explained that its occupant was the grandson of the great Baba Farid Ganj-i Shakar ('Sugar-Store') of Pakpattan, now across the border in Pakistan. In the *pir*-charts, Baba Farid was up there with Nizam al-Din of Delhi. In fact, so popular was he that according to a newspaper report I'd just read, thirty-two fans had been killed in a stampede for the tomb at his recent *urs*, or deathday party. He was no less a celebrity in IB's day, and the Moroccan had visited Baba Farid's tomb and been the guest of Kamal Mawla's first cousin. Looking now at Kamal's tomb I felt the fleeting pleasure of a distant connection made, like the man who danced with the girl who danced with the Prince of Wales.

There was a further link, too, into that wider parageography of saints. IB's visit to Baba Farid's tomb had been predicted by another holy man, Burhan al-Din of Alexandria, and that was even before he had his dream in the Nile Delta . . .

'Mr Tim-sir . . . am I asking imam-sahib about melons farming?'

Carried away across the saintly Internet, I'd momentarily lost the plot of our melodrama. The imam, Mr Salim had said, was a repository of local knowledge. The name of Shaykh Ibrahim the Maldivian, however, meant nothing to him. I could see him mouthing '*Maldives?*'

'Tell him . . . ' But Dewan had already begun to tell him about the melons.

Kamal Mawla's tomb had the usual splendid acoustic, and the dome rang with the sound of dropping pennies: '*Kharbuz-wala!*' And then (I reconstruct), 'All this "Shaykh Ibrahim" nonsense! The Maldives my foot. Why didn't you tell me in the first place? Honestly, the *Maldives* . . . ' He put his arm round a grinning Dewan and rattled on as if they'd just rediscovered a long-lost mutual friend. Somewhere in the flow of words I heard another name: Muhammad Shah Tughluq.

'Imam-sahib saying', Dewan explained when released from his hug, 'your Mr Shaykh Ibrahim is name Qurban Shah Wali. He is also calling him *kharbuz-wala* meaning "melons-man". And saying he give melons to Muhammad Shah.'

Between us we'd joined up some more dots.

Some time later – numb with the history and genealogy of Kamal

Mawla's neighbours in death, both indoors and out in the surrounding graveyard – I stood on an elevation near the mausoleum of Changal and looked across the plateau. Three or four miles off rose a little conical tor, and at its base I could just make out the small white *mazar*, the 'place of visitation', of Qurban Shah Wali, 'Saint Sacrifice-King' the melon-*wala*. This being the City of Saints, he had of course been enshrined. We didn't visit him: I was tombed out. Travelling with IB, repetitive shrine injury is an occupational hazard.

I spent the rest of the day writing my diary in a shriek of parrots on the terrace of our hotel, the Maharaja of Dhar's Jhira Bagh Palace, then exploring its small but rewarding library. There were game books, textbooks on revenue collection, various European *Baedekers*, a book of cocktail recipes, Islamic prayerbooks and an interesting-looking manuscript entitled *Bahar-e aysh ma'ruf bi ladhdhat al-nisa (The Springtime of Delight, Better Known as the Pleasures of Women)*. This did not disappoint, for it contained miniatures, their corners stained by licked fingers, of big-thighed ladies getting rogered – extremely graphically – by moustachioed gentlemen. Manuals of penetration, administration and cocktail-mixing: one might infer a lot from a maharaja's library.

Martin had been hard at it in the grounds, recording the waning day in oils. In his final canvas the setting sun hung dead centre, like a turmeric *tilak* mark.

*

Flags of tattered green gauze hung limp in the forenoon heat. They marked the beginning of the track that led to the conical tor and the melon-*wala*'s shrine. But we drove on, drawn by one of the great Indian tourist attractions, or repulsions: sati.

The sati, the 'excellent woman', is also the widow who burns herself to death on her husband's funeral pyre. Probably no other spectacle on earth can arouse simultaneously the feelings generated by a good wedding, a grand funeral and a gruesome public execution. Horror, death, love, faith are an irresistible combination; writers on and visitors to India from Diodorus Siculus onwards have been fascinated with what is, at one end of the scale of emotional response, a live snuff-movie and, at the other, the strictest Aristotelian tragedy inspiring pity, terror and catharsis. In *Hobson-Jobson* (that peerless cyclopaedia of the Indies, with which Sir Henry Yule redeems himself for his tart remarks on my Tangerine friend) 'Suttee', at five double-column pages, is the third-longest article, after 'Upas' and 'Pardao'; it outquotes even these, citing nearly fifty authorities. The burning obsession continues. The most celebrated or notorious sati of recent decades, Roop Kanwar, who burned herself in a Rajasthan village in 1987, split the nation and has fuelled many hundreds of thousands of words both in the Indian press and from outside commentators. At the site of her fiery apotheosis, reporters gathered as eagerly as worshippers.

In all this vast literature IB's description of a sati ceremony is the first piece of eye-witness reportage. It stands in sharp contrast to the blurred second-hand accounts of earlier, European writers. It was written in what might be called the classical age of the sati, when the associated ritual had reached its full development, in the century of Narayani Devi, the teen widow-turned-goddess whose shrine at Jhunjhunu in Rajasthan is the most famous sati temple in India. IB's piece is, in short, the scoop of sati journalism.

Briefly, it goes like this. The act of self-cremation is seen as commendable but not compulsory, although widows who do not take up the option are despised for the rest of their lives. The ceremony IB saw followed a three-day party. On the fourth day the widow, one of three whose warrior husbands had been killed in an encounter with local Muslims and their Hindu allies, mounted a horse and rode to the place of cremation. She was gorgeously dressed, and held a coconut in her right hand and a looking-glass in her left. Brahmans surrounded her; a band of trumpets and drums preceded her. On reaching the site she bathed in a tank then changed into a garment of coarse white cotton, distributing her finery as alms. Meanwhile the pyre was lit and sesame oil poured on to it to feed the flames. As she approached it a sheet was held up to conceal the blaze. Her response was haughty: 'Is it fire that you would frighten me with? I know it is a burning fire! Let me be!' Greeting the flames with a two-handed salutation, she leapt in. The onlookers placed heavy balks of wood on her and, as the blaze grew fiercer, the noise from the band and the chants of the participants rose in a great clamour. 'When I beheld this,' IB ends, 'I almost fell off my horse, but my companions rushed to sprinkle water on my face, after which I withdrew.'

IB's accuracy is not in question. Later reports confirm every detail of his account, with only minor differences, omissions or additions. Conti (c. 1430) substitutes a linen garment for IB's coarse cotton, and adds that the remains were preserved in a sepulchre. Varthema (*c.* 1505) has the widow chewing betel, and places the sheet or firescreen on poles. Barbosa's fire (*c.* 1510) is fuelled by ghee as well as by oil. Balbi (1583) has the sati holding a lemon and a looking-glass, as does della Valle (*c.* 1620; a plate in his Dutch edition of 1664–5 shows the scene convincingly, even if the lady is a Lelyesque creature, fashionably fleshy like the Windsor Beauties). Leaping forward another three centuries, IB's tragedy plays again at the burning of Roop Kanwar. The bridal finery, the drums, trumpets and chanting, the balks of wood are all there; even that sang-froid when the heat is on – Mrs Kanwar complained about the disgracefully mean amount of ghee and firewood, says Tully (1987; although when you think about it, it would be preferable for more than one reason to go out in a blaze of glory than to end up half-baked).

The continuity is remarkable but not, in India, astonishing. What interested me more than the drama – what, in effect, I wanted to test IB on – was the backdrop to this *locus classicus* of sati narrative. It was another precisely memorized setting, like that of his Doab adventures. This in itself was off-putting. I foresaw another hunt for decayed fragments – if I was lucky; for neither the commentators on the *Travels*, nor the exiguous antiquarian jottings on the area possibly concerned, offered any clues as to whether even fragments might exist. Leaving Martin in Dhar to paint the solid, sausagemeat-coloured certainty of its fort, I had set off with Dewan into the unknown.

What we were looking for was 'a dark place with much water and many trees, thick with shadows. Set among the trees were four pavilions, each containing a stone idol; between the pavilions lay a tank, covered in so deep and dense a shade that no sunlight could penetrate it. The place might have been a spot in hell – from which God preserve us.' The three pyres, IB adds, had been built on 'a piece of low-lying ground near the tank'. It was a brief description yet, unlike that of Ujjain, it had depth, detail and shading. In my mind's eye I saw it as one of those steel engravings, heavily cross-hatched and inked, in Victorian newspapers; with, of course, a suitable caption – 'The Scene of the Tragic Events'. I may be over-impressionable, but from the very first reading it had made my flesh creep.

But where was it? In the *Travels* the picture is torn from its geographical context and pasted, together with rhinos, jackfruit and other exotica, into a sort of frontispiece to India which IB insets in his

journey from the frontier to Delhi. During one of his halts in the Punjab, he returned from an excursion – the visit to Baba Farid 'Sugar-Store' – to find his companions hurrying out of the camp. Perhaps temporarily tombed out, he didn't follow. When they reappeared they told him they had watched the cremation of a sati. IB was not to be outdone: 'Then, some time later, I happened to be in a town inhabited mostly by infidels, called Amjari . . .'; his sati site was about three miles outside this town. Professor Gibb had no hesitation in locating Amjari – not in a bet-hedging footnote but between square brackets that brooked no argument – as '[Amjhera, near Dhar]'. I wasn't convinced. 'Then, some time later' was more than a little elliptical for the seven and a half years it apparently took IB to get from the Punjab to Dhar. But in the absence of anywhere else in the gazetteer even remotely near to 'Amjari', I had given in to the obvious.

Before we'd even started out, the obvious had become the nebulous. As we were leaving the Jira Bagh Palace, the manager called out to us to say that he'd made his own inquiries and found a place called Anjari. It lay south-east of Dhar, in the opposite direction to Amjhera; and it was, as he pointed out, rather closer in sound to IB's 'Amjari'. The Beast of Barwan/Barwa/Barauni/Parvan/Narwar slunk ominously back into my thoughts. That elusive quarry had at least been constrained by the exigencies of IB's route within an area of 10,000 square miles. In contrast, there could be any number of mutant Amjaris on the loose, and they had a whole subcontinent of back-roads to lurk in. Tails and donkeys came to mind.

Still, we had to start somewhere. I felt a slight bias in favour of the new-found Anjari: Jourdain, the early seventeenth-century English traveller and merchant, noted the particular frequency of satis in the region where it lay. I consulted possibly-psychic Dewan, and he plumped for Amjhera. In the end I tossed a coin. Amjhera it was.

★

The first thing we saw after passing the track to the melon-farmer's shrine was a line of women carrying brass vessels on their heads, erect and graceful as caryatids. Each vessel contained a nest of greenery and, sitting in this, a coconut. A promising augury. But as we approached the side-road to Amjhera my optimism faded. Time and again – I gave up counting at number ten – we stopped to ask if there

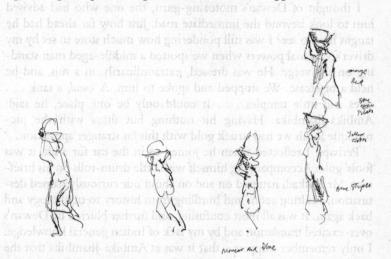

was a tank nearby, surrounded by trees and by sati monuments, which was what I supposed IB's four pavilions to be. All the men we questioned were variations on a theme of dhotis, kurtas, whiskers and turbans. The variations were played out in the last two features: handlebar moustaches that ranged from sit-up-and-beg to dropped Tour de Madhya Pradesh and included one upstanding, almost

Daliesque, chopper; and turbans of Day-Glo hue that resembled outsize scoops of sorbet – mostly lime or lemon, with the odd *neapolitano*. Their answers, too, were variations on a theme: No. There were a few looks of incomprehension, others of suspicion (since the Roop Kanwar furore, foreigners in search of satis are apt to be looked on askance). The wearer of a particularly elaborate *bombe glacée* thought there might be somewhere answering our description near Indore – halfway back to Ujjain.

By now we were about three miles from Amjhera, the distance of IB's sati site from his Amjari, and it seemed as if we'd been through all the handlebars imaginable plus a tutti-frutti of turbans. If the spot from hell were anywhere near here, it seemed hardly credible that so distinctive a place could have escaped so many notices. I was ready to turn back and make for the hotel manager's Anjari before the day was lost. But Dewan counselled giving Amjhera itself a chance. 'I am one hundred per cent certain we find sati place,' he said, matter-of-factly.

I thought of Dewan's motoring-guru, the one who had advised him to look beyond the immediate road. Just how far ahead had he taught him to see? I was still pondering how much store to set by my driver's vaticinal powers when we spotted a middle-aged man standing on the verge. He was dressed, extraordinarily, in a suit, and he held a briefcase. We stopped and spoke to him. A *kund*, a tank . . . trees and little temples . . . It could only be one place, he said: Ambika-Jhambika. Having hit nothing but dross with the picturesque locals we had struck gold with this far stranger apparition.

Perhaps, I reflected when he joined us in the car for a lift, it was fools' gold. Accompanying himself with little drum-rolls on his briefcase, Mr Mukadi nattered on and on about our curiously named destination, vaulting aeons and hurdling from history to mythology and back again. It was all most confusing, and further blurred by Dewan's over-excited translation and by my lack of Indian general knowledge. I only remember snippets – that it was at Ambika-Jhambika that the Lord Krishna captured and ravished Rupmati – or was it Rukmani? – and that the British – or was it the Mughals, or Muhammad Shah? – captured Maharaja Something Singh, presumably for different reasons. There was also a somnambulating statue and a tunnel to Mandu (I looked at the map: twenty-three miles). How could such an action-packed spot have failed to register in the turbaned collective memory of the sons of Amjhera's soil, when it featured so richly in that of someone who looked like a travelling salesman astray? I was about to butt in and ask when, at an outlying village on the far side of Amjhera, Mr Mukadi told Dewan to stop. Ambika-Jhambika wasn't far down the road, he said between thanks. We would see a gateway among some trees. He added that this village was called Satipura; and disappeared into it before the name hit home.

The ground began to fall away, to draw us down, past a cement works, past an electricity substation, towards the lip of the scarp, till Dewan said, 'This is the place. I know it,' and we pulled over by the trees. I looked at the odometer: a little under three miles from Amjhera. Uncharacteristically accurate of IB, if . . .

There was no if. Had he known the phrase – and not himself been silenced by what lay through the gate – Dewan would have asked me if I'd seen a ghost. But the scene was more unnerving than anything in the spirit world. When I was a child my father told me about a strange experience. He had just been to an exhumation (graveyards, you see, are in the blood). When they opened the lead-lined coffin they saw the face of a woman, perfect in every feature from her long red-gold hair to the smallpox that had killed her. 'I stood there and thought, "I'm looking at a face that's three hundred years old." It was rather a beautiful face. When they moved her she crumbled away.' What was a ghost compared to that? The vision now before us was as chilling and as thrilling as that seventeenth-century face.

It was a sudden depression in the ground perhaps 150 yards across and rimmed with rock walls twenty-five feet high. The rim was broken only at the south, where a track descended through an opening; the rest was ringed with trees, enormous, crook-backed and club-footed, leaning this way and that like a crowd of crippled giants and clenching the rock with obscenely knobbled roots. The crater looked less the result of geology than of arboreal assault, a conspiracy by the trees to prise crust from bedrock. That monstrous tree of Barwa smothered; these ripped, slowly and patiently. I had no doubt that some of them, as gnarled and thickset as the oldest English oaks, had been at it since IB was here. Their branches spread an impasto gloom over the structures in the bottom of the gulch. There were four of these – to east and south two little temples with squat spires and domed antechambers, each flying tomato-red pennants, to the west a stepped platform, to the north-west a simple domed cube – and between them a deep slot-like tank. The tank was dry, and beside it stood the only significant addition to the scene IB described, a bicycle.

'Before all, to make you *see*.' After the first jolt of déjà vu I realized that here, in this obscure corner of Madhya Pradesh, was the picture I was after. The three dimensions; not a speaking but a shrieking likeness. It was just as I'd remembered it, illogical though that may sound; and, even without the snap and crackle of the pyre, the pop of exploding skulls, just as terrifying. In fact more so: mutability and decay are merely nasty; the picture of Dorian Gray is cheap sensation, knock-down Hammer horror. The true terror is when the image stays the same and all the world around grows old.

It seemed all the stranger, after those interminable invisible miles since Khajuraho, broken only by hazy cities and dim worthies, to come upon such sudden clarity of vision. But I remembered now what Martin said when I read him IB's tale of torture and death in the Thousand-Column Hall – 'He was still terrified when he wrote that.' Here, too, some photochemistry of fear had seared the scene into his mind's retina – just as the legendary snake retains within its eye the image of an attacker, until the day comes for revenge. Today, I felt, IB was avenged, vindicated before all those who have doubted his accuracy as an observer of India – the slanderers of Fez, the libellous plagiarist al-Ziyani and his Indian 'scholars', Klaproth, Yule and occasionally – I must admit – me. There was no need to dispute with him the dimensions of elephants or reservoirs, to reconstruct hills or lakes or palaces on his behalf, to question the bona fides of informants or cultivate a donnish scepticism. This was not a question of faith. It was what he saw. All it needed was a smoking pyre. And there, standing on the steps of the eastern temple in a saffron skirt, was someone who might lead me to it.

'Please to mind your head on the ledge as you stand,' said the guardian of the spot from hell. Baburaoji had learned his English from missionaries in the 1920s, when tigers stalked the shadowed margins of Ambika-Jhambika and the rains had been more generous. 'There was much water here in the days of my youth. Now, we have not enjoyed the blessings of a decent downpour for two to three years past.' Hence, he added, the emptiness of the Brahma Kund, the tank between the four temples.

I noted down the name. It was satisfying to be able to add substantial detail to IB's sketch, where he had left off 650 years ago. Baburaoji

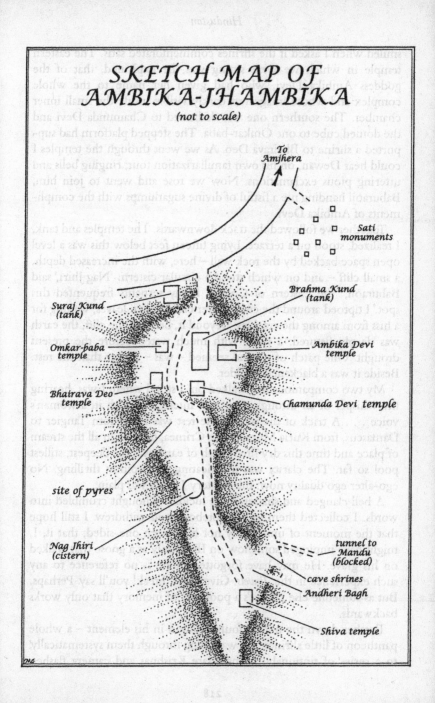

SKETCH MAP OF
AMBIKA-JHAMBIKA
(not to scale)

To
Amjhera

*Sati
monuments*

Brahma Kund
(tank)

Suraj Kund
(tank)

Omkar-baba
temple

Ambika Devi
temple

Bhairava Deo
temple

Chamunda Devi temple

site of pyres

Nag Jhiri
(cistern)

tunnel to
Mandu
(blocked)

cave shrines

Andheri Bagh

Shiva temple

smiled when I asked if the shrines commemorated satis. The eastern temple in which we were sitting was, he explained, that of the goddess Ambika Devi, who had given her name to the whole complex and whose image was darkly visible inside the small inner chamber. The southern one was dedicated to Chamunda Devi and the domed cube to one Omkar-baba. The stepped platform had supported a shrine to Bhairava Deo. As we went through the temples I could hear Dewan, on his own familiarization tour, ringing bells and uttering pious exclamations. Now we rose and went to join him, Baburaoji handing me a fistful of divine sugarlumps with the compliments of Ambika Devi.

Together we followed the track downwards. The temples and tank, I realized, stood on a terrace. Lying fifteen feet below this was a level open space backed by the rock wall – here, with the increased depth, a small cliff – and on which stood a circular cistern. 'Nag Jhiri,' said Baburaoji, 'the Cistern of Cobras. Many serpents frequented this spot.' I tiptoed around the cistern over crispy fallen leaves, waiting for a hiss from among the crackles. Beyond it, beneath the cliff, the earth was deeply fissured; a place with much water, before the present drought. One patch of ground seemed – was – darker than the rest. Beside it was a blackened boulder.

My two companions had walked on. I stood where I was, hearing the whisper of air through trees and, interleaved with it, a woman's voice . . . A trick of the wind. The rest was real. From Tangier to Damascus, from Kuria Muria to the Crimea, to here, in all the stream of place and time this dry fired patch of earth was the deepest, stillest pool so far. The clarity was intoxicating, the coition thrilling. No ego-alter ego duality now: the mystery *I am he* was plain.

A bell clanged and shattered the lucidity. Thought crumbled into words. I collected them in my notebook and withdrew. I still hope that the moment of union may not have been one-sided; that it, I, might have impinged somehow on IB, if only as a goose that walked on his grave. He may have forgotten; there is no reference to any such experience in the *Travels*. Give him a break! you'll say. Perhaps. But as someone else said, it's a poor sort of memory that only works backwards.

Further down the track I found Dewan in his element – a whole pantheon of little shrines. He was going through them systematically, to a series of tintinnabulations, Hare Krishnas and camera flashes.

(More systematically than I knew: that evening he presented me unbidden with a sketch map showing every feature of this idol-crowded spot, set within a frame of rocks and roots. Compared with my own bald effort it was baroque in its detail.) Baburaoji looked on contentedly: another happy customer. I broached once more the subject of satis.

Again, the old man smiled. 'This place is known as "Andheri Bagh",' he said, indicating the surrounding shrine-park, 'which means "Dark Garden". Many years ago it was filled with jungle. Even during my lifetime, when I was a youngster, the forest began over there.' He pointed down the track, where it fell out of sight. 'It was impenetrable.'

Like you, I thought.

*

The darkened earth, the blackened stone . . . No, I hadn't imagined them. But as we pulled out of the gateway, up from the deep allusive gloom of Ambika-Jhambika into the prosaic light of afternoon, I realized there could be any number of explanations. It was that dual-purpose portal through which the sati had gained heaven and IB had glimpsed hell, no doubt of that; but the fires were long burnt out. There was no memory of that day, no smoking pyre. And I wanted my lunch.

'Mr Tim . . .'

Dewan was pulling over to another, smaller gateway. I hadn't noticed it when we first arrived. It led to yet another group of shrines and – my stomach rumbled – to a further session of ding-a-lings and Hare Krishnas. 'Goodness! I didn't know it was that time,' I said, looking pointedly at my watch.

'Mr Tim-sir . . .'

'Do you think we'll find anything to eat in Amjhera?' I thought of Martin, lone and splendid in the marble hall of the Jhira Bagh, probably tucking at this very moment into the first of half a dozen exquisite courses. I would have to put my foot down. After all, *I* was meant to be the tourist, not Dewan.

'Mr Tim-sir-sahib . . .' Strange, I thought, looking through the gate. Perhaps they weren't shrines. More like graves. But I hadn't seen any trace of Muslims in the area. Amjhera seemed to be an entirely Hindu district, as it was in IB's day. Hindus didn't have graves. ' . . . I am thinking here are satis ladies.'

There were about twenty of them. Most were plain square stone platforms approached by a few steps. Two were finished off with small pavilions, domed and whitewashed. One of these, although clearly old, bore a recent plaque: 'Sati Mata Pancholi Parivar,' Dewan read – the Pancholi Family Sati Mother. The other contained several amorphous stones, thickly smeared with vermilion and further decorated with squares of shiny silver leaf and with garlands, dry but intact, of marigolds. Nearly all the monuments also supported stelae the size of gravestones. These showed couples standing side by side; one depicted a man on a horse, in profile, and a woman standing on a dais, head on – the head inflated into a giant, pop-eyed ball. A few of the couples wore crimson *tilak* marks on their foreheads, recently applied. One feature of the stelae never varied: each showed in its upper section a disc and a crescent. I remembered one of the many accounts of the cremation of Roop Kanwar. It said that as the pyre blazed up the crowd had circled it, chanting that her name would last as long as sun and moon endure.

'They put heavy balks of wood on top of her to stop her moving, and a great clamour of voices rose from them.' The name they chanted that day, as IB swooned in the saddle, hasn't endured. Which of these monuments commemorated its owner I couldn't tell. But there was a group of four platforms, standing together and precisely identical. IB said that three women were burned. Could there have been a fourth, widowed soon after by a lingering death from wounds? I noticed a movement from the corner of my eye: Dewan, prostrating himself to the anonymous ancestress of the Pancholi family.

I was sombrely satisfied. I'd found the smoking pyre; more pyres than I'd ever dared to hope for. I'd also seen marigolds and silver leaf, vermilion, Dewan falling down in worship. It all belied the official line – that the rites are barbarous and criminal, that widows are forced on to the pyre by reactionary brahmans and scheming relatives. It is a line followed religiously by a few, toed half-heartedly by rather more, sidestepped by many, and ignored by most. Since Roop Kanwar there have been several more satis – reported ones, that is. As I write, the most recent was an elderly widow who cremated herself a year ago in a village in north-eastern Madhya Pradesh. She is said to have acted voluntarily. Whether volition is the same as free will, whether individual will is separable – in an Indian village of all places – from that of society, are not for the conjecture of amateurs. But I suspect there were other forces at work: the pressure, if not of people, then of propriety; the weight of a tradition far heavier than balks of wood. Part of me admires that tradition, the glorious pathetic devotion of the excellent woman. But most of me is sickened by the thought of all that barbecued humanity, and I know that if I had been there that day at Ambika-Jhambika I would have fainted too.

*

'Satis ladies *very* good thing!' Dewan enthused as we drove away.

I looked at his shining face, guileless and transparent. It wasn't just a lack of connection. I was looking across a gulf far wider than all the centuries back to IB. Dewan must have sensed the distance, for he fell silent. Neither of us spoke until the outskirts of Dhar, where I saw a roadside shop and told him to slow down. I was dizzy with hunger, but the store sold only devotional odds and ends – idols, incense and marigolds; mirrors and coconuts. 'It's OK. Drive on.'

The Dome of the Sultan's Tooth

'It behoves a man in search of wonders sometimes to go out of his way.'

Sir John Mandeville, *Travels*

'**Y**OU ARE A coward,' Dr Amjad said.

I tried to think of worse situations I'd been in . . . wrestling in the dark with a drunken gunman; reeling in the blast of an exploding Scud; doing aerobatics with an ex-Rhodesian Air Force pilot and a hangover – the plane was a single-seater, and he had the seat. But they were nothing beside the exquisite torture of having a miniature bradawl probing the innermost recesses of my mandible. The dentist's chair was my own spot in hell.

Muhammad Shah ibn Tughluq wasn't so lucky. The crystallized melons, the sherbets, sweetmeats and *pan*, and lately IB's *bouchées du juge* and other sugar-rich *douceurs*, took their toll: in 1336 or 1337, during his return from a failed expedition to stamp out a rebellion in Coromandel, the sweet sultanic tooth finally blew up. No root-extractions then; he had the offending molar out near the town of Bid, in what is now central Maharashtra. Then he gave it a decent burial. This last fact, which was apparently in accordance with the tenets of the Hanafi school of Islam to which the sultan subscribed, I had learned from a note in Mahdi Husain's *The Rise and Fall of Muhammad bin Tughluq*. 'A magnificent tomb', added Professor Husain, 'was reared over it, which still stands, and is known as "the dome of the tooth of Sultan Tughluq".'

'All over,' said Dr Amjad. I looked up at my gentle torturer. He'd recently shaved his head and cultivated a bushy beard, which made him look like one of those reversible faces of Rex Whistler's – useful for someone who spends so much time being viewed from abnormal angles. 'This is your *asab*.' He held a miniscule object in his tweezers, the root of all recent evil.

'So you're not going to bury it,' I said, as he transferred it to a tissue and dropped it in the bin.

'*Kayf?*'

I told him about the interment of Muhammad Shah's tooth. Since reading about it I had also learned that some schools of Islamic law have advocated committing all discarded body parts to the earth, even hair and fingernail clippings. Perhaps the Hanafis – to whom my Syrian dentist belonged, like IB's sultan – drew the line at a root. As it happened, Amjad hadn't even heard of tooth burials. 'Hanafi doctrine has never been fossilized,' he explained. 'Perhaps the official line has changed. These days we'd bury a hand, certainly; a finger too. But teeth get chucked in the rubbish.' He thought Muhammad Shah's odontophorous monument highly eccentric, if not heretical.

This conversation of some months earlier had made the magnificent mausoleum more intriguing still. It would mean a sidetrack off IB's route; but the building boasted a high rarity value. It wasn't in Welch and Crane's terse catalogue raisonné of Tughluqid architecture, and the only other reference I'd found to it was a fleeting mention in the *Imperial Gazetteer*. This entry also stated that Bid was renowned for the manufacture of sword-sticks. So, while the idea of going there had drawn a unanimous response from my Delhi friends – '*Where?*' closely followed, when I showed them on the map, by '*Why?*' – for me the place was invested with the irresistible allure of the curious.

Besides, I told myself – as if further excuses were necessary – the molar mausoleum was a nice metaphor for what I was doing. It embodied the extraction of something small – one man's life in India, both sweet and painful – and the construction around it of a monument. And a visit to the tomb would be an ideal way to say a final farewell to Muhammad Shah; not least since there is some debate about where the rest of him is buried.

But first we had to go rat-hunting.

*

223

We motored south from Dhar on what Dewan classed as an '*in sha Allah* road', one grade up from a glory-be road. It passed through level wheat-and-potato land with haystacks in trees, then fell, down clefts and scarps, to a cattle-rich underplateau that reminded Martin of Corot's Campagna. But not for long, for we crossed two boundaries. The first was the Narmada River, the trail of a particularly mighty slug that slithered over lettuce-green meadows and marked the end of Hindustan. An arbitrary end, it seemed, since nothing changed at first – more cattle, more Corot, a dry selvage of wrinkled hills. Then, suddenly, Madhya Pradesh gave way to Maharashtra, tile to thatch, wheat to sugar cane, aridity to humidity. The cane fields sucked the River Tapti to a trickle then transpired it into the atmosphere; sugar refineries simmered in a syrupy fug. A pervasive stickiness impeded even sounds, and we passed convoy after convoy of cane-laden bullock carts, their bells playing downward Doppler scales, orchestras of drunken gamelans. And there was another change: since we'd crossed the state border there hadn't been a peep from the gonk.

It was all, as Dewan put it, 'areawise and roadwise very different'. To me it smelt and felt of South. But not, again, for long. A looming massif; hairgrip bends and gripping overtakes; and we were on another plateau, neither North nor South but the elevated middle earth of the Deccan. The sun set as we reached the lip of the pass.

I read Martin his bedtime story in our lodgings near Khuldabad, 'Paradise City'. The tale was set only a few miles away in Khuldabad's sister Dawlatabad, 'State City', Muhammad Shah's relocated capital. IB had heard it from Malik Khattab, a high-ranking Afghan officer of the sultan's and, like all the best bedtime stories, it was a shocker. Khattab had the distinction of having been incarcerated by Muhammad in the nastiest dungeon in Deogiri, the castle of Dawlatabad – the notorious Pit of Rats. His furry fellow-occupants, he pointed out, were not the oversized mice that pass for rats in most places. The 'rats, rats, rats as big as cats' of the marching song had nothing on them: these were *bigger* than cats, IB confirmed, 'and cats run away from them. They cannot fight them because the rats would overcome them . . . I saw them there and was amazed by their size.' (By the late seventeenth century they had become bigger still: the English traveller Fryer saw 'the strongest huge Rats as big as our Pigs'.) 'The rats', Khattab continued, 'used to gang up at night in order to devour me, and I fought them off only with great difficulty.' But the Afghan had a lucky escape: 'The reason for my release was that Malik Mall was imprisoned in a dungeon adjacent to mine; he fell ill and the rats ate his fingers and his eyes and he died. When news of this reached the sultan he said, "Let Khattab go before he suffers the same fate."'

Reading the passage for the first time, I'd been reminded of Southey's wicked Bishop Hatto of Mainz. During a famine, this unsavoury prelate is said to have burned to death a barnful of peasants on the grounds that they were 'rats that only consume the corn'. The bishop's come-uppance compensates in horror for what it lacks in poetry, for the *echt*-rats

> whetted their teeth against the stones,
> And now they pick the Bishop's bones:
> They gnawed the flesh from every limb,
> For they were sent to do judgement on him!

As IB describes it the setting of Malik Mall's tragic end, a castle on an isolated rock in a plain, sounded not unlike that of Bishop Hatto's demise, a tower on an island in the Rhine. Next door to it, however, was something far more to the traveller's taste – another Tarababad or 'Music City' where, as in its namesake in Delhi, the singing-girls congregated. Each diva had a richly carpeted booth furnished with a swing in which she would rock, warbling arias. It all sounded rather Bollywood; so too the next sequence, a lingering close-up followed by IB's equivalent of the wet-sari dance: 'The people of the region of Dawlatabad belong to the Maratha tribe, whose women God has endued with a singular beauty, and in particular in the figure of their noses and eyebrows. As to their deliciousness in bed and their knowledge of the movements employed in copulation, no other women excel them . . .' (IB's comment inspired a marginal note from the owner of one manuscript of the *Travels* – 'O God, give me a taste of this delight!')

Dewan confirmed IB's data, adding his own interpretation: 'Many peoples living here Muslims. They non-veg, killing and eating the animals. So the womens very hot, *very* sexy!' Martin and I doubted whether we'd get a chance to do any proper fieldwork on the carnivorous Maratha ladies. But at least there might be eyebrows and noses to contemplate – perhaps to record, if Martin felt inspired to draw these features – and, I hoped, some equally carnivorous rats.

In the illustrated Windsor Castle copy of the Mughal *Badshahnama* there is a double representation of Dawlatabad, a bird's-eye view and, beside it, an elevation. Our first sight of the place, from the ghat overlooking the plain, was a compromise between the two angles. It showed the Mughal artist to be an accurate observer of detail. But he had prettified the view, underplaying the sheer height and mass of the castle rock and turning it into an innocuous cake wrapped in ribbons of wall.

The reality was not pretty. The black, sarcophagus-shaped rock rose suddenly out of the plain to a height of 800 feet, the suddenness of nature improved on by a vicious man-made scarp along its base. As if this were not enough to deter unwanted visitors, it was enclosed by no fewer than three walls, the first and second near the rock itself, the third – Muhammad Shah's city wall – further out. This last was furnished with fat-bottomed bastions and finished off with crenellations, ruinous and blackened, that gave the wall the look of a long, horribly decayed grin. Within it was a scrubby waste dotted with brick kilns, each emitting a column of smoke – 'fire-fog', in Dewan's picturesque coinage; dust-devils zigzagged between the standing columns like dancing partners in a reel. The whole scene, with those concentric circles of wall enclosing the fortress perched on its slag-black, shag-black crag, suggested some terrestrial Inferno. Deogiri, 'the Hill of the Gods' of its earlier Hindu masters, might have been better named the Hill of Lucifer.

The under-worldliness of the prospect seemed to magnify the distance of Muhammad Shah's new metropolis from Delhi. I thought of the unfortunate blind man IB said was dragged here from the old capital, scattering parts of himself across India like the *disjecta membra* of the goddess Sati, and marvelled to think that so much as his foot made it. The journey usually took forty days, but VIP travellers could do it by inter-city palankeen, flat out in both senses, in a week. Allowing ten hours a day for sleep, food, prayer and other necessities, that would mean an average speed of about 8 m.p.h., which compares respectably with that of some country trains today.

Although for us the journey had taken closer to the standard-class forty days, all the other visitors we spoke to were locals on a day-trip from nearby Aurangabad. There were one or two eye-catching eye-brows and notable noses beneath the baseball caps worn by most of today's Maratha maidens; but it was hard to concentrate on them, let alone speculate on the deliciousness of other members, for the first circle of Inferno pullulated with pedlars of the most importunate type. The most persistent was a man trying to dispose of a heavy coffee-table book entitled *Visions of India by Soviet Artists*. He'd bought a stack of them, he said, hence the bargain price. It was indeed remarkably cheap – and having seen a few of the plates we decided pulping would be too good for it. 'Poor man,' Martin sighed, as we escaped. 'I wonder what he's done to deserve that.'

'He's probably a publisher who didn't pay his authors,' I said, thinking of one such of my acquaintance for whom Dante himself could not have designed a more perfect punishment.

We ran the gauntlet of the postcard men, the Kama Sutra-keyring-*walas* and the would-be guides, and made it into the second, hawker-free circle. Here was Muhammad Shah's cantonment; nothing identifiable remains of it, or of Music City. But there was a big old mosque, and I went to explore it while Martin drew. How old the mosque was I couldn't immediately tell, for like so many Islamic monuments I'd seen in India it lacked inscriptions. I entered the colonnaded prayer-hall and made for the mihrab, the Mecca-ward niche where an epigraph might have survived. More Persian spaghetti to unravel . . .

Anyone watching on CCTV would have thought some unseen hand had hit Pause, quickly followed by Rewind: what I had seen stopped me in my tracks then took me, in reverse, back to the shelter of a column. Replay. I emerged once more. It was still there. The mihrab contained a life-sized idol. Not some tasteful Vishnu but the full iconodule monty, with eight arms, in mandrill-arse technicolor. I had to sit down.

It was the shock of finding a deity so liberally accoutred with limbs, colours, gender and other attributes – she held a trident, a sword, flames and various obscurer items – in a place designed for one devoid of all physical qualities, a cerebral Absolute signified by an empty niche. I rubbed my eyes. I pinched myself. I told myself that places of worship had been recycled ever since He was in short trousers; that the game of musical shrines had never been played more keenly than in India; that, for all I knew, this might have been a temple site to start with (it was, I found out later – first Jain, then Hindu). I reminded myself of those wise words of Nizam al-Din – that every people has its own *din* and *qiblah*, its own religion and direction of worship. But it was no good. This was blatant *qiblah-barging*, and the result was strange to the point of kinkiness.

I suppose I was shocked partly on IB's behalf. As it was, lost in his reverie of noses, eyebrows and pelvic thrusts, he was silent on the mosque. And he also failed to convey the complexity, the sheer theatricality, of the castle that hung above it. The way up, through a twisting sequence of gateways supplied with tunnel-like guard-houses, platforms for chamberlains and spiked anti-elephant gates, was at once suspenseful, triumphal and dreamlike. With its full cast of sentries and flunkeys, the drama of entry must have rivalled that of the Thousand-Column Hall in Delhi. For a foe it would have been a strategic Rubik cube, with booby-traps. But all this was only the prologue. Having passed through the lower gateways we were out in the open again, by a massive Mughal siege-gun with a ram's head on the butt, two lions at the breech and a small boy, Kim-like, astride the business end. Then, across a sheer-sided moat, we entered a cavernous chamber hewn out of the granite. Here, 'in the heart of the rock,' wrote the author of the *Badshahnama*, 'there is a dark and tortuous passage like the ascent of a minaret, and a light is required there even at mid-day'. With perfect timing, Mr and Mrs Borkar and family of Aurangabad turned up with a couple of birthday-cake candles. We latched on to them, climbing up through the black granite bowels of the hill in a din of ghost-train wails and screams. Forget about erotic movements, I thought as we re-emerged, pink and panting, into the daylight. If it was strenuous exercise and climactic thrills you were after, this was as good as anything the Maratha ladies could provide. Well, almost.

Several hundred external stairs on, we reached the top. As in Gwalior, the entire acropolis was so generously riddled with crypts and vaults, dungeons and oubliettes, that I'd already despaired of identifying IB's hole. Besides, although there were belfryfuls of bats we hadn't spotted a single rodent. But at the very summit, beneath a diminutive keep, was a highly plausible Rat Pit. Steps descended to an underground room. Opening off this were two adjacent chambers, their only entrances set six feet off the ground and just big enough to admit a man. I hauled myself up to one of these and tossed lighted matches in. The floor level was several feet below that of the outer room; other than that I could make out only spectral walls, dim, leathery movements and the ammoniac stink of flittermouse shit. I wondered if the chamber might have had some innocent purpose – the storage of water or grain, perhaps. But it was no cistern, for there was no way in for water; and it would have made a useless granary with that tiny high-set entrance. To my mind it could only be a dungeon – a maximum-security one. Two dungeons, side by side, one for Khattab, the other for the unfortunate Mall . . . I thought I saw something scuttle across the floor, in the final flicker of my last match.

Crouching in the corner of the outer room, just visible in the light of a small lamp, was a human figure. I approached, and saw it to be that of an old witch. She had the face of a puckered crab apple and was in charge of a tiny shrine, the centrepiece of which was a pair of baby-sized, baby-pink feet. These she prevailed on us to tickle, for a reasonable fee.

I wanted that lamp. More important, I wanted its owner's services as an informant. Although it was yet another long shot, some folk-memory of Mall's demise could have survived, like that of Bishop Hatto in his Mäuseturm on the Rhine. But there was the language problem – Dewan, no mountaineer, had stayed with the car. I turned to Martin. 'How do you say, "I think an Afghan may have been nibbled to death by rats in there" in sign language?' He rolled his eyes.

'OK. Forget that . . . I know! Could you draw a quick rat?' This time he obliged, and I showed the sketch to the old hag.

'*Ah*,' she cackled, '*machchli!*'

'*Achchha!*' I replied, delighted she'd got the point so quickly. Martin hadn't won the Ondaatje Prize for nothing. I indicated the two holes in the rock wall. '*Machchli hai?*'

If it were possible, the crab-apple visage puckered even more. It also gave me a very funny look. '*Nahin!*' she said, firmly. '*Machchli nahin!*'

'Oh,' I said. Perhaps she thought I was casting aspersions on the health-and-safety record of her shrine. I briefly considered asking for a loan of the shrine-lamp but, judging by repeated frowns in my direction, she'd decided I was a rum customer. I let the matter drop. In any case, knowing the Archaeological Survey they would have done a rodent purge ages ago. None of this, however, shook my conviction that we had found IB's Pit, if not his Rats. And since the old lady then sat for Martin, to whom she had obviously taken a shine, we left with one visual record of Dawlatabad womanhood.

'I think not too much sexy womens here,' said Dewan, wistfully, when we reconvened at the end of the afternoon. Good chap, I thought. He must have been doing some research on our behalf. 'But too much cheaters, hawkers and policemens.' He farted disapprovingly.

Following our respective exertions, we were restoring our strength with Super Stud beer. I gave Dewan an account of our investigations in the castle, ending with the wrinkled keeper of the two holy feet. 'Anyway,' I concluded, 'she seemed absolutely certain there weren't any er . . . What do you say for "rats"?'

'*Chuha*,' said Dewan.

'Oh, she used another word.' I looked in my notebook. 'That's it. *Machchli.*'

Now Dewan gave me a funny look. 'Mr Tim-sir, *machchli* meaning "fish".'

We studied Martin's drawing. Come to think of it, it did look a bit ambiguous. In fact, positively amphibious.

'She must have thought you were barking mad,' said Martin.

*

The road into Khuldabad was lined with stately banyan trees, the nave of a grow-your-own cathedral. These, and the rest of the prevailing verdure, recalled the old name of the place – Rawdah, the Arabic for a garden or meadow. The new name, bestowed on it when the Mughal Emperor Aurangzeb was buried here in 1707, was also apt: 'Paradise City' has always been a spiritual foil to the grimly temporal 'State City' of Dawlatabad. But while Stateville is now a fallen Babylon, Paradiseville remains the Mecca of the Deccan. IB didn't mention it, and I wanted to fill the gap in his catalogue of wonders.

To avoid sepulchre-fatigue, it will suffice to mention only a few features of Khuldabad; although it must be said that in the *Which Shrine?* guide I'm thinking of compiling it would earn the maximum five-cupola rating. Not only is there a Cloak of the Prophet and a Hair of the Beard of the Prophet; there is also a gem-encrusted threshold leading to the tomb of Burhan al-Din, the local saint who died a few years before IB's visit to the region; and, next to this, a patio suffering from what may best be described as an outbreak of silver zits.

The surface of the paving was smooth, grey and unnaturally hot. Here and there, bubbles gave the impression that the stone was simmering on a low flame. Some of the bubbles had burst, and inside them were little nodules of silver. Our guide, a descendant of Burhan al-Din, explained that they were the remnant of a shrubbery of silver bushes that had sprouted up after the saint's death and paid for the construction of his tomb. The growth was much reduced now, he added, although new nodules regularly popped up in the small hours. Less convincing was his explanation of the presence, on the gem-set threshold, of an abandoned Indian takeaway. The tomb-complex catered for weddings, he said; the plate of curry and rice ensured blessings on the marriage, and was a safeguard against 'dangers with the madam'.

Before any further information forthcame, he steered us into his ancestor's tomb. The interior had the look of an upmarket opium den, with a tented ceiling in silver plush and other opulent orientalia. An elderly gentleman was stroking the saint's cenotaph with that multi-purpose tool, a peacock-feather *morchal*. This he stuck out of an aperture in the wall between strokes; outside, a line of ladies, banned from entering the mausoleum, queued for a touch of the old man's tickling-stick. As part of the pampering at this spiritual resort, our guide had already stroked us with feathers at a nearby tomb; he had also invested us with scented turbans of green gauze. But here the pampering was replaced by a stricter regime. Having dealt with his women, the greybeard motioned to us to bend over then, after lulling us with a few forehand tickles, whacked us backhand and so hard that the shafts of his feather fascicle clattered together. As he did so I heard him reciting some Qur'anic verses about 'the woeful scourge'.

When the session was over we all went out and sat by the silver zits. While Martin drew the flagellant sacristan, my mind went back to Khajuraho, to Matanga-baba and his distribution of blessings with sharp blows of a palm-frond besom. Perhaps the feather duster was an Islamic equivalent, or improvement. Or was it just the case that elderly Indian gentlemen develop a taste for flogging?

These idle speculations led to no conclusion. Besides, the excitements of Khuldabad were not over. Outside the sanctuary, a brass band announced the arrival of a wedding party. I went on to the street for a look, and was induced to skip, solo, around an enormous floral tribute composed of jasmine, roses and tinsel – which, I realized on my third circuit, was the bridegroom.

*

'Do you know the significance of the number 786?' asked Dr Zayne, a few miles down the road in Aurangabad.

As it happened, I did. At first, seeing it written in Indian numerals on everything from shops to sheep, I'd been mystified. Then someone told me it was the sum of *bismi 'ullah al-rahman al-rahim*, 'In the name of God, the Compassionate, the Merciful', using the *abjad* reckoning in which every Arabic letter has a numerical value. Indian Muslims therefore regard 786 as supremely auspicious. A car licence plate containing it is worth a nabob's ransom.

'Well,' the doctor continued, 'multiply by 10. Now, 7,860 seconds equals 131 minutes, or 2 hours and 11 minutes. And –' he paused, portentously '– 2 hours and 11 minutes after sunset is the precise moment at which al-Qiyamah al-Sughra, the Lesser Resurrection, will occur! Am I right?'

'You are most *certainly* right,' piped Mr Kazi, Dr Zayne's small and birdlike companion.

The doctor wanted confirmation from me, too. 'I'll take your word for it . . . . But on which day?'

'Ah . . .' said Dr Zayne. He had no lower teeth, and a pronounced and mobile chin that almost met the tip of his nose when it flapped shut, as it did now. Martin later compared him to a glove-puppet. But in his cream suit, cream, green and pink tie and immaculately Brylcreemed hair, he belonged rather to Menton or Palm Beach than to the Sooty and Sweep Show. 'On which *day* . . . Of that we are not certain.'

Dr Zayne Lukmani, numerologist and Nostradamus *de nos jours*, was also according to his card a specialist in mental and chronic diseases. But the walls of his clinic, otherwise the Divine Academy (41), bespoke other interests too: there were Chishti saints and charm squares, as in Sabirah's green room in Ujjain; also, interspersed with these and with advertisements for Rex's Remedies and several acupuncture charts, there were Arabic and Persian exhortations of a Shi'ite nature, a Happy Diwali poster and a Ganesh calendar, and a recurring device, familiar yet unplaceable –

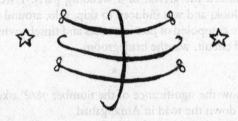

It was a surprising mixture. But, unlike the idol in the *qiblah* at Dawlatabad, it didn't shock: the fusion, or confusion, was a happy one. Clearly Dr Zayne, like Dewan, was into the joy of sects. Perhaps he was even a full-blown syncretist, a credenda-bender.

While I browsed this divine curiosity shop, Martin enthused to its proprietor about the famous cave-temple sculptures of Ellora. They too were a mixture – Buddhist, Jain, Hindu – and they were right next door to Khuldabad. I had missed them, confined to quarters by the dictatorial diary, and was now regretting it. 'You must go and have a look,' Martin had told me, excitedly. 'They're better than Michelangelo. They really knock him off his bloody pedestal. He'd have done his nut if he'd seen them!' But I didn't; we had to press on to the magnificent tomb of Muhammad Shah's tooth. I had allowed a brief stop here in Aurangabad to look for a post office; or it would have been brief had Dewan, with his unerring nose for interesting people, not asked for directions from Dr Zayne.

'By the way,' I asked the doctor, 'what exactly is the Lesser

Resurrection?' If I was going to be steeling myself for it on a daily basis, 2 hours and 11 minutes after sunset, I wanted some idea of what I was in for.

'It is that which precedes the Greater Resurrection,' he replied, going on to explain the difference between the two events according to Baha'i doctrine – which, on balance, was what he seemed to incline to. It was then that I remembered what that curious loopy pictogram was and where I'd seen it: it was a Baha'i device, and it appeared in that most fascinating of nineteenth-century travel books, E.G. Browne's *A Year Amongst the Persians*. I mentioned this to Dr Zayne. '*Browne*,' he said, nose and chin nearly meeting again. 'Browne was a Babi. The Babis are very . . . *militant*. Am I right?'

'You are *absolutely* right,' chirped Mr Kazi.

For a time we spoke of Babis and Shaykhis, then of acupuncture and moxibustion – Dr Zayne's comments invariably earning the vigorous endorsement of Mr Kazi, whose sole function, like that of the stooge in a Socratic dialogue, was to agree. But the doctor's overriding passion was for numbers. ' . . . And do you know where the Muslims got the science of numerology from? From the *Jews*! From the *cabbala*! Am I right?'

There was an unnerving silence, until Mr Kazi, who had been involved in a struggle with a pocket handkerchief, got his line out.

'Very good. Let us return to 786, the number of the *basmalah* . . .' The sum of 7+8+6, Dr Zayne pointed out, was 21. Apparently, years that gave the same total – 1947 (Independence in India) and 1956 (the Suez Crisis), for example – always witnessed momentous events. Such a date would not now occur again until 2199, which suggested two centuries of boring history to come.

'Phew,' I said.

'Indeed. But now is the time for the nitty-gritty. Please write your name in block capitals.' I did so. My cabbalistical total was 59; 5+9 = 14, and 1+4 = 5. 'Anything with 5 is very lucky indeed. And you have it *twice!*' An almanac was consulted: the prognostications were promising. 'But', said the doctor, 'you never think about the future.'

'I find it comes quickly enough anyway.'

'That may be so. But at least you should think more about the immediate future, about today. "Pass therefore not today in vain, / For it shall never come again." And', he looked at me with great concern, 'gentleman, please abstain from sex.'

For a few moments I did my own impression of a glove-puppet, one that had lost its voice. Eventually, I managed to protest that I led a sober life, one that revolved around books, IB and other friends. 'Yes; but I see that you are *thinking* about sex too much. Sex is God-given, and you must direct it into the correct *channels*. Am I right?'

'You are one *hundred* per cent right!' chirruped Mr Kazi, looking particularly beady-eyed.

My session on the dissecting slab was over. I got down, feeling flayed, and my place was taken – very unwillingly – by Martin. His number was 40. He had been successful in his youth, was still successful; had enjoyed many pleasures. 'But . . .' Martin braced himself for the personalized ghastly revelation, 'you are inclined to be quarrelsome. And in your middle and old age you will suffer. *Like a dog*.'

It was said with enormous vehemence. The seconds crept by; no one spoke.

'You have two options,' the doctor continued. 'You could spell your first name M-*double*-a-r-t-i-n. This would produce a highly fortuitous 41, as is the case with my Divine Academy. Or you could simply use your surname on its own.'

'But that's what I do anyway!' Martin cried, looking like a man who'd escaped the gallows. 'I always sign my paintings "Yeoman"!' There was a general sigh of relief.

This seemed an appropriate note on which to resume our journey to the Tooth Tomb. But for some time more the doctor expatiated on the Number of the Basmalah, the Number of the Beast and, above all, on his particular numeral obsession, 5. (I have since sent him a copy of the fifth and climactic chapter of *The Garden of Cyrus*, the master-work of that even more illustrious Browne, Sir Thomas. It is all there: the mystical mathematics, the relentless quincunxes; Abram's addition of the fifth Hebrew letter, *he*, to his name to make it total 5; Scaliger's derivation of the Latin for 'five' from the Greek for 'four and one' – this explained in my edition, eerily, in footnote number 41. It is pleasing to introduce two pentomanes, to enlarge, I hope, the circle of Browne studies.)

We finally left the Divine Academy (41) covered in the doctor's embraces and with prayers both Islamic and Baha'i, and armed with his pessoptimistic advice: Hope for the best, prepare for the worst.

*

Although neither Dr Zayne nor Mr Kazi knew of Muhammad Shah's dental edifice, another chance dropper-in at the Academy, a prominent local historian, had confirmed that it was extant. He had seen it from a distance, crowning a majestic hill overlooking the Bendsura River. Such a situation added to the allure of the monument; we were hoping for the best. But hope dissipated in the long dull plain beyond Aurangabad, in which the only objects of remark were a number of brick kilns that reeked of old socks and jock-straps. The

Godavari River, an inviting blue stripe on the map, was an almost waterless smear. Beyond it the plain was, if anything, flatter and duller. Even Martin couldn't magic anything from the tedium. I remembered our Delhi friends: *Where? . . . Why?*

Not long before Bid the land condescended to undulate slightly. Our hopes rose; then fell, for the sword-stick capital of India was clearly all it was cracked up not to be. It was a village trying to be a city, with the advantages of neither and the drawbacks of both. 'I'm sure it'll be character-forming,' I said as we entered a mini-miasma of diesel fumes.

'My character's already formed,' Martin replied, through clenched teeth.

We checked into the best hotel in town. It was a long process. 'I think we're the first tourists in Bid,' I whispered.

Eventually Dewan handed us our passports. 'Hotel manager saying you are first tourists in Bid!' he said, proudly.

To be fair, Bid was improved by the morning light. And we found the tomb of Muhammad Shah's tooth with surprising ease. There it was: a whitewashed cupola on the summit of a dome-shaped hill. Together, hill and tomb had something of the look of a Buddhist stupa – rather appropriate, I thought, recalling that one of Gautama's blessed gnashers had been similarly enshrined. Beneath the hill was a lake formed by a dam across the Bendsura River, a tributary of the Godavari. The words BENDSURA PROJECT, written on the hill in gigantic letters, were somewhat unsultanic. But Muhammad Shah had chosen well, for nothing could have detracted from the ensemble of tomb and hill. It was, as Professor Husain wrote, magnificent.

We left the car, crossed the dry river bed and began the ascent of the hill. I'm not as unfit as I thought, I reflected, for I was on the flattened summit in no time. Must be the adrenalin. Martin and Dewan soon joined me, and we admired the view: the lake to the south, to the east a cultivated plain; to the west a range of hills, similar in altitude to ours but none so geometrically perfect, with a lone figure in saffron descending a track – the figure magnified, it seemed, by the clarity of light; Bid in its micro-climate of smog to the north. We then inspected a low masonry platform, topped by some tatty green flags and by a score or so of green glass bangles. The ground all about was strewn with broken bits of coconut shell. 'Muslim peoples having no sons or wanting good salary or *bakhshish*, breaking the coconuts,' Dewan explained. 'Same like Hindu peoples at temples.' I was surprised. I knew of the Hindu practice of nut-sacrifice; but it was so overtly pagan, the nuts with their hair and eyes standing in for human heads, that I'd have expected Muslims to be coconut-shy. Besides, why here?

We now approached the tomb itself. It was a domed, inward-sloping cube with the same profile as our first Tughluqid monument, the Red Tomb in Delhi. The walls were topped by equally period scutiform crenellations. The edifice was in a good state of repair, the whitewash fairly fresh, although the dome was missing its finial. Beside the doorway stood a tree with a spindly trunk . . .

Something extraordinary happened. It must be the sun, I thought . . . a softening of the brain. I looked from the tomb to Martin. Perhaps our dubious 'whisky' of the night before had contained some delayed-action hallucinogen, for he had a strange expression on his face – one, like mine, of confusion and disbelief: Dewan, standing by the door of the tomb, had turned into a giant.

On second thoughts, the world had shrunk.

Several oscillations on – enormous, momentary swings – the pendulum of perception came to a sudden halt at the only sane conclusion: that the magnificent Maqbara-ye Dandan-e Muhammad Shah Tughluq was about the size of a Wendy house. Without Dewan, there had been nothing to give the building scale. Only now, with the top of its doorway not quite level with his crotch, did its dimensions become apparent. Dewan went down on all fours and squeezed through the door.

Martin was laughing. 'Is this it? I thought you said it was "magnificent". Must have been one of his milk teeth. We've come a bloody long way . . .' Mumbling excuses – it wasn't my fault, I'd read about it in a book, size wasn't everything, it was perfectly formed – I walked the remarkably short distance to the tomb and started measuring. The height of the door was a fraction over two feet, that of the roof about six. The apex of the dome soared another three or four feet above. (Martin drew me as I carried out my survey, entitling the result – rather cruelly, I thought – the Tooth Fairy.)

Dewan emerged arse-first and covered in cobwebs. I took his place, feeling like Alice on 'Eat Me' pills. The interior was kennel-sized; but all the features of a grand and venerated Islamic tomb were there – a mihrab showing the *qiblah* of Mecca, a selection of incense burners, a cenotaph covered in layers of green palls. I lifted these, disturbing several leggy spiders and a slim brown reptile – a lizard, I think, but it was too fast to tell. The seventh and final pall bore the legend 'Tip-Tip 100% Polyester Texturised Filament'. Otherwise the Toy Town cenotaph was devoid of inscriptions, as was the entire building. I tucked up the sultan's tooth and extracted myself, arsy-versy, through the door.

Viewing the tomb again from a few yards off, the eye was trumped once more: without scale, the building might have been huge. I recalled how IB's pre-perspective vision had distorted minarets and elephants. Here, it was we who had been deceived – not just by misleading reports but also by our own post-trecento way of seeing. The hill was a very relative *jabal* indeed, a mere pimple; and yet it managed to create an illusion of distance, an expectation of mass. And, in relation to it, the building *was* big. In seeing an enormous tomb we were both relatively right and absolutely wrong.

So why, I wondered, did Muhammad Shah build this miniature

folie de grandeur? After the Hall of a Thousand Columns and the great wall of Delhi, it was utter bathos. But then, where were hall and wall now? This had survived intact. Seven hundred miles from his capital, his empire collapsing about him, the sultan might well have concluded that the rest of his mortal self was heading for defeat and an unmarked grave. At least posterity could stand here and mourn – or curse – a partial Muhammad Shah ibn Tughluq, Master of the World.

Dewan interrupted my thoughts. 'Mr Tim, the tree by the door is *neem*. Very suitable.' I asked why. '*Neem* sticks very good for *dant*. Every morning Indians taking them and colgating tooths!' We all laughed. Our farewell gesture to the tomb was unintentionally suitable too. Inside, I had spotted some palm-frond brooms. I now crawled in again, passed a couple out, and in less than a minute we swept the interior and the tiny forecourt clean. It was Martin who realized we'd just brushed the sultan's tooth.

There was one last surprise. At the bottom of the knoll we met a local man walking along the track with a dog and a goat, and fell into conversation. The tomb was venerated not only by Muslims, he said, but also by Hindus. Lots of people of both faiths took coconuts up the hill to Dargah Pir Baba.

I stared at Dewan. 'To *what*?'

The Shrine of the Holy Father. That was what they called it, the man explained; but of course they were only village people and they didn't know history.

IB's Caveman had become 'Holy Old Grandad', his Maldivian melon farmer of Dhar 'Saint Sacrifice-King'. And Muhammad Shah's rotten tooth had gained a courtesy title worthy of the Pope of Rome. I pointed out to Dewan that Muhammad Shah was no holy man – not by the most elastic stretch of the very wildest imagination.

'But', he replied, 'he is last-600-years-old man. So *altogether* holy man.' Time, then, sanctifies a tooth; even sanctifies a tyrant.

We turned our backs on him and headed for the coast.

Malabar

From the Gulf of Cambay the diplomatic party sailed via present-day Goa down to Calicut in Kerala, the coastal state roughly coterminous with the Malabar of IB's time. The Hindu principalities of Malabar lay beyond the rule of Muhammad Shah but enjoyed friendly relations with their powerful neighbour. Calicut and its ruler, the Zamorin (IB's 'al-Samari'), were especially welcoming to official visitors from Delhi, and no less so to the many merchants who visited the port from around the Indian Ocean. IB and his companions stayed there for three months as the Zamorin's guests before embarking, probably in April 1342, on a junk bound for China.

At this point disaster struck in the shape of a violent storm. IB, who by good fortune was ashore when the storm hit, survived. But he was now alone; for a year and a half he wandered the coast between Kollam, in the far south of Malabar, and Goa. His Indian career was finished, and he was once again as hard up as he had been when he left Tangier nearly twenty years before.

Like Mountains on the Sea

'Scarcely any change in India, since the days of our travellers, is more remarkable than the decay of the numerous ports, flourishing with foreign as well as domestic trade, which then lined the shores of the country. The commencement of this decay appears to date nearly from the arrival of the Portuguese.'

Sir Henry Yule, *Cathay and the Way Thither*

AT FIRST SIGHT, Mangalore spoke with the same grim pungency as Delhi. 'May The Twin Towers Of Your Prosperity Remain Standing For Ever!' exclaimed a roadside hoarding in the outskirts. 'Happy New Year!' (With the recent attack on New York, Dr Zayne's two tedious centuries had got off to an all too interesting start.) But the wish came from far away, from the Bank of Baroda in Gujarat. The authentic voices of Mangalore were the riffle of wind in the palms and the ripple of waves on the quay. Between them, an after-thought, was a laid-back, low-rise town, a city of cottages called 'Jenifer', 'Lakshadweep' and other such whimsies. Even the crows and auto-rickshaws seemed muted.

Following our journey down through Hindustan to the Deccan, the inescapable demands on a society portraitist – society in its broad sense, from bishops to strippers – had called Martin back to England; I'd returned to Yemen to add a new *qat*-chewing eyrie to my house and to digest our first, rich Indian course. We had agreed to regroup in Mangalore, each travelling to that tantalizing destination by aeroplane. We would take the Malabar Express south, deep into Kerala, then turn about and head north, non-express, by boat and Ambassador, making for Gujarat. There, in the ancient port of Cambay, we would visit the tomb of 'the King of the Merchants', a local magnate who makes a brief appearance in the *Travels*. It was the only Battutian monument I knew for certain to be extant in this entire stretch. The rest was a thousand miles of possibilities.

We were taking a liberty with IB's route; in fact, reversing it. Leaving Dawlatabad and its giant rats, he had proceeded uneventfully to Gujarat and taken ship. The ambassadorial party sailed direct to Goa then port-hopped down to Calicut, where they re-embarked on a Chinese junk for the long voyage east. At this point calamity struck. It was the very finest of all IB's Indian messes, a Candidesque reversal of fortune that deprived him of an itinerary – of everything, in fact, short of his life and his love of travel. The disaster that altered our plans was negligible in comparison, but it too had meant a rejigging of routes. Of all the possibilities of those thousand miles, the one I was most eager to explore was an island south of Goa. IB's strangest meetings often seemed to happen on islands, and Anjidiv was the setting for the very strangest of them all. It was also, I had discovered, being turned into the Indian Navy's most important and impenetrable base on the Arabian Sea.

'Absolutely no problem,' said a well-connected friend in Delhi. 'Just bang off a letter to the Chief of Naval Intelligence and I'll make sure he gets it pronto. It may take a few weeks for him to do the needful, of course. I think you know the score.'

I thought I did too. The only thing was to put those ominous-sounding few weeks to profitable use in the creeks and pepper-groves of Malabar.

*

As the airport taxi drew up by our rendezvous, the unpalatial Navaratna Palace Hotel, a dreadful thought occurred: what if Martin had booked himself not to Mangalore but to Bangalore? I'd only just escaped that mix-up myself. Mangalore wasn't high on the list of international airline destinations, particularly if like Martin you were buying your ticket in Dorset; indeed I doubted whether either place featured in the consciousness of Shaftesbury travel agents. Martin, unlike me, was not a compulsive checker of travel documents. Besides, it was the season of colds in England. I could picture a nasal block-up, a consonantal cock-up, and my friend wandering the streets of the state capital 200 miles away, easel in hand, searching for a non-existent Navaratna Palace.

'I think you may have a Mr Yeoman staying,' I said to the receptionist, doubtfully. He looked puzzled. 'A British guest?'

'There is only one. Mr . . .' he peered at the register '. . . Martin.'

Stanley and Livingstone met with less warmth, and with hardly more relief.

Martin, never a light traveller, had brought all his sketchbooks and pastel albums from the year before. We sat on a bed and looked through them – at the 'notes', controlled scribbles that caught the tilt of a turban, the turn of a bullock's horn, the twist of a shawl; at pastels, shadowed and shimmering, done in the *longueurs* of Delhi, at langur-haunted Orchha, by the lingam-lake of Barwa; portraits, of Matanga-baba, stoned, of Titoo with his Ganesh eyes; landscapes, of the infernal plain of Dawlatabad, the magical-ordinary ploughman of Dhar, detailed images ('explained', Martin called them) labelled with private colours that no dictionary contained; the Tooth Fairy – a whole stream of moments, not discrete, particular, but confluent, flooding now across the gap of months until it seemed as if there'd been no interruption in our journey.

Like Martin, I was carrying a portfolio of images that ranged from scribbled notes to detailed explanations, but recorded in the cruder medium of words. Unlike him, I had seen my images second-hand, or second-eye. I was not artist but picturer-restorer, and I had to deal with a whole history of techniques from pre-perspective minarets and miniaturist elephants via the dreamlike, Samuel Palmeresque landscape of the Doab to the frightening photorealism of Ambika-Jhambika. With the exception of the last, each image had suffered more or less from the ravages of time and from the distortions of IB's memory. Or more then less: for it seemed that as we'd moved away from Delhi, from those shattered, shat-upon fragments of the Thousand-Column Hall, the clarity increased; as if we'd passed down a long gallery that began deep in decay and gloom, dominated by that great dark portrait of Muhammad Shah, and ended in bright and terrible visibility.

I also carried another set of images: a pebble on a brick, a secret semaphore of sculpted limbs in Khajuraho, Dewan worshipping a burnt widow. All as simple and transparent as water if you only follow the thread. I hadn't even found the beginning of the thread. No long gallery here; only a labyrinth, increasing in obscurity. It would all be perfectly clear, al-Biruni wrote, if there were more connection. But I hadn't made the connection, and at Ambika-Jhambika the gap had become an abyss.

*

Our ticket for the Malabar Express was an impressive document that even stated our ages – '41 NV, 49 NV'; non-vintage, we assumed. The train, equally impressively, pulled out on the dot of 5.50 p.m. 'Never, ever privatize the railways,' I said to the guard.

The only other passenger in our compartment was a Tamil coconut consultant bound for Trivandrum. Coals and Newcastle came to mind. Kerala, roughly the old Malabar, is the Coconut State. Our companion explained his mission. In Tamil Nadu the yield was 150 n.p.p.p.a. (nuts per palm per annum), in Kerala currently only 80 n.p.p.p.a. owing to a beetle-borne disease. A council of insecticidal war was to be held at the Coconut Research Station, where a bunch of like-minded experts hung out. 'Sounds like a tough one,' I said; then, knowing I would probably never bump into a coconut consultant again, I tried out IB's account of the coco-palm's origin on him. To put it in a nutshell, the first specimen sprouted from a date-stone planted in a severed human head. The story proved to be a conversation-damper. I went to join Martin, who was hanging out of the open door between carriages.

'He probably thinks you're a nutter,' he said when I reported the exchange. Behind him, the sun collided with the Arabian Sea, disgorging a slick of fire.

Martin went to get a sketchbook. 'Express' is a relative term, and from this one he could take notes in the dying light. Not for the first time, I envied him his directness of observation. And IB his. The traveller's Malabar album is as slim as the land itself – twenty pages on a strip of land squeezed between the Western Ghats and the sea – and as dense with detail and people: manners and customs, Muslim merchants and Hindu rulers, a string of seaside statelets with strange names. The prospect of exploring all this, even at a remove of centuries, was exciting; or it would have been, had I not read Yule's comments on the decay of the Malabar ports. His words were echoed by others – 'destroyed', 'changed beyond recognition', 'unidentifiable', 'lost'. I shut them out of my mind and tried to look at the present.

6.35 p.m. The sea, through bent bars of palm-trunks, is matt silver turning to lead. The tops of the palms are bronzed. 'It's like a lake,' Martin says, 'it's so calm.' A fragment of the call to prayer, from somewhere over by the shore. For a moment, Arabia could be just behind the horizon.

It used to be; and China, Africa, the world. But I knew that the frail spontaneous tissue of traffic that interwove Mangalore with Mecca and Malacca, Calicut with Cairo and Canton, was torn apart 500 years ago. That over the first decades of the sixteenth century the Malabar IB knew changed as irrevocably as did the Gulf in the latter years of the twentieth. That what started with round-shot from the Lisbon arsenal continues with the soft but deadly burger bun.

6.45 p.m. Down down into the downy tropical depth, chasing the palmy, balmy night towards its equinox. The day gutters away, the picture fades; lamps flicker to life from an undergrowth of villas beneath the palms, some scarcely bigger than bathing huts or potting sheds. We're passing through a vast inhabited garden.

This, at least, hadn't changed. 'Not a patch of ground, be it as small as a span in breadth, is left uncultivated,' IB wrote. 'Every man has his own separate palm-grove with his house in the middle . . . And this continues for a journey of two months.' It gave a pleasing impression of continuity. It was not enough. I wanted to see the things IB had seen. I wanted detail, not generality – explained pictures. But we had turned a corner in the gallery, and impressions were the best I could hope for. The rest was abstract: palmline, shoreline, skyline, three flickering lines of colour.

6.55 p.m. And now not even that. Still, though, an afterglow, a bloom on grape-black clouds. Palm trunks show black against house lights, a hall of a thousand thousand vegetable columns.

*

In Kollam it wasn't only the wind and the waves that riffled and rippled. The people did too. After the parade-ground harangue of Hindi, everyone here seemed to be talking very rapidly in scat. Politically we were in a different state; linguistically we seemed to have arrived on another planet.

The torrent of Malayalam syllables continued in the library of Mr Cheriyil Sukumuran Nair, an Ayurvedic practitioner who ran the Kerala History Research Centre. He was discussing IB's account of Kollam with a fellow-historian, Mr Jonakapuram Thaha Kutty. (The first element of their names came, in Kerala fashion, from their place of birth. I quite liked the idea of being 'Mr Bristol Tim Mackintosh-Smith': it had a solid, dependable ring to it.) I enjoyed letting the alien sounds flow over me, a phonemic flood of liquids and palatals in which the occasional log of an identifiable word flashed past – 'sultan' . . . 'Ibn Battutah' . . . 'qadi'.

IB's 'Kawlam', they agreed – now back in the calmer waters of English – was a better reflection of their city's name than the 'Quilon' of the Portuguese and British. But they ticked him off for his 'sultan of Kawlam, who is an infidel called Tirawari'. 'It is not strictly a name,' said Mr Kutty. 'It is rather a dynastic title meaning holy or respected lord.'

'And his spelling is not one hundred per cent,' added Mr Nair. He wrote the title in Malayalam script, then Latin: 'Tirawaḍi'. In defence of IB I said that to me, too, that dotted *d* sounded almost indistinguishable from the *r*. Mr Nair admitted that Dravidian consonants were tricky for foreigners. 'Malayalam', he said, 'has fifty-six alphabets.' I supposed he meant 'characters'; even so it seemed a little on the short side.

There were still Tirawaris at large, in the shape of the former royal family of Travancore. The names of IB's Muslim hosts in Kollam, however, meant nothing to the two historians. 'In some ways,' said Mr Nair, 'in its language and its customs for example, Kerala is an island separated from the rest of India by hills. But it is joined to the rest of the world by the sea. People, and not only Muslims, have come from across the globe, married and settled down here. They have natural feelings for getting a lady; this is a biological necessity.'

I smiled.

'There is a ninth-century copper-plate grant,' Mr Kutty continued quickly, perhaps sensing that the conversation might lose its gravity, 'made by the Hindu ruler to a Syrian Christian church here in Kollam. It is witnessed by Muslims and Jews, in both the Arabic and Hebrew scripts.' Even if the Jews had gone, there were still plenty of Muslims in Kollam – Mappillas, as they are called in Kerala; but from what the two gentlemen told me, any descendants of IB's Kollam acquaintances – assuming they had submitted to biological necessity – would have been lost long ago in a patronymic melting-pot of Kuttys, Koyas and other local Muslim surnames.

Having failed on genetic survivals from fourteenth-century Islamic Kollam, I asked about concrete ones. Mr Nair's response confirmed my fears: there was nothing left. But, following another rippling exchange, Mr Kutty took me to the Friday mosque of his native Jonakapuram, the old Muslim quarter on the seashore. The mosque was undeniably concrete, but in the wrong sense: it was a recent cement structure in the Legoland-Islamic taste. But Mr Kutty steered me to a smaller building nearby. It had a façade of pierced breeze-blocks and resembled an elaborate bus shelter. 'This is the tangled tomb,' Mr Kutty said; or that is what I thought he said. It was, in fact, the *tangal's* tomb – *tangal* being the Malayalam title for a descendant of the Prophet. 'It is the last resting-place of Bappachi Tangal,' he went on. Bappachi didn't sound a particularly Islamic name. Equally puzzling was a plate of curry and rice that someone had left on the threshold. Then I remembered Khuldabad, and asked if there was to be a wedding. After disentangling our cross-purposes, Mr Kutty told me that the food belonged to Bappachi's cats. On cue, a strapping tabby emerged and did a slow slalom through our legs.

Inside were more cats, mostly of the tabby race.* There was also an old man, the muezzin of the mosque, reciting the Qur'an by Bappachi's cenotaph. At the end of a chapter, Mr Kutty spoke to him. The muezzin bobbed down behind the cenotaph. I heard an annoyed miaow, then a harsh grating sound – and the muezzin reappeared with a stone slab. This he set down in front of me. He then produced another slab and slid it on top of the first – scrunch! I frowned at the freshly scarred surface of the stone and opened my mouth to remonstrate . . .

My mouth remained open while my brain exploded in several directions at once: South Arabia; South Kensington; Gujarat. In the first of these, four years earlier, I had tried to visit an old graveyard to see the tomb of IB's host. The place was out of bounds in the Sultan of Oman's back garden; to make up for the disappointment, I had found the tombstone in the Victoria and Albert Museum. It had been carved, however, not in Arabia but in Gujarat. The Gujarati tomb of IB's 'King of the Merchants' – that sole Battutian monument I knew to exist on the whole west coast of India – had a gravestone of precisely the same appearance. And now, in front of me, were two large fragments of identical design: hanging lamps in cusped niches, the niches separated by pagoda-like columns, the row of columns and niches ending in a palm tree bearing a baggy bunch of dates. Comparing my sketch now with the V&A photographs, I see that the Arabic script running along the top of the Kollam stones is spindlier than that of the Dhofar examples, the Kollam dates plumper and riper. But if not by the same hand or hands, then the stones are from

---

* Not an inappropriate breed. One Attab, a scion of the early Umayyad dynasty of caliphs and thus a distant collateral of the *tangal's*, gave his name to a quarter of Baghdad, which gave its name to a type of stripey cloth woven there – *attabi*, the English 'tabby', which gave its name to the cat.

the same workshop – the workshop that, it seems, had cornered the market in high-class Islamic monumental masonry from South Arabia to South India. (Islamic; but according to my learned friend Venetia Porter the design derives in part from local Hindu styles in Gujarat, which derive in part from Hellenistic prototypes, which derive . . . But that, as they say, is another story.)

I collected my scattered brains, sat down by the stones and tried to make out the inscription. The period looked absolutely right. Could the characters contain the name of one of IB's Kollam contacts? Perhaps it would disclose the identity of that unIslamic-sounding 'Bappachi'. The words began to make sense: 'Allah and His Prophet . . . and Allah is King of heaven and earth . . .' The youngest of Bappachi's cats, a tiny gummy-eyed kitten, came and sat in my lap. '. . . He forgives whom He wishes and punishes whom He wishes . . .' Qur'anic verses; no names. I finished transcribing and asked the questions I would have asked before, but for my temporary brainburst: Where did the stones come from? From the original tomb of Bappachi?

Mr Kutty smiled. 'No. Bappachi Tangal is not very old. Perhaps 200 years. The stones come from a mosque, and the mosque is under the sea.' I stared at him. 'The sea has invaded on the land, perhaps for a distance of two miles. Some fishermen pulled the stones up in their nets.' I'd heard of fishermen catching jinns in bottles; but mosques? With soft advice against further damaging the stones, we took our leave of the muezzin and of Bappachi and his cats, and walked down to the beach. I looked out over the sea and wondered if they ever heard ghostly calls to prayer, burbling up from beneath the waves.

Kerala may be joined by the sea to Gujarat, Arabia and London SW7 but the sea, as I had just learned, has extracted its price. Not only did it bring the Portuguese; it has also taken land away, rearranging the coastline like a child playing in a sand-pit. In his office, beneath a plaster bust of the last Maharaja of Travancore,* Mr Nair told me about the legend of Parasurama. An avatar of Vishnu, he implemented a miraculous land consolidation project, stamping gold dust into the Kerala coastline to reclaim it from the waves. Since then a persistent current, sweeping clockwise around the Indian Ocean from Madagascar, has undone some of Parasurama's work; in addition

---

* The descendant of IB's Tirawari via a long line of nephews. As the traveller noted, 'In these lands sovereignty passes to the son of the sultan's sister, not to his own offspring.'

the occasional snappish monsoon had caused the disappearance of some ports and the formation of entirely new ones. Cochin for example, now the most important harbour of Kerala, was born in a violent storm in 1341, a year or so before IB's visit. All fascinating stuff; but I was beginning to fear that much of the traveller's Malabar had gone the way of Atlantis; that I would find nothing but drowned ports, a coast of a dozen Kollams.

One part of IB's Malabar, however, could be seen through my host's window. Mr Nair's Ayurvedic physic garden contained the complete Battutian botanica of Malabar: brazil-wood – its grey and thorny bark protecting a purple heart, source of a valuable dye – and cinnamon ('They burn them for fuel,' wrote IB of these two trees, astounded at the prodigality); jack-fruit, bananas and colocasia; coco-palms, of course, and delicate areca palms; and, spiralling up the latter in weedy helices punctuated by heart-shaped leaves, the insignificant plant that had excited more lust than all the diamonds of Golconda: pepper. I had to look hard to see the sprigs of miniature fruit, hidden in leaf-shadows. *Piper nigrum* was such a diffident creature that it was difficult to believe it had been the most important commodity of Old World intercontinental trade; that it had launched navies, and empires – not least its own, a culinary colonialism that stretches from

Apicius to Delia Smith, from the grandest banquet to the greasiest spoon. How could they ever pick enough of those fiddly little bunches to fill the untold millions of pepper-pots? Malabar must be full of people picking pecks of *Piper*, but we never saw them.

Some of the early geographers credited the pepper plant with unusual properties. Ibn Khurradadhbih, for example, said that its leaves acted as miniature umbrellas that automatically opened over the pepper clusters in time of rain. But for IB the extraordinary thing about Malabar pepper was its quantity: 'I have seen it, in the city of Calicut, being measured by the bushel, like sorghum in our country!' For a native of the western edge of the world, pepper was something to be counted by the grain.

Pepper and Malabar were only part of the Indian Ocean trade. There were other spices, and textiles galore. Timber, especially teak, was a major commodity exported not only from India but also from further east. One of the oldest surviving mosque-pulpits in the world is the ninth-century one at Qayrawan in Tunisia: its prefabricated panels were probably carved in Iraq, but the timber had come all the way from Java. The ocean and its hinterland were a huge warehouse of trade goods. Not long after the Qayrawan pulpit was installed, al-Mas'udi listed some of the products of the region: 'In the depths of its seas are pearls, in its mountains mines of gemstones, gold, silver, lead and tin; from the jaws of its beasts comes ivory, and from its forests ebony, bamboos and rattans, brazil-wood, teak and aloes-wood; from those lands come camphor, coconuts, cloves and sandal-wood, and all the other aromatics, perfumes and spices; thence too come parrots white and green and peacocks great and small, some the size of ostriches; and in the Indies the civet cat is as common as the puss-cat in the lands of Islam.' All through this vast terraqueous treasure-house and beyond, merchants plied the land- and sea-roads unconstrained. ' "I shall take Persian sulphur to China," ' a trader of Kish in the Arabian Gulf mused to the poet Sa'di, ' "then Chinese porcelain to Byzantium, Byzantine brocade to India, Indian steel to Aleppo, mirrors of Aleppo to Yemen, striped cloth of Yemen to Persia . . ." He continued for some time rambling in this strain until he had not the power to utter more.' That is Free Trade for you, not the WTO.

It isn't hard to find reminders of that old organic commerce: a party of lady suitcase-merchants from my adoptive home of San'a, for instance, who had taken frankincense and hyrax dung (dried, for medicinal use) to Bombay and were heading back laden with brocades; a knife seen in the San'a *suq*, its blade made in Solingen and counter-stamped in Arabic by a Saudi trader whose ancestors hailed from Kashgar in Chinese Turkestan, its hilt the work of a Jewish Yemeni silversmith, hammered and filigreed from Austro-Hungarian thalers minted in Bombay or Birmingham – eight inches that took in most of Eurasia and all the three revealed faiths; those grubby jobbing dhows on the Sharjah quay. Not everything and everyone can be container-shipped, globally positioned and remotely controlled. But golden roads and quinquiremes have had their day.

It was all very well, this musing on fag-ends of transoceanic traffic, of a submarine mosque. As for more substantial, perhaps visitable, survivals from IB's Malabar chapter – his hilltop settlement of Jews, his revered mosque of Budfattan, his miraculous tree of Dahfattan . . . Sunk without trace, if the notes to Mr Nair's Malayalam version of the chapter were to be believed. It was strange, listening to the passages he read aloud, to hear IB's lumpish Arabic liquefied into that tumbling phonemic stream; strange to think that here, as in the *zamindar*'s house in the Doab a year before and far to the north, the traveller's tales had come home. But what was left of them now, except words?

*

For a start, lunch. IB, staying further up the coast with the Sultan of Honavar, began the meal with a ladleful of rice drizzled with ghee and surrounded by little mounds of lemon and mango chutney, green ginger, and vegetables cooked in more ghee. 'One first eats a mouthful of the rice, and then a little of one of the side-dishes to follow,' he explained to his couscous-eating countrymen. Another ladleful of rice, this time accompanied by a fowl; more rice, with another species of fowl; ditto, with fish, as the last course. The side-dishes too were constantly replenished.

As befitted the Sultan of Delhi's envoy to the Emperor of China, IB got the *menu dégustation*. But although we had lentils instead of fowl, in all other respects the food was identical: rice, a ladleful at a time, surrounded by lemon pickle, ginger, vegetables in ghee; a final course of fish. Tamarind and coconut were ingredients that seem to have slipped IB's memory; another one, curry-leaf, probably evaded his vocabulary. Other than these forgivable omissions on his part – and the addition on ours of a post-Columbian pineapple – it was, if not the visitable, then the edible past.

There were greater differences in presentation. Since IB was the guest of a sultan, lunch came on a brass *ṭālam*. ('Ar. *ṭulm*, a pastry board,' said Professor Beckingham in a footnote. No. It is pure South Indian, down to the emphatic *ṭ* which Arabic shares with the Dravidian tongues. A *ṭālam* is a large plate, a *ṭālī* a small one – and by extension the meal served on it.) On less exalted occasions IB made do, like us, with banana leaves: with their brilliant splodges of colour and flavour, they were palettes for the palate. The other difference was that the 'beautiful slave-girl draped in a robe of silk' who served IB was, in our case, a horny-handed boatman called Melvin.

IB's journey into southern Malabar was made by boat along the network of backwaters that join Calicut to Kollam. After the calamity that had taken place in the former city, his ten-day trip was mercifully disaster-free – except for his hired servant who, although a Muslim, 'would drink wine with the infidels when we went ashore and then would start to pick quarrels with me, which all added to my misery'. We decided to emulate IB. Our water-journey began with an exploratory moonlit paddle in a dugout around a finger of Kollam's Ashtamudi Lake – 'the Loch Lomond of Travancore State', as the Victorian tourist literature called it; 'a Whistler – just like being in a Whistler!' Martin whispered. We also emulated IB's servant, in his drinking if not his quarrelling, for our boatman plied us with toddy. Coconutty, *pétillant*, this was surely IB's 'wine'.

The following morning, we upgraded to a Kerala Department of Tourism houseboat for the backwater voyage north to Cochin. It had an outboard motor and a collection of erotic daubs, inspiration for the honeymooners who were its usual passengers. But in one respect it was the acme of authenticity: like most other craft we were to see on the backwaters, and like every indigenous vessel in the western Indian Ocean of IB's time, its hull was not nailed but sewn. Inside it the coir stitches joining the planks showed as a line of Xs; beneath these, more coconut fibre caulked the seams. The exterior was painted with a gloopy and authentically noisome varnish made from cashew oil and fish guts. I had only seen three sewn boats before – a pair of dinghy-sized craft rotting on an Arabian beach, and Tim Severin's *Sindbad*, now a roundabout adornment in suburban Muscat. I'd never dreamed I'd travel in one.

For Martin, the houseboat was a mobile studio more perfect even than Titoo's auto or Dewan's Ambassador. A mile or so out of Kollam, we moored by a Chinese net. These fishing-engines, their meshes hung from enormous, mantis-like wooden pivots fixed on the bank or in the shallows, are named after their supposed country of origin. (IB, who was here at the height of the trade with China, didn't mention this most notable feature of the Malabar backwaters – a fact which proves nothing, since he also omitted tea from his account of China.) The gimcrack geometry of the Chinese net occupied Martin for the rest of the day; after our Battutian lunch, I went ashore to wander in the palmeries.

Tracks of beaten red dust meandering through coconut groves; little open-fronted shelters with thatched roofs; those potting-shed houses, each in its own garden surrounded by fences of hurdles lashed together with coir twine – nothing much had changed since IB described it. Nor, I supposed, had the sounds: the giggle of a girl on a swing, the groan of a Chinese net, the flutter-whistle of an unseen kite; the constant seamless ripple of water, wind, words.

One aspect of Malabar which does seem to have changed is its prodigiously complex, all-pervading apartheid. 'If his customer is an infidel, he lets him drink from a cup,' IB wrote of the water-carriers who supplied those thatched rest-houses; 'but if he is a Muslim he pours the water into his hands.' Similar restrictions applied to eating and sleeping, and Muslims could only lodge with their coreligionists. (IB would have felt at home in the hamlet where I spent part of the afternoon, writing in the dust with a stick to test the children of the Anvarulislam Madrasa on their Arabic verbs.) This, however, was only the tip of a dizzy pyramid of taboos, a fuller picture of which emerged from my later reading in William Logan's indispensible *Malabar Manual* of 1887. Among upper-caste Malabar Hindus the concept of untouchability was elaborated to extraordinary lengths. Jonaka- and Nasrani-Mappillas, that is Muslims and Christians, polluted by direct touch; so did 'foreign' brahmans – those from outside Malabar. But certain castes polluted via the surrounding air. Fishermen for example were forbidden to approach within eight yards of a member of the higher castes; for the unfortunate Nayadi, or 'Dog-eaters', it was twenty-four yards on pain of death. This phobia of contact afflicted the dead as well as the living – corpses were both polluting and pollutable – and applied to inanimate objects: 'If a Muslim happens to eat from an infidel's vessels,' said IB, 'they break them or give them to the Muslims.' Broken pots were nothing beside the *faux pas* of Dr Hamilton of the East India Company. In 1707, he wrote, while visiting a raja's palace, 'I chanced to touch the Thatch with my Hat which polluted it so much that as soon as I went away he stript it of its covering.' As well as untouchability, there was a concept of unutterability: there were, for instance, fourteen different words for 'house' depending on the caste of the owner, and woe betide him who inadvertently referred to his *pura* as a *pushpottu*. No wonder Malabar ended up as one great scattered village with hardly any towns. For a society riddled with such angst, the idea of next-door neighbours must have been terrifying.

Judging by handshakes given and received in Kollam, the old multi-storey apartheid has fallen into decay. So too have several Malabar practices that survived from IB's day almost into Logan's century. 'When a sultan in the land of Malabar wishes to stop someone buying and selling he orders one of his slaves to hang over the man's shop branches of trees with their leaves,' IB noted. 'No one trades while these branches are in place.' The East India Company issued the same rustic closure orders in its early days in Malabar, and on one occasion in Calicut placed the Queen Mother under house arrest by means of a leafy interdict. Another custom noted by the traveller and still practised at the end of the eighteenth century (not, of course, by the Honourable Company) was that of impaling criminals alive. So tough on crime were the authorities that sometimes, IB says, the theft of a fallen coconut could result in this punishment. The stakes, fitted with cross-pieces, combined spitting with crucifixion. One nut-thief he saw 'was placed on the stake so that it entered his stomach and came out of his back; he was left like that as an example to all who should see him'. Such draconian penalties seemed to work: IB had never travelled, he says, in a more secure land. Logan records that the instrument of execution was known from its shape as the *kalu*, or eagle, and condemns it as barbarous. IB, the detached anthropologist, offers no moral judgement. But when speaking of the impalement of prisoners by a fellow-Muslim, the ruler of a short-lived dynasty in Coromandel, he outdoes Logan in his revulsion: 'So foul a deed as this I have heard imputed to no other ruler, and because of it God hastened his death.' Muslims should have known better.

I was relieved that the 'eagles' were extinct, that no one shrank – or at any rate not visibly – from my touch; and delighted that the happier aspects of IB's Malabar had survived – the landscape, that endless village, and the waterscape. We were tourists; but our miniature gin-, or toddy-, palace floated on a workaday stream, still the major highway it had been six centuries ago. While Martin painted and drew from his little sterncastle, I watched the traffic: elegant barges like scaled-down Viking war vessels, a bamboo cabin amidships between two minor Fujis of sand; floating islands of coconut husks, propelled on their way to coir factories by men with punt poles; lilac-painted waterbuses; watermilkmen and waterironmongers; a bicycle in a canoe, so low in the water that it seemed to be performing the miracle of Galilee. The waterway was busy with boats and nobody was messing about in them, except me.

Night fell with the soft thud of the tropics. The Chinese net dipped and rose, groaned and dripped. Voices, of watermen or waterbirds, sounded clear across the lake, now near, now far: 'Uwee! Uwweee!' Martin pulled out a harmonica and answered, very quietly, with 'Schoolgirl Blues'.

★

I dreamed I was at the organ. I was struggling with Messiaen's 'Chants des Oiseaux', and had too many fingers. Then I realized it was real, a dawn chorus, *mezzo piano*, water music in a myriad of parts that no ganja-clarity could have unravelled. I drifted off again, until human voices woke me and I – and sparrow-fart, widgeon-quack and coot-toot – drowned in an amplified surge of cries. They were calling on God, all at once, and it wasn't Messiaen, *mezzo*, but Berio, *fortissimo*. Devi, Allah, God, Shiva, Krishna, listen to me! *Me*! ME! Like monoglot memsahibs in the cookhouses of old, the various faithful seemed to think that the way to get the message over to Him, or Her, was to say it as loudly as possible. The Hindus made the biggest noise but then they, and their addressees, were in the majority. Clearly the ancient multi-faith society of the Kollam copper-plate Mr Kutty had told me about was alive and in fine voice; with one exception – where were the Jews?

I wasn't surprised that the cantor's chant was missing. I knew that the only Jews left in Malabar were those of Cochin, and that all but an elderly handful of these had been inveigled to Israel and other fleshpots. But even in IB's day Hebrews were thin on the ground. He mentions them only once, halfway along his backwater journey from Calicut to Kollam: 'We arrived at Kunji Kari, which is on top of a hill. It is inhabited by Jews, who have one of their own number as *amir* and pay a poll-tax to the Sultan of Kawlam.' At first I'd wondered whether 'Kunji' could be a version of 'Kochi', the Malayalam name of Cochin; but from Mr Nair's copy of the *Cochin State Manual* I'd learned that the Jewish presence there dated only from 1567. In that year the Jewish community moved to Cochin from Cranganore, twenty miles to the north. A footnote drew attention to IB's Jews, and suggested that their settlement may have lain inland from Cranganore at a village called Chennamangalam; it added that this place stood on a backwater called Kanjirapuzha, the first element of which seemed to account for 'Kunji', the first part of IB's place-name.

It all sounded persuasive, until I remembered the precision with which IB tried to render other words – Kawlam, Tirawari, *talam* and so on. Why Kunji *Kari*? Mr Nair had been unable to provide any further clues about the place. Now, though, I realized that in our boatmen I might well have the best informants possible. They knew the backwaters inside-out; if anyone could lead me to Kunji Kari it would be them. 'Melvin,' I asked, as he served breakfast, 'what does *kunji* mean in Malayalam?' An indirect approach seemed best.

'*Kunji*? It is "bronze".'

This was interesting. 'What about *kunji kari*?'

'It is "bronze curry".'

'*Bronze curry*?'

He smiled, as one might at a slow child. 'Yes. Bronze, muscles. All are selfish.' Another indulgent smile at my incomprehension, now total. 'Look. Man is getting selfish.'

I looked. The man stood in the shallows, bobbing down into the water and coming up with small, purplish objects which he dropped into a bucket. 'Oh, mussels! Shellfish . . . *prawns* curry!' Melvin beamed: I was learning fast.

The rest of the crew now began to contribute. *Kunji* also meant 'small'. That was the original meaning – prawns were called *kunji* because they were small shellfish. Or did I mean *kunchi*? *Kunchi* was the back of the neck. Before things got out of hand, I revealed that Kunji Kari was a place-name. 'Perhaps the second word is *karai*,' Melvin suggested. 'This meaning "bank of river, boat-landing place".' The others agreed; we came to the conclusion that the name probably signified 'the Small Landing-place'.

This was all promising. 'Now, at this place called Kunji Kari, or Karai,' I went on, 'there were Jews. You know "Jews"?'

Oh yes, they said. Mango Jews, pineapple Jews . . .

We were still on Ashtamudi Lake, moving slowly northward. The further end of this vast irregular sheet of water was sprinkled with fishing craft. We passed near one – three men in a boat, their bodies on the diagonal as they hauled on a net, grunting and straining as if they meant to drag up the very bottom of the lake. 'Rubens,' said Martin, '*The Miraculous Draught of Fishes*.' It wasn't: the net came up with a couple of tiddlers.

Into a narrow waterway, the sea to the west across a shaving of land. Another lake, Kayankulam; another day. Martin drew and painted, and our rate of progress slowed, for the first time, to sub-Battutian.

On the third day we passed through a lock on a second narrow channel and crossed from salt water to fresh – to water so placid, so pellucid that the banks resembled heads of lutes, every palm-tree and its reflection a pair of opposing pegs. Boats slid along the narrow water-mirror, each with a slender violin-scroll carved at stem and stern, each joined at an invisible waterline to its inverted consort. Domestic chores – the slapping of laundry, the scouring of pots – were *pas de deux* performed with underwater partners. 'Rembrandt,' I said, spotting my own Old Master – a raised skirt, a pear-shaped buttock cling-wrapped in dripping drapery – '*The Toilet of Bathsheba*.' And all along the busy banks they smiled and waved, the smaller children in their parents' arms, prompted – 'Look! Look at the foreigners!' – round-eyed, raising hesitant hands; and I thought of their child-ancestors, waving, wavering, receding, back six centuries and more, and of children and travellers to come, and saw one wave rippling out from this mirrored moment.

★

Among the tattier vehicles on the ferry from Cochin to Vypin Island the Ambassador stood out like a duchess in a dole queue; a rather tarty duchess, for her paintwork was metallic beige. Abhilesh, our new driver, told me the proper term was 'Symphonic Gold'. 'It is the most modern colour in the range,' he said, snootily. But modernity was only paint-deep, for Abhilesh's golden Ambassador was the same old Aga-on-wheels as Dewan's white one. Even before the ferry had completed the five-minute crossing, however, I had concluded that Abhilesh himself was not as colourful as hectic, eclectic Dewan. Trying to find a chink in his social armour, I asked if he liked cricket. 'No.' 'Films?' 'No.' 'Music?' 'No.' 'What do you like then?' 'I like only tourism.' I thought back to Dewan and his merry farts. Something about Abhilesh told me he probably didn't even break wind in private.

We drove up Vypin Island. When IB passed through the back-waters inland from here, it would have been a nude and oozy mudbank fifteen miles long, thrown up shortly before by the storm of 1341 (its name means 'New Deposit'). Now it was a suburb of the endless village of Malabar. We stopped for a breakfast of pea curry and crumpets; only the two of us, for Martin had declined to come looking for defunct Hebrews in favour of painting Cochin.

Frankly, he was welcome to the place. We'd spent a sweaty, mozzy, extortionate night in Ye Olde Colonial Experience, a 'heritage hotel' with the very latest range of antique furniture, glossy mags in the loo, gels in harem pants, gazpacho on the menu. It even had a 'library' (O fat bad novel that nobody reads, I thought, glancing at the books). Outside, the streets of Old Cochin were busy with shop-signs offering Internet services and Ayurvedic massage – in a few cases, simultaneously – and with pinched, north European, Cranach faces. It had suddenly struck me there that, other than in Khajuraho and on my unscheduled day-trip to Agra, it was the only time in India that I'd seen foreign tourists. 'What are they here for?' I asked Martin, meaning What are we here for?

'Oh, I suppose they're trying to discover themselves.'

'Well they're succeeding. I mean, they're discovering a load of other people exactly like themselves.'

Cochin, however, was highly paintable, so one of us was happy. We'd left him in a ginger godown. Now I was happy too, back on the road and full of curried peas. Abhilesh had perked up as well. He even managed a kind of grin – or half-grin, with one side of his mouth – when I mused aloud on the idea of sending an e-mail while being Ayurvedically massaged.

We crossed back to the mainland by a bridge. More bridges, over waterways threaded with slim peninsulas and bounded by paddy fields. I'd never been in such an indecisive landscape, one so torn between earth and water. For a time it seemed to plump for earth, and we entered a momentary confusion of lanes; this resolved in our immediate goal, Chennamangalam, and a watery dead-end.

Abhilesh knew of the handful of Jews remaining in Cochin. He had never heard of any in this area, however, nor of Kunji Kari. My further conversations with the boatmen concerning that elusive place had ended up various creeks and garden paths, two features in which Malabar abounds. Before returning to India, I had combed the geographers and travellers and found nothing even remotely like the name; but several works of the period did mention a Jewish community at a place called, according to the mood of the copyists, Shinkali, Singly, or similar. No such toponym exists in the area, and it seems likely that the word abbreviated one of the tonguenumbingly agglutinating place-names in which the Dravidians revel. (Gangaikondacholapuram, Periyanayakampalaiyam and other cartographers' nightmares litter the map. Asking the way must result in *Mahabharata*-sized monologues; is this why people have to talk so fast?) The learned Dr Gundert suggested that Shinkali and its variants represent the last three syllables of Thiruvanchikulam, an outlying area of the ancient port of Cranganore. I hesitate to contradict the great nineteenth-century Malayalam scholar, but to me it seems just as plausible that Shinkali could be a mangling of Chennamangalam. It would be a similar deformation to the one by which the Kerala state capital, Thiruvananthapuram, has become the slimmed-down, syncopated Trivandrum. And Chennamangalam, as I knew from the *Cochin State Manual*, had been home to a Jewish community. Faced with a maze of byways, waterways and polysyllables, it seemed as good a place to start as any.

The first people I met in Chennamangalam were Hepzibah, about five years old and stark naked, her blind father, and a smaller, clothed girl named Blessing. 'Are you a believer?' the man asked.

What could one say? 'Yes.'

'Praise the Lord! Alleluia!' he cried, laughing. By the time we'd all praised Him several times, I'd discovered that the blind man was a Pentecostal preacher. Between further alleluias, we were joined by more Chennamangalans and I learned that in an area 300 yards square there were places of worship for three Christian denominations plus Muslims, Hindus – and Jews.

We all circumambulated the synagogue, a big abandoned building. It stood in a walled compound and, with its plain gables and severe arched windows, might have been a prosperous dissenting chapel in the Welsh valleys but for the jungle of jackfruit and other tropical trees that had smothered it. There was only one clue to its identity. At the entrance there stood a rectangular slab of stone – a greyer and harder stone than the corned-beef-coloured laterite from which the synagogue was built – inscribed with nine lines of characters. It had the time-baked look of a cuneiform tablet, and the script was Hebrew. My guides said it was 800 years old. To my eyes it might have dated from before the Flood.

The Chennamangalans weren't far off in their dating. Much later, at the Indian Institute in Oxford, I tracked down a transcription of the tablet made in the 1930s by M. le grand rabbin Israël Lévi. It was the gravestone of a woman, Sara bat-Israel, who died on 28 Kislev in the year 1581 of the Seleucid era. This corresponds with AD 1269, and makes it the oldest Hebrew inscription on stone in India. The mason earned a rabbinical rap on the knuckles for several *fautes grossières*. I wasn't bothered by the grossness of his grammar. For me the mason's work – like those stones from the undersea mosque of Kollam – was a precious, a miraculous survival from IB's Malabar. (Elsewhere on the Institute's shelves I found a date for the synagogue as well – AD 1614, but built on an earlier foundation. The authority for this is the oddest entry in my IB bibliography: Yehudi, Adv. Prem Doss Swami Doss [Honorary Kerala Correspondent of the *Jewish Telegraph*, Manchester, etc. etc.], *The Shingly Hebrews*, Trivandrum, 5750 [= 1989/1990].)

There were more discoveries on the ground, too. Overlooking Chennamangalam was a prominent knoll, covered with more jungle and with jumbled masonry. I saw no more inscriptions, nor any sense in the scattered stones. But one of my companions assured me that this was the site of 'the Jewish chief's house'. So all the elements were there – Jews, suitably long-dead; a hill; a Jewish chief, perhaps IB's *amir*.

All the elements but one: Kunji Kari. My guides didn't know 'Kanjirapuzha', the reputed name of the backwater that flowed past Chennamangalam, although they said it meant 'the river of the *kanjira* tree'. But there was a big village on the far bank, they said, called Kunnu Karai, 'the Landing-place of the Small Hill'; and on the way back – scribbling excitedly, I almost missed this – we could call on the last of the Jews of Chennamangalam.

Abhilesh and I – and the Ambassador, an auto-rickshaw, several motorbikes and a group of pedestrians – crossed the backwater to Kunnu Karai on three sewn boats. These supported a raft and were towed by a launch called *St Antony*. We alighted from this promiscuous conveyance and soon found the *kunnu*, or small hill; but no trace of habitation on it, and not a memory of Jews in Kunnu Karai itself. Several villagers, though, had suggestions to make, and my ears pricked up at another name – Kunjunni Karai. It was an island a few miles east of here; but it was flat and had been so as long as anyone could remember. My last hope of solving definitively the riddle of the name resided in that solitary Israelite.

A decaying shack; a penniless Methuselah, bearded and ringleted, guarding ancient Torah scrolls from termites and time . . . Not a bit of it. The last of the possibly Shingly Hebrews lived along the backwater in a double-bow-fronted villa approached by an avenue of coco- and areca-palms – arboreal fireworks, each long smooth ascent ending in a starburst of green – was about fifty years old and, judging by the house and by a weighty gold six-pointed star that hung at her neck, she wasn't short of a shekel.

We stood at the door; inside, the villa was being repainted. Through Abhilesh I told her about my search for Kunji Kari. Her eyes narrowed and she appraised me closely, head to one side. She then told us to come back in ten minutes, after she had seen to the painters' lunch. 'Now she doesn't think we're after prawns curry, does she?' I said to Abhilesh, worried by her suspicious look.

He gave one of his semi-grins. 'I have explained.'

After loitering outside the gate for the period stated, we reappeared at the door – and were told by one of the men that Madam had been called, quite unexpectedly, to a funeral.

*

According to tradition, the first Jews of Malabar landed on the coast near Cranganore. According to tradition, the first Christians of Malabar landed on the coast near Cranganore. According to tradition, the first Muslims . . . But you have guessed! Three waves of pilgrim fathers, all washed up on the same beach. The names of those earliest Jews are not preserved. The founder of Christianity here was, we are told, St Thomas the Apostle, who arrived from the Holy Land (via, in one account, Brazil); the founder of Islam, I had learned, was Malik ibn Dinar, who arrived from the Muslim Holy Land. To commemorate Thomas's coming the Christians have built a spanking new Renaissance-Disney church by the seaside, populated by life-sized saints and with giant white rabbits and chimpanzees, zoomorphic litter-bins. The Muslim monument was in Cranganore itself. A sign on the gate said, 'Cheraman Perumal Juma Masjid, Est. AD 629'. The date struck me as a little enthusiastic: were people really building mosques here while the Prophet Muhammad was still mopping up pagan resistance in Mecca? We entered a small building by the gate – Abhilesh, I noticed, with some reluctance.

As it turned out I didn't need an interpreter since Faysal, the man in charge of the little office at the gate, spoke excellent English. I introduced myself. My name elicited a sympathetic look, and an apology. 'I'm afraid non-Muslims may not enter the mosque.'

I didn't try to hide my disappointment. The building was said to be ancient and beautiful; perhaps not as ancient as it claimed, but still the oldest Islamic monument in Malabar. I was asking if he could make an exception when, through a corner of a window, I caught sight of the mosque. Disappointment gave way to shock: the ancient and beautiful building was no more, and in its place stood another Legoland monstrosity.

'I'm sorry,' said Faysal in answer to my plea. 'You see, we have become a little strict.' I nodded, glancing once more at the dreary cement building across the courtyard. Dancing Delhi dervishes and peacock-feather tickling-sticks seemed a universe away.

Faysal was visibly embarrassed. To cover the awkwardness, I asked about that surprising date on the gate. 'Ah, yes,' he said, smiling even more uncomfortably, 'AD 629. Well, the story behind it goes like this . . .' It was a strange tale. One night Cheraman Perumal, the last sole ruler of Malabar, dreamed that the full moon split in two. Some time after this a party of Muslim pilgrims touched at Cranganore on their way to visit the Footprint of Adam in Ceylon. They called on the king, and happened to tell him of a miracle which had lately occurred in Arabia and caused the conversion to Islam of many unbelievers: the moon had been seen to split in two. The phenomenon, they said, had been predicted in their scriptures. On hearing this Cheraman Perumal resolved to become a Muslim and to travel to Arabia. Before setting sail he divided his lands and honours among several trusted deputies, chief among them a young man who was given the region of Calicut and Cheraman Perumal's most revered title, 'Samudari'. Later, after his arrival in Mecca, the old king dispatched Malik ibn Dinar and his followers to propagate Islam in Malabar. '. . . And the first mosque they founded', Faysal concluded, 'was this one.'

Cheraman Perumal and his heavenly sign reminded me of the Magi and the Star of Bethlehem. I could picture him on the road to Mecca, singing 'I one king of orient am'. 'Of course,' Faysal went on, 'all this is only a legend. Over the centuries almost every religious group in Kerala has claimed that Cheraman Perumal converted to their faith. And that date on the gate is, ahem, nonsense.' He looked at the floor.

I tried to cheer him up. Dates weren't everything, I said; cherished beliefs about the past, even if factitious, had a certain validity of their own – history was written in hearts as well as books. Since he seemed to rally at this, I asked if there was any more to the legend. Faysal told me that Malik ibn Dinar's followers stayed on in Malabar, building mosques up and down the coast. He opened a well-used copy of the *Malabar Manual* and read out a list of their locations, several of which were familiar to me from IB. We were now back on more factual ground. But I wanted to know what had happened to the hero of the story. 'And Cheraman Perumal?'

'He never returned. There is said to be a tomb. Somewhere in Oman, I think.'

At this my mind did a back-flip and landed four years earlier – it must have been almost to the day – on the coast of Dhofar; to be precise, in the office of al-Hammadi Fisheries in Salalah. More details came back: the kindly Keralan manager, Mr Joseph, who had told me of his spiritual journey from Syrian Orthodoxy to the Plymouth Brethren; talk of other spiritual journeys; and a short physical one to the tomb of an early Indian convert to Islam. The long-deceased gentleman, Mr Joseph said, had once ruled Kerala. Before his conversion, his name had been . . . something exotic that I never caught. His old title became his Arabic name . . .

'Al-Samari,' I said, recalling it aloud. I could see why the Arabs, with their lack of *ch*s and *p*s, had preferred 'Samudari' to 'Cheraman Perumal'. And al-Samari was a name IB knew well. Before, I hadn't made the connection. Mr Joseph's tomb had been a passing curiosity, noted down and shelved. 'I've visited the grave.'

Legend or no, Faysal looked impressed. We, too, had connected, and we now wandered amicably around Islam, Malabar and the Indian Ocean in general. I happened to mention that more recent Malabar–Arabia link that I'd found, the carved stones at the tomb-cattery of Bappachi in Kollam.

'You mean Ba Faqih,' Faysal interrupted.

'*Ba Faqih*?'

'Arabic pronunciation is difficult for Malayalam speakers. The Ba Faqihs are one of the old *tangal* families of Calicut – descendants of the Prophet, peace be upon him.'

And Ba Faqih was a name that *I* knew well: the Ba Faqihs were an aristocratic family of Hadramawt, in Yemen. Another connection across the sea.

There were more to come. By now, Faysal seemed to have decided that I was an honorary Muslim. While Abhilesh, relieved, went to buff up the Symphonic Gold, my host led me across the courtyard and into the mosque. In an antechamber we washed our feet, drawing the water from a cistern in dippers with long wooden handles (an old Indian Ocean arrangement – IB remembered doing the same in Mombasa). We then passed through a doorway.

My eyes soon adjusted to the darkness; my mind took longer, for instead of the high ceiling, cement and pastel paint I'd expected, we were in a low chamber, heavy with teak. It was unlike any mosque I'd ever been in: it might almost have been the lower deck of a galleon but for the pulpit, a short, steep staircase leading to a platform, all gal-leried with balusters stained dull yellow, apple green and cinnabar red. I recognized the colours and the shapes immediately. In the *suqs* in Yemen you can occasionally find old turned boxes in the same style, and they call them *munaybari* work. Munaybar, IB's Mulaybar, is the old Arabic version of 'Malabar'. The wooden columns that sup-ported the ceiling, with their scrolled capital-T-shaped capitals, I had also seen in my adoptive land, in Hadramawt. A cabin-like room filled with ocean-going features: more links across the sea.

The old mosque hadn't been demolished. It had been sheathed in a new, pan-Islamic façade. But why? They were obviously proud of having the oldest mosque in Malabar. Why hide it away beneath car-buncular concrete? As I turned the question over I noticed some circular wooden bosses on the door that were reminiscent of Mamluk work in Syria and Egypt. 'I think they're actually more like forms you'll find in the cave-temples of Ellora and Ajanta,' Faysal said when I mentioned the similarity. 'And look at this.' He patted an enormous bronze lamp, sitting on a small platform and shaped rather like a dumb waiter. The upper tier was scalloped, each projection designed to hold a wick; the lower tier must have caught oil drips. 'It was a gift from one of the Samudari Rajas. We used to light it when the stu-dents recite the Holy Qur'an. But not long ago we stopped using it . . . It is of the same form as the Hindu temple lamps.'

It was then that I saw a glimmer of what might be going on. The temple lamp and the Hindu-style carvings were embarrassing, a touch of the doctrinal tar-brush. The mosque, this dark and distinguished beauty, had been put in purdah, clad in a style which wouldn't have looked out of place in any modern Islamic setting from Luzon to Luton. They were proud of its age, but not of the Indian, pagan elements in its ancestry. It was a kind of self-consciousness, and going by Faysal's comment on the lamp it had come on recently. I was, of course, leaping to a conclusion.

'Oh. Here's the imam,' whispered Faysal. I turned.

If anything, the imam's appearance showed that I'd made the right leap. While Faysal wore the usual ankle-length Kerala dhoti, the imam affected a silky Gulf-style *dishdashah*. He had a very small mobile telephone that warbled immediately and gave me more time to study him: flashy Rado watch, fleshy face, Wahhabi-wispy beard. He was the walking equivalent of the new mosque façade . . . The phone clicked shut and, for a moment, the imam studied me. Faysal did a little shuffle and studied the ceiling. I felt like a schoolboy caught out of bounds.

The imam whisked me into his office, where he swiftly established my interloping status and told me, quoting the Qur'an (his Arabic was rather good), that my infidelity was not acceptable to Allah, that I would be one of the losers in the afterlife. I responded with another verse: 'Those who believe [in the Qur'an], and Jews, *and Christians*, and Sabians – any who believe in God and the Last Day, and do what is right – they shall have their reward with their Lord. They have nothing to fear or to regret.' (Needless to say the italics were mine, not the Almighty's.) We went several more rounds of scriptural sparring; then, as I was starting to flag, the imam looked at his watch and apologized. 'I must go and look over some accounts. I'm in ladies' veils, you see.' He handed me a card; I congratulated him on the name of his veil emporium, 'The Purdah Palace'. 'And next door to it I've got an ice-cream parlour . . .'

'Glory be to Him Who conjoined like with unlike!' I interjected.

'. . . twelve flavours!'

And, I said privately, the veils come in any colour as long as it's black.

It had been a busy day. On the way back to Cochin two questions rose to the surface of my simmering brain. The first, concerning the precise origin of 'Kunji Kari', was probably unanswerable. The second involved the conversion of Cheraman Perumal. At first hearing it sounded, as Faysal implied, no more than a pious jackanory. But there was that tomb in Dhofar; besides, IB also told a tale he heard further up the coast – the story of an early ruler inspired by a miracle to convert to Islam. The miracle was different, and yet the account seemed to be an echo of the legend of Cheraman Perumal. Before I travelled north to investigate it *in situ*, I wanted to find out more about that ancient potentate. And since my breed of history on the hoof entailed resorting where possible to the horse's mouth, then I needed to find a man whose ancestor IB had seen under an

umbrella on a beach, who still bore the old king's honorific – that name on the tomb across the sea, the name in the *Travels* – al-Samari, better known to Europeans by the Portuguese version of his title, the Zamorin. As far as I knew there was still such a thing as a Zamorin. But how would I find him? And would I even be able to see him if I did? IB's Zamorin provided board and lodging for the traveller in Calicut but, except for that sighting on the beach, remained an invisible host, hidden behind the heavy purdah of caste.

*

'The Zamorin? Samudari Raja? I will try, sir. Please take a seat and I will look for his number.' It couldn't be this easy, I thought as I crossed the reception lounge and joined Martin on a leatherette banquette. The Hyson Heritage Hotel in Calicut was devoid of heritage, of gels, gazpacho and gilded paperback novels. Instead it offered plump plastic, well-stuffed businessmen and, it turned out, some of the best food we were to eat in India. It charged a fraction of the place in Cochin, and any mosquito daring to cross its threshold would have been instantly deep-frozen by the air-conditioning. The staff were exemplary. Even when Martin trod a human turd – brought from the beach in the interstices of his commando sole – into the royal blue, deep-pile carpet of our room, the chambermaid brushed it off with a smile.

Martin had eventually gone off Cochin too, after an experience with an auto-rickshaw-*wala* he'd hired to take him to his ginger godown. 'Do you know what he said? He said, "Now I'm in front of the building, I know what your sketch is showing. If I wasn't here I'd have to see a snap, to tell me what it is." A *snap*. I ask you . . .' He was soon back on form, however. 'It looks just like Donegal round here,' he said as we drove up the coast north of Vypin Island.

'*Uh?*'

'It's all the paddy fields.'

Not long after, Abhilesh came out with his first and last pleasantry. As we negotiated a particularly cow-ridden village, I asked if the animals ever got knocked over. 'No,' he said. 'We always drive round their backside. Cows do not have reverse gear.'

Between Cranganore and Calicut we passed through an over-whelmingly Muslim area of mosques and veils where, in place of the usual 'Bisleri' brand, the mineral water at our lunch-stop was called 'Bismillahri'. Other amusements along the way were probably unintentional. I noticed a Police Punching Station and, among the many 'hotels' or roadside eateries, a Naive Hotel, a Pee Pee Hotel, and even a Hotel Runs. In Calicut, however, the charming gave way to the disturbing. A shop selling electric fans was called, inexplicably, 'Mask and Ripper'; a lunatic spotted us, stuck in the traffic, and came across to gibber and screech through the windscreen. Even the sea looked sinister.

Perhaps it was the associations. After coasting down from Gujarat, IB and the ambassadorial party arrived in Calicut, 'one of the great ports. It is the destination of ships from China, Sumatra, Ceylon, the Maldives, Yemen and Persia, and in it gather merchants from every corner of the earth. Its anchorage is one of the largest in the world.' A reception committee made up of local Muslim VIPs and a representative of the Zamorin escorted them ashore, flags fluttering and brass bands honking in welcome. 'But', IB continued darkly, 'our joy was to end in tears.'

To start with it all went swimmingly. First the diplomats called on the chief Muslims of Calicut, including the *shahbandar* or 'port-king' – a title with resonances, for it was bestowed on Sindbad and is still born by harbourmasters in many parts of the Indian Ocean – and the *nakhudah* or 'ship-master' Mithqal, 'the owner of great riches and of many vessels that ply his trade with India, China, Yemen and Persia'.* The visitors were given lodgings, courtesy of 'Sultan al-Samari', until the season for the China run began. At last, the Zamorin himself overseeing arrangements from a suitable distance, the embassy and their present were put aboard a huge ocean-going junk. There was a palaver about cabins. IB's set was poky and lacked an *en suite* lavatory, but he managed to wheedle a transfer to a smaller and less crowded vessel. His considerable dunnage and several slave-girls – one of whom, his favourite, was pregnant – were embarked. IB himself spent the final night ashore so he could attend Friday prayers the following day. He was probably glad of the excuse. The Prince of Travellers was never the keenest of sailors; in fact, although a native of one of the great Mediterranean ports, he had got as far as Jeddah and the age of twenty-six without ever going to sea.

'Now,' IB goes on, 'it happens every afternoon that the sea here grows so rough that no one can cross it to embark.' That Friday evening, however, the weather had not improved and IB found himself stuck on shore. By Saturday morning the storm was more violent still, and the junk and the smaller vessel were driven off their anchorages. Then:

---

* Mithqal is an unusual name for a free man – like Camphor, Spikenard, Ruby and so on it is usually given to slave-eunuchs. Appropriately for an Indian Ocean Onassis it signifies a type of large gold coin.

When night came, the junk carrying the sultan's present was driven on to the shore, with the loss of all who were on board. The following morning I went to inspect the aftermath, and saw Zahir al-Din [a fellow-envoy] with his head split in two and his brains scattered; Malik Sumbul had a nail driven through one of his temples and coming out of the other. Having prayed over them we buried them. I saw the infidel, the Sultan of Calicut, wearing a large white cloth round his waist, folded from his navel to his knee, and a small turban on his head. His feet were bare, and a slave held the parasol of state over him. A fire had been lit in front of him on the beach, and his police were beating the people to stop them looting what the sea cast up.

Of the smaller vessel, the one carrying IB's concubines and other possessions, there was no trace. She had last been seen running before the storm, God alone knew where. IB was left on the beach with nothing but a prayer-rug, ten dinars and one freed slave. The slave promptly bolted.

Even for a seasoned misadventurer like IB, this was bad luck. For a while he considered returning to Delhi to face Muhammad Shah's music. His decision not to do so was probably a wise one. As the poet Sa'di said, 'The service of the king is like a sea-voyage at once profitable and fraught with peril; where you will either acquire a treasure, or perish amid the billows.' IB had both lost a treasure and failed to perish, dutifully, amid the billows. This was the sort of occasion when a wise man cut his cable and ran before the sultanic storm; his cable, and his losses, for IB the career courtier was now a castaway.

One, at least, of the *dramatis personae* of this tragedy was still there: the villain of the piece, the sea. It was, I found out later from the *Malabar Manual*, thoroughly consistent in its villainy. The passage is worth quoting in full:

The squalls which usher in the south-west monsoon are at times terrific in their violence, and do much damage to ships which have incautiously remained too long on the coast to complete their lading. These squalls are accompanied by mountainous seas, and the wind and waves together generally smash the strongest cables of the best equipped ships. With their anchors gone, the ships usually attempt to set sail, but, the squall being past, the seamen find there is a lull in the wind, while the sea runs as high as ever. If the attempt to make an offing is persisted in, the ship generally drifts slowly into the breakers.

Perhaps the crew of the treasure-junk were lubbers; perhaps its outlandish construction ('*Nails?* Fall apart at a tap, this one . . .') was the cause of its undoing as well as of the spiking of poor Spikenard. In any case, Logan's is probably a fair description of what happened to IB's ships. The timing works too. The great elemental battle in which the north-east monsoon gives way to the south-west begins in April. From early times, navigators knew that to go south from Malabar and make enough offing to double Ceylon they needed the north-east monsoon, while to sail from Ceylon to the Strait of Malacca they needed the south-west. According to the late-fifteenth-century navigator Ahmad ibn Majid the porthole of opportunity, the time to catch the tail of one wind and the head of the other, lasts from 11 April to its end. This, as far as I can make out from IB's sparse chronology, is when the disaster happened, around the middle of that cruellest month.

IB doesn't tell us what the sea cast up of those nautch girls and eunuchs, cut velvets and cashmeres, marquees and thoroughbreds; but as I stood on the beach I wondered if the odd piece of gold plate might have survived, undigested, in the belly of the sea. I also remembered that perfidiously placid lake that we had seen from the Malabar Express, so pretty in the sunset. Here the lake was beginning to lick its chops, innumerable grey-green mouths slavering yellowish spume. It was now late afternoon, the time that IB noted, and it was getting hungry. Fishermen were beaching their boats. I watched the waves; Martin drew. Nothing happened. Yet the evidence was there: two piers, one with its end snapped off, the other with a hole bitten out of its middle. In a couple of months this sea, now merely cross-grained, would turn vicious – into a monster that snacked on dhows, guzzled ports, and had a particular taste for junk food.

Quite apart from these teatime tantrums of the sea, Calicut has always been a rotten port. Shoals, reefs and foul ground loom in Ahmad ibn Majid's notes on the place as they do on modern charts. What made it into one of the largest anchorages in the world, as IB called it, was another of the actors in his tragedy – al-Samari, the Zamorin, friend to Arab merchants, protector of wrecks; Kunnalakonatiri to his own people, among many other titles – Lord of the Hills and Waves. And now – the receptionist was calling me, and smiling – I knew that he too had survived.

*

'His Highness is very aged and tires quickly. I ask you to take this into account.' Mr Varma, the Zamorin's nephew by marriage, spoke in a low courtierly voice, hard to hear against the test-match commentary that blared from a television in the corner of the room. It was a small room in a very modest house, an ordinary suburban bungalow in fact, with a couple of scooters and a line of shoes parked at the front door. Only the presence of some incongruously large objects – several bronze lamps like the one I'd seen in Cranganore, a full-length portrait of a stout and handsome woman with bare shoulders and heavy bangles – showed that we were in the right place; that, and a board by the gate: 'Zamorin Raja of Calicut'.

I had read in the sixteenth-century *Book of Duarte Barbosa* that one should approach the Zamorin with one's left hand in one's right armpit, one's right hand covering one's mouth. Mr Varma smiled when I mentioned this. 'We are now more relaxed,' he whispered, opening a door.

Relaxed was the word: we were in the Zamorin's bedroom. And then, as the details came into focus, my heart – and Martin's, he admitted later – missed a beat. The body on the cot, tiny, pale, arms and legs like twigs, dressed only in a white cloth folded over from knees to waist, might have been that of a sick and emaciated child; above it, separated by a surgical collar, was the face of a corpse at peace – or of a man so old that he had already made his peace with death. It was a face that mapped mortality in every plane and hollow of bone. With that plinth-like collar it reminded me of a portrait head Martin had once shown me in his studio, a living face being translated from the inside out into inert clay – a work in progress, caught at the mid-point between quick and dead.

For a time we stood and looked. Then the eyes opened and turned to us, a light spread across the face, and HH Sri Puthiya Kovilakam Etanunni Raja Manavikraman Raja Samudari Raja, as he is known informally, sat up. He patted the cot; I went to sit by him, embarrassed by my size.

At first the Zamorin was unable to talk. But after an attendant had spent some time rubbing his chest and head, he began to speak in a faint but clear voice. It was like listening to a wax phonograph; the intonation, like the Zamorin himself, was Edwardian. 'I used to have thirty-six temples. Now I have not got even *one* . . .'

I looked at him with appropriate sympathy; and saw that the Zamorin was amused by his faneless state. 'We saw a very fine temple on our way here,' I said. 'The one by the big tank.'

'The Talli Temple. I really should put in an appearance there every day. But, unfortunately . . . *anno domini*. You see, I am supposed to worship the sword of Cheraman Perumal, which is kept there.'

'*The* Cheruman Perumal?'

'The very one. It is said that he entrusted it to the first Zamorin when he left for Mecca.' I was popping to find out more, but the Zamorin leapt forward in time. 'Our history began with the Perumal and the division of his kingdom, and finished, in effect, with the Honourable Company. Since their time we have reigned, but not ruled. But we still have our *malikhana*. That is, our pension from the Company.'

'I thought the Company was dissolved in Victorian times.'

'That is so. However, the *malikhana* was assigned in perpetuity. The Crown took over its payment and, following Independence, the Government of India.' A pause for a cough and a rub; I wondered if I could steer things back to Mecca . . . 'Rs. 5,000 a month, give or take. It has not been increased since it was granted, which was in 1806, I believe. They calculated it at twenty per cent of our former revenues.' Most people would complain about a non-inflation-linked pension fixed in the year after Trafalgar that was now little more than pocket money – and this in exchange for a kingdom; but once again, I noticed, the Zamorin seemed amused. The words 'Cheraman Perumal' were on my lips, but he continued with his theme. 'It would have been more if there were not five of us rajas, each with his share. Quite apart from all the feudatories.'

'*Five* rajas?'

The Zamorin explained. Not only was inheritance matrilineal, as IB pointed out, titles and properties passing to sisters' sons; the Calicut dynasty also worked on a system of rolling rajaships. When a Zamorin died the raja of the second degree, the Eralpad Raja, took his place, the third-ranking Munnalpad became Eralpad, and so on. As the family were long-lived the highest honour usually came late in life. The current Zamorin had been installed, he told me, at the age of eighty-seven. We went through the photograph albums of the ceremony. Despite the presence of a caparisoned elephant and the occasional green-faced demon it was, the Zamorin admitted, a rather scaled-down version of the ceremonies of former years. (A description of these takes up a dozen pages of Ayyar's history of the Zamorins, a copy of which Mr Varma later gave me. Reading this fascinating work now I wonder if the East India Company, when calculating pensions, took into account all of the odder royal perquisites – proceeds from the sale of lewd outcaste women, for example, and the right to claim wild hogs that had fallen into wells and cows with three or five teats to their udders.) Martin, meanwhile, began to draw His Highness. I heard my friend's whispered protest when Mr Varma offered to remove the surgical collar.

So far the Zamorin, who seemed to maintain the rare and admirable old convention of not questioning a guest, hadn't asked why we were here. I now showed him the English *Travels* with its description of his predecessor. ' "The Sultan of Calicut is an infidel, known as al-Samari," ' he read. ' "He is an aged man . . ." Ah, yes, how true.' The small turban and parasol of state, identified as the *tala-pavan* and *venkottakoda*, elicited an apology: 'I fear you are seeing me in circumstances which are . . . less than formal.' The voice was becoming fainter, the phonograph winding down.

'Do you have a question you would like to ask?' said Mr Varma in his discreet voice.

A score of questions came to mind, but I knew I could only ask one. 'You said that Cheraman Perumal went to Mecca. I've seen a tomb, in Arabia, which is said to be his. I assume it's no more than a legend, a myth – I mean the idea that he became a Muslim.'

The Zamorin smiled, and perked up. 'But of *course* he became a Muslim. And . . .' he paused; the smile became what I could only interpret as naughty, '. . . and so did my father!' He waited while the bombshell burst, then continued, 'Albeit it was a forced conversion. The Musulmans revolted in, I believe it was 1921. They wanted to found a Mappilla state – a Maplistan, like Pakistan – and they compelled hundreds of Hindus to convert. Of course many reconverted afterwards. The family wanted my father to do so. But he didn't. He had married some . . . additional wives, and *they* wouldn't let him!' His eyes sparkled. He was the former master of thirty-six temples, in an ultra-conservative corner of Hindu India; his father had died a Muslim, and he was tickled pink by the thought of it. 'I myself am a confirmed bachelor,' he added, as if to make up for the paternal fit of uxoriousness.

The sparkle was still there as we bid our farewells. But when we left the little cluttered room and I turned to look for the last time at that tiny figure, I saw that the light had dimmed. He was a king without a kingdom, a man almost without a body, and what was left of that was frighteningly frail. Now the glow had gone too. But something else remained: an essence distilled over centuries – legend aside, there has been a Zamorin as long as there has been an England – from majesty, mystery, ceremony. It was impalpable, invisible, perhaps pointless, but it was something that Bushes and Blairs, all the hollow noisy flashy shrill ephemeral men, *ignes fatui* that flick across the TV screen, who rule but do not reign, could never buy, not even for an empire.

*

We passed the Talli Temple once more, repository of that palladium of the Zamorins, the sword of Cheraman Perumal. The temple precinct was guarded by a beefy laterite wall, the wall punctuated by a two-storey gatehouse of unusual design. The first storey stood on a stepped plinth and was colonnaded with ochre-stained pillars. The second was smaller in area and height; its wooden walls, raked outwards and built of strakes and ribs, had a shipyard look. Each storey supported a hipped, tiled roof with wide overhanging eaves, and at the very top was a miniature gable end, set on the hip like a dormer. This was decorated with fretted bargeboards and turned balusters and topped by a finicky finial bearing a trident; it gave the gatehouse a cuckoo-clock levity. The building suggested – if such a conceit can be envisaged – Hansel and Gretel in Shangri-La, with a nautical twist.

I would dearly have loved to see the sword. But entry was forbidden, a sign on the gatehouse said, not only to non-Hindus but to those wearing 'trousers, shirts, lungies, pyjamas etc.' (we dress up to go to church or mosque; they dress down, in nothing but a dhoti). The sword was out of reach in a private, impenetrable world elaborate with taboos. At the same time, it pointed to quite another world, a world wide open: it was a constant reminder of the benefactor of the Zamorins – their ancestor, the historian Ayyar believes, arguing that the first of the dynasty was Cheraman Perumal's son – who sailed away to the land where the date-palm grows, and of that vital bond with Arabia.

The bond was older than the Perumal. The king's alleged departure, according to Ayyar and other authorities, may date if not to the time of the Prophet Muhammad then to 200 years later, in the first half of the ninth century. But there were already Arabs in western and southern India, and there had been since at least the time of Pliny. And despite other trading links, to China, Persia and elsewhere, the Arabian relationship was special. Not long after the probable time of Cheraman Perumal, Sulayman the Merchant wrote of a belief among the Indian kings that the Arabs were 'lucky', and that association with the foreigners blessed them with long lives and reigns. Captain Buzurg noted that one of the Indian rulers had commissioned for his palace a portrait of a famous Arab navigator.

The Arabian trade flourished under the kingly parasol of the Zamorins. Not only did they protect wrecks – unlike the other Malabar rulers, IB points out – but they were also scrupulously honest in other ways. An old Kerala chronicle tells of a merchant of Muscat sending identical presents of pickles to each of the kings of Malabar. The pickle jars concealed quantities of gold coins. 'I think there must be some mistake,' the Zamorin said, returning the gold; the other rulers quietly pocketed the cash. As a result, the merchant settled in Calicut and prospered. So did thousands of others like him.

Each arrival added a filament to the web of trade that stretched across the Arabian Sea.

And then the Portuguese came and tore it to pieces. The story has been told often – the wooing of the Zamorin with presents, his refusal to bow to a Portuguese monopoly on trade, Gama's horrific revenge – but the details never fail to shock: the Muslim merchant grandee captured, fed with excrement and gagged with bacon; the Zamorin's brahman envoy sent back ashore with his ears cut off and those of a dog sewn on; the boatload of ears, hands and noses hacked from captive Muslim crews, from which the Zamorin was invited to make a curry. One is reminded by Gama of Muhammad Shah, minus his good side.

*

We met Mr Varma once more. Our appointment was in the Zamorin's College, a school founded in the nineteenth century by an earlier ruler and incorporating a wing of an old palace, a long airy gallery overlooking the tank by the Talli Temple. Here Mr Varma showed us the Crown Jewel of Calicut. It was an oval pendant set with cabochon diamonds and rubies, suspended from a chain interlaced with seed pearls. Something Mr Varma said made me want to fling it into the temple tank: 'It was a gift from Vasco da Gama.'

Et dona ferentes. The end of IB's world, in the palm of my hand.

*

For all the best efforts of the Portuguese, the 'Moors', as they called them, are still there. The southern end of the Calicut shore, with its straggle of low houses and small mosques, its light complexions and elegant Arab noses, might have been a small town on the coast of Yemen or Oman. It ended at an inlet. While Martin painted I sat on a sea wall and watched boys diving for mussels. Somewhere here, beneath the waves, were the remains of a fort built by the Portuguese during a brief occupation of the Calicut shore in the 1520s. What hope was there that anything tangible had survived from the Calicut of IB, of nearly two centuries earlier? The ceaseless suck and gulp of the sea said None.

But it was the thought of watery graves that took my mind back to Kollam, to the stones from the submarine mosque, and to the cat-filled tomb of Bappachi: Ba Faqih, Faysal had told me at Cranganore, 'one of the old *tangal* families of Calicut' – and one, I knew, of the old *sayyid* families of Hadramawt, across the Arabian Sea. And it was that most useful authority, the Calicut telephone directory, that led me that evening to the Bafakyh Export House (Mom's Choice) and to Sayyid Hamza.

Sayyid Hamza's business interests included a hospital, a toyshop, and a hookah factory whose products he exported to the land of his ancestors. The Water-Pipe Suq in San'a has long been flooded with Indian-made models designed for Yemeni tastes. I had probably smoked Sayyid Hamza's pipes: he is, by general consent, the Hookah King. He was shakier on history, however, than on hookahs, and he didn't know of his fellow Ba Faqih buried in Kollam. 'But there is someone who will be able to tell you about him,' he said. 'Sayyid Fazal. You'll find no genealogist in Malabar to equal him.' Hamza drove me south from downtown Calicut, into ever dimmer, narrower lanes. A sudden gaping blackness to our right – a tank, he said; more lanes, even narrower, and then a gate. The headlights showed a sign: 'Jiffri House'.

If there was a magic word to conjure back the old web of trade, it was this name. The Portuguese – and after them the Dutch and the English – notwithstanding, some Arab traders had survived, and thrived. The Jiffris, another Hadrami *sayyid* family, worked the ocean as *nakhudahs* until well into the nineteenth century. One, Sayyid Mohsin, was among the richest merchants of nascent Singapore, with agents in steamy places from Suez to Surabaya – a descendant in all but blood of IB's Calicut tycoon, Nakhudah Mithqal. Joseph Conrad served on a Jiffri ship; Gavin Young, tracking Conrad as I was following IB, found Jiffris – or Joofrees, as they call themselves – in Borneo, still trading in rattans, birds' nests and aloes-wood. Now, judging by the evidence before us – several great barn-like houses, a private mosque – it seemed that their Calicut cousins had prospered too. A servant scuttled to the gate and let us in.

Sayyid Fazal, like Professor Habib of Aligarh, was hard to date. He might also have been nearing eighty, but he moved and thought with the suppleness of a much younger man. The identity of the saintly Ba Faqih of Kollam having been confirmed, we were off up Sayyid Fazal's own family tree: Jiffris on his mother's side, Shihab al-Dins on his father's – a nineteenth-century namesake of his was, he said, a kind of proto-Osama bin Laden, accused by the British of inspiring suicidal attacks by the Mappillas – and into the further branches of the Hadrami *sayyids*. Aydids in Mogadishu, East Indian Kaffs and Saqqafs, Ba Faqihs of al-Madinah, Colombo and Hyderabad. It was the human equivalent of that great holy banyan tree of Barwa Sagar, a diasporic growth extending around the Indian Ocean and down through the centuries to the Prophet.

And beyond. We moved to Sayyid Fazal's library where Burhan, a small grandson, was doing his Arabic prep. With the help of a large manuscript genealogy, I tested the child on his numbers: we counted the generations back from Burhan himself (a recent addition in biro) via the Prophet, to Adam. '*Sittatun wa thamanun*,' he said, with perfect case-endings and glowing eyes. Six-and-eighty.

Since we could hardly go any further with Sayyid Fazal's own family, I tried out IB's Calicut acquaintances on him – Ibrahim the *shahbandar* and Mithqal the *nakhudah*. There was still a Shahbandar House down by the shore, he said. Other than that . . . A brief exchange in Malayalam between the two *sayyids*, then Hamza, smiling, said I had to see the old mosque.

The family chapel turned out to be of the mortuary sort. It was a ritzy place, hung with Victorian chandeliers and earthly home to a Jiffri forebear of Sayyid Fazal. This ancestor, he explained, had been the spiritual preceptor of Tippu Sultan of Mysore, that bane of the British in India. He was also something of a saint. In front of the cenotaph was a high wooden bench inscribed in black Arabic characters: 'This is the seat of the noble Sayyid Shaykh Muhammad al-Jiffri, may God have mercy on his soul and profit us by his example.' 'Feel underneath the bench,' Sayyid Fazal instructed. I did so. The tips of my fingers came out black. 'Sayyid Muhammad spent the last ten years of his life on this bench,' he explained, 'day and night.' My eyes widened. 'Except, of course, when he prayed or answered the call of nature. The underside of the wood, as you see, is charred – from the heat of his learning.'

Further up the coast in Mangalore, IB saw a Muslim ascetic who spent long periods on a wooden platform. But never, in nearly thirty years of collecting saints and their miracles, did he find anything remotely like Sayyid Muhammad's superheated fundament.

As we left the Jiffri House, I reflected on the remarkable family that built it. In their mobility, in their navigation of those twin streams of matter and spirit – so successful in their case – they resembled IB. In them, something of the human and mystical geography of his world had survived the irruption of the Portuguese. As for physical survivals from that world . . . well, if the nineteenth-century Jiffri tomb-mosque was considered old, I might as well give up.

Driving back past the blackness of the tank, Hamza pointed to an even blacker blackness, a pile of hipped temple roofs rising ahead of us in silhouette. 'There it is,' he said. 'The old mosque. Miskal Masjid.'

A moment later, there was a soft but surprising clunk of recognition as the name dropped into place.

*

Even by daylight I could have been deceived into thinking that Mithqal, the Onassis of the Pepper Coast, had built a mistake for a *masjid*. It began with the same stepped plinth, went through the same succession of tiled overhangs, and ended in the same fretted and fussy gable as the Talli Temple gatehouse. It gave that same impression of an almighty but ultimately happy blunder over blueprints, in which bits of pagoda and Black Forest cottage had run away to sea – in this case in a four-decker, fit for the biggest shipping magnate of Malabar. If that venerable mosque at Cranganore had looked anything like this, then I could just about understand why they'd put it in purdah, in that faceless, Islamic-international cladding. The Mithqal Mosque looked embarrassingly like a temple. All it lacked was Shiva's trident on the gable end. (Speaking of which, we made a brief visit to Ponnani, down the coast from Calicut and a famous centre of Islamic learning. The gabled front of the Friday mosque there reaches the apex of kitsch: one expects it to erupt at prayer-time in a chorus of cuckoos. Looking now at the snap I took of it, I see – although I can hardly believe my eyes, for this is the bastion of the orthodox in Malabar and the place where, according to a tract I was given, 'tramendous inquisitive persons from Mecca, Madeena, Malasia, Iran, Iraque, Indonesia, Egypt and Sreelanka Streamed to satiate their spiritual thirst' – I see that it culminates in an indubitably Shaivite trident. It is as astonishing as a crescent would be on a steeple, or a crucifix on a synagogue.)

Perhaps, on second thoughts, I was mistaken in assuming Miskal was Mithqal. The mosque was in remarkably shipshape condition for a fourteenth-century building mostly made of wood. But an Arabic-speaker turned up and dispelled my doubts. Together we inspected the cool blue-painted prayer-hall, then went outside and sat together on the stepped platform, where he took me through a history of fires and reconstructions. 'But this', he concluded, patting our seat, 'is original, and so is the big tank. They were built nearly 700 years ago by Miskal Nahod.' Mithqal the *nakhudah*.

To keep it prayerworthy, Mithqal's monument had undergone so many refits that its former self was only a shadow – except for that massive reservoir (if you want to be remembered, dig a hole) and the steps beneath my backside, no mere impression of IB's age but as solid a relic as any. I sat on until my buttocks ached – wondering if it was here that IB had prayed on that black Friday, with a freshening wind beginning to moan through the wooden superstructure of the mosque, and the sea, a few hundred yards beyond the *qiblah*, starting to get hungry for junks; and the congregation whispering in the sermon – 'Sounds as if it's coming on to blow'; and the preacher's voice rising with the swelling of the elements, his text a thought-provoking one I like to think – most topical for the season of China sailings – from the Chapter of Counsel: 'And among His signs are the ships which sail upon the sea like mountains. If He will, He calms the wind and they lie motionless upon the back of the ocean . . . Or if He will, He causes them to founder, in punishment for their people's deeds.'

No Admission Without Permission

'"A shrine of Durga" Malcolm thought, but he was wrong, it
was Moslem: one was always going to be wrong.'

E.M. Forster, *The Hill of Devi*

'**Y**ET MANY', concludes the conjectural text of that Friday sermon
in Calicut, 'are the sins that He forgives.'

This time He was forgiving, to some extent. Months later, IB
heard that the vessel carrying his companions had survived the storm.
It must have been some storm, for his goods and fellow-travellers
were 'scattered to China, Java and Bengal'. His concubines had
washed up at a princely court in Sumatra; all but one – 'The pregnant
slave-girl, on whose account I was feeling miserable, had died.'

That sentence is about as near as IB gets to a cry from the heart. I
sometimes wonder if he even has much of a heart, can almost believe
Derek Walcott's dictum, that 'the traveller cannot love, since love is
stasis and travel is motion'. Certainly writers of travel, and not least of
fourteenth-century Arabic travel, do not often admit to being in love.
In fact IB does, a few dozen pages on – and, as it happens, in another
shipwreck: 'You two get out,' he says to his companions on the sinking
ship, 'and take the slave girl that I love.' *Allati uhibbuha*. Extraordinary.
No: travellers can love, and do, but they try not to for reasons of self-
preservation. A later Arab travel writer, Muhammad al–Musawi, hinted
at the dangers in a verse, the appropriate vehicle for such thoughts:

How long until my overburdened heart-strings start
to fray and sever?

290

Ah, me! each day I love and lose, desire and part;
and so for ever.

*

After the disaster in Calicut, Mithqal and the other magnates must
have held a whip-round for IB; he wouldn't have got very far on a
prayer rug and ten dinars. Besides, the dinars were no ordinary currency. IB, as we shall see, would rather have starved than spent them.

The neat line of progress from Delhi to Calicut now became a
desultory scribble as IB sponged his way up and down the coast of
Malabar and beyond – down to Kollam, back to Calicut, up to the
small Muslim-ruled state of Honavar. This time the *menu dégustation*
and the silk-clad slave-girl were off – 'The Sultan of Honavar gave
me lodgings, but', he adds woundedly, 'no servant.' After several
straitened months he embarked on a new but brief career when,
incredibly, the sultan appointed him commander of an expedition
against Hindu Goa. Even more incredibly the expedition was a
success – but not for long, for the ousted raja's forces regrouped and
besieged the Muslims. IB did a runner back to Calicut and then, like
some jaded jetsetter, 'decided to go to the Maldives, of which I had
heard' . . . One almost expects him to go on, 'from the Snookses next
door, who went there last year with Club Med, and had a lovely
time'; but it is the end of the chapter (and, except for a quick return
trip to Malabar, a short visit to Coromandel and a flying one to
Bengal, of his Indian career).

It was probably during his post-disaster wanderings that IB gathered most of his topographical data on Malabar, not on the original
port-hop down the coast in which he presents them. (We all do it.
My chapter on Aligarh, a linear progression of discoveries, is the
result of three separate visits. There! the illusion is broken.) Of all the
places he describes, one that interested me in particular was
Dahfattan, a large town on an inlet in the territories of a Hindu ruler
he calls Kuwayl. Here, beside a Friday mosque that overlooked a
large tank surrounded by pavilions, stood a remarkable tree. Every
autumn, IB heard from a local Islamic scholar, a leaf fell from the tree
'on which was written by the pen of the divine power *There is no god
but God; Muhammad is the apostle of God*'. Each year a group of
eminent Muslims and Hindus would sit under this prodigy, known as
the Creed Tree, and wait for the leaf to fall. 'The Muslims take half of

the leaf, while the other half is placed in the treasury of the infidel sultan, who uses it for healing the sick.' One of the ancestors of Kuwayl, IB's informant continued, had been inspired by this recurring miracle to convert to Islam. The convert's son, a zealous idolator, had the Creed Tree uprooted; but it sprouted up again, 'and the infidel died soon after'. IB prayed in a small enclosure beneath the tree, which at the time of his visit was as vigorous as ever.

IB's Dahfattan – the Malayalam Dharmapattanam – was still there, fifty miles north of Calicut, although it had shrunk in common usage to a more manageable 'Dharmadam'. But as we crossed the bridge over the inlet I wondered what remained of it, apart from the name and the setting. At the start of the sixteenth century there were still fine mosques here according to Duarte Barbosa, an official at the Portuguese factory in nearby Cannanore; there were also, this sober and reliable authority adds, large numbers of crocodiles whose breath smelled sweetly of civet. I could picture the place – the tank and pavilions and mosque, an Islamic Ambika-Jhambika without the darkness, Listerine-fresh crocodiles basking in the sun. I could picture the Creed Tree too. (It was not unique. Captain Buzurg wrote of an Indian bush with red flowers which were similarly inscribed; no conversions are recorded, but the bush did inspire a passage in a tale by Borges. Even today the divine pen leaves its mark on a wide range of objects, animal and mineral as well as vegetable, to the delight of sub-editors short on harder news. The diabolical pen, meanwhile, has allegedly written a sort of anti-creed on Coca-Cola bottles: look at the English logo in a mirror, read it as Arabic, and you will – if you wish to do so – see the words *There is no Muhammad; there is no Mecca*.)

I could picture Dahfattan; Dharmadam dispelled the image. Its Friday mosque turned out to be another well-meant carbuncle and its imam, the present repository of Islamic scholarship, could offer only disappointments. The Portuguese had razed Dharmadam in 1525, he said; he had never been close enough to a crocodile's smile to test the reptilian ring of confidence; the Creed Tree had been cut down.

'*Cut down?*'

'Unfortunately, all sorts of people were coming and taking the leaves. They all had the creed written on them, in the veins. People would use them as medicine and it all became a . . .' his Arabic faltered

'. . . a nuisance.' He spoke in Malayalam to Abhilesh, who later explained that 'all sorts of people' had included Hindus and Christians.

So not only the tree but also the inter-communal sharing of its leaves had survived IB's visit by more than six centuries. Remembering the lamp in the mosque at Cranganore, I wondered if the tree too had been the victim of a new Islamic self-consciousness. The imam confirmed my suspicions when he told me that it had been a pipal. I'd seen plenty of open-air Hindu shrines set up in the capacious boles of pipals – *Ficus religiosa*, also the bo-tree of the Buddha's enlightenment. To puritan minds, an Islamic prayer enclosure by one of them must have looked dangerously heterodox, if not wholly dendolatrous.

The Creed Tree, then, was lost. If it had sprouted up again, as it had after that earlier extirpation, the imam didn't let on. But he did provide some clues about the miraculous conversion mentioned by IB. He agreed that the name of IB's convert, Kuwayl, looked very much like Kovil, 'Palace' – an element of at least one of the Zamorin's many titles and, his nephew-in-law Mr Varma told me, of those of the Kolattiri Rajas who ruled Dharmadam and the surrounding area (Mr Varma was an impeccable source: he himself was a member of the Kolattiri family). And we spoke of Cheraman Perumal, that other old Hindu ruler converted by a miracle. Dharmadam, the imam said, was the port from which the Perumal left on his one-way trip via Arabia to Paradise; it was also one of the places where the missionaries he sent back founded mosques. On the evidence available, I could only guess that IB had heard a version of the Cheraman Perumal story, grafted the Creed Tree on to it, and produced his own hybrid. But it was a woolly sort of solution, and it niggled me.

Down on the quay I unearthed a few more fragments of IB's Dahfattan from the deep compost of the older fishermen's memories. The original *palli* or mosque, one of them said, had stood at a spot still known as Pallipuram. Another disagreed: Pallipuram was named after a *pallikodam* or Buddhist college. One was always going to be wrong. But there was a consensus on Kulikulam, an area of gardens next to Pallipuram. They occupied the site of a big tank, now buried; the name meant 'the Tank of the Spirits of the Dead'. Thanks to the Portuguese, there were no visible remains at either place. My informants left me to record these spectral data and went back to the more important business of watching Martin paint.

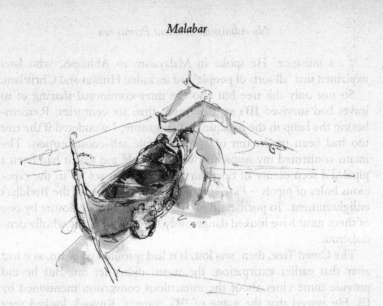

*

The Portuguese had a hell of a lot to answer for. Indulging their pepper-lust, they not only wiped IB's Dahfattan from the map but also blew apart that tissue of Old World trade with the violence of a duchess's sneeze. The explosion was felt far away. 'Where', the Bolognese traveller Varthema asked a citizen of Mecca, 'are the jewels and spices?' They no longer came, he was told, 'and the King of Portugal is the cause'. In Egypt, sand buried the tracks of the last pepper caravans. In Venice, the clink of ducats began its long *diminuendo*. Cumberland put it all nicely in his *Historical Fragments*:

> Arabia mourned
> And saw her spicy caravans return
> Shorn of their wealth; the Adriatic bride,
> Like a neglected beauty, pined away.
> Europe, which by her hand of late received
> India's rich fruits, from the deserted mart
> Now turned aside, and plucked them as they grew.

Roland Miller, a historian of the Kerala Muslims, said that for them 'The results of the Portuguese period may be summarized as: economic retrogression, estrangement from Hindus, bitterness against Christians, and a new militancy. Each of these was passed forward in some measure into modern times.' I had seen estrangement in that temple lamp in Cranganore, extinguished; heard it in the story of the Creed Tree, axed. Worse still, that first, Portuguese big bang set off a long chain of other superpower explosions. We are in the middle of one now. Estrangement, bitterness, militancy, far beyond Malabar. When will it all end?

Most of all, I felt on the quay at Dharmadam, the Portuguese had to answer for the wrecking of my research. But Malabar did sometimes get its own back, as I discovered during a fruitless search for IB's mosque of Budfattan, another 'big town on a large inlet'. The commentators have found Budfattan in Valarapattanam, north of Cannanore, or not found it at all. My own homework pointed to Puthupanam, 'Newport', on the north bank of the Kottapuzha River. But there was no old mosque there, nor even the ghost of one. Either the Portuguese had been up to their tricks or my identification was wrong. The only glimmer of hope came when somebody said there was an old mosque in Kottakal, on the south side of the inlet.

The glimmer was swiftly snuffed. 'About 450 years ago,' said one of the elders of Kottakal when I asked when their mosque was built. But even if the date was wrong it was a fine building of the cuckoo-clock-cum-temple variety, set near the river among palms, and my Arabic gained me admittance. Another of those dark and cabin-like interiors; another temple lamp. A round wooden object hung above the lamp, painted in red and black concentric rings like a target. The imam unhooked it. 'Kunjali Marakkar built this mosque,' he said. 'He fought the Portuguese. This is a Portuguese . . .' the Arabic word eluded him; Abhilesh, to his obvious relief, hadn't been allowed in to interpret. But the imam grasped a handle at the back of the wooden disc and, his other hand holding an imaginary sword, began to mime energetic blows and feints.

'*Turs!*' I said. A shield.

I didn't know enough about sixteenth-century Lusitanian weaponry to be certain that it really was Portuguese. But the shield was followed by a stone cannon-ball, a six-pounder or so, and then by a real sword, brought out from its cobwebby hiding place behind the pulpit. 'For the *khatib*,' the imam explained. Traditionally, some *khatibs*, preachers, would deliver their sermons leaning on a sword. This one, however, was not of the type one would expect to see in a mosque: it was no scimitar or yataghan but a rapier, and one of an early design, closer to a claymore than to the enlarged bodkin of later centuries. I searched every inch of the pitted four-foot blade and basket hilt for inscriptions. There were none; but I didn't doubt now that this and the other objects were trophies of battle with the Portuguese.

'Also Portuguese,' the imam said, indicating a gleam of gold at the top of the pulpit. He led me up the wooden steps. By now I was prepared for anything – but not for what I saw when my guide removed a prayer-rug that was draped over the back panel of the pulpit: from the centre of a mass of carved and gilded arabesques and inset in a halo, or aureole, appeared the figure of a classically draped man, full-face, with long straight hair . . .

Christ. In Majesty. On the pulpit of a mosque.

It was even more astonishing than the idol in the mihrab at Dawlatabad: this was a working mosque. Though perhaps not as astonishing as that trident on the Friday mosque of Ponnani – unlike Shiva, Jesus is a prophet of Islam. Still, any representation of man or beast was anathema in a Muslim place of prayer – even if, as here, the features had been carefully erased and the blank face regilded. The imam may have mistaken my surprise for disapproval, for he quickly replaced the prayer-rug. I looked at the turned supports that framed the panel, still visible on either side of the rug. They seemed to be the sidepieces of a chair-back . . . an episcopal throne? 'It came from Samudari Raja,' the imam said, descending the stairs.

It is quite possible. When the Portuguese weren't making war on the Zamorin they were making advances to him, and gifts. I'd already seen that crown jewel of Calicut, Gama's pendant. Later, back in the library at Aligarh, I found out that Gama's other presents to the Zamorin had indeed included some pieces of gilded furniture. Equally important, I discovered that the mosque-building Kunjali Marakkar, who was eventually captured by the Portuguese and executed in Goa in 1600, had been the last in a line of hereditary Muslim admirals of the Zamorins. A terrifyingly powerful man, he had once sliced an opponent in two, lengthways, with one blow – of that captured sword? He was a hero to the people of Malabar, a pirate to the Portuguese. (The freedom-fighter/terrorist question is an old one.) My final library discovery, tucked away in Dr Ibrahim Kunju's *Studies in Medieval Kerala History*, was the most pleasing. The present Puthupanam is in fact a new Newport. The old Newport, IB's Budfattan, had been renamed Kottakal when the Zamorin's admiral chose the place to build his *kotta*, or fort. It wasn't a wild guess to suppose that IB's mosque had stood on the site of the one I visited.

All this book-history, however, was in the future. That afternoon in the Kottakal mosque I had seen history itself with my eyes, touched it with my hands, held objects that throbbed with it, that oozed it. And I knew that, here at least, IB's world hadn't gone down without a fight.

*

Next day, back in Dharmadam, I found another significant piece of history. Again the period was wrong; but like those relics in the mosque Mr Ramunny embodied his age, which spanned most of the twentieth century. He had been a young civil servant on the North West Frontier in British days, a Hurricane pilot in Burma in the Second World War, and had served as ADC to Jawaharlal Nehru. Now he was a polymath of the palm-groves. Having written on Nagaland and the Laccadives, both of which he had administered, he was currently at work on a history of cricket in India. I managed to ease him back in time from Colonel Wellesley's first match, a few miles down the coast at Tellicherry, to our immediate surroundings in earlier centuries. He could add nothing to my findings on Dharmadam, but he shared my views on the Portuguese. 'Do you know, they were going to celebrate the 500th anniversary of Vasco da Gama's arrival! Everything worked perfectly before he came. The Portuguese brought only violence and destruction. What is there to celebrate in that? I wrote to the PM and gave him a piece of my mind, I can tell you.'

Later in our conversation Mr Ramunny asked if IB had included the Muslim Ali Raja of Cannanore in his list of Malabar potentates. No, I said: the only west-coast Muslim ruler he mentioned was the Sultan of Honavar. 'I only wondered,' Mr Ramunny went on, 'since the Ali Raja dynasty was in existence at that time. It still is, in a manner of speaking.' He then told me about the origin of this ancient line, whose title means 'King of the Sea' and who once, like Mr Ramunny himself, had governed the Laccadives. Its founder, the story went, saved the daughter of the Kolattiri Raja from drowning. By touching the girl, her Muslim saviour made her lose caste; the ending was happy, however, for the raja married the princess to her rescuer and gave her a gratifying dowry – an eighth part of his kingdom. (I made a mental note to look out for bathing ladies in distress, especially those of good family.) 'Hence,' he concluded, 'the Ali Rajas' family name, Arakkal, which means "Half-a-Quarter". Of course, this is only the romantic version of events. Perhaps we should look at Logan.'

Like all the best households in Malabar, Mr Ramunny's had a well-thumbed copy of Logan's *Manual*. Its account of the founding father of the Ali Rajas was short on romance: he was probably a minister of the Kolattiri Raja; he converted to Islam in about AD 1100; the ministerial job stayed in the family and his descendants, being adept at commerce as well as politics, built up a capital that enabled them to run their own army and free themselves from their Kolattiri lords. Logan guessed that their independence began in the time of Mammali (Muhammad Ali) the Great, who was head of the family from about 1364. Twenty-plus years after IB's visit, which would explain why they hadn't got into his Good Sultans Guide.

Later that afternoon, lounging in a Bombay Fornicator, I reread the passage in our hotel's copy of Logan. As I did so another thought occurred: the Kolattiri Raja was IB's Kuwayl; might the convert in the Creed Tree story have been not Kuwayl's ancestor but his ancestor's *minister*, the progenitor of the Ali Rajas? The hypothesis was impossible to test. But then . . . Mr Ramunny had said that the Ali Raja family were still in existence. Why not go and ask them?

I was clutching at straws; no, trying to catch chaff. But IB's mystery convert still niggled me, and in any case there had been no more solid Battutiana since the Mithqal Mosque in Calicut. Then fate intervened – the paternal uncle of Mr Moosa, the owner of our hotel, just happened to be the brother-in-law of the current head of the Ali Raja family – and I knew the idea was meant to be pursued.

'Yes, she'll be delighted to grant you an audience,' said Mr Moosa as he put the receiver down.

'She?' In Islamic dynastic history, female rulers are only slightly less rare than camels' eggs.

'Yes. It's the custom that the eldest member of the family holds the title, whether male or female. You Brits have got a queen; we've got a bibi.'

'A *bibi!*' IB's Court and Social columns included khans, amirs and sultans by the score; even an ilkhan and an atabeg. But he only ever met one female monarch, the Sultana of the Maldives. And he never called on a bibi; or only on a dead one – Bibi Maryam of Hurmuz and Qalhat, whose tomb we had both visited in Oman. For once, with the real live Bibi of Cannanore, whose line had also been masters of the Laccadives and of Minicoy, the Indian Ultima Thule, I was going to out-hobnob IB.

★

If, that is, we could find her. It was so much easier to locate one's potentate in IB's day, what with all the fanfares and drum-rolls and that sensible habit of living in palaces. Even now it isn't hard in most of the rest of India, with the more authentic heritage hotels offering bed, breakfast and maharaja. Judging by the Zamorin, however, the latter-day princes of Malabar were an unostentatious lot. The Bibi of Cannanore turned out to be no exception. Everyone knew where she lived, which was somewhere beyond the railway line; no one could explain how to get there.

We found ourselves, for the third time, back on the Cannanore sea front. A long street followed the curve of the bay, lined with decaying rust-coloured godowns and with arcades of empty shops. The buildings were all of a piece, a model bazaar constructed at a time when the Ali Rajas still reaped the fruits of the sea (their monopolies, I learned later, included Laccadivian sea-slugs). It must have been a distant time. I had noted from the *Imperial Gazetteer* that Cannanore was 'in melancholy decline'; that was in the 1907 edition, and the decline had clearly not been reversed since then. There were hints of gaiety among the melancholy, though – a perky Victorian-looking mosque at one end of the street and a godown, now the Universal Gym, that sported a mural of a muscle-man in the manner of Tom of Finland.

Towards the mosque end of the street stood a gateway with a large sign: No Admission Without Permission. On our first reconnaissance we had swept through this – *audentis Fortuna iuvat* – into a large quadrangle formed by warehouse-backs and house-fronts. Knocks on the door of the grandest house, a ramshackle palazzo, went unanswered. On the far side of the quadrangle was a gatehouse topped by a belfry (belfries and Muslims do not go together; in Malabar I had learned not to be surprised). Here, we found out from the gatekeeper that this was indeed the Ali Rajas' compound, but that the Bibi herself lived on the outskirts of town. He gave us directions.

So too did a dozen other kind citizens of Cannanore. Eventually, back in the back-lanes and thoroughly lost again, we found a person – a man sitting on a motor-cycle – who *didn't* know where the Bibi lived; who, in fact, had never heard of her. Behind him was a gate with a name-board: Sulthana Adi Raja Ayisha Beebi.

The Bibi's residence, like the Zamorin's, was a modest bungalow. Also like the Zamorin's, it contained a number of palace-sized objects – items of bulbous and impractical furniture, maces, halberds and swords, a set of plate for a banquet. Some of the objects bore the Ali Rajas' coat of arms. The charges on the shield included a Hindu-style sun with a face and what, with hindsight, may have been a sea-slug, proper; the crest was an Islamic star and crescent atop an esquire's helmet, the supporters a pair of heraldic sea-horses; and the whole assembly floated aboard what might have been either a ship or a hip-bath.

Also like the Zamorin, the Bibi gave audiences in her boudoir, a small room behind a knobbly screen through which we caught a gleam of red and gold. We were led behind the screen, and the colours resolved into an elderly lady sitting on a bed, her legs straight out in front of her, dressed entirely in scarlet silk plush and dripping with gold – anklets, bangles, earrings, a fringe of gold beads on her head-cloth. From beneath the last, out of a face mottled with age, she regarded us with her single eye. It was an imperious eye, as befitted the Queen of Cannanore, Minicoy, the Laccadives and the Sea.

Two chairs were brought in for Martin and me, filling the remaining space in the little bedchamber. With her permission, granted with a slight inclination of the head, and with her grandsons standing behind us to interpret, I questioned the Bibi on her dynasty's origins. She seemed to need prompting, so I went through the fabulous tale of Mr Ramunny, then Logan's down-to-earth account, and finally added my own footnotes from IB's story of the Creed Tree. 'My idea', I concluded, 'is that the convert Ibn Battutah mentioned may have been the same person as your ancestor.'

Spoken aloud, my theory sounded dreadfully implausible. The Bibi smiled, slightly and inscrutably, like a sibyl about to impart mysteries. I waited for my theory to be crushed. But she said nothing.

At last one of the young men spoke. 'The truth is, she doesn't know. And neither do we.' His brother thought he had heard something about a rescue from the sea. And that, as far as my hypothesis went, seemed to be that.

Martin did better. With another little inclination of her head, the Bibi agreed to sit for him. Tea was served, and the grandsons showed me various large objects inscribed in Arabic, which they were unable to read. (Creaking sounds emanated from the bedroom – the Bibi laughing, Martin assured me afterwards. He seemed to have a way with elderly Indian ladies.) I provided translations, and by the end of the session had been acknowledged as the world's foremost authority on both the Arabic language and the history of the Ali Rajas.

Some time later I found out that the real expert on the Ali Rajas, K.K.N. Kurup, had published some of their dynastic archives. Among the documents is one that gives the family's own account of their beginnings – the authoritative statement that I'd failed to get. To cut a long story short the first Ali Raja, it says, reigned at Dharmadam and was a sister's son of none other than the ubiquitous Cheraman Perumal.

By now you may be confused. I certainly am. But neither of us is as confused as the traditional Malayalam and Sanskrit chronicles of the region. I looked into translated fragments of these for clues about the convert of Dharmadam, and found firearms and 'men of round hats' – the Inkiriss, or English, and others – popping up in eighth-century Kerala; Muslims and mosques suddenly turning into Buddhists and *viharas*, and vice versa; a Buddhist king of Dharmadam going to Mecca to worship Vishnu.

Even without the dubious benefit of this knowledge, I realized that the conundrum of IB's convert would probably never be solved. I left the Bibi's bungalow still niggled by it. Martin, however, was ecstatic. 'She's wonderful!' he whispered on the way to the garden gate. 'She's a Rembrandt! A Delacroix!'

*

Landscape, for the first time. Not those three unending abstract lines of shore and palm and sky, not that half-drowned world of waterways and paddy fields, but a real panorama – a lake of green trees with floating islands of pink laterite. For weeks we had moved in scarcely more than two dimensions, trapped in a flickering corridor of palm-columns. And ever since Martin had sung a snatch of 'I've got a luvverly bunch of cokernuts', I'd been possessed by that silly song . . . 'Some as big as yer 'ead!'

Now, ninety miles north of Calicut, we had risen above the incessant coconuts. The problem was that our landscape appeared to be one without IB. He might have been there at Mount Dely, the Malayalam Ezhimala, in a mosque he mentioned. If so we didn't get the chance to find out: the hill and adjacent coastline had been swallowed up by the Ezhimala Naval Academy, and the rule of No Admission Without Permission was more strictly applied than in Cannanore. As we were turned away from the gate I gave silent thanks for my advance warning about the naval take-over of the island of Anjidiv. ('Permission should forthcome pretty soon,' said my helpful Delhi friend last time I'd called. 'But keep your fingers crossed, just for the nonce.') To make up for the disappointment we discovered, on the landward slope of the hill, a variant species of Creed Tree. Paper plates hung from its branches, inscribed not by the pen of the divine power but by that of the Communist Party of India (Marxist), usually almighty in Kerala but currently out of power. Slogans about the proletariat rustled in the breeze. And at Etikulam, a village at the south end of the hill, we found a Battutian relic that even IB had forgotten about.

The sun was almost at its height, and a group of men had gathered in the shade of a tea-house to wait for Friday prayers. I wished them, in Arabic, the blessings of the day. One of them responded in kind, a prosperous-looking man in a Friday-best *dishdashah* that came, like his own Arabic, from Abu Dhabi. He confirmed what I thought –

that there were old mosques within the perimeter fence of the Naval Academy. I then explained why we were here: a Moroccan traveller had visited the area in the fourteenth century, he had written a book . . . My Arabic-speaker studied his watch, his mind on the coming devotions. Then he looked up and smiled. 'You mean Ibn Battutah. There is a little mosque here, down by the shore, where they say he copied Qur'ans.'

As he spoke the call to prayer sounded and the men rose to go to the big Friday mosque across the road. I followed the *dishdashah*-wearer, tossing questions into his wake – where? who says? how do they know?

He pointed to an opening in the trees. 'Down there.'

'But how do they *know*?'

The man turned, shrugged, smiled again, and disappeared through the mosque door in a swish of robe.

The Talakal Mosque stood on a low terrace in the pied light of a palm-grove, a few yards from the beach. Not being a Friday mosque it was deserted. And it was undecorated, undatable; almost unidentifiable, for it might have been a Scout hut but for the project-ing niche that showed the *qiblah* of Mecca. It gave nothing away. It just sat among the palms, an empty box waiting to be filled with prayers. I looked at it and thought Why here? It had to be one of those false traditions Professor Habib had warned me about back in Aligarh, a back-projected memory. Then again, Why *not* here? No one could prove that IB hadn't copied Qur'ans in this place. It was just the sort of thing he might have done to make some cash, on the road again after the calamity at Calicut. Besides, an educated Arab, the ex-qadi of Delhi . . . the people of Etikulam would have pounced on him, would have told their grandchildren about him in years to come. But would the grandchildren have told their grandchildren, and so on for 660 years to come?

*

We travelled on, over rising land where the foothills of the Ghats came down to the sea, into a new state, a new language, into the land of ear-hair – it was Martin who noticed this genetic peculiarity of southern Karnataka, a tendency to luxuriant lugholes. We'd left Malabar proper and, I felt, IB. From what I'd already seen of Mangalore I had no hopes of relics there; nor even of questions like the ones I'd brought away from Etikulam. That unconfirmable sighting of him at the little mosque by the shore now looked like a farewell, the last glimpse of a half-regained Eurydice. There remained one chance of grasping him again before the long blank stretch to Cambay – on Anjidiv, that scene of his own strangest meeting.

The island had been the first port of call for the ambassadorial party on their voyage from Gujarat to Calicut. Going ashore, IB found a palm-grove, a tank and a small temple with a yogi sitting on a wall between two idols. The yogi did not reply to the travellers' greetings; instead, he suddenly 'yelled very loudly, at which a nut fell from a coco-palm in front of him'. He presented the nut to his visitors but refused a return gift of coins. 'I had in my hand a string of prayer-beads from Zayla,' IB remembered. 'The yogi began to examine the beads so I gave them to him, whereupon he rubbed them with his fingers, sniffed them, kissed them, and pointed to the sky then to the *qiblah* of Mecca. My companions did not understand his gestures. I, on the contrary, knew that he was a Muslim . . . As we were leaving him I kissed his hand. My companions disapproved of this, but the yogi understood the reason for their disapproval and kissed my hand in return. Then he smiled and indicated that we should depart.' As they were walking away, IB felt a tug on his cloak: it was the yogi, and he pressed into the traveller's hand a further gift – ten gold dinars. 'I could not get over my amazement at this yogi,' IB concludes, 'and I made sure that I kept safely those dinars that he had given me.' Together with his prayer-rug, they were all he had left after the disaster at Calicut.

The first time I'd read the story of the yogi's island in my dire and noteless Lebanese edition of the *Travels* it had seemed as fabulous as Prospero's isle. It lay uncharted between one religion and another, between religion and magic. One element, however, was familiar – the prayer-beads of Zayla. That place lies on the Somali coast in the crook of the Gulf of Aden, a source of black coral. The most prized material for Islamic rosaries, *yusr*, as it is called in Arabic, gives off a peculiar faint scent when rubbed in the hand. The scent never fades: a Yemeni friend has a *yusr* rosary of great age which still releases its distinctive odour, slightly sweet with a note of iodine. On smelling it one prays for blessings on the Prophet; a kiss, like the yogi's, is also acceptable form.

Since that first encounter, the Gibb-Beckingham *Travels* had given me a name for the island and a place on the map, off Karwar and just south of the Karnataka-Goa border. Later I gathered more notes on Anjidiv. It was about half a square mile in area. In 1664 the English force sent to take possession of Bombay for Charles II had to take shelter on the island, and 400 of them 'succumbed to an unhealthy monsoon'. Two decades on, the Portuguese built a fort there, and the island eventually became the penal colony for Goa. The fort, I then learned, was not the first one to be built. As early as 1505 the viceroy Almeida had used the island as a naval base and put up some minor defences. While digging the foundations for these, the Portuguese unearthed stones inscribed with crosses. Anjidiv had been home to Christians!

Most likely the crosses were Hindu swastikas, Almeida a victim of the same confusion that, a few years earlier, had led Vasco da Gama to fall to his knees before a statue of Devaki with the infant Krishna. I can sympathize with them. What with tridents on mosques and temple lamps inside them (I take Jesus on the pulpit to be a one-off), the west coast of India is still confusing. Indeed, from what I'd seen of it, India as a whole had a habit of sliding in and out of that borderland between faith and faith, creed and conjury. The yogi's island no longer seemed as strange as on that first reading. Confusion was now familiar territory.

Other travellers have given in to the confusion. Afanasii Nikitin, a fifteenth-century Russian merchant stranded in southern India, lost track of the Christian calendar and ended up performing his Lenten fast in Ramadan. 'I am between two faiths,' he admitted, proving the point with a Russo-Turco-Perso-Arabo-nonsense litany: '*Bog ollo, Bog karym, Bog garym, Bog khudo, Bog Akber, God, King of Glory, Ollovareno ollo garymello, sensen olloty.*' (Count Wielhorsky, who did his best to put Nikitin into English, admitted that the merchant's text is sometimes 'utterly unintelligible; a circumstance which could not fail to be apparent in the translation'. Perhaps Mr Postnikov, who is working on a new one, will make more sense of it.) Yet others, however, thrived on confusion. At about the time of Nikitin, overt syncretists were coming out of the closet – men who lived simultaneously as yogis and Sufis. And, back in Aligarh, IG had told me of a later west-coast tradition of *lashkar-babas*, Muslim seamen who had ended up on land and redesigned themselves as sadhus. Perhaps IB's yogi of Anjidiv had begun a trend. And yet doctrinal amphibiousness, or the idea of it, was much older. 'My heart is capable of every form,' said the Andalusian visionary Ibn Arabi, early in the thirteenth century,

> A cloister for the monk, a fane for idols,
> A pasture for gazelles, the pilgrim's Ka'bah,
> The Tables of the Torah, the Qur'an.
> Love is the faith I hold: wherever turn
> His camels, still the one true faith is mine.

IB's companions were blind to such possibilities. IB himself was partially sighted. Like the Portuguese and their crosses on that same island, he saw what he wanted to see.

As I mentioned during my search for the Caveman in Delhi, the yogi's tale comes to a conclusion, or an inconclusion, in China. IB was visiting Canton when he heard of an ascetic who lived in a grotto outside the city. The hermit was over 200 years old; no one knew what religion he followed. IB went to the cave and found him at its entrance. 'I gave him the Muslim greeting, at which he took my hand, sniffed it, and said to the interpreter, "This man is from one end of the world and we are from the other." Then he said to me, "You have witnessed a prodigy. Do you remember the day you arrived at an island where there was a temple and a man sitting among the idols who gave you ten gold dinars?" I said, "Yes." He said, "I am that man." ' He then entered his cave. IB ran in after him; the hermit had vanished.

There is an epilogue. In 1498, seven years before Almeida made Anjidiv his base, Vasco da Gama called there and careened his ship on the beach after the long voyage from Lisbon. The earliest account of the journey mentions a tank and idol-house nearby. Correa's later *Lendas da India* adds a detail: 'There were no inhabitants, only a beggar man whom they called *Joguedes*.'

The tank and temple must be those that IB saw. Was Yogi Das – if that is what Correa's word represents – IB's yogi? If he was over 200 years old in IB's time, he would have been 350 in Gama's. A good innings, but not unique among Indian holy men. The celebrated Shah Madar died at the age of 383. Yogi Balundai seems to have made a similar total, if not more. He was at large in IB's fourteenth century and according to Simon Digby, an authority on Indian Sufism, was encountered by 'Emperor Akbar, the Jesuit Montserrate and the Zoroastrian leader Mubad Shah. The Tibetan traveller sTags-tan

Ras-pa met him on the road to Swat at the beginning of the seventeenth century.' He also turned up in the Salt Range a hundred years later. In our time the yogi Devraha Baba, who is said to subsist on nothing but air, has made a triple century.

If Correa had written the epilogue, I wanted to add the envoi. Even after its long stint as the Devil's Island of Portuguese Goa, I was convinced that some trace of the tank and temple would have survived on Anjidiv. I also had a sneaking suspicion that I'd find a yogi . . . too much to hope to meet IB's man; but then, he did exist outside the normal bounds of space and time. The problem was, so did the Indian Navy. Anjidiv was out of bounds, and my permission was taking a bloody long time to forthcome.

'Don't worry,' said my helpful Delhi friend. 'I'll see if I can chivvy the admiral a bit.' Why not try killing him? I thought as I put the phone down; it might encourage the others.

*

We were back in Mangalore. Martin was painting on the beach, the empty strand of the long outer spit. His beginning was abstract – a huge oblong of sky, a wide-based triangle of sand racing thinner triangles of sea and palms to the vanishing-point; but as I watched, white became wind, filling a topsail of cloud, and waves, pulling at the land, and the wake of a man, wading in the middle distance.

I tried to swim, but the undertow was terrific. I sat on the sand and wondered what to do next. IB had walked off my picture, abstracted himself. As I'd expected, he'd left no footprints in Mangalore, no impressions at all. The constant tide of comings and goings had swept them away. Not for the first time I envied Martin. He saw; I was always having to look. Now I had to look beyond the *Travels*.

When I did, I found signs that pointed to Anjidiv. The first was a Muslim seaman who had become not a mere sadhu, but a god. From some of his devotees, a pair of fishermen at a shrine on a headland south of Mangalore, I picked up a partial and confused account of the sailor's career change. His name is Bobbariya. He was a Muslim who came from the sea. He died at sea. He didn't die – he went into a room and when they opened the door he had gone. He became very big, very strong. He is now a *bhuta*. He stood with one foot in the mountains and one in the sea. This happened 400 years ago. This happened 1,000 years ago.

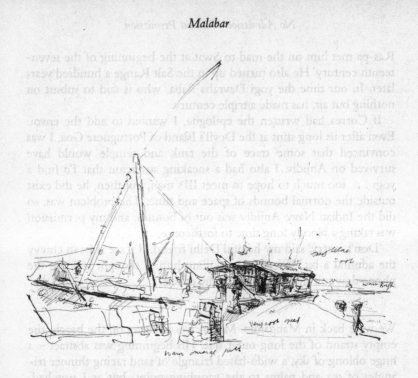

Perhaps Bobbariya approved of my visit to his shrine; in any case, some force was with me for I was led to Mr M.M. Prabhu, an authority on the worship of *bhutas*, or demons. From him I learned that Bobbariya, like Krishna and other originally local deities, had been welcomed into the open house of the Hindu pantheon; also that he was a Barbari – that is, from the region of Berbera on the Somali coast – hence his name. I also learned more about his colossal feat of the splits. The most reliable sources agree that Bobbariya stood with one foot in Malabar and the other on his native Horn of Africa. He had outstraddled even our forefather Adam who, when cast down from Paradise, landed with one foot on the eponymous Peak in Sri Lanka and the other at Pantalayini, north of Calicut. (I had measured the little-noticed Pantalayini print – IB went there too, but missed it – and found it to be five feet two inches long. The celebrated pair to it, according to the best authority, measures five foot seven: not a bad match.)

Mr Prabhu also put me on to the second intimation of the yogi's island, another example of the permeability of religious borders. It lay twenty miles north of Calicut and, unlike Bobbariya's small shrine, was a large temple-complex dedicated to Durga Parameshvari. It was known by the name of its founder, Bappa Byari. Bappa, you will not be amazed to hear, was a Muslim.

The precinct of the temple reminded Martin, who has a small son and is an expert on such things, of the Postman Pat Village at Longleat. There were various jolly wooden heads with curly moustaches, Krishna fishing in a pond in his garden-gnome manifestation, a jaunty wooden alligator ('Roald Dahl's Enormous Crocodile,' said Martin), a real goose in a cage. Nearby, a coach-house contained a pair of towering chariots with elephant-head bumpers, the larger of them two storeys tall.

Since the Karnataka border Abhilesh had been almost as lost, linguistically, as us. Two students of English, however, were able to tell us the story of Bappa Byari – Bappa the Merchant. One day he was sailing along the coast here, his ship filled with valuable goods, when the vessel struck a rock. She had impaled herself on an *udbavalingam*, a naturally occurring example of the emblem of Shiva, and it was bleeding all over the place. Blood and water began to rise in the well of the ship. Bappa was devastated – his entire cargo would be lost. Eventually, exhausted by his vain attempts to save it, he fell asleep on the deck of the drowning vessel. Durga, Shiva's consort and guardian of the sea shore, appeared to him in a dream. She made a proposal: she would save his ship if he would build her a temple. Bappa agreed, and awoke to find that the sea had retreated, the ship was on dry land, and his cargo was safe. True to his word he built a temple around the lingam, which to this day bears the scars of its accident with the ship's bottom. 'This was 700 or 800 years ago,' said Vishwas, one of the students. 'But Bappa's family are still living near here, in Mulki.'

'And they are still Muslims,' added his friend, Bhojraj. 'Every year we have a festival and they put Durga on a chariot, and the people pull her to the house of Bappa's family. The priests ride with her and give Bappa's family flowers and sweets.'

'There is also another chariot,' Vishwas said. 'They put statues of Bappa and his servants on it and pull it around. Everybody is coming – Hindus, Muslims, Christians. It is very beautiful!'

★

It was more beautiful than words can describe.

Inevitably you have seen what I want you to see. I have made you look through a pinhole, at IB and the remains of his days, and at the narrow periphery of now. I will pull back for a page or two, show you what lay beyond the verge of his road and the field of your vision; but not beyond mine, although I tried so hard to cut it out. You may have noticed something was wrong – 'The only other passenger in our compartment,' I wrote near the start of the chapter before this one. An Indian train not packed to bursting?

The reason was this. The morning before we went aboard the Malabar Express a group of men had joined another express, the Sabarmati, and firebombed one of the coaches. Fifty-eight volunteers allied to the Vishwa Hindu Parishad, or World Hindu Council, were burned – 'charred', as Indo-journalese puts it – to death. The incident happened at Godhra in eastern Gujarat. The volunteers, all from that state, had been returning from a ceremony 600 miles away at Ayodhya. There, ten years earlier, militants like them had razed the Mughal Babri Mosque: it was built, they alleged, on the site of an ancient temple marking the birth-place of the Lord Ram, and their intention was to build a new one. The highest court in the land had clapped a ban on this; undeterred, the Gujarat volunteers had gone to take part in a ceremony preparing for the foundation of the new temple. They were, as Sir Thomas Browne said, too great friends unto fire. They played with it, and they died by it.

If the razing of the mosque had ignited the worst communal violence since Partition, the events that now took place came a close second. With remarkable speed, retribution for the murdered Hindus was extracted from what the euphemists referred to as 'members of one community' and the less delicate called – with some irony, as it is the Qur'anic term for unbelievers – *kafirs*. In plain words this meant that Gujarati Muslims were dragged from their houses and killed, the favourite method being 'torching' with petrol or kerosene. ('Petrol Price To Rise. Rs. 1.50 More For Kerosene' said the headline below in the *Times of India*, no doubt unintentionally.) At first it was reported that the police stood by and twirled their lathis. The allegation of apathy is unfair: a reliable source (the head of Human Rights Watch in India) stated later that the police often reached the scene of an attack before the torch-mob arrived, in order to hand out supplies of fuel. Even as the pogrom was going on, debates began about whether the (entirely BJP) state government had merely acquiesced in, or encouraged, or actively planned it. The same government is still in charge as I write. Gujarat is a democratic state.

As we travelled south down that palmy coast with our lone coconut consultant, 2,000 people were being killed behind us, nearly all of them Muslims; tens of thousands of Muslims were losing their homes; hundreds of Islamic monuments were being wrecked. The arithmetic, of course, only emerged later. But despite attacks on reporters – 'lensmen', the papers said, were being 'strangulated' – enough came out of Gujarat over the next few days to know that the sum of death would be appalling. Among the screams of revenge, the printed cries of indignation, the crackle of combusting flesh, I heard two voices: those of IG, warning of brinks and chasms, and of Kabir, poet laureate of the borderland between the two great faiths of India – 'The Hindu says Ram is the beloved, the Muslim says Rahim. Then they kill each other.' I say *kafir*, and you say martyr.

It hardly touched us. Once there was a mob on the road, just this side of violence, and a hasty retreat. And there was a suspicion at the Talakal Mosque, IB's scriptorium among the palms: was I scouting out targets for attack? That was about it. But fear was pandemic; except at Bappa Byari's temple, which seemed to lie outside the bounds of that mad time.

The heart of Bappa's complex was a dark courtyard lined with murals of deities, garish even in the gloom. At the centre of this, ringed by bells and recitations, was the *sri kovil* – the *sanctum sanctorum*, Bappa's original temple. It was a low building with a fussy little gable like those of the temples and mosques in Kerala. I stood before the door, looking in, and made out a further, silver door frame; beyond that more frames, lined with candles, black with smoke, receding frame within frame within frame; then the dim idea of an idol. The injured lingam was invisible.

I wondered how Bappa had seen his temple, their temple. From the Muslim point of view, I supposed – it was a *budkhanah*, an idol-house. But I could imagine that for him, as for me, his view and theirs might have converged in possibility, two *qiblahs* that – if one might only see far enough – would come together, at the vanishing-point where idol and Allah, god and God, connect.

*

I think I held the beginning of the thread, for a moment. Soon afterwards it seemed I'd picked up IB's thread again as well. 'I've had a confab with the admiral', said my helpful Delhi friend, 'and, touch wood, it'll all be done and dusted in a day or two.'

Inching to Anjidiv

'I have tasted the bitter and the sweet of affairs
And walked over the rough and smooth path of days.
I have come to know all about time.'

al-Mutanabbi

IB BEGAN HIS Indian career in the Hall of a Thousand Columns with a boil on the bottom. Before we reach the yogi's island, it would be appropriate to explain how he ended it on a beach in Karnataka in his underpants.

Some time ago we left him setting off for a well-earned mini-break in the Maldives. It had all spiralled out of control: the islanders wheedled him into becoming their qadi; he left, eight months and four marriages later, under a cloud of multiple divorce and mutual disdain. His later jaunt to Coromandel, one of the rash of statelets that had broken out on the dying empire of Muhammad Shah, was a family affair of sorts – the local sultan was married to a sister of one of IB's Delhi ex-wives. But IB didn't hit it off with his in-law (he was the one who turned captured enemies into live shish kebabs) and the visit ended with the sultan's death from an aphrodisiac overdose and IB's own near-death from a fever. Only the interlude to these holidays in hell, a trip to Ceylon, had been a success: IB visited the Foot of Adam and was showered with gems by the ruler of Jaffna. But Time had more daughters in store. IB was on his way by sea back to the west coast of India when, 'at the small island between Honavar and Barkur, the infidels fell upon us in twelve warships, fought fiercely against us and boarded us. They took everything I had put by for emergencies. They took the rubies and other gems given me by the King of Ceylon. They took my clothes and the supplies given me on the road by pious persons and saints. They left me no covering except my drawers. They stripped us all and set us down on the shore.' Among the saintly supplies IB lost were those ten talismanic dinars, given him seventy miles to the north and several calamities ago by the Islamic yogi of Anjidiv.

We didn't try to identify the scene of IB's scantily clad marooning. But we visited Honavar, a busy seaside bazaar where a variant on the sola topi was all the rage – a scented kepi, woven from vetiver roots. Nothing was left of the town where the silken slave-girl had served that signature South India lunch. The Portuguese again, I thought; but according to the proprietor of the Kamat Readymade Garment Centre it was Tippu Sultan who had done the razing here. I couldn't summon up much animosity towards the Tiger of Mysore. Our next destination, Anjidiv, was all that mattered now.

And there it was – long, low and lumpy, like a basking sea-slug. I was surprised how near the shore it was; surely nearer than on the map. As the yogi's island came fully into view, I saw I wasn't wrong: the shore itself was stretching out to touch it, extending a long thin arm that bristled with derricks. More cranes stood about the bay. For miles on either side the coast was a building site – 'Project Sea Bird', said a board by a heavily guarded gate – and at the centre of it all was that spiky tentacle, a causeway inching out to Anjidiv. It had almost ceased to be an island.

It still lay, however, beyond the normal bounds of time. 'I, er, don't quite know how to put this,' said my helpful Delhi friend when I rang from Karwar, our Anjidiv Expedition base a few miles up the coast. 'Your . . . your application has been *misplaced*. I mean . . .'

There was a twenty-rupee silence before I could speak. 'You mean it's lost.'

'Well, to be frank, the long and the short of it is, er, yes.'

Over the coming days, thanks to the satellite TV in my hotel room in Karwar, I caught up on movies both Bolly- and Hollywood, on the latest music videos, and on the latest charring and strangulation statistics from Gujarat; I confirmed beyond reasonable doubt Martin's theory that 'old Veg-Pie' – otherwise the Prime Minister, Mr Vajpayee – is a long-lost twin of the British comedian Ronnie Barker; and I became progressively pickled in Kingfishers and self-pity – alone, since Martin had gone to paint Goa – as I followed the painful progress of my resubmitted letter, from the head of Naval Intelligence to the Vice Admiral to the Ministry of Defence and back to where it started. While the application followed its cyclical transmigration, my friend's predictions remained linear: ten days, four to five days, two to three, tomorrow or the day after, it would be in the bag. I was back in Dhow Time, in Zeno's First Paradox; except that the final measure never halved — it was always tomorrow, and tomorrow, and tomorrow.

To say, as did the fifteenth-century Persian envoy Abd al-Razzaq when he was going through a bad patch in India, that through the effect of so many vicissitudes (and in my case beers) the mirror of my understanding had become covered with rust, and the hurricano of so many painful circumstances had extinguished the lamp of my mind, so that I might declare, in one word, that I had fallen into a condition of apathetic stupidity, would be to understate things. The only relief came from the appearance one day at breakfast time of a walking, talking temple. She wore a shrine on her head — the statue of a god flanked by a pair of silver hands and topped by a plume of peacock feathers. No Ascot lady was arrayed as one of these.

★

'You'll never guess how they make Indian Yellow,' Martin said. 'They feed cows nothing but mangoes, then they boil up their piss.' It was good that one of us was making discoveries. Rather than go crazy on my own in Karwar, I had followed him to Goa. It would be just as easy to keep an eye on the sorry saga of my permission from there. I could also look for survivals from Sandabur, as IB called Goa. I even thought in a moment of madness that I might find some fragment of the enormous mosque he had visited there.

Not surprisingly, the Portuguese had wiped out nearly all traces of their predecessors. The churches of the conquerors, in pink laterite topped with creamy plaster, were magnificent ('rhubarb and custard,' said Martin). But through them history had been so thoroughly rewritten — even the winsome St Sebastian in the Se Cathedral was being shot at, with gay anachronism, by turbaned and bearded 'Moors' — that the real Muslim Goa was hardly even a memory. A few bits of Islamic palace lay dejected beside St Cajetan's, but that was all I found, and they were a hundred years later than IB.

The library of the Xavier Centre, which contains all one might ever wish to know about the Goan past, only proved the point with its single small shelf labelled 'Pre-Portuguese Goa'. I looked through a couple of things on the Kadamba dynasty, temporarily ousted by IB's expeditionary force from Honavar. Curiously, a memento of the Moroccan's moment of martial glory did exist – a battered *viragal* or hero-stone which I had seen in the museum and which, I now learned, probably commemorated a feudatory of the Kadambas killed in the battle. All else swirled in obscurity. Even the derivation of IB's Sandabur was disputed – hotly, I discovered as I struggled through P. Pissurlencar and D.M. Ermelinda dos Stuarts Gomes, who in the 1930s published paper and counter-paper on the problem and worked themselves into a lather of *insinuações, invectivas e insultos*.

Between shushing a noisy tomcat and rescuing an ant from the sugar-bowl, Father Cajetan Coelho admitted he preferred Dona Ermelinda's Chandrapur to Senhor Pissurlencar's Sindapur. I couldn't, however, see the gentle Jesuit getting worked up over so parochial a question. He ran the Xavier Centre, but his interests went far wider than Goa: his worldly doctorate was on the gem trade between India and the Netherlands; his theology came from Louvain. Oxford, Lisbon and South Africa were also on his academic itinerary. He was heir to the old travelling Jesuit scholars, who were heirs, in spirit, to the older Muslim ones. He smiled when I pointed this out. 'These days, we have to look beyond Goa. There are too many priests here as it is, and not enough for them to do. Couples are living together, so there aren't as many marriages. They're using contraceptives, so there aren't as many births. And people live longer, so there aren't even as many funerals.' Eventually we made it, via tea and comparative religion, to Anjidiv. Father Cajetan knew IB's account of the island and its ambiguous yogi. 'Hmm. I think you may be half a Muslim too,' he said with an inquisitive, perhaps inquisitorial look; then a grin: 'I've been to Anjidiv. The tank is still there, down by the shore. And the temple.'

'And the yogi?' O God, I thought; he probably thinks he's asked a fruit-cake to tea.

'It was very crowded,' he said. 'There's an old church there, and the Navy had an open day a month or two ago. We celebrated mass for a thousand pilgrims.' A thousand pilgrims. And I was only one.

'*In sha Allah* you will visit Anjidiv,' said Father Cajetan to my Muslim half, as we parted at the gate.

'*Deo volente*,' I replied, dubiously.

*

For the rest of our time in Goa He showed no sign of volition. I deluded myself into thinking I might remove some mountains by going back to Delhi. Nothing, however, not even a kindly arms dealer who had the ear of admirals, would shift that inert and adamant massif. The permission would certainly come, my helpful friend told me; but tomorrow became the day after, then three or four, then another seven to ten, at least. The Zenonian time-line had gone into reverse. Anjidiv receded. By now it will be an island no longer. And with the continuing violence in Gujarat even that last certainty, the grave of the King of the Merchants, was unvisitable. I was most welcome to try, everyone said, but I might be dropping into my own grave on the way.

My Indian journey seemed to be winding up as it began, back on the shores of the Gulf – in failure. There was a drop of cold comfort in knowing that IB's Indian days had also ended in grief, on that beach in Karnataka. 'Few men leave India with their riches,' he sighed. 'And when one does, God sends him some calamity that turns all he has to nought.' The gold, the jewels, the judge's robes, the gorgeous palaces had dissolved.

Then again, neither of us was exactly empty-handed. IB had a treasure of tales as rich as any in the history of travel. I'd found enough of the stuff of his dreams, and his nightmares, to prove that they were real.

There remained the immediate question of what to do next. In IB's position, I might have been tempted to set up as a hermit: from the yogi of Anjidiv to the present time, the coast around Goa has provided an ideal environment for transcendental beach-bums. Another possibility would be an island in some agreeable Maldivian atoll. The idea had in fact crossed IB's mind, as he was sailing out of the Maldives. 'We came to a little island on which there was but one house, belonging to a weaver. He had his wife and children, a few coco-palms and banana trees, and a small boat . . . And I swear to God that I wished I had what that man had, and that the island might be mine, to be my retreat from the world until the hour that comes to all of us.'

IB didn't end up cultivating his garden, like Candide, on what is now probably some Hilton Coral Reef. For whatever else he had lost, his oldest travelling companion was still there, dogging his steps, snapping at his heels – *al-nafs al-lajuj*, his worldly and importunate spirit. There was no choice:

> Onward he pressed and paced the path of Destiny,
> A man whose load was loosed and bound by God's decree.
> And if Time lent him coursers swift enough, he'd seize
> The reins at dawn – and dine in the Antipodes!

It was all quite exhausting. Still, I had to press on after him. Apart from anything else, there was a cave outside Canton that needed looking into.

*

For the time being I went more modestly to Aligarh to lecture on IB. I spoke in anecdotes and in allusions, of peeling and portioning my Tangerine and, like MacNeice, finding the world incorrigibly plural; of the kindness of strangers. Professor Habib didn't come; I was relieved.

It was later that day, towards the end of my final session in the History Department library – looking, of course, for something else – that I came across Shaykh Ahmad al-Maghribi. He was a Sufi saint, born in Delhi in 1338 and abandoned while an infant . . . the zing of the mosquitoes ceased, and the rustle of readers, and the song of crickets in the ganja-patch – all suddenly silent: my Maghribi, IB, had fathered a child in Delhi at that time; the boy's name was Ahmad; IB had left him behind and did not know what God had done with him. *I did*.

And I had jumped to precisely the sort of conclusion that Professor Habib would deplore. Besides, when I read on I found that the boy was the adopted son of another Maghribi. So that was that.

Or was it? The accounts that I found were in total disagreement on the question of his parentage. In any case, Islamic law frowns on children assuming the names of adoptive parents – wasn't there a Qur'anic verse about it? . . . like as not the boy was born a Maghribi . . . it would be quite natural for IB's child to be passed on to a fellow-countryman . . . My thoughts whirled, then took on an extra spin: the boy, I read, had arrived at his new home in the eye of a tornado. IB's possible son sounded like some friend of Dorothy from Kansas. Perhaps a visit to his shrine would clarify things . . . It was at Ahmadabad, the eye of the storm in Gujarat.

I watched IG waving, receding with the station platform, and decided to follow his advice against braving that storm. I still wonder if Shaykh Ahmad was one of those lost children; whether the son had succeeded where the father failed, on the journey of the spirit. Another grave to visit.

*

Back in Delhi I found Martin painting Safdarjang's tomb, lost in the Mughal twilight. An overblown sun slid down behind the dome, disappearing on its daily journey to the Maghrib. Martin pressed on after the last of the light. A guard hovered, telling us time was finished. I stood there, wondering how my friend could see, until at last I heard a sigh, and the scraping of the palette.

'Come on then. Let's get going.'

Appendix

Sultans of Delhi Mentioned in the Text

Shamsid Dynasty

Shams al-Din Iltutmish (1210–36)

Ghiyathid Dynasty

Ghiyath al-Din Balaban (1266–87)

Khalji Dynasty

Jalal al-Din Firuz Shah (1290–6)
Ala al-Din Muhammad Shah (1296–1316)
Shihab al-Din Umar (1316)
Qutb al-Din Mubarak Shah (1316–20)

Usurpation of

Nasir al-Din Khusraw Shah (1320)

Tughluqid Dynasty

Ghiyath al-Din Tughluq Shah (1320–4)
Muhammad Shah (1324–51)
Firuz Shah (1351–88)

Acknowledgements

A LTHOUGH PART OF me has the distinction of appearing in *Hobson-Jobson* – 'By another curious corruption *Mackintosh* becomes *Makkhanī-tosh*, "buttered toast"!' – I am in every other respect a griffin, 'One newly arrived in India, and unaccustomed to Indian ways and peculiarities'. I therefore have an even greater debt of gratitude to pay than in my previous book on IB. Some of those whom I owe particular thanks have already appeared but should do so again in this formal colophon; others have yet to be mentioned.

In the Gulf (India, for the old Arab traders, began at Basra) I was the guest of Robert and Laura Sykes in Abu Dhabi, Anderson Bakewell aboard *Sanjeeda* and Jay Butler in Sharjah; Jay was also my guide to the high-rise wadis of Arabia Concreta, not her natural habitat. In Delhi I would have been lost and homeless without Justine Hardy, who has also kindly answered queries on everything from the jujube season to the orthography of insults; Captain Paddy Singh provided untiring hospitality and, in the persona of Paddy's Treks & Tours Pvt. Ltd., drivers; Yashwant Singh Rathor and Salman and Kusum Haidar were also most generous hosts, and I was fortunate indeed to have access to Salman's wide-ranging wisdom and contacts. In Aligarh I was the guest of Hamid Ansari, then Vice-Chancellor of Aligarh Muslim University; Professors Irfan Habib, Shireen Moosvi and other members of the Department of History were liberal with their time and knowledge. As for the many others met on the road, I should like to thank in particular Anurag Shukla of Khajuraho, Murkot Ramunny of Dharmadam, M. Mukunda Prabhu of Mangalore and Father Cajetan Coelho of the Xavier Centre in Goa.

I should also like to thank Bernard Haykel and Francine Stone for help in planning my journey; Nile Green, Hasan al-Shamahi, Christopher Smith, Bruce Wannell and Janet Watson for assistance with aspects of the text, and John Keay for subjecting the whole thing to his expert scrutiny; Dr Simon Lawson and Helen Topsfield of the Indian Institute Library in Oxford; the Centre for Middle Eastern and Islamic Studies in Durham, for keeping me on as an absentee Honorary Research Fellow; and Anthony Sattin, the late Professor Martin Esslin, Professor Ross E. Dunn and Dr Abdelhadi Tazi, IB's Arabic editor, for their enthusiastic words about the predecessor to this volume. Caroline Knox has given much encouragement from afar; Gail Pirkis, that paragon among editors, has once more weeded the ranker patches of my prose. Carolyn Whitaker, my agent, continues to be an indispensable anchorwomen in London, the Morrises of Oxford and Monica Esslin to provide beds and other forms of entertainment. Dr Abdulla Abdul Wali Nasher and Dr Rashad al-Alimi maintain their kind support in San'a.

The verses on pp. 306 and 313 were translated by Reynold Nicholson and Franz Rosenthal respectively; quotations from al-Biruni are taken from the 1888 version of his India book by Edward Sachau. All other translations from the Arabic are mine unless stated.

God is ever kind to those who travel, says a Tradition of the Prophet. The kindness usually comes in human form, and in India it was manifest most unforgettably in the late Dr Iqbal Ghani Khan of Aligarh – IG. To him, and to Martin Yeoman, friend and fellow-traveller, this book is jointly dedicated.

Index

Note: Arabic *ibn/bin*, 'son of . . .', is abbreviated to b., the Indian states of Madhya Pradesh and Uttar Pradesh to MP and UP respectively.

Horizon   weapons

Panama

Cool Buff

Water taff

C

overall cool tones col...
smokey blue greys o...

grey tow entows

ple greys shadows   10:45   17.5.2001

Read more . . .

Tim Mackintosh-Smith

YEMEN: Travels in Dictionary Land

Winner of the Thomas Cook / *Daily Telegraph* Travel Book Award: an Arabian grand tour in which every page is dashed – like the land it describes – with the marvellous

Arguably the most fascinating but least known country in the Arab world, Yemen has a way of attracting comment that ranges from the superficial to the wildly fictitious. Crossing mountain, desert, ocean and three millennia of history, Tim Mackintosh-Smith portrays hyrax hunters and dhow skippers, a noseless regicide and a sword-wielding tyrant with a passion for Heinz Russian salad.

'This book is a classic' *Independent*

'Masterful' *Sunday Times*

'*Yemen* . . . is assured and agile: witty, quirky, gossipy, learned, poetic . . . [Tim Mackintosh-Smith] has created a work that will endure' *The Times*

'Mackintosh-Smith seems incapable of writing a dull sentence, and in him the scholar, the linguist and the storyteller swap hats with marvellous speed' *New York Times*

Order your copy now by calling Bookpoint on 01235 827716 or visit your local bookshop quoting ISBN 978-0-7195-9740-4
www.johnmurray.co.uk